How to use your Connected Casebook

Step 1: Go to **www.CasebookConnect.com** and redeem your access code to get started.

Access Code:

Step 2: Go to your **BOOKSHELF** and select your Connected Casebook to start reading, highlighting, and taking notes in the margins of your e-book.

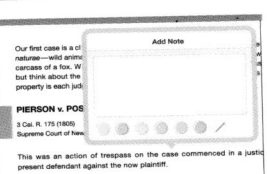

Step 3: Select the **STUDY** tab in your toolbar to access a variety of practice materials designed to help you master the course material. These materials may include explanations, videos, multiple-choice questions, flashcards, short answer, essays, and issue spotting.

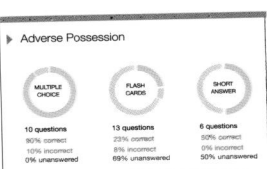

Step 4: Select the **OUTLINE** tab in your toolbar to access chapter outlines that automatically incorporate your highlights and annotations from the e-book. Use the My Notes area for copying, pasting, and editing your book notes or creating new notes.

Step 5: If your professor has enrolled your class, you can select the **CLASS INSIGHTS** tab and compare your own study center results against the average of your classmates.

Is this a used casebook? Access code already scratched off?

You can purchase the Digital Version and still access all of the powerful tools listed above.
Please visit CasebookConnect.com and select Catalog to learn more.

PIN: 9111149547

01087

DEFINING CRIMES

ASPEN CASEBOOK SERIES

DEFINING CRIMES

Third Edition

Joseph L. Hoffmann
Harry Pratter Professor of Law
Indiana University Maurer School of Law

William J. Stuntz
Henry J. Friendly Professor of Law
Late of Harvard University

 Wolters Kluwer

Printed in the United States of America.

1 2 3 4 5 6 7 8 9 0

ISBN 978-1-4548-7574-1

Library of Congress Cataloging-in-Publication Data

Names: Hoffmann, Joseph L., 1957- author. | Stuntz, William J., author.
Title: Defining crimes / Joseph L. Hoffmann, Harry Pratter Professor of Law,
  Indiana University Maurer School of Law, William J. Stuntz, Henry J.
  Friendly Professor of Law, Late of Harvard University.
Description: Third Edition | New York: Wolters Kluwer, [2017] | Series:
  Aspen casebook series
Identifiers: LCCN 2016059834 | ISBN 9781454875741
Subjects: LCSH: Criminal law—United States. | LCGFT: Casebooks.
Classification: LCC KF9219.S78 2017 | DDC 345.73—dc23
LC record available at https://lccn.loc.gov/2016059834

About Wolters Kluwer Legal & Regulatory U.S.

To my wife, Mary, and my children, Becky, Maureen, and Michael.

—Joe Hoffmann

Summary of Contents

Contents

Preface to the First Edition

Defining Crimes is a new casebook that has been under development for almost a decade. But the genesis of this project occurred much earlier. Since 1986, we have been teaching the introductory course in Criminal Law to our students at Harvard Law School, Indiana University Maurer School of Law, and (before that) the University of Virginia School of Law. For most of that time, we have shared the feeling that something important was missing.

Most of the available materials for teaching criminal law (including the leading casebooks we have regularly used in our own classes) are rich with interesting issues of blame, culpability, voluntariness, and free will—in short, the stuff of moral philosophy. That makes them fun to teach. But those materials tend to lack an essential connection with the equally rich and intellectually challenging issues that arise from the everyday practice of criminal law.

Defining Crimes is intended to help remedy that disconnect. This casebook provides a set of teaching materials that moves the study of criminal law out of the classic law-and-philosophy framework ("Why do we punish?") and into the real world ("How is criminal law defined, interpreted, and applied in today's criminal justice system?"). Although in terms of both coverage and content this casebook certainly resembles most others in common use today, our fundamental shift in perspective is reflected in the following key features that make our book distinctive:

(1) Emphasis on the political economy of criminal justice—the complex relationships between the key institutional players (legislatures, prosecutors, police, judges, and juries) that share responsibility for defining, interpreting, and applying criminal law. This casebook reveals to students how criminal justice institutions sometimes reinforce and support each other's efforts, but at other times come into conflict over both the goals and the methods of criminal law.

(2) A balanced presentation of the Model Penal Code and the traditional common-law approach to criminal liability, illustrating both the advantages *and* the disadvantages of the MPC and the common law that it sought (but has largely failed) to replace. This casebook explains how the MPC, in its pursuit of analytical precision, tried to eliminate much of the discretion that allowed common-law judges and juries to use their moral intuitions to "do justice"—which is a big part of the reason why the MPC never managed to occupy the field.

(3) Introduction of many of the important general concepts of criminal law—such as causation, omission liability, attempt, conspiracy, and accomplice liability—in the specific legal contexts where those concepts are most frequently applied.

(4) Coverage of drug crimes and other "low-level" crimes (such as vandalism and prostitution) that are most often used by local governments as instruments of social control, and that often lead to serious concerns about arbitrary and discriminatory law enforcement.

(5) Discussion of core aspects of federal criminal law, such as federal jurisdictional elements, strict liability for at least some federal regulatory offenses, and requirements of factual and legal knowledge for others, that raise interesting issues not discussed in most criminal law casebooks.

(6) Full treatment of sentencing law, including sentencing discretion, guideline sentencing, "three-strikes" laws, and victim restitution, demonstrating how the line between "crime" and "punishment" is largely arbitrary and increasingly has become subject to legislative manipulation.

We have constructed this casebook around contemporary cases—most of them decided since 2000, and many since 2005—that raise issues as timely as today's headlines. The traditional "chestnuts" of criminal law are here (indeed, the casebook begins with the famous 1884 cannibalism case of *Dudley & Stephens*), but the primary focus on modern cases provides a rich and challenging set of materials that shows how American criminal law continues to evolve in today's world. We have also included the most compelling empirical studies and journalistic accounts that depict current issues in criminal law.

Chapter 1, The Character of Criminal Law, opens with a discussion of one of the casebook's major themes: the political economy of criminal justice. In Chapter 1, we explore the respective primary roles of the legislature and the judiciary in defining and applying the Criminal Law. Chapter 1 next introduces two constitutional doctrines, proportionality and vagueness, that—at least in theory, if not so often in practice—allow the judiciary to exercise some control over the legislature's definition of crimes. Chapter 1 concludes with a brief overview of the relationship between criminal law and crime.

Chapters 2 and 3 address the two core subjects within the so-called general part of the criminal law (i.e., those general rules, principles, and doctrines that apply across many different crimes). Chapter 2, Defining Criminal Conduct (or, to use the old Latin terminology, *actus reus*), focuses primarily on the statutory interpretation of conduct elements on crimes, especially the modern rise of formalism. Chapter 3, Defining Criminal Intent (in Latin, *mens rea*), contains an extensive discussion of both the common law's traditional "general intent" and "specific intent" approach to criminal intent, and the Model Penal Code's alternative "element" approach, allowing students to draw their own informed conclusions about the relative strengths and weaknesses of each competing approach.

Chapter 4 deals with some unusual (and, in certain cases, unique) aspects of Federal Criminal Law. We believe that federal criminal law raises interesting issues that can contribute to a fuller understanding of the criminal law in general. But the chapter is designed to be enriching, rather than essential, to the rest of the casebook—and thus may be omitted, if the professor so chooses.

Chapter 5 begins the coverage of the so-called special part of the criminal law—those specific rules, doctrines, and issues that arise from the definitions of specific crimes. Chapter 5 is about Property Crimes: vandalism, theft (including burglary), extortion, and fraud. Chapter 6 addresses Drug Crimes, including drug possession (with and without the intent to distribute), special *mens rea* issues, the relationship between drug crimes and the practice of medicine, and the new frontier of medical marijuana.

In Chapter 7, we take a break from the "special part" of the criminal law to introduce the concepts of Inchoate Crimes and Accomplice Liability. These concepts, although generally applicable, arise so frequently in connection with drug crimes that we think it makes sense to discuss them immediately after the Drug Crimes chapter. However, Chapter 7 also can be taught earlier in the course, right after the chapters on Defining Criminal Conduct (Chapter 2) and Defining Criminal Intent (Chapter 3), if the professor so chooses.

Chapter 8 returns to the coverage of specific crimes by addressing crimes of Sex and Sexual Violence. In Chapter 8, we start with "sex for money" (prostitution, pimping, and pandering), and then proceed to fraudulent sex, and finally to coerced sex (rape). The latter section includes extensive coverage of date rape as well as the role of intoxication in rape law. Chapter 8 concludes with a brief treatment of contemporary child pornography laws.

Chapter 9 is about Homicide Crimes: murder (in the first and second degrees), manslaughter (both voluntary—"in the heat of passion"—and involuntary), and negligent homicide. Chapter 9 also deals with causation, a topic that tends to arise primarily in homicide cases, and reprises the general concepts of inchoate crimes and accomplice liability that were introduced back in Chapter 7.

Chapters 10 deals with Defenses, including self-defense, duress, necessity, entrapment, public authority, and insanity. Along the way, we also introduce imperfect self-defense, the "battered spouse" defense, and diminished capacity. Chapter 11, Sentencing, demonstrates how the line that divides crime from punishment is largely arbitrary and subject to legislative manipulation; the contemporary shift from traditional discretionary sentencing to modern guideline sentencing has helped to dissolve that line and has forced legislatures, courts, and litigants to address sentencing issues as part of the everyday practice of criminal law. Finally, in Chapter 12, we present several

Constitutional Limits on the Criminal Law—including a brief reprise of vagueness and proportionality (first discussed back in Chapter 1), the right of privacy, the issue of "constitutionalized intent," and equal protection.

Of course, not all of the above chapters and subjects can be taught adequately in a one-semester Criminal Law course of 3 credit hours; most likely, even 4 or 5 credit hours would be insufficient to cover it all. We hope, however, that we have provided professors (and, by extension, their students) with enough material to be able to pick and choose, and to end up with a course that illuminates the range and depth of the criminal law. Criminal law is a wonderful subject to teach and to learn. We hope you enjoy it!

Throughout the casebook, wherever our own footnotes might be confused with those contained in the primary material, our own footnotes are identified by asterisks. This casebook contains court decisions and legislative materials current through December 2010.

William J. Stuntz
Joseph L. Hoffmann

February 2011

Preface to the Second Edition

You are holding in your hands (or are viewing on your tablet or laptop) the Second Edition of *Defining Crimes*, a casebook that we continue to hope will help to redefine the study of Criminal Law in the United States.

The main revisions from the First Edition are not numerous, but they are significant:

In Chapter 3, we have expanded the coverage of "malice" as part of the common law of *mens rea*;

In Chapter 5, we have added a new section on criminal trespass, focusing on its frequent and controversial use as a proxy crime for drug dealing in public housing;

In Chapter 6, we have added a new section on drug laws that increase punishments based on the location of the drug possession or sale (e.g., "drug-free school zones") — laws that often have disparate impacts based on race and class;

In Chapter 8, we have included expanded coverage of "acquaintance rape";

In Chapter 10, we have added new sections on the "battered spouse defense" and "Stand Your Ground" laws.

In addition, the Second Edition has been updated throughout, with new empirical data as well as new material on hot topics like the legalization of marijuana, racial bias in police stop-and-frisk actions, and mandatory minimum sentences, all in keeping with the desire for *Defining Crimes* to continue to reflect the issues and controversies that are most important in contemporary criminal justice.

As with the First Edition, wherever our own footnotes might be confused with those contained in the primary material, our footnotes are identified by asterisks. This Second Edition of the casebook contains court decisions and legislative materials current through March 2014.

Finally, a brief personal word about my beloved co-author, Bill Stuntz, who passed away shortly after the First Edition of this casebook was published. Although Bill is no longer with us, he will always be fondly remembered, not only for his intellect and his keen insight — which were without peer among criminal law and criminal procedure scholars of his generation — but also, and even more so, for his humanity. Bill was one of the warmest human beings I have ever had the pleasure to know, and I miss him every day. His ideas, as well as his spirit, will continue to animate this casebook in the years to come.

Joseph L. Hoffmann

May 2014

Preface to the Third Edition

This Third Edition of *Defining Crimes* preserves the structure and content of the First and Second Editions, while adding a few new subjects and expanding on a couple of others:

(1) There's a new Chapter 8, on Gun Crimes, designed to provide a brief introduction to this important aspect of modern American criminal law. The new chapter covers both stand-alone gun crimes and the role that guns can play in enhancing other crimes and punishments. The original Chapters 8 through 12 have been renumbered to become Chapters 9 through 13.

(2) There's a new subsection in the chapter on Defenses—which is now numbered as Chapter 11—about Police Use of Force, a subject that has become highly controversial due to a number of recent police-involved shootings of young black men. This new subsection addresses the general issue of criminal liability for police officers, and the special defenses they may have for the use of deadly force.

(3) The discussion of Acquaintance Rape in the chapter on Crimes of Sex and Sexual Violence—which is now numbered as Chapter 9—has been updated to reflect the continuing evolution of legal and societal views about consent to sex, and especially the current debate about "no means no" versus "yes means yes" policies.

(4) The original section of Chapter 6, Drug Crimes, on Drugs and Medicine—which was deleted from the Second Edition—has been restored, in light of the recent societal and political focus on the problem of opioid addiction.

(5) Chapter 4, on Federal Criminal Law, has been partially rewritten to incorporate two recent U.S. Supreme Court decisions: *Taylor v. United States* (2016), on federal jurisdiction under the Hobbs Act, and *Elonis v. United States* (2015), on *mens rea* for federal crimes.

Last but not least, in conjunction with this Third Edition, new student assessment questions will be made available – including a number of questions written by the current casebook author. It is hoped that these new student assessment questions will prove helpful to both the students themselves and the teachers who continually strive to improve student learning.

As always, I want to recognize my dear friend, the late Bill Stuntz, with whom I co-authored the First Edition of this casebook, and whose intellect and spirit still inhabit every page of the book. My mission is to carry on Bill's legacy by keeping the book fresh and up-to-date, while always remaining true to what Bill and I originally designed this book to do: introduce students to the wonderful and often strange world of criminal law, in a manner that's both fun and interesting for students and teachers, and with a special focus on the way that criminal law actually works in the real world and the real-world institutions that define it.

Joseph L. Hoffmann

March 2017

Acknowledgments

We are grateful to the following sources for permission to reprint excerpts of their work:

Lon Fuller, The Case of the Speluncean Explorers. Used with permission of the Harvard Law Review Association, from The Case of the Speluncean Explorers, by Lon Fuller, 62, no. 4, February 1949.

Republished with permission of The University of Chicago Law Review, from A Separate Crime of Reckless Sex, Ian Ayres and Katharine K. Baker, 72, 2005; permission conveyed through Copyright Clearance Center, Inc.

Republished with permission of The University of Chicago Law Review, from A Separate Crime of Reckless Sex, Ian Ayres and Katharine K. Baker, 72, 2005; permission conveyed through Copyright Clearance Center, Inc.

Republished with permission of Harvard Law Review, from The Secret Ambition of Deterrence, Dan Kahan, 113(2), 1999; permission conveyed through the Copyright Clearance Center, Inc.

Zachary Price, The Rule of Lenity as a Rule of Structure, 72 Fordham L. Rev. 885, 891-94 (2004). Reprinted with permission.

DEFINING CRIMES

1

The Character of Criminal Law

The subject of this book is American criminal law: the body of law that defines crimes and sentences in the United States. In many respects, that body of law resembles the law of tort or contract. Like those bodies of legal doctrine, criminal law exists in large measure to resolve disputes between contending litigants, one of whom is called a "defendant." In criminal cases, as in tort and contract cases, the party who alleges that her opponent has behaved illegally bears the burden of proving that allegation. As is true of the large majority of tort and contract cases, the large majority of criminal cases are settled by an agreement between the contending parties. Last but not least, as is true of tort law and contract law, criminal law has its origin in the common law: In other words, its origins lie in decisions of (mostly English) judges whose judgments, over time, came to define the body of legal rules enforced in criminal cases.

Those are the chief similarities. There are also several important differences. Civil lawsuits, including those that allege torts or breaches of contract, are usually brought by private parties called "plaintiffs." In criminal cases, the equivalent to a civil complaint—usually called an "indictment" or "information"*—is brought in the government's name by a prosecutor whom the government employs. Civil plaintiffs must prove the allegations in their complaints by a preponderance of the evidence; prosecutors must prove the crimes they charge beyond a reasonable doubt. Settlement agreements in civil cases are called, conveniently, "settlement agreements." In criminal cases, such agreements usually end in guilty pleas and are called "plea bargains." When plaintiffs win in tort or contract cases, they usually get money damages. When prosecutors win in criminal cases, at least serious ones, the usual result

---

*Indictments are charges that have been voted by grand juries. Informations are issued by prosecutors. In practice, the difference is small, since prosecutors also draft the charges that grand juries authorize.

is a term of incarceration.** Finally, though criminal law began as common law — indeed, centuries ago, criminal law and tort were a single field — in America, it is now almost entirely a matter of statute. Judges still define most tort law and much of contract law. Legislators are the primary authors of American criminal law.

Two of these differences are especially important. The first is the role of public prosecutors. Because successful civil plaintiffs usually get money damages, those plaintiffs are likely to litigate to the margins of the law: They are paid when they win, so they have an incentive to bring all winning claims in which success would be profitable. Prosecutors, by contrast, are salaried government employees; they get no bonuses when defendants are convicted. Which means there is bound to be a gap, usually a large one, between criminal law as it is written and criminal law as it is enforced. Marijuana possession is still a crime in most states and also under federal law, yet — except for those the government believes are guilty of selling the drug, and not merely possessing small quantities of it — most people who commit the crime face little risk of criminal prosecution. Such enforcement patterns are bound to be common in a system that gives broad discretion to prosecutors who are paid a salary, rather than paid by the victory.

The second key difference is the source of the relevant legal doctrine: common law in torts and contracts, statutes in criminal law. Common law is made by judges; statutes are enacted by legislators. The fact that criminal law is statutory, like the fact that it is enforced by public prosecutors, means that criminal law is much more politicized than tort or contract law. Criminal law is enforced by politicians (the heads of most local prosecutors' offices, usually called District Attorneys, are elected officials), and the laws they enforce are defined by other politicians (both state legislators and members of Congress are also elected officials). At the same time, judges still play an important role in defining crimes, since judges must interpret and apply criminal statutes. Thus, criminal law is the combined product of two very different kinds of lawmaking: legislation and judicial decisions. Still, legislation — and hence the legislature — occupies the driver's seat. That makes criminal law very different than the other bodies of law that are usually studied in the first year of law school.

This special character of criminal lawmaking has large consequences because criminal law itself has large consequences. At the end of 2014, more than 2.2 million inmates made their beds in prisons and jails in the United

---

**In 2006, the most recent year studied by the U.S. Bureau of Justice Statistics, there were roughly 1.1 million felony convictions per year in the United States, and roughly 700,000 prison sentences of one year or longer were imposed. (Due to decreasing crime rates and recent sentencing reforms, most notably in California, felony prison sentences have declined slightly over the past several years.) The number of jail sentences — offenders usually serve sentences of less than one year in local jails, not in state prisons — is large but unknown. The same is true of the number of misdemeanor convictions, which runs in the millions. Roughly, felonies are crimes punishable by substantial prison sentences of more than one year; misdemeanors carry less severe punishments.

States. In 1970, the figure was a little over 300,000. Today, America's overall state and federal imprisonment rate stands at 693 per 100,000 total population. Although this figure is down slightly from the peak of more than 750 per 100,000 in 2009, our nation's modern incarceration rate is the second highest in the world (behind only the Seychelles, a tiny island nation of 92,000 people). Before 1980, the highest imprisonment rate in American history was 137; the average rate in Western Europe today is less than 100. China's imprisonment rate is below 120. Even Russia and Rwanda, both of which have reputations as prison-happy states, imprison fewer than 500 per 100,000. Not counting tiny Seychelles, the United States is the most punitive country in the world, and probably the most punitive democracy in history.

Why? One answer is, because the statutes that define crimes and sentences helped make it so. Broad and severe criminal laws lead to more convictions and more lengthy prison sentences, which leads to more inmates in prison cells. Might that breadth and severity have something to do with the nature of criminal lawmaking? Keep that question in mind as you read the materials that follow.

American punitiveness is not only extreme, it also disproportionately impacts the poor and people of color. For example, a comprehensive report published in 2016 revealed that whites in America are incarcerated at the rate of 275 per 100,000; Hispanics at the rate of 378 per 100,000; and blacks at the rate of 1,408 per 100,000. In 12 states—Alabama, Delaware, Georgia, Illinois, Louisiana, Maryland, Michigan, Mississippi, New Jersey, North Carolina, South Carolina, and Virginia—more than half of the state prison population is black. See The Sentencing Project, "The Color of Justice: Racial and Ethnic Disparity in State Prisons," available online at http://www.sentencingproject.org/wp-content/uploads/2016/06/The-Color-of-Justice-Racial-and-Ethnic-Disparity-in-State-Prisons.pdf. These disturbing statistics reflect in part the way that criminal laws get enforced by police, prosecutors, judges, and juries. But they also reflect the substance of the criminal law itself; as we shall see, the very way that crimes are defined can contribute substantially to such disparities.

A brief note on casebook organization is in order. In Chapter 1, Section A below deals with two related issues: the allocation of lawmaking power between legislators and judges, and the reasons why those different lawmakers choose to punish the offenders whose conduct they criminalize. Section B introduces two constitutional doctrines—proportionality and vagueness—that are only rarely invoked by courts, but that nevertheless serve to limit (at least in theory) the legislature's power to define crimes and to authorize punishments for those crimes. Section C briefly discusses the relationship between criminal law and crime.

Chapter 2 covers the basic principles that govern judicial interpretation of conduct terms in criminal statutes. Chapter 3 covers the same ground with respect to intent terms. And Chapter 4 examines special aspects of federal criminal law, including federal jurisdiction and the intent requirements for federal crimes.

Chapters 5 through 10 deal with particular kinds of crimes: Chapter 5 discusses property crimes. Chapter 6 covers drug crimes. Chapter 7 introduces the law of criminal attempts, criminal conspiracies, and accomplice liability. Chapter 8 provides an introduction to the subject of gun crimes. Chapter 9 addresses crimes involving sex, both violent and otherwise. And Chapter 10's subject is the law of homicide; that chapter also contains a reprise of the law of attempt, conspiracy, and complicity.

Chapter 11 covers the major defenses to criminal liability: self-defense, duress, necessity, entrapment, public authority, and insanity. Chapter 12 addresses the substantive law of criminal sentencing. Chapter 13 concludes with a look at several additional constitutional doctrines that restrain (barely) the definition of crimes.

Like most law casebooks, this casebook is filled with cases — written decisions rendered by state and federal appellate courts. Learning how to read cases, and how to decipher their meaning and significance, are important goals for law students. In reading the cases that follow, you may often find yourself challenged to figure out the legal rules and principles that underlie the judges' opinions. Hang in there — you will get better at it over time. Be sure to consult the notes that follow each case; we have frequently included therein background and supplemental information that might help you to better to understand the case.

At the same time, always keep in mind that modern American criminal law is governed by statutes. For this reason, with respect to every main case in this casebook (except for the very first one, which predates the modern era), we have made sure to include the relevant portions of the governing criminal statute. You will find the statute either in the text of one of the judicial opinions, or in a footnote supplied by one of the judges or by us. Sometimes it may be hard to find, but it will be there. Use the statute as the starting point for your analysis of the case; ignore or overlook it at your peril. In many (perhaps even most) cases, the statute will be crucial to understanding the decision.

Welcome to a fascinating and extremely important field of study. Enjoy the ride.

A. WHO DEFINES CRIMES? — THE ROLE OF COURTS AND LEGISLATURES

The three cases excerpted below — two real, one fictitious — kick off the exploration. The first of those cases comes not from contemporary America but from nineteenth-century England. Regina v. Dudley & Stephens, 14 Q.B.D. 273 (1884), was a homicide prosecution that arose from a strange and sad turn of events on a voyage through the South Atlantic. *Dudley & Stephens* is a famous example of the common law at work. The third of the three cases arises from a twenty-first-century California prosecution; the case is People v. Kellogg, 14 Cal. Rptr. 3d 507 (4th Dist. App. 2004). The defendant in *Kellogg* was a homeless alcoholic who had been repeatedly arrested and punished for public drunkenness — in other words, for being a homeless alcoholic. *Kellogg* offers a useful picture of criminal law in a system in which legislative authority is paramount. In between *Dudley & Stephens* and *Kellogg* is the imaginary set of judicial opinions in the imaginary case imagined by Lon Fuller, The Case of the Speluncean Explorers, 62 Harv. L. Rev. 616 (1949). Fuller's article offers a mix of common law and statutory interpretation; the central issue in Fuller's hypothetical case is the allocation of power between judges and legislators.

Regina v. Dudley & Stephens

Queen's Bench
14 Q.B.D. 273 (1884)

The judgment of the Court (Lord COLERIDGE, C.J., GROVE and DENMAN, JJ., POLLOCK and HUDDLESTON, B-B.) was delivered by Lord COLERIDGE, C.J.

The two prisoners, Thomas Dudley and Edwin Stephens, were indicted for the murder of Richard Parker on the high seas on the 25th of July in the present year. They were tried before my Brother Huddleston at Exeter on the 6th of November, and under the direction of my learned Brother, the jury returned a special verdict, the legal effect of which has been argued before us, and on which we are now to pronounce judgment.

The special verdict . . . [was] as follows. [The jury found:]

> "that on July 5, 1884, the prisoners, Thomas Dudley and Edward Stephens, with one Brooks, all able-bodied English seamen, and the deceased also an English boy, between seventeen and eighteen years of age, the crew of an English yacht, a registered English vessel, were cast away in a storm on the high seas 1600 miles from the Cape of Good Hope, and were compelled to put into an open boat belonging to the said yacht. That in this boat they had no supply of water and no supply of food, except two 1 lb. tins of turnips, and for three days they had nothing else to subsist upon. That on the fourth day they caught a small turtle, upon which they subsisted for a few days, and this was the only food they had up to the twentieth day when the act now in question was committed.
>
> That on the twelfth day the turtle were entirely consumed, and for the next eight days they had nothing to eat. That they had no fresh water, except such rain as they from time to time caught in their oilskin capes. That the boat was drifting on the ocean, and was probably more than 1000 miles away from land. That on the eighteenth day, when they had been seven days without food and five without water, the prisoners spoke to Brooks as to what should be done if no succour came, and suggested that some one should be sacrificed to save the rest, but Brooks dissented, and the boy, to whom they were understood to refer, was not consulted. That on the 24th of July, the day before the act now in question, the prisoner Dudley proposed to Stephens and Brooks that lots

should be cast who should be put to death to save the rest, but Brooks refused consent, and it was not put to the boy, and in point of fact there was no drawing of lots. That on that day the prisoners spoke of their having families, and suggested it would be better to kill the boy that their lives should be saved, and Dudley proposed that if there was no vessel in sight by the morrow morning the boy should be killed. That next day, the 25th of July, no vessel appearing, Dudley told Brooks that he had better go and have a sleep, and made signs to Stephens and Brooks that the boy had better be killed. The prisoner Stephens agreed to the act, but Brooks dissented from it. That the boy was then lying at the bottom of the boat quite helpless, and extremely weakened by famine and by drinking sea water, and unable to make any resistance, nor did he ever assent to his being killed. The prisoner Dudley offered a prayer asking forgiveness for them all if either of them should be tempted to commit a rash act, and that their souls might be saved. That Dudley, with the assent of Stephens, went to the boy, and telling him that his time was come, put a knife into his throat and killed him then and there; that the three men fed upon the body and blood of the boy for four days; that on the fourth day after the act had been committed the boat was picked up by a passing vessel, and the prisoners were rescued, still alive, but in the lowest state of prostration. That they were carried to the port of Falmouth, and committed for trial at Exeter. That if the men had not fed upon the body of the boy they would probably not have survived to be so picked up and rescued, but would within the four days have died of famine. That the boy, being in a much weaker condition, was likely to have died before them. That at the time of the act in question there was no sail in sight, nor any reasonable prospect of relief. That under these circumstances there appeared to the prisoners every probability that unless they then fed or very soon fed upon the boy or one of themselves they would die of starvation. That there was no appreciable chance of saving life except by killing some one for the others to eat. That assuming any necessity to kill anybody, there was no greater necessity for killing the boy than any of the other three men. But whether upon the whole matter by the jurors found the killing of Richard Parker by Dudley and Stephens be felony and murder the jurors are ignorant, and pray the advice of the Court thereupon, and if upon the whole matter the Court shall be of opinion that the killing of Richard Parker be felony and murder, then the jurors say that Dudley and Stephens were each guilty of felony and murder as alleged in the indictment."

From these facts, stated with the cold precision of a special verdict, it appears sufficiently that the prisoners were subject to terrible temptation, to sufferings which might break down the bodily power of the strongest man and try the conscience of the best. . . . But nevertheless this is clear, that the prisoners put to death a weak and unoffending boy upon the chance of preserving their own lives by feeding upon his flesh and blood after he was killed, and with the certainty of depriving *him* of any possible chance of survival. The verdict finds in terms that "if the men had not fed upon the body of the boy they would *probably* not have survived," and that, "the boy being in a much weaker condition was *likely* to have died before them." They might possibly have been picked up next day by a passing ship; they might possibly not have been picked up at all; in either case it is obvious that the killing of the boy would have been an unnecessary and profitless act. It is found by the verdict that the boy was incapable of resistance, and, in fact, made none; and it is not even suggested that his death was due to any violence on his part attempted against, or even so much as feared by, those who killed him. Under these circumstances the jury say that they are ignorant whether those who killed him were guilty of murder, and have referred it to this Court to determine what is the legal consequence which follows from the facts which they have found. . . .

[T]he real question in the case [is] whether killing under the circumstances set forth in the verdict be or not be murder. The contention that it could be anything else was, to the minds of us all, both new and strange, and we stopped the Attorney General['s oral] argument in order that we might hear [from defense counsel] what could be said in support of a proposition which appeared to us to be at once dangerous, immoral, and opposed to all legal principle and analogy. . . . [I]t is said that it follows from various definitions of murder in books of authority, which definitions imply, if they do not state, the doctrine, that in order to save your own life you may lawfully take away the life of another, when that other is neither attempting nor threatening yours, nor is guilty of any illegal act whatever towards you or any one else. But if these definitions be looked at they will not be found to sustain this contention. . . .

[T]he doctrine contended for receives no support from the great authority of Lord Hale. It is plain that in his view the necessity which justified homicide is that only which has always been and is now considered a justification. . . . Lord Hale regarded the private necessity which justified, and alone justified, the taking the life of another for the safeguard of one's own to be what is commonly called "self-defence." Hale's Pleas of the Crown, i. 478.

But if this could be even doubtful upon Lord Hale's words, Lord Hale himself has made it clear. For in the chapter in which he deals with the exemption created by compulsion or necessity he thus expresses himself: "If a man be desperately assaulted and in peril of death, and cannot otherwise escape unless, to satisfy his assailant's fury, he will kill an innocent person then present, the fear and actual force will not acquit him of the crime and punishment of murder, if he commit the fact, for he ought rather to die himself than kill an innocent; but if he cannot otherwise save his own life the law permits him in his own defence to kill the assailant, for by the violence of the assault, and the offence committed upon him by the assailant himself, the law of nature, and necessity, hath made him his own protector. . . ." Hale's Pleas of the Crown, i. 51.

But further still, Lord Hale in the following chapter deals with the position asserted by the casuists, and sanctioned, as he says, by Grotius and Puffendorf, that in a case of extreme necessity, either of hunger or clothing[,] theft is no theft, or at least not punishable as theft. . . . "But," says Lord Hale, "I take it that here in England, that rule, at least by the laws of England, is false; and therefore, if a person, being under necessity for want of victuals or clothes, shall upon that account clandestinely and animo furandi steal another man's goods, it is felony, and a crime by the laws of England punishable with death." Hale, Pleas of the Crown, i. 54. If, therefore, Lord Hale is clear—as he is—that extreme necessity of hunger does not justify larceny, what would he have said to the doctrine that it justified murder? . . .

Is there, then, any authority for the proposition which has been presented to us? Decided cases there are none. . . . The American case cited by my Brother Stephen in his Digest, from Wharton on Homicide, in which it was decided, correctly indeed, that sailors had no right to throw passengers overboard to save themselves, but on the somewhat strange ground that the proper mode of determining who was to be sacrificed was to vote upon the subject by ballot, can hardly, as my Brother Stephen says, be an authority satisfactory to a court in this country. . . .

The one real authority of former time is Lord Bacon, who, in his commentary on the maxim, "necessitas inducit privilegium quoad jura private," lays down the law as follows: "Necessity carrieth a privilege in itself. Necessity is of three sorts—necessity of conservation of life, necessity of obedience, and necessity of the act of God or of a stranger. First of conservation of life; if a man steal viands to satisfy his present hunger, this is no felony nor larceny. So if divers be in danger of drowning by the casting away of some boat or barge, and one of them get to some plank, or on the boat's side to keep himself above water, and another to save his life thrust him from it, whereby he is drowned, this is neither se defendendo nor by misadventure, but justifiable." On this it is to be observed that Lord Bacon's proposition that stealing to satisfy hunger is no larceny . . . is expressly contradicted by Lord Hale in the passage already cited. And for the proposition as to the plank or boat, it is said to be derived from the canonists. At any rate he cites no authority for it, and it must stand upon his own. Lord Bacon was great even as a lawyer; but it is permissible to much smaller men, relying upon principle and on the authority of others, the equals and even the superiors of Lord Bacon as lawyers, to question the soundness of his dictum. There are many conceivable states of things in which it might possibly be true, but if Lord Bacon meant to lay down the broad proposition that a man may save his life by killing, if necessary, an innocent and unoffending neighbour, it certainly is not law at the present day. . . .

. . . Now it is admitted that the deliberate killing of this unoffending and unresisting boy was clearly murder, unless the killing can be justified by some well-recognised excuse admitted by the law. It is further admitted that there was in this case no such excuse, unless the killing was justified by what has been called "necessity." But the temptation to the act which existed here was not what the law has ever called necessity. Nor is this to be regretted. Though law and morality are not the same, and many things may be immoral which are not necessarily illegal, yet the absolute divorce of law from morality would be of fatal consequence; and such divorce would follow if the temptation to murder in this case were to be held by law an absolute defence of it. It is not so. To preserve one's life is generally speaking a duty, but it may be the plainest and the highest duty to sacrifice it. War is full of instances in which it is a man's duty not to live, but to die. The duty, in case of shipwreck, of a captain to his crew, of the crew to the passengers, of soldiers to women and children[;] . . . these duties impose on men the moral necessity, not of the preservations but of the sacrifice of their lives for others, from which in no country, least of all, it is to be hoped, in England, will men ever shrink. . . . It is not correct, therefore, to say that there is any absolute or unqualified necessity to preserve one's life. . . .

It would be a very easy and cheap display of commonplace learning to quote from Greek and Latin authors, from Horace, from Juvenal, from Cicero, from Euripides, passage after passage, in which the duty of dying for others has been laid down in glowing and emphatic language as resulting from the principles of heathen ethics; it is enough in a Christian country to remind ourselves of the Great Example whom we profess to follow. It is not needful to point out the awful danger of admitting the principle which has been contended for. Who is to be the judge of this sort of necessity? By what measure is the comparative value of lives to be measured? Is it to be strength, or intellect, or what? It is plain that the principle leaves to him who is to profit by it to determine the necessity which will justify him in deliberately taking another's life to save his own. In this case the weakest, the youngest, the most unresisting, was chosen. Was it more necessary to kill him than one of the grown men? The answer must be "No" —

"So spake the Fiend, and with necessity,
The tyrant's plea, excused his devilish deeds."

It is not suggested that in this particular case the deeds were devilish, but it is quite plain that such a principle once admitted might be made the legal cloak for unbridled passion and atrocious crime. There is no safe path for judges to tread but to ascertain the law to the best of their ability and to declare it according to their judgment; and if in any case the law appears to be too severe on individuals, to leave it to the Sovereign to exercise that prerogative of mercy which the Constitution has intrusted to the hands fittest to dispense it.

It must not be supposed that in refusing to admit temptation to be an excuse for crime it is forgotten how terrible the temptation was; how awful the suffering; how hard in such trials to keep the judgment straight and the conduct pure. We are often compelled to set up standards we cannot reach ourselves, and to lay down rules which we could not ourselves satisfy. But a man has no right to declare temptation to be an excuse, though he might himself have yielded to it, nor allow compassion for the criminal to change or weaken in any manner the legal definition of the crime. It is therefore our duty to declare that the prisoners' act in this case was willful murder, that the facts as stated in the verdict are no legal justification of the homicide; and to say that in our unanimous opinion the prisoners are upon this special verdict guilty, of murder. —

— The Court then proceeded to pass sentence of death upon the prisoners.

Notes on Dudley & Stephens

1. According to historian Brian Simpson's book about the case—A.W. Brian Simpson, Cannibalism and the Common Law (1984); it's a terrific read—Tom Dudley at no time hid the facts of *Dudley & Stephens.* On the contrary, the elaborate findings by the jury are largely based on his statements, freely given after he and his shipmates reached shore. Dudley was so forthcoming partly because it never occurred to him that he would face criminal charges. Given Dudley's subsequent conviction, seamen who later found themselves in similar circumstances were bound to be less talkative. Meaning, the knowledge of the facts in such cases was bound to be less complete. Does that affect your view of Lord Coleridge's opinion?

2. Recall these words from Coleridge's opinion: "By what measure is the comparative value of lives to be measured? Is it to be strength, or intellect, or what?" The reader is invited to think: No one can fairly choose which of the stranded seamen should live and which should die. But is that really true? Try using different yardsticks than "strength, or intellect": say, illness and numbers. Richard Parker was about to die anyway when the defendants killed him. And if the defendants had not derived their sustenance from his body, all four would have died. If those propositions are correct, the defendants' choice was between four deaths and only one—and the one was bound to die soon either way. Seen in those terms, the decision to kill Parker doesn't seem so clearly wrong, does it? How do you suppose Coleridge would respond?

3. Reread the last paragraph of Coleridge's opinion, and note the phrase: "We are often compelled to set up standards we cannot reach ourselves." That is an odd idea, no? It becomes all the more odd if one considers the empirical data on crimes and criminal prosecutions. More than 650,000 robberies are committed in the United States each year, according to the National Crime Victimization Survey. Fewer than 400,000 of these are reported to the police. Roughly 40,000 robbers are tried and convicted each year. As those numbers make plain, our criminal justice system does not (and surely cannot afford to) punish even a large minority of serious offenses. Plainly, "standards we cannot reach ourselves" cannot be enforced with any degree of consistency in such a system—even far more lax standards cannot be enforced consistently.

This leads to a crucial point about the character of criminal law. Tort law draws lines between good conduct and bad. *Dudley & Stephens* notwithstanding, criminal law draws few such lines. Instead of distinguishing good conduct from bad, the criminal justice system must primarily distinguish bad conduct from worse—at least with respect to crimes that are less heinous than homicide.

4. If *Dudley & Stephens* is any indication, judge-made criminal law is made chiefly through moral reasoning: Judges consider the parties' arguments and then decide which result better comports with fairness and justice, or which one creates the proper incentives for those whose conduct criminal law regulates. Is that the right way to decide criminal cases? Are there any good alternatives?

5. Shortly after the decision in *Dudley & Stephens*, Queen Victoria commuted the prisoners' sentences to six months' imprisonment. Was she right to do so? Coleridge seems to have anticipated the Queen's decision—*Dudley & Stephens* attracted enormous publicity at the time, and there was widespread speculation that a commutation was in the offing. The line about the Queen's "prerogative of mercy" was probably meant to suggest that the court believed the prerogative ought to be exercised in this case. Was that the right outcome: legal severity coupled with executive clemency? Does clemency undermine the rule of law, or does it make the rule of law tolerable?

Notes on the Purposes of Criminal Punishment

1. Among lawyers and judges, criminal punishment is usually justified in one of three ways. The first justification is moral; the customary term is *retribution*. The second is economic; the most common label is *deterrence*. The third justification is psychiatric; the relevant term is *rehabilitation*. Retributivists believe that punishment for crime is a moral good because crime is a moral wrong. Deterrence aficionados look not to moral rights and wrongs but to social costs and benefits: Crime is socially destructive, and socially destructive behavior is best reduced by raising the price those who engage in such behavior must pay. Believers in rehabilitation seek to use criminal punishment not to punish offenders but to treat them, so that they keep their noses clean after they are released. Retribution is the moral or philosophical theory of criminal punishment. Deterrence is the economic or empirical theory. Rehabilitation is the medical or psychiatric theory. In nineteenth-century England (as in nineteenth-century America), rehabilitation was not part of the law's intellectual furniture; it was a theory that no one embraced.

2. These theories are often discussed as though they were substitutes, not complements—as though one must choose one of the three, and only one. *Dudley & Stephens* suggests that view is mistaken. Lord Coleridge's opinion discusses the defendants' moral duty at length, using clear retributivist language. Coleridge also notes the deterrent rationale for the court's decision: Hence the idea that the defendants' argument, if successful, "might be made the legal cloak for unbridled passion and atrocious crime"—deterrence talk, using nineteenth-century language. Such an eclectic approach to theories of criminal punishment remains common, and not only in England. Criminal punishment might be seen as a means of imposing moral order where disorder has reigned; punishment might also be seen as the price criminal defendants pay for their crimes, imposed in the hope that future would-be offenders will be unwilling to pony up. Or, punishment might be seen as *both* retributive *and* deterrent. (And, perhaps, even as rehabilitative.) When judges are told to choose among these rationales, the choice is often "all of the above."

3. Consider the strength or weakness of these standard rationales for punishment in the context of *Dudley & Stephens*. Retributivists believe that the degree of the moral wrong ought to determine the severity of the subsequent punishment. Coleridge acknowledged that the defendants faced enormous temptation to behave as they did. It would seem to follow that, at worst, Dudley and Stephens committed a modest wrong — for which they presumably deserved only a modest punishment, meaning something well shy of a murder conviction. As for deterrence, anyone stranded in the middle of the Atlantic Ocean facing imminent death is unlikely to concern himself with legal rules, and it was wildly improbable that Dudley or Stephens would ever again find themselves in a similar situation. There is no obvious deterrent justification for punishing a crime committed in such unusual circumstances. For the same reason, rehabilitation made little sense in this context: The defendants did not need rehabilitating, since they had displayed no propensity to commit crimes in the future.

4. Do you agree with the propositions just stated? If so, consider: History is filled with examples of men and women who have starved to death without killing and eating their neighbors. Which suggests that the temptation Dudley and Stephens faced was less than overwhelming. Besides, even were it true that most of us would behave no better under similar circumstances, it does not follow that Dudley and Stephens committed no great wrong. According to Immanuel Kant and many others, killing innocents for one's own convenience is *always* wrong: the worst wrong criminal law punishes. Retributive justice therefore required punishment in this case. So did deterrence — if the law excused Dudley and Stephens, the message to would-be offenders would be that killing is excused when the killers offer a sufficiently sympathetic account of their circumstances. Since their victims are dead, killers are often the only ones who know the relevant circumstances. Thus, even if these defendants were undeterrable, they needed to be punished in order to deter others. As for rehabilitation: There was something sick (wasn't there?) about killing and eating Richard Parker. It seems likely that Dudley and Stephens could have used some therapy. A spell of confinement might have been therapeutic in itself. Do you agree with *those* propositions? The lesson of these dueling arguments seems clear: The standard theories of criminal punishment do not yield clear results.

5. As you read the judicial opinions in Lon Fuller's imaginative reconception of *Dudley & Stephens*, consider which of the above arguments Fuller's fictitious judges might embrace.

Lon Fuller, The Case of the Speluncean Explorers

62 Harvard Law Review 616 (1949)

In the Supreme Court of Newgarth, 4300

The defendants, having been indicted for the crime of murder, were convicted and sentenced to be hanged by the Court of General Instances of the County of Stowfield. They bring a petition of error before this Court. The facts sufficiently appear in the opinion of the Chief Justice.

TRUEPENNY, C.J.

The four defendants are members of the Speluncean Society, an organization of amateurs interested in the exploration of caves. Early in May of 4299 they, in the company of Roger Whetmore, then also a member of the Society, penetrated into the interior of a limestone cavern of the type found in the Central Plateau of this Commonwealth. While they were in a position remote from the entrance to the cave, a landslide occurred. Heavy boulders fell in such a manner as to block completely the only known opening to the cave. When the men discovered their predicament they settled themselves near the obstructed entrance to wait until a rescue party should remove the detritus that prevented them from leaving their underground prison. On the failure of Whetmore and the defendants to return to their homes, the Secretary of the Society was notified by their families. It appears that the explorers had left indications at the headquarters of the Society concerning the location of the cave they proposed to visit. A rescue party was promptly dispatched to the spot.

The task of rescue proved one of overwhelming difficulty. . . . A huge temporary camp of workmen, engineers, geologists, and other experts was established. The work of removing the obstruction was several times frustrated by fresh landslides. In one of these, ten of the workmen engaged in clearing the entrance were killed. . . . Since it was known that the explorers had carried with them only scant provisions, . . . anxiety was early felt that they might meet death by starvation before access to them could be obtained. On the twentieth day of their imprisonment it was learned for the first time that they had taken with them into the cave a portable wireless machine capable of both sending and receiving messages. A similar machine was promptly installed in the rescue camp and oral communication established with the unfortunate men within the mountain. They asked to be informed how long a time would be required to release them. The engineers in charge of the project answered that at least ten days would be required even if no new landslides occurred. The explorers then asked if any physicians were present, . . . described their condition and the rations they had taken with them, and asked for a medical opinion whether they would be likely to live without food for ten days longer. The chairman of the committee of physicians told them that there was little possibility of this. . . . Whetmore, speaking on behalf of himself and the defendants, asked whether they would be able to survive for ten days longer if they consumed the flesh of one of their number. The physicians' chairman reluctantly answered this question in the affirmative. . . . When the imprisoned men were finally released it was learned that on the twenty-third day after their entrance into the cave Whetmore had been killed and eaten by his companions.

. . . [I]t appears that it was Whetmore who first proposed that they might find the nutriment without which survival was impossible in the flesh of one of their own number. It was also Whetmore who first proposed the use of some method of casting lots, calling the attention of the defendants to a pair of dice he happened to have with him. The defendants were at first reluctant to adopt so desperate a procedure, but . . . they finally agreed on the plan proposed by Whetmore. . . .

Before the dice were cast, however, Whetmore declared that he withdrew from the arrangement, as he had decided on reflection to wait for another week before embracing an expedient so frightful and odious. The others charged him with a breach of faith and proceeded to cast the dice. When it came Whetmore's turn, the dice were cast for him by one of the defendants, and he was asked to declare any objections he might have to the fairness of the throw. He stated that he had no such objections. The throw went against him, and he was then put to death and eaten by his companions.

After the rescue of the defendants, and after they had completed a stay in a hospital where they underwent a course of treatment for malnutrition and shock, they were indicted for the murder of Roger Whetmore. At the trial, after the testimony had been concluded, the foreman of the jury (a lawyer by profession) inquired of the court whether the jury might not find a special verdict, leaving it to the court to say whether on the facts as found the defendants were guilty. After some discussion, both the Prosecutor and counsel for the defendants indicated their acceptance of this procedure, and it was adopted by the court. In a lengthy special verdict the jury found the facts as I have related them above, and found further that if on these facts the defendants were guilty of the crime charged against them, then they found the defendants guilty. On the basis of this verdict, the trial judge ruled that the defendants were guilty of murdering Roger Whetmore. The judge then sentenced them to be hanged, the law of our Commonwealth permitting him no discretion with respect to the penalty to be imposed. After the release of the jury, its members joined in a communication to the Chief Executive asking that the sentence be commuted to an imprisonment of six months. . . .

It seems to me that in dealing with this extraordinary case the jury and the trial judge followed a course that was not only fair and wise, but the only course that was open to them under the law. The language of our statute is well known: "Whoever shall willfully take the life of another shall be punished by death." N.C.S.A. §12-A. This statute permits of no exception applicable to this case, however our sympathies may incline us to make allowance for the tragic situation in which these men found themselves.

In a case like this the principle of executive clemency seems admirably suited to mitigate the rigors of the law, and I propose to my colleagues that we follow the example of the jury and the trial judge by joining in the communications they have addressed to the Chief Executive. . . . [If] some form of clemency [is] extended to these defendants . . . , then justice will be accomplished without impairing either the letter or spirit of our statutes. . . .

FOSTER, J.

. . . I believe something more is on trial in this case than the fate of these unfortunate explorers; that is the law of our Commonwealth. If this Court declares that under our law these men have committed a crime, then our law is itself convicted in the tribunal of common sense, no matter what happens to the individuals involved in this petition of error. . . .

For myself, I do not believe that our law compels the monstrous conclusion that these men are murderers. I believe . . . that it declares them to be innocent of any crime. . . .

Now it is, of course, perfectly clear that these men did an act that violates the literal wording of the statute which declares that he who "shall willfully take the life of another" is a murderer. But one of the most ancient bits of legal wisdom is the saying that a man may break the letter of the law without breaking the law itself. Every proposition of positive law, whether contained in a statute or a judicial precedent, is to be interpreted reasonably, in the light of its evident purpose. . . . In *Commonwealth v. Staymore* the defendant was convicted under a statute making it a crime to leave one's car parked in certain areas for a period longer than two hours. The defendant had attempted to remove his car, but was prevented from doing so because the streets were obstructed by a political demonstration in which he took no part and which he had no reason to anticipate. His conviction was set aside by this Court, although his case fell squarely within the wording of the statute. Again, in *Fehler v. Neegas* there was before this Court for construction a statute in which the word "not" had plainly been transposed from its intended position in the final and most crucial section of the act. . . . This Court refused to accept a literal interpretation of the statute, and in effect rectified its language by reading the word "not" into the place where it was evidently intended to go.

. . . Centuries ago it was established that a killing in self-defense is excused. There is nothing in the wording of the statute that suggests this exception. Various attempts have been made to reconcile the legal treatment of self-defense with the words of the statute, but in my opinion these are all merely ingenious sophistries. The truth is that the exception in favor of self-defense cannot be reconciled with the words of the statute, but only with its purpose.

The true reconciliation of the excuse of self-defense with the statute making it a crime to kill another is to be found in the following line of reasoning. One of the principal objects underlying any criminal legislation is that of deterring men from crime. Now it is apparent that if it were declared to be the law that a killing in self-defense is murder such a rule could not operate in a deterrent manner. A man whose life is threatened will repel his aggressor, whatever the law may say. Looking therefore to the broad purposes of criminal legislation, we may safely declare that this statute was not intended to apply to cases of self-defense.

. . . [T]he same reasoning is applicable to the case at bar. If in the future any group of men ever find themselves in the tragic predicament of these defendants, . . . their decision whether to live or die will not be controlled by the contents of our criminal code. Accordingly, if we read this statute intelligently it is apparent that it does not apply to this case. . . .

I therefore conclude that on any aspect under which this case may be viewed these defendants are innocent of the crime of murdering Roger Whetmore, and that the conviction should be set aside.

TATTING, J.

. . . I find myself torn between sympathy for these men and a feeling of abhorrence and disgust at the monstrous act they committed. I had hoped that I would be able to put these contradictory emotions to one side. . . . Unfortunately, this deliverance has not been vouchsafed me. . . .

The gist of my brother [Foster's] argument may be stated in the following terms: No statute, whatever its language, should be applied in a way that contradicts its purpose. One of the purposes of any criminal statute is to deter. The application of the statute making it a crime to kill another to the peculiar facts of this case would contradict this purpose, for it is impossible to believe that the contents of the criminal code could operate in a deterrent manner on men faced with the alternative of life or death. . . .

. . . It is true that a statute should be applied in the light of its purpose, and that one of the purposes of criminal legislation is recognized to be deterrence. The difficulty is that other purposes are also ascribed to the law of crimes. It has been said that one of its objects is to provide an orderly outlet for the instinctive human demand for retribution. *Commonwealth v. Scape.* It has also been said that its object is the rehabilitation of the wrongdoer. *Commonwealth v. Makeover.* Other theories have been propounded. Assuming that we must interpret a statute in the light of its purpose, what are we to do when it has many purposes or when its purposes are disputed?

. . . [A]lthough there is authority for my brother's interpretation of the excuse of self-defense, there is other authority which assigns to that excuse a different rationale. . . . The taught doctrine of our law schools . . . runs in the following terms: The statute concerning murder requires a "willful" act. The man who acts to repel an aggressive threat to his own life does not act "willfully," but in response to an impulse deeply ingrained in human nature. . . . [That] familiar explanation for the excuse of self-defense . . . obviously cannot be applied by analogy to the facts of this case. These men acted not only "willfully" but with great deliberation and after hours of discussing what they should do. . . .

I recognize the relevance of the precedents cited by my brother concerning the displaced "not" and the defendant who parked overtime. But what are we to do with one of the landmarks of our jurisprudence, which again my brother passes over in silence? This is *Commonwealth v. Valjean.* . . . [T]he defendant was indicted for the larceny of a loaf of bread, and offered as a defense that he was in a condition approaching starvation. The court refused to accept this defense. If hunger cannot justify the theft of wholesome and natural food, how can it justify the killing and eating of a man? Again, if we look at the thing in terms of deterrence, is it likely that a man will starve to death to avoid a jail sentence for the theft of a loaf of bread? My brother's demonstrations would compel us to overrule *Commonwealth v. Valjean*, and many other precedents that have been built on that case. . . .

I have given this case the best thought of which I am capable. . . . When I feel myself inclined to accept the view of my brother Foster, I am repelled by a feeling that his arguments are intellectually unsound and approach mere rationalization. On the other hand, when I incline toward upholding the conviction, I am struck by the absurdity of directing that these men be put to death when their lives have been saved at the cost of the lives of ten heroic workmen. It is to me a matter of regret that the Prosecutor saw fit to ask for an indictment for murder. If we had a provision in our statutes making it a crime to eat human flesh, that would have been a more appropriate charge. If no other charge suited to the facts of this case could be brought against the defendants, it would have been wiser, I think, not to have indicted them at all. . . .

Since I have been wholly unable to resolve the doubts that beset me about the law of this case, . . . I declare my withdrawal from the decision of this case.

Keen, J.

I should like to begin by setting to one side two questions which are not before this Court.

The first of these is whether executive clemency should be extended to these defendants if the conviction is affirmed. Under our system of government, that is a question for the Chief Executive, not for us. . . . The second question that I wish to put to one side is that of deciding whether what these men did was "right" or "wrong," "wicked" or "good." That is also a question that is irrelevant to the discharge of my office as a judge sworn to apply, not my conceptions of morality, but the law of the land. . . .

The sole question before us for decision is whether these defendants did, within the meaning of N.C.S.A. §12-A, willfully take the life of Roger Whetmore. The exact language of the statute is as follows: "Whoever shall willfully take the life of another shall be punished by death." Now I should suppose that any candid observer, content to extract from these words their natural meaning, would concede at once that these defendants did "willfully take the life" of Roger Whetmore.

Whence arise all the difficulties of the case, then, and the necessity for so many pages of discussion about what ought to be so obvious? The difficulties, in whatever tortured form they may present themselves, all trace back to a single source, and that is a failure to distinguish the legal from the moral aspects of this case. To put it bluntly, my brothers do not like the fact that the written law requires the conviction of these defendants. Neither do I, but unlike my brothers I respect the obligations of [my] office. . . .

There was a time in this Commonwealth when judges did in fact legislate very freely, and all of us know that during that period some of our statutes were rather thoroughly made over by the judiciary. . . . [C]ivil war . . . arose out of the conflict between the judiciary, on the one hand, and the executive and the legislature, on the other. There is no need to recount here the factors that contributed to that unseemly struggle for power. . . . It is enough to observe that those days are behind us, and that in place of the uncertainty that then reigned we now have a clear-cut principle, which is the supremacy of the legislative branch of our government. . . .

Though the principle of the supremacy of the legislature has been accepted in theory for centuries, such is the tenacity of professional tradition and the force of fixed habits of thought that many of the judiciary have still not accommodated themselves to the restricted role which the new order imposes on them. My brother Foster is one of that group; his way of dealing with statutes is exactly that of a judge living in the 3900's. . . .

We are all familiar with the process by which the judicial reform of disfavored legislative enactments is accomplished. . . . [That process] requires three steps. The first of these is to divine some single "purpose" which the statute serves. This is done although not one statute in a hundred has any such single purpose. . . . The second step is to discover that a mythical being called "the legislator," in the pursuit of this imagined "purpose," overlooked something or left some gap or imperfection in his work. Then comes the final and most refreshing part of the task, which is, of course, to fill in the blank thus created. . . .

My brother Foster's penchant for finding holes in statutes reminds one of the story told by an ancient author about the man who ate a pair of shoes. Asked how he liked them, he replied that the part he liked best was the holes. That is the way my brother feels about statutes; the more holes they have in them the better he likes them. In short, he doesn't like statutes.

. . . My brother thinks he knows exactly what was sought when men made murder a crime, and that was something he calls "deterrence." . . . I doubt very much whether our statute making murder a crime really has a "purpose" in any ordinary sense of the term. Primarily, such a statute reflects a deeply-felt human conviction that murder is wrong and that something should be done to the man who commits it. If we were forced to be more articulate about the matter, we would probably take refuge in the more sophisticated theories of the criminologists, which, of course, were certainly not in the minds of those who drafted our statute. We might also observe that men will do their own work more effectively and live happier lives if they are protected against the threat of violent assault. . . .

If we do not know the purpose of §12-A, how can we possibly say there is a "gap" in it? How can we know what its draftsmen thought about the question of killing men in order to eat them? My brother Tatting has revealed an understandable, though perhaps slightly exaggerated revulsion to cannibalism. How do we know that his remote ancestors did not feel the same revulsion to an even higher degree? . . . Perhaps it was for that very reason that our ancestors expressed their prohibition in so broad and unqualified a form. All of this is conjecture, of course, but it remains abundantly clear that [none of us] knows what the "purpose" of §12-A is.

. . . As in dealing with the statute, so in dealing with the exception, the question is not the conjectural purpose of the rule, but its scope. Now the scope of the exception in favor of self-defense as it has been applied by this Court is plain: it applies to cases of resisting an aggressive threat to the party's own life. It is therefore too clear for argument that this case does not fall within the scope of the exception, since it is plain that Whetmore made no threat against the lives of these defendants. . . .

I conclude that the conviction should be affirmed.

HANDY, J.

. . . The problem before us is what we, as officers of the government, ought to do with these defendants. That is a question of practical wisdom, to be exercised in a context, not of abstract theory, but of human realities. When the case is approached in this light, it becomes, I think, one of the easiest to decide that has ever been argued before this Court. . . . In order to demonstrate this I shall have to introduce certain realities that my brothers in their coy decorum have seen fit to pass over in silence, although they are just as acutely aware of them as I am.

The first of these is that this case has aroused an enormous public interest, both here and abroad. . . . One of the great newspaper chains made a poll of public opinion on the question, "What do you think the Supreme Court should do with the Speluncean explorers?" About ninety per cent expressed a belief that the defendants should be pardoned or let off with a kind of token punishment. It is perfectly clear, then, how the public feels about the case. We could have known this without the poll, of course, on the basis of common sense, or even by observing that on this Court there are apparently four-and-a-half men, or ninety per cent, who share the common opinion.

This makes it obvious, not only what we should do, but what we must do if we are to preserve between ourselves and public opinion a reasonable and decent accord. Declaring these men innocent need not involve us in any undignified quibble or trick. . . . Certainly no layman would think that in letting these men off we had stretched the statute any more than our ancestors did when they created the excuse of self-defense. . . .

Now I know that my brothers will be horrified by my suggestion that this Court should take account of public opinion. They will tell you that public opinion is emotional and capricious. . . . They will tell you that the law surrounds the trial of a case like this with elaborate safeguards, designed to insure that the truth will be known and that every rational consideration bearing on the issues of the case has been taken into account. They will warn you that all of these safeguards go for naught if a mass opinion formed outside this framework is allowed to have any influence on our decision.

But let us look candidly at some of the realities of the administration of our criminal law. When a man is accused of crime, there are, speaking generally, four ways in which he may escape punishment. One of these is a determination by a judge that under the applicable law he has committed no crime. This is, of course, a determination that takes place in a rather formal and abstract atmosphere. But look at the other three ways in which he may escape punishment. These are: (1) a decision by the Prosecutor not to ask for an indictment; (2) an acquittal by the jury; (3) a pardon or commutation of sentence by the executive. Can anyone pretend that these decisions are held within a rigid and formal framework of rules that prevents factual error, excludes emotional and personal factors, and guarantees that all the forms of the law will be observed?

. . . In the normal course of events the case now before us would have gone on all of its issues directly to the jury. Had this occurred we can be confident that there would have been an acquittal or at least a division that would have prevented a conviction. . . . Of course the only reason that didn't occur in this case was the fortuitous circumstance that the foreman of the jury happened to be a lawyer. His learning enabled him to devise a [procedure] that would allow the jury to dodge its usual responsibilities. . . .

I come now to the most crucial fact in this case, a fact known to all of us . . . [but] that my brothers have seen fit to keep under the cover of their judicial robes. This is the frightening likelihood that if the issue is left to him, the Chief Executive will refuse to pardon these men or commute their sentence. As we all know, our Chief Executive is a man now well advanced in years, of very stiff notions. Public clamor usually operates on him with the reverse of the effect intended. . . . [H]e is firmly determined not to commute the sentence if these men are found to have violated the law. . . .

. . . I conclude that the defendants are innocent of the crime charged, and that the conviction and sentence should be set aside. . . .

* * *

The Supreme Court being evenly divided, the conviction and sentence of the Court of General Instances is affirmed. It is ordered that the execution of the sentence shall occur at 6:00 A.M., Friday, April 2, 4300, at which time the Public Executioner is directed to proceed with all convenient dispatch to hang each of the defendants by the neck until he is dead.

POSTSCRIPT

Now that the court has spoken its judgment, the reader puzzled by the choice of date may wish to be reminded that the centuries which separate us from the year 4300 are roughly equal to those that have passed since the Age of Pericles. There is probably no need to observe that the Speluncean Case itself is intended neither as a work of satire nor as a prediction in any ordinary sense of the term. As for the judges who make up Chief Justice Truepenny's court, they are, of course, as mythical as the facts and precedents with which they deal. . . . The case was constructed for the sole purpose of bringing into a common focus certain divergent philosophies of law and government. These philosophies presented men with live questions of choice in the days of Plato and Aristotle. Perhaps they will continue to do so when our era has had its say about them. If there is any element of prediction in the case, it does not go beyond a suggestion that the questions involved are among the permanent problems of the human race.

Notes and Questions

1. As Fuller's postscript suggests, *Speluncean Explorers* was written to highlight "certain divergent philosophies of law and government," not to discuss the manner in which courts decide whether criminal defendants deserve to be punished. In *Dudley & Stephens*, the moral character of the defendants' conduct and the utility of punishing them were the chief issues before the court. The chief issue before the Supreme Court of Newgarth, by contrast, was the allocation of power between judges and legislators. *Dudley & Stephens* exemplifies common-law crime definition. *Speluncean Explorers* exemplifies the debate — there is no clear resolution, either in Fuller's imaginary world or in our real one — about the enterprise of defining crimes in a system in which legislators are the primary lawmakers.

2. Recall that, when judges decide criminal cases, they write opinions to justify their decisions. Legislators cast votes but are not required to justify those votes. Judges cite precedents for their decisions; legislators need not do so. Should these differences affect the manner in which judges interpret statutes? Justice Keen would say no: Judges should follow the relevant statutory text, regardless of its underlying principles (or lack thereof). How would the other justices on Fuller's fictitious court answer the same question?

3. Arguably, one fact underlies all criminal legislation—the same fact that motivated Justice Handy: public opinion. To say that criminal law should be governed by legislatures rather than courts is to say that criminal law should be defined democratically. Should it be? Or should crimes be defined according to moral principle rather than voters' preferences? Perhaps those are the wrong questions to ask: Outside New England and Hawaii, judges too are elected officials, as are the District Attorneys whose offices prosecute the overwhelming majority of criminal cases in the United States. It would seem to follow that criminal law follows public opinion regardless of who defines it. Is there any reason to care whether elected judges or elected legislators define criminal law?

4. In a portion of his hypothetical opinion not excerpted above, Justice Foster argued that the defendants should be judged only by the contract they made with one another. Foster maintained that all law is the product of social contracts by which men and women agree to be bound by the rules that the majority of the voting population enacts. Given the extreme circumstances in which the defendants found themselves, Foster argued, they were no longer bound by the contract that gave rise to the laws of Newgarth:

> Had the tragic events of this case taken place a mile beyond the territorial limits of our Commonwealth, no one would pretend that our law was applicable to them. . . . If we look to the purposes of law and government, and to the premises underlying our positive law, these men when they made their fateful decision were as remote from our legal order as if they had been a thousand miles beyond our boundaries.

Judged by their own agreement, he concluded, the defendants were innocent of any crime. Are you persuaded? Few crimes happen in circumstances as extreme as those in *Dudley & Stephens* or *Speluncean Explorers*, but many crimes happen in circumstances the legislature never considered when enacting the relevant criminal statutes. That would seem to be an argument for giving judges a great deal of leeway when interpreting criminal statutes. Is the argument sound? Is it fair to hold defendants like Whetmore's killers to laws they cannot obey, made for circumstances that lawmakers never imagined?

5. Judges are bound to see cases in which a legally valid statute requires a decision the judges believe is wrong. What should a conscientious judge do in such a case? The late Robert Cover wrote an excellent book about this subject. See Robert Cover, Justice Accused: Antislavery and the Judicial Process (1975). As his title suggests, Cover studied the behavior of antislavery judges in pre-Civil War America. A few such judges resigned rather than enforce the law of slavery; many enforced that law as they would enforce any other body of law. The judges on whom Cover focuses the most attention are those who used the law to defeat the law—that is, they used legal procedures and formalities to promote freedom in the teeth of legal rules that protected slavery.

6. The questions raised in *Speluncean Explorers* arise not only in law review articles and old English cases, but in contemporary American court decisions as well. Consider the form those issues take in the next case.

People v. Kellogg

California Court of Appeals, Fourth Appellate District
119 Cal. App. 4th 593; 14 Cal. Rptr. 3d 507 (2004)

HALLER, J.

Thomas Kellogg contends his public intoxication conviction constitutes constitutionally proscribed cruel and/or unusual punishment because his status as an involuntarily homeless, chronic alcoholic makes it impossible for him to avoid being intoxicated in public. We reject this contention. . . .

FACTUAL AND PROCEDURAL BACKGROUND

. . . On January 10, 2002, Officer Heidi Hawley, a member of the Homeless Outreach Team,[1] responded to a citizen's complaint of homeless persons camping under bridges and along State Route 163. She found Kellogg sitting on the ground in some bushes on the embankment off the freeway. Kellogg appeared inebriated and was largely incoherent. He was rocking back and forth, talking to himself and gesturing. Officer Hawley arrested Kellogg for public intoxication. He had $445 in his pocket from [a recently cashed disability check]. . . .

After his arrest . . . , Kellogg posted $104 cash bail and was released. Because he was homeless, he was not notified of his court date and he did not appear for his January 31 arraignment. A warrant for his arrest was issued on February 11, 2002; he was arrested again for public intoxication on February 19 and 27 and subsequently charged with three violations of [Penal Code] section 647(f). . . .

Kellogg pleaded not guilty and filed a motion to dismiss the charges based on his constitutional right to be free of cruel and unusual punishment.

[At a hearing on that motion,] psychologist Gregg Michel and psychiatrist Terry Schwartz testified on behalf of Kellogg. These experts explained that . . . [i]n addition to his severe alcohol dependence, which causes him

---

1. The Homeless Outreach Team consists of police officers, social services technicians, and psychiatric technicians.

to suffer withdrawal symptoms if he stops drinking, [Kellogg] suffers from dementia, long-term cognitive impairment, schizoid personality disorder, and symptoms of post-traumatic stress disorder. He has a history of seizure disorder and a closed head injury, and reported anxiety, depressive symptoms and chronic pain. He is estranged from his family. Physically, he has peripheral edema, gastritis, acute liver damage, and ulcerative colitis requiring him to wear a colostomy bag. To treat his various conditions and symptoms he has been prescribed Klonopin and Vicodin and may suffer from addiction to medication.

Dr. Michel opined that Kellogg was gravely disabled and incapable of providing for his basic needs, and that his degree of dysfunction was life-threatening. His mental deficits impeded his executive functioning (planning, making judgments) and memory. Dr. Michel described Kellogg as having "good immediate reality contact," struggling to express himself but lacking the ability to do so. . . .

Drs. Michel and Schwartz opined that Kellogg's homelessness was not a matter of choice but a result of his gravely disabled mental condition. His chronic alcoholism and cognitive impairment made it nearly impossible for him to obtain and maintain an apartment without significant help and support. Dr. Michel stated Kellogg would not be a suitable candidate for out-patient treatment but required long-term in-patient treatment at a locked facility. Because Kellogg needed a program geared towards a person with dual conditions of substance dependence and mental disorder, he was not an appropriate candidate for a typical in-patient substance abuse program. . . .

. . . Dr. Schwartz stated that Kellogg had been offered various forms of treatment and housing but had not made use of those resources. . . . Dr. Schwartz explained that for a person with Kellogg's conditions, crowded homeless shelters can be psychologically disturbing and trigger post-traumatic stress or anxiety symptoms, causing the person to prefer to hide in a bush where minimal interactions with people would occur. Additionally, a homeless person such as Kellogg, particularly when intoxicated, might refuse offers of assistance from authorities because he has difficulty trusting people and fears his situation, although bad at present, will worsen.

In Dr. Michel's view, Kellogg's incarceration provided some limited benefit in that he obtained medication for seizures, did not have access to alcohol, received some treatment, and was more stable during incarceration than he was when homeless on the streets. However, such treatment was insufficient to be therapeutic, and medications prescribed for inmate management purposes can be highly addictive and might not be medically appropriate. Dr. Schwartz opined that incarceration was not an effective form of treatment. Although incarceration provided a period of abstention from alcohol, it did not provide the necessary additional treatments, especially for individuals with mental disorders. . . .

Testifying for the prosecution, Physician James Dunford stated that at the jail facility, medical staff assess the arrestee's condition and provide treatment as needed, including vitamins for nutritional needs and medication to control alcohol withdrawal symptoms or other diseases such as hypertension, seizure disorders, and diabetes. Consistent with this protocol, on February 28, 2002, Kellogg was evaluated at intake by the jail nursing staff, who found him covered with feces and resisting efforts to assess his medical condition. On March 2, the jail medical staff delineated a treatment plan for Kellogg, which included assistance with his colostomy bag, ongoing treatment of his alcohol withdrawal, medication to address his reports of pain, evaluation of the existence of and appropriate medication for seizure disorder, and support to overcome the conditions that cause him to become disheveled and foul-smelling. On March 7, the medical staff assessed that Kellogg appeared well and in no distress and no longer had alcohol withdrawal as his primary complaint. . . . Dr. Dunford opined that between March 2 and 7, Kellogg's condition had improved because his seizure medicine was restarted, his alcohol withdrawal was treated, his vital signs were stable, his colostomy bag was clean and intact, his overall cleanliness was restored, and he was interacting with people in a normal way.

After the presentation of evidence, the trial court found that Kellogg suffers from both chronic alcohol dependence and a mental disorder and was homeless at the time of his arrests. Further, his alcohol dependence is both physical and psychological and causes him to be unable to stop drinking or to engage in rational choice-making. Finding that before his arrest Kellogg was offered assistance on at least three occasions and that his medical condition improved while in custody, the court denied the motion to dismiss the charges.

On April 2, 2002, the court found Kellogg guilty of one charge of violating section 647(f) arising from his conduct on January 10, 2002. . . . [The court sentenced Kellogg to 180 days in jail, but suspended the sentence on condition that Kellogg complete an alcohol treatment program and return to court on June 4 to report on his status. Kellogg did not satisfy those conditions, and was arrested for public drunkenness twice more in May 2002. The court therefore ordered that Kellogg serve the 180-day sentence of incarceration. Kellogg appealed.]

DISCUSSION

Section 647(f) defines the misdemeanor offense of disorderly conduct by public intoxication as occurring when a person

> "is found in any public place under the influence of intoxicating liquor . . . in such a condition that he or she is unable to exercise care for his or her own safety or the safety of others, or by reason of his or her being under the influence of intoxicating liquor . . . interferes with or obstructs or prevents the free use of any street, sidewalk, or other public way."

Kellogg argues that this statute, as applied to him, constitutes cruel and/or unusual punishment prohibited by the Eighth Amendment to the federal Constitution and article 1, section 17 of the California Constitution. He asserts that his chronic alcoholism and mental condition have rendered him involuntarily homeless and that it is impossible for him to avoid being in public while intoxicated. He argues because his public intoxication is a result of his illness and beyond his control, it is inhumane for the state to [punish him for the results of] his condition. . . .

It is well settled that it is cruel and unusual punishment to impose criminal liability on a person merely for having the disease of addiction. Robinson v. California, 370 U.S. 660, 666-67 (1962). In *Robinson*, the United States Supreme Court invalidated a California statute which made it a misdemeanor to "be addicted to the use of narcotics." Id. at 660. The *Robinson* Court recognized that a state's broad power to provide for the public health and welfare made it constitutionally permissible for it to regulate the use and sale of narcotics, including, for example, such measures as penal sanctions for addicts who refuse to cooperate with compulsory treatment programs. But the Court found the California penal statute unconstitutional because it did not require possession or use of narcotics, or disorderly behavior resulting from narcotics, but rather imposed criminal liability for the mere status of being addicted. Id. at 665-66. . . .

In Powell v. Texas, 392 U.S. 514 (1968), the United States Supreme Court, in a five-to-four decision, declined to extend [*Robinson*] to . . . a chronic alcoholic [convicted] of public intoxication, reasoning that the defendant was not convicted merely for being a chronic alcoholic, but rather for being in public while drunk. Id. at 532. That is, the state was not punishing the defendant for his mere status, but rather was imposing "a criminal sanction for public behavior which may create substantial health and safety hazards, both for [the defendant] and for members of the general public." Ibid. In [Justice Marshall's plurality opinion], four justices rejected the proposition set forth by four dissenting justices that it was unconstitutional to punish conduct that was involuntary or "occasioned by a compulsion."

The fifth justice in the *Powell* [majority], Justice White, concurred in the result only, . . . [in part because] the record did not show the defendant (who had a home) suffered from any inability to refrain from drinking in public. Id. at 553-54 (White, J., concurring in the judgment). Justice White opined that punishing a homeless alcoholic for public drunkenness could constitute unconstitutional punishment if it was impossible for the person to resist drunkenness in a public place. Id. at 551. Relying on Justice White's concurring opinion, Kellogg argues Justice White, who was the deciding vote in *Powell*, would have sided with the dissenting justices had the circumstances of his case (i.e., an involuntarily homeless chronic alcoholic) been presented. . . .

We are not persuaded. Although in *Robinson* the United States Supreme Court held it was constitutionally impermissible to punish for the mere *condition* of addiction, the court was careful to limit . . . its decision by pointing out that a state may permissibly punish disorderly conduct resulting from the use of narcotics. This limitation was recognized and refined by the plurality opinion in *Powell,* where the court held it was permissible for a state to impose criminal punishment when the addict engages in *conduct* which spills into public areas. . . .

Here, the reason Kellogg was subjected to misdemeanor [liability] for being intoxicated in public was not because of his *condition* of being a homeless alcoholic, but rather because of his *conduct* that posed a safety hazard. If Kellogg had merely been drunk in public in a manner that did *not* pose a safety hazard (i.e., if he was able to exercise care for his own and the public's safety and was not blocking a public way), he could not have been adjudicated guilty under section 647(f). The state has a legitimate need to control public drunkenness when it creates a safety hazard. It would be neither safe nor humane to allow intoxicated persons to stumble into busy streets or to lie unchecked on sidewalks, driveways, parking lots, streets, and other such public areas where they could be trampled upon, tripped over, or run over by cars. The facts of Kellogg's public intoxication in the instant case show a clear potential for such harm. He was found sitting in bushes on a freeway embankment in an inebriated state. It is not difficult to imagine the serious possibility of danger to himself or others had he wandered off the embankment onto the freeway. . . .

. . . [A]lthough the California Supreme Court has not expressly decided the issue of whether section 647(f) may be unconstitutional as applied to certain chronic alcoholics, it has rejected an attempt to civilly enjoin enforcement of the statute based on an argument that the statute resulted in cruel and/or unusual punishment as applied to chronic, homeless alcoholics. Sundance v. Municipal Court, 42 Cal. 3d 1101, 1119-21, 729 P.2d 80 (1986). The *Sundance* court acknowledged the trial court's finding that "[m]any alcoholics . . . cannot refrain from appearing in public while intoxicated" because "they are indigent and homeless." Id. at 1114. Nevertheless, . . . the court concluded that section 647(f) did not impose constitutionally excessive sentences based on the repeated convictions of chronic alcoholics for public intoxication. The court noted the maximum sentence that could be imposed for a single violation of section 647(f) was six months. While recognizing that civil detoxification facilities may be a wiser policy choice, the *Sundance* court also concluded it was not *constitutionally* mandated that chronic alcoholics be sent to such facilities in lieu of jail. . . . Id. at 1125-27, 1131-32 & n.13.

Based on the guidance provided by *Powell* and *Sundance,* we conclude that the California Legislature's decision to allow misdemeanor culpability for public intoxication, even as applied to a homeless chronic alcoholic such as Kellogg, is neither disproportionate to the offense nor inhumane. . . . To the extent Kellogg has no choice but to be drunk in public given the nature of his impairments, his culpability is low; however, the penal sanctions imposed on him under section 647(f) are correspondingly low. Given the state's interest in providing for the safety of its citizens, including Kellogg, imposition of low-level criminal sanctions for Kellogg's conduct does not tread on the federal or state constitutional proscriptions against cruel and/or unusual punishment. . . .

. . . It may be true that the safety concerns arising from public intoxication can be addressed by means of civil custody rather than penal sanctions. . . . However, the Legislature has not seen fit to remove the option of criminal prosecution and conviction. Absent a constitutional violation, it is not our role to second-guess this policy determination. . . .

The judgment is affirmed.

McDONALD, J., dissenting.

. . . The scope of the California Constitution's prohibition of cruel or unusual punishment is not well-defined. . . . Nevertheless, the California Supreme Court has consistently followed the principle that "a sentence is cruel or unusual as applied to a particular defendant . . . [when] the punishment shocks the conscience and offends fundamental notions of human dignity. . . ." People v. Cox, 30 Cal. 4th 916, 969-70, 70 P.3d 277 (2003). . . .

A section 647(f) public intoxication offense, both in the abstract and as committed by Kellogg, is a nonviolent, fairly innocuous offense. . . . Kellogg was found intoxicated sitting under a bush in a public area. He was rocking back and forth, talking to himself and gesturing. The record does not show that Kellogg's public intoxication posed a danger to other persons or society in general. His motive in drinking presumably was merely to fulfill his physical and psychological compulsion as an alcoholic to become intoxicated. Because Kellogg . . . did not have the alternative of being intoxicated in private, he did not have any specific purpose or motive to be intoxicated in a *public* place. Rather, it was his only option.

. . . [T]he record shows Kellogg is involuntarily homeless and a chronic alcoholic with a past head injury who suffers from dementia, severe cognitive impairment, and a schizoid personality disorder.[17] As an involuntarily homeless person, Kellogg cannot avoid appearing in public. As a chronic alcoholic, he cannot stop drinking and being intoxicated. Therefore, Kellogg cannot avoid being intoxicated in a public place.

Based on the nature of the offense and the offender, Kellogg's section 647(f) public intoxication conviction "shocks the conscience and offends fundamental notions of human dignity," and therefore constitutes cruel or unusual punishment in violation of article I, section 17 of the California Constitution. . . .

---

17. At the time of the instant offense, Kellogg was 44 years old. His extensive criminal history consists primarily of public intoxication offenses.

Notes and Questions

1. For the most part, the Eighth Amendment's ban on "cruel and unusual punishments" limits criminal sentences, not the definition of particular crimes. Along with *Kellogg*, Robinson v. California, 370 U.S. 660 (1962), and Powell v. Texas, 392 U.S. 514 (1968), are among the small number of court decisions that discuss the possibility that *any* punishment for some offenses would be "cruel and unusual." Under *Robinson*, the government cannot criminalize drug addiction, though it can criminally punish the possession or purchase of illegal drugs. *Powell* held that the government could criminally punish public drunkenness, in a case in which the defendant had a home. Because of his alcohol addiction, *Robinson* seemed to help Kellogg's Eighth Amendment claim. Because of his homelessness, *Powell* seemed not to foreclose that argument—at least, not until the Fourth District Court of Appeals decided *Kellogg*. *Robinson* and *Powell* are discussed in more detail infra, at pages 57-59.

2. Notice two key differences between *Kellogg* and *Dudley & Stephens*. Where Tom Dudley argued that his conduct did not constitute murder and hence did not violate the relevant criminal law, Kellogg (or more precisely, his lawyer) argued that the state could not punish him even though his conduct *did* violate the relevant criminal law. Since England had no written constitution, no such argument was possible in *Dudley & Stephens*. The second key difference follows from the first. Justice Haller's majority opinion in *Kellogg* says little about why punishing the defendant is fair or appropriate. Instead, Justice Haller—a former prosecutor himself—took for granted that, if the state and federal constitutions did not forbid Kellogg's punishment, section 647(f) required it. The question whether punishing Kellogg was morally reasonable or economically sound was answered not by the court but by the California legislature. In *Dudley & Stephens*, the appropriateness of criminal punishment was the court's decision.

3. Suppose the California legislature that enacted Penal Code §647(f) could decide whether Kellogg should be punished. How would the legislators vote? Should the answer matter? Suppose the public could be polled about their views on the question whether homeless alcoholics should be subject to criminal punishment. Should those poll results matter? Was Lon Fuller's fictitious Justice Handy right about public opinion and criminal law?

4. Now suppose the *Kellogg* court had held that homeless alcoholics cannot be convicted of public drunkenness, since that crime is largely the consequence of their condition, not their moral choices. As a practical matter, California's ban on public drunkenness would then apply to most Californians but not to Kellogg. Is that fair? Imagine that some future defendant with Kellogg's condition is charged with theft; defense counsel argues that the defendant could not possibly avoid stealing, since he had no other means of obtaining the food and liquor his body craves. If Kellogg had won, that argument might win too. Is *that* fair?

5. The use of criminal sanctions against homeless persons is common in modern America. So, increasingly, are constitutional challenges to the existence or enforcement of such laws. In addition to public intoxication statutes like the one at issue in *Kellogg*, state laws and municipal ordinances frequently prohibit sleeping or camping in public places, sleeping in cars, sitting or lying down at certain times in certain public places (such as parks), storing personal possessions in public places, "aggressive" begging or panhandling (the modifier has been added because panhandling as such has been held to be protected speech under the First Amendment), loitering, and even distributing food to the homeless in public places. See National Law Center on Homelessness & Poverty, "No Safe Place: The Criminalization of Homelessness in U.S. Cities" (2014) (listing current state and local criminal laws addressing such "undesirable" public behaviors of homeless persons), available online at https://www.nlchp.org/documents/No_Safe_Place.

In August 2015, the U.S. Department of Justice filed a "Statement of Interest" in the case of *Bell v. City of Boise*, a lawsuit filed in federal district court by homeless persons against the city of Boise, Idaho. The lawsuit challenged city ordinances that, inter alia, criminalized "camping"—defined as "the use of public property as a temporary or permanent place of dwelling . . . or as a living accommodation at any time between sunset and sunrise . . . ." According to the Justice Department's filing:

> On any given night in the United States, half a million people are likely to be experiencing homelessness. Homeless individuals are a diverse population, including children, families, veterans, and the elderly. The causes of homelessness are also varied. In recent years, some people who were affected by the economic downturn and foreclosure crisis have become homeless. Some homeless individuals have serious and persistent physical or behavioral health conditions that neither they nor the communities in which they live have sufficient services to accommodate. As a result, these individuals are unable to obtain permanent housing. Other individuals are homeless because of circumstances beyond their control; they are victims of domestic violence and trafficking, or youth who are separated from their families. These individuals must find space in a public shelter or sleep on the street.
>
> For many homeless people, finding a safe and legal place to sleep can be difficult or even impossible. In many cities, shelters are unable to accommodate all who are homeless. In 2014, 42% of homeless individuals slept in unsheltered, public locations—under bridges, in cars, in parks, on the sidewalk, or in abandoned buildings.
>
> In this case, Plaintiffs are homeless individuals who were convicted of violating certain city ordinances that prohibit camping and sleeping in public outdoor places. They claim that the City of Boise and the Boise Police Department's ("BPD") enforcement of these ordinances against homeless individuals violates their constitutional rights because there is inadequate shelter space available in Boise to accommodate the city's homeless population. Plaintiffs argue that criminalizing public sleeping in a city without adequate

shelter space constitutes criminalizing homelessness itself, in violation of the Eighth Amendment.

. . . [T]he Court should consider whether conforming one's conduct to the ordinance is possible for people who are homeless. If sufficient shelter space is unavailable because (a) there are inadequate beds for the entire population, or (b) there are restrictions on those beds that disqualify certain groups of homeless individuals (e.g., because of disability access or exceeding maximum stay requirements), then it would be impossible for some homeless individuals to comply with these ordinances. As set forth below, in those circumstances enforcement of the ordinances amounts to the criminalization of homelessness, in violation of the Eighth Amendment.

See Statement of Interest, U.S. Department of Justice, available online at https://www.justice.gov/crt/file/761211/download.

On September 29, 2015, the federal lawsuit was dismissed. The district court based the dismissal on a lack of standing by any of the named plaintiffs, because there was "no known citation of a homeless individual under the Ordinances for camping or sleeping on public property on any night or morning when he or she was unable to secure shelter due to a lack of shelter capacity." The court explained, however, that the dismissal "does not reach the underlying merits of the Plaintiffs' Eighth Amendment claims." See Memorandum of Decision and Order, Martin v. City of Boise, Case No. 1:09-cv-00540-REB, available online at https://cases.justia.com/federal/district-courts/idaho/iddce/1:2009cv00540/24902/298/0.pdf?ts=1443613543.

If you were a state or local legislator, how would you deal with constituent complaints about the public behavior of homeless persons? If you were a judge — and assuming that there was no problem of standing — how would you deal with the merits of a constitutional challenge like the one in *Bell v. City of Boise*? Is criminal law really the best solution for the problem of homelessness in America?

Notes on the Purposes of Criminal Punishment (Reprise)

1. Recall the trio of standard justifications for criminal punishment: retribution, deterrence, and rehabilitation. Those justifications do not easily fit cases like *Kellogg*. Kellogg committed no serious moral wrong that requires punishment; hence there is no need for retribution in his case. As for deterrence, homeless alcoholics are not likely to respond well to deterrent signals. If Dudley and Stephens were effectively undeterrable, surely Kellogg is. Rehabilitation is hard to imagine: Kellogg might be cleaned up for a time, but as soon as he is released, the behavior that prompted his arrest will recur.

2. Perhaps those familiar purposes of punishment do not fit the facts of *Kellogg* because the California legislature did not have those purposes in mind when it enacted section 647(f). Three very different justifications for locking up criminals probably matter more to legislators: avoiding private vengeance, regulating the otherwise hard-to-regulate misconduct of the poor, and defining a society's values and culture. That second trio of justifications explains *Kellogg* a good deal better than the first.

3. Take them in turn. One of the most basic functions of organized government is the suppression of private violence. If the government declined to punish private misconduct, the victims of that misconduct and their friends might do the punishing. That leads to rule by vigilantes carrying out personal vendettas. Private "justice" of that sort is likely to be rough at best: Vigilantes are not scrupulous about affording their victims due process, so their error rate is likely to be high. One reason why governments might punish crime is to avoid that state of affairs. In other words, criminal punishment is designed not just to protect the law-abiding portion of society from criminals, but also to protect criminals—and those who might be mistaken for criminals—from the law-abiding portion of society.

At first blush, that idea seems to apply to classic street crimes like robbery or murder, but not to *Kellogg*. If the state does not avenge serious wrongs to personal safety and private property, the victims of those wrongs will. But Kellogg hasn't injured anyone or stolen any private property. His crimes appear to be victimless: His behavior harmed himself, but no one else. The truth is more complicated. If homeless alcoholics can set up residence in public spaces and behave as Kellogg did, most ordinary citizens will avoid those public spaces. People who own businesses in or near those spaces will lose customers. That will generate anger. Plus, some people *can't* avoid those public spaces, and some of them will find Kellogg's presence frightening. (Would you find it frightening?) In large measure, fear stems from unpredictability, and people who abuse drugs and alcohol seem unpredictable to the rest of the population. If the government tolerates behavior like Kellogg's, business owners and frightened individuals might take matters into their own hands. That would not be good news for the Kelloggs of the world.

4. This leads to the second justification. Kellogg has no significant assets and has difficulty making rational decisions. Financial penalties cannot deter him. Some economists argue that criminal punishment is a necessary deterrent only when conventional civil penalties like money damages cannot work—as is the case when the targets of regulation are judgment-proof (meaning that they do not have enough assets to pay damages or a substantial fine). If the justice system followed that logic rigidly, prisons and jails would be filled with poor people. The crimes of the middle and upper classes would not be crimes at all—they would be dealt with by civil liability rules.

That would strike many people as offensive. Why should the rich be punished with damage bills when the poor are locked up? It's a fair question. Whatever the right answer may be, in practice, America's justice system adheres more closely to that economic model than one might suppose. Theft and criminal violence are torts as well as crimes, but one rarely sees civil lawsuits arising from such incidents—the lawsuits would do no good, since the offenders rarely have assets sufficient to pay damage bills, and most insurance policies bar payment for the consequences of criminal conduct. Meanwhile, financial misconduct is usually dealt with through civil fines and lawsuits. Prosecutors tend to go light on behavior that the civil justice system can handle, and focus their energies on conduct that won't be deterred unless it is criminally punished.

Once again, that principle seems not to apply to Kellogg—his condition makes him undeterrable. But there are different forms of deterrence. Kellogg's conduct may not be affected by the *threat* of legal penalties. But his conduct is powerfully affected when he is actually locked up. Even when criminal punishment's threat value is low, there may be sizeable social benefits from incapacitating individual defendants who cannot be deterred in any other fashion. That proposition tends to apply most strongly to the poor and sick—that is, to people like Kellogg.

5. The third justification—the use of criminal punishment to reaffirm society's values and to define its public culture—may be the most important one. Societies define themselves by their cultures: Because different civilizations value different things, the character of art, commerce, politics, and social life all vary widely across time and place. Free societies tend to leave most such matters to individual choice. But even the freest societies regulate a wide range of consensual conduct in the interest of promoting particular kinds of culture and suppressing other kinds. For most of American history, consensual sex outside of heterosexual marriage was a crime. A wide range of vices—gambling, prostitution, the production of pornography, the manufacture and sale of alcohol, the purchase and possession of various narcotics—have been criminalized over the past two centuries, and many of them still are.

At some periods, including our own, some of those vices have dominated criminal litigation: During Prohibition, one-quarter of all prison inmates were incarcerated on liquor charges. A slightly smaller proportion of today's prison population is incarcerated for drug crimes. Perhaps the prison system of the future will incarcerate large numbers of cigarette smokers—smoking is already banned in most public places, and while banning it everywhere seems implausible today, the same was true of other vices before their prohibitions were enacted. Criminal laws such as the ones just mentioned might be defended on many grounds, but the primary reason why vices are criminalized is the belief that the behavior in question is wrong, along with the desire to avoid having the wrong infect the culture.

In theory, protecting the culture need not require regulating private conduct. What people do behind closed doors with like-minded friends and lovers has no effect on the society that surrounds them—again, in theory. In practice, the line between private and public conduct is murkier than that. High-end prostitution networks conduct business by phone and behind closed doors, but the business still affects local street life. Nearby residents are not as tolerant of the relevant transactions as liberal political theory suggests they should be. The same is true of the other vices mentioned in the preceding paragraph. America's criminal justice system has long devoted a substantial amount of energy and resources to cultural regulation. Such regulation ensures that criminal law will define the line between public and private life.

6. Recall that roughly 90 percent of robberies reported to the police go unpunished. That percentage was probably similar in nineteenth-century England. Does it make sense to punish people like Dudley, Stephens, and Kellogg when the large majority of serious crimes escape punishment? Is *all* criminal punishment unfair, given how selectively the government prosecutes and punishes crime?

B. PROPORTIONALITY AND VAGUENESS

In America today, as a general matter, legislatures play the dominant role in initially defining crimes and in establishing the range of applicable sentences for those crimes. Judges, however, must interpret and apply the criminal statutes that legislatures enact. Moreover, judges also possess a special kind of power that allows them—if they so choose—to impose limits on the legislature's choices. That special power is the power to decide whether or not a challenged statute violates either the United States Constitution or, in state criminal cases, the relevant state constitution. If the statute is held unconstitutional, either on its face or as applied to the facts of the particular case, then the defendant's conviction will be overturned. We saw an example of this kind of issue in *Kellogg*, where the defendant argued—unsuccessfully—that the criminal statute in question violated both the Eighth Amendment to the United States Constitution and a similar provision in the California state constitution. Such constitutional challenges to criminal statutes are extremely rare, and successful ones even more so. Nevertheless, the possibility exists.

Although a more complete account of various constitutional doctrines that might be asserted as limits on legislative authority must wait for later, see Chapter 13, infra, there are two particular constitutional challenges that are worth mentioning now, at the beginning of our journey. The first of these is proportionality. The proportionality doctrine arises from the Eighth Amendment's "cruel and unusual punishments" clause. Although that clause clearly was intended to prohibit certain punishments in the abstract, without regard to the particular crimes for which they might be imposed, the Supreme Court has held that the Eighth Amendment also requires a very rough correspondence between the severity of a crime and the severity of the punishment imposed against those who commit that crime. To give a relatively clear example, although a sentence of life imprisonment might be appropriate for first degree murder, the same sentence would be inappropriate for the crime of jaywalking—because it would be grossly disproportionate to the seriousness of that particular crime, and thus "cruel and unusual punishment" in violation of the Eighth Amendment. The constitutional issue in *Kellogg* was much the same; Kellogg essentially argued that his "crime" was so benign that *any* criminal punishment, no matter how small, would be disproportionate.

Over the past 40 years, proportionality has evolved into two very differ-ent doctrines applicable in two very different contexts. In the context of cap-ital cases, the proportionality doctrine has been used by the Supreme Court on numerous occasions to regulate the imposition of the death penalty for certain crimes and certain categories of criminals. Thus the Court has held that the death penalty is disproportionate, in violation of the Eighth Amendment, for the crime of rape, Coker v. Georgia, 433 U.S. 584 (1977); for those who commit felony murder but do not actually kill their victims nor exhibit extreme recklessness with respect to their deaths, Tison v. Arizona, 481 U.S. 137 (1987); for defendants who are mentally retarded, Atkins v. Virginia, 536 U.S. 304 (2002); and for defendants who commit their mur-ders before turning age 18, Roper v. Simmons, 543 U.S. 551 (2005). In *Roper v. Simmons*, the Court cited not only psychology research showing that juve-niles as a class are generally less culpable for their crimes than adults, and the recent trend in the states to exempt juveniles from the death penalty, but also the fact that most other modern, industrialized democracies around the world have abolished the death penalty for juveniles. This caused Justice Scalia to object that "the meaning of our Eighth Amendment . . . should [not] be determined by the subjective views of five Members of this Court and like-minded foreigners." Id. at 608 (Scalia, J., dissenting).

In the context of noncapital cases, by contrast, the Court has been far less willing to invoke the proportionality doctrine to strike down criminal statutes. For example, in Harmelin v. Michigan, 501 U.S. 957 (1991), the Court upheld a law mandating a sentence of life imprisonment without pos-sibility of parole for simple possession of 672 grams of cocaine. (The law was later repealed by the Michigan legislature.) And in Ewing v. California, 538 U.S. 11 (2003), the Court rejected a challenge to California's "three strikes" law; the defendant, who had four prior convictions for burglary and rob-bery, had been sentenced to a prison term of 25 years to life for his "third strike" felony of stealing three golf clubs, worth $399 each, by walking (actu-ally, limping) out of a pro shop with the golf clubs hidden in his pants. The Court noted that—at least outside the death penalty context—"the Eighth Amendment does not require strict proportionality between crime and sen-tence. Rather, it forbids only extreme sentences that are 'grossly dispropor-tionate' to the crime." Id. at 23.

More recently, in Graham v. Florida, 560 U.S. 48 (2010), the Court struck down the use of life imprisonment without parole for juveniles who commit nonhomicide crimes. And in the companion cases of Miller v. Alabama and Jackson v. Hobbs, 567 U.S. ___ (2012), the Court held that *mandatory* life-without-parole sentences are unconstitutional for *all* crimes committed by juveniles (including murder)—although the decision did *not* prohibit the *discretionary* imposition of life without parole for such crimes. These deci-sions, however, may be more about the specialness of juveniles (as in *Roper v. Simmons*) than about signaling that the Court intends to begin applying the Eighth Amendment more aggressively to noncapital crimes in general.

At least until the next big proportionality case comes along, it seems fair to conclude that the Court continues to believe that the proportionality doctrine has relatively little bite outside the special context of capital cases.

A second, and perhaps more important, constitutional limit on defining crimes concerns not the content of criminal prohibitions, but the specificity with which those prohibitions are defined. The "void-for-vagueness doctrine"—which derives from the Constitution's Due Process Clause*—requires that crimes be defined with enough precision to inform potential offenders how to avoid criminal punishment. The vagueness doctrine also requires that crimes be defined in a manner that does not invite arbitrary and discriminatory enforcement. What those propositions mean in practice is far from clear.

The first main case below, Nash v. United States, 229 U.S. 373 (1913), shows why vagueness doctrine is less radical than first appears. Nash was tried for and convicted of violations of the Sherman Antitrust Act, one of the most vaguely defined criminal prohibitions in American law. No matter: Nash knew that his own conduct might land him in hot water—or, as Justice Oliver Wendell Holmes put it, "common social duty would, under the circumstances, have suggested a more circumspect conduct." That proposition is enough to sustain Nash's conviction. The notes after *Nash* explore vagueness doctrine's unusual history. The second main case, Gray v. Kohl, 568 F. Supp. 2d 1378 (S.D. Fla. 2008), offers a good picture of contemporary vagueness doctrine in action; the court in that case invalidated a law banning loitering in the vicinity of a school. As you read these cases and the notes that follow them, ask yourselves: Why are some—but only some—vague criminal laws impermissible? What problem is vagueness doctrine designed to solve? Does the solution work?

Nash v. United States

Supreme Court of the United States
229 U.S. 373 (1913)

Mr. Justice HOLMES delivered the opinion of the court.

This is an indictment in two counts—the first for a conspiracy in restraint of trade, the second for a conspiracy to monopolize trade, contrary to the act of July 2, 1890, . . . commonly known as the Sherman Act.** . . .

---

*Actually, there are two such clauses: one in the Fifth Amendment that regulates the federal government, and another in the Fourteenth Amendment that applies to the states.

**[Section 1 of the Act provided: "Every contract, combination in the form of trust or otherwise, or conspiracy, in restraint of trade or commerce among the several States, or with foreign nations, is declared to be illegal." Section 2 provided: "Every person who shall monopolize, or attempt to monopolize, or combine or conspire with any other person or persons, to monopolize any part of the trade or commerce among the several States, or with foreign nations, shall be deemed guilty of a felony . . . ."—EDS.]

The allegations of fact in the two counts are alike. . . . The American Naval Stores Company, a West Virginia corporation having its principal office in Savannah and branch offices in New York, Philadelphia, Chicago, etc., was engaged in buying, selling, shipping and exporting spirits of turpentine in and from Southern States to other States and abroad. Nash was the president; Shotter, chairman of the board of directors; Myers, vice-president; Boardman, treasurer; DeLoach, secretary, and Moller, manager of the Jacksonville, Florida, branch. The National Transportation and Terminal Company, a New Jersey corporation, had warehouses and terminals for handling spirits of turpentine and naval stores at Fernandina, and other places named, in Florida, Alabama, Mississippi, etc., and was engaged in storing such turpentine and rosin and issuing warehouse receipts for the same. Myers was the president; DeLoach the secretary and Moller manager of the Jacksonville branch. On May 1, 1907, it is alleged, these corporations and individuals conspired to restrain commerce in the articles named, among the States and with foreign nations—the restraint to be effected in the following ways among others: (1) by bidding down turpentine and rosin so that competitors could sell them only at ruinous prices; (2) by causing naval stores receipts that naturally would go to one port to go to another; (3) by purchasing . . . supplies at ports known as closed ports and, with intent to depress the market, refraining from purchasing any appreciable part at Savannah, the primary market in the United States for naval stores, where purchases would tend to strengthen prices, . . . (4) by coercing factors and brokers into contracts with the defendants for the storage and purchase of their receipts and refusing to purchase from such factors and brokers unless such contracts were entered into; (5) by circulating false statements as to naval stores production and stocks on hand; (6) by issuing fraudulent warehouse receipts; (7) by fraudulently grading, regrading and raising grades of rosins and falsely gauging spirits of turpentine; (8) by attempting to bribe employes of competitors so as to obtain information concerning their business and stocks; (9) by inducing consumers, by payments and threats of boycotts, to postpone dates of delivery of contract supplies and thus enabling defendants to postpone purchasing when to purchase would tend to strengthen the market; (10) by making tentative offers of large amounts of naval stores to depress the market, accepting contracts only for small amounts and purchasing when the market had been depressed by the offers; (11) by selling far below cost in order to compel competitors to meet prices ruinous to everybody; (12) by fixing the price of turpentine below the cost of production—all the foregoing being for the purpose of driving competitors out of business and restraining foreign trade or, in the second count, of doing the same and monopolizing the trade.

The two counts before us were demurred to on the grounds that the statute was so vague as to be inoperative on its criminal side. . . . The demurrer was overruled and this action of the court raises the important questions of the case. . . .

The objection to the criminal operation of the statute is thought to be warranted by The Standard Oil Co. v. United States, 221 U.S. 1, and United States v. American Tobacco Co., 221 U.S. 106. Those cases may be taken to have established that only such contracts and combinations are within the act as, by reason of intent or the inherent nature of the contemplated acts, prejudice the public interests by unduly restricting competition or unduly obstructing the course of trade. And thereupon it is said that the crime thus defined by the statute contains in its definition an element of degree as to which estimates may differ, with the result that a man might find himself in prison because his honest judgment did not anticipate that of a jury of less competent men. The kindred proposition that "the criminality of an act cannot depend upon whether a jury may think it reasonable or unreasonable. There must be some definiteness and certainty," is cited from the late Mr. Justice Brewer sitting in the Circuit Court. Tozer v. United States, 52 Fed. Rep. 917, 919.

But apart from the common law as to restraint of trade . . . the law is full of instances where a man's fate depends on his estimating rightly, that is, as the jury subsequently estimates it, some matter of degree. If his judgment is wrong, not only may he incur a fine or a short imprisonment, as here; he may incur the penalty of death. "An act causing death may be murder, manslaughter, or misadventure according to the degree of danger attending it" by common experience in the circumstances known to the actor. . . . "[Thus,] a man might have to answer with his life for consequences which he neither intended nor foresaw." Commonwealth v. Pierce, 138 Mass. 165, 178. The criterion in such cases is to examine whether common social duty would, under the circumstances, have suggested a more circumspect conduct. If a man should kill another by driving an automobile furiously into a crowd he might be convicted of murder however little he expected the result. If he did no more than drive negligently through a street he might get off with manslaughter or less. And in the last case he might be held although he himself thought that he was acting as a prudent man should. . . . We are of opinion that there is no constitutional difficulty in the way of enforcing the criminal part of the act. . . .

Mr. Justice PITNEY dissents.

Notes on the Void-for-Vagueness Doctrine

1. As *Nash* illustrates, the notion that criminal prohibitions must be defined with some degree of precision is an old one. The rationale behind that notion is likewise old: The defendants' argument—that, absent a more precise definition of unlawful restraint of trade, "a man might find himself in prison because his honest judgment did not anticipate that of a jury"—captures it well. If men and women can be imprisoned for unexpected "crimes," even the most law-abiding among us cannot reliably avoid criminal punishment. The void-for-vagueness doctrine excuses defendants from criminal liability if the crime charged is so vaguely defined that "[people] of common intelligence must necessarily guess at its meaning." Connally v. General Construction Co., 269 U.S. 385, 391 (1926).

2. That proposition sounds both simple and persuasive. But its implications are potentially enormous—again, as *Nash* illustrates. The Sherman Act, the source of the criminal charges in *Nash*, uses sweeping language the definition of which Congress left to the courts. The Act's crucial sentence reads as follows: "Every contract, combination in the form of trust or otherwise, or conspiracy, in restraint of trade or commerce among the several States, or with foreign nations, is declared to be illegal." 15 U.S.C. §1. If those words are taken literally, the Act forbids nearly every employment contract—by agreeing to work for one employer, any given worker is prevented from negotiating terms of employment with rival employers, which sounds like a "contract . . . in restraint of trade." Plainly, the law was not meant to reach so far. But if the Act's language is not to be given its ordinary meaning, what should be the boundaries of criminal liability? By the time *Nash* was decided, the Supreme Court had held that only "unreasonable" restraints of trade were forbidden, see Standard Oil Co. of New Jersey v. United States, 221 U.S. 1 (1911)—leaving reasonableness undefined. Nash and his co-defendants might fairly ask: How are corporate officers supposed to know what conduct will constitute an unreasonable restraint of trade?

The problem is not limited to Sherman Act cases. Uncertain legal boundaries are common in criminal law: Consider the definition of "causing death" in homicide cases, see infra at Chapter 10, or the meaning of "consent" in the law of rape, see infra at Chapter 9. No American judge is likely to invalidate her jurisdiction's homicide and rape statutes on vagueness grounds—which leaves entirely unclear the degree of vagueness that criminal law can tolerate. Vagueness doctrine is itself remarkably vague. Constitutional law is not without a sense of irony.

3. Connally v. General Construction Co., 269 U.S. 385, 391 (1926), began as a suit to enjoin enforcement of an Oklahoma statute that required "that not less than the current rate of per diem wages in the locality where the work is performed shall be paid to laborers." Violations were punishable by fine and up to six months in jail, and each underpaid worker each day constituted a separate violation. The construction company brought suit when state officials announced their intent to prosecute. The Supreme Court found the statute unconstitutionally vague:

> . . . [T]he words "current rate of wages" do not denote a specific or definite sum, but minimum, maximum and intermediate amounts, indeterminately, varying from time to time and dependent upon the class and kind of work done, the efficiency of the workmen, etc. . . . The statutory phrase reasonably cannot be confined to any of these amounts, since it imports each and all of them. The "current rate of wages" [extends] from so much (the minimum) to so much (the maximum), including all between; and to direct the payment of an amount which shall not be less than one of several different amounts,

without saying which, is to leave the question of what is meant incapable of any definite answer.

269 U.S. at 393-94. Notice the difference between *Connally* and *Nash*. The employer in *Connally* had no way to determine what wage the law required him to pay. Notwithstanding the Sherman Act's vagueness, the *Nash* defendants could hardly be surprised that the attempt to rig the market in naval stores (meaning the goods used to make wooden ships) would be deemed a "conspiracy in restraint of trade." In short, the criminal law of antitrust defines a clear core with a vague periphery. With respect to the minimum wage law at issue in *Connally*, even the core was unclear.

4. Regulated actors in cases like *Nash* and *Connally* have access to high-quality legal counsel who can explain to them just where the relevant legal lines fall. Most criminal defendants are situated differently: They must make their judgments about their behavior in the absence of detailed legal knowledge. Few defendants read criminal statutes and court decisions. Why, then, does it matter how specifically (or not) those statutes and court decisions define criminal liability?

5. Until the middle of the twentieth century, vagueness claims chiefly arose in cases like *Nash* and *Connally*: prosecutions—or, as in *Connally*, threatened prosecutions—of regulated businesses and their officers. Two law review articles helped to change that state of affairs: Caleb Foote, Vagrancy-Type Law and Its Administration, 104 U. Pa. L. Rev. 603 (1956), and William O. Douglas, Vagrancy and Arrest on Suspicion, 70 Yale L.J. 1 (1960). Foote's article examined the enforcement of crimes like vagrancy and public drunkenness in Philadelphia in the 1950s:

> Philadelphia magistrates . . . viewed their function as a deterrent one to banish "bums" from Philadelphia and keep them out ("After this you stay where you belong"), or as a form of civic sanitation ("I'll clean up this district if I have to stay here until 5 o'clock every afternoon"), or as control of suspicious persons ("There have been a lot of robberies around here. I'm going to have you investigated—three months"), or as humanitarian ("I'm saving his life by sending him where he can't booze"). . . .
>
> Administratively, vagrancy-type statutes are regarded as essential criminal preventives, providing a residual police power to facilitate the arrest, investigation and incarceration of suspicious persons. . . . [T]hese statutes are sufficiently indefinite to give the police wide scope. They permit arrest . . . and summary prosecution . . . before a justice of the peace. . . . Unwanted drunkards, panhandlers, gamblers, peddlers or paupers are committed or banished, a procedure that is alleged to deter other like persons from entering or remaining in a given locality.

104 U. Pa. L. Rev. at 613-15. Justice Douglas' article criticized the use of such laws to justify arrest based on mere suspicion—hence less than probable cause, the standard the Fourth Amendment requires for arrests—of other, more serious crimes. Foote's and Douglas' articles led to a number of challenges to

the constitutionality of such laws, which were sometimes called "street clean-ing statutes" because they were used to clear city streets of "undesirables."

6. The offense that lies at the heart of Foote's and Douglas' articles is vagrancy. The criminal law of vagrancy began in the aftermath of the four-teenth century's outbreak of the bubonic plague. In the wake of the plague, wages for agricultural workers rose sharply, since the population of those workers had fallen sharply (in some places, by more than half). In England, would-be laborers who refused work at wages landowners were willing to pay were deemed vagrants, and could be either criminally punished or enslaved. The subsequent history of vagrancy law is similarly scandalous:

> . . . In 16th-century England, . . . the "Slavery acts" provided for a 2-year enslavement period for anyone who "liveth idly and loiteringly." . . . [M]any American vagrancy laws were patterned on these Elizabethan poor laws. These laws went virtually unchallenged in this country until attorneys became widely available to the indigent following [the Supreme Court's] decision in Gideon v. Wainwright, 372 U.S. 335 (1963). In addition, vagrancy laws were used after the Civil War to keep former slaves in a state of quasi-slavery. In 1865, for example, Alabama broadened its vagrancy statute to include "any runaway, stubborn servant or child" and "a laborer or servant who loiters away his time, or refuses to comply with any contract for a term of service without just cause." T. Wilson, Black Codes of the South 76 (1965).

Chicago v. Morales, 527 U.S. 41, 53 n.20 (1999). In Papachristou v. Jacksonville, 405 U.S. 156 (1972), the Justices considered the constitutional-ity of one city's vagrancy ordinance, which read as follows:

> "Rogues and vagabonds, or dissolute persons who go about begging, common gamblers, persons who use juggling or unlawful games or plays, common drunkards, common night walkers, thieves, pilferers or pickpockets, traders in stolen property, lewd, wanton and lascivious persons, keepers of gambling places, common railers and brawlers, persons wandering or stroll-ing around from place to place without any lawful purpose or object, habitual loafers, disorderly persons, persons neglecting all lawful business and habitu-ally spending their time by frequenting houses of ill fame, gaming houses, or places where alcoholic beverages are sold or served, persons able to work but habitually living upon the earnings of their wives or minor children shall be deemed vagrants and, upon conviction in the Municipal Court shall be pun-ished as provided for Class D offenses."

Id. at 156-57 n.1. The defendants in *Papachristou* were two black men and two white women arrested while driving down one of Jacksonville's main streets. Justice Douglas authored the majority opinion invalidating the ordinance:

> Persons "wandering or strolling" from place to place have been extolled by Walt Whitman and Vachel Lindsay. The qualification "without any lawful pur-pose or object" may be a trap for innocent acts. Persons "neglecting all lawful business and habitually spending their time by frequenting . . . places where alcoholic beverages are sold or served" would literally embrace many mem-bers of golf clubs. . . .

Walkers and strollers and wanderers may be going to or coming from a burglary. Loafers or loiterers may be "casing" a place for a holdup. Letting one's wife support him is an intra-family matter, and normally of no concern to the police. Yet it may, of course, be the setting for numerous crimes.

The difficulty is that these activities are historically part of the amenities of life as we have known them. They are not mentioned in the Constitution or in the Bill of Rights. These unwritten amenities have been in part responsible for giving our people the feeling of independence and self-confidence, the feeling of creativity. These amenities have dignified the right of dissent and have honored the right to be non-conformists and the right to defy submissiveness. They have encouraged lives of high spirits rather than hushed, suffocating silence.

Id. at 164.

7. The crime of loitering has raised similar vagueness concerns. In Kolender v. Lawson, 461 U.S. 352 (1982), the Court reviewed a California statute that provided: "Every person who commits any of the following acts is guilty of disorderly conduct, a misdemeanor: . . . (e) Who loiters or wanders upon the streets or from place to place without apparent reason or business and who refuses to identify himself and to account for his presence when requested by any peace officer so to do, if the surrounding circumstances are such as to indicate to a reasonable man that the public safety demands such identification." The defendant, Edward Lawson, was a 36-year-old business consultant from San Francisco. Lawson was also black, wore his hair in dreadlocks, and liked to dress in unconventional ways. On a number of business trips to San Diego, Lawson took walks in largely white neighborhoods late at night. Lawson was detained or arrested for disorderly conduct on 15 separate occasions within a two-year period; he was prosecuted twice, and convicted once. Lawson filed a lawsuit challenging the California statute as unconstitutionally vague. The Court agreed, based not on the lack of specificity in the term "loiter" but instead on the California courts' interpretation of the identification requirement in the statute:

As construed by the California Court of Appeal, §647(e) requires that an individual provide "credible and reliable" identification when requested by a police officer who has reasonable suspicion of criminal activity. . . . *People v. Solomon*, 33 Cal. App. 3d 429, 108 Cal. Rptr. 867 (1973). "Credible and reliable" identification is defined by the State Court of Appeal as identification "carrying reasonable assurance that the identification is authentic and providing means for later getting in touch with the person who has identified himself." *Id.* at 438, 108 Cal. Rptr. at 873. In addition, a suspect may be required to "account for his presence . . . to the extent that it assists in producing credible and reliable identification . . . ." *Id.* at 438, 108 Cal. Rptr. at 872 . . . .

Section 647(e), as presently drafted and as construed by the state courts, contains no standard for determining what a suspect has to do in order to satisfy the requirement to provide a "credible and reliable" identification. As such, the statute vests virtually complete discretion in the hands of the police to determine whether the suspect has satisfied the statute and must be permitted to go on his way in the absence of probable cause to arrest . . . .

We conclude §647(e) is unconstitutionally vague on its face because it encourages arbitrary enforcement by failing to describe with sufficient particularity what a suspect must do in order to satisfy the statute.

Id. at 355-57, 358, 361.

8. Since the days of *Papachristou* and *Lawson*, the Supreme Court has become more explicit about the two distinct (but related) dimensions of vagueness doctrine, as this passage from Chicago v. Morales, 527 U.S. 41 (1999), shows: "Vagueness may invalidate a criminal law for either of two independent reasons. First, it may fail to provide the kind of notice that will enable ordinary people to understand what conduct it prohibits; second, it may authorize and even encourage arbitrary and discriminatory enforcement." Id. at 79-80. The statute at issue in *Morales* was a modern, modified version of a loitering statute, aimed at groups of persons standing around in a public place with no apparent lawful object and including at least one person believed by police to be a criminal street gang member. The next case involved another modern, modified version of a loitering statute.

Gray v. Kohl

United States District Court for the Southern District of Florida
568 F. Supp. 2d 1378 (2008)

MOORE, District Judge.

. . . This action arises from Defendants' prohibition of Plaintiff Thomas Gray's distribution of Bibles on a public sidewalk within 500 feet of Key Largo School, a school safety zone pursuant to the Florida School Safety Zone Statute. Fla. Stat. §810.0975. Gray claims the statute is unconstitutional for vagueness and overbreadth. The School Safety Zone Statute states, in relevant part:

(a) Each principal or designee of each public or private school in this state shall notify the appropriate law enforcement agency to prohibit any person from loitering in the school safety zone who does not have legitimate business in the school safety zone or any other authorization, or license to enter or remain in the school safety zone or does not otherwise have invitee status in the designated safety zone.

(b) During the period from 1 hour prior to the start of a school session until 1 hour after the conclusion of a school session, it is unlawful for any person to enter the premises or trespass within a school safety zone or to remain on such premises or within such school safety zone when that person does not have legitimate business in the school safety zone or any other authorization, license, or invitation to enter or remain in the school safety zone. Any person who violates this subsection commits a misdemeanor of the second degree. . . .

(c) Any person who does not have legitimate business in the school safety zone or any other authorization, license, or invitation to enter or remain in the school safety zone who shall willfully fail to remove himself or herself from the school safety zone after the principal or designee, having a reasonable belief that he or she will commit a crime or is engaged in harassment or intimidation of students entering or leaving school property, requests him or her to leave the school safety zone commits a misdemeanor of the second degree. . . . Nothing in this section shall be construed to abridge or infringe upon the right of any person to peaceably assemble and protest.

(d) This section does not apply to residents or persons engaged in the operation of a licensed commercial business within the school safety zone.

Fla. Stat. §810.0975(2). Section 810.0975(1) defines a "school safety zone" as being "within 500 feet of any real property owned by or leased to any public or private elementary, middle, or high school or school board and used for elementary, middle, or high school education."

The following facts are set forth in the Complaint. Gray, a resident of Key Largo, Florida, and member of Gideons International, feels a religious desire and obligation to share his religion with others. One way Plaintiff shares his religion is by distributing Bibles in public. Complaint ¶¶25-27.

Key Largo has one road, US 1, that spans its entire length. Monroe County built and maintains a public bike path/sidewalk that abuts the east side of US 1 for approximately twenty miles in Key Largo. This public bike path/sidewalk is open and accessible to the public and is regularly used by community members for walking, running, biking, and other activities. The public bike path/sidewalk runs in front of commercial businesses, government buildings, personal residences, and public and private schools. Id. ¶¶37-40.

Many activities occur within 500 feet of Key Largo School between one hour prior to school beginning and one hour after school ends. The public bike path/sidewalk abutting US 1 and Key Largo School is located within 500 feet of the school to both the north and south and is routinely used by community members as they talk, walk, bike, and jog. Many businesses are located within 500 feet of Key Largo School, including a pet motel, a gas station, "The Cracked Conch" restaurant, and a plumbing business. Also within 500 feet of the school is a church, as well as a building where trucks are housed. Numerous residences are also located within 500 feet of the school. Id. ¶¶41-47, 53-54.

The Gideons' procedure for handing out Bibles from the public [areas near] school grounds is as follows: (1) approximately two weeks prior to the distribution, a member calls the appropriate police department to notify them of distribution; (2) ten to fifteen minutes prior to distribution, a few Gideon members give school administrators notice that they will be handing out Bibles after classes are dismissed; (3) Gideon members are instructed that they must stand on the public bike path/sidewalk during distribution and are not permitted on school grounds; and (4) Gideon members are instructed not to force Bibles on anyone. Id. ¶58. . . .

. . . [O]n January 19, 2007, Gray and other Gideons distributed Bibles at Key Largo School. Approximately two weeks prior to the distribution at Key Largo School, Gray contacted Deputy Williams to inform him of the planned distribution at Key Largo School. . . . Deputy Williams told Gray that the planned distribution from the public bike path/sidewalk at Key Largo School was permissible. . . . Gray arrived at Key Largo School at approximately 2:00 P.M. on January 19. Gray and another Gideon member then went to the school administration building to inform the Principal of the planned Bible distribution, but the Principal was not available. Gray also spoke with Florida State Patrol Officer, Gretchen Glenn, who was in the school office at this time, and Officer Glenn gave no indication that the Bible distribution was problematic. Id. ¶¶69-73, 76-78, 81-82.

Gray then returned to the other Gideons on the public bike path/ sidewalk and positioned himself on the public bike path/sidewalk by the school crosswalk. Shortly after Gray took his position by the crosswalk, the Principal came out of the school and stared at Gray for a few minutes. She did not approach or speak to Gray and she did not witness Plaintiff handing out any Bibles. . . . For the duration of the time he distributed Bibles at the school, Gray stood on the public bike path/sidewalk and did not cross onto school grounds. Id. ¶¶83-85, 88-90.

At approximately 3:30 P.M., Gray received a call on his cell phone from a fellow Gideon member who was distributing Bibles at the school that day. The caller informed Gray that he and another Gideon member were being arrested. Gray stopped distributing Bibles, put them back in his truck, and walked up to the school's north exit. There were approximately five to six Sheriff's Officers present. Gray identified himself as the Gideon member in charge and asked the officers who was in charge. They all indicated that Officer John Perez was the arresting Officer. Gray approached Officer Perez and asked what the charges were. Officer Perez was highly agitated and said that Gray would know in forty-eight hours when he received the report. Id. ¶¶91-98. . . . Gray immediately ceased his Bible distribution. Gray has not returned to distribute Bibles on public sidewalks within 500 feet of school property due to his fear of arrest and prosecution. Id. at ¶¶101-106, 123-124. The Gideons who Officer Perez arrested were charged with violating the School Safety Zone Statute but were never convicted.

On April 20, 2007, Gray filed the Verified Complaint in this case, [claiming] . . . violation of the Due Process Clause of the Fourteenth Amendment. . . .

ANALYSIS

Gray facially challenges §810.0975 (the "School Safety Zone Statute") on grounds that it is unconstitutionally vague, in violation of the Due Process Clause of the Fourteenth Amendment. "Vagueness may invalidate a criminal law for either of two independent reasons. First, it may fail to provide the kind of notice that will enable ordinary people to understand what conduct it prohibits; second, it may authorize and even encourage arbitrary and discriminatory enforcement." Chicago v. Morales, 527 U.S. 41, 56 (1999); see Kolender v. Lawson, 461 U.S. 352, 357 (1983); Papachristou v. Jacksonville, 405 U.S. 156, 162 (1972). "In evaluating a facial challenge to a state law, a federal court must . . . consider any limiting construction that a state court or enforcement agency has proffered." *Kolender*, 461 U.S. at 355. Criminal penalties are scrutinized more closely for vagueness than civil penalties because the consequences of imprecise criminal statutes are more severe. Hoffman Estates v. Flipside, 455 U.S. 489, 499-500 (1982). "[A] scienter requirement may mitigate a law's vagueness, especially with respect to the adequacy of notice to the complainant that his conduct is proscribed." Id.

1. Notice

"It is established that a law fails to meet the requirements of the Due Process Clause if it is so vague and standardless that it leaves the public uncertain as to the conduct it prohibits." *Morales*, 527 U.S. at 56. "[B]ecause we assume that man is free to steer between lawful and unlawful conduct, we insist that laws give the person of ordinary intelligence a reasonable opportunity to know what is prohibited, so that he may act accordingly." *Hoffman Estates*, 455 U.S. at 498. "[A] statute which either forbids or requires the doing of an act in terms so vague that men of common intelligence must necessarily guess at its meaning and differ in its application violates the first essential of due process of law." Connally v. General Construction Co., 269 U.S. 385, 391 (1926). "No one may be required at peril of life, liberty or property to speculate as to the meaning of penal statutes." Lanzetta v. New Jersey, 306 U.S. 451, 453 (1939).

a. Subsection (2)(b)

Subsection (2)(b) of the School Safety Zone Statute prohibits any person from entering the school safety zone during certain hours of the day unless they have "legitimate business" within the school safety zone. "Legitimate business" is not defined in the statute and there is no scienter requirement. . . . Violation of this portion of the statute contains no prerequisite that a person refuse to leave the area once notified that they have no "legitimate business" in the school safety zone. An individual is in violation of subsection (2)(b) as soon as they enter the school safety zone during an applicable time of day without "legitimate business" to justify their presence. Because the school safety zone extends 500 feet outward from the perimeter of school property, the school safety zone around Key Largo School encompasses residential neighborhoods, businesses and sidewalks on both sides of US 1. Therefore, people in any of these areas who are not exempt may be convicted of a second degree misdemeanor unless they are in the school safety zone on "legitimate business."

. . . Florida's appellate courts have never had occasion to define, clarify or narrow the meaning of "legitimate business" within the context of §810.0975. . . . Therefore, . . . this Court must rely solely on the text of the statute to determine if it is unconstitutionally vague.

This Court finds that subsection (2)(b) of the School Safety Zone Statute is unconstitutionally vague because it does not provide citizens of ordinary intelligence with reasonable notice of the types of acts that the statute criminalizes. The term "legitimate business" requires citizens to guess at the conduct that falls within the statute's ambit. . . . The vagueness that dooms this statute is not the product of uncertainty about the normal meaning of "legitimate business," but rather about what "legitimate business" is covered by the statute and what is not. *Morales*, 527 U.S. at 60; see Allen v. Bordentown, 524 A.2d 478 (N.J. Super. Ct. 1987) (finding curfew statute unconstitutionally vague because the words "legitimate business" are unduly subjective and fail to provide fair notice of proscribed conduct). . . . Such "[u]ncertain meanings inevitably lead citizens to steer far wider of the unlawful zone . . . than if the boundaries of the forbidden areas were clearly marked." Grayned v. Rockford, 408 U.S. 104, 109 (1972).

With respect to the imprecise scope of conduct proscribed by the School Safety Zone Statute, the statute is similar to the ordinance held unconstitutionally vague in Coates v. Cincinnati, 402 U.S. 611 (1971). In *Coates*, the Court assessed the constitutionality of a Cincinnati ordinance making it a criminal offense for "three or more persons to assemble . . . on any of the sidewalks . . . and there conduct themselves in a manner annoying to persons passing by." Id. The Court held that the ordinance's prohibition against annoying behavior was unconstitutionally vague because it provided an unascertainable standard . . . , especially since "conduct that annoys some people does not annoy others." Id. at 614. As a result, enforcement of the statute would necessarily depend on whether or not a policeman was annoyed. Id.

. . . The term "legitimate business" describes conduct at least as imprecisely as does the word "annoying." . . . Therefore, the School Zone Safety Statute is unconstitutionally vague because it fails "to provide the kind of notice that will enable ordinary people to understand what conduct it prohibits." *Morales*, 527 U.S. at 56.

b. Subsection (2)(c)

Subsection (2)(c) gives rise to a criminal penalty if a person fails to vacate the school safety zone after being instructed to do so by a principal or designee who reasonably believes a crime is about to be committed or that the person is engaged in harassment or intimidation. . . . An argument could therefore be made that subsection (2)(c) provides sufficient notice of proscribed conduct because a person will always . . . have an opportunity to leave the school safety zone before the conduct becomes a crime.

However, the vagueness of a statute . . . cannot be remedied by a provision that permits a potential offender to cease the activity once they are advised that their conduct is proscribed. . . . See *Morales*, 527 U.S. at 58 (rejecting city's assertion that gang [loitering] ordinance provided fair notice of proscribed conduct where no violation of the ordinance occurred until a person failed to respond to an order of dispersal). This is so for two reasons. First, . . . the statute fails to provide the advance notice that will protect a citizen from being ordered to leave the school safety zone in the first instance. Id. at 59. "Such an order cannot retroactively give adequate warning of the boundary between the permissible and the impermissible applications of the law." Id. Second, the School Safety Zone Statute fails to define how long a person must leave the covered area or whether they can return by simply subjectively deciding that they have a reason that better approximates "legitimate business." . . .

Unlike subsection (2)(b), however, in addition to being present within a school safety zone without "legitimate business," no offense results under subsection (2)(c) unless a person refuses an order . . . to leave the school safety zone. No order to vacate may issue unless the principal or designee has "a reasonable belief that [the person] will commit a crime or is engaged in harassment or intimidation." Fla. Stat. §810.0975(2)(c). . . .

. . . This Court finds that subsection (2)(c)'s requirement that a principal or designee have "a reasonable belief that [the person] will commit a crime or is engaged in harassment or intimidation" prior to issuing an order to leave the school safety zone resolves the unconstitutional vagueness fatal to subsection (2)(b). . . . [T]he terms "reasonable belief," "harassment" and "intimidation" provide sufficient notice to enable ordinary people to understand what kind of conduct subsection (2)(c) prohibits.

Of these terms, "harassment" is perhaps the least specific and most subjective. However, unlike the terms "legitimate business" and "annoy," which are not defined in any of Florida's penal statutes, the term "harassment" is defined as "engag[ing] in a course of conduct directed at a specific person that causes substantial emotional distress in such person and serves no legitimate purpose." Fla. Stat. §784.048(1)(a). . . . [T]his statutory definition of harassment . . . is sufficiently specific to put an ordinary person on notice. . . . See United States v. Eckhardt, 466 F.3d 938, 943-44 (11th Cir. 2006) (finding that federal statute criminalizing harassing phone calls was not unconstitutionally vague).

This Court is cognizant that subsection (2)(c)'s applicability may be unclear in some situations. However, the test for unconstitutional vagueness is not whether the statute is unclear in some of its applications. A statute is only unconstitutional if it is "impermissibly vague in all of its applications."

Hoffman Estates, 455 U.S. at 497. . . . Therefore, subsection (2)(c) is not unconstitutionally vague. . . .

2. Arbitrary and Discriminatory Enforcement

A statute is unconstitutionally vague if it authorizes or encourages arbitrary and discriminatory enforcement. *Morales*, 527 U.S. at 56. A legislature enacting a penal statute must "establish minimal guidelines to govern law enforcement." *Kolender*, 461 U.S. at 358. . . .

Subsection (2)(b) of the School Safety Zone Statute contains no standard for law enforcement to ascertain when a person within a school safety zone is there on "legitimate business." As such, the statute vests virtually complete discretion in the hands of the police to determine whether the suspect has satisfied the statute and must be permitted to go on his way in the absence of probable cause to arrest. Subsection (2)(b) therefore grants law enforcement with unbridled discretion and "entrusts lawmaking to moment-to-moment judgment of the policeman on his beat." Smith v. Goguen, 415 U.S. 566, 575 (1974). As a result, subsection (2)(b) of the School Safety Zone Statute "furnishes a convenient tool for harsh and discriminatory enforcement by local prosecuting officials, against particular groups deemed to merit their displeasure." *Papachristou*, 405 U.S. at 170. Although the necessity of providing children with safe and secure environs within and around educational areas is an interest of great importance, "it cannot justify legislation that would otherwise fail to meet constitutional standards for definiteness and clarity." *Kolender*, 461 U.S. at 357. "Although due process does not require impossible standards of clarity, this is not a case where further precision in the statutory language is either impossible or impractical." Id. Therefore, subsection (2)(b) of the School Safety Zone Statute is unconstitutionally vague because it authorizes and encourages arbitrary enforcement. For the reasons stated above . . . , subsection (2)(c) does not create the same potential for arbitrary enforcement. . . .

CONCLUSION

For the foregoing reasons, it is ordered and adjudged that Plaintiff's Motion for Summary Judgment is granted in part. [Subsection 2(b)] of Florida Statutes §810.0975 [is] declared unconstitutionally vague. The State of Florida and its officers are hereby permanently enjoined from enforcing [that subsection]. . . .

Notes and Questions

1. As noted previously, Chicago v. Morales, 527 U.S. 41 (1999), arose from a local ordinance barring loitering by and with "criminal street gang

members." The ordinance read:

> (a) Whenever a police officer observes a person whom he reasonably believes to be a criminal street gang member loitering in any public place with one or more other persons, he shall order all such persons to disperse and remove themselves from the area. Any person who does not promptly obey such an order is in violation of this section.
>
> (b) It shall be an affirmative defense to an alleged violation of this section that no person who was observed loitering was in fact a member of a criminal street gang.
>
> (c) As used in this section:
>
> (1) "Loiter" means to remain in any one place with no apparent purpose.
>
> (2) "Criminal street gang" means any ongoing organization, association in fact or group of three or more persons, whether formal or informal, having as one of its substantial activities the commission of one or more of the criminal acts enumerated in paragraph (3), and whose members individually or collectively engage in or have engaged in a pattern of criminal gang activity. . . .
>
> (5) "Public place" means the public way and any other location open to the public, whether publicly or privately owned. . . .
>
> (e) Any person who violates this Section is subject to a fine of not less than $100 and not more than $500 for each offense, or imprisonment for not more than six months, or both. . . .

Chicago Municipal Code §8-4-015, quoted in *Morales*, 527 U.S. at 47 n.2. The Court held that this ordinance violated both prongs of vagueness doctrine: It failed to provide adequate notice to those who might become subject to police "dispersal orders," and it invited arbitrary and discriminatory police enforcement of the law. In the words of the Court:

> [T]he ordinance does not provide sufficiently specific limits on the enforcement discretion of the police "to meet constitutional standards for definiteness and clarity."... We recognize the serious and difficult problems testified to by the citizens of Chicago that led to the enactment of this ordinance. "We are mindful that the preservation of liberty depends in part on the maintenance of social order." Houston v. Hill, 482 U.S. 451, 471-472 (1987). However, in this instance the city has enacted an ordinance that affords too much discretion to the police and too little notice to citizens who wish to use the public streets.

Id. at 64.

The very next year, Chicago's City Council enacted a new version of the ordinance, based on language in a *Morales* concurring opinion written by Justice O'Connor suggesting that certain changes might render the ordinance constitutional. The current Revised Antigang Loitering Ordinance is different from the original in several ways. First, it provides a new definition of "gang loitering": "remaining in one place under circumstances that would warrant a reasonable person to believe that the purpose or effect of that behavior is to enable a criminal street gang to establish control over identifiable areas, to intimidate others from entering those areas, or to conceal illegal activities." Chicago Municipal Code §8-4-015. Second, the ordinance is now limited to specific areas within the city designated by the Superintendent of Police as "gang hot spots"; these "hot spots," which are not required to be disclosed publicly, have tended to be located in poor minority areas on the South and West Sides of Chicago. (One study found that between 2000 and 2010, the Revised Ordinance led to 1,815 dispersal orders against blacks; 1,082 dispersal orders against Hispanics; and only 61 dispersal orders against whites. See Jane Penley, Comment, Urban Terrorists: Addressing Chicago's Losing Battle with Gang Violence, 61 DePaul L. Rev. 1185, 1201 (2012).) And the new ordinance specifies that, after receiving a dispersal order, the persons subject to the order must not be "within sight or hearing of the place at which such an order was issued during the eight-hour period following the time the order was issued." The Revised Ordinance survived a constitutional challenge in state court in 2002, and to date has not been ruled upon by the federal courts. Do you think the Revised Ordinance adequately constrains police discretion?

2. Laws like the ones at issue in *Morales* and *Gray* are not designed primarily to send criminals to jail. Rather, their chief purpose is to permit the police to keep the relevant paths and street corners clear and free of trouble. Why is notice of the relevant legal standard so important when it comes to laws of this sort? The question is especially puzzling in *Morales*: Under Chicago's gang loitering ordinance, only those who disobeyed police orders to move along could be prosecuted. By definition, all who were subjected to such police orders received individual, personalized notice that their failure to disperse could lead to criminal punishment. Why doesn't that notice suffice? On the other hand, should local police officers have the power to order people who are causing no clear harm to find someplace else to stand?

3. Consider vagueness doctrine's second prong: the potential for arbitrary and discriminatory enforcement. What feature of vague criminal statutes gives rise to that potential? The most natural answer is, the statutes' breadth, not their vagueness. The core problem with vagrancy and loitering laws is that they might plausibly apply to a sizeable fraction of the population using city streets and sidewalks. Any statute that applies to a large number of offenders, and from which police officers select a small number of arrestees, creates the potential for arbitrariness and discrimination. Such a statute need not be vague for those dangers to exist. In most of the United States, criminal bans on marijuana possession are rarely enforced; again in most of the United States, a large minority of the local population uses that drug. Enforcement of marijuana laws may be as arbitrary and discriminatory as enforcement of Chicago's gang loitering law—yet marijuana bans are not vague. Should specifically defined crimes that invite discriminatory enforcement be declared unconstitutionally vague? Should vagueness doctrine abandon its concern with vagueness?

C. CRIME AND CRIMINAL LAW

Criminal law is an important part of the criminal justice system, and from the point of view of the politicians who supervise it, that system's chief end is to control and, if possible, reduce the incidence of crime. How does criminal law help the system achieve that goal? Do criminal liability rules have any predictable effect on crime rates? If so, what is the nature of the effect?

One might suppose that these questions have clear answers. Surprisingly, they don't. Consider two sets of crimes with very different recent histories. Before 1980, drunk driving was usually treated as a minor offense, akin to speeding. When a drunk driver killed a pedestrian or another driver, serious punishment was sometimes imposed; otherwise, the crime was considered small potatoes. In 1980, a woman whose daughter was killed by a drunk driver formed the organization Mothers Against Drunk Driving. Over the next decade, tougher laws against drunk driving were enacted. The frequency of arrest and prosecution rose, as did sentences. The incidence of drunk driving fell substantially. Today, roughly 10,000 fewer people are killed each year by drunk drivers than in the 1970s, even though the number of miles driven is vastly greater now than then. That is an enormous deterrent effect.

America's experience with drug crime is very different. In the mid-1970s, the number of prison and jail inmates incarcerated for drug crime was fewer than 50,000. That number is close to a half-million today: a tenfold increase. Yet the incidence of illegal drug use is roughly what it was in the mid- to late 1970s. In one instance, deterrence triumphed. In the other, it failed spectacularly. Why the difference? No one knows.

One more connection between crime and criminal law deserves mention, and on this score, scholars all agree—though politicians and, it appears, voters don't: The *likelihood* of punishment affects the level of deterrence much more than the *amount* of punishment. Voters continue to demand and politicians continue to enact tough sentencing laws, but social scientists overwhelmingly believe those laws—at least unless coupled with increased rates of apprehension and conviction—have only slight deterrent impact. Crime fell in the 1990s, not when legislators began to raise average sentences—they had been doing that for nearly 20 years—but when criminal punishment became more consistent, when a larger fraction of serious crimes led to arrest, prosecution, and punishment. Perhaps the consistency brought crime rates down.

   "Perhaps" is the appropriate word in this context; the relationship between crime definition and crime remains mysterious. Legislators and judges must make decisions and lawyers must make arguments in conditions of radical uncertainty—yet those decisions and arguments may have large social effects. How should lawmakers respond? Is it appropriate to guess at the social effects of legal rules, or should the justice system concern itself solely with doing justice? What does justice mean in criminal cases? What does it mean in *Dudley & Stephens*? In *Kellogg*?

2

Defining Criminal Conduct

The conventional definition of "crime" is a voluntary, affirmative act that causes harm, done with culpable intent that coincides with the act, and defined by a statute to be a "crime." The last feature of that definition—the requirement that crimes be defined by statute—accurately describes American criminal law. Most of the rest of the definition doesn't, as even a cursory examination of the criminal law of narcotics suggests. Habitual users of illegal drugs are often addicted to the drugs they use (remember *Kellogg*); for them, the acquisition of drugs is not "voluntary" in the usual sense of that word. Defendants charged with possession of illegal drugs are punished for an omission—failing to get rid of the drugs they have—not for the affirmative act of purchasing those drugs. (Do you see why?) Any given drug transaction causes no harm as the law customarily defines "harm." The transaction is consensual; neither buyer nor seller seeks police intervention. Nevertheless, drug cases account for more than one-fifth of the United States' enormous prison population.

A better definition of "crime" would focus more on institutional practice: A crime is any combination of conduct and intent that violates a criminal statute, as enforced by a prosecutor and interpreted by a court (and, in those very few cases that go to trial, as applied by a jury). Below, Section A briefly explains why the definition in the preceding paragraph is incorrect for most crimes—why voluntariness, affirmative conduct, harm, and causation are, for the most part, non-issues in American criminal law. Section B is the bulk of the chapter; its focus is on the interpretation of criminal statutes: or, to put it another way, on the scope of legislators' and judges' power to define criminal conduct.

A. VOLUNTARY ACTS THAT CAUSE HARM

Return to the classic definition of criminal conduct: a voluntary, affirmative act that causes harm, done with culpable intent, and defined by a statute.

We will return to intent in the next chapter. The subject of this chapter is the rest of the definition. Here is the key point: The last element in that definition—the idea that legislatures, not courts, define crimes—undermines the rest of the definition. Legislators are not required to explain or justify the choices they make when drafting statutes. Often, those choices have more to do with political advantage than with legal principle. The law of criminal conduct fits the principled definition given above if, and only if, legislators decide to stick to the relevant principles. Sometimes that happens. Often, it doesn't.

1. Voluntary Acts

It is often said that American criminal law bars punishment without voluntary, affirmative conduct—in other words, that (1) save for a few carefully defined exceptions, no one may be convicted of crime for failing to act but only for acting, and (2) no one may be punished for conduct that was not freely chosen.

Those propositions would be very important if true. But both are false. Take omissions first. There is a governing common-law doctrine on criminal liability for omissions, but apart from the law of homicide, it means very little—and within the law of homicide, it is redundant. The doctrine holds that a defendant may not be held criminally liable for inaction unless the defendant had a legal duty to act, which is roughly akin to saying that omissions do not lead to criminal liability, except when they do. Again according to the doctrine, the relevant sources of legal duties to act include criminal statutes, many of which create such duties. Criminal tax laws oblige taxpayers to pay their taxes, or go to prison if they don't. Criminal drug laws impose liability on anyone who knowingly possesses illegal drugs, even if the possessor took no affirmative steps to obtain the drugs—in effect, one who has controlled substances is under a legal duty to get rid of them, on pain of criminal punishment. There are many other examples in both state and federal criminal codes. Criminal liability for omissions is common, perfectly legal and, usually, governed by the same legal principles that govern other forms of criminal liability.

To the extent that there is a "law of criminal omissions," that law is largely a subset of the law of homicide. As long as people have sought to kill each other, they have found creative ways to do so without appearing to do so. One of those ways is by standing back and permitting some other person or some other force to take the life in question. We address such cases later, in the first assignment of the homicide chapter, Chapter 10.

As for the requirement that criminal conduct must be voluntary, that "requirement" likewise means less than first appears. The reason is nicely captured by the leading case on the subject: Martin v. State, 17 So. 2d 427 (Ala. App. 1944). The defendant was drunk in his home, where police officers arrested him and took him to a public highway—after which he was charged with public drunkenness. Unsurprisingly, the court held "that an accusation of drunkenness in a designated public place cannot be established by proof that the accused, while in an intoxicated condition, was involuntarily and forcibly carried to that place by the arresting officer."

Cases like *Martin* are easy: The opposite result would seem Kafkaesque. Few readers will be surprised to learn that the government may not punish someone for what a police officer physically caused him to do. If the voluntariness requirement means only that, however, it means very little. On the other hand, if voluntariness means that criminal liability must be freely chosen in the strong sense of that phrase — that, for example, a drug addict may not be criminally punished for possessing drugs, or for stealing to support his habit — then it means quite a lot.

The Supreme Court briefly flirted with that broad principle in Robinson v. California, 370 U.S. 660 (1962). The defendant in *Robinson* was convicted of violating a California statute that stated: "No person shall use, or be under the influence of, or be addicted to the use of narcotics, excepting when administered by or under the direction of a person licensed by the State to prescribe and administer narcotics. . . ." The statute carried a minimum sentence of 90 days in jail, and a maximum of one year. The Justices overturned both the defendant's conviction and the statute on which it was based:

> . . . [W]e deal with a statute which makes the "status" of narcotic addiction a criminal offense. . . . California has said that a person can be continuously guilty of this offense, whether or not he has ever used or possessed any narcotics within the State, and whether or not he has been guilty of any antisocial behavior there.
>
> It is unlikely that any State at this moment in history would attempt to make it a criminal offense for a person to be mentally ill, or a leper, or to be afflicted with a venereal disease. A State might determine that the general health and welfare require that the victims of these and other human afflictions be dealt with by compulsory treatment, involving quarantine, confinement, or sequestration. But, in the light of contemporary human knowledge, a law which made a criminal offense of such a disease would doubtless be universally thought to be an infliction of cruel and unusual punishment in violation of the Eighth and Fourteenth Amendments.
>
> We cannot but consider the statute before us as of the same category. In this Court counsel for the State recognized that narcotic addiction is an illness. Indeed, it is apparently an illness which may be contracted innocently or involuntarily. We hold that a state law which imprisons a person thus afflicted as a criminal, even though he has never touched any narcotic drug within the State or been guilty of any irregular behavior there, inflicts a cruel and unusual punishment in violation of the Fourteenth Amendment. To be sure, imprisonment for ninety days is not, in the abstract, a punishment which is either cruel or unusual. But the question cannot be considered in the abstract. Even one day in prison would be a cruel and unusual punishment for the "crime" of having a common cold.

370 U.S. at 666-67.

Of course, states need not penalize drug addiction in order to attack the drug trade: Most drug statutes use possession as a proxy for purchase, and possession of more-than-user-quantity as a proxy for sale. *Robinson* raised the question whether such laws are unconstitutional as applied to drug addicts—or, alternatively, whether the problem with California's statute was technical only.

Just a few years later, in Powell v. Texas, 392 U.S. 514 (1968), the Court backed away from broadest potential implications of *Robinson*, suggesting instead that the problem was merely technical. Like the defendant in *People v. Kellogg*, page 23 supra, the defendant in *Powell* was an alcoholic charged with public drunkenness. Writing for a plurality of four Justices, Thurgood Marshall concluded that *Robinson* offered Powell no help:

> On its face the present case does not fall within [*Robinson*'s] holding, since appellant was convicted, not for being a chronic alcoholic, but for being in public while drunk on a particular occasion. The State of Texas thus has not sought to punish a mere status, as California did in *Robinson*; nor has it attempted to regulate appellant's behavior in the privacy of his own home. Rather, it has imposed upon appellant a criminal sanction for public behavior which may create substantial health and safety hazards, both for appellant and for members of the general public, and which offends the moral and esthetic sensibilities of a large segment of the community. This seems a far cry from convicting one for being an addict, being a chronic alcoholic, being "mentally ill, or a leper. . . ."
>
> *Robinson* so viewed brings this Court but a very small way into the substantive criminal law. And unless *Robinson* is so viewed it is difficult to see any limiting principle that would serve to prevent this Court from becoming, under the aegis of the Cruel and Unusual Punishment Clause, the ultimate arbiter of the standards of criminal responsibility, in diverse areas of the criminal law, throughout the country.

392 U.S. at 532-33 (plurality opinion). Justice White, who provided the fifth vote to affirm Powell's conviction, stressed the fact that, while Powell's illness may have compelled him to drink, it did not compel him to drink in public:

> If it cannot be a crime to have an irresistible compulsion to use narcotics, Robinson v. California, [370 U.S. 660 (1962)], I do not see how it can constitutionally be a crime to yield to such a compulsion. Punishing an addict for using drugs convicts for addiction under a different name. Distinguishing between the two crimes is like forbidding criminal conviction for being sick with flu or epilepsy but permitting punishment for running a fever or having a convulsion. Unless *Robinson* is to be abandoned, the use of narcotics by an addict must be beyond the reach of the criminal law. Similarly, the chronic alcoholic with an irresistible urge to consume alcohol should not be punishable for drinking or for being drunk. . . .
>
> The trial court said that Powell was a chronic alcoholic with a compulsion not only to drink to excess but also to frequent public places when intoxicated.

Nothing in the record before the trial court supports the latter conclusion, which is contrary to common sense and to common knowledge. The sober chronic alcoholic has no compulsion to be on the public streets; many chronic alcoholics drink at home and are never seen drunk in public. Before and after taking the first drink, and until he becomes so drunk that he loses the power to know where he is or to direct his movements, the chronic alcoholic with a home or financial resources is as capable as the non-chronic drinker of doing his drinking in private, of removing himself from public places and, since he knows or ought to know that he will become intoxicated, of making plans to avoid his being found drunk in public. For these reasons, I cannot say that the chronic alcoholic who proves his disease and a compulsion to drink is shielded from conviction when he has knowingly failed to take feasible precautions against committing a criminal act, here the act of going to or remaining in a public place. On such facts the alcoholic is like a person with smallpox, who could be convicted for being on the street but not for being ill, or, like the epileptic, who could be punished for driving a car but not for his disease.

Id. at 549-50 (White, J., concurring in the judgment). Although in the quoted passage Justice White might appear to favor a stronger voluntariness principle than the plurality, it is important to note that he *dissented* in *Robinson*. In other words, Justice White presumably *wanted Robinson* to be "abandoned." For this reason, *Powell* is generally viewed as having narrowly limited *Robinson* to the rare situation where a criminal statute seeks to punish addiction itself, rather than some behavior that results from the addiction.

The last line in the quoted portion of Justice White's opinion refers to cases in which drivers suffered epileptic seizures and were subsequently convicted of reckless driving or of some form of homicide, on the theory that they knew or should have known they were prone to such seizures, and so should have abstained from driving. Are those convictions fair? Do they represent wise policy? What result do they suggest in *Kellogg*?

Since *Powell*, the constitutional law of voluntariness has been essentially dormant. The years after *Powell* saw prosecutions for drug offenses explode. Throughout the explosion, arguments based on *Robinson* and the "voluntary act" doctrine have been rarely made and never successful. It seems fair to say that, insofar as the principle of voluntariness is respected, it is respected by the terms of state and federal criminal statutes, not by federal constitutional law.

2. Causing Harm

In most civil suits, the plaintiff must show that the defendant's conduct caused the plaintiff harm; causation and injury are key issues in civil litigation. The same is sometimes true in criminal litigation: Homicide cases can turn on whether the government has proved that the defendant caused the victim's death. But homicide is the exception. The majority of criminal statutes do not require proof that the defendant caused anything—instead, criminal statutes usually require proof of specified conduct and of a particular mental state. Causation and injury are large issues in the law of homicide, but small issues elsewhere. We therefore defer our coverage of causation to the homicide chapter, Chapter 10, as well.

A large body of philosophical literature argues that causing harm should be a prerequisite for criminal punishment. The argument is most famously associated with John Stuart Mill, who wrote:

> The object of this Essay is to assert one very simple principle, as entitled to govern absolutely the dealings of society with the individual in the way of compulsion and control, whether the means used be physical force in the form of legal penalties, or the moral coercion of public opinion. That principle is, that the sole end for which mankind are warranted, individually or collectively, in interfering with the liberty of action of any of their number, is self-protection. That the only purpose for which power can be rightfully exercised over any member of a civilized community, against his will, is to prevent harm to others. His own good, either physical or moral, is not sufficient warrant. He cannot rightfully be compelled to do or forbear because it will be better for him to do so, because it will make him happier, because, in the opinion of others, to do so would be wise, or even right. . . . The only part of the conduct of anyone, for which he is amenable to society, is that which concerns others. In the part which merely concerns himself, his independence is, of right, absolute. Over himself, over his own body and mind, the individual is sovereign.

John Stuart Mill, On Liberty 10-11 (David Spitz ed., 1975) (1859). If the law followed Mill's harm principle, criminal punishment would be barred in *Kellogg* (supra, at page 23), in prostitution cases, and in the large majority of drug cases. Criminalizing the possession of unregistered guns would be impermissible, as would a range of regulatory offenses. And that is only a partial list.

In other words, Mills' argument would transform American criminal justice — if it were adopted. But it hasn't been adopted, neither in Mill's home country (Great Britain) nor in ours, neither in the nineteenth century nor today. Americans have a long history of punishing vices that are, especially in the view of those who participate in them, harmless. There is no comparable tradition of listening to philosophers when drafting criminal statutes.

B. INTERPRETING CONDUCT TERMS IN CRIMINAL STATUTES

Criminal conduct is defined by criminal statutes. Statutes, criminal and otherwise, are subject to judicial interpretation. As those propositions suggest, legislators and judges share power over the definition of crimes. How is that power shared? How thoroughly do statutory texts determine the scope of criminal liability? Should judges defer to legislative judgments in criminal cases, or should they exercise their own judgment about the proper definition of crimes? Consider the different ways appellate judges answer those questions in the cases that follow.

1. Greater and Lesser Crimes

The concept of greater and lesser offenses plays no significant role in most areas of law. The reason is straightforward: In most civil cases, any given plaintiff can get only one damages bill from any given defendant, no matter how many different legal theories the plaintiff presents. Putney kicked Vosburg in a nineteenth-century schoolyard fight that prompted a famous tort case. See Vosburg v. Putney, 56 N.W. 480 (Wis. 1893). Whether Putney was liable for battery or for negligence or on some other theory that none of the lawyers in the case imagined, the damages bill is the same: Putney must pay the costs associated with Vosburg's amputated leg.

Criminal law is different. The next two cases—In re Joseph G., 667 P.2d 1176 (Cal. 1983), and People v. Cleaves, 280 Cal. Rptr. 146 (4th Dist. Ct. App. 1991)—raise the question whether the defendants should be punished for murder or for assisting a suicide. If the former, defendants' punishment would be severe; if the latter, much less so. The degree of criminal defendants' punishment does not depend on the measure of the harm the defendant caused: Many crimes cause no harm at all, as is the case with most drug offenses. Rather, the measure of punishment depends primarily on the seriousness of the crime(s) the defendant committed, as determined by the legislature that enacted the relevant criminal statutes.

That difference between criminal law and the bodies of law that define civil liability produces other important differences. The large majority of tort and contract cases define the line between legal liability and its absence. In *Joseph G.* and *Cleaves*, criminal liability is clear; the relevant line is drawn between more criminal liability and less, not between some criminal liability and none. That is true of most of the cases you will read in this book.

An important corollary follows. One might suppose that criminal defendants always seek to read criminal statutes narrowly. Not so: Sometimes, defendants benefit because a court construes a criminal statute broadly. *Joseph G.* is an example: The California Supreme Court read the assisting suicide statute more broadly than the prosecution wished; that decision led to less punishment for the defendant than the prosecution wished. The broad reading of the statute favored the defense; the narrow reading favored the government. That is a consequence of the fact that Joseph G. was seeking less criminal liability rather than no criminal liability.

In re Joseph G.

Supreme Court of California
34 Cal. 3d 429; 667 P.2d 1176 (1983)

Opinion of Mosk, J.

Joseph G., a minor, was charged in a juvenile court petition . . . with murder (Penal Code §187) and aiding and abetting a suicide (Penal Code §401). At the contested adjudication hearing, the court sustained the petition as to the murder count but dismissed the aiding and abetting charge as inapplicable; the court further found that the murder was in the first degree.

In the case before us a genuine suicide pact was partially fulfilled by driving a car over a cliff; the primary issue is whether the survivor, who drove the vehicle, is guilty of aiding and abetting the suicide rather than the murder of his deceased partner. We conclude that, under the unusual, inexplicable and tragic circumstances of this case, the minor's actions fall more properly within the statutory definition of the former.

I

The minor and his friend, Jeff W., both 16 years old, drove to the Fillmore library one evening and joined a number of their friends who had congregated there. During the course of the two hours they spent at the library talking, mention was made of a car turnout on a curve overlooking a 300- to 350-foot precipice on a country road known as "the cliff." Both the minor and Jeff declared that they intended to "fly off the cliff" and that they meant to kill themselves. The others were skeptical but the minor affirmed their seriousness, stating "You don't believe us that we are going to do it. We are going to do it. You can read it in the paper tomorrow." The minor gave one of the girls his baseball hat, saying firmly that this was the last time he would see her. Jeff repeatedly encouraged the minor by urging, "let's go, let's go" whenever the minor spoke. One other youth attempted to get in the car with Jeff and the minor but they refused to allow him to join them "because we don't want to be responsible for you." Jeff and the minor shook hands with their friends and departed.

The pair then drove to a gas station and put air in a front tire of the car, which had been damaged earlier in the evening; the fender and passenger door were dented and the tire was very low in air pressure, nearly flat. Two of their fellow students, Keith C. and Craig B., drove up and spoke with Jeff and the minor. The minor said, "Shake my hand and stay cool." Jeff urged, "Let's go," shook their hands and said, "Remember you shook my hand." The minor then drove off in the direction of the cliff with Jeff in the passenger seat; Keith and Craig surreptitiously followed them out of curiosity. The minor and Jeff proceeded up the hill past the cliff, turned around and drove down around the curve and over the steep cliff.

Two other vehicles were parked in the turnout, from which vantage point their occupants watched the minor's car plummeting down the hill at an estimated 50 miles per hour. The car veered off the road without swerving or changing course; the witnesses heard the car accelerate and then drive straight off the cliff. No one saw brake lights flash. The impact of the crash killed Jeff and caused severe injuries to the minor, resulting in the amputation of a foot.

Investigations following the incident revealed there were no defects in the steering or brake mechanisms. There were no skid marks at the scene, but a gouge in the pavement apparently caused by the frame of a motor vehicle coming into contact with the asphalt at high speed indicated that the car had gone straight over the cliff without swerving or skidding.

A few weeks after the crash, another friend of the minor discussed the incident with him. The minor declared he had "a quart" before driving over the cliff; the friend interpreted this to mean a quart of beer. The minor told his friend that he had "no reason" to drive off the cliff, that it was "stupid" but that he "did it on purpose." Just before the car went over the cliff, the minor told Jeff, "I guess this is it [Jeff]. Take it easy."

II

The minor maintains that, under the peculiar circumstances presented here, he can be convicted only of aiding and abetting a suicide and not of murder. We begin by reviewing the development of the law relevant to suicide and related crimes.

At common law suicide was a felony, punished by forfeiture of property to the king and ignominious burial. Essentially, suicide was considered a form of murder. Under American law, suicide has never been punished and the ancient English attitude has been expressly rejected. Rather than classifying suicide as criminal, suicide in the United States "has continued to be considered an expression of mental illness." Hendin, Suicide in America 23 (1982). As one commentator has noted, "punishing suicide is contrary to modern penal and psychological theory." Victoroff, The Suicidal Patient: Recognition, Intervention, Management 173-174 (1982).

Currently no state, including California, has a statute making a successful suicide a crime. . . . Contemporary England, by abolishing its criminal penalties for suicide, has also adopted this more modern approach. English Suicide Act of 1961; Barry, Suicide and the Law, 5 Melb. U. L. Rev. 1, 7 (1965).

Attempted suicide was also a crime at common law. A few American jurisdictions have adopted this view, but most, including California, attach no criminal liability to one who makes a suicide attempt. . . . [A]s one commentator has noted, "[the] current psychiatric view is that attempted suicide is a symptom of mental illness and, as such, it makes no more sense to affix criminal liability to it than to any other symptom of any other illness. . . ."

Note, The Punishment of Suicide—A Need for Change, 14 Vill. L. Rev. 463, 469 (1969). Finally, it has been said that "all modern research points to one conclusion about the problem of suicide—the irrelevance of the criminal law to its solution." Id. at 473.

The law has, however, retained culpability for aiding, abetting and advising suicide. At common law, an aider and abettor was guilty of murder . . . because he [assisted in] the self-murder of the other. Most states provide, either by statute or case law, criminal sanctions for aiding suicide, but few adopt the extreme common law position that such conduct is murder. Some jurisdictions instead classify aiding suicide as a unique type of manslaughter. But the predominant statutory scheme, and the one adopted in California, is to create a *sui generis* crime of [assisting] suicide. "This latter structure . . . reflects a fundamental shift in the understanding of the law. Since public morals are no longer imposed upon the would-be suicide, the traditional rationale that would support the proscription of assisting suicide as the assistance of a crime is accordingly eroded." Englehardt & Malloy, Suicide and Assisting Suicide: A Critique of Legal Sanctions, 36 Sw. L.J. 1003, 1019-1020 (1982). The modern trend reflected by [California's] statutory scheme is therefore to mitigate the punishment for assisting a suicide by removing it from the harsh consequences of homicide law and giving it a separate criminal classification more carefully tailored to the actual culpability of the aider and abettor.

The California aiding statute, in effect since 1873, provides simply that "Every person who deliberately aids, or advises or encourages another to commit suicide, is guilty of a felony." Penal Code, §401. . . . The sole California decision which . . . considers criminal liability for assisting suicide under this statute is People v. Matlock, 51 Cal. 2d 682, 336 P.2d 505 (1959). . . .

The defendant in *Matlock* was convicted of murder and robbery. Although admitting that he strangled the victim and took his money, the defendant claimed he did so solely at the victim's insistence. According to the defendant, the victim, who had only six months to live and had been recently convicted of a federal crime, sought a way to die but could not commit suicide without forfeiting the benefits of his insurance policy; the victim therefore induced the defendant to kill him and take his property so that it would appear to be a robbery-murder.

The defendant contended that the trial court erred in refusing his requested instructions on aiding and abetting suicide under section 401 of the Penal Code. Relying on the Oregon decision in People v. Bouse, 199 Ore. 676, 264 P.2d 800 (1953), we held that the defendant's active participation in the final overt act causing the victim's death, i.e., strangling him, precluded the application of the aiding suicide statute.

In *Bouse*, the defendant's wife drowned in a bathtub; there was evidence that she had told the defendant she wanted to die and that he attempted suicide shortly after her death. On the evidence, the jury could have found that the defendant held his wife's head underwater, despite her struggles, until she died, thereby committing murder. On the other hand, the jury might have found that the defendant merely ran the water and assisted his wife into the tub, and was therefore guilty of only manslaughter under the Oregon assisting statute. In upholding the manslaughter instruction, the court reasoned that the latter statute

> does not contemplate active participation by one in the overt act directly causing death. It contemplates some participation in the events leading up to the commission of the final overt act, such as furnishing the means for bringing about death — the gun, the knife, the poison, or providing the water, for the use of the person who himself commits the act of self-murder. But where a person actually performs, or actively assists in performing, the overt act resulting in death, such as shooting or stabbing the victim, administering the poison, or holding one under water until death takes place by drowning, his act constitutes murder, and it is wholly immaterial whether this act is committed pursuant to an agreement with the victim, such as a mutual suicide pact.

People v. Bouse, supra, at 812; quoted in *Matlock*, supra, 51 Cal. 2d at 694. . . .

Under *Matlock* and *Bouse*, the key to distinguishing between the crimes of murder and of assisting suicide is the active or passive role of the defendant in the suicide. If the defendant merely furnishes the means, he is guilty of aiding a suicide; if he actively participates in the death of the suicide victim, he is guilty of murder. If this literal formulation were to be applied mechanically to the facts in the case at hand, it would be difficult not to conclude that the minor, by driving the car, "actively participated" in the death of his friend Jeff. It must be remembered, however, that *Matlock* did not involve a suicide pact but instead dealt with the more straightforward situation in which a suicide victim is killed as a result of direct injury that the defendant inflicts on him, i.e., strangling. The reasoning which justified the application of the active/ passive distinction in *Matlock* is therefore not wholly apposite to the peculiar facts shown here. The present case requires us instead to consider an entirely distinct situation to determine whether the minor's actions fall most appropriately within the conduct sought to be proscribed by Penal Code section 401.

It has been suggested that "[states] maintaining statutes prohibiting aiding . . . suicide attempt to do so to discourage the actions of those who might encourage a suicide in order to advance personal motives." Note, Criminal Aspects of Suicide in the United States, 7 N.C. Cent. L.J. 156, 162 (1975). . . . "[A]lthough the evidence indicates that one who attempts suicide is suffering from mental disease, there is not a hint of such evidence with respect to the aider and abettor. . . . [The] justifications for punishment apply to the aider and abettor, while they do not apply to the attempted suicide." Note, Punishment of Suicide, supra, 14 Vill. L. Rev. at 476.

The mutual suicide pact situation, however, represents something of a hybrid between the attempted suicide and the aiding suicide scenarios. In essence, it is actually a double attempted suicide, and therefore the rationale for not punishing those who attempt suicide would seem to apply. "Although there may have been aiding and abetting involved in the suicide pact, the survivor is distinguishable from a non-suicide pact aider and abettor in the sense that he was also a potential victim." Id. at 480.

> Suicides in pursuance of a pact are merely cases of double or multiple suicides. There can be no more justification for punishing an attempted double suicide than for punishing an attempted individual suicide. As in the case of an attempt at individual suicide, punishing the survivor of a genuine pact can serve no deterrent purpose, may hinder medical treatment, and is merely useless cruelty. It can do no more than strengthen the will to succeed in the act of self-destruction.

Williams, The Sanctity of Life and the Criminal Law 305 (1957). Dostoevski wrote, "the law of self-destruction and the law of self-preservation are equally strong in humanity." Dostoevski, The Idiot 356 (Modern Library edition, 1935). As we have noted, attempted suicide is not a crime in California.

On the other hand, it cannot be denied that the individuals involved in the pact aid . . . each other in committing suicide: Although such individuals are thus not totally lacking in blameworthiness, their criminal responsibility would appear to fall far short of the culpability of one who actively kills another at the request of the victim, such as the defendant in *Matlock*. We are thus faced with a dilemma: Should one who attempts suicide by means of a mutual suicide pact be liable for first degree murder at one extreme, or at the other, only for aiding and abetting a suicide? The current law in California provides no options save these.

Traditionally under the common law the survivor of a suicide pact was held to be guilty of murder. . . . It has been suggested that

> [surviving] a suicide pact gives rise to a presumption . . . that the participant may have entered into the pact in less than good faith. Survival, either because one party backed out at the last minute or because the poison, or other agent, did not have the desired effect, suggests that the pact may have been employed to induce the other person to take his own life.

Brenner, Undue Influence in the Criminal Law: A Proposed Analysis of the Criminal Offense of "Causing Suicide," 47 Alb. L. Rev. 62, 85-86 (1982). . . .

Under the facts presented here, these concerns are not particularly appropriate. First, the trial judge was satisfied there was a genuine suicide pact between Jeff and the minor. By "genuine," we mean simply that the pact was freely entered into and was not induced by force, duress or deception. There is no evidence in the present case that Jeff's participation in the pact was anything but fully voluntary and uncoerced. Second, because of the instrumentality used there was no danger of fraud: the potential consequences for the minor of driving the car off the cliff were identical to the potential consequences for Jeff, his passenger. Finally, the suicide and the attempted suicide were committed simultaneously by the same act.

These factors clearly distinguish the present case from the murder-suicide pact situation in which one party to the agreement actively kills the other (e.g., by shooting, poison, etc.) and then is to kill himself. The active participant in that scenario has the opportunity to renege on the agreement after killing the other or to feign agreement only for the purpose of disposing of his companion and without any true intention to commit suicide himself. By contrast, in the case at hand the minor and Jeff, because of the instrumentality chosen, necessarily were to commit their suicidal acts simultaneously and were subject to identical risks of death. The potential for fraud is thus absent in a genuine suicide pact executed simultaneously by both parties by means of the same instrumentality. The traditional rationale for holding the survivor of the pact guilty of murder is thus not appropriate in this limited factual situation.

The anomaly of classifying the minor's actions herein as murder is further illustrated by consideration of Jeff's potential criminal liability had he survived. If Jeff, the passenger, had survived and the minor had been killed, Jeff would be guilty, at most, of a violation of Penal Code section 401. In order to commit suicide by this means, i.e., a car, only one of the parties to the pact, the driver, can be said to "control" the instrumentality. To make the distinction between criminal liability for first degree murder and merely [assisting] suicide turn on the fortuitous circumstance of which of the pair was actually driving serves no rational purpose. The illogic of such a distinction has been similarly recognized in the classic example of the parties to the pact agreeing to commit suicide by gassing themselves in a closed room. If the party who turns on the gas survives, he is guilty of murder; if on the other hand, the other person survives, that person's criminal liability is only that of an aider and abettor. "It would be discreditable if any actual legal consequences were made to hinge upon such distinctions." Williams, supra, at 299.

In light of the foregoing analysis we decline to ritualistically apply the active/passive distinction of *Matlock* to the genuine suicide pact situation in which the suicides are undertaken simultaneously by a single instrumentality. Given the inapplicability of *Matlock*, the actions of the minor constitute no more than a violation of Penal Code section 401.

The order declaring the minor a ward of the court is reversed and the cause is remanded to the trial court for further proceedings not inconsistent with this opinion.

People v. Cleaves

Court of Appeal of California, Fourth Appellate District
229 Cal. App. 3d 367; 280 Cal. Rptr. 146 (1991)

Opinion of WORK, J.

John Cleaves appeals a judgment convicting him of second degree murder (Penal Code, §187), primarily contending the court erred by failing to honor his request to instruct on a lesser related offense of aiding and abetting a suicide (§401). . . . For the following reasons, we find his [contention] meritless and affirm the judgment.

I

. . . [T]o evaluate whether aiding and abetting suicide instructions were warranted on the facts presented to the trial court, we set forth Cleaves's version of the events in detail.

Cleaves was especially sensitive to the sufferings associated with AIDS. He was living with and helping a friend who was in an advanced stage of illness from AIDS. Another of Cleaves's friends had died of AIDS. Around 3 A.M., as Cleaves was walking down the street, Eaton drove alongside and invited Cleaves to his apartment. At Eaton's apartment they twice engaged in sex over a period of hours. After they had sex, Eaton told Cleaves he had AIDS. During the day Eaton and Cleaves talked seriously about AIDS and death; Eaton telling Cleaves he had once tried to kill himself in New Orleans, and wanted to die. Eaton asked Cleaves how he looked, and when Cleaves responded he looked fine, Eaton told him he did not feel that way. Cleaves stayed with Eaton because he was concerned and was trying to help him. Eaton talked about the suffering a person goes through in the final stages of the illness, which he wanted to avoid.

Eaton talked of a service called the Black Mask that killed people with AIDS for money. Eaton offered various items of his personal property to Cleaves which he placed in the living room.[3] When Eaton stated he wanted to kill himself by strangulation Cleaves agreed to help him "do it." Later they knelt and prayed, and Eaton repeated his resolve to commit suicide.

Eaton tied a sash from his bathrobe around his neck, lay down on the bed, and asked Cleaves to tie his hands with the sash from his neck and to his feet. Cleaves tied Eaton's wrists behind his back with a belt, and tied the sash tautly from his neck to his wrists. Eaton bent his knees up, and Cleaves tied Eaton's feet to his hands with a soft sash or belt. Thus trussed, Eaton's body was arched with his feet in the air, his thighs still on the bed, with some distance between his feet and his hands. Eaton's face was down in a pillow. Eaton "pulled down"; and, when requested, Cleaves put his hands on Eaton's back to steady him on the bed. Eaton did not roll over on his side and Cleaves did not try to prevent him from doing so. Cleaves did not have to exert pressure to hold him down; his role was to steady him as he rocked up and down to prevent him from falling off the bed which Eaton feared would prevent him from completing the act of suicide. Eaton proceeded to strangle himself by "just straightening up," with his face staying down in the pillow.

---

3. These included a pair of pants, two shirts, a jacket, a belt, a collar, a ring, some change, a pair of cuff links, a toiletry bag, and a teddy bear.

When the sash slipped from Eaton's neck, Cleaves rewrapped it at Eaton's request and retied it to his hands. Cleaves never pulled on the sash or attempted to strangle Eaton; he did not exert pressure on the sash or on any tie; he did nothing to directly strangle Eaton; and he did not hold Eaton's face in the pillow. Eaton did not start choking when Cleaves tied the sash from his neck to his hands; rather Eaton began choking when he (Eaton) started "pushing" back on the sash with his hands and feet. Eaton was in sole control of how tight the sash was around his neck by straightening out his body with his feet.

Cleaves told the police that after the tie around his neck broke, he had to "extra hold him down," and he "laid on him." When asked by the police if he was helping Eaton out by putting enough weight on his back to where it started to choke him, because Eaton was not doing "it" himself, Cleaves answered, "yes." When asked if he put his full weight on Eaton, Cleaves told the police no, variously describing his conduct as placing his hands and pushing him down on the bed; just holding him down without putting a lot of weight on him; just holding him to keep him from bucking; holding him while standing along side of the bed; and holding him without putting any pressure on him. . . .

Cleaves acknowledged at trial that he knew Eaton was going to die when he tied him up; he wanted to help him die; and he knew if he did not tie him up and hold him on the bed he was not going to die.

After Eaton's death, Cleaves fixed himself a drink, put on a pair of pants and shoes Eaton had given him, and as Eaton had requested, took the bindings off Eaton and threw them away. Eaton had told Cleaves his wallet containing his automatic teller machine (ATM) card was in the glove compartment of his car, and had given Cleaves his ATM number. Cleaves took the wallet and withdrew money from the ATM machine over the next three days. Because he did not drive, Cleaves had a friend pick up Eaton's car.

When arrested, Cleaves at first denied involvement in Eaton's death, insisting he fell asleep and woke up to find Eaton dead. After continued interrogation, Cleaves finally admitted he tied Eaton up and held him down. . . .

The coroner found a type of cancer in Eaton's intestines which indicated infection with the AIDS virus, but the quantity and smallness of the infected cells suggested Eaton would not have known he had the cancer or suffered from any symptoms. Eaton tested positive for the AIDS virus, but the coroner did not find evidence of any other illnesses. The cause of Eaton's death was determined to be asphyxia by ligature strangulation, as evidenced by ligature marks on his neck and wrists, abrasions on his lips, chin and nose, and biting of the lower lip and tongue. There was no other evidence of trauma to his body. The coroner acknowledged the ligature marks could be consistent with Eaton attempting to pull on his neck or strangle himself, noting it does not take much pressure to cause asphyxiation and it is possible for a person to strangle himself with a ligature tied from his neck to his wrists. On the other hand, the coroner stated a person lapses into unconsciousness prior to death during strangulation, and once unconscious it was doubtful the person could maintain the pressure necessary to cause the tension to a ligature from his neck to his wrists.

II

A defendant is entitled to a lesser related offense instruction when there is some basis on which the jury could find the lesser offense, when the offense is closely related to the offense charged and shown by the evidence, and when the defendant is relying on a theory of defense consistent with the lesser offense. Although the trial court allowed the defense to present evidence on its aiding and abetting suicide theory, it ultimately refused to instruct the jury on the lesser related offense. . . .

. . . Accordingly, the jury was instructed as to first and second degree murder only, and convicted Cleaves of the latter. Further, the trial court fashioned an instruction addressing the evidence pertaining to suicide as follows:

> "There has been evidence that the defendant killed the victim at the victim's request. You are the exclusive judges of whether or not this is true and, if true, what impact it will have on your verdict. However, if you find beyond a reasonable doubt that the offense of murder in the first or second degree was committed by the defendant as defined in these instructions, it is immaterial whether the acts of the defendant were committed pursuant to an agreement with the victim."

Section 401 provides: "Every person who deliberately aids, or advises, or encourages another to commit suicide, is guilty of a felony."[6]

As explained by our Supreme Court, the "key to distinguishing between the crimes of murder and of assisting suicide is the active or passive role of the defendant in the suicide. If the defendant merely furnishes the means, he is guilty of aiding a suicide; if he actively participates in the death of the suicide victim, he is guilty of murder." In re Joseph G., 34 Cal. 3d 429, 436, 667 P.2d 1176 (1983).[7] The statute providing for a crime less than murder

> "does not contemplate active participation by one in the overt act directly causing death. It contemplates some participation in the events leading up to the commission of the final overt act, such as furnishing the means for bringing about death—the gun, the knife, the poison, or providing the water, for

---

6. The felony is punishable by a state prison term of 16 months, 2 years, or 3 years (§18), whereas second degree murder is punishable by a term of 15 years to life (§190).

7. *In re Joseph G.* declines to apply this active/passive distinction to a genuine suicide pact situation, where—although the defendant actively participates in the death—the suicides are undertaken simultaneously by a single instrumentality. Id. at 436, 440.

the use of the person who himself commits the act of self-murder. But where a person *actually performs, or actively assists in performing, the overt act resulting in death,* such as shooting or stabbing the victim, administering the poison, or holding one under water until death takes place by drowning, his act constitutes murder, and it is wholly immaterial whether this act is committed pursuant to an agreement with the victim. . . ." People v. Matlock, 51 Cal. 2d 682, 694, 336 P.2d 505 (1959) (emphasis added).

In *Matlock,* the defendant put a cord around the victim's neck, the victim adjusted the cord, and the defendant choked him. Id. at 689. The court held aiding and abetting suicide instructions were properly refused since the defendant "actively strangled" the victim. Id. at 694.

Here, viewing the facts most favorably to the defense, there are no facts which would support the requested instruction. Although Cleaves may not have applied pressure to the ligature itself, he admits his holding Eaton to keep him from falling off the bed was designed to assist Eaton to complete the act of strangulation. This factual scenario indisputably shows active assistance in the overt act of strangulation, and the instruction was not warranted. . . .

. . . *In re Joseph G.* observes [that] suicide and attempted suicide are [widely] viewed as symptoms of mental illness and not crimes, and although some jurisdictions classify aiding and abetting suicide as manslaughter, most jurisdictions, including California, create a *sui generis* crime for aiding suicide, "removing it from the harsh consequences of homicide law and giving it a separate criminal classification more carefully tailored to the actual culpability of the aider and abettor." *In re Joseph G.,* 34 Cal. 3d at 434-435. . . . [C]urrent law in California provides no options between the two extremes of murder at one end, and aiding and abetting suicide at the other. . . .

The judgment is affirmed.

Notes on Joseph G. and Cleaves

1. The opinions in both *Joseph G.* and *Cleaves* discuss the question whether the defendants in those cases are guilty of "aiding and abetting" the victims' suicides. For present purposes, you should treat those terms as synonyms for "assisting" the victims' suicides, and you should assume that "assisting" carries its ordinary meaning. The meaning of "aiding and abetting" (otherwise known as complicity, or accomplice liability) is addressed later, in Chapter 7.

2. As a general matter, a single incident may lead to multiple criminal charges. *Joseph G.* and *Cleaves,* however, begin with the following proposition: Under California law, a criminal defendant may be convicted of assisting suicide or homicide, but not both. To put it another way, under California law assisting suicide is a "lesser included" offense of the "greater" offense of homicide, such that no one can be punished for both in a case arising out of a single death. That is a common phenomenon in American criminal law. A defendant may be convicted of either possessing a given quantity of illegal drugs or possessing those drugs with intent to distribute them, but not for both. Under most state criminal codes, a defendant may be convicted of rape or of a lesser form of sexual assault, but not both. All state criminal codes include degrees of homicide: first degree murder, second degree murder, voluntary manslaughter, involuntary manslaughter, and negligent homicide—and often there are more items on the list, such as the assisting suicide offense at issue in *Joseph G.* and *Cleaves*. A homicide defendant charged with killing a single victim may be punished for only one of these offenses.

Note that the situation of greater and lesser included crimes might arise for two different reasons: First, the enacting legislature might have intended the relevant criminal statutes to be interpreted in that way. This seems to be what the *Joseph G.* court concluded: "The modern trend reflected by this statutory scheme is therefore to mitigate the punishment for assisting a suicide by removing it from the harsh consequences of homicide law and giving it a separate criminal classification." Second, no matter what the legislature might have intended, two statutory crimes might be so closely related to one another that they *must* be treated as "the same offence" for purposes of applying the Double Jeopardy Clause in the Fifth Amendment to the U.S. Constitution. The constitutional test is whether or not the two statutes each require proof of at least one unique element that the other statute does not require. Blockburger v. United States, 284 U.S. 299 (1932). If two criminal statutes overlap to such an extent that there is *not* at least one unique element for each crime, then with respect to a single incident, the Double Jeopardy Clause bars the defendant from being punished for both crimes.*

3. Joseph G. drove his car over a cliff because he wanted to die. That act—Joseph G.'s act—directly caused his friend's death. On Cleaves' version of the facts, Cleaves helped Eaton strangle himself because Eaton asked him to do so; Eaton's conduct caused his own death as much as Cleaves' conduct did. Why, then, is Joseph G. liable only for assisting suicide, while Cleaves is liable for murder? The *Matlock* test does not answer the question: Joseph G.'s conduct was at least as "active" as Cleaves'. Perhaps the answer, again, goes to the risk that evidence was being manipulated by the defendant. Only Cleaves knows what happened in *Cleaves*; not so in *Joseph G.* Is it fair to base criminal punishment on such factors?

4. Justice Mosk's opinion in *Joseph G.* is unusual in that it makes very little legal doctrine. The *Matlock* test continues to apply in assisted suicide cases,

---

* This sentence is true only for two criminal statutes enacted by the same sovereign. Due to the unique nature of American federalism, two different sovereigns—either two states, or a state and the federal government—may constitutionally punish a person for the exact same crime. See Heath v. Alabama, 474 U.S. 82 (1985).

but that test is deemed inapplicable on the facts of *Joseph G.* The result is a "rule" that applies only to those facts. In a sense, Mosk's opinion resembles a typical jury verdict more than it resembles a typical appellate opinion: somewhat like Justice Handy's opinion in *Speluncean Explorers.* Is Handy a good model to follow in this context? Does Mosk's opinion trouble you? Should it?

Notes on Statutory Interpretation

Both *Joseph G.* and *Cleaves* involve the judicial interpretation of criminal statutes enacted by the California legislature. What should a judge do, when faced with such a daunting task? Although reasonable minds might disagree about what to do in any particular case, there is general agreement about both the ultimate goal and the basic steps in the process of statutory interpretation.

The goal of statutory interpretation is to determine, to the extent possible, the intent of the legislature that enacted the particular statute in question. Note that it is the particular legislature that existed at the time of statutory enactment whose intent matters most. The views of prior and subsequent legislatures matter only indirectly, in the sense that they may help the judge to figure out the intent of the legislature that actually enacted the statute (unless, of course, the subsequent legislature has actually amended the statute in question, in which case it *becomes* the relevant legislature).

How does a judge determine legislative intent? The first step in the process is to look at the language of the statute itself, for that is usually the best gauge of legislative intent. If the language is clear and unambiguous, then no further "interpreting" need occur. If the statutory language is unclear, however, then the judge might get lucky and find something authoritative in the legislative history, that is, the official record of proceedings relating to the bill as it moved its way through the legislature. This record might include earlier drafts of the bill, amendments, statements by co-sponsors, committee hearings and reports, and—best of all—the report of any conference committee or similar entity charged with the responsibility to develop a consensus version of the bill capable of being passed by both legislative chambers. In Congress, legislative histories tend to be extensive, but in many states, they are anything but. So this second step in the process of statutory interpretation is one that only rarely turns out to be very useful.

Beyond statutory language and legislative history, a judge has several additional methods that can be used to determine legislative intent. One is to examine more broadly the overall statutory framework within which the particular statute in question resides, which may reveal structural evidence of the legislature's intent. *Joseph G.* and *Cleaves* involved such an inquiry, since the "assisting suicide" statute had to be interpreted in light of another criminal statute prohibiting murder. Another method is to apply "rules of construction" that have been developed by judges based on reasonable assumptions about what legislatures usually mean when they enact statutes containing particular language. So, for instance, judges sometimes resort to the rule, "*expressio unius est exclusio alterius*," meaning that items in a statutory list are assumed to be exclusive, and any items not mentioned are assumed not to be covered by the statute. Another well-known rule of construction is "*ejusdem generis*," meaning that general terms listed in a statute should be interpreted in light of any specific terms included in the same list. Still another such rule is that statutes should be interpreted in a manner that will not give rise to a serious constitutional issue; judges usually assume that legislatures do not intend to enact statutes that might be held unconstitutional.

As we saw in the *Speluncean Explorers* case, some judges (like Justice Foster) believe that they are authorized to interpret statutes on the basis of sound public policy, or some other important normative consideration, on the ground that legislatures should be assumed to intend to enact statutes that make sense and that will operate for the overall good of society. Other judges (such as Justice Keen), however, draw the line at such reasoning, viewing it as nothing more than thinly disguised judicial legislating.

What happens if, after all of the available and appropriate methods of statutory construction have been exhausted, a judge still cannot decide what the legislature intended? What is the judge to do in such a situation?

2. The Not-Quite-Rule of Lenity

Ambiguities in criminal statutes are to be resolved in defendants' favor. So holds the "rule of lenity." The rule might be seen as a heightened burden of persuasion with respect to statutory interpretation: If the issue is doubtful, defendant wins, just as the beyond-a-reasonable-doubt standard of proof holds that doubts about the facts must be resolved in criminal defendants' favor as well.

That proposition sounds important: One might think that statutory ambiguity is fairly common—recall *Joseph G.* and *Cleaves*—so that any doctrine requiring that doubtful cases go defendants' way would have large consequences. That is not so of the rule of lenity: In practice, it means much less than first appears. The next case may help to explain why.

Brogan v. United States

Supreme Court of the United States
522 U.S. 398 (1998)

Justice SCALIA delivered the opinion of the Court.

This case presents the question whether there is an exception to criminal liability under 18 U.S.C. §1001 for a false statement that consists of the mere denial of wrongdoing, the so-called "exculpatory no."

While acting as a union officer during 1987 and 1988, petitioner James Brogan accepted cash payments from JRD Management Corporation, a real estate company whose employees were represented by the union. On October 4, 1993, federal agents from the Department of Labor and the Internal Revenue Service visited petitioner at his home. The agents identified themselves and explained that they were seeking petitioner's cooperation in an investigation of JRD and various individuals. They told petitioner that if he wished to cooperate, he should have an attorney contact the U.S. Attorney's Office, and that if he could not afford an attorney, one could be appointed for him.

The agents then asked petitioner if he would answer some questions, and he agreed. One question was whether he had received any cash or gifts from JRD when he was a union officer. Petitioner's response was "no." At that point, the agents disclosed that a search of JRD headquarters had produced company records showing the contrary. They also told petitioner that lying to federal agents in the course of an investigation was a crime. Petitioner did not modify his answers, and the interview ended shortly thereafter.

Petitioner was indicted for accepting unlawful cash payments from an employer in violation of 29 U.S.C. §§186(b)(1), (a)(2), (d)(2), and making a false statement within the jurisdiction of a federal agency in violation of 18 U.S.C. §1001. He was tried, along with several co-defendants, before a jury in the United States District Court for the Southern District of New York, and was found guilty. The United States Court of Appeals for the Second Circuit affirmed the convictions. . . .

At the time petitioner falsely replied "no" to the Government investigators' question, 18 U.S.C. §1001 (1988 ed.) provided:

> "Whoever, in any matter within the jurisdiction of any department or agency of the United States knowingly and willfully falsifies, conceals or covers up by any trick, scheme, or device a material fact, or makes any false, fictitious or fraudulent statements or representations, or makes or uses any false writing or document knowing the same to contain any false, fictitious or fraudulent statement or entry, shall be fined not more than $10,000 or imprisoned not more than five years, or both."

By its terms, 18 U.S.C. §1001 covers "any" false statement. . . . The word "no" in response to a question assuredly makes a "statement," and petitioner does not contest that his utterance was false or that it was made "knowingly and willfully." In fact, petitioner concedes that under a "literal reading" of the statute he loses. Brief for Petitioner 5.

Petitioner asks us, however, to depart from the literal text that Congress has enacted, and to approve the doctrine adopted by many Circuits which excludes from the scope of §1001 the "exculpatory no." The central feature of this doctrine is that a simple denial of guilt does not come within the statute. There is considerable variation among the Circuits concerning, among other things, what degree of elaborated tale-telling carries a statement beyond simple denial. In the present case, however, the Second Circuit agreed with petitioner that his statement would constitute a "true 'exculpatory no' as recognized in other circuits," 96 F.3d at 37, but aligned itself with the Fifth Circuit . . . in categorically rejecting the doctrine.

Petitioner's argument in support of the "exculpatory no" doctrine proceeds from the major premise that §1001 criminalizes only those statements to Government investigators that "pervert governmental functions"; to the minor premise that simple denials of guilt to government investigators do not pervert governmental functions; to the conclusion that §1001 does not criminalize simple denials of guilt to Government investigators. Both premises seem to us mistaken. As to the minor: We cannot imagine how it could be true that falsely denying guilt in a Government investigation does not pervert a governmental function. Certainly the investigation of wrongdoing is a proper governmental function; and since it is the very purpose of an investigation to uncover the truth, any falsehood relating to the subject of the investigation perverts that function. It could be argued, perhaps, that a disbelieved falsehood does not pervert an investigation. But making the existence of this crime turn upon the credulousness of the federal investigator (or the persuasiveness of the liar) would be exceedingly strange; such a defense to the analogous crime of perjury is certainly unheard-of. Moreover, as we shall see, the only support for the "perversion of governmental functions" limitation is a statement of this Court referring to the possibility (as opposed to the certainty) of perversion of function—a possibility that exists whenever investigators are told a falsehood relevant to their task.

In any event, we find no basis for the major premise that only those falsehoods that pervert governmental functions are covered by §1001. Petitioner derives this premise from a comment we made in United States v. Gilliland, 312 U.S. 86 (1941), a case involving the predecessor to §1001. . . . The defendant in *Gilliland* . . . argued that the statute should be read to apply only to matters in which the Government has a financial or proprietary interest. In rejecting that argument, we noted that Congress had specifically amended the statute to cover "any matter within the jurisdiction of any department or agency of the United States," thereby indicating "the congressional intent to protect the authorized functions of governmental departments and agencies from the perversion which might result from the deceptive practices described." Id., at 93. Petitioner would elevate this statement to a holding that §1001 does not apply where a perversion of governmental functions does not exist. But it is not, and cannot be, our practice to restrict the unqualified language of a statute to the particular evil that Congress was trying to remedy—even assuming that it is possible to identify that evil from something other than the text of the statute itself. . . .

Petitioner repeats the argument made by many supporters of the "exculpatory no," that the doctrine is necessary to eliminate the grave risk that §1001 will become an instrument of prosecutorial abuse. The supposed danger is that overzealous prosecutors will use this provision as a means of "piling on" offenses—sometimes punishing the denial of wrongdoing more severely than the wrongdoing itself. The objectors' principal grievance on this score, however, lies not with the hypothetical prosecutors but with Congress itself, which has decreed the obstruction of a legitimate investigation to be a separate offense, and a serious one. It is not for us to revise that judgment. . . .

A brief word in response to the dissent's assertion that the Court may interpret a criminal statute more narrowly than it is written: Some of the cases it cites for that proposition represent instances in which the Court . . . applied what it thought to be a background interpretive principle of general application. Staples v. United States, 511 U.S. 600, 619 (1994) (construing statute to contain common-law requirement of *mens rea*); Sorrells v. United States, 287 U.S. 435, 446 (1932) (construing statute not to cover violations produced by entrapment); United States v. Palmer, 16 U.S. 610, 631 (1818) (construing statute not to apply extraterritorially to noncitizens). Also into this last category falls the dissent's correct assertion that the present statute does not "make it a crime for an undercover narcotics agent to make a false statement to a drug peddler." Criminal prohibitions do not generally apply to reasonable enforcement actions by officers of the law. See, e.g., 2 P. Robinson, Criminal Law Defenses §142(a), at 121 (1984) ("Every American jurisdiction recognizes some form of law enforcement authority justification").

It is one thing to acknowledge and accept such well defined (or even newly enunciated), generally applicable, background principles of assumed legislative intent. It is quite another to espouse the broad proposition that criminal statutes do not have to be read as broadly as they are written, but are subject to case-by-case exceptions. The problem with adopting such an expansive, user-friendly judicial rule is that there is no way of knowing when, or how, the rule is to be invoked. As to the when: The only reason Justice Stevens adduces for invoking it here is that a felony conviction for this offense seems to him harsh. Which it may well be. But the instances in which courts may ignore harsh penalties are set forth in the Constitution, and to go beyond them will surely leave us at sea. And as to the how: There is no reason in principle why the dissent chooses to mitigate the harshness by saying that §1001 does not embrace the "exculpatory no," rather than by saying that §1001 has no application unless the defendant has been warned of the consequences of lying, or indeed unless the defendant has been put under oath. We are again at sea. . . .

In sum, we find nothing to support the "exculpatory no" doctrine except the many Court of Appeals decisions that have embraced it. . . . Courts may not create their own limitations on legislation, no matter how alluring the policy arguments for doing so, and no matter how widely the blame may be spread. Because the plain language of §1001 admits of no exception for an "exculpatory no," we affirm the judgment of the Court of Appeals.

Justice Souter, concurring in part and concurring in the judgment.

I join the opinion of the Court except for its response to petitioner's argument premised on the potential for prosecutorial abuse of 18 U.S.C. §1001 as now written. On that point I have joined Justice Ginsburg's opinion espousing congressional attention to the risks inherent in the statute's current breadth.

Justice Ginsburg, with whom Justice Souter joins, concurring in the judgment.

Because a false denial fits the unqualified language of 18 U.S.C. §1001, I concur in the affirmance of Brogan's conviction. I write separately, however, to call attention to the extraordinary authority Congress, perhaps unwittingly, has conferred on prosecutors to manufacture crimes. . . .

At the time of Brogan's offense, §1001 made it a felony "knowingly and willfully" to make "any false, fictitious or fraudulent statements or representations" in "any matter within the jurisdiction of any department or agency of the United States." That encompassing formulation arms Government agents with authority not simply to apprehend lawbreakers, but to generate felonies, crimes of a kind that only a Government officer could prompt.

This case is illustrative. Two federal investigators paid an unannounced visit one evening to James Brogan's home. The investigators already possessed records indicating that Brogan, a union officer, had received cash from a company that employed members of the union Brogan served. (The agents gave no advance warning, one later testified, because they wanted to retain the element of surprise.) When the agents asked Brogan whether he had received any money or gifts from the company, Brogan responded "No." The agents asked no further questions. After Brogan just said "No," however, the agents told him: (1) the Government had in hand the records indicating that his answer was false; and (2) lying to federal agents in the course of an investigation is a crime. Had counsel appeared on the spot, Brogan likely would have received and followed advice to amend his answer, to say immediately: "Strike that; I plead not guilty." But no counsel attended the unannounced interview, and Brogan divulged nothing more. Thus, when the interview ended, a federal offense had been completed — even though, for all we can tell, Brogan's unadorned denial misled no one.

A further illustration. In United States v. Tabor, 788 F.2d 714 (CA11 1986), an Internal Revenue Service agent discovered that Tabor, a notary public, had violated Florida law by notarizing a deed even though two signatories had not personally appeared before her (one had died five weeks before the document was signed). With this knowledge in hand, and without "warning Tabor of the possible consequences of her statements," id., at 718, the agent went to her home with a deputy sheriff and questioned her about the transaction. When Tabor, regrettably but humanly, denied wrongdoing, the Government prosecuted her under §1001. See id., at 716. An IRS agent thus turned a violation of state law into a federal felony by eliciting a lie that misled no one. (The Eleventh Circuit reversed the §1001 conviction, relying on the "exculpatory no" doctrine. Id., at 719.)

As these not altogether uncommon episodes show,[4] §1001 may apply to encounters between agents and their targets "under extremely informal circumstances which do not sufficiently alert the person interviewed to the danger that false statements may lead to a felony conviction." United States v. Ehrlichman, 379 F. Supp. 291, 292 (DC 1974). . . . Unlike proceedings in which a false statement can be prosecuted as perjury, there may be no oath, no pause to concentrate the speaker's mind on the importance of his or her answers. As in Brogan's case, the target may not be informed that a false "No" is a criminal offense until after he speaks.

At oral argument, the Solicitor General forthrightly observed that §1001 could even be used to "escalate completely innocent conduct into a felony." . . . If the statute of limitations has run on an offense—as it had on four of the five payments Brogan was accused of accepting—the prosecutor can endeavor to revive the case by instructing an investigator to elicit a fresh denial of guilt. Prosecution in these circumstances . . . [amounts to] Government generation of a crime when the underlying suspected wrongdoing is or has become nonpunishable. . . .

Congress has been alert to our decisions in this area, as its enactment of the False Statements Accountability Act of 1996 (passed in response to our decision in Hubbard v. United States, 514 U.S. 695 (1995)) demonstrates. Similarly, after today's decision, Congress may advert to the "exculpatory no" doctrine and the problem that prompted its formulation. . . .

Justice STEVENS, with whom Justice BREYER joins, dissenting.

. . . The mere fact that a false denial fits within the unqualified language of 18 U.S.C. §1001 is not, in my opinion, a sufficient reason for rejecting a well-settled interpretation of that statute. It is not at all unusual for this Court to conclude that the literal text of a criminal statute is broader than the coverage intended by Congress. See, e.g., Staples v. United States, 511 U.S. 600, 605, 619 (1994); Williams v. United States, 458 U.S. 279, 286 (1982) (holding that statute prohibiting the making of false statements to a bank was inapplicable to depositing of a "bad check" because "the Government's interpretation . . . would make a surprisingly broad range of unremarkable

---

4. See, e.g., United States v. Stoffey, 279 F.2d 924, 927 (CA7 1960) (defendant prosecuted for falsely denying, while effectively detained by agents, that he participated in illegal gambling; court concluded that "purpose of the agents was not to investigate or to obtain information, but to obtain admissions," and that "they were not thereafter diverted from their course by alleged false statements of defendant"); see also United States v. Goldfine, 538 F.2d 815, 820 (CA9 1976) (agents asked defendant had he made any out-of-state purchases, investigators already knew he had, he stated he had not; . . . defendant was prosecuted for violating §1001).

conduct a violation of federal law"); Sorrells v. United States, 287 U.S. 435, 448 (1932) ("We are unable to conclude that it was the intention of the Congress in enacting [a Prohibition Act] statute that its processes of detection and enforcement should be abused by the instigation by government officials of an act on the part of persons otherwise innocent in order to lure them to its commission and to punish them"); United States v. Palmer, 16 U.S. 610, 631 (1818) (holding that although "words 'any person or persons,' [in maritime robbery statute] are broad enough to comprehend every human being . . . general words must not only be limited to cases within the jurisdiction of the state, but also to those objects to which the legislature intended to apply them") (Marshall, C. J.). Although the text of §1001, read literally, makes it a crime for an undercover narcotics agent to make a false statement to a drug peddler, I am confident that Congress did not intend any such result. . . .

Accordingly, I respectfully dissent.

Notes and Questions

1. You might be wondering whether the behavior of the federal agents who came to Brogan's house violated his Fifth Amendment right not to be compelled to incriminate himself. The short answer is no. As the Court explained in a portion of its opinion not reproduced above, Brogan had the right to invoke his Fifth Amendment privilege, after which he could have safely remained silent in the face of the agents' incriminating questions. But the Fifth Amendment gave Brogan no right to lie.

2. Compare *Brogan* with United States v. Bronston, 409 U.S. 352 (1973). Here are the facts in *Bronston*:

> Petitioner is the sole owner of Samuel Bronston Productions, Inc., a company that between 1958 and 1964, produced motion pictures in various European locations. For these enterprises, Bronston Productions opened bank accounts in a number of foreign countries; in 1962, for example, it had 37 accounts in five countries. As president of Bronston Productions, petitioner supervised transactions involving the foreign bank accounts.
>
> In June 1964, Bronston Productions petitioned for an arrangement with creditors under Chapter XI of the Bankruptcy Act. On June 10, 1966, a referee in bankruptcy held a [hearing] to determine, for the benefit of creditors, the extent and location of the company's assets. Petitioner's perjury conviction was founded on the answers given by him as a witness at that bankruptcy hearing, and in particular on the following colloquy with a lawyer for a creditor of Bronston Productions:
>
> "**Q:** Do you have any bank accounts in Swiss banks, Mr. Bronston?
> "**A:** No, sir.
> "**Q:** Have you ever?

"**A:** The company had an account there for about six months, in Zurich.
"**Q:** Have you any nominees who have bank accounts in Swiss banks?
"**A:** No, sir.
"**Q:** Have you ever?
"**A:** No, sir."

It is undisputed that for a period of nearly five years, between October 1959 and June 1964, petitioner had a personal bank account at the International Credit Bank in Geneva, Switzerland, into which he made deposits and upon which he drew checks totaling more than $180,000. It is likewise undisputed that petitioner's answers were literally truthful. Petitioner did not at the time of questioning have a Swiss bank account. Bronston Productions, Inc., did have the account in Zurich described by petitioner. Neither at the time of questioning nor before did petitioner have nominees who had Swiss accounts. The Government's prosecution for perjury went forward on the theory that in order to mislead his questioner, petitioner answered the second question with literal truthfulness but unresponsively addressed his answer to the company's assets and not to his own—thereby implying that he had no personal Swiss bank account at the relevant time.

409 U.S. at 353-55. The relevant portion of the federal perjury statute covers anyone who, under oath in a federal case, "willfully and contrary to such oath states or subscribes any material matter which he does not believe to be true." 18 U.S.C. §1621. The government argued that unresponsive answers that imply false propositions fall within the perjury statute.

The Supreme Court held otherwise:

. . . Beyond question, petitioner's answer to the crucial question was not responsive if we assume, as we do, that the first question was directed at personal bank accounts. There is, indeed, an implication in the answer to the second question that there was never a personal bank account; in casual conversation this interpretation might reasonably be drawn. But we are not dealing with casual conversation and the statute does not make it a criminal act for a witness to willfully state any material matter that *implies* any material matter that he does not believe to be true.

. . . We might go beyond the precise words of the statute if we thought they did not adequately express the intention of Congress, but we perceive no reason why Congress would intend the drastic sanction of a perjury prosecution to cure a testimonial mishap that could readily have been reached with a single additional question by counsel alert . . . to the incongruity of petitioner's unresponsive answer. Under the pressures and tensions of interrogation, it is not uncommon for the most earnest witnesses to give answers that are not entirely responsive. Sometimes the witness does not understand the question, or may in an excess of caution or apprehension read too much or too little into it. It should come as no surprise that a participant in a bankruptcy proceeding may have something to conceal and consciously tries to do so, or that a debtor may be embarrassed at his plight and yield information reluctantly. . . . If a witness evades, it is the lawyer's responsibility to recognize the evasion and to bring the witness back to the mark, to flush out the whole truth with the tools of adversary examination.

409 U.S. at 357-59.

The government claimed that Bronston's conduct was the functional equivalent of perjury—Bronston told no out-and-out lies, but it seems clear that he tried to (and did) mislead his questioner—even though that conduct did not fit the terms of the perjury statute. Brogan argued that his conduct differed from most false statements to government officials—his lie was unplanned, disbelieved, and harmless—even though it did fit the terms of the false statements statute. The question in both cases would seem to be: Does criminal law follow functional lines, or formal ones? In both cases, form wins.

3. More precisely, statutory text wins. In *Bronston*, the government argued that "states or subscribes" should be read (at least in some cases) as "states, subscribes, or implies." In *Brogan*, the defense maintained that the false statements statute should be read to include an exception for false denials of guilt—an exception that wasn't and isn't in the statutory text. In both cases, the side that wants to read language into a criminal statute loses. Why? One answer is, because Congress commanded both results: Federal judges' job is to apply the laws Congress writes, not to rewrite those laws to suit judges' sensibilities. But that answer has a problem: Members of Congress probably did not consider cases like *Bronston* and *Brogan* when drafting and enacting the perjury and false statements statutes. Why should judges follow legislative commands that legislators do not intend to make?

4. The more willing legislators are to fix problems with criminal statutes once those problems emerge, the less judges may feel the need to remedy those problems themselves. Recall that Justices Ginsburg and Souter voted to affirm Brogan's conviction but went on to suggest, not very subtly, that Congress revise section 1001 to exclude "exculpatory no" cases from its coverage. Congress didn't take the hint; *Brogan* remains good law today. In Hubbard v. United States, 514 U.S. 695 (1995), the Supreme Court held that section 1001 covers only lies told to agents of the executive branch. A year later, Congress passed the False Statements Accountability Act of 1996, reinstating coverage of lies told to judges, members of Congress, and their agents.

Congressional silence in *Brogan*'s wake, together with Congress's speedy overruling of *Hubbard*, suggests that members of Congress are more likely to overturn pro-defense decisions than pro-government ones. The data reported in William N. Eskridge, Jr., Overriding Supreme Court Statutory Interpretation Decisions, 101 Yale L.J. 331 (1991), support that proposition. Between 1978 and 1984, the Supreme Court decided 34 cases interpreting statutes unfavorably to criminal defendants. Congress overturned just one of those 34 decisions. During the same six years, Congress overturned 5 of 24 statutory interpretation decisions that were unfavorable to the federal government. Id. at 348 tbl. 7, 351 tbl. 9. Most judicial decisions stand, regardless of which side the decision favors. Still, Congress—state legislatures probably behave the same way, though the issue has not been studied in detail—is far more likely to reverse decisions that favor criminal defendants than decisions that favor the government.

5. Brogan was charged and convicted both of lying to FBI agents and of labor racketeering. (The latter charge is the one covered by 29 U.S.C. §186, the other statute mentioned in *Brogan.* Union officials like Brogan are allowed to take money from the employers with whom the union bargains, but only if the money is payment for their labor—they may not accept bribes in exchange for adopting a bargaining stance that favors employers.) With rare exceptions (the prosecution of Martha Stewart was a notable exception), federal prosecutors charge violations of the false statements statute only in cases in which other, more serious charges are likely to be brought. Is that fair? Al Capone, then the nation's most famous mobster, was not charged with illegally selling beer and whiskey—which is how Capone made his money in the 1920s and early 1930s—nor with ordering the murders of various rivals. Instead, Capone was charged with and convicted of failing to pay federal income taxes. Was *that* fair? For two different takes on the Capone problem, see Harry Litman, Pretextual Prosecution, 92 Geo. L.J. 1135 (2004); Daniel C. Richman & William J. Stuntz, Al Capone's Revenge: An Essay on the Political Economy of Pretextual Prosecution, 105 Colum. L. Rev. 583 (2005).

Notes on the Rule of Lenity

1. The rule of lenity suggests that statutory interpretation in criminal cases must be *asymmetric*: If the rule has any bite, at least some arguments that win when made by defendants must lose when offered by the government. *Brogan* and *Bronston,* by contrast, seem to suggest that statutory interpretation is *symmetric.* In each case, one side argued that the statute should be read to include or exclude a particular class of cases; in each case, the side that sought, in effect, to add language to the relevant statute lost.

2. Perhaps the rule doesn't apply in *Brogan* because, as Justice Scalia points out, the relevant ambiguity does not arise from the statute's language. For another case to the same effect, see United States v. Wells, 519 U.S. 482 (1997), in which the defendant was charged with fraud in connection with a loan application; the relevant statute barred "knowingly mak[ing] any false statement or report . . . for the purpose of influencing in any way the action of" any of a wide range of financial institutions. 18 U.S.C. §1014. The question before the Supreme Court was whether the relevant crime required proof that the defendant's misrepresentation was material—meaning, roughly, that the misrepresentation was about a matter of some importance. The statute in *Wells* did not include the word "material," so the Court held that proof of materiality is not required; the majority opinion reads a good deal like Scalia's majority opinion in *Brogan*. (Do you see why?)

As in *Brogan*, Justice Stevens dissented in *Wells*; the heart of his dissent was a passage in which Stevens listed 96 fraud and misrepresentation statutes, roughly half of which contained the word "material"; the other half did not. There is no discernible pattern to the inclusion (or not) of materiality in those statutes. The most reasonable conclusion, Stevens argues, is that "Congress simply assumed . . . that the materiality requirement would be implied wherever it was not explicit." 519 U.S. at 509 (Stevens, J., dissenting). Does that sound right? The statutes cited in Stevens' *Wells* dissent suggest that members of Congress take little care when drafting criminal statutes. How much deference should courts give to carelessly drafted statutory texts?

3. *Brogan* and *Wells* suggest that the rule of lenity does not apply when the statutory language is clear, even if legislators gave no thought to the question whether the relevant statute applied to cases like the one at hand. If that is the correct reading of those cases, one might expect more generous results when defendants argue that the statutory language itself is unclear. Yet such arguments rarely succeed. Consider State v. Lutters, 853 A.2d 434 (Conn. 2004). Connecticut General Statutes §29-35(a) states that "[n]o person shall carry any pistol or revolver upon one's person, except when such person is within the dwelling house or place of business of such person, without a permit to carry the same. . . ." The statute does not define "place of business." Lutters, who did not have a permit, was charged with carrying a pistol for self-protection in his taxicab; he argued that the taxi was his "place of business." The Connecticut Supreme Court not only disagreed; the court found the statute unambiguously favored the prosecution:

> Although the word "place," like virtually all words, has different connotations, we are persuaded that the term "place *of business*" implies a particular or fixed location. . . . In other words, we generally think of a motor vehicle as mobile personal property that, at any point in time, *occupies* a particular place but that is not, *itself*, a place. . . . Thus, as we noted in State v. Vickers, 260 Conn. 219, 796 A.2d 502 (2002), one's place of business is "the premises in which the business one owns or controls is located." Id. at 225. A motor vehicle generally is not considered the premises in which a business is located.

853 A.2d at 440. The *Lutters* dissent pointed out that a number of other states with similar statutes use the phrase "fixed place of business" to describe the analogous exemption from their gun registration requirement. The dissenters argued that, since it would have been easy for Connecticut's legislators to use the more precise language, the language they did use should—at the very least—be seen as ambiguous. That argument did not persuade the *Lutters* majority. Does it persuade you?

4. For a federal case that deals with the rule of lenity in a manner similar to *Lutters*, see Muscarello v. United States, 524 U.S. 125 (1998). The defendants in *Muscarello* were charged under a federal statute that applied to anyone who "uses or carries a firearm" "during and in relation to" a "drug trafficking offense." 18 U.S.C. §924(c)(1). The defendants drove their respective vehicles to the site of the relevant drug transactions, where they were arrested and searched. One defendant had a handgun in the locked glove compartment of his pickup truck; two other defendants had a bag filled with guns in the trunk of their car. The question was whether these three defendants were "carr[ying]" the guns at the time of the drug sales. The Court split 5-4 on the meaning of "carries": The majority held that one "carries" a weapon when it is accessible in a nearby vehicle; the dissenters argued that one "carries" only the items on one's person. Both Justice Breyer's majority opinion and Justice Ginsburg's dissent cited dictionaries, usage guides, and the Bible for their preferred interpretations—yet reached different conclusions. Even so, the *Muscarello* majority did not find the statutory term sufficiently ambiguous to trigger the rule of lenity:

> Finally, petitioners and the dissent invoke the "rule of lenity." The simple existence of some statutory ambiguity, however, is not sufficient to warrant application of that rule, for most statutes are ambiguous to some degree. "The rule of lenity applies only if, after seizing everything from which aid can be derived, . . . we can make no more than a guess as to what Congress intended." United States v. Wells, 519 U.S. 482, 499 (1997). To invoke the rule, we must conclude that there is "a grievous ambiguity or uncertainty in the statute." Staples v. United States, 511 U.S. 600, 619 n.7 (1994). Certainly, our decision today is based on much more than "a guess as to what Congress intended," and there is no "grievous ambiguity" here. The problem of statutory interpretation in this case is indeed no different than in many of the criminal cases that confront us. Yet, this Court has never held that the rule of lenity automatically permits a defendant to win.

524 U.S. at 138-39.

5. The origins of the rule of lenity are a little mysterious. In the United States, the so-called rule dates at least to 1820, when Chief Justice John Marshall wrote that the rule of lenity was "perhaps not much less old than" judicial interpretation of statutes. United States v. Wiltberger, 18 U.S. 76, 95 (1820). Wiltberger was charged with manslaughter; the relevant events happened on board an American ship which was then in a river in China, 35 miles from that nation's coast. The governing statute, passed by the First Congress in 1790, read: "[I]f any seaman, or other person, shall commit manslaughter on the high seas, . . . such person or persons so offending, and being thereof convicted, shall be imprisoned not exceeding three years, and fined not exceeding one thousand dollars." The same statute barred murders "on the high seas, or in any river, haven, basin or bay, out of the jurisdiction of any particular state." There was no apparent reason for the different coverage of murder and manslaughter. Nevertheless, the Chief Justice read the manslaughter provision, with its limited geographic scope, as it was written:

> The rule that penal laws are to be construed strictly is perhaps not much less old than construction itself. It is founded on the tenderness of the law for the rights of individuals, and on the plain principle that the power of punishment is vested in the legislative, not in the Judicial Department. It is the legislature, not the court, which is to define a crime and ordain its punishment.
>
> . . . [T]hough penal laws are to be construed strictly, they are not to be construed so strictly as to defeat the obvious intention of the legislature. . . . The intention of the legislature is to be collected from the words they employ. Where there is no ambiguity in the words, there is no room for construction. . . . It would be dangerous indeed to carry the principle that a case which is within the reason [for] a statute is within its provisions so far as to punish a crime not enumerated in the statute because it is of equal atrocity or of kindred character with those which are enumerated. . . .
>
> . . . The crimes of murder and manslaughter, when committed on water, are also described as two distinct offenses in two sections. . . . [T]he argument chiefly relied on to prove that the words of one section descriptive of the place ought to be incorporated into another is the extreme improbability that Congress could have intended to make those differences with respect to place, which their words import. We admit that it is extremely improbable. But probability is not a guide which a court, in construing a penal statute, can safely take. We can conceive no reason why other crimes which are not comprehended in this act should not be punished. But Congress has not made them punishable, and this Court cannot enlarge the statute. . . .

18 U.S. at 95-96, 104-06. Notice the following language: "It would be dangerous indeed to carry the principle that a case which is within the reason [for] a statute is within its provisions so far as to punish a crime not enumerated in the statute because it is of equal atrocity or of kindred character with those which are enumerated." In *Joseph G.*, the court maintained that the defendant's behavior was more excusable than typical murders—that is, that the defendant's behavior was *not* "of equal atrocity" or "of kindred character" with most murders—and therefore should not be covered by the state's murder statute. Are *Joseph G.* and *Wiltberger* consistent?

6. *Wiltberger* read an illogical statute (there is no reason to cover murders but not manslaughters in foreign rivers) exactly as it was written; the statute's plain language favored the defendant. The defendant in McBoyle v. United States, 283 U.S. 25 (1931), was charged with taking a stolen airplane across a state line, under a statute that barred interstate transport of the following stolen goods: "an automobile, automobile truck, automobile wagon, motor cycle, or any other self-propelled vehicle not designed for running on rails." This time, the statute's plain language favored the government: An airplane is a "self-propelled vehicle not designed for running on rails," is it not? And there was no illogic in the statutory text. Nevertheless, a unanimous Supreme Court held that the statute did not apply to McBoyle. Justice Oliver Wendell Holmes explained why:

> Although it is not likely that a criminal will carefully consider the text of the law before he murders or steals, it is reasonable that a fair warning should be given to the world, in language that the common world will understand, of what the law intends to do if a certain line is passed. To make the warning fair, so far as possible, the line should be clear. When a rule of conduct is laid down in words that evoke in the common mind only the picture of vehicles moving on land, the statute should not be extended to aircraft simply because it may seem to us that a similar policy applies, or upon the speculation that, if the legislature had thought of it, very likely broader words would have been used.

283 U.S. at 27. Why did Congress have to use "broader words" than the ones in the statute?

7. Another famous application of the rule came in Keeler v. Superior Court of Amador County, 470 P.2d 617 (Cal. 1970). Keeler was charged with murder after assaulting his pregnant ex-wife; the assault killed the fetus she was carrying. (That was Keeler's goal: Before the assault, he glared at his ex-wife's swollen abdomen and said, "I'm going to stomp it out of you.") At the time of the assault, the victim's pregnancy was in its ninth month; doctors testified that there was a greater than 90 percent chance the fetus would be born alive. The court found that Keeler could not be convicted of murder because a viable fetus was not "a human being" under California law. Justice Mosk, the author of *Joseph G.*, wrote the majority opinion in *Keeler*:

> . . . Although the Penal Code commands us to construe its provisions "according to the fair import of their terms, with a view to effect its objects and to promote justice," Penal Code §4, it is clear the courts cannot go so far as to create an offense by enlarging a statute, by inserting or deleting words, or by giving the terms used false or unusual meanings. Penal statutes will not be made to reach beyond their plain intent; they include only those offenses coming clearly within the import of their language. . . .
>
> Applying [that principle] to the case at bar, we would undoubtedly act in excess of the judicial power if we were to adopt the People's proposed construction of section 187. . . . [T]he Legislature has defined the crime of murder in California to apply only to the unlawful and malicious killing of one who has been born alive. We recognize that the killing of an unborn but viable fetus may be deemed by some to be an offense of similar nature and gravity; but as Chief Justice Marshall warned long ago, "It would be dangerous, indeed, to carry the principle, that a case which is within the reason or mischief of a statute, is within its provisions, so far as to punish a crime not enumerated in the statute, because it is of equal atrocity, or of kindred character, with those which are enumerated." United States v. Wiltberger, 18 U.S. (5 Wheat.) 76, 96 (1820). Whether to thus extend liability for murder in California is a determination solely within the province of the Legislature.

470 P.2d at 624-25. Notice that the California legislature has expressly instructed state judges to construe criminal statutes "according to the fair import of their terms, with a view to effect [those statutes'] objects and to promote justice." That sounds like a legislative repeal of the rule of lenity. Mosk and his colleagues thought otherwise.

8. What are the reasons for the rule of lenity? One answer is the separation of powers: Legislators, not judges, should determine the scope of criminal liability. Why? Most states elect both trial and appellate judges. Since voters choose legislators and (most) judges in a similar manner, is there good reason to draw sharp lines between legislative and judicial power? Why aren't elected judges as good lawmakers as elected legislators? The other standard justification is the one Justice Holmes used to justify *McBoyle*: "[A] fair warning should be given to the world, in language that the common world will understand, of what the law intends to do if a certain line is passed." As Justice Mosk put the point in *Keeler*:

> The first essential of due process [of law] is fair warning of the act which is made punishable as a crime. . . . "No one may be required at peril of life, liberty or property to speculate as to the meaning of penal statutes. All are entitled to be informed as to what the State commands or forbids." Lanzetta v. New Jersey, 306 U.S. 451, 453 (1939). The law of California is in full accord. . . .
>
> This requirement of fair warning is reflected in the constitutional prohibition against the enactment of *ex post facto* laws. U.S. Const., art. I, §§9, 10; Cal. Const., art. I, §16. . . . When a new penal statute is applied retrospectively to make punishable an act which was not criminal at the time it was performed, the defendant has been given no advance notice consistent with due process. And precisely the same effect occurs when such an act is made punishable under a preexisting statute but by means of an unforeseeable *judicial* enlargement thereof. . . .
>
> Turning to the case law, we find no reported decision of the California courts which should have given petitioner notice that the killing of an unborn but viable fetus was prohibited by section 187. . . .

We have previously discussed the idea of "fair warning" as a part of the constitutional "vagueness" doctrine. See supra Chapter 1, at pages 43 and 51. Here, consider Mosk's argument as a principle relevant to statutory interpretation in criminal cases. What is the principle's source? Why is surprising criminal liability unfair? No principle of unfair surprise limits the scope of civil liability—no body of tort doctrine seeks to ensure that defendants have "notice" of the damages liability their conduct might produce. Why is criminal liability different?

9. A few months after the decision in *Keeler*, the California legislature amended the state's murder statute to read: "Murder is the unlawful killing of a human being, or a fetus, with malice aforethought." The amendment added language establishing an exception for consensual abortions. Three years later, the Supreme Court established a constitutional right to abortion

in Roe v. Wade, 410 U.S. 113 (1973). Do these subsequent events suggest that *Keeler* was wrongly decided, or do they suggest the opposite?

10. Zachary Price says the rule of lenity has three possible meanings:

> The first possibility is a view that has recently gained favor in both state and federal courts. This approach ranks lenity dead last in the interpretive hierarchy. The rule comes into operation at the end of the process of construing [the statute]. . . . On this view, judges are free to indulge a broad reading based on legislative history or policy even though the text could mean something narrower. Or they may take a literal view of a statute's broad language, though common sense or legislative policy might suggest a narrow reading. Lenity comes into play only in the unlikely event that other conventions yield an interpretive "tie."
>
> Recent decisions by the Supreme Court have endorsed this first approach to lenity. "We have always," the Court said recently in Moskal v. United States, "reserved lenity for those situations in which a reasonable doubt persists about a statute's intended scope even after resort to the language and structure, legislative history, and motivating policies' of the statute."[32] . . . [L]enity tends to appear in opinions only as a supplemental rationale when narrow readings are chosen for other reasons. . . .
>
> The second rendition of lenity is a theory that Justice Scalia has sketched in a series of dissents. On this view, lenity operates to cut off broad readings based on policy, legislative history, or other extra-textual sources whenever the text standing alone supports a narrower view. . . . As Scalia puts it, "if the rule of lenity means anything, it means that the Court ought not . . . use an ill-defined general purpose to override an unquestionably clear [statutory] term." . . .
>
> Of course, the rule of lenity might also mean confining the reach of criminal statutes even in cases where textualism would support a broader view. A third rendition of lenity would achieve that result. Under this theory . . . the judge's first step in interpreting a criminal statute would be to identify all the plausible readings of the statute, employing all accepted interpretive techniques. Lenity would then compel the judge to select the narrowest interpretation within that set of plausible options. . . . Arguments about policy and legislative history . . . could narrow the statute's coverage, but never broaden it.

Zachary Price, The Rule of Lenity as a Rule of Structure, 72 Fordham L. Rev. 885, 891-94 (2004). Which of these three approaches does *Brogan* take? Which one did Mosk follow in *Keeler*?

---

32. 498 U.S. 103, 108 (1990).

3

Defining Criminal Intent

Criminal conduct is defined by a stunningly long list of federal and state criminal statutes: There are thousands of separate federal criminal prohibitions and at least several hundred such prohibitions in every state code. The law of criminal intent (or, in the traditional Latin terminology, *mens rea*) is somewhat more orderly, but also harder to understand. Early state criminal statutes said little about fault or intent; most criminal prohibitions defined the banned conduct and left it at that. Congress has often done the same with federal crimes. Thus, if the law of criminal intent followed the actual language of criminal statutes—if courts approached intent cases the same way the Supreme Court analyzed criminal conduct elements in *Brogan*, *Wells*, and *Muscarello*—many crimes would impose strict liability: There would be no intent requirements at all, and even accidental violations would lead to prison terms. State and federal courts have historically chosen a different doctrinal path, however, treating criminal intent as a more appropriate subject for common-law development. Some statutes define intent standards, but many do not; and even when statutes speak clearly, judges are less likely to hew closely to statutory text than when defining conduct terms. While the law of criminal conduct is mostly an exercise in statutory interpretation, the law of criminal intent is only partly that, and partly a species of common law.

In most states, courts still use the concepts and terminology of the common law to define the relevant intent standards. The core concepts, and the core terms, come from two standards: "general intent" and "specific intent." The definition of those terms, along with related doctrines on mistakes of fact and law, are the subjects of Section A. A much smaller number of states—the number is disputed, but today it probably lies between a half-dozen and a dozen—adhere closely to some version of the criminal intent standards defined by the Model Penal Code, a proposal for a comprehensive criminal code drafted by the American Law Institute and promulgated in 1962. The MPC's intent standards are the subject of Section B. Finally, federal criminal law tends to use its own *mens rea* terminology and concepts; these will be discussed in greater detail later, in Chapter 4. As you read these materials, consider which of the various approaches to defining criminal intent works best, and why.

A. COMMON-LAW CULPABILITY STANDARDS

Some bodies of legal doctrine—contract law is a good example—require no showing of fault for legal liability. Parties must abide by their agreements or pay damages when they don't. In most other areas—tort law is the most obvious example—the law usually requires that plaintiffs show that defendants acted negligently, meaning that the defendant's conduct must fall below the standard of a reasonable person in her circumstances.

In criminal law, a third norm applies: Usually, the government must prove that the defendant acted *intentionally*—that he meant to do what he did. Unfortunately, the standard is not that simple. Common-law courts require different forms of intent in different criminal cases. And the concept of negligence plays a large part in criminal law as well, though that term means something different in criminal cases than elsewhere. The following cases explore these propositions. Welcome to the strange world of criminal intent.

1. General Intent

The word "general" in the phrase "general intent" means "ordinary." General intent is the intent standard that applies to most crimes—the intent standard that courts presume unless there is good reason to use a different standard. Since general intent is the most common intent standard, it applies to a great many different crimes. Unsurprisingly, the definition varies across time, across different jurisdictions, and across different crimes even within the same jurisdiction, as the next two cases show.

People v. Stark

Court of Appeal of California, Third Appellate District
26 Cal. App. 4th 1179; 31 Cal. Rptr. 2d 887 (1994)

Opinion of PUGLIA, Presiding Judge.

A jury convicted defendant of willful diversion of construction funds (Penal Code, §484b) and found the taking exceeded $25,000 (Penal Code, §12022.6(a)). Imposition of sentence was suspended and defendant was granted probation for five years.

. . . [W]e shall reject defendant's contention that the trial court erred in instructing the jury that willful diversion of construction funds is a general intent crime. Finding no error, we shall affirm.

In 1989, Doctors Steven Johnson and Douglas Martin contracted with defendant, doing business as Stark Construction, to build a medical facility for approximately $350,000. The project was begun in October 1989, and as various phases of the project were completed, defendant received partial payment from a construction loan obtained by the doctors. With these payments defendant was to pay the subcontractors and materialmen who had either performed work or provided materials for the job.

By February 15, 1990, defendant had received three draws from the construction loan, totaling about $245,000. On March 1, the doctors received several calls from subcontractors and materialmen informing the doctors they had not been paid. The doctors discussed the matter with defendant and it was agreed the doctors would thereafter write the checks to the subcontractors and materialmen. The building was completed on March 1. On March 16 the doctors issued approximately $70,000 in checks to subcontractors and material suppliers from the fourth draw.

When the doctors continued to receive calls from people who were supposed to have been paid, but had not been paid, from the first three draws, they again confronted defendant. Defendant informed the doctors he had been experiencing financial difficulties on other jobs and some of the money from the medical building project had been spent to defray costs incurred for those jobs. Defendant promised to repay the money as the other jobs progressed.

Months later, when money owed subcontractors and material suppliers still had not been paid, the doctors contacted the Contractor's State License Board and the district attorney. The doctors estimated defendant's diversion of the funds cost them approximately $46,000. [Defendant admits] he used the money from the medical building project to defray costs on some of his other jobs. However, he [claims,] he always intended to pay the money back.

Penal Code §484b provides in pertinent part:

> "Any person who receives money for the purpose of obtaining or paying for services, labor, materials or equipment and willfully fails to apply such money for such purpose by either willfully failing to complete the improvements for which funds were provided or willfully failing to pay for services, labor, materials or equipment provided incident to such construction, and wrongfully diverts the funds to a use other than that for which the funds were received, shall be guilty of a public offense. . . ."

Relying on People v. Dollar, 228 Cal. App. 3d 1335, 279 Cal. Rptr. 502 (1991), and arguing here as he did in the trial court, defendant contends Penal Code §484b defines a specific intent crime. Therefore, he continues, the trial court prejudicially erred when it instructed the jury the offense was one requiring only general criminal intent. We conclude Penal Code §484b defines a general intent crime and that *Dollar* is inapposite.

In People v. Whitfield, 7 Cal. 4th 437, 868 P.2d 272 (1994), the court reiterated the general rule for differentiating between specific and general criminal intent offenses:

> "[As a] general rule [when] the definition of a crime consists of only the description of a particular act, without reference to intent to do a further act or achieve a future consequence, we ask whether the defendant intended to do the proscribed act. This intention is deemed to be a general criminal intent. When the definition refers to defendant's intent to do some further act or achieve some additional consequence, the crime is deemed to be one of specific intent."

Id. at 449. Defendant concedes there was a wrongful diversion of the construction funds and that this act requires only general criminal intent, i.e., merely the intent to do the [criminal] act. He contends there must exist in the mind of the defendant the additional intent either to fail to complete the work or, as in this case, not to pay either material suppliers or subcontractors. Therefore, defendant argues, the offense is one of specific intent.

The only "act" described by Penal Code §484b is the wrongful diversion, i.e., "a diversion to a use other than bona fide project costs," People v. Butcher, 185 Cal. App. 3d 929, 938, 229 Cal. Rptr. 910 (1986), of funds accepted for one or more of the specific purposes set forth in Penal Code §484b. Nothing in §484b suggests that when the defendant wrongfully diverts the funds that he [must] intend to do a further act or to achieve a future consequence. The offense is complete if the wrongful diversion was the cause of failure either to complete the improvement or, as here, to pay for services, labor, materials or equipment. It is immaterial whether defendant intended that there be a failure either to complete the project or to pay subcontractors or material suppliers. Consequently, the offense defined by §484b is one of general criminal intent, and the trial court did not err in so instructing the jury.

People v. Dollar, supra, does not aid defendant. In that case the accused, who had previously been convicted of committing a lewd and lascivious act upon the victim, was thereafter convicted of threatening her (Penal Code, §139) after he had unsuccessfully attempted to grab her and, as she was running away, yelled, "I'll get you soon, bitch." 228 Cal. App. 3d at 1338. On appeal, the accused contended the trial court erred in instructing the jury the offense was a general rather than specific intent crime.

In pertinent part, Penal Code section 139 reads:

> "(a) Except as provided in Sections 71 and 136.1, any person who has been convicted of any felony offense specified in Section 12021.1 who willfully and maliciously communicates to a witness to, or a victim of, the crime

for which the person was convicted, a credible threat to use force or violence upon that person or that person's immediate family, shall be punished by imprisonment in the county jail not exceeding one year or by imprisonment in the state prison. . . .

"(c) As used in this section, 'a credible threat' is a threat made with the intent and the apparent ability to carry out the threat so as to cause the target of the threat to reasonably fear for his or her safety or the safety of his or her immediate family."

In concluding the offense was one requiring a specific intent, the court stated:

"A threat as defined in section 139 would be a general intent crime if it is merely the threat itself that is being proscribed by the statute. If section 139 falls within the category of general intent crimes, it cannot proscribe additional future goals or consequences beyond the act of making the threat itself. . . .

"Section 139 draws a distinction between an idle threat, a joke or a threat that no one would believe, and a credible threat, which the section defines. For a threat to be credible, the criminal actor must have the apparent ability to carry out the threat and must have the additional criminal intent to cause the victim of the threat fear. . . . The communication of the threat itself is the act. The intent to create a future or additional consequence is the intent to cause the victim to feel fear or intimidation."

228 Cal. App. 3d at 1341.

As noted above, in cases arising under §484b it is immaterial whether at the time of the wrongful diversion the defendant intends or desires that the improvement not be completed or the suppliers and subcontractors not be paid. To violate the statute all that it required is the wrongful diversion of the funds, which means not applying the funds for the purpose for which they were disbursed, and that the diversion be the cause of at least one of the described failures. In contrast, a violation of Penal Code §139 requires the making of the threat coupled with the intent to cause fear in the target of the threat, thus defining an additional mental state not required by Penal Code §488b. . . . *Dollar* is of no assistance to defendant. . . .

The judgment is affirmed.

Notes on the Meaning of "General Intent"

1. *Stark* captures the usual meaning of general intent: In Judge Puglia's words, that standard means "the intent to do the [criminal] act."

Crimes are generally composed of some combination of three different kinds of elements: (1) conduct elements, meaning those elements that describe the defendant's prohibited act (in *Stark*, the "diversion" of funds); (2) circumstance elements, meaning those elements that describe the factual conditions under which the defendant acted (in *Stark*, this would include the fact that the funds originally were given to the defendant for the purpose of "obtaining or paying for services, labor, materials or equipment"); and, for a relatively smaller subset of crimes, (3) result elements, meaning the specific harmful consequences caused by the defendant's prohibited act (in *Stark*, the crime required that, in the court's words, "the improvement not be completed or the suppliers and subcontractors not be paid"). The common-law standard of general intent focuses entirely on the first kind of element. The defendant need not have intended the result of his conduct; instead, he must only be shown to have intended to do the act proscribed by the relevant criminal statute.

To meet the general intent standard in *Stark*, the government must prove that the defendant intended to pay the wrong contractors with the money supplied by Drs. Martin and Johnson — not the contractors working on the doctors' building, but other contractors to whom the defendant owed money. Stark appears to have been going bankrupt: He did not have enough money to pay all his creditors. Under California Penal Code §484b, his crime was to pay the wrong ones with money from the wrong source. Proof of general intent means proof that Stark engaged in that conduct intentionally, or consciously — by design, not by accident.

2. Criminalizing such behavior may seem odd, but it is actually commonplace. The reason has to do with the incentives of soon-to-be bankrupt debtors. When the owner of a business is about to go belly-up, her incentive is to take unreasonable risks: If the risk pays off, she may make enough money to return to solvency; if not, the business' creditors will pay the price. By criminalizing conduct like Stark's, California's criminal code forces insolvent general contractors into bankruptcy sooner rather than later, before they can drag down too many creditors with them. Of course, one might use fines or civil damages to send that deterrent message, but insolvent debtors can't pay large fines or damages bills. Criminal punishment may be the only legal tool the government can use in this context.

3. Stark argued that the government should be required to prove specific intent — usually defined as the intent to bring about a legally forbidden result — rather than general intent. Specific intent is the customary standard applied in theft cases; there, the forbidden result is the permanent deprivation of the victim's property, and the defendant must be shown to have intended that result. If specific intent *were* the governing standard in *Stark*, the forbidden result would likely be the same as in theft cases: not just the temporary nonpayment of the contractors working on the doctors' building, but the permanent loss of the money to which those contractors are entitled. It is not hard to understand why Stark would want such a standard applied in his prosecution: In order to convict, the government would be required to prove that Stark planned *never* to pay the unpaid contractors. Odds are, the government could not prove that intent. Like many bankrupt debtors, Stark *wanted* to pay all of his debts. He simply didn't have the money to do so.

4. Why did Stark's specific intent argument lose? By making California Penal Code §484b a general intent offense, the Court of Appeal makes it possible to punish debtors who are guilty of nothing worse than staying out of bankruptcy court a little too long: hardly a serious crime. Making section 484b a specific intent offense would fix the problem: Defendants could be convicted and punished if, but only if, they intended never to pay their contractors. To put the point another way, as a general intent offense, section 484b criminalizes a form of unlawful borrowing: Stark was using one set of contractors' money to pay off another set, in the hope that he would soon be in a position to make good the rest of his obligations. As a specific intent offense, section 484b would criminalize a form of theft. Punishment for unlawful borrowing by a soon-to-be bankrupt debtor sounds like imprisonment (or, as in Stark's case, probation) for debt, a practice abolished in the United States in the 1820s. Incarcerating thieves is routine. At first blush, Stark's argument seems strong.

But consider the argument again: If specific intent is the governing standard, section 484b catches only theft cases—and theft is already criminalized, in California and everywhere else. The legislature must have wished to punish something more than theft; otherwise, the statute is redundant. And section 484b captures that "something more" only if general intent is the applicable *mens rea*. To put the point more starkly (sorry), Stark did precisely the act that the statute forbids: He "willfully fail[ed] to apply" the money he received from the two doctors for the purpose for which that money was paid. If he is not guilty of violating section 484b, that statute is pointless.

5. In Volume 4 of his Commentaries on the Law of England, published in 1769, William Blackstone wrote that "a vicious will" is part of the definition of all crimes. Did Stark act with a vicious will? That seems a stretch; Stark's conduct is fairly typical of debtors on the brink of bankruptcy. Intent standards, one might suppose, are designed to ensure that only those defendants who deserve criminal punishment receive it—to ensure that only those who act with a "vicious will," to use Blackstone's evocative phrase, face criminal punishment. What gives? One answer goes like this: Proof of general intent cannot by itself distinguish between blameworthy and non-blameworthy defendants. Instead, the definition of criminal conduct—the legislature's job, not Judge Puglia's—does most of the work of separating those two categories. If the legislature defines innocuous conduct as a crime, requiring proof that the defendant intentionally engaged in that conduct will not help matters much. On the other hand, if the legislature criminalizes only seriously wrongful behavior, requiring proof that the behavior was performed intentionally *does* ensure that only blameworthy actors are punished.

To put the point another way, general intent is unlike, say, negligence in tort law. Proof of negligence guarantees a measure of fault in tort cases: Such proof amounts to a showing that the defendant failed to take adequate account of the risks his conduct imposed on others. Proof of general intent guarantees fault only when the legislature criminalizes the sort of conduct that, if done intentionally, can fairly be called wrongful.

6. Before you read further, it may help to have some definitions of frequently used terms in mind. Following is a brief glossary on the terminology of criminal intent:

Mens rea: Latin for "guilty mind." Courts use this term generically, to refer to any form of culpability or mental state that the law requires the government to prove in order to convict.

Intent: This word is used in two distinct ways; you must pay attention to context to determine which meaning of the term applies in any particular instance. First, "intent" is often a synonym of *mens rea*. When lawyers refer to "criminal intent" without specifying any particular intent standard, this is usually what they mean. Second, "intent" is often used as a synonym for "purpose." One might say that the defendant in *Stark* intentionally diverted funds from subcontractors on his current job to subcontractors on previous construction jobs: meaning, the defendant purposely did what he did; his actions were not accidental.

General intent: This phrase may take on different meanings in different cases — see *Sargent*, the next main case — but its standard definition is the one used in *Stark*. A defendant acted with general intent if he consciously chose the physical acts that constitute the relevant crime — in other words, if he meant to do what he did; his acts were choices, not accidents. Importantly, proof of general intent does *not* mean proof that the defendant tried to cause the victim harm or tried to produce some legally forbidden outcome; that is the conventional meaning of "specific intent."

Specific intent: Here too, the conventional definition is the one used in *Stark*. A defendant acted with specific intent if he tried to cause some injury or to bring about some harmful or legally forbidden result. For example, in the *Dollar* case (discussed in *Stark*), the defendant tried to cause the victim to fear for her safety — precisely the result forbidden by the relevant criminal statute. Hence, the defendant in *Dollar* acted with specific intent.

Scienter: Sometimes used as a synonym of "*mens rea*" (that is how the term is used in *Sargent*, see below), and sometimes as a synonym of "specific intent." One must pay attention to context to determine the meaning of the term in any particular judicial opinion.

Willfully: At common law, this is a synonym for acting "purposely" or "intentionally," in the "general intent" sense that the act itself was willed and not accidental. Stark willfully failed to use the payments he received to pay his subcontractors because he chose not to do so. In *Sargent*, the next case, the defendant willfully shook his young child because he intended to shake the child. As we will see later, the Model Penal Code and, especially, federal criminal law tend to use a different interpretation for this term.

Criminal negligence: Roughly, criminal negligence means gross or severe negligence; it is a more serious level of wrongful risk-taking than tort-law negligence. See Note 3 following *Sargent* for further explanation.

Malice: Roughly, malice means wrongfulness—which can include deliberately doing something known to be wrongful, without a justification or an excuse, as well as the wrongful creation of risk to others. This term will be dealt with in more detail below, in the main case of *In re V.V.* and the notes that follow.

7. In *Stark*, the meaning of "general intent" is clear. Not so in the next case; there, the central question is whether something more needs to be added to the customary definition. Why might something extra—think of it as a general intent "plus factor"—be necessary? When is it necessary? Consider these questions as you read.

People v. Sargent

Supreme Court of California
19 Cal. 4th 1206; 970 P.2d 409 (1999)

Opinion of BROWN, J.

In this case we determine the required *mens rea* for a conviction of felony child abuse based on direct infliction of unjustifiable physical pain and mental suffering. Penal Code, §273a(1), now §273a(a).[2] The Court of Appeal concluded criminal negligence is required. We disagree, and therefore reverse its judgment.

---

2. . . . At the time of defendant's crime, former section 273a provided:

"(1) Any person who, under circumstances or conditions likely to produce great bodily harm or death, willfully causes or permits any child to suffer, or inflicts thereon unjustifiable physical pain or mental suffering, or having the care or custody of any child, willfully causes or permits the person or health of such child to be injured, or willfully causes or permits such child to be placed in such situation that its person or health is endangered, is punishable by imprisonment in the county jail not exceeding one year, or in the state prison for 2, 4, or 6 years.

"(2) Any person who, under circumstances or conditions other than those likely to produce great bodily harm or death, willfully causes or permits any child to suffer, or inflicts thereon unjustifiable physical pain or mental suffering, or having the care or custody of any child, willfully causes or permits the person or health of such child to be injured, or willfully causes or permits such child to be placed in such situation that its person or health may be endangered, is guilty of a misdemeanor." Stats. 1984, ch. 1423, §2, at 4994-95.

FACTS AND PROCEDURAL BACKGROUND

Michael Sargent, Jr. (Michael), defendant's son, was born on March 24, 1993, three months premature. He weighed two pounds, four ounces, and spent the first three months of his life in the hospital. By August 19, 1993, he was the equivalent of a four to six-week-old infant in terms of neck muscle development. On that date, Marysville Fire Department personnel and a paramedic responding to a 911 call found Michael in a deep coma and close to death on defendant's apartment floor. He was not breathing, had no heartbeat, no eye or motor movement, and no response to verbal stimuli. There was bright red blood coming from his nose and mouth.

Michael was ultimately airlifted to the University of California at Davis Medical Center. While Michael's subsequent condition was not made clear at trial, it appears he survived and was released from the hospital on September 3, 1993.

Defendant's explanation of Michael's injuries varied. On August 19, 1993, defendant told a neighbor, paramedic, and hospital personnel Michael had rolled off the couch and fallen 18 to 20 inches to a carpeted floor. On August 24, 1993, defendant was interviewed by the police. He denied dropping Michael or losing his temper.

On August 25, 1993, defendant was again interviewed by the police. He stated he had dropped Michael while throwing him up in the air to stop him from crying, causing Michael to strike his head on the linoleum kitchen floor. The interviewing officers told defendant a consulting physician had concluded Michael was a victim of shaken baby syndrome. Defendant initially denied Michael was ever shaken. He then changed his story a third time. He said he and Michael's mother had an argument, and she dropped defendant and Michael off at the house. Defendant carried Michael in his car seat into the house. The infant was crying inconsolably. Defendant started to try to make a bottle for Michael. When Michael continued crying, defendant shook him front to back as Michael sat in his car seat. Defendant then returned to making the bottle. When Michael continued to cry, and refused a pacifier, "that's when I was shaking him more hard." Defendant shook Michael four or five times, causing the infant's head to lose contact with the car seat "a couple of times." Michael stopped

---

The current version of section 273a is substantively identical. As relevant here, the sole difference between the two subdivisions is that former subdivision (1), now subdivision (a), punishable as a felony or misdemeanor, requires that the proscribed conduct occur in "circumstances or conditions likely to produce great bodily harm or death"; former subdivision (2), now subdivision (b), a misdemeanor, has no such requirement.

crying. He "had this weird look in his eyes . . . like [he] was going to sleep you know like he was falling or something." When defendant picked him up, Michael's back bowed. His eyes closed, and he appeared to have difficulty breathing.

Defendant was charged with felony child abuse (§273a(1)), alleged to be a serious felony because it involved the personal infliction of great bodily injury. §§667(a), 1192.7(c)(8). It was further alleged that defendant had suffered a prior serious felony conviction for burglary, and served two prior prison terms.

At trial, Dr. John McCann, a pediatrician and director of the Davis Medical Center's child protection program, testified as a medical expert on child abuse for the prosecution. When Michael arrived at the Davis Medical Center he was sedated and consequently paralyzed because he appeared to be having seizures. No bruises or other external trauma, except for swelling around the eyes, were observed. A CAT (computerized axial tomography) scan revealed bilateral subdural hematomas, or blood over the surface of Michael's brain on both sides behind his ears. In addition, his brain was swollen. During his examination of Michael, Dr. McCann observed flame-shaped retinal hemorrhages in both eyes.

Based on all of this information, Dr. McCann opined Michael was a victim of shaken baby syndrome. Seventy to seventy-five percent of the children injured by shaking suffer either severe long-term disabling injury, such as blindness, seizures, and difficulty walking or talking, or death. McCann stated that shaking Michael was a circumstance likely to result in great bodily injury or death. For a fall to have caused the injuries sustained, Michael would have to fall out a second-story window, not off the couch or from his father's arms.

Dr. Todd Brandtman testified as a defense medical expert. He was an emergency room physician who had neither treated nor examined Michael. He did not have expertise in child abuse. He testified Michael's injuries could have resulted from being dropped, and that photographs of Michael taken two days after he left the hospital showed a swollen spot on the back of his head. . . .

The jury was instructed that it could find defendant guilty of violating section 273a(1) based on general criminal intent if it found defendant willfully inflicted unjustifiable physical pain or mental suffering on Michael. In addition, the jury was required to find the infliction occurred under circumstances or conditions likely to produce great bodily harm or death. The jury was further instructed that permitting a child to suffer unjustifiable physical pain or mental suffering, or when having the care or custody of a child permitting the child to be injured, or permitting the child to be placed in a situation that endangers the child's person or health in violation of section

273a(1) required criminal negligence. Both general criminal intent and criminal negligence were defined.[3]

The prosecutor argued that the jury could conclude defendant committed child abuse whether it found defendant had shaken Michael with general criminal intent, or dropped Michael with criminal negligence, and that this crime was a felony if it was committed under circumstances or conditions likely to produce great bodily harm or death.

The jury found defendant guilty of a violation of section 273a(1). The verdict did not indicate which branch of section 273a(1) the jury found defendant had violated, that is, whether defendant had directly inflicted the abuse by shaking Michael, or had been criminally negligent in dropping him. In a bifurcated court trial, the enhancement allegations were found true. The court sentenced defendant to the upper term of six years for the felony child abuse count, with a consecutive five-year enhancement.

The Court of Appeal, with one justice dissenting, concluded criminal negligence must be demonstrated to convict a defendant of infliction of unjustifiable physical pain or mental suffering, and the evidence did not support the inference that defendant was criminally negligent. The court relied on cases involving other branches of section 273a(1) that generally required criminal negligence. It disagreed with [cases holding otherwise],

---

3. The jury was instructed [as follows]:

"In the crime charged in Count I of the Information and in the lesser [included] crime there must exist a union or joint operation of act or conduct and general criminal intent. To constitute general criminal intent, it's not necessary that there exist an intent to violate the law. When a person intentionally does that which the law declares to be a crime he or she is acting with general criminal intent[] [e]ven though he or she may not know that the act or conduct is unlawful.

"When a person commits an act or makes an omission through misfortune or by accident under circumstances that show neither criminal intent nor purpose nor criminal negligence, he or she does not thereby commit a crime.

"The Defendant is accused in Count I of the Information of having violated Section 273(a)(1) of the Penal Code, a crime. Every person who under circumstances or conditions likely to produce great bodily harm or death, one, willfully inflicts unjustifiable physical pain or mental suffering on a child or, two, willfully causes or as a result of criminal negligence permits a child to suffer unjustifiable physical pain or mental suffering or, three, has care or custody of a child and, A, willfully causes or . . . as a result of criminal negligence, permits the child to be injured or, B, willfully causes or as a result of criminal negligence permits the child to be placed in a situation that endangers the child's person or health is guilty of a violation of Section 273(a)(1) of the Penal Code, a crime. The word 'willfully' as used in this instruction means with knowledge of the consequences or purposefully.

"In the crime charged in the Information there must exist a union or joint operation of act or conduct and either general criminal intent or criminal negligence. To establish general criminal intent, it's not necessary that there should exist an intent to violate the law. A person who intentionally does that which the law declares to be a concluding their interpretation of section 273a(1) "reads out of the statute the element which embodies criminal negligence, the requirement that the culpable conduct occur in circumstances likely to produce great bodily harm or death."

The court further concluded that "[t]here is nothing in the record from which it can be inferred that the defendant knew or should have known of the risk of great bodily harm or death from shaking the infant, e.g., attendance at a prenatal education session concerning this risk. . . . Nor can we take judicial notice that such a risk is generally known. . . . The defendant denied knowledge of the syndrome and the record is devoid of evidence showing that he knew or should have known of the syndrome. Accordingly, there is no basis for a finding that he knew or should have known that great bodily injury or death is likely to result from shaking his baby."

---

crime is acting with general criminal intent even though he may not know that such act or conduct is unlawful.

"Unjustifiable physical pain or mental suffering is the infliction of pain or suffering which cannot be defended or excused under the circumstances as reasonable, both as to necessity and to degree.

"Great bodily harm refers to significant or substantial injury and does not refer to trivial or insignificant injury. If a child is placed in a situation likely to produce great bodily harm or death it is not necessary that . . . actual bodily injury occur in order to constitute the offense. However, if such bodily injury does occur, its nature and extent are to be considered in connection with all of the evidence in determining whether the circumstances were such as were likely to produce great bodily harm or death.

"In order to prove such a crime each of the following elements must be proved: A person willfully inflicted unjustifiable physical pain or mental suffering on a child or a person willfully causes or as a result of criminal negligence permitted a child to suffer unjustifiable physical pain or mental suffering or, one, a person having care or custody of a child, A, willfully caused or as a result of criminal negligence permitted the child to be injured or, B, willfully caused or as a result of criminal negligence permitted the child to be placed in a situation that endangered the child's person or health. And, two, such conduct occurs under circumstances likely to produce great bodily harm or death.

"Criminal negligence means conduct which is more than ordinary negligence. Ordinary negligence is the failure to exercise ordinary or reasonable care. Criminal negligence refers to a negligent act which is aggravated, reckless and gross and which is such a departure from that which would be the conduct of an ordinarily, prudent, careful person under the same circumstances as to be contrary to a proper regard for human life or to constitute indifference to the consequences of such act. The facts must be such that the consequences of the negligent act could reasonably have been foreseen and it must appear that the danger to human life was not the result of inattention, mistaken judgment or misadventure but the natural and probable result of an aggravated, reckless or grossly negligent act. . . .

"The word 'willfully' when applied to the intent with which an act is done or omitted means with a purpose or willingness to commit the act or make the omission in question. The word 'willfully' does not require any intent to violate the law or to injure another or to acquire any advantage."

Finally, the court concluded that "defendant was convicted under the second branch of section [273a(1)], the 'inflict[ion of] . . . unjustifiable physical pain or mental suffering' upon a child 'under circumstances or conditions likely to produce great bodily harm or death. . . .'" The prosecution was not predicated on criminal negligence in dropping Michael. While defendant testified "he dropped the child and that is how the child was injured . . . there was no evidence of fracture or bruises which would support that theory and the prosecution introduced extensive evidence to refute the claim. Given that strong evidence supporting the prosecution's theory of the mechanism of injury, it is entirely unlikely that the conviction was predicated upon dropping the baby." Rather, "there is far more than a 'reasonable probability' that the jury in fact found the defendant guilty solely on the shaken baby syndrome theory. Accordingly, we conclude that the defendant's felony conviction cannot be affirmed." The court modified the judgment to a conviction of violation of section 273a, former subdivision (2), a misdemeanor, and remanded to the trial court for resentencing. The judgment was otherwise affirmed. . . .

We granted the Attorney General's petition for review.

DISCUSSION

A. Background

Section 20 [of the Penal Code] provides, "In every crime or public offense there must exist a union, or joint operation of act and intent, or criminal negligence." . . . Intent can be either general or specific.

> "When the definition of a crime consists of only the description of a particular act, without reference to intent to do a further act or achieve a future consequence, we ask whether the defendant intended to do the proscribed act. This intention is deemed to be a general criminal intent. When the definition refers to defendant's intent to do some further act or achieve some additional consequence, the crime is deemed to be one of specific intent."

People v. Hood, 1 Cal. 3d 444, 456-457, 462 P.2d 370 (1969). General criminal intent thus requires no further mental state beyond willing commission of the act proscribed by law.

Criminal negligence is "aggravated, culpable, gross, or reckless, that is, . . . such a departure from what would be the conduct of an ordinarily prudent or careful [person] under the same circumstances as to be incompatible with a proper regard for human life. . . ." People v. Penny, 44 Cal. 2d 861, 879, 285 P.2d 926 (1955). "Under the criminal negligence standard, knowledge of the risk is determined by an objective test: [I]f a reasonable person in defendant's position would have been aware of the risk involved, then defendant is presumed to have had such an awareness." Williams v. Garcetti, 5 Cal. 4th 561, 574, 853 P.2d 507 (1993). . . .

Section 273a(1) . . . proscribes . . . four branches of conduct. At the time of defendant's crimes, and in substantively identical form currently, it provided:

> "Any person who, under circumstances or conditions likely to produce great bodily harm or death, [1] willfully causes or permits any child to suffer, or [2] inflicts thereon unjustifiable physical pain or mental suffering, or [3] having the care or custody of any child, willfully causes or permits the person or health of such child to be injured, or [4] willfully causes or permits such child to be placed in such situation that its person or health is endangered, is punishable by imprisonment in the county jail not exceeding one year, or in the state prison for 2, 4, or 6 years."

We have observed that violation of section 273a(1) "can occur in a wide variety of situations: the definition broadly includes both active and passive conduct, i.e., child abuse by direct assault and child endangering by extreme neglect." People v. Smith, 35 Cal. 3d 798, 806, 678 P.2d 886 (1984). We have also observed, however, that "[t]wo threshold considerations . . . govern all types of conduct prohibited by this law: first, the conduct must be willful; second, it must be committed 'under circumstances or conditions likely to produce great bodily harm or death.' Absent either of these elements, there can be no violation of the statute." Ibid. . . .

We have not previously addressed the question of the appropriate *mens rea* for direct infliction of abuse cases under section 273a. In Walker v. Superior Court, 47 Cal. 3d 112, 135, 763 P.2d 852 (1988), we did not dispute the defendant's broad statement that section 273a requires criminal negligence. However, in *Walker*, a Christian Science parent declined to obtain medical treatment for her four-year-old child suffering from meningitis, who eventually died. 47 Cal. 3d at 118-119. Hence, that case involved indirect abuse or child endangerment, not direct infliction of abuse. . . .

In People v. Peabody, 46 Cal. App. 3d 43, 119 Cal. Rptr. 780 (1975), the defendant's four-month-old infant suffered multiple nonaccidental fractures. Id. at 45-46. There was no evidence that the defendant, as opposed to the baby's father, had inflicted the injuries on her child. Id. at 46. Thus, "the conviction can stand only under that portion of the statute which proscribes a person from willfully causing or permitting a child to be placed in a health endangering situation under circumstances likely to produce great bodily harm or death." Ibid., italics omitted. The court held that under these circumstances, section 273a(1) "requires proof of criminal negligence." Id. at 48. . . .

. . . [O]ther than the Court of Appeal opinion in this case, those cases which impose a criminal negligence requirement involve indirect abuse, such as failing to seek medical treatment, child endangerment, or willfully permitting situations that imperil children. See, e.g., Walker v. Superior Court, supra, 47 Cal. 3d at 118, 135 (failure to obtain medical care resulting in 4-year-old's death); People v. Hansen, 59 Cal. App. 4th 473, 476-478, 68 Cal. Rptr. 2d 897 (1997) (34-year-old man encouraged 14-year-old neighbor to play fatal game of Russian roulette); People v. Rippberger, 231 Cal. App. 3d 1667, 1673, 1682, 283 Cal. Rptr. 111 (1991) (failure to seek medical treatment for child suffering from meningitis); People v. Odom, 226 Cal. App. 3d 1028, 1031, 1032, 277 Cal. Rptr. 265 (1991) (children living in squalor, and surrounded by highly dangerous drug lab and weapons); People v. Pointer, 151 Cal. App. 3d 1128, 1131-1134, 199 Cal. Rptr. 357 (1984) (failure to provide proper nutrition and medical care); Cline v. Superior Court, 135 Cal. App. 3d 943, 945-946, 948-949, 185 Cal. Rptr. 787 (1982) (father endangered toddler by throwing him into a car driven by another and then encouraging or knowingly permitting dangerous ride). . . .

. . . [A] number of cases involving indirect abuse and child endangerment broadly state, as did Walker v. Superior Court, supra, 47 Cal. 3d at 135, that section 273a is a criminal negligence statute. In each case, the statement is supported by citation to other endangerment or indirect abuse cases. . . .

B. Appropriate *Mens Rea* When Child Abuse Directly Inflicted

We first consider whether a violation of section 273a(1) based on direct infliction of unjustifiable physical pain or mental suffering requires proof of general criminal intent or criminal negligence. As noted above, the Court of Appeal concluded that criminal negligence is required; defendant urges us to adopt this view. The Attorney General argues that only general criminal intent is required.

. . . We begin with the language of the statute. The language "inflicts [on a child] unjustifiable physical pain or mental suffering" is most readily interpreted as requiring general criminal intent. That is, the statute describes "a particular act, without reference to intent to do a further act or achieve a future consequence." People v. Hood, 1 Cal. 3d at 456-457.

Moreover, the language of section 273a(1) is similar to that of section 273d, which proscribes corporal punishment or child beating.[7] . . . Section 273d has been interpreted as a general intent statute. People v. Atkins, (1975) 53 Cal. App. 3d 348, 358, 125 Cal. Rptr. 855 (1975) ("[t]here need not be found a deliberate intent to cause a traumatic condition, but only the more general intent to inflict upon a child any cruel or inhuman corporal punishment or injury"). . . . Given the similarities between section 273a(1) and section 273d, the *mens rea* element should be the same. . . .

Defendant asserts that section 273a(1) and section 273d differ significantly because section 273a(1), but not section 273d, requires that the

7. Section 273d, subdivision (a), provides in relevant part: "Any person who willfully inflicts upon a child any cruel or inhuman corporal punishment or injury resulting in a traumatic condition is guilty of a felony. . . ."

culpable conduct occur "under circumstances or conditions likely to produce great bodily harm or death." . . .

. . . Section 273a does not provide that a defendant must "know or reasonably should know that his or her actions occur under circumstances or
conditions likely to produce great bodily harm or death." Rather, the statute
proscribes the infliction of unjustifiable physical pain or mental suffering on
a child . . . "under circumstances or conditions likely to produce great bodily
harm or death." . . . The scienter for any crime is inextricably linked to the
proscribed act or omission. The *actus reus* for section 273a(1) is infliction of
unjustifiable physical pain or mental suffering on a child. Hence, the scienter requirement applies to such an act. There is no separate scienter which
attaches to the phrase "circumstances or conditions likely to produce great
bodily harm or death."

We note this inquiry, as a practical matter, will in most cases not differ
significantly from the imposition of a criminal negligence *mens rea* element
into the language "under circumstances or conditions likely to produce
great bodily harm or death." Thus in this case, while defendant denied any
awareness that his actions were likely to harm Michael, any reasonable person would recognize that shaking a four-and-a-half-month-old infant, who
had been born three months prematurely and had the neck development
of a four- to six-week-old, with the force equivalent to dropping him out of
a second-story window, was a circumstance or condition likely to result in
great bodily harm or death. . . .

Nor, contrary to defendant's assertion, will section 273a(1) be tantamount to a strict liability crime if we do not conclude criminal negligence
is a required element of the statute. Generally speaking, a strict liability
offense is one which dispenses with a *mens rea*, scienter, or wrongful intent
element. Felony child abuse requires a *mens rea*: the defendant must willfully
inflict unjustifiable physical pain or mental suffering on a child.

At oral argument, defendant's counsel asserted that concluding [that
the requisite *mens rea* for] the second branch of section 273a(1) [is general
intent] . . . would result in parents being prosecuted for shaking a child or
slapping it on the back to save it from choking. However, shaking or slapping a choking child, whatever physical pain or mental suffering that may
involve, is justified. Section 273a(1) sanctions only the infliction of *unjustifiable* physical pain or mental suffering.

In sum, we conclude that when the conduct at issue involves the direct
infliction of unjustifiable physical pain or mental suffering on a child, criminal negligence is not an element of the offense. Rather, the defendant must
have a *mens rea* of general criminal intent to commit the proscribed act. In
addition, the trier of fact must determine whether the infliction of the unjustifiable physical pain or mental suffering on a child was under circumstances
or conditions likely to produce great bodily harm or death. If so, the crime
is punishable as a felony. If not, it is punishable solely as a misdemeanor. . . .

DISPOSITION

The judgment of the Court of Appeal is reversed and the matter is remanded for further proceedings consistent with this opinion.

[Justice MOSK's concurring opinion is omitted.]

Notes and Questions

1. In all criminal cases, the government must prove the conduct and circumstance elements that the relevant criminal statute specifies; some statutes also require proof that the defendant caused a particular harmful result. In *Sargent*, the criminal statute required the government to prove that the defendant "inflict[ed] . . . unjustifiable physical pain or mental suffering" on Michael, "under circumstances or conditions likely to produce great bodily harm or death." The question in *Sargent* is: What *else* must the government prove to convict? The language of California's child abuse statute doesn't seem to require the government to prove *anything* else. That is fairly common in American criminal codes; statutes often define criminal conduct but are completely silent with respect to criminal intent. Nevertheless, as *Sargent* illustrates, courts tend to require proof of *some* intent or culpability, in addition to the conduct described in the relevant criminal statute. Why?

Some of the cases you read in Chapter 2—remember *Brogan*, for example, the case that decided there is no "exculpatory no" exception to criminal liability for false statements to federal agents—treat judicial crime-definition as dangerous, even potentially oppressive. Why is judicially defining criminal *intent* somehow less dangerous or oppressive than judicially defining criminal *conduct*?

2. Under the governing California statute, felony child abuse can be directly inflicted—as in active child abuse cases, in which the abuser is charged with the crime—or indirectly inflicted as in passive child abuse cases, in which the defendant is charged with permitting someone else to abuse the child. Both forms of child abuse are general intent crimes. But general intent means different things in those two settings. Under *Sargent*, prosecutors in active child abuse or direct infliction cases must prove only that the defendant intended his physical acts: the same standard applied in *Stark*, supra at page 92. Under Walker v. Superior Court, 763 P.2d 852 (Cal. 1988) (cited and discussed in *Sargent*), however, prosecutors in passive abuse cases must prove *both* that the defendant intended his physical acts *and* that the defendant's conduct was criminally negligent. Sargent claimed he didn't realize that shaking Michael could cause the kind of injury the child suffered, and that other parents in his circumstances might likewise be ignorant of the relevant danger. The trial judge apparently believed that claim. Had *Sargent* been a passive child abuse case, that would have been enough to win Sargent an acquittal.

3. The preceding sentence is true in part because of the meaning of criminal negligence. The relevant paragraph of the jury instructions — see footnote 3 in *Sargent* — calls criminal negligence "aggravated, reckless, and gross." Similar language appears in standard jury instructions in other states. For purposes of tort law, one behaves negligently whenever she values others' interests too lightly. A defendant behaves with *criminal* negligence when she values others' interests not at all, or close to it: when she acts not just selfishly, but with extreme selfishness, enough to constitute "indifference" (again, using the jury instruction's language) to the risks her conduct imposes on others. In *Sargent*, the defendant claimed that shaking his child may have been negligent in the tort-law sense of the word, but was not "aggravated, reckless, and gross" — because parents (including, allegedly, the defendant) do not always realize that shaking small children can cause serious injury.

4. As noted above, "general intent" means simply the intent to carry out one's physical actions. For some general intent crimes, however, courts require something more — some kind of "plus factor" that the government must prove in addition to the ordinary general intent standard. (Why didn't the court require such a "plus factor" in *Stark* or *Sargent*?) Usually, that "plus factor" has to do with either the risk of harm the defendant's conduct wrongfully created, or the deliberate commission of an act known by the defendant to be wrongful. Criminal negligence is one such "plus factor," as seen in the passive child abuse cases that the court discussed (but chose to distinguish) in *Sargent*. Another "plus factor" that sometimes gets added to general intent crimes is *malice* — which sounds very different from criminal negligence, but in many situations may turn out to mean nearly the same thing.

In re V.V.

Supreme Court of California
51 Cal. 4th 1020; 252 P.3d 979 (2011)

Opinion of CHIN, J.

In this case, V.V. and J.H., minors, set off a firecracker on a brush-covered hillside in Pasadena, causing a fire that burned five acres of forest land. At a combined adjudicatory hearing, the juvenile court determined that V.V. and J.H. had committed arson. The court found that, although they did not intend to set the hillside on fire, the evidence satisfied the mental state required for arson.

In V.V.'s case, the Court of Appeal affirmed the juvenile court's order, finding that the evidence sufficiently established the requisite mental state of malice because V.V. deliberately and intentionally set off a firecracker on a brush-covered hill. In J.H.'s case, a different division of the Court of Appeal found that the intentional act of setting off a firecracker on a brush-covered hill without intent to do harm is insufficient to establish the element of malice.

We conclude that under the circumstances of this case, V.V.'s and J.H.'s acts of intentionally igniting and throwing a firecracker amid dry brush on a hillside, although done without intent to cause a fire or other harm, were sufficient to establish the requisite malice for arson.

I. FACTS AND PROCEDURAL HISTORY

On the afternoon of July 18, 2008, V.V. and J.H. (both 17-year olds) joined a friend to climb a steep hill located behind a residential street in Pasadena. V.V. lit a large firecracker, which J.H. threw onto the brush-covered hillside. The firecracker exploded and caused a five-acre brush fire.

Abel Ramirez, a Pasadena resident, heard a "very loud explosion" from his backyard patio. He immediately saw smoke rising from the hillside and saw flames several minutes later. Shortly thereafter, Ramirez saw three young men running down the hill from the fire's point of origin. The fire was rapidly spreading, coming within 60 to 75 feet of a residence. Ramirez called 911 to report the fire and described the three young men . . . .

Ara Moujoukian, Ramirez's neighbor, heard kids laughing, yelling, and "having a good time" outside his house. He heard them exclaiming "Wow," "Look," "Did you see that," and "Fire." Moujoukian went outside and saw three boys laughing and "high-fiving" each other. When Moujoukian asked, "What are you guys doing?" they immediately ran away. One of the three boys "smacked" Moujoukian's car as he ran off. Moujoukian turned around and saw a fire on the hill behind his house. He called 911 to report the fire and gave descriptions of the three boys . . . .

Pasadena police officers responded to the 911 calls. About one-quarter mile from the scene of the fire, they saw three people matching the description of the suspects and detained them. Officer Brian Bozarth patted down V.V. and found a lighter and "a large firecracker that would be described as a cherry bomb," which was about the size of a golf ball and had a fuse coming out of the top. When Officer Bozarth discovered the firecracker, V.V. declared, "That's what caused the fire." V.V. admitted that he had caused the brush fire by setting off a firecracker on the hillside. Officer Bozarth saw a gray substance on J.H.'s fingers that appeared to be gunpowder from fireworks.

Firetrucks arrived and climbed three-fourths of the way up the hill. The fire burned five acres of brush-covered hillside behind a housing development.

At the police station, Detective Jesse Carrillo read V.V. and J.H. their *Miranda* rights and interviewed them separately. During the interviews, V.V. and J.H. admitted that they had been playing with firecrackers and had set the hillside on fire. They stated they had gone to the hill with the intention of climbing it. J.H. admitted that he had brought six firecrackers "because we wanted to blow them up." V.V. and the third minor knew J.H. had the firecrackers with him. But the third minor did not want to participate in lighting the firecrackers because he feared that someone might get injured.

V.V. acknowledged that, although J.H. brought the firecrackers to the hill, they both had the idea of lighting one. The minors stated that J.H. held the firecracker, V.V. lit it with J.H.'s lighter, and J.H. threw it. V.V. stated that they tried to throw the firecracker onto a green area on the hillside. On the other hand, J.H. said he told V.V. he was going to throw the firecracker onto a concrete area. V.V. claimed that he lit the firecracker "[j]ust to make a lot of noise," and that he did not think the green areas on the hillside would ignite. After the fire started, they "got kind of scared" because the fire could have reached them. They then discarded the other fireworks into a sewer. The three minors ran down the hill without stopping to report the fire to anyone.

Detective Carrillo testified that the brush fire's point of origin was below the minors' position on the hillside. He stated that the concrete area J.H. said he was aiming for was even further down the hillside, about 150 yards from the fire's point of origin.

The Los Angeles County District Attorney filed petitions under Welfare and Institutions Code section 602 alleging that V.V. and J.H. committed the crimes of arson of a forest land (Pen. Code, §451, subd. (c)) and recklessly causing a fire (§452, subd. (c)). The juvenile court found that V.V. and J.H. understood what they were doing and that they knew "the natural consequence could be setting the hill on fire because they're trying to throw the thing into a patch of green or into a cement area. So they're trying to avoid setting the hill on fire." The court further found that V.V. and J.H. did not intend to set the hill on fire, but concluded that because they intentionally ignited and threw the firecracker that caused the fire, the requisite mental state for arson was met, as construed in People v. Atkins (2001) 25 Cal. 4th 76, 18 P.3d 660 (*Atkins*). The court found the arson allegation to be true, dismissed the lesser offense of unlawfully causing a fire, declared V.V. and J.H. wards of the state, and placed them on home probation.

In affirming V.V.'s wardship order, Division One of the Court of Appeal, Second Appellate District, in an unpublished opinion, concluded that arson's malice requirement was met under *Atkins*. The court reasoned that "[u]ndisputed evidence established that V.V. intentionally ignited the firecracker with the knowledge and intent that his companion would throw the firecracker onto the hillside and it would explode amidst dry brush. This was not an accidental ignition, but a deliberate and intentional act of igniting and exploding the firecracker 'under such circumstances that the direct, natural, and highly probable consequences would be the burning of dry brush on the hill when the firecracker exploded."

In setting aside the arson finding in J.H.'s case, Division Eight of the Court of Appeal, Second Appellate District, in a published opinion, concluded that, under *Atkins*, the act of lighting and throwing a firecracker without the intent to do harm was not malicious conduct because it was not done with "an intent to do a wrongful act." The court struck the arson finding as to J.H. and modified the judgment to reflect a finding that J.H. committed the lesser offense of recklessly causing a fire.

We granted review in both cases to determine the correct application of *Atkins.*

II. DISCUSSION

V.V. and J.H. argue that there is insufficient evidence of malice, as defined in the arson statutes (§§450, 451), because they lit and threw the firecracker without intent to cause a fire or any other harm. As explained below, the evidence supports the juvenile court's finding that V.V. and J.H. acted with malice.

Our review of the minors' substantial evidence claim is governed by the same standard applicable to adult criminal cases. "In reviewing the sufficiency of the evidence, we must determine 'whether, after viewing the evidence in the light most favorable to the prosecution, any rational trier of fact could have found the essential elements of the crime beyond a reasonable doubt.'" (People v. Davis (1995) 10 Cal. 4th 463, 509; 896 P.2d 119.) . . .

"A person is guilty of arson when he or she willfully and maliciously sets fire to or burns or causes to be burned or who aids, counsels, or procures the burning of, any structure, forest land, or property." (§451.) "Willfully" is defined not in the arson chapter, but in section 7, item 1: "The word 'willfully,' when applied to the intent with which an act is done or omitted, implies simply a purpose or willingness to commit the act, or make the omission referred to. It does not require any intent to violate law, or to injure another, or to acquire any advantage." The arson chapter defines "maliciously" as involving "a wish to vex, defraud, annoy, or injure another person, or an intent to do a wrongful act, established either by proof or presumption of law." (§450, subd. (e).) This is the same definition as found in section 7, item 4, except for the inclusion of "defraud" in section 450.

In *Atkins*, we held that arson requires only a general criminal intent and that the specific intent to set fire to, burn, or cause to be burned the relevant structure or forest land is not an element of arson. In reaching that conclusion, we examined the statutory terms "willfully" and "maliciously," and explained: "'[T]he terms "willful" or "willfully," when applied in a penal statute, require only that the illegal act or omission occur "intentionally," without regard to motive or ignorance of the act's prohibited character.' 'Willfully implies no evil intent; "it implies that the person knows what he is doing, intends to do what he is doing and is a free agent."'' The use of the word 'willfully' in a penal statute usually defines a general criminal intent, absent other statutory language that requires 'an intent to do a further act or achieve a future consequence.'" (*Atkins*, supra, 25 Cal. 4th at p. 85.) Similarly, the statutory definition of "maliciously," in the context of arson, requires no specific intent to do a further act or achieve a future consequence. Other language in the arson statute "does not require an additional specific intent to burn a 'structure, forest land, or property.' . . ."

In *Atkins*, the defendant admitted that he poured a mixture of oil and gasoline on a pile of weeds and lit the weeds with a disposable lighter in a cleared area in a canyon that had heavy brush, trees, and grass. He claimed that he had been drinking most of that day. Although the prosecution presented evidence that he had previously threatened to burn down a nearby house, the defendant asserted that he meant no harm and that the resultant brush fire was an accident. (*Atkins*, supra, 25 Cal. 4th at pp. 79-80.) We held that because arson is a general intent crime, evidence of voluntary intoxication was not admissible on the issue of whether the defendant formed the required mental state for arson. We stated that the arson statute does not require the intent to cause the resulting harm, but "rather requires only [a general] intent to do the act that causes the harm."

Here, the evidence shows that V.V. and J.H. willfully and intentionally ignited and threw a large firecracker onto the brush-covered hillside, that the firecracker exploded in the dry brush, and that the explosion caused a brush fire. Thus, the actus reus element of section 451 was met because V.V. and J.H. willfully and intentionally committed the act that "cause[d] to be burned . . . forest land." (§451.) However, V.V. and J.H. argue that their acts were not malicious. They agree that an intent to commit the resulting harm is not an element of arson, but argue there must be evidence they intended to cause a fire or some other harm or "evil result."

The statutory definition of arson is derived from the common law crime of arson as a willful and malicious burning. (*Atkins*, supra, 25 Cal. 4th at pp. 86-87.) Although "[m]alice as universally understood by the popular mind has its foundation in ill-will" (Davis v. Hearst (1911) 160 Cal. 143, 157; 116 P. 530), it need not take the form of malevolence or ill will (1 Witkin & Epstein, Cal. Criminal Law (3d ed. 2000), p. 213; Perkins & Boyce, Criminal Law (3d ed. 1982), p. 275; see also People v. Ah Toon (1886) 68 Cal. 362, 363; 9 P. 311 ["'malice, in common accept[ance], means ill-will against a person, but in its legal sense it means a wrongful act, done intentionally, without just cause or excuse'"]). Malice in fact—defined as "a wish to vex, annoy, or injure" (§7, item 4)—consists of actual ill will or intent to injure. However, "'[t]here is still another malice, the presumption of the existence of which is raised by the law in certain cases upon certain proofs.'" (Davis v. Hearst, supra, 160 Cal. at p. 158.) This type of malice—malice in law—is defined in section 7, item 4 as "an intent to do a wrongful act, established either by proof or presumption of law." Malice in law may be "presumed" or "implied" from the intentional doing of the act without justification or excuse or mitigating circumstances. (See Davis v. Hearst, supra, 160 Cal. at p. 158.)

In determining whether the second type of malice ("intent to do a wrongful act") is established for arson, malice will be presumed or implied from the deliberate and intentional ignition or act of setting a fire without a legal justification, excuse, or claim of right. (*Atkins*, supra, 25 Cal. 4th at pp. 88-89; accord, U.S. v. Doe (9th Cir. 1998) 136 F.3d 631, 635 [common law arson].) " 'An intentional act creating an *obvious fire hazard* . . . done without justification . . . would certainly be malicious. . . . '" (U.S. v. Doe, supra, 136 F.3d at p. 635, fn. 4, italics added.)

As we stated in *Atkins*, arson's "willful and malice requirement ensures that the setting of the fire must be a deliberate and intentional act, as distinguished from an accidental or unintentional ignition or act of setting a fire; 'in short, a fire of incendiary origin.' (People v. Green [(1983) 146 Cal. App. 3d 369,] 379; accord, U.S. v. Doe, supra, 136 F.3d at p. 635.) 'Because the offensive or dangerous character of the defendant's conduct, by virtue of its nature, contemplates such injury, a general criminal intent to commit the act suffices to establish the requisite mental state.' Thus, there must be a general intent to willfully commit the act of setting on fire under such circumstances that the direct, natural, and highly probable consequences would be the burning of the relevant structure or property." (*Atkins*, supra, 25 Cal. 4th at pp. 88-89.) . . .

Substantial evidence supports the juvenile court's finding of malice. V.V. and J.H. were equal participants. Although J.H. brought large "cherry bombs" to the hill, both J.H. and V.V. had the idea of lighting one. J.H. held the firecracker while V.V. lit it with J.H.'s lighter. J.H. then threw the ignited firecracker into dry brush on the hillside.

The juvenile court further found that, despite their intentional acts, V.V. and J.H. did not intend to set the hillside on fire and tried to avoid such a consequence. Nevertheless, the court correctly recognized "that's not the issue." V.V. and J.H. were not required to know or be subjectively aware that the fire would be the probable consequence of their acts. (See U.S. v. Doe, supra, 136 F.3d at p. 635 [common law arson does not require proof of intent to burn down building, or of knowledge this would be the probable consequence of defendant's act]; cf. People v. Wyatt (2010) 48 Cal. 4th 776, 781; 229 P.3d 156 [defendant need not know or be subjectively aware his assaultive act is capable of causing great bodily injury]; see also People v. Hayes, supra, 120 Cal. App. 4th at p. 803, fn. 3 ["[t]he second definition—intent to do a *wrongful* act—has never been construed, so far as we can determine, to require knowledge by the defendant that his or her conduct violated social norms"].) A defendant may be guilty of arson if he or she acts with awareness of facts that would lead a reasonable person to realize that the direct, natural, and highly probable consequence of igniting and throwing a firecracker into dry brush would be the burning of the hill-side. Here, V.V. and J.H. were aware of such facts.

Although V.V. and J.H. did not intend to set the hillside on fire, they knew that their intentional acts created a fire hazard. J.H. told the police he attempted to throw the firecracker onto a concrete area on the hillside, while V.V. said they wanted to throw the firecracker onto a green area on the hillside. The juvenile court reasonably inferred that because V.V. and J.H. tried to avoid the dry brush, they knew a fire could result from setting off the large "cherry bomb" on the brush-covered hillside. V.V. and J.H. also told the police that the third minor did not want to participate in lighting the firecrackers because he feared that someone might get injured. Thus, the third minor alerted V.V. and J.H. beforehand to the dangers of playing with firecrackers.[4] Moreover, the concrete area was about 150 yards from the fire's point of origin and more than 150 yards away from V.V. and J.H.. A reasonable person would not have objectively believed that a firecracker thrown from V.V. and J.H.'s position would reach the concrete area. Thus, V.V. and J.H. were aware of facts that would lead a reasonable person to real-ize that the direct, natural, and highly probable consequence of throwing a lit "cherry bomb" from their location would be its landing in the dry brush short of the concrete area and causing a fire.

Indeed, the record supports an inference that V.V. and J.H. were not sur-prised or upset that the firecracker exploded in dry brush and caused a fire. Ara Moujoukian testified that V.V. and J.H. were yelling, laughing, "high-fiving," and seemingly having a good time moments after they realized the hillside was on fire. When Moujoukian asked what they were doing, V.V. and J.H. ran away and did not notify the authorities about the brush fire. These facts suggest that V.V. and J.H. did not realistically expect that the thrown "cherry bomb" would reach the concrete area. From the above evidence, the juvenile court reasonably inferred that V.V. and J.H. acted with malice.[6]

---

4. V.V.'s interview with the police reflects that the third minor alerted V.V. and J.H. to the dangers of playing with firecrackers before setting off the firecracker on the hillside:

"[Officer]: Alright, so you guys climbed the mountain and then what happened?
"V.V.: We got to the top and we're like and . . . we got to the top and we're kinda like (unintelligible) because it is hard getting to the top.
"[Officer]: Um-hum.
"V.V.: We, *Ivan didn't want to because he said what if someone gets injured.*
"[Officer]: Was everyone gonna light one?
"V.V.: No, no just one. Just to make a lot of noise. And . . .
"[Officer]: Whose idea was it to light one?
"V.V.: Ah, [J.H.'s], both of us, me and [J.H.]."

6. In arguing that the majority opinion does not comport with the law, Justice Werdegar's dissent repeatedly asserts that the majority presumes malice simply from the commission of the volitional act that causes a fire to start. In making these assertions, the dissent never rec-ognizes that, in upholding the juvenile court's malice finding, we have applied the standard of malice as stated in *Atkins*. There, we stated "[T]here must be a general intent to willfully

V.V. and J.H. claim that the evidence supports a finding only that they had committed the offense of unlawfully causing a fire (§452) because their conduct was reckless and resulted in an accidental fire. "[T]he offense of unlawfully causing a fire covers reckless accidents or unintentional fires, which, by definition, is committed by a person who is 'aware of and consciously disregards a substantial and unjustifiable risk that his or her act will set fire to, burn, or cause to burn a structure, forest land, or property.' (§452.)" (*Atkins*, supra, 25 Cal. 4th at p. 89.) We disagree.

This was not an accidental or unintentional ignition. A similar situation occurred in U.S. v. Doe, supra, which we cited with approval in *Atkins*, supra. There, a juvenile intentionally set fire to paper towels in a dispenser in the girls' bathroom of a school. With a lighter, the juvenile lit one corner of a paper towel from the dispenser, let the towel burn for a few seconds, blew out the flame, and put the burned towel in the sink. She then lit the left corner of a paper towel protruding from the dispenser, let the flame burn for a second, and blew it out. She lit the right corner of the same towel in the dispenser, blew it out, and left the bathroom. The building caught fire. An investigation revealed that the fire originated in the girls' bathroom. In affirming the juvenile's arson conviction, the court did not base its decision on whose paper towels were set on fire and left smoldering in the bathroom. Instead, in construing the common law definition of arson, the court reasoned that the "elements of willfulness and maliciousness are established by proof that the defendant set the fire intentionally and without justification or lawful excuse" with "no suggestion that the fire started as a result of accident or negligence." (U.S. v. Doe, supra, 136 F.3d at pp. 635-636.)[7]

As in U.S. v. Doe, supra, 136 F.3d 631, the evidence here supports the juvenile court's finding that V.V.'s and J.H.'s intentional conduct of setting

---

commit the act of setting on fire *under such circumstances that the direct, natural, and highly probable consequences would be the burning of the relevant structure or property.*" (*Atkins*, supra, 25 Cal. 4th at p. 89, italics added.) The unitalicized language describes arson's willful requirement, or as the dissent characterizes it, the "volitional act" requirement, i.e., that the act of setting fire to, of burning, or that causes to be burned (§451) is intentional. The italicized language describes arson's malice requirement, i.e., that the willful and intentional act is committed under circumstances that create an obvious fire hazard. Thus, a willful act that causes a fire without further evidence of the underlying circumstances would be insufficient to establish malice.

7. In *Atkins*, supra, 25 Cal. 4th 76, 89, we observed that "reckless accidents or unintentional fires may include those caused by a person who recklessly lights a match near highly combustible materials." Defendants argue that their conduct was more akin to this type of reckless conduct. The Attorney General responds that the affirmative acts of lighting *and* throwing a firecracker into dry brush is qualitatively different from merely lighting a match near combustible materials. She counters that more apt examples of reckless behavior would be an instance of a person who carves open a firecracker to check for gunpowder, next to a lit cigarette—and it explodes in a location of obvious fire danger; or a person who lights a

fire to and throwing a large "cherry bomb" that exploded in dry brush, causing a fire, was willful and malicious.[8]

III. Disposition

We affirm the judgment of the Court of Appeal relating to the arson finding in V.V.'s case. We reverse the judgment of the Court of Appeal relating to the arson finding in J.H.'s case and remand the case to that court for further proceedings consistent with this opinion.

Kennard, J., dissenting.

. . . As Justice Werdegar's dissent (which I have signed) persuasively explains, the evidence is insufficient to show that V.V. and J.H. acted with malice, a necessary element of the crime of arson. Instead, they were guilty only of reckless fire setting (§452), which is a serious crime but not so serious as arson. I write to comment on the majority's erroneous assertion that the fire started by V.V. and J.H. was not accidentally set.

As this court explained in People v. Atkins (2001) 25 Cal. 4th 76; 18 P.3d 660, California's arson statute applies only to fires that are set deliberately, not to those set accidentally. The statutory requirement that the defendant act willfully and with malice, we said, "ensures that the setting of the fire must be a deliberate and intentional act, as distinguished from an accidental or unintentional ignition or act of setting a fire." (Id. at p. 88.) . . .

Here, the court commissioner hearing the matter expressly found that V.V. and J.H. did not intend to set the fire that resulted when the cherry bomb exploded on the hillside. Nevertheless, the majority concludes: "This was not an accidental or unintentional ignition." The majority's only explanation for that bald assertion is to say that the facts here are comparable to those of U.S. v. Doe (9th Cir. 1998) 136 F.3d 631 (*Doe*), a case cited with

---

firecracker, but instead of throwing it, fumbles with it, and it falls on dry brush; or a farmer who burns crops on a very windy and dry day.

In U.S. v. Doe, supra, 136 F.3d 631, the court compared the facts of that case to other types of conduct, such as the burning of a building caused by a smoldering cigarette butt tossed into a trash can or caused by lighted candles placed too close to drapes. The court distinguished those hypotheticals, commenting that "the present case . . . is more analogous to intentionally setting fire to the drapes and then walking away in the (erroneous) belief that the fire had been blown out. While one can argue that that is a close case for the trier of fact, on that evidence the trier of fact would be entitled to return a verdict of guilty." (U.S. v. Doe, supra, 136 F.3d at p. 635, fn. 5.) Similarly, defendants' conduct here is more analogous to intentionally throwing a lighted match on a brush-covered hill, unsuccessfully aiming for a concrete area amidst the dry brush, and causing a brush fire.

8. Contrary to the Justice Werdegar's dissent, our holding would not "render every unlawful fire under section 452 also an arson under section 451." (Dis. opn. of Werdegar, J., post, at p. 1039.) "[T]hat defendant's willful and malicious conduct may *also* have been reckless does not suggest that he may not be convicted of arson . . . or that his culpability is the same as someone who [performs the act] recklessly . . . ." (People v. Fry, 19 Cal. App. 4th at p. 1339.)

approval in *Atkins,* supra, at page 88. In *Doe,* a juvenile intentionally set fire to several paper towels from a dispenser in a school restroom. Although she blew out the flame, sparks remained, which eventually set the building on fire. The federal court of appeals upheld the juvenile's arson conviction, reasoning that she had acted maliciously because she "set the fire intentionally and without justification or lawful excuse." (*Doe,* supra, at p. 635.)

But the facts here are not comparable to those of *Doe,* supra, 136 F.3d 631. The minor in *Doe* intentionally and illegally set fire to the school's property (the paper towels) and the fire thereafter spread. Intentionally setting that fire was the illegal act that furnished the requisite malice to support the arson conviction in that case. Here, by contrast, V.V. and J.H. did not intentionally set a fire; they exploded a cherry bomb. That act, under the circumstances in which they did it, was criminally reckless, and it therefore violated section 452 (reckless fire setting). But because the fire that resulted from the explosion was accidental, they were not guilty of arson of forest land, the offense the court commissioner found them to have committed. . . .

WERDEGAR, J., dissenting.

. . . The minors in this case played with fireworks on the edge of the Angeles National Forest shortly after July 4th, when fireworks were plentiful and the brush was dry. Their reckless conduct would, if committed by adults, have constituted the felony of unlawfully causing a fire. (See Pen. Code, §452.) Contrary to the majority, however, I conclude the minors' conduct did not amount to arson. (§451.)

A person is guilty of arson when he or she "willfully and maliciously sets fire to . . . forest land . . . ." (§451.) "Willfully," for all practical purposes, means nothing more than that the prohibited act was intentionally done. (See *Atkins.*) The term "implies simply a purpose or willingness to commit the act. . . . It does not require any intent to violate law, or to injure another . . . ." (§7, par. 1.) There is no dispute that the minors "willfully"—that is intentionally—lit the firecracker that started the fire. In contrast, the term "maliciously" imports an additional element, namely, "a wish to vex, defraud, annoy, or injure another person, or an intent to do a wrongful act, established either by proof or presumption of law." (§450, subd. (e).)

The court commissioner who conducted the juvenile hearing in this case expressly found the minors did not intend to set the hillside on fire. He believed the dispositive question was simply whether "the natural and probable consequence or highly probable consequence of lighting a firecracker on a hillside and throwing it some distance away trying to hit a patch of green or a patch of cement" satisfied the statutory definition of arson. (§451.) Certainly the minors lit the firecracker "willfully"; the act was clearly volitional. But nothing in the record justifies the majority's conclusion the minors also lit the firecracker "maliciously." No evidence was introduced to show the minors had "a wish to vex, defraud, annoy, or injure another person, or an intent to do a *wrongful* act . . . ." (§450, subd. (e), italics added.) The only evidence concerning the minors' purpose in lighting fireworks comes from their statements to police and reflects nothing more than a common youthful enthusiasm for loud noises.[2] Had the minors lit fireworks in violation of an ordinance prohibiting them, their conduct would certainly have been "wrongful," and thus malicious (§450, subd. (e)), but the People do not claim the minors violated any such ordinance.

The majority offers various analytical paths to the conclusion that the minors acted with malice. I find all of them unsupportable. At one point, the majority seems to presume malice *"from the deliberate and intentional ignition or act of setting a fire* without a legal justification, excuse, or claim of right." This approach has two problems. First, the minors did not intend to set a fire at all, as the commissioner expressly held, let alone maliciously. What they intended was to explode a firecracker. The majority does not argue the minors committed arson by setting fire to *the firecracker*, as that view of the facts would implicate not the general prohibition of arson (§451), but a different provision punishing those who set fire to their own property and thereby cause injury to forest land (§451, subd. (d)). Second, the authority the majority offers as support for presuming malice under these circumstances provides no support. What we actually stated in *Atkins* is that "[a]rson's malice requirement ensures that the act is 'done with a design to do an intentional *wrongful* act . . . without any legal justification, excuse or claim of right.'" (Id., at p. 88, italics added.) Malice thus requires, in addition to an intentional (i.e., volitional, willful) act, a *wrongful* one. Or, to quote the relevant California statute, "a wish to vex, defraud, annoy, or injure another person, or an intent to do a wrongful act . . . ." (§450, subd. (e).) Today, the majority ignores the requirement of wrongfulness and presumes malice simply from the commission of the volitional act that causes a fire to start, thus eviscerating the statutory requirement of malice. . . .

To presume malice from nothing more than the volitional act that causes a fire to start could render every unlawful fire under section 452 also an arson under section 451. The Legislature, which we assume does not perform idle acts or enact superfluous legislation, could not have intended this result. Evidently anxious to avoid any such logical, albeit extreme, extension of its holding, the majority offers hypothetical fire-starting scenarios to demonstrate that not all recklessly started fires will qualify as arson. I find the scenarios either contrived and implausible, as that of "a person who carves open a firecracker to check for gunpowder, next to a lit cigarette" (maj. opn., ante, at fn. 7), or practically indistinguishable from the

---

2. V.V. told police that he and J.H. had lit the firecracker "just to make a lot of noise." J.H. explained he had gotten the fireworks on "July, 4th of July. And . . . there was a bunch of fireworks in Compton and I just saw some guys, like a [round] of guys throwing some fireworks. Boom! And they were like exploding and it was like wow!"

case before us, as that of "a person who lights a firecracker, but instead of throwing it, fumbles with it, and it falls on dry brush" (ibid.). To attribute special significance to the fact a firecracker is thrown, as the majority does, seems odd, because one does not ordinarily continue to hold a firecracker that is about to explode. Had the minors deliberately thrown the firecracker into dry brush, the throwing might have had special significance. But the commissioner expressly found the minors had not intended to set a fire and expressly based his ruling on the assumption they were "trying to hit a patch of green or a patch of cement."

In summary, I find the majority's reasoning and conclusion unsupportable. Accordingly, I dissent.

Notes and Questions

1. A majority of the California Supreme Court concluded that V.V. and J.H. acted with "malice," and thus committed arson, when one of them threw a "cherry bomb" and set fire to a grassy hillside. (Note that arson is a serious crime: The particular kind of arson committed by the two juveniles, arson of "forest land," would—if committed by an adult—be punished by either two, four, or six years in state prison.) The dissenters disagreed, largely because the two juveniles never intended to start the fire—they were merely trying to make a big "boom."

Do you think V.V. and J.H. acted with "malice"? How does their culpability compare with that of the defendant in *Atkins*? Or in *U.S. v. Doe*?

2. In two footnotes to a portion of his dissenting opinion not reproduced above, Justice Werdegar quoted one of the juveniles, J.H., as telling the police shortly afterwards:

> "After that we were like, 'Dude, we should just give ourselves in 'cause we did it.' He's like, and someone might get hurt. We were like damn, we started a fire . . . . And when we got down there, we were like, 'Dude, we, we should just . . .' like 'cause like even if . . . like we knew the cops were coming and we, like, we didn't even ran, like we ran at first and then we were like, 'Dude, naw. We're gonna stop and we're gonna give ourselves in.' And then like when the cops came, we were just like stop them and were like ok yeah we did it. It was us. He didn't even ask us anything. We were like, 'we started the fire, it was us.'"

51 Cal. 4th, at 1038 nn.6 & 7. Do these statements by J.H. make you more likely or less likely to agree with the majority's finding of "malice"?

3. The meaning of "malice" was also at the heart of People v. Fennell, 677 N.W.2d 66 (Mich. Ct. App. 2004). The defendant in that case was found guilty of 19 counts of violating the following statute: "A person who willfully, maliciously and without just cause or excuse kills, tortures, mutilates, maims, or disfigures an animal . . . is guilty of a felony, punishable by imprisonment for not more than 4 years." The facts were as follows:

> The Grosse Pointe Hunt Club is a private equestrian facility that maintained two stables to house horses. On July 7-8, 2001, one of the stables at the hunt club burned to the ground. Nineteen of the twenty-four horses kept in that stable died as a result of the fire. The fire began when a firecracker exploded inside the stable.
>
> Joseph Evola lived at his parents' home across the street from the hunt club in July 2001. On the night in question, several of Joseph's friends, including defendant, had gathered at the Evola residence. Joseph claimed that defendant possessed a variety of firecrackers that he had purchased in Ohio. Several people in the group recalled overhearing defendant mention something about throwing firecrackers to scare the horses. And Joseph testified that he saw defendant light a firecracker and make an arm movement to throw it toward the hunt club barn. He then observed the firecracker go over the hunt club's fence. The firecracker was described as a "mortar," the kind that goes up into the air and sparks. Gregory Grosfield, another individual in the group, testified that he saw a firework hit the hunt club barn at approximately 4:15 a.m., and begin to spark.
>
> When defendant threw the [firecracker], everyone ran inside. Within minutes, several witnesses inside the Evola residence claimed that they could see a light glow coming from the barn and that it was obvious the barn was on fire. But defendant dissuaded them from calling for help by saying it would look suspicious. Instead, he suggested that they claim that they were asleep when the fire began.
>
> Raymond Neal, the night watchman for the hunt club, was on duty the night in question. He recalled going out to the barn to close the doors because someone was setting off fireworks in the area. As he was closing the doors, Mr. Neal claimed he felt something go past his head and then saw flames going up the barn walls. Although he was able to let some of the horses out, Mr. Neal testified that the fire was too intense for him to rescue the remainder of the horses in the barn. Further inspection of the barn revealed no evidence of electrical or mechanical failure that might have caused the fire.

677 N.W.2d at 68-69.

The issue on appeal was whether Michigan's animal torture statute required proof of general intent or specific intent, and whether the jury instructions accurately described the governing standard. The court held that animal torture was indeed a general intent offense—and, therefore, that Fennell was guilty even if he did not specifically intend to torture, maim, or kill the dead horses. Still, something more was required than simply proof that Fennell intended to throw the firecracker:

> . . . [I]n People v. Iehl, 299 N.W.2d 46 (Mich. App. 1980), this Court held that the element of malice . . . "requires only that the jury find that defendant committed the act, while knowing it to be wrong, without just cause or excuse,

and did it intentionally or with a conscious disregard of known risks to the property of another." . . .

. . . [S]everal witnesses testified that defendant intentionally threw fireworks at the hunt club stable in an attempt to scare the horses. The record further shows that as a result of his actions, nineteen horses were either tortured or killed in the ensuing fire. Defendant presented no justifications or excuses for his actions. And as evidenced by his behavior after throwing the fireworks, defendant clearly knew his actions were wrong. Accordingly, we find that there was sufficient evidence to support defendant's conviction. . . .

Fennell, 677 N.W.2d at 71-72.

The definition of "malice," according to the *Fennell* court, consists of (1) an awareness by the defendant that his conduct was wrongful in general (even if he may not have been aware of the specific harmful result that actually occurred), combined with (2) either an intent to do the wrongful act despite such awareness, or a "conscious disregard" of the risk that his wrongful conduct created to the property (or, presumably, the person) of others. Fennell claimed he had no idea that the barn would burn down and the horses would die. Why wasn't that claim, if believed, enough to merit an acquittal?

4. For some crimes (like those in *V.V.* and *Fennell*), malice is required by the text of the relevant crime statute. For others, malice is added as a "plus factor" by the courts—even though the relevant statute says nothing about it—based on the judicial feeling that something extra is needed to ensure that defendants don't get convicted unfairly for general intent crimes in which the prohibited act might not sufficiently speak for itself, in terms of establishing the defendant's moral culpability.

In Dauphine v. United States, 73 A.3d 1029 (D.C. 2013), the D.C. Court of Appeals (that's the highest appellate court for cases originating in the D.C. judicial system—not to be confused with the U.S. Court of Appeals for the D.C. Circuit) discussed malice as an implied element of the crime of animal cruelty:

D.C. Code §22-1001(a)(1) (2001) provides, in pertinent part, that any person who "knowingly . . . tortures, torments, . . . or mutilates, any animal, or knowingly causes or procures any animal to be so . . . tortured, tormented, . . . or mutilated," will be guilty of a misdemeanor. Prior to 2001, the language of the statute was essentially the same except the word "knowingly" was omitted. This court has not had occasion to apply this statute since its language was amended, and we take the opportunity now to clarify that our jurisprudence remains intact.

Here, appellant contends that there was insufficient evidence for the fact finder to conclude that she committed the crime knowingly with malice as required. Appellant acknowledges that our decision in Regalado v. United States, 572 A.2d 416 (D.C. 1990), established the mens rea for this crime as general intent with malice, but contends that because the statute changed, *Regalado* no longer controls. Appellant posits that the addition of the term "knowingly" changes the statute from a crime of general intent with malice into a specific intent crime.

The primary case in this area of the law is *Regalado,* supra. Appellant in that case was convicted of cruelty to animals, then codified at D.C. Code §22-801 (1989 Repl.), for beating a puppy while he hung it upside down from a tree. Appellant's defense was that he was disciplining the dog for urinating inside and that the beating as testified to by an eyewitness did not happen. *Regalado,* supra, 572 A.2d at 418-19. He appealed his conviction, claiming that the evidence was insufficient because the government "failed to prove that he had the specific intent to harm the puppy." Id. at 419.

The statute, as then-written, did not expressly specify a mens rea, and the trial court instructed the jury that it had to find appellant had "willfully" mistreated the animal, borrowing language from the instruction for cruelty to children. Id. at 419 (citing D.C. Code §22-901 (1989 Repl.)). This court had previously held that cruelty to children was a "general intent crime . . . requiring proof of malice." Id. at 419. Thus, we stated cruelty to children requires more than general intent, but less than specific intent, which "offers children the protection of the statute . . . while . . . not undermining the domestic authority of parents." Id.

Similar to the statute against cruelty to children, the statute prohibiting cruelty to animals recognizes the need for flexibility, permitting an owner to discipline an animal while preventing "beating[s] and the needless infliction of pain accompanied by a cruel disposition." Id. at 420. While making clear that children are obviously deserving of more protection than animals, the *Regalado* court noted that like the statute in place to protect children, the statute protecting animals was "not intended to place unreasonable restrictions on the infliction of such pain as may be necessary for the training or discipline of an animal." Id. at 420. Thus, the court rejected appellant's claim that specific intent was required, holding that cruelty to animals only required a showing of general intent with malice. Id.

Appellant contends that *Regalado* no longer applies because the amended language in the statute changed the crime of cruelty to animals from general intent with malice to a crime of specific intent. Our review of the Committee Reports discloses that the legislative history does not address appellant's contention. The stated purpose of the 2000 amendment was to add a felony provision and to broaden the definition of cruelty to animals to include "cruelly chaining" an animal. D.C. Council, Report on Bill 13-473, the "Freedom from Cruelty to Animals Protection Amendment Act of 2000" at 2 (May 11, 2000).

The addition of "knowingly" to the statute does not alter our reliance on the holding in *Regalado. Regalado* established the mens rea for cruelty to animals as general intent with malice. It is well settled that the general intent to commit a crime means the intent to do the act that constitutes the crime. Stroman v. United States, 878 A.2d 1241, 1245 (D.C. 2005) ("general intent . . . may be inferred from doing the act that constituted" the crime). The meaning of malice is malleable. This court recently endeavored to explain the meaning of legal malice in the context of malicious destruction of property in Russell v. United States, 65 A.3d 1172 (D.C. 2013). After a thorough discussion of the roots of its usage, *Russell* recognized that malice incorporates two levels of intent, specific and "conscious disregard." Id. at 1183. This is reflected in the jury instructions for malicious destruction of property and in the formal definition of legal malice this court adopted in Charles v. United States, 371 A.2d 404, 411 (D.C. 1977).[5] For our purposes, since *Regalado* made clear cruelty to animals is a general intent crime, the addition of malice to general intent merely means that the actor had no "justification, excuse or recognized mitigation" for his actions and that he was at least aware of the "plain and strong likelihood that [the resulting] harm may result." *Russell*, supra, 65 A.3d at 1184 (quoting *Charles*, supra, 371 A.2d at 411).

73 A.3d at 1031-33. The discussion in *Dauphine* highlights how the concept of malice allows for consideration of claims of justification or excuse (e.g., disciplining a child or a puppy) for the defendant's behavior—something that the general intent standard essentially precludes. This is what the *Dauphine* court means when it says that the addition of a malice requirement makes a crime like cruelty to children "more than general intent, but less than specific intent."

5. In State v. Lomba, 37 A.3d 615 (R.I. 2013), the defendant was convicted of the simple assault of one Susan Rocheleau during an altercation about a car. On appeal, he argued that his use of physical force was without "malice":

> A gray Chrysler Pacifica stands at the center of an encounter between the defendant, John Lomba, and Joseph and Susan Rocheleau, the son and daughter-in-law of his friend, Leonard Rocheleau. The circumstances of this case constitute but one chapter in what appears to have been an ongoing feud between the defendant and Joseph and Susan. The increasing enmity between the parties escalated into a brawl that occurred on July 11, 2008, after the defendant discovered Joseph and Susan tampering with the license plate affixed to the Pacifica while the vehicle was parked in the dirt parking lot of the Little Rhody Beagle Club in Warwick, Rhode Island. During the melee that ensued, the defendant struck Susan in the shoulder, and slashed Joseph's arm with a utility knife. . . .
>
> Before this Court, defendant . . . contends that the trial justice erred when he denied his motion for judgment of acquittal on the charge of simple assault because the state failed to introduce evidence of malice or wantoness . . . .
>
> The defendant asserts that his offer of force did not constitute an assault since it was not made with a wicked or malicious intention to cause injury to Mrs. Rocheleau. . . . Rather, he reasons that any blow that he may have directed

---

5. "Malice in the legal sense imports (1) the absence of all elements of justification, excuse or recognized mitigation, and (2) the presence of either (a) an actual intent to cause the particular harm which is produced or harm of the same general nature, or (b) the wanton and willful doing of an act with awareness of a plain and strong likelihood that such harm may result."

Charles, supra, 371 A.2d at 411 (quoting Perkins, Criminal law, 769-70 (2d ed. 1969).

at Susan Rochealeau was lawful because "she deliberately tried to block [him] from getting into his car after he emphatically warned her and her husband to get away from the vehicle." In other words, he argues that because his actions were undertaken "in order to be able to do what he had every right to do," the state failed to demonstrate in its case-in-chief that he possessed the necessary mens rea for simple assault. . . .

We have defined simple assault as an "unlawful attempt or offer, with force or violence, to do a corporal hurt to another, whether from malice or wantonness."* State v. Pope, 414 A.2d 781, 788 (R.I. 1980) (quoting State v. Baker, 20 R.I. 275, 277, 38 A. 653, 654 (1897)). In addition, we have held that simple assault is a general intent crime. See In re Michael, 423 A.2d 1180, 1183 (R.I. 1981). In its most plain and ordinary sense, malice means "wrongful intention." See Black's Law Dictionary 1042 (9th ed. 2009). The primary legal definition is "[t]he intent, without justification or excuse, to commit a wrongful act." Id. In addition, legal malice is defined simply as "ill will" or "wickedness of the heart." Id. We are convinced that this definition is appropriate in the context of simple assault. This conclusion is consistent with this Court's construction of the term "maliciously" more than one hundred years ago in the context of malicious destruction. See State v. Gilligan, 23 R.I. 400, 408, 50 A. 844, 847 (1901) (defining malicious as "[t]he doing [sic] a wrongful act intentionally without just cause or excuse; a wicked and mischievous purpose which characterizes the perpetration of an injurious act without lawful excuse.").

As the learned trial justice ruled, whether defendant acted with malice was a question of fact to be determined by the jury. At trial, Susan and Joseph Rocheleau testified that it was defendant who approached them, coming out of the darkness from the bushes that surrounded the parking lot. Each testified that defendant was screaming obscenities, and that he escalated what began as a verbal argument into a physical encounter by trying to kick Joseph. There is no dispute that defendant then pushed or punched Susan. Furthermore, Sgt. Tainsh testified that defendant attempted to hide from police by ducking behind a dirt berm in the woods, which certainly may be interpreted as consciousness of guilt. In our opinion, after considering this evidence in the light most favorable to the state, a reasonable juror could conclude beyond a reasonable doubt that defendant acted with "wrong intention" or "ill will" when he struck Susan Rocheleau. Therefore, the trial justice did not err in denying defendant's . . . motion for judgment of acquittal.

Id. at 617, 619-21. What was the nature of the malice issue in *Lomba*? Did the defendant claim that he didn't intend to "cause injury" to Susan when he "pushed or punched" her? (Not to mention when he slashed Joseph with a utility knife—although the jury didn't convict for the slashing, presumably

---

*[The Rhode Island statute under which the defendant was convicted defines "simple assault or battery," rather unhelpfully, as follows: "[E]very person who shall make an assault or battery or both shall be imprisoned not exceeding one year or fined not exceeding one thousand dollars ($1,000), or both." R.I. Gen. Laws §11-5-3.—Eds.]

because there was a question about who was the aggressor at that point in the brawl.) Surely such a claim would have been implausible. Instead, the defendant seems to have claimed that any injury (or threat thereof) to Susan was somehow justified by the fact that she was blocking his path to his car.

Legal ownership of the car, however, was one of many issues in dispute between the parties. Shouldn't the court have to resolve the dispute about the car in order to determine whether or not the defendant acted with malice? But wouldn't that turn malice into a vehicle (sorry!) for litigating property rights? Or the rights of an owner to use "self-help" to reclaim his property? The court doesn't seem to feel the need to address any of those matters. Why not? Is that fair to the defendant?

Note that the defendant's behavior *after* the alleged assault is cited by the court as evidence of malice. As the court explains in a footnote: "It is axiomatic that evidence of a defendant's flight is admissible to show 'consciousness of guilt.'" Id. at 620, fn. 6.

6. The concept of malice reaches far back into the common law. In fact, at common law, malice was the essential element that traditionally distinguished murder from other, lesser forms of criminal homicide. In the special context of homicide law, malice has gradually evolved into a legal term of art that encompasses a wide variety of different culpability levels — including intent to kill (so long as the intent was not the product of legally adequate provocation); intent to cause serious bodily injury (in the sense of an injury that would usually, or at least frequently, prove lethal); extreme recklessness manifesting indifference to the value of human life; and intent to commit any felony crime that is considered inherently dangerous to human life. We will return to the subject of malice in homicide law later, in Chapter 10.

7. In the end, the flexibility of the common law's general intent standard — especially when coupled with the fact that courts also possess the power, even in the absence of any statutory language on the subject, to require proof of a "plus factor" (like criminal negligence or malice) for at least some crimes — seems to render the law of criminal intent rather vague. Is this a problem? Or is it instead an asset — because it allows judges (and juries) a considerable degree of "wiggle room" to achieve a just result on the facts of the particular case? Keep this in mind as you continue to explore the common law of criminal intent.

2. Specific Intent

Crimes of physical violence, like the ones prosecuted in *Sargent*, *Fennell*, and *Dauphine*, are usually general intent offenses. Crimes like theft and fraud, by contrast, usually require proof of specific intent — as the following two cases involving stolen pickup trucks suggest.

State v. Schminkey

Supreme Court of Iowa
597 N.W.2d 785 (1999)

Opinion of Ternus, J.

The defendant, William Schminkey, entered *Alford* pleas to the offenses of homicide by vehicle, see Iowa Code §707.6A(1) (1997), and theft of a motor vehicle, see id. §§714.1, 714.2(2). See generally North Carolina v. Alford, 400 U.S. 25, 37 (1970) (holding that an accused may consent to the imposition of a prison sentence even if he is unwilling or unable to admit his participation in the acts constituting the crime). The court sentenced him to consecutive ten-year and five-year terms of imprisonment, respectively. Schminkey now claims that the record lacks a sufficient factual basis for a finding that he was guilty of the theft offense. . . .

We agree that the record does not show a factual basis for Schminkey's conviction of the crime of theft of a motor vehicle. . . . Accordingly, we vacate the sentence on the theft conviction and remand for further proceedings.

The underlying facts of the tragic episode culminating in Schminkey's convictions are undisputed. . . .

Schminkey spent the evening of May 17, 1997 drinking, first at a party and then at a bar. Although Schminkey has no recollection of leaving the bar or of what happened after he left, witnesses established that he departed the bar and then drove a pickup owned by Dale Kimm, a man Schminkey did not know. Schminkey did not have Kimm's permission to drive the pickup. Several witnesses observed the pickup being driven erratically and in excess of the speed limit. They saw the vehicle heading north, approaching a controlled intersection in the town of Van Horne at an excessive rate of speed. The pickup went through the intersection without slowing down and struck two vehicles, facing south, that were stopped at the intersection stop sign. The driver and only occupant of the first vehicle, nineteen-year-old Jason Kray, died en route to the hospital.

Notwithstanding the collision, the driver of the pickup appeared to be fleeing the scene, accelerating the engine and proceeding down the road for another block or so before crashing into a fence. Witnesses who assisted in extricating Schminkey from the pickup said he smelled strongly of alcohol. A later urine test showed his blood alcohol level to be .189, significantly over the legal limit of .10. See Iowa Code §321J.2(1).

Schminkey was charged with homicide by vehicle in violation of Iowa Code section 707.6A(1), involuntary manslaughter in violation of Iowa Code section 707.5(1), and theft of a motor vehicle in violation of Iowa Code sections 714.1 and 714.2(2). Claiming he was unable to recall the events of the evening due to his intoxication, Schminkey entered into a plea agreement with the State, whereby, in exchange for his *Alford* plea to the theft and homicide charges, the State would dismiss the involuntary manslaughter charge and recommend that Schminkey's sentences on the remaining charges run concurrently.

The State dismissed the manslaughter charge. At the plea hearing, the district court made a determination that a factual basis for the pleas appeared in the record and then accepted Schminkey's guilty pleas. Schminkey was subsequently sentenced to consecutive ten-year and five-year terms of incarceration. . . .

The district court may not accept a guilty plea without first determining that the plea has a factual basis. See Iowa R. Crim. P. 8(2)(b); State v. Burtlow, 299 N.W.2d 665, 668 (Iowa 1980). This requirement exists even where the plea is an *Alford* plea. See *Alford*, 400 U.S. at 38 n.10. . . . In deciding whether a factual basis exists, we consider the entire record before the district court at the guilty plea hearing, including any statements made by the defendant, facts related by the prosecutor, the minutes of testimony, and the presentence report.

The offense of theft is defined in section 714.1(1), which states that a person commits theft when he "takes possession or control of the property of another, or property in the possession of another, *with the intent to deprive the other thereof*" (emphasis added). Schminkey challenges the factual basis for the intent element of this crime.

The intent required for the commission of a theft is an intent to deprive the owner of his or her property. See Eggman v. Scurr, 311 N.W.2d 77, 79 (Iowa 1981). Schminkey argues that this element of the crime requires proof that he intended to *permanently* deprive the owner of his vehicle. He contrasts the theft statute, section 714.1(1), with Iowa Code section 714.7, defining the crime of operating a vehicle without the owner's consent. The latter statute prohibits the "possession or control of . . . any self-propelled vehicle . . . without the consent of the owner of such, *but without the intent to permanently deprive the owner thereof.*" Iowa Code §714.7 (emphasis added). This crime, operating a vehicle without the owner's consent, is expressly made a lesser included offense of the crime of theft. See id.

Schminkey correctly argues that an intent to permanently deprive the owner of his property is an essential element of theft under section 714.1(1). The legislature's distinction of the crime of theft from the crime of operating a vehicle without the owner's consent—the existence or absence of an intent to permanently deprive the owner—supports this conclusion. In addition, this interpretation of section 714.1(1) is consistent with the crime of larceny as it was defined prior to the revision of Iowa's criminal laws in 1978. . . . Prior to the criminal code revisions, the crime of larceny, see Iowa Code §709.1 (1977), and the separate crime of larceny of a motor vehicle, see id. §321.82, required proof of an intent to permanently deprive the owner of the stolen property or vehicle. In one of the few cases in which this court has addressed the issue of intent since the criminal code revisions, we held that the record must demonstrate more than an intent to temporarily deprive the owner of the property in order to prove a theft. See [State v. Fluhr, 287 N.W.2d 857, 867 (Iowa 1980), overruled on other issues by State v. Kirchoff, 452 N.W.2d 801, 804-05 (Iowa 1990)].

Because proof that the defendant acted with the specific purpose of depriving the owner of his property requires a determination of what the defendant was thinking when an act was done, it is seldom capable of being established with direct evidence. . . . Accordingly, we examine the record for facts and circumstances that would support an inference that Schminkey intended to permanently take possession of the truck. . . .

. . . Because Schminkey entered an *Alford* plea, he made no admissions with respect to his commission of this crime. The county attorney made no factual statements. The presentence report had not been completed. The court merely had before it the minutes of testimony.

From the minutes of testimony, it can be established that at 7 P.M. on the day of the accident, Schminkey accompanied a friend to a party where he consumed several beers. He eventually left that party and went to a bar where he drank more alcohol. Later in the evening, at approximately 10:45 P.M., Schminkey was seen driving a pickup from Blairstown to Van Horne. Minutes later, he was involved in the accident described above, and then crashed the vehicle into a fence a block or two from the accident scene. The minutes also show that the owner of the pickup had parked the vehicle in Blairstown and had not given Schminkey permission to drive it.

We find no facts or circumstances in this recitation that would allow an inference that Schminkey intended to permanently deprive the owner of his vehicle. In a similar case that arose under Iowa's old larceny statute, . . . the defendant admitted in the plea colloquy that he took another's automobile without permission. [Brainard v. State, 222 N.W.2d 711, 720.] He denied that he intended to sell the car, but he admitted that he did not intend to bring it back. Id. This court stated that "the essential question as to [the defendant's] intent is whether he intended to deprive the owner permanently of his automobile." Id. at 721. We concluded the record did not show a factual basis for finding that the defendant had that intent. Id. Without that intent, we noted, he would at most be guilty of the lesser offense of operating a motor vehicle without the owner's consent. Id.

Under analogous circumstances, the court of appeals has also concluded the record lacked a factual basis for a finding of intent. State v. Henning, 299 N.W.2d 909, 911 (Iowa App. 1980). In *Henning*, the defendant pled guilty to a charge of assault with intent to inflict serious injury. Id. at 909. During the plea colloquy, he acknowledged being involved in a fight, but stated that he did not otherwise remember the event. Id. at 911. The court of appeals found the record adequate to show a factual basis for the defendant's acts, but not to show a factual basis for the requisite intent. Id. . . .

We acknowledge the general statements made in some of our prior cases that possession of stolen property creates an inference supporting a conviction of larceny. See State v. Everett, 157 N.W.2d 144, 146 (Iowa 1968), overruled on other grounds by State v. Hawkins, 203 N.W.2d 555, 556 (Iowa 1973); State v. Brightman, 110 N.W.2d 315, 318 (Iowa 1961); State v. Girdler, 102 N.W.2d 877, 879 (Iowa 1960). In none of these cases, however, was the defendant's intent at issue. In *Brightman*, a suit stolen from a dry cleaning business was discovered in the defendant's home six months after it had been taken. 252 Iowa at 1280-81, 110 N.W.2d at 316. The defendant claimed that he had purchased the suit from an over-the-road trucker. Id. at 1285, 110 N.W.2d at 319. The element of larceny at issue in this case was whether the defendant took the suit from the cleaners; there was no discussion of his intent. . . . [W]e also think the *Everett* case is not helpful. In that case, the defendant was accused of taking a vehicle from a used car lot. *Everett*, 157 N.W.2d at 145. The defendant claimed he had borrowed the vehicle from a bartender with whom he was acquainted. Id. at 146. Although the court discusses the sufficiency of the evidence with respect to the defendant's "intent to steal" the vehicle, id., it is apparent from the discussion of the evidence that the real dispute was whether he took the vehicle from the used car lot or legitimately borrowed it from a friend. Thus, the court did not really focus on the precise issue that confronts us in the present case, namely, where there is an admitted taking, is that sufficient, standing alone, to support an inference of an intent to permanently deprive the owner of his vehicle.

Because the *Brainard* and *Henning* cases are more on point factually and because the courts in those cases focused on the evidence necessary to support a finding of intent, we conclude the principles applied in *Brainard* and *Henning* should govern our analysis here. Accordingly, the mere fact that Schminkey took the pickup without the owner's consent does not give rise to an inference that he intended to permanently deprive the owner of the vehicle.

In our search for other facts or circumstances that might reveal Schminkey's intent in taking the pickup, we find none indicating that he intended to do anything more than temporarily use the vehicle to go home or to another bar. Because Schminkey wrecked the pickup before he could dispose of it, we do not have the typical inferences that can be drawn from a defendant's actions subsequent to the taking. Compare [Slay v. State, 241 So. 2d 362, 364 (Miss. 1970)] (holding the evidence was insufficient to prove that the defendant had an intent to permanently deprive the owner of his car, stating "the extent of damage to the car was of no probative value on the issue of specific intent, since its wrecking was not purposeful"), with People v. Graham, 327 N.E.2d 261, 264 (Ill. App. 1975) (finding evidence of intent to permanently deprive owner of vehicle sufficient where defendant had changed the license plates on the car); State v. Keeler, 710 P.2d 1279, 1283 (Kan. 1985) (holding evidence sufficient to prove intent to permanently deprive owner of car where defendant used the vehicle for several days and then abandoned it); State v. Winkelmann, 761 S.W.2d 702, 708 (Mo. App. 1988) (finding sufficient evidence of an intent to permanently deprive owner of her car where the defendant intentionally drove the car into a brick wall, inflicting severe damage to the vehicle). Furthermore, the record contains no admissions by the defendant or statements from other witnesses that would indicate Schminkey's purpose in taking the vehicle. Under these circumstances, we conclude the record does not show a factual basis for Schminkey's guilty plea to the charge of theft of a motor vehicle. . . .

. . . There may be additional facts and circumstances that do not appear in the minutes of testimony that would support an inference that the defendant intended to permanently deprive the pickup's owner of his vehicle. Therefore, we vacate the sentence entered on the theft charge and remand for further proceedings at which time the State may supplement the record to establish a factual basis for the crime of theft of a motor vehicle. If a factual basis is not shown, the defendant's plea must be set aside. . . .

CARTER, J., dissenting.

. . . The record made before the district court during the guilty-plea proceeding adequately demonstrated a factual basis for the charge of theft of a motor vehicle. The minutes of testimony indicated that (1) the owner of a 1978 brown and tan Chevrolet pickup truck would testify that the vehicle was taken without permission on the evening of May 17, 1997; and (2) a Benton County deputy sheriff would testify that he was close enough to a fatal collision involving the stolen pickup to hear the sound of the impact and moments later arrived at the crash scene to find defendant sitting crossways, by himself, in the front seat of the missing pickup. . . .

. . . As a general proposition in prosecutions charging theft, possession of property recently taken without permission establishes a prima facie case that a theft has been perpetrated by the possessor of the missing property. See State v. Brightman, 110 N.W.2d 315, 316-18 (Iowa 1961). This court has consistently applied this rule in cases involving prosecutions for theft of a motor vehicle. State v. Rosewall, 239 N.W.2d 171, 173-74 (Iowa 1976); State v. Everett, 157 N.W.2d 144, 146 (Iowa 1968), overruled on other issues by State v. Hawkins, 203 N.W.2d 555, 556-57 (Iowa 1973); State v. Girdler, 102 N.W.2d 877, 879 (Iowa 1960).

A helpful illustration of the application of this principle in a vehicle theft situation similar to the present case is found in *Everett*. There, the evidence showed that a motor vehicle had been left on the lot of a used car dealer at the close of business on October 18, 1965. On that evening, that vehicle was observed being driven on the streets of Cedar Rapids and later parked behind a tavern in Cedar Rapids. Still later in the evening, defendant was apprehended while driving the vehicle. Defendant was convicted at trial of larceny of a motor vehicle. On appeal the presumption of guilt to which I have referred was utilized as the basis for upholding the conviction notwith-standing defendant's testimony that he had only borrowed the car.

The majority attempts to distinguish these cases on the basis that the intent to keep the property was not made an issue on those appeals. This overlooks the fact that the inference of guilt applied therein encompassed *all* elements of the offense of larceny of a motor vehicle. This was expressly recognized in *Rosewall* in which this court states:

> Under our holding in *Everett* the admitted possession by defendants of the recently stolen motorcycle creates an inference barring a motion for directed verdict. The inference is not limited to any particular element of larceny. When it arises guilt of the crime of larceny is inferred.

Rosewall, 239 N.W.2d at 174. The elements of the former statutory crime of larceny of a motor vehicle are sufficiently similar to the present statutory crime of theft that the principle established in the cases under discussion should be applied in the same manner. . . .

. . . I would hold that the showing of factual basis in the present case was adequate and proceed to consider the other issues raised on appeal.

McGiverin, C.J., and Harris and Larson, JJ., join this dissent.

Note on Guilty Pleas and Alford *Pleas*

In the large majority of cases you will read in this book, the defendant was tried and convicted and then appealed his conviction. Not so in *Schminkey*: There, the defendant entered what is called "an *Alford* plea." The defendant in North Carolina v. Alford, 400 U.S. 25 (1970), was charged with capital murder. Prosecutors offered to let the defendant plead guilty to a lesser homicide charge and thereby avoid the death penalty. The defendant chose to accept the offer but refused to admit guilt. Such cases are unusual: Ordinarily, defendants pleading guilty must "allocute"—meaning, they must confess to the crime in open court as part of the plea proceeding. In the usual case, the required factual basis for the plea comes from the defendant's allocution. In *Alford* cases, the required factual basis comes from a government "proffer": The prosecutor summarizes the evidence she would have introduced if the case had gone to trial. In *Schminkey,* the court found that factual basis insufficient to support the plea.

Guilty pleas are mostly invisible in criminal law casebooks. But they constitute the overwhelming majority of criminal cases: Roughly 19 out of every 20 felony convictions in the United States stem from guilty pleas, most of them pursuant to "plea bargains" in which the defendant receives a promised benefit—such as the dropping of additional charges, or a reduced sentence—in return for pleading guilty. The chief effect of the reported decisions you read in this book is felt not in the few cases that go to trial, but in the many cases that plead out. One might say that pleas are made in the shadow of these reported decisions, because any plea will be influenced by the likely outcome if the case *did* go to trial. Keep that in mind as you assess the merits of the legal doctrines that define crimes.

State v. Morris

Supreme Court of Iowa
677 N.W.2d 787 (2004)

PER CURIAM.

Defendant, Willis Elbert Morris, appeals from judgment and sentence convicting him of second-degree theft as a habitual offender in violation of Iowa Code sections 714.2(2), 902.8, and 902.9(3). The alleged theft involved a motor vehicle. He contends that the state failed to produce sufficient evidence that he intended to permanently deprive the owner of possession of the motor vehicle, an essential element of theft involving a motor vehicle. The court of appeals agreed with that contention and reversed defendant's conviction for theft. After reviewing the record and considering the arguments presented, we affirm the decision of the court of appeals. The judgment of the district court is reversed and remanded.

On October 6, 2001, at 4:30 A.M., Brian Gonzales started the engine on his truck parked on the street in front of his home. He intended to let it warm up before driving to work. Gonzales reentered his home leaving the engine running. Shortly thereafter, he heard a "revving" of the truck's engine, looked outside, and saw someone driving his truck away.

Gonzales called Waterloo police and reported the taking of the vehicle. Officer Aaron McClelland arrived at the scene and took the necessary information from Gonzales, including a description of the truck. The officer then put out an "attempt to locate" call to Waterloo patrol officers for the location of a brown Ford Ranger pickup truck.

Approximately thirty minutes later, McClelland came upon the missing truck about five miles from Gonzales's residence. The truck was being driven in the opposite direction from that of the officer's vehicle. McClelland turned his police vehicle around and gave pursuit. The person driving Gonzales's truck stopped the vehicle, got out, and fled on foot toward nearby houses. Officer McClelland radioed for backup and a K-9 unit responded. One of the dogs alerted police to the presence of a person hiding on a porch of a house. McClelland identified this person as the man who had fled from the truck. That person was ultimately determined to be defendant, Willis Elbert Morris.

Defendant was arrested and charged with second-degree theft pursuant to Iowa Code section 714.2(2), a class "D" felony. He was also charged as a habitual offender, pursuant to Iowa Code section 902.8. The second-degree theft charge was submitted to the jury along with the lesser-included offense of operating a motor vehicle without the owner's consent in violation of Iowa Code section 714.7. The jury found defendant guilty of second-degree theft. He ultimately stipulated to the prior offenses on which the habitual-offender sentencing enhancement was based.

The court of appeals, relying on our decision in State v. Schminkey, 597 N.W.2d 785 (Iowa 1999), concluded that the mere fact that defendant took Gonzales's pickup truck without consent of the owner did not give rise to an inference that he intended to permanently deprive the owner of the vehicle. The court further concluded that the evidence, viewed in its entirety, was insufficient to permit a finding of the requisite intent beyond a reasonable doubt. We agree with the court of appeals' reading of *Schminkey* and its application to the present facts.

Although apprehension of the suspect within a short time of the taking of the vehicle does not defeat the possibility that there was an intent to permanently deprive the owner of the property at the time of the taking, it is a circumstance that severely limits the circumstantial evidence from which that intent can be inferred. The State urges that the circumstances under which the defendant abandoned the vehicle, i.e., stopping it and running away, are indicative of the requisite intent. We disagree. Abandoning the vehicle and fleeing upon observing the presence of police was an act that would ordinarily assure that the truck would be returned to its owner. We affirm the decision of the court of appeals holding that the evidence was insufficient to support a conviction for second-degree theft.

The court of appeals simply remanded the case for further proceedings not inconsistent with its opinion. We believe a more specific remand mandate is warranted. The offense of operating a motor vehicle without the owner's consent in violation of Iowa Code section 714.7 was submitted to the jury as a lesser-included offense. The jury did not reach a verdict on that offense because it found that the State had established all elements of the greater offense. In so doing, the jury necessarily found that the State had established all elements of the included offense. In such instances, we have approved entering an amended judgment of conviction with respect to the lesser-included offense. State v. Pace, 602 N.W.2d 764, 774 (Iowa 1999). We order that this be done following remand in the present case. Defendant shall then be resentenced. . . .

CARTER, J., concurring.

Although I am troubled with the decision of the court in State v. Schminkey, 597 N.W.2d 785 (Iowa 1999), . . . I do not agree that that decision only applies to guilty pleas, as the dissent in the present case suggests.

Schminkey involved the taking of an *Alford* plea in which the defendant refused to admit guilt. When this occurs, the court, before accepting the plea, must determine whether the evidence available to the State would be sufficient to sustain a guilty verdict at trial. That is the same analysis that must be undertaken in ruling on a motion for judgment of acquittal. For this reason, *Schminkey* is valid authority for the issue presently before the court.

I believe *Schminkey* failed to recognize the strength of the inference that arises from taking an automobile without the owner's consent. An individual's intent is synonymous with what he wants to do. What he wants to do is usually motivated by and derived from the actor's own best interests. It is in the best interests of one taking another's automobile without permission that the vehicle not be returned to the owner because this may aid in the identification of the perpetrator.

Notwithstanding my conclusions in this regard, I concur in the result because I am unable to find that the totality of the evidence in the present case, including the presumption to which I refer, is sufficient to sustain a verdict of guilty on the greater charge. The defendant should be declared guilty of the lesser included offense.

LARSON, J., joined by CADY and STREIT, JJ., dissenting.

I dissent because the majority fails to recognize and apply the well-established principle that a defendant's possession of recently stolen property creates an inference that the defendant stole it. In concluding that proof of intent was not established in this case, the majority expressly relies on State v. Schminkey, 597 N.W.2d 785 (Iowa 1999), stating, "we agree with the court of appeals' reading of *Schminkey* and its application to the present facts."

While I agree with the holding in *Schminkey*, I disagree with the majority's reliance on it in this case. Both *Schminkey* and the present case involve the sufficiency of evidence on the element of intent to deprive the owner of possession of a vehicle. With that, however, the similarity ends. *Schminkey* was a guilty-plea case, while the present case was tried to a jury. In a guilty-plea case, the State may not rely on inferences to establish a factual basis. In contrast, a jury-tried case is one in which inferences are standard stock-in-trade. . . . "It is often necessary for the trier of fact to determine the existence of an element of the crime — that is, an 'ultimate' or 'elemental' fact — from the existence of one or more 'evidentiary' or 'basic' facts." Court of Ulster County, New York v. Allen, 442 U.S. 140, 156 (1979). . . .

The facts presented at trial are briefly stated in the majority opinion. It is undisputed that Morris took the truck, at about 4:30 A.M., without the owner's consent. The owner immediately called the police who soon located the vehicle and began to give chase. When the police stopped the vehicle, Morris fled on foot. These facts are clearly sufficient to give rise to an inference of guilt, including the element of intent. . . .

The majority points to facts it contends militate against proof of an intent to deprive the owner of possession. These facts include the distance Morris traveled with the truck (approximately five miles) before he was apprehended and the time he had the truck (approximately thirty minutes). These facts are not necessarily helpful to Morris's case, however; his relatively short time of possession might well have been viewed by the jury to be the result of speedy police work—not evidence that he lacked the intent to keep it. In any event, that was a question for the jury. While the facts relied on by Morris may affect the strength of the inference, they do not preclude, as a matter of law, an inference of intent. . . .

I believe the majority erred in relying on *Schminkey*, in refusing to recognize the inference of intent, and in failing to conclude that sufficient evidence supports the conviction. I would vacate the decision of the court of appeals and affirm the judgment of the district court.

Notes on the Meaning of Specific Intent

1. *Schminkey* and *Morris* show what specific intent ordinarily means: that the defendant not only intended to do the act he did—in both of these cases, drive someone else's truck—but also intended to bring about some specific harm the law forbids. In these cases, the forbidden harm is the permanent deprivation of the victim's property.

2. In general intent cases, courts often combine two very different concepts. First, the defendant must have intended to do what he did—throw the firecracker onto the grassy hillside in *V.V.*, shake the injured child in *Sargent*, divert the doctors' payments in *Stark* to a construction project other than the one for which they were intended. Second, courts at least sometimes hold that the defendant also must have behaved with either "malice" or "criminal negligence," or some comparably vague phrase or label. In specific intent cases, by contrast, courts rarely mention the second concept; there is no "plus factor" in such cases. Why the difference?

One possibility is that the intent to bring about the forbidden result obviates the need for adding anything like a criminal negligence or malice standard. The point of those "plus factors" is to ensure that convicted defendants intended to do something wrong. If Schminkey and Morris really intended to take and keep trucks that didn't belong to them, then they clearly *did* intend to do something wrong. The "plus factor" demonstrating an "evil mind" would be superfluous, because it would always be satisfied: All thieves are, by definition, indifferent to the property rights of those from whom they steal. On the other hand, if state legislators choose to criminalize the intentional causing of results that are only trivially harmful, then proof of intent to cause the relevant forbidden result will not amount to much. Once again, the statutory definition of the criminal conduct does most of the work in separating blameworthy defendants from non-blameworthy ones.

3. Because guilty defendants cannot be relied on to confess to the crimes they commit, criminal intent—both general and specific—must be inferred from the defendant's conduct under the circumstances under which the defendant engaged in that conduct. At most criminal trials, the government puts on evidence of what the defendant did, and asks the jury to infer that anyone who did *that*, under the relevant circumstances, must have intended *this*. A large part of a prosecutor's job is to identify and support the most plausible inferences, just as a defense lawyer's job is to try to poke holes in the prosecutor's arguments, to explain why the inferences the state wants the jury to draw are weakly supported or do not fit the evidence. Notice that Schminkey's guilty plea wasn't overturned because Schminkey denied having the requisite intent. Rather, it was overturned because, in the court's view, his conduct didn't establish a sufficient "factual basis" for the requisite intent. The same result obtained in *Morris*, on the majority's view, even though *Morris* involved a trial rather than a guilty plea.

4. Did the court get the two cases right? Does *Morris* follow from *Schminkey*? Obviously, three members of the Iowa Supreme Court didn't think so. The disagreement between the majority and dissent in *Morris*, and to some degree in *Schminkey* as well, concerns a question that arises frequently in criminal cases: Since intent generally must be inferred from conduct, how aggressive should judges and juries be in drawing the relevant inferences? Should Schminkey and Morris be convicted only if their intent was absolutely clear? Or should judges and juries start from the assumption that defendants' intentions were probably what they seemed, and force the defense to prove otherwise?

The familiar rule that the government must prove guilt "beyond a reasonable doubt" suggests that the answer to that last question is no. And, indeed, as a matter of constitutional due process law, jurors may not be told to "presume" any element of a crime from proof of some other fact, see Francis v. Franklin, 471 U.S. 307 (1985); permissive "inferences" are permitted, but mandatory "presumptions," even if rebuttable, are not.

But whatever a jury may or may not be told, consistent with due process standards, it seems pretty clear that jurors probably do a fair amount of "presuming" whenever they are trying to determine a defendant's intentions. Isn't it perfectly natural for jurors to rely on the assumption (or is it a "presumption"?) that the defendant intended to do what he actually did?

Moreover, even the meaning of "reasonable doubt" is far from clear; in practice, that phrase leaves a great deal of flexibility to juries (and to judges, in bench trials). That flexibility probably matters more when deciding on the presence or absence of criminal *intent* than when deciding whether the defendant engaged in the relevant criminal *conduct*—because conduct is often proved more directly, whereas intent requires fact finders to draw inferences from conduct and circumstances. Sometimes, drawing the proper inferences is hard.

5. Why do some crimes require proof of specific intent and others require only proof of general intent? One reason is grading: Criminal law might punish a specific-intent version of a crime more harshly than the general-intent version. The criminal law of assault does precisely that. In all jurisdictions, it is a crime to strike another person in a manner likely to cause injury, whether or not the defendant intends to injure the victim. Likewise, in all jurisdictions, it is a worse grade of offense, carrying a heavier sentence, to strike another person with the intent to kill or cause serious injury. As *Schminkey* and *Morris* illustrate, something similar is true of the law of auto theft. It is a crime to take someone else's car, drive it for a while, then return or abandon it—the offense is usually called "joyriding." Taking someone else's car with the intent to keep or sell it is a more serious crime carrying a harsher sentence. Joyriding is usually defined as a general intent offense; auto theft is a specific intent crime.

But grading does not explain all the uses of these two different intent standards. Again, consider the bodies of law that define theft and assault. Ordinarily, picking up someone else's briefcase by mistake is not a crime; in order to prove theft, the government must show that the defendant intended to keep or sell the victim's property: to "convert" it to the defendant's use. But assaulting another person *is* a crime, even if the defendant intended no harm; intending to do the prohibited act is all that is required for assault. Does that difference make sense? Why do you suppose the law evolved in that way?

6. In his classic discussion of the common law of criminal intent, Oliver Wendell Holmes offered the following answer to those questions:

> There remain to be considered certain substantive crimes, which differ in very important ways from murder and the like. . . .
>
> The type of these is larceny. Under this name acts are punished which of themselves would not be sufficient to accomplish the evil which the law seeks to prevent, and which are treated as equally criminal, whether the evil has been accomplished or not. Murder, manslaughter, and arson, on the other hand, are not committed unless the evil is accomplished, and they all consist of acts the tendency of which under the surrounding circumstances is to hurt or destroy person or property by the mere working of natural laws.
>
> In larceny the consequences immediately flowing from the act are generally exhausted with little or no harm to the owner. Goods are removed from his possession by trespass, and that is all, when the crime is complete. But they must be permanently kept from him before the harm is done which the law seeks to prevent. A momentary loss of possession is not what has been guarded against with such severe penalties. What the law means to prevent is the loss of it wholly and forever, as is shown by the fact that it is not larceny to take for a temporary use without intending to deprive the owner of his property. If then the law punishes the mere act of taking, it punishes an act which will not of itself produce the evil effect sought to be prevented, and punishes it before that effect has in any way come to pass.
>
> The reason is plain enough. The law cannot wait until the property has been used up or destroyed in other hands than the owner's, or until the owner

has died, in order to make sure that the harm which it seeks to prevent has been done. And for the same reason it cannot confine itself to acts likely to do that harm. For the harm of permanent loss of property will not follow from the act of taking, but only from the series of acts which constitute removing and keeping the property after it has been taken. After these preliminaries, the bearing of intent upon the crime is easily seen.

According to Mr. Bishop, larceny is "the taking and removing, by trespass, of personal property which the trespasser knows to belong either generally or specially to another, with the intent to deprive such owner of his ownership therein. . . ."

There must be an intent to deprive such owner of his ownership therein, it is said. But why? Is it because the law is more anxious not to put a man in prison for stealing unless he is actually wicked, than it is not to hang him for killing another? That can hardly be. The true answer is, that the intent is an index to the external event which probably would have happened, and that, if the law is to punish at all, it must, in this case, go on probabilities, not on accomplished facts. The analogy to the manner of dealing with attempts is plain. Theft may be called an attempt to permanently deprive a man of his property, which is punished with the same severity whether successful or not. If theft can rightly be considered in this way, intent must play the same part as in other attempts. An act which does not fully accomplish the prohibited result may be made wrongful by evidence that but for some interference it would have been followed by other acts co-ordinated with it to produce that result. This can only be shown by showing intent. In theft the intent to deprive the owner of his property establishes that the thief would have retained, or would not have taken steps to restore, the stolen goods. Nor would it matter that the thief afterwards changed his mind and returned the goods. From the point of view of attempt, the crime was already complete when the property was carried off.

Oliver Wendell Holmes, The Common Law 70-72 (1881). Note Holmes' analogy to the law of criminal attempts. As you will see in Chapters 7 and 9, see infra pages 454-471 and 635-648, the law of attempts permits the punishment of conduct that does not amount to a completed crime — but only when the perpetrator specifically intends to complete the crime in question. The usual rationale for that standard goes like this: Since the defendant intended to commit the completed crime, he probably would have succeeded in doing so had he not been apprehended before his criminal conduct was finished. In Holmes' view, the rationale for specific intent is similar: one who specifically intended a given harm was likely to cause that harm if given the opportunity. One might wonder at the enterprise of punishing criminal defendants based on predictions of future conduct, but whatever the wisdom of that course of action, the law has taken it many times over a period of centuries.

7. The facts in State v. Orsello, 554 N.W.2d 70 (Minn. 1996), are as follows:

> Paul and Diane Orsello were married for over nine years, but were divorced in 1992. Diane Orsello received custody of their three children. Appellant was granted visitation and the right to phone his children on certain days of the week. However, the record reflects that he continued to contact his wife and children frequently via the phone and in writing. Often appellant suggested reconciliation, or at least social contact, with his former wife. While the tenor of these contacts was often affectionate, sometimes appellant was threatening or angry. On one occasion, appellant showed his ex-wife a gun, stating he hoped "it wouldn't go off," and later told her she could "burn in hell."
>
> Diane Orsello sought and received a harassment restraining order in June 1992, prohibiting appellant from contact with his family in any manner other than that allowed by a previous court order. Repeated contacts with his family resulted in his conviction for violating the harassment order in 1993. His contact with his wife and children continued and . . . he was charged with stalking under Minn. Stat. §609.749.

554 N.W.2d at 71. Here is the stalking statute Orsello violated:

> Subd. 1. Definition. As used in this section, "harass" means to engage in intentional conduct in a manner that (1) would cause a reasonable person under the circumstances to feel oppressed, persecuted, or intimidated; and (2) causes this reaction on the part of the victim.
>
> Subd. 2. Harassment and stalking crimes. A person who harasses another by committing any of the following acts is guilty of a gross misdemeanor:
>
> > (1) directly or indirectly manifests a purpose or intent to injure the person, property, or rights of another by the commission of an unlawful act;
> >
> > (2) stalks, follows, or pursues another;
> >
> > (3) returns to the property of another if the actor is without claim of right to the property or consent of one with authority to consent;
> >
> > (4) repeatedly makes telephone calls, or induces a victim to make telephone calls to the actor, whether or not conversation ensues;
> >
> > (5) makes or causes the telephone of another repeatedly or continuously to ring;
> >
> > (6) repeatedly uses the mail or delivers or causes the delivery of letters, telegrams, packages, or other objects; or
> >
> > (7) engages in any other harassing conduct that interferes with another person or intrudes on the person's privacy or liberty.

Minn. Stat. §609.749.

Since the statute did not specify an intent standard, the Minnesota Supreme Court had to choose between general and specific intent. The court opted for specific intent, on two grounds. First, several of the listed examples of impermissible harassment were crimes even before the state legislature enacted the stalking statute — and those crimes required proof of specific intent. The court described the second reason this way:

> . . . [T]he language of subdivision 1 reinforces our conclusion that specific intent is required by the text of the stalking statute. Subdivision 1 states that:

"as used in this section, 'harass' means to engage in intentional conduct in a manner that: (1) would cause a reasonable person under the circumstances to feel oppressed, persecuted, or intimidated; and (2) causes this reaction on the part of the victim." Minn. Stat. §609.749, subd. 1. Canons of statutory construction require us to give effect to each word in the statute, to avoid any interpretation that characterizes any portion of the statute as surplusage. The legislature needed only itemize the actions to be criminalized to create a general intent crime. It did not need to qualify further the type of action required. In other words, a general intent version of this statute did not need either the adjective "intentional" or the phrase "in a manner that." The addition of these words, we believe, further demonstrates that the stalking statute must require specific intent, for how does one act "in a manner that would cause a reasonable person to feel oppressed" unless one acts with at least the knowledge, if not the purpose, to cause such a reaction? To conclude otherwise would be to admit the possibility that one might be guilty of accidentally stalking and that seems inconsistent with the legislative background and intent of the statute.

554 N.W.2d at 75-76. In dissent, Justice Stringer objected to this reasoning:

. . . The majority's conclusion that Minn. Stat. §609.749 requires proof that the defendant intended to cause the victim to feel oppressed, persecuted or intimidated, as opposed to proof that the defendant intended to engage in conduct that caused the victim's reaction, regardless of whether the defendant had the specific intent to cause the reaction, is an unwarranted rewrite of a clear and unambiguous statute. . . .

. . . [N]ow the state will not only be required to prove intent to oppress, persecute or intimidate; it must also prove that a hypothetical, reasonable person would so react, and that the victim did so react. . . . But the [statute] already had a protective device incorporated in it to prevent its unwarranted application — that the conduct must be of a nature to cause a reasonable person to feel oppressed.

554 N.W.2d at 77-78 (Stringer, J., dissenting). Which side has the more persuasive argument? Is the majority in *Orsello* saying that any time a crime statute requires a defendant to cause a particular harm, the defendant also must be proved to have *specifically intended* to cause that harm? If so, is *Orsello* consistent with *Sargent*? If not, is there a better way to explain the majority's position? Is stalking in Minnesota defined more like active child abuse in California, or does the definition above more closely resemble passive child abuse?

Notes on Intoxication and Proof of Criminal Intent

1. Intoxication wasn't an issue in *Schminkey* because he decided to plead guilty. Had the case gone to trial, however, the likeliest defense argument would have turned on Schminkey's drinking. Intoxication is not a defense to crime, but sometimes it can be helpful to defendants when the crime charged requires proof of specific intent. Not so with respect to crimes that require only general intent. See, for example, the discussion of the *Atkins* case in *V.V.,* supra at page 113, where the court notes that evidence of the defendant's voluntary intoxication was "inadmissible" on the issue of general intent.

2. Chief Justice Roger Traynor of the California Supreme Court, widely regarded as one of the leading American judges of the twentieth century, famously argued that intoxication is in fact the *only* reason criminal law distinguishes between specific and general intent. The case in which Traynor made that argument was People v. Hood, 462 P.2d 370 (Cal. 1969). While Hood was being arrested for another offense, he grabbed the arresting officer's gun and fired it twice, hitting the officer once in each leg. Hood was charged with assault with a deadly weapon, battery on a police officer, and assault with intent to kill. At the time of the relevant events, Hood was thoroughly drunk. The question before the court was whether, and if so how, his drunkenness might be relevant to the first and third of the charges just listed. Here is what Chief Justice Traynor had to say on the subject:

> The distinction between specific and general intent crimes evolved as a judicial response to the problem of the intoxicated offender. . . . On the one hand, the moral culpability of a drunken criminal is frequently less than that of a sober person effecting a like injury. On the other hand, it is commonly felt that a person who voluntarily gets drunk and while in that state commits a crime should not escape the consequences.
>
> Before the nineteenth century, the common law refused to give any effect to the fact that an accused committed a crime while intoxicated. The judges were apparently troubled by this rigid traditional rule, however, for there were a number of attempts during the early part of the nineteenth century to arrive at a more humane, yet workable, doctrine. The theory that these judges explored was that evidence of intoxication could be considered to negate intent, whenever intent was an element of the crime charged. As Professor Hall notes, however, such an exculpatory doctrine could eventually have undermined the traditional rule entirely, since some form of *mens rea* is a requisite of all but strict liability offenses. Hall, Intoxication and Criminal Responsibility, 57 Harv. L. Rev. 1045, 1049. To limit the operation of the doctrine and achieve a compromise between the conflicting feelings of sympathy and reprobation for the intoxicated offender, later courts both in England and this country drew a distinction between so-called specific intent and general intent crimes.
>
> Specific and general intent have been notoriously difficult terms to define and apply, and a number of text writers recommend that they be abandoned altogether. Hall, General Principles of Criminal Law 142 (2d ed. 1960); Williams, Criminal Law—The General Part §21, at 49 (2d ed. 1961). Too often the characterization of a particular crime as one of specific or general intent is determined solely by the presence or absence of words describing psychological phenomena—"intent" or "malice," for example—in the statutory language defining the crime. When the definition of a crime consists of only the description of a particular act, without reference to intent to do a further act or achieve a future consequence, we ask whether the defendant intended to do the proscribed act. This intention is deemed to be a general criminal intent. When the definition refers to defendant's intent to do some further

act or achieve some additional consequence, the crime is deemed to be one of specific intent. . . .

. . . Even if assault requires an intent to commit a battery on the victim, it does not follow that the crime is one in which evidence of intoxication ought to be considered in determining whether the defendant had that intent. . . . Since the definitions of both specific intent and general intent cover the requisite intent to commit a battery, the decision whether or not to give effect to evidence of intoxication must rest on other considerations.

A compelling consideration is the effect of alcohol on human behavior. A significant effect of alcohol is to distort judgment and relax the controls on aggressive and anti-social impulses. Alcohol apparently has less effect on the ability to engage in simple goal-directed behavior, although it may impair the efficiency of that behavior. In other words, a drunk man is capable of forming an intent to do something simple, such as strike another, unless he is so drunk that he has reached the stage of unconsciousness. What he is not as capable as a sober man of doing is exercising judgment about the social consequences of his acts or controlling his impulses toward anti-social acts. He is more likely to act rashly and impulsively and to be susceptible to passion and anger. It would therefore be anomalous to allow evidence of intoxication to relieve a man of responsibility for the crimes of assault with a deadly weapon or simple assault, which are so frequently committed in just such a manner. As the court said in Parker v. United States, 359 F.2d 1009, 1012-13 (D.C. Cir. 1966), "Whatever ambiguities there may be in distinguishing between specific and general intent to determine whether drunkenness constitutes a defense, an offense of this nature is not one which requires an intent that is susceptible to negation through a showing of voluntary intoxication."

Those crimes that have traditionally been characterized as crimes of specific intent are not affected by our holding here. The difference in mental activity between formulating an intent to commit a battery and formulating an intent to commit a battery for the purpose of raping or killing may be slight, but it is sufficient to justify drawing a line between them and considering evidence of intoxication in the one case and disregarding it in the other. Accordingly, on retrial the court should not instruct the jury to consider evidence of defendant's intoxication in determining whether he committed assault with a deadly weapon on a peace officer or any of the lesser assaults included therein. . . .

Elsewhere in his opinion, Traynor indicated that evidence of intoxication *was* relevant to the charge of assault with intent to kill, a specific intent crime.

3. Traynor's account of the relevant history is contested; not everyone believes that general and specific intent evolved simply as means of distinguishing between cases in which intoxication might negate intent and cases in which it cannot do so. (Recall that Oliver Wendell Holmes believed the distinction rests on the greater need to predict future behavior when specific intent crimes are at issue. See pages 48-49 supra.) But the line Traynor describes in *Hood* has been remarkably stable. Not all states use it, and there are differences of detail. Some states hold that intoxication is relevant only to show that the defendant may have lacked the *capacity* to form specific intent; others hold that intoxication may negate specific intent itself, a more generous standard. And a growing fraction of states hold that intoxication may *never* be used to negate *mens rea*, regardless of the intent standard at issue. Notwithstanding these differences, all jurisdictions agree that evidence of intoxication may not be used to negate general intent. The basic idea that intoxication does not negate culpability for most crimes has a powerful hold on American criminal law.

Why? Recall the key passage in *Hood*:

> What [the intoxicated defendant] is not as capable as a sober man of doing is exercising judgment about the social consequences of his acts or control-ling his impulses toward anti-social acts. He is more likely to act rashly and impulsively and to be susceptible to passion and anger. It would therefore be anomalous to allow evidence of intoxication to relieve a man of responsibility for the crimes of assault with a deadly weapon or simple assault, which are so frequently committed in just such a manner.

The premise seems to be that acting "rashly and impulsively" out of "passion and anger" is a culpable mental state, whether the actor is drunk or sober. One might even think of it as another "plus factor" that makes a defendant deserving of criminal punishment.

Do you agree that impulsive behavior is inherently wrongful? Doesn't the answer depend on the nature of the impulse or the object of the passion? To be sure, Hood's impulses seem clearly wrong and destructive. But that doesn't resolve the issue. Suppose Hood were to testify that, though he had been drunk before, he had never committed any crime while drunk; suppose further that other evidence corroborated his claim. Now suppose Hood argues that he did not *choose* to grab the officer's gun and fire it, for he did not choose to do anything; he was too drunk to make meaningful choices. Should he be punished? For what? On the facts hypothesized, the only culpa-ble choice Hood made was the choice to get drunk—and that choice wasn't really culpable under the terms of the hypothetical, since Hood had no way of knowing that his drunkenness would lead him to behave as he did.

All American states would reject the argument sketched above, but why? Holmes would say that the law requires people to live up to reason-able standards of behavior and punishes them when they fail, whether they could have done better or not. But that description doesn't fit the cases. The intent standards applied in the cases excerpted earlier in this chapter seem designed to punish only those who could have behaved better but chose not to. By and large, American criminal law punishes only those who make culpable choices. It isn't obvious that a defendant with no history of violence who assaults someone while drunk has made a culpable choice.

4. Does it matter whether the choice to get drunk was legal or not? Recall People v. Kellogg: Many jurisdictions have criminal statutes prohibit-ing public drunkenness. Hood committed his assault in a private home, so his conduct would not be covered by that statute. Suppose the incident had happened in a bar. Should that affect the result?

5. Consider a different line of argument. A large fraction of the adult population has been drunk in the presence of other people; only a small fraction of that population has assaulted anyone while drunk. What separates that small fraction from the larger one? Some defendants who behave as Hood did might find their own behavior surprising after the fact. Others' behavior might be perfectly predictable: Hood may have known full well that he tended to be an angry, out-of-control drunk. In which case, getting drunk really *was* a culpable choice—a little like a decision by one who is prone to sudden seizures to drive a car on a busy highway. If so, it makes perfect sense not to allow Hood to excuse his conduct by pointing to his intoxication.

But if that is the law's rationale, why not force the government to prove that Hood had been an angry drunk in the past? The answer is: That approach would give the Hoods of the world one free bite at the apple. Anyone with no history of violence could plan an assault, get drunk (perhaps to muster up courage), commit the crime, and then claim that he had no idea he would behave so badly. Such claims are hard to refute, since the effect of a given quantity of alcohol (the point applies to other drugs as well) varies from person to person. And unless the police apprehended the defendant at the time of the crime and tested his blood alcohol level promptly, it would be hard to disprove defendants' claims about how much they drank.

6. Note that even when defendants are charged with crimes that require proof of specific intent, the fact of intoxication itself—even if clearly established by the evidence—is never a defense to crime. At most, the defendant may use evidence of intoxication to try to negate specific intent; the fact that the defendant was drunk does not *by itself* excuse criminal behavior. A drunken car thief is not excused simply because he would not have stolen the victim's car if sober. But the defendant *can* argue (in most states) that he didn't *know* he was taking someone else's car—that, for example, he was too drunk to recognize that the car wasn't his, or too drunk to form any purpose at all. Does that distinction make sense? Is there a more appropriate way to handle evidence of intoxication in criminal cases?

7. One of the most important implications of the line discussed in *Hood* concerns sexual assault cases. The defendant in People v. Vigil, 127 P.3d 916 (Colo. 2006), was charged with sexual assault of a seven-year-old child. The defendant argued that his intoxication negated *mens rea*; the relevant state statute specified that the defendant must commit the assault "knowingly." The Colorado Supreme Court held that child sexual assault was a general intent crime, and that voluntary intoxication could not negate such intent. The result in *Vigil* is typical; for the most part, sexual assault is deemed to be a general intent crime, meaning that intoxication is not relevant to negate intent. That has a large practical effect on rape prosecutions, as we shall see in Chapter 9, at pages 673-679. Is *Vigil* rightly decided? Why should intoxication be relevant to negate criminal intent in theft cases, but not in assault or rape cases?

3. Mistakes of Fact

General intent refers to defendants' mental state with respect to their conduct. Specific intent refers to defendants' mental state with respect to the results caused by their conduct. What kind of "intent" (if that word even fits) must defendants have with respect to the factual circumstances surrounding their conduct? At common law, the answer to that question is governed primarily by mistake doctrine. In general intent cases, a defendant has a valid mistake-of-fact defense if he made an *honest and reasonable* mistake about the surrounding circumstances *that negates his culpability*. In specific intent cases, a mistake-of-fact defense is available if the defendant's error was merely *honest*—it need not be reasonable. The following cases explore the meaning of these different mistake standards.

United States v. Oglivie

United States Army Court of Military Review
29 M.J. 1069 (1990)

FOREMAN, Senior Judge:

A military judge sitting as a special court-martial convicted the appellant, in accordance with his plea of guilty, of altering a public record in violation of Article 134, Uniform Code of Military Justice, 10 U.S.C. §934 (1982) [hereinafter UCMJ]. Contrary to his pleas, the military judge also convicted the appellant of signing a false official statement (two specifications), wrongful appropriation of a copy of a divorce decree, and bigamy, in violation of Articles 107, 121 and 134, UCMJ, 10 U.S.C. §§907, 921 and 934 (1982). His approved sentence provides for a bad-conduct discharge, confinement for three months, and reduction to Private E1.

The appellant married his first wife, Amparo, in December 1986, while stationed in Panama. In January 1987, the appellant was reassigned from Panama to Germany, but his wife remained in Panama. While in Germany, the appellant did not know Amparo's address or telephone number, but sent letters to a friend, who passed them on to her. The appellant returned from Germany in March 1988 and was reassigned to Fort Sill, Oklahoma. In August 1988, the appellant sent his wife a money order with his telephone number written on it. The appellant filed for divorce in Oklahoma and sent a copy of the petition to a friend's post office box in Panama for delivery to his wife. In September or October 1988, Amparo called the appellant from Panama and informed him that she had filed for divorce in Panama, that there was "nothing between the two of us" and that he "didn't have to worry about her anymore." The appellant testified that he thought he was divorced at that point. In November 1988, the Red Cross notified the appellant that Amparo had been hospitalized. The Red Cross referred to Amparo as his "ex-wife." On 9 November 1988, the appellant requested that his basic allowance for quarters (BAQ) at the "with dependents" rate be terminated because he was divorced. The finance clerk told him that she could not stop the BAQ without a divorce decree. Since the appellant did not have a copy of a divorce decree, he took another sergeant's divorce decree, made a copy of it, inserted his name and Amparo's in the text (but neglected to change the caption) and attached it to his request to terminate his BAQ. In December 1988, the appellant married Jackeline, and requested that his BAQ at the "with dependents" rate be reinstated.

The appellant was charged with making two false official statements to officials of the Fort Sill finance office, first that he was divorced from Amparo (Specification 1 of Charge II) and second that he was married to Jackeline (Specification 2 of Charge II). He contends that the evidence was insufficient to prove both specifications because he honestly believed that he was divorced from Amparo.

This court specified the following issues: (1) whether creation of an altered copy of a public record without altering the original constitutes the offense of altering a public record, and (2) whether the appellant's plea of guilty to altering a public record was provident to the offense charged or any lesser included offense.

I. FALSE OFFICIAL STATEMENTS

Making a false official statement in violation of UCMJ, Article 107, 10 U.S.C. §907 (1982),* is a specific intent crime. An honest mistake of fact regarding the truth of the statement made is a defense. United States v. Rowan, 4 U.S.C.M.A. 430 (C.M.A. 1954); Manual for Courts-Martial, United States, 1984, Rule for Courts-Martial 916(j) [hereinafter M.C.M., 1984 and R.C.M.]; M.C.M., Part IV, ¶31c(5). The evidence establishes that Amparo told the appellant she had filed for divorce, that the appellant received correspondence from the Red Cross referring to Amparo as his "ex-wife," and that he attempted to terminate his entitlement to BAQ, on the ground that he was divorced. He then participated in a marriage ceremony and received a marriage certificate indicating that he was married to Jackeline. Based upon the entire record, we find that the defense of an honest mistake of fact was raised and not overcome by the government's evidence. R.C.M. 916(b). Accordingly, we find that the evidence is insufficient to prove appellant's guilt of making false official statements (Charge II and its two specifications).

---

 * ["Any person subject to this chapter who, with intent to deceive, signs any false record, return, regulation, order, or other official document, knowing it to be false, or makes any other false official statement knowing it to be false, shall be punished as a court-martial may direct."—EDS.]

II. Bigamy

Bigamy is a general intent crime.** To constitute a defense to bigamy, a mistake of fact must be both honest and reasonable. M.C.M., 1984, Part IV, ¶65c. While the appellant may have honestly believed that he was divorced from Amparo, we find that he did not take the steps which a reasonable man would have taken to determine the validity of his honest belief. He was not reasonable in assuming that he was divorced. See United States v. Bateman, 8 U.S.C.M.A. 88, 23 C.M.R. 312 (C.M.A. 1957) (knowledge that wife intended to proceed with divorce proceedings insufficient); United States v. Avery, 9 C.M.R. 648 (A.F.B.R. 1953) (reliance on attorney's prediction that divorce would occur on a given date not reasonable). Accordingly, we find that the evidence is sufficient to prove bigamy.

III. Altering a Public Record

The offense of altering a public record in violation of UCMJ, Article 134 . . . is committed by altering, concealing, removing, mutilating, obliterating, destroying, or taking a public record with the intent to do any of the foregoing. M.C.M., 1984, Part IV, ¶99b. A public record is defined as including "records, reports, statements, or data compilations, in any form, of public offices or agencies, setting forth the activities of the office or agency, or matters observed pursuant to duty imposed by law as to which there was a duty to report." M.C.M., 1984, Part IV, ¶99c. . . .

. . . In the case before us the appellant created and altered an unofficial, unauthenticated photocopy of a public record, but did not disturb the integrity of the public record itself. We hold that the unofficial, unauthenticated photocopy altered by the appellant was not a public record. . . . While intentional introduction of the altered unauthenticated photocopy into government channels may have violated another proscription, e.g., UCMJ, Article 132 or 18 U.S.C. §1001, it did not constitute the crime of altering a public record in violation of UCMJ, Article 134, or any lesser included offense. Accordingly, we hold that the appellant's plea of guilty to altering a public record in violation of UCMJ, Article 134 was improvident.

The findings of guilty of Charge II and its two Specifications (false official statements), and Specification 2 of Charge IV (altering a public record) are set aside. Charge II and its two Specifications, and Specification 2 of Charge IV are dismissed. The remaining findings of guilty are affirmed. The

---

** [Bigamy is punished in the military justice system under U.C.M.J. Article 134, a general provision that prohibits, among other things, "all disorders and neglects to the prejudice of good order and discipline in the armed forces" as well as "all conduct of a nature to bring discredit upon the armed forces." This provision effectively picks up the traditional common-law definition of bigamy, which includes any person who enters into a marriage while already married to another person. Military justice precedent—consistent with the majority rule in the states—treats bigamy as a general intent crime.—Eds.]

sentence is set aside. A rehearing on the sentence may be ordered by the same or a different convening authority.

United States v. Binegar

United States Court of Appeals for the Armed Forces
55 M.J. 1 (2001)

Judge SULLIVAN delivered the opinion of the court.

In March of 1997, appellant was tried by a general court-martial composed of officer members at Hanscom Air Force Base in Massachusetts. Contrary to his pleas, he was found guilty of four specifications of stealing contact lenses which were military property of the United States, and one specification of conspiring to steal those contact lenses, in violation of Articles 121 and 81, Uniform Code of Military Justice, 10 USC §§921 and 881, respectively. On March 28, 1997, he was sentenced to a bad-conduct discharge, 3 months of hard labor without confinement, and forfeiture of $300 pay per month for 3 months. The convening authority approved this sentence on July 24, 1997, and the Court of Criminal Appeals affirmed on November 1, 1999, in an unpublished opinion. . . .

Evidence was admitted in this case that shows that in September 1995, appellant began work in the Medical Logistics Office at Hanscom Air Force Base. . . . One of his duties was to order contact lenses for servicemembers who brought a prescription from the base Optometry Clinic to the Medical Logistics Office. Personnel who needed contact lenses to perform their duties or for a medical condition were entitled to receive them free of charge. Other personnel had to obtain contact lenses off-base and pay for the lenses themselves.

It was also shown that Air Force regulations governed the process of ordering contact lenses at the Medical Logistics Office. The Optometry Clinic was required to produce a purchase letter for all prescriptions sent to the Medical Logistics Office. If the lenses were required "for the performance of duties," the Logistics Office was to code the purchase order with a "fund cite" indicating the servicemember's section. If, however, the lenses were required for a medical condition, the Optometry Clinic fund cite was used. Once a month, the office generated reports of how many lenses had been billed to each account.

Evidence was further admitted that appellant's supervisors neglected to follow these procedures with any regularity. The Optometry Clinic rarely generated purchases letters, and Medical Logistics would order contact lenses without them. One of appellant's supervisors, Senior Master Sergeant Kremer, testified that he believed at one time that all clinic personnel were entitled to free contact lenses, even if not medically required. In fact, SMSgt Kremer instructed appellant to sign a purchase order for him to get free lenses soon after appellant began work at Medical Logistics. SMSgt Kremer did not provide appellant with a purchase letter or prescription for his lenses, although he testified that he later discussed with appellant a clarified command policy requiring a medical reason for contact lenses with some exceptions.

Finally, evidence was admitted that appellant continued to order contact lenses, filing the appropriate purchase orders and keeping his paperwork in order. Appellant's supervisors never reviewed the monthly reports to determine whether lenses were being billed to the proper accounts. Moreover, appellant's supervisors failed to provide appellant with formal training or specific guidelines for any of these procedures. The next supervisor of the office, Staff Sergeant Smith, even authorized appellant to sign purchase orders for him between October 1995 to January 1996. Appellant signed SSgt Smith's name to over 90% of the purchase orders filed between September 1995 and March 1996. Neither SSgt Smith nor his predecessor, SMSgt Kremer, ever told appellant that he was doing his job improperly. Furthermore, appellant had public conversations concerning his conduct in ordering contact lenses with the servicemembers for whom he ordered those lenses. . . .

The military judge gave the following instructions in this case:

> As to the various charges, the evidence has raised the issue of ignorance or mistake on the part of the accused concerning whether he was under the mistaken belief that he was authorized to order contact lenses at government expense with a purchase order from military members who provided him only a prescription from the Optometry Clinic. If the accused mistakenly believed that he was authorized to order contact lenses at government expense with a purchase order for military members who provided him only a prescription from the Optometry Clinic, he is not guilty of the offense of larceny or conspiracy to commit larceny if his ignorance or belief was reasonable. To be reasonable, the ignorance or belief must have been based upon information or lack of it which would indicate to a reasonable person that he was authorized to order contacts at government expense. Additionally, the ignorance or mistake cannot be based on a negligent failure to discover the true facts. . . .

Appellant contends that the military judge at his court-martial erred in refusing to give an "honest" mistake-of-fact instruction as requested by the defense. We note that the military judge made this ruling because he concluded appellant's purported mistake of fact went to a matter unrelated to the specific intent required for conviction of larceny under Article 121, UCMJ. Accordingly, . . . he concluded that an honest and reasonable mistake as to such a fact was required and so instructed the members. The Court of Criminal Appeals likewise concluded that this was a correct instruction because the purported mistake "concerned the wrongfulness of the appellant's taking, whether he had permission to order the contacts [, and] this is a general intent element and appellant's belief must have been reasonable under all the circumstances." We disagree. United States v. Turner, [27 M.J. 217, 220 (CMA 1988)]. . . .

Article 121, UCMJ, states:

> (a) Any person subject to this chapter who wrongfully takes, obtains, or withholds, by any means, from the possession of the owner or of any other person any money, personal property, or article of value of any kind—
>
>> (1) with intent permanently to deprive or defraud another person of the use and benefit of property or to appropriate it to his own use or the use of any other person other than the owner, steals that property and is guilty of larceny;

We have long recognized that this . . . article requires the Government to prove beyond a reasonable doubt that an accused had a specific intent to steal. Moreover, it also has long been recognized that an honest mistake of fact as to a soldier's entitlement or authorization to take property is a defense to a charge of larceny under this [provision]. See United States v. Sicley, 6 U.S.C.M.A. 402 (1955); . . . United States v. Turner, supra.

The military judge in appellant's case did not acknowledge this case law. . . . Moreover, he did not explain why appellant's averred mistake as to his authority to issue contact lenses did not undermine a specific intent on his part to permanently deprive the Government of this property. His exclusive reliance on the relevance of the mistaken fact to a so-called general "intent" element was misplaced. The pertinent inquiry is whether the purported mistake concerns a fact which would preclude the existence of the required specific intent.

This Court's opinions in [United States v. Peterson, 47 M.J. 231 (1997)] (mistake as to consent in housebreaking case) and [United States v. Garcia, 44 M.J. 496 (1996)] (mistake as to sexual consent in indecent assault case) also do not support the trial judge's ruling. They addressed mistakes as to facts which were completely unrelated to the specific intents at issue in those non-larceny cases. Moreover, those decisions do not suggest in any way that a military superior's permission to his subordinate to dispose of government property to other servicemembers is that type of fact, i.e., one unrelated to a specific intent of that subordinate to steal from the Government. Accordingly, we must find legal error.

Turning to the question of harmless error, we conclude that appellant was materially prejudiced by the "honest and reasonable" mistake-of-fact instruction actually given in this case. First of all, the prosecution-requested instruction placed a lesser burden on the Government to prove appellant's guilt because it could now secure his conviction by disproving either the honesty or the reasonableness of appellant's mistake. Moreover, trial counsel exploited the erroneous instruction by calling this government option to the attention of the members during deliberations. He said:

> And that leads us to the defense of mistake of fact for all of these contacts. As the judge instructed you, there must be two different things here: One is, was

this mistake honest; namely, did Airman Binegar really have this mistake? And, number two is: Was this mistake reasonable? Because regardless of whether Airman Binegar thought this, if it was not reasonable, the defense still does not exist. The government has disproven this mistake beyond a reasonable doubt.

Finally, the Government presented a substantial case on the unreasonableness of appellant's conduct in this case, creating a reasonable possibility that the members resolved this case against appellant on this basis.

The decision of the United States Air Force Court of Criminal Appeals is reversed. The findings of [guilt] and the sentence are set aside. . . .

[Judge GIERKE's opinion concurring in the result is omitted.]

CRAWFORD, C.J., dissenting.

I would hold that the military judge did not abuse his discretion by instructing the members that appellant's mistake related to the general intent element of "wrongful taking" and that the mistake had to be both "honest and reasonable." Giving tens of free contact lenses to individuals not entitled to government contact lenses was neither honest nor reasonable. If the judge did err, any error was harmless because the record does not support the conclusion that appellant ever made an honest mistake of fact. . . .

Notes on Mistakes of Fact

1. The defendant in United States v. Bankston, 57 M.J. 786 (U.S.C.M.A. 2002), took some items from a local P.X. on an army base—the total value was a little over $1,100—without paying for them; he claimed the cashier and her husband (another soldier) had both told him that they would pay for the goods later. They didn't. At his trial for larceny, the defendant claimed that his honest mistake was a defense. The trial judge ruled that the mistake needed to be both honest and reasonable. The Court of Military Appeals reversed, citing and relying on *Binegar*, and stating that the crime was one of specific intent, and hence that an honest mistake about the defendant's authority to take the goods in question was a defense.

2. *Oglivie*, *Binegar*, and *Bankston* accurately describe the standard common-law doctrines concerning mistakes of fact. As *Oglivie* states, a mistake of fact that would negate general intent is a defense only if the mistake is both honest and reasonable: The defendant loses on the bigamy charge because the court found that his error was unreasonable. Recall *Hood*, supra at page 142; among the charges brought against the defendant in that case was assault with a deadly weapon, a general intent crime. If the defendant had claimed, for example, that he believed the gun he reached for was a toy instead of a weapon, his mistake would have had to be both honest and reasonable in order to succeed.*

As all three military cases also state, however, a mistake of fact that negates specific intent is a defense if the mistake is merely honest: Under that standard, Oglivie prevailed on the charge of making a false official statement, and both Binegar and Bankston prevailed on theft charges.

3. Why is a separate doctrine of mistake necessary? The short answer is, because neither general intent nor specific intent defines any particular level of culpability that convicted defendants must have with respect to the factual circumstances surrounding their crimes. General intent requires proof that the defendant's conduct, but not the results of that conduct, be intentional. Specific intent requires proof that both the conduct and the results be intentional. Neither standard speaks to knowledge of relevant underlying facts, like whether Oglivie's first wife had ever really finalized their divorce in Panama, or the true ownership of the goods Bankston took from the P.X.

4. Why is mistake doctrine so stingy? If Oglivie genuinely believed that his first marriage had ended before he married a second time, why not excuse the mistake? If Bankston had no clue, one way or the other, about whether the goods he took from the P.X. were rightfully his, why punish him for theft? The answer to the first question is that someone else might have been harmed by Oglivie's mistake, in which case Oglivie arguably ought to be held to a higher standard than honest belief. As for *Bankston*, suppose the defendant in that case thought it was *possible*, but not *probable*, that the cashier would pay for the merchandise in question. In other words, suppose that he didn't *know* that the property was the government's — he was uncertain, in the sense that there was a decent chance that taking the stuff without paying for it was permissible. Should that be enough to negate criminal liability? The more natural expectation is probably that someone in Bankston's position ought to have behaved differently, if he thought there was even a modest chance that the P.X. would go uncompensated.

Mistake-of-fact doctrine appears to solve both problems. In specific intent cases, the mistake must be honest — meaning, Binegar and Bankston must actually *believe* they were authorized to behave as they did — if the defendant is to have a defense. Thinking they *might have been* or *probably were* authorized isn't good enough. In general intent cases, however, the mistake must be both honest *and* reasonable — meaning, a defendant in Oglivie's shoes must *reasonably believe* that the earlier marriage was no longer valid. That's a tougher standard for defendants than simply the absence of

---

*Assuming that a toy gun was not deemed a "deadly weapon" for purposes of the California statute. That assumption is not necessarily correct. See Merritt v. Commonwealth, 386 S.W.2d 727 (Ky. 1965) (holding that a toy gun *is* a deadly weapon if it appears to be and if its user wishes others to believe it is).

"malice" or an "evil mind." In this context, "reasonable" means what it says: Oglivie's mistake about the divorce is a defense only if most soldiers in his shoes would have made it. The absence of *criminal* negligence isn't enough to save Oglivie; he must have behaved at least as well as most people would behave in the same circumstances.

5. In each of these cases, the effect of mistake doctrine is to make it harder for criminal defendants to escape liability based on their own testimony. Oglivie can say that he didn't know he was still married, but his claim will succeed only if he can persuade a judge and jury that most people would have made the same mistake in his circumstances. Bankston can claim that he was sure the cashier would pay for the goods, but his argument probably won't fly without additional proof, such as corroboration from the cashier (or her husband). Binegar might testify that he assumed it was OK to hand out contact lenses to any soldiers who asked for them, but his argument will prevail only if we believe him, which might come down to whether others who worked in the Medical Logistics Office will testify that they made the same assumption. As a practical matter, mistake-of-fact doctrine seems designed to require a measure of skepticism about defendants who claim not to have understood what they were doing as a means of defending themselves against criminal charges.

Is that wise? Is it fair? Appellate judges of the nineteenth and early twentieth centuries—they are the ones who largely defined the criminal law of mistake—seem to have thought so. On the one hand, most of those judges believed strongly in the idea that defendants should not be criminally punished for mere accidents or errors in judgment. Hence the two main common-law intent standards: general intent and specific intent, both of which condition criminal liability on the defendant's actual state of mind. But the same judges who crafted those standards worried that, by doing so, they might make it too easy for guilty defendants to take the witness stand, claim ignorance of the relevant facts, and thereby win unmerited acquittals. So a large portion of what the law seemed to give defendants through the general and specific intent standards, it took back from them with its less-than-generous mistake rules.

6. To put the point another way, the law of criminal intent seems to define different standards depending on the kind of evidence used to satisfy those standards. When the defendant's conduct and the surrounding circumstances are used to prove intent—as is ordinarily the case in criminal trials—the governing standards are more favorable to the defense; when the evidence of the defendant's intent (or lack thereof) comes from the defendant's own testimony, as in mistake cases, the governing standards tilt more toward the prosecution.

7. In light of that general principle, consider Stagner v. State, 842 P.2d 520 (Wyo. 1992). The defendant in *Stagner* was charged with receiving stolen property. The facts as stated in the court's opinion were as follows:

. . . [A] high school teacher testified he had a 1973 Lincoln Continental Mark IV stolen from his locked garage in Huntley, Montana. A Wyoming rancher from Fremont County testified that he had called the Bureau of Indian Affairs (BIA) in the early hours of January 10, 1989 to report two vehicles heading onto his absent neighbor's ranch.

The two BIA agents testified that they responded to the rancher's call. They discovered an area that was cluttered with junk vehicles when they arrived at the neighboring property. There they spotted a pickup in pretty good shape that had new Wyoming license plates. One agent approached the pickup on foot and had to peer inside before seeing two people lying down on the seat. He identified Stagner as one of those people. . . . One agent testified that a tribal game warden, who had showed up to assist them, spotted a Lincoln Continental Mark IV. The engine was still warm but had no license plates. When they checked the vehicle identification numbers, they discovered that the car had been stolen. When they searched Stagner pursuant to her arrest, they discovered the keys to the Lincoln in her coat pocket. They also found three handguns in the pickup which Stagner indicated were hers.

Notwithstanding the keys in her pocket, Stagner denied knowing anything about the Lincoln or its owner when the police questioned her shortly after her arrest.

The statute Stagner was charged with violating reads:

A person who buys, receives, conceals or disposes of property which he knows, believes or has reasonable cause to believe was obtained in violation of law is guilty of [a] felony punishable by imprisonment for not more than ten years, a fine of not more than ten thousand dollars, or both, if the value of the property is five hundred dollars or more. . . .

The man who sold Stagner the Lincoln, one Les Kilwein, testified that he told her the car was stolen at the time of the sale. Stagner told a different story; she testified that Kilwein had told her he bought the car for an old Camaro plus $150. Stagner asked the trial judge to instruct the jury that an honest and reasonable belief that Kilwein legally owned the car before selling it to her would require an acquittal. (Under Wyoming law, receiving stolen property is a general intent offense.) The judge refused the requested instruction, and Stagner was convicted.

The Wyoming Supreme Court reversed:

. . . It is for no one but the jury to decide who is credible. . . . [T]he weight and sufficiency of the evidence to establish a fact in issue are a question for the jury. It is generally recognized that any evidence which will authorize the jury to find on it, although in the opinion of the court it may be weak, inconclusive, or unworthy of belief, is sufficient to justify an instruction on the issue raised by such evidence. . . .

Claiming that "[i]t is inconceivable that a jury would find that Stagner did not know the vehicle was stolen in light of all the evidence to the contrary," and hence that no mistake instruction was appropriate, Chief Justice Macy dissented. Justice Thomas (no, not *that* Justice Thomas) dissented as well, claiming that the majority had misunderstood mistake doctrine:

> Mistake of fact is concerned with something entirely different from what Stagner contended. In Stagner's case, virtually all of the circumstances proclaimed that the car was stolen, and the person who had possession of that stolen car testified that he told Stagner the car was stolen. Her contrary testimony in her defense was that Kilwein told her the car was his. This is not a "mistake of fact" situation. It simply presents the opportunity for the jury to resolve the credibility of the witnesses in favor of a finding of guilt or innocence. . . .

Was Stagner's testimony believable? Who got the law right in *Stagner*—the majority, Chief Justice Macy, or Justice Thomas?

8. Recall the facts of *Binegar*: The defendant regularly supplied contact lenses to soldiers who ordered them, free of charge, regardless of whether the lenses were necessary to the performance of the soldiers' jobs. That course of action was plainly contrary to the relevant Air Force regulations. Equally plainly, the regulations were widely ignored. About what "fact" was Binegar mistaken? Was he mistaken about *any* fact? Might the mistake instead have been about the content of legal rules—or, rather, about which legal rules he was supposed to follow and which ones he was free to ignore? If the mistake was really one of law rather than fact, why did the *Binegar* court treat it as one of fact rather than law?

4. Mistakes of Law

Binegar may be written as it is because mistakes of law are treated even less generously than mistakes of fact. As a mistake of fact, Binegar's error wins his case; had his error been classified as a mistake of law, Binegar would have lost. That much probably comes as no surprise. One of the most familiar principles of American criminal law—a legal proposition most students know well before their first day of law school—is captured by the Latin maxim, *ignorantia legis* (sometimes written *ignorantia juris*) *neminem excusat*: in English, "ignorance of the law is no excuse." That familiar phrase exaggerates; legal mistakes sometimes *do* excuse criminal conduct. But the basic idea behind the phrase is correct, at least as a descriptive matter. Usually, ignorance or misunderstanding of the governing criminal law is no defense to criminal charges.

The next three cases stand for three distinct doctrines governing legal mistakes. The first doctrine is captured by People v. Marrero, 507 N.E.2d 1068 (N.Y. 1987): A mistake about the meaning of a criminal prohibition is not a defense to criminal charges for violating that prohibition. The second doctrine is captured by Darab v. United States, 623 A.2d 127 (D.C. 1993): Belief that one's conduct was morally right is likewise no defense. State v. Varszegi, 635 A.2d 816 (Conn. App. 1993), is an example of the third doctrine in action: An honest claim of legal right to allegedly stolen property *does* excuse a defendant from liability, *if* the crime charged requires proof of specific intent. As you read, ask yourself: Are these doctrines fair? Are they workable?

People v. Marrero

Court of Appeals of New York
69 N.Y.2d 382; 507 N.E.2d 1068 (1987)

Judge BELLACOSA delivered the opinion of the Court.

The defense of mistake of law is not available to a Federal corrections officer arrested in a Manhattan social club for possession of a loaded .38 caliber automatic pistol who claimed he mistakenly believed he was entitled, pursuant to the interplay of [Criminal Procedure Law (CPL)] §§2.10, 1.20 and Penal Law §265.20, to carry a handgun without a permit as a peace officer. . . .

On the trial of the case, the court rejected the defendant's argument that his personal misunderstanding of the statutory definition of a peace officer is enough to excuse him from criminal liability under New York's mistake of law statute (Penal Law §15.20). The court refused to charge the jury on this issue and defendant was convicted of criminal possession of a weapon in the third degree. We affirm the Appellate Division order upholding the conviction.

Defendant was a Federal corrections officer in Danbury, Connecticut. . . . He claimed at trial that there were various interpretations of fellow officers and teachers, as well as the peace officer statute itself, upon which he relied for his mistaken belief that he could carry a weapon with legal impunity.

The starting point for our analysis is the New York mistake statute. . . . The central issue is whether defendant's personal misreading or misunderstanding of a statute may excuse criminal conduct in the circumstances of this case. . . .

. . . Penal Law §15.20 . . . provides in pertinent part:

> "§15.20. EFFECT OF IGNORANCE OR MISTAKE UPON LIABILITY.
> . . . 2. A person is not relieved of criminal liability for conduct because he engages in such conduct under a mistaken belief that it does not, as a matter of law, constitute an offense, unless such mistaken belief is founded upon an official statement of the law contained in (a) a statute or other enactment . . . (d) an interpretation of the statute or law relating to the offense, officially made or issued by a public servant, agency, or body legally charged or empowered with the responsibility or privilege of administering, enforcing or interpreting such statute or law."

This section was added to the Penal Law as part of the wholesale revision of the Penal Law in 1965. When this provision was first proposed, commentators viewed the new language as codifying "the established common law maxim on mistake of law, while at the same time recognizing a defense when the erroneous belief is founded upon an 'official statement of the law.'" Note, Proposed Penal Law of New York, 64 Colum. L. Rev. 1469, 1486 (1964).

The defendant claims as a first prong of his defense that he is entitled to raise the defense of mistake of law under section 15.20(2)(a) because his mistaken belief that his conduct was legal was founded upon an official statement of the law contained in the statute itself. Defendant argues that his mistaken interpretation of the statute was reasonable in view of the alleged ambiguous wording of the peace officer exemption statute, and that his "reasonable" interpretation of an "official statement" is enough to satisfy the requirements of subdivision (2)(a). . . .

The prosecution . . . counters defendant's argument by asserting that one cannot claim the protection of mistake of law under section 15.20(2)(a) simply by misconstruing the meaning of a statute but must instead establish that the statute relied on actually permitted the conduct in question and was only later found to be erroneous. To buttress that argument, the People analogize New York's official statement defense to the approach taken by the Model Penal Code (MPC). Section 2.04 of the MPC provides:

> "SECTION 2.04. IGNORANCE OR MISTAKE.
> ". . . (3) A belief that conduct does not legally constitute an offense is a defense to a prosecution for that offense based upon such conduct when . . . (b) he acts in reasonable reliance upon an official statement of the law, *afterward determined to be invalid or erroneous*, contained in (i) a statute or other enactment" (emphasis added).

Although the drafters of the New York statute did not adopt the precise language of the Model Penal Code provision with the emphasized clause, it is evident and has long been believed that the Legislature intended the New York statute to be similarly construed. . . .

It was early recognized that the "official statement" mistake of law defense was a statutory protection against prosecution based on reliance of a statute that did *in fact* authorize certain conduct. "It seems obvious that society must rely on some statement of the law, and that conduct which *is in fact* 'authorized' . . . should not be subsequently condemned. The threat of punishment under these circumstances can have no deterrent effect unless the actor doubts the validity of the official pronouncement— *a questioning of authority that is itself undesirable*." Note, 64 Colum. L. Rev. at 1486 (emphasis added). While providing a narrow escape hatch, the idea was simultaneously to encourage the public to read and rely on official statements of the law, not to have individuals conveniently and personally question the validity and interpretation of the law and act on that basis. If later the statute was invalidated, one who mistakenly acted in reliance on the authorizing statute would be relieved of criminal liability. That makes sense and is fair. To go further does not make sense and would create a legal chaos. . . .

In the case before us, the underlying statute never in fact authorized the defendant's conduct; the defendant only thought that the statutory exemptions permitted his conduct when, in fact, the primary statute clearly forbade his conduct. . . . It would be ironic at best and an odd perversion at worst for this court now to declare that the same defendant is nevertheless free of criminal responsibility.

The "official statement" component in the mistake of law defense in both paragraphs (a) and (d) adds yet another element of support for our interpretation and holding. Defendant tried to establish a defense under Penal Law §15.20(2)(d) as a second prong. But the interpretation of the statute relied upon must be "officially made or issued by a public servant, agency or body legally charged or empowered with the responsibility or privilege of administering, enforcing or interpreting such statute or law." . . . [N]one of the interpretations which defendant proffered meets the requirements of the statute. . . .

. . . [W]hile our construction of Penal Law §15.20 provides for narrow application of the mistake of law defense, it does not, as the dissenters contend, "rule out *any* defense based on mistake of law." To the contrary, mistake of law is a viable exemption in those instances where an individual demonstrates an effort to learn what the law is, relies on the validity of that law and, later, it is determined that there was a *mistake in the law itself.*

The modern availability of this defense is based on the theory that where the government has affirmatively, albeit unintentionally, misled an individual as to what may or may not be legally permissible conduct, the individual should not be punished as a result. . . . [It] follows that where, as here, the government is not responsible for the error (for there is none except in the defendant's own mind), mistake of law should not be available as an excuse. See Jeffries, Legality, Vagueness and the Construction of Penal Statutes, 71 Va. L. Rev. 189, 208 (1985).

We recognize that some legal scholars urge that the mistake of law defense should be available more broadly where a defendant misinterprets a potentially ambiguous statute not previously clarified by judicial decision and reasonably believes in good faith that the acts were legal. Professor Perkins, a leading supporter of this view, has said: "[if] the meaning of a statute is not clear, and has not been judicially determined, one who has acted 'in good faith' should not be held guilty of crime if his conduct would have been proper had the statute meant what he 'reasonably believed' it to mean, even if the court should decide later that the proper construction is otherwise." Perkins, Ignorance and Mistake in Criminal Law, 88 U. Pa. L. Rev. 35, 45. In support of this conclusion Professor Perkins cites two cases:

State v. Cutter, 36 N.J.L. 125, and Burns v. State, 123 Tex. Crim. 611, 61 S.W.2d 512. In both these cases mistake of law was viewed as a valid defense to offense where a specific intent . . . was an element of the crime charged. In *Burns*, the court recognized mistake of law as a defense to extortion. The statute defining "extortion" made the "willful" doing of the prohibited act an essential ingredient of the offense. The court, holding that mistake of law is a defense only where the mistake negates the specific intent required for conviction, borrowed language from the *Cutter* case: "In State v. Cutter . . . the court said: 'The argument goes upon the legal maxim *ignorantia legis neminem excusat*. But this rule, in its application to the law of crimes, is subject . . . to certain important exceptions. Where the act done is *malum in se*, or where the law which has been infringed was settled and plain, the maxim, in its rigor, will be applied; but where the law is not settled, or is obscure, *and where the guilty intention, being a necessary constituent of the particular offence, is dependent on a knowledge of the law, this rule, if enforced, would be misapplied.*'" 61 S.W.2d, at 513 (emphasis added). Thus, while Professor Perkins states that the defense should be available in cases where the defendant claims mistaken reliance on an ambiguous statute, the cases he cites recognize the defense only where the law was ambiguous *and* the ignorance or mistake of law negated the requisite intent. In this case, the forbidden act of possessing a weapon is clear and unambiguous, and only by the interplay of a double exemption does defendant seek to escape criminal responsibility, i.e., the peace officer statute and the mistake statute.

We conclude that the better and correctly construed view is that the defense should not be recognized, except where specific intent is an element of the offense or where the misrelied-upon law has later been properly adjudicated as wrong. Any broader view fosters lawlessness. . . .

Accordingly, the order of the Appellate Division should be affirmed.

HANCOCK, J., with whom WACHTLER, C.J., and SIMONS and TITONE, JJ. join, dissenting.

. . . The basic difference which divides the court may be simply put. Suppose the case of a man who has committed an act which is criminal not because it is inherently wrong or immoral but solely because it violates a criminal statute. He has committed the act in complete good faith under the mistaken but entirely reasonable assumption that the act does not constitute an offense because it is permitted by the wording of the statute. Does the law require that this man be punished? The majority says that it does and holds that (1) Penal Law §15.20(2)(a) must be construed so that the man is precluded from offering a defense based on his mistake of law and (2) such construction is compelled by prevailing considerations of public policy and criminal jurisprudence. We take issue with the majority on both propositions. . . .

The maxim *"ignorantia legis neminem excusat"*[3] finds its roots in Medieval law when the "actor's intent was irrelevant since the law punished the *act itself,*" United States v. Barker, [514 F.2d 208, 228] (Bazelon, C.J., concurring) (emphasis in original), and when, for example, the law recognized no difference between an intentional killing and one that was accidental. Ames, Law and Morals, 22 Harv. L. Rev. 97, 98 (1908). Although the common law has gradually evolved from its origins in Anglo-Germanic tribal law (adding the element of intent . . . and recognizing defenses based on the actor's mental state [such as] justification, insanity, and intoxication) the dogmatic rule that ignorance or mistake of law is no excuse has remained unaltered. Various justifications have been offered for the rule, but all are frankly pragmatic and utilitarian—preferring the interests of society (e.g., in deterring criminal conduct, fostering orderly judicial administration, and preserving the primacy of the rule of law)[5] to the interest of the individual in being free from punishment except for intentionally engaging in conduct which he knows is criminal. See White, Reliance on Apparent Authority as a Defense to Criminal Prosecution, 77 Colum. L. Rev. 775, 784-89 (1977); Perkins, Ignorance and Mistake in Criminal Law, 88 U. Pa. L. Rev. 35, 40, 41 (1939).

Today there is widespread criticism of the common-law rule mandating categorical preclusion of the mistake of law defense. The utilitarian arguments for retaining the rule have been drawn into serious question, but the fundamental objection is that it is simply wrong to punish someone who, in good-faith reliance on the wording of a statute, believed that what he was doing was lawful. It is contrary to "the notion that punishment should be conditioned on a showing of subjective moral blameworthiness." White, [77 Colum. L. Rev.] at 784. This basic objection to the maxim *"ignorantia legis neminem excusat"* may have had less force in ancient times when most crimes consisted of acts which by their very nature were recognized as evil (*malum in se*). In modern times, however, with the profusion of legislation making otherwise lawful conduct criminal (*malum prohibitum*), the "common law

---

3. Although *"ignorantia legis"* does not literally refer to mistake of law, the maxim is ordinarily understood, as we use it here, to include both ignorance and mistake of law. See, e.g., Jeffries, Legality, Vagueness, and the Construction of Penal Statutes, 71 Va. L. Rev. 189, 208 (1985); Note, Proposed Penal Law of New York, 64 Colum. L. Rev. 1469, 1485 (1977); Keedy, Ignorance and Mistake in the Criminal Law, 22 Harv. L. Rev. 75, 81 (1908).

5. The societal interests mentioned in the literature include: facilitating judicial administration, encouraging knowledge and obedience to law and preservation of integrity of legal norms. 77 Colum. L. Rev. [at] 787. Justice Holmes, for example, stressed society's interest in deterrence, noting that acceptance of ignorance or mistake of law as a defense would encourage ignorance at the expense of the public good. See Holmes, The Common Law, at 48 (1881). John Austin justified *"ignorantia legis"* on the ground that if the defense were permitted, the courts would be confronted with questions about defendant's mental state which they could not solve. Austin, Lectures on Jurisprudence, at 496-501 (4th ed. 1873). For a discussion of the societal interest in maintaining primacy of the law as a reason for the common-law maxim, see Hall, General Principles of Criminal Law, at 382, 383 (2d ed. 1960).

fiction that every man is presumed to know the law has become indefensible in fact or logic." Id.[6]

With this background we proceed to a discussion of our disagreement with the majority's construction of Penal Law §15.20(2)(a) and the policy and jurisprudential arguments made in support of that construction. . . .

Penal Law §15.20, in pertinent part, provides:

> "2. A person is not relieved of criminal liability for conduct because he engages in such conduct under a mistaken belief that it does not, as a matter of law, constitute an offense, unless such mistaken belief is founded upon an official statement of the law contained in (a) a statute or other enactment. . . ."

It is fundamental that in interpreting a statute, a court should look first to the particular words of the statute in question, being guided by the accepted rule that statutory language is generally given its natural and most obvious meaning. Here, there is but one natural and obvious meaning of the statute: that if a defendant can establish that his mistaken belief was "founded upon" his interpretation of "an official statement of the law contained in . . . [a] statute," he should have a defense. . . .

. . . Defendant stands convicted after a jury trial of criminal possession of a weapon in the third degree for carrying a loaded firearm without a license (Penal Law §265.02). He concedes that he possessed the unlicensed weapon but maintains that he did so under the mistaken assumption that his conduct was permitted by law. Although at the time of his arrest he protested that he was a Federal corrections officer and exempt from prosecution under the statute, defendant was charged with criminal possession of a weapon in the third degree. On defendant's motion before trial the court dismissed the indictment, holding that he was a peace officer as defined by CPL 2.10(25) and, therefore, [exempt from prosecution].[7] The People appealed and the

---

6. Professor LaFave notes the unfairness of never recognizing ignorance or mistake of law as a defense to offenses which are purely regulatory:

> "The early criminal law was well integrated with the mores of the time, so that a defendant's mistake as to the content of the criminal law . . . would not ordinarily affect his moral guilt. But the vast network of regulatory offenses which make up a large part of today's criminal law does not stem from the mores of the community, and so moral education no longer serves us as a guide as to what is prohibited. Under these circumstances, where one's moral attitudes may not be relied upon to avoid the forbidden conduct, it may seem particularly severe for the law *never* to recognize ignorance or mistake of the criminal law as a defense. . . ."

LaFave and Scott, Substantive Criminal Law §5.1, at 587-588 (emphasis in original). . . .

7. By virtue of Penal Law §265.20(a)(1)(a) "peace officers," as defined in . . . CPL 1.20, are expressly exempt from criminal liability under Penal Law §265.02. CPL 1.20 incorporates the definition of "peace officer" in CPL 2.10, which includes "correction officers of any state correction facility or of any penal correctional institution." . . .

Appellate Division reversed and reinstated the indictment by a 3-2 vote.[8] Defendant's appeal to this court was dismissed for failure to prosecute and the case proceeded to trial. The trial court rejected defendant's efforts to establish a defense of mistake of law. . . . He was convicted and the Appellate Division has affirmed.

Defendant's mistaken belief that, as a Federal corrections officer, he could legally carry a loaded weapon without a license was based on the express exemption from criminal liability under Penal Law §265.02 accorded in Penal Law §265.20(a)(1)(a) to "peace officers" as defined in the Criminal Procedure Law and on his reading of the statutory definition for "peace officer" in CPL 2.10(25) as meaning a correction officer "of *any* penal correctional institution" (emphasis added), including an institution not operated by New York State. Thus, he concluded erroneously that, as a corrections officer in a Federal prison, he was a "peace officer" and, as such, exempt by the express terms of Penal Law §265.20(a)(1)(a). This mistaken belief, based in good faith on the statute defining "peace officer," is, defendant contends, the precise sort of "mistaken belief . . . founded upon an official statement of the law contained in . . . a statute or other enactment" which gives rise to a mistake of law defense under Penal Law §15.20(2)(a). He points out, of course, that when he acted in reliance on his belief he had no way of foreseeing that a court would eventually resolve the question of the statute's meaning against him and rule that his belief had been mistaken, as three of the five-member panel at the Appellate Division ultimately did in the first appeal. See People v. Marrero, 71 A.D.2d 346.

The majority, however, has accepted the People's argument that to have a defense under Penal Law §15.20(2)(a) "a defendant must show that the statute *permitted his conduct*, not merely that he believed it did." Respondent's brief, at 26 (emphasis added). Here, of course, defendant cannot show that the statute permitted his conduct. To the contrary, the question has now been decided by the Appellate Division and it is settled that defendant was not exempt under Penal Law §265.20(a)(1)(a). Therefore, the argument goes, defendant can have no mistake of law defense. While conceding that reliance on a statutory provision which is later found to be invalid would constitute a mistake of law defense, the People's flat position is that "one's mistaken reading of a statute, no matter how reasonable or well intentioned, is not a defense." Respondent's brief, at 27. . . .

[That position] leads to an anomaly: only a defendant who is *not mistaken* about the law when he acts has a mistake of law defense. . . . In other words, a defendant can assert a defense under Penal Law §15.20(2)(a) only when his

---

8. The majority held that Penal Law §265.20(a)(1)(a) included only State correction officers. The dissenters agreed with [the trial court] that under the unambiguous language of CPL 2.10 defendant was a "peace officer" within the meaning of Penal Law §265.20(a)(1)(a) and exempt from prosecution under Penal Law §265.02.

reading of the statute is *correct*. . . . The statute is of no benefit to a defendant who has proceeded in good faith on an erroneous but concededly reasonable interpretation of a statute, as defendant presumably has. An interpretation of a statute which produces an unreasonable or incongruous result and one which defeats the obvious purpose of the legislation and renders it ineffective should be rejected.

. . . It is self-evident that in enacting Penal Law §15.20(2) as part of the revision and modernization of the Penal Law [in 1965,] the Legislature intended to effect a needed reform by abolishing what had long been considered the unjust archaic common-law rule totally prohibiting mistake of law as a defense. Had it not so intended it would simply have left the common-law rule intact. In place of the abandoned "*ignorantia legis*" common-law maxim the Legislature enacted a rule which permits *no defense for ignorance of law* but *allows a mistake of law defense* in specific instances, including the one presented here: when the defendant's erroneous belief is founded on an "official statement of the law." . . .

The majority construes the statute, however, so as to rule out *any* defense based on mistake of law. In so doing, it defeats the only possible purpose for the statute's enactment and resurrects the very rule which the Legislature rejected in enacting Penal Law §15.20(2)(a). . . . It is fundamental that a construction of a statute which does not further the statute's object, spirit and purpose must be rejected. . . .

. . . [T]he majority bases its decision on an analogous provision in the Model Penal Code and concludes that despite its totally different wording and meaning Penal Law §15.20(2)(a) should be read as if it were Model Penal Code §2.04(3)(b)(i). But New York in revising the Penal Law did not adopt the Model Penal Code. As in New Jersey, which generally adopted the Model Penal Code but added one section which is substantially more liberal,[10] New York followed parts of the Model Penal Code provisions and rejected others. In People v. Goetz, 68 N.Y.2d 96, we said that the Legislature's rejection of the verbatim provisions of the Model Penal Code was crucial in determining its intent in drafting the statute. The significance of the alterations here can be no different.

While Penal Law §15.20(2) and Model Penal Code §2.04 are alike in their rejection of the strict common-law rule, they are not alike in wording and differ significantly in substance. . . . The Model Penal Code does not permit a defense for someone who acts in good faith upon a *mistaken belief*

---

10. In addition to permitting defenses based on ignorance of the law and reasonable reliance on official statements afterward determined to be invalid or erroneous, the New Jersey statute provides a defense, under the following broad provision, when:

"(3) The actor otherwise diligently pursues all means available to ascertain the meaning and application of the offense to his conduct and honestly and in good faith concludes his conduct is not an offense in circumstances in which a law-abiding and prudent person would also so conclude." N.J. Stat. Ann. §2C:2-4(c)(3).

that a specific statute authorizes his conduct. The defense is limited to an act in reliance on an official statement of law in a statute "afterward determined to be *invalid or erroneous.*" Model Penal Code §2.04(3)(b) (emphasis added). The New York statute, in contrast, specifically permits the defense when the actor proceeds under "a *mistaken belief*" that his conduct does not "constitute an offense" when that "*mistaken belief* is founded upon an official statement of the law contained in . . . a statute." Penal Law §15.20(2)(a) (emphasis added). . . . How the Legislature can be assumed to have enacted the very language which it has specifically rejected is not explained. . . .

If defendant's offer of proof is true, his is not the case of a "free agent confronted with a choice between doing right and doing wrong and choosing freely to do wrong." Pound, Introduction to Sayre, Cases on Criminal Law (1927). He carried the gun in the good-faith belief that, as a Federal corrections officer, it was lawful for him to do so under the words of the statute. That his interpretation of the statute as exempting corrections officers (whether or not employed in a State facility) was a reasonable one can hardly be questioned. If the statute does not plainly say that corrections officers are exempt, as defendant contends, the statute at the very least is ambiguous and clearly susceptible to that interpretation. Indeed, the Supreme Court in dismissing the indictment (94 Misc. 2d 367) and two of the five-member panel in the first appeal to the Appellate Division (71 A.D.2d 346) read the statute as it was read by defendant and the police officials and others whose opinions he sought. We believe that under our present Penal Law and the policies underlying its revision (L. 1965, ch. 1030) this defendant should not be found guilty of violating Penal Law §265.02 if he can establish that his conduct was based on a good-faith mistake of law founded on the wording of the statute.

We do not believe that permitting a defense in this case will produce the grievous consequences the majority predicts. The unusual facts of this case seem unlikely to be repeated. . . . New Jersey, which adopted a more liberal mistake of law statute in 1978, has apparently experienced no such adversity. . . .

But these questions are now beside the point, for the Legislature has given its answer by providing that someone in defendant's circumstances should have a mistake of law defense. Penal Law §15.20(2)(a). Because this decision deprives defendant of what . . . the Legislature intended that he should have, we dissent. . . .

Notes on Mistakes of Law

1. Should Marrero have been prosecuted? Why do you suppose he *was* prosecuted?

2. Was Marrero's mistake "founded upon an official statement of the law"? At first blush, the question seems easy: The answer is plainly yes.

Marrero misunderstood the terms of the relevant statutes, and the statutes themselves are indisputably "official statements of the law." What is the majority's answer to this argument?

One answer might go like this. Marrero's mistake was "founded upon" the relevant statutes only if the statutes were the *source* of his mistake. And the source of Marrero's mistake, the majority might say, was his own misunderstanding, not the law itself.* If that position sounds harsh, consider the consequences of the alternative. Imagine a defendant charged with the same violation as in *Marrero* who says he believed he was a "peace officer" because he's an officer in the local Elks Club and he's a peaceful guy. The argument is ludicrous—but under the dissent's reading of section 15.20, it's a valid claim if the defendant is telling the truth. The allegedly peaceful Elks Club officer's mistake is "founded upon" the language of the relevant statute in the same manner that Marrero's mistake was: He misunderstood the governing legal rule, thought it exempted him from liability when it didn't. And there is no language in section 15.20 stating that, in order to qualify, mistakes of law must be reasonable—or even that such mistakes must be something other than laughable.

That is a telling omission. Why would the New York legislature create a defense for unreasonable mistakes of law, when even reasonable mistakes had not been a defense in the past? The dissenters have no good answer to this question. But from the majority's point of view, the answer is simple: *All* mistakes that are "founded upon" official statements of the law by competent legal authorities are reasonable by definition. If, for example, Marrero had relied on a legal definition of "peace officer" that had been valid in the past but that was (unbeknownst to him) recently repealed, his reliance would surely be deemed reasonable. Likewise if an intermediate appellate court had declared the relevant criminal statute unconstitutional—but (again, unbeknownst to Marrero) that court ruling had just been overturned. Or if the local district attorney had written Marrero a letter, on official stationery, stating that the relevant statute did not apply to Marrero. In all these scenarios, Marrero's mistake is "founded upon" an official statement of the law in the strong sense of that phrase—the source of the mistake is not Marrero's mind but the legal document on which he relied. And in all these situations, the mistake is reasonable. The majority's position grants a defense to defendants who make reasonable mistakes like the ones just described, but not to defendants like the allegedly peaceful Elks Club officer.

3. The dissenters might respond that the majority's position is vulnerable as well—it leaves the real Marrero out in the cold. And Marrero's

---

* Actually, it was a combination of Marrero's personal mistake and the mistake of his New York City gun dealer, Eugene DiMayo. DiMayo sold Marrero the gun in question, and told Marrero that he didn't need a New York permit for it because he was a "peace officer." DiMayo apparently knew other prison guards who had bought guns without a New York permit. See Paul H. Robinson & Michael T. Cahill, Law Without Justice: Why Criminal Law Doesn't Give People What They Deserve 29 (Oxford U. Press 2005).

mistake seems as reasonable as the mistakes described above, or nearly so. Is there any way out of this box? How can courts grant a defense to those who, like Marrero, reasonably, but mistakenly, assume their behavior is legal, without also granting a defense to those who seem less deserving?

4. Had Marrero won, the prohibition of gun possession in public would mean different things for different people — one law for Marrero, perhaps another for someone with a different understanding of "peace officer," yet a third for those who understand the rule correctly. Can the rule of law function if different laws bind different people? On the other hand, if innocent mistakes like Marrero's can land you in prison, even the most upright citizens cannot reliably avoid incarceration. Can a society call itself free if even honest and reasonable mistakes of law lead to criminal punishment? In *Marrero*, the rule of law is on one side of the scales of justice and freedom is on the other side. How are judges to choose? How would you choose?

5. Footnotes 5 and 6 in the dissent list the standard justifications for the idea that ignorance of the law should not excuse criminal conduct. It isn't clear which of those justifications (or perhaps some other argument that has been lost to history) drove courts to adopt the rule. But it is reasonably clear that a general ban on defenses of legal mistake did not arise because such defenses were common. Rather, the ban arose precisely because such claims were so rare. The common law of crimes was more spare than contemporary American criminal codes. With few exceptions, the crimes it included were those that all mentally competent adults knew not to commit. Defendants claiming they did not know that burglary or arson or murder were crimes would have been laughed out of court. Banning such arguments may have been little more than an acknowledgment of that obvious truth. "Ignorance of the law is no excuse" might have arisen not as a legal principle, but as an empirical truth.

During the course of the twentieth century, American criminal codes expanded considerably; today, those codes criminalize a good deal of behavior that ordinary citizens might find surprising. (Is the crime in *Marrero* an example of that phenomenon?) Unsurprisingly, claims of legal mistake have multiplied. The debate in *Marrero* is more common now than in the past, and it is not likely to go away anytime soon.

6. Which way does Marrero's job cut? On the one hand, it seems natural enough to assume that he falls within the exemption for "peace officers": Corrections officers like Marrero are basically cops who patrol prison inmates. On the other hand, Marrero's job does not entitle him to police ordinary citizens. Perhaps Marrero of all people should know to make certain of his legal status before carrying his gun into a nightclub. When white-collar offenders charged with crimes like securities fraud argue that *they* misunderstood the governing law, they generally lose: Courts say that, as sophisticated actors familiar with the relevant business, they ought to have made sure they were staying within the law's bounds. Is that argument sound as applied to investment bankers? Federal corrections officers?

7. Notice that the limited defense for legal mistakes concerns *official* statements of the law—meaning that, had Marrero sought the advice of a private attorney and received a letter from his lawyer stating that he was a "peace officer" under New York law, the lawyer's advice would do him no good in any subsequent criminal prosecution. That result is nearly universal, in state and federal law alike. Why? Isn't consulting a lawyer in order to discover one's legal obligations a good thing? (Lawyers certainly think so.) Why shouldn't mistakes "founded upon" such consultations be a defense against later criminal charges?

Darab v. United States

District of Columbia Court of Appeals
623 A.2d 127 (1993)

ROGERS, Chief Judge.

These twenty-four appeals arise from appellants' convictions by a jury of unlawful entry, D.C. Code §22-3102,* at the Islamic Center located at 2551 Massachusetts Avenue, N.W., Washington, D.C., on July 11, 1983. . . .

I

The Islamic Center is owned and operated by an organization incorporated as the Islamic Center. In November 1982, the Board of Governors named Dr. Samuel Hamoud the administrator and program planner of the Islamic Center. In his capacity as administrator, Dr. Hamoud was responsible primarily for secular matters involving the Center, including daily operations and security.

July 11, 1983, was significant to the Islamic Center for two reasons. First, a service was scheduled to celebrate a major Islamic holiday, the Eid Al-Fitr or the Feast of the Breaking of the Fast following Ramadan. In addition, it was the first day that the Mosque was open to the public following a three to four month renovation period. The Board of Governors of the Center had announced, in a newspaper advertisement, the reopening of the Mosque and invited Muslims to join in the Eid prayer to be held on July 11th. Dr. Hamoud testified that the center was expecting 1,500 to 3,000 people; the capacity of the Mosque was only 850 to 1,000 people.

The disturbance at issue arose from a schism within the Muslim community. According to the testimony of appellants Mohammed Asi and Tariq

---

* ["Any person who, without lawful authority, shall enter, or attempt to enter, any public or private dwelling, building, or other property, or part of such dwelling, building, or other property, against the will of the lawful occupant or of the person lawfully in charge thereof, or being therein or thereon, without lawful authority to remain therein or thereon shall refuse to quit the same on the demand of the lawful occupant, or of the person lawfully in charge thereof, shall be deemed guilty of a misdemeanor, and on conviction thereof shall be punished by a fine not exceeding $100 or imprisonment in the Jail for not more than 6 months, or both, in the discretion of the court."—EDS.]

Khan, for several years members of the Muslim community in the Washington metropolitan area were displeased with the appointed leadership at the center and wanted to have a greater role in its administration. An election was held on November 11, 1981, to choose a Counsel of Guidance and an Imam, who serves as the religious leader for the congregation. Approximately 400 to 500 members voted, and appellant Asi was chosen by 250 votes to be Imam. From the time of his election through March of 1983, appellant Asi delivered the Friday sermons at the Center. On March 5, 1983, however, Asi was evicted from his apartment in the Islamic Center and the Center was closed. Nevertheless, Muslims continued attending services led by Asi outside the center. This set the stage for the reopening of the Mosque at the celebration of the Eid on July 11, 1983.

The administrator of the Center, Dr. Hamoud, made special security arrangements for the event. He hired ushers to help seat people, H&H investigators (a private security company under contract with the Center since it had closed in March of 1983), and fourteen additional private security officers. Dr. Hamoud testified that he had made these special arrangements for two main reasons. First, he was concerned about the size of the crowd expected in view of the coincidence of the reopening and the holiday. Secondly, he anticipated that a confrontation might occur between those leading the service conducted by the appointed Imam and the dissatisfied segment of the Muslim community led by Imam Asi. He based his concern on a newsletter circulated by the dissatisfied group which stated that only Mohammed Asi would lead the prayer.

On July 11, 1983, the Islamic Center opened at 7:00 A.M. for the ritual chanting. The Center's appointed Imam, Dr. Al-Aseer,[6] testified regarding the format of the Eid ceremony. He explained that the ritual chanting, or the "takbiraat," is supposed to stop once the Imam issues the order for the person in charge to give a prelude to the prayer. The prelude normally takes one to three minutes, at which point the worshipers rise and the Imam begins the prayer, which is in two parts. The first prayer begins with the takbiraat, which is repeated seven times, followed by a recitation from the Koran. The second unit of prayer involves a similar sequence. According to Dr. Hamoud, the chanting was scheduled to begin at 7:00 A.M. followed by the prayer at 8:00 A.M.

Dr. Al-Aseer arrived at the Center between 7:30 and 8:00 A.M. in order to lead the prayer and deliver the sermon. He went into the Mosque and shared the takbiraat with the Muslims present who were already performing the ritual chanting. A few minutes after 8:00 A.M. he signaled to the officer in the Mosque to begin the prelude. According to Dr. Al-Aseer, as that person stood up to deliver the prelude, someone moved toward him and took

---

6. The Board of Governors of the Center, which also chooses the Imam, appointed Dr. Adil Al-Aseer as the new Imam. July 11, 1983, was to be his first opportunity to lead the prayer as the new Imam.

the microphone, another person sat in the mihrab, and a third person sat on the mimbar.[8] The person who took the microphone then led a chant of takbeer, in which approximately fifty people joined. At some point after that, Dr. Al-Aseer was hit and his turban was knocked to the floor. As he moved to pick up his turban, he saw two worshipers fighting with someone close to him. He left the Mosque and returned later, at 10:00 A.M., to lead a second ceremony.

Dr. Hamoud testified that when he first entered the mosque that morning it was "jammed with people like sardines." Shortly after 8:00 A.M., he was standing in the courtyard when he heard people yelling that fighting was taking place inside the Center. Upon entering the Mosque for a second time, he heard the shouting and observed an unauthorized man sitting on the mimbar with a microphone in his hand. Dr. Hamoud approached that person and asked twice for the microphone. The man refused and continued chanting. When Dr. Hamoud held out his hand for the microphone, the man swung the microphone at him, hitting him in the arm. Dr. Hamoud then grabbed the man with his left hand and felt himself being pushed by others. He also noticed that two Muslim worshipers were defending the appointed Imam and that "there were blows being struck." As he continued to push, Dr. Hamoud was knocked to the ground, and he observed more fighting and arguing. He was unable to stand up, despite several efforts to do so, because he was being hit and kicked.[9] He crawled toward the back of the Mosque and ran out in order to call the police.

As he ran out of the Mosque, Dr. Hamoud saw Sadiq Hassan-Bey of H&H security and requested that he go in and attempt to quiet the disturbance. Hassan-Bey testified that when he went to the front door of the Mosque, he saw "basically pandemonium. I saw individuals at the rear of the mosque being involved in some type of multiple struggles. I observed an individual sitting on what is known as the mimbar. I observed others individuals involved in shouting matches." According to Dr. Hamoud, Hassan-Bey responded that police assistance was needed, and Dr. Hamoud approached Lieutenant Parker of the Metropolitan Police Department, who was standing outside the gates of the Center. Dr. Hamoud asked Lieutenant Parker to take his officers into the mosque and break up the disturbance. After Lieutenant Parker radioed for assistance, Dr. Hamoud conferred again with

8. The mimbar is a Muslim pulpit. The mihrab is the area in the mosque which identifies which direction the Muslims are to pray and also serves as the traditional seating place for the Imam prior to the start of religious services.

9. Special Police Officer David Merrill Diggs II, an employee of Honor Guard who had been assigned to assist H&H Security, corroborated this part of Dr. Hamoud's testimony, stating that he saw him receive several blows to the back of his head and body. Diggs also testified that earlier he had heard people hollering in the mosque as to who were the good Muslims and heard some say "we're going to take the Mosque back."

Hassan-Bey in the courtyard in order to assess the situation. According to Dr. Hamoud, Hassan-Bey informed him that they had to keep the situation under control until the rest of the police officers arrived.

In arriving at a decision on how to handle the situation, Dr. Hamoud consulted with various sources. In addition to discussing the matter with Hassan-Bey, Dr. Hamoud had a conversation with Deputy Chief Connors and Lieutenant Parker about how to handle the situation. He concluded that the police and security officers would have to clear the Mosque and that the service would be restarted later. Dr. Hamoud testified that this was his decision to make because the Board of Governors had given him "the authority to run the security operation, and if necessary, to have people evicted from the Mosque. . . ."[13]

Upon making the decision to have the Mosque cleared, Dr. Hamoud instructed Hassan-Bey to go into the Mosque and warn those inside that if they did not leave peacefully, arrests would have to be made. Hassan-Bey testified that he gave the warnings in a "clear and distinct" voice at around 9:00 A.M., and that he specifically warned appellant Al Asi to have his people leave or they would be arrested. Dr. Hamoud, from about thirty feet away, heard Hassan-Bey give the warnings and recite the Code provisions over the bullhorn. . . . After three warnings had been issued by Hassan-Bey, and no one left the Mosque, Dr. Hamoud asked the police to enter the Mosque and assist with the arrests.

Most of the appellants who testified claimed that they never heard the warnings to leave the Mosque. Specifically, Appellant Asi testified that he "definitely" did not hear the announcement by Hassan-Bey; he attributed this to the fact that about sixty people were chanting the takbiraat at the time and that they were located a distance from the speaker. In addition, most of the appellants who testified claimed that they were operating under a belief that they had the right to remain in the Mosque because no one had the authority to interfere with a religious service.

Regarding their right to remain, appellant Asi explained:

My belief was that the services . . . the prayer services at the Islamic Center and the Islamic Center, itself, was a place of worship for all Muslims. And that no one, no group of people whatever their characterization might be, had the right to interfere in the religious services designated for this place of worship. . . .

---

13. On cross-examination of Dr. Hamoud, the defense attempted to elicit evidence of a dispute between Dr. Hamoud and Hassan-Bey in an attempt to demonstrate that it was unclear who had lawful authority. According to Dr. Hamoud, he shouted at Hassan-Bey in the presence of appellants before the arrests were made. Apparently, Dr. Hamoud and Hassan-Bey disagreed about whether the private security forces should wait for police assistance before intervening.

This belief was based on a "fatwa,"[17] which appellant Asi had obtained from the Al-Azhar University in Cairo, Egypt, and circulated and discussed with fellow Muslims in the community. The fatwa stated:

> Once (a piece of) land is endowed for the purpose of constructing a mosque upon it, then it is not permissible for anyone to own that mosque nor to claim an ownership of the mosque. It remains in the ownership of God forever. No one — Muslim or non-Muslim — may ban anyone from praying within the mosque. And no individual, organization or group may exercise control of admission for prayers in it, nor may restrict prayers.

The jury found appellants guilty of unlawful entry.

II

In appealing their convictions of unlawful entry, appellants first contend that their prosecutions violated the Free Exercise and Establishment Clauses of the First Amendment. Second, they maintain that because they had the lawful authority to remain in the Mosque, the government failed to meet its burden of proof to sustain the unlawful entry convictions. Third, they assert that even if the elements of unlawful entry were proven beyond a reasonable doubt, their convictions cannot be upheld because they had a bona fide belief in their right to remain in the Mosque.

. . . The Supreme Court has recently addressed the interplay between state criminal laws and the exercise of religion. In Employment Division Department of Human Resources v. Smith, 494 U.S. 872 (1990) (*Smith II*), the Court considered whether an Oregon criminal statute prohibiting the religious use of the drug peyote violated the Free Exercise Clause. In concluding that it did not, the Court rejected the argument that the religious motivation underlying the defendants' conduct placed them beyond the reach of a criminal law that was not specifically aimed at religion and was admittedly constitutional as applied to others. Id. at 1599. . . .

Like the criminal law in *Smith II*, the District's unlawful entry statute is a neutral and generally applicable law. It is not directly aimed at religious practice. As invoked here, the unlawful entry statute was used to quell a disturbance, not a religious service. Thus, it was used to regulate conduct, not beliefs, a goal vindicated by the Supreme Court in . . . *Smith II*. . . . The Free Exercise Clause cannot be used as a means to escape civic duties. [Id.] at 888-89. . . .

---

17. According to appellant Asi, "fatwas are considered the cornerstone . . . of the Muslim world. In other words, if there were an equivalent in Islam to a Vatican . . . that would be it." Asi testified that he secured the opinion after the closure of the Center on March 5, 1983, in order to determine whether they could properly be prohibited from entering the Mosque. He also stated that the opinion was published in English translation in a newspaper distributed in the Muslim community.

Appellants also contend that the government's evidence was insufficient to prove beyond a reasonable doubt that appellants did not have lawful authority to remain in the Mosque after being asked to leave by officials of the Center.[19] We disagree.

In [Riley v. District of Columbia, 283 A.2d 819 (1971)], . . . the court concluded that there was sufficient evidence of guilt where the defendants had disobeyed the warning issued at the beginning of the mass by the pastor, acted contrary to the customs of the Church by handing out leaflets during the offertory, and caused the prayers to be interrupted and the mass stopped. Id. at 824.

. . . [E]ven appellant Asi supported the conclusion that the conduct which occurred that day was not within the bounds of the customs of the Muslim religion when he testified that if a person came into the Mosque and caused a disturbance, "he could be requested to leave the Mosque, no doubt about it."

In addition, the government . . . offered sufficient evidence to show that Dr. Hamoud and Sadiq Hassan-Bey qualified as persons legally authorized to demand that those involved in the disturbance leave. Evidence relating to any disagreement between Dr. Hamoud and Sadiq Hassan-Bey about precisely when persons inside should be told to leave is irrelevant to the issue of whether appellants were ordered to leave by a person or persons with the legal authority to do so. See Woll v. United States, 570 A.2d 819, 821 (D.C. 1990) ("a person may be lawfully in charge even though there are other persons who could, if they chose to do so, countermand or override his authority"). In addition, *Woll*, supra, 570 A.2d at 822, makes clear that even a person without a possessory interest in the property can issue the order to leave, and consequently, there is no need to scrutinize precisely the limits of Dr. Hamoud's authority. The evidence showed that the Board of Governors vested Dr. Hamoud with considerable authority with respect to managing the daily affairs of the Center and maintaining security, and he was given the express authority to remove unauthorized persons from the Center and keep "troublemakers" out. . . . [A] reasonable jury could find that appellants did not have a right to remain thereafter in the Mosque. . . .

Appellants also contend that the government could not prove that they had the requisite intent to commit the crime of unlawful entry because they had a reasonable belief in their right to enter and remain in the Mosque. While a bona fide belief defense to the crime of unlawful entry does exist, appellants' contention, while not without some merit, is ultimately unpersuasive.

---

19. In order to convict appellants under the unlawful entry statute the government had the burden of proving that: (1) they were present at the mosque; (2) they were instructed to leave by the lawful occupant or person lawfully in charge of the mosque; (3) at the time they were instructed to leave, they did not have lawful authority to remain; and (4) upon being directed to leave the mosque, they refused to do so. See Criminal Jury Instructions for the District of Columbia No. 4.44(B) (3d ed. 1978).

When a person enters a place with a good purpose and a bona fide belief in his or her right to enter, that person lacks the requisite criminal intent for unlawful entry. Smith v. United States, 281 A.2d 438, 439 (D.C. 1971). A defendant is entitled to an instruction, where the existence of such a belief is "genuinely questionable," to the effect that the government must prove beyond a reasonable doubt that the defendant did not have a reasonable, good faith belief in his lawful authority to stay. Id. at 439. However, "to warrant an instruction it is not sufficient that an accused merely claim a belief to the right to enter. A bona fide belief must have some justification — some reasonable basis." [Id.] As elaborated in Gaetano v. United States, 406 A.2d 1291, 1294 (D.C. 1979), the court stated:

> The clear rule of law . . . is that a reasonable belief in an individual's right to remain on property not owned or possessed by that individual must be based in the *pure indicia of innocence*. There must be some evidence that, for example, the individual had no reason to know that he was trespassing on the rights of others. Perhaps the individual could reasonably believe that he had title or a possessory interest in the land, or that the land was publicly owned. Perhaps he could believe that he was invited onto the land.

The court further stated in Morgan v. District of Columbia, 476 A.2d 1128, 1133 (D.C. 1984), that "the belief must be based on a reasonable mistake of fact, or on a reasonable mistake as to a non-penal property law which, if not a mistake, would justify remaining on the property. . . . General intent is not negated by a mistaken belief about the applicability of a penal law." In the instant case, the government presented sufficient evidence from which a reasonable jury could conclude that appellants' motivation did not rise to the level of a reasonable, good faith belief in lawful authority to remain in the Mosque after being asked to leave.

First, appellants based their defense on their reliance on the fatwa and the Koran, arguing that such reliance negated the criminal intent necessary for the crime of unlawful entry.[24] However, the government presented evidence to raise a reasonable question regarding whether appellants had a bona fide belief in their lawful, as opposed to religious, authority to remain in the Mosque. The jury could fairly have credited the testimony of the five government witnesses who stated that they heard the warnings issued by Hassan-Bey. . . .

The touchstone of the bona fide belief defense is the belief in lawful authority to stay, not moral or religious authority. Yet each defense witness

---

24. The two appellants aside from appellant Asi who did testify at trial also stated that they believed that no one could own or possess a Mosque and that no one had the right to order anyone out of a Mosque who was praying. Both testified that the basis of their belief was the Koran and the fatwa contained in the newsletter. Another defense witness testified to the same belief and basis. . . .

who was asked the basis of his belief that he could not be ejected from the Mosque cited the Koran and the fatwa. Furthermore, by acknowledging that the Board of Governors constituted the "true" owner of the Center in the eyes of the law, appellant Asi undercut appellants' claim of a bona fide belief in their lawful authority to stay.

Second, appellants could not prevail simply by reciting their belief in the fatwa and Koran since *Gaetano* makes clear that they had to demonstrate that the belief in their lawful right to stay was reasonable and based in the "pure indicia of innocence." Evidence of awareness of a request to leave will defeat a bona fide belief claim. See Jackson v. United States, 357 A.2d 409, 411 (D.C. 1976) (where girlfriend had ordered defendant to leave her apartment, "any grounds for a bona fide belief in his right to remain lapsed"). At trial, government witnesses testified that they were able to hear the warnings to persons inside the Mosque given by Hassan-Bey. Although appellants testified that they did not hear the warnings, this was an issue well within the jury's province to resolve. . . .

Finally, appellants do not suggest that their reasonable belief was rooted in either a reasonable mistake of fact or a reasonable mistake of non-penal property law. Their reliance on the fatwa does not operate as a mistake of fact, nor does it represent a form of property law. Consequently, appellants' bona fide belief claim ultimately fails. . . .

Notes and Questions

1. Was criminal prosecution appropriate in *Darab*? If so, why? If not, are there any circumstances under which behavior like the defendants' *should* give rise to criminal punishment?

2. As a practical matter, the chief issue underlying *Darab* has to do not with criminal punishment but with police authority. Ordinarily, police officers may not restrain anyone's freedom of movement without reasonable grounds for suspecting the individual in question has committed or is about to commit a crime. See Terry v. Ohio, 392 U.S. 1 (1968). American law gives police officers no general entitlement to tell people to "move along" or to go home, even when such orders might make sense. With few exceptions, police officers' authority to restrain individuals tracks prosecutors' authority to prosecute crimes.

3. Most mistake-of-law claims fall into one of two categories. Defendants in theft cases sometimes claim they believed the property they took was theirs—see the next main case for an example. (Notice the reference to these cases in the last paragraph of Chief Judge Rogers' opinion in *Darab*.) And, like Marrero, some defendants claim that they didn't realize their behavior constituted a crime. The *Darab* defendants' mistake doesn't obviously fall into either category. Defendant Asi acknowledged that "in the eyes of the law" his opponents owned the mosque, and none of the protesters claimed ignorance of the law of criminal trespass or "unlawful entry." Rather, they claimed that their religious duty required them to behave as they did — to stay in the mosque after they were told to leave. How should that "mistake" be categorized? Is it a mistake?

4. Here is one way to approach those questions. Begin with a proposition that even the prosecutor in *Darab* would accept: If the defendants had honestly and reasonably believed that they owned the mosque under the governing property law, their behavior would not constitute "unlawful entry." Why not? Presumably the answer is that someone who behaves consistently with widely held legal assumptions is not committing a serious moral wrong and is unlikely to harm others. If that is true of people who behave consistently with common assumptions about property law, might it also be true of people who behave consistently with common assumptions about religious doctrine? Does the answer depend on the particulars of the doctrine? On how common the assumptions are? Should conduct motivated by religious doctrine be treated the same as conduct motivated by some secular philosophy? Should courts make such judgments? Perhaps claims like those made by the *Darab* defendants lose because the alternative would require courts to judge the reasonableness of the claimants' religious convictions. See Jones v. Wolf, 443 U.S. 595 (1979) (courts resolving church property disputes must employ "neutral principles" analysis that is "completely secular in operation"); "Faith in Court," The Economist, Vol. 398, No. 8715 (Jan. 8, 2011), at p. 59 (available at www.economist.com/node/17849169?story_id=17849169& CFID=160002310&CFTOKEN=67210666).

5. Marrero misunderstood the legal rule that governed his conduct; had he known the rule would be interpreted as it was, he plainly would have left his gun at home when he entered the social club. The *Darab* defendants may well have known the governing legal rule; even if they didn't, such knowledge probably would not have changed their behavior. It is more accurate to say that the *Darab* defendants *disagreed with* the governing legal rule than that they misunderstood it. At least, they disagreed with the rule's application to their behavior. How should the law treat such disagreements?

6. Had the jury believed that the *Darab* defendants didn't hear the order to leave the mosque, those defendants would have been acquitted. Why not apply the same rule to defendants who believe that violating such commands is not a crime? What about defendants who believe that violating such commands is not wrong?

7. The issue of balancing individual claims of religious liberty and the rule of law continues to arise in modern America — seemingly with increasing frequency (and increasing ferocity) since the U.S. Supreme Court's decision in Obergefell v. Hodges, 576 U.S. ___ (2015), which held that states must recognize and allow same-sex marriages. Acts of resistance to the *Obergefell* decision, often based explicitly on religious objections, persist.* Perhaps the most infamous religion-based resistance was the prolonged refusal of Kim Davis, the Clerk of Rowan County, Kentucky, in the months following the *Obergefell* decision, to issue marriage licenses to gay couples. Davis eventually was sent to jail by a federal district judge for refusing to follow binding federal law; a week later, she finally consented to allow her office to issue the disputed licenses without her signature, and she was released from custody. In April 2016, Kentucky passed a new state statute removing the previous legal requirement for county clerks to sign marriage licenses; shortly after the new statute went into effect, Kim Davis agreed to drop her remaining legal appeals. See http://www.nbcnews.com/news/us-news/kentucky-clerk-kim-davis-who-refused-issue-marriage-licenses-gays-n596476.

The Kim Davis saga, like the *Darab* case, raised concerns about the scope of First Amendment's Free Exercise Clause. But as the *Darab* court explained, the Supreme Court has previously performed the necessary constitutional balancing, and has held that the First Amendment provides no basis for avoiding neutral and generally applicable secular laws. See Employment Division Department of Human Resources v. Smith, 494 U.S. 872 (1990) (*Smith II*). In 1993, however, Congress responded to the Court's decision in *Smith II* by enacting the Religious Freedom Restoration Act of 1993 (RFRA). See Pub. L. No. 103-141, 107 Stat. 1488 (Nov. 16, 1993), codified at 42 U.S.C. §2000bb through 42 U.S.C. §2000bb-4. The federal RFRA raises the bar for any federal government actions that "substantially burden" religious freedom, requiring a showing by the government that such actions are designed to serve a "compelling government interest" and employ the "least restrictive means" to further that government interest. Many states have enacted their own state versions of RFRA, some of them even more protective of religious rights than the federal RFRA.

RFRA statutes appeared on the legal scene too late to have any impact on the *Darab* decision. But it seems unlikely that RFRA would have made any difference in the *Darab* result anyway. As a general matter, neither the federal nor state RFRAs should pose much of an impediment to the enforcement of criminal law, because most crime statutes (except perhaps for so-called "victimless" crimes, like drug possession) will pass muster under even the most stringent

---

* In January 2016, Alabama Supreme Court Chief Justice Roy S. Moore issued an administrative order to Alabama probate judges, instructing them to continue enforcing Alabama's ban on same-sex marriages. Moore based his order not on religious beliefs, but instead on a tortured interpretation of the scope of *Obergefell* (Moore claimed that *Obergefell* didn't apply to Alabama, since Alabama was not a party to the *Obergefell* litigation). Moore was charged in a complaint filed by the Alabama Judicial Inquiry Commission with violating the Alabama Canons of Judicial Ethics. On September 30, 2016, the Alabama Court of the Judiciary ruled against Moore and suspended him from the bench for the remainder of his term. See http://judicial.alabama.gov/judiciary/COJ46FinalJudgment_09302016.pdf. Moore will be unable to run for reelection after his suspension (he was reelected under similar circumstances once before, after being removed from the bench in 2003 due to his refusal to remove the Ten Commandments monument from the state's judicial building) because at that point he will be too old to serve.

"compelling government interest" and "least restrictive means" analysis. How RFRAs might affect the enforcement of other laws (such as laws that prohibit discrimination based on sexual orientation) remains much less clear.

State v. Varszegi

Appellate Court of Connecticut
635 A.2d 816 (1993)

Opinion of O'CONNELL, J.
The defendant was initially charged with larceny in the first degree in violation of General Statutes §§53a-122(a)(2) and 53a-119, and criminal coercion in violation of General Statutes §53a-49(a)(2). Following a jury trial, he was convicted of the lesser included offense of larceny in the third degree in violation of General Statutes §53a-124[3] and acquitted of the coercion charge. The defendant appeals from his larceny conviction. The defendant claims that there was insufficient evidence to support the larceny conviction. . . . We reverse.

The jury could have reasonably found the following facts. The defendant was the landlord of commercial property at 1372 Summer Street in Stamford. One of the defendant's tenants was Executive Decisions Support, Inc., a computer software company headed by Catherine Topp. Topp, in her capacity as president of the company, personally signed the lease with the defendant. The lease contained a default clause authorizing the defendant to enter the tenant's premises, seize the tenant's personal property and sell it as a way of recovering unpaid rent or other charges.[4] The defendant claimed Topp had failed to pay her rent for March, April and May, 1990.

On Saturday, May 5, 1990, the defendant entered Topp's office by picking the lock. He proceeded to remove two of Topp's computers and attached

---

3. General Statutes §53a-124 provides in relevant part: "A person is guilty of larceny in the third degree when he commits larceny as defined in section 53a-119 and . . . (2) the value of the property or service exceeds one thousand dollars. . . ."

4. Paragraph twelve, section (b) of the defendant's lease reads as follows:

"*If Lessee defaults under this Lease, Lessor may without further notice to the Lessee: (i) terminate this Lease; (ii) re-enter and take possession of the Leased Premises, remove all persons and property therefrom and disconnect any telephone lines installed for the benefit of Lessee, all without being deemed to have committed any trespass; (iii) impound Lessee's property and sell it at auction or private sale,* applying the proceeds thereof to any unpaid rent or other charges, including costs of collection, and holding the Lessee responsible for any deficiency; (iv) recover, in addition to any rent and other charges already due and payable, all rent for the entire unexpired balance of the Term of this Lease and all costs incurred by Lessor to recover such sums from Lessee, including reasonable attorney's fees. All rights and remedies of Lessor under this Lease shall be cumulative and in addition to any other rights or remedies available at law or in equity."

printers. On Monday May 7, 1990, Topp arrived at work and noticed that the lock on her office door had been tampered with. Upon entering and noticing her computers were missing, Topp called the Stamford police. After the completion of an initial investigation at the scene by Officer Frank Pica, Topp telephoned the defendant, who admitted that he had taken her computers as a consequence of her failure to pay three months rent. Pica then took the phone from Topp and identified himself. The defendant advised Pica that he was Topp's landlord and expressed his belief that his actions were proper and legal. Upon hearing this, Pica expressed doubt as to the lawfulness of the defendant's conduct, at which point the defendant reiterated his belief that his actions were in accordance with his lease.

At this point, Pica called his supervisor, Sergeant Ralph Geter. Geter arrived shortly thereafter and telephoned the defendant, who again identified himself as Topp's landlord and again admitted having taken the computers in question. Geter informed the defendant that he had no right under the law to confiscate Topp's computer equipment and that he should make arrangements with Topp to return the goods. No such arrangements were made and the defendant sold the computers on May 23, 1990.

On May 25, 1990, a detective contacted the defendant and inquired whether they could meet to discuss the matter as part of his investigation. As he had from the start, the defendant admitted during this telephone conversation that he had taken and retained the computers pursuant to his lease. On June 6, 1990, the defendant met with the detective at the Stamford police station and was asked for a formal statement. The defendant requested an attorney and the conversation ended. The defendant was subsequently arrested on June 28, 1990.

The defendant . . . claims that the state did not prove beyond a reasonable doubt that he was guilty of larceny. . . .

Larceny is defined in General Statutes §53a-119 as follows: "A person commits larceny when, with intent to deprive another of property or to appropriate the same to himself or a third person, he wrongfully takes, obtains or withholds such property from an owner. . . ." This crime has three elements and all three must be established beyond a reasonable doubt. It must be shown that (1) there was an intent to do the act complained of, (2) the act was done wrongfully, and (3) the act was committed against an owner. . . . Because larceny is a specific intent crime, the state must show that the defendant acted with the subjective desire or knowledge that his actions constituted stealing. A specific "intent to deprive another of property or to appropriate the same to himself . . . is an essential element of larceny . . . and as such must be proved beyond a reasonable doubt by the state." State v. Fernandez, 198 Conn. 1, 20, 501 A.2d 356 (1985).

. . . Hornbook law articulates the same premise. "Since the taking must be with felonious intent . . . taking under a bona fide claim of right, however unfounded, is not larceny. . . . Although ignorance of the law is, as a rule, no excuse, it is an excuse if it negatives the existence of a specific intent. Therefore, even if the taker's claim of right is based upon ignorance or mistake of law, it is sufficient to negative a felonious intent. A fortiori, a mistake of fact, if it is the basis of a bona fide claim of right, is sufficient." J. Miller, Handbook of Criminal Law (1934) §114(a), at 367; see also 2 W. LaFave & A. Scott, Substantive Criminal Law (1986) §8.5(a), at 358. . . .

Particularly apposite to the present case is the comment in American Jurisprudence that, "it is generally held that because of lack of a felonious intent, one is not guilty of larceny who, in the honest belief that he has the right to do so, openly and avowedly takes the property of another without the latter's consent, as security for a debt bona fide claimed to be due him by the owner, or even to apply or credit it to the payment thereof." Id., 205-206.

"A defendant who acts under the subjective belief that he or she has a lawful claim on property lacks the required felonious intent to steal. Such a defendant need not show his mistaken claim of right was reasonable, since an unreasonable belief that he had a right to take another's property will suffice so long as he can establish his claim was made in good faith." 50 Am. Jur. 2d, Larceny §41, relying on People v. Romo, 269 Cal. Rptr. 440 (1990). . . .

Our Supreme Court has . . . considered the scenario of a landlord who, like the defendant in the present case, seizes his tenant's property as security for a debt. State v. Sawyer, 95 Conn. 34, 35-36, 110 A. 461 (1920). In *Sawyer*, a landlady took possession of a tenant's handbag on the ground that the tenant was liable to her for damage done to the demised premises. The court held that the defendant had not committed a larceny because she believed that her claim justified refusal to return the handbag unless the tenant paid for the damage. Id. at 38. The court based its decision on the absence of felonious intent and the presence of a color of right. The court held that "one is not guilty of theft without consciousness of the wholly unlawful and inexcusable nature of his act. The grave character of the necessary intent makes that clear. His belief in his right to take the thing involved, *even though a mistaken belief, or one entertained upon insufficient grounds*, is essentially inconsistent with the presence of an intent to steal, and the terms 'colour of right or excuse' obviously demand a construction consonant with that point of view." Id. (emphasis added). . . .

In the present case, the defendant claims that he did not possess the specific felonious intent to commit larceny but rather acted in good faith pursuant to a lease that gave him, as the landlord, authority to enter the premises, impound the lessee's property, sell it and apply the proceeds to the unpaid rent or other charges. The state claims that it introduced evidence from which the jury could reasonably have inferred that the defendant intended to steal the computer equipment.

We hold that there was insufficient evidence introduced at trial to prove that the defendant knew that he had no right to take the lessee's computers. During the initial phone conversation with Topp, the defendant made no attempt to conceal either his identity or that he had in fact taken the computers. The defendant emphatically stated during this conversation that the default clause in the lease provided him with the authority to impound her property based on her failure to pay the three months rent due. Moreover, the officers testifying at trial each stated that the defendant never wavered from his contention that his actions were lawful, even when faced with the threat of criminal prosecution. The defendant's unfaltering and consistent statements to all parties involved that he acted in good faith in seizing Topp's computers were not contradicted by the testimony of any witness. . . .

. . . The state contends . . . that the defendant's weekend entry into Topp's office by picking the lock and his subsequent impounding of the computers without leaving a note was enough evidence from which the jury could have reasonably found the requisite intent. . . . In fact, the defendant testified that he entered the office on the weekend so as to avoid an awkward confrontation. When asked by Topp where the computers were on the following Monday, the defendant concealed nothing. Notwithstanding the state's claim to the contrary, the record is devoid of any evidence that the jury could have reasonably relied upon in finding the defendant acted with the requisite culpability. The state's bald and conclusory assertion that the jury simply rejected the defendant's consistent claim that the rental agreement served as justification for his action is not enough to prove beyond a reasonable doubt the specific intent requirement for larceny.

Moreover, the state contends that even if the defendant believed in good faith that he had the right to take his tenant's personal property to secure overdue rent payments, once he was told by three members of the police force that he was acting illegally, he could no longer reasonably maintain an honest though mistaken belief that he was acting lawfully. We do not agree. Police officers are not imbued with the authority or prerogative to declare provisions of civil contracts void, thereby converting good faith to a felonious intent. . . .

The judgment is reversed and the case is remanded with direction to render judgment of not guilty of larceny in the third degree.

Notes on Color of Right Mistakes

1. *Varszegi* is representative of the one category of mistake-of-law claims that regularly succeeds: Theft defendants' claims that they honestly (even if unreasonably) believed they owned the "stolen" property. Why should those claims succeed? Why not tell Varszegi that he must seek legal remedies for the unpaid debt—and if he insists on helping himself to his tenant's property, he risks criminal liability on the same terms as would anyone else? What would be the likely consequences of such a rule?

2. Notice that the court dismisses the fact that Varszegi was clearly informed by three police officers that he was not legally authorized to keep the tenant's computer equipment. Why doesn't that matter? Should we be encouraging people like Varszegi to act on their own personal views about their legal rights, even if those views might be unreasonable? Isn't Varszegi essentially a vigilante, enforcing his own interpretation of the law? How can we possibly square the decision in *Varszegi* with the broad policy arguments behind the *Marrero* decision?

3. Perhaps the rule in *Varszegi* has survived because pursuing an effective legal remedy for collecting money from tenants has become a good deal harder than it was in times past. The law of landlords and tenants historically favored landlords, but beginning roughly a half-century ago, it took a sharp turn in tenants' favor. Collecting unpaid rent and evicting defendants who do not pay up are more difficult and more expensive than in generations past. If legal assistance is harder to come by, landlords like Varszegi will naturally find self-help more attractive. Is that a healthy state of affairs? Might it make more sense to give landlords broader legal remedies—and, at the same time, tell them that claims like Varszegi's will not excuse trespass or theft?

4. Why should a merely honest mistake of law excuse a theft defendant? (Or a larceny defendant—the historic differences between theft and larceny, which have largely disappeared in most states, certainly don't matter for present purposes.) Why not require that the mistake be both honest and reasonable?

That was the position taken by a divided panel of the Massachusetts Appeals Court in the interesting case of Commonwealth v. Liebenow, 84 Mass. App. Ct. 387; 997 N.E.2d 109 (2013):

> The defendant was convicted of larceny under $250 for the theft of steel pipes and metal plates from a construction site. G.L. c. 266, §30. At a bench trial, the defendant claimed as an affirmative defense that he lacked the requisite specific intent to steal because he honestly believed that the metal property was abandoned. This defense was unsuccessful. The trial judge determined that the defendant's stated belief that the pieces of metal were abandoned property—notwithstanding that these metal construction materials were being stored on private property posted with no trespassing signs—even if considered as honest in the defendant's subjective mind, was not objectively reasonable based on the case evidence. . . .
>
> The construction site from which the defendant took the pieces of metal was private property located in Pittsfield. The property was known as Amy Court. There was active, ongoing construction on a townhouse development, with large construction machines, a work trailer, the raising of a building, and the clearing of land. There were several "no trespassing . . . private property" signs posted throughout the site. The defendant drove his pickup truck onto Amy Court during midmorning. The defendant then took several lengths of

steel pipe and metal plates and loaded them into the back of his pickup truck. An employee at the site inquired what the defendant was doing. The defendant replied that he was just picking up some junk steel. The defendant drove away from the Amy Court construction site. The police were notified. Shortly thereafter, a police officer stopped the defendant. The bed of the defendant's pickup truck still contained numerous pieces of pipe, plates, and other metal. When inquired of by the police officer where he had gotten the metal, the defendant first denied that any of the metal came from the Amy Court construction site.

The defendant later changed this story and admitted that the metal property was taken from the construction site. However, the defendant testified that he honestly believed the metal was abandoned. In finding the defendant guilty, the trial judge stated, "As far as I'm concerned, the presence of the no trespassing sign puts you on notice that the property was not for you to take. Your honest belief at that point would not be relevant. So I find you guilty, sir."

The dissent sees this statement as error of law. We think not. . . . The dissent far too finely parses and interprets the judge's remark in such a way that would compel a reversal that is entirely unwarranted by the trial evidence. As the trial transcript reveals, the judge referenced the no trespassing signs as "put[ting] [the defendant] on notice" that the scrap metal was not abandoned. Add to this that the defendant lied when first confronted by the police, denying that he had taken the metal pieces from within the Amy Court construction site. These two incriminating pieces of evidence, when added to the totality of the other evidence at trial, support the judge's rejection of the affirmative defense of mistake of fact with regard to property abandonment. . . .

As recast under the dissent's construction, a defendant's mistaken belief regarding property ownership or abandonment would compel a trial judge to instruct that the jury must acquit (or a judge sitting as fact finder must acquit), even if a defendant's subjectively expressed honest belief that property is abandoned is, objectively, totally unreasonable. Such acquittals under the dissent's theory would be compelled so long as a defendant claims — even without any reasonable basis to so believe — that the property had no owner or was abandoned. . . .

Finally, and of import, the dissent's recast of the affirmative defense of mistake concerning abandonment of property will lead to instructing a jury (and defining the law to be applied by a judge as fact finder) that the jury (or judge) must enter a not guilty verdict (or finding) — even if such an acquittal is contrary to the trial evidence, and even if the acquittal is virtually nonsensical because the defendant's belief that the subject property was abandoned is entirely irrational and unreasonable, if viewed objectively. . . .

84 Mass. App. Ct. at 388-91. Justice Milkey, in dissent, commented: "Neither the Commonwealth nor the majority has identified any case holding that a defendant may be found to possess the specific intent to steal property that he honestly believed he had the legal right to take. We are now the first appellate court anywhere to reach that conclusion." Id. at 408 (Milkey, J., dissenting).

That conclusion didn't last for long. Just one year later, the Massachusetts Supreme Judicial Court reversed the Appeals Court. See Commonwealth v. Liebenow, 470 Mass. 151 (2014). Here's what the Supreme Judicial Court had to say:

> The defendant claimed as an affirmative defense at trial that he lacked the requisite specific intent to steal because he honestly, albeit mistakenly, believed that the property he removed from the site was abandoned. The judge, however, erroneously viewed the affirmative defense as requiring proof that the defendant's belief was objectively reasonable. This misperception appears to have arisen from the conflation of two distinct concepts that have appeared over time in our jurisprudence: the concept of good faith belief, which is subjective, and the concept of reasonable belief, which is objective. We take this opportunity to resolve the resulting confusion.

Id. at 151-52. The Supreme Judicial Court attributed the "confusion" to an earlier Appeals Court decision in Commonwealth v. White, 5 Mass. App. Ct. 483 (1977), which had been cited by the Appeals Court in *Liebenow*. *White* involved a defendant who walked into a bar with a gun and demanded from his employer what he apparently believed to be $50 in wages owed to him. The employer threw the money down onto the bar, and the defendant took the money and left. The Appeals Court threw out the larceny conviction in *White*, but wrote in its opinion — in dictum, the issue of "reasonableness" never having been raised — that the jury must acquit in a larceny case if they find "that the defendant honestly *and reasonably* believed that the money he took from [the victim] represented a debt actually due from [the victim] to the defendant." Id. at 488. The Supreme Judicial Court continued:

The offense of larceny is defined in G.L. c. 266, §30 (1), as follows:

> "Whoever steals, or with intent to defraud obtains by a false pretense, or whoever unlawfully, and with intent to steal or embezzle, converts, or secretes with intent to convert, the property of another as defined in this section, whether such property is or is not in his possession at the time of such conversion or secreting, shall be guilty of larceny . . . ."

To convict a defendant of larceny requires that the Commonwealth prove that a defendant took the personal property of another without the right to do so, and "with the specific intent to deprive the other of the property permanently." Commonwealth v. Murray, 401 Mass. 771, 772 (1988). . . .

A defendant has sufficiently raised the defense of mistaken belief "if any view of the evidence" would support a factual finding that the defendant honestly believed that the items he took were abandoned. Commonwealth v. Vives, 447 Mass. 537, 541 (2006).

Here, in addition to the defendant's testimony that he believed that the property he took had been abandoned, there was evidence at trial, viewed favorably to the defendant, from which a fact finder could have inferred that, notwithstanding the presence of the no trespassing signs, the paved cul-de-sac named Amy Court, as well as the construction site surrounding it, were open to the public to permit inspection of the lots on which town-houses were to be constructed. The evidence also permitted the inference that the defendant's denials to Parise of having taken anything from "Amy Court" reflected a misunderstanding as to the location the officer meant when he referred to "Amy Court"; there was evidence that the defendant was unaware that the paved cul-de-sac was private property, or that the dirt trail at the end of that cul-de-sac was part of the Amy Court development then under construction. The left-over lengths of steel pipe taken by the defendant were behind a pile of soil, in an area where no construction was then taking place. . . .

It has been long established that the specific intent to steal is negated by a finding that a defendant held an honest, albeit mistaken, belief that he was entitled to the property he took. See, e.g., Commonwealth v. Brisbois, 281 Mass. 125, 128-129 (1932) (jury correctly instructed that, if defendant "honestly thought" he had legal right to remove wooden building, "then there was no criminal intent to steal"); Commonwealth v. McDuffy, 126 Mass. 467, 469, 471 (1879) (trial judge erred in excluding evidence "competent upon the issue of the defendant's belief" that money he took was due him); Commonwealth v. Stebbins, 8 Gray 492, 495 (1857) (court noted as "clearly unexceptional" jury instruction "that the defendant was not guilty of larceny, if she took the money under an honest belief that she had a legal right to take it"). See also Commonwealth v. Weld, Thacher's Crim. Cas. 157, 163 (Boston Mun. Ct. 1827) (judge instructed, "if [the defendant] honestly thought he had a right to the paper, it excludes the idea of a felonious taking"). . . .

[W]e do not think that the Appeals Court in Commonwealth v. White, supra at 488, intended to depart from the long-established principle that an honest belief need not be objectively reasonable to negate the specific intent required for larceny, despite its use of the phrase "honestly and reasonably believed.". . .

Evidence of reasonableness may, however, be considered by the jury to assist in their determination whether to credit a defendant's honest belief. "Neither juries nor judges are required to divorce themselves of common sense, but rather should apply to facts which they find proven such reasonable inferences as are justified in the light of their experience as to the natural inclinations of human beings." United States v. Tejeda, 974 F.2d 210, 213 (1st Cir. 1992), quoting United States v. Batista-Polanco, 927 F.2d 14, 18 (1st Cir. 1991). . . .

A defendant may raise an honest, yet mistaken, belief as an affirmative defense.[15] See Commonwealth v. Vives, 447 Mass. at 540-541. A defendant's

---

15. Although we use the term affirmative defense, in this context the Commonwealth nonetheless bears the burden of proof because the defense addresses an element of the offense of larceny, the defendant's specific intent to steal. Once a defendant meets the burden of production, the burden of proof shifts to the Commonwealth to disprove the defense.

honest belief that the property he took was abandoned constitutes an affirmative defense to larceny.

Liebenow, 470 Mass. at 156-62.

Surely the Massachusetts Supreme Judicial Court eventually got to the right answer in *Liebenow.* But didn't the Appeals Court have a good point? Does Liebenow seem like someone who ought to be able to get away with what he did? Does the law of larceny seem just?

5. How should legal mistakes be classified? One might argue that Marrero made a mistake not about whether it was a crime to carry a gun to a New York social club, but about whether New York's definition of "peace officers" (in the state's criminal procedure law, not in its criminal code) included federal corrections officers. As for Varszegi, one could argue that *his* mistake concerned the legal definition of theft—he believed, wrongly, that landlords are permitted to satisfy their tenants' debts by stealing their tenants' property. Are those characterizations fair? Why should Varszegi be treated better than Marrero?

And why should Varszegi be treated better than the defendants in *Darab*? The *Darab* defendants were arguably acting out of conscience—they genuinely believed the right thing to do was to stay in the mosque, not because doing so served their interests but because doing so served their God. Varszegi's motive was purely selfish: He wanted to recover the money he was owed. If he had any other goal, it was probably to punish his recalcitrant tenant. Why should the law excuse selfishness and a desire to get even with one's enemies, but punish the exercise of religious duty? Is that a fair description of *Varszegi* and *Darab*? Is mistake-of-law doctrine just?

6. Now that you have a better understanding of mistake-of-law doctrine, return to the question asked at the very end of the mistake-of-fact materials: What kind of mistake did Binegar make? Was it a mistake of fact, because he mistook the fact that he was allowed to dispense those contact lenses? Or was it really a mistake of law, because his mistake was that he did not think he was bound to follow the legal rules under which he acted?

For that matter, what kind of mistake did Oglivie make, with respect to his first marriage? Was it a mistake of fact, because he was wrong about the fact that his first wife had finalized his divorce in Panama? Or was it instead a mistake about his legal status (i.e., his legal status as either "married" or "divorced")? How was Oglivie's mistake any different from Marrero's, who also made a mistake about his legal status (i.e., whether or not he was classified under N.Y. law as a "peace officer")? Why is one treated as a mistake of fact, and the other as a mistake of law?

Clearly, the common-law line between "mistake of fact" and "mistake of law" can be pretty unclear (if not entirely nonexistent). Is this a problem for the common law? Or is it, once again, an advantage — precisely because it provides judges with still more flexibility that they can use to achieve just results?

5. Strict Liability

State v. Loge

Supreme Court of Minnesota
608 N.W.2d 152 (2000)

Opinion by GILBERT, J.

This case presents the question of whether knowledge is an element of the crime under the open bottle law when the driver is the sole occupant of a motor vehicle. Appellant Steven Mark Loge was cited on September 2, 1997, for a violation of Minn. Stat. §169.122(3), which makes it unlawful for the driver of a motor vehicle, when the owner is not present, "to keep or allow to be kept in a motor vehicle when such vehicle is upon the public highway any bottle or receptacle containing intoxicating liquors or 3.2 percent malt liquors which has been opened." Violation of the statute is a misdemeanor. See Minn. Stat. §169.122(4). After a bench trial, the district court held that [section 169.122(3)] imposed "absolute liability" on the driver/owner. Loge appealed. The court of appeals affirmed the conviction, holding that proof of knowledge that the open container was in the motor vehicle was not required. We affirm.

On September 2, 1997, Loge borrowed his father's pick-up truck to go to his evening job. Driving alone on his way home from work, he was stopped by two . . . police officers on County Road 18 at approximately 8:15 P.M. because he appeared to be speeding. Loge got out of his truck and stood by the driver's side door. While one officer was talking with Loge, the second officer, who was standing by the passenger side of the truck, observed a bottle, which he believed to be a beer bottle, sticking partially out of a brown paper bag underneath the passenger's side of the seat. He retrieved that bottle, which was open and had foam on the inside. He searched the rest of the truck and found one full, unopened can of beer and one empty beer can. After the second officer found the beer bottle, the first officer asked Loge if he had been drinking. Loge stated that he had two beers while working and was on his way home. Loge passed all standard field sobriety tests. The officers gave Loge [a citation] . . . for a violation of the open bottle statute but not for speeding. . . .

The trial on the open bottle charge took place on January 29, 1998. Loge testified that the bottle was not his, he did not know it was in the truck and had said that to one of the officers. That officer did not remember any such statements. . . . The trial court found that one of the police officers "observed the neck of the bottle, which was wrapped in a brown paper sack, under the pickup's seat of the truck being operated by defendant." Based on an analysis of section 169.122 as a whole, the trial court held that subdivision 3 creates "absolute liability" on a driver/owner to "inspect and determine . . . whether there are any containers" in the motor vehicle in violation of the open bottle law and found Loge guilty. Loge was sentenced to five days in jail, execution stayed, placed on probation for one year, and fined $150 plus costs of $32.50.

Loge appealed the verdict. . . . [T]he court of appeals affirmed the decision of the trial court finding that the evidence . . . was sufficient to support Loge's conviction. The court of appeals held that proof of knowledge that the bottle was in the truck is not required to sustain a conviction. Loge's petition for further review was granted. . . .

Loge is seeking reversal of his conviction because, he argues, the trial court and court of appeals erroneously interpreted subdivision 3 of the open bottle statute[1] not to require proof of knowledge. Loge argues that the words "to keep or allow to be kept" implicitly and unambiguously require a defendant to have knowledge of the open container in the motor vehicle in order for criminal liability to attach. He argues that "keep" means "to maintain, or cause to stay or continue, in a specified condition, position, etc." Loge argues that that definition suggests that a person must purposely

---

1. Minnesota Statutes §169.122 reads in part:

Subdivision 1. No person shall drink or consume intoxicating liquors or 3.2 percent malt liquors in any motor vehicle when such vehicle is upon a public highway.

Subdivision 2. No person shall have in possession while in a private motor vehicle upon a public highway, any bottle or receptacle containing intoxicating liquor or 3.2 percent malt liquor which has been opened, or the seal broken, or the contents of which have been partially removed. For purposes of this section, "possession" means either that the person had actual possession of the bottle or receptacle or that the person consciously exercised dominion and control over the bottle or receptacle. This subdivision does not apply to a bottle or receptacle that is in the trunk of the vehicle if it is equipped with a trunk, or that is in another area of the vehicle not normally occupied by the driver and passengers if the vehicle is not equipped with a trunk.

Subdivision 3. It shall be unlawful for the owner of any private motor vehicle or the driver, if the owner be not then present in the motor vehicle, to keep or allow to be kept in a motor vehicle when such vehicle is upon the public highway any bottle or receptacle containing intoxicating liquors or 3.2 percent malt liquors which has been opened, or the seal broken, or the contents of which have been partially removed except when such bottle or receptacle shall be kept in the trunk of the motor vehicle when such vehicle is equipped with a trunk, or kept in some other area of the vehicle not normally occupied by the driver of passengers, if the motor vehicle is not equipped with a trunk. A utility compartment or glove compartment shall be deemed to be within the area occupied by the driver and passengers. . . .

choose to continue possession. Further, Loge argues that the word "allow" from the phrase "allow to be kept" means "to permit; to grant license to," suggesting awareness at the minimum.

The state argues that the language of subdivision 3 creates a strict liability offense. The statute was enacted in 1959 and subdivision 3 has not had any substantive change since its enactment. The state relies heavily on the presumption that the legislature intends the statute as a whole to be effective and certain, with no surplusage. State v. Orsello, 554 N.W.2d 70, 75-76 (Minn. 1996). The state argues that subdivision 3's "keep or allow to be kept" language must mean more than mere possession of alcohol because owners/drivers are already subject to liability under subdivision 2 for mere possession, which applies to all persons in the motor vehicle. The state further argues that to read subdivision 3 as requiring conscious or continuing possession would make it mere surplusage. . . .

. . . We must . . . look to all subdivisions of section 169.122 together to help us determine whether the legislature intended to impose liability under subdivision 3 on a driver/owner without proof of knowledge. Subdivision 1 prohibits the consumption of alcohol by any person in a motor vehicle on a public highway. Subdivision 2 prohibits the actual possession of, or conscious exercise of dominion and control over, an open bottle of alcohol by any person in the vehicle. In contrast, subdivision 3 provides that the owner, or if the owner is not present, the driver is responsible for ensuring that no open bottles of alcohol are present in a vehicle on a public highway, regardless of consumption, actual possession or conscious exercise of dominion and control. Consumption, possession and presence of an open container of alcohol in a motor vehicle are each separate risks. The legislature separately addressed each risk in section 169.122(1-3) in an effort to promote highway safety by decreasing the opportunity for alcohol consumption and drunken driving. . . .

We are mindful of Loge's argument that, as a criminal statute, section 169.122 must be strictly construed. Where we have found a statute ambiguous, we have said, "if criminal liability, particularly gross misdemeanor or felony liability, is to be imposed for conduct unaccompanied by fault, the legislative intent to do so should be clear." State v. Neisen, 415 N.W.2d 326, 329 (Minn. 1987). However, . . . where, as here, we have interpreted the statute and find no ambiguity, "the so-called 'rule of lenity,' which holds that *ambiguity* concerning the ambit of criminal statutes should be resolved in favor of lenity towards the defendant," has no application. *Orsello*, 554 N.W.2d at 74 (emphasis added). . . .

The legislature has made . . . distinctions within its traffic statutes that also guide our interpretation. For example, with respect to marijuana in a motor vehicle, the Minnesota legislature has used language similar to the language found in §169.122(3) ("keep or allow to be kept") but added a knowledge requirement. An owner, or if the owner is not present, the driver, is guilty of a misdemeanor if he "*knowingly* keeps or allows to be kept" marijuana in a motor vehicle. Minn. Stat. §152.027(3) (emphasis added). The use of the word "knowingly" . . . indicates that the legislature does not perceive the word "keep" alone to imply or contain a knowledge element. . . .

. . . [T]he parallels between subdivision 3 and other non-alcohol related traffic statutes also support our holding. The phrases "it shall be unlawful" or "no person shall" appear throughout the traffic code and have never been understood to require a showing of intent to prove a violation of the statute. See generally Minn. Stat. §169.14 (1998) (speeding); Butler v. Engel, 68 N.W.2d 226, 238 (Minn. 1954). . . . Loge concedes that other provisions of the traffic code that use such language are strict liability offenses. . . .

Though the dissent acknowledges the authority of the legislature to create criminal statutes without regard to intent or knowledge, it cites . . . the rule enunciated in *Kremer*[6] as a limitation: "it is not essential that the wrongdoer should intend to commit the crime to which his act amounts, but it is essential that he should intend to do the act which constitutes the crime." State v. Kremer, 114 N.W.2d 88, 89 (Minn. 1962). . . . [A]lthough dicta, we also stated:

> If the defendant . . . went through a stop light that he did not see, and was defending on the ground that he did so without any criminal intent, a court could be justified in finding him guilty of a violation of the ordinance involved. When the driver intends to proceed forward, or is negligent in any way, he can be held liable for his acts.

Id. at 89. . . . [E]ven though Loge did not see the open bottle and argues therefore that he had no criminal intent, he, as the driver, intended to proceed forward. . . . In order to avoid violating this statute, Loge had an affirmative duty to ensure that there were no open containers in the area of a motor vehicle normally occupied by the driver or passenger on a public highway. He . . . was in the best position to find out the fact of the open bottle's presence "with no more care than society might reasonably expect and no more exertion than it might reasonably exact from one who assumed his responsibilities." Id. . . . [A]ll Loge had to do was observe an open beer bottle protruding from a bag under the passenger's seat, which the trial court found was visible . . . to the officer who was standing outside the truck looking in.

---

6. The dissent also cites State v. Dombroski, 176 N.W. 985 (Minn. 1920) . . . for support for this rule. In *Dombroski*, we held that with respect to a statute criminalizing the rape of an incompetent woman, the legislature had "clearly eliminated the element of knowledge and intent" about a victim's incompetence. See 176 N.W. at 986. . . . *Dombroski* involved construing the language of [a] specific [statute; it did not alter] our basic understanding of the rule enunciated in *Kremer*.

The "to keep" an open bottle language of subdivision 3 means more than knowingly continuing possession because such conduct is already made illegal by subdivision 2. Any other interpretation would render subdivision 3 mere surplusage and would violate the statutory presumption that the legislature intends an entire statute to be effective and certain. See Minn. Stat. §645.17(2); *Orsello*, 554 N.W.2d at 75-76. Therefore, we hold that in a prosecution under §169.122(3), the state need not prove that the driver and sole occupant of a motor vehicle on a public highway knew of the existence of the open bottle containing intoxicating liquors in the motor vehicle.

ANDERSON, PAUL H., J., with whom PAGE and STRINGER, JJ. join, dissenting.

. . . [W]hen the legislature intends . . . to impose criminal sanctions without any requirement of intent or knowledge, it must do so clearly. See State v. Neisen, 415 N.W.2d 326, 329 (Minn. 1985). Further, the legislature's authority to impose criminal sanctions without any requirement of knowledge or intent is subject to another important limitation. . . . We have stated that "it is not essential that the wrongdoer should intend to commit the crime to which his act amounts, [but] it is essential that he should intend to do the act which constitutes the crime." State v. Kremer, 114 N.W.2d 88, 89 (Minn. 1962).[1] The United States Supreme Court, confronted with a similar issue, noted: "Historically, our substantive criminal law is based upon a theory of punishing the vicious will. It postulates a free agent confronted with a choice between doing right and doing wrong and choosing freely to do wrong." Morissette v. United States, 342 U.S. 246, 250 (1952). . . .

. . . The majority attempts to avoid the implications of the phrase "[keep or] allow to be kept" . . . on the grounds that Loge was the sole occupant of the vehicle. . . . In other contexts, we have held that the inclusion of words like "permit" (a synonym of "allow") clearly indicates a legislative intent to require some level of knowledge or intent. See, e.g., Peterson v. Pawelk, 263 N.W.2d 634, 637 (Minn. 1978) (stating that the use of the term "permit" in a statute clearly indicates that the legislature did not intend to impose strict liability). While it is possible to find definitions of "keep" that do not [imply] knowledge or intent, there are, as Loge points out, many definitions of "keep" that imply some level of conscious knowledge or intent. The multiple definitions of the word "keep" cited by the parties underscore the lack of clarity in the statute's language. . . .

---

1. The majority responds to this argument by noting that we also stated in *Kremer* that a person could be held liable for driving through a stop sign that he failed to see. However, the majority misses the essential point of *Kremer*. A wrongdoer must intend to do the act *that constitutes the crime*. As we went on to point out in *Kremer*, while operating a motor vehicle in a negligent manner (i.e., failing to observe traffic signs) can support a level of intent (negligence) to support criminal liability, running a stop sign due to unexpected brake failure would not. See *Kremer*, 114 N.W.2d at 89. . . . Loge's situation is more analogous to brake failure than to a negligent failure to observe the rules of the road.

The majority asserts that because the legislature used the similar language "keeps or allows to be kept" in Minn. Stat. §152.027, but added the word "knowingly," the lack of the word "knowingly" in Minn. Stat. §169.122 means that no knowledge requirement was intended. While we do presume that the legislature uses words in a consistent manner, here such analysis yields no clear answers. It is clear that the use of the word "knowingly" in §152.027 indicates that the legislature intended to require knowledge for the possession of marijuana in a vehicle. However, the fact that it is not included in §169.122, a law passed some 20 years earlier and on a different subject, does not indicate that the legislature intended to disregard any requirement of knowledge or intent.

The majority's analysis also disregards those situations where there is more than one person in the vehicle. . . . [For example, a] driver could be held responsible for the acts of passengers that they conceal from him. An absent owner could be held liable for acts of passengers he has never met. . . .

The majority also implies that in this case the bottle was in plain sight and that under the circumstance of this case, Loge actually knew (or should have known) that the open bottle was in the truck. The district court made no such finding nor is it our province to do so. . . .

. . . In State v. Dombroski, 176 N.W. 985, 985-86 (Minn. 1920), we noted that the legislature clearly and unambiguously manifested its intent to impose criminal liability for the statutory rape of an incompetent female without regard to whether the accused knew that the victim was incompetent. . . . [T]he statute did not require knowledge that the victim was incompetent, but it required intent to commit an act that, in combination with the victim's status, would constitute statutory rape. . . .

. . . [U]nder the majority's holding, we now will impose criminal liability on a person, not simply for an act that the person does not know is criminal, but also for an act the person does not even know he is committing. While the district court and the majority seem to assume that everyone who drives a motor vehicle knows that he or she is obligated to search the entire passenger compartment of the vehicle before driving on the state's roads, the law imposes no such requirement. Most drivers would be surprised to discover that after anyone else used their vehicle — children, friends, spouse — they are criminally liable for any open containers of alcohol that are present, regardless of whether they know the containers are there. This also means that any prudent operator of a motor vehicle must also carefully check any case of packaged alcohol before transport and ensure that each container's seal is not broken. See Minn. Stat. §169.122 (defining an open bottle as a container that is open, has the contents partially removed, or has the seal broken). Under the majority's interpretation, all of these situations would render the driver criminally liable under Minn. Stat. §169.122. Without a more clear statement by the legislature that this is the law, I cannot agree with such an outcome.

Notes and Questions

1. Was Loge treated fairly? Was strict liability appropriate given the crime charged? Does your answer depend on Loge's modest sentence? If so, would your answer change if Loge had actually served his five-day jail sentence? How much jail time is too much to be justified by a strict liability crime?

2. There is good reason to believe that Loge actually knew about the open bottle of beer in the truck: The police officer who found it saw the bottle from outside the truck and the bottle had foam in it, suggesting that someone opened it and drank some of the contents shortly before the traffic stop. Is strict liability appropriate in cases like *Loge* on the ground that, even though the state need not *prove* knowledge, the defendant will nearly always *have* it?

3. *Loge* suggests that strict liability is often the governing standard for traffic offenses. Why? Suppose a defendant is charged with driving more than 20 miles per hour above the governing speed limit, which is 70 miles per hour. Suppose further that the defendant testifies that he believed he was driving only 88 miles per hour, not 95 as the state trooper's radar gun showed. Finally, suppose that the defendant can show that his car's speedometer was faulty, that at high speeds, it reads several miles per hour more slowly than the car is actually traveling. If general intent were the governing standard, the defendant would have a valid mistake of fact defense. In most jurisdictions, the standard is strict liability, meaning that no such defense exists. Again, why?

4. The defendant in State v. Kremer, 114 N.W.2d 88 (Minn. 1962), cited in *both* the majority and dissenting opinions in *Loge*, was charged with running a red light. The defendant testified that he tried to stop but that the brakes on his vehicle were broken. The court found strict liability inappropriate:

> The theory behind statutes which impose absolute liability is well explained in Morissette v. United States, 342 U.S. 246, 256. As to some activities, even though a person does not criminally intend the harm caused by his acts, he "usually is in a position to prevent it with no more care than society might reasonably expect and no more exertion than it might reasonably exact from one who assumed his responsibilities." But when there is no negligence, and no intent to do the act which turned out to be criminal, this rationale does not apply.
>
> If the defendant here went through a stop light that he did not see, and was defending on the ground that he did so without any criminal intent, a court could be justified in finding him guilty of a violation of the ordinance involved. When the driver intends to proceed forward, or is negligent in any way, he can be held liable for his acts. However, we have a different situation here where the court found that he was unable to stop because the brakes on his car failed to operate; that he had experienced no prior brake trouble; and

that he had no knowledge that his brakes were defective. A conviction under those facts and circumstances cannot stand.

114 N.W.2d at 191-92. A portion of the second of those two paragraphs is quoted by the majority opinion in *Loge*. Is *Loge* consistent with *Kremer*? If not, which case is rightly decided?

State v. T.R.D.

Supreme Court of Connecticut
286 Conn. 191; 942 A.2d 1000 (2008)

Opinion of VERTEFEUILLE, J.

The defendant, T.R.D., appeals from the judgment of conviction, rendered after a jury trial, of failing to register as a sex offender in violation of General Statutes §54-251[3] and General Statutes §54-257.[4] He was sentenced to three years imprisonment, execution suspended after one year, and five years probation.

On appeal, the defendant claims that . . . the trial court improperly instructed the jury regarding the elements of the crime of which the defendant was ultimately convicted. . . .

The following facts and procedural history are relevant to this appeal. On April 2, 1998, the defendant entered pleas of *nolo contendere* to charges of sexual assault in the first degree in violation of General Statutes §53a-70(a)(2) and risk of injury to a child in violation of General Statutes §53-21(2). The court accepted the defendant's pleas and sentenced him to a total effective term of twelve years imprisonment, execution suspended after five years, followed by ten years of probation.

---

3. General Statutes §54-251(a) provides in relevant part: "Any person who has been convicted . . . of a criminal offense against a victim who is a [child] or a nonviolent sexual offense . . . and is released into the community on or after October 1, 1998, shall . . . register such person's name, identifying factors, criminal history record and residence address with the Commissioner of Public Safety, on such forms and in such locations as the commissioner shall direct, and shall maintain such registration for ten years except that any person . . . who is convicted of a violation of subdivision (2) of subsection (a) of section 53a-70 shall maintain such registration for life. . . . If such person changes such person's address such person shall, within five days, register the new address in writing with the Commissioner of Public Safety. . . . During such period of registration, each registrant shall complete and return forms mailed to such registrant to verify such registrant's residence address. . . ."

4. General Statutes §54-257(c) provides in relevant part: "[T]he Department of Public Safety shall verify the address of each registrant by mailing a non-forwardable verification form to the registrant at the registrant's last reported address. Such form shall require the registrant to sign a statement that the registrant continues to reside at the registrant's last reported address and return the form by mail by a date which is ten days after the date such form was mailed to the registrant. The form shall contain a statement that failure to return the form or providing false information is a violation of section 54-251. . . . Each person required to register under section 54-251 . . . shall have such person's address verified in such manner every ninety days after such person's initial registration date. . . ."

The defendant was released from incarceration on November 15, 2002. Prior to being released from incarceration, the defendant met with the coordinator for sex offender registration at the correctional institution where he was being held, who informed the defendant of his responsibilities under the Connecticut sex offender registration law, commonly referred to as Megan's Law, General Statutes §54-250 et seq. One such responsibility is to return address verification letters, which are sent by the sex offender registry unit (unit) of the department of public safety every ninety days. Prior to his release from incarceration, the defendant signed several forms stating that he understood his responsibilities under the registration law, and further, that he understood that noncompliance with these responsibilities would constitute a crime.

The unit sent the first letter to the defendant in its first round[7] of ninety day address verification letters on February 8, 2003, approximately ninety days after the defendant's release from incarceration. Although the defendant did not return the first letter sent by the unit for address verification purposes, he did return the second letter, which the unit received on February 27, 2003. The defendant was thus in compliance with his registration responsibilities for the first ninety day period. The unit sent the first letter in its next round of address verification letters on May 23, 2003. When the unit did not receive a response from the defendant, it subsequently sent two additional address verification letters. After the unit did not receive a response to any of the three letters it sent in its address verification attempts for the period beginning May 23, 2003, the defendant's status changed to "failure to verify his address" and his address was considered unknown. The defendant was arrested for failure to comply with the registration requirements on February 24, 2004. . . .

The case was tried to a jury, which found the defendant guilty of failing to register as a sex offender in accordance with §§54-251 and 54-257. On December 5, 2005, the trial court sentenced the defendant to three years incarceration, execution suspended after one year, and five years probation. This appeal followed. . . .

. . . Prior to the defendant's release from prison . . . , the defendant met with Scott Tetreault, the coordinator for sex offender registration, at the Brooklyn correctional institution. At that meeting, Tetreault obtained the defendant's post-release address and gave the defendant a number of

---

7. The unit sends non-forwardable letters to individuals on the sex offender registry every ninety days for address verification purposes. For each ninety day period, the unit's practice is to send up to three letters to an individual's address. The second and third letters become necessary only if the individual does not promptly return the first letter sent within the ninety day period. Thus a "round" of letters can include up to three letters sent within any particular ninety day period for purposes of verifying a convicted sex offender's current address.

forms to complete, two of which were entitled "Sex Offender Advisement of Registration Requirement" and "Sex Offender Registry—Registration Form."

The form entitled "Sex Offender Advisement of Registration Requirement" contained a section captioned "Notice To Registrant," which provided as follows:

> "As a person who has been convicted of any crime specified in [§]54-250 . . . or as one who is required to register . . . with the State of Connecticut Sex Offender Registry, you must report in person to the [unit]. Failure to comply with this requirement is a Class D Felony. After completing the initial registration you will further be required to return address verification forms that will be mailed to you at your last known address. These address verification forms must be returned to the Department of Public Safety at P.O. Box 2794, Middletown, CT 06457-9294, by first class mail. You must also notify the Department of Public Safety Sex Offender Registry within five days of changing your address and you must notify the appropriate law enforcement authorities if you move into another state. Failure to comply with any of these requirements will make you subject to arrest for a Class D Felony."

Both the defendant's and Tetreault's signatures appear at the bottom of the form.

The defendant also signed a form captioned "Sex Offender Registry—Registration Form" at the meeting with Tetreault. The bottom of this form contained the following information: "Full registration requires all of the following: completion of this form, a full set of fingerprints and a photograph taken at the time of registration, and a blood sample taken for the purposes of DNA analysis. Failure to complete ALL registration requirements is a Class D felony." Both the defendant's and Tetreault's signatures appear on this form. After the meeting, Tetreault forwarded the aforementioned forms to the unit. The unit received both forms containing the defendant's signature on November 15, 2002, the same day the defendant was released from incarceration.

In accordance with its policy on address verification, the unit sent the first letter in its first round of correspondence on February 8, 2003, approximately ninety days after the defendant was released from incarceration. This letter was not returned. The unit then sent a second letter to the defendant in an effort to verify his address. The second paragraph of this letter provides, with the bold face text included:

> "The . . . [unit] is required to verify your residence address every [ninety] days. This verification of your address will be accomplished via the mail every [ninety] days until you are relieved of your registration requirement. ***You must return this address verification letter within ten (10) days of the postmark.*** The address that appears with your name at the top of this letter is the address of record for you. If you move you must notify the [unit], in writing, within five (5) days of such a change. If the address is incorrect as it appears, make the necessary corrections in the residence address correction space below."

On February 27, 2003, the unit received from the defendant a completed copy of the second letter. In the space on the form following the words "[r]esidence address correction," the defendant wrote the word "same." The defendant's signature appears at the bottom of the form, followed by the date of February 25, 2003, and his telephone number. The defendant's signature appears below a paragraph stating: "My current address is correct as it appears above. I understand that failure to comply with any of the registration requirements, including the address verification and above listed notifications, is a Class 'D' Felony."

The unit sent the first letter in its next round of address verification letters on May 23, 2003. When this letter was not returned by the defendant, the unit subsequently sent two additional letters, on June 13, 2003, and June 24, 2003, respectively. When neither of these letters was returned to the unit, the unit identified the defendant's status as "failure to verify his address," and the address was considered unknown. The defendant was arrested for failure to comply with the registration requirements on February 24, 2004. Three days after his arrest, on February 27, 2004, the unit received a typewritten letter from the defendant, dated February 25, 2004, informing it that his address had remained the same. . . .

. . . [T]he defendant asserts that the trial court improperly failed to include an element of *mens rea* in its instruction regarding §§54-251 and 54-257, and that the defendant was entitled to [have the jury informed] that the state must prove that the defendant had a duty to return the address verification forms and that he actually knew of this duty. The state responds that the trial court's charge on the elements of failure to register as a sex offender was correct . . . because failure to register is a strict liability offense, and because [the defendant's knowledge that] he was obligated to verify his address is not an element of the offense. We agree with the state. . . .

A plain reading of §§54-251 and 54-257 reveals that neither [contains] an element of intent. Although there is generally a presumption that crimes having their origin in the common law contain an element of intent, the registry statutes do not have their origin in the common law and this presumption therefore does not apply. See State v. Swain, 245 Conn. 442, 454 n.16, 718 A.2d 1 (1998).

The absence of a *mens rea* element in a statute does not necessarily mean, however, that the statute [imposes] strict liability. . . . As explained by the Appellate Court in State v. Charles, 78 Conn. App. 125, 826 A.2d 1172 (2003):

> "General intent is the term used to define the requisite *mens rea* for a crime that has no stated *mens rea*; the term refers to whether a defendant intended deliberate, conscious or purposeful action, as opposed to causing a prohibited result through accident, mistake, carelessness, or absent-mindedness. Where a particular crime requires only a showing of general intent, the prosecution need not establish that the accused intended the precise harm or precise result which resulted from his acts."

Id. at 131. In *Charles*, the court considered the defendant's claim that the trial court violated the defendant's due process rights by failing to charge the jury that intent was a necessary element of the crime of violating a protective order. The Appellate Court . . . [found proof of] general intent to be required. . . .

In contrast, strict liability offenses dispense with . . . *mens rea* . . . , meaning that the possession of a "guilty mind" is not essential [to] conviction. . . . [Such statutes do] "not require [. . .] that the defendant know the facts that make his conduct fit the definition of the offense." Id. The United States Supreme Court outlined the reasoning for imposing strict criminal liability for public welfare offenses . . . in Morissette v. United States, 342 U.S. 246, 254-56 (1952):

> "While many of these [regulations on activities that affect public health, safety or welfare] are sanctioned by . . . civil liability, lawmakers, whether wisely or not, have sought to make such regulations more effective by invoking criminal sanctions. . . . This has confronted the courts with a multitude of prosecutions, based on statutes or administrative regulations, for what have aptly been called 'public welfare offenses.' These cases do not fit neatly into any of such accepted classifications of common-law offenses, such as those against the state, the person, property, or public morals. Many of these offenses are not in the nature of positive aggressions or invasions, with which the common law so often dealt, but are in the nature of neglect where the law requires care, or *inaction where it imposes a duty*. . . . [W]hatever the intent of the violator, the injury is the same, and the consequences are injurious or not according to fortuity. Hence, legislation applicable to such offenses, as a matter of policy, does not specify intent as a necessary element. The accused, if he does not will the violation, usually is in a position to prevent it with no more care than society might reasonably expect and no more exertion than it might reasonably exact from one who assumed his responsibilities."

(Emphasis added.)

Given the legislative purpose of the sex offender registry . . . , we conclude that the crime of failing to comply with the sex offender registry requirements is a strict liability offense. The goal of Megan's Law is to "alert the public by identifying potential sexual offender recidivists when necessary for public safety." State v. Pierce, 69 Conn. App. 516, 522, 794 A.2d 1123 (2002). . . . [T]he United States Supreme Court has noted that Connecticut's version of Megan's Law was created in response to the fact that "[s]ex offenders are a serious threat in this [n]ation" and that "[t]he victims of sexual assault are most often juveniles. . . ." Dept. of Public Safety v. Doe, 538 U.S. 1, 4 (2003). The Supreme Court noted that . . . "[w]hen convicted sex offenders reenter society, they are much more likely than any other type of offender to be rearrested for a new rape or sexual assault." Id.

Two well reasoned decisions from Illinois and New York support our conclusion that failing to register is a strict liability offense. In People v. Molnar, 222 Ill. 2d 495, 857 N.E.2d 209 (2006), and People v. Patterson,

185 Misc. 2d 519, 708 N.Y.S.2d 815 (2000), the Illinois Supreme Court and the New York Criminal Court, respectively, interpreted sex offender registry statutes similar to ours and found them to impose strict liability. In *Molnar*, supra, the Illinois Supreme Court reviewed a sex offender registry scheme that requires the state police to send non-forwardable verification letters that the sex offender must complete and return within ten days. The provision stating the consequences of not registering provides as follows: "A sex offender shall register in person annually within one year after his or her last registration. Failure to comply with any provision of the [Sex Offender Registration] Act shall extend the period of registration by ten years beyond the period otherwise required." 222 Ill. 2d at 509, quoting 20 Ill. Admin. Code title 20, §1280.40(a). The Illinois Supreme Court concluded that the offense of violating the state's registration act was a strict liability offense. Crucial to the court's analysis was the notion that "the imposition of strict liability for failing to register was not as harsh as it first appeared, given that [the statute as a whole] required an offender to be given notice of his obligation to register." *Molnar*, supra, at 523. For that reason, the court found that "the concern that a person might be subject to a severe penalty for an offense that he might unknowingly commit is not present. . . ." Id.

In so ruling, the *Molnar* court relied heavily on the reasoning of *Patterson*, supra, 185 Misc. 2d 519, wherein the New York Criminal Court considered, inter alia, whether failure to register as a sex offender under New York's Sex Offender Registration Act was a strict liability crime. Although violation of the statute could result in the revocation of parole and/or a felony conviction upon a second offense, the court reasoned that the state's registration act is "not a traditional criminal statute aimed primarily at punishing wrongdoing" but is instead "in essence a regulatory statute . . . [which] proceeds from a legislative finding that convicted sex offenders exhibit heightened rates of recidivism and that sex offenders therefore present a special danger to the public and, in particular, to vulnerable women and children." . . . Id. at 530.

In light of the legislative purpose of the statute, the New York Criminal Court reasoned that strict liability was appropriate:

> "Viewed in the light of the important public safety concerns that are at the heart of [the Sex Offender Registration Act], the Legislature's decision to impose strict liability for failure to register was altogether appropriate and consistent with precedent. The power of a Legislature to enact a criminal statute imposing strict liability for an essentially regulatory offense involving the public safety, health or welfare has long been recognized. . . . In dealing with such offenses, the urgent public interest in protecting the community's welfare may require[,] in the prohibition or punishment of particular acts[,] . . . that he who shall do them shall do them at his peril and will not be heard to plead in defense good faith or ignorance."

Id. at 530-31.

The policy justifications for imposing strict liability are compelling as well. Like the sex offender registry examined in *Patterson*, our registration requirements are "not intended as a punitive measure.... State v. Waterman, 264 Conn. 484, 489, 825 A.2d 63 (2003)." The imposition of strict liability for failure to register as a sex offender "strikes a careful balance between [the] defendant's due process rights and the community's interest in protecting its most vulnerable citizens from truly terrible crimes." *Patterson*, supra, 185 Misc. 2d at 534. That is, although §54-256 requires that a convicted sex offender be notified of his obligations regarding the sex offender registry, the strict liability nature of the offense ensures that a sex offender will not be able to defeat prosecution under §54-257 "simply by claiming that he did not know about [the relevant registration statute], or that he unintentionally overlooked its requirements, or that he had adopted some privately held interpretation of the statute under which he was not required to register." Id. Thus, we conclude that interpreting our registration statute to be one of strict liability is more appropriate than reading it as requiring general intent, where "accident, mistake, carelessness, or absent-mindedness" could potentially serve as a defense. State v. Charles, supra, 78 Conn. App. at 131. We thus reject the defendant's argument that the jury instructions were improper because they omitted . . . *mens rea*.

The fact that the penalty for violation of §54-257 results in further incarceration for the defendant does not [change that conclusion]. "Neither the United States Supreme Court nor [this court] has held that the magnitude of the penalty determines the constitutionality of strict liability statutes." State v. Nanowski, 56 Conn. App. 649, 656-57, 746 A.2d 177 (2000) (rejecting defendant's argument that General Statutes §31-71a et seq. regarding payment of wages was unconstitutional as strict liability offense where amendments to statute increased penalty for conviction from misdemeanor to felony); see State v. Kirk R., 271 Conn. 499, 515 n.20, 857 A.2d 908 (2004) (noting that crime of sexual assault in first degree [under] §53a-70 is strict liability crime, which does not require state to prove actor's knowledge or intent as element of offense).

Because we conclude that the statutes in question impose strict liability, it follows that the trial court was not required to include a *mens rea* element in its jury charge. . . .

The defendant also claims that the trial court improperly failed to instruct the jury that the state must prove that the defendant [knew he] had a duty to return the address verification forms [in order to convict under] §54-257.[22] [Because] §54-257 is a strict liability statute, we conclude that

---

22. The defendant cites Lambert v. California, 355 U.S. 225 (1957), in support of this claim. We, however, find *Lambert* to be inapposite. In *Lambert*, the defendant was arrested under a Los Angeles general municipal ordinance requiring registration of convicted felons if they remained in the city for more than five days. Id. at 226. When the defendant was arrested on "suspicion of another offense," the police discovered that the defendant had been a resident of Los Angeles for more than seven years and, within that period, had been convicted of a felony offense, but had not registered with the chief of police, as required under the municipal code. Id. Consequently, the defendant was convicted of failing to register in violation of the

actual notice to the defendant is not an element of §54-257, and that the trial court's instructions were not constitutionally deficient. . . .

[Justice SCHALLER's dissenting opinion, joined by Justice NORCOTT, is omitted.]

Notes and Questions

1. The 1994 murder of 10-year-old Megan Kanka by a convicted sex offender led to a wave of statutes known as "Megan's Laws." Such laws—the Connecticut statute at issue in *T.R.D.* is one of them—require that sex offenders or child abusers register with the government so that their identities and whereabouts are known. As *T.R.D.* indicates, strict liability is usually the governing standard when defendants are charged with violating Megan's Laws.

2. *T.R.D.* involves punishment that is much more severe than the sentence Loge received. Is strict liability ever appropriate in crimes punished with such long terms of incarceration? On the other hand, given the forms the defendant signed before his release, was T.R.D.'s liability really "strict"?

For that matter, think about *Loge* once again. What, exactly, was Loge punished for? Wasn't it because, when he borrowed his father's pickup truck and drove it, he acquired the responsibility to check and make sure that no open containers of alcohol were in the vehicle? And isn't that the whole point of the open container law? If so, then was the liability in *Loge* really "strict"?

3. If T.R.D. and Loge weren't actually punished in the complete absence of fault or moral culpability, but instead because they culpably failed to live up to their responsibilities under the law (meaning that they actually exhibited, at a minimum, some form of negligence), then what's the big deal about strict liability? (Notice, by the way, that the one "strict liability" defendant we've encountered who really *did* seem to lack all moral culpability, Kremer, eventually won an acquittal. See Note 4, supra, at page 193.) Why would legislatures choose to enact such laws? What purpose do they actually serve?

4. According to the court, T.R.D. is subject to strict liability because the law he violated defines a "public welfare offense"; such offenses "are not in the nature of positive aggressions or invasions, with which the common law so often dealt, but are in the nature of neglect where the law requires care, or inaction where it imposes a duty." That language, borrowed from Justice Robert Jackson in Morissette v. United States, 342 U.S. 246, 255 (1952) (see

---

municipal ordinance. Id. at 227. The defendant appealed her conviction to the United States Supreme Court, claiming that the municipal ordinance, as applied, denied her due process of law. The Supreme Court held that the defendant's conviction violated the due process provisions of the fourteenth amendment because her conduct in failing to register was "wholly passive" and because "circumstances which might move one to inquire as to the necessity of registration [were] completely lacking." Id. at 228-29. The court ruled that due process requires "actual knowledge of the duty to register or proof of the probability of such knowledge and subsequent failure to comply. . . ." Id. at 229. Unlike the defendant in *Lambert*, the defendant in the present case had ample notice of his registration requirements, as we have discussed previously.

page 252, infra), suggests that public welfare offenses are more like torts than crimes. Why, then, should they be punished like crimes, with prison terms—and not like torts, with damages?

5. In State v. Kirk R., 857 A.2d 908 (Conn. 2004), the court held that no *mens rea* need be proved in order to establish liability for statutory rape, defined as sex with a minor under the age of 13; under Connecticut law, the perpetrator must also be at least two years older than the victim. State v. Dombroski, 176 N.W. 985, 985-86 (Minn. 1920), applied strict liability to the crime of sex with a mentally incompetent adult. (*Kirk R.* is cited in *T.R.D.*; *Dombroski* is cited and discussed in *Loge*.) Were both of these cases rightly decided? Why should strict liability apply to sex with preteens and with mentally disabled partners, but not to other forms of sexual assault? We will return to this subject later, in Chapter 9.

B. THE MODEL PENAL CODE CULPABILITY STRUCTURE

Model Penal Code §2.02—General Requirements of Culpability

(1) Minimum Requirements of Culpability. Except as provided in Section 2.05, a person is not guilty of an offense unless he acted purposely, knowingly, recklessly or negligently, as the law may require, with respect to each material element of the offense.

(2) Kinds of Culpability Defined.

(a) Purposely. A person acts purposely with respect to a material element of an offense when:

(i) if the element involves the nature of his conduct or a result thereof, it is his conscious object to engage in conduct of that nature or to cause such a result; and

(ii) if the element involves the attendant circumstances, he is aware of the existence of such circumstances or he believes or hopes that they exist.

(b) Knowingly. A person acts knowingly with respect to a material element of an offense when:

(i) if the element involves the nature of his conduct or the attendant circumstances, he is aware that his conduct is of that nature or that such circumstances exist; and

(ii) if the element involves a result of his conduct, he is aware that it is practically certain that his conduct will cause such a result.

(c) Recklessly. A person acts recklessly with respect to a material element of an offense when he consciously disregards a substantial and unjustifiable risk that the material element exists or will result from his conduct. The risk must be of such a nature and degree that, considering the nature and purpose of the actor's conduct and the circumstances known to him, its disregard involves a gross deviation from the standard of conduct that a law-abiding person would observe in the actor's situation.

(d) Negligently. A person acts negligently with respect to a material element of an offense when he should be aware of a substantial and unjustifiable risk that the material element exists or will result from his conduct. The risk must be of such a nature and degree that the actor's failure to perceive it, considering the nature and purpose of his conduct and the circumstances known to him, involves a gross deviation from the standard of care that a reasonable person would observe in the actor's situation.

(3) Culpability Required Unless Otherwise Provided. When the culpability sufficient to establish a material element of an offense is not prescribed by law, such element is established if a persona acts purposely, knowingly or recklessly with respect thereto.

(4) Prescribed Culpability Requirement Applies to All Material Elements. When the law defining an offense prescribes the kind of culpability that is sufficient for the commission of an offense, without distinguishing among the material elements thereof, such provision shall apply to all the material elements of the offense, unless a contrary purpose plainly appears.

(5) Substitutes for Negligence, Recklessness and Knowledge. When the law provides that negligence suffices to establish an element of an offense, such element also is established if a person acts purposely, knowingly or recklessly. When recklessness suffices to establish an element, such element also is established if a person acts purposely or knowingly. When acting knowingly suffices to establish an element, such element also is established if a person acts purposely.

(6) Requirement of Purpose Satisfied If Purpose Is Conditional. When a particular purpose is an element of an offense, the element is established although such purpose is conditional, unless the condition negatives the harm or evil sought to be prevented by the law defining the offense.

(7) Requirement of Knowledge Satisfied by Knowledge of High Probability. When knowledge of the existence of a particular fact is an element of an offense, such knowledge is established if a person is aware of a high probability of its existence, unless he actually believes that it does not exist.

(8) Requirement of Willfulness Satisfied by Acting Knowingly. A requirement that an offense be committed willfully is satisfied if a person acts knowingly with respect to the material elements of the offense, unless a purpose to impose further requirements appears.

(9) Culpability as to Illegality of Conduct. Neither knowledge nor recklessness or negligence as to whether conduct constitutes an offense or as to the existence, meaning or application of the law determining the elements of an offense is an element of such offense, unless the definition of the offense or the Code so provides.

(10) Culpability as Determinant of Grade of Offense. When the grade or degree of an offense depends on whether the offense is committed purposely, knowingly, recklessly or negligently, its grade or degree shall be the lowest for which the determinative kind of culpability is established with respect to any material element of the offense.

Notes on Criminal Intent and the Model Penal Code

1. As its name suggests, the Model Penal Code is a model criminal code designed to be used by state governments. The MPC was written over many years—its initial drafts starting coming out in the early 1950s; it was finished in 1962. Its authors continued to make minor revisions to the text; the current version was published in 1985. Some 34 states revised their criminal codes during the 1960s, 1970s, and 1980s; in 22 of those states, legislators used the MPC as their model. But only loosely—legislatures in those 22 states adopted a few MPC provisions unchanged, adopted some others after amending them, and ignored many others. Appellate courts in all but a few of those states continue today to use the common law's *mens rea* terminology: Courts routinely speak of specific and general intent, and mistakes of fact and law, even though the MPC hoped to render those terms obsolete. In short, the MPC never became, as its drafters had hoped, the source of a general American criminal law that would govern in most jurisdictions. Instead, the MPC is the source of scattered legal rules that some, but not most, states have adopted.

2. But we are getting ahead of the story. The MPC's official author was the American Law Institute. The ALI is an organization devoted to law reform; its members were and are drawn from among elite judges, law professors, and practicing lawyers—an odd group to take a stab at writing a criminal code. They did so primarily because of one person: Columbia Law Professor Herbert Wechsler, the MPC's chief drafter and intellectual mastermind, a longtime critic of state criminal law who sought to rationalize the field. "Rationalize" is the right word here: Wechsler's chief complaint about American criminal law was its chaotic, irrational character. According to Wechsler, the common law's approach to criminal intent was to throw meaningless labels at the problem. Words and phrases like "general intent," "specific intent," "malice," and "evil mind" were, Wechsler believed, at once empty and confusing. As for the law of criminal conduct, Wechsler and his colleagues believed that state criminal codes were filled with overlapping, poorly defined offenses that covered too much ground. In drafting the MPC, they sought to offer an example of a code that defined criminal culpability clearly and effectively, and that defined criminal conduct more narrowly than is customary.

3. Section 2.02 is the MPC's heart. That provision does away with the common law's two main criminal intent standards—general and specific intent—as well as the mass of subsidiary intent terms traditionally used in criminal cases. The MPC replaces all those doctrinal standards with four, and only four, intent standards: purpose, knowledge, recklessness, and negligence.

The definitions of purpose and knowledge are straightforward. Purpose means "conscious object"; one acts purposely with respect to a given element of a crime if one is trying to do what that element describes.* Knowledge means awareness of a "practical certainty" of the relevant proposition.** Importantly, a fact *need not be true* for a defendant to "know" it in the Code's sense of that word—as long as the defendant *believes* the relevant proposition is practically certain, he "knows" it, even if the proposition is actually false. Otherwise, the Code's definitions of purpose and knowledge generally conform to the popular understanding of those words.***

The definition of recklessness combines two very different ideas. First, the defendant must be aware of ("consciously disregard[. . .]") the risks his conduct poses. The second idea concerns not the defendant's conscious thoughts but the moral character of his conduct in light of the relevant risks. The risks in question must have been "substantial"; ignoring them must have been both "unjustifiable" and—crucially—"a gross deviation from the standard of care that a reasonable person would observe in the actor's situation." The "gross deviation" language roughly tracks conventional definitions of criminal negligence. (Recall footnote 3 in *Sargent,* supra at page 102.) Section 2.02's definition of negligence adopts the second half of the meaning of recklessness, while leaving off the first. A negligent defendant need not be consciously aware of the relevant risk, but his conduct still must amount to a "gross deviation" from any reasonable standard of care. MPC negligence, in other words, equates to the common law's "criminal" or "gross" negligence.

---

*In its "General Definitions" section, the Code also defines "intentionally" or "with intent" to mean "purposely." See MPC 1.13(12).

**This definition was drafted to include cases in which a defendant is aware of facts showing that a circumstance element of a crime is "practically certain" to be true, but chooses to remain ignorant of the existence of the element. Being "willfully blind" to the existence of a circumstance element is treated by the Code as having "knowledge" of that element.

***Notice, however, that in section 2.02(8) the Code defines "willfulness" as the equivalent of "knowledge"; this is somewhat of a departure from the common law approach, which usually treats "willfully" as a synonym for "intentionally" or "purposely." See the definition at page 203.

4. Aside from these four terms, the other key innovation in section 2.02 was the use of "element analysis"—an unfamiliar phrase before the MPC was written but a common one in criminal law scholarship today. As several of the cases earlier in this chapter show, state courts traditionally applied a given intent standard to each *crime*. The MPC, by contrast, applies a given intent standard to each *element* in a given crime.**** If a theft statute forbids taking the property of another, and if the criminal code in which the statute appears uses some form of MPC §2.02, the question is not what *mens rea* standard applies to theft in general. Rather, there are at least three separate questions: What *mens rea* term attaches to the element, "takes"? What term attaches to "property"? And what term applies to "of another"?

5. Three key default rules in section 2.02 help to answer questions of that sort. Section 2.02(3) holds that, whenever a criminal statute contains *no* culpability or *mens rea* term whatsoever that could be applied to a particular element of the crime, then the governing standard for that particular element is recklessness. That rule is very important: The Code's drafters hoped and expected that the most common criminal intent standard—that is, the new MPC standard that would take the place of general intent—would be recklessness. Section 2.02(4) states a simple drafting convention: Whenever a criminal statute contains but a single *mens rea* term, that term presumptively applies to *all* elements of the crime, "unless a contrary purpose plainly appears" (i.e., unless there is plain legislative intent to the contrary). Since most Code provisions either contain no culpability term or only one such term, sections 2.02(3) and 2.02(4) resolve most cases. Last but definitely not least, section 2.02(5) states that the government may always prove the existence of a "lower" *mens rea* term by proving the existence of a "higher" one.

Focus on the last of these default rules, and think of the four possible *mens rea* standards of section 2.02 as rungs on a ladder, with negligence at the bottom and purpose at the top. If a statute requires the government to climb to the second rung (by proving recklessness), section 2.02(5) holds that the government may, if it wishes, climb to the third (knowledge) or fourth (purpose) rungs instead. Negligence may be proved by proving it directly; or the government may choose to prove recklessness, knowledge, or purpose. Recklessness may be proved directly or by proving knowledge or purpose. If the law requires proof of knowledge, proof of either knowledge or purpose will suffice.

**** To be a bit more precise, the MPC requires *mens rea* only with respect to "material" elements of crimes—the kinds of elements with which we have mostly been dealing, and that impact the defendant's moral blameworthiness or "wrongfulness." Non-material elements (for which *mens rea* is not necessarily required) would include such technical matters as jurisdiction, venue, and the relevant statute of limitations. See MPC §1.13(10).

Note that, in section 2.02(1), the Model Penal Code rejects the idea of "strict liability" for any material element of any crime; in MPC-land, *all* material elements require a corresponding culpable mental state. The MPC makes a separate provision for "strict liability" that is strictly limited to "violations"—low-level offenses that cannot be called "crimes," cannot trigger legal disabilities that are based on criminal convictions, and cannot carry any risk of incarceration. See MPC §2.05(1), §1.04(5).

6. With these default rules in mind, consider two cases with a single fact pattern: The defendant takes a flat-screen television worth $1,000 from an apartment that several of his friends share. The defendant does not know who owns the TV, but he knows that the owner is one of the three roommates who live in that apartment. In both cases the question is whether, on the facts just described, the government can prove that the defendant has the *mens rea* required for the circumstance element that the TV is "of another." Here are the two hypothetical theft statutes; you should assume that your jurisdiction has adopted MPC section 2.02:

> "Whoever takes the property of another without the owner's consent shall be liable for theft in the second degree if the value of the property taken exceeds $500."

> "Whoever purposely takes the property of another without the owner's consent shall be liable for theft in the second degree if the value of the property taken exceeds $500."

Take the two cases in turn, and begin by asking what *mens rea* term applies to the "of another" element under the relevant statute. In the first case, the answer is recklessness. No *mens rea* is specified, so the default rule of section 2.02(3) applies; recklessness is the *mens rea* for all the elements of the crime. By the terms of the hypothetical, the defendant knows that the TV is owned by another person: Nothing in the statute suggests that the defendant must know specifically *which* other person owns it. So the case boils down to the simple question whether proof of knowledge satisfies the statutory recklessness standard. Section 2.02(5) says it does—knowledge is a higher *mens rea* standard than recklessness, and the Code allows the government to meet a lower *mens rea* standard by proving a higher one. The defendant has the required *mens rea* for "of another."

The same is true in the second case, but for different reasons. The second statute includes one *mens rea* term—"purposely"—modifying one conduct element: "takes." Since no other *mens rea* term appears in the statute, MPC section 2.02(4) holds that the purpose standard presumptively applies to all of the elements of the crime. The *mens rea* for the "of another" element thus appears to be purpose. But that conclusion doesn't seem quite right. It would seem strange to ask whether a defendant had a "purpose" with respect to a factual circumstance like the legal ownership of stolen property. Ownership of the property isn't something the defendant either *does* or *causes*; it isn't something that the defendant has any power to alter. Rather, it's a verifiable, non-legal fact external to the defendant's conduct. The TV is either the property "of another," or it's not. People do not have "purposes" with respect to such facts. The MPC's definition of "purposely" implicitly recognizes this problem; the MPC definition says that, when applied to circumstance elements—meaning, those factual elements of the crime external to the defendant's conduct or the results of that conduct—"purpose" means either that the defendant is aware of that fact, or he believes or hopes that it is so. So the question in the second case is whether the defendant was aware (or believed or hoped) that the television belonged to someone else. He was (and he did). The *mens rea* for "of another" is once again satisfied.

7. Now suppose the defendant breaks into his friends' apartment one evening, takes the television, and leaves. He is charged with violating one of the hypothetical theft statutes quoted above, and also with violating a separate burglary statute that covers "anyone who enters a closed dwelling at night, with purpose to commit a crime therein." What is the *mens rea* for "at night"? The temptation is to say knowledge: The statute uses only one *mens rea* term ("purpose"), so section 2.02(4) would seem to require that purpose be the required *mens rea* for all elements of the crime. And we have already established that purpose, as applied to a factual circumstance element like the "at night" element, means either awareness (or belief or hope) — in other words, knowledge.

While that answer is textually plausible, the MPC takes a different tack. The phrase "with purpose to commit a crime therein" is not treated like a *mens rea* term attached to a particular element of the crime, since the phrase includes no such element. Instead, the phrase describes a *collateral mental state*—a mental state that stands apart from the definition of the rest of the crime. This kind of collateral mental state is often called the defendant's *motive*; he must satisfy the specified motive in order to be found guilty of the crime, but he does not actually have to fulfill his intended purpose (i.e., he does not actually have to "commit a crime therein").

For purposes of applying sections 2.02(3) and 2.02(4), statutory interpreters are supposed to pretend that the collateral mental state, or motive, does not appear in the statute. Without considering the "with purpose" phrase, there is no *mens rea* term in the statute, so the governing standard for "at night" — along with the other elements "enters," "closed," and "dwelling" — is the default standard of recklessness. If the government proves that the defendant's behavior was at least reckless with respect to those elements, and also proves that the defendant acted "with purpose to commit a crime therein," he is guilty.

The MPC doctrine with respect to collateral mental states is confusing in principle, but it is not that hard to apply. As the MPC is written, a collateral mental state is nearly always a phrase separated by commas (or semi-colons, or other grammatical breaks in the statute) that describes a mental state *without describing any other facts.* Compare these two hypothetical statutes:

> "Anyone who purposely strikes another person and thereby causes serious bodily injury is guilty of a felony."

> "Anyone who strikes another person, with the purpose of causing serious bodily injury, is guilty of a felony."

Under the first statute, the presumptive *mens rea* for each element — "strikes," "another person," "without that person's consent," "thereby causes," and "serious bodily injury" — is purpose. The government must prove *both* that the victim suffered the result of "serious bodily injury," *and* that the defendant intended to cause that result, in order to convict. Under the second statute, the *mens rea* for each of the conduct and circumstance elements is recklessness. There is no result element in the second statute: The government need *not* prove that the victim suffered "serious bodily injury," or indeed any injury at all—only that the defendant acted "*with the purpose* of causing" such injury.

To make the point more concrete, imagine a defendant who tries to attack his victim with a golf club. (In Chapter 10, you will read a case with these facts: State v. Robinson, 934 P.2d 38 (Kan. 1997), excerpted infra at page 772.) The defendant swings the club at the victim once, but because the victim moves quickly, the club barely touches him and causes no injury. After that one blow, the defendant is arrested. Under the first statute, that defendant is innocent, since he actually caused no "serious bodily injury." Under the second statute he is guilty—he was *trying* to cause serious harm but failed, and the second statute is designed to capture such a case.

8. If all that sounds complicated, it is. But it is complicated in different ways than common-law *mens rea* analysis. The common law offers a mix of complexity and uncertainty. The meaning of specific intent and (especially) general intent, the interpretation of vague statutory terms like "willfully" and "maliciously," the ins and outs of mistake doctrine—these things are certainly confusing, but they are also flexible, open to multiple understandings. So the lawyers and judges who must apply them argue not only about formal legal texts, but also about the character of a fair justice system and the goals of criminal punishment. Traditionally, the law of criminal intent has been the legal space where such arguments do battle.

In doing away with those terms, the Model Penal Code sought above all to make *mens rea* doctrine clear and certain. So the complexity of MPC *mens rea* analysis is the complexity of a high-school algebra class: Crunch through the appropriate formulas in the proper order and you get the right answers; skip a step, or plug in the wrong variable, and you don't. Bottom lines are not wise or foolish but correct or incorrect, and they turn not on arguments about justice or fairness but on purely formal, mechanical criteria. In the world of the Model Penal Code, policy argument is largely banished from legal debate—because the relevant policies are already specified in the Code, not supplied later by judges deciding what *mens rea* standards to apply to a particular crime or case, as in the common-law cases excerpted earlier in this chapter.

9. In other words, the Model Penal Code sought to make criminal law more statutory. Traditionally, the definition of criminal conduct has been primarily a matter of interpreting the language in criminal statutes, but criminal intent has been defined through common-law argument and judicial decisions. In those jurisdictions that adopted some form of MPC §2.02, the law of criminal intent is no different than the law of criminal conduct—legislators, not judges, define the relevant terms. Indeed, legislators' power over intent might be even greater than their power over conduct, since section 2.02 defines the relevant intent terms so precisely; most of the Code's conduct terms do not have similarly elaborate statutory definitions. To put the point more simply, the Model Penal Code represents an effort to shift power over criminal law from judges to legislators.

For an example of the Model Penal Code in action, consider the following case:

State v. Ducker

Court of Criminal Appeals of Tennessee
1999 WL 160981; 1999 Tenn. Crim. App. LEXIS 288
(Mar. 25, 1999)

Honorable DAVID G. HAYES:

The appellant, Jennie Bain Ducker, was indicted in June, 1995, on two counts of first degree murder resulting from the aggravated child abuse* of her two children, ages 13 months and 23 months. A Warren County jury, on October 3, 1995, found the appellant guilty of two counts of the lesser charged offense of aggravated child abuse. Concurrent sentences of eighteen years were imposed for each of the class A felony convictions. In this appeal as of right, the appellant [argues, *inter alia*, that] the evidence is insufficient to support convictions for two counts of aggravated child abuse because the trial court failed to properly instruct the jury as to the definition of "knowingly." . . .

After a review of the record and the applicable law, we affirm the judgment of the trial court.

[The evidence showed that appellant, who was married but estranged from her husband, spent much of the evening of June 5, 1995, with her two infant children, Dustin and Devin, at the home of a boyfriend, Jimmy Turner. In the early morning hours, she left with the children to travel to a nearby Holiday Inn, where she entered the hotel room of another boyfriend, Micah Majors. Also present were three of Majors' male friends. Appellant left her children in her car, strapped in their car seats with the windows closed and the doors locked, while she hung out and drank with the four men in the hotel room.

---

* [The relevant Tennessee statutes, at the relevant time, provided as follows:

Tenn. Code Ann. §39-15-401. Child Abuse and neglect.—(a) Any person who knowingly other than by accidental means, treats a child under eighteen (18) years of age in such a manner as to inflict injury or neglects such a child so as to adversely affect the child's health and welfare is guilty of a Class A misdemeanor provided, that if the abused child is six (6) years of age or less, the penalty is a class D felony.

Tenn. Code Ann. §39-15-402. Aggravated child abuse.—(a) A person is guilty of the offense of aggravated child abuse who commits the offense of child abuse as defined in §39-15-401 and; (1) The act of abuse results in serious bodily injury to the child.

—EDS.]

She never mentioned her children. At around 5 A.M., Majors' three friends left; appellant followed them out to the parking lot, but immediately returned to Majors' hotel room without checking on the children in her car. Appellant then confronted Majors about their relationship, but Majors fell asleep. Majors awoke around 12 noon or 1 P.M. the next day, and found appellant still in the hotel room; she then said that she had to leave. Shortly thereafter, appellant showed up at a local hospital emergency room, frantically seeking help for her two "dehydrated" children. The children, however, were already dead. A two-thirds-empty bottle of whiskey was found under appellant's car seat. Tests administered at 2 P.M. showed that appellant had a blood-alcohol level of .06; a doctor testified that, assuming she had stopped drinking at 5 A.M., her blood-alcohol level at that time was likely almost .20. The same doctor opined that the children died of hyperthermia sometime between 6 A.M. and 12 noon; he testified that, as of 12 noon, the inside of appellant's car would have reached about 120 degrees. Defense witnesses established that appellant suffered from bi-polar disorder as well as a sleep disorder. Appellant testified that she "did not see any danger in leaving her thirteen-month-old and twenty-three-month old sons in her locked car for over nine hours." A prosecution witness testified that she frequently babysat for appellant's children, and that on one occasion in March 1995, appellant was gone for more than 24 hours without ever checking on her children; upon her return, appellant explained that she had been out with friends and needed to "sober up" before picking up the children.]

Based upon this evidence, the jury returned guilty verdicts as to two counts of aggravated child abuse. . . .

The appellant . . . contends that the evidence is insufficient to support her convictions for aggravated child abuse because the State failed to prove "knowing conduct" beyond a reasonable doubt, *i.e.*, that she "was actually aware that her conduct was reasonably certain to cause the resulting injury to her children." Specifically, the appellant challenges the trial court's instructions to the jury as they relate to the requisite mental state of "knowing" as the definition of this term applies to the offense of aggravated child abuse.[8] She argues that the erroneous charge altered the State's burden of proving the elements of the offense beyond a reasonable doubt.

We begin our analysis of the appellant's issue by first noting that the implications of this issue extend beyond the boundaries of this case. The appellant's challenge assails the method by which juries are currently instructed as to the requisite mental state of the charged offense. With this in mind, we write not with the purpose of reaching a desired result but, rather, of effecting the intent of our legislature as expressed in its enactment of our criminal code.

---

8. We note that the appellant's sufficiency argument also encompasses her challenge to the trial court's instruction on the definition of "knowingly." As one issue cannot be addressed without logical reference to the other, both will be considered in our analysis of the sufficiency of the evidence.

A. THEORIES OF CULPABLE MENTAL STATES

Central to the concept of criminal liability is that, before there can be a crime, there must be an act, or *actus reus*, which must be accompanied by a criminal mind, or *mens rea*. The early concept of *mens rea* meant little more than a "general notion of blameworthiness," or an "evil meaning mind." See 21 AM. JUR. 2d *Criminal Law* §129 (1981). Over time, this general concept shifted from this vague notion of wickedness to a more definite requirement of a specific state of mind to do that which is prohibited by the criminal law. Thus, no longer could the requirement of "wickedness" suffice. Rather, a different state of mind was required for each crime. This development in the common law culminated in the creation of eighty or so culpability terms. See generally Paul H. Robinson, *Element Analysis in Defining Criminal Liability: The Model Penal Code and Beyond*, 35 Stan. L. Rev. 681, 691 (1983). Even with a specific mental state existing for each offense, under this "offense analysis," of culpability, it was soon recognized that each specific mental state was multifaceted. Id. In a traditional "offense analysis" offenses were referred to simply in terms of one encompassing mental state for the offense, *i.e.*, an intentional offense, a knowing offense or a reckless offense. Prior to the enactment of our 1989 code, this state employed "offense analysis." However, where different culpability requirements are appropriate for different elements, offense analysis fosters definitions that obscure the requisite mental state. Id. As in the case of the offense of possession of a controlled substance with the intent to sell, Tenn. Code Ann. §39-17-417(4) (1997), proof of different mental states are required for the respective elements of (1) the knowing possession of a controlled substance and (2) the intent to sell the same.

The plethora of *mentes reae* originating from the common law created much confusion and ambiguity. Thus, . . . the drafters of the Model Penal Code sought to eliminate this confusion and narrowed the multitude of existing culpability terms to four: purpose, knowledge, recklessness, and negligence. See MODEL PENAL CODE §2.02 (1985); see also Tenn. Code Ann. §39-11-301(a)(1) (1991) (delineating the levels of culpability and providing that "a person commits an offense who acts intentionally, knowingly, recklessly, or with criminal negligence"). In furtherance of this

---

11. [R]elevant portions of the Tennessee Code provide:

Tenn. Code Ann. §39-11-201 — (a) No person may be convicted of an offense unless each of the following is proven beyond a reasonable doubt:
(1) The conduct, circumstances surrounding the conduct, or a result of the conduct described in the definition of the offense;
(2) The culpable mental state required.
Tenn. Code Ann. §39-11-301 — (a)(1) A person commits an offense who acts intentionally, knowingly, recklessly or with criminal negligence, as the definition of the offense requires, with respect to each element of the offense. . . .
Tenn. Code Ann. §39-11-302 — . . . (b) "Knowing" refers to a person who acts knowingly with respect to the conduct or to circumstances surrounding the conduct when the person is aware of the nature of the conduct or that the circumstances exist. A person acts knowingly with respect to a result of the person's conduct when the person is aware that the conduct is reasonably certain to cause the result. . . .

concept, the Model Penal Code and, subsequently the Tennessee Criminal Code,[10] provide that, with the exception of strict liability offenses, some mental culpability "must be faced separately with respect to each material element of the crime," otherwise, no valid conviction may be obtained.[11] COMMENTS, MODEL PENAL CODE §2.02; Tenn. Code Ann. §39-11-301(a)(1). Moreover, the Model Penal Code and the Tennessee Criminal Code both require that one of four levels of culpability must be proven with respect to each "material element" of the offense. . . .

The definition of each culpability term with respect to each [element] of an offense reflects a fundamental and critical principle of the Model Penal Code's culpability scheme, the application of an "element analysis" of culpability requirements, *i.e.*, different degrees of culpability may be required with respect to different elements of the same offense. See Robinson, *Element Analysis in Defining Criminal Liability: The Model Penal Code and Beyond*, 35 Stan. L. Rev. at 699. Judicial construction or interpretation is not necessary to determine whether our legislature intended to employ "element analysis" within our criminal code. Rather, the legislature's enactment of Tenn. Code Ann. §39-11-301(a)-(b), requiring proof of a culpable mental state "with respect to each element of the offense," expressly provides for the application of element analysis. We acknowledge that our conclusion is in accord with the decisions reached by other Model Penal Code states . . . which have likewise incorporated the Code's innovation of element analysis into their statutory schemes. Accordingly, we proceed utilizing an element analysis approach.[14]

B. ELEMENT ANALYSIS

As stated previously, the Model Penal Code recognizes that each culpability term is defined in relation to . . . (1) nature of the conduct; (2) the circumstances at the time; and (3) the result of the conduct. The first element, conduct, involves the nature of the proscribed act or the manner in which the defendant acts, *e.g.*, the physical act of committing an assault, or the physical restraint of another person (kidnapping). See Feinberg, *Toward a New Approach to Proving Culpability: Mens Rea and the Proposed Federal Criminal Code*, 18 Am. Crim. L. Rev. 123, 128 (1980). The second element, circumstances surrounding the conduct, refers to a situation which relates to the actor's culpability, *e.g.*, lack of victim's consent or stolen status of property. The result of the defendant's conduct constitutes the final element, in other

---

10. On November 1, 1989, Tennessee enacted a new criminal code which was in large part an adoption of the American Law Institute's Model Penal Code. . . .

14. We acknowledge that, although supposedly a simplified approach to understanding culpability, element analysis has produced similar confusion and ambiguity as its counterpart, offense analysis. Legal scholars recognize that to rectify such problems state legislators must initiate necessary revisions to current criminal codes to express each element as a separate word to negate confusion as to which conduct element the element references. Until such a time, however, the courts are duty bound to separate the elements by interpretation.

words, the accused's conduct must at least be a physical cause of the harmful result, *e.g.*, causing the death of another.

Many crimes are made up of not only . . . an act or omission, but also some specific result of that act or omission, or some prescribed attendant circumstances, or perhaps both result and circumstances. See WAYNE R. LaFAVE & AUSTIN W. SCOTT JR., SUBSTANTIVE CRIMINAL LAW §3.4(d) (1986). In other words, an offense may contain one or more of these . . . elements which, alone or in combination with the others, form the overall behavior which the Legislature has intended to criminalize, and it is those essential . . . elements to which a culpable mental state must apply. Correspondingly, each culpability term is defined with respect to . . . conduct, circumstances, and result. MODEL PENAL CODE §2.02. See also Tenn. Code Ann. §39-11-302. For example, where a specific act is criminalized because of its very nature, a culpable mental state must apply to committing the act itself, *i.e.*, awareness of conduct. On the other hand, unspecified conduct which is criminalized because of the result requires culpability as to that result, *i.e.*, result of conduct. Finally, where otherwise innocent behavior is criminalized due to the circumstances under which it occurs, a culpable mental state is required as to those surrounding circumstances, *i.e.*, awareness of circumstances. In other words, the analysis of the applicable *mens rea* varies according to the . . . elements of the offense.

In the present offense, the applicable *mens rea* is "knowingly." Tenn. Code Ann. §39-11-302(b) defines "knowing" as:

> [A] person who acts knowingly with respect to the conduct or to circumstances surrounding the conduct when the person is aware of the nature of the conduct or that the circumstances exist. A person acts knowingly with respect to a result of the person's conduct when the person is aware that the conduct is reasonably certain to cause the result.

When a criminal statute requires a *mens rea* of knowingly, it may speak to conduct, or to circumstances, or to result, or to any combination thereof, but not necessarily to all three. WAYNE R. LaFAVE & AUSTIN W. SCOTT JR., SUBSTANTIVE CRIMINAL LAW §3.4(d). In essence, three theories of "knowingly" exist, *i.e.*, (1) conduct; (2) circumstances; and (3) result of conduct, to correspond to the . . . elements of a criminal offense. See Tenn. Code Ann. §39-11-302. . . . [T]here may be different *mens rea* requirements as to the different [elements] that constitute the crime, even if the required culpability is the same, *e.g.* "knowingly."

Because the applicable definition of "knowing" is element specific, a blanket instruction as to each theory, generally, will invite error. In other words, the court cannot instruct the jury that it could employ either (1) conduct; or (2) circumstances; or (3) result of conduct. To do so would effectively alter the State's burden of proving each element of the offense beyond a reasonable doubt. See State v. Lambert, 280 Mont. 231, 929 P.2d 846, 850 (Mont. 1996). For example, the offense of second degree murder is a result of conduct offense, that is, the intent of the legislature is to punish a person for the killing of another. The trial court may only instruct the jury as to the result of conduct theory of knowingly. If the court instructed the jury as to "awareness of conduct" or "awareness of circumstances," the jury could find a defendant guilty on less proof than that needed to show that the defendant engaged in conduct with knowledge that his conduct is reasonably certain to cause the result.

The dangers of a full instruction of the applicable *mens rea* diminishing the State's burden was illustrated in Alvarado v. State, 704 S.W.2d 36 (Tex. Crim. App. 1994), the same case that the appellant contends that this court is bound to follow, *infra*. In *Alvarado*, the defendant was charged with injury to her child by placing the child in a bathtub of scalding water. At trial, she defended on the ground that she did not know that the water was hot enough to cause burning, even though she admitted that she was angry at her child for resisting his bath and refusing to disrobe, and placed him, fully clothed, into the water, without first testing it. Id. at 39. The trial court provided a general instruction as to the applicable culpability requirement and refused to instruct on the result of the conduct definition. The appellate court reversed the defendant's conviction finding that the court's charge permitted the jury to convict the defendant if they found that she knowingly placed the child in "a tub of hot water" without requiring a finding that she intended or knew serious bodily injury would result. Id. at 39-40. . . .

We agree with the appellant that to provide the jury with the option that the appellant was aware of her conduct, aware of the circumstances, or was reasonably aware that her conduct was reasonably certain to cause the result, is to relieve the State of their burden of proof. To prove that a defendant is aware of her conduct is one thing; to prove that the defendant's conduct is reasonably certain to produce a certain result is, although subtle, another. *Alvarado*, 704 S.W.2d at 39. The court cannot give the jury the choice of which definition to apply to the crime charged, rather the statute defining the crime dictates which definition of "knowingly" is appropriate as to each element. . . .

The appellant asserts that the offense of "aggravated child abuse," as defined in Tenn. Code Ann. §39-15-402 and as charged in the present case, only contains the element of "result of conduct," as was determined in *Alvarado*. We do not agree. Upon analysis of our statutory provision, a purview into the legislative intent behind the enactment of the offense leads us to conclude that the offense, as charged in the case presently before this court, contains the elements of (1) awareness of conduct; (2) awareness of circumstances; and (3) result of conduct.

The trial court provided the jury with the following instruction:

> Any person who commits the offense of aggravated child abuse is guilty of a felony. For you to find the Defendant guilty of this offense, the State must have proven beyond a reasonable doubt the existence of the following essential elements:
>
> (1) The Defendant acted knowingly; AND

(2) That the Defendant did:

     a. Other than by accidental means, treat a child in such a manner as to inflict injury; OR

     b. Other than by accidental means, neglect a child so as to adversely affect the child's health and welfare; AND

(3) a. The Defendant used a deadly weapon to accomplish the act of abuse; OR

     b. The act of abuse resulted in serious bodily injury to the child.

The requirement of "knowingly" is also satisfied if it is shown that the Defendant acted intentionally.

A person acts "knowingly" if that person acts with an awareness either:

     (1) That his or her conduct is of a particular nature; or

     (2) That a particular circumstance exists.

A person acts knowingly with respect to a result of the person's conduct when the person is aware that the conduct is reasonably certain to cause a result.

A reading of this instruction implies that, for a jury to find that the defendant acted knowingly, the jury must find that the defendant was (1) aware of her conduct or aware of the circumstances and (2) aware that the conduct was reasonably certain to cause a certain result as to each material element of the offense. Although this instruction is erroneous in that it did not charge the specific *mens rea* definition applicable to each [element], we conclude that any such error is harmless. Tenn. R. App. P. 36(a).

The prejudice in not providing an [element-]specific definition of the applicable *mens rea* is the alteration of the State's burden of proof. The instruction in the present case did not relieve the State's burden of proof. The jury was instructed that it must find each element of the offense beyond a reasonable doubt. The definition of "knowingly" provided by the court supplied a two-prong definition of the term, resulting in an added burden of proof upon the State, for which the appellant cannot now complain. Although the preferred instruction would be one that is [element-]specific, we conclude that the instruction provided in the present case did not prejudice the appellant. Accordingly, any such error in the instruction is harmless.

Because we have determined that the jury instruction constitutes harmless error, we must determine whether the evidence is sufficient to sustain the conviction. A jury conviction removes the presumption of innocence with which a defendant is initially cloaked and replaces it with one of guilt, so that on appeal a convicted defendant has the burden of demonstrating that the evidence is insufficient. State v. Tuggle, 639 S.W.2d 913, 914 (Tenn. 1982). It is the appellate court's duty to affirm the conviction if the evidence viewed under these standards was sufficient for any rational trier of fact to have found the essential elements of the offense beyond a reasonable doubt. Jackson v. Virginia, 443 U.S. 307, 317 (1979); State v. Cazes, 875 S.W.2d 253, 259 (Tenn. 1994); Tenn. R. App. P. 13(e). On appeal, the State is entitled to the strongest legitimate view of the evidence and all legitimate or reasonable inferences which may be drawn therefrom. State v. Harris, 839 S.W.2d 54, 75 (Tenn. 1992).

Before a jury can find a defendant guilty of aggravated child abuse as charged in the present case, the State must prove beyond a reasonable doubt that the defendant "knowingly, other than by accidental means, treats a child under eighteen (18) years of age in such a manner as to inflict injury or neglects such a child so as to adversely affect the child's health and welfare . . ." and such abuse results in serious bodily injury.[21] See Tenn. Code Ann. §39-15-401, -402. "Knowing" is applicable to the situations in which the accused, while not having the actual intent to accomplish a specific wrongful purpose, is consciously aware of the existence of facts which makes his conduct unlawful. See People v. Weiss, 263 Ill. App. 3d 725, 635 N.E.2d 635, 639 (Ill. App. 1994). "Knowing" is ordinarily established by circumstantial evidence rather than by direct proof. People v. Hall, 273 Ill. App. 3d 838, 652 N.E.2d 1266, 1269 (Ill. App.). The undisputed proof reveals that the appellant strapped her two children, Dustin and Devin, into their car seats, secured the windows and doors, and left her children alone in the car for over nine hours, never returning to check on them. The children died as a result of systemic hyperthermia triggered by being locked in the hot vehicle. Obviously, by returning a guilty verdict, the jury did not accredit the appellant's theory of the case that the deaths of her children were an accident. Nor did the jury accredit defense testimony of the appellant's psychological problems. We conclude that a rational trier of fact could find that the appellant knew the ages of her children (circumstances), knowingly strapped her children in the car (conduct), knowingly neglected them over the next nine hours (conduct), and was aware that her conduct was reasonably certain to cause harm or injury to her children (result of conduct). Thus, the facts are sufficient to support a conviction for aggravated child abuse on each count. Tenn. R. App. P. 13(e). This issue is without merit.

Notes and Questions

1. The issue in *Ducker* is nearly identical to the one in *Sargent*, see supra page 99. Both cases involved defendants, convicted of serious crimes

---

21. "Serious bodily injury" is defined as bodily injury which involves:

    (A) A substantial risk of death;
    (B) Protracted unconsciousness;
    (C) Extreme physical pain;
    (D) Protracted or obvious disfigurement; or
    (E) Protracted loss or substantial impairment of function of a bodily member, organ or mental faculty.

Tenn. Code Ann. §39-11-106(a)(33).

involving child abuse, who claimed that they lacked the appropriate *mens rea* with respect to the harm that befell the children. Both defendants claimed that they didn't realize that their actions would cause such serious harm, and that to hold them criminally liable without such awareness would be unjust and tantamount to strict liability.

Beyond the obvious factual differences between the two cases, the main legal difference is that *Sargent* arose in a jurisdiction that followed the common law of criminal intent, whereas *Ducker* arose in a Model Penal Code jurisdiction. In *Sargent*, the court found the California felony child abuse statute to require no particular *mens rea* with respect to the likelihood of serious harm caused to a child by the active, direct infliction of pain and suffering to the child. The court justified its decision on the basis of statutory language, statutory structure, legislative purpose, comparisons with prior cases, and general public policy (e.g., the court stressed that its holding would create no appreciable risk that good and loving parents might unfairly be convicted of felony child abuse merely for slapping the back of a choking child).

In *Ducker*, by contrast, the court emphasized that "we write not with the purpose of reaching a desired result but, rather, of effecting the intent of our legislature as expressed in its enactment of our criminal code." The *Ducker* court found the Tennessee aggravated child abuse statute (which applies, see supra at page 210, whenever a defendant "knowingly, other than by accidental means, treats a child under eighteen (18) years of age in such a manner as to inflict injury or neglects such a child so as to adversely affect the child's health and welfare . . ." and thereby causes serious bodily injury) to require "knowledge" that such harm or injury would result from the defendant's actions. The court did not discuss either the soundness of this result as a matter of public policy, or the fairness of this result to the defendant; instead, the court simply parsed the language of the relevant statute (which included the single MPC *mens rea* term "knowingly"), thus effectively deciding the issue.

Having read both cases, which method of *mens rea* analysis do you prefer? The one that allows judges to consider all relevant variables when determining the appropriate criminal intent standards for a particular crime and case, or the one that essentially limits judges to a grammatical analysis of the statutory text?

2. After first deciding that the Tennessee statute required the defendant to "know" (i.e., be aware) that her conduct, under the circumstances, was "reasonably certain" to cause the specific harmful result required by the statute—which, for the crime of aggravated child abuse, is "serious bodily injury" to a child—the court proceeded to hold that (1) the trial judge's instructions to the jury were defective; (2) this defect in the instructions, however, was "harmless error" (i.e., could not have affected the jury's verdict); and (3) the evidence was legally sufficient to sustain the defendant's conviction, because the jury reasonably could have found that the defendant satisfied the Model Penal Code's "knowledge" standard, based on reasonable inferences drawn from her conduct under the circumstances.

Do you think that Jennie Bain Ducker actually "knew" that her behavior would seriously injure her children, as that term was defined in the Tennessee statute? Was there any evidence in the case from which one could reasonably infer such knowledge? Beyond a reasonable doubt? If not, then how did the *Ducker* court manage to find the evidence legally sufficient to sustain the verdict?

Or did the Court of Criminal Appeals even require such "knowledge" at all? Notice that the court, at the very end of its opinion, didn't actually repeat the statutory language of "serious bodily injury"—instead, the court simply concluded that Ducker "was aware that her conduct was reasonably certain to cause *harm or injury* to her children." Was that a last-minute bait and switch? What if Ducker, at the time when she left her children alone, believed that the worst thing that could happen to them was some discomfort? Would that be enough to find "knowledge," and thereby convict Ducker of aggravated child abuse, when instead the children actually died? Wouldn't that effectively hold Ducker strictly liable for the much greater harm that actually occurred—in contravention of the MPC's strict prohibition on strict liability (see footnote **** at page 206)?

3. The decision of the Tennessee Court of Criminal Appeals in *Ducker* subsequently was affirmed by the Tennessee Supreme Court. See State v. Ducker, 27 S.W.3d 889 (Tenn. 2000). According to the Tennessee Supreme Court:

> The defendant was found guilty of aggravated child abuse, which requires either child abuse or neglect under Tenn. Code Ann. §39-15-401 and the additional element that the abuse or neglect resulted in *serious* bodily injury. We will next address whether the knowing mens rea required in the child abuse statute applies to the conduct of the defendant or to the result of that conduct. The defendant argues that the child abuse statute defines a result-of-conduct offense and, therefore, the statute requires that one must actually be aware that her conduct would result in serious bodily injury to the child victim. We disagree. . . .
>
> [T]he Tennessee child abuse and neglect statute is clear that "knowingly" modifies "treats" or "neglects." The actus reus is modified by the clause "other than by accidental means." Accordingly, the statute requires that the act of treating a child in an abusive manner or neglecting the child must be knowing conduct. For instance, the defendant must have knowingly left or abandoned her children in the car for more than eight hours. If the defendant had been unaware that her children were present in the car when she left her car parked in front of the hotel, the neglect of her children would have been accidental or unknowing. Contrary to the defendant's assertions, application of the mens rea to the actus reus of this statute precludes this statute from being a strict liability statute.
>
> Once the knowing mens rea is established, the next inquiry under the plain language of the statute is simply whether the child sustained an injury or, in the case of child neglect, whether the child suffered an adverse effect to the child's health or welfare. The legislature has employed the phrases "so as

to injure" and "so as to adversely affect" when defining the injury aspect of the child abuse statute. These phrases clearly indicate that if an injury results from knowing abuse or neglect, the actor has committed child abuse.

As a practical matter, the defendant's argument could render the child abuse statute ineffectual. Defendants in child abuse cases could argue that, while they in fact knowingly punished or spanked the child, they did not know harm would occur. . . . We, therefore, reject the defendant's argument and hold that the mens rea of "knowing" refers only to the conduct elements of treatment or neglect of a child under the child abuse statute and conclude that the child abuse offenses are not result-of-conduct offenses.

In the case now before us, the defendant was convicted of aggravated child abuse. The record establishes that the defendant knowingly parked her car, rolled up the windows, securely fastened the children in the car, locked the car and left them inside the parked car from approximately 3:45 A.M. to between 12 and 1 P.M. on June 6. The children died of hyperthermia. The evidence supports a finding that the defendant knowingly and other than by accidental means neglected the children. The evidence also supports a finding that the neglect adversely affected the children's health and welfare. Accordingly, the evidence of the children's deaths overwhelmingly supports a finding of aggravated child abuse. We conclude a rational trier of fact could have found the defendant guilty of aggravated child abuse beyond a reasonable doubt based upon the evidence presented.

Id. at 895-97.

Did the Tennessee Supreme Court do any better, in terms of faithfully applying the Model Penal Code, than the Tennessee Court of Criminal Appeals? What does the court mean when it says that "the child abuse offenses are not result-of-conduct offenses"? Does that mean that *no* level of culpability is required with respect to the element of "serious bodily injury" in aggravated child abuse cases? Or even with respect to the elements of "injury" or "adversely affect[ing] the child's health and welfare," in non-aggravated child abuse cases? Perhaps so, given that the court never mentions any requirement of any such culpability. But how can that be, in a state governed by the Model Penal Code?

Is it possible that both of the *Ducker* courts, having found themselves boxed in by the apparent outcome of the MPC's culpability analysis of the relevant Tennessee statute, simply found ways to fudge the application of the MPC's "knowledge" standard so that they could still reach what they believed to be the just result on the facts of the case? If that is what really happened, then—at least on the basis of *Ducker*—is the MPC really a step forward or a step backward?

To put it another way: The Model Penal Code was designed to transform *mens rea* analysis, making it more predictable, rational, and ultimately fair. Having read both *Sargent* and the two court opinions in *Ducker*, does the MPC's approach truly seem to represent a more predictable, rational, and ultimately fair method of making *mens rea* decisions?

Notes on Cognitive Fault and Moral Fault

1. One more feature of MPC §2.02 deserves mention here. Recall section 2.02(5), which holds that evidence of a higher *mens rea* standard may be used to prove a lower standard. Recall too the hierarchy of MPC *mens rea* standards: Negligence occupies the ladder's bottom rung, with recklessness just above it, knowledge above recklessness, and purpose on the ladder's top rung. The assumption behind section 2.02(5) is that each of those higher *mens rea* standards necessarily represents a more blameworthy state of mind than the standards on the rungs below it. But that assumption may be false. Consider two hypothetical homicides:

Case 1. The defendant is the husband of a 75-year-old woman who suffers from a serious, chronic illness. The illness is incurable, and causes great pain, but is unlikely to prove fatal (at least not in the near term). The defendant is distraught that his beloved wife, to whom he has been married for more than 50 years, is suffering. He wants to put an end to her pain. Although the relevant state law does not recognize a "right to die"—and, indeed, the situation would not qualify even in states like Oregon that recognize such a right—the husband, after many months of anguish and deep reflection, decides to give his wife a lethal dose of tranquilizers, thus helping her to die a peaceful death.

Case 2. The defendant owns a one-acre lot in a suburban neighborhood. The back half of his lot is part of a large wooded area. Much of that area is public property, though some of it belongs to other property owners in the neighborhood. A large number of children live in this neighborhood, and many of them like to play in the wooded area. They are not always careful to stay on public property, and often wander onto defendant's lot. The defendant finds this intrusion annoying, and often chases the children away. The defendant has a rifle, and one day he decides to attach a target to one of the trees on his property to use for target practice. He does not know whether any children are playing nearby, nor does he try to find out. Instead, he assumes that he probably won't hit anyone and, if he does, perhaps it would serve the victim right for trespassing. Unfortunately, some children *are* playing in the woods. The defendant's first shot misses the target (and the tree) and hits a child, who dies soon afterward.

Assume both defendants are charged with murder under a statute that covers "anyone who purposely or knowingly causes the death of another human being." Assume further that MPC §2.02 applies in the relevant jurisdiction. How are the two cases resolved?

Under the *mens rea* analysis of MPC §2.02, the first defendant is guilty of murder, and the second one is not—the opposite of the result most people would instinctively reach. The first defendant made an enormously difficult choice that—whether morally correct or not—was intended to serve the best interests of his "victim." Nevertheless, applying section 2.02 to the terms of the hypothetical statute, he loses, because he acted with the "purpose" to cause the death of the woman he loved. The fact that he had a good reason (i.e., motive) for acting as he did is, at least under section 2.02, irrelevant to his moral culpability. The second defendant acted out of either indifference or spite, which seems morally monstrous given the risk his conduct created. He wins anyway, because he did *not* "know" that his actions would cause the death of the child his bullet struck. The fact that he acted for terrible reasons is again irrelevant.*

Now suppose that the two defendants are prosecuted under a "negligent homicide" statute that uses criminal negligence as its *mens rea* standard. What result? Under MPC §2.02, the answer is that *both* defendants now lose. The loving husband might not have caused death negligently—although the risk in question was "substantial," it may not have been "unjustifiable," nor is it 100 percent clear that his conduct was a "gross deviation" from ordinary and reasonable standards of care. None of that matters to section 2.02: The husband caused death purposefully, and under section 2.02(5), proof of purpose suffices to prove either recklessness or negligence. The second defendant loses because he *was* reckless: Plainly, firing a gun into a wooded area where children often play is an unjustifiable and gross deviation from any reasonable-person standard of care, and the second defendant was consciously aware of the risk.

The point here is *not* that MPC §2.02 necessarily compels a different *result* in the two hypothetical cases than would be reached at common law. In fact, under most existing homicide statutes, in both MPC and non-MPC states, both defendants probably would be found guilty of murder. (As we will see later, in Chapter 10, the crime of murder usually includes both intentional killings and killings that result from extreme recklessness.) The same would be true under the MPC's own homicide statutes (the Code contains a full set of proposed crime statutes, in addition to its general provisions about *mens rea* and other such matters). See MPC §210.2(1), discussed further infra, in Chapter 10.

Instead, the point here is simply that the MPC's rigid hierarchy of mental states, as expressed in section 2.02(5), might not always accurately reflect moral blameworthiness—because in some situations, "recklessness" might be morally worse than "knowledge" or even "purpose." Under the common law approach to *mens rea*, as we have seen, judges (and juries) at least possess the flexibility to think about such matters of moral blameworthiness—in the first

---

* Interestingly, in its own homicide statutes, the Model Penal Code followed the lead of the common law by introducing a new, hybrid form of *mens rea* applicable *only* to murder—"recklessly under circumstances manifesting an indifference to the value of human life." See MPC §210.2(1)(b). Isn't this a tacit acknowledgement that the four-part *mens rea* scheme in MPC §2.02 might be insufficient to capture the full range and depth of moral blameworthiness? If homicides cannot be graded fairly without the introduction of a more nuanced *mens rea* scheme, might not the same also be true for other crimes?

hypothetical above, for example, a creative common law judge might well ask whether or not the loving husband acted with "malice." Under MPC §2.02, however, the judge's hands are tied; only the legislature can speak to the issue of moral culpability. Once the legislature has spoken (or not, in which case the default *mens rea* applies), the role of the judge is limited to determining whether or not the defendant satisfied the legislature's *mens rea* prescription.

2. The specific problem with section 2.02(5) is that the MPC's drafters may have misunderstood their own handiwork: The four *mens rea* standards contained therein actually define two different culpability ladders, not one, and the two ladders deal with two very different sets of criteria. Purpose and knowledge, along with the subjective awareness component of recklessness, all deal with what one might call cognitive fault. During the Senate Watergate hearings that eventually led to President Richard Nixon's resignation, Senator Howard Baker defined the central question in the scandal this way: "What did the President know, and when did he know it?" Baker's famous line captures the sensibility underlying cognitive fault standards—the goal is to evaluate the defendant's behavior based on what the defendant did and didn't know, on his subjective understanding of his conduct and of the surrounding circumstances, and on his subjective intentions as to the results of his conduct. Recklessness and negligence rest on a different sensibility altogether: The central question is not the degree of the defendant's knowledge but the moral quality of her conduct—how selfish or unselfish her choices were, how much or how little she valued the costs her risky behavior imposed on others.

A well-functioning system of criminal law inevitably must use a mix of the two types of standards. When prosecuting tax cheats, the law might focus on whether defendants understood the relevant tax rules, in order to avoid treating honest but foolish conduct the same as conscious cheating. On the other hand, when punishing homicide and assault, it may be wiser to focus more on the defendant's level of indifference toward the victim than on the defendant's cognitive understanding. On that scale, the defendant in Case 1 seems positively virtuous—he valued the victim highly, so much so that he willingly broke the law to try to help her. The defendant in Case 2 looks like a monster—he valued *his* victim's life less than he valued his own interests in target shooting and perhaps deterring harmless trespassers.

But while both the cognitive and moralist approaches to criminal culpability are useful, they are not substitutes for each other. Self-interested behavior is the norm when paying taxes; the goal of even honest taxpayers is to pay as little as possible. To punish selfishness in such contexts is to punish nearly everyone. Far better to separate taxpayers who pay too little tax into two groups—those who *knew* they were paying less than they were supposed to, and those who didn't—and punish only the former. When designing dangerous products like automobiles, imposing serious risks on others is inherent in the enterprise. In settings like that, punishing those who know the most about the risks they impose means punishing the *best* actors, not the worst ones. Far better to punish those who value the risks they impose too lightly, and let the others go free. Cognitive intent standards work for some crimes but not others; the same is true of moralist intent standards. Neither standard readily translates into the other's terms. Wechsler and his colleagues failed to see that point.

3. Under MPC §2.02, cognitive fault is deemed inherently more blameworthy than the more moralist kind of fault embodied in the definitions of recklessness and negligence. Notice which standards occupy the ladder's highest rungs—knowledge and purpose, the standards that have the most to do with cognition and the least to do with moral blame or fault. The Code's drafters sought to push American criminal law further away from its roots in the common-law concept of an "evil mind" and a "vicious will," and toward a more narrowly cognitive (and more psychologically sophisticated) understanding of criminal culpability.

In doing so, the drafters thought they were helping criminal defendants. But it hasn't worked out that way in practice. Consider a crime that was of minor importance when the MPC was first drafted, but that occupies a large fraction of criminal litigation today: possession of illegal drugs. Violations of drug laws are almost always knowing and purposeful, as the Model Penal Code defines those terms. People who buy and use drugs generally understand what drugs they are buying and using, and usually try to do exactly what they do: buy and use drugs. On the other hand, a large fraction of illegal drug users might argue plausibly that their conduct was not a "gross deviation from the standard of care" of most ordinary people in the communities in which they live. An even larger number of defendants might be able to argue that their conduct was not "malicious," in that it does not reflect an "evil mind" or a "vicious will."

In the past 35 years, the number of inmates incarcerated on drug charges has risen from fewer than 50,000 to nearly a half-million. One reason for that staggering increase is that the criminal law of drugs has, with rare exceptions, used purely cognitive fault standards—the same standards that the Model Penal Code's authors believed necessary to protect against excessive criminal punishment. American criminal law is often criticized for being too moralist. Ironically, had the law of *mens rea* followed a *more* explicitly moralist path, we might have seen many fewer drug prisoners, and much less severe criminal law.

Notes on Mistakes and Intoxication Under the MPC

1. The Model Penal Code provision governing mistakes of fact is section 2.04(1)(a), which reads: "Ignorance or mistake as to a matter of fact or law is a defense if . . . the ignorance or mistake negatives the purpose, knowledge, recklessness, or negligence required to establish a material element of the offense." That provision effectively abolishes mistake-of-fact doctrine.

In jurisdictions that adopt section 2.04(1)(a), the law of factual mistakes is simply folded into the law of *mens rea*. Mistake arguments are relevant in precisely the same way, and to precisely the same degree, as any other *mens rea* arguments. Whether this provision is wise policy depends on one's view of the common law of mistake, but it certainly makes *mens rea* analysis easier.

2. Note that section 2.04(1)(a) refers to "[i]gnorance or mistake as to a matter of fact *or law*" (emphasis added). That sounds like a command to treat legal mistakes no differently than factual errors, which would be a large gift to criminal defendants. But section 2.02(9) takes back a large portion of the gift. That provision reads:

> Neither knowledge nor recklessness nor negligence as to whether conduct constitutes an offense or as to the existence, meaning, or application of the law determining the elements of an offense is an element of such offense, unless the definition of the offense or the Code so provides.

That cumbersome wording essentially reaffirms the common-law view that ignorance of *criminal* law is no defense: No level of awareness of the "existence, meaning, or application" of any part of the criminal code is required in order for a defendant to be held liable for violating that part of the code.

3. How is one to determine when section 2.04(1)(a) applies, and when section 2.02(9) defines the governing standard? The former provision seems to give defendants broad leeway to raise mistake-of-law arguments; the latter appears to shut the door on those arguments. In this regard, the MPC largely follows the common law. Errors about the meaning of the criminal statute under which the defendant is charged are covered by section 2.02(9); mistakes about relevant non-criminal law, on the other hand, are covered by section 2.04(1)(a). Mistakes about criminal law are no defense, period. Mistakes about non-criminal law are treated like ordinary *mens rea* arguments—as are mistakes of fact. Thus, if a thief wished to testify, implausibly, that he had no idea that theft was a crime, the testimony would be inadmissible under both the MPC and the common law. On the other hand, if the same thief wished to testify that he believed he owned the property in question, that testimony would be perfectly proper, again under both the MPC and the common law—though the MPC would treat the defendant's argument a little more generously than would the common law (assuming the common law treated it as a mistake of law).

4. If *Marrero* (see supra, page 157) were decided in a Model Penal Code jurisdiction in which both sections 2.02(9) and 2.04(1)(a) were valid law, how would the case come out? What about *Varszegi* (supra, page 178)? The answers may be harder to discern than you think. Marrero believed it was legal to take his gun into a New York City social club, just as Varszegi may have believed it was legal to grab his defaulting tenant's computer. Neither defendant parsed his belief or otherwise identified its precise legal source—since

neither was a lawyer, such parsing would have been impossible; non-lawyers
don't think about legal rules in that manner. And the mistakes themselves
could easily be assigned either to the definition of the relevant crime or to
some piece of non-criminal law. Did Marrero make a mistake about the definition of the gun crime for which he was prosecuted? Or was his mistake
about the definition of "peace officer" in another part of New York's code?
Did Varszegi misunderstand the definition of the crime of theft, or did he
misperceive the governing civil property rules? These questions have no ana-
lytically correct answers—either under the common law or under the MPC.
The categories of mistake governed by MPC §§2.04(1)(a) and 2.02(9) are
both unclear and manipulable: the opposite of Wechsler's goal.

5. Another significant MPC provision is section 2.08, which governs the
complicated relationship between intoxication and *mens rea*. Section 2.08
reads:

> SECTION 2.08. INTOXICATION.
>
> (1) Except as provided in Subsection (4) of this Section, intoxica-
> tion of the actor is not a defense unless it negatives an element of the
> offense.
>
> (2) When recklessness establishes an element of the offense, if the
> actor, due to self-induced intoxication, is unaware of a risk of which he
> would have been aware had he been sober, such unawareness is immaterial.
>
> (3) Intoxication does not, in itself, constitute mental disease within
> the meaning of Section 4.01.
>
> (4) Intoxication that (a) is not self-induced or (b) is pathological is
> an affirmative defense if by reason of such intoxication the actor at the time
> of his conduct lacks substantial capacity either to appreciate its criminality
> [wrongfulness] or to conform his conduct to the requirements of law.
>
> (5) Definitions. In this Section unless a different meaning plainly
> is required:
>
>> (a) "intoxication" means a disturbance of mental or physical
>> capacities resulting from the introduction of substances into the body;
>>
>> (b) "self-induced intoxication" means intoxication caused by sub-
>> stances that the actor knowingly introduces into his body, the tendency
>> of which to cause intoxication he knows or ought to know, unless he
>> introduces them pursuant to medical advice or under such circum-
>> stances as would afford a defense to a charge of crime;
>>
>> (c) "pathological intoxication" means intoxication grossly exces-
>> sive in degree, given the amount of the intoxicant, to which the actor
>> does not know he is susceptible.

Section 2.08(1) applies the same principle to intoxication that the
MPC applies to mistakes: Just as mistakes of fact or law provide no defense
unless they negate some conduct or intent term that is part of the relevant
crime's definition, the same is true of the defendant's intoxication. Section
2.08(2) is a convoluted way of expressing a simple idea: As a matter of law,
evidence of the defendant's intoxication cannot negate the subjective awareness component of recklessness. As long as a sober person under the same

circumstances would have been consciously aware of the risk, a drunk person is held to have the same awareness—even if he actually didn't. Recall that recklessness is the default *mens rea* under the MPC, the standard that applies unless the legislature specifies otherwise—that is, recklessness plays the same role under the MPC that general intent plays in most states. In essence, the MPC's authors applied the same intoxication rule to offenses that require proof of recklessness as is traditionally applied by the common law to offenses that require proof of general intent: For such crimes, evidence of intoxication is inadmissible to negate *mens rea.*

Section 2.08(3) bars using intoxication as the basis for an insanity defense; MPC §4.01 (discussed later, in Chapter 11) is the Code provision that defines that defense. Section 2.08(4) provides for an equivalent to the insanity defense—but only when the defendant did not know that he was consuming the substance that caused his intoxication, or when the defendant had a pathological (i.e., unforeseen and unforeseeable) reaction to the substance in question. These are very rare circumstances. Notice that, under these provisions (as the Commentaries to the Model Penal Code make clear), alcoholism does *not* serve as a defense to crime.

Notes on the Model Penal Code's Influence

1. Initially, the Model Penal Code seemed popular with state legislatures. Beginning in the early 1960s—the MPC was formally issued in 1962—there was a wave of state criminal code revision. For the first time in American history, legislators in many states sought to rationalize their bodies of criminal law, and most of them used the MPC as a model. It seemed to most criminal law scholars that the MPC was in the process of displacing the common law. America seemed to be establishing a reasonably uniform national body of criminal law—not by act of Congress, but through the influence of law reformers in the ALI. Consequently, for the past generation, most law students have been taught (as this casebook's authors were taught in the early 1980s) that the MPC was increasingly coming to dominate the interpretation of criminal statutes and, especially, the analysis of criminal intent.

2. Those predictions have proved false. Fewer than half the states—22—ended up modeling their revised criminal codes on the MPC,* and that number is no longer growing. Even those states that originally did use the MPC as their template have substantially changed their criminal codes in the years since first revising them. Illinois, one of the first states to revise its criminal code in response to the MPC, offers a useful case study. In 1856,

---

* This is the number of states that have adopted MPC §2.02, at least in revised form. Since the Code is built around that provision, it seems fair to use its presence or absence as a benchmark for the Code's influence. About a dozen other states revised their criminal codes but declined to use the MPC as a model. The rest of the states have not undertaken systematic revisions of their criminal codes.

Illinois' criminal code contained 131 separate crimes, most of them taken verbatim from Blackstone's Commentaries. By 1874, the number of distinct offenses had climbed to 220. The number topped 300 by the beginning of the twentieth century; it reached 460 by 1951. The 1961 code revision dramatically reduced the number of separate crimes, to 263. But the reduction was only temporary. Since 1961, the Illinois legislature has added more than 150 new criminal statutes. Many of these statutes, like Illinois' general drug law, contain a long list of separate offenses; the total number of new crimes created since 1961 probably exceeds 500. Other states have seen similar waves of expansion in their lists of criminal prohibitions. Even in states that purport to follow the MPC, then, the definition of criminal conduct is both different and a great deal more expansive than in Wechsler's Code.

3. That proposition is equally true of the law of criminal intent. Only a small minority of the states whose codes are allegedly modeled on the MPC adopted section 2.02 in its entirety. Most states have retained common-law concepts like specific and general intent, malice, and willfulness. A Colorado Supreme Court decision illustrates the point. The defendant in People v. Vigil, 127 P.3d 916 (Colo. 2006), was charged with sexually assaulting his child; he sought to introduce evidence of his voluntary intoxication to negate *mens rea*. The court held that he could not do so, because the crime in question is a general intent crime. All of which sounds unsurprising — except for the fact that Colorado's criminal code *is modeled on the MPC*. The intent standard for the Colorado crime charged in *Vigil* is knowledge; the words "general intent" do not appear anywhere in that statute. Decisions like *Vigil* are commonplace. The common law's terminology seems to have a more durable hold on the legal imagination than the drafters of the MPC ever imagined.

And it is not just a matter of vocabulary. By most accounts, the single most important proposition in MPC §2.02 is the default rule of section 2.02(3), which holds that recklessness is the presumptive *mens rea* standard for all crimes. Only half of the 22 states that originally adopted some form of section 2.02 — or about one-fifth of the states in total — retained that presumption. In six states, negligence is the presumptive *mens rea* standard. In another five, the presumptive standard is intentional *conduct* — the same as general intent. Kansas' criminal code is fairly typical; its intent provision is modeled only loosely on MPC §2.02:

> SECTION 21-3201. CRIMINAL INTENT.
>
> (a) Except as otherwise provided, a criminal intent is an essential element of every crime defined by this code. Criminal intent may be established by proof that the conduct of the accused person was intentional or reckless. Proof of intentional conduct shall be required to establish criminal intent, unless the statute defining the crime expressly provides that the prohibited act is criminal if done in a reckless manner.
>
> (b) Intentional conduct is conduct that is purposeful and willful and not accidental. As used in this code, the terms "knowing," "willful," "purposeful," and "on purpose" are included within the term "intentional."

(c) Reckless conduct is conduct done under circumstances that show a realization of the imminence of danger to the person of another and a conscious and unjustifiable disregard of that danger. The terms "gross negligence," "culpable negligence," "wanton negligence" and "wantonness" are included within the term "recklessness" as used in this code.

Kan. Stat. Ann. §21-3201. Notice that knowing and purposeful conduct are treated the same; likewise, recklessness and criminal negligence are treated as a single standard. The Kansas legislators who drafted the state's reformed criminal code evidently believed that the MPC's four intent terms — purpose, knowledge, recklessness, and negligence — sliced *mens rea* too finely; the lines that distinguish those four mental states from one another cannot be drawn reliably. As you read the cases in the chapters that follow, ask yourself whether that suspicion is correct. Criminal liability rules are useful only if judges and juries can apply those rules with a reasonable measure of accuracy. The MPC's *mens rea* rules — and American criminal law more generally — may not satisfy that condition.

The bottom line is fairly straightforward: The MPC never became the universal template for state criminal law. At most, it was a jumping-off point that state legislators used as they reworked their criminal codes. Today, state criminal law consists of 50 distinct bodies of legal doctrine, just as it did before Wechsler's Code was written. The vast majority of those states continue to use the common law's *mens rea* vocabulary; the number that use the MPC's terminology and approach is small and shrinking. Measured by Wechsler's goals, Wechsler's project failed.

4. Even so, the MPC's approach to *mens rea* analysis *has* had a great deal of influence over American criminal law, in three crucial respects. The first has already been mentioned: Because of the MPC, cognitive fault standards have become increasingly common in state criminal law, and more moralist fault standards have become less so. For crimes like drug offenses, the effect may have been to make criminal liability rules broader, and to make the law of criminal intent more severe.

5. The second influential feature of the MPC is the use of "element analysis." Before the MPC, intent standards were usually applied crime by crime: Most offenses required proof of general intent, while some called for specific intent. The MPC applies *mens rea* terms not crime by crime, but element by element: For any given crime, two or three different *mens rea* standards might apply — purpose for these elements and recklessness for those, or knowledge for this circumstance and negligence for that portion of the criminal conduct. In a large fraction of criminal cases today, judges do *mens rea* analysis based on element analysis, as the MPC does, breaking criminal offenses down into their component parts and arguing about the proper intent term for each part of the crime, not for the crime as a whole. That is true even in jurisdictions whose criminal codes have not been modified to fit the MPC's template.

6. The third key aspect of the MPC's influence is captured by a case excerpted in Chapter 2: Brogan v. United States, 522 U.S. 398 (1998). Recall that in *Brogan*, the Court rejected the "exculpatory no" doctrine because that doctrine did not derive from any language in 18 U.S.C. §1001, the federal false statements statute. *Brogan* was a federal case, and the federal criminal code was not modeled on the MPC. But *Brogan*'s approach to the interpretation of criminal statutes closely resembles the approach the MPC takes. In *Brogan*, statutory interpretation is a formal, mechanical process—the question is not whether it is fair to punish the defendant for the relevant conduct or even whether Congress intended that such conduct be punished, but only whether the words of the statute cover the defendant's behavior. Arguments of justice and fairness and sound policy are put aside, on the ground that those arguments are for Congress to address and not appropriate subjects for judges to consider.

In a *Brogan*-like system, law is not the product of a dialogue between different lawmakers—it's more like a monologue in which legislators speak and judges listen. As Justice Scalia's majority opinion in *Brogan* recognized, that approach to criminal law has one large virtue: It effectively constrains the power of judges, especially appellate judges. But by constraining judicial power, *Brogan* increases the authority of the other two branches of government: legislators and prosecutors. Perhaps it is more than coincidental that this power shift occurred during a generation when America's prison population rose to unprecedented heights—state and federal prisons housed fewer than 200,000 inmates in 1970 but more than 1.4 million by 2005. Legislators writing criminal statutes do not hear from well-funded interest groups explaining why crimes ought to be defined more narrowly. A few areas aside (chiefly those involving high-end financial crime), such interest groups do not exist. The only groups with influence over the legislative process in this area are groups that favor *broader* criminal liability: chiefly, police and prosecutors.

Judges, by contrast, hear arguments from both sides. Reported criminal cases are filled with moral arguments like the "exculpatory no" claim Brogan made—arguments that are not tied to statutory language because no one made them when the relevant statutes were being drafted. Because of the rise of Model Penal Code–style criminal justice formalism, judges increasingly are not permitted to consider such arguments. And if judges cannot hear arguments like Brogan's, no one else will.

On the surface, the law of criminal intent is not dramatically different than it was 50 years ago, before the Model Penal Code arrived on the scene. Specific intent and general intent still survive and even thrive, as does the confusing welter of culpability terms (e.g., "willfulness," "criminal negligence," "malice") that the MPC sought to displace. Under the surface, though, the change has been substantial. Judicial opinions in the area are a good deal more formalist and textualist, and a good deal less interested in open-ended arguments about policy and principle, than before the MPC arose. The rise of legal formalism is a broad trend in American law, with roots far outside the criminal justice system. But the MPC has contributed more than a little bit to bringing that movement *inside* the realm of criminal justice. The consequence is a system in which defendants find it harder to argue that they do not deserve punishment, and in which the government finds it easier to convict defendants who might plausibly raise such arguments, than in the past. That is not a recipe for a more just criminal justice system.

4

Federal Criminal Law

To this point, you have read a mix of state and federal criminal cases. Many of the issues these cases raise are common to state and federal criminal law. That is so because most federal crimes are also crimes under state law; the converse is probably true as well. Federal prosecutors prosecute a mix of violent felonies, thefts, frauds, drug cases, and immigration-related crimes; save for the last category, the same is true of local district attorneys. The mix of these cases differs somewhat: Federal prosecutors charge proportionally fewer theft cases and more frauds than do local D.A.s, while organized crime cases are more common in the federal justice system than in state courts. Notwithstanding these qualifications, the two bodies of law cover similar ground, and cover it in a similar manner.

Similar, but not identical. Three major differences distinguish the federal criminal justice system from its state and local counterparts. First, all the key actors who enforce and interpret federal criminal law—FBI agents, U.S. Attorneys and their Assistants, federal judges (including Supreme Court Justices)—are appointed, not elected. State criminal law is enforced by District Attorneys elected by the counties in which they work. The large majority of state judges, both those who try cases and those who hear and decide appeals, are elected as well. The same is true of local sheriffs. While urban police chiefs are usually appointed, their officers are supervised by elected mayors and city council members. Electoral politics plays a larger role in state-court criminal litigation than in federal criminal cases.

Second, the federal portion of America's criminal justice system is much smaller than the portion that state and local officials govern. There are roughly 750,000 full-time local police officers in the United States. The number of FBI agents is fewer than 14,000—which is less than the number of state and local law enforcement *agencies* (over 17,000) that employ at least one police officer. Roughly 30,000 local prosecutors are available to handle the prosecution of state-law crimes; the number of federal prosecutors stands at around 6,000. Each year in the United States, roughly 1.1 million felony cases and several million misdemeanors are prosecuted. Federal officials prosecute about 85,000 felonies and fewer than 13,000 misdemeanors each year. Save for homicide laws, all criminal statutes are enforced selectively. But the federal justice system is, of necessity, far more selective than its local counterparts. To take just one example, those 96 federal misrepresentation statutes listed in Justice Stevens' footnotes in *Wells* (see supra, at page 84), taken together, generate fewer than 1,000 federal prosecutions each year. No one knows how often those statutes are violated each year, but the answer is probably in the hundreds of thousands, perhaps even higher. Only a tiny fraction of federal *crimes* lead to actual federal criminal *cases*.

The third major difference arises from constitutional law. State governments possess what lawyers call "plenary power" over crime—meaning that, with few exceptions, state and local officials may punish all crimes that happen within their borders. The federal government's power is more constrained. The Framers of the United States Constitution set up a balanced system of government in which sovereignty is divided between the states (which, in terms of the original 13, preexisted the Constitution) and the federal government. The federal government's sovereign powers are limited to those matters that are specified, or "enumerated," in the Constitution—and the plenary power to define and punish crimes was never granted to the federal government.

This constitutional limit on federal power to make and enforce criminal law gives rise to two special considerations. The first is that, in order to ensure compliance with the Constitution, most federal crimes contain a special kind of conduct or result element that is not required for comparable state crimes—specifically, a conduct or result element that clearly establishes the constitutional basis for federal jurisdiction. The second is that, because many federal crimes tend to arise from the federal government's constitutional authority to regulate various kinds of economic activity, federal courts have developed a special approach to *mens rea* that differs significantly from both the common-law approach and the Model Penal Code's approach. The remainder of this chapter will address these two special aspects of federal criminal law.

A. FEDERAL JURISDICTION

Under the Framers' concept of balanced government and dual sovereignty, Congress may enact statutes, criminal and otherwise, only when those statutes fall within the scope of some power specifically granted by the Constitution of the United States. The majority of those constitutional grants of authority appear in Article I, Section 8, which lists the permissible subjects of federal lawmaking. Here is the list:

The Congress shall have Power To lay and collect Taxes, Duties, Imposts and Excises, to pay the Debts and provide for the common Defence and general Welfare of the United States; but all Duties, Imposts and Excises shall be uniform throughout the United States;

To borrow Money on the credit of the United States;

To regulate Commerce with foreign Nations, and among the several States, and with the Indian Tribes;

To establish a uniform Rule of Naturalization, and uniform Laws on the subject of Bankruptcies throughout the United States;

To coin Money, regulate the Value thereof, and of foreign Coin, and fix the Standard of Weights and Measures;

To provide for the Punishment of counterfeiting the Securities and current Coin of the United States;

To establish Post Offices and post Roads;

To promote the Progress of Science and useful Arts, by securing for limited Times to Authors and Inventors the exclusive Right to their respective Writings and Discoveries;

To constitute Tribunals inferior to the supreme Court;

To define and punish Piracies and Felonies committed on the high Seas, and Offences against the Law of Nations;

To declare War, grant Letters of Marque and Reprisal, and make Rules concerning Captures on Land and Water;

To raise and support Armies, but no Appropriation of Money to that Use shall be for a longer Term than two Years;

To provide and maintain a Navy;

To make Rules for the Government and Regulation of the land and naval Forces;

To provide for calling forth the Militia to execute the Laws of the Union, suppress Insurrections and repel Invasions;

To provide for organizing, arming, and disciplining, the Militia, and for governing such Part of them as may be employed in the Service of the United States, reserving to the States respectively, the Appointment of the Officers, and the Authority of training the Militia according to the discipline prescribed by Congress;

To exercise exclusive Legislation in all Cases whatsoever, over such District . . . as may . . . become the Seat of the Government of the United States, and to exercise like Authority over all Places purchased by the Consent of the Legislature of the State in which the Same shall be, for the Erection of Forts, Magazines, Arsenals, dock-Yards, and other needful Buildings; — and

To make all Laws which shall be necessary and proper for carrying into Execution the foregoing Powers, and all other Powers vested by this Constitution in the Government of the United States, or in any Department or Office thereof.

Most of the items on that list have nothing to do with criminal law. Congress must collect taxes, which necessarily involves punishing the occasional tax cheat. Likewise, Congress is supposed to punish counterfeiters, pirates, and "Felonies committed on the high Seas, and Offences against the Law of Nations." And it is expressly given exclusive authority "in all cases whatsoever" in the District of Columbia. Otherwise, criminal law seems a constitutional afterthought. Indeed, if there is a primary theme to the list of congressional powers quoted above, the theme is military — 8 of the 18 items on the list refer to some form of military force.

Afterthought or not, the grants of congressional power in Article I, Section 8 have produced large bodies of federal criminal law. The power "To establish Post Offices and post Roads" led to the mail fraud statute, which bars the use of the mails in furtherance of "any scheme or artifice to defraud." 18 U.S.C. §1343. The federal-program bribery statute bars, roughly, bribery of anyone administering federal funds, 18 U.S.C. §666 — which is permissible because of the power "to pay the Debts and provide for the common Defence and general Welfare of the United States." Federal gun laws bar possession of a firearm by a convicted felon, if the possession was "in or affecting commerce," which courts have construed to mean that the gun has crossed a state line. See Scarborough v. United States, 431 U.S. 563 (1977). The congressional power that applies to the most federal crimes is the same one that authorizes those gun laws: the power to regulate "Commerce . . . among the several States." Federal drug laws rest on the same power, usually called the "interstate commerce" power, as do the federal statutory bans on robbery, extortion, and racketeering.

The next case deals with one of those bans: the Hobbs Act, 18 U.S.C. §1951, which forbids robbery and extortion — as long as it "obstructs, delays or affects commerce or the movement of any article or commodity in commerce." That inartful phrase defines what is called a "jurisdictional element": the portion of the crime definition that establishes the federal government's constitutional power to prosecute. Most federal crimes have such elements; state-law crimes do not, because they need not, due to the states' plenary power over crime.

The most common jurisdictional elements in federal crimes require federal prosecutors to prove — in addition to the usual conduct, circumstance, and/or result elements that define the particular crime in question—that the defendant's conduct affected interstate commerce. These jurisdictional elements essentially define the legal boundary between federal and state criminal law enforcement. As you read, ask yourself: Is the boundary defined well? Is this really the best way to divide power over crime and criminal punishment between the federal government and the states?

Taylor v. United States

Supreme Court of the United States
579 U.S. ___ (2016)

Justice ALITO delivered the opinion of the Court.

The Hobbs Act makes it a crime for a person to affect commerce, or to attempt to do so, by robbery. 18 U.S.C. §1951(a). The Act defines "commerce" broadly as interstate commerce "and all other commerce over which the United States has jurisdiction." §1951(b)(3). This case requires us to decide what the Government must prove to satisfy the Hobbs Act's commerce element when a defendant commits a robbery that targets a marijuana dealer's drugs or drug proceeds.

The answer to this question is straightforward and dictated by our precedent. We held in Gonzales v. Raich, 545 U.S. 1 (2005), that the Commerce Clause gives Congress authority to regulate the national market for marijuana, including the authority to proscribe the purely intrastate production, possession, and sale of this controlled substance. Because Congress may regulate these intrastate activities based on their aggregate effect on interstate commerce, it follows that Congress may also regulate intrastate drug *theft*. And since the Hobbs Act criminalizes robberies and attempted robberies that affect any commerce "over which the United States has jurisdiction," §1951(b)(3), the prosecution in a Hobbs Act robbery case satisfies the Act's commerce element if it shows that the defendant robbed or attempted to rob a drug dealer of drugs or drug proceeds. By targeting a drug dealer in this way, a robber necessarily affects or attempts to affect commerce over which the United States has jurisdiction.

In this case, petitioner Anthony Taylor was convicted on two Hobbs Act counts based on proof that he attempted to rob marijuana dealers of their drugs and drug money. We hold that this evidence was sufficient to satisfy the Act's commerce element.

I

[Here Justice Alito described the facts and procedural history of the case: The "Southwest Goonz" gang committed a series of home-invasion robberies targeting drug dealers—who tended to keep lots of cash and illegal drugs in their homes, and who usually wouldn't report robberies to the police—near Roanoke, Virginia. Defendant Anthony Taylor participated in two such home invasions during late 2009; in both instances, the gang did not find any illegal drugs to steal, but took other property and cash. Taylor was charged with two counts of Hobbs Act robbery, in violation of 18 U.S.C. §1951(a), and one count of using a firearm in furtherance of a crime of violence, in violation of 18 U.S.C. §924(c). Taylor's first trial ended in a hung jury. At the retrial, the judge barred Taylor from introducing evidence that the drug dealers he robbed dealt only in locally grown marijuana. The judge also denied Taylor's motion for a judgment of acquittal on Commerce Clause grounds, holding that the evidence that Taylor attempted to rob drug dealers of their illegal drugs was sufficient, as a matter of law, to establish the required element of "affects commerce . . . or attempts or conspires so to do" under the Hobbs Act. Taylor was convicted, and he appealed the sufficiency of the evidence to prove the "affects commerce" element. The Fourth Circuit affirmed.—Eds.]

II

A

The Hobbs Act provides in relevant part as follows:

> "Whoever in any way or degree obstructs, delays, or affects commerce or the movement of any article or commodity in commerce, by robbery . . . or attempts or conspires so to do . . . shall be fined under this title or imprisoned not more than twenty years, or both." 18 U.S.C. §1951(a).

The Act then defines the term "commerce" to mean

> "commerce within the District of Columbia, or any Territory or Possession of the United States; all commerce between any point in a State, Territory, Possession, or the District of Columbia and any point outside thereof; all commerce between points within the same State through any place outside such State; and all other commerce over which the United States has jurisdiction." §1951(b)(3).

The language of the Hobbs Act is unmistakably broad. It reaches any obstruction, delay, or other effect on commerce, even if small, and the Act's definition of commerce encompasses "all . . . commerce over which the United States has jurisdiction." Ibid. We have noted the sweep of the Act in past cases. United States v. Culbert, 435 U.S. 371, 373 (1978) ("These words do not lend themselves to restrictive interpretation"); Stirone v. United States, 361 U.S. 212, 215 (1960) (The Hobbs Act "speaks in broad language, manifesting a purpose to use all the constitutional power Congress has to punish interference with interstate commerce by extortion, robbery or physical violence").

B

To determine how far this commerce element extends—and what the Government must prove to meet it—we look to our Commerce Clause cases. We have said that there are three categories of activity that Congress may regulate under its commerce power: (1) "the use of the channels of interstate commerce"; (2) "the instrumentalities of interstate commerce, or persons or things in interstate commerce, even though the threat may come only from intrastate activities"; and (3) "those activities having a substantial relation to interstate commerce, . . . *i.e.*, those activities that substantially affect interstate commerce." United States v. Lopez, 514 U.S. 549-559 (1995). We have held that activities in this third category—those that "substantially affect" commerce—may be regulated so long as they substantially affect interstate commerce in the aggregate, even if their individual impact on interstate commerce is minimal. See Wickard v. Filburn, 317 U.S. 111, 125 (1942) ("[E]ven if appellee's activity be local and though it may not be regarded as commerce, it may still, whatever its nature, be reached by Congress if it exerts a substantial economic effect on interstate commerce").

While this final category is broad, "thus far in our Nation's history our cases have upheld Commerce Clause regulation of intrastate activity only where that activity is economic in nature." United States v. Morrison, 529 U.S. 598, 613 (2000).

In this case, the activity at issue, the sale of marijuana, is unquestionably an economic activity. It is, to be sure, a form of business that is illegal under federal law and the laws of most States. But there can be no question that marijuana trafficking is a moneymaking endeavor—and a potentially lucrative one at that.

In *Raich*, the Court addressed Congress's authority to regulate the marijuana market. The Court reaffirmed "Congress' power to regulate purely local activities that are part of an economic 'class of activities' that have a substantial effect on interstate commerce." 545 U.S., at 17. The production, possession, and distribution of controlled substances constitute a "class of activities" that in the aggregate substantially affect interstate commerce, and therefore, the Court held, Congress possesses the authority to regulate (and to criminalize) the production, possession, and distribution of controlled substances even when those activities occur entirely within the boundaries of a single State. Any other outcome, we warned, would leave a gaping enforcement hole in Congress's regulatory scheme. Id., at 22.

The case now before us requires no more than that we graft our holding in *Raich* onto the commerce element of the Hobbs Act. The Hobbs Act criminalizes robberies affecting "commerce over which the United States has jurisdiction." §1951(b)(3). Under *Raich*, the market for marijuana, including its intrastate aspects, is "commerce over which the United States has jurisdiction." It therefore follows as a simple matter of logic that a robber who affects or attempts to affect even the intrastate sale of marijuana grown within the State affects or attempts to affect commerce over which the United States has jurisdiction.

C

Rejecting this logic, Taylor takes the position that the robbery or attempted robbery of a drug dealer's inventory violates the Hobbs Act only if the Government proves something more. This argument rests in part on the fact that *Raich* concerned the Controlled Substances Act (CSA), the criminal provisions of which lack a jurisdictional element. See 21 U.S.C. §§841(a), 844. The Hobbs Act, by contrast, contains such an element—namely, the conduct criminalized must affect or attempt to affect commerce in some way or degree. See 18 U.S.C. §1951(a). Therefore, Taylor reasons, the prosecution must prove beyond a reasonable doubt either (1) that the particular drugs in question originated or were destined for sale out of State or (2) that the particular drug dealer targeted in the robbery operated an interstate business. The Second and Seventh Circuits have adopted this same argument. See United States v. Needham, 604 F.3d 673, 681 (CA2 2010); United States v. Peterson, 236 F.3d 848, 855 (CA7 2001).

This argument is flawed. It confuses the standard of proof with the meaning of the element that must be proved. There is no question that the Government in a Hobbs Act prosecution must prove beyond a reasonable doubt that the defendant engaged in conduct that satisfies the Act's commerce element, but the meaning of that element is a question of law. And, as noted, *Raich* established that the purely intrastate production and sale of marijuana is commerce over which the Federal Government has jurisdiction. Therefore, if the Government proves beyond a reasonable doubt that a robber targeted a marijuana dealer's drugs or illegal proceeds, the Government has proved beyond a reasonable doubt that commerce over which the United States has jurisdiction was affected. . . .

This conclusion does not make the commerce provision of the Hobbs Act superfluous. That statute, unlike the criminal provisions of the CSA, applies to forms of conduct that, even in the aggregate, may not substantially affect commerce. The Act's commerce element ensures that applications of the Act do not exceed Congress's authority. But in a case like this one, where the target of a robbery is a drug dealer, proof that the defendant's conduct in and of itself affected or threatened commerce is not needed. All that is needed is proof that the defendant's conduct fell within a category of conduct that, in the aggregate, had the requisite effect.

D

. . . As long as Congress may regulate the purely intrastate possession and sale of illegal drugs, Congress may criminalize the theft or attempted theft of those same drugs.

We reiterate what this means. In order to obtain a conviction under the Hobbs Act for the robbery or attempted robbery of a drug dealer, the Government need not show that the drugs that a defendant stole or attempted to steal either traveled or were destined for transport across state lines. Rather, to satisfy the Act's commerce element, it is enough that a defendant knowingly stole or attempted to steal drugs or drug proceeds, for, as a matter of law, the market for illegal drugs is "commerce over which the United States has jurisdiction." And it makes no difference under our cases that any actual or threatened effect on commerce in a particular case is minimal. See Perez v. United States, 402 U.S. 146, 154 (1971) ("Where the class of activities is regulated and that class is within the reach of federal power, the courts have no power 'to excise, as trivial, individual instances' of the class" (emphasis deleted)).

E

In the present case, the Government met its burden by introducing evidence that Taylor's gang intentionally targeted drug dealers to obtain drugs and drug proceeds. One of the victims had been robbed of substantial quantities of drugs at his residence in the past, and the other was thought to possess high-grade marijuana. The robbers also made explicit statements in the course of the robberies revealing that they believed that the victims possessed drugs and drug proceeds. . . . Both robberies were committed with the express intent to obtain illegal drugs and the proceeds from the sale of illegal drugs. Such proof is sufficient to meet the commerce element of the Hobbs Act.

Our holding today is limited to cases in which the defendant targets drug dealers for the purpose of stealing drugs or drug proceeds. We do not resolve what the Government must prove to establish Hobbs Act robbery where some other type of business or victim is targeted. See, *e.g.*, *Stirone*, supra, at 215 (Government offered evidence that the defendant attempted to extort a concrete business that actually obtained supplies and materials from out of State).

* * *

The judgment of the Fourth Circuit is affirmed.

Justice THOMAS, dissenting.
. . . Under the Court's decision today, the Government can obtain a Hobbs Act conviction without proving that the defendant's robbery in fact affected interstate commerce—or any commerce. The Court's holding creates serious constitutional problems and extends our already expansive, flawed commerce-power precedents. I would construe the Hobbs Act in accordance with constitutional limits and hold that the Act punishes a robbery only when the Government proves that the robbery itself affected interstate commerce.

I

. . .To determine the Hobbs Act's reach, I start by examining the limitations on Congress' authority to punish robbery under its commerce power. In light of those limitations and in accordance with the Hobbs Act's text, I would hold that the Government in a Hobbs Act case may obtain a conviction for robbery only if it proves, beyond a reasonable doubt, that the defendant's robbery itself affected interstate commerce. The Government may not obtain a conviction by proving only that the defendant's robbery affected intrastate commerce or other intrastate activity.

A

Congress possesses only limited authority to prohibit and punish robbery. "The Constitution creates a Federal Government of enumerated powers." United States v. Lopez, 514 U.S. 549, 552 (1995); see Art. I, §8; Marbury v. Madison, 1 Cranch 137, 176 (1803) (Marshall, C.J.) ("The powers of the legislature are defined, and limited; and that those limits may not be mistaken, or forgotten, the constitution is written"). As with its powers generally, Congress has only limited authority over crime. . . . The Constitution expressly delegates to Congress authority over only four specific crimes: counterfeiting securities and coin of the United States, Art. I, §8, cl. 6; piracies and felonies committed on the high seas, Art. I, §8, cl. 10; offenses against the law of nations, ibid.; and treason, Art. III, §3, cl. 2. Given these limited grants of federal power, it is "clea[r] that Congress cannot punish felonies generally." Cohens v. Virginia, 6 Wheat. 264, 428 (1821) (Marshall, C.J.). Congress has "no general right to punish murder committed within any of the States," for example, and no general right to punish the many crimes that fall outside of Congress' express grants of criminal authority. Id., at 426. "The Constitution," in short, "withhold[s] from Congress a plenary police power." Lopez, supra, at 566; see Art. I, §8; Amdt. 10.

Beyond the four express grants of federal criminal authority, then, Congress may validly enact criminal laws only to the extent that doing so is "necessary and proper for carrying into Execution" its enumerated powers or other powers that the Constitution vests in the Federal Government. Art. I, §8, cl. 18. As Chief Justice Marshall explained, "the [federal] government may, legitimately, punish any violation of its laws" as a necessary and proper means for carrying into execution Congress' enumerated powers. McCulloch v. Maryland, 4 Wheat. 316, 416 (1819); see id., at 416-421. But if these limitations are not respected, Congress will accumulate the general police power that the Constitution withholds.

The scope of Congress' power to punish robbery in the Hobbs Act—or in any federal statute—must be assessed in light of these principles. The Commerce Clause—the constitutional provision that the Hobbs Act most clearly invokes—does not authorize Congress to punish robbery. That

Clause authorizes Congress to regulate "Commerce . . . among the several States." Art. I, §8, cl. 3. Robbery is not "Commerce" under that Clause. . . .

Because Congress has no freestanding power to punish robbery and because robbery is not itself "Commerce," Congress may prohibit and punish robbery only to the extent that doing so is "necessary and proper for carrying into Execution" Congress' power to regulate commerce. Art. I, §8, cl. 18. To be "necessary," Congress' prohibition of robbery must be "plainly adapted" to regulating interstate commerce. *McCulloch*, supra, at 421. . . .

B

With those principles in mind, I turn to the Hobbs Act. . . .

In keeping with Congress' authority to regulate certain commerce—but not robbery generally—the central feature of a Hobbs Act crime is an effect on commerce. The Act begins by focusing on commerce and then carefully describes the required relationship between the proscribed conduct and commerce: The Act uses active verbs—"obstructs," "delays," "affects"—to describe how a robbery must relate to commerce, making clear that a defendant's robbery must affect commerce. . . .

[F]or the Hobbs Act to constitutionally prohibit robberies that interfere with intrastate activity, that prohibition would need to be "necessary and proper for carrying into Execution" Congress' power to regulate interstate commerce, Art. I, §8, cls. 3, 18. Punishing a local robbery—one that affects only intrastate commerce or other intrastate activity—cannot satisfy that standard. . . . Permitting Congress to criminalize such robberies would confer on Congress a general police power over the Nation—even though the Constitution confers no such power on Congress. *Lopez*, 514 U.S., at 566; see *Raich*, 545 U.S., at 65 (Thomas, J., dissenting). Allowing the Federal Government to reach a simple home robbery, for example, would "encroac[h] on States' traditional police powers to define the criminal law and to protect . . . their citizens." Id., at 66. This would "subvert basic principles of federalism and dual sovereignty," id., at 65, and would be inconsistent with the "letter and spirit" of the Constitution, *McCulloch*, 4 Wheat., at 421.

Thus, the Hobbs Act reaches a local robbery only when that particular robbery "obstructs, delays, or affects" *interstate* commerce. §§1951(a), 1951(b)(3). So construed, the Hobbs Act validly punishes robbery. . . . If construed to reach a robbery that does not affect interstate commerce, however, the Hobbs Act exceeds Congress' authority because it is no longer "necessary and proper" to the execution of Congress' power "[t]o regulate Commerce . . . among the several States," Art. I, §8, cls. 3, 18.

Robberies that might satisfy these principles would be those that affect the channels of interstate commerce or instrumentalities of interstate commerce. A robbery that forces an interstate freeway to shut down thus may form the basis for a valid Hobbs Act conviction. So too might a robbery of a truck driver who is in the course of transporting commercial goods across state lines. But if the Government cannot prove that a robbery in a State affected interstate commerce, then the robbery is not punishable under the Hobbs Act. Sweeping in robberies that do not affect interstate commerce comes too close to conferring on Congress a general police power over the Nation.

Given the Hobbs Act's text and relevant constitutional principles, the Government in a Hobbs Act robbery case (at least one that involves only intrastate robbery) must prove, beyond a reasonable doubt, that the defendant's robbery itself affected interstate commerce.

C

On this interpretation of the Hobbs Act, petitioner David Anthony Taylor's convictions cannot stand. The Government cites no evidence that Taylor actually obstructed, delayed, or affected interstate commerce when he committed the two intrastate robberies here. The Government did not prove that Taylor affected any channel of interstate commerce, instrumentality of commerce, or person or thing in interstate commerce. See *Lopez*, supra, at 558-559 (describing these core areas of commerce regulation). Nor did the Government prove that Taylor affected an actual commercial transaction—let alone an interstate commercial transaction. . . . Under the principles set forth above, that is not sufficient to bring Taylor's robberies within the Hobbs Act's reach. We should reverse Taylor's Hobbs Act convictions. . . .

Notes on Federalism and Criminal Law

1. The number of local prosecutors is roughly five times the number of U.S. Attorneys and their Assistants. The number of local police officers is more than 50 times the number of FBI agents. There are 1.2 million inmates housed in state penitentiaries, compared to 185,000 in federal prisons. As these numbers show, America's criminal justice system is hardly in danger of becoming a centralized, nationalized system like those in most other countries. Yet language like Justice Thomas's in *Taylor*, with its image of an all-powerful federal justice system prosecuting simple, garden-variety home invasions, is fairly common in judicial opinions in federal criminal cases. What is Justice Thomas worried about? What, if anything, *should* federal judges worry about when deciding cases like *Taylor*?

2. Most of the Supreme Court (save Justice Thomas) found *Taylor* to be a relatively easy federal jurisdiction case, because Congress had previously indicated its desire to regulate illegal drugs to the maximum extent of its Commerce Clause power. (See Gonzales v. Raich, 545 U.S. 1 (2005), reproduced in full later in the casebook, at the end of Chapter 6.) But what about Hobbs Act cases that *don't* involve the robbery of illegal drugs?

In *United States v. Shavers*, 693 F.3d 363 (3d Cir. 2012), defendant Glorious Shavers and two compatriots were convicted, inter alia, of violating the Hobbs Act when they robbed the patrons of an unlicensed "speakeasy" operating out of a single-family home in North Philadelphia, obtaining two cell phones, a wallet, and $121 in cash. On appeal, after noting the "rather low hurdle" faced by the government in Hobbs Act cases, the Third Circuit found the commerce clause connection to be sufficiently established. The speakeasy, despite its location in a home, was a profit-making business that had operated for years; alcohol sold there came from out of state; and although the speakeasy's owner was not directly victimized by the robbery, she was so frightened by it that she thereafter limited her patrons to friends and family, and three months later, closed the joint altogether. The court acknowledged, however, that the case "stands at the outer limit of Hobbs Act jurisdiction and it is far from obvious which cases are purely matters for state prosecution." Id. at 376.

In *United States v. Jimenez-Torres*, 435 F.3d 3 (1st Cir. 2006), defendant Hector Jimenez-Torres (along with five others) broke into the home of Carlos Flores-Rodriguez, the sole proprietor of a Texaco gas station in Puerto Rico. Flores-Rodriguez was killed during the robbery, and the robbers got away with about $600 in daily receipts from the gas station (which Flores-Rodriguez had stashed in a kitchen cabinet). The First Circuit held that the robbery "affect[ed]" interstate commerce because (1) the robbery depleted the assets of a business that operated in interstate commerce (or, to be more precise, inter-territorial; the gas station bought its gas from a refinery located in the U.S. Virgin Islands); and (2) the robbery caused the gas station to close, primarily due to the sudden and untimely death of its owner. The court noted that "Jimenez may not have intended to cause these effects but his intent is irrelevant to establishing the commerce element of a Hobbs Act offense." Judge Torruella wrote a strongly worded concurring opinion:

> We are not faced here with the robbery of decedent's local *gas station*. . . . Nor is this a case of Jimenez waylaying the decedent on his way to the bank with the proceeds of interstate sales. It is not even a case of robbers intercepting decedent and forcibly depriving him of the local gas station's receipts while he was on the way home. Although all of these scenarios would cause me to hesitate as to the impact of such criminal activity on interstate commerce, certainly these examples would be closer to providing the required constitutional jurisdictional nexus [than] the present case. Here, all criminal activity took place in decedent's *home*, the stolen funds had come to rest in decedent's *kitchen*, and there is no evidence that Jimenez or his cohorts even knew of their existence before decedent's *home* was fortuitously picked to be burglarized. There was in fact no connection between the perpetrators of the robbery and decedent's business. . . .
>
> . . . At the rate we are going, perhaps the day will come when the federal government will see fit to prosecute the robbery of a child's roadside lemonade stand because the lemons came from California, the sugar was refined in Philadelphia, and the paper cups were manufactured in China. . . .

I cannot agree that the federal government has the constitutional power to prosecute Jimenez for a violation of the Hobbs Act given the facts proven in this case. However, because precedent binds me until such time as the Supreme Court puts an end to the fictions that allow the apparently limitless aggrandizement of federal power into areas reserved to the states by the Constitution, I have no choice but to concur in the affirmance of Jimenez's conviction.

Id. at 15-16 (Torruella, J., concurring). It seems reasonable to suppose that Judge Torruella would not be a huge fan of the Supreme Court's decision in *Taylor*. Does he have a valid point?

3. As *Taylor*, *Shavers*, and *Jimenez-Torres* all demonstrate, jurisdiction over robberies is divided between federal and state governments based largely on the class of the robbery victim. When businesses (legitimate or not), owners of businesses, or rich individuals are robbed, the robbers most likely can be charged in either federal *or* state court; when less-than-rich individuals are robbed, only state law governs and only local prosecutors may prosecute. That seems a strange way to divide authority over criminal law enforcement. Is there any way to make sense of it?

4. The law of federal jurisdiction has changed a great deal over time—in both directions. A century ago in Champion v. Ames, 188 U.S. 321 (1903), the Supreme Court upheld a federal statute barring the interstate transportation of lottery tickets. Under *Champion*, interstate *movement* of people or goods would give the federal government power to prosecute and punish, but the *effects* of intrastate transactions would not: meaning, the federal government probably would have had no jurisdiction over crimes like the one in *Taylor*. Like much else in American law, that changed in the 1930s and 1940s. The scope of federal power increased substantially as the federal government sought to battle the Great Depression and fight World War II. For nearly 60 years, any crime that had economic effects—as virtually all crimes do—appeared to fall within the scope of the federal power to regulate interstate commerce. That state of affairs was captured by Perez v. United States, 402 U.S. 146 (1971), in which the Supreme Court held that a small-time loan shark, whose transactions all occurred within the boundaries of the city where he worked, affected interstate commerce enough to justify federal jurisdiction.

Perez was the high-water mark of federal criminal jurisdiction. Indeed, when the authors of this casebook went to law school back in the 1980s, they were taught that federalism (meaning dual sovereignty, or the balance of state and federal government powers) was dead and had been relegated to the realm of legal history—that the federal government could regulate anything it wanted to regulate, always justifying its actions on the ground that the subject of the regulation affected interstate commerce. Such broad conclusions seemed accurate, given that from the 1940s to the mid-1990s, the Supreme Court never once invalidated a federal statute that was based on a Congressional assertion of the interstate commerce power.

The pendulum began to swing back in United States v. Lopez, 514 U.S. 549 (1995). The particular federal statute at issue in *Lopez* was the Gun-Free

School Zones Act, which barred possession of firearms within one thousand feet of a school. By a 5-4 vote, the Supreme Court invalidated the Act, on the ground that it exceeded the scope of Congress' authority under the Commerce Clause. The Court explained that most of the statutes previously upheld had involved regulation of "economic activity"; the Gun-Free School Zones Act, on the other hand, did not involve "economic activity," since it applied to all gun possession (even, for example, the possession of a gun that had been home-built with materials obtained entirely within the state). Moreover, while reiterating that Congress can enact federal regulations that go beyond interstate *movement* of people and goods, the Court limited the broader reach of the Commerce Clause to regulation of activities that "*substantially* affect" interstate commerce. Since *Lopez*, federal courts have paid closer attention to the boundaries of federal power over crime and punishment than in the past—although, as *Taylor* indicates, that doesn't necessarily mean that federal criminal jurisdiction will actually be restricted.

Today, we may be witnessing another significant expansion of federal power, in response to three new crises that rocked the nation in the early years of the twenty-first century: (1) the War on Terror that commenced on September 11, 2001; (2) major natural and man-made disasters, with impacts on a scope never before seen in the United States, and well beyond the capacity of the individual states to address (i.e., Hurricane Katrina and the Gulf Oil Disaster); and (3) the massive global economic downturn that began in 2008. These crises led to new and unprecedented assertions of federal power (e.g., the USA Patriot Act, the Department of Homeland Security, and stricter federal regulations of the financial industry). The ever-changing balance of federalism seems to be changing once again. Will this lead to renewed growth in federal criminal law? Stay tuned.

B. FEDERAL *MENS REA* DOCTRINE

Federal criminal cases do not consistently follow the common-law doctrines on intent and mistake. Nor does federal criminal law consistently follow the Model Penal Code. Instead, federal crimes tend to offer more generous *mens rea* standards than the crimes in most states—including both states that use common-law intent standards and states that have adopted the MPC intent framework. The next three subsections address three separate questions about the distinctive federal law of *mens rea*: First, how did that federal criminal law come to be? Second, what level of factual knowledge does federal law require in criminal cases? Third and most important, what level of legal knowledge does federal criminal law require? As you read the following cases, consider also a fourth question: Are federal *mens rea* standards more just than the standards used by state courts?

1. History

In the years following Franklin D. Roosevelt's New Deal, the legal conventional wisdom held that federal criminal law would be largely a strict liability field, filled with regulatory statutes that required the punishment of regulated actors regardless of their state of mind. The next case, United States v. Dotterweich, 320 U.S. 277 (1943), shows what that field would have looked like. But the field didn't turn out the way FDR's admirers planned—as the second main case below, Morissette v. United States, 342 U.S. 246 (1952), illustrates.

United States v. Dotterweich

Supreme Court of the United States
320 U.S. 277 (1943)

Mr. Justice FRANKFURTER delivered the opinion of the Court.

This was a prosecution begun by two informations, consolidated for trial, charging Buffalo Pharmacal Company, Inc., and Dotterweich, its president and general manager, with violations of the Act of Congress of June 25, 1938, 52 Stat. 1040, 21 U.S.C. §§301-392, known as the Federal Food, Drug, and Cosmetic Act. The Company, a jobber in drugs, purchased them from their manufacturers and shipped them, repacked under its own label, in interstate commerce. . . . The informations were based on §301 of that Act (21 U.S.C. §331), paragraph (a) of which prohibits "The introduction or delivery for introduction into interstate commerce of any . . . drug . . . that is adulterated or misbranded." "Any person" violating this provision is, by paragraph (a) of §303 (21 U.S.C. §333), made "guilty of a misdemeanor." Three counts went to the jury—two, for shipping misbranded drugs in interstate commerce, and a third, for so shipping an adulterated drug. The jury disagreed as to the corporation and found Dotterweich guilty on all three counts. . . . The Circuit Court of Appeals . . . reversed the conviction on the ground that only the corporation was the "person" subject to prosecution. . . .

. . . The Food and Drugs Act of 1906 was an exertion by Congress of its power to keep impure and adulterated food and drugs out of the channels of commerce. By the Act of 1938, Congress extended the range of its control over illicit and noxious articles and stiffened the penalties for disobedience. The purposes of this legislation thus touch phases of the lives and health of people which, in the circumstances of modern industrialism, are largely beyond self-protection. Regard for these purposes should infuse construction of the legislation if it is to be treated as a working instrument of government. . . . The prosecution to which Dotterweich was subjected is based on a now familiar type of legislation whereby penalties serve as effective means of regulation. Such legislation dispenses with the conventional requirement for criminal conduct—awareness of some wrongdoing. In the interest of the larger good it puts the burden of acting at hazard upon a person otherwise innocent but standing in responsible relation to a public danger. United States v. Balint, 258 U.S. 250. And so it is clear that shipments like those now in issue are "punished by the statute if the article is misbranded [or adulterated], and that the article may be misbranded [or adulterated] without any conscious fraud at all. It was natural enough to throw this risk on shippers with regard to the identity of their wares. . . ." United States v. Johnson, 221 U.S. 488, 497-98.

The statute makes "any person" who violates §301(a) guilty of a "misdemeanor." It specifically defines "person" to include "corporation." §201(e). But the only way in which a corporation can act is through the individuals who act on its behalf. And the historic conception of a "misdemeanor" makes all those responsible for it equally guilty. . . . If, then, Dotterweich is not subject to the Act, it must be solely on the ground that individuals are immune when the "person" who violates §301(a) is a corporation, although from the point of view of action the individuals *are* the corporation. . . . To hold that the Act of 1938 freed all individuals, except when proprietors, from the culpability under which the earlier legislation had placed them is to defeat the very object of the new Act. Nothing is clearer than that the later legislation was designed to enlarge and stiffen the penal net and not to narrow and loosen it. This purpose was unequivocally avowed by the two committees which reported the bills to the Congress. The House Committee reported that the Act "seeks to set up effective provisions against abuses of consumer welfare growing out of inadequacies in the Food and Drugs Act. . . ." (H. Rep. No. 2139, 75th Cong., 3d Sess., at 1.) And the Senate Committee explicitly pointed out that the new legislation "must not weaken the existing laws," but on the contrary "it must strengthen and extend that law's protection of the consumer." (S. Rep. No. 152, 75th Cong., 1st Sess., at 1.) . . .

. . . Hardship there doubtless may be under a statute which thus penalizes the transaction though consciousness of wrongdoing be totally wanting. Balancing relative hardships, Congress has preferred to place it upon those who have at least the opportunity of informing themselves of the existence of conditions imposed for the protection of consumers before sharing in illicit commerce, rather than to throw the hazard on the innocent public who are wholly helpless.

It would be too treacherous to define or even to indicate by way of illustration the class of employees which stands in such a responsible relation. To attempt a formula embracing the variety of conduct whereby persons may responsibly contribute in furthering a transaction forbidden by an Act of Congress, to wit, to send illicit goods across state lines, would be mischievous futility. In such matters the good sense of prosecutors, the wise guidance of trial judges, and the ultimate judgment of juries must be trusted. Our system of criminal justice necessarily depends on "conscience and circumspection in prosecuting officers," Nash v. United States, 229 U.S. 373, 378, even when the consequences are far more drastic than they are under the provision of law before us. See United States v. Balint, supra (involving a maximum sentence of five years). For present purpose it suffices to say that . . . the District Court properly left the question of the responsibility of Dotterweich for the shipment to the jury, and there was sufficient evidence to support its verdict. . . .

Mr. Justice MURPHY, dissenting.

. . . There is no evidence in this case of any personal guilt on the part of the respondent. There is no proof or claim that he ever knew of the introduction into commerce of the adulterated drugs in question, much less that he actively participated in their introduction. Guilt is imputed to the respondent solely on the basis of his authority and responsibility as president and general manager of the corporation.

It is a fundamental principle of Anglo-Saxon jurisprudence that guilt is personal and that it ought not lightly to be imputed to a citizen who, like the respondent, has no evil intention or consciousness of wrongdoing. It may be proper to charge him with responsibility to the corporation and the stockholders for negligence and mismanagement. But in the absence of clear statutory authorization it is inconsistent with established canons of criminal law to rest liability on an act in which the accused did not participate and of which he had no personal knowledge. Before we place the stigma of a criminal conviction upon any such citizen the legislative mandate must be clear and unambiguous. . . .

. . . To erect standards of responsibility is a difficult legislative task and the opinion of this Court admits that it is "too treacherous" and a "mischievous futility" for us to engage in such pursuits. But the only alternative is a blind resort to "the good sense of prosecutors, the wise guidance of trial judges, and the ultimate judgment of juries." Yet that situation is precisely what our constitutional system sought to avoid. . . . The legislative power to restrain the liberty and to imperil the good reputation of citizens must not rest upon the variable attitudes and opinions of those charged with the duties of interpreting and enforcing the mandates of the law. I therefore cannot approve the decision of the Court in this case.

Mr. Justice ROBERTS, Mr. Justice REED, and Mr. Justice RUTLEDGE join in this dissent.

Notes and Questions

1. Had the law required the government to prove that Dotterweich knew the drugs were adulterated, Dotterweich and a host of other regulated actors like him would have been unconvictable. If the law *didn't* require proof of knowledge, criminal punishment might have been imposed even in cases with "no evidence . . . of any personal guilt." Both results seem problematic: The government has a strong interest in requiring that drugs be safe, but individual defendants have a strong interest in avoiding prison sentences for merely negligent conduct. Is there a way out of this box?

Of course there is. The law can regulate the conduct of people like Dotterweich without criminally punishing them. Civil regulations that impose strict liability and hefty fines for violators — including, perhaps, individual violators like Dotterweich — can ensure reasonably high levels of safety without the need for criminal prosecutions. Criminal law can require substantial proof of criminal intent without disabling the regulatory state.

2. That proposition seems obvious today — but to the New Deal generation, it was anything but. Today, criminal punishment is seen as a special form of government power, limited in special ways. That was less true in 1943. Most of the New Deal's core regulatory statutes included provisions criminalizing violations. Pro-New Deal politicians and judges (like Felix Frankfurter, author of the majority opinion in *Dotterweich*, former Alabama Senator Hugo Black, and former Securities and Exchange Commission Chair William O. Douglas; note that Black and Douglas joined Frankfurter's opinion) feared that, if the law restricted criminal prosecution too much, the regulatory state would be unable to regulate effectively. For their part, anti-New Deal politicians and judges often embraced restrictions on criminal prosecution and punishment because they sought to limit government power generally — and hoped to limit the authority of the many government agencies that FDR and his followers had created.

3. Though *Dotterweich* was the product of New Deal-era debates, it is more than a historical curiosity. The defendant in United States v. Hong, 242 F.3d 528 (4th Cir. 2001), ran a company called Avion Environmental Group; the company in turn ran a wastewater treatment facility in Richmond, Virginia. The company purchased an inadequate filtration system that Hong was told could not handle the amount of waste the facility processed. The system soon became clogged, leading some of Avion's employees to dump untreated waste into Richmond's sewer system, in violation of Avion's permit and of the Clean Water Act. Hong was charged and convicted of 13 counts of illegal discharge of waste under the Act; he was fined $300,000 and sentenced to three years in prison. The Fourth Circuit affirmed the conviction and sentence, citing *Dotterweich* for the proposition that Hong was a "responsible corporate officer" and consequently could be held liable for illegal discharges that he neither committed nor supervised: "Under the [Clean Water Act], a person is a 'responsible corporate officer' if the person has authority to exercise control . . . over the activity that is causing the discharges." 242 F.3d at 531. "The government may satisfy its burden of proof by introducing evidence sufficient to warrant a finding . . . that the defendant had, by reason of his position in the corporation, responsibility and authority either to prevent in the first instance, or promptly to correct, the violation complained of, and that he failed to do so." Id.

4. Was Hong fairly treated? Was Dotterweich? When, if ever, is it appropriate to punish defendants who unknowingly violate criminal statutes? See the next case.

Morissette v. United States

Supreme Court of the United States
342 U.S. 246 (1952)

Mr. Justice JACKSON delivered the opinion of the Court.

This would have remained a profoundly insignificant case to all except its immediate parties had it not been so tried and submitted to the jury as to raise questions both fundamental and far-reaching in federal criminal law, for which reason we granted certiorari.

On a large tract of uninhabited and untilled land in a wooded and sparsely populated area of Michigan, the Government established a practice bombing range over which the Air Force dropped simulated bombs at ground targets. These bombs consisted of a metal cylinder about forty inches long and eight inches across, filled with sand and enough black powder to cause a smoke puff by which the strike could be located. At various places about the range signs read "Danger—Keep Out—Bombing Range." Nevertheless, the range was known as good deer country and was extensively hunted.

Spent bomb casings were cleared from the targets and thrown into piles "so that they will be out of the way." They were not stacked or piled in any order but were dumped in heaps, some of which had been accumulating for four years or upwards, were exposed to the weather and rusting away.

Morissette, in December of 1948, went hunting in this area but did not get a deer. He thought to meet expenses of the trip by salvaging some of these casings. He loaded three tons of them on his truck and took them to a nearby farm, where they were flattened by driving a tractor over them. After expending this labor and trucking them to market in Flint, he realized $84.

Morissette, by occupation, is a fruit stand operator in summer and a trucker and scrap iron collector in winter. An honorably discharged veteran of World War II, he enjoys a good name among his neighbors and has had no blemish on his record more disreputable than a conviction for reckless driving.

The loading, crushing and transporting of these casings were all in broad daylight, in full view of passers-by, without the slightest effort at concealment. When an investigation was started, Morissette voluntarily, promptly and candidly told the whole story to the authorities, saying that he had no intention of stealing but thought the property was abandoned, unwanted and considered of no value to the Government. He was indicted, however, on the charge that he "did unlawfully, willfully and knowingly steal and convert" property of the United States of the value of $84, in violation of 18 U.S.C. §641, which provides that "whoever embezzles, steals, purloins, or knowingly converts" government property is punishable by fine and imprisonment.[1] Morissette was convicted and sentenced to imprisonment for two months or to pay a fine of $200. The Court of Appeals affirmed. . . .

On his trial, Morissette, as he had at all times told investigating officers, testified that from appearances he believed the casings were cast-off and abandoned, that he did not intend to steal the property, and took it with no wrongful or criminal intent. The trial court, however, was unimpressed, and ruled: "He took it because he thought it was abandoned and he knew he was on government property. . . . That is no defense. . . . I don't think anybody can have the defense they thought the property was abandoned on another man's piece of property." The court stated: "I will not permit you to show this man thought it was abandoned. . . . I hold in this case that there is no question of abandoned property." The court refused to submit or to allow counsel to argue to the jury whether Morissette acted with innocent intention. It charged: "And I instruct you that if you believe the testimony of the government in this case, he intended to take it. . . . He had no right to take this property. . . . And it is no defense to claim that it was abandoned, because it was on private property. . . . And I instruct you to this effect: That if this young man took this property (and he says he did), without any permission (he says he did), that was on the property of the United States Government (he says it was), that it was of the value of one cent or more (and evidently it was), that he is guilty of the offense charged here. If you believe the government, he is guilty. . . . The question on intent is whether or not he intended to take the property. He says he did. Therefore, if you believe either side, he is guilty." Petitioner's counsel contended, "But the taking must have been with a felonious intent." The court ruled, however: "That is presumed by his own act."

---

1. 18 U.S.C. §641, so far as pertinent, reads:

"Whoever embezzles, steals, purloins, or knowingly converts to his use or the use of another, or without authority, sells, conveys or disposes of any record, voucher, money, or thing of value of the United States or of any department or agency thereof, or any property made or being made under contract for the United States or any department or agency thereof; . . . [s]hall be fined not more than $10,000 or imprisoned not more than ten years, or both; but if the value of such property does not exceed the sum of $100, he shall be fined not more than $1,000 or imprisoned not more than one year, or both."

The Court of Appeals [affirmed]. . . . This conclusion was thought to be required by . . . this Court's decisions in United States v. Behrman, 258 U.S. 280, and United States v. Balint, 258 U.S. 250.

I

In those cases this Court did construe mere omission from a criminal enactment of any mention of criminal intent as dispensing with it. If they be deemed precedents for principles of construction generally applicable to federal penal statutes, they authorize this conviction. Indeed, such adoption of the literal reasoning announced in those cases would do this and more — it would sweep out of all federal crimes, except when expressly preserved, the ancient requirement of a culpable state of mind. We think a resume of their historical background is convincing that an effect has been ascribed to them more comprehensive than was contemplated and one inconsistent with our philosophy of criminal law.

The contention that an injury can amount to a crime only when inflicted by intention is no provincial or transient notion. It is as universal and persistent in mature systems of law as belief in freedom of the human will and a consequent ability and duty of the normal individual to choose between good and evil. A relation between some mental element and punishment for a harmful act is almost as instinctive as the child's familiar exculpatory "But I didn't mean to," and has afforded the rational basis for a tardy and unfinished substitution of deterrence and reformation in place of retaliation and vengeance as the motivation for public prosecution.[5] Unqualified acceptance of this doctrine by English common law in the Eighteenth Century was indicated by Blackstone's sweeping statement that to constitute any crime there must first be a "vicious will." Common-law commentators of the Nineteenth Century early pronounced the same principle. . . .

Crime, as a compound concept, generally constituted only from concurrence of an evil-meaning mind with an evil-doing hand, was congenial to an intense individualism and took deep and early root in American soil. As the states codified the common law of crimes, even if their enactments were silent on the subject, their courts assumed that the omission did not signify disapproval of the principle but merely recognized that intent was so inherent in the idea of the offense that it required no statutory affirmation. Courts, with little hesitation or division, found an implication of the requirement as to offenses that were taken over from the common law.

---

5. In Williams v. New York, 337 U.S. 241, 248, we observed that "Retribution is no longer the dominant objective of the criminal law. Reformation and rehabilitation of offenders have become important goals of criminal jurisprudence." We also there referred to ". . . a prevalent modern philosophy of penology that the punishment should fit the offender and not merely the crime." Id., at 247. Such ends would seem illusory if there were no mental element in crime.

The unanimity with which they have adhered to the central thought that wrongdoing must be conscious to be criminal is emphasized by the variety, disparity and confusion of their definitions of the requisite but elusive mental element. However, courts of various jurisdictions, and for the purposes of different offenses, have devised working formulae, if not scientific ones, for the instruction of juries around such terms as "felonious intent," "criminal intent," "malice aforethought," "guilty knowledge," "fraudulent intent," "willfulness," "scienter," to denote guilty knowledge, or "*mens rea*," to signify an evil purpose or mental culpability. By use or combination of these various tokens, they have sought to protect those who were not blameworthy in mind from conviction of infamous common-law crimes.

However, the *Balint* and *Behrman* offenses belong to a category of another character, with very different antecedents and origins. The crimes there involved depend on no mental element but consist only of forbidden acts or omissions. This, while not expressed by the Court, is made clear from examination of a century-old but accelerating tendency, discernible both here and in England, to call into existence new duties and crimes which disregard any ingredient of intent. The industrial revolution multiplied the number of workmen exposed to injury from increasingly powerful and complex mechanisms, driven by freshly discovered sources of energy, requiring higher precautions by employers. Traffic of velocities, volumes and varieties unheard of came to subject the wayfarer to intolerable casualty risks if owners and drivers were not to observe new cares and uniformities of conduct. Congestion of cities and crowding of quarters called for health and welfare regulations undreamed of in simpler times. Wide distribution of goods became an instrument of wide distribution of harm when those who dispersed food, drink, drugs, and even securities, did not comply with reasonable standards of quality, integrity, disclosure and care. Such dangers have engendered increasingly numerous and detailed regulations which heighten the duties of those in control of particular industries, trades, properties or activities that affect public health, safety or welfare.

While many of these duties are sanctioned by a more strict civil liability, lawmakers, whether wisely or not, have sought to make such regulations more effective by invoking criminal sanctions to be applied by the familiar technique of criminal prosecutions and convictions. This has confronted the courts with a multitude of prosecutions, based on statutes or administrative regulations, for what have been aptly called "public welfare offenses." These cases do not fit neatly into any of such accepted classifications of common-law offenses, such as those against the state, the person, property, or public morals. Many of these offenses are not in the nature of positive aggressions or invasions, with which the common law so often dealt, but are in the nature of neglect where the law requires care, or inaction where it imposes a duty. Many violations of such regulations result in no direct or immediate injury to person or property but merely create the danger or probability of it which the law seeks to minimize. While such offenses do not threaten the security of the state in the manner of treason, they may be regarded as offenses against its authority, for their occurrence impairs the efficiency of controls deemed essential to the social order as presently constituted. In this respect, whatever the intent of the violator, the injury is the same, and the consequences are injurious or not according to fortuity. Hence, legislation applicable to such offenses, as a matter of policy, does not specify intent as a necessary element. The accused, if he does not will the violation, usually is in a position to prevent it with no more care than society might reasonably expect and no more exertion than it might reasonably exact from one who assumed his responsibilities. Also, penalties commonly are relatively small, and conviction does no grave damage to an offender's reputation. Under such considerations, courts have [held] that the guilty act alone makes out the crime. . . .

In overruling a contention that there can be no conviction on an indictment which makes no charge of criminal intent but alleges only making of a sale of a narcotic forbidden by law, Chief Justice Taft wrote:

> "While the general rule at common law was that the scienter was a necessary element in the indictment and proof of every crime, and this was followed in regard to statutory crimes even where the statutory definition did not in terms include it . . . , there has been a modification of this view in respect to prosecutions under statutes the purpose of which would be obstructed by such a requirement. It is a question of legislative intent to be construed by the court. . . ." United States v. Balint, supra, 251-52.

He referred, however, to "regulatory measures in the exercise of what is called the police power where the emphasis of the statute is evidently upon achievement of some social betterment rather than the punishment of the crimes as in cases of *mala in se*," and drew his citation of supporting authority chiefly from state court cases dealing with regulatory offenses. Id., at 252.

On the same day, the Court determined that an offense under the Narcotic Drug Act does not require intent, saying, "If the offense be a statutory one, and intent or knowledge is not made an element of it, the indictment need not charge such knowledge or intent." United States v. Behrman, supra, at 288. Of course, the purpose of every statute would be "obstructed" by requiring a finding of intent, if we assume that it had a purpose to convict without it. Therefore, the obstruction rationale does not help us to learn the purpose of the omission by Congress. And since no federal crime can exist except by force of statute, the reasoning of the *Behrman* opinion, if read literally, would work far-reaching changes in the composition of all federal crimes. . . .

It was not until recently that the Court took occasion more explicitly to relate abandonment of the ingredient of intent, not merely with considerations of expediency in obtaining convictions, nor with the *malum prohibitum* classification of the crime, but with the peculiar nature and quality of the offense. We referred to ". . . a now familiar type of legislation whereby penalties serve as effective means of regulation," and continued, "such legislation dispenses with the conventional requirement for criminal conduct—awareness of some wrongdoing. In the interest of the larger good it puts the burden of acting at hazard upon a person otherwise innocent but standing in responsible relation to a public danger." But we warned: "Hardship there doubtless may be under a statute which thus penalizes the transaction though consciousness of wrongdoing be totally wanting." United States v. Dotterweich, 320 U.S. 277, 280-281, 284.

Neither this Court nor, so far as we are aware, any other has undertaken to delineate a precise line or set forth comprehensive criteria for distinguishing between crimes that require a mental element and crimes that do not. We attempt no closed definition, for the law on the subject is neither settled nor static. The conclusion reached in the *Balint* and *Behrman* cases has our approval and adherence for the circumstances to which it was there applied. A quite different question here is whether we will expand the doctrine of crimes without intent to include those charged here.

Stealing, larceny, and its variants and equivalents, were among the earliest offenses known to the law that existed before legislation; they are invasions of rights of property which stir a sense of insecurity in the whole community and arouse public demand for retribution, the penalty is high and, when a sufficient amount is involved, the infamy is that of a felony, which, says Maitland, is ". . . as bad a word as you can give to man or thing." State courts of last resort, on whom fall the heaviest burden of interpreting criminal law in this country, have consistently retained the requirement of intent in larceny-type offenses. . . .

Congress, therefore, omitted any express prescription of criminal intent from the enactment before us in the light of an unbroken course of judicial decision in all constituent states of the Union holding intent inherent in this class of offense, even when not expressed in a statute. Congressional silence as to mental elements in an Act merely adopting into federal statutory law a concept of crime already so well defined in common law and statutory interpretation by the states may warrant quite contrary inferences than the same silence in creating an offense new to general law, for whose definition the courts have no guidance except the Act. Because the offenses before this Court in the *Balint* and *Behrman* cases were of this latter class, we cannot accept them as authority for eliminating intent from offenses incorporated from the common law. . . .

We hold that mere omission from §641 of any mention of intent will not be construed as eliminating that element from the crimes denounced.

II

. . . Congress, by the language of this section, has been at pains to incriminate only "knowing" conversions. . . . Had the statute applied to conversions without qualification, it would have made crimes of all unwitting, inadvertent and unintended conversions. Knowledge, of course, is not identical with intent and may not have been the most apt words of limitation. But knowing conversion requires more than knowledge that defendant was taking the property into his possession. He must have had knowledge of the facts, though not necessarily the law, that made the taking a conversion. In the case before us, . . . it is not apparent how Morissette could have knowingly or intentionally converted property that he did not know could be converted, as would be the case if it was in fact abandoned or if he truly believed it to be abandoned and unwanted property.

It is said, and at first blush the claim has plausibility, that, if we construe the statute to require a mental element as part of criminal conversion, it becomes a meaningless duplication of the offense of stealing, and that conversion can be given meaning only by interpreting it to disregard intention. But here again a broader view of the evolution of these crimes throws a different light on the legislation. It is not surprising if there is considerable overlapping in the embezzlement, stealing, purloining and knowing conversion grouped in this statute. What has concerned codifiers of the larceny-type offense is that gaps or crevices have separated particular crimes of this general class and guilty men have escaped through the breaches. The books contain a surfeit of cases drawing fine distinctions between slightly different circumstances under which one may obtain wrongful advantages from another's property. The codifiers wanted to reach all such instances. Probably every stealing is a conversion, but certainly not every knowing conversion is a stealing. . . . Conversion . . . may be consummated without any intent to keep and without any wrongful taking, where the initial possession by the converter was entirely lawful. Conversion may include misuse or abuse of property. It may reach use in an unauthorized manner or to an unauthorized extent of property placed in one's custody for limited use. Money rightfully taken into one's custody may be converted without any intent to keep or embezzle it merely by commingling it with the custodian's own, if he was under a duty to keep it separate and intact. . . . It is not difficult to think of intentional and knowing abuses and unauthorized uses of government property that might be knowing conversions but which could not be reached as embezzlement, stealing or purloining. . . .

We find no grounds for inferring any affirmative instruction from Congress to eliminate intent from any offense with which this defendant was charged.

III

As we read the record, this case was tried on the theory that even if criminal intent were essential its presence (a) should be decided by the court (b) as a presumption of law, apparently conclusive, (c) predicated upon the isolated act of taking rather than upon all of the circumstances. In each of these respects we believe the trial court was in error. . . .

The court thought the only question was, "Did he intend to take the property?" That the removal of them was a conscious and intentional act was admitted. But that isolated fact is not an adequate basis on which the jury should find the criminal intent to steal or knowingly convert, that is, wrongfully to deprive another of possession of property. Whether that intent existed, the jury must determine, not only from the act of taking, but from that together with defendant's testimony and all of the surrounding circumstances. Of course, the jury, considering Morissette's awareness that these casings were on government property, his failure to seek any permission for their removal and his self-interest as a witness, might have disbelieved his profession of innocent intent and concluded that his assertion of a belief that the casings were abandoned was an afterthought. Had the jury convicted on proper instructions it would be the end of the matter. But juries are not bound by what seems inescapable logic to judges. They might have concluded that the heaps of spent casings left in the hinterland to rust away presented an appearance of unwanted and abandoned junk, and that lack of any conscious deprivation of property or intentional injury was indicated by Morissette's good character, the openness of the taking, crushing and transporting of the casings, and the candor with which it was all admitted. They might have refused to brand Morissette as a thief. Had they done so, that too would have been the end of the matter. . . .

Mr. Justice DOUGLAS concurs in the result.

Notes and Questions

1. *Morissette* and *Dotterweich* represent two very different models for the federal law of *mens rea*. Which model seems more practical? Which seems more just? Do your answers to those two questions differ?

2. Why do you suppose the government prosecuted Morissette? There is no evidence that, had Morissette left the bomb casings where they were, any government official would have collected and sold them for scrap. More likely, they would have stayed where they were and rusted. What was the point of punishing Morissette for taking a small piece of property to which its owner attached no value?

3. Reread Justice Jackson's description of United States v. Balint, 258 U.S. 250 (1922), along with the quoted passage from Chief Justice Taft's opinion in that case. Before the enactment of the Harrison Act—the statute Balint was charged with violating—the use of various opium products was both legal and common in the United States. Doctors often prescribed such drugs. Those things did not immediately cease to be true when the Act took effect. It takes time for ordinary people to understand that the rules have changed, that older conduct patterns are now impermissible. Naturally, the government tried to speed that process along, by prosecuting (for example) doctors who prescribed drugs without the relevant federal licenses. What should happen in such cases? The defendants may claim, justifiably, that they cannot be expected to know about every legal change that might affect their conduct. The government may contend, also justifiably, that if defendants can excuse their violations by claiming ignorance of the new legal rule, then new legal rules will be unenforceable. As between the rock and the hard place, which should prevail?

Balint seemed to answer that question in the federal government's favor. *Morissette* suggested that the answer was less certain, and the cases that follow have leaned more in *Morissette*'s direction than in *Balint*'s. This question arises more often in federal cases than in state-law criminal cases. Why might that be so? What makes strict liability more attractive in federal cases? What makes it more problematic?

4. How would *Morissette* be decided under the common law of criminal intent? Theft is traditionally a specific intent crime, so the government would have to prove that Morissette specifically intended to take the spent bomb casings and to keep or sell them as his own. It seems pretty clear that Morissette wanted to take the bomb casings and make them his own. But did he make any mistake of fact or law that might undermine a finding of specific intent?

Does the nature of the "mistake" matter? For example, did Morissette mistakenly believe that he legally owned the bomb casings, as Varszegi mistakenly believed that he was legally entitled (pursuant to the lease agreement) to take his deadbeat tenant's computer (see supra page 178)? Probably not—Morissette made no claim of legal right to the bomb casings before the moment when he took them.

Or did Morissette mistakenly believe that, although the bomb casings still belonged to the government, no government official would really mind his taking the bomb casings? Isn't that akin to saying that Morissette knew exactly what he was *doing*, but simply didn't know that what he was doing was a *crime? That* kind of mistake would not be a defense, even to a specific intent crime, at common law.

But there's one other possibility: Maybe Morissette's mistake was that he believed the bomb casings had been legally abandoned by the government, which would make them fair game for anyone to take. In other words, perhaps Morissette's mistake is best characterized not as a mistake about the criminal law, but as a mistake about the law of abandoned property. *That* characterization might well give Morissette a defense. And maybe that's what Justice Jackson meant when he wrote, "it is not apparent how Morissette could have knowingly or intentionally converted property that he did not know could be converted, as would be the case if it was in fact abandoned or if he truly believed it to be abandoned and unwanted property."

5. Morissette's mistake resembles Binegar's (see supra page 149), does it not? Both defendants broke rules that they assumed, plausibly, were no big deal. In both cases, the assumption seemed reasonable but turned out to be wrong. Finally, both defendants won, in part because the court chose to characterize the defendant's claim in an unusual manner: In *Binegar,* Judge Sullivan described the defendant's legal error as a mistake of fact; in *Morissette,* Justice Jackson seemingly ignored traditional mistake doctrine entirely and asked, instead, whether the relevant crime required proof of *any* intent. Why do appellate judges find such cases so hard to describe?

6. Jackson defined the issue in *Morissette* as whether or not proof of criminal intent is required in prosecutions for theft of government property. Why did he frame the issue that way? After all, the statute expressly forbade the knowing conversion of government property; Jackson might have concluded that proof of knowledge is implicitly required for conviction of the other forms of theft the statute covers. Isn't knowledge a form of criminal intent? What was Jackson talking about?

The answer is that, even if the statute in *Morissette* were read to require proof of knowledge for all covered offenses, the resulting *mens rea* standard seemed less substantial than the norm under the common law—even for general intent crimes. This was so in two distinct senses. Recall the definition of "general intent": A defendant acts with general intent when he acts purposely, that is, when he intends to do what he does. A defendant acts with specific intent, by contrast, when she intends to cause the particular result that the relevant criminal statute forbids. Both standards require that conduct be purposeful, not merely knowing. Knowing conversion of the spent bomb casings thus seemed to Jackson the equivalent of a strict liability crime, because it did not meet the *mens rea* standards required for nearly all crimes in all American states.

But there is another, broader meaning that often attaches to the phrase "general intent": Recall from *V.V.* and *Fennell* (supra page 109), or the passive child abuse cases discussed in *Sargent* (supra page 99), the idea that the defendant's conduct and intent, taken together, were morally blameworthy. Those phrases seem to require that the defendant act not only purposely but also in a morally reprehensible manner. The government argued that Morissette was guilty of stealing the spent bomb casings simply because he knew they were located on government property and they weren't his. Proof of an "evil mind" or a "vicious will" would require something more—as Jackson notes, Morissette did nothing to hide his behavior, but instead acted as though he assumed no one would mind him taking the bomb casings and selling them for scrap. The absence of concealment suggests that Morissette assumed his behavior was consistent with governing moral standards. According to Jackson, that fact alone should be enough to produce an acquittal. Is he right?

2. Factual Knowledge

Morissette, not *Dotterweich,* eventually became the template for most of the federal law of *mens rea.* The next case shows what that template means to defendants who would, at common law, raise claims of mistake of fact.

Staples v. United States

Supreme Court of the United States
511 U.S. 600 (1994)

Justice THOMAS delivered the opinion of the Court.

The National Firearms Act makes it unlawful for any person to possess a machinegun that is not properly registered with the Federal Government. Petitioner contends that, to convict him under the Act, the Government should have been required to prove beyond a reasonable doubt that he knew the weapon he possessed had the characteristics that brought it within the statutory definition of a machinegun. We agree and accordingly reverse the judgment of the Court of Appeals.

I

The National Firearms Act (Act), 26 U.S.C. §§5801-5872, imposes strict registration requirements on statutorily defined "firearms." The Act includes within the term "firearm" a machinegun, §5845(a)(6), and further defines a machinegun as "any weapon which shoots, . . . or can be readily restored to shoot, automatically more than one shot, without manual reloading, by a single function of the trigger," §5845(b). Thus, any fully automatic weapon is a "firearm" within the meaning of the Act. Under the Act, all firearms must be registered in the National Firearms Registration and Transfer Record maintained by the Secretary of the Treasury. §5841. Section 5861(d) makes it a crime, punishable by up to 10 years in prison, see §5871, for any person to possess a firearm that is not properly registered.

Upon executing a search warrant at petitioner's home, local police and agents of the Bureau of Alcohol, Tobacco and Firearms (BATF) recovered, among other things, an AR-15 rifle. The AR-15 is the civilian version of the military's M-16 rifle, and is, unless modified, a semiautomatic weapon. The M-16, in contrast, is a selective fire rifle that allows the operator, by rotating a selector switch, to choose semiautomatic or automatic fire. Many M-16 parts are interchangeable with those in the AR-15 and can be used to convert the AR-15 into an automatic weapon. No doubt to inhibit such conversions, the AR-15 is manufactured with a metal stop on its receiver that will prevent an M-16 selector switch, if installed, from rotating to the fully automatic position. The metal stop on petitioner's rifle, however, had been filed away, and the rifle had been assembled with an M-16 selector switch and several other M-16 internal parts, including a hammer, disconnector, and trigger. Suspecting that the AR-15 had been modified to be capable of fully automatic fire, BATF agents seized the weapon. Petitioner subsequently was indicted for unlawful possession of an unregistered machinegun in violation of §5861(d).

At trial, BATF agents testified that when the AR-15 was tested, it fired more than one shot with a single pull of the trigger. It was undisputed that the weapon was not registered as required by §5861(d). Petitioner testified that the rifle had never fired automatically when it was in his possession. He insisted that the AR-15 had operated only semi-automatically, and even then imperfectly, often requiring manual ejection of the spent casing and chambering of the next round. According to petitioner, his alleged ignorance of any automatic firing capability should have shielded him from criminal liability for his failure to register the weapon. He requested the District Court to instruct the jury that, to establish a violation of §5861(d), the Government must prove beyond a reasonable doubt that the defendant "knew that the gun would fire fully automatically."

The District Court rejected petitioner's proposed instruction and instead charged the jury as follows:

> "The Government need not prove the defendant knows he's dealing with a weapon possessing every last characteristic [which subjects it] to the regulation. It would be enough to prove he knows that he is dealing with a dangerous device of a type as would alert one to the likelihood of regulation." Tr. 465.

Petitioner was convicted and sentenced to five years' probation and a $5,000 fine.

The Court of Appeals affirmed. . . .

II

Whether or not §5861(d) requires proof that a defendant knew of the characteristics of his weapon that made it a "firearm" under the Act is a question of statutory construction. As we observed in Liparota v. United States, 471 U.S. 419 (1985), "the definition of the elements of a criminal offense is entrusted to the legislature, particularly in the case of federal crimes, which are solely creatures of statute." Id., at 424 (citing United States v. Hudson, 11 U.S. 32, 7 Cranch 32 (1812)). Thus, we have long recognized that determining the mental state required for commission of a federal crime requires "construction of the statute and . . . inference of the intent of Congress." United States v. Balint, 258 U.S. 250, 253 (1922). The language of the statute, the starting place in our inquiry, provides little explicit guidance in this case. Section 5861(d) is silent concerning the *mens rea* required for a violation. It states simply that "it shall be unlawful for any person . . . to receive or possess a firearm which is not registered to him in the National Firearms Registration and Transfer Record." 26 U.S.C. §5861(d). Nevertheless, silence on this point by itself does not necessarily suggest that Congress intended to dispense with a conventional *mens rea* element, which would require that the defendant know the facts that make his conduct illegal. See n.3, infra. . . .

According to the Government, however, the nature and purpose of the Act suggest that the presumption favoring *mens rea* does not apply to this case. The Government argues that Congress intended the Act to regulate and restrict the circulation of dangerous weapons. Consequently, in the Government's view, this case fits in a line of precedent concerning what we have termed "public welfare" or "regulatory" offenses, in which we have understood Congress to impose a form of strict criminal liability. . . .

For example, in *Balint*, we concluded that the Narcotic Act of 1914, which was intended in part to minimize the spread of addictive drugs by criminalizing undocumented sales of certain narcotics, required proof only that the defendant knew that he was selling drugs, not that he knew the specific items he had sold were "narcotics" within the ambit of the statute. See *Balint*, supra, at 254. Cf. United States v. Dotterweich, 320 U.S. 277, 281 (1943) (stating in dicta that a statute criminalizing the shipment of adulterated or misbranded drugs did not require knowledge that the items were misbranded or adulterated). As we explained in *Dotterweich*, *Balint* dealt with "a now familiar type of legislation whereby penalties serve as effective means of regulation. Such legislation dispenses with the conventional requirement for criminal conduct—awareness of some wrongdoing." 320 U.S. at 280-81. Such public welfare offenses have been created by Congress, and recognized by this Court, in limited circumstances. Typically, our cases recognizing such offenses involve statutes that regulate potentially harmful or injurious items. In such situations, we have reasoned that as long as a defendant knows that he is dealing with a dangerous device of a character that places him "in responsible relation to a public danger," *Dotterweich*, supra, at 281, he should be alerted to the probability of strict regulation, and we have assumed that in such cases Congress intended to place the burden on the defendant to "ascertain at his peril whether [his conduct] comes within the inhibition of the statute." *Balint*, supra, at 254. . . .[3]

The Government argues that §5861(d) defines precisely the sort of regulatory offense described in *Balint*. In this view, all guns, whether or not they are statutory "firearms," are dangerous devices that put gun owners on notice that they must determine at their hazard whether their weapons

---

3. By interpreting such public welfare offenses to require at least that the defendant know that he is dealing with some dangerous or deleterious substance, we have avoided construing criminal statutes to impose a rigorous form of strict liability. See, e.g., United States v. International Minerals & Chemical Corp., 402 U.S. 558, 563-564 (1971) (suggesting that if a person shipping acid mistakenly thought that he was shipping distilled water, he would not violate a statute criminalizing undocumented shipping of acids). True strict liability might suggest that the defendant need not know even that he was dealing with a dangerous item. Nevertheless, we have referred to public welfare offenses as "dispensing with" or "eliminating" a *mens rea* requirement or "mental element," see, e.g., Morissette v. United States, 342 U.S. 246, 263 (1952); United States v. Dotterweich, 320 U.S. 277, 281 (1943), and have described them as strict liability crimes, United States v. United States Gypsum Co., 438 U.S. 422, 437 (1978). While use of the term "strict liability" is really a misnomer, we have interpreted statutes defining public welfare offenses to eliminate the requirement of *mens rea*; that is, the requirement of a "guilty mind" with respect to an element of a crime. Under such statutes we have not required that the defendant know the facts that make his conduct fit the definition of the offense. . . .

come within the scope of the Act. On this understanding, the District Court's instruction in this case was correct, because a conviction can rest simply on proof that a defendant knew he possessed a "firearm" in the ordinary sense of the term. . . .

. . . [T]he Government ignores the particular care we have taken to avoid construing a statute to dispense with *mens rea* where doing so would "criminalize a broad range of apparently innocent conduct." *Liparota*, 471 U.S. at 426. . . . [T]here is a long tradition of widespread lawful gun ownership by private individuals in this country. Such a tradition did not apply . . . to the selling of dangerous drugs that we considered in *Balint*. . . . Guns in general are not "deleterious devices or products or obnoxious waste materials," [United States v. International Minerals and Chemical Corp., 402 U.S. 558, 565 (1971)], that put their owners on notice that they stand "in responsible relation to a public danger," *Dotterweich*, 320 U.S. at 281.

The Government protests that guns, unlike food stamps, but like . . . narcotics, are potentially harmful devices. Under this view, it seems that *Liparota*'s concern for criminalizing ostensibly innocuous conduct is inapplicable whenever an item is sufficiently dangerous—that is, dangerousness alone should alert an individual to probable regulation and justify treating a statute that regulates the dangerous device as dispensing with *mens rea*. But that an item is "dangerous," in some general sense, does not necessarily suggest, as the Government seems to assume, that it is not also entirely innocent. Even dangerous items can, in some cases, be so commonplace and generally available that we would not consider them to alert individuals to the likelihood of strict regulation. As suggested above, despite their potential for harm, guns generally can be owned in perfect innocence. Of course, we might surely classify certain categories of guns—no doubt including the machineguns, sawed-off shotguns, and artillery pieces that Congress has subjected to regulation—as items the ownership of which would have [a suspect character]. But precisely because guns falling outside those categories traditionally have been widely accepted as lawful possessions, their destructive potential . . . cannot be said to put gun owners sufficiently on notice of the likelihood of regulation to justify interpreting §5861(d) as not requiring proof of knowledge of a weapon's characteristics.

On a slightly different tack, the Government suggests that guns are subject to an array of regulations at the federal, state, and local levels that put gun owners on notice that they must determine the characteristics of their weapons and comply with all legal requirements. But regulation in itself is not sufficient to place gun ownership in the category of the sale of narcotics in *Balint*. The food stamps at issue in *Liparota* were subject to comprehensive regulations, yet we did not understand the statute there to dispense with a *mens rea* requirement. Moreover, despite the overlay of legal restrictions on gun ownership, we question whether regulations on guns are sufficiently intrusive that they impinge upon the common experience that owning a gun is usually licit and blameless conduct. Roughly 50 percent of American homes contain at least one firearm of some sort, and in the vast majority of States, buying a shotgun or rifle is a simple transaction that would not alert a person to regulation any more than would buying a car. . . .

Here, there can be little doubt that, as in *Liparota*, the Government's construction of the statute potentially would impose criminal sanctions on a class of persons whose mental state—ignorance of the characteristics of weapons in their possession—makes their actions entirely innocent. The Government does not dispute the contention that virtually any semiautomatic weapon may be converted, either by internal modification or, in some cases, simply by wear and tear, into a machinegun. . . . Such a gun may give no externally visible indication that it is fully automatic. But in the government's view, any person who has purchased what he believes to be a semiautomatic rifle or handgun, or who simply has inherited a gun from a relative and left it untouched in an attic or basement, can be subject to imprisonment, despite absolute ignorance of the gun's firing capabilities, if the gun turns out to be an automatic. . . .

The potentially harsh penalty attached to violation of §5861(d)—up to 10 years' imprisonment—confirms our reading of the Act. Historically, the penalty imposed under a statute has been a significant consideration in determining whether the statute should be construed as dispensing with *mens rea*. Certainly, the cases that first defined the concept of the public welfare offense almost uniformly involved statutes that provided for only light penalties such as fines or short jail sentences, not imprisonment in the state penitentiary. See, e.g., Commonwealth v. Raymond, 97 Mass. 567 (1867) (fine of up to $200 or six months in jail, or both); People v. Snowburger, 113 Mich. 86, 71 N.W. 497 (1897) (fine of up to $500 or incarceration in county jail). . . .

As commentators have pointed out, the small penalties attached to such offenses logically complemented the absence of a *mens rea* requirement: In a system that generally requires a "vicious will" to establish a crime, 4 W. Blackstone, Commentaries *21, imposing severe punishments for offenses that require no *mens rea* would seem incongruous. . . .

In rehearsing the characteristics of the public welfare offense, we, too, have included in our consideration the punishments imposed and have noted that "penalties commonly are relatively small, and conviction does no grave damage to an offender's reputation." Morissette v. United States, 342 U.S. 246, 256 (1952). We have even recognized that it was "under such considerations" that courts have construed statutes to dispense with *mens rea*. Ibid.

Our characterization of the public welfare offense in *Morissette* hardly seems apt, however, for a crime that is a felony, as is violation of §5861(d). After all, "felony" is, as we noted in distinguishing certain common-law crimes from public welfare offenses, "'as bad a word as you can give to man or thing.'" Id., 342 U.S. at 260 (quoting 2 F. Pollock & F. Maitland, History of English Law 465 (2d ed. 1899)). Close adherence to the early cases described above might suggest that punishing a violation as a felony is simply incompatible with the theory of the public welfare offense. In this view, absent a clear statement from Congress that *mens rea* is not required, we should not apply the public welfare offense rationale to interpret any statute defining a felony offense as dispensing with *mens rea*.

We need not adopt such a definitive rule of construction to decide this case, however. Instead, we note only that where, as here, dispensing with *mens rea* would require the defendant to have knowledge only of traditionally lawful conduct, a severe penalty is a further factor tending to suggest that Congress did not intend to eliminate a *mens rea* requirement. In such a case, the usual presumption that a defendant must know the facts that make his conduct illegal should apply.

III

. . . We emphasize that our holding is a narrow one. As in our prior cases, our reasoning depends upon a commonsense evaluation of the nature of the particular device or substance Congress has subjected to regulation and the expectations that individuals may legitimately have in dealing with the regulated items. In addition, we think that the penalty attached to §5861(d) suggests that Congress did not intend to eliminate a *mens rea* requirement for violation of the section. . . . [I]f Congress had intended to make outlaws of gun owners who were wholly ignorant of the offending characteristics of their weapons, and to subject them to lengthy prison terms, it would have spoken more clearly to that effect. . . .

[Justice GINSBURG's opinion concurring in the judgment, joined by Justice O'CONNOR, and Justice STEVENS' dissent, joined by Justice BLACKMUN, are omitted.]

Notes and Questions

1. *Staples* announces a clear standard for judging factual errors in federal criminal cases: "[A] defendant must know the facts that make his conduct illegal." Is that a wise standard? The answer matters a great deal. Technically speaking, *Staples* is a piece of the law of statutory interpretation; its holding applies only to the particular gun statute at issue in the case. Practically, however, given the Court's analysis, *Staples* establishes a *mens rea* doctrine that applies to all federal criminal statutes, save when Congress speaks "more clearly to that effect."

2. Justice Thomas' opinion in *Staples* misdescribes the common law of *mens rea*. According to the majority opinion in *Staples*, proof that the defendant knew "the facts that make his conduct illegal" amounts to the equivalent of proof of general intent. That isn't true. Were *Staples* a general intent case, the defendant would have to prove that his mistake about the gun's capability to fire automatically was both "honest" and "reasonable"—which is much more than having to raise a mere reasonable doubt about whether the defendant knew of his gun's automatic firing capability. Whatever else federal *mens rea* doctrine may be, it is different from the common law.

3. Like the Food, Drug, and Cosmetic Act at issue in *Dotterweich*, the National Firearms Act of 1934 was a New Deal-era regulatory statute. But the regulated actors were very different. In the Food, Drug, and Cosmetic Act of 1938, the targets were businessmen (in 1938, they were all men) who manufactured and shipped pharmaceuticals. The regulated actors Congress sought to punish under the National Firearms Act were, as Justice Stevens put it in his dissenting opinion in *Staples*, "professional gangsters"—is that really a profession?—"like Al Capone, Pretty Boy Floyd, and their henchmen." Notice two things about that target audience. First, the Act targeted criminals, not crimes. Second, the criminals in question were traditionally the responsibility of local police and local prosecutors, not FBI agents and United States Attorneys. The New Dealers did not try to displace those local officials or the state laws they enforced, but instead sought to supplement them—and, along the way, to grab some political credit for fighting crime. Is that a legitimate goal? Is it fair to criminalize easily proved misconduct in order to punish harder-to-prove crimes indirectly? One's answer to those questions may determine one's view of the wisdom of the rule announced in *Staples*.

4. The defendant in United States v. X-Citement Video, Inc., 513 U.S. 64 (1994), shipped pornographic videos showing an underage actress (Traci Lords) to a federal undercover agent. The defendant was charged under the Protection of Children Against Sexual Exploitation Act of 1977; the relevant provision read as follows:

> (a) Any person who—
> (1) knowingly transports or ships in interstate or foreign commerce by any means including by computer or mails, any visual depiction, if (A) the producing of such visual depiction involves the use of a minor engaging in sexually explicit conduct; and (B) such visual depiction is of such conduct;
> (2) knowingly receives, or distributes, any visual depiction that has been mailed, or has been shipped or transported in interstate or foreign commerce, or which contains materials which have been mailed or so shipped or transported, by any means including by computer, or knowingly reproduces any visual depiction for distribution in interstate or foreign commerce or through the mails, if (A) the producing of such visual depiction involves the use of a minor engaging in sexually explicit conduct; and (B) such visual depiction is of such conduct; . . .
> shall be punished as provided in subsection (b) of this section.

18 U.S.C. §2252(a). In a decision issued a few months after *Staples*, the Supreme Court held that, in order to convict under this statute, the government must prove knowledge that at least one of the actors in the video was a minor:

> The critical determination . . . is whether the term "knowingly" in subsections (1) and (2) modifies the phrase "the use of a minor" in subsections (1)(A) and (2)(A). The most natural grammatical reading, adopted by the Ninth Circuit, suggests that the term "knowingly" modifies only the surrounding verbs: transports, ships, receives, distributes, or reproduces. . . . But we do not think this is the end of the matter. . . .
>
> . . . If we were to conclude that "knowingly" only modifies the relevant verbs in §2252, we would sweep within the ambit of the statute actors who had no idea that they were even dealing with sexually explicit material. For instance, a retail druggist who returns an uninspected roll of developed film to a customer "knowingly distributes" a visual depiction and would be criminally liable if it were later discovered that the visual depiction contained images of children engaged in sexually explicit conduct. Or, a new resident of an apartment might receive mail for the prior resident and store the mail unopened. If the prior tenant had requested delivery of materials covered by §2252, his residential successor could be prosecuted for "knowing receipt" of such materials. Similarly, a Federal Express courier who delivers a box in which the shipper has declared the contents to be "film" "knowingly transports" such film. We do not assume that Congress . . . intended such results. . . .
>
> Our reluctance to simply follow the most grammatical reading of the statute is heightened by our cases interpreting criminal statutes to include broadly applicable scienter requirements, even where the statute by its terms does not contain them. . . .
>
> Liparota v. United States, 471 U.S. 419 (1985), posed a challenge to a federal statute prohibiting certain actions with respect to food stamps. The statute's use of "knowingly" could be read only to modify "uses, transfers, acquires, alters, or possesses" or it could be read also to modify "in any manner not authorized by [the statute]." . . . [T]he Court was concerned with the broader reading which would "criminalize a broad range of apparently innocent conduct." 471 U.S. at 426. . . .
>
> Applying these principles, we think the Ninth Circuit's plain language reading of §2252 is not so plain. First, §2252 is not a public welfare offense. Persons do not harbor settled expectations that the contents of magazines and film are generally subject to stringent public regulation. In fact, First Amendment constraints presuppose the opposite view. Rather, the statute is more akin to the common-law offenses against the "state, the person, property, or public morals," [Morissette v. United States, 342 U.S. 246, 255 (1952),] that presume a scienter requirement in the absence of express contrary intent. Second, *Staples'* concern with harsh penalties looms equally large respecting §2252: Violations are punishable by up to 10 years in prison as well as substantial fines and forfeiture. . . .

X-Citement Video, 513 U.S. at 68-72.

5. With *X-Citement Video,* compare United States v. Jones, 471 F.3d 535 (4th Cir. 2006). Jones was convicted of transporting an underage girl across state lines "to act as a prostitute at a truck stop." The relevant federal statute applies to

> [any] person who knowingly transports an individual who has not attained the age of 18 years in interstate or foreign commerce, or in any commonwealth, territory or possession of the United States, with intent that the individual engage in prostitution, or in any sexual activity for which any person can be charged with a criminal offense. . . .

18 U.S.C. §2423(a). Writing for a unanimous panel, Judge Wilkinson decided that "knowingly" modifies only "transports":

> . . . Adverbs generally modify verbs, and the thought that they would typically modify the infinite hereafters of statutory sentences would cause grammarians to recoil. We see nothing on the face of this statute to suggest that the modifying force of "knowingly" extends beyond the verb to other components of the offense. . . .
>
> The defendant's interpretation, meanwhile, would strip the statute of its clear purpose: the protection of minors. If the prosecution were required to prove knowledge with regard to the victim's age, it would be the rare defendant who would not claim to have mistaken the victim for an adult. Imposing such a *mens rea* requirement would be tantamount to permitting adults to prey upon minors so long as they cultivate ignorance of their victims' age. But "the statute is intended to protect young persons who are transported for illicit purposes, and not transporters who remain ignorant of the age of those whom they transport." [United States v. Taylor, 239 F.3d 994, 996 (9th Cir. 2001).] It would be nonsensical to require proof of knowledge of the victim's age when the statute exists to provide special protection for all minors, including, if not especially, those who could too easily be mistaken for adults. . . .

Jones, 471 F.3d at 539-40. So far, *Jones* sounds squarely at odds with *Staples* and *X-Citement Video.* But Judge Wilkinson founds those cases easily distinguishable:

> In this case, the reasoning of *X-Citement Video* and *Staples* is inapposite. . . . [Those cases are] "directed at awareness of the elements that define circumstances upon which criminality turns." [United States v. Bostic, 168 F.3d 718, 723 (4th Cir. 1999).] But in §2423(a), the minority of the victim is hardly a factor that distinguishes the defendant's actions from "innocent conduct." *X-Citement Video,* 513 U.S. at 72. To the contrary, "the transportation of *any* individual for purposes of prostitution or other criminal sexual activity is already unlawful under federal law." *Taylor,* 239 F.3d at 997.

471 F.3d at 541. Is *Jones* rightly decided? Is it consistent with *Staples* and *X-Citement Video*? When should federal judges pay attention to statutory grammar and plain language, and when should they focus on policy arguments?

6. The defendants in United States v. Feola, 420 U.S. 671 (1975), were charged with assaulting federal officers who, at the time of the assault, were posing as drug buyers as part of an investigation into a heroin distribution ring. The defendants claimed, plausibly, that they had no idea the victims were federal agents, and so lacked the intent necessary for criminal conviction. The Supreme Court rejected the argument—using very different reasoning than in either *Staples* or *X-Citement Video*:

> This interpretation poses no risk of unfairness to defendants. It is no snare for the unsuspecting. Although the perpetrator of a narcotics "rip-off," such as the one involved here, may be surprised to find that his intended victim is a federal officer in civilian apparel, he nonetheless knows from the very outset that his planned course of conduct is wrongful. The situation is not one where legitimate conduct becomes unlawful solely because of the identity of the individual or agency affected. In a case of this kind the offender takes his victim as he finds him. The concept of criminal intent does not extend so far as to require that the actor understand not only the nature of his act but also its consequence for the choice of a judicial forum.

420 U.S. at 685. Is shooting a rival drug dealer as blameworthy as shooting a police officer or a federal agent? If the answer is yes, why do many death penalty states treat the killing of a police officer as an aggravating factor sufficient to authorize capital punishment? If the answer is no, why was *Feola* decided as it was?

3. Legal Knowledge

Federal *mens rea* doctrine on mistakes of fact differs from the common law, but not radically so: Federal law assesses mistake-of-fact claims more generously than does the common law, but both systems of doctrine acknowledge such claims.

Federal doctrine on legal mistakes, by contrast, differs radically from traditional state law. One of the longstanding bedrock propositions of American criminal law is that "ignorance of the law is no excuse." In federal criminal cases, ignorance of the law often *is* an excuse, as the following cases show.

Notes on Mistakes of Law in Federal Criminal Cases

1. Federal law in this area begins with *Morissette*, supra at page 252. Joe Morissette understood what he was doing when he took the spent bomb casings, and he knew that he was on federal land when he took them. He *didn't* understand that the taking was illegal: a classic mistake-of-law claim. As you have seen, although mistake-of-law claims rarely prevail, they *may* succeed at common law when the crime requires specific intent. (They may also succeed under the Model Penal Code, depending on the specific elements of the crime and the *mens rea* required for those specific elements.) And in the U.S. Supreme Court, Morissette's claim carried the day.

2. Thirty years later, the law Justice Jackson made in *Morissette* began to take root in federal criminal law more generally. The defendant in Liparota v. United States, 471 U.S. 419 (1985), was prosecuted for food stamp fraud, under a statute providing that "whoever knowingly uses, transfers, acquires, alters, or possesses coupons or authorization cards in any manner not authorized by [the statute] or the regulations" is subject to a fine and imprisonment. 7 U.S.C. §2024(b)(1). The facts were as follows:

> Petitioner Frank Liparota was the co-owner with his brother of Moon's Sandwich Shop in Chicago, Illinois. He was indicted for acquiring and possessing food stamps in violation of §2024(b)(1). The Department of Agriculture had not authorized petitioner's restaurant to accept food stamps.[2] At trial, the Government proved that petitioner on three occasions purchased food stamps from an undercover Department of Agriculture agent for substantially less than their face value. On the first occasion, the agent informed petitioner that she had $195 worth of food stamps to sell. The agent then accepted petitioner's offer of $150 and consummated the transaction in a back room of the restaurant with petitioner's brother. A similar transaction occurred one week later, in which the agent sold $500 worth of coupons for $350. Approximately one month later, petitioner bought $500 worth of food stamps from the agent for $300.

471 U.S. at 421-22. Liparota could not claim that he didn't know he was buying food stamps. Instead, he argued that he didn't know his conduct was "not authorized by" the governing statute and regulations.

The Supreme Court bought Liparota's legal argument—though not necessarily his application of that argument to the facts:

> Absent indication of contrary purpose in the language or legislative history of the statute, we believe that §2024(b)(1) requires a showing that the defendant knew his conduct to be unauthorized by statute or regulations. "The contention that an injury can amount to a crime only when inflicted by intention is no provincial or transient notion. It is as universal and persistent in mature systems of law as belief in freedom of the human will and a consequent ability and duty of the normal individual to choose between good and evil." [Morissette v. United States, 342 U.S. 246, 250 (1952)]. . . . [T]he failure of Congress explicitly and unambiguously to indicate whether mens rea is required does not signal a departure from this background assumption of our criminal law.

2. Food stamps are provided by the Government to those who meet certain need-related criteria. See 7 U.S.C. §§2014(a), 2014(c). They generally may be used only to purchase food in retail food stores. 7 U.S.C. §2016(b). If a restaurant receives proper authorization from the Department of Agriculture, it may receive food stamps as payment for meals under certain special circumstances not relevant here.

This construction is particularly appropriate where, as here, to interpret the statute otherwise would be to criminalize a broad range of apparently innocent conduct. For instance, §2024(b)(1) declares it criminal to use, transfer, acquire, alter, or possess food stamps in any manner not authorized by statute or regulations. The statute provides further that "[coupons] issued to eligible households shall be used by them only to purchase food in retail food stores which have been approved for participation in the food stamp program at prices prevailing in such stores." 7 U.S.C. §2016(b). This seems to be the only authorized use. A strict reading of the statute with no knowledge-of-illegality requirement would thus render criminal a food stamp recipient who, for example, used stamps to purchase food from a store that, unknown to him, charged higher than normal prices to food stamp program participants. Such a reading would also render criminal a nonrecipient of food stamps who "possessed" stamps because he was mistakenly sent them through the mail due to administrative error, "altered" them by tearing them up, and "transferred" them by throwing them away. . . . [W]e are reluctant to adopt such a sweeping interpretation. . . .

. . . [T]he Government contends that the §2024(b)(1) offense is a "public welfare" offense, which the Court defined in Morissette v. United States, 342 U.S., at 252-253, to "depend on no mental element but consist only of forbidden acts or omissions." Yet the offense at issue here differs substantially from those "public welfare offenses" we have previously recognized. In most previous instances, Congress has rendered criminal a type of conduct that a reasonable person should know is subject to stringent public regulation and may seriously threaten the community's health or safety. Thus, in United States v. Freed, 401 U.S. 601 (1971), we examined the federal statute making it illegal to receive or possess an unregistered firearm. In holding that the Government did not have to prove that the recipient of unregistered hand grenades knew that they were unregistered, we noted that "one would hardly be surprised to learn that possession of hand grenades is not an innocent act." Id., at 609. Similarly, in United States v. Dotterweich, 320 U.S. 277, 284 (1943), the Court held that a corporate officer could violate the Food, Drug, and Cosmetic Act when his firm shipped adulterated and misbranded drugs, even "though consciousness of wrongdoing be totally wanting." See also United States v. Balint, 258 U.S. 250 (1922). The distinctions between these cases and the instant case are clear. A food stamp can hardly be compared to a hand grenade, see *Freed*, nor can the unauthorized acquisition or possession of food stamps be compared to the selling of adulterated drugs, as in *Dotterweich*.

We hold that in a prosecution for violation of §2024(b)(1), the Government must prove that the defendant knew that his acquisition or possession of food stamps was in a manner unauthorized by statute or regulations. This holding does not put an unduly heavy burden on the Government in prosecuting violators of §2024(b)(1). To prove that petitioner knew that his acquisition or possession of food stamps was unauthorized, for example, the Government need not show that he had knowledge of specific regulations governing food stamp acquisition or possession. Nor must the Government introduce any extraordinary evidence that would conclusively demonstrate petitioner's state of mind. Rather, as in any other criminal prosecution requiring *mens rea*, the Government may prove by reference to facts and circumstances surrounding the case that petitioner knew that his conduct was unauthorized or illegal.[17] . . .

471 U.S. at 425-34.

Read footnote 17 carefully. How much of a victory did Liparota actually win?

3. John Cheek was a tax protester who regularly failed to file income tax returns. When charged with "willfully" failing to pay his taxes, Cheek claimed, among other things, that his non-payment was not "willful" because he honestly believed (1) that ordinary wages were not taxable "income,"* and (2) that the tax laws were unconstitutional.** At Cheek's trial, the District Judge told the jurors that negligent misunderstandings of the law amounted to willfulness. The Supreme Court disagreed:

> The proliferation of statutes and regulations has sometimes made it difficult for the average citizen to . . . comprehend the extent of the duties and obligations imposed by the tax laws. Congress has accordingly softened the impact of the common-law presumption [that every person knows the law] by making specific intent to violate the law an element of certain federal criminal tax offenses. . . .
>
> . . . In United States v. Bishop, 412 U.S. 346, 360 (1973), we described the term "willfully" [as used in federal criminal tax statutes] as connoting "a voluntary, intentional violation of a known legal duty." . . .
>
> Willfulness, as construed by our prior decisions in criminal tax cases, [thus] requires the Government to prove that the law imposed a duty on the defendant, that the defendant knew of this duty, and that he voluntarily and intentionally violated that duty. . . . In this case, if Cheek asserted that he truly believed that the Internal Revenue Code did not purport to treat wages as income, and the jury believed him, the Government would not have carried its

17. In this case, for instance, the Government introduced evidence that petitioner bought food stamps at a substantial discount from face value and that he conducted part of the transaction in a back room of his restaurant to avoid the presence of the other patrons. Moreover, the Government asserts that food stamps themselves are stamped "nontransferable." A jury could have inferred from this evidence that petitioner knew that his acquisition and possession of the stamps were unauthorized.

* Cheek had been taught, at tax-protestor seminars (yes, there are such things, and sadly enough, they are often taught by lawyers), that wages were received as "barter" for work, and thus did not constitute "income," because "income" was limited to returns on passive investments.

** Here, the claims were that the Sixteenth Amendment—which was ratified in 1913 and provides, *inter alia*, "The Congress shall have power to lay and collect taxes on incomes, from whatever source derived"—does not include "wages" as "income," and in any event was never properly ratified. Such claims, like the one mentioned in the preceding footnote, have long been rejected by the federal courts as "frivolous"—including in four civil cases to which Cheek had been a named party. In addition, Cheek had attended two criminal trials at which tax-protestor friends had been found guilty of violating the federal tax laws.

burden to prove willfulness, however unreasonable a court might deem such a belief. . . .

Cheek v. United States, 498 U.S. 192, 200-02 (1991). Do you agree? Was this a case of a good-hearted "average citizen" who made an honest mistake of law because the U.S. tax code is too difficult to understand? Should a committed tax protestor like Cheek be able to avoid criminal liability simply because he continues to adhere, despite overwhelming evidence to the contrary (of which he was personally aware, see *supra* footnotes * and **), to a massively unreasonable view about what the law actually requires of him? Given the Court's framing of the issue, could the jury have found Cheek guilty? If not, is there anything else that the tax authorities—or anybody else—could do to render Cheek subject to the criminal statute in question?

With respect to Cheek's constitutional misunderstandings, the Court was less generous:

> Claims that some of the provisions of the tax code are unconstitutional are submissions of a different order. They do not arise from innocent mistakes caused by the complexity of the Internal Revenue Code. Rather, they reveal full knowledge of the provisions at issue and a studied conclusion, however wrong, that those provisions are invalid. . . . [I]n this case, Cheek paid his taxes for years, but after attending various seminars and based on his own study, he concluded that the income tax laws could not constitutionally require him to pay a tax.
>
> We do not believe that Congress contemplated that such a taxpayer, without risking criminal prosecution, could ignore the duties imposed upon him by the Internal Revenue Code. . . . Cheek . . . was free to pay the tax that the law purported to require, file for a refund and, if denied, present his claims of [constitutional] invalidity . . . to the courts. See 26 U.S.C. §7422. Also, without paying the tax, he could have challenged claims of tax deficiencies in the Tax Court, §6213, with the right to appeal to a higher court if unsuccessful. §7482(a)(1). Cheek took neither course in some years, and when he did was unwilling to accept the outcome. As we see it, he is in no position to claim that his good-faith belief about the validity of the Internal Revenue Code negates willfulness or provides a defense to criminal prosecution under §§7201 and 7203. Of course, Cheek was free in this very case to present his claims of invalidity and have them adjudicated, but like defendants in criminal cases in other contexts, who "willfully" refuse to comply with the duties placed upon them by the law, he must take the risk of being wrong.

Id. at 205-06. Justice Scalia concurred in the judgment in *Cheek*; he agreed with the Court that negligent errors about the meaning of "income" negated willfulness—but he went even further, arguing that Cheek's alternate claim that the tax code is unconstitutional (if an honest claim, albeit an incredibly unreasonable one) likewise negates *mens rea*.

4. Waldemar Ratzlaf was a gambler who had won a considerable sum of money in a Las Vegas casino. Federal law requires the keeping of elaborate records of bank deposits of $10,000 or more. At the casino's suggestion—should that fact matter?—Ratzlaf broke his winnings into smaller portions and made a series of bank deposits, each of which was slightly under the $10,000 threshold. Unbeknownst to Ratzlaf, federal law also forbade "willfully" structuring cash transactions in a manner designed to avoid federal reporting requirements. Ratzlaf was charged and convicted under that anti-structuring statute. The Supreme Court overturned the conviction, holding that the word "willfully" required the government to prove Ratzlaf knew that breaking up his winnings into smaller cash deposits violated the law. Ratzlaf v. United States, 510 U.S. 135 (1994). In support, the Court cited *Cheek* as well as a series of lower-court decisions that had previously found other parts of the federal money laundering statute (of which the anti-structuring statute was also a part) to require "both knowledge of the reporting requirement *and* a specific intent to commit the crime, *i.e.*, a purpose to disobey the law." Id. at 141 (emphasis in original; internal quote marks omitted).

The Supreme Court's decision in *Ratzlaf* prompted outrage in Congress, which promptly amended the anti-structuring statute to remove the word "willfully." Thus, *Ratzlaf*'s holding, as applied to future defendants like Ratzlaf, is no longer good law—but it remains good law as to other defendants charged with violating other federal criminal statutes. Does that make sense? State criminal statutes that use the word "willfully" do not require proof that the defendant knew that his conduct was illegal. Nor does the criminal law of *mens rea*—either at common law or under the Model Penal Code—generally require such proof. Why should federal criminal statutes be so different?

Bryan v. United States

Supreme Court of the United States
524 U.S. 184 (1998)

Justice STEVENS delivered the opinion of the Court.

Petitioner was convicted of "willfully" dealing in firearms without a federal license. The question presented is whether the term "willfully" in 18 U.S.C. §924(a)(1)(D) requires proof that the defendant knew that his conduct was unlawful, or whether it also requires proof that he knew of the federal licensing requirement.

In 1968 Congress enacted the Omnibus Crime Control and Safe Streets Act. In Title IV of that Act Congress . . . amended the Criminal Code to include detailed provisions regulating the use and sale of firearms. As amended, 18 U.S.C. §922 defined a number of "unlawful acts"; subsection (a)(1) made it unlawful for any person except a licensed dealer to engage in the business of dealing in firearms.[2] Section 923 established the federal licensing program and repeated the prohibition against dealing in firearms without a license, and §924 specified the penalties for violating "any provision of this chapter." Read literally, §924 authorized the imposition of a fine of up to $5,000 or a prison sentence of not more than five years, "or both," on any person who dealt in firearms without a license even if that person believed that he or she was acting lawfully.[3] As enacted in 1968, §§922(a)(1) and 924 omitted an express scienter requirement and therefore arguably imposed strict criminal liability on every unlicensed dealer in firearms. The 1968 Act also omitted any definition of the term "engaged in the business" even though that conduct was an element of the unlawful act prohibited by §922(a)(1).

In 1986 Congress enacted the Firearms Owners' Protection Act (FOPA), in part, to cure these omissions. The findings in that statute explained that additional legislation was necessary to protect law-abiding citizens with respect to the acquisition, possession, or use of firearms for lawful purposes. FOPA therefore amended §921 to include a definition of the term "engaged in the business,"[5] and amended §924 to add a scienter requirement as a condition to the imposition of penalties for most of the unlawful acts defined in §922. For three categories of offenses the intent required is that the defendant acted "knowingly"; for the fourth category, which includes "any other

---

2. 82 Stat. 228. The current version of this provision, which is substantially the same as the 1968 version, is codified at 18 U.S.C. §922(a)(1)(A). It states:

> "(a) It shall be unlawful—(1) for any person (A) except a licensed importer, licensed manufacturer, or licensed dealer, to engage in the business of importing, manufacturing, or dealing in firearms, or in the course of such business to ship, transport, or receive any firearm in interstate or foreign commerce."

3. "§924. PENALTIES

> "(a) Whoever violates any provision of this chapter . . . shall be fined not more than $5,000 or imprisoned not more than five years, or both."

82 Stat. 233.

5. "Section 921 of title 18, United States Code, is amended—. . . .

> "(21) The term 'engaged in the business' means—
>
> . . . .
>
>   "(C) as applied to a dealer in firearms, as defined in section 921(a)(11)(A), a person who devotes time, attention, and labor to dealing in firearms as a regular course of trade or business with the principal objective of livelihood and profit through the repetitive purchase and resale of firearms, but such term shall not include a person who makes occasional sales, exchanges, or purchases of firearms for the enhancement of a personal collection or for a hobby, or who sells all or part of his personal collection of firearms. . . ." 100 Stat. 449-450.

provision of this chapter," the required intent is that the defendant acted "willfully." [18 U.S.C. §924(a)(1)(D).] The §922(a)(1)(A) offense at issue in this case is an "other provision" in the "willfully" category.

The jury having found petitioner guilty, we accept the Government's version of the evidence. That evidence proved that petitioner did not have a federal license to deal in firearms; that he used so-called "straw purchasers" in Ohio to acquire pistols that he could not have purchased himself; that the straw purchasers made false statements when purchasing the guns; that petitioner assured the straw purchasers that he would file the serial numbers off the guns; and that he resold the guns on Brooklyn street corners known for drug dealing. The evidence was unquestionably adequate to prove that petitioner was dealing in firearms, and that he knew that his conduct was unlawful.[7] There was, however, no evidence that he was aware of the federal law that prohibits dealing in firearms without a federal license.

Petitioner was charged with a conspiracy to violate 18 U.S.C. §922(a)(1)(A), by willfully engaging in the business of dealing in firearms, and with a substantive violation of that provision. After the close of evidence, petitioner requested that the trial judge instruct the jury that petitioner could be convicted only if he knew of the federal licensing requirement, but the judge rejected this request. Instead, the trial judge gave this explanation of the term "willfully":

> "A person acts willfully if he acts intentionally and purposely and with the intent to do something the law forbids, that is, with the bad purpose to disobey or to disregard the law. Now, the person need not be aware of the specific law or rule that his conduct may be violating. But he must act with the intent to do something that the law forbids."

Petitioner was found guilty on both counts. On appeal he argued that the evidence was insufficient because there was no proof that he had knowledge of the federal licensing requirement, and that the trial judge had erred by failing to instruct the jury that such knowledge was an essential element of the offense. The Court of Appeals affirmed. It concluded that the instructions were proper and that the Government had elicited "ample proof" that petitioner had acted willfully. . . .

The word "willfully" is sometimes said to be "a word of many meanings" whose construction is often dependent on the context in which it appears. Most obviously it differentiates between deliberate and unwitting conduct, but in the criminal law it also typically refers to a culpable state of mind. . . . As a general matter, when used in the criminal context, a "willful" act is one undertaken with a "bad purpose." In other words, in order to establish a

---

7. Why else would he make use of straw purchasers and assure them that he would shave the serial numbers off the guns? Moreover, the street corner sales are not consistent with a good-faith belief in the legality of the enterprise.

"willful" violation of a statute, "the Government must prove that the defendant acted with knowledge that his conduct was unlawful." Ratzlaf v. United States, 510 U.S. 135, 137 (1994). . . .

With respect to the three categories of conduct that are made punishable by §924 if performed "knowingly," the background presumption that every citizen knows the law makes it unnecessary to adduce specific evidence to prove that "an evil-meaning mind" directed the "evil-doing hand."[15] More is required, however, with respect to the conduct in the fourth category that is only criminal when done "willfully." The jury must find that the defendant acted with an evil-meaning mind, that is to say, that he acted with knowledge that his conduct was unlawful.

Petitioner . . . argues that we must read §924(a)(1)(D) to require [particularized] knowledge of the law because of our interpretation of "willfully" in two other contexts. In certain cases involving willful violations of the tax laws, we have concluded that the jury must find that the defendant was aware of the specific provision of the tax code that he was charged with violating. See, e.g., Cheek v. United States, 498 U.S. 192, 201 (1991). Similarly, in order to satisfy a willful violation in *Ratzlaf,* we concluded that the jury had to find that the defendant knew that his structuring of cash transactions to avoid a reporting requirement was unlawful. See 510 U.S. at 138, 149. Those cases, however, are readily distinguishable. Both the tax cases and *Ratzlaf* involved highly technical statutes that presented the danger of ensnaring individuals engaged in apparently innocent conduct. As a result, we held that these statutes "carve out an exception to the traditional rule" that ignorance of the law is no excuse and require that the defendant have knowledge of the law. The danger of convicting individuals engaged in apparently innocent activity that motivated our decisions in the tax cases and *Ratzlaf* is not present here because the jury found that this petitioner knew that his conduct was unlawful.

Thus, the willfulness requirement of §924(a)(1)(D) does not carve out an exception to the traditional rule that ignorance of the law is no excuse; knowledge that the conduct is unlawful is all that is required. . . .

Justice SCALIA, with whom Chief Justice REHNQUIST and Justice GINSBURG join, dissenting.

Petitioner Sillasse Bryan was convicted of "willfully" violating the federal licensing requirement for firearms dealers. The jury apparently found, and the evidence clearly shows, that Bryan was aware in a general way that some aspect of his conduct was unlawful. The issue is whether that general knowledge of illegality is enough to sustain the conviction, or whether a "willful"

---

15. Justice Jackson's translation of the terms *mens rea* and *actus reus* is found in his opinion for the Court in Morissette v. United States, 342 U.S. 246, 251 (1952).

violation of the licensing provision requires proof that the defendant knew that his conduct was unlawful specifically because he lacked the necessary license. On that point the statute is, in my view, genuinely ambiguous. Most of the Court's opinion is devoted to confirming half of that ambiguity by refuting Bryan's various arguments that the statute clearly requires specific knowledge of the licensing requirement. The Court offers no real justification for its implicit conclusion that either (1) the statute unambiguously requires only general knowledge of illegality, or (2) ambiguously requiring only general knowledge is enough. Instead, the Court curiously falls back on "the traditional rule that ignorance of the law is no excuse" to conclude that "knowledge that the conduct is unlawful is all that is required." In my view, this case calls for the application of a different canon—"the familiar rule that, where there is ambiguity in a criminal statute, doubts are resolved in favor of the defendant." Adamo Wrecking Co. v. United States, 434 U.S. 275, 284-85 (1978).

Section 922(a)(1)(A) of Title 18 makes it unlawful for any person to engage in the business of dealing in firearms without a federal license. That provision is enforced criminally through §924(a)(1)(D), which imposes criminal penalties on whoever "willfully violates any other provision of this chapter." The word "willfully" has a wide range of meanings, and "its construction [is] often . . . influenced by its context." Ratzlaf v. United States, 510 U.S. 135, 141 (1994). In some contexts it connotes nothing more than "an act which is intentional, or knowing, or voluntary, as distinguished from accidental." United States v. Murdock, 290 U.S. 389, 394 (1933). In the present context, however, inasmuch as the preceding three subparagraphs of §924 specify a *mens rea* of "knowingly" for other firearms offenses, see §§924(a)(1)(A)-(C), a "willful" violation under §924(a)(1)(D) must require some mental state more culpable than mere intent to perform the forbidden act. The United States concedes (and the Court apparently agrees) that the violation is not "willful" unless the defendant knows in a general way that his conduct is unlawful. Brief for United States 7-9; ante, at 9 ("The jury must find that the defendant acted with an evil-meaning mind, that is to say, that he acted with knowledge that his conduct was unlawful").

That concession takes this case beyond any useful application of the maxim that ignorance of the law is no excuse. Everyone agrees that §924(a)(1)(D) requires some knowledge of the law; the only real question is which law? The Court's answer is that knowledge of any law is enough—or, put another way, that the defendant must be ignorant of every law violated by his course of conduct to be innocent of willfully violating the licensing requirement. The Court points to no textual basis for that conclusion other than the notoriously malleable word "willfully" itself. Instead, it seems to fall back on a presumption (apparently derived from the rule that ignorance of the law is no excuse) that even where ignorance of the law is an excuse, that excuse should be construed as narrowly as the statutory language permits.

I do not believe that the Court's approach makes sense of the statute that Congress enacted. I have no quarrel with the Court's assertion that "willfully" in §924(a)(1)(D) requires only "general" knowledge of illegality—in the sense that the defendant need not be able to recite chapter and verse from Title 18 of the United States Code. It is enough, in my view, if the defendant is generally aware that the *actus reus* punished by the statute—dealing in firearms without a license—is illegal. But the Court is willing to accept a *mens rea* so "general" that it is entirely divorced from the *actus reus* this statute was enacted to punish. That approach turns §924(a)(1)(D) into a strange and unlikely creature. Bryan would be guilty of "willfully" dealing in firearms without a federal license even if, for example, he had never heard of the licensing requirement but was aware that he had violated the law by using straw purchasers or filing the serial numbers off the pistols. The Court does not even limit (for there is no rational basis to limit) the universe of relevant laws to federal firearms statutes. Bryan would also be "acting with an evil-meaning mind," and hence presumably be guilty of "willfully" dealing in firearms without a license, if he knew that his street-corner transactions violated New York City's business licensing or sales tax ordinances. (For that matter, it ought to suffice if Bryan knew that the car out of which he sold the guns was illegally double-parked, or if, in order to meet the appointed time for the sale, he intentionally violated Pennsylvania's speed limit on the drive back from the gun purchase in Ohio.) Once we stop focusing on the conduct the defendant is actually charged with (i.e., selling guns without a license), I see no principled way to determine what law the defendant must be conscious of violating.

Congress is free, of course, to make criminal liability under one statute turn on knowledge of another, to use its firearms dealer statutes to encourage compliance with New York City's tax collection efforts, and to put judges and juries through the kind of mental gymnastics described above. But these are strange results, and I would not lightly assume that Congress intended to make liability under a federal criminal statute depend so heavily upon the vagaries of local law—particularly local law dealing with completely unrelated subjects. If we must have a presumption in cases like this one, I think it would be more reasonable to presume that, when Congress makes ignorance of the law a defense to a criminal prohibition, it ordinarily means ignorance of the unlawfulness of the specific conduct punished by that criminal prohibition. . . .

Notes and Questions

1. Bryan plainly knew he was violating *some* law (otherwise, why file off the serial numbers?), but he may not have known he was violating the *particular* law that gave rise to criminal charges. The relevant statutory texts do not clearly state which kind of legal knowledge Bryan must have in order to violate 18 U.S.C. §§922(a)(1) and 924. Accordingly, Justice Scalia argues, this is an appropriate case in which to apply the rule of lenity: Since either of two statutory interpretations is plausible, the interpretation that favors the defendant must prevail. Is that the right analysis in *Bryan*? Does Scalia reach the right bottom line?

Recall that in *Brogan*, Justice Scalia refused to apply the rule of lenity to an argument that the federal false statements statute should not cover false denials of guilt, on the ground that the no statutory language suggested such an exemption. Does the word "willfully" suggest knowledge of the *particular* illegality with which the defendant is charged? Are the majority opinion in *Brogan* and the dissent in *Bryan* consistent?

2. Justice Stevens, on the other hand, maintains that the rule of *Cheek* and *Ratzlaf*—that federal statutes that use the word "willfully" require the government to prove the defendant's knowledge of illegality—is an exception to the standard common-law principle that "ignorance of the law is no excuse." In general, he argues, exceptions to such general principles should be construed narrowly, in order to avoid undermining those principles. Thus, given a choice between requiring knowledge of the particular illegality at issue and requiring only knowledge of some more generalized illegality, the Court should opt for the latter. Is *that* the right analysis in *Bryan*? Does Stevens reach the right bottom line?

3. A cynic might interpret the bottom line of *Cheek, Ratzlaf,* and *Bryan* as follows: White-collar criminal defendants (like Cheek and Ratzlaf) who are charged under a federal criminal law that requires "willfulness," and who don't possess actual knowledge that their conduct violates the law, are generally not guilty. But street criminals (like Bryan) who lack the exact same kind of actual knowledge about the illegality of their conduct *are* guilty of crimes requiring "willfulness," simply because we can usually find that they've done *something else* that they knew* was either wrong or illegal. Is this interpretation correct? If not, why not?

4. Perhaps the Enron debacle further supports the cynical view suggested above. In 2001, Enron Corporation—an enormous multinational energy company based in Houston, Texas—suddenly declared bankruptcy. This not only put more than 20,000 employees out of work, but also wiped

---

* Or should have known? Should it matter here that the federal gun registration laws that Bryan violated, like the tax code in *Cheek* and the money laundering statutes in *Ratzlaf*, are (like much of federal law) extremely complicated?

By the way, how certain are you that Bryan actually *knew* that his conduct was illegal under *any* law, state or federal (see footnote 7 in *Bryan*, supra)? Isn't it possible that he sold the guns on street corners, and shaved off their serial numbers, not because he had actual knowledge of the illegality of his conduct (although he may well have suspected it), but because that's what his customers wanted?

out virtually all of the retirement funds of those employees as well as Enron retirees, since their retirement accounts were heavily invested in Enron stock. Eventually it was learned that several top Enron officials, including Kenneth Lay and Jeffrey Skilling, had conspired to prop up the value of the failing company long enough to cash out their own stock and leave the rest of the shareholders holding the bag. Enron was one of the largest corporate scandals in U.S. history, and helped motivate Congress to enact the Sarbanes-Oxley Act of 2002, which established tough new standards for corporate auditing and accountability.

Enron's primary accounting firm during the scandal was Arthur Andersen LLP, at the time one of the "Big Eight" largest U.S. accounting firms. Pursuant to directions from several high-ranking Arthur Andersen officials—but apparently contrary to firm policy—Arthur Andersen employees began destroying documents related to Enron shortly after the company learned that the SEC was launching an investigation of accounting improprieties at Enron. The destruction of documents continued right up to the very day when Arthur Andersen received official notice of an SEC subpoena for Enron-related documents. The next day, the head of Arthur Andersen's Enron "engagement team" sent around an e-mail that read: "Per Dave—No more shredding. . . . We have been officially served for our documents."

Arthur Andersen LLP was indicted for violating 18 U.S.C. §§1512(b)(2)(A) and (B). These statutes made it a federal crime to "knowingly use intimidation or physical force, threaten, or corruptly persuade another person . . . with intent to . . . cause" that person to "withhold" documents from, or "alter" documents for use in, an "official proceeding." A jury found Arthur Andersen guilty, and the Fifth Circuit affirmed.

The U.S. Supreme Court, however, reversed the conviction. According to the Court, the trial judge failed to instruct the jury properly on the elements of the statute — including the *mens rea* elements. The Court, per Chief Justice Rehnquist, explained its decision thusly:

> . . . [R]estraint is particularly appropriate here, where the act underlying the conviction—"persuasion"—is by itself innocuous. Indeed, "persuading" a person "with intent to . . . cause" that person to "withhold" testimony or documents from a Government proceeding or Government official is not inherently malign. Consider, for instance, a mother who suggests to her son that he invoke his right against compelled self-incrimination, or a wife who persuades her husband not to disclose marital confidences.
>
> Nor is it necessarily corrupt for an attorney to "persuade" a client "with intent to . . . cause" that client to "withhold" documents from the Government. In Upjohn Co. v. United States, 449 U.S. 383 (1981), for example, we held that Upjohn was justified in withholding documents that were covered by the attorney-client privilege from the Internal Revenue Service. See id., at 395. No one would suggest that an attorney who "persuaded" Upjohn to take that step

acted wrongfully, even though he surely intended that his client keep those documents out of the IRS' hands. . . .

. . . Section 1512(b) punishes not just "corruptly persuading" another, but "*knowingly* . . . corruptly persuading" another. (Emphasis added.) The Government suggests that "knowingly" does not modify "corruptly persuades," but that is not how the statute most naturally reads. . . . The Government suggests that it is "questionable whether Congress would employ such an inelegant formulation as 'knowingly . . . corruptly persuades.' " Brief for United States 35, n.18. Long experience has not taught us to share the Government's doubts on this score, and we must simply interpret the statute as written.

The parties have not pointed us to another interpretation of "knowingly . . . corruptly" to guide us here. In any event, the natural meaning of these terms provides a clear answer. "Knowledge" and "knowingly" are normally associated with awareness, understanding, or consciousness. "Corrupt" and "corruptly" are normally associated with wrongful, immoral, depraved, or evil. Joining these meanings together here makes sense both linguistically and in the statutory scheme. Only persons conscious of wrongdoing can be said to "knowingly . . . corruptly persuade.". . .

The outer limits of this element need not be explored here because the jury instructions at issue simply failed to convey the requisite consciousness of wrongdoing. Indeed, it is striking how little culpability the instructions required. For example, the jury was told that, "even if [petitioner] honestly and sincerely believed that its conduct was lawful, you may find [petitioner] guilty." . . .

The instructions also were infirm for another reason. They led the jury to believe that it did not have to find any nexus between the "persuasion" to destroy documents and any particular proceeding. In resisting any type of nexus element, the Government relies heavily on §1512(e)(1), which states that an official proceeding "need not be pending or about to be instituted at the time of the offense." It is, however, one thing to say that a proceeding "need not be pending or about to be instituted at the time of the offense," and quite another to say a proceeding need not even be foreseen. A "knowingly . . . corrupt persuader" cannot be someone who persuades others to shred documents under a document retention policy when he does not have in contemplation any particular official proceeding in which those documents might be material. . . .

For these reasons, the jury instructions here were flawed in important respects. The judgment of the Court of Appeals is reversed, and the case is remanded for further proceedings consistent with this opinion.

Arthur Andersen v. United States, 544 U.S. 696, 703-08 (2005).

As a matter of pure statutory interpretation, *Arthur Andersen* seems more persuasive than *Bryan*, does it not? The combination of "knowingly" and "corruptly" suggests, at the least, that the defendants must have known that their conduct was improper. And, as Chief Justice Rehnquist suggests, destroying documents is not always improper—often, it is a routine business practice.

It would appear to follow that, in order to be liable, defendants must have known that their conduct was illegal.

But even assuming the result in *Arthur Andersen* is legally correct, is it also fair? On the one hand, it is hard to know exactly where the legal line falls, and it seems unfair to punish defendants for guessing wrong about the scope of vague criminal statutes. On the other hand, these defendants plainly knew that they faced potentially serious legal liability (both civil and criminal), and equally plainly tried to limit the scope of the evidence that would be used against them in any subsequent litigation. Why isn't that sufficiently "corrupt" to violate the law? Why isn't it sufficiently "knowing"? Do you find their *mens rea*—however we might label it—any less culpable than that of Bryan?

4. The Future of Federal *Mens Rea* Doctrine?

So far, the law of federal *mens rea* looks something like this:

(1) For some federal crimes, such as the criminal provisions contained in statutes addressing heavily regulated industries or professions like the pharmaceutical industry (*Dotterweich*), strict liability is the default standard—because such crimes are intended mostly to protect the innocent consumer or innocent citizen, and it seems reasonable to assume that Congress meant to impose a duty upon "responsible" actors in those industries or professions to do whatever reasonably can be done to avoid the harm.

(2) For other federal crimes, such as the federal version of a traditional *mala in se* common-law crime like theft or conversion (*Morissette*), federal *mens rea* looks a lot like common law *mens rea*—because it seems reasonable to assume that Congress would have wanted it that way, and that the relevant statutes were premised on adhering to the traditional requirements of common-law *mens rea*.

(3) For still other federal crimes, such as the relatively complicated provisions of the federal firearms laws (*Staples*), the Internal Revenue Code (*Cheek*), or the laws requiring the reporting of certain financial transactions (*Ratzlaf*), the government generally must prove not only that the defendant knew of the *facts* that made his behavior unlawful, but also—at least where the relevant crime statute contains the word "willfully"—that the defendant knew of the *law* that imposed upon him the relevant duty. This is because it seems reasonable to assume that Congress would not want to snare "ordinary citizens" in the net of complicated federal criminal laws without proof of such knowledge. But even where a defendant lacks knowledge about the specific criminal law under which he was charged, he can still be convicted if he knew that he was doing *something* illegal (*Bryan*).

As you read the next case, think about what effect it might have on this overall picture.

Elonis v. United States

Supreme Court of the United States
575 U.S. ___ (2015)

Chief Justice ROBERTS delivered the opinion of the Court.

Federal law makes it a crime to transmit in interstate commerce "any communication containing any threat . . . to injure the person of another." 18 U.S.C. §875(c). Petitioner was convicted of violating this provision under instructions that required the jury to find that he communicated what a reasonable person would regard as a threat. The question is whether the statute also requires that the defendant be aware of the threatening nature of the communication, and—if not—whether the First Amendment requires such a showing.

I

A

Anthony Douglas Elonis was an active user of the social networking Web site Facebook. Users of that Web site may post items on their Facebook page that are accessible to other users, including Facebook "friends" who are notified when new content is posted. In May 2010, Elonis's wife of nearly seven years left him, taking with her their two young children. Elonis began "listening to more violent music" and posting self-styled "rap" lyrics inspired by the music. App. 204, 226. Eventually, Elonis changed the user name on his Facebook page from his actual name to a rap-style nom de plume, "Tone Dougie," to distinguish himself from his "on-line persona." The lyrics Elonis posted as "Tone Dougie" included graphically violent language and imagery. This material was often interspersed with disclaimers that the lyrics were "fictitious," with no intentional "resemblance to real persons." Elonis posted an explanation to another Facebook user that "I'm doing this for me. My writing is therapeutic." Id., at 329; see also id., at 205 (testifying that it "helps me to deal with the pain").

Elonis's co-workers and friends viewed the posts in a different light. Around Halloween of 2010, Elonis posted a photograph of himself and a co-worker at a "Halloween Haunt" event at the amusement park where they worked. In the photograph, Elonis was holding a toy knife against his co-worker's neck, and in the caption Elonis wrote, "I wish." Elonis was not Facebook friends with the co-worker and did not "tag" her, a Facebook feature that would have alerted her to the posting. But the chief of park security was a Facebook "friend" of Elonis, saw the photograph, and fired him.

In response, Elonis posted a new entry on his Facebook page:

> "Moles! Didn't I tell y'all I had several? Y'all sayin' I had access to keys for all the f***in' gates. That I have sinister plans for all my friends and must have taken home a couple. Y'all think it's too dark and foggy to secure your facility from a man as mad as me? You see, even without a paycheck, I'm still the main

attraction. Whoever thought the Halloween Haunt could be so f***in' scary?" App. 332.

This post became the basis for Count One of Elonis's subsequent indictment, threatening park patrons and employees.

Elonis's posts frequently included crude, degrading, and violent material about his soon-to-be ex-wife. Shortly after he was fired, Elonis posted an adaptation of a satirical sketch that he and his wife had watched together. In the actual sketch, called "It's Illegal to Say . . . ," a comedian explains that it is illegal for a person to say he wishes to kill the President, but not illegal to explain that it is illegal for him to say that. When Elonis posted the script of the sketch, however, he substituted his wife for the President. The posting was part of the basis for Count Two of the indictment, threatening his wife:

"Hi, I'm Tone Elonis.

Did you know that it's illegal for me to say I want to kill my wife? . . .

It's one of the only sentences that I'm not allowed to say. . . .

Now it was okay for me to say it right then because I was just telling you that it's illegal for me to say I want to kill my wife. . . .

Um, but what's interesting is that it's very illegal to say I really, really think someone out there should kill my wife. . . .

But not illegal to say with a mortar launcher.

Because that's its own sentence. . . .

I also found out that it's incredibly illegal, extremely illegal to go on Facebook and say something like the best place to fire a mortar launcher at her house would be from the cornfield behind it because of easy access to a getaway road and you'd have a clear line of sight through the sun room. . . .

Yet even more illegal to show an illustrated diagram.

[diagram of the house]. . . ." Id., at 333.

The details about the home were accurate. At the bottom of the post, Elonis included a link to the video of the original skit, and wrote, "Art is about pushing limits. I'm willing to go to jail for my Constitutional rights. Are you?" Id., at 333.

After viewing some of Elonis's posts, his wife felt "extremely afraid for [her] life." Id., at 156. A state court granted her a three-year protection-from-abuse order against Elonis (essentially, a restraining order). Elonis referred to the order in another post on his "Tone Dougie" page, also included in Count Two of the indictment:

"Fold up your [protection-from-abuse order] and put it in your pocket

Is it thick enough to stop a bullet?

Try to enforce an Order

that was improperly granted in the first place

Me thinks the Judge needs an education

on true threat jurisprudence

And prison time'll add zeros to my settlement . . .

And if worse comes to worse

I've got enough explosives

to take care of the State Police and the Sheriff's Department." Id., at 334.

At the bottom of this post was a link to the Wikipedia article on "Freedom of speech." Elonis's reference to the police was the basis for Count Three of his indictment, threatening law enforcement officers.

That same month, interspersed with posts about a movie Elonis liked and observations on a comedian's social commentary, Elonis posted an entry that gave rise to Count Four of his indictment:

"That's it, I've had about enough

I'm checking out and making a name for myself

Enough elementary schools in a ten mile radius

to initiate the most heinous school shooting ever imagined

And hell hath no fury like a crazy man in a Kindergarten class

The only question is . . . which one?" Id., at 335.

Meanwhile, park security had informed both local police and the Federal Bureau of Investigation about Elonis's posts, and FBI Agent Denise Stevens had created a Facebook account to monitor his online activity. After the post about a school shooting, Agent Stevens and her partner visited Elonis at his house. Following their visit, during which Elonis was polite but uncooperative, Elonis posted another entry on his Facebook page, called "Little Agent Lady," which led to Count Five:

"You know your s***'s ridiculous

when you have the FBI knockin' at yo' door

Little Agent lady stood so close

Took all the strength I had not to turn the b**** ghost

Pull my knife, flick my wrist, and slit her throat

Leave her bleedin' from her jugular in the arms of her partner

[laughter]

So the next time you knock, you best be serving a warrant

And bring yo' SWAT and an explosives expert while you're at it

Cause little did y'all know, I was strapped wit' a bomb

Why do you think it took me so long to get dressed with no shoes on?

I was jus' waitin' for y'all to handcuff me and pat me down

Touch the detonator in my pocket and we're all goin'

[BOOM!]

Are all the pieces comin' together?

S***, I'm just a crazy sociopath

that gets off playin' you stupid f***s like a fiddle

And if y'all didn't hear, I'm gonna be famous

Cause I'm just an aspiring rapper who likes the attention

who happens to be under investigation for terrorism

cause y'all think I'm ready to turn the Valley into Fallujah

But I ain't gonna tell you which bridge is gonna fall

into which river or road

And if you really believe this s***

I'll have some bridge rubble to sell you tomorrow

[BOOM!] [BOOM!] [BOOM!]" Id., at 336.

B

A grand jury indicted Elonis for making threats to injure patrons and employees of the park, his estranged wife, police officers, a kindergarten class, and an FBI agent, all in violation of 18 U.S.C. §875(c). In the District Court, Elonis moved to dismiss the indictment for failing to allege that he had intended to threaten anyone. The District Court denied the motion, holding that Third Circuit precedent required only that Elonis "intentionally made the communication, not that he intended to make a threat." App. to Pet. for Cert. 51a. At trial, Elonis testified that his posts emulated the rap lyrics of the well-known performer Eminem, some of which involve fantasies about killing his ex-wife. In Elonis's view, he had posted "nothing . . . that hasn't been said already." The Government presented as witnesses Elonis's wife and co-workers, all of whom said they felt afraid and viewed Elonis's posts as serious threats.

Elonis requested a jury instruction that "the government must prove that he intended to communicate a true threat." The District Court denied that request. The jury instructions instead informed the jury that

> "A statement is a true threat when a defendant intentionally makes a statement in a context or under such circumstances wherein a reasonable person would foresee that the statement would be interpreted by those to whom the maker communicates the statement as a serious expression of an intention to inflict bodily injury or take the life of an individual."

The Government's closing argument emphasized that it was irrelevant whether Elonis intended the postings to be threats — "it doesn't matter what he thinks." A jury convicted Elonis on four of the five counts against him, acquitting only on the charge of threatening park patrons and employees. Elonis was sentenced to three years, eight months' imprisonment and three years' supervised release.

Elonis renewed his challenge to the jury instructions in the Court of Appeals, contending that the jury should have been required to find that he intended his posts to be threats. The Court of Appeals disagreed, holding that the intent required by Section 875(c) is only the intent to communicate words that the defendant understands, and that a reasonable person would view as a threat. 730 F.3d 321, 332 (CA3 2013). . . .

II

A

An individual who "transmits in interstate or foreign commerce any communication containing any threat to kidnap any person or any threat to injure the person of another" is guilty of a felony and faces up to five years' imprisonment. 18 U.S.C. §875(c). This statute requires that a communication be transmitted and that the communication contain a threat. It does not specify that the defendant must have any mental state with respect to these elements. In particular, it does not indicate whether the defendant must intend that his communication contain a threat.

Elonis argues that the word "threat" itself in Section 875(c) imposes such a requirement. According to Elonis, every definition of "threat" or "threaten" conveys the notion of an intent to inflict harm. E.g., 11 Oxford English Dictionary 353 (1933) ("to declare (usually conditionally) one's intention of inflicting injury upon"); Webster's New International Dictionary 2633 (2d ed. 1954) ("*Law*, specif., an expression of an intention to inflict loss or harm on another by illegal means"); Black's Law Dictionary 1519 (8th ed. 2004) ("A communicated intent to inflict harm or loss on another").

These definitions, however, speak to what the statement conveys — not to the mental state of the author. For example, an anonymous letter that says "I'm going to kill you" is "an expression of an intention to inflict loss or harm" regardless of the author's intent. A victim who receives that letter in the mail has received a threat, even if the author believes (wrongly) that his message will be taken as a joke.

For its part, the Government argues that Section 875(c) should be read in light of its neighboring provisions, Sections 875(b) and 875(d). Those provisions also prohibit certain types of threats, but expressly include a mental state requirement of an "intent to extort." See 18 U.S.C. §875(b) (proscribing threats to injure or kidnap made "with intent to extort"); §875(d) (proscribing threats to property or reputation made "with intent to extort"). According to the Government, the express "intent to extort" requirements in Sections 875(b) and (d) should preclude courts from implying an unexpressed "intent to threaten" requirement in Section 875(c). . . .

The Government takes this *expressio unius est exclusio alterius* canon too far. The fact that Congress excluded the requirement of an "intent to extort" from Section 875(c) is strong evidence that Congress did not mean to confine Section 875(c) to crimes of extortion. But that does not suggest that Congress, at the same time, also meant to exclude a requirement that a defendant act with a certain mental state in communicating a threat. The most we can conclude from the language of Section 875(c) and its neighboring provisions is that Congress meant to proscribe a broad class of threats in Section 875(c), but did not identify what mental state, if any, a defendant must have to be convicted.

In sum, neither Elonis nor the Government has identified any indication of a particular mental state requirement in the text of Section 875(c).

B

The fact that the statute does not specify any required mental state, however, does not mean that none exists. We have repeatedly held that "mere omission from a criminal enactment of any mention of criminal intent" should not be read "as dispensing with it." Morissette v. United States, 342 U.S. 246, 250 (1952). . . . Although there are exceptions, the "general rule" is that a guilty mind is "a necessary element in the indictment and proof of every crime." United States v. Balint, 258 U.S. 250, 251 (1922). We therefore generally "interpret[ ] criminal statutes to include broadly applicable scienter requirements, even where the statute by its terms does not contain them." United States v. X-Citement Video, Inc., 513 U.S. 64, 70 (1994).

This is not to say that a defendant must know that his conduct is illegal before he may be found guilty. The familiar maxim "ignorance of the law is no excuse" typically holds true. Instead, our cases have explained that a defendant generally must "know the facts that make his conduct fit the definition of the offense," Staples v. United States, 511 U.S. 600, n.3 (1994), even if he does not know that those facts give rise to a crime. . . .

When interpreting federal criminal statutes that are silent on the required mental state, we read into the statute "only that *mens rea* which is necessary to separate wrongful conduct from 'otherwise innocent conduct.' " Carter v. United States, 530 U.S. 255, 269 (2000). In some cases, a general requirement that a defendant *act* knowingly is itself an adequate safeguard.... In other instances, however, requiring only that the defendant act knowingly "would fail to protect the innocent actor." Id., at 269....

C

Section 875(c), as noted, requires proof that a communication was transmitted and that it contained a threat. The "presumption in favor of a scienter requirement should apply to *each* of the statutory elements that criminalize otherwise innocent conduct." *X-Citement Video*, 513 U.S., at 72 (emphasis added). The parties agree that a defendant under Section 875(c) must know that he is transmitting a communication. But communicating *something* is not what makes the conduct "wrongful." Here "the crucial element separating legal innocence from wrongful conduct" is the threatening nature of the communication. Id., at 73. The mental state requirement must therefore apply to the fact that the communication contains a threat.

Elonis's conviction, however, was premised solely on how his posts would be understood by a reasonable person. Such a "reasonable person" standard is a familiar feature of civil liability in tort law, but is inconsistent with "the conventional requirement for criminal conduct— *awareness* of some wrongdoing." *Staples*, 511 U.S., at 606-607 (quoting United States v. Dotterweich, 320 U.S. 277, 281 (1943); emphasis added). Having liability turn on whether a "reasonable person" regards the communication as a threat—regardless of what the defendant thinks—reduces culpability on the all-important element of the crime to negligence, and we "have long been reluctant to infer that a negligence standard was intended in criminal statutes," Rogers v. United States, 422 U.S. 35, 47 (1975) (Marshall, J., concurring) (citing *Morissette*, 342 U.S. 246).... Under these principles, "what [Elonis] thinks" does matter....

* * *

In light of the foregoing, Elonis's conviction cannot stand. The jury was instructed that the Government need prove only that a reasonable person would regard Elonis's communications as threats, and that was error. Federal criminal liability generally does not turn solely on the results of an act without considering the defendant's mental state. That understanding "took deep and early root in American soil" and Congress left it intact here: Under Section 875(c), "wrongdoing must be conscious to be criminal." *Morissette*, 342 U.S., at 252.

There is no dispute that the mental state requirement in Section 875(c) is satisfied if the defendant transmits a communication for the purpose of issuing a threat, or with knowledge that the communication will be viewed as a threat. In response to a question at oral argument, Elonis stated that a finding of recklessness would not be sufficient. Neither Elonis nor the Government has briefed or argued that point, and we accordingly decline to address it. . . . Given our disposition, it is not necessary to consider any First Amendment issues. . . .

Justice Alito . . . suggests that we have not clarified confusion in the lower courts. That is wrong. Our holding makes clear that negligence is not sufficient to support a conviction under Section 875(c), contrary to the view of nine Courts of Appeals. There was and is no circuit conflict over the question Justice Alito and Justice Thomas would have us decide—whether recklessness suffices for liability under Section 875(c). No Court of Appeals has even addressed that question. We think that is more than sufficient "justification," post, at 2 (opinion of Alito, J.), for us to decline to be the first appellate tribunal to do so. . . .

We may be "capable of deciding the recklessness issue," post, at 2 (opinion of Alito, J.), but following our usual practice of awaiting a decision below and hearing from the parties would help ensure that we decide it correctly.

The judgment of the United States Court of Appeals for the Third Circuit is reversed. . . .

Justice ALITO, concurring in part and dissenting in part.

In Marbury v. Madison, 1 Cranch 137, 177 (1803), the Court famously proclaimed: "It is emphatically the province and duty of the judicial department to say what the law is." Today, the Court announces: It is emphatically the prerogative of this Court to say only what the law is not.

The Court's disposition of this case is certain to cause confusion and serious problems. Attorneys and judges need to know which mental state is required for conviction under 18 U.S.C. §875(c), an important criminal statute. This case squarely presents that issue, but the Court provides only a partial answer. The Court holds that the jury instructions in this case were defective because they required only negligence in conveying a threat. But the Court refuses to explain what type of intent was necessary. Did the jury need to find that Elonis had the *purpose* of conveying a true threat? Was it enough if he *knew* that his words conveyed such a threat? Would *recklessness* suffice? The Court declines to say. Attorneys and judges are left to guess.

This will have regrettable consequences. While this Court has the luxury of choosing its docket, lower courts and juries are not so fortunate. They must actually decide cases, and this means applying a standard. If purpose or knowledge is needed and a district court instructs the jury that recklessness suffices, a defendant may be wrongly convicted. On the other hand, if recklessness is enough, and the jury is told that conviction requires proof of more, a guilty defendant may go free. We granted review in this case to resolve a disagreement among the Circuits. But the Court has compounded—not clarified—the confusion. . . .

. . . In the hierarchy of mental states that may be required as a condition for criminal liability, the *mens rea* just above negligence is recklessness. Negligence requires only that the defendant "should [have] be[en] aware of a substantial and unjustifiable risk," ALI, Model Penal Code §2.02(2)(d), while recklessness exists "when a person disregards a risk of harm of which he is aware," Model Penal Code §2.02(2)(c). And when Congress does not specify a *mens rea* in a criminal statute, we have no justification for inferring that anything more than recklessness is needed. It is quite unusual for us to interpret a statute to contain a requirement that is nowhere set out in the text. Once we have reached recklessness, we have gone as far as we can without stepping over the line that separates interpretation from amendment.

There can be no real dispute that recklessness regarding a risk of serious harm is wrongful conduct. . . . Someone who acts recklessly with respect to conveying a threat necessarily grasps that he is not engaged in innocent conduct. He is not merely careless. He is aware that others could regard his statements as a threat, but he delivers them anyway.

Accordingly, I would hold that a defendant may be convicted under §875(c) if he or she consciously disregards the risk that the communication transmitted will be interpreted as a true threat. . . .

[B]ecause the jury instructions in this case did not require proof of recklessness, I would vacate the judgment below and remand for the Court of Appeals to decide in the first instance whether Elonis's conviction could be upheld under a recklessness standard. . . .

Justice THOMAS, dissenting.

We granted certiorari to resolve a conflict in the lower courts over the appropriate mental state for threat prosecutions under 18 U.S.C. §875(c). Save two, every Circuit to have considered the issue—11 in total—has held that this provision demands proof only of general intent, which here requires no more than that a defendant knew he transmitted a communication, knew the words used in that communication, and understood the ordinary meaning of those words in the relevant context. The outliers are the Ninth and Tenth Circuits, which have concluded that proof of an intent to threaten was necessary for conviction. . . .

Rather than resolve the conflict, the Court casts aside the approach used in nine Circuits and leaves nothing in its place. Lower courts are thus left to guess at the appropriate mental state for §875(c). All they know after today's decision is that a requirement of general intent will not do. But they can safely infer that a majority of this Court would not adopt an intent-to-threaten requirement, as the opinion carefully leaves open the possibility that recklessness may be enough.

This failure to decide throws everyone from appellate judges to everyday Facebook users into a state of uncertainty. This uncertainty could have been avoided had we simply adhered to the background rule of the common law favoring general intent. Although I am sympathetic to my colleagues' policy concerns about the risks associated with threat prosecutions, the answer to such fears is not to discard our traditional approach to state-of-mind requirements in criminal law. Because the Court of Appeals properly applied the general-intent standard, and because the communications transmitted by Elonis were "true threats" unprotected by the First Amendment, I would affirm the judgment below. . . .

General intent divides those who know the facts constituting the *actus reus* of this crime from those who do not. For example, someone who transmits a threat who does not know English—or who knows English, but perhaps does not know a threatening idiom—lacks the general intent required under §875(c). Likewise, the hapless mailman who delivers a threatening letter, ignorant of its contents, should not fear prosecution. A defendant like Elonis, however, who admits that he "knew that what [he] was saying was violent" but supposedly "just wanted to express [him]self," App. 205, acted with the general intent required under §875(c), even if he did not know that a jury would conclude that his communication constituted a "threat" as a matter of law. . . .

Requiring general intent in this context is not the same as requiring mere negligence. Like the mental-state requirements adopted in many of the cases cited by the Court, general intent under §875(c) prevents a defendant from being convicted on the basis of any *fact* beyond his awareness. See, e.g., United States v. X-Citement Video, Inc., 513 U.S. 64, 73 (1994) (knowledge of age of persons depicted in explicit materials); *Staples*, supra, at 614-615 (knowledge of firing capability of weapon); Morissette v. United States, 342 U.S. 246-271 (1952) (knowledge that property belonged to another). In other words, the defendant must *know*—not merely be reckless or negligent with respect to the fact—that he is committing the acts that constitute the *actus reus* of the offense.

But general intent requires *no* mental state (not even a negligent one) concerning the "fact" that certain words meet the *legal* definition of a threat. That approach is particularly appropriate where, as here, that legal status is determined by a jury's application of the legal standard of a "threat" to the contents of a communication. And convicting a defendant despite his ignorance of the legal—or objective—status of his conduct does not mean that he is being punished for negligent conduct. . . .

. . . Not only does [today's] decision warp our traditional approach to *mens rea*, it results in an arbitrary distinction between threats and other forms of unprotected speech. Had Elonis mailed obscene materials to his wife and a kindergarten class, he could have been prosecuted irrespective of whether he intended to offend those recipients or recklessly disregarded that possibility. Yet when he threatened to kill his wife and a kindergarten class, his intent to terrify those recipients (or reckless disregard of that risk) suddenly becomes highly relevant. That need not—and should not—be the case.

Nor should it be the case that we cast aside the mental-state requirement compelled by our precedents yet offer nothing in its place. Our job is to decide questions, not create them. Given the majority's ostensible concern for protecting innocent actors, one would have expected it to announce a clear rule—any clear rule. Its failure to do so reveals the fractured foundation upon which today's decision rests.

I respectfully dissent.

Notes and Questions

1. The *Elonis* decision would seem to represent yet another different approach to federal *mens rea*. Although the Supreme Court in *Elonis* cites a number of its prior decisions in support of the general propositions that "a guilty mind is 'a necessary element'" for every crime, and that "wrongdoing must be conscious to be criminal," the Court's ultimate holding stops short of resolving the *mens rea* issue. What the Court actually holds in *Elonis* is this: (1) the government doesn't have to prove that a defendant like Elonis *intended* to communicate a "threat"; but (2) the government also can't get away with proving only that such a defendant was *negligent*, i.e., *should have known* that the communication would be interpreted as a "threat."

What *does* the government have to prove in order to convict a defendant under section 875(c)? The Court doesn't say. One possibility, of course, is *knowledge* that the communication would be interpreted as a "threat." That would be roughly consistent with how the Court came down in *Staples*, where (as you will recall) the Court held that a defendant "must know the facts that make his conduct illegal." Another possibility, supported here by Justice Alito, is *recklessness*, meaning a conscious awareness of the risk that the communication might be so taken. But the Court—seemingly at least a bit more aware of the subtler nuances of *mens rea* than was apparent in the *Staples*, *Cheek*, *Ratzlaf*, and *Bryan* decisions, and perhaps therefore a bit more cautious—decides to leave the final resolution of the *mens rea* issue for another day.

2. Meanwhile, Justice Thomas continues (as he did in *Staples*) to obfuscate the common law of *mens rea*. Thomas claims in *Elonis* that general intent "divides those who know the facts constituting the *actus reus* of this crime from those who do not." He adds that general intent "prevents a defendant from being convicted on the basis of any *fact* beyond his awareness," citing *X-Citement Video*, *Staples*, and *Morissette*. (Note, by the way, that *Morissette* actually involved not general intent, but a classic specific intent crime.) And he finishes up by explaining that general intent "requires *no* mental state (not even a negligent one) concerning the 'fact' that certain words meet the *legal* definition of a threat."

As we have previously learned, however, general intent is not really about either "the facts" or "the law." Instead, general intent is about the defendant's intent—that is, his "willful" decision—to perform the *conduct*, or *actus reus*, of the crime. The common law developed entirely separate doctrines to deal with claims of "mistake of fact" and "mistake of law."

3. So how *would* the common law have resolved the *Elonis* case? The key issue would be whether Elonis, when he said that he didn't think anybody else would interpret his words as a true "threat," was claiming to have made a "mistake of fact" or a "mistake of law." If the nature of a communication as a "threat" is treated by the courts as a question of "fact," then mistake doctrine *might* provide a defense, but only if Elonis's mistaken belief was both "honest" and "reasonable." In short, Elonis would be held to a negligence standard. If, on the other hand, the nature of a communication as a "threat" is held to be a question of "law" (i.e., if it's simply a matter of how to interpret properly the relevant crime statute), then Elonis (like Marrero, see page 157) surely would lose.

4. And what about the Model Penal Code? In MPC-land, Justice Alito's view would prevail. Because the crime statute contains no *mens rea* words at all, we would use the default *mens rea* of recklessness, and Elonis would be guilty as long as he was consciously aware of a substantial and unjustifiable risk that others would interpret his words as a true "threat." (Do you think he was "consciously aware" of that risk?)

5. In the end, then, *Elonis* leaves just about as many questions unanswered as it answers. But at a minimum, we can say that the Court in *Elonis* at least managed to avoid the worst of the *mens rea* pitfalls into which it so easily fell in *Staples, Cheek, Ratzlaf,* and *Bryan.* Perhaps that should give us hope for the future of federal *mens rea* doctrine.

5

Property Crimes

We now move from the so-called "general part" of the criminal law—those general rules, principles, and doctrines that apply to all (or at least most) crimes—to the "special part," where we will examine specific crimes and their specific characteristics. (We will return to the "general part" briefly in Chapter 7, and more extensively at the end of the casebook, in Chapters 11-13.) Actually, we have already learned a great deal about a number of specific crimes: Arson, see page 112; Assault (often, although not always, linked with Battery), see page 125; Auto Theft (and the related crime of Joyriding), see page 128; Bigamy, see page 148; Child Abuse, see page 99; Vagrancy and Loitering, see page 41; and in Chapter 4, various federal crimes.

This chapter focuses on property crimes. Property crimes occupy a large place in any criminal justice system, and America's is no exception, as these data show: One-fourth of felony convictions and one-fifth of prison sentences are for criminal violations of property rights. Interestingly, a large fraction of those cases deal with conduct that threatens something other than property owners' interest in keeping what they own. Robbery and burglary punish not theft but the creation of fear—chiefly the fear of criminal violence. Criminal trespass and vandalism laws often are used indirectly to punish those who are suspected of dealing or possessing drugs, or who are seen as generally disrespecting other social norms. The merged law of blackmail and extortion seems aimed at protecting private parties' reputations as much as their wallets. And the federal law of fraud often protects the public's "intangible right of honest services," which basically means the interest in trusting those whose job it is to be trustworthy.

As you read the cases involving these different kinds of property crime, consider the ways in which protecting property also protects other values—and the ways in which property rights may conflict with those other values. When property and liberty clash, which side wins? What about property and equality? Consider, too, the boundary line between criminal punishment and civil damages. When should the criminal justice system assume primary responsibility for protecting property rights? When should property owners take that responsibility themselves, using civil lawsuits to protect their property rights?

A. TRESPASS

People v. Luke (Derek)

Supreme Court of New York, Appellate Term, First Department
37 Misc. 3d 73; 955 N.Y.S.2d 465 (2012)

Opinion of HUNTER, JR., J.:

. . . On the evening of December 19, 2008, defendant was arrested for trespass at Manhattan's Taft Houses, a public housing development consisting of nine almost identical brown brick buildings. According to defendant, he was there to visit a long-time family friend for dinner and provide her with computer assistance, but mistakenly entered the wrong building directly across the street. Following his arrest, defendant was charged by misdemeanor complaint with second-degree criminal trespass (Penal Law §140.15), but in a subsequent prosecutor's information, the charge was reduced to one count of criminal trespass in the third degree (Penal Law §140.10[a]).*

At the non-jury trial, the arresting officer, Raquel Marte, was the prosecution's sole witness. She testified, inter alia, that on December 19, 2008, she was on "vertical patrol" at one of the Taft Houses buildings, located at 65 East 112th Street. She testified that tenants would access the building by using a key or the intercom and that there were "no trespassing" signs posted. She could not recall if the locks on the entrance doors to the building were working that day and could not recall exactly where the "no trespassing" signs were posted. She went on to testify that the entrance doors to

---

* ["A person is guilty of criminal trespass in the third degree when he knowingly enters or remains unlawfully in a building or upon real property (a) which is fenced or otherwise enclosed in a manner designed to exclude intruders . . . ." Penal Law §140.10[a]. A separate definition section of the statute provides, in relevant part: "A person 'enters or remains unlawfully' in or upon premises when he is not licensed or privileged to do so. A person who, regardless of his intent, enters or remains in or upon premises which are at the time open to the public does so with license and privilege unless he defies a lawful order not to enter or remain, personally communicated to him by the owner of such premises or other authorized person. A license or privilege to enter or remain in a building which is only partly open to the public is not a license or privilege to enter or remain in that part of the building which is not open to the public . . . ." Penal Law §140.00[5].—EDS.]

the building were not always locked. She observed the defendant enter the building but was not able to state how the defendant gained entry. She then observed defendant board an elevator within a minute of his entering the building. She and her partner boarded an adjacent elevator to the 19th floor. However, she stated that the elevator stopped on the 11th floor, at which time she observed defendant standing in the hallway. Marte and her partner continued up to the 19th floor where they patrolled the roof before taking the stairs down to the 18th floor. Marte testified that she then observed defendant standing in the hallway of the 18th floor. She approached him and asked him if he lived in the building. Defendant informed her that he did not live in the building but was visiting an aunt who was a tenant in the building and that he also had friends in the building. Defendant could not provide an apartment number or the name of his aunt or friends. Defendant was then arrested and searched. No drugs or weapons were found on his person.

Defendant testified that while he was a student at the State University of New York at Albany, he became close friends with a classmate named Charee Walker and subsequently developed a close relationship with her mother, Laurie Holder, whom he referred to as his "aunt." Defendant testified that Ms. Holder lived in the Taft Houses and he visited her ten to fifteen times over a ten-year period prior to December 2008. However, he had not visited her in 2008.

Defendant further testified that he had spoken to Ms. Holder by telephone on December 18, 2008, and arranged to visit her the next day to help her with some computer problems and to have dinner. The next day, he took the subway to Taft Houses to see Ms. Holder and when he got off the subway at 110th Street, "it was dark" and he had not been "in that area a while." He "did notice some changes" but stated that "for the most part everything was the same." He proceeded to walk to 112th Street and stated that he crossed a parking lot connected to a walkway which was significant to him because a similar parking lot and walkway was in front of 1695 Madison Avenue where Ms. Holder lives. However, he instead entered 65 East 112th Street.

Defendant testified that he gained access to 65 East 112th Street as another individual exited the building and he took the elevator to the 18th floor. He exited on the 18th floor and "realized that it probably wasn't the right floor" as it did not look familiar to him. He knocked on the door to an apartment he believed was Ms. Holder's, but no one answered, and by that time he "was pretty sure that it wasn't the right floor." He took the stairs down to the 14th floor and exited the staircase to see if it "looked like the right one," since that one did not look familiar to him, he continued to go down the stairs and exited on the 11th floor to call Ms. Holder because he "didn't think it would be safe to go all the way downstairs."

While he was searching for Ms. Holder's number on his cell phone, he was approached by Marte and her partner who asked him if he lived in the building, what he was doing in the building and if he knew anyone who lives in the building. Defendant informed them that he was "visiting friends" and that his "aunt" lived in the building. When asked where his aunt lived, he testified that he told the officers, "I thought she lived on the 18th floor but I am calling her right now to go check because I had the floor wrong." He testified that Marte did not permit him to make a phone call. He informed her that he was on probation and if he was permitted to make a phone call it would "clear everything up." She refused and he was arrested.

Defendant admitted that there was no blood relation between him and Ms. Holder. He explained that he referred to her as his "aunt" at the time of the arrest "to create an understanding" that it was "somebody older" and not just a "buddy" or "pal," but he was nevertheless arrested.

Ms. Holder also testified for the defense and essentially corroborated defendant's assertions. Ms. Holder confirmed that she had known defendant since 1997 and that he was the "son" she never had. She testified that he called her "mom" and confirmed that she invited defendant to her apartment on the evening of December 19, 2008 to fix her computer and have dinner. Ms. Holder also testified that she lives on the 18th floor of 1694 Madison Avenue, not 1695 Madison Avenue and that defendant "constantly called" her to confirm what floor she lived on. She testified that Taft Houses is comprised of at least ten buildings that are the same shape and height and arrangement with the only visible difference being a colored strip "in the middle" that is "not very visible" and to notice it one would "have to know it to look for it."

Ms. Holder further testified that there is a parking lot in front of her building and acknowledged that there was one in front of 65 East 112th Street. The only difference is that the one in front of her building is "directly in front" and the parking lot in front of 65 East 112th Street is "slightly to the side." She also testified that the intercom system in her building does not work and the directory listing residents was incomplete and she did not know whether or not her name was listed. She also testified that the door to her building "hasn't been locked in years." Ms. Holder testified that after receiving the telephone call from defendant notifying her of his arrest, she contacted 311 and eventually filed a complaint with the "complaint bureau" about the fact that her invited guest had been arrested for trespassing. Following the trial, Criminal Court convicted defendant of criminal trespass in the third degree. This appeal ensued, and we reverse.

. . . Th[is] court must determine, viewing the evidence in the light most favorable to the prosecution, whether there is a valid line of reasoning and permissible inferences from which the fact-finder could have found the elements of the crime proved beyond a reasonable doubt . . . . A conviction based on legally sufficient evidence is [also] subject to this court's factual review power to assure that the verdict is supported by the weight of the evidence. "If based on all the credible evidence a different finding would not have been unreasonable, then the appellate court must, like the trier of fact below, weigh the relative probative force of conflicting testimony and the relative strength of conflicting inferences that may be drawn from the testimony'" (People v. Bleakley, 69 N.Y.2d 490, 495, 508 N.E.2d 672 [1987]) . . . .

Upon a factual review of the record, I find that defendant's conviction for criminal trespass in the third degree was against the weight of the evidence. An individual, "who enters upon the premises accidentally, or who honestly believes that he is licensed or privileged to enter, is not guilty of any degree of criminal trespass" (People v. Basch, 36 N.Y.2d 154, 159, 325 N.E.2d 156 [1975]).

It was the prosecution's burden to prove unlawful entry or remaining, and the testimony of Marte, standing alone, was insufficient to prove beyond a reasonable doubt that defendant "knowingly enter[ed] or remain[ed] unlawfully," without license or privilege, in the subject building. Although Marte testified that defendant was unable to provide the apartment number for his "aunt," the inability to provide the arresting officer with the explanation she sought, "has no logical bearing on the adequacy of the proof" that defendant remained unlawfully in the building (Matter of James C., 23 A.D.3d 262, 805 N.Y.S.2d 13 [1st Dept. 2005]). Moreover, it was not his obligation to provide the arresting officer with an explanation for his presence in the building.

Defendant's testimony at trial was corroborated by Ms. Holder in that he was her invited guest on the day he was arrested. His testimony that he was visiting his "aunt" and mistakenly believed she lived on the 18th floor of that building coupled with Ms. Holder's testimony was sufficient to support his reasonable belief that he was licensed or privileged to be in the building. Therefore, his belief, even if mistaken, negated the element of "knowing and unlawfully remaining" (see People v. Basch, 36 N.Y.2d at 159).

Accordingly, the judgment of conviction is reversed, the accusatory instrument is dismissed, and the fine and surcharge, if paid, are remitted. In light of this determination, we need not reach defendant's remaining contentions.

SHULMAN, J. (dissenting):

Defendant was convicted, after a bench trial, of third-degree criminal trespass upon evidence, largely undisputed: that police officers conducting a "vertical sweep" of a drug prone building in a public housing development known as the Taft Houses, observed defendant enter the building at about 6:50 P.M. on a December evening, proceed through the lobby to an elevator and, within a 10-minute period, appear in three different hallways on the building's upper floors; that "No Trespassing" signs were displayed near the building's entranceways and that the entrance doors generally were locked; and that defendant, in response to police inquiries, acknowledged that he did not live in the building, explaining that he intended to visit his aunt—though unable to provide her name or apartment number—and that he had an unnamed friend or friends in the building.

The primary defense asserted at trial, as defense counsel framed it in her opening statement, was whether defendant had "made a mistake by walking into the wrong building." In this connection, defendant testified that he had previously made arrangements to have dinner with his "very good friend," one Laurie Holder, in her apartment at 6:00 P.M. on the evening in question. The trial record shows, and it is undisputed, that Holder actually lives in a Taft Houses building known as 1694 Madison Avenue, located across the street from the building (65 East 112th Street) in which defendant was arrested. Despite admittedly having visited the Holder residence on no fewer than 10 to 15 prior occasions and being "completely familiar" with the surrounding area, defendant maintained that he mistakenly entered the wrong building, gaining access "as another tenant or guest was exiting." Defendant came to realize his mistake when, after taking the elevator to the 18th floor and walking down the staircase to the 14th floor,[1] he could not find Holder's apartment. Defendant testified as follows as to what occurred next: "I figured I was in the wrong building so I had started to exit the building by the stairs because to wait . . . the elevator just takes [too] long. So I was going to take the stairs down and while I was taking the stairs I . . . got out on the 11th floor so I could make the phone call [to explain his tardy arrival to Holder] because I didn't really think that the stairs would be safe to go all the way downstairs and also I had to make the phone call anyway." The police approached defendant in the 11th floor hallway before he could call Holder and, in response to their questioning about his presence in the building, defendant told the officers that he was visiting a "close friend," that his "aunt lives in the building," and that he "had a place to be," but "had the floor wrong." Asked on direct examination to "clarify" the nature of his relationship with Holder, defendant stated that, while there is no "blood relation" between them, Holder is the mother of a close female friend of his and that he generally calls Holder "mom," because she is older than he is and "that is how [Holder's] daughter introduced her to [him]." As to why he referred to Holder as his "aunt" in response to police questioning, defendant testified that he used that term so as to convey to the officers that "it was more than . . . a buddy of mine or a pal that I was visiting. It was somebody older who was very close to me." Defendant acknowledged on cross-examination that this occasion marked the "only time" he ever referred to Holder as his aunt. Defendant also testified that, immediately prior to his arrest, he "humbly" asked the police "for some courtesy because [he] was on probation."

---

1. Defendant's testimony on this point diverged from that of the arresting police officer, who stated that defendant, after being sighted in the lobby, was next seen on the 11th floor hallway and then, about eight minutes later, on the 18th floor hallway.

Called as a defense witness, Holder offered testimony tending to essentially confirm defendant's account of the timing and purpose of the (allegedly) planned apartment visit and the nature of her relationship with defendant. As to the latter point, Holder appeared to waffle, initially characterizing their relationship as merely "pretty close," but ultimately describing defendant as the "son [she] never had," a "son", it bears mention, whose precise age or birth date Holder could not identify. Further, Holder conceded that, despite defendant's failure to appear at the appointed hour, she did not call his cell phone at any point that evening to find out if he was all right, and only came to know of defendant's arrest some time after 8:30 P.M. that night, when she (or, more precisely, her husband) received a call from an officer at the police precinct.

The arresting police officer, in testimony elicited on rebuttal, denied defendant ever indicated he was lost.

. . . When the evidence is viewed in the light most favorable to the prosecution and given the benefit of every favorable inference, it clearly sufficed to establish beyond a reasonable doubt that the dwelling premises was "fenced or otherwise enclosed in a manner designed to exclude intruders" (Penal Law §140.10[a]) and that defendant knowingly entered or remained unlawfully there (see Matter of Lonique M., 93 A.D.3d 203, 939 N.Y.S.2d 341 [2012]; see also People v. Williams, 16 A.D.3d 151, 790 N.Y.S.2d 458 [2005] [probable cause for criminal trespass arrest found where defendant claimed to be visiting his cousin in a Housing Authority building, but was unable to provide an apartment number and falsely identified a woman in the lobby as his cousin]). The credited police testimony detailing defendant's suspicious behavior in the hallways of the public housing building, his ready admission that he did not live in the building and his inability to identify the name(s) or apartment number(s) of the person(s) he purportedly was attempting to visit, was sufficient to establish, at least circumstantially, that he entered or remained unlawfully in the building without the requisite license or privilege (see Penal Law §140.00[5]). I find unavailing defendant's apparent argument that the trial court, in determining whether the prosecution met its burden to establish guilt beyond a reasonable doubt, could not properly rely on defendant's on-the-scene statements. Having, by his own account, affirmatively explained his presence in the building in response to police questioning, and indeed having relied on that explanation as the centerpiece of his defense at trial, defendant may not now be heard to argue that the trial court was precluded from drawing any inferences adverse to him from that evidence on the theory that it was not his obligation, in the first instance, to explain his presence.

Nor, respectfully, can I join the majority's conclusion that defendant's conviction was against the weight of the evidence. In conducting an independent review of the weight of the evidence, a reviewing court must assess in a neutral light "all the credible evidence" (People v. Bleakley, 69 N.Y.2d 490,

495, 508 N.E.2d 672 [1987]), including evidence presented by the defense, to ascertain whether such evidence was accorded the proper weight by the factfinder, here the trial court. Under a weight-of-evidence analysis, the court "does not take the place of the [factfinder] in passing on questions of the reliability of witnesses and the credibility of testimony" (People v. Griffin, 63 A.D.3d 635, 638, 882 N.Y.S.2d 406 [2009]), and instead must give "[g]reat deference . . . to the factfinder's opportunity to view the witnesses, hear the testimony and observe demeanor" (see People v. Mateo, 2 N.Y.3d 383, 410, 811 N.E.2d 1053 [2004], quoting People v. Bleakley, 69 N.Y.2d at 495]).

Upon reviewing the record here, I am satisfied that defendant's conviction comported with the weight of the credible evidence. To be sure, a person who "honestly believes that he is licensed or privileged to enter[ ] is not guilty of any degree of criminal trespass" (People v. Basch, 36 N.Y.2d 154, 159, 325 N.E.2d 156 [1975]). The central question put before the trial judge, then, was whether defendant, assuming he was invited to visit Holder's apartment, "honestly believe[d]" he had lawfully entered the building housing that apartment pursuant to Holder's consent. Resolution of that issue required the trial judge to make a credibility call, pure and simple. The court, in the end, rejected—justifiably, in my view—defendant's explanation as to how it came about that, despite his avowed familiarity with the Taft Houses and their environs, he managed to get lost in the hallways and stairwells on the upper floors of the "wrong" Taft Houses building. The trial court's decision to reject defendant's trial testimony was well within its province as factfinder, particularly considering the various unanswered questions raised by the defense accounts, including why defendant (mis)identified Holder as his "aunt" to police; why, in initially attempting to exit the building, he initially chose to eschew the elevator in favor of descending at least 14 flights of stairs when he was already late for a dinner engagement; why he ultimately paused in his descent on the 11th floor hallway; and why Holder, if she in fact invited defendant to eat dinner at her apartment, made no effort whatsoever to call her supposed surrogate son to determine his whereabouts and safety.

Because it does not "appear[ ] that the trier of fact has failed to give the evidence the weight it should be accorded" (People v. Bleakley, 69 N.Y.2d at 495), and given the lack of merit to defendant's challenge to the facial sufficiency of the information, I respectfully dissent and vote to affirm the judgment of conviction.

Notes and Questions

1. What exactly is going on here? Why do you think the defendant became the subject of police scrutiny and, eventually, arrest and criminal prosecution?

As a general matter, criminal trespass is a crime that is almost never prosecuted. Except, that is, when it is used as a proxy crime for something else: suspected drug dealing or drug possession, suspected membership in a criminal street gang, or other kinds of suspected behaviors that are seen as violating various social norms. Is this an appropriate use of the criminal law? Might your answer to that question depend, at least in part, on whether you are more or less likely to be suspected by the police of such violations?

2. Criminal trespass, in short, often functions in practice very much like the crimes of vagrancy and loitering—providing the police with great discretion to act preemptively in situations where they might suspect, but perhaps cannot prove, more serious criminal conduct. We have already seen that the U.S. Supreme Court has expressed serious concerns about the constitutionality of vagrancy and loitering. See, e.g., the discussions of *Papachristou*, at page 41, and of *Morales*, at page 49. How does criminal trespass resemble those other traditional "public order" crimes? How is it different? Should those differences matter?

The usual constitutional problem with vagrancy and loitering statutes is vagueness. Do you find the New York criminal trespass statute vague? Or is the real problem that the statute too easily could be applied to conduct that—while relatively clearly defined—should not be criminalized? That problem is usually described as "overbreadth," to distinguish it from the lack of fair notice that usually characterizes "vagueness."

Or maybe the real problem is that the statute's overbreadth gives too much discretion to the police (and prosecutor) to decide whom to treat as a criminal. Is that concern adequately addressed by the fact that the New York criminal trespass statute requires defendants to be proven to have acted "knowingly"?

3. In New York City, the police have long run a program known as "Operation Clean Halls" (now called "Trespass Affidavit Program," or TAP). The program is designed to fight crime and bring law and order to public housing projects and other large apartment buildings in various parts of the city, especially those located in high-crime areas. The program includes, among other police tactics, "vertical patrols" (i.e., floor-by-floor sweeps, of the kind that occurred in the *Luke* case) and aggressive police use of "stop-and-frisk" authority pursuant to Terry v. Ohio, 392 U.S. 1 (1968) (i.e., stopping, questioning, and patting down for weapons anyone "reasonably believed" by the police to be suspicious).

In March 2012, the N.Y Civil Liberties Union, the Bronx Defenders, LatinoJustice PRLDEF, and civil rights attorney Chris Fabricant filed a federal civil-rights lawsuit against the City of New York on behalf of residents of buildings enrolled in the "Trespass Affidavit Program" (the plaintiffs alleged there were almost 4,000 such buildings in Manhattan alone, although the lawsuit was focused instead on the Bronx, where in some neighborhoods virtually every apartment building was on the list), and individuals who allegedly were unlawfully stopped and arrested on criminal trespassing charges through the program. The lawsuit claimed, inter alia, that discretionary police enforcement of New York's criminal trespass laws violated the Fourth Amendment and Equal Protection Clause of the U.S. Constitution, along with provisions of the N.Y. Constitution, the federal Fair Housing Act, and New York common law. According to the NYCLU's website: "Many tenants who live in Clean Halls buildings are restricted in their ability to maintain familial ties and friendships due to the use of aggressive police tactics in their homes. The program is part of a citywide practice of suspicionless police stops and arrests that primarily impact communities of color." See http://www.nyclu.org/case/ligon-v-city-of-new-york-challenging-nypds-aggressive-patrolling-of-private-apartment-building.

The case, Ligon v. City of New York (S.D.N.Y., 12 Civ. 2274 (S.A.S.)), was litigated in tandem with another lawsuit, Floyd v. City of New York (S.D.N.Y., 08 Civ. 1034 (S.A.S.)), challenging directly the discretionary use of "stop-and-frisk" authority by New York City police officers. In January 2013, U.S. District Judge Shira Scheindlin issued a preliminary injunction in favor of the *Ligon* plaintiffs, based on finding police violations of their Fourth Amendment rights. On August 12, 2013, Judge Scheindlin handed down two decisions: one ruling on the merits in favor of the plaintiffs in *Floyd*, and the other ordering the City of New York to implement a variety of corrective remedies to stop the abuses of rights alleged in both *Floyd* and *Ligon*. The remedies included appointment of an independent monitor and extensive revamping of the city's training program for police officers. The city appealed both decisions. On October 31, 2013, the U.S. Court of Appeals for the Second Circuit issued a stay of the remedial decision, and remanded the case to the District Court with instructions to replace Judge Scheindlin on the grounds that her comments about the case, both in and outside of court, gave rise to an "appearance" of partiality.

Meanwhile, the wheel of politics turned. On November 5, 2013, the city elected a new mayor: Bill de Blasio, the Democratic candidate and former New York City Public Advocate. Fewer than three weeks later, the Second Circuit ordered all pending motions in the two cases temporarily held in abeyance. On January 30, 2014, Mayor de Blasio announced that the city would drop its appeal of Judge Scheindlin's decisions, and asked for a full remand to the District Court so that the city could reach and implement an agreement with the plaintiffs to make the reforms contemplated in Judge Scheindlin's remedial decision. According to the city's website:

CITY TO FULLY EMBRACE STOP-AND-FRISK REFORM, PLEDGES RESPECT FOR EVERY NEW YORKER'S CONSTITUTIONAL RIGHTS

[T]he mayor pledged to reunite police with communities across the city and to respect the constitutional rights of every New Yorker.

"This is a defining moment in our history. It's a defining moment for millions of our families, especially those with young men of color. And it will lay the foundation for not only keeping us the safest big city in America, but making us safer still. This will be one city, where everyone's rights are respected, and where police and community stand together to confront violence," said Mayor Bill de Blasio.

"We will not break the law to enforce the law. That's my solemn promise to every New Yorker, regardless of where they were born, where they live, or what they look like. Those values aren't at odds with keeping New Yorkers safe — they are essential to long-term public safety. We are committed to fulfilling our obligations under this agreement as we protect and serve this great city," said Police Commissioner Bill Bratton.

Under the agreement with plaintiffs announced today, a court-appointed monitor will serve for three years, overseeing the NYPD's reform of its stop-and-frisk policy. The monitor is empowered to report to federal court on the city's progress meeting its obligation to abide by the United States Constitution. The city will also take part in a joint process with community stakeholders to ensure people affected by stop-and-frisk play an active role in shaping reform.

See http://www1.nyc.gov/office-of-the-mayor/news/726-14/mayor-de-blasio-agreement-landmark-stop-and-frisk-case#/0.

4. In *Luke*, the defendant was convicted under Penal Law §140.10[a], which covers real property "fenced or otherwise enclosed in a manner designed to exclude intruders." Other sections of the same law apply "where the building is used as a public housing project" and the defendant acts "in violation of conspicuously posted rules or regulations governing entry and use thereof" (Penal Law §140.10[e]) and "where a building is used as a public housing project in violation of a personally communicated request to leave the premises from a housing police officer or other person in charge thereof" (Penal Law §140.10[f]). Why do you think those other sections, which seem more directly applicable to Taft Houses, weren't used here?

5. Another crime that is rarely prosecuted, but can be useful as a proxy crime, is vandalism. Tennessee's vandalism statute is typical:

> Vandalism. (a) Any person who knowingly causes damage to or the destruction of any real or personal property of another or of the state, the United States, any country, city, or town knowing that the person does not have the owner's effective consent is guilty of an offense under this section.
>
> (b) For purposes of this section:
>
> (1) "Damage" includes, but is not limited to:
>
> (A) Destroying, polluting or contaminating property; or
>
> (B) Tampering with property and causing pecuniary loss or substantial inconvenience to the owner or a third person; and
>
> (2) "Polluting" is the contamination by manmade or man-induced alteration of the chemical, physical, biological or radiological

integrity of the atmosphere, water, or soil to the material injury of the right of another . . . .

Tenn. Code Ann. §39-14-408. Under the above definition, the Tennessee Court of Criminal Appeals affirmed the vandalism conviction of a defendant who was arrested and then, in an apparent act of defiance, urinated in the back seat of the police car: "By doing this, the appellant *damaged* the patrol car by contaminating it. Further, by his conduct he *tampered* with the patrol car in a manner that caused substantial inconvenience to the person who had to clean up the mess that he made." State v. McAnally, 209 S.W.3d 639 (2006). The court also upheld the defendant's sentence of 60 days in jail and almost one year of probation.

Many vandalism cases are brought against suspected or wannabe street gang members—often believed to have committed much more serious crimes, including murder, assault, robbery, and drug dealing—who deface private or public property in order to define the gang's territory, or "turf." Does the definition of vandalism adequately capture what is really wrong with "gang graffiti"? Does the punishment for vandalism fit *that* kind of crime? Once again, as in the case of criminal trespass, should we be concerned about the pretextual use of a relatively low-level crime like vandalism to address a much more serious kind of crime problem?

6. Another situation that can give rise to a vandalism prosecution is a domestic dispute. In People v. Kahanic, 196 Cal. App. 3d 461, 241 Cal. Rptr. 722 (1987), a wife who was in the process of divorcing her husband (but was not yet legally divorced) drove her Corvette to a residence where her husband was seeing another woman. She proceeded to throw a beer bottle through the back window of her husband's Mercedes. She was convicted of misdemeanor vandalism, and argued on appeal that her conviction should be reversed because—California being a so-called community property state in which all marital property is considered co-owned by both spouses—she couldn't legally vandalize her own property.

The California Court of Appeals disagreed:

We are well aware that conduct of this kind may be better resolved in family law courts than by criminal prosecution. Nevertheless we conclude the community property status of the Mercedes automobile did not preclude the application of criminal law which refers to personal property "not his own," as the property damaged by the criminal act. . . .

Section 594, subdivision (a), provides: "(a) Every person who maliciously (1) defaces with paint or any other liquid, (2) damages or (3) destroys any real or personal property *not his own*, in cases otherwise than those specified by state law, is guilty of vandalism." (Italics added.) . . .

By way of analogy, the Attorney General directs us to People v. Sobiek, 30 Cal. App. 3d 458, 106 Cal. Rptr. 519 (1973). In *Sobiek*, the court held a partner could be guilty of embezzling or stealing partnership property. The court reasoned: "It is both illogical and unreasonable to hold that a partner cannot steal from his partners merely because he has an undivided interest in the partnership property. Fundamentally, stealing that portion of the partners' shares which does not belong to the thief is no different from stealing the property of any other person." *Id.* at 468. . . .

It is true *Sobiek* was concerned only with partnership interests which, though similar in some respects, are not identical to community property ownership. . . . The court noted . . . that the effort of the criminal law is "to deter deprivations of other people's economic interests." *Id.* at 466. We agree. Whether the statute refers to property "not his own," or "property of another," the sense of the descriptive words excludes criminality only when the actor-defendant is involved with property wholly his or her own.

It is of no consequence defendant wife may have had a community property right to share possession of the Mercedes. We do not determine this issue based on the husband's possession of the car at the particular time. The criminal wrong may occur irrespective of who physically "possessed" the Mercedes when the act occurred. The essence of the crime is in the physical acts against the ownership interest of another, even though that ownership is less than exclusive. . . . Each community property owner has an equal ownership interest and, although undivided, one which the criminal law protects from unilateral nonconsensual damage or destruction by the other marital partner.

Id. at 463-66.

B. THEFT

Theft takes a host of different forms. The criminal law of theft has traditionally focused on three main ones: robbery, burglary, and larceny or embezzlement. Robbery is theft by direct, person-to-person force. As defined at common law, burglary is a form of trespass rather than theft, though it is chiefly used in theft cases; like robbery, burglary traditionally required proof of force—but the force is directed against a home or an apartment, not against a person. Larceny and embezzlement are instances of (usually) nonviolent theft: Stealth rather than threatened violence is the means by which property is taken. Over the course of the past two generations, lawmakers have blurred these categories, to the point where the distinctions among them seen less than clear. Consider, when reading the cases that follow, whether these redefined crimes improve on their more distinctly defined predecessors.

1. Robbery

At common law, robbery was defined as the taking and carrying away of property, with the intent permanently to deprive its owner thereof, by force or threat of force. In other words, robbery was defined as theft by force. The next case addresses the meaning of "by force."

State v. Keeton

Supreme Court of Iowa
710 N.W.2d 531 (2006)

Opinion of CADY, J.

In this appeal, the defendant claims there was insufficient evidence to support the assault element of his conviction for second-degree robbery of a convenience store, during which the store clerk confronted him at the door of the store as he was attempting to exit following a theft. In resolving the issue, the State asks that we declare the crime of assault to be a general-intent offense and submits a well-researched and thorough brief to support its position. We conclude substantial evidence supports the conviction and decline to consider the additional question raised by the State. We affirm the judgment and sentence of the district court.

On March 28, 2004, Larry Keeton entered a convenience store in Marshalltown and purchased a pack of cigarettes. When the store clerk opened the cash register drawer to make change, Keeton reached over the counter and grabbed the twenty-dollar bills from the register. He stated: "I'll take that." Keeton then attempted to exit the store, but the clerk rushed to the door and blocked his path by standing in front of the double doors. She also tried to grab the cash from Keeton's hand as he approached, but he would not release the money from his hand. Their hands touched when she attempted to retrieve the money. Keeton then briefly backed away from the door and extended his arm. The clerk realized she could not keep him in the store until police arrived, and stepped aside to allow Keeton to leave the store. As he exited through the door, she snatched the hat from his head in anger. The incident was recorded by surveillance video.

Keeton was arrested and charged with robbery in the second degree in violation of Iowa Code section 711.1(1) (2003). He waived his right to a jury trial, and the case proceeded to a bench trial. The district court found Keeton guilty of second-degree robbery and sentenced him to a term of imprisonment not to exceed ten years.

Keeton appeals. He claims there was insufficient evidence presented at trial to support the assault element of robbery. . . .

Section 711.1 defines robbery as follows:

"A person commits a robbery when, having the intent to commit a theft, the person does any of the following acts to assist or further the commission of the intended theft or the person's escape from the scene thereof with or without the stolen property: 1. Commits an assault upon another. . . ."

The State . . . claimed at trial that Keeton committed an assault on the store clerk in furtherance of his escape from the convenience store.

We look to the definition of assault in section 708.1 to consider whether a robbery occurred under section 711.1(1). See State v. Spears, 312 N.W.2d 79, 80 (Iowa 1981). Section 708.1 provides, in relevant part:

> An assault as defined in this section is a general intent crime. A person commits an assault when, without justification, the person does any of the following:
>
> 1. Any act which is intended to cause pain or injury to, or which is intended to result in physical contact which will be insulting or offensive to another, coupled with the apparent ability to execute the act.
> 2. Any act which is intended to place another in fear of immediate physical contact which will be painful, injurious, insulting, or offensive, coupled with the apparent ability to execute the act.
> 3. Intentionally points any firearm toward another, or displays in a threatening manner any dangerous weapon toward another.

Iowa Code §708.1. In this case, the State relied upon the first two alternatives of assault, and the district court found Keeton committed assault under both alternatives.

Although the State asks us to resolve the sufficiency-of-evidence claim by considering section 708.1(1)-(2) to only require a general intent element, the specific issue on appeal in this case only requires us to decide if the evidence in the case satisfies the statutory elements of the crime of assault. This question can be decided without considering whether the statutory language used to define the crime of assault requires a specific or general intent. See Scott A. Anderegg, Note, The Voluntary Intoxication Defense in Iowa, 73 Iowa L. Rev. 935, 935 (1988) (noting confusion regarding concepts of specific and general intent); see also Model Penal Code §2.02, at 230 & n.3 (1985) (stating the Model Penal Code employed four culpability distinctions in lieu of the specific-intent/general-intent dichotomy, "which has been such an abiding source of confusion and ambiguity in the penal law"). . . .

Accordingly, we decline to revisit the issue whether assault is a general- or specific-intent crime in this case. Regardless of which label is attached to the offense, the State was still required to prove Keeton possessed the *mens rea* required by the statute, and we turn to decide if it did so. State v. Taylor, 689 N.W.2d 116, 132 (Iowa 2004) ("Regardless of whether assault is a specific intent or general intent crime, the State must prove by evidence beyond a reasonable doubt that the defendant intended his act to cause pain or injury to the victim or to result in physical contact that would be insulting or offensive to the victim."). The State had to prove that Keeton . . . intended either: (1) to cause the clerk pain or injury, (2) to make insulting or offensive physical contact with the clerk, or (3) to make the clerk fear immediate painful, injurious, insulting, or offensive physical contact. Iowa

Code §708.1(1)-(2). We turn to the evidence in the record that bears upon this intent element.

Keeton testified that he did not intend to touch, hurt, insult, or offend the clerk. However, intent required by the statute "may be inferred from the circumstances of the transaction and the actions of the defendant." 21 Am. Jur. 2d Criminal Law §128, at 214-15 (1998); see also *Taylor*, 689 N.W.2d at 132 ("An actor will ordinarily be viewed as intending the natural and probable consequences that usually follow from his or her voluntary act.").

We begin by considering the actions of the parties to the incident. The surveillance video of the incident offered into evidence at trial showed that the clerk blocked one of the double doors as Keeton tried to exit by standing in front of the door. After the clerk attempted to retrieve the money, Keeton moved in the direction of the other door to exit, and the clerk lunged in front of that door to block Keeton from leaving. Keeton then backed up and began to walk toward the clerk with his hand extended, holding the money. He then pulled his hand to his chest at the same time as the clerk moved off to the side of the doors to permit Keeton to exit.

This evidence could support an inference of intent to place the clerk in fear of immediate physical contact that would be painful, injurious, insulting, or offensive. Similarly, the evidence could support an inference that the actions of Keeton were intended to result in physical contact which would be insulting or offensive to the clerk. Keeton wanted to leave the store, and his outstretched hand could evidence his intent to push the clerk out of his path.

Furthermore, the testimony of Keeton and the testimony of the clerk at trial provided further evidence of the intent to support the conviction under the statute. The clerk testified she felt Keeton was "bound and determined to keep the money," and she realized there was "no way" she could keep him from leaving. While this testimony is not dispositive, these perceptions are properly considered in determining intent. Moreover, Keeton acknowledged on cross-examination that he "would have pushed past [the clerk] and went out the door" if the clerk failed to move from the exit. Although Keeton tried to retract this testimony on redirect examination, it was nevertheless evidence of intent.

We conclude that the record, viewed in the light most favorable to the State, reveals substantial evidence to satisfy the intent element of the crime of assault under section 708.1(1) and (2). . . . We understand Keeton's argument that he was only attempting to leave the store to complete his theft, not to commit an assault. Yet, this is not a case where proof of intent depends upon a single piece of evidence from which two reasonable inferences could be drawn. See State v. Truesdell, 679 N.W.2d 611, 618-19 (Iowa 2004) ("When two reasonable inferences can be drawn from *a piece* of evidence, we believe such evidence only gives rise to a suspicion, and, without additional evidence, is insufficient to support guilt.") (emphasis added). The multiple actions of the participants in this case and the inferences derived from those actions, as well as their testimony, are together sufficient to support a finding of the intent element of an assault under our statutory definition. . . .

We conclude there was substantial evidence presented at trial that Keeton committed an assault on the clerk. We affirm his conviction for robbery in the second degree.

Notes and Questions

1. It seems clearer that the store clerk assaulted Keeton than that Keeton assaulted the store clerk, does it not? When Keeton extended his hand—with the stolen money in it—then pulled it back to his chest, did that constitute a threat? Or did it instead amount to a statement that Keeton intended to keep the money? (No surprise there: Few thieves take money only to return it when asked.) If the latter is the more natural interpretation, why did the court find that Keeton meant to assault the store clerk by that strange hand motion? To put the point another way: Assaults prompt fear in their victims. Did the store clerk seem afraid?

2. Robbery means theft plus assault. There was no doubt that Keeton was guilty of some form of theft; the only question was whether Keeton's conduct and intent were sufficiently violent to satisfy the assault element of the crime. Was it? Keeton might plausibly argue that he took care *not* to harm or threaten anyone: If this is a robbery, then Keeton could not possibly steal money from the cash register *without* committing robbery. Is that conclusion correct?

3. The prosecution might respond as follows: Keeton took the money knowing that there were other people in the store. If he planned on simply giving himself up to anyone who blocked the door, it made no sense to take the money in the first place. Unless he is crazy, Keeton's act of theft logically implied a threat to do whatever was necessary to escape with the cash in hand—including assaulting and, if need be, injuring anyone who got in his way. If that implied threat suffices to show robbery, public theft is *always* robbery. Should it be?

4. The *Keeton* court explicitly declined to decide whether assault is a general intent offense—but quoted the relevant statute, which plainly says that assault *is* a general intent offense. What gives? The explanation lies in the odd language of this particular statute. On the one hand, the statute does say that assault is a general intent crime; on the other hand, the statute also says that the state may prove the requisite intent by proving (among other alternatives) that the defendant intended to injure or frighten the victim—which sounds like specific intent. The governing law in Iowa assault cases is a strange mix of general and specific intent: The government may prove either that the defendant intended to behave in a particular manner, or that he intended to cause particular results. Perhaps the *Keeton* court decided that the labels attached to these different categories of intent are not important; the question is whether the government sufficiently proved at least one of them.

Notes on the Federal Law of Robbery

1. As explained in Chapter 4, the federal government's authority to engage in any act or regulation is limited by the powers enumerated in the Constitution. The Constitution contains no general authorization for the enactment and enforcement of federal criminal law. Nevertheless, there is a relatively well-developed federal criminal law of robbery.

For one thing, the federal government may (and does) punish robberies that are proven to affect "interstate commerce." The relevant federal statute is the Hobbs Act, which applies to "whoever in any way or degree obstructs, delays or affects commerce or the movement of any article or commodity in commerce, by robbery, or extortion, or attempts or conspires to do so, or commits or threatens physical violence to any person or property in further-ance of a plan or purpose to do anything in violation of this section." See 18 U.S.C. §1951(a). The *Taylor* case, in Chapter 4, supra at page 237, was an example of a Hobbs Act prosecution.

Another source of authority for federal robbery law is the fact that the federal government, through the Federal Deposit Insurance Corporation (FDIC) (an independent federal agency created in 1933), insures all bank deposits under $250,000 in the United States. Based on this special federal role within the U.S. banking system—a role that is itself authorized by the Commerce Clause—the federal government may (and does) punish bank robberies. The relevant federal statute is 18 U.S.C. §2113(a), which applies to "[w]hoever, by force and violence, or by intimidation, takes, or attempts to take, from the person or presence of another, or obtains or attempts to obtain by extortion any property or money or any other thing of value belonging to, or in the care, custody, control, management, or possession of, any bank, credit union, or any savings and loan association. . . ."

Note that whenever a particular robbery falls within the scope of the Hobbs Act, or the federal bank robbery statute, that robbery will also be a violation of state robbery law. This means that the robbery may be investigated by either federal police (i.e., the FBI) or state and local police, and may be charged by either federal or state prosecutors in either federal or state court, respectively.

2. The federal bank robbery statute (18 U.S.C. §2113(a)) is part of a larger federal law about bank crimes that also defines several related crimes, including federal bank larceny (18 U.S.C. §2113(b)), which applies to "[w]hoever takes and carries away, with intent to steal or purloin, any property or money or any other thing of value exceeding $1,000 belonging to, or in the care, custody, control, management, or possession of any bank, credit union, or any savings and loan association . . . ", as well as the federal crime of receiving stolen bank property (18 U.S.C. §2113(c)). The next case explores the relationship between federal bank robbery, under §2113(a), and federal bank larceny, under §2113(b).

Carter v. United States

Supreme Court of the United States
530 U.S. 255 (2000)

Justice THOMAS delivered the opinion of the Court.

. . . On September 9, 1997, petitioner Floyd J. Carter donned a ski mask and entered the Collective Federal Savings Bank in Hamilton Township, New Jersey. Carter confronted a customer who was exiting the bank and pushed her back inside. She screamed, startling others in the bank. Undeterred, Carter ran into the bank and leaped over the customer service counter and through one of the teller windows. One of the tellers rushed into the manager's office. Meanwhile, Carter opened several teller drawers and emptied the money into a bag. After having removed almost $16,000 in currency, Carter jumped back over the counter and fled from the scene. Later that day, the police apprehended him. [Carter was charged with, and convicted of, federal bank robbery under 18 U.S.C. §2113(a). On appeal, he claimed that he should have been entitled to a jury instruction on the crime of federal bank larceny under 18 U.S.C. §2113(b) as well, because it is a "lesser included offense" of §2113(a).* The Third Circuit affirmed Carter's conviction.]

. . . A textual comparison of the elements of these offenses suggests that the Government is correct [that federal bank larceny is not a "lesser included offense" of federal bank robbery]. First, whereas subsection (b) requires that the defendant act "with intent to steal or purloin," subsection (a) contains no similar requirement. Second, whereas subsection (b) requires that the defendant "take and carry away" the property, subsection (a) only requires that the defendant "take" the property. Third, whereas the first paragraph of subsection (b) requires that the property have a "value exceeding $1,000," subsection (a) contains no valuation requirement. . . .

---

* [At common law, Carter's claim likely would have succeeded; the common law crime of robbery includes everything necessary to be guilty of common law larceny, except for the additional element that the "taking" of property must be accomplished by force, violence, or a threat of the same that places the victim in fear. And as a matter of due process, defendants are legally entitled to a jury instruction on any lesser included offense that is plausibly applicable, given the evidence and the facts of the case. — EDS.]

[Carter] submits that, insofar as subsections (a) and (b) are *similar* to the common-law crimes of robbery and larceny, we must assume that subsections (a) and (b) require the *same* elements as their common-law predecessors, at least absent Congress' affirmative indication (whether in text or legislative history) of an intent to displace the common-law scheme. While we (and the Government) agree that the statutory crimes at issue here bear a close resemblance to the common-law crimes of robbery and larceny, see Brief for United States 29 (citing 4 W. Blackstone, Commentaries *229, *232), that observation is beside the point. The canon on imputing common-law meaning applies only when Congress makes use of a statutory *term* with established meaning at common law, and Carter does not point to any such term in the text of the statute.

Here, it is undisputed that "robbery" and "larceny" are terms with established meanings at common law. But neither term appears in the text of §2113(a) or §2113(b). . . . Accordingly, the canon on imputing common-law meaning has no bearing on this case.

We turn now to Carter's more specific arguments concerning the "extra" elements of §2113(b). While conceding the absence of three of §2113(b)'s requirements from the text of §2113(a) — (1) "intent to steal or purloin"; (2) "takes *and carries away*," i.e., asportation; and (3) "value exceeding $1,000" (first paragraph) — Carter claims that the first two should be deemed implicit in §2113(a), and that the third is not an element at all.

As to "intent to steal or purloin," it will be recalled that the text of subsection (b) requires a specific "intent to steal or purloin," whereas subsection (a) contains no explicit *mens rea* requirement of any kind. Carter nevertheless argues that such a *specific intent* requirement must be deemed implicitly present in §2113(a) by virtue of "our cases interpreting criminal statutes to include broadly applicable scienter requirements, even where the statute by its terms does not contain them." United States v. X-Citement Video, Inc., 513 U.S. 64, 70 (1994). Properly applied to §2113, however, the presumption in favor of scienter demands only that we read subsection (a) as requiring proof of *general intent* — that is, that the defendant possessed knowledge with respect to the *actus reus* of the crime (here, the taking of property of another by force and violence or intimidation).

Before explaining why this is so under our cases, an example, United States v. Lewis, 628 F.2d 1276, 1279 (CA10 1980), will help to make the distinction between "general" and "specific" intent less esoteric. In *Lewis,* a person entered a bank and took money from a teller at gunpoint, but deliberately failed to make a quick getaway from the bank in the hope of being arrested so that he would be returned to prison and treated for alcoholism. Though this defendant knowingly engaged in the acts of using force and taking money (satisfying "general intent"), he did not intend permanently to deprive the bank of its possession of the money (failing to satisfy "specific intent").

The presumption in favor of scienter requires a court to read into a statute only that *mens rea* which is necessary to separate wrongful conduct from "otherwise innocent conduct." *X-Citement Video*, supra, at 72. In Staples v. United States, 511 U.S. 600 (1994), for example, to avoid criminalizing the innocent activity of gun ownership, we interpreted a federal firearms statute to require proof that the defendant knew that the weapon he possessed had the characteristics bringing it within the scope of the statute. Id. at 611-12. . . .

In this case, as in *Staples*, a general intent requirement suffices to separate wrongful from "otherwise innocent" conduct. Section 2113(a) certainly should not be interpreted to apply to the hypothetical person who engages in forceful taking of money while sleepwalking (innocent, if aberrant activity), but this result is accomplished simply by requiring, as *Staples* did, general intent—*i.e.*, proof of knowledge with respect to the *actus reus* of the crime. And once this mental state and *actus reus* are shown, the concerns underlying the presumption in favor of scienter are fully satisfied, for a forceful taking—even by a defendant who takes under a good-faith claim of right—falls outside the realm of the "otherwise innocent." Thus, the presumption in favor of scienter does not justify reading a specific intent requirement—"intent to steal or purloin"—into §2113(a). . . .

Turning to the second element in dispute, it will be recalled that, whereas subsection (b) requires that the defendant "take and carry away the property," subsection (a) requires only that the defendant "take" the property. Carter contends that the "takes" in subsection (a) is equivalent to "takes and carries away" in subsection (b). While Carter seems to acknowledge that the argument is at war with the text of the statute, he urges that text should not be dispositive here because nothing in the evolution of §2113(a) suggests that Congress sought to discard the asportation requirement from that subsection.

But, again, our inquiry focuses on an analysis of the textual product of Congress' efforts, not on speculation as to the internal thought processes of its Members. Congress is certainly free to outlaw bank theft that does not involve asportation, and it hardly would have been absurd for Congress to do so, since the taking-without-asportation scenario is no imagined hypothetical. See, e.g., State v. Boyle, 970 S.W.2d 835, 836, 838-839 (Mo. Ct. App. 1998) (construing state statutory codification of common-law robbery to apply to defendant who, after taking money by threat of force, dropped the money on the spot). . . . No doubt the common law's decision to require asportation . . . has its virtues. But Congress adopted a different view in §2113(a), and it is not for us to question that choice.

There remains the requirement in §2113(b)'s first paragraph that the property taken have a "value exceeding $1,000"—a requirement notably absent from §2113(a). . . . The structure of subsection (b) strongly suggests that its two paragraphs—the first of which requires that the property taken have "value exceeding $1,000," the second of which refers to property of "value not exceeding $1,000" — describe distinct offenses [rather than a single offense containing two sentencing factors]. . . .

We hold that §2113(b) is not a lesser included offense of §2113(a), and therefore that petitioner is not entitled to a jury instruction on §2113(b). The judgment of the Third Circuit is affirmed.

Justice GINSBURG, with whom Justice STEVENS, Justice SOUTER, and Justice BREYER join, dissenting.

. . . At common law, as the Government concedes, robbery was an aggravated form of larceny. Specifically, the common law defined larceny as "the felonious taking, and carrying away, of the personal goods of another." 4 W. Blackstone, Commentaries *230 (Blackstone) (internal quotation marks omitted). Robbery, in turn, was larceny effected by taking property from the person or presence of another by means of force or putting in fear. Brief for United States 29-30 (citing 2 W. LaFave & A. Scott, Substantive Criminal Law §8.11, at 437-38 (1986)). Larceny was therefore a lesser included offense of robbery at common law. See 4 Blackstone *241 (robbery is "open and violent larciny from the person"); 2 E. East, Pleas of the Crown §124, at 707 (1803) (robbery is a species of "aggravated larceny").

Closer inspection of the common-law elements of both crimes confirms the relationship. The elements of common-law larceny were also elements of robbery. First and most essentially, robbery, like larceny, entailed an intentional taking. See 4 Blackstone *241 (robbery is "the felonious and forcible taking, from the person of another, of goods or money to any value, by putting him in fear"). Second, . . . the taking in a robbery had to be "felonious," a common-law term of art signifying an intent to steal. And third, again like larceny, robbery contained an asportation requirement. See 2 LaFave & Scott §8.11, at 439 ("Just as larceny requires that the thief both 'take' (secure dominion over) and 'carry away' (move slightly) the property in question, so too robbery under the traditional view requires both a taking and an asportation (in the sense of at least a slight movement) of the property." Unlike larceny, however, robbery included one further essential component: an element of force, violence, or intimidation. See 4 Blackstone *242.

Precedent thus instructs us to presume that Congress has adhered to the altogether clear common-law understanding that larceny is a lesser included offense of robbery, unless Congress has affirmatively indicated its design, in codifying the crimes of robbery and larceny, to displace their common-law meanings and relationship. . . .

Prior to 1934, federal law did not criminalize bank robbery or larceny; these crimes were punishable only under state law. Congress enacted the precursor to §2113(a) in response to an outbreak of bank robberies committed by John Dillinger and others who evaded capture by state authorities by moving from State to State. In bringing federal law into this area,

. . . Congress chose language that practically jumped out of Blackstone's Commentaries:

> "Whoever, by force and violence, or by putting in fear, feloniously takes, or feloniously attempts to take, from the person or presence of another any property or money or any other thing of value belonging to, or in the care, custody, control, management, or possession of, any bank shall be fined not more than $5,000 or imprisoned not more than twenty years, or both." Act of May 18, 1934, ch. 304, §2(a), 48 Stat. 783.

It soon became apparent, however, that this legislation left a gap: It did not reach the thief who intentionally, though not violently, stole money from a bank. Within a few years, federal law enforcers endeavored to close the gap. In a letter to the Speaker of the House, the Attorney General . . . cited the example of a thief apprehended after taking $11,000 from a bank while a teller was temporarily absent. Id. at 1-2. See H. R. Rep. No. 732, 75th Cong., 1st Sess., 1-2 (1937) (reprinting letter). He therefore asked Congress to amend the bank robbery statute . . . to add a larceny provision shorn of any force, violence, or fear requirement. Id. at 2. Congress responded by passing an Act "to amend the bank robbery statute to include burglary and larceny." Act of Aug. 24, 1937, ch. 747, 50 Stat. 749. The Act's new larceny provision . . . punished "whoever shall take and carry away, with intent to steal or purloin," property, money, or anything of value from a bank. Ibid. . . .

In its 1948 codification of federal crimes, Congress delineated the bank robbery and larceny provisions of §§2113(a) and 2113(b) and placed these provisions under the title "Bank robbery and incidental crimes." Act of June 25, 1948, §2113, 62 Stat. 796-97. In this codification, Congress deleted the word "feloniously" from the robbery provision, leaving the statute in substantially its present form. That 1948 deletion forms the basis of the Government's prime argument against characterizing §2113(b) as a lesser included offense of §2113(a), namely, that robbery unlike larceny no longer requires a specific intent to steal. The Government concedes that to gain a conviction for robbery at common law, the prosecutor had to prove the perpetrator's intent to steal. . . . But the Government contends that the 1948 removal of "feloniously" from §2113(a) showed Congress' purpose to dispense with any requirement of intent to steal.

. . . Guided by the historical understanding of the relationship between robbery and larceny both at common law and as brought into the federal criminal code, I conclude that the offense of bank robbery under §2113(a), like the offense of bank larceny under §2113(b), has always included and continues to include a requirement of intent to steal.

This traditional reading of the robbery statute makes common sense. The Government agrees that to be convicted of robbery, the defendant must resort to force and violence, or intimidation, to accomplish his purpose. But what purpose could this be other than to steal? The Government describes two scenarios in which, it maintains, a person could commit bank robbery while nonetheless lacking intent to steal. One scenario involves a terrorist who temporarily takes a bank's money or property aiming only to disrupt the bank's business; the other involves an ex-convict, unable to cope with life in a free society, who robs a bank because he wants to be apprehended and returned to prison. Brief for United States 22, n.13.

The Government does not point to any cases involving its terrorist scenario, and I know of none. To illustrate its ex-convict scenario, the Government cites United States v. Lewis, 628 F.2d 1276 (CA10 1980), which appears to be the only reported federal case presenting this staged situation. . . . I resist the notion—apparently embraced by the Court—that Congress' purpose in deleting the word "feloniously" from §2113(a) was to grant homesick ex-convicts like Lewis their wish to return to prison. Nor can I credit the suggestion that Congress' concern was to cover the Government's fictional terrorist, or the frustrated account holder who "withdraws" $100 by force or violence, believing the money to be rightfully his, or the thrill seeker who holds up a bank with the intent of driving around the block in a getaway car and then returning the loot, or any other defendant whose exploits are seldom encountered outside the pages of law school exams.

Indeed, there is no cause to suspect that the 1948 deletion of "feloniously" was intended to effect any substantive change at all. Nothing indicates that Congress removed that word in response to any assertion or perception of prosecutorial need. Nor is there any other reason to believe that it was Congress' design to alter the elements of the offense of robbery. . . .

Having accepted the Government's argument concerning intent to steal, the Court goes on to agree with the Government that robbery, unlike larceny, does not require that the defendant carry away the property. As with intent to steal, the historical linkage of the two crimes reveals the Court's error. It is true that §2113(b) includes the phrase "takes and carries away" while §2113(a) says only "takes." Both crimes, however, included an asportation requirement at common law. . . . I note, moreover, that the asportation requirement, both at common law and under §2113, is an extremely modest one: even a slight movement will do. See LaFave & Scott §8.11, at 439. . . . [N]othing in the evolution of the statute suggests that "Congress adopted a different view in §2113(a)," [as the Court states,] deliberately doing away with the minimal asportation requirement in prosecutions for bank robbery. . . .

[Justice Ginsburg agreed with the majority that the "value exceeding $1,000" requirement of the first paragraph of §2113(b) is an element of the crime of federal bank larceny, but concluded that this was an insufficient basis for depriving Carter of the right to have the jury instructed on that crime.—EDS.]

. . . I would therefore hold that a defendant charged with the felony of bank robbery is not barred as a matter of law from requesting and receiving an instruction describing as a lesser included offense the felony grade of bank larceny. . . . In reaching the opposite conclusion, the Court gives short shrift to the common-law origin and statutory evolution of §2113. The Court's woodenly literal construction . . . effectively shrinks the jury's choices while enlarging the prosecutor's options. I dissent.

Notes and Questions

1. The Supreme Court's holding in *Carter* affects more than jury instructions on lesser included offenses. Because bank larceny is not a lesser included offense, defendants like Carter can be punished for *both* larceny *and* robbery for a single criminal incident. The Double Jeopardy Clause bars punishing a defendant twice for "the same offence." As we have seen previously at page 72, under Blockburger v. United States, 284 U.S. 299 (1932), which is still good law, two crimes are not "the same" for double jeopardy purposes—hence punishment for both is permissible—if each crime requires proof of at least one unique fact. As the *Carter* majority defines the crimes, bank robbery and bank larceny are not "the same." Would it seem fair to punish Carter for both? Do you think Congress so intended?

2. *Carter* includes a substantial discussion of the meaning of asportation: the carrying away of stolen property. People v. Lardner, 133 N.E. 375 (Ill. 1921), captures the conventional definition of this element. The defendant in *Lardner* entered a store, took several small handbags and stuffed them into an overcoat, then placed the overcoat a few feet away; the Illinois Supreme Court held that this conduct amounted to the "carrying away" of the handbags:

> . . . [I]f the goods were actually carried away even the least distance it was sufficient to constitute larceny. . . . Taking goods and putting them into a place for convenient removal is the taking of property, and if one takes the goods of another out of the place where they are put, although he is detected before they are actually carried from the owner's premises, the crime is complete, as in case of the removal of an article from one place to another in the same house. State v. Wilson, 1 N.J.L. 439. Any change of location whereby complete control of the article is transferred from the true owner to the thief is sufficient evidence of the taking away. . . . The removal of goods from their accustomed place to another place in the same store is carrying away. State v. Higgins, 88 Mo. 354. If an article is secured by a string or chain which is not broken there is no taking which will constitute larceny. So taking a coat from a dummy figure in a store, which was not carried away because it was attached to the dummy by a chain and the dummy attached to the building, did not constitute larceny. People v. Meyer, 75 Cal. 383.

133 N.E. at 376. The facts in State v. Spears, 196 P.3d 1037 (Or. App. 2008), are similar:

Central Freight Lines is a freight moving facility in Multnomah County. When freight arrives at the facility, it is transferred either directly to a delivery unit for final delivery, or to "trap trailers" where it is stored until the appropriate time to move it to a final delivery unit.

On Friday, April 22, 2005, a shipment of computers arrived at the facility and was transferred into one of the trap trailers for storage until final delivery, scheduled for the following Monday. At around 6:00 the next morning, employees at the facility discovered a hole in the perimeter fence, which was then temporarily repaired.

Shortly after midnight on Sunday morning, April 24, two Portland police officers were called to the facility after employees inside the warehouse heard suspicious noises coming from outside. Upon arriving, one of the officers saw a man stepping down from one of the trailers while carrying a box. The officers approached that area, but did not see the man. The officers then looked under several of the trailers with their flashlights, and discovered five unopened boxes containing computers concealed behind the wheels of one of the trailers. As they checked under other trailers, one of the officers spotted the legs of two people under another trailer—and, ultimately, after repeated demands to come out, defendant and another man emerged from beneath that trailer. Defendant was dressed in dark clothes with a dark cap, gloves, and a flashlight; he also had a small cutting tool next to him.

Spears was arrested and charged with first-degree theft—which, under Oregon law, required the taking of property, but not that it be carried away. The Oregon Court of Appeals concluded that the difference did not matter; the defendant's conduct constituted both "taking" and "carrying away."

One more example: The defendant in State v. Boyle, 970 S.W.2d 835 (Mo. App. 1998), a case cited in *Carter*, pointed a gun at a store clerk and demanded the money in the cash register. Boyle then dropped some of the money; when he leaned down to pick it up, he was struck in the head by the store's owner. Missouri law requires that the robber "appropriate" the stolen property; the crime includes no asportation element. Boyle's robbery conviction was upheld on appeal. The court assumed that Boyle's conduct would not constitute asportation.

3. Courts often say that even a slight movement of the goods in question satisfies the requirement of asportation. But the magnitude of the movement is not the point; rather, the key to asportation is whether the movement of the goods "show[s] that the thief had indeed gained possession and control of the property." People v. Olivo, 420 N.E.2d 40, 44 (N.Y. 1981). (Why does that matter?) Given the point of the asportation element as defined in *Olivo*, the element is plainly satisfied in *Carter*. What about *Lardner*, *Spears*, and *Boyle*? Suppose Keeton had been arrested before exiting the store. On those facts, did Keeton "carry away" the stolen money?

4. A growing number of states have consolidated their theft statutes. The Oregon statute at issue in *Spears* reads: "A person commits theft when, with intent to deprive another of property or to appropriate property to the person or to a third person, the person . . . [t]akes, appropriates, obtains or withholds such property from an owner thereof." Or. Rev. Stat. §164.015. Typically, such statutes go on to authorize greater or lesser punishment depending on the value of the stolen property and the degree of violence used in obtaining it. These consolidated theft statutes are designed to eliminate the "technicalities" of the common-law definitions of different grades of theft. Is asportation a technicality?

2. Burglary

At common law, burglary "was defined as breaking and entering the dwelling house of another in the nighttime with intent to commit a felony." People v. Sparks, 47 P.3d 289, 293 (Cal. 2002). What purpose did that definition serve? Several of those common-law elements are missing from the definition of the crime used in *Sparks*, which is the next case. Is California's definition an improvement on the common law?

People v. Sparks

Supreme Court of California
28 Cal. 4th 71; 47 P.3d 289 (2002)

George, C.J.

Section 459 of the Penal Code provides, in part, that one who "enters *any* house, *room,* apartment, . . . store, . . . or other building . . . with intent to commit . . . larceny or any felony is guilty of burglary." (Italics added.) We granted review to address a conflict in Court of Appeal decisions concerning whether a defendant's entry into a bedroom within a single-family house with the requisite intent can support a burglary conviction if that intent was formed only after the defendant's entry into the house. We conclude that such an entry can support a burglary conviction under section 459, and hence reverse the judgment of the Court of Appeal, which reached a contrary conclusion.

I

At approximately noon on April 20, 1999, 22-year-old Ana I. answered defendant's knock at the door of her single-family home in Vista. Defendant, then 25 years of age, attempted to sell Ana some magazines, but she stated she was not interested. Defendant asked Ana for a glass of water, which she provided to him as he remained outside the house. Defendant eventually asked Ana whether he could enter the house, and he did so. . . .

Defendant sat at the dining room table while Ana stood in the "area where the door to the kitchen was." Eventually Ana sat at the table with defendant.

Defendant persisted in his attempt to sell a magazine subscription, but soon changed the subject, asking Ana whether she had a boyfriend. When told that she did not, defendant asked her why she did not. Ana revealed that she had broken up with her boyfriend. Ana felt nervous because she did not speak English well and "did not know how to answer the questions he was asking."[2] Ana asked defendant to leave, telling him that she had to depart to pick up her niece. . . . [W]hen he still did not leave the house, Ana got up, walked to the living room to turn off the stereo, and again told defendant that she had to depart to pick up her niece.

At this point, defendant had been in the house, talking with Ana at the dining room table, for about 15 minutes. Defendant rose from the dining room table, walked to the living room where Ana was standing near the stereo, and asked her whether she liked the music that was playing. Ana replied that she did, and walked down the hall to her bedroom to find outdoor shoes to wear upon leaving the house.

Although Ana did not ask defendant to go with her into the bedroom, he followed her into that room. (There was no testimony that the bedroom door was closed, or that Ana opened it.) As Ana retrieved her shoes from the floor of the closet, she realized that defendant was in the bedroom with her, standing just inside the bedroom doorway. . . . Defendant blocked Ana's exit, diverted her attention by telling her to look out a window, and then shoved her face down onto the bed, pressing a pillow on top of her head as she began to scream. During her struggles, Ana began to see white spots and had difficulty breathing. . . . [D]efendant raped her, and then walked into the bathroom. Ana closed her bedroom door and locked it. When defendant exited from the bathroom, he knocked on Ana's door. She told him to leave and stated that she was "not going to tell anybody, but he should leave."

Ana left the house through her bedroom window and walked to a school to meet her niece, who noticed that Ana had red splotches on her face. Later that day Ana told her mother and her sister that she had been attacked, and that evening Ana went to a hospital, where she described the assault to a police officer. A later medical examination revealed the presence of defendant's semen in Ana's vagina. Ana also showed signs of petechiae (pinpoint hemorrhaging) on her face, a condition consistent with asphyxia.

The trial court instructed the jury on the offense of burglary . . . as follows:

"The defendant is accused in count one of having committed the crime of burglary, a violation of section 459 of the Penal Code. Every person who enters a building or *any room within a building* with the specific intent to commit rape,

2. Ana testified with the assistance of a court interpreter.

a felony, is guilty of the crime of burglary in violation of Penal Code section 459." (Italics added.)

Based upon these and related instructions, the prosecution argued to the jury that defendant could be found guilty of burglary if he formed the intent to rape either (i) prior to entering the house, or (ii) after entering the house, but prior to entering the bedroom in which the sexual assault occurred.

The jury convicted defendant of first degree burglary and forcible rape, and found true the allegations that defendant personally used a deadly weapon (the pillow). The jury also found true the allegation that the forcible rape was committed during the commission of a residential burglary with the intent to commit forcible rape. The trial court imposed a sentence of 29 years to life in prison.[5]

The Court of Appeal upheld defendant's conviction for forcible rape, but in a split decision reversed the burglary conviction for instructional error. . . . We granted the Attorney General's petition for review.

II

The Attorney General asserts that the plain words of section 459 (defining as burglary the entry of "any . . . room . . . with intent to commit . . . larceny or any felony") establish that the court's instructions were correct and that the elements of the offense of burglary were established in this case.

Defendant contends . . . that the Legislature could not have intended for the circumstances presented here to constitute a burglary. He maintains that the word "room" in section 459 applies only to those rooms as to which there is an expectation of protection from intrusion—from room to room—that is comparable to the expectation of protection from intrusion into a house from outside the house. In other words, defendant argues that the term "any . . . room" as used in section 459 was intended to encompass only certain types of rooms—for example, a locked room within a single-family house or a separate dwelling unit within a boarding house, entry into which is generally unauthorized even for other legal occupants of the house.

. . . During the past few decades, the legislatures of many of our sister states have been quite active in amending their respective burglary statutes. . . . [S]tatutes in most jurisdictions, consistent with the recommendation of the

---

5. The court imposed a sentence of 25 years to life for rape committed during a residential burglary with intent to rape, plus a consecutive four-year term for personally using the deadly weapon while committing the forcible rape. Defendant was not separately sentenced for the burglary conviction standing alone.

Model Penal Code,[6] make clear that the burglary statutes in these jurisdictions apply only to entry of a "room" that constitutes a "separate unit" or a "separately secured" or "separately occupied" portion of a building or structure.[7]

As noted, the interpretation proposed by defendant would focus upon the nature of the room entered and would inquire whether an occupant's reasonable expectation of protection from intrusion into that room *from the other rooms* is comparable to the expectation of protection from intrusion *into a house from outside the house*. . . . In other words, the limiting gloss proposed by defendant essentially would embrace the "separately secured or occupied" standard endorsed by the Model Penal Code and adopted, in one form or another, in most (but not all) other jurisdictions.[8]

Although the interpretation of the statute proposed by defendant (and endorsed by the majority in the Court of Appeal below) is not unreasonable, . . . we do not write on a clean slate. In view of the history and prior interpretation of the California statute, we are not free to adopt [an interpretation of] the term "room" that has been explicitly established in other jurisdictions only by explicit legislative action. Instead, . . . we conclude that section 459 reasonably must be interpreted in the manner urged by the Attorney General.

III

At common law, the offense of burglary was defined as breaking and entering the dwelling house of another in the nighttime with intent to commit a

---

6. Model Penal Code §221.1(1), first adopted in 1962, reads in relevant part: "A person is guilty of burglary if he enters a building or occupied structure, *or separately secured or occupied portion thereof*, with purpose to commit a crime therein. . . ." (Italics added.) As explained in the comment to this section,

> "[t]he provision in Subsection (1) as to separately secured or occupied portions of buildings and occupied structures takes care of the situation of apartment houses, office buildings, hotels, steamships with a series of private cabins, etc., where occupancy is by unit. It is the individual unit as well as the overall structure that must be safeguarded. Thus, while it would violate this section for a person to make an unprivileged entry into an apartment house for the purpose of stealing money or other valuables from a common safe, it also would violate the burglary provision if an intrusion is made into a single unit, even by an occupant of another unit of the same structure." Model Penal Code & Commentaries, comment 3(b) to §221.1, at 73.

7. A typical statute provides that, for purposes of the offense of burglary, "each unit of a building consisting of two or more units separately secured or occupied is a separate building." Hawaii Rev. Stat., §708-800. . . .

8. A minority of jurisdictions have statutes similar to California's, listing without qualification the word "room" (or a variant of that term) as a place, the entry into which, with the requisite intent, may constitute burglary. See Ga. Code Ann., §16-7-1(a); Idaho Code, §18-1401; Okla. Stat. tit. 21, §1435; Wis. Stat., §943.10(1)(f). Defendant has not cited, nor have we found, any decision from these jurisdictions limiting such a statute in the manner presently suggested by defendant. . . .

felony. See 2 LaFave & Scott, Substantive Criminal Law §8.13, at 464 (1986). "Across the intervening centuries these elements have been expanded or discarded to such an extent that the modern-day offense commonly known as burglary bears little relation to the common-law ancestor." Id. In California, the metamorphosis of common law burglary into statutory burglary began in 1850 with the adoption of section 58 of the Act Concerning Crimes and Punishments, from which today's Penal Code section 459 is derived. This first statute defined burglary as entering, in the nighttime and with the requisite intent, "any dwelling house, or any other house whatever. . . ." Stats. 1850, ch. 99, §58, at 235.

Eight years later, in 1858, section 58 was amended by substituting for the phrase "any dwelling house, or any other house whatever," the phrase that exists today in Penal Code section 459, "*any* house, *room*, apartment or tenement." Stats. 1858, ch. 245, §58, at 206 (italics added). Upon being codified into the Penal Code in 1872, the statute read essentially the same and, as relevant here, section 459 continues to read the same today:

> "Every person who enters *any* house, *room*, apartment, tenement, shop, warehouse, store, mill, barn, stable, outhouse or other building . . . with intent to commit . . . larceny or any felony is guilty of burglary." (Italics added.)[12]

Section 460(a) currently specifies that "[e]very burglary of an inhabited dwelling house . . . is burglary of the first degree." . . .

This court directly ruled upon the meaning of the word "room," as used in section 459, for the first time in People v. Young, 65 Cal. 225, 3 P. 813 (1884). In that case, the defendant entered a public railway station and thereafter entered a ticket office (which apparently had walls that were eight to nine feet high but did not reach the ceiling) located within the station. We rejected the theory that section 459 required the defendant to have

---

12. As most recently amended in 1991, section 459 now provides in full:

"Every person who enters any house, room, apartment, tenement, shop, warehouse, store, mill, barn, stable, outhouse or other building, tent, vessel, as defined in Section 21 of the Harbors and Navigation Code, floating home, as defined in subdivision (d) of Section 18075.55 of the Health and Safety Code, railroad car, locked or sealed cargo container, whether or not mounted on a vehicle, trailer coach, as defined in Section 635 of the Vehicle Code, any house car, as defined in Section 362 of the Vehicle Code, inhabited camper, as defined in Section 243 of the Vehicle Code, vehicle as defined by the Vehicle Code, when the doors are locked, aircraft as defined by Section 21012 of the Public Utilities Code, or mine or any underground portion thereof, with intent to commit grand or petit larceny or any felony is guilty of burglary. As used in this chapter, 'inhabited' means currently being used for dwelling purposes, whether occupied or not. A house, trailer, vessel designed for habitation, or portion of a building is currently being used for dwelling purposes if, at the time of the burglary, it was not occupied solely because a natural or other disaster caused the occupants to leave the premises." Stats. 1991, ch. 942, §14, at 4290.

formed the required intent prior to entering the railway station, so long as he formed that intent prior to entering a room within that structure—the ticket office. . . . We stated: "One who enters, with burglarious intent, a room of a house enters the house with such intent. . . ." *Young*, supra, at 226. In this regard, *Young* reflected the prevailing common law understanding that entry from inside a structure into a room within that structure could constitute a burglary.

Subsequent to *Young*, a number of California appellate court decisions have held that entry into various types of rooms can constitute burglary. Most of these cases, like *Young*, concern entry into private rooms within public or commercial buildings. E.g., People v. Elsey, 81 Cal. App. 4th 948, 97 Cal. Rptr. 2d 269 (2000) (entry into separate, locked school classrooms); People v. Church, 215 Cal. App. 3d 1151, 264 Cal. Rptr. 49 (1989) (entry into separately leased and locked offices in an office building); People v. Edwards, 22 Cal. App. 3d 598, 99 Cal. Rptr. 516 (1971) (entry into women's restroom inside hospital). In other decisions, courts have upheld burglary convictions based upon the defendant's (i) entry into a private room within a multi-unit lodging facility, e.g., People v. O'Keefe, 222 Cal. App. 3d 517, 271 Cal. Rptr. 769 (1990) (entry into separate student dormitory rooms), (ii) entry from the garage of a single-family home into a locked kitchen, People v. Thomas, 235 Cal. App. 3d 899, 1 Cal. Rptr. 2d 434 (1991), and (iii) entry, from inside a home, into a rented and locked bedroom within the home, People v. Wilson, 208 Cal. App. 3d 611, 256 Cal. Rptr. 422 (1989).

Of all the cases applying section 459, only one, People v. McCormack, 234 Cal. App. 3d 253, 285 Cal. Rptr. 504 (1991), concerns the precise type of entry we face here—entry, by an ostensible guest in the home, from inside the living quarters of a single-family home, into the unsecured bedroom of a member of a family living in the home. Most of the other recent decisions described above—specifically, *Elsey*, *Thomas*, and *O'Keefe*—have made a point of distinguishing *McCormack* and the normal single-family-home setting. . . .

The defendant in *McCormack* entered a single-family home through an unlocked door, assertedly at the occupant's invitation. The occupant—the brother of the homeowner—observed the defendant in the kitchen and asked him to leave the house, but the defendant refused to do so. Instead, the defendant asked the occupant whether he wanted a beer and requested permission to use the telephone. 234 Cal. App. 3d at 255. The occupant departed and telephoned the police from a neighbor's residence. When the police arrived, they found the defendant (in a hallway of the home) holding items taken from bedrooms. The defendant was charged with a single count of burglary. The trial court instructed that the "intent [to steal the personal property of another] need not be in the mind of the person at the time of the initial entry into the structure, if he subsequently forms the intent and enters a room within the structure." Ibid. (bracketed material in original). . . . The defendant was convicted of burglary and appealed.

. . . Relying upon our decision in *Young*, 65 Cal. 225, and some of the Court of Appeal decisions cited [above], the court held that because "the plain language of the code includes entry into a room within the definition of burglary," the instruction was proper. *McCormack*, supra, at 256. . . .

One year prior to *McCormack*, the Court of Appeal in *O'Keefe* addressed whether entries into separate rooms in a college dormitory supported convictions for separate burglary counts. . . . The defendant . . . [argued] that the student dormitory rooms were analogous to rooms in a single-family home (as to which, the defendant assumed, multiple convictions under §459 would not be proper). Without endorsing the defendant's assumption, the court in *O'Keefe* rejected the attempted analogy between dormitory rooms and bedrooms of a single-family home. First, it observed, a student dormitory is "analogous to a hotel or apartment complex" and not to a single-family home. *O'Keefe*, 222 Cal. App. 3d at 521. . . . [The court noted] that although the dormitory residents

> "may share kitchen and bathroom facilities . . . , this does not make them one big family. . . . [E]ach student lives and enjoys separate privacy in each of their individual dormitory rooms. These rooms are their homes while attending school. Unauthorized entry into each dormitory room presents a new and separate danger to each of the occupants. Accordingly, individual dormitory rooms and the students who occupy them are entitled to protection under the meaning of section 459." Id. at 521.

Shortly after *McCormack* was filed, the Court of Appeal decided *Thomas*. In that case the defendant first entered the garage of a single-family residence and then, while still in the garage, forcibly entered locked living quarters of the home — the kitchen. The prosecutor in *Thomas* argued that the jury could convict the defendant of burglary if he formed an intent to steal in the garage but prior to entry into the kitchen. . . . The court [agreed]. . . .

As in *O'Keefe*, however, the court in *Thomas* proceeded to distinguish the entry there at issue from other entries of rooms within single-family homes. The court emphasized that the defendant's

> "forcible and unauthorized entry into the living quarters of the [victims'] home [from the garage] was precisely the evil that the burglary statute is designed and intended to prevent. *The kitchen was separate from the garage.* It was protected and secured by a locked door which [the defendant] forced open with a crowbar. The [victims'] expectation of privacy and security within their living quarters *was clearly greater than that in their garage*, even if the garage may be considered part of the entire dwelling for burglary purposes. In our opinion, it would defeat the purposes of the burglary statute to hold in this case that [the defendant] could not be found guilty of burglary unless it was shown that he conceived his felonious intent prior to entering the garage." . . . *Thomas*, 235 Cal. App. 3d at 906-07, italics added.

In the course of its discussion, the court in *Thomas* also asserted in a footnote: "[W]here a burglar enters several rooms in a single structure, each with felonious intent, and steals something from each, ordinarily he or she cannot be charged with multiple burglaries and punished separately for each room burgled *unless* each room constituted a separate, individual dwelling place within the meaning of sections 459 and 460." Id. at 906 n.2, italics in original.

Most recently, the court in *Elsey* addressed the defendant's entry into six classrooms, some of them located in the same building, on a single school campus. The court, distinguishing "entry into multiple rooms of a single-family house [from] the entries into multiple secured classrooms," id., at 960, upheld the resulting six burglary convictions. . . .

IV

Defendant asserts that the interpretation of section 459 set out in *McCormack*, 234 Cal. App. 3d 254, will produce bizarre results. He echoes the Court of Appeal majority below, which observed that . . . if the defendant had formed the requisite intent while in the kitchen and yet thereafter did not enter any other room, he would not have been guilty of burglary[17] — but if the defendant had gone into another room and then reentered the kitchen, this time with the requisite intent, he would have been guilty of burglary. The Court of Appeal majority also asserted that allowing a conviction of burglary on the present facts . . . would subject defendants to [a separate burglary conviction] for every room in the house entered with the requisite intent.

Justice Benke, dissenting in the Court of Appeal below, conceded that under *McCormack*'s interpretation of the statute, whether a particular entry into a room constitutes burglary will depend upon "the location of an actor when the requisite intent is formed," but further observed that this consequence "is not the result of the *McCormack* rule but of the nature of the crime of burglary itself as defined in section 459." Moreover, Justice Benke noted that even if the interpretation of the statute set out in *McCormack* may "allow[. . .] the creative mind to formulate disconcerting hypotheticals about the application of the law of burglary," the rule proposed by defendant would do so as well:

> "For example, a person may enter a residence without the intent to commit a theft. He walks down a hall off of which there are two indistinguishable

17. The statutes in some jurisdictions provide otherwise and include in their definition of burglary the situation where one enters *or remains* with the requisite intent. See, e.g., Fla. Stat. ch. 810, §10.02(1); Me. Rev. Stat., tit 17-A, §401; N.J. Rev. Stat., §2C:18-2; N.Y. Penal Law §140.00(5); N.D. Cent. Code, §12.1-22-02(1); Vt. Stat. Ann. tit. 13, §1201. Section 459, by contrast, requires an *entry* with requisite intent. Accordingly, in the present case, defendant would not have committed burglary if, after entering the home as a guest, he formed the requisite intent in the dining room or in the living room, but thereafter did not enter another room within the home with that intent.

bedrooms. The first is the bedroom of a family member, the second the bed-room rented by a family friend. Under the [rule proposed by defendant and the majority below], if the person enters the first with the intent to commit a theft, he commits no burglary [because he has not invaded a separate posses-sory interest]. If he enters the second [with the intent to commit a theft], he commits a first degree burglary. This distinction makes no sense . . . and does not serve the policy basis of the crime."

Accordingly, Justice Benke concluded that the rule proposed by defen-dant "simply exchanges one set of potential anomalies . . . for another," and she asserted that "[i]f I must choose my anomalies . . . , then I believe I am duty bound to choose those created by the Legislature."

V

. . . As noted above, California decisions applying section 459 have upheld burglary convictions based upon entry into diverse types of rooms—among them ticket offices, liquor cages, business offices, enclosed counter areas, school classrooms, hotel rooms, apartments, a kitchen in a single-family home, and, in *McCormack*, a bedroom within a single-family home. These decisions—and *McCormack* in particular—are consistent with common law cases from other jurisdictions, recognizing as burglary the entry (with requisite intent), from within a home, into a bedroom inside the home.[18] Although the burglary statute historically has been the subject of frequent amendments, our Legislature has not revised section 459 to disapprove any of these decisions. . . .

. . . [T]reating the entry at issue here as an entry for burglary is consis-tent with the personal security concerns of the burglary statute, because entry, from inside a home, into a bedroom of the home "raise[s] the level of risk that the burglar will come into contact with the home's occupants with the resultant threat of violence and harm." *McCormack*, supra, at 257. Here, the 22-year-old victim, living in her family's home, reasonably could expect signifi-cant additional privacy and security when she retreated into her own bedroom. Accordingly, . . . consistent with the common law and the history of section 459, we conclude that the unadorned word "room" in section 459 reasonably must be given its ordinary meaning. It follows that the trial court did not err in this case by instructing the jury that entry into Ana's bedroom with the specific intent to commit rape constitutes a burglary in violation of section 459.

---

18. The common law is well illustrated by State v. Contreras-Cruz, 765 A.2d 849 (R.I. 2001). In that case the defendant was charged with burglary for entering the bedroom of his brother and the brother's girlfriend, while the brother was absent, with intent to sexu-ally assault the girlfriend. The defendant claimed that he had his brother's permission to be inside the house. . . . The court observed: "It has long been held that while one may have permission to enter parts of a dwelling, entry into a room within that dwelling that a person does not have permission to enter can constitute burglary." [Id.] at 854.

In light of California decisions construing section 459, the policy under-lying that statute, common law antecedents, and the history of section 459, we conclude that the trial court did not err in defining burglary to include entry into the victim's bedroom with the specific intent to commit rape. . . .

Notes and Questions

1. Though burglary is usually seen as a species of theft, the actual taking of someone else's property is no part of its definition. Rather, burglary stat-utes criminalize the trespass that precedes thefts (and other crimes) com-mitted inside private homes. Is burglary really the same thing as a trespass, or is it different? Does the answer help to explain the crime's definition?

2. How many separate burglaries did Sparks commit? Applying the California Supreme Court's definition (and assuming he formed the intent to commit rape beforehand), each time Sparks walked into a different room in Ana's home, he committed burglary. Does that definition of burglary make sense? Does any other definition make sense?

3. Burglary plays much the same role in *Sparks* as the false statements charge plays in Brogan v. United States, page 74 supra. As you may recall, Brogan was a union official suspected of taking bribes from an employer to sell out the union's members. Brogan was convicted of labor racketeering, but during its investigation, the government was not certain a conviction on that charge would be possible. So FBI agents confronted Brogan in his home and asked him a question (to which they already knew the answer) that was likely to prompt a dishonest response. When Brogan lied, he was charged under the false statements statute — thereby guaranteeing a convic-tion. *Sparks* appears similar: Prosecutors may have been less than confident that they could convict Sparks of rape; if so, the burglary charge was a con-venient backstop. Assuming that is what happened, was Sparks treated fairly? Should backstop charges be permitted in criminal cases? Does the answer depend on what charge is used as a backstop?

4. *Sparks* and *Brogan* are similar in another respect. To prove Brogan guilty of lying to FBI agents, the government had to show that Brogan had indeed accepted money from his members' employer — which was also one of the elements of the labor racketeering charge. To prove Sparks guilty of burglary, the prosecution had to show that Sparks had the specific intent to commit rape when he walked into Ana's room. In both cases, proof of the backstop crime suggests that the "real" crime — the offense that is the reason for the criminal investigation and prosecution — happened as well. Indeed, in *Sparks*, the government carries a heavier burden of proof for burglary than for rape. Rape is a general intent offense, and the requisite intent need not be formed in advance of the act. To convict on the burglary charge, the government must prove specific intent — and must prove it existed in advance of the act of rape. In this sense, convicting Sparks of burglary may have been harder, not easier, than convicting him of rape.

5. At common law, walking through an open bedroom doorway could not constitute burglary, regardless of the defendant's intent: The government had to prove "breaking" as well as entering, and the entry that mattered was entry into the victim's "dwelling"—meaning a house or apartment, not a bedroom. In other words, to win a burglary conviction, a prosecutor had to show that the defendant used force of some kind (say, breaking a window or picking a door lock) in order to gain access to the victim's home. What is the point of such a requirement?

6. In most jurisdictions, there is a backstop charge for burglary: possession of burglars' tools. Consider the facts in People v. Southard, 152 Cal. App. 4th 1079, 62 Cal. Rptr. 3d 48 (2007). After a high-speed chase, the defendant abandoned his car and was then captured on foot.

> [Officer Paul Arnett] conducted a full inventory of the Oldsmobile after it had been towed from the scene and found a myriad of tools, including a steel pry bar, a crowbar, five pairs of pliers, a large pair of boltcutters, a sledge hammer, an unspecified number of screwdrivers and hammers, and a tool box. . . . At trial, Arnett opined that the items were for possible use in a burglary. . . . Arnett explained . . . that although none of the individual items was illegal to possess, the sum of items made them suspicious because, collectively, the tools would be useful for breaking into a building. . . .
>
> Karen Olson, a chief deputy district attorney, also testified at trial. According to Olson, some time in April 2005, she had a conversation with defendant in which he requested "his burglary tools, a release for his burglary tools." . . . Olson explained at trial that "[i]t struck me as odd. I actually found it amusing. I thought he was joking."

62 Cal. Rptr. 3d at 51-52. Defendant was convicted of violating California Penal Code §466:

> Every person having upon him or her in his or her possession a picklock, crow, keybit, crowbar, screwdriver, vise grip pliers, water-pump pliers, slidehammer, slim jim, tension bar, lock pick gun, tubular lock pick, floor-safe door puller, master key, ceramic or porcelain spark plug chips or pieces, or other instrument or tool with intent feloniously to break or enter into any building . . . is guilty of a misdemeanor.

On the burglars' tools charge, Southard was sentenced to six months in the local jail. On appeal, the key issue was whether there was sufficient evidence of Southard's intent to support the conviction. The court said there was, relying on two facts: Southard tried to evade capture when first spotted, and—in what must be one of the most foolish moves any criminal defendant has made—Southard asked the district attorney's office to return his "burglary tools."

7. Notice that both robbery and burglary are typically defined in ways that cover many incomplete offenses. Even if the defendant is caught before exiting the site of the robbery, he may still be convicted of having "taken" and "carried away" the stolen goods. Sparks was guilty of burglary the moment he walked into a room with the requisite intent. Southard was guilty of possessing burglars' tools from the moment he acquired the various items seized from his car. Prosecutors rarely need charge *attempted* robbery or *attempted* burglary—since even unsuccessful efforts to commit robbery and burglary usually fall within the definitions of those crimes, or within the definition of a backstop charge such as possession of burglars' tools.

3. Larceny and Embezzlement

The common-law definition of larceny is the taking and carrying away of the property of another, with the intent to deprive the owner of that property permanently. Unlike robbery, no use of force is required; unlike burglary, the government need not prove the defendant guilty of any trespass. Embezzlement is usually defined as the conversion of another's property after that property was entrusted to the defendant; embezzlers are guilty of *keeping* property that is not theirs rather than *taking* it.

Robbery and burglary cases rarely raise any question about the line between criminal punishment and civil sanctions like money damages; all societies with functioning criminal justice systems use those systems to punish forcible thefts and trespasses. Such questions arise more frequently in cases of non-violent theft. As you read the next two cases, consider the question whether such disputes should be handled by the criminal justice system or by civil litigation.

State v. Moon

Supreme Judicial Court of Maine
755 A.2d 527 (2000)

Opinion of WATHEN, C.J.

Defendant John R. Moon appeals from a judgment entered in the Superior Court following a jury verdict finding him guilty of theft (Class B), 17-A Maine Rev. Stat. Ann. §353.[1] Defendant contends that the court

---

1. The statute provides as follows:

1. A person is guilty of theft if he obtains or exercises unauthorized control over the property of another with intent to deprive him thereof.

2. As used in this section, "exercises unauthorized control" includes but is not necessarily limited to conduct heretofore defined or known as common law larceny by trespassory taking, larceny by conversion, larceny by bailee and embezzlement.

erred in limiting his expert's testimony, in instructing the jury concerning the charges of theft by unauthorized taking or transfer and theft by misapplication of property, in instructing the jury concerning the time at which an intention to deprive must exist, and in allowing overly remote evidence of the mental element. Finding no error, we affirm.

The relevant facts may be summarized as follows: Defendant, while working on his M.B.A. degree at the University of Maine at Orono, was recruited to be a resident advisor of the Sigma Chi Fraternity house. After the local chapter of the Sigma Chi was closed, he was again recruited by alumni of the Rho Rho Chapter of Sigma Chi to resurrect the chapter at the University. He was hired as director of the fundraising campaign, project manager of the renovation project, and live-in resident advisor. He also served, without compensation, as treasurer of the Rho Rho Chapter. During the period defendant was treasurer, he transferred funds from the fraternity's bank accounts on numerous occasions to either himself personally or to Marsh Island Development Company (MIDCO), a corporation in which he was a significant shareholder. He used the funds primarily to renovate a four-story brick townhouse located at 137 Main Street, Bangor, with the intention of then obtaining conventional residential financing. In the end, he was unable to obtain residential financing. He concealed these transfers from the Board of Trustees of the fraternity and obtained no authorization from the Board. During the period defendant was taking the funds, his personal bank balances were low and he incurred substantial debt, the proceeds of which he used in part to repay the fraternity. Defendant continued to take funds even when he knew that obtaining the residential financing would be difficult. He admits that from 1991 to 1994 he took approximately $120,000.00, returned over $100,000.00, and still owes $19,972.41.

His defense at trial focused on demonstrating that he had no intent to deprive. He argued that he always intended to repay the money and that he believed he had $110,000.00 in equity in his Main Street property to cover the money he had taken. To support his defense, defendant testified himself as to his intent and also introduced the testimony of Gregory Noonan, a certified fraud examiner, certified public accountant and attorney. Noonan

---

17-A Maine Rev. Stat. Ann. §353. "Intent to deprive" is defined by statute as follows:

> "Intent to deprive" means to have the conscious object: A. To withhold property permanently or for so extended a period or to use under such circumstances that a substantial portion of its economic value, or the use and benefit thereof, would be lost; or B. To restore the property only upon payment of a reward or other compensation; or C. To use or dispose of the property under circumstances that make it unlikely that the owner will recover it or that manifest an indifference as to whether the owner will recover it.

17-A Maine Rev. Stat. Ann. §352(3).

testified before the jury as follows: Defendant kept a separate account entitled "accounts receivable—other" in the journal and properly recorded each transaction in which defendant either took funds from the fraternity or returned funds. It was significant that defendant included no other receivables within the "accounts receivable—other" account, in accordance with generally accepted accounting principles, and important that he included none of these transfers in the general accounts receivable account, which would have been improper because he was an employee. As a result, according to Noonan, defendant left a very good audit trail so that it was easy for an auditor to trace the transactions back to the check register and determine that the funds were made payable to John Moon or MIDCO. Noonan's review of the records confirmed that during the period from 1991 to 1994 the total amount that went to defendant was $123,477.86 and the amount repaid by defendant was approximately $103,505.00, leaving a balance of approximately $19,000.00.

Defendant was indicted in 1997 for theft by unauthorized taking or transfer in violation of 17-A Maine Rev. Stat. Ann. §353 and subsequently indicted for theft by misapplication of property. . . . [D]efendant was found guilty of theft in violation of §353 and now appeals.

I. EXCLUSION OF EXPERT TESTIMONY

. . . Defendant . . . argues that the court erred by refusing to let him introduce the expert testimony of Noonan that would explain to the lay person how the financial records were kept, how the records created an audit trail, and how the audit trail was inconsistent with all methods of obscuring theft in the books of a business. In fact, the court excluded only the last element of Noonan's testimony. In voir dire, Noonan testified that there are four basic "embezzlement schemes," i.e., lapping a/k/a kiting, fictitious receivables, diverting payments in old written off receivables, and borrowing against receivables; that in fourteen years of experience he has not seen a situation of account receivable or cash fraud that fell outside of these four categories; and this case is distinguished because "every transaction was documented right to the T."

The court refused to allow this portion of Noonan's testimony on the basis of relevancy [and] . . . jury confusion. . . . The court determined that the expert's testimony dealt with embezzlement schemes, that defendant was charged with theft, and that embezzlement and theft are not necessarily co-extensive. It further found that the testimony could confuse the jurors because Noonan's audit standards for the embezzlement schemes differ from the statutory elements of theft.

We review evidentiary rulings on relevancy and prejudicial effect for clear error or an abuse of discretion. . . . Evidence is relevant if it has "any tendency to make the existence of any fact that is of consequence to the determination of the action more probable or less probable than it would be without the evidence." Maine Rule of Evidence 401. . . .

The jury had the expert's testimony, without the proffered portion, that explained how the financial records were kept and how the records created an audit trail. This evidence . . . supported defendant's argument that because of his meticulous recordkeeping and because he returned a substantial portion of the funds, he did not intend to deprive the fraternity of the funds permanently, but instead intended to repay the debt. . . . [But] whether defendant's conduct [resembles] historical patterns of embezzlement is irrelevant to whether defendant committed theft by unauthorized taking. . . .

. . . Simply because a person is clever enough to devise a new method of committing a theft that does not [resemble] a known existing embezzlement scheme, or foolhardy enough to document his activity, does not make it less probable that the crime of theft was committed. Although defendant and his expert witness focused on his intent to repay the money to support his contention that he did not intend to deprive the fraternity of the funds permanently, see 17-A Maine Rev. Stat. Ann. §352(3)(A), they ignored the patent possibility that he committed theft in violation of the statute by using the fraternity's money "under circumstances that make it unlikely that the owner will recover it." 17-A Maine Rev. Stat. Ann. §352(3)(C). Accordingly, the expert's testimony . . . does not tend to prove that defendant lacked the intent to deprive based on the complete statutory definition of theft.

II. JURY INSTRUCTIONS

. . . Defendant also argues that the court erred because it refused to provide his proposed jury instructions which emphasized that the necessary mental element of intent to deprive must exist "at the time of the taking." Defendant's proposed instruction stated in relevant part:

> This intent to deprive the true owner of the property must have existed at the time that the unauthorized control first took place. . . . If you find that the Defendant exercised unauthorized control over the fraternity's money, you must then examine the evidence whether, at the time Defendant began exercising unauthorized control, he then and there had the intent to deprive the fraternity of that money.

The court instructed the jury as follows:

> A person commits the crime of theft . . . if that person obtains or exercises unauthorized control over the property of another with the intent, at the time he obtains or exercises unauthorized control over the property, to deprive the owner thereof.

The difference between the instructions is that defendant sought to limit the criminal act to a single point in time, namely, "the time Defendant *began exercising* unauthorized control," for the purpose of determining the presence of the required mental element. The distinction, however, if any, is not relevant in this case. Even if defendant intended to repay the funds at the precise moment he took them, he nonetheless consciously used the money in a way which the jury could find made it unlikely that the fraternity would recover it, in violation of section 352(3)(C). . . .

III. REMOTE EVIDENCE

Defendant also argues that the court erred in allowing evidence that he filed bankruptcy years after he took the funds and that he had not repaid the fraternity up until the time of the trial. He argues that the evidence was too remote and thus prejudicial because the intent to deprive must be at the time of initially obtaining possession or control. This argument also focuses on his intent to repay the money at the time of the taking and thus lacks merit because it does not negate the particular variant of intent to deprive involved in this case. In any event, the jury could have inferred that defendant had not repaid the fraternity based on his testimony on direct examination that he owes the fraternity $19,972.41.

Judgment affirmed.

Notes and Questions

1. Reread the definition of "intent to deprive" in section 353, quoted in footnote 1 in *Moon*. Did the defendant have the requisite intent? If so, when?

2. Ordinarily, in order to convict, the prosecution must prove that the defendant committed the relevant criminal acts with the prescribed criminal intent. Acts and intent usually must coincide; the defendant must have the necessary mental state at the same time he engages in the prohibited conduct. Moon argues that, if he had the necessary intent to deprive the fraternity of its money, he formed that intent long after he acquired control over the money. Assuming Moon is right, does that justify his acquittal? Note that the statute forbids not only acquiring control of another's property, but also exercising such control. Did Moon have the required intent at any point when he was exercising control over the fraternity's property? The question is not easily answered. When Moon declared bankruptcy, he presumably no longer had the $20,000 in fraternity funds that he had not repaid.

3. Recall *Stark*, page 92 supra. As in *Moon*, the defendant in *Stark* took money to which someone else was entitled and used it for his own purposes; again as in *Moon*, the defendant in *Stark* maintained that he intended to repay his victims—the fraternity in *Moon*, the doctors and subcontractors in *Stark*. To put the point another way, both defendants were convicted of, in effect, unlawful borrowing. Should the criminal justice system punish such behavior, or is it a problem best handled by civil lawsuits? Consider the next case.

People v. Perry

Supreme Court of Illinois
224 Ill. 2d 312; 864 N.E.2d 196 (2007)

Justice GARMAN delivered the opinion of the court.

After a jury trial in the circuit court of Du Page County, defendant Michael L. Perry was convicted of theft by deception (720 Ill. Cons. Stat. §5/16-1(a)(2)). Based on the value of the stolen property, his crime was classified as a Class 2 felony and he was sentenced to a term of six years' imprisonment and ordered to pay restitution. 720 Ill. Cons. Stat. §5/16-1(b)(5). On appeal, the court held that he could be convicted only of the lesser offense of theft of property valued in excess of $300, but less than $10,000 (720 Ill. Cons. Stat. §5/16-1(b)(4)), a Class 3 felony, and remanded for a new sentencing hearing. We granted the State's petition for leave to appeal, to determine whether defendant was properly convicted of theft of property valued in excess of $10,000 when the property at issue was the occupancy of a hotel room for a period of more than three months. . . .

BACKGROUND

Defendant, along with his wife and children, occupied a suite at the Embassy Suites hotel in Lombard, Illinois, from January through April 2000. The testimony at trial revealed that after staying at the hotel for several weeks, defendant sought to negotiate a reduced rate for the room. He also requested that the cost of his stay be billed to a company of which he was the president, Prolific Development Corporation (Prolific). He provided several trade references and a credit card in the name of Bryan Green.

The hotel manager drafted a document headed "RATE AGREEMENT February 2000-December 30, 2000." The agreement provided for a rate of $130 per night for a two-room suite, with a minimum stay of 100 nights "on an annual basis." Both parties signed the agreement. Several days thereafter, the hotel controller sent a letter to defendant at the address he had provided for Prolific, confirming that billing statements would be sent to the corporate address and that the hotel's "net terms are 30 days from each statement date."

After four bills sent to the business address went unpaid, the hotel's controller slid a letter under defendant's hotel room door. The letter noted that payment was more than 60 days past due and that the balance on the account was over $12,000. Defendant did not respond to the letter.

Eventually, it was revealed that the person defendant identified as the contact person for Prolific was not actually connected with the company. The hotel was also unable to contact the company using the e-mail address provided by defendant. Bills and letters that had been sent to the business address were returned to the hotel by the post office in a single envelope marked "Address Unknown." When the trade references were eventually contacted, one reported that defendant did not have a valid account. Another reported that defendant was not in good standing and owed it money.

At various times, defendant explained to members of the hotel staff that he was having problems with the post office, that he had submitted the bill to his accountant for payment, that payment would be made by May 9, 2000, that payment would arrive "any day," and that the check was being "cut from another company" about which he was unable to provide any information. . . .

During the night shift on May 13, 2000, defendant and his family vacated the hotel room without checking out or settling the bill. Although defendant paid a small portion of his bill by credit card during the early part of his stay, the unpaid balance for the room, restaurant, laundry services, telephone, and other charges exceeded $15,000. An attempt by the hotel to charge some of these expenses to the credit card in the name of Bryan Green, which defendant had provided earlier, was unsuccessful because the individual named on the credit card disputed the charges.

A Du Page County grand jury returned an indictment charging defendant with theft by deception "of property exceeding $10,000 and not exceeding $100,000 in value." 720 Ill. Cons. Stat. §5/16-1(a)(2), (b)(5). . . . After a jury trial, defendant was convicted of the theft and sentenced accordingly. 720 Ill. Cons. Stat. §5/16-1(b)(5). . . .

ANALYSIS

. . . Article 16 [of the criminal code] defines theft and related offenses. Defendant was charged with theft under section 16-1: "(a) A person commits theft when he knowingly . . . (2) obtains by deception control over property of the owner; . . . and (A) intends to deprive the owner permanently of the use or benefit of the property." 720 Ill. Cons. Stat. §5/16-1(a)(2)(A).

. . . "Theft of property exceeding $10,000 and not exceeding $100,000 in value is a Class 2 felony." 720 Ill. Cons. Stat. §5/16-1(b)(5). . . . "Property" is defined in section 15-1 as follows:

> "'[P]roperty' means anything of value. Property includes real estate, money, commercial instruments, admission or transportation tickets, written instruments representing or embodying rights concerning anything of value, labor, or services, or otherwise of value to the owner; things growing on, affixed to, or found or land, or part of or affixed to any building; electricity, gas and water; telecommunications services; birds, animals and fish, which ordinarily are kept in a state of confinement; food and drink; samples, cultures,

microorganisms, specimens, records, recordings, documents, blueprints, drawings, maps, and whole or partial copies, descriptions, photographs, computer programs or data, prototypes or models thereof, or any other articles, materials, devices, substances and whole or partial copies, descriptions, photographs, prototypes, or models thereof which constitute, represent, evidence, reflect or record a secret scientific, technical, merchandising, production or management information, design, process, procedure, formula, invention, or improvement." 720 Ill. Cons. Stat. §5/15-1.

Relying on People v. Davis, 203 Ill. App. 3d 838, 561 N.E.2d 165 (1990), the appellate court concluded that the occupancy of a hotel room is not "property" as that term is defined in section 15-1. As a result, the stolen property consisted only of food and other incidentals obtained by defendant, valued at over $300, but less than $10,000, and punishable as a Class 3 felony. 720 Ill. Cons. Stat. §5/16-1(b)(4). The *Davis* defendants were indicted for theft of property after it was alleged that they instructed city employees to engage in political activities such as the collection of absentee ballots during time that they were being paid by the City of East St. Louis to work on a public works project. *Davis*, 203 Ill. App. 3d at 841. The trial court dismissed the indictments on the basis that the labor of an employee is not the property of the employer and, thus, diversion of the employee's labor is not a theft. *Davis*, 203 Ill. App. 3d at 841-42.

[In *Davis*, the court] . . . concluded that the statutory definition of property in section 15-1 includes only tangible personal property that was subject to larceny at common law, indicated by the phrase "anything of value," and those other items specifically enumerated in the following sentence. Further, the court stated that section 15-1 "only lists items which may be physically possessed and carried away." *Davis*, 203 Ill. App. 3d at 845. . . .

In the present case, the appellate court noted that except for the subsequent addition of the term "telecommunications services," section 15-1 is identical to the statute at issue in *Davis*. . . .

. . . Because the use of a hotel room is neither tangible personal property nor one of the items specifically enumerated in section 15-1, the appellate court held that the right to use a hotel room is not property that can be stolen by deception under section 16-1. . . .

Whether the Occupancy of a Hotel Room Is "Property"

At common law, the crime of larceny was "the felonious stealing, taking and carrying, leading, riding or driving away the personal goods of another . . . with the felonious intent to deprive the owner of his property." People v. Pastel, 306 Ill. 565, 568, 138 N.E. 194 (1923). Under this traditional definition of larceny, the occupancy of a hotel room clearly could not have been the subject of the crime.

Eventually, the common law crimes were codified by statute. As the State correctly notes, for at least 50 years prior to the adoption of the Criminal

Code of 1961, some items that would not have been subject to the crime of larceny at common law were nevertheless property subject to statutory theft. For example, in Moline Water Power Co. v. Cox, 252 Ill. 348, 96 N.E. 1044 (1911), this court held that water power created by a waterfall was property under the theft statute at the time. This court explained:

> "[Water] [p]ower is not a chattel. It is not a tangible entity. It manifests itself only by its results. But it is property, and is bought and sold in the market as freely as the products of the farm. . . . The use of a fall of water artificially impounded is [the] taking of that which has been produced by the combination of artificial means and natural forces. . . . It is, in fact, an interest in the aggregate of rights constituting the water power, which is real estate." [Id.,] at 357.

Similarly, in People v. Menagas, 367 Ill. 330, 336, 11 N.E.2d 403 (1937), this court held that the defendant was properly charged with larceny of electrical energy because larceny under the Criminal Code had wider application than at common law. The larceny statute then said, " 'Larceny shall embrace every theft which deprives another of his money or other personal property, or those means . . . by which the right and title to property, real or personal, may be ascertained.' " *Menagas*, 367 Ill. at 336, quoting Ill. Rev. Stat. 1935, ch. 38, ¶380.

Our Criminal Code underwent revision in 1961 and the section dealing with crimes against property was entirely reorganized.

> "Formerly, in Illinois, there were some seventy-four separate sections which dealt in one form or another with the obtaining of property of another with the intent to permanently deprive such other or the true owner of the property or its beneficial use. All lawyers and judges are too familiar with the highly technical differences between larceny, larceny by trick, embezzlement, false pretenses, confidence game, and the many variations to require detailed comment. Suffice to say that, with the exception of robbery, burglary, arson, and criminal damage and trespass to property, . . . the Committee intended to codify the entire range of offenses against property into Articles 16 and 17, and to abolish completely the labels and highly technical distinctions which had developed through centuries of case law and statutory amendments." People v. McCarty, 94 Ill. 2d 28, 34, 445 N.E.2d 298 (1983), quoting Ill. Ann. Stat., ch. 38, art. 16, Committee Comments — 1961, at 18.

With this background in mind, we turn to the question of whether the use of a hotel room is property that can be the subject of theft by deception under section 16-1. . . . [T]his inquiry requires the interpretation of two separate statutes. First, we must determine whether the use of a hotel room is property under section 15-1. Second, if the answer to the first question is yes, we must determine whether one who obtains such property by deception can be charged under section 16-1. . . .

The first sentence of section 15-1 states that the word "property" . . . "means anything of value." The appellate court, relying on *Davis*, limited the meaning of "anything" to items of tangible personal property. . . .

The legislature's inclusion, in 1961, of real estate and electricity and, in 1994, of telecommunications services in the statutory definition of property encompassed by the theft statute did away with this ancient rule. Real estate cannot be taken and carried away, yet it is "property" under section 15-1. Similarly, electricity and telecommunications services can be stolen but cannot be taken and carried away.

The phrase "anything of value" is unambiguous. Clearly, the legislature intended to expand the definition of property to include not only items of tangible personal property but also other things of value such as real estate, electricity, and telecommunications services. The hospitality industry provides lodging to the public for profit. The market for hotel and motel rooms is vast. The use of a hotel room does have value. See *Moline Water Power*, 252 Ill. at 357 (stating that water power is property because it "is bought and sold in the market as freely as the products of the farm"). We conclude that the use of a hotel room is a thing of value as that phrase is used in the first sentence of section 15-1. . . .

In light of this statutory [phrase], we reject the appellate court's suggestion that the term "includes" in section 15-1 is ambiguous because the words "but is not limited to" are not present. . . . [E]ven in the absence of the phrase "but is not limited to," the plain, ordinary, and popularly understood meaning of the term "includes" does not support the appellate court's conclusion. . . . According to Black's Law Dictionary, "include" means:

> "To contain as a part of something. The participle *including* typically indicates a partial list [the plaintiff asserted five tort claims, including slander and libel]. But some drafters use phrases such as *including without limitation* and *including but not limited to*—which mean the same thing." Black's Law Dictionary 777-78 (8th ed. 2004) (emphases in original).

. . . [T]he absence of additional verbiage such as "but not limited to" does not render section 15-1 ambiguous. In this section, the word "includes" is used to introduce a list of things of value that illustrate the meaning of the general term "property." . . .

In the present case, the statutory terms "property" and "includes" are unambiguously defined. . . . [Consequently,] the rule of lenity need not be employed. Under this canon of statutory construction, "penal statutes, where ambiguous, should be construed to afford lenity to the accused." People v. Hicks, 164 Ill. 2d 218, 222, 647 N.E.2d 257 (1995). . . . Because section 15-1 is not ambiguous, there is no need for construction and the rule of lenity is not implicated.

The Requirement of Permanent Deprivation of Property

Having concluded that section 15-1 was intended to broaden the definition of property and that the use of a hotel room is property within the meaning of this statute, we turn to the separate question of whether such property may be the subject of theft by deception under section 16-1 of the Criminal Code.

Section 16-1(a)(2) provides that a person commits theft when he knowingly obtains control of the property of another by deception. 720 Ill. Cons. Stat. §5/16-1(a)(2). So long as one of the three required mental states is present, the crime of theft is complete. Defendant was charged under section 16-1(a)(2)(A), the intent "to deprive the owner permanently of the use or benefit of the property." 720 Ill. Cons. Stat. §5/16-1(a)(2)(A). . . .

The parties do not dispute that the hotel is the owner of the property, the meaning of the term "deception," or that defendant obtained control over the hotel room during the period of his occupancy. The question is whether, when the property at issue is the use of a hotel room, it is possible to permanently deprive the owner of its use or benefit. If not, defendant cannot be convicted under section 16-1(a)(2)(A) for its theft.

"Permanent Deprivation," as used in part C of the Criminal Code, means to:

> "(a) Defeat all recovery of the property by the owner; or
> (b) Deprive the owner permanently of the beneficial use of the property; or
> (c) Retain the property with intent to restore it to the owner only if the owner purchases or leases it back, or pays a reward or other compensation for its return; or
> (d) Sell, give, pledge, or otherwise transfer any interest in the property or subject it to the claim of a person other than the owner." 720 Ill. Cons. Stat. §5/15-3.

In the present case, only (a) or (b) are potentially applicable. . . .

The property at issue here is the use of a hotel room. The hotel's complement of rooms can be analogized to a store's inventory of goods. The hotel has a finite number of rooms, which it can rent to members of the public 365 nights each year. One night in one room is a thing of value. When this thing of value is taken by deception, the owner has permanently lost the benefit of one night's income. We, therefore, hold that each night of occupancy that is obtained by deception permanently deprives the owner of the beneficial use of the hotel room within the meaning of section 15-3(b).

Defendant acknowledges that even though the hotel "was deprived of the rental value it should have received for the room on each of the nights" that he and his family occupied the suite, the record does not provide a basis to conclude that the suite would have been rented to another guest who would have paid at least $130 per night. He cites no authority for the proposition that in addition to proving that the value of the property involved exceeded $10,000, the State has the burden of proving that the suite would have been occupied by a paying customer if defendant and his family had not been there.

It is well-settled law that the value of stolen property is the fair cash market value at the time and place of the theft. See, e.g., People v. Josephine, 165 Ill. App. 3d 762, 764, 520 N.E.2d 745 (1987). The rate of $130 per night negotiated by defendant was a discounted rate. The record supports a finding that the value of the stolen property exceeded $10,000.

Theft Versus Use of Property

Defendant also argues that he cannot be prosecuted under section 16-1 for the theft by deception of the use of a hotel room because that offense is codified at section 16-3(a) and must be charged as such.

Section 16-3(a) provides:

> "A person commits theft when he obtains the temporary use of property, labor or services of another which are available only for hire, by means of threat or deception or knowing that such use is without the consent of the person providing the property, labor or services." 720 Ill. Cons. Stat. §5/16-3.

Violation of this section is punishable as a Class A misdemeanor. 720 Ill. Cons. Stat. §5/16-3(c). . . .

Section 16-1(a)(2)(A) requires that the defendant: (1) knowingly obtain control, (2) over the property of the owner, (3) by deception, (4) with the intent to permanently deprive the owner of the use or benefit of the property. The State must also prove (5) the value of the stolen property in order to establish the grade of the offense. Section 16-3(a) requires that he (1) obtain the temporary use of property, (2) that is available only for hire, (3) by threat or deception or knowing that the owner has not consented.

Each offense requires proof of one or more elements not required of the other. To convict a defendant of section 16-1 theft, the State need not prove that the property is available only for hire. To convict a defendant of section 16-3 theft, the State need not prove either the intent to permanently deprive the owner of the use or benefit of the property or the value of the property.

Nevertheless, defendant argues that the use of deception to obtain the temporary use of property that is available only for hire, such as a hotel suite, may be prosecuted *only* under section 16-3. He asserts that section 16-3 is "directed at precisely the sort of conduct" in which he allegedly engaged and that the legislature intended such conduct to be punished as a Class A misdemeanor. *Davis*, 203 Ill. App. 3d at 844 (section 16-3 is "intended to protect businesses from the unscrupulous practices of prospective customers"). . . .

. . . [Section 16-3 is descended from] the first section of "An Act to define and punish frauds upon hotel, inn, boarding and eating-house keepers." The act was approved in 1889. That section provided:

"[A]ny person who shall obtain food, lodging or other accommodation at any hotel, inn, boarding or eating house, with intent to defraud the owner or keeper thereof, shall be deemed guilty of a misdemeanor, and upon conviction, shall be punished by a fine not exceeding one hundred dollars or imprisoned in the county jail not exceeding thirty days." See Ill. Rev. Stat 1933, ch. 38, ¶300.

Defendant also points to the provisions of the Innkeeper Protection Act, which, although contained in the Code of Civil Procedure, parallels the language of section 16-3 of the Criminal Code:

"Any person who, with intent to defraud, shall obtain lodging, food, money, property or other accommodations at a hotel, inn, boarding house or lodging house without paying therefor shall be guilty of a Class A misdemeanor. In case of a second conviction of the offense described, the punishment shall be that provided for a Class 4 felony." 740 Ill. Cons. Stat. §90/5.

. . . The State responds that sections 16-1 and 16-3 are not mutually exclusive. . . . Thus, the State argues, if it can prove the elements of a section 16-1 theft, it may prosecute under that section, even if the property is available for hire and the defendant's conduct might otherwise meet the elements of section 16-3.

. . . [T]he State has the better argument. First, although the Innkeeper Protection Act and the forerunners of section 16-3 have been the law in Illinois for many decades, the legislature has not expressed any intent that these statutes are intended to be the exclusive basis for the prosecution of theft by deception of the use of a hotel room.

Second, the prosecutor has broad discretion in determining whether to charge an individual with a criminal offense and the nature of the offense to be charged. Both this court and the United States Supreme Court have held that the prosecutor has the discretion to decide which of two offenses to charge where two different statutes prohibit the same criminal conduct but prescribe different punishments. People v. McCollough, 57 Ill. 2d 440, 443-44, 313 N.E.2d 462 (1974) (same set of facts may constitute separate offenses under different statutes); United States v. Batchelder, 442 U.S. 114, 123-24 (1979) ("when an act violates more than one criminal statute, the Government may prosecute under either so long as it does not discriminate against any class of defendants").

Where, as here, proof of theft under section 16-1 requires proof of elements not required under section 16-3, it is clear that the prosecutor has the exclusive discretion to decide which charge to bring. People v. Jamison, 197 Ill. 2d 135, 161-62, 756 N.E.2d 788 (2001); see also People v. Barlow, 58 Ill. 2d 41, 44, 317 N.E.2d 49 (1974) (when conduct violates more than one statute and the statutes require different proof or provide different defenses, a defendant is not denied equal protection of the law if he is prosecuted under the statute that provides the greater penalty). . . .

CONCLUSION

In sum, we hold that the occupancy of a hotel room is "property" within the meaning of section 15-1 of the Criminal Code and that the taking of such property by deception can result in the owner's being permanently deprived of its use or benefit. We further hold that the offenses defined in sections 16-1 and 16-3 are not mutually exclusive and that, in the present case, the State properly charged the defendant with theft under section 16-1. Because these questions of law are resolved against the defendant and because a rational trier of fact could have found that defendant intended to permanently deprive the hotel of the use or benefit [of] a suite of rooms, we reverse the judgment of the appellate court as to defendant's conviction of theft. . . .

Justice FITZGERALD, dissenting.

. . . I believe the legislature was careful to exclude the mere "use" of property from the definition of "property" in section 15-1. 720 Ill. Cons. Stat. §5/15-1. That section defines "property" to mean "anything of value." It includes: money, food and drink, real estate, fixtures, telecommunications services, electricity, gas, water, tickets, documents, photographs, computer programs, drawings, models, commercial instruments, and "written instruments representing or embodying rights concerning anything of value, labor, or services, or otherwise of value to the owner." 720 Ill. Cons. Stat. §5/15-1. Notably, the statutory definition of property does not cover labor or services themselves, only written instruments embodying the rights to such services. This definition also does not include the right to temporarily use property. Therefore, the defendant cannot be found guilty of theft by deception of the use of a hotel room under section 16-1 (720 Ill. Cons. Stat. §5/16-1).

I further disagree with [the proposition that] the phrase "anything of value" unambiguously supports the majority's holding. . . . The majority opinion ignores the underlying premise of the sole citation for this proposition. The premise of [the quoted statement in Moline Water Power Co. v. Cox, 252 Ill. 348, 96 N.E. 1044 (1911),] was that one buys and sells the ownership of the electricity in the market, not the right to temporarily use that electricity. In other words, it is not the *rental* of these things which is "bought and sold on the market"; it is the thing itself.

. . . By . . . equat[ing] the mere "use" of a hotel room with a "store's inventory of goods," the majority . . . ignore[s] the distinction between rental, in which the owner allows another temporarily to possess a thing, and the sale of a thing, where ownership of the thing itself changes hands. The [problem with] the majority's analogy is that a store is not in the habit of renting its inventory of goods for temporary use. Because [of] failure to recognize this distinction, I believe the majority has [expanded] section 15-1 . . . beyond the legislature's intention.

Moreover, it is unclear that the Embassy Suites would have otherwise obtained the money for the night's lodging used by defendant. The majority cites no specific evidence that defendant denied the hotel the opportunity to rent the room to another customer. Further, there is no basis to conclude that there were any nights when the hotel was full and another party would have taken the suite. In this context, the mere opportunity that the hotel might have had to take in other money for the suite cannot be found to constitute "property" for purposes of the general theft statute.

The majority's expansive interpretation is problematic for several other reasons. First, tenants and landlords could potentially apply the court's reasoning concerning "use" to criminalize breaches of leases. Commentators have criticized similar approaches because of "the possibility of theft prosecutions in cases of holdover or eviction in a landlord-tenant relationship" and the "problem . . . of distinguishing between theft and criminal trespass." Model Penal Code §223.2, Comment, at 173-74 (1980). Commentators also state that obstacles to theft prosecution in these situations makes sense, for "the immobility and virtual indestructibility of real estate makes unlawful occupancy of land a relatively minor harm for which civil remedies supplemented by mild criminal sanctions for trespass should be adequate." Id. at 172. . . . "Relations between a landlord and a tenant are so minutely regulated and constitute such a delicate socio-political problem that it would be wrong to introduce the possibility of a theft prosecution for unauthorized occupancy by a tenant or improper eviction by a landlord." Id. . . .

. . . Consider three common, hypothetical cases. The first situation is the typical failure of a landlord to provide habitable rental property, even for a short period of time. For instance, a landlord may lack the money or desire to sufficiently winterize the building. Nevertheless, the landlord accepts rent from various tenants in the building, knowing full well that the facilities to provide the building's heat and hot water are inadequate. But he decides to wait until the facilities actually break down in the dead of winter before he fixes the problem. Consequently, the landlord has denied the tenants the benefit of their bargain. The tenants have lost their contractual right to "use" of the apartment, and also the opportunity to rent another apartment before the onset of winter. . . . Under normal circumstances, the landlord would be subject to civil remedies such as a suit by the municipality seeking an injunction to repair the property, and for fines for ordinance violations, or a tenant's suit directly against the landlord for whatever value that the property has been diminished. Following the majority's reasoning, however, the landlord has committed a theft because he consciously deprived the tenants of their rightful "use" of the property to which the tenants were entitled under the lease. . . .

Perhaps clearer is a typical "self-help" eviction. A tenant has not paid rent for three months. Instead of initiating a proceeding for forcible entry and detainer, the landlord deliberately changes the locks on the tenant's apartment, permanently barring the tenant from the property. Because the tenant still retains the right to the "use" of the property for the remainder of the lease, a landlord would be guilty of theft of the tenant's right to "use" the property under the lease.

The third case is one of a holdover tenant. The family's breadwinner has lost his job and is unable to pay rent. The family knows that it is unlikely or unwilling to pay the arrears on the rent and holds out in the apartment until the landlord institutes civil proceedings for forcible entry and detainer. The family avoids the landlord and deprives the landlord of his ability to rent the property to another tenant. Under all normal circumstances, the legislature has given the tenant the benefit of civil legal processes of forcible entry and detainer, which begins with a five-day notice, service of process, and, eventually, a day in court. Thus, the tenant has the legal right to "use" the premises until a court finds that the landlord has the right of possession. This opinion theoretically entitles the landlord to submit a complaint for prosecution upon the tenants for a felony offense punishable by six years in prison in lieu of or in addition to the normal course of civil proceedings. I do not know what the deleterious effects of this additional remedy may be, but I believe that it is best considered by the legislature.

Next, this decision implicates the legislative judgment not to criminalize ordinary cases sounding in contract. I believe the legislature should act with caution in imposing criminal penalties on a hotel guest, landlord, tenant, or any party which has the right to "use" property where contractual remedies remain available. As Judge Posner has stated,

> "[U]nder the common law (including the common law of Illinois . . .), a breach of contract is not considered wrongful activity in the sense that a tort or a crime is wrongful. When we delve for reasons, we encounter Holmes's argument that practically speaking the duty created by a contract is just to perform or pay damages, for only if damages are inadequate relief in the particular circumstances of the case will specific performance be ordered. In other words, and subject to the qualification just mentioned, the entire practical effect of signing a contract is that by doing so one obtains an option to break it. The damages one must pay for breaking the contract are simply the price if the option is exercised. See Holmes, The Path of the Law, 10 Harv. L. Rev. 457, 462 (1897).
>
> "Why such lenity? Perhaps because breach of contract is a form of strict liability. Many breaches are involuntary and so inapt occasions for punishment. Even deliberate breaches are not necessarily culpable, as they may enable an improvement in efficiency. . . . The option of which Holmes spoke was the option not to perform because performance was impossible or because some more valuable use of the resources required for performance arose after the contract was signed." Zapata Hermanos Sucesores, S.A. v. Hearthside Baking Co., 313 F.3d 385, 389-90 (7th Cir. 2002).

Here, the hotel seeks criminal punishment because of the inability, at least initially, to screen out defendant as a customer and thereafter to be made whole through adequate contractual remedies. . . . The holding today calls into question whether a person who deliberately breaches a contract may also be subject to significant criminal penalties.

Lastly, the legislature has already addressed the [relevant] concerns in other statutes. In these provisions, the legislature has specifically outlawed the act of unlawfully using a hotel by employing words such as "use," "lodging," or "accommodations." The legislature has prohibited defendant's behavior in section 16-3(a), which [defines] a Class A misdemeanor. . . . [T]he legislature could have explicitly employed words such as "accommodation," "lodging," or "use" of property in its definition of "property" in section 15-1. [The fact that it did not do so] demonstrates that the legislature intend[s] that defendant's behavior receive punishment as a Class A misdemeanor [only]. . . .

Because of the foregoing reasons, I respectfully dissent.

Justice KILBRIDE joins in this dissent.

Notes and Questions

1. Does punishing Perry amount to criminalizing breaches of contract? Or was Perry's conduct worse than most contractual violations? Should the answers to these questions matter? What, precisely, is wrong with criminally punishing persistent, purposeful breaches of contract?

2. Note Judge Posner's characterization of contractual obligations: "[T]he entire practical effect of signing a contract is that by doing so one obtains an option to break it. The damages one must pay for breaking the contract are simply the price if the option is exercised." This view was classically articulated by Oliver Wendell Holmes in The Path of the Law, 10 Harv. L. Rev. 457 (1897), the Holmes essay cited in Posner's *Zapata* opinion. Holmes' essay is famous for articulating what is known as the "bad man" theory of legal rules—because Holmes described the law as it would be understood by a bad man (or woman: Are only men bad?), someone interested only in the price to be paid for illegality.

3. Perhaps the "bad man" theory is right as applied to contractual obligations. But no one uses language like Holmes' or Posner's to characterize criminal law: Even Judge Posner would hesitate to characterize criminal prohibitions as giving a would-be offender the option of committing the relevant crimes as long as the offender is willing to pay the penalty the legislature specified. To put the point another way, one might argue that the optimal number of breaches of contract is very large. But the optimal number of crimes is presumably zero.

Robert Cooter discusses the distinction between these two types of legal rules in Prices and Sanctions, 84 Colum. L. Rev. 1523 (1984). Cooter's point is that some legal rules do indeed establish a price for engaging in a given kind of conduct; as long as the regulated actor is willing to pay the price, decisions to violate such rules are morally neutral. Other legal rules define behavior that should never happen. According to Cooter, the penalties attached to such behavior are not prices that create options that regulated actors can exercise or not as they wish. Rather, those penalties are sanctions, meant to send the signal that the behavior in question is unacceptable. If Cooter is right, what kind of rule is appropriate in *Perry*?

4. How would most long-term hotel guests answer that question? Such guests might want strict punishment of the Perrys of the world, because that makes it easier to convince hotel managers to strike deals like the one that Perry broke. Are you persuaded? If so, is that a good reason to criminally punish Perry's conduct? One might make a similar argument about a wide range of contract breaches—by submitting oneself to criminal punishment in case of breach, one makes one's contractual promises more reliable, hence more valuable. Is that a good reason to criminally punish breaches of contract generally? Only when the contracting parties agree to the punishment in advance?

5. Recall the cases, excerpted in the notes after *Carter*, discussing the meaning and application of "asportation." Does *Perry* shed light on those issues? Perhaps asportation matters because requiring it limits the kinds of property that can be stolen. Electrical power or hotel room rates cannot be put in one's pocket and carried away. Consequently, appropriating those forms of property did not give rise to criminal penalties; the civil justice system handled such disputes. Now that the alleged technicalities of the common law of theft have been displaced, such disputes *are* subject to criminal penalties. Is that a step forward, or back?

4. Mistake and Abandonment

United States v. Coffmann

United States Navy-Marine Corps Court of Criminal Appeals
62 M.J. 677 (2006)

DORMAN, Chief Judge.

A military judge sitting as a special court-martial convicted the appellant, pursuant to his pleas, of a false official statement and larceny. The appellant's crimes violated Articles 107 and 121, Uniform Code of Military Justice, 10 U.S.C. §§907 and 921. The adjudged and approved sentence consists of a bad-conduct discharge, confinement for 45 days, and reduction to pay grade E-1. . . .

This case was initially submitted without assignment of error. In our initial review of the record, we specified an issue to counsel concerning whether the appellant's guilty plea to larceny was provident. We have carefully considered the record of trial, and the briefs submitted by counsel in response to the specified issue. We conclude that the appellant's plea to larceny was not provident. . . .

The appellant pleaded guilty to the theft of several items of special operations equipment, such as a force vest, canteen covers, and a duty belt (hereinafter referred to as "gear"). The total value of the stolen gear exceeded $500. The gear belonged to another Marine. . . .

The appellant was serving in Al Hillah, Iraq, when he took the gear he was charged with stealing. The gear was located in an open box, and, at the time he took it, the appellant did not know who owned the gear. The appellant found the box in a room that he and others had been told to clean out in preparation for another platoon's arrival. Unit personnel had previously used this room to store their packs. The room contained several boxes that they had been instructed to dispose of, including the box containing the gear. As they cleaned out the room, they discovered items that were never picked up by their owners and appeared to have been left behind for trash. The appellant took the box from a room where unit personnel had been storing their packs and he brought it to his rack. There was no name on the gear, but the appellant knew it did not belong to him. The appellant was the first one to find the box containing the gear. The appellant also knew that the items should not have been discarded. He went up and down the passageway asking whether anyone had left a box of gear in the room. He asked almost the entire platoon. When he could not determine who owned the gear, he decided to use it himself.

The appellant used the gear for about a month while going on patrols. The use continued until his section leader confronted him about whether the gear belonged to him. Initially, the appellant told the section leader that he had purchased the gear. This false statement was prosecuted under Article 107, UCMJ. The appellant did not learn who owned the gear until after he had surrendered it. The owner was a member of the appellant's battalion, and the appellant was acquainted with him. The appellant informed the military judge that if he had not been confronted by the command, he would have continued to use the gear.

As the providence inquiry continued, the appellant then answered "yes" or "no" to a series of questions dealing with the legality of his actions. He admitted that he knew it was wrongful to take the gear, that the gear was not abandoned, that he intended to permanently deprive the owner of the gear, that he had no legal justification or excuse for his actions, and that he took and retained the gear with a criminal state of mind. Record at 13-22. . . . The appellant now argues that his plea is improvident because the military judge failed to adequately inquire into the "apparent defense of ignorance or mistake of fact as to whether the gear . . . was abandoned, lost, or mislaid." Appellant's Brief at 6. The Government counters . . . that the pleas are provident, with no discussion of the law concerning abandoned, lost or mislaid property.

. . . Before accepting a guilty plea, the military judge must explain the elements of the offense and ensure that a factual basis for the plea exists. . . . Mere conclusions of law recited by the accused are insufficient to provide a factual basis for a guilty plea. The accused "must be convinced of, and able to describe all the facts necessary to establish guilt." Rule for Courts-Martial 910(e), Manual for Courts-Martial, Discussion. Acceptance of a guilty plea requires the accused to substantiate the facts that objectively support his plea.

. . . The standard of review to determine whether a plea is provident is whether the record reveals a substantial basis in law and fact for questioning the plea. United States v. Prater, 32 M.J. 433, 436 (C.M.A. 1991). Such rejection must overcome the generally applied waiver of the factual issue of guilt inherent in voluntary pleas of guilty. . . . An abuse of discretion standard is applied in reviewing the question of whether a military judge erred in accepting a guilty plea. . . .

In our review of the record, we determined that the military judge accurately listed the elements of larceny and defined the terms relevant to those elements. Record at 11-13. We also determined that the appellant indicated an understanding of the elements of the offense and that he acknowledged that they correctly described what he did. Id. at 13. Thereafter, the military judge conducted an inquiry with the appellant to determine whether a factual basis for the plea existed. The inquiry went well until such time as the appellant essentially informed the military judge that the gear he took had been left in the room as trash. After that point, most of the questions asked by the military judge called for a "yes" or "no" answer, and many called for legal conclusions. Id. at 19-22.

Abandoned property cannot be the subject of a larceny. United States v. Malone, 14 M.J. 563, 564 (N.M.C.M.R. 1982). The appellant's statement to the military judge that the gear had been left there as trash raised the issue of mistake of fact. Furthermore, since larceny is a specific intent offense, if the appellant had an honest belief that the property was abandoned, he has a complete defense. *Malone*, 14 M.J. at 565.

For a complex offense such as conspiracy, robbery, or murder, a failure to discuss and explain the elements of the offense during the providence inquiry has been held to be fatal to the guilty plea on appeal. United States v. Pretlow, 13 M.J. 85, 88-89 (C.M.A. 1982). Similarly, a military judge should explain the elements of defenses, such as mistake of fact and abandonment, if raised by the appellant during the providence inquiry. If during the plea inquiry an accused "reasonably raises the question of a defense," United States v. Timmins, 45 C.M.R. 249, 253 (C.M.A. 1972), or "'sets up matter inconsistent with the plea' . . . the military judge must either resolve the apparent inconsistency or reject the plea." United States v. Garcia, 44 M.J. 496, 498 (C.A.A.F. 1996) (quoting Art. 45(a), UCMJ). . . .

In the case before us, the military judge failed to explain the mistake of fact defense to the appellant. Although the military judge did ask the appellant if he believed the gear was abandoned, he did not provide the appellant with the legal definition of abandoned property. A reading of the case law with respect to this issue makes clear that the legal significance of the term "abandoned" is not one that would be commonly known and understood by service members.

. . . [W]e conclude that the record reveals a substantial basis in law and fact to question the appellant's guilty plea to larceny. Thus, we conclude that the military judge erred by failing to inform the appellant of the defense of mistake of fact and the definitions and legal significance of abandoned property. . . . When the appellant informed the military judge that the gear had been left behind as trash, the military judge inappropriately asked the appellant "yes" or "no" type questions that called for legal conclusions. By not explaining the relevant legal terms, the military judge denied the appellant the ability to make an informed decision concerning the answers he provided. In light of these errors, we conclude that the appellant's guilty pleas to Charge II and its specification are not provident. . . .

Accordingly, the findings to Charge II and its specification are set aside. The remaining findings are affirmed. In light of our action on the findings, the case is returned to the Judge Advocate General for referral to an appropriate convening authority. . . .

Notes and Questions

1. The requirement that guilty pleas must have a factual basis applies in federal and state law as well as in military law. But military courts generally take the requirement more seriously than civilian courts. In most American jurisdictions, cases like *Coffmann* would slip through the cracks. That fact matters, since guilty pleas are so common in state and federal criminal cases: More than 95 percent of all state-court felony convictions happen by guilty plea; in federal court, the figure is 96 percent. *Coffmann* offers a nice example of a guilty plea process that actually doubles as a fact-finding process. In most places in the United States, guilty pleas are far more casual — meaning that innocent defendants like Coffman go to prison.

2. The court in United States v. Malone, 14 M.J. 563, 564 (N.M.C.M.R. 1982), one of the cases cited in *Coffmann*, offered the following summary of the law of lost or abandoned property and its relationship to the law of theft:

> *Abandoned personal property* is that property which the owner has thrown away. In doing so, the owner relinquishes all right to, and possession of, the goods with no intent to reclaim them. Property which has been abandoned by the owner may be acquired by the first finder. Such a first finder is not a thief.
>
> *Lost personal property* is property which the owner has *involuntarily* parted with because of negligence, carelessness, or other nonvoluntary means (e.g., theft). There is no intent to part with the ownership of such property. Personal property is lost when "accidentally dropped in any public place, public

thoroughfare, or street. . . . In short, property will not be considered to have been lost unless the circumstances are such that considering the place where and the conditions under which it is found, there is an inference that it was left there unintentionally." [1 Am. Jur. 2d, Abandoned, Lost, and Unclaimed, Property, §3 (1962).]

Mislaid personal property is property which the owner voluntarily and *intentionally* lays down in a place where he can again resort to it—then he forgets where he left it. Further,

> If the owner laid the property down in a public place, in a place of business, as in a private compartment of a safe-deposit company, or other place, and then forgets that he has done so, and hence cannot find it . . . it is not lost, but mislaid, property which is still in the constructive possession of the owner.

Id. §3.

An individual who finds *mislaid* personal property, such as the radio and scanner in this case, has no right to its initial possession. . . . [A] finder of mislaid property may be guilty of larceny even though there are no clues that would assist in locating the owner. In the instant case, the occupants of the cubicle had a superior right of possession as against any finder except the true owner.

The finder of *lost* personal property is not in as precarious a position as the finder of *mislaid* personal property. Paragraph 200a(8) of the Manual for Courts-Martial notes:

> A taking or withholding of lost property by the finder is larceny if accompanied by an intent to steal and if a clue to the identity of the . . . owner, or through which such identity may be traced, is furnished by the character, location, or marking of the property, or by other circumstances.

. . . The [property at issue in this case] may have been left by its owner next to the couch with an intent to later retrieve it. In such a case, although the owner has exposed the property to theft, he has not given up possession nor consented to the taking. Cf. Anderson, 2 Wharton's Criminal Law and Procedure §465 (1957) and cases cited therein (for the proposition that property in the constructive, as well as actual, possession of the victim may be the subject of larceny).

Into which category did the allegedly stolen property in *Coffmann* fall? Recall the facts of *Morissette*, excerpted in Chapter 4 at page 252. Into which category did the spent bomb casings in that case fall? Do the categories make sense? How does mistake doctrine interact with the legal rules that define the property rights in each of these categories?

3. Fact patterns like the one in *Coffmann* happen all the time in the civilian world. One person finds property that belongs to another, where the property was accidentally dropped or forgotten. In the military, keeping such property is a crime if the finder has "a clue to the identity of the . . . owner." Should that rule apply to civilians? If, after class, you found a hundred-dollar bill on the floor under the seat next to you, would you keep it? If the person sitting in that seat later discovered that you had her money and reported the incident to the police, would you expect to be held criminally liable for theft?

4. It is fairly easy to tell what happened in *Coffmann*—the defendant gave a detailed account of the facts, and given his plea, that account appears not to have been self-interested. That is not always the case. Defendants charged with theft have good reason to lie, and often do. (Witnesses sometimes lie too, and frequently err.) So the legal standards applied in *Coffmann* and *Malone* rest on two competing concerns. The first is obvious: The court in those cases sought to avoid punishing innocent defendants. The second concern is less obvious but (perhaps) no less important: The court in those cases, and American courts generally, seek to define the law of abandonment in a manner that does not allow *guilty* defendants to escape liability by telling plausible but false stories about how they came to possess the allegedly stolen property. How well does the doctrine described in *Coffmann* and *Malone* address those two competing concerns?

Simms v. District of Columbia

District of Columbia Court of Appeals
612 A.2d 215 (1992)

ROGERS, Chief Judge.

Following a bench trial before Hearing Commissioner John W. King, appellant was found guilty of tampering with a vehicle in violation of 18 DCMR §1105.2(a),* and sentenced . . . to a $160 fine and ten days imprisonment; the sentence was suspended and appellant was placed on six months probation. The trial judge affirmed the commissioner's decision. Appellant now contends that the hearing commissioner erroneously refused to consider appellant's defenses of abandonment and mistake of fact. We affirm.

I

At approximately 7:30 P.M. on May 3, 1990, Captain Joseph Amady of the Metropolitan Police Department observed a group of people attempting to

---

    * [The text of the statute reads:

    It shall be unlawful for any person except members of the police and fire departments in connection with the performance of their official duties to tamper with or move a parked vehicle of any other person unless such person has the permission of the owner or operator of such vehicle. Any person violating this section shall, upon conviction, be fined not more than $300 or imprisoned for not more than 10 days, or both.

—EDS.]

raise a parked Volkswagen Jetta automobile onto the crane of a tow truck. Appellant was standing near a jack and he was placing boards underneath the car. Captain Amady also testified that the police department previously had recovered numerous stolen cars in the same location and that the Jetta being towed did not appear to have been there long. After a computerized check identified the Jetta as a stolen vehicle,[4] Captain Amady charged appellant with tampering with a vehicle.

Linda Hancock, who was present at the time of appellant's arrest, testified that after she had told appellant that she needed a grill and fender for her own Jetta, he escorted her to the stolen Jetta. According to her, before the police arrived appellant examined the stolen Jetta's fender and said, "It might work." He then placed a tire on the Jetta so the tow truck could move it. Ms. Hancock described the car as "an abandoned Jetta in the bushes."

Shawn Clayton, a defense witness, testified that the Jetta looked abandoned to him, since he had seen it a couple of times over the period of a month. He also testified that he overheard appellant talking to someone named Darryl about a request for Jetta parts; appellant told Darryl that he had seen the Jetta in Brandywine Alley, that the "windows are busted out of it . . . [and] it looked like it's brand new," and that he did not know if it was stolen or not.

Appellant also testified about his conversation with Darryl, and that when Linda Hancock asked if he could acquire parts for her Jetta, he told her that he had noticed "a Jetta abandoned" in the same place for "approximately three weeks to a month, [and that] the windows are all busted out and the car is totally destroyed." He had told her that "I don't know if it's been stolen or abandoned, as far as I know it's abandoned. No wheels on it and all that. It's in bad condition." She responded that she would get a tow truck driver, and less than two hours later she returned with a tow truck, and her two brothers had tried to get the Jetta hooked up to the tow truck to pull the Jetta out of the bushes. On cross-examination, when asked if he had said he did not know if the Jetta was stolen or abandoned, appellant explained that he knew the Jetta did not belong to him and that he had seen the Jetta five or six times over the three-weeks-to-a-month period.

The government, in rebuttal, called Officer Simmons who testified that he believed that the Jetta might have had a current Maryland tag on its rear, and that it "was basically pretty much stripped" at the time of appellant's arrest.

In finding appellant guilty, the hearing commissioner rejected appellant's . . . defense that he believed the Jetta had been abandoned by its owner. The hearing commissioner ruled that, in general, abandonment had to be proved by unequivocal, clear and decisive evidence but that since appellant

---

4. Ms. Evelyn Stewart testified that her 1988 Jetta had been stolen in 1990. When she recovered the car, the tires, radio, and seats had been removed.

was not a member of any statutory class permitted under 18 DCMR §1105.2 to touch a vehicle (i.e., the vehicle's owner, the vehicle owner's representative or a government official), abandonment in the nature of a mistake of fact was not a defense. Alternatively, the commissioner ruled that "under either the Government's theory or even the Defense theory, [appellant,] based on the evidence and the facts that I have found beyond a reasonable doubt[,] must be found guilty." Appellant raised [his] abandonment [claim] in a . . . motion before the trial judge, who affirmed the decision of the hearing commissioner without opinion upon entering the judgment and commitment order.

II

Appellant contends that the hearing commissioner erroneously rejected his defense of mistake of fact based on the evidence that appellant thought the stolen Jetta had been abandoned by its owner. He maintains that although the hearing commissioner recognized that tampering under 18 DCMR §1105.2 was a general intent crime, the commissioner concluded that the offense was one of strict liability.

The prohibition against tampering does not ban all forms of contact with a vehicle by individuals not within one of the statutorily exempted groups. See In re R.F.H., 354 A.2d 844 (D.C. 1976). This court has construed the word "tampering" as limiting the regulation's applicability to those who physically contact another's vehicle with "an improper purpose or intent." Id. at 847 (concluding that the regulatory prohibition against tampering with a vehicle was not unconstitutionally vague). The court distinguished lawful and unlawful contact as follows:

> [The definition of tampering] excludes from its coverage the Good Samaritan who is caught turning off the lights of another, because he does not possess an unlawful purpose in acting. It would, however, include those individuals apprehended for prying open or picking a vehicle's lock. . . . It would also include those individuals caught while attempting to pick the lock of an automobile.

Id. at 847.

Appellant's defense that he believed the Jetta was abandoned is essentially a defense of mistake of fact.[6] Williams v. United States, 337 A.2d 772, 774 (D.C. 1975). In general intent crimes, such as tampering with another's vehicle, see R.F.H., 354 A.2d at 847 n.7, a defendant may interpose a mistake

---

6. Although appellant contends that the hearing commissioner rejected two defenses—abandonment and mistake of fact—these are one and the same defense in the instant case. Appellant never raised a mistake of fact defense that was separate and distinct from his abandonment defense. Furthermore, the hearing commissioner never addressed a second mistake of fact defense, but instead, characterized the abandonment defense as being in the nature of a mistake of fact defense.

of fact defense if the defendant proves "to the satisfaction of the fact finder that the mistake was both (1) honest and (2) reasonable." *Williams*, 337 A.2d at 774-75. Thus, appellant's mistake of fact defense is a proper defense to tampering with an automobile because it can negate appellant's general intent to commit the crime, thereby demonstrating that appellant did not physically make contact with the stolen Jetta with an "unlawful purpose." *R.F.H.*, 354 A.2d at 847.

However, where the mistake of fact is based on a claim that the defendant mistakenly believed property had been abandoned by its owner, the court has also stated that:

> An abandonment must be made to appear affirmatively by the party relying on it, and an intention to abandon will not ordinarily be presumed, and this is particularly true if the conduct of the owner can be explained consistently with a continued claim. Proof of abandonment must be made by the one asserting it by clear, unequivocal and decisive evidence.

Peyton v. United States, 275 A.2d 229, 230 (D.C. 1971). The precise relationship between the requirement that an abandonment must be shown by clear, unequivocal and decisive evidence, and the requirement that a defendant demonstrate that his belief that property was abandoned was honest and reasonable, is not immediately clear. *Peyton*'s . . . language might suggest that the focus should be on whether the lawful owner intended to abandon the property, and that a mistake of fact defense resting on a belief that the property was abandoned is somehow different from other mistake of fact defenses, requiring the defendant to satisfy a more burdensome standard of proof. . . . But that is not, and indeed, could not be, the case. See Mullaney v. Wilbur, 421 U.S. 684, 702 (1975) (fact that intent is "peculiarly within the knowledge of the defendant" does not justify shifting burden to defendant); In re Winship, 397 U.S. 358, 364 (1970) (Due Process Clause places burden on government to prove every element of a crime beyond a reasonable doubt). . . .

A mistake of fact defense based on a defendant's belief that property was abandoned by its owner necessarily turns on the defendant's reasonable belief and not on the lawful owner's actual intention to abandon his or her property.[9] See W. LaFave & A. Scott, Substantive Criminal Law §5.1(b), at 581 ("the general principle [is] that ignorance or mistake of fact or law is a defense only if it negates a required mental state [of defendant]"). Therefore, as with any other mistake of fact defense to a general intent crime, the defense of abandonment rests on whether the defendant's belief was

---

9. Objective evidence available to the defendant suggesting that the property had been abandoned would, of course, offer further support for the reasonableness of defendant's belief.

honest and reasonable, see *Williams*, 337 A.2d at 774-75, and is not a special kind of mistake of fact defense placing a heavier burden on the defendant.

The question remains whether the hearing commissioner's ruling that appellant could not interpose a mistake of fact defense was harmless error. The commissioner did not state that appellant's only burden was to show that his mistake was both honest and reasonable. Rather, the commissioner focused initially on the fact that appellant would not have been entitled to a jury instruction because he did not fall within one of the three statutory classes of people entitled to touch a vehicle. Therefore, the commissioner concluded that no such defense was available to appellant. However, thereafter the commissioner made an alternative ruling, that even under the defense theory the evidence established beyond a reasonable doubt that appellant was guilty. The only theory presented by the defense . . . was that appellant had thought that the Jetta was abandoned.

The factual findings underlying the commissioner's ruling are supported by the evidence and are not clearly erroneous. The findings relevant to the mistake of fact defense were that, according to appellant and Mr. Clayton, the Jetta had been in the alley for about a month and did not have any windows or wheels and looked like it needed parts. Further, appellant had stated that he did not know whether the car was abandoned or stolen. The transcript makes clear that appellant did not testify that he believed the car was abandoned by its owner. Rather, just prior to the tampering incident, he admitted to others that he did not know whether the car had been abandoned or stolen. The commissioner could reasonably infer that appellant's admission reflected that he knew there was an alternative explanation for the vehicle's condition that was consistent with a continuous claim of ownership by the Jetta's owner. The fact that the Jetta had been stripped of its tires and radio and had its windshield broken, much less its location in the bushes, did not require the commissioner to credit appellant's defense.[11] Abandonment cannot be presumed merely because of the location and condition of the car since those circumstances "[could] be explained consistently with a continued claim" by the owner. *Peyton*, 275 A.2d at 230. The Jetta was only about two years old, and had a current registration tag on the rear. Appellant never disputed that the car had a current license plate on it. The Jetta also was in an area where numerous stolen vehicles had previously

---

11. As noted by the court in Kearns v. McNeill Bros. Moving & Storage Co., 509 A.2d 1132 (D.C. 1986):

> Abandoned property is that to which the over has voluntarily relinquished all right, title, claim, and possession, with the intention of terminating his [or her] ownership, but without vesting it in any other person and with the intention of not reclaiming future possession or resuming its ownership, possession, or enjoyment.

Id. at 1136. A thief does not acquire ownership interest in the goods he or she steals, and thus cannot abandon them in the legal sense of the word.

been recovered by the police, although, admittedly, there was no showing that appellant had reason to be aware of this fact. However, there also was no testimony of any structural damage to the body of the car that would suggest that the Jetta's damage resulted from an automobile accident. Thus, there was sufficient evidence for the commissioner to find that appellant realized that the car might not be abandoned.

Accordingly, we affirm the judgment.

Notes and Questions

1. If *Coffmann* is a good example of the type of abandoned property claim a middle-class theft defendant might raise, *Simms* offers a good picture of the kind of claim poorer defendants sometimes raise. Notice that Coffmann's claim wins, while Simms' claim loses. Are those results fair? Was Simms' conduct more culpable than Coffmann's or less so? Add another case to the comparison—State v. Varszegi, 635 A.2d 816 (Conn. 1993), excerpted in Chapter 3—and the pattern seems even more stark. In *Varszegi*, a landlord broke into the tenant's office on leased property and took the tenant's computer because the tenant was behind on her rent. The defendant's claim that he believed he was entitled to take the computer allowed him to escape criminal liability. Whose claim seems stronger, Varszegi's or Simms'? Perhaps the best explanation of the doctrine is that property rights are better protected when threatened by poor people than when threatened by middle-class defendants.

2. On the other hand, *Simms* might actually be better for the residents of poor neighborhoods than the opposite result. Poor city neighborhoods suffer from a lack of business investment. One reason for low investment is fear of crime—owners of stores and other businesses fear opening up shop in places where thefts and criminal violence are common. That deprives local residents of needed jobs. And those local residents likewise bear the brunt of local crime—rates of burglary, robbery, and auto theft (the crime that gave rise to *Simms*) are much higher in poor neighborhoods than in their middle- and upper-class counterparts. Strict enforcement of the relevant property rights might be bad news for Simms, but it might be good news for his neighbors. Does *that* sound right?

3. Assume that the Jetta was stolen, as the *Simms* court suggests. Assume further that the thief drove the car for a time, was in an accident, managed to put the car in the bushes, and left it there. Should the Jetta be considered abandoned property? Its owner hadn't abandoned it, but the thief may well have done so. In a prosecution of someone other than the thief—Simms, for example—should it matter who did the abandoning? From Simms' point of view, the only relevant question is whether the car is likely to be reclaimed before it is stripped. Even if the owner would like her car back, she can't reclaim it if she has no idea where it is. Functionally, the Jetta may stand in much the same posture as the abandoned bomb casings in *Morissette v. United States*, 342 U.S. 246 (1952), excerpted in Chapter 4. There too, the property owner—in *Morissette*, the Army—wished not to relinquish its claims to the property in question. At the same time, the Army was unlikely to *do* anything with its property. Morissette took the bomb casings because he assumed, rightly, that if he didn't, they would be either left to rust or taken by someone else. Simms started to remove the Jetta's fender because he assumed that if he didn't, the car would either be left to rust or stripped by someone else. Morissette won. If Simms' assumption was reasonable, shouldn't he win too? What explains the different results in the two cases?

4. Perhaps the answer to the last question is simply a matter of formal legal doctrine: Simms was charged with a general intent crime, whereas Morissette, Varszegi, and Coffmann were all charged with crimes requiring proof of specific intent. So any mistake of fact in *Simms* had to be honest and reasonable, while a merely honest mistake was enough to excuse the other three defendants. But that explanation explains less than it seems. Judging by the court's opinion, Simms lost not because his mistake was unreasonable but because he was mistaken about the wrong thing. Assume Simms believed the Jetta was stolen, wrecked, and then abandoned by the thief; assume further that such vehicles are rarely recovered from the area in question. Under *Simms*, that belief—it seems wrong to call it a "mistake," since it probably wasn't mistaken—would not excuse the defendant from criminal liability, because he did not believe the car was abandoned *by its owner*. Accordingly, Simms could be liable not only for tampering, but for theft as well: He was preparing to remove the car's grill and fender for his friend Linda Hancock. The reasonableness, even the correctness, of his belief turns out not to matter.

Does that result make sense? Do you think it made sense to Simms?

C. EXTORTION

United States v. Zhou

United States Court of Appeals for the Second Circuit
428 F.3d 361 (2005)

MINER, Circuit Judge.

Defendants-appellants . . . appeal from judgments of conviction entered in the United States District Court for the Southern District of New York, following a jury trial, convicting each of the Appellants, under a superseding indictment, of one count of conspiracy to commit extortion, in violation of 18 U.S.C. §1951; one count of extortion, in violation of 18 U.S.C. §§2 and 1951; three counts of conspiracy to commit robbery, in violation of 18 U.S.C. §1951; [and] three counts of robbery, in violation of 18 U.S.C. §§2 and 1951. . . .

Appellants contend that the evidence adduced at trial to prove their guilt in connection with the charged counts of extortion and of conspiracy to commit extortion was insufficient as a matter of law. We agree and, accordingly, reverse the convictions of Appellants under Counts One and Two. . . .

BACKGROUND

. . . The charges in the Indictment have their genesis in a series of robberies and related incidents that occurred in Manhattan's "Chinatown" during a six-month period between the summer of 2001 and the early months of 2002. The first such incident occurred in or around July 2001 at 75 Eldridge Street—an illegal gambling parlor located behind a clothing store. On or about July 23, 2001, at approximately 6:00 P.M., an unknown caller telephoned Chen Tin Hua ("Hua"), a "shareholder" in the gambling operation, and identified himself as being associated with "Vietnamese Boy"—presumably, co-defendant/cooperating witness Xiao Qin Zhou ("Xiao"). The caller stated that Vietnamese Boy would come to the gambling parlor later that day to pick up $10,000, which the caller instructed Hua to place in a red envelope. Hua told the caller that he had no money and hung up.

Later that evening, while in the parlor, Hua was summoned outside by a group of men demanding to speak with him. Awaiting Hua were Appellants—Chen and Lin—along with Xiao and co-defendant Li Wei. All four pointed guns at Hua, and Xiao demanded that he give them $10,000. Hua told the group that he had no money. Xiao struck Hua on the head, and Li Wei, using his gun, struck Hua in the stomach. Xiao then ripped a necklace from around Hua's neck, and the group fled the scene in a vehicle. . . .

DISCUSSION

As noted above, Appellants contend that the evidence adduced at trial was insufficient to sustain the convictions of Appellants on the extortion-related crimes charged in Counts One and Two and, concomitantly, on the firearm crime charged in Count Three. . . .

In order to prove a conspiracy, the Government must show that two or more persons entered into an agreement to commit the substantive offense as charged and that an overt act in furtherance of the conspiracy was committed. "In order to convict a given defendant of conspiracy, the Government must prove that he knew of the conspiracy and joined it with the intent to commit the offenses that were its objectives, that is, with the affirmative intent to make the conspiracy succeed." United States v. Ceballos, 340 F.3d 115, 123-24 (2d Cir. 2003). . . .

Here, the object of the alleged conspiracy was to commit extortion, which, in the context of federal crimes, in relevant part, "means the obtaining of property from another, *with his consent*, induced by wrongful use of actual or threatened force, violence, or fear." 18 U.S.C. §1951(b)(2) (emphasis added). Extortion is frequently exemplified by "revenue-producing measures . . . utilized by organized crime to generate income"—measures "such as shakedown rackets and loan-sharking." United States v. Nardello, 393 U.S. 286, 295 (1969). . . .

Choice on the part of the victim is a common theme in all extortion cases. As noted above, "the Hobbs Act definition of coercion speaks of obtaining property from another 'with his consent.'" United States v. Arena, 180 F.3d 380, 394 (2d Cir. 1999). [The Hobbs Act's proponents] "understood extortion to encompass situations in which a victim is given the option of relinquishing some property immediately or risking unlawful violence resulting in other losses, and he simply *chooses* what he perceives to be the lesser harm." Id. at 395 (emphasis added). "In order to foreclose any argument by an extortionist that the relinquishment of property in such circumstances was [truly] voluntary, [however,] the Hobbs Act definition of extortion simply prohibits the extortionist from forcing the victim to make such a choice." Id.

. . . [U]ndeniably, the victim of an extortion acts from fear. . . . But both the language of the statute and the relevant precedents make clear that he or she always retains some degree of choice in whether to comply with the extortionate threat, however much of a Hobson's choice that may be. . . . [T]his element of consent is the razor's edge that distinguishes extortion from robbery, which, in contrast, is defined in pertinent part as

> the unlawful taking or obtaining of personal property from the person or in the presence of another, *against his will*, by means of actual or threatened force, or violence, or fear of injury, immediate or future, to his person or property, or property in his custody or possession, or the person or property of a relative or member of his family or of anyone in his company at the time of the taking or obtaining.

18 U.S.C. §1951(b)(1) (emphasis added).

Among the essential elements of the federal crime of extortion, then, are (i) the defendant's "use of actual or threatened force, violence, or fear," and (ii) the victim's consent—however forced—to the transfer of the property. 18 U.S.C. §1951(b)(2). And . . . essential to a determination of conspiracy to commit extortion are (i) an agreement to use actual or threatened force to obtain property with the consent of the victim and (ii) actions taken in affirmative furtherance of that agreement.

Here, the Government's theory is that Appellants conspired to extort—and in fact committed extortion, and not robbery—when they "informed Hua by telephone that [Xiao] was coming to the gambling parlor to collect $10,000 from him," instructing him to leave the money for Xiao's pick-up in a red envelope, and, later, when they "summoned Hua outside the parlor and attempted to collect the money that had been demanded in the extortionate telephone call." The Government contends that "this call clearly represented a request, albeit under duress, for the money, rather than a forcible taking." "After all," the Government observes, "robbers typically do not telephone in their requests to victims ahead of time." In making this distinction between robbery and extortion, however, the Government fails to identify any element of "duress," either express or implied, in the telephone call, thus calling into question whether the Government has proved each and every element of the extortion-related crimes charged in the Indictment. . . .

Hua, the victim of the 75 Eldridge Street crime, testified as follows regarding the above-noted telephone call that he received on July 23, 2001:

> **Q:** Did you receive any telephone calls at the gambling parlor on July 23, 2001?
> **A:** Yes.
> **Q:** How many telephone calls did you receive that day?
> **A:** One call. . . .
> **Q:** Did [the caller] identify himself by name?
> **A:** He did. He identified himself as Vietnamese Boy,[1] and he demanded money from me. . . .
> **Q:** And what specifically did he say to you?
> **A:** He said Vietnamese Boy, he will come over to me to pick up money and I should give him $10,000. . . .
> **Q:** Did he say anything about how Vietnamese Boy [would] pick up that money?
> **A:** He said that I should put it in the red envelope, $10,000 worth, inside the red envelope.
> **Q:** What, if anything, did you say to the caller?
> **A:** I said I have no money.
> **Q:** Did the caller say anything back to you at that point?
> **A:** No. I hung up the phone.

Hua further testified that four individuals came to 75 Eldridge Street at approximately 8:00 P.M. on July 23, 2001. These individuals asked another employee of the gambling parlor to summon Hua outside. When Hua went outside, four individuals were waiting, pointing guns at him. Thereafter, Xiao, aka "Vietnamese Boy," asked Hua for $10,000. When Hua said that he had no money, one of the other men poked Hua in the side with his gun, and Xiao hit Hua on his head. Xiao then ripped the necklace from Hua's neck, after which all four of the men got into a car and drove off. . . .

---

1. "Vietnamese Boy" is an alias of Xiao.

. . . The Indictment clearly and expressly charges Appellants with conspiring "to commit extortion, as the term is defined in [18 U.S.C. §1951(b)(2)], by conspiring to obtain property from and with the consent of others, . . . which consent would be and was induced by the wrongful use of actual and threatened force, violence and fear." The jury charge, too, expressly recited "the victim's consent" as an element of extortion. There is nothing in the Record, however, to suggest that there was an agreement to obtain the property of either Hua or the gambling operation at 75 Eldridge by consent—forced or otherwise. An inference may fairly be drawn that Appellants and others agreed to visit the 75 Eldridge Street parlor to rob it, but that is all.

. . . [T]he evidence establishes that on at least eight separate occasions, Xiao discussed an agreement between himself, Appellants, and others. But each time the criminal conduct was discussed, it was in terms of a robbery. Extortion was neither spoken of nor apparently ever contemplated. Indeed, not a single fact was elicited from Xiao that could lead to an inference that a co-conspirator planned, or agreed, to *extort*—as opposed to rob—the gambling parlor at 75 Eldridge Street or any individual at that location.

Again, absent from the Record is any indication that Appellants thought, or sought, to obtain property from Hua, or anyone else at 75 Eldridge Street, by means of a forced consent. Rather, the Record supports an agreement among, and an actual effort by, Appellants and others to get a person at that location to open a door so that Appellants and others could enter the establishment and rob it. . . . [T]he only evidence that even arguably [indicated] extortion came from Hua, who testified that he was gambling at the 75 Eldridge Street parlor when he received a phone call, either from Xiao or someone on Xiao's behalf.

Hua testified that the caller demanded $10,000. Hua refused and hung up the phone. Later, Hua was summoned to come outside the parlor, where he was confronted by Xiao, Appellants, and another gangster, all of whom were pointing guns at Hua. Xiao demanded $10,000, and Hua refused, informing the gangsters that he had no money. Xiao then hit Hua in the head, grabbing the chain from around his neck, and the gang fled. Xiao testified that the chain was later sold and that he, Appellant, and Li Wei then split the proceeds. It seems inescapable that this incident was nothing more nor less than a classic robbery.

. . . [As for] the alleged extortionate phone call[,] . . . absent from Hua's testimony is any suggestion that the call itself conveyed any degree of threat—implied or express, violent or otherwise. Thus, . . . the evidence does not support any inference of a threat in the phone call.

The Government contends, however, that the fact of the phone call *combined* with the facts surrounding the gang's visit to 75 Eldridge reasonably supports the inference that the purpose of the call was to extort, since the demand for $10,000, which was initially made by telephone, was then repeated by the gang in person before they resorted to violence and took the chain. Thus, concludes the Government, the phone call was both an attempted extortion and an act in furtherance of an extortion conspiracy. But again, there was no testimony that the call itself was threatening in any way. . . .

The caller recited no consequences—deleterious or otherwise—of a failure to tender the $10,000, and no evidence was put before the jury suggesting that any such consequences were implied by the caller or understood implicitly by Hua. Moreover, there was nothing in Hua's testimony from which one could reasonably infer that he was placed in a subjective state of fear, or felt threatened in any way, by the call. Hua testified that Xiao "was somewhat familiar" to him; that he had seen Xiao "once or twice in Chinatown"; and that he knew Xiao by the name "Vietnamese Boy." But Hua said nothing from which a juror could reasonably infer that Xiao was feared in the neighborhood or known to be involved in criminal activities; nor was there anything else in the Record to support such an inference. . . . If the name "Vietnamese Boy" was intended to strike fear in the heart of Hua, there is simply no evidence that it in fact did so. . . . [The fact] that Hua hung up the phone after stating simply that he had no money suggests that he saw no negative consequences in refusing to consent to the demand or, for that matter, in ignoring the call altogether. . . .

A robbery plus a cryptic and ambiguous phone call does not equal extortion—at least, not on the facts presented to us in this case. . . .

. . . [W]e conclude that the evidence put forward by the Government to prove the charged extortion and conspiracy to extort, even viewed in the light most favorable to the prosecution, was insufficient as a matter of law to prove the crimes charged in Counts One and Two of the Indictment. At best, the evidence proves an uncharged conspiracy to rob, and the robbery of, an individual at 75 Eldridge Street. Accordingly, we reverse the convictions of Appellants under Counts One and Two, for the crimes of conspiracy to extort and extortion, respectively. . . .

Notes on the Meaning of Extortion

1. The Hobbs Act, 18 U.S.C. §1951, is the chief federal extortion statute (as well as a major federal robbery statute). It reads:

> (a) Whoever in any way or degree obstructs, delays, or affects commerce or the movement of any article or commodity in commerce, by robbery or extortion or attempts or conspires so to do, or commits or threatens physical violence to any person or property in furtherance of a plan or purpose to do anything in violation of this section shall be fined under this title or imprisoned not more than twenty years, or both.
>
> (b) As used in this section—

(1) The term "robbery" means the unlawful taking or obtaining of personal property from the person or in the presence of another, against his will, by means of actual or threatened force, or violence, or fear of injury, immediate or future, to his person or property, or property in his custody or possession, or the person or property of a relative or member of his family or of anyone in his company at the time of the taking or obtaining.

(2) The term "extortion" means the obtaining of property from another, with his consent, induced by wrongful use of actual or threatened force, violence, or fear, or under color of official right. . . .

18 U.S.C. §1951. *Zhou* deals with the line between robbery and extortion under this federal statute.

2. What makes the incident in *Zhou* robbery rather than extortion? The fact that the victim had no choice? In *Zhou* itself, that line works: The robbers "ripped a necklace from around Hua's neck, and the group fled the scene. . . ." But in many robbery cases, the victim hands the money over in order to avoid being shot or stabbed. Those victims have a choice: They can refuse to cooperate with their victimizers and take the consequences. Yet courts routinely call such cases robberies. Why? If victim "consent" is not the source of the robbery-extortion line, what is?

Stuart Green argues that the defining feature of extortion and blackmail is not the presence of consent but its absence: Green calls extortion "theft by coercion"—which appears to be the *Zhou* court's definition of robbery. See Stuart P. Green, Theft by Coercion: Extortion, Blackmail, and Hard Bargaining, 44 Washburn L.J. 553 (2005). Green's theory plainly finds support in the Hobbs Act, which defines extortion as "the obtaining of property" through "force, violence, or fear." Yet the Act also requires that property be obtained "with [the victim's] consent." How can a taking be both coerced and consensual?

3. Maybe the answer is that a given criminal transaction can have different characteristics at different times. Suppose the phone conversation in *Zhou* had been more explicitly threatening, as the defendants probably intended. Suppose further that Hua had given the defendants some cash when they arrived at his club. On those facts, the property would have been obtained consensually, if one looks only at the moment when the cash is handed over. Viewed from a larger time frame (i.e., one that includes the phone call), the transfer in that hypothetical case is plainly coerced. Perhaps the strange definition of extortion aims to capture those two conclusions. The "consent" in robbery cases follows immediately after the threat: The robber says "your money or your life," and the victim hands over his wallet. Extortion cases are different: The threat happens at one time and place; the money changes hands later and elsewhere. From this perspective, extortion is slow robbery.

Speed and time are not the only factors in drawing the robbery-extortion line. In robbery cases, consent is obviously fictive, and the threats are not subtle. That is why robberies look like robberies to those who witness them—there is little ambiguity to the crime. Again, extortion is different. When the threat comes at one time and place and property changes hands at another, the transfer may look entirely legitimate. In short, extortionate transactions do not identify themselves. Witnesses see money pass from one set of hands to another, but the passing may not indicate that a crime has been committed. That captures the essence of the offense: It is the functional equivalent of robbery, but is (often) designed to look like an ordinary legal exchange of money for goods and services. To put the point another way, extortion is deceptive robbery; the crime tends to combine elements of force and fraud. The crime in *Zhou* was pure force.

4. At common law, extortion was a close relative not of robbery, but of bribery. Blackstone defined extortion as "an abuse of public justice, which consists in an officer's unlawfully taking, by colour of his office, from any man, any money or thing of value, that is not due to him, or more than is due, or before it is due." 4 W. Blackstone, Commentaries *141. That public-sector branch of extortion doctrine still survives; in the Hobbs Act, it is covered by the language barring extortion "under color of official right." 18 U.S.C. §1951(b)(2). Many contemporary extortion cases likewise involve no hint of violence: Threats of economic and reputational harm may supply the necessary element of force.

5. The original impetus for the Hobbs Act was labor violence. But in United States v. Enmons, 410 U.S. 396 (1973), the Supreme Court held that acts of violence by union members during a strike did not constitute "extortion" within the meaning of the Hobbs Act, because although the strikers' chosen *means* may have been unlawful, their *end*—higher wages—was not "wrongful." *Enmons* placed ordinary labor violence outside the scope of the Hobbs Act (where it still remains today), but the Court's reasoning has broader implications. Because of the decision in *Enmons*, "actual or threatened force, violence, or fear" can be defined broadly—because only the "wrongful" use of those things is forbidden. Consider the relevance of that proposition to the next case.

United States v. Jackson

United States Court of Appeals for the Second Circuit
180 F.3d 55 (1999)

KEARSE, Circuit Judge.

Defendants Autumn Jackson, Jose Medina, and Boris Sabas appeal from judgments of conviction entered in the United States District Court for the Southern District of New York following a jury trial. . . . Jackson and Medina were convicted of threatening to injure another person's reputation with the intent to extort money, in violation of 18 U.S.C. §875(d); all three defendants were convicted of traveling across state lines to promote extortion, in violation of the Travel Act, 18 U.S.C. §1952(a)(3), and conspiring to commit extortion, in violation of 18 U.S.C. §371. Sabas was found not guilty of making extortionate threats. Jackson, Medina, and Sabas were sentenced principally to 26, 63, and 3 months' imprisonment, respectively. . . . On appeal, defendants contend chiefly that the district court failed to give proper jury instructions as to the nature of extortion. For the reasons that follow, we agree, and we accordingly vacate the judgments and remand for a new trial.

BACKGROUND

The present prosecution arises out of defendants' attempts to obtain up to $40 million from William H. ("Bill") Cosby, Jr., a well-known actor and entertainer, by threatening to cause tabloid newspapers to publish Jackson's claim to be Cosby's daughter out-of-wedlock. . . . Taken in the light most favorable to the government, the evidence showed the following.

In the early 1970s, Cosby had a brief extramarital affair with Jackson's mother, Shawn Thompson. After Jackson was born in 1974, Thompson told Cosby that he was the father. Cosby disputed that assertion, and according to Jackson's birth certificate, her father was one Gerald Jackson. Jackson's grandmother testified, however, that she and Thompson told Jackson, as Jackson was growing up, that Cosby was her biological father. The grandmother told Jackson that Cosby had said that, so long as they "didn't tell anyone about it, that he would take care of her mother and her, and take care of his responsibility."

For more than 20 years after Jackson's birth, Cosby provided Thompson with substantial sums of money, provided her with a car, and paid for her admission to substance-abuse treatment programs. . . . Between 1974 and mid-1994, Cosby gave Thompson a total of more than $100,000, typically having traveler's checks or cashier's checks issued in the name of an employee rather than his own name. In 1994, Cosby established a trust fund for Thompson, which was administered by John P. Schmitt, a partner in the New York City law firm that represented Cosby. The trust fund provided Thompson with $750 a week for as long as Cosby chose to fund the trust. Thompson received approximately $100,000 in payments from this fund from mid-1994 until the fund was exhausted, and not replenished, in early 1997.

In addition, Cosby, who had funded college educations for some 300 persons outside of his own immediate family, . . . had offered to pay for the education of Jackson and of Thompson's other two children. In about 1990, after a telephone conversation with Jackson's grandmother, Cosby became concerned that Jackson's education was being hampered by conditions at her California home, and he arranged to have Jackson finish high school at a preparatory school in Florida associated with a Florida college. Cosby thereafter also created a trust to pay for Jackson's college tuition and for certain personal expenses such as food, rent, utilities, and medical costs while Jackson was attending college. This trust was administered by Schmitt's law partner Susan F. Bloom. Jackson subsequently enrolled in a community college in Florida. While Jackson was in school, Cosby spoke with her by telephone approximately 15 times to encourage her to pursue her education, telling her that although he was not her father, he "loved her very, very much" and would be a "father figure" for her. . . .

In April 1995, Bloom learned that Jackson had dropped out of college, and Bloom therefore ceased making payments to Jackson from the college education trust. . . .

In the fall of 1996, Jackson and her then-fiancé Antonay Williams were living in California and working for a production company in Burbank, California, headed by Medina. Medina's company, which operated out of his hotel suite, was attempting to produce a children's television show. Jackson, Williams, and Sabas had acting roles in the show; along with cooperating witness Placido Macaraeg, they also had administrative positions. Jackson worked without pay, but she expected to receive a commission when the television show was sold.

In December 1996, Jackson reinitiated contact with Cosby. Within a four-day period, she telephoned him seven times and left urgent messages asking him to return her calls. In one instance, Jackson identified herself as "Autumn Cosby," a message that Cosby perceived as "some sort of threat." When he returned Jackson's call, he reproached her for using his name. Jackson described the project on which she was working, told Cosby that she was homeless, and asked him to lend her $2100. Cosby initially refused and suggested that she instead get an advance from the person for whom she was working. After further reflection, Cosby called Jackson back and agreed to send her the $2100 she had requested, plus an additional $900; he urged her to return to school, and he renewed his offer to pay for her education. Cosby directed his attorneys to tell Jackson that he would pay for her education and related expenses if she returned to school, maintained a B average, and got a part-time job. . . .

On January 2 and 3, 1997, Jackson spoke with Bloom and Schmitt by telephone and asked that she be sent money for food, lodging, and tuition. Bloom responded that Jackson had not shown that she was enrolled in school. Bloom and Schmitt reiterated that Cosby would not pay for Jackson's support until she enrolled in school and secured employment for eight hours a week; they advised her that her unpaid work at Medina's production company did not satisfy the condition that she get a part-time job. . . .

. . . [O]n January 6, Jackson left a voice-mail message for Peter Lund, president and chief executive officer of CBS, whose television network currently carried Cosby's prime-time program. Stating that her name was Autumn Jackson, Jackson said: "I am the daughter of Doctor William Cosby, Jr. I need to speak with you . . . regarding this relationship . . . that he and I have, and how this will affect CBS if I go to any tabloids." . . .

. . . [O]n January 7, Jackson telephoned Schmitt and asked if there was any chance that Cosby "would send her money to live on." When Schmitt responded in the negative, Jackson said that if she did not receive money from Cosby, she would have to go to the news media. Schmitt testified that he replied that if Jackson meant that "she was planning to go to the news media with what she believed was damaging information and would refrain from doing so only if Mr. Cosby paid her money, that that was extortion, that was both illegal and disgraceful." . . . Jackson stated that she had "checked [it] out and she knew what she was doing."

During the week of January 6, Jackson and Medina discussed ways to intensify the pressure on Cosby and his corporate sponsors. . . . [Those] discussions resulted in . . . the mailing on January 10 and 11 of company solicitation letters that . . . included a paragraph referring to Jackson as the daughter of a "CBS megastar" who was "CBS's most prized property," and stating that, contrary to the star's public image as an advocate of parenting, the star had left Jackson "cold, penniless, and homeless." Letters containing this paragraph were sent to the President and Vice President of the United States, the Governor of California, the Mayor of New York City, CBS, Eastman Kodak, Philip Morris Company, which was another Cosby sponsor, two publishing companies that had published Cosby's books, and many other companies. . . .

On January 15, 1997, after the telephone calls and letters of the week before had failed to produce the desired results, Medina and Jackson contacted Christopher Doherty, a reporter for The Globe tabloid newspaper. Medina and Jackson told Doherty that Cosby was Jackson's father and asked what her story would be worth. To support the story, Medina described for Doherty an affidavit in which Jackson had stated (falsely) that Cosby admitted his paternity. Medina faxed Doherty a copy of Bloom's December 13, 1996 letter to Jackson setting out the terms under which Cosby offered to pay Jackson's tuition. After some negotiation of terms, Doherty agreed that The Globe would purchase the rights to Jackson's story of her relationship to Cosby for $25,000.

That evening, Doherty brought to Medina's hotel a "source agreement," for the signatures of both Jackson and Medina, setting forth the terms under which The Globe would buy the rights to Jackson's story. . . .

The agreement with The Globe was never signed. Instead, on the following morning, January 16, Jackson faxed a copy of the agreement, after obliterating the $25,000 price, to Schmitt. In addition, Jackson faxed Schmitt a letter stating, "I need monies and I need monies now." Jackson's letter . . . concluded:

If I don't hear from you by today for a discussion about my father and my affairs, then I will have to have someone else in CBS to contact my father for me. I want to talk to my father because I need money and I don't want to do anything to harm my father in any way. . . . Enclosed you will find a copy of a contract that someone is offering monies for my story, which is the only property I have to sell in order to survive.

The fax cover letter directed Schmitt to "R.S.V.P." to Jackson in Medina's hotel suite.

Schmitt called Jackson later that morning. Medina, Jackson, Williams, Sabas, and Macaraeg were present. . . . With Medina mouthing words and passing notes to Jackson, Jackson and Schmitt had the following conversation . . . :

SCHMITT: I, I received your letter, Autumn.
JACKSON: Okay.
SCHMITT: [Clears throat] How, how much money are you asking for, Autumn?
JACKSON: I'm wanting to settle, once and finally.
SCHMITT: What, what are you asking for?
JACKSON: I'm asking for 40 million, to settle it completely.
SCHMITT: And if our answer to that is no?
JACKSON: Well, like I said, I have offers, and I will go through with those offers.
SCHMITT: And those offers are to sell your story to the Globe? [Pause.] Autumn, are you there?
JACKSON: Yes I am.
SCHMITT: Is that what you're referring to, the contract that you sent me, that, for sale to the Globe of your story?
JACKSON: Them, as well as any others. [Pause.]
SCHMITT: Well, I'm, I'm sure you know the answer to that is no, Autumn. Thank you very much.

Jackson asked to have her "father" call her; Schmitt responded that Jackson's father was "Mr. Jackson," and that she should "not expect a call from Mr. Cosby." Macaraeg testified that when the conversation ended, Jackson looked frustrated and told the group that Schmitt "doesn't understand the meaning of the term settlement," and Medina said, "if [Cosby] doesn't want this to get out, he's going to have to pay a lot of money." . . .

Some hours later, Jackson and Medina faxed a letter to CBS president Lund. They attached a copy of the unsigned source agreement with The Globe, again with the price redacted. In the letter, which was signed "Autumn J. Jackson-Cosby" and bore the heading "ATTENTION: PLEASE FORWARD THIS LETTER TO MY FATHER, WILLIAM H. COSBY, JR.," Jackson said that Cosby's failure to acknowledge her as his daughter had left her mentally anguished and financially impoverished. . . . Jackson's letter to Lund concluded: "I am willing to decline this offer and all others upon a fair settlement. . . . [Cosby's] show and his private life just happens [sic] to be one of your best properties and this disclosure . . . could undoubtedly effect [sic] your ratings negatively."

When Schmitt informed Cosby of Jackson's demand for $40 million[], Cosby responded that he would not pay. . . . That afternoon, Cosby instructed Schmitt to report Jackson's threats to the Federal Bureau of Investigation.

At the direction of the FBI agents, Schmitt telephoned Jackson for the purpose of allowing the agents to hear and record her demands. In that conversation, Schmitt told Jackson that Cosby had changed his mind and now wanted to come to an arrangement with her. Schmitt asked Jackson how much money she needed, saying her $40 million demand was unreasonable. Schmitt and Jackson negotiated and eventually arrived at the figure of $24 million. Schmitt told Jackson that she and Medina would have to come to New York to pick up a check. Jackson said that Medina was to receive 25 percent of the money and asked Schmitt to make out one check for $18 million and the other for $6 million. Schmitt . . . asked Jackson to meet him in his office [in New York] the next morning to execute a written agreement and pick up the checks.

That evening, Sabas drove Jackson, Medina, and Williams to the airport. Only Jackson and Medina flew to New York; Williams remained in Los Angeles, and Sabas allowed him to use Sabas's credit card to pay for tickets for Jackson's and Medina's return flight to California.

On the morning of January 18, 1997, Jackson and Medina met Schmitt at the offices of his law firm in Manhattan. Jackson and Medina reviewed a draft agreement, prepared by Schmitt under the direction of the FBI, which provided that, in consideration for $24 million, Jackson and Medina would "refrain from providing any information whatsoever about Mr. Cosby to any third party," would "terminate any and all discussion with . . . The Globe," and would "not initiate any further discussions with The Globe or any other media outlet, with respect to Ms. Jackson's story that she is the daughter of Mr. Cosby." When Jackson and Medina had signed, Schmitt left the room on the pretense of getting the checks, and FBI agents entered and arrested Jackson and Medina. . . .

. . . The . . . indictment alleged three counts against each defendant: (1) conspiracy to violate 18 U.S.C. §875(d) and the Travel Act, 18 U.S.C. §1952(a)(3), in violation of 18 U.S.C. §371; (2) interstate transmission of threats to injure another person's reputation with the intent to extort money, in violation of 18 U.S.C. §§875(d) and 2; and (3) interstate travel in order to promote extortion, as prohibited by §875(d) and the New York State extortion statute, N.Y. Penal Law §155.05(2)(e)(v), in violation of the Travel Act, 18 U.S.C. §1952(a)(3). Following a jury trial, Jackson and Medina were convicted on all three counts. Sabas was convicted of conspiracy and violating the Travel Act but was acquitted on the §875(d) extortion count.

In a post-trial motion defendants moved for dismissal of their convictions on the ground that §875(d) and the New York State extortion statute, as interpreted in the district court's jury instructions, are unconstitutionally overbroad or vague. . . . [T]he district court denied the motion. . . . Judgments of conviction were entered, defendants were sentenced as indicated above, and these appeals followed.

DISCUSSION

On appeal, Jackson and Medina contend principally that the district court gave an erroneous jury charge on the elements of extortion as prohibited by §875(d) because it omitted any instruction that, in order to convict, the jury must find that the threat to injure Cosby's reputation was "wrongful." . . . Finding merit in the challenge to the district court's instructions, we vacate and remand for a new trial.

Section 875(d), the extortion statute under which Jackson and Medina were convicted, provides as follows:

> Whoever, with intent to extort from any person . . . any money or other thing of value, transmits in interstate or foreign commerce any communication containing any threat to injure the property or reputation of the addressee or of another . . . shall be fined under this title or imprisoned not more than two years, or both.

18 U.S.C. §875(d). This statute does not define the terms "extort" or "intent to extort." At trial, Jackson asked the court to instruct the jury that to act with intent to "extort" means to act with the intent to obtain money or something of value from someone else, with that person's consent, but caused or induced by the wrongful use of fear, and to explain that

> the term "wrongful" in this regard means that the government must prove beyond a reasonable doubt, first, that the defendant had no lawful claim or right to the money or property he or she sought or attempted to obtain, and, second, that the defendant knew that he or she had no lawful claim or right to the money or property he or she sought or attempted to obtain.
>
> If you have a reasonable doubt as to whether a defendant's object or purpose was to obtain money or other thing of value to which he or she was lawfully entitled, or believed he or she was lawfully entitled, then the defendant would not be acting in a "wrongful" manner and you must find him or her not guilty.

The court informed the parties that it would not give these requested instructions, stating its view that "threatening someone's reputation for money or a thing of value is inherently wrongful." Consistent with that view, after instructing the jury that a §875(d) offense has four elements, to wit, (1) an interstate communication, (2) containing a threat to reputation, (3) with intent to communicate such a threat, (4) with intent to extort, the court described the "intent to extort" element as follows, without mentioning any ingredient of wrongfulness:

> . . . The final element that the government must prove beyond a reasonable doubt is that the defendant you are considering acted with the intent to extort money or a thing of value from Bill Cosby. You should use your common sense to determine whether the defendant you are considering had the requisite intent to extort. In this connection, to extort means to obtain money or a thing of value from another by use of threats to reputation. . . .
>
> . . . It is not a defense that the alleged threats to another's reputation are based on true facts. In other words, it is irrelevant whether Bill Cosby in fact is the father of Autumn Jackson. Rather, you must determine whether the defendant you are considering communicated a threat to injure Bill Cosby's reputation, and whether that defendant did so with intent to extort money from Bill Cosby. In addition, if you find that the government has proved beyond a reasonable doubt a particular defendant threatened to injure Bill Cosby's reputation in order to obtain money from him, it makes no difference whether the defendant was actually owed any money by Bill Cosby or thought he or she was. That is because the law does not permit someone to obtain money or a thing of value by threatening to injure another person's reputation.

Although in connection with the counts charging conspiracy and violations of the Travel Act the court instructed the jury that the government was required to prove that the defendant acted with the intent to engage in "unlawful" activity, the court did not use the words "unlawful" or "wrongful" or any equivalent term in its instructions as to the scope of §875(d).

The government contends that §875(d) contains no "wrongfulness" requirement, and that even if such a requirement is inferred, threats to injure another person's reputation are inherently wrongful. These arguments are not without . . . support. The subsection itself contains no explicit wrongfulness requirement, and it parallels a subsection that prohibits, with intent to extort, a "threat to kidnap" a person, 18 U.S.C. §875(b), and a "threat to injure the person of another," id. Given the inherent wrongfulness of kidnaping and assault, the parallelism of subsection (b)'s prohibitions with §875(d)'s prohibition against threats to injure reputation or property may support an inference that Congress considered threats to injure reputation to be inherently wrongful methods of obtaining money. Such an inference would be consistent with the established principle that, when a threat is made to injure the reputation of another, the truth of the damaging allegations underlying the threat is not a defense to a charge of extortion under §875(d). Cf. United States v. Pascucci, 943 F.2d 1032, 1033-34, 1036-37 (9th Cir. 1991) (§875(d) conviction upheld where defendant threatened to send genuine tape of extramarital sexual encounter to victim's employer). . . .

. . . [Still,] we are troubled that §875(d) should be interpreted to contain no element of wrongfulness, for plainly not all threats to engage in speech that will [harm] another person's reputation, even if a forbearance from speaking is conditioned on the payment of money, are wrongful. For example, the purchaser of an allegedly defective product may threaten to complain to a consumer protection agency or to bring suit in a public forum if the manufacturer does not make good on its warranty. . . . Or a private club may threaten to post a list of the club members who have not yet paid their dues. We doubt that Congress intended §875(d) to criminalize acts such as these. . . .

. . . The Hobbs Act prohibits, inter alia, obstructing, delaying, or affecting commerce "by robbery or extortion," id. §1951(a), and it defines extortion as . . . "the obtaining of property from another, with his consent, induced by wrongful use of actual or threatened force, violence, or fear, or under color of official right. . . . " Id. §1951(b)(2). The Travel Act refers to "extortion" without defining it. That Act has nonetheless been interpreted as using the term in its generic sense, a sense that inherently signifies wrongfulness. Thus, in determining whether the term "extortion" as used in [18 U.S.C.] §1952 was meant to encompass acts that at common law were classified as blackmail but not as extortion (because not committed by a public official), the Supreme Court accepted the

> Government['s] . . . suggestion that Congress intended that extortion should refer to those acts prohibited by state law which would be generically classified as extortionate, i.e., obtaining something of value from another with his consent induced by the wrongful use of force, fear, or threats.

United States v. Nardello, 393 U.S. 286, 290 (1969).

In sum, in sections of the Criminal Code other than §875(d), the words "extort," "extortionate," and "extortion" either are defined to have a wrongfulness component or implicitly contain such a component. If Congress had meant the word "extort" in §875(d) to have a different connotation, we doubt that it would have chosen to convey that intention by means of silence. . . .

Under the Hobbs Act definition of extortion, which includes obtaining property from another through a wrongful threat of force or fear, the use of a threat can be wrongful because it causes the victim to fear a harm that is itself wrongful, such as physical injury, or because the means is wrongful, such as violence. . . . [T]he Hobbs Act may also be violated by a threat that causes the victim to fear only an economic loss. Yet as we discussed in United States v. Clemente, 640 F.2d 1069, 1077 (2d Cir. 1981), a threat to cause economic loss is not inherently wrongful; it becomes wrongful only when it is used to obtain property to which the threatener is not entitled.

In *Clemente*, we considered challenges to Hobbs Act convictions on the ground that the trial court's instructions permitted the jury to "convict [Clemente] solely upon finding that he used fear of economic loss to obtain money," and that as a matter of law "the use of fear of economic loss is not inherently wrongful." 640 F.2d at 1077. We rejected the challenge because Clemente's factual premise was erroneous. The trial court had in fact informed the jury . . . that "extortion" means obtaining property from another, with his consent, induced by the "wrongful" use of actual or threatened force or fear, id. at 1076, and had instructed that "wrongful" meant that the defendant in question had instilled in his victim the fear of economic loss of property to which the defendant "had no lawful right," id. at 1077. . . .

We are persuaded that a similar interpretation of §875(d) is appropriate. Given Congress's contemporaneous consideration of the predecessors of §875(d) and the Hobbs Act, both of which focused on extortion, we infer that Congress's concept of extortion was the same with respect to both statutes. . . . And since, like threats of economic harm, not every threat to make a disclosure that would harm another person's reputation is wrongful, we adopt an interpretation of §875(d) similar to *Clemente*'s interpretation of the Hobbs Act. We conclude that not all threats to reputation are within the scope of §875(d), that the objective of the party employing fear of economic loss or damage to reputation will have a bearing on the lawfulness of its use, and that it is material whether the defendant had a claim of right to the money demanded.

We do, however, view as inherently wrongful the type of threat to reputation that has no nexus to a claim of right. There are significant differences between, on the one hand, threatened disclosures of such matters as consumer complaints and nonpayment of dues, as to which the threatener has a plausible claim of right, and, on the other hand, threatened disclosures of such matters as sexual indiscretions that have no nexus with any plausible claim of right. In the former category of threats, the disclosures themselves—not only the threats—have the potential for causing payment of the money demanded; in the latter category, it is only the threat that has that potential, and actual disclosure would frustrate the prospect of payment. Thus, if the club posts a list of members with unpaid dues and its list is accurate, the dues generally will be paid; if the consumer lodges her complaint and is right, she is likely to receive her refund; and both matters are thereby concluded. In contrast, if a threatener having no claim of right discloses the victim's secret, regardless of whether her information is correct she normally gets nothing from the target of her threats. And if the victim makes the demanded payment, thereby avoiding disclosure, there is nothing to prevent the threatener from repeatedly demanding money even after prior demands have been fully met. . . .

Within this framework, we conclude that the district court's instruction to the jury on the meaning of "extort" as that term is used in §875(d) was erroneous. The court instructed simply that "to extort means to obtain money or a thing of value from another by use of threats to reputation." The court gave no other explanation of the term "extort" and did not limit the scope of that term to the obtaining of property to which the defendant had no actual, or reasonable belief of, entitlement. . . .

The evidence at trial was plainly sufficient to support verdicts of guilty had the jury been properly instructed. Even if Jackson were Cosby's child, a rational jury could find that her demand, given her age (22) and the amount ($40 million), did not reflect a plausible claim for support. The evidence supported an inference that Jackson had no right to demand money from Cosby pursuant to a contract or promise and no right to insist that she be included in his will. The jury thus could have found that her threat to disclose was the only leverage she had to extract money from him; that if she sold her story to The Globe, she would lose that leverage; and that if Cosby had capitulated and paid her in order to prevent disclosure, there was no logical guarantee that there would not be a similar threat and demand in the future. . . .

We conclude, however, that the court's failure to inform the jury of the proper scope of the intent-to-extort element of §875(d) erroneously allowed the jury to find defendants guilty of violating that section on the premise that any and every threat to reputation in order to obtain money is inherently wrongful. Accordingly, Jackson and Medina are entitled to a new trial on the §875(d) count. . . .

Notes and Questions

1. Assuming that, as she claims, Autumn Jackson is Bill Cosby's biological daughter, what made her threat "wrongful"? Was it the $40 million demand? If so, would a more gently worded request for $1 million be permissible? How about $100,000? Do your answers depend on whether Jackson has any viable state-law claims for support? If so, how viable must those claims be?

2. Suppose, as often happens, a tabloid owns some embarrassing pictures of a celebrity. This tabloid expects to make $50,000 in extra sales and advertising revenue by publishing these pictures. As an act of kindness (he claims), the owner of the tabloid contacts the celebrity and offers to destroy the pictures in exchange for $75,000. Is the offer extortionate? Does the answer depend on the nature of the pictures?

3. In many extortion cases, the defendant sells something he does not own, as where mobsters charge a fee for "protecting" charged businesses from harm. In paradigmatic blackmail cases, the defendant seeks to sell something she *does* own: the right to disclose embarrassing information about the victim. Autumn Jackson was free to speak or keep quiet, and free to sell her story to the highest bidder. But she may not sell her silence to Bill Cosby, at least under some circumstances. Why not?

That is the puzzle of blackmail. It is the subject of a massive literature; for a sampling, see Mitchell N. Berman, The Evidentiary Theory of Blackmail, 65 U. Chi. L. Rev. 795 (1998); Leo Katz, Blackmail and Other Forms of Arm-Twisting, 141 U. Pa. L. Rev. 1567 (1993); George N. Fletcher,

Blackmail: The Paradigmatic Crime, 141 U. Pa. L. Rev. 1617 (1993); Richard Epstein, Blackmail, Inc., 50 U. Chi. L. Rev. 553 (1983). The real puzzle, though, is the persistence of the problem. The legal concept of blackmail has been around for a very long time. One might suppose that, long before now, the law would have arrived at a consensus rationale for the concept. Why hasn't it?

4. The defendants in United States v. Nardello, 393 U.S. 286 (1969), participated in "a 'shakedown' operation whereby individuals would be lured into a compromising homosexual situation and then threatened with exposure unless [victims'] silence was purchased." The defendants were charged under the Travel Act, 18 U.S.C. §1952, which forbids "travel[ing] in interstate or foreign commerce . . . with intent to . . . carry on . . . any unlawful activity." "Unlawful activity" is defined to include "extortion, bribery, or arson in violation of the laws of the State" where the relevant acts were committed. In *Nardello*, the relevant conduct committed in Pennsylvania; under Pennsylvania law, the defendants would have been guilty of blackmail but not extortion—those are different crimes in some states, as they were at common law. The District Court had accordingly dismissed the indictment. The Supreme Court overturned that decision, on the grounds that (1) some states do define blackmail to fall within their criminal extortion laws, and (2) the conduct in question did violate Pennsylvania law. After *Nardello*, Travel Act extortion is defined by a species of federal common law—as is true of extortion under section 875(d) in *Jackson*, and also, in large measure, under the Hobbs Act. Is common law-style crime definition a good fit for extortion? Can this crime be defined with any more specificity? Who should decide those questions?

D. FRAUD

Durland v. United States

Supreme Court of the United States
161 U.S. 306 (1896)

[The defendants in *Durland* were late-nineteenth-century con artists—they used the mails to advertise "bonds" that would return profits of 50 percent in six months, with no intention of paying even the principal, much less any interest. Surprisingly (at least to twenty-first-century readers), the common law of fraud did not cover such conduct. Common-law fraud required proof of false statements of material fact; false promises of future performance—such as Durland's promise to pay interest on the bonds in question—did not suffice. The government nevertheless prosecuted Durland

and his colleagues for mail fraud, and the Supreme Court concluded that the mail fraud statute extended further than the common law.—Eds.]

Mr. Justice BREWER, after stating the case, delivered the opinion of the Court.

Inasmuch as the testimony has not been preserved, we must assume that it was sufficient to substantiate the charges in the indictments; that this was a scheme and artifice to defraud, and that the defendant did not intend that the bonds should mature, or that although money was received any should be returned, but that it should be appropriated to his own use. In other words, he was trying to entrap the unwary, and to secure money from them on the faith of a scheme glittering and attractive in form, yet unreal and deceptive in fact, and known to him to be such. So far as the moral element is concerned it must be taken that the defendant's guilt was established.

But the contention on his part is that the statute reaches only such cases as, at common law, would come within the definition of "false pretenses," in order to make out which there must be a misrepresentation as to some existing fact and not a mere promise as to the future. It is urged that there was no misrepresentation as to the existence or solvency of the corporation, the Provident Bond and Investment Company, or as to its modes of doing business, no suggestion that it failed to issue its bonds to any and every one advancing the required dues, or that its promise of payment according to the conditions named in the bond was not a valid and binding promise. . . .

. . . The statute is broader than is claimed. Its letter shows this: "Any scheme or artifice to defraud." Some schemes may be promoted through mere representations and promises as to the future, yet are none the less schemes and artifices to defraud. Punishment because of the fraudulent purpose is no new thing. As said by Mr. Justice Brown, in Evans v. United States, 153 U.S. 584, 592, "if a person buy goods on credit in good faith, knowing that he is unable to pay for them at the time, but believing that he will be able to pay for them at the maturity of the bill, he is guilty of no offence even if he be disappointed in making such payment. But if he purchases them, knowing that he will not be able to pay for them, and with an intent to cheat the vendor, this is a plain fraud, and made punishable as such by statutes in many of the States."

But beyond the letter of the statute is the evil sought to be remedied, which is always significant in determining the meaning. It is common knowledge that nothing is more alluring than the expectation of receiving large returns on small investments. Eagerness to take the chances of large gains lies at the foundation of all lottery schemes, and, even when the matter of chance is eliminated, any scheme or plan which holds out the prospect of receiving more than is parted with appeals to the cupidity of all.

In the light of this the statute must be read, and so read it includes everything designed to defraud by representations as to the past or present, or suggestions and promises as to the future. The significant fact is the intent and purpose. . . . If the testimony had shown that this Provident company, and the defendant, as its president, had entered in good faith upon that business, believing that out of the moneys received they could by investment or otherwise make enough to justify the promised returns, no conviction could be sustained, no matter how visionary might seem the scheme. The charge is that in putting forth this scheme it was not the intent of the defendant to make an honest effort for its success, but that he resorted to this form and pretence of a bond without a thought that he or the company would ever make good its promises. It was with the purpose of protecting the public against all such intentional efforts to despoil, and to prevent the post office from being used to carry them into effect, that this statute was passed; and it would strip it of value to confine it to such cases as disclose an actual misrepresentation as to some existing fact, and exclude those in which is only the allurement of a specious and glittering promise. . . .

[A second objection] . . . is that the indictment is defective in that it avers that in pursuance of this fraudulent scheme twenty letters and circulars were deposited in the post office, without in any way specifying the character of those letters or circulars. It is contended that the indictment should either recite the letters, or at least by direct statements show their purpose and character, and that the names and addresses of the parties to whom the letters were sent should also be stated. . . .

It may be conceded that the indictment would be more satisfactory if it gave more full information as to the contents or import of these letters, so that upon its face it would be apparent that they were calculated or designed to aid in carrying into execution the scheme to defraud. But still we think that as it stands it must be held to be sufficient. There was a partial identification of the letters by the time and place of mailing, and the charge was that defendant "intending in and for executing such scheme and artifice to defraud and attempting so to do, placed and caused to be placed in the post office," etc. This, it will be noticed, is substantially the language of the statute. If defendant had desired further specification and identification, he could have secured it by demanding a bill of particulars. Rosen v. United States, 161 U.S. 29.

We do not wish to be understood as intimating that in order to constitute the offence it must be shown that the letters so mailed were of a nature calculated to be effective in carrying out the fraudulent scheme. It is enough if, having devised a scheme to defraud, the defendant with a view of executing it deposits in the post office letters, which he thinks may assist in carrying it into effect, although in the judgment of the jury they may be absolutely ineffective therefor. . . .

Notes and Questions

1. The mail fraud statute was probably designed to punish fraudulent mailings—that is, mailings that obtain money for their authors by means of false statements of material facts. Had it been limited to such cases, the statute would have had small effects on America's unsystematic criminal justice system. Thanks to *Durland*, it was not limited to such cases, and so became the heart of the law of white-collar crime.

2. *Durland* has two major holdings: first, that mailings need not themselves be fraudulent in order to establish liability for mail fraud; and second, that the common law of fraud does not define the *federal* law of fraud. At common law, proof of fraud meant proof of knowingly false statements of material fact, on which the victim relied, that caused the victim's loss and the perpetrator's gain. In combination, those elements are hard to prove, as *Durland* illustrates: The case arose from a classic financial con game that, despite its obviously fraudulent character, does not fit the common-law definition of fraud. *Caveat emptor*—Latin for "let the buyer beware"—became a famous piece of legal conventional wisdom because business cheats bore so little risk of legal sanctions. After *Durland*, the risk was at least modestly higher.

3. The mail fraud statute, 18 U.S.C. §1341, reads as follows:

> Whoever, having devised or intending to devise any scheme or artifice to defraud, or for obtaining money or property by means of false or fraudulent pretenses, representations, or promises, or to sell, dispose of, loan, exchange, alter, give away, distribute, supply, or furnish or procure for unlawful use any counterfeit or spurious coin, obligation, security, or other article, or anything represented to be or intimated or held out to be such counterfeit or spurious article, for the purpose of executing such scheme or artifice or attempting so to do, places in any post office or authorized depository for mail matter, any matter or thing whatever to be sent or delivered by the Postal Service, or deposits or causes to be deposited any matter or thing whatever to be sent or delivered by any private or commercial interstate carrier, or takes or receives therefrom, any such matter or thing, or knowingly causes to be delivered by mail or such carrier according to the direction thereon, or at the place at which it is directed to be delivered by the person to whom it is addressed, any such matter or thing, shall be fined under this title or imprisoned not more than 20 years, or both. . . .

That must be one of the longest sentences in the U.S. Code. Wade through the verbiage, and you'll find that the only criminal act required by this statute is mailing a letter or causing one to be mailed: the federal jurisdictional element. (The mail fraud statute falls within the postal power—Congress' Article I power "To establish Post Offices and post Roads.") All the rest is intent. Technically, the "scheme or artifice to defraud" can remain entirely in the defendant's head without negating the defendant's criminal liability.

4. In practice, the focus of mail fraud cases is the fraud, not the mailing. That is so because the relationship between the mailing and the fraud can be tenuous and still satisfy the statute. The defendant in Schmuck v. United States, 489 U.S. 705 (1989)—Wayne T. Schmuck, surely one of the best-named criminal defendants in legal history—was a crooked used car salesman; he bought used cars, dialed back the odometers, then resold the cars to dealers. The requisite mailings were title application forms the dealers submitted to the Wisconsin Department of Motor Vehicles. Those forms, which Schmuck did not mail, had only a slight relationship to Schmuck's fraudulent scheme. No matter: Schmuck's scheme involved the sale of used cars, and those sales caused the mailing of the forms. That sufficed to establish federal jurisdiction. Since there are few frauds that don't involve the mailing of at least one letter, the mail fraud statute amounts to a nationwide fraud prohibition.

And in those rare cases of mail-free frauds, federal prosecutors can usually charge wire fraud instead. See 18 U.S.C. §1343, which is violated whenever a defendant "transmits or causes to be transmitted by means of wire, radio, or television communication in interstate or foreign commerce, any writings, signs, signals, pictures, or sounds for the purpose of executing such scheme or artifice. . . . " The wire fraud statute is based on the federal government's power to regulate, under the Commerce Clause, the means of electronic communication; note the statute's requirement that the prosecution prove that the transmission was "in interstate or foreign commerce."

5. *Durland* was decided near the beginning of the age of laissez-faire in American law. One year earlier, the Supreme Court invalidated the federal income tax. Pollock v. Farmers' Loan and Trust Co., 157 U.S. 429 (1895) (subsequently overturned by the ratification of the Sixteenth Amendment). Two years later, the Justices invalidated a Nebraska law setting rates railroads could charge for shipping farm products. Smyth v. Ames, 171 U.S. 361 (1898). Seven years after that, the Court overturned a New York statute barring bakers from working more than 60 hours per week. Lochner v. New York, 198 U.S. 45 (1905). Laws barring employers from contractually prohibiting union organizing by their employees were struck down in Adair v. United States, 208 U.S. 161 (1907), and Coppage v. Kansas, 236 U.S. 1 (1915). Minimum wage laws were invalidated in Adkins v. Children's Hospital, 261 U.S. 525 (1923), and Morehead v. New York ex rel. Tipaldo, 298 U.S. 587 (1936). The liberty of private parties to make contracts free of government control was constitutionally protected. Legal regulation of business was constitutionally suspect.

But not all legal regulation. The broad federal prohibition of fraud—considerably broader than the common law—was deemed permissible in *Durland*. So were the federal ban on the interstate transportation of lottery tickets in Champion v. Ames, 188 U.S. 321 (1903), the federal prohibition on interstate movement of young women for the purpose of engaging in "prostitution, debauchery, and other immoral practices," Caminetti v. United States, 242 U.S. 470 (1917), and the federal ban on the interstate shipment of liquor in United States v. Hill, 248 U.S. 420 (1919). The federal statutes at issue in *Champion*, *Caminetti*, and *Hill* had two things in common:

First, they were criminal prohibitions; second, they barred conduct widely believed to be immoral. In the early twentieth century, federal economic regulation was constitutionally questionable (this would change dramatically during the New Deal), but morals laws fell into a different category. Laissez-faire did not extend to dishonesty and vice.

Carpenter v. United States

Supreme Court of the United States
484 U.S. 19 (1987)

Justice WHITE delivered the opinion of the Court.

Petitioners Kenneth Felis and R. Foster Winans were convicted of violating §10(b) of the Securities Exchange Act of 1934, 15 U.S.C. §78j(b), and Rule 10b-5. They were also found guilty of violating the federal mail and wire fraud statutes, 18 U.S.C. §§1341, 1343, and were convicted for conspiracy under 18 U.S.C. §371. David Carpenter, Winans' roommate, was convicted for aiding and abetting. . . .

I

In 1981, Winans became a reporter for the Wall Street Journal (the Journal) and in the summer of 1982 became one of the two writers of a daily column, "Heard on the Street." That column discussed selected stocks or groups of stocks, giving positive and negative information about those stocks and taking "a point of view with respect to investment in the stocks that it reviews." Winans regularly interviewed corporate executives to put together interesting perspectives on the stocks that would be highlighted in upcoming columns, but, at least for the columns at issue here, none contained corporate inside information or any "hold for release" information. Because of the "Heard" column's perceived quality and integrity, it had the potential of affecting the price of the stocks which it examined.

The official policy and practice at the Journal was that prior to publication, the contents of the column were the Journal's confidential information. Despite the rule, with which Winans was familiar, he entered into a scheme in October 1983 with Peter Brant and petitioner Felis, both connected with the Kidder Peabody brokerage firm in New York City, to give them advance information as to the timing and contents of the "Heard" column. This permitted Brant and Felis and another conspirator, David Clark, a client of Brant, to buy or sell based on the probable impact of the column on the market. Profits were to be shared. The conspirators agreed that the scheme would not affect the journalistic purity of the "Heard" column, and the District Court did not find that the contents of any of the articles were altered to further the profit potential of petitioners' stock-trading scheme. Over a 4-month period, the brokers made prepublication trades on the basis of information given them by Winans about the contents of some 27 "Heard" columns. The net profits from these trades were about $690,000.

In November 1983, correlations between the "Heard" articles and trading in the Clark and Felis accounts were noted at Kidder Peabody and inquiries began. Brant and Felis denied knowing anyone at the Journal and took steps to conceal the trades. Later, the Securities and Exchange Commission began an investigation. Questions were met by denials both by the brokers at Kidder Peabody and by Winans at the Journal. As the investigation progressed, the conspirators quarreled, and on March 29, 1984, Winans and Carpenter went to the SEC and revealed the entire scheme. This indictment and a bench trial followed. Brant, who had pleaded guilty under a plea agreement, was a witness for the Government.

. . . The Court is evenly divided with respect to the convictions under the securities laws and for that reason affirms the judgment below on those counts. For the reasons that follow, we also affirm the judgment with respect to the mail and wire fraud convictions.

II

Petitioners assert that their activities were not a scheme to defraud the Journal within the meaning of the mail and wire fraud statutes; and that in any event, they did not obtain any "money or property" from the Journal, which is a necessary element of the crime under our decision last Term in McNally v. United States, 483 U.S. 350 (1987). We are unpersuaded by either submission and address the latter first.

We held in *McNally* that the mail fraud statute does not reach "schemes to defraud citizens of their intangible rights to honest and impartial government," id. at 355, and that the statute is "limited in scope to the protection of property rights." Id. at 360. Petitioners argue that the Journal's interest in prepublication confidentiality for the "Heard" columns is no more than an intangible consideration outside the reach of §1341; nor does that law, it is urged, protect against mere injury to reputation. This is not a case like *McNally*, however. The Journal, as Winans' employer, was defrauded of much more than its contractual right to his honest and faithful service, an interest too ethereal in itself to fall within the protection of the mail fraud statute, which "had its origin in the desire to protect individual property rights." *McNally*, supra, at 359, n.8. Here, the object of the scheme was to take the Journal's confidential business information — the publication schedule and contents of the "Heard" column — and its intangible nature does not make it any less "property" protected by the mail and wire fraud statutes. *McNally* did not limit the scope of §1341 to tangible as distinguished from intangible property rights.

. . . Confidential business information has long been recognized as property. "Confidential information acquired or compiled by a corporation in the course and conduct of its business is a species of property to which the corporation has the exclusive right and benefit, and which a court of equity will protect through the injunctive process or other appropriate remedy." 3 W. Fletcher, Cyclopedia of Law of Private Corporations §857.1, at 260 (rev. ed. 1986) (footnote omitted). The Journal had a property right in keeping confidential and making exclusive use, prior to publication, of the schedule and contents of the "Heard" column. As the Court has observed before:

> "[N]ews matter, however little susceptible of ownership or dominion in the absolute sense, is stock in trade, to be gathered at the cost of enterprise, organization, skill, labor, and money, and to be distributed and sold to those who will pay money for it, as for any other merchandise." International News Service v. Associated Press, 248 U.S. 215, 236 (1918).

Petitioners' arguments that they did not interfere with the Journal's use of the information or did not publicize it and deprive the Journal of the first public use of it miss the point. The confidential information was generated from the business, and the business had a right to decide how to use it prior to disclosing it to the public. Petitioners cannot successfully contend based on *Associated Press* that a scheme to defraud requires a monetary loss, such as giving the information to a competitor; it is sufficient that the Journal has been deprived of its right to exclusive use of the information, for exclusivity is an important aspect of confidential business information and most private property for that matter.

We cannot accept petitioners' further argument that Winans' conduct in revealing prepublication information was no more than a violation of workplace rules and did not amount to fraudulent activity that is proscribed by the mail fraud statute. Sections 1341 and 1343 reach any scheme to deprive another of money or property by means of false or fraudulent pretenses, representations, or promises. . . . The concept of "fraud" includes the act of embezzlement, which is "the fraudulent appropriation to one's own use of the money or goods entrusted to one's care by another." Grin v. Shine, 187 U.S. 181, 189 (1902).

The District Court found that Winans' undertaking at the Journal was not to reveal prepublication information about his column, a promise that became a sham when in violation of his duty he passed along to his co-conspirators confidential information belonging to the Journal, pursuant to an ongoing scheme to share profits from trading in anticipation of the "Heard" column's impact on the stock market. In Snepp v. United States, 444 U.S. 507, 515, n.11 (1980), . . . we noted the similar prohibitions of the common law, that "even in the absence of a written contract, an employee has a fiduciary obligation to protect confidential information obtained during the course of his employment." As the New York courts have recognized:

> "It is well established, as a general proposition, that a person who acquires special knowledge or information by virtue of a confidential or fiduciary relationship with another is not free to exploit that knowledge or information

for his own personal benefit but must account to his principal for any profits derived therefrom." Diamond v. Oreamuno, 24 N.Y.2d 494, 497, 248 N.E. 2d 910, 912 (1969).

See also Restatement (Second) of Agency §§388, Comment c, 396(c) (1958). . . .

Lastly, we reject the submission that using the wires and the mail to print and send the Journal to its customers did not satisfy the requirement that those mediums be used to execute the scheme at issue. The courts below were quite right in observing that circulation of the "Heard" column was not only anticipated but an essential part of the scheme. Had the column not been made available to Journal customers, there would have been no effect on stock prices and no likelihood of profiting from the information leaked by Winans.

Notes on "Money or Property" Fraud

1. Given *Durland*'s expansive definition of fraud, most private-sector fraudulent schemes raise no serious interpretive issues. The scheme at issue in *Carpenter* is unusual in that respect, because the Wall Street Journal was defrauded neither of cash nor of other liquid assets, but of information. What, exactly, was the Journal's property interest in that information? The Journal owned Winans' column, which it sold along with all the other news and commentary in its daily issues. But Winans didn't steal "Heard on the Street." He continued to write the column, and buyers of the newspaper continued to pay the Journal for the privilege of reading it. Again, of what property interest was the Journal defrauded?

2. While Winans did not steal his column in the conventional sense of that word, he did appropriate its value by taking bribes and, in exchange, disclosing the column's contents before the newspaper's subscribers could read it. But that answer is likewise problematic. The value to the Journal of Winans' column did not diminish during the course of Winans' fraudulent scheme. It may have increased, given the degree to which trading was influenced by the column's contents. Winans might argue that, in effect, he was paid twice for doing his job: once by his employer, and once by the parties who bought advance notice of the information in the column. In a sense, he was moonlighting. As long as the "journalistic purity" of Winans' column was unaffected, as he claimed, how did his employer suffer from his receipt of that second salary?

Carpenter does not answer that question. Perhaps it needs no answer: The Journal owns the information in its news stories and columns, and the Journal is free to sell that information (or not) in whatever manner it chooses. By also selling his columns on the side, Winans took the traditional property owner's right to define the terms on which property can be sold. That is harm enough, even if the property owner has suffered no financial loss.

3. On the other hand, isn't there something wrong with the federal government prosecuting crimes that cause no tangible harm? Why can't the Wall Street Journal protect its own intangible property interests? What role does the criminal law of fraud play in *Carpenter*? Is it the right role?

Notes on "Honest Services" Fraud

1. As seen in *Carpenter*, the federal mail and wire fraud statutes are not strictly limited to deprivations of money or tangible property. Those statutes also apply to deprivations of intangible rights (in *Carpenter*, the intangible property right of the owner of intellectual property to control the profits from selling that property).

The "intangible rights" theory of fraud actually began as a means of punishing official corruption. The first case to rely on the theory was Shushan v. United States, 117 F.2d 110 (5th Cir. 1941), involving the mail fraud prosecution of a public official who took bribes from entrepreneurs in exchange for supporting official acts on their behalf. According to the court: "A scheme to get a public contract on more favorable terms than would likely be got otherwise by bribing a public official would not only be a plan to commit the crime of bribery, but would also be a scheme to defraud the public. . . . It is not true that because the [city] was to make and did make a saving by the operations there could not have been an intent to defraud." Id. at 115, 119.

Over time, the lower federal courts gradually evolved the concept of "honest services" fraud as a way to identify and describe exactly what was being taken from the victims of official corruption, that is, the public. See United States v. States, 488 F.2d 761 (8th Cir. 1973) (affirming the mail fraud convictions of participants in a fraudulent voter registration scheme in St. Louis). At the time, there was no federal statute specifically barring bribery of state or local government officials. The chief obstacle to attacking official misconduct by means of the federal fraud statutes was the requirement that "money or property" be "obtain[ed]" from the victim of the fraud. In cases like *States*, the true victims were the local voters, who were deprived of honest elections and honest government. But even under the broad definition used in *Carpenter*, such interests would not qualify as property.

On the other hand, as the Eighth Circuit noted in *States*, the mail fraud statute does not actually require "the obtaining of money or property" from the fraud's victims: The relevant statutory language applies to all those "having devised or intending to devise any scheme or artifice to defraud, *or* for obtaining money or property by means of false or fraudulent pretenses, representations, or promises . . ." (emphasis added). The phrase following the word "or" appears to cover schemes that make money for the defendants, without requiring proof that the money in question actually came out of the pockets of those victimized by the defendants' dishonesty.

2. After the Eighth Circuit's decision in *States*, the "honest services" theory of fraud took off, and a number of prominent public officials were prosecuted and punished under that theory. Then, in McNally v. United States, 483 U.S. 350 (1987), a case cited and discussed in *Carpenter*, the Supreme Court rejected the theory, holding that it strayed too far from the text of the mail fraud statute. Congress promptly overruled *McNally* by enacting what became 18 U.S.C. §1346: "For purposes of this chapter, the term 'scheme or artifice to defraud' includes a scheme or artifice to deprive another of the intangible right of honest services." Note that section 1346 does not distinguish between public-sector and private-sector corruption. In the years since its passage, section 1346 has worked in combination with the mail and wire fraud statutes to produce a robust federal criminal law that covers both commercial (e.g., corporate officers, employees, and other such fiduciaries) and public-official bribery.

3. In some cases, the "honest services" theory might be the only way to fit the case within the scope of the fraud statutes. See, for example, United States v. Frost, 125 F.3d 346 (6th Cir. 1997), in which two engineering professors awarded graduate degrees for plagiarized work; in exchange, the graduate students worked for the professors' consulting company. Following is an excerpt from the jury instruction in *Frost*:

> What the government must prove is that there was a failure by Walter Frost and Robert Turner to disclose something which in their knowledge or contemplation posed a business risk of harm or loss to their employer, the University of Tennessee. If you find that the nondisclosure of a conflict of interest by Walter Frost and Robert Turner furthered a scheme by them to abuse the trust of their employer in a manner that made an identifiable harm to the University of Tennessee reasonably foreseeable, then you may find that Walter Frost and Robert Turner had the intent to defraud under Section 1341. The key determination is whether you can find from the evidence presented in this case that Walter Frost and Robert Turner might reasonably have contemplated or understood that the University of Tennessee would suffer some harm to its business arising out of or resulting from their failure to disclose their alleged conduct and conflict of interest to the University of Tennessee. However, the government is not required to prove that the intended victim, the University of Tennessee, actually suffered a loss of money or property.

Notice the curious status of economic harm in *Frost*: On the one hand, the instruction states that the fraudulent scheme must have contemplated "identifiable harm" to the university; on the other hand, there is no requirement that the university "actually suffered a loss of money or property."

Here is what the Sixth Circuit had to say about the quoted passage from the jury instructions in *Frost*:

We believe that the above instructions captured the proper standard for determining whether an employee has committed mail fraud by depriving his employer of honest services. The prosecution must prove that the employee intended to breach a fiduciary duty, and that the employee foresaw or reasonably should have foreseen that his employer might suffer an economic harm as a result of the breach.

What is the difference between the theory of fraud used in *Carpenter* and the theory used in *Frost*? What work does the idea of an intangible right of "honest services" do in *Frost*?

4. The Supreme Court has narrowed the permissible scope of the "honest services" fraud theory. Jeffrey K. Skilling was the CEO of Enron Corporation just before the company collapsed into bankruptcy in 2001, causing $74 billion in losses to investors, including tens of thousands of then-current and former Enron employees, many of whom lost their entire retirement savings. (The Enron debacle—at the time, the largest bankruptcy in U.S. history—was also the underlying subject of the *Arthur Andersen* case discussed in Chapter 4, at page 283, supra.) Skilling was accused of conspiring with other Enron officials to hide the financial problems of the company and artificially prop up its stock prices, in large part so that Skilling and his co-conspirators could buy the time to unload (at huge profits) their own massive holdings of Enron stock. Skilling was charged with one count of conspiracy to commit securities and wire fraud; the conspiracy charge was based in part on the theory that he "depriv[ed] Enron and its shareholders of the intangible right of [his] honest services." He was also charged with more than 25 additional counts of securities fraud, wire fraud, false representation, and insider trading. At trial, he was convicted on the conspiracy count as well as 19 of the additional counts, and was sentenced to more than 24 years in prison plus $45 million in restitution. On appeal, Skilling argued that his conspiracy conviction should be reversed because the "honest services" wire fraud statute on which it was partially based, 18 U.S.C. §1346, was unconstitutionally vague because it (1) failed to provide fair notice to defendants about the definition of the crime, and (2) created unconstitutionally broad discretion for prosecutors, judges, and juries to decide whom to convict for the crime.

The Supreme Court agreed with Skilling's argument that the "honest services" theory should be rejected, although the Court reached this conclusion as a matter of statutory interpretation in order to avoid the constitutional issues. Skilling v. United States, 561 U.S. 358 (2010). Justice Ginsburg wrote the majority opinion:

> There is no doubt that Congress intended §1346 to refer to and incorporate the honest-services doctrine recognized in Court of Appeals' decisions before *McNally* derailed the intangible-rights theory of fraud. . . . Congress enacted §1346 on the heels of *McNally* and drafted the statute using that decision's terminology. . . .

... While the honest-services cases preceding *McNally* dominantly and consistently applied the fraud statute to bribery and kickback schemes—schemes that were the basis of most honest-services prosecutions—there was considerable disarray over the statute's application to conduct outside that core category. ...

... Although some applications of the pre-*McNally* honest-services doctrine occasioned disagreement among the Courts of Appeals, these cases do not cloud the doctrine's solid core: The "vast majority" of the honest-services cases involved offenders who, in violation of a fiduciary duty, participated in bribery or kickback schemes. ... Indeed, the *McNally* case itself, which spurred Congress to enact §1346, presented a paradigmatic kickback fact pattern. ... Congress' reversal of *McNally* and reinstatement of the honest-services doctrine, we conclude, can and should be salvaged by confining its scope to the core pre-*McNally* applications. ...

... [T]here is no doubt that Congress intended §1346 to reach *at least* bribes and kickbacks. Reading the statute to proscribe a wider range of offensive conduct, we acknowledge, would raise the due process concerns underlying the vagueness doctrine. To preserve the statute without transgressing constitutional limitations, we now hold that §1346 criminalizes *only* the bribe-and-kickback core of the pre-*McNally* case law.[44] ...

The Government did not, at any time, allege that Skilling solicited or accepted side payments from a third party in exchange for making these misrepresentations. See Record 41328 (May 11, 2006 Letter from the Government to the District Court) ("[T]he indictment does not allege, and the government's evidence did not show, that [Skilling] engaged in bribery."). It is therefore clear that, as we read §1346, Skilling did not commit honest-services fraud.

Id. at 404-13. The Supreme Court remanded to determine whether any of Skilling's convictions should be reversed. On remand, the U.S. Court of Appeals for the Fifth Circuit concluded that none of the convictions—including the conspiracy conviction, which the court found to be amply supported by evidence that Skilling conspired to commit securities fraud, even if he

---

44. Justice Scalia charges that our construction of §1346 is "not interpretation but invention."*Post*, at 8. Stating that he "know[s] of no precedent for . . . 'paring down'" the pre-*McNally* case law to its core, *ibid.*, he contends that the Court today "wield[s] a power we long ago abjured: the power to define new federal crimes,"*post*, at 1. . . . [C]ases "paring down" federal statutes to avoid constitutional shoals are legion. These cases recognize that the Court does not *legislate*, but instead *respects the legislature*, by preserving a statute through a limiting interpretation. See United States v. Lanier, 520 U.S. 259, 267-268, n.6 (1997) (This Court does not "create a common law crime" by adopting a "narrow[ing] constru[ction]." (internal quotation marks omitted)). Given that the Courts of Appeals uniformly recognized bribery and kickback schemes as honest-services fraud before *McNally*, and that these schemes composed the lion's share of honest-services cases, limiting §1346 to these heartland applications is surely "fairly possible." Boos v. Barry, 485 U.S. 312, 331 (1988); cf. Clark v. Martinez, 543 U.S. 371, 380 (2005) (opinion of the Court by Scalia, J.) (when adopting a limiting construction, "[t]he lowest common denominator, as it were, must govern"). So construed, the statute is not unconstitutionally vague. Only by taking a wrecking ball to a statute that can be salvaged through a reasonable narrowing interpretation would we act out of step with precedent.

did not conspire to commit wire fraud—were tainted by the prosecution's improper use of the "honest services" theory of fraud.

The heart of the disagreement between the majority and the dissent in *Skilling* is contained in footnote 44, supra. Do you agree with Justice Ginsburg that significantly limiting the scope of a statute, on the ground that most of the cases decided prior to the statute's enactment implicitly defined a "core" or "heartland" of factual scenarios that Congress probably intended the statute to cover, is judicial interpretation rather than judicial invention? Do you believe that Congress really thought about all of this when deciding whether to enact the "honest services" fraud statute? If not, then isn't the new version of "honest services" fraud that emerges from the *Skilling* decision an example (as Justice Scalia suggests) of a new common-law federal crime?

5. The Justice Department took another hit, with respect to both the "honest services" theory of fraud and the scope of Hobbs Act extortion, in the case of McDonnell v. United States, 579 U.S. ___ (2016). Robert McDonnell was the former Governor of Virginia. While he was Governor, McDonnell received $175,000 in loans, gifts, and other benefits (including a Rolex watch, designer clothing, and the use of a Ferrari) from Virginia businessman Jonnie Williams, the CEO of Star Scientific, a Virginia-based company that had developed a nutritional supplement from anatabine, a compound found in tobacco. Williams wanted Governor McDonnell's help to get Virginia public universities to conduct research studies on anatabine.

McDonnell was indicted by the federal government on one count of conspiracy to commit "honest services" fraud, three counts of "honest services" fraud, one count of conspiracy to commit Hobbs Act extortion, six counts of Hobbs Act extortion, and two counts of making a false statement. (His wife, Maureen McDonnell, was also indicted on similar charges.) The fraud charges were based on the notion that Governor McDonnell had accepted bribes. Both sides agreed, before trial, that all of the charges would depend on whether or not McDonnell had committed or agreed to commit "official acts" as defined in the federal bribery statute, 18 U.S.C. §201(a)(3)—"any decision or action on any question, matter, cause, suit, proceeding or controversy, which may at any time be pending, or which may be law be brought before any public official, in such official's official capacity, or in such official's place of trust or profit"—in exchange for whatever he received from Jonnie Williams.

At trial, the prosecution argued that (1) arranging meetings for Williams with other Virginia public officials; (2) hosting events for Star Scientific at the Governor's Mansion; (3) contacting other government officials about studies of anatabine; (4) promoting Star Scientific's products by allowing Williams to invite his business contacts to exclusive events at the Governor's Mansion; and (5) recommending that senior government officials meet with Star Scientific executives all constituted "official acts"—especially since all of these activities related to the general subject of economic development in

Virginia, which was one of McDonnell's top priorities as Governor. The jury convicted McDonnell on the fraud and extortion charges, but acquitted him on the false statement charges, and McDonnell was sentenced to two years in prison. The Fourth Circuit affirmed.

The U.S. Supreme Court unanimously reversed. The Court rejected the government's broad argument that the statutory term "official acts" includes "*any* decision or action, on *any* question or matter, that may at *any time* be pending, or which may by law be brought before *any* public official, in such official's official capacity." Rather, according to the Court:

> [A] decision or action to initiate a research study—or a decision or action on a qualifying step, such as narrowing down the list of potential research topics—would qualify as an "official act." A public official may also make a decision or take an action . . . by using his official position to exert pressure on *another* official to perform an "official act." In addition, if a public official uses his official position to provide advice to another official, knowing or intending that such advice will form the basis for an "official act" by another official, that too can qualify as a decision or action for purposes of §201(a)(3). . . .
>
> Under this Court's precedents, a public official is not required to actually make a decision or take an action on a "question, matter, cause, suit, proceeding or controversy"; it is enough that the official agree to do so. The agreement need not be explicit, and the public official need not specify the means that he will use to perform his end of the bargain. Nor must the public official in fact intend to perform the "official act," so long as he agrees to do so. A jury could, for example, conclude that an agreement was reached if the evidence shows that the public official received a thing of value knowing that it was given with the expectation that the official would perform an "official act" in return. It is up to the jury, under the facts of the case, to determine whether the public official agreed to perform an "official act" at the time of the alleged *quid pro quo*. The jury may consider a broad range of pertinent evidence, including the nature of the transaction, to answer that question.
>
> Setting up a meeting, hosting an event, or calling an official (or agreeing to do so) merely to talk about a research study or to gather additional information, however, does not qualify as a decision or action on the pending question of whether to initiate the study. Simply expressing support for the research study at a meeting, event, or call—or sending a subordinate to such a meeting, event, or call—similarly does not qualify as a decision or action on the study, as long as the public official does not intend to exert pressure on another official or provide advice, knowing or intending such advice to form the basis for an "official act." Otherwise, if every action somehow related to the research study were an "official act," the requirement that the public official make a decision or take an action on that study, or agree to do so, would be meaningless. . . .
>
> In addition to being inconsistent with both text and precedent, the Government's expansive interpretation of "official act" would raise significant constitutional concerns. . . . [C]onscientious public officials arrange meetings for constituents, contact other officials on their behalf, and include them in events all the time. The basic compact underlying representative government

assumes that public officials will hear from their constituents and act appropriately on their concerns—whether it is the union official worried about a plant closing or the homeowners who wonder why it took five days to restore power to their neighborhood after a storm. The Government's position could cast a pall of potential prosecution over these relationships if the union had given a campaign contribution in the past or the homeowners invited the official to join them on their annual outing to the ballgame. Officials might wonder whether they could respond to even the most commonplace requests for assistance, and citizens with legitimate concerns might shrink from participating in democratic discourse. . . .

A related concern is that, under the Government's interpretation, the term "official act" is not defined "with sufficient definiteness that ordinary people can understand what conduct is prohibited," or "in a manner that does not encourage arbitrary and discriminatory enforcement." *Skilling*, 561 U.S., at 402-403. . . .

The Government's position also raises significant federalism concerns. A State defines itself as a sovereign through "the structure of its government, and the character of those who exercise government authority." Gregory v. Ashcroft, 501 U.S. 452, 460 (1991). That includes the prerogative to regulate the permissible scope of interactions between state officials and their constituents. Here, where a more limited interpretation of "official act" is supported by both text and precedent, we decline to "construe the statute in a manner that leaves its outer boundaries ambiguous and involves the Federal Government in setting standards" of "good government for local and state officials." McNally v. United States, 483 U.S. 350, 360 (1987). . . .

There is no doubt that this case is distasteful; it may be worse than that. But our concern is not with tawdry tales of Ferraris, Rolexes, and ball gowns. It is instead with the broader legal implications of the Government's boundless interpretation of the federal bribery statute. A more limited interpretation of the term "official act" leaves ample room for prosecuting corruption, while comporting with the text of the statute and the precedent of this Court.

The judgment of the Court of Appeals is vacated, and the case is remanded for further proceedings consistent with this opinion.

Id. at ___-___.

What, exactly, is wrong with zealous federal prosecution of public officials who engage in "tawdry" exchanges of personal favors for Rolex watches? Or, for that matter, with zealous federal prosecution of corporate officials who sell out the interests of their shareholders? Why does the Court feel the need to protect people like Jeffrey Skilling and Robert McDonnell? Do you agree that they should be protected?

6

Drug Crimes

In 2014, more than 1.5 million persons were arrested in the United States for drug crimes—more than for any other single category of crimes, including property crimes and violent crimes. One-third of all felony convictions in the United States—more than 300,000 per year—are for drug crimes. In many places, drug cases dominate criminal dockets; nearly everywhere, they occupy a large portion of police officers' and prosecutors' time and attention. Drug crimes also account for a large part—more than 20 percent—of America's massive prison population, and an even larger part of the modern growth in that population. The total number of persons incarcerated for drug offenses has increased dramatically since the inception of the "war on drugs," from 40,000 in 1980 to nearly half a million today; more Americans are incarcerated for drug crimes today than were incarcerated for *all* crimes back in 1980.

These statistics, sobering as they may be, understate the real impact that America's "war on drugs" has had on the criminal justice system and on society as a whole. Arrests, prosecutions, and convictions for drug offenses are distributed unevenly across racial lines. In 2014, blacks comprised about 13 percent of the overall U.S. population, and a roughly similar proportion of all users and sellers of illegal drugs. But 31 percent of those arrested for drug crimes, and nearly 40 percent of those incarcerated in state prisons for committing such crimes, were black. In 2013, about one out of every ten black men between the ages of 30 and 39 was incarcerated in prison or jail; in some cities (including Washington, D.C., our nation's capital), the overwhelming majority of adult black men were under the direct or indirect supervision of the criminal justice system. About one out of every three black men can expect to end up in prison or jail during his lifetime; for Hispanic men, the comparable ratio is about one in six.*

The criminal laws that give rise to these drug convictions and sentences have received remarkably little attention. One could easily fill a good-sized library with articles and books about the merits of legalizing or criminalizing drug use. But drug *law*—the definition of illegal conduct and intent, along with the virtues and vices of alternative definitions—is rarely studied.

This inattention is puzzling. In part, it may be due to the perception that the criminal law of drugs is easy: Possess them and the state will lock you up; sell them and it will lock you up and throw away the key. But that perception is wrong. Actually, the definition of both the relevant conduct and the intent that goes along with it are contested, as the cases below suggest. That should come as no surprise, for drugs raise two fundamental problems of crime definition.

First, the relevant transactions are hidden, and often remain so even after offenders have been caught and convicted. Because drug transactions are consensual, no victim with an incentive to report the crime exists. Consequently, the government must either prosecute defendants based on radically incomplete information, or gin up phony drug transactions with undercover agents and punish defendants for those. Save perhaps for the law of terrorism, nowhere else is the definition of criminal conduct so driven by the need to define crimes the government can prove—because there is so much it *can't* prove.

Second, drug cases present challenging problems of grading: separating more serious offenses from less serious ones so that punishment may be allocated fairly. One might try punishing defendants more (or less) based on the relative size of the harm they cause. But how does one measure the harm? Some statutes focus on the quantity of drugs possessed or sold; two of the main cases below deal with such statutes, from Colorado and New York, and most other states have similar laws. But defendants who carry large quantities of "merchandise" are often relatively minor players in drug distribution rings; the bigger fish are rarely caught with the drugs on them. More recently, many states have tried to assess harm by focusing on the location of the drug possession or sale; we will see two examples of such "drug-free zone" statutes, from Minnesota and Indiana, among the main cases that follow. But location is also, at least sometimes, a poor proxy for the kind of relative harm that really matters.

The core problem with grading drug crimes is that the most common approach for grading most crimes—using different intent or *mens rea* standards

* The statistics in this and the preceding paragraph are drawn mostly from the FBI's 2014 Uniform Crime Reports, available at https://ucr.fbi.gov/crime-in-the-u.s/2014/crime-in-the-u.s.-2014/persons-arrested/main, and from Marc Mauer, The Changing Racial Dynamics of the War on Drugs, The Sentencing Project (April 2009), available at http://sentencingproject.org/doc/dp_raceanddrugs.pdf. The Mauer Report contains one bright spot: Racial disparity in drug conviction and incarceration rates seems to have moderated ever so slightly since 2000, partly (the author suggests) as a result of deliberate efforts, in both legal and public policy realms, to address and ameliorate the problem.

to distinguish cases meriting long prison terms from those that receive lighter sentences—doesn't work well for drug crimes. That is because the most obvious *mens rea* standard—"knowledge" of the nature of the substances bought or sold—is not much help, since almost all defendants have such knowledge. In the context of drug crimes, it is hard to come up with a better approach that actually distinguishes between more and less culpable actors.

Finally, as you read the cases and materials in this chapter, keep thinking about the striking statistics on racial disparity reported above. Why are the serious negative consequences of convictions for drug crimes—including imprisonment, probation, and disenfranchisement (in many states, felons lose the right to vote)—visited so disproportionately on people of color? Some of the answers may involve the exercise of police discretion. That's a subject largely within the realm of criminal procedure rather than criminal law—although we have already seen that the existence of vague or overbroad criminal statutes, such as loitering or criminal trespass laws, may give rise to such problems as well. But some of the answers may involve the (perhaps unforeseen) discriminatory impacts of reasonably clear, facially neutral criminal statutes. Laws that substantially increase punishments based on the location of a drug buy, or on the particular form of the drug possessed, may contribute to racial disparity. To what extent should this be a matter of societal concern, and a reason for law reform?

A. POSSESSION, WITH OR WITHOUT INTENT TO DISTRIBUTE

Kier v. State

Court of Appeals of Georgia
292 Ga. App. 208, 663 S.E.2d 832 (2008)

Opinion by MILLER, J.

Following a bench trial, Lavashiae Kier was convicted of a single count of possession of less than one ounce of marijuana. . . . She now appeals, claiming that the evidence was insufficient to sustain her conviction. . . . Finding that the State failed to prove Kier's possession of marijuana beyond a reasonable doubt, we reverse.

"On appeal from a criminal conviction, the evidence must be viewed in the light most favorable to support the verdict, and [the defendant] no longer enjoys a presumption of innocence." Jackson v. State, 252 Ga. App. 268, 555 S.E.2d 908 (2001). So viewed, the evidence shows that on January 20, 2007, Sergeant Zack Tanner of the Baldwin County Sheriff's Department observed a vehicle traveling at a very low rate of speed while flashing its emergency lights. Tanner conducted a traffic stop to see if the driver needed assistance, and he found that the car was owned and driven by Cory Dixon. A juvenile was sitting in the front passenger seat next to Dixon; Kier was seated in the rear seat behind Dixon; and Kier's friend, Chiquita Baker, was seated next to Kier in the back seat.

After Tanner approached the driver's side door, Dixon rolled down his window, and Tanner noticed both the scent of marijuana coming from the vehicle and smoke inside of it. In investigating the possible presence of marijuana in the car, Tanner found a bag containing 16 "rocks" of crack cocaine in the compartment of the driver's door. Tanner then arrested Dixon, and he asked the other occupants of the car to exit the same. After the passengers were outside the car, police observed a hand-rolled marijuana cigarette on the rear floorboard, just behind the center console, and observed that the same had been recently smoked. Based on this cigarette, Tanner arrested all three passengers for possession of marijuana.

The only defense witness was Baker, who stated that on the evening in question, she and Kier had gone to a local nightclub, where she encountered Dixon, whom she knew from school. Baker asked Dixon if he could give Kier and her a ride home, and Dixon agreed. During that ride, Dixon and his juvenile passenger smoked a marijuana cigarette, which they disposed of when the police stopped the car. Baker, however, did not see what they did with that cigarette, because she was preoccupied with hiding her personal marijuana, obtained at the nightclub, in her underwear. Baker further stated that Kier did not smoke the marijuana cigarette belonging to Dixon and his juvenile passenger, that Kier was unaware that Baker had marijuana on her person, and that she never saw Kier in possession of marijuana that night.

After the trial court found Kier guilty, she filed this appeal. Kier first asserts that the evidence was insufficient to sustain her conviction. We agree.

Because no evidence showed Kier in actual possession of the marijuana, the State relied on circumstantial evidence to show she had constructive possession of the same. To prove constructive possession, the State was required to show some connection between Kier and the marijuana cigarette other than spatial proximity. "Evidence of mere presence at the scene of the crime . . . is insufficient to support a conviction." Hodges v. State, 277 Ga. App. 174, 626 S.E.2d 133 (2006). Rather, the State needed to demonstrate beyond a reasonable doubt that Kier "knowingly had both the power and intention at a given time to exercise control over the [marijuana]. Power may be inferred from access to the drugs, while the matter of intent may be derived from the surrounding circumstances." Castillo v. State, 288 Ga. App. 828, 830, 655 S.E.2d 695 (2007).

Circumstances showing an intent to exercise control over the drugs include a defendant's attempts to flee or elude police, inconsistent explanations by the defendant for her behavior; the presence of significant amounts of contraband and drug paraphernalia in plain view; the defendant's possession of large amounts of cash, other indicia of the sale of drugs, or drug-related paraphernalia; evidence that the defendant was under the influence of drugs; or drug residue found on the defendant. The evidence shows no such circumstances in this case. Specifically, there was no evidence that Kier was uncooperative, attempted to flee police, behaved erratically, or appeared to be under the influence of drugs. Sergeant Tanner testified that the evidence indicated that the juvenile sitting in the front passenger seat had rolled the marijuana cigarette. Sergeant Tanner further admitted that while marijuana residue was found on the floor and on the front passenger seat, no such residue was found in the area near Kier, on her seat, or on her person, and that Kier possessed no drug paraphernalia. . . .

The circumstantial evidence presented at trial was entirely consistent with Kier's theory of innocence — i.e., that she was merely a passenger in Dixon's car and had nothing to do with the marijuana cigarette found therein. Accordingly, we find no evidentiary basis on which the trial court could find beyond a reasonable doubt that Kier was in constructive possession of that marijuana. See Mitchell v. State, 268 Ga. 592, 593, 492 S.E.2d 204 (1997) (noting there is no presumption of possession by a mere passenger in an automobile, even where the drugs are found near that passenger). . . .

United States v. Hunte

United States Court of Appeals for the Seventh Circuit
196 F.3d 687 (1999)

KANNE, Circuit Judge.

Defendant Cheryl A. Hunte appeals her conviction and sentence for her role in an attempt to transport narcotics from Arizona to New York in 1997. The trial court sentenced Hunte to concurrent terms of thirty-three months imprisonment, two years supervised release and a $500 fine. On appeal, Hunte challenges the sufficiency of the evidence against her. . . .

I. HISTORY

In March 1997, Hunte decided to accompany her boyfriend, co-defendant, Joseph Richards, on a trip to California with an acquaintance known as Luis Gonzalez. Richards was a known drug dealer, and there was little mystery that the purpose of the trip was to purchase and bring back a load of narcotics. Richards supplied a minivan for the trip, and Gonzalez was to be the driver. Richards agreed to pay Gonzalez seven pounds of marijuana for help driving the van, purportedly to California. Hunte, on the other hand, stood to gain nothing from the deal. She apparently went along for the ride.

Richards directed the trip and made all or most of the decisions. Once on the road, he told Gonzalez that they were headed for Arizona, not

California, and that he planned to pick up as much marijuana as he could get and bring it back to New York. Gonzalez would get his share and sell it for $8,000 to $9,000. Richards warned Gonzalez to drive safely and obey the speed limit and other rules of the road.

The three drove to Tulsa, Oklahoma, where they rented a motel room. They showered but did not stay the night. Instead, leaving Hunte behind, Richards and Gonzalez went to meet Johnathan Warwick. Warwick was a Tulsa resident who rented a room from a man to whom Richards owed $3,000 for past drug dealings. Richards asked Warwick to help him drive to Phoenix (apparently not telling him for what purpose). Warwick agreed, believing that if the trip was successful, Richards would pay his friend the $3,000 Richards owed, and the friend would stop taking Warwick's disability checks for room and board. The three men picked up Hunte at the motel and left for Arizona.

Once back on the highway, Richards changed the plan again and said they were headed for Tucson, not Phoenix, and that their ultimate destination was Virginia, not New York. Warwick eventually figured out they were going to pick up drugs, but by this time they were in Texas. In Tucson, Richards made some calls from a pay phone at a convenience store, and eventually a man in a Chevy Blazer arrived who then escorted them to a house. Several hours later, a man came and took the minivan, returning it later loaded with marijuana. Richards asked Gonzalez and Warwick to help him carry the marijuana into the kitchen. During this time, Hunte remained in the living room watching television. With Hunte in the other room, the three men weighed the bundles of marijuana. Richards cut one bundle open to make sure it was all marijuana and extracted some buds for sampling. Gonzalez testified at trial that Richards took precautions to keep Hunte out of the business aspects of the deal.

Hunte helped roll the buds into a joint and closed the window blinds while the group smoked some of the marijuana. Warwick, Richards and Gonzalez re-wrapped the marijuana and loaded it into the van. Richards' brother then arrived in a burgundy Nissan Maxima. After dropping off Richards' brother in Phoenix, Richards and Hunte drove to Tulsa in the Maxima, followed by Gonzalez and Warwick in the van. Hunte registered for a motel room for herself and Richards, while Gonzalez and Warwick registered for another room. Richards paid all expenses, including the motels, throughout the trip.

The next morning, March 25, 1997, the group awoke and continued to New York. In Illinois, state police pulled the minivan over and a search revealed the bundles of marijuana. Warwick and Gonzalez admitted they were following another car, and based on the information they supplied, the police radioed ahead and were able to pull over Hunte and Richards. Before they were stopped by police but after the minivan had been pulled over, Hunte and Richards had switched positions so that Hunte was driving. Hunte and Richards initially denied that they were traveling with the mini-van and told police they had been traveling around the Midwest looking for farm equipment for Richards' Jamaican chicken farm. As their grasp of basic geography deteriorated, so did their cover story. Police matched fingerprints on the marijuana to Richards, but not to Hunte.

Richards, Warwick and Gonzalez pleaded guilty to conspiracy and possession with intent to distribute almost 45 kilograms of marijuana. Hunte, like the others, was charged with . . . possession of marijuana with intent to distribute, 21 U.S.C. §841(a)(1). Gonzalez and Warwick agreed to testify against Hunte at trial in exchange for one-third off their sentences. At trial, Hunte's primary defense was that she never possessed the marijuana because Richards was in charge and only he, Gonzalez and Warwick ever handled the bundles. . . .

II. ANALYSIS

. . .

Sufficiency of the Evidence

Possession with intent to distribute marijuana requires the Government prove beyond a reasonable doubt that Hunte (1) knowingly or intentionally possessed the marijuana, (2) possessed the marijuana with the intent to distribute it, and (3) knew the marijuana was a controlled substance. The first element, possession, can be satisfied by direct or circumstantial evidence of constructive or joint possession. Constructive possession applies when "a person does not have actual possession but instead knowingly has the power and the intention at a given time to exercise dominion and control over an object, either directly or through others." United States v. Garrett, 903 F.2d 1105, 1110 (7th Cir. 1990); see also United States v. DiNovo, 523 F.2d 197, 201 (7th Cir. 1975).

Hunte challenges her conviction on the theory that she did not exercise "dominion and control" over the marijuana because at all times Richards, as the group's leader, had exclusive control over the contraband. *DiNovo* stands for the proposition that "mere proximity to the drug, mere presence on the property where it is located, or mere association, without more, with the person who does control the drug or the property on which it is found, is insufficient to support a finding of possession." *DiNovo*, 523 F.2d at 199. This line of cases protects the "ordinary bystander" who happens to be unlucky enough to be near someone who possesses contraband. United States v. Windom, 19 F.3d 1190, 1200 (7th Cir. 1994). To this end, we have required that in non-exclusive possession cases, the evidence must show some nexus between the defendant and the drugs. See United States v. Hernandez, 13

F.3d 248, 252 (7th Cir. 1994); United States v. Galiffa, 734 F.2d 306, 316 (7th Cir. 1984).

Galiffa appears especially instructive in this case. In *Galiffa*, Stuart Ashenfelter and Thomas Galiffa rented a truck, Ashenfelter bought some boxes and the two drove to a forest preserve. Ashenfelter then proceeded alone to a hiding place where he retrieved the marijuana. He picked up Galiffa in the forest preserve and the two returned to their house. While Ashenfelter, Galiffa and another man were unloading the contraband, they were arrested. Galiffa challenged the sufficiency of the evidence on his conviction for possession. Galiffa argued that his mere presence in the truck, presence at the rear of the truck during unloading and flight from law enforcement officers were insufficient to establish his possession of the marijuana or his knowledge of the contents of the packages. This court held that "residence in a house used as a drug distribution center, and evidence of direct access to and participation in the marijuana distribution on the day of his arrest is enough to establish this nexus and, therefore, marijuana possession under 21 U.S.C. §841(a)." Id. at 315.

As convincing as the proof against Galiffa, the evidence against Hunte more than substantiates the nexus between her and the contraband. There can be no doubt of her knowledge of the marijuana because she was present when it was delivered, unloaded, sampled and loaded. Although the evidence of her direct access to the drugs and participation in the transportation is minimal, it can hardly be said that she was in any sense an ordinary bystander. She registered for the hotel room, drove at least one of the vehicles, helped hide their activities from view and aided in the sampling of the drugs. She can no more claim to be a mere bystander than could Thomas Galiffa.

. . . Hunte argues that no evidence shows "she ever touched the bundles of marijuana," but that argument only refutes actual possession and is not dispositive of constructive possession. Hunte further argues that only Richards had constructive possession of the marijuana, as shown by his offer to pay Gonzalez from the stash and to let Hunte sample some of it. While those facts provide strong evidence that Richards exercised control over the drugs, it does not necessarily mean Hunte and the others did not jointly possess them as well. As discussed above, control need not be exclusive.

The evidence showed that all four defendants were engaged in a plan to transport narcotics and that Richards was the leader of the group. The fact that one person leads and the others follow does not mean that only the leader has possession of the contraband. All four had access to the drugs at various times and assisted in their concealment and transportation. As a group, the four each exercised joint possession of the narcotics by virtue of their individual acts consistent with non-exclusive dominion and control over the contraband. . . .

Notes on Drug Possession

1. For the most part, drug crimes are proxy crimes: The statutes that define the crimes do not accurately define the conduct the crimes aim to suppress. The law's real target is the manufacture, purchase, and sale of the relevant substances. Purchase is punished by prosecutions for possession of those substances. Manufacture and sale are punished, usually, by prosecutions for possession "with intent to distribute" — meaning, possession of quantities larger than ordinary users possess for their own personal use. The meaning of possession is at the heart of both crimes.

2. *Kier* and *Hunte* define the conduct that leads to punishment for drug possession. In *Kier,* the defendant wins because she lacked control over the drugs; the court emphasizes that "the State was required to show some connection between Kier and the marijuana cigarette other than spatial proximity." In *Hunte,* the defendant loses mostly because of spatial proximity — the very fact that *Kier* says does not suffice to show constructive possession. Why the different standards? Are *Kier* and *Hunte* consistent?

3. At trial, Kier was convicted of the possession crime, based on "constructive possession," because she was found in a car that contained (in close proximity to her location within the car) a partially smoked marijuana joint. The appellate court overturns the conviction, largely because Kier was lucky enough to have a *really* good friend in Chiquita Baker, who was willing to take the rap herself and testify that Kier had nothing whatsoever to do with the marijuana. Not all defendants like Kier are so lucky.

What does this mean for persons who may inadvertently find themselves in situations — in cars, in homes or apartments or dorm rooms, at parties — where illegal drugs are visibly present? If the police suddenly show up, aren't they likely to infer that everyone present shares both access to (i.e., "power") and "intent to control" the drugs, which means that everyone present is subject to being arrested and charged with possession? (Note, by the way, that the *Kier* court identifies attempted flight from the police as one of the facts that can help *establish* "constructive possession" — so running away when the police arrive can only make matters worse!) Certainly a person in such a situation who lacks the actual intent to exercise control over the drugs *should* not be convicted based solely on "mere proximity," but is that a risk worth taking? Does this suggest that one must choose one's friends and roommates carefully? Doesn't this seem like guilt by association? Does it seem fair?

On the general subject of guilt by association, compare the U.S. Supreme Court's criminal procedure decision in Maryland v. Pringle, 540 U.S. 366 (2003), where the Court unanimously held that a police officer's discovery of $763 in cash (in the glove compartment) and five glassine baggies of cocaine (from between the back-seat armrest and the back seat) in a lawfully stopped car provided sufficient probable cause to arrest not only the *driver* of the car, but also the two *passengers.* As the Court explained, "a car passenger . . . will often be engaged in a common enterprise with the driver, and have the same interest in concealing the fruits or the evidence of their wrongdoing." See also Wyoming v. Houghton, 526 U.S. 295 (1999), where the Court allowed the warrantless search of a *passenger's* purse based upon the admission of the *driver* of the car to the police that he used illegal drugs.

4. Hunte had a closer relationship with her boyfriend than with the drugs. Was that the real reason she was convicted? Was it the reason she was prosecuted? Notice that one consequence of imposing criminal liability on Hunte is that, in future cases, girlfriends like Hunte will have a significant incentive to cooperate with the prosecutor and provide evidence against their drug-dealing boyfriends.

5. Tens of millions of Americans use marijuana each year. The number of prosecutions for simple possession of marijuana is probably in the low tens of thousands, and most of those prosecutions happen when prosecutors have reason to believe the defendants are guilty of selling the drug, not just using it. Given those statistics, is it appropriate to prosecute even the passenger who actually rolled the joint in *Kier*?

Garcia v. Florida

Supreme Court of Florida
901 So. 2d 788 (2005)

Opinion of QUINCE, J.

. . . The facts of this case are thoroughly set forth in the [Second District Court of Appeal's] decision as follows:

> In the early morning hours on June 9, 2001, Pasco County Deputy Sheriff Joseph Irizarry observed Garcia driving a truck. Garcia's vehicle first came to Deputy Irizarry's attention when it passed through a flashing yellow light without slowing down. Thereafter, Deputy Irizarry saw Garcia's vehicle go off the road while making a right-hand turn and then weave off the roadway onto the grassy shoulder three times. After observing this behavior and following Garcia's vehicle for approximately a quarter of a mile, Deputy Irizarry decided to stop Garcia's vehicle.
>
> After the vehicle stopped and Deputy Irizarry approached the driver's window of the vehicle, he smelled alcohol and observed that Garcia's eyes were bloodshot and that Garcia's speech was slurred. Garcia was alone in the truck. Deputy Irizarry proceeded to conduct field sobriety tests. After conducting the tests, Deputy Irizarry arrested Garcia for driving under the influence.
>
> In the meantime, Deputy Wilkins and Deputy Banner arrived at the scene. In the course of searching Garcia's truck incident to his arrest, Deputy Wilkins found an item—which looked like a softball wrapped in black electrical tape—underneath the passenger's seat of Garcia's truck. Garcia told the deputies at the scene that he did not know what the item was, that he had not

seen it before, and had not known that it was in the truck. He also stated that his truck had recently been stolen and that some friends had been in his truck earlier that night. Subsequent tests conducted by the FDLE crime laboratory determined that an off-white powder contained within the item was a mixture containing methamphetamine and a cutting agent.

Garcia was charged by information with trafficking in methamphetamine, driving under the influence, and obstructing or resisting an officer without violence. In his testimony at trial, Garcia stated that the night of his arrest he had the truck at a party from about 7:00 P.M. until 2:00 A.M. His truck was used at the party for playing CDs. Garcia also used the truck on two occasions during the party to take friends to buy beer. Garcia denied using drugs. He testified that he did not put the tape-covered item in the truck, know it was there, or know what it contained. Finally, Garcia testified that his truck had been stolen on Wednesday, May 31, from a shop where he had taken it. The truck was recovered the following Monday in a dirty condition and containing items that did not belong to Garcia. After recovering the truck, he returned it to the shop for the installation of a stereo. When he later picked up the truck, it was clean.

Garcia was found guilty of the driving under the influence charge and guilty of the lesser-included crime of possession of methamphetamine on the trafficking offense. He was found not guilty of the obstructing or resisting charge.

During the trial, at the close of the State's evidence and at the close of all the evidence, Garcia moved for a judgment of acquittal on the trafficking charge pursuant to Florida Rule of Criminal Procedure 3.380(a). The motion was denied.

854 So. 2d 758, 760-61 (Fla. 2d DCA 2003). At the jury charge conference, Garcia objected to the standard jury instruction that permitted the jury to infer or assume knowledge of the presence of the methamphetamine based on exclusive possession. The trial court overruled the objection, rejected Garcia's proposed special instructions, and read the standard instructions on trafficking. In listing the elements of trafficking, the trial court instructed the jury that "the defendant's knowledge 'that the substance was methamphetamine or a mixture containing methamphetamine' was a material element of the offense of *trafficking*." Id. at 764 (emphasis added). The trial court also instructed the jury concerning actual and constructive possession and stated as follows:

If a thing is in a place over which the person does not have control, in order to establish constructive possession, the State must prove the person has control over the thing, knowledge of the thing which was in the person's presence, and the *knowledge of the illicit nature of the thing*.

Id. at 765 (emphasis in original). The trial court then gave an instruction on the elements of the lesser included offense of simple possession. That instruction omitted any reference to the requirement that the defendant have knowledge of the illicit nature of the substance. However, the trial court did state that the prior instruction regarding the "definition of possession . . . applies to the lesser charge as it did to the greater charge." Id. at 765. . . .

During deliberations, the jury submitted a question to the court: "What is the difference between trafficking and possession of methamphetamine?" The court then reread the instructions on possession and trafficking, but not the instructions concerning actual and constructive possession. The jury acquitted Garcia of trafficking but found him guilty of the lesser included offense of possession. Garcia renewed his motion for judgment of acquittal and moved for a new trial. Both motions were denied.

Garcia raised several claims on appeal. The district court summarily denied all but the following two claims: (1) the trial court erred when it denied Garcia's motion for judgment of acquittal based on his contention that there was insufficient evidence to establish knowledge of the illicit nature of the substance, and (2) the trial court erred in giving a jury instruction on the lesser included offense of possession that did not include the "knowledge of the illicit nature of the substance" element, i.e., the "guilty knowledge element."

The district court held that the illicit nature of the substance is an indisputable element of the crime of drug possession pursuant to Chicone v. State, 684 So. 2d 736, 737 (Fla. 1996) (holding that guilty knowledge is an element of possession of a controlled substance and possession of drug paraphernalia). The district court rejected the State's argument that the holding in *Chicone* was superseded by Fla. Stat. §893.101. That statute provides that knowledge of the illicit nature of a controlled substance is not an element of drug offenses, but lack of knowledge is an affirmative defense. The statute became law after Garcia committed the offense in this case. The district court then concluded that the instruction given was clearly inadequate and erroneous. However, the court also found that Garcia [failed to object to the erroneous instruction on the possession offense]. The error was not preserved, and the district court found that it was not fundamental. . . .

LAW AND ANALYSIS

In 1973, this Court established a presumption of the scienter element of drug charges arising from actual possession. See State v. Medlin, 273 So. 2d 394 (Fla. 1973). In *Medlin*, the defendant gave a capsule to another person, and it contained an illegal substance. Despite the fact that Medlin told the other person that the capsule would make her "go up," Medlin argued that there was no proof at trial to show that he delivered the capsule with knowledge that it contained a barbiturate. Medlin was convicted of delivery of an unlawful barbiturate. . . . On review, this Court . . . held that the State was not required to prove knowledge or intent since both were presumed from the doing of the prohibited act. . . . [T]he *Medlin* presumption was incorporated into [the standard jury instructions for the crime of possession] by the following language: "If a person has exclusive possession of a thing, knowledge of its presence may be inferred or assumed." However, the instruction did not list knowledge of the illicit nature of the substance as an element [of the crime]. . . .

In 1987, this Court addressed whether the jury instructions on trafficking offenses were erroneous because they did not include knowledge of the nature of the substance as an element. See State v. Dominguez, 509 So. 2d 917 (Fla. 1987). . . . The Court . . . expressly amended the jury instructions on trafficking offenses to include a fourth element: that the defendant "knew the substance was (specific substance alleged)." Id. at 918.

In 1996, the Court applied the rationale of *Dominguez* to possession offenses. See Chicone v. State, 684 So. 2d 736 (Fla. 1996). In *Chicone*, the defendant was convicted of possession of cocaine. The trial court refused Chicone's request to instruct the jury that the State had to prove he knew the substance he possessed was cocaine. On review, this Court held that guilty knowledge is part of the statutory offense charged. Id. at 738. . . . In *Chicone*, the State was required to prove the defendant knew of the *illicit nature* of the items in his or her possession. . . . However, the trial court was only required to "expressly indicate to jurors that guilty knowledge means the defendant must have knowledge of the illicit nature of the substance allegedly possessed" if "specifically requested by a defendant." Id. at 745-46.

. . . In Scott [v. State, 808 So. 2d 166 (Fla. 2002)], the defendant was convicted of possession of contraband (cannabis) in a correctional facility. At trial, Scott's defense was that he . . . had no knowledge of [the drug's] presence in his locker, where it was found. He requested an instruction pursuant to *Chicone* that the guilty knowledge element includes knowledge of the illicit nature of the substance. The trial court denied the request. On review, this Court held that the trial court's failure to give the requested instruction was reversible error. This Court explained that the *Chicone* decision stood for the proposition that both knowledge of the presence of the substance and knowledge of the illicit nature of the substance are essential elements of the crime of possession of an illegal substance. Id. at 169. . . . [We] further found that it is error to fail to give the requested instruction even if the defendant did not explicitly say he did not have knowledge of the illicit nature of the substance. Id. at 172. . . .

. . . *Medlin*, *Chicone*, and *Scott* stand for the proposition that "guilty knowledge" is an element of the offense of possession and must be proven beyond a reasonable doubt. The guilty knowledge element includes knowledge of both the *presence* of, and the *illicit nature* of, the substance possessed, and the jury should be instructed on both. . . .

In this case, the element of knowledge of the illicit nature [of the relevant substance] is in dispute. A challenge to that element is encompassed in Garcia's argument that he did not know the container existed at all and he had never seen it before. By arguing that he did not have knowledge that the black taped package existed, the defendant in this case is implicitly arguing that he did not have knowledge of the illicit nature of the substance inside of it. See, e.g., *Scott*, 808 So. 2d at 169 (holding that Scott's argument that he did not possess the drugs and had no knowledge of the drug's presence in his locker encompasses the argument that he was unaware of the illicit nature of the substance). . . . Thus, when a defendant argues that he or she had no knowledge that an illegal substance was in his or her possession, that defendant also disputes that he or she had knowledge of the nature of the illegal substance. When an essential element of a crime is in dispute at trial, such as the knowledge of the illicit nature of the substance in a possession case, the failure to instruct the jury on that element is fundamental error. . . .

[The dissenting opinion of Justice Wells, joined by Justices Cantero and Bell, is omitted.]

Notes on Mens Rea *with Respect to Drug Possession*

1. Shortly after the Florida Supreme Court's opinion in *Scott*—and shortly after the events that gave rise to Garcia's prosecution—the Florida legislature enacted the following statute, altering the doctrine described in *Garcia*:

§893.101. LEGISLATIVE FINDINGS AND INTENT.

> (1) The Legislature finds that . . . Scott v. State, 808 So. 2d 166 (Fla. 2002), and Chicone v. State, 684 So. 2d 736 (Fla. 1996), holding that the state must prove that the defendant knew of the illicit nature of a controlled substance found in his or her actual or constructive possession, were contrary to legislative intent.
>
> (2) The Legislature finds that knowledge of the illicit nature of a controlled substance is not an element of any offense under this chapter. Lack of knowledge of the illicit nature of a controlled substance is an affirmative defense to the offenses of this chapter.
>
> (3) In those instances in which a defendant asserts the affirmative defense described in this section, the possession of a controlled substance, whether actual or constructive, shall give rise to a permissive presumption that the possessor knew of the illicit nature of the substance. It is the intent of the Legislature that, in those cases where such an affirmative defense is

raised, the jury shall be instructed on the permissive presumption provided in this subsection.

Fla. Stat. §893.101. Under the statute, knowledge of possession remains part of the definition of the crime, while lack of knowledge of the nature of the substance possessed becomes an affirmative defense (meaning that the defendant bears the burden of proving it). Why do you suppose the legislature treated those two *mens rea* issues differently?

2. What is the best approach to culpability in a case like *Garcia*? How is the state supposed to prove what Garcia did or didn't know? The answers to those questions are not obvious. Drug purchase and use are consensual activities; no crime victim reports the offense to the police, and the only witnesses to the relevant conduct are usually guilty of crimes themselves. In short, both victims and witnesses lack the natural incentive to cooperate with the police or testify in a later criminal trial. The government generally deals with this problem by the use of informants—people who buy and/or sell drugs themselves, and who therefore come in contact with other buyers and sellers. In order to overcome an informant's natural tendency to lie or clam up, the police and prosecutors use both threats and bribes. The most common threat is criminal punishment—often an officer can "turn" an arrestee against whom the government has a strong case. (As noted above, this may have been the true motivation behind the prosecution in *Hunte.*) Bribes can take the form of immunity (the flip side of the threat) or money; cash payment for information about drug violations is common.

3. Obviously, there is enormous potential for error and injustice in a system that extensively relies on informants. Informants may provide information in part to eliminate rivals or settle scores, or simply to get the police off their backs. Those motives may be served by providing false testimony as well as the truthful kind. Plus, the informants who have the most information to sell to the government—and, therefore, the ones who can expect to receive the biggest payments in return—tend to be not just participants in drug distribution rings, but often major figures in those organizations. In the strange world of drug offenses, crime often pays, and pays well.

4. All of which brings us back to the definition of the offense in *Garcia*. The chief alternative to the use of informants is prosecution of defendants who are caught with illegal drugs on them—in their pockets, in their cars, and in their homes. The harder it is for the government to convict in such cases, the more tempting it will be to rely instead on informants and government stings, which carry their own problems.

Given that Hobson's choice, what is the best way to define the crime in *Garcia*? What should the government have to prove in order establish possession? What should it have to prove in order to show criminal intent?

State v. Pigford

Supreme Court of Louisiana
922 So. 2d 517 (2006)

PER CURIAM.

Defendant was charged by bill of information with possession of marijuana with intent to distribute in violation of La. Rev. Stat. §40:966(A)(1).* After trial in which defendant represented himself . . . a jury returned a verdict of guilty as charged. The court . . . sentenced [the defendant] to eight years imprisonment at hard labor. On appeal, the Second Circuit reversed his conviction and sentence on grounds that the state's evidence failed to prove that he had constructive possession of the marijuana found in the trailer of an 18-wheel truck he had driven from California into Louisiana, where it was stopped in Caddo Parish en route to either Pennsylvania or New York. This Court granted review because we agree with the state that the court of appeal erred by substituting its view of the evidence for that of the jury. . . . We therefore reverse the decision below and reinstate defendant's conviction and sentence.

The evidence adduced at trial showed the following: On September 25, 2000, a computer weight monitoring system set up on Interstate 20 in Caddo Parish by state police registered an eastbound Volvo 18-wheeler 3,000 pounds over the state weight limit of 80,000 pounds. The vehicle, driven by defendant, was directed to pull over into the nearest weigh station where the truck was weighed on the stationary scales and again registered 3,000 pounds over the legal limit. Sergeant Brierre Thomas, with the Louisiana Department of Transportation, Weights and Standard Unit, and Deputy Danny Williams, a K-9 officer with the Caddo Parish Sheriff's Office, interviewed defendant. Defendant told them that he was traveling to New York; however, the bill of lading showed that he was hauling a load of grapes from Reedley, California to Pittsburgh, Pennsylvania.

Because they were concerned about the discrepancy in the destination for the load of grapes and about defendant's seemingly wayward route from California to either New York or Pennsylvania, Sergeant Thomas and Deputy Williams asked him to open the back of the trailer so they could see what he had as cargo. Defendant refused to open the trailer, telling the officers he

* [The relevant portion of the statute reads as follows:

§40:966. . . . Except as authorized by this Part, it shall be unlawful for any person knowingly or intentionally:

(1) To produce, manufacture, distribute or dispense or possess with intent to produce, manufacture, distribute, or dispense, a controlled dangerous substance or controlled substance analogue classified in Schedule I. . . .

—EDS.]

was a member of the NAACP and that he knew he had a right to refuse to allow the search.

Immediately after defendant refused to open the trailer, Sergeant Thomas called Peggy Adley, an agent with the Public Service Commission. Sergeant Thomas testified that he called Adley because she would need to know what was in the trailer and that she would need to check defendant's [registration] and insurance, and inspect his load to see if it matched his bill of lading. Officer Adley arrived and told defendant that she had the right to inspect the trailer without his consent. Defendant produced a key, unlocked the padlock, and opened the trailer's doors. At the request of Officer Adley, Officer Thomas climbed up onto the back of the trailer to inspect the load. The officer testified that as he stood up at the back of the trailer he saw in plain view the end of a large package sitting on top of the boxes of grapes, less than an arm's length from the back end of the load. Officer Thomas turned his head and asked defendant what the object was, and defendant indicated that he knew nothing about it. The officer then reached over the stacked boxes of grapes and pulled the package towards him. The package was wrapped in clear plastic wrap and duct tape; it measured approximately a foot wide and six-and-a-half to seven feet long. According to Adley, who stood outside at the rear of the truck, despite its size, the package was not visible from her vantage point when she looked through the opened doors of the trailer.

After Thomas removed the package, Deputy Williams cut a slit in the side and determined that the bundle contained marijuana. In all, the package contained approximately 52 pounds of marijuana possessing a street value of $52,000. Both officers testified at trial that the sheer amount of marijuana, its value, and the manner of its packaging, were all consistent with an intent to distribute. However, no fingerprints were found on the package and the officers had otherwise determined that defendant's bill of lading for his cargo was in good order.

. . . [At trial, defendant] urged jurors to consider that he was not off route because Interstate 20 runs to California, and he promised to produce a map to prove the point. Defendant also urged jurors to consider that no evidence would establish that he had witnessed the loading of the trailer in California. Defendant prompted Deputy Williams to admit that it was possible that someone loading the load could have placed the marijuana into the truck while he was sorting out the paperwork before leaving California with the load, and that someone else could have taken the marijuana off at the other end, and ". . . the defendant would never have known what he was carrying." . . . It was therefore entirely possible, defendant suggested, that persons unknown to him had concealed the marijuana in the trailer without his knowledge and far enough back from the trailer door that it was not visible to anyone standing outside, and then alerted other conspirators in New York waiting to off-load the contraband that the shipment was on its way. As for the discrepancy in the load's ultimate destination, defendant suggested that he had been transporting a "blind shipment," one intended by the broker for a destination other than the one listed on the bill of lading.

In reversing the defendant's conviction, the Second Circuit panel emphasized that Sergeant Thomas found the marijuana not in the cab of the tractor but in the trailer, on top of the truck's legal cargo of grapes and positioned out of the plain view of anyone standing, as Adley had, in the opened doors at the rear of the vehicle. On the premise that "one cannot apply private vehicle case law regarding constructive possession to drugs found in the cargo area of a common carrier involving the transportation of goods or persons," 892 So. 2d at 730, the court of appeal reasoned that defendant's access to the cargo area did not [necessarily] indicate that he had knowledge of the contraband concealed in the trailer. In the appellate court's view, the state needed to present additional evidence demonstrating defendant's guilty knowledge "to preclude the possibility that the contraband was put there by third persons during the loading of the cargo, or evidence proving the driver's knowledge of the contraband in the cargo area." Id. The court of appeal ultimately concluded that the state's evidence did not exclude the reasonable hypothesis that persons responsible for loading the trailer placed the marijuana on top of the grapes and out of sight for unloading by other members of the conspiracy at [the end of the trip]. In addition, . . . the state presented no evidence at trial as to the ownership of the cargo trailer. The state's case therefore did not "preclude the possibility that the defendant may have backed his Volvo tractor up to someone else's loaded trailer, hitched the trailer to his tractor, locked the trailer doors, and driven off." 892 So. 2d at 731.

. . . In reviewing the sufficiency of evidence, an appellate court must determine that the evidence, whether direct or circumstantial, or a mixture of both, viewed in the light most favorable to the prosecution, was sufficient to convince a rational trier of fact that all of the elements of the crime have been proven beyond a reasonable doubt. Jackson v. Virginia, 443 U.S. 307 (1979); State v. Captville, 448 So. 2d 676, 678 (La. 1984). . . .

In the present case, the court of appeal justified its decision to reverse in part on grounds that the state failed to negate the possibility that defendant simply hooked his tractor up to the wrong trailer and unwittingly drove off with over $52,000 worth of marijuana and someone else's legal load of grapes. That alternative hypothesis of innocence may have been possible, but it clearly was not so probable that reasonable jurors would necessarily . . . entertain a reasonable doubt of defendant's guilt. As to the hypothesis of innocence actually advanced by defendant at trial through his cross-examination of the state's witnesses, i.e., that he did not load the trailer and therefore remained unaware of the marijuana stashed by someone else on top of his legal load and out of sight to a casual observer, defendant clearly had dominion and control over the trailer and its contents as well as his tractor. The trailer had been padlocked only and Officer Thomas's testimony at trial informed jurors of the difference between a trailer sealed by the shipper to deny the driver or anyone else access to the contents during transportation and a trailer merely padlocked, as to which the driver retains access to the interior and cargo. . . .

Defendant's dominion and control over the trailer and access to its contents did not alone establish his guilty knowledge of the marijuana bundle placed on top of the grape pallets. Nevertheless, guilty knowledge, an essential component of any showing that a defendant has constructive possession of contraband, i.e., dominion and control over it although the contraband is not in his actual possession, may be inferred from the circumstances of the transaction. State v. Major, 888 So. 2d 798, 803 (La. 2004).

In the present case, the court of appeal feared that "to convict a driver only on the evidence that he had access to the cargo area creates a dangerous precedent for the many drivers involved in commercial transportation of goods. . . ." 892 So. 2d at 730. [But] . . . the state provided jurors with additional evidence from which a rational trier of fact could infer defendant's guilty knowledge. . . . Sergeant Thomas testified that a citation for an overweight load was a "common occurrence" on the interstate but that the defendant appeared unusually nervous for such a routine violation. Defendant also appeared to have gone considerably off course, given his bill of lading indicating that the trailer had been loaded in California with pallets of grapes for delivery in the Northeast, either in Pennsylvania or New York. . . .

Defendant's apparently wayward course and attempt to conceal his ultimate destination gave rise to a reasonable inference that he had a particular and not-so-innocent reason for traveling far out of his way although engaged in interstate shipment of perishable cargo. The marijuana may not have been in plain view from outside the trailer but anyone with access to the cargo could have found the package in the same way that Officer Thomas discovered it, simply by standing in the back of the trailer and inspecting the load. The supposed conspirators loading the trailer had therefore chosen the least likely spot to conceal the six-to-seven-foot-long marijuana package inside a trailer that was not sealed by the shipper but padlocked only. In fact, the location of the marijuana packet on top of the grape pallets at the rear of the trailer clearly suggested that the contraband had been placed in the trailer after it was fully loaded and not during the loading process, a scenario entirely consistent with the state's theory of the case that at some point after loading defendant used his key to unlock the trailer and stash his marijuana shipment.

Finally, rational jurors could also consider the likelihood that a person would commit over $50,000 worth of marijuana to a carrier completely oblivious of the conspiracy to ship the contraband, although the load had not been sealed but merely padlocked and the driver therefore retained access to the trailer's interior and could easily find the package placed on top of the legal load. See Major, 888 So. 2d at 803 ("The quantity of drugs and cash in the car indicated the likelihood of drug dealing, an enterprise to which a dealer would be unlikely to admit an innocent person with the potential to furnish evidence against him."); see also United States v. Serrano-Lopez, 366 F.3d 628, 635 (8th Cir. 2004) ("The large quantity of drugs involved is evidence of the defendants' knowledge. Even if the drugs were not owned by the defendants, it is unlikely that the owner would place approximately $130,000 worth of cocaine in the hands of people who do not even know it is there.").

Under these circumstances, we conclude that jurors reasonably rejected the hypothesis of innocence advanced by defendant, and that the evidence presented at trial suggested no other hypothesis necessarily giving rise to reasonable doubt as to defendant's guilty knowledge. . . . The evidence otherwise supported the jury's finding that defendant had dominion and control over the contraband by virtue of his access to the interior of the trailer and that he therefore had constructive possession of the marijuana, in an amount and value sufficient to support an inference of intent to distribute. Accordingly, the decision below is vacated [and] defendant's conviction and sentence are reinstated. . . .

Notes and Questions

1. Notice the punishment in *Pigford*: eight years at hard labor. Does that seem a reasonable sentence for transporting $50,000 worth of marijuana across the country?

2. Speaking of transporting drugs across the country, why was Pigford prosecuted in a Louisiana state court? He was not a local marijuana dealer; indeed, he apparently was not a local resident. His real crime was interstate transportation, which sounds like a federal offense. *Pigford* and *Whitaker* (the next main case) both look like the sort of offenses that federal prosecutors should handle; by contrast, *Hurwitz* and *Ruiz*—two federal cases later in this chapter and the next—both look like classic state-court cases, with defendants whose conduct was restricted to a single jurisdiction. Is there any discernible pattern to the exercise of jurisdiction in these cases?

3. *Pigford* captures the basic structure of the law of drug distribution. Prosecutors focus on drug dealing, but the most frequently charged offense is not distribution, which is hard to prove. Instead, the usual way prosecutors go after dealers is to charge possession with intent to distribute: meaning, in practice, possession of more-than-user-quantity of the relevant drug. There are only two potentially difficult questions in such cases—proving possession, and proving "guilty knowledge." In *Pigford*, as in many possession-with-intent cases, those two issues wind up collapsing into one. The defendant's possession is proved by his control over and access to the back of the truck. The defendant's "guilty knowledge" is proved in the same manner. Is the evidence persuasive? Is there any substantial chance that Pigford is telling the truth—that the package with marijuana was placed on the truck by someone else without Pigford's knowledge or consent? If he *is* telling the truth, how likely is it that he can establish that fact in court? If he's lying, how likely is it that the government can prove *that* fact in court?

4. Assuming the government is right in *Pigford* (and it probably is), how much do you know about the defendant's crime? With respect to most crimes and in cases that go to trial, the prosecution and the court know a great deal. In homicide cases, the court generally knows who killed whom, when, how, and why; in robbery or assault cases, much the same is true. In rape cases, the problem isn't that the relevant transactions are hidden but that different parties offer conflicting versions of the facts. Nevertheless, anyone who reads appellate opinions in rape cases cannot help being struck by the level of factual detail those opinions offer.

Not so in drug cases. There, most of the relevant facts *are* hidden—even after the defendant is convicted. The source of Pigford's drugs, the drugs' destination, Pigford's previous drug transactions, the identities of his colleagues and employers—all that is invisible, at least to the court. Prosecutors and the police might know some of those things (or might think they do), but the law doesn't require the government to paint a detailed picture in order to convict, so the incentive is to hold as much information in reserve as possible, to maximize its value to other investigations. And sometimes, the government doesn't know those things at all. That is particularly likely with defendants like Pigford who refuse to plead out and insist on going to trial. Drug defendants are regularly sentenced to long prison terms not because the government knows what they've done, but because it doesn't—the defendant refused to give the police and/or prosecutors the information they wanted (either because he didn't want to or because he couldn't), so the government tries to make an example of him, in order to convince future defendants to be more cooperative.

Perhaps that is the best the system can do. (Can you think of a better way?) And Pigford is very probably guilty of the charge against him. But he might not be as guilty as his prosecutor imagines. And his sentence surely reflects the imagined crimes as much as it reflects the one the state actually proved.

B. THE AMOUNT OF THE DRUG POSSESSED OR SOLD

Whitaker v. People

Supreme Court of Colorado
48 P.3d 555 (2002)

Justice HOBBS delivered the opinion of the Court.

A jury convicted the defendant, David Whitaker, of possessing with intent to distribute over 1,000 grams of methamphetamine, a schedule II controlled substance, and importing methamphetamine into Colorado.

Whitaker claimed that his conviction should be reversed because the trial judge did not instruct the jury to apply the *mens rea* of "knowingly" to both the quantity and the importation of the drug. The court of appeals upheld Whitaker's conviction. We agree.

We hold that the General Assembly, in section 18-18-405, did not intend to apply a culpable mental state to the quantity of drugs the defendant distributed, manufactured, dispensed, sold, or possessed. We also hold that importation under Colorado's special offender statute, section 18-18-407, does not include a *mens rea* requirement. . . .

I

On January 14, 1998, David Whitaker was a passenger on a Greyhound bus en route from Los Angeles, California to Denver, Colorado. The bus stopped in Grand Junction, Colorado for routine service and to change drivers. Passengers were required to leave the bus during this stop. After the passengers had reboarded, three Grand Junction Police Department officers entered the bus, identifying themselves as police officers. Two of the officers began talking to each of the bus passengers, including Whitaker.

The officers testified that Whitaker appeared nervous while talking to them. When asked about his luggage, Whitaker told the police that he had none. The officers pointed to a black bag near Whitaker and asked if it was his. Whitaker responded that it was not his bag, but said he had placed his jacket and a few other items inside it because no one else appeared to be using it. Whitaker then consented to a search of the bag. The officers discovered 8.8 pounds of uncut methamphetamine contained in several duct tape covered packages inside the bag.

The prosecution charged Whitaker with several drug offenses. At trial, Whitaker argued that he did not possess the drugs and did not know that the packages of drugs were in the bag. The defense did not dispute the facts that the bag contained 8.8 pounds of methamphetamine and that the drugs came across Colorado's state lines via the Greyhound bus. The jury convicted Whitaker of possessing 1,000 grams or more of a schedule II controlled substance with intent to distribute and importation of a schedule II controlled substance. The trial court sentenced him to twenty years in state prison.

The court of appeals affirmed Whitaker's conviction and sentence. People v. Whitaker, 32 P.3d 511 (Colo. App. 2000). . . . It held that the prosecution need not prove that Whitaker "knowingly" imported the controlled substance, nor that the defendant "knew" the drugs weighed more than 1,000 grams. Id. at 517-19. . . .

II

We hold that the General Assembly, in section 18-18-405, did not intend to apply a culpable mental state to the quantity of drugs the defendant distributed, manufactured, dispensed, sold, or possessed. We also hold that importation under Colorado's special offender statute, section 18-18-407, does not include a *mens rea* requirement. The jury found beyond a reasonable doubt that the defendant possessed the drug quantity specified by section 18-18-405(3)(a)(III), and imported the drugs across state lines as specified by section 18-18-407(1)(d). Accordingly, we uphold Whitaker's conviction and sentence.

Section 18-18-405 and Quantity of Drug

. . . Section 18-18-405(3)(a)(III) defines the required sentence for a defendant convicted of unlawful distribution, manufacturing, dispensing, sale or possession of 1,000 grams or more of a schedule I or II controlled substance.[3]

Whitaker argues that the quantity of drugs contained in section 18-18-405(3)(a)(III) is an essential element of the crime of possession with intent to distribute, and the *mens rea* contained in section 18-18-405(1)(a), "knowingly," must apply to it. . . . [W]hether the quantity of drugs involved in the offense requires a *mens rea* is a matter of statutory interpretation. "Our fundamental responsibility in interpreting a statute is to give effect to the General Assembly's purpose and intent in enacting the statute." Empire Lodge Homeowners' Ass'n v. Moyer, 39 P.3d 1139, 1152 (Colo. 2001). . . .

Here, section 18-18-405(1)(a) defines the offense, and the provisions of 18-18-405(2), (3), (5) and (6) set forth the applicable punishment levels. This statutory structure demonstrates the General Assembly's intent to separate sentencing factors, such as drug type and quantity, from the elements of the crime. Section 18-18-405(3)(a) does not prescribe drug quantity as an element of the offense, nor does it require proof of a culpable mental state [with regard] to it. . . .

Although section 18-18-405(1)(a) requires the prosecution to prove that the defendant "knowingly" distributed, manufactured, dispensed, sold or

---

3. 6 C.R.S. §18-18-405(3)(a)(III) provides:

> (3)(a) Except as otherwise provided in section 18-18-407 relating to special offenders, any person convicted pursuant to paragraph (a) of subsection (2) of this section for knowingly manufacturing, dispensing, selling, distributing, possessing, or possessing with intent to manufacture, dispense, sell, or distribute, or inducing, attempting to induce, or conspiring with one or more other persons, to manufacture, dispense, sell, distribute, possess, or possess with intent to manufacture, dispense, sell, or distribute an amount that is or has been represented to be:
> . . . (III) One thousand grams or one kilogram or more of any material, compound, mixture, or preparation that contains a schedule I or schedule II controlled substance as listed in section 18-18-203 or 18-18-204 shall be sentenced to the department of corrections for a term greater than the maximum presumptive range but not more than twice the maximum presumptive range provided for such offense in section 18-1-105(1)(a).

possessed the controlled substance, nothing in the statute's language suggests that the prosecution must show that the defendant "knew" the actual weight of the drugs. . . . To the contrary, section 18-18-405(3)(a) triggers the level of punishment upon proof that the drug quantity involved in the offense was "an amount that is or has been represented to be" the amount specified by subsections (I), (II), or (III) thereunder. . . .

The statute thereby sets forth the drug quantity separately from the elements, with no *mens rea* requirement and with the apparent design of separating the applicable punishment from the creation and definition of the offense. People v. Ramirez, 997 P.2d 1200, 1208 (Colo. App. 1999) (holding that quantity of a controlled substance possessed is not a substantive element of the offense), aff'd by an equally divided court, 43 P.3d 611 (Colo. 2001).[5]

Any amount of drugs, even less than a usable quantity, can support a conviction under 18-18-405(1)(a). Richardson v. People, 25 P.3d 54, 58 (Colo. 2001) ("In a possession case, a jury may return a verdict of guilty if it finds, beyond a reasonable doubt, that the defendant knowingly possessed any quantity of a controlled substance."). The quantity of drugs turns on objective standards and requires no inquiry into the defendant's state of mind. See United States v. Normandeau, 800 F.2d 953, 956 (9th Cir. 1986) (stating that proof of the amount of drugs is far different from proof that the defendants knew of the amount).

The underlying purpose of section 18-18-405(3) is to punish more severely those offenders who deal with large quantities of controlled substances. The legislature's choice to do so is within its prerogative. Section 18-18-405(3)(a) does not create an additional element for the underlying substantive offense; rather, it defines circumstances that, if proven beyond a reasonable doubt, may require a sentence greater than the presumptive minimum contained in section 18-1-105(1)(a). See People v. Ceja, 904 P.2d 1308, 1310 (Colo. 1995) (stating that Colorado Supreme Court cases "have turned not on the quantity of substance found but rather on the knowing possession of that substance"); *Ramirez*, 997 P.2d at 1208 ("Section 18-18-405(3)(a), in itself, does not make possession unlawful and, therefore, does not set forth an offense.").

Here, the issue of drug quantity went to the jury and the possession with intent to distribute more than 1,000 grams of a schedule II controlled substance jury instruction clearly included the quantity of drugs as a fact that must be proven beyond a reasonable doubt. Thus, we find no error.

5. Because the quantity of drugs is not an element of the offense under this statutory design, section 18-1-503(4) does not apply. See 6 C.R.S. §18-1-503(4) (providing that where a statute defining an offense contains a culpable mental state, that mental state applies to every element of the offense, unless an intent to limit its application clearly appears).

Section 18-18-407 and Importation of the Drug

The jury found beyond a reasonable doubt that Whitaker imported a controlled substance into Colorado, a special offender factual finding for the jury to make under section 18-18-407(1)(d).[7] Whitaker . . . contends that: (1) the Colorado special offender statute creates a separate substantive offense or, alternatively, an additional element for the underlying offense; and (2) the *mens rea* of "knowingly" must apply to the special offender statute. We disagree.

The plain language of Colorado's special offender statute with regard to importation does not include a culpable mental state. See §18-18-407, 6 C.R.S. Rather, this provision deals with the level of punishment. Vega v. People, 893 P.2d 107, 112 (1995) (stating that importation provision addresses punishment, not the creation of a substantive offense). The plain language of the statute indicates that "(1) it is triggered only after a felony drug conviction, and (2) its effect is to increase the required sentencing range upon a finding of one of the specified 'aggravating circumstances.'" *Vega*, 893 P.2d at 113. "Once a jury has determined that a defendant possessed the mental state required for conviction of the substantive offense, an enhanced sentence must be imposed whether or not the defendant fully knew of the circumstances leading to the special offender finding." *Ramirez*, 997 P.2d at 1205.

The legislative history of the special offender provision demonstrates the General Assembly's intent to address punishment rather than defining the elements of an offense. *Vega*, 893 P.2d at 113 ("During discussion of the motion to adopt the amendment, Joseph Mackey, one of its drafters, testified that the special offender provision is 'not a substantive charge'. . . ."). The General Assembly added this provision to the Controlled Substances Act to allow greater penalties for drug traffickers. Id. . . . Colorado law requires the fact-finder to enter a special finding in regard to the existence of the special offender circumstance. *Ramirez*, 997 P.2d at 1206 ("Notice is required, trial by jury is not eliminated, and a finding of the existence of the [special offender circumstance] beyond a reasonable doubt is required before a defendant's sentence is increased.").

In this case, the jury was instructed to find the presence or absence of the special offender importation fact only if it found Whitaker guilty of the underlying crime, possession with intent to distribute. Whitaker argues that the jury verdict form violated his due process rights because it did not apply a *mens rea* to the importation of methamphetamine charge. We disagree. The special offender statute's importation feature does not include a *mens rea* requirement. We find no error. . . .

7. Section 18-18-407(1)(d) provides: "The defendant unlawfully introduced, distributed, or imported into the state of Colorado any schedule I or II controlled substance (contained in part 2 of this article)."

Notes and Questions

1. The premise of possession-with-intent statutes, and of the sentencing laws that attach to them, is that those defendants caught with the largest quantities of the relevant drug are responsible for selling the largest quantities of that drug. That proposition sounds sensible enough. Is it correct? Do major dealers take Greyhound buses? Is Whitaker more likely a large-scale dealer, or is he more likely a run-of-the-mill mule?

2. Colorado's rules requiring strict liability as to drug quantities and importation seem, and are, harsh. (They are not unusual.) But are those strict liability rules responsible for the result in *Whitaker*? Suppose knowledge of at least the rough amount the defendant possessed were an element of the crime charged. How would the government prove such knowledge? The most likely answer—at least for a drug like methamphetamine—is by first proving the amount possessed, and then asking the jury to infer that the defendant surely knew the contents of his bag. In many cases that would be enough; juries would routinely convict defendants like Whitaker.

In the few rare cases in which juries might be more skeptical, another *mens rea* concept—willful blindness—would make convictions likely, maybe certain. It has long been the case that when defendants consciously choose *not* to discover or evaluate information in an effort to escape legal responsibility for their actions, they are treated as if they knew the information. Those who are willfully blind are treated like those who see perfectly. Together with willful blindness, the ordinary inference that people know what their luggage contains would more than suffice in most cases. The *mens rea* rule in *Whitaker* may, in most situations, be small potatoes.

3. The idea of willful blindness suggests a deeper problem with cases like *Whitaker*. *Mens rea* standards aim to distinguish between more and less culpable conduct. Would a knowledge standard in *Whitaker* serve that function? Is it clear that defendants who know more are more culpable in this context? Consider the importation charge: Would the absence of knowledge that Whitaker crossed a state line lessen his culpability in any way? Would the presence of such knowledge increase it? If knowledge is not the right *mens rea* standard to use in cases of this sort, what is?

4. Note that even though the *Whitaker* court holds that no proof of *mens rea* is required, with respect to either the quantity of the drug possessed or the fact of importation, those two facts must still be proven in order to convict and sentence a defendant in the manner that Whitaker was convicted and sentenced. This is true notwithstanding the *Whitaker* court's labeling of the quantity possessed as a "sentencing factor," and the fact of importation as a "special offender factual finding."

The U.S. Supreme Court has held, in a series of important recent cases, that *all* facts legally necessary to the imposition of a more severe criminal sentence—no matter what those facts may be labeled—must be proven to a jury, beyond a reasonable doubt. See United States v. Booker, 543 U.S.

220 (2005); Blakely v. Washington, 542 U.S. 296 (2004); Apprendi v. New Jersey, 530 U.S. 466 (2000). In *Whitaker*, that would not have posed a problem; as the *Whitaker* court notes, the jury *did* make the necessary factual findings about the quantity possessed and the importation, using a "beyond a reasonable doubt" standard. (Note the apparent anomaly here: The jury was required at trial to make the factual finding about the quantity of the drug possessed, which suggests that this was an element of the crime charged—yet the *Whitaker* court held that it was, instead, a "sentencing factor.") But in many other states, *Apprendi* and its progeny have necessitated a major change, requiring those states either to begin placing such factual issues before the jury (either at trial or at a separate sentencing hearing), or to change the criminal law so that the maximum sentence faced by the defendant no longer legally depends on such facts.

In case you were wondering, the *Whitaker* court's actual holding—that the defendant need not possess any *mens rea* with respect to either the quantity of the drug possessed or the fact of importation—does *not* create any *Apprendi* problems. Keep in mind that *Apprendi* applies *only* to those facts that are legally necessary to impose a higher sentence. The *Whitaker* court's holding means that *mens rea*, with respect either to quantity or to importation, is *not* such a fact—and *Apprendi*, therefore, is not implicated by the court's decision.

5. Colorado is generally classified as one of the minority of states that has adopted the Model Penal Code's culpability framework (although Colorado's courts do not always follow the Code's culpability approach; see the discussion of the *Vigil* case, supra, at page 228). One specific aspect of the Code that is *not* replicated in Colorado's statutes is the Code's general prohibition of strict liability that appears at MPC sections 2.02(3) and 2.05. But the same "*mens rea* with respect to the quantity of the drug possessed" issue addressed in *Whitaker* also arises, of course, in those jurisdictions (roughly a dozen or so) that *have* adopted the Model Penal Code's strict liability provisions. Such jurisdictions are prohibited, at least in theory, from applying strict liability to *any* element of *any* crime. (Assuming, for sake of argument, that we characterize the issue in *Whitaker* as such.) How should this issue be resolved in such a jurisdiction? The next case shows how one particular court, in a more strongly MPC-influenced jurisdiction, resolved it—in a different factual context where it would be difficult, if not impossible, to infer that the defendant actually *knew* the quantity of the illegal drug he possessed.

People v. Ryan

Court of Appeals of New York
82 N.Y.2d 497, 626 N.E.2d 51 (1993)

Chief Judge KAYE:

Penal Law §220.18(5) makes it a felony to "knowingly and unlawfully possess . . . six hundred twenty-five milligrams of a hallucinogen." The question of statutory interpretation before us is whether "knowingly" applies to the weight of the controlled substance. We conclude that it does and that the trial evidence was insufficient to satisfy that mental culpability element. . . .

I

Viewed in a light most favorable to the People, . . . the trial evidence revealed that on October 2, 1990 defendant asked his friend David Hopkins to order and receive a shipment of hallucinogenic mushrooms on his behalf. Hopkins agreed, and adhering to defendant's instructions placed a call to their mutual friend Scott in San Francisco and requested the "usual shipment." Tipped off to the transaction, on October 5 State Police Investigator Douglas Vredenburgh located the package at a Federal Express warehouse in Binghamton. The package was opened (pursuant to a search warrant) and resealed after its contents were verified. The investigator then borrowed a Federal Express uniform and van and delivered the package to Hopkins, the addressee, who was arrested upon signing for it.

Hopkins explained that the package was for defendant and agreed to participate in a supervised delivery to him. In a telephone call recorded by the police, Hopkins notified defendant that he got the package, reporting a "shit load of mushrooms in there." Defendant responded, "I know, don't say nothing." At another point Hopkins referred to the shipment containing two pounds. The men agreed to meet later that evening at the firehouse in West Oneonta.

At the meeting, after a brief conversation, Hopkins handed defendant a substitute package stuffed with newspaper. Moments after taking possession, defendant was arrested. He was later indicted for attempted criminal possession of a controlled substance in the second degree.

. . . The case proceeded to trial, where the evidence summarized above was adduced. Additionally, the police chemist testified that the total weight of the mushrooms in Hopkins' package was 932.8 grams (about two pounds), and that a 140-gram sample of the package contents contained 796 milligrams of psilocybin, a hallucinogen (Penal Law §220.00 [9]; Public Health Law §3306 [schedule I] [d] [19]). He did not know, however, the process by which psilocybin appears in mushrooms, whether naturally, by injection or some other means. Nor was there any evidence as to how much psilocybin would typically appear in two pounds of mushrooms.

At the close of the People's case, defendant moved to dismiss for insufficient proof that he knew the level of psilocybin in the mushrooms. . . . [D]efendant was convicted as charged, and he was sentenced as a second felony offender to 10 years-to-life.

The Appellate Division affirmed. The court held that a defendant must know the nature of the substance possessed, and acknowledged that the weight of the controlled substance is an element of the crime. The court declined, however, to read the statute as requiring that a defendant have actual knowledge of the weight. Instead, the court held that "the term 'knowingly' should be construed to refer only to the element of possession and not to the weight requirement." (184 A.D.2d 24, 27.)

Finding ample evidence that defendant intended and attempted to possess psilocybin while knowing the nature of the substance, and that the weight of the psilocybin ultimately proved to be more than 625 milligrams, the Appellate Division sustained the conviction. . . .

We now reverse.

II

Although the present case involves an attempt, analysis begins with the elements of the completed crime, second degree criminal possession of a controlled substance. Penal Law §220.18(5) provides:

> "A person is guilty of criminal possession of a controlled substance in the second degree when he knowingly and unlawfully possesses: . . .
>
> > "5. six hundred twenty-five milligrams of a hallucinogen."

It is undisputed that the knowledge requirement of the statute applies to the element of possession, and that defendant must also have "actual knowledge of the nature of the possessed substance." At issue is whether defendant must similarly know the weight of the material possessed. That is a question of statutory interpretation, as to which the Court's role is clear: our purpose is not to pass on the wisdom of the statute or any of its requirements, but rather to implement the will of the Legislature as expressed in its enactment.

In effectuating legislative intent, we look first of course to the statutory language. Read in context, it seems evident that "knowingly" does apply to the weight element. Indeed, given that a defendant's awareness must extend not only to the fact of possessing something ("knowingly . . . possesses") but also to the nature of the material possessed ("knowingly . . . possesses . . . a hallucinogen"), any other reading would be strained. Inasmuch as the knowledge requirement carries through to the end of the sentence, eliminating it from the intervening element—weight—would rob the statute of its obvious meaning. We conclude, therefore, that there is a *mens rea* element associated with the weight of the drug.

That reading is fortified by two rules of construction ordained by the Legislature itself. First, a "statute defining a crime, unless clearly indicating a legislative intent to impose strict liability, should be construed as defining a crime of mental culpability" (Penal Law §15.15[2]). If any material element of an offense lacks a *mens rea* requirement, it is a strict liability crime (Penal Law §15.10). Conversely, a crime is one of "mental culpability" only when a mental state "is required with respect to every material element of an offense" (*id.*).

By ruling that a defendant need not have knowledge of the weight, the Appellate Division in effect held, to that extent, that second degree criminal possession is a strict liability crime (*see*, Penal Law §15.10). That is an erroneous statutory construction unless a legislative intent to achieve that result is "clearly indicat[ed]" (Penal Law §15.15[2]).

In a similar vein, the Legislature has provided in Penal Law §15.15(1):

"CONSTRUCTION OF STATUTES WITH RESPECT TO CULPABILITY REQUIREMENTS.

> "1. When the commission of an offense defined in this chapter, or some element of an offense, requires a particular culpable mental state, such mental state is ordinarily designated in the statute defining the offense by use of the terms 'intentionally,' '*knowingly*,' 'recklessly' or 'criminal negligence,' or by use of terms, such as 'with intent to defraud' and 'knowing it to be false,' describing a specific kind of intent or knowledge. *When one and only one of such terms appears in a statute defining an offense, it is presumed to apply to every element of the offense unless an intent to limit its application clearly appears*." (Emphasis added.)

Accordingly, if a single *mens rea* is set forth, as here,[2] it presumptively applies to all elements of the offense unless a contrary legislative intent is plain.

We discern no "clear" legislative intent to make the weight of a drug a strict liability element, as is required before we can construe the statute in that manner (Penal Law §15.15[1], [2]). Moreover, the over-all structure of the drug possession laws supports the view that a defendant must have some knowledge of the weight.

There are six degrees of criminal possession of a controlled substance, graded in severity from a class A misdemeanor (Penal Law §220.03 [seventh degree]) up to an A-I felony (Penal Law §220.21 [first degree]). The definition of each begins identically: "A person is guilty of criminal possession of a controlled substance in the degree when he knowingly and unlawfully possesses. . . ." The primary distinctions between one grade or another relate to the type and weight of the controlled substance, and in some instances the existence of an intent to sell (*e.g.*, Penal Law §220.16[1]) or intent to sell combined with a prior drug conviction (*e.g.*, Penal Law §220.09[13]).

Taking hallucinogens as an example, knowing and unlawful possession of any amount, even a trace (*see*, People v. Mizell, 72 NY2d 651, 655) is seventh degree possession (Penal Law §220.03); 25 milligrams or more, fourth degree (Penal Law §220.09[6]); 125 milligrams or more, third degree (Penal Law §220.16[10]); and 625 milligrams, second degree (Penal Law

---

2. "Unlawfully" is not a term of mental culpability but means "in violation of article thirty-three of the public health law" (Penal Law §220.00[(2)]).

§220.18[5]). The maximum penalty for these crimes ranges from one-year incarceration to a life sentence, yet the only statutory difference relates to the weight of the drugs. To ascribe to the Legislature an intent to mete out drastic differences in punishment without a basis in culpability would be inconsistent with notions of individual responsibility and proportionality prevailing in the Penal Law (*see, e.g.,* Penal Law §1.05[4]). . . .

In sum, the plain language of the statute, rules of construction, the format of the drug possession laws and our cases all lead to the conclusion that the Appellate Division erred in holding that there is no *mens rea* requirement associated with the weight of a controlled substance.

III

The People's contrary argument is based in part on a concern that it would be "prohibitively difficult," if not impossible, to secure convictions if they were required to prove that a defendant had knowledge of the weight. We disagree.

Often there will be evidence from which the requisite knowledge may be deduced, such as negotiations concerning weight, potency or price (*see, e.g.,* People v. Acosta, 80 NY2d 665, 668, n.1, *and* 672-673). Similarly, for controlled substances measured on an "aggregate weight" basis (*see, e.g.,* Penal Law §220.06[2]), knowledge of the weight may be inferred from defendant's handling of the material, because the weight of the entire mixture, including cutting agents, is counted. . . .

By contrast, that same inference may be unavailable for controlled substances measured by "pure" weight, like psilocybin. The effective doses of these drugs may be minuscule, and they are customarily combined with other substances to facilitate handling and use. In these circumstances it may indeed be difficult to show defendant's knowledge of the weight. Although we cannot simply read the knowledge requirement out of the statute, these "compelling practical considerations" may inform our interpretation of that element (*see,* People v. Mizell, 72 N.Y.2d, at 654).

The Legislature has decided that persons who illegally possess larger quantities of controlled substances should be punished more severely; their conduct is more repugnant and presents a greater threat to society. Because drug possession is not a strict liability crime, however, an individual is not deserving of enhanced punishment unless he or she is aware that the amount possessed is greater. A purpose of the knowledge requirement, then, is to avoid overpenalizing someone who unwittingly possesses a larger amount of a controlled substance than anticipated.

That legislative purpose can be satisfied, among other ways, with evidence that the pure weight of the controlled substance possessed by defendant is typical for the particular form in which the drug appears. This correlation between the pure weight typically found, and the pure weight actually possessed, substantially reduces the possibility that a person will unjustly be convicted for a more serious crime.

To illustrate: a person may knowingly possess 50 doses of LSD on blotter paper but, understandably, have no awareness what the pure LSD weighs; upon chemical analysis it is determined that defendant actually possessed 2.5 milligrams. If there is evidence that a typical dose of LSD weighs .05 milligrams, the jury could conclude, within the meaning of the statute, that defendant knowingly possessed more than 1 milligram, and convict of fourth degree possession (Penal Law §220.09[5] [1 mg or more]). If, however, because of some manufacturing defect unknown to defendant those 50 doses weighed 10 milligrams, defendant should not be convicted of more serious third degree possession (Penal Law §220.16[9] [5 mg or more]).

There may of course be other ways of proving defendant's knowledge within the meaning of the statute. Our purpose today, however, is not to survey all of the permissible methods but to clarify that the statute does in fact contain a weight-related mental culpability element.

IV

With the foregoing principles in mind, we consider whether there was sufficient evidence to convict defendant of attempted second degree possession, an A-II felony.

Certainly there was sufficient evidence from which the jury could conclude, beyond a reasonable doubt, that defendant attempted and intended to possess a two-pound box of hallucinogenic mushrooms. It is also undisputed that, upon testing, the mushrooms in the particular box defendant attempted to possess—the one sent to Hopkins by Scott—contained more than 650 milligrams of psilocybin. The issue we must decide, however, is whether sufficient evidence was presented at trial from which it could be inferred that defendant had the requisite knowledge of the weight.

We disagree with the People's suggestion that the evidence of defendant's knowing attempt to possess two pounds of mushrooms, without more, could satisfy their burden of proof. The controlled substance here is psilocybin; had defendant ordered a specific quantity of that drug, plainly that would satisfy the knowledge element. But defendant attempted to possess two pounds of mushrooms, only a small portion of which was pure psilocybin.

Although in these circumstances defendant could properly be convicted of attempting to possess the amount of psilocybin that would typically appear in two pounds of hallucinogenic mushrooms, there was no evidence linking psilocybin weight to mushroom weight. Indeed, there was no evidence indicating whether psilocybin grows naturally or is injected into the mushrooms, or of the usual dose of the drug—matters not within the ken of the typical juror. We thus conclude on this record that there was insufficient evidence to satisfy the knowledge requirement within the meaning of the statute.

That deficiency does not absolve defendant of all criminal liability. There is sufficient evidence to sustain a conviction for the lesser-included offense of attempted criminal possession of a controlled substance in the seventh degree (Penal Law §220.03), which does not have a weight element.

. . . Accordingly, the order of the Appellate Division should be reversed and the indictment dismissed with leave to the People to institute such proceedings as they deem appropriate respecting the lesser-included offense of attempted criminal possession of a controlled substance in the seventh degree.

Judges SIMONS, TITONE, HANCOCK, Jr., and SMITH concur with Chief Judge KAYE; Judge BELLACOSA dissents and votes to affirm for the reasons stated in the [lower court] opinion; Judge LEVINE taking no part.

Order reversed. . . .

Notes and Questions

1. Whitaker received 20 years in prison for carrying about nine pounds of meth into Colorado on a Greyhound bus. Ryan originally was sentenced, under a recidivist statute, to 10-years-to-life in prison for possessing (with no proof of intent to distribute) a "shit load" of magic mushrooms. Ryan's conviction was overturned on appeal, but the court made clear that the *next* Ryan to come along could be lawfully convicted and sentenced in that way. Do these seem like the kinds of crimes, and criminals, that deserve such draconian punishments? Is there a problem with using "quantity of the drug possessed" as *both* indirect proof of "intent to distribute" *and* evidence of the relative harm caused by the defendant's crime?

2. One of the most significant real-world impacts of the kinds of severe prison sentences faced by many relatively low-level drug defendants like Whitaker and Ryan is that prosecutors thereby acquire immense leverage to force such defendants to plead guilty *and* turn in their suppliers. Indeed, some believe that this may be the most important reason behind the modern proliferation of draconian drug laws: They help prosecutors to pressure the street dealers and thereby nail the drug kingpins and other high-level drug criminals who are almost impossible to catch any other way. Is this a proper purpose for criminal law? Does it seem fair to *over*-punish less heinous criminals in order to catch more heinous criminals who might otherwise go *under*-punished?

3. *Whitaker* and *Ryan* illustrate, once again, the fundamental difference in approach between the Model Penal Code and the common law when it comes to *mens rea* issues. In *Whitaker*, the court spends most of its opinion talking about the intent of the legislature and the purpose behind the statute. In *Ryan*, by contrast, most of the opinion is devoted to a technical analysis of grammar, statutory structure, and statutory language; only at the very end, once the game is basically over (in terms of deciding the governing legal rule), does the *Ryan* court begin to discuss the impact of its decision on the fulfillment of the legislature's purpose.

4. In *Ryan*, the New York Court of Appeals (widely viewed as one of the very best state courts in the nation), properly applying the technical *mens rea* analysis outlined by the Model Penal Code, reaches the following set of conclusions:

(1) the relevant criminal statute contains an element involving the amount of the pure drug possessed;

(2) the single *mens rea* term in the statute, "knowingly," must be applied to that element;

(3) the prosecution therefore must prove that the defendant "knew" the amount of the pure drug he possessed (i.e., the amount of the psilocybin, not merely the amount of the magic mushrooms);

(4) this defendant's conviction must be reversed, because no such proof ever was introduced; and

(5) in the future, however, other similar defendants can be proven guilty by showing that the substance they possessed (e.g., the magic mushrooms) "typically" would contain a given amount of the pure drug (e.g., the psilocybin).

The court justifies this last conclusion with the mysterious statement that "'compelling practical considerations' may inform our interpretation of th[e] [knowledge] element."

Isn't the *Ryan* court's view—that a conviction can be based on proof of what a given substance "typically" contains, in terms of pure psilocybin—essentially a judicial redefinition of what MPC knowledge means? Doesn't the court redefine knowledge to mean something like, "this is the amount of pure psilocybin that a reasonable person (or, perhaps, a reasonable drug purchaser) should expect to find in the shipment of magic mushrooms the defendant purchased"? But isn't that actually what the MPC would call negligence?

On the other hand, would there be any way to convict anyone of possessing psilocybin, if MPC knowledge of the amount of the pure psilocybin contained in the mushrooms were required? Anyone short of a Ph.D. chemist, that is? The problem is that it's highly unreasonable to infer that anyone without an advanced chemistry degree (and perhaps some high-tech scientific equipment to boot) actually knows how much pure psilocybin is in any particular shipment of magic mushrooms. Does this illustrate a defect in the New York psilocybin statute? Or in the MPC?

5. Shortly after the *Ryan* decision, the New York legislature overturned the court's ruling (at least for future defendants committing future crimes). The legislature enacted the following amendment to New York's "mistake" statute (a statute otherwise based on the MPC's mistake provision, section 2.04):

EFFECT OF IGNORANCE OR MISTAKE UPON LIABILITY.
. . .

> 4. Notwithstanding the use of the term "knowingly" in any provision of this chapter defining an offense in which the aggregate weight of a controlled substance or marihuana is an element, knowledge by the defendant of the aggregate weight of such controlled substance or marihuana is not an element of any such offense and it is not, unless expressly so provided, a defense to a prosecution therefor that the defendant did not know the aggregate weight of the controlled substance or marihuana.

N.Y. Penal Law §15.20. Given that New York generally follows the Model Penal Code's approach to culpability analysis, what is the effect of this statutory amendment? What would the impact of such a statute be, in the much larger number of states that *don't* follow the Model Penal Code's approach?

C. THE LOCATION OF THE DRUG POSSESSION OR SALE: "DRUG-FREE ZONES"

State v. Benniefield

Supreme Court of Minnesota
678 N.W.2d 42 (2004)

Opinion by HANSON, J.

Appellant was convicted of third-degree possession of a controlled substance within a school zone. He argues that punishing possession within a school zone more harshly than possession outside a school zone violates the equal protection guaranty of the Minnesota Constitution. Alternatively, he argues that a conviction of this crime requires proof that he either knew he was in a school zone or intended to commit the crime in a school zone. Because there is a rational basis to enhance the crime where possession occurs within a school zone, and the plain language of the statute does not impose a mens rea requirement on the location element of the crime, we affirm.

On December 17, 2001, at approximately 11:00 P.M., police officer John Fishbauger noticed appellant Steven Allen Benniefield walking at the corner of 7th Avenue and 6th Street Southeast in Rochester, Minnesota, within approximately 61 feet of the Riverside School property line. The officer recognized Benniefield from previous encounters and checked with police dispatch to see if there were any outstanding warrants for his arrest. After being informed that there was an outstanding warrant for Benniefield, Officer Fishbauger stopped Benniefield and placed him under arrest. During a pat-down search, the officer discovered a makeshift crack pipe in Benniefield's pocket.

Benniefield was placed in another officer's squad car and taken directly to the adult detention center. When the transporting officer searched his squad car, he found a baggie containing small off-white colored "rocks." These rocks were later identified as containing 1.10 grams of cocaine.

Benniefield was charged with violation under Minn. Stat. §152.023, subd. 2(4) (2000), a third-degree controlled substance offense for possession of any amount of a Schedule II narcotic drug "in a school zone, a park zone, a public housing zone, or a drug treatment facility." Cocaine is a Schedule II narcotic drug. Minn. Stat. §152.01, subd. 10 (2002). A school zone is defined as:

(1) any property owned, leased, or controlled by a school district or an organization operating a nonpublic school, as defined in section 123B.41, subdivision 9, where an elementary, middle, secondary school, secondary vocational center or other school providing educational services in grade one through grade 12 is located, or used for educational purposes, or where extracurricular or cocurricular activities are regularly provided;

(2) the area surrounding school property as described in clause (1) to a distance of 300 feet or one city block, whichever distance is greater, beyond the school property; and

(3) the area within a school bus when that bus is being used to transport one or more elementary or secondary school students.

Minn. Stat. §152.01, subd. 14a (2002).

Benniefield represented himself at trial. In his opening statement, Benniefield informed the jury that he had not intended to be in a school zone, that he was merely on his way home from work, and that this was the most direct route to his home. The state filed a motion in limine requesting that the court not allow Benniefield to argue that intent to be in a school zone or knowledge of being in the school zone was a necessary element of the crime. The district court granted the motion in limine. Benniefield presented no witnesses and did not testify himself.

The jury returned a verdict of guilty. The court denied Benniefield's motion for a new trial and sentenced him to 37 months in prison for third-degree possession, a severity VI level offense. According to the sentencing guidelines in effect at that time, the presumptive sentence with a criminal history score of 3 was from 37 to 41 months. See Minnesota Sentencing Guidelines IV.

On direct appeal, Benniefield argued that punishing for possession of a controlled substance in a school zone more harshly than possession outside a school zone violates equal protection and that the district court erred in failing to instruct the jury that the offense required proof of intent to be in a school zone. See State v. Benniefield, 668 N.W.2d 430, 433 (Minn. App. 2003). The court of appeals affirmed the conviction. Id. at 435-38.

I.

Benniefield challenges the constitutionality of Minn. Stat. §152.023, subd. 2(4), on equal protection grounds. Unless a fundamental right or suspect class is involved, statutes are presumed to be constitutional. Rio Vista Non-Profit Housing Corp. v. Ramsey County, 335 N.W.2d 242, 245 (Minn. 1983). We will hold a statute unconstitutional "only when absolutely necessary." State v. Behl, 564 N.W.2d 560, 566 (Minn. 1997). We review the constitutionality of a statute de novo. State v. Machholz, 574 N.W.2d 415, 419 (Minn. 1998). A defendant, claiming that a statute is unconstitutional, bears the burden of showing that the statute is unconstitutional beyond a reasonable doubt. Scott v. Minneapolis Police Relief Ass'n, Inc., 615 N.W.2d 66, 73 (Minn. 2000).

Benniefield did not challenge the constitutionality of the statute at trial. We need not consider issues that were not presented to the district court but may choose to do so where the interests of justice so require. State v. Sorenson, 441 N.W.2d 455, 457 (Minn. 1989). The court of appeals considered the equal protection claim in the interests of justice. *Benniefield*, 668 N.W.2d at 435. We do likewise.

Benniefield argues that Minn. Stat. §152.023, subd. 2(4), "violates the equal protection component of the Minnesota Constitution because there is no genuine and substantial distinction between those who receive longer sentences for possession of a controlled substance in a school zone and those who possess the substance outside such a zone." Benniefield reinforces his argument by pointing out that the statute does not require that school children actually be present and does not distinguish between mere possession and the manufacture or sale of drugs in a school zone. Benniefield concludes, "without some greater connection to the statute's purpose, such as children being present or a requirement tied to the time of day, the greater penalty for mere possession in the school zone does not relate to the purported goals to be achieved, that is protecting children."

Benniefield acknowledges that federal courts have determined that similar federal drug statutes that enhance drug crimes that occur within a school zone are constitutional. He argues that the Minnesota Constitution provides greater protection than the federal constitution when reviewing equal protection challenges and the federal enhancement statute is distinguishable because it requires the sale, distribution or manufacture of drugs within the school zone, not mere possession.

The state counters that drug activity in a school zone, even at times when children are not present, can have adverse consequences for children and thus the enhancement of the crime for possession in a school zone has a rational basis. The state suggests the example that if Benniefield had disposed of the drugs when he was first observed by the officer, the drugs could have later been found and used by children. The state concludes that the possible consequences of the presence of any kind of drug activity in a school zone provides "a rational basis for the legislature trying to deter possession or use of drugs in a school zone at any time of day."

When a statute does not involve a suspect classification or a fundamental right, this court reviews the constitutional challenge to the statute under a rational-basis test. *Scott*, 615 N.W.2d at 74. Benniefield does not claim that Minn. Stat. §152.023, subd. 2(4), involves a suspect classification or a fundamental right. Thus, Minn. Stat. §152.023, subd. 2(4), will be presumed to be constitutional and should be sustained "if the classification drawn by it is rationally related to a legitimate governmental interest." Kolton v. County of Anoka, 645 N.W.2d 403, 411 (Minn. 2002).

This court employs a three-pronged rational-basis test as follows:

> (1) The distinctions which separate those included within the classification from those excluded must not be manifestly arbitrary or fanciful but must be genuine and substantial, thereby providing a natural and reasonable basis to justify legislation adapted to peculiar conditions and needs; (2) the classification must be genuine or relevant to the purpose of the law; that is there must be an evident connection between the distinctive needs peculiar to the class and the prescribed remedy; and (3) the purpose of the statute must be one that the state can legitimately attempt to achieve. State v. Russell, 477 N.W.2d 886, 888 (Minn. 1991).

Benniefield does not claim that the definition of a school zone is arbitrary or capricious, but that the imposition of a more severe sentence for third-degree possession, based solely on the location in a school zone and with no limitations as to the time of day or the actual presence of children, does not further the public safety goal of the legislature.[2] It is true that conviction of third-degree possession under Minn. Stat. §152.023, subd. 2(4), carries a significantly greater penalty than conviction of fifth-degree possession for possession of the same quantity of drugs outside a school zone. The maximum prison term for third-degree possession is 20 years and the presumptive sentence, with a criminal history score of 2, is 33 months. Minn. Stat. §152.023, subd. 3; Minnesota Sentencing Guidelines IV. The maximum prison sentence for fifth-degree possession is 5 years and the presumptive sentence, with a criminal history score of 2, is 13 months stayed. Minn. Stat. §152.025, subd. 3(a) (2002); Minnesota Sentencing Guidelines IV, V.

Applying the three-prong test, we must first determine whether there is a genuine or substantial reason to differentiate between those who possess drugs within a school zone and those who possess drugs outside a school

---

2. Benniefield also observes that the distinction for possession in a school zone would produce the irrational result that a person merely traveling through a school zone on a city bus could be prosecuted for the greater offense. But this fact pattern is not before us and we need not determine whether the statute would be constitutional as applied to those facts. Benniefield does not contest that he was on foot within 61 feet of school property while in the possession of a controlled substance.

zone. See *Russell*, 477 N.W.2d at 888. We conclude that there is a rational connection between the goal of protecting children from drugs and deterring the possession of drugs in a school zone. There is a genuine risk that those involved in illegal drug use, whether selling or merely possessing a controlled substance, could bring the dangers associated with illegal drugs into school zones. For example, abandoned drugs or discarded drug paraphernalia might be found in or around areas of drug use. The desire to provide an area for schoolchildren, free of illegal drugs and the possible accessories that go with illegal drug use, is a genuine and substantial reason for enhancing the crime to deter criminals who choose to bring illegal drugs within 300 feet of school property. See, e.g., Polk v. State, 683 N.E.2d 567, 571 (Ind. 1997) (concluding that "it is within the legislature's prerogative to determine that a drug-free zone deters possible spillover effects, and to provide enhanced penalties for controlled substance violations in proximity to schools.").

We must next determine whether differentiating between those who possess controlled substances in a school zone and those who possess them outside a school zone is relevant to the purpose of the law. See *Russell*, 477 N.W.2d at 888. Both parties acknowledge that the purpose of the statute is to provide for public safety, especially that of schoolchildren on their way to or while at school. Preventing illegal drugs from being present near schools is relevant to the purpose of protecting school children from the dangers associated with illegal drug use.

Finally, we must determine whether the objective of achieving a safe area for school children is a legitimate one for the state. Id. Benniefield concedes, and it is apparent, that the state can legitimately take measures to provide a safe area for children to attend school.

We conclude that there is a rational basis for the legislature to enhance the crime for those who possess illegal drugs in a place where children are likely to be present on a regular basis in order to protect children from discarded drugs or drug paraphernalia. Thus, we conclude that Minn. Stat. §152.023, subd. 2(4), as applied to the present facts, does not violate the guaranty of equal protection contained in the Minnesota Constitution.

II.

Benniefield argues that the district court erred in not allowing him to argue lack of intent to be in a school zone and in not including intent to be in a school zone as a necessary element of the crime in the jury instructions. Benniefield argues that the dramatic increase in the penalty associated with possession of a controlled substance in a school zone compels the court to imply the requirement that the state prove not only the intent to possess but also the intent to possess in this particular location. The state argues that the plain language of the statute does not require proof of an intent to be in a school zone. The state points out that the statute does have a mens rea requirement, the intent to possess an illegal drug, and argues that a mens rea requirement need not attach to every element of the crime.

In In re C.R.M., 611 N.W.2d 802 (Minn. 2000), we examined the language of a somewhat similar criminal statute that makes it a felony offense to possess a dangerous weapon on school property. At that time, the statute was silent on any mens rea requirement.[3] Minn. Stat. §609.66, subd. 1d (1998). A juvenile was convicted of the crime based on his possession on school property of a folding knife with a 4-inch blade. In re C.R.M., 611 N.W.2d at 803. We observed that knives are not inherently dangerous or anti-social and thus that the possessor would not necessarily be put on notice that mere possession could be a crime. We declared that "great care is taken to avoid interpreting statutes as eliminating mens rea where doing so criminalizes a broad range of what would otherwise be innocent conduct." Id. at 809. We concluded that the state was required to prove that the appellant "knew he possessed the knife on school property." Id. at 810.

In re C.R.M. can be distinguished from the present case and is not controlling. In fact, in In re C.R.M. we distinguished possession that only becomes criminal in certain locations from possession that is criminal independent of the location. We observed that items such as knives "are certainly not as inherently anti-social as *illegal drugs* and hand grenades." Id. (emphasis added). Because the mere possession of illegal drugs is a crime, the possessor is already on notice of the illegality of his actions, without regard to location.

We have implied a mens rea requirement for the possession of a controlled substance. In State v. Florine, 303 Minn. 103, 104, 226 N.W.2d 609, 610 (1975), a case charging the defendant with possession of cocaine, we held that the "state must prove that defendant consciously possessed . . . the substance and that defendant had actual knowledge of the nature of the substance." Having established that mens rea is an implied element in the statute with respect to possession, we see no basis for requiring the state to demonstrate an additional mens rea element with respect to location. See *Florine*, 303 Minn. at 104, 226 N.W.2d at 610. The possessor of the illegal drug who is already on notice that his conduct is criminal can reasonably be expected to assume the risk that he might enter a location that will make the consequences of his crime more severe. *Polk*, 683 N.E.2d at 572.

Finally, we recognize that proof of a defendant's intent to be in a specified location would be difficult. Benniefield was charged with possession of a

---

3. This statute was amended in 2003 to expressly state "while knowingly on school property."

controlled substance for which possession was a crime even outside the protected area. The district court correctly ruled that the state was not required
to prove that Benniefield also knew that he was in a school zone or intended
to commit the crime in a school zone.

This conclusion is consistent with federal and other state decisions that
have consistently held that, although the government must prove an intent
to sell illegal drugs, it need not prove an intent to do so in the prohibited
location of a school zone. See, e.g., United States v. Dimas, 3 F.3d 1015,
1022 (7th Cir. 1993); United States v. Falu, 776 F.2d 46, 50 (2d Cir. 1985);
State v. Denby, 235 Conn. 477, 668 A.2d 682, 685 (Conn. 1995). See also
Tracy A. Bateman, Validity, Construction and Application of State Statutes
Prohibiting Sale or Possession of Controlled Substances Within Specified
Distance of Schools, 27 A.L.R. 5th 593 §31 (1995 & Supp. 2003) (com-
piling cases from Florida, Indiana, Ohio, and Pennsylvania holding that
intent to be or knowledge of being in a school zone is not necessary for
conviction).

We hold that Minn. Stat. §152.023, subd. 2(4), does not require proof
that a defendant intended to be or knew that he was in a school zone.

Affirmed.

Whatley v. State

Supreme Court of Indiana
928 N.E.2d 202 (2010)

Opinion by SULLIVAN, J.

The Legislature has declared that if a person commits certain drug
offenses within 1,000 feet of a "youth program center," the penal consequences
are enhanced. Defendant Walker Whatley committed such an offense within
1,000 feet of a church with an active youth program. The church constituted
a "youth program center" for purposes of the enhancement.

BACKGROUND

The facts most favorable to the conviction indicate that in March, 2008,
Whatley was arrested at his home on a warrant issued in an unrelated case.
During a search incident to arrest, the arresting officer discovered a bag
containing 3.2459 grams of cocaine in Whatley's pocket. In relevant part,
the State charged Whatley with possession of cocaine as a Class A felony.
Possession of cocaine is ordinarily a Class C felony, but possession of three
grams or more of cocaine within 1,000 feet of a youth program center
elevates the offense to a Class A felony. Ind. Code §35-48-4-6. Whatley's
home, where the arrest occurred, was located approximately 795 feet from
Robinson Community Church ("RCC"). Whether RCC qualifies as a "youth

program center" for the purpose of triggering the elevation to a Class A felony is the central issue of this appeal.

The jury found that the enhancement was supported by the evidence and the court sentenced Whatley to a term of 35 years.[1] Whatley appealed and the Court of Appeals reversed his conviction on the grounds that RCC did not qualify as a "youth program center." The Court of Appeals found that RCC's hosting of various programs for children did not change its status as a church; thus, removing it from the ambit of the statute's intended coverage for purposes of the sentence enhancement. Whatley v. State, 906 N.E.2d 259 (Ind. Ct. App. 2009). The Court of Appeals remanded the case with instructions to enter the conviction as a Class C felony and sentence Whatley accordingly.

The State sought, and we granted, transfer. Ind. Appellate Rule 58(A).

---

1. The full text of the statute Whatley was convicted under is as follows:

(a) A person who, without a valid prescription or order of a practitioner acting in the course of the practitioner's professional practice, knowingly or intentionally possesses cocaine (pure or adulterated) or a narcotic drug (pure or adulterated) classified in schedule I or II, commits possession of cocaine or a narcotic drug, a Class D felony, except as provided in subsection (b).

(b) The offense is:

(1) a Class C felony if:

(A) the amount of the drug involved (pure or adulterated) weighs three (3) grams or more; or

(B) the person was also in possession of a firearm (as defined in IC 35-47-1-5);

(2) a Class B felony if the person in possession of the cocaine or narcotic drug possesses less than three (3) grams of pure or adulterated cocaine or a narcotic drug:

(A) on a school bus; or

(B) in, on, or within one thousand (1,000) feet of:

(i) school property;

(ii) a public park;

(iii) a family housing complex; or

(iv) a youth program center; and

(3) a Class A felony if the person possesses the cocaine or narcotic drug in an amount (pure or adulterated) weighing at least three (3) grams:

(A) on a school bus; or

(B) in, on, or within one thousand (1,000) feet of:

(i) school property;

(ii) a public park;

(iii) a family housing complex; or

(iv) a youth program center.

I.C. §35-48-4-6.

DISCUSSION

I

Whatley first contends that his conviction for Class A felony possession of cocaine, grounded on his possession being within 1,000 feet of a youth program center, should be reversed because the criminal statute and the statute defining a youth program center are unconstitutionally vague as applied to him. He asserts that there was nothing about RCC that would put a person of ordinary intelligence on notice that it was a youth program center. Specifically, Whatley argues that RCC bears no objective indicia signaling its designation as a protected area; therefore, the statute is unconstitutional as applied to him because there was no way for him to know that he was within the proscribed distance of an "unmarked youth program center." (Appellant's Br. 7.) Relying on Indiana case law, Whatley insists that due process demands a bright-line rule for what structures will trigger the sentence enhancement when the protected area is a youth program center.

The phrase "youth program center" is defined by statute as "(1) A building or structure that on a regular basis provides recreational, vocational, academic, social, or other programs or services for persons less than eighteen (18) years of age[;] (2) [t]he real property on which a building or structure described in subdivision (1) is located." I.C. §35-41-1-29.

Relying on our decision in Walker v. State, 668 N.E.2d 243 (Ind. 1996), the Court of Appeals rejected Whatley's vagueness claim on grounds that the law does not require knowledge of presence within a school-zone in order to trigger the sentence enhancement. In *Walker*, we held that presence in a school-zone was a strict-liability element. Id. at 244-45. While the Court of Appeals correctly notes that *Walker* established that drug offenders need not be aware of their presence within a protected area, Whatley's vagueness claim cannot be disposed of on this ground alone.

Walker addressed whether the school-zone elevation in the dealing in cocaine statute, Indiana Code section 35-48-4-1(b)(3), required proof of any *mens rea* to obtain an enhanced sentence. But the need for proof of *mens rea*—the precise issue addressed and answered in *Walker*—is not the same as the constitutional requirement against vagueness. For a statute to avoid constitutional infirmity on vagueness grounds, it must provide the person of ordinary intelligence with notice of what conduct is prohibited.

In Polk v. State, 683 N.E.2d 567 (Ind. 1997), we addressed the defendant's argument that an earlier version of the school-zone statute was unconstitutionally vague as applied to him. Polk argued that the statute did not reasonably inform average people that they would be subject to enhanced penalties for possessing drugs while stopped for a traffic violation in a protected area. Addressing his vagueness claim, we held that "[t]he school-zone enhancement, far from being unconstitutionally vague, quite clearly communicates to drug offenders a bright[-]line rule as to what conduct is proscribed. Thus a federal constitutional challenge on this ground is meritless." Id. at 572 (citing Kolender v. Lawson, 461 U.S. 352, 357 (1983)).[5]

Whatley's vagueness claim focuses on the statute's requirement that programs or services be provided on a "regular" basis. While it is true that "regular" is susceptible to numerous meanings, the Constitution does not demand a statute free of ambiguities, but instead one that will put a person of ordinary intelligence on notice or provide objective criteria for determining whether one is within a protected area. See State v. Winot, 294 Conn. 753, 988 A.2d 188, 194 (Conn. 2010) ("Because perfect precision is neither possible nor required . . . the [vagueness] doctrine does not mandate the invalidation of all imprecisely drafted statutes. Simply put, [w]hile some ambiguous statutes are the result of poor draftsmanship, it is apparent that in many instances the uncertainty is merely attributable to a desire not to nullify the purpose of the legislation by the use of specific terms which would afford loopholes through which many could escape." (citations and internal quotation marks omitted)).

There are likely hypothetical scenarios in which the definition of "youth program center" would be unconstitutionally vague, but vagueness challenges are challenges that statutes are unconstitutional as-applied, not on their faces. See Evangelatos v. Superior Court, 44 Cal. 3d 1188, 246 Cal. Rptr. 629, 753 P.2d 585, 592 (Cal. 1988) ("Many, probably most, statutes are ambiguous in some respects and instances invariably arise under which the application of statutory language may be unclear. So long as a statute does not threaten to infringe on the exercise of First Amendment or other constitutional rights, however, such ambiguities, even if numerous, do not justify the invalidation of a statute on its face."). Here, Whatley could have objectively discovered RCC's status as a youth program center by observing young people entering and exiting the building on a regular basis—in fact,

---

5. The Court of Appeals has upheld the current version of the school-zone statute against a vagueness claim. See Manigault v. State, 881 N.E.2d 679, 687-88 (Ind. Ct. App. 2008) (applying the penalty enhancement where there was a high density of protected locations in a particular area). And as best as we are able to determine, there is unbroken authority from other jurisdictions as well. See, e.g., People v. Townsend, 62 Cal. App. 4th 1390, 73 Cal. Rptr. 2d 438 (1998) (concluding that a school-zone statute that was ambiguous and susceptible to more than one reasonable interpretation, was not impermissibly vague because it did not invite arbitrary and discriminatory enforcement by those who administer the statute); State v. Brown, 648 So.2d 872 (La. 1995) (statute was not unconstitutionally vague as it was readily understandable, gave adequate notice of what conduct was proscribed, and provided adequate standards for determining guilt or innocence of the accused); Fluellen v. State, 104 S.W.3d 152 (Tex. App. 2003) (penalty enhancement statute was not unconstitutionally vague despite defendant's lack of knowledge that he was in a proscribed area); State v. Davis, 93 Wn. App. 648, 970 P.2d 336 (Wash. Ct. App. 1999) (penalty enhancement statute was not unconstitutionally vague despite defendant's lack of knowledge that he was in a proscribed area). We have found no authority to the contrary and Whatley cites none in opposition.

his residence faced RCC's entrance. Whatley could have contacted RCC to inquire whether programs were offered for youth on a regular basis. And under *Walker*, it is of no import here that Whatley was unaware of the existence of a youth program center. It is, therefore, not dispositive that RCC did not have a sign indicating it was a youth program center, or that Whatley did not realize that RCC regularly provided services and programs to young people; an objective observer could discern that the activities occurring at RCC qualified it as a youth program center by observing children entering and exiting the building on a regular basis or by contacting RCC to determine whether it offered programs to young people on a regular basis. The statute is not vague as applied to these facts.

II

Whatley contends that his Class A felony conviction is not supported by sufficient evidence. Specifically, Whatley argues that because the State failed to prove that RCC qualifies as a youth program center under Indiana Code section 35-41-1-29, his sentence should be reduced to a Class C felony.

Relying on principles of zoning law, the Court of Appeals held that the principal character and use of a structure "is not changed by some ancillary or accessory use." *Whatley*, 906 N.E.2d at 262. Applying these principles to RCC, the Court of Appeals found it significant that evidence at trial revealed that all of the youth program services and events were essentially faith based. Thus, it held that RCC's principal identity or purpose was as a church; it was not converted into a youth program center by reason of its incidental and auxiliary faith-based activities for young people.

We disagree with our colleagues and find that neither the religious content of the programs offered by RCC nor the other uses of the building are relevant to whether RCC meets the statutory definition of a "youth program center." The statute neither explicitly nor implicitly places any limitation on the content of the programs offered or the purposes for which children are present. The only relevant characteristic of the programs and services offered by RCC were whether they were programs provided on a regular basis for persons less than eighteen years of age.

The evidence produced at trial showed that RCC regularly held the following youth programs:

(1) "Amani (sic) church services" several Sundays out of the month, targeted for young people age 5-11, to "teach them the purpose of worship and why we worship the way we do";
(2) "Boys to Men" and "Girls to Women" programs which are mentoring programs "so that the kids have positive role models";
(3) A Girl Scout troop made up of girls who are members of the church and a few from the community, meeting twice a month;

(4) "Wednesday Bible Circle" for teens, youth and children broken into age appropriate classes "so that they might learn the Bible and the principles therein";

(5) "Family Fun Night" every Friday from 6 P.M. to 9 P.M. where parents and children meet together at church to "get them to find positive ways to interact one with another. Give children opportunities to see how other kids react and interact with their parents. And give all of them positive role models"; and

(6) Monday night Teen Choir (ages 13-18) and Wednesday night Children's Choir (age 5-12).

(Tr. at 30-33.)

Whatley himself, "in the interest of candor, . . . concede[s] that the Robinson Community Church does offer activities for children [and] [t]his was clearly established at trial and cannot reasonably be disputed." (Appellant's Resp. in Opp'n to Transfer 5.) In light of these facts, a jury could properly find that RCC was a "youth program center" because it provided a building or structure that on a regular basis offered recreational, social, or other programs or services for persons less than 18 years of age.

III

Because we find that the statute is constitutional as applied to Whatley and that his conviction was supported by sufficient evidence, we turn to his final contention that his 35-year sentence is inappropriate in light of the nature of the offense and his character. Pursuant to Indiana Appellate Rule 7(B), an appellate court "may revise a sentence authorized by statute if, after due consideration of the trial court's decision, the Court finds that the sentence is inappropriate in light of the nature of the offense and the character of the offender." The defendant bears the burden of persuading us that his sentence meets the inappropriateness standard of review. Anglemyer v. State, 868 N.E.2d 482, 494 (Ind. 2007), clarified on reh'g, 875 N.E.2d 218. "[R]egarding the nature of the offense, the advisory sentence is the starting point the Legislature has selected as an appropriate sentence for the crime committed." Id. In this case, "[a] person who commits a Class A felony shall be imprisoned for a fixed term of between twenty (20) and fifty (50) years, with the advisory sentence being thirty (30) years." I.C. §35-50-2-4.

Regarding the nature of his offense, Whatley argues that he was at home when he was arrested pursuant to an unrelated warrant, he surrendered without incident, and that he was found in possession of a quantity of cocaine only 0.2459 grams above the statutory threshold of 3.0 grams of cocaine for a Class A felony. Regarding his character, Whatley contends that the trial court noted only three adult convictions: one misdemeanor charge for possession of marijuana, a Class C felony conviction for cocaine possession, and a revocation of probation.

The record indicates that at the time of Whatley's arrest, he was in possession of a small plastic baggie in his pocket; the baggie contained sixteen smaller baggies "which contained a substance . . . [later confirmed] to be crack cocaine" totaling over three grams. (Tr. at 40-41, 85-86, 88-89, 92-93; State's Ex. 1, 5.) Beyond this, Whatley's possession occurred within 1,000 feet of a statutorily protected area—a youth program center. The trial court also found that Whatley had prior convictions for possession of cocaine, a Class C felony, and possession of marijuana, a Class A misdemeanor. In both cases he had received the opportunity for probation, and in both cases, his probation had been revoked and previously suspended sentences had been ordered executed.

In addition to prior convictions, the record reveals that at the time of sentencing, Whatley faced pending charges in two separate cases. The first included two counts of dealing cocaine, a Class B felony, and two counts of possession of cocaine, one as a Class C felony and one as a Class D felony. The second case included three counts of stalking, two as Class C felonies and one as a Class D felony, two counts of invasion of privacy, a Class A misdemeanor, and two counts of criminal mischief, a Class A misdemeanor. In light of the nature of Whatley's offense and his character as reflected by his criminal history, we cannot say that a sentence five years in excess of the advisory term of 30 years is inappropriate.

CONCLUSION

The opinion of the Court of Appeals is vacated. Whatley's conviction and sentence is affirmed.

BOEHM, J., dissenting.

I respectfully dissent. Whatley was convicted of possession of 3.24 grams of cocaine. The penalty for this crime was enhanced from a C felony carrying a maximum sentence of eight years to an A felony with a maximum penalty of fifty years due to the proximity of Whatley's home to Robinson Community Church. The statute here provides for this dramatic enhancement of a sentence if the possession occurs:

> (A) on a school bus; or
> (B) in, on, or within one thousand (1,000) feet of:
>> (i) school property;
>> (ii) a public park;
>> (iii) a family housing complex; or
>> (iv) a youth program center.

Ind. Code §35-48-4-6. Notably, this short list does not include "church," "place of worship" or other terms that might much more plainly include Robinson Community Church. Nor is there anything in this record indicating that the exterior of the Church revealed the nature or regularity of its youth programs.

I agree with the majority that the statutory definition of "youth program center" as a structure "that on a regular basis provides . . . programs or services" for people under age eighteen turns only on the activities "provided" by the structure. I.C. §35-41-1-29. But in my view that definition must be confined to comply with basic principles of due process of law. Due process requires that a criminal statute give everyone reasonable notice of what is prohibited. Healthscript, Inc. v. State, 770 N.E.2d 810, 813 (Ind. 2002). It also requires notice of the consequences of violation so the facts warranting the enhanced penalty at issue here are equally subject to the requirement of fair notice. United States v. Batchelder, 442 U.S. 114, 123 (1979); Coleman v. Ryan, 196 F.3d 793, 797 (7th Cir. 1999) ("'[T]he notice requirements of the Due Process Clause' require that a criminal law 'clearly define the conduct prohibited' as well as 'the punishment authorized.' A statute is constitutionally defective if it 'do[es] not state with sufficient clarity the consequences of violating a given criminal statute.'" (quoting *Batchelder*, 442 U.S. at 123)); United States v. Samaniego-Rodriguez, 32 F.3d 242, 244 (7th Cir. 1994) ("The fair notice requirement of the Due Process Clause is satisfied if the criminal statute clearly defines the conduct prohibited and the punishments authorized.").

I agree with the majority that there are many buildings that are easily identified as housing "regular . . . programs or services" for persons under age eighteen. But the statute under the majority's rationale here looks only to the activities conducted in the structure to determine whether it is a youth program center, and not to whether a casual observer could readily discern that the structure provides those services. This reasoning would make a youth program center of every residence housing a Cub Scout weekly meeting. Any other building could become a "youth program center" regardless of its appearance or signage. I would confine the term as the legislature has written it to those structures identifiable from their appearance as likely to house youth programs. These would include Boys and Girls Clubs, YMCAs, YWCAs, sports facilities and the like, but not structures principally identified with other activities, at least without some external signage or other clear indication that the structure houses regularly conducted youth programs.

The State makes no claim that the structure here was readily identifiable as a youth program center. Rather, the State argues that this enhancement applies irrespective of the appearance of the structure. Because I disagree, I believe the Court of Appeals correctly held that the enhanced sentence should be set aside.

Notes and Questions

1. Minnesota law substantially enhances the punishment (from a maximum of five years in prison to a maximum of 20 years) for possessing or selling certain illegal drugs "in a school zone, a park zone, a public housing zone, or a drug treatment facility"; a "school zone" is defined as including any real estate on which any K-12 school (or any extracurricular or cocurricular activity) is located, as well as the surrounding areas up to 300 feet away from such a property. Indiana applies a similar sentence enhancement (increasing the maximum prison sentence from eight years to 50 years) for any locations up to 1000 feet away from "school property, a public park, a family housing complex, or a youth program center." Does this seem like a reasonable way to grade drug crimes and drug criminals? Especially if, as in both Minnesota and Indiana (and almost all other jurisdictions with such laws—they have become quite common these days), no proof is required that the defendant even was aware that he was in such a location?

2. If you are familiar with the geography of almost any large city, think about this: How many urban locations are *not* within 1000 feet (that's about 1/5 of a mile) of a school property, a public park, a family housing complex, or a youth program center? Especially given the hugely expansive reading of "youth program center" provided by the Indiana Supreme Court, which would apply to most (if not all) churches—not to mention a significant number of private homes as well, if the home happens to be the location of, e.g., a day-care center or "Cub Scout weekly meeting"? Doesn't this create a special kind of problem, in that residents of densely settled urban areas are far more likely to violate such sentence-enhancing laws than those who live in spread-out suburbs or rural areas? Does it matter that residency in such densely settled urban areas tends to correlate pretty closely with both socio-economic class and race?

At least one state legislature seems to have thought so. On August 2, 2012, the Massachusetts legislature amended its "drug-free school zone" law (which added two years of additional imprisonment to the sentence for the underlying drug crime) to reduce the relevant distance from 1000 feet to 300 feet (i.e., the length of a football field). The amendment also limited the temporal scope of the law to cases of drug possession occurring between the hours of 5:00 A.M. and 12:00 midnight. In November 2013, the Massachusetts Supreme Judicial Court held that the amendment should be applied partially retroactively—meaning to any case in which a conviction had not yet been entered as of August 2, 2012—because the legislature's clear purpose was to remedy a serious and troubling disparity:

> The legislative purpose of §32J when it was first enacted in 1989 was to protect school children from drug dealers by creating drug-free school zones. But since its enactment, various studies have shown that the 1,000-foot radius was overbroad, and that its overbreadth has had an unfair impact on those living in urban communities. As one study summarized:
>
>> "Though the statute aims to protect children, its patterns of conviction indicate that it has more effectively created a two-tiered system of drug sentencing in Massachusetts. Because schools are more numerous

in dense urban areas, most urban residents—including most of the state's Black and Latino residents—face longer mandatory minimum sentences for drug offenses than the state's rural residents, who are predominantly White."

A Kajstura, P. Wagner, & W. Goldberg, The Geography of Punishment: How Huge Sentencing Enhancement Zones Harm Communities, Fail to Protect Children (2008). A study of Hampden County "found that residents of urban cities and towns are five times as likely to live in a sentencing enhancement zone as rural residents." Id. Because African-Americans and Latinos comprised most of Hampden County's urban population, they were more likely to live in school zones. Id. (finding majority—fifty-two per cent—of African-American and Latino residents in Hampden County lived in school zones compared to only twenty-nine per cent of white residents).

At least in part because of the greater likelihood that African-American and Latino residents live in school zones, in 2011, seventy-three per cent of those convicted of school zone offenses in Massachusetts were racial or ethnic minorities even though they comprise less than one quarter of the Massachusetts population and do not have a higher rate of illicit drug use. See Massachusetts Sentencing Commission, Survey of Sentencing Practices: FY 2011, at 85 (May 2012); United States Census Bureau, 2012 State & County QuickFacts, Massachusetts; Massachusetts Department of Public Health, Alcohol Use, Illicit Drug Use, and Gambling in Massachusetts, 2002, at 35-36 (July 2005). See generally J. Greene, K. Pranis, & J. Ziedenberg, Disparity by Design: How Drug-Free Zone Laws Impact Racial Disparity—and Fail to Protect Youth (2006).

Moreover, because of the overbreadth of the 1,000-foot school zone radius, few school zone cases involved the sale or distribution of drugs to minors or minors' participation in drug-dealing activities. A study of drug-dealing in three cities in Massachusetts—Fall River, New Bedford, and Springfield—found that seventy-one per cent of drug-dealing incidents within school zones occurred when school was not in session. W.N. Brownsberger, S.E. Aromaa, C.N. Brownsberger, & S.C. Brownsberger, An Empirical Study of the School Zone Anti-Drug Law in Three Cities in Massachusetts, Journal of Drug Issues, at 936 (2004). Of the 340 drug-dealing incidents that occurred within a school zone, no more than four cases "involved charges of dealing to minors or using minors in sales." Id. at 945 (Table 8) & 946.

The legislative history of §30 demonstrates that the Legislature was aware of the school zone's overbreadth and the disparate impact that resulted. The chair of the House Judiciary Committee, Representative Eugene O'Flaherty, told the House chamber when it considered the conference committee report that included §30:

"I hope you will understand what some of the urban districts have been dealing with. In Charlestown and Chelsea, you can't stand anywhere in my district and not be in a school zone. If you are in Worthington, you can stand in Worthington and you are probably not going to be in a school zone . . . . In urban areas all the individuals have this minimum mandatory sentence hanging over their head . . . . It has resulted in disparate sentencing."

State House News Service, July 18, 2012, at 10-11. Similar arguments were made in the State Senate. During a debate regarding the radius of the school zone, Senator James Eldridge noted that the existing school zone law punished city dwellers more harshly. State House News Service, Nov. 10, 2011, at 8. Senator Stephen Brewer claimed that the entire city of Boston is a school zone. Id. at 9. Senator Daniel Wolf argued that the existing school zone law fostered the discriminatory incarceration of the urban population and of minorities. Id. Perhaps because the existing G.L. c. 94C, §32J, was recognized to be overbroad, the focus of the debate on §30 was not whether, but by how much, the school zone radius was to be narrowed. The Senate bill proposed that the radius be reduced to 500 feet, id. at 3, and the Governor proposed 100 feet. State House News Service, Nov. 2, 2011, at 1. The conference committee settled on 300 feet.

Where the radius of the school zone was reduced from 1,000 feet to 300 feet at least in part because the broader radius was recognized to create an unfair disparate impact on those residing in urban areas and, consequently, on minority residents, and where the broader radius did not better protect school children from drug dealers, we conclude that it would be "repugnant to the context of [that] statute" to apply the §30 amendment to §32J prospectively and prolong the unfair disparate impact that the preamendment §32J was having on urban and minority residents. We recognize that, generally, when the Legislature narrows the statutory definition of a crime or reduces the possible sentence for a crime, prospective application "may be, in the defendant's view, an unfair consequence . . . , but it does not rise to the level of repugnancy." What distinguishes this amendment is that it was enacted to diminish the unfair disparate impact of the prior statute on urban and minority residents. Prospective application, therefore, affects more than the individuals charged with school zone violations; it affects all urban communities by subjecting their residents to a greater likelihood of a school zone sentencing enhancement than residents in suburban and rural communities . . . .

We recognize . . . that retroactive application will create its own set of disparities. With retroactive application, a person who committed a school zone violation before August 2, 2012, and pleaded guilty to that violation before that date will have his case adjudicated under the preamendment G.L. c. 94C, §32J, while another person who committed the same school zone violation on the same date but whose case was still pending on August 2, 2012, will have his case adjudicated under the amended §32J. We acknowledge this unfortunate disparity, but, if the price of avoiding it is to prolong the unfair disparate impact on urban communities in matters of sentencing by declining to apply §30 retroactively, we think the price is too high.

Commonwealth v. Bradley, 466 Mass. 551, 556-61, 998 N.E.2d 774 (Mass. 2013).

Notes on Crack Cocaine and Powder Cocaine

1. Still another way in which legislatures often have tried to grade different drug crimes is by focusing on the particular drugs involved. Federal drug laws, for example, lump certain drugs together as "Schedule I controlled substances"—meaning that the federal government finds them to have "no currently accepted medical use and a high potential for abuse." The federal Drug Enforcement Agency (DEA) calls these "the most dangerous drugs," with "potentially severe psychological or physical dependence." By contrast, "Schedule II controlled substances" involve "less abuse potential than Schedule I drugs." Schedule I drugs include heroin, LSD, and marijuana (?!). Schedule II drugs include cocaine, methadone, and methamphetamine; Dilaudid, Demerol, and OxyContin (pain medications); and Adderall and Ritalin (medications used to treat ADHD). See the official DEA website at www.justice.gov/dea/druginfo/ds.shtml.

All unauthorized possession, distribution, or use of controlled substances is prohibited by the federal Controlled Substances Act. The same law, however, contains very different punishments based on the particular drugs involved—and the differences don't always correspond with the particular Schedule on which the drug in question appears. Sometimes the differences in punishment seem to reflect political considerations more than thoughtful criminal justice policy.

The early 1980s witnessed a so-called "epidemic" of crack cocaine that swept America's large cities, including Washington, D.C. Partly in response, Congress enacted the Anti-Drug Abuse Act of 1986. Part of the Act created special "mandatory minimum" sentencing laws that required the imposition of extraordinarily severe punishments for possession of relatively small amounts of crack cocaine. For example, under the Act, possession of five grams of crack cocaine triggered a "mandatory minimum" sentence of five years in prison. Powder cocaine was not subjected to such harsh treatment—to get the same five-year "mandatory minimum" prison sentence, a person would have to possess 500 grams of powder cocaine. See 21 U.S.C. §841(b)(1)(A).

Scientific research eventually established that many of the purported reasons for imposing harsher punishment for crack cocaine than for powder cocaine are untrue. In particular, studies have shown that crack cocaine is not necessarily more addictive than powder cocaine; although there is a chemical difference (crack cocaine is a form of "cocaine base," whereas powder cocaine is cocaine in the form of a salt), the physiological and psychotropic effects are largely the same. The practical difference is that crack cocaine is simply a more efficient (and less expensive) method of delivery of the drug into the human body.

Meanwhile, over time, the disparate impact upon inner-city communities of the Act's sharp crackdown on crack cocaine became gradually apparent—and increasingly controversial. The Act's sentencing disparity (often described as "100-to-1," meaning that the law required 100 times as much powder cocaine to trigger the same level of mandatory punishment as crack cocaine) led to a dramatic increase in the federal imprisonment rates of urban black men. One study found that approximately 80 percent of the defendants who were convicted of possessing crack cocaine were black. By the mid-1990s, the United States Sentencing Commission, the entity charged with the responsibility to draft and study sentencing guidelines for federal crimes, reached the conclusion that something had to be done to reduce the 100-to-1 sentencing ratio. See http://www.ussc.gov/Legislative_and_Public_Affairs/Congressional_Testimony_and_Reports/Drug_Topics/199502_RtC_Cocaine_Sentencing_Policy/EXECSUM.PDF.

After more than a decade of additional discussion and debate, Congress finally enacted—and President Barack Obama signed into federal law—the Fair Sentencing Act of 2010 (FSA). The FSA reduced, but did not eliminate, the crack-powder cocaine sentencing disparity. Under the FSA, the five-year mandatory minimum sentence now applies to those caught with 500 grams of powder cocaine or 28 grams of crack cocaine—or a ratio of about 18 to 1.

2. In Dorsey v. United States, 567 U.S. __ (2012), the U.S. Supreme Court ruled by 5-4 that the Fair Sentencing Act of 2010 applies partly retroactively, granting relief to the limited class of defendants whose crack cocaine crimes were committed before the Act's effective date of August 3, 2010, but who were not sentenced until after that date. (*Dorsey* was relied upon heavily by the Massachusetts Supreme Judicial Court in its *Bradley* decision, see supra at page 447.) Every federal court of appeals to address the question so far, however, has rejected full retroactive application of the Act. See, e.g., United States v. Blewett, 2013 U.S. App. LEXIS 24018, 2013 FED App. 0336P, 2013 WL 6231727 (6th Cir. Dec. 3, 2013) (en banc); see also Linda Greenhouse, "Crack Cocaine Limbo," New York Times, Jan. 5, 2014, available online at http://www.nytimes.com/2014/01/06/opinion/greenhouse-crack-cocaine-limbo.html?_r=0.

3. The Anti-Drug Abuse Act of 1986 used the term "cocaine base," not "crack cocaine," in its mandatory minimum sentencing provisions. And although the Fair Sentencing Act of 2010 changed the amounts that triggered those mandatory minimum sentences, it did not change the statutory term "cocaine base." As used by chemists, the term "cocaine base" actually includes not only crack cocaine, but also coca paste (the substance from which powder cocaine is made) and yet another form of cocaine known as "freebase" cocaine. (If you insist on knowing more, powder cocaine is converted into crack cocaine by using baking soda, and into freebase cocaine by using ammonia.) Does the statutory term "cocaine base" also include both crack cocaine and freebase cocaine, or does it include only crack cocaine?

In DePierre v. United States, 564 U.S. __ (2011), the defendant (who was caught selling "freebase" cocaine) argued that the statute includes only crack cocaine; his argument relied in large part on the U.S. Sentencing Commission's 1993 decision to issue federal sentencing guidelines that limited the more severe mandatory minimum sentence to crimes involving crack cocaine. The U.S. Supreme Court unanimously disagreed, concluding that the statutory term's "most natural reading" includes all base forms of cocaine, and noting that the Sentencing Commission's interpretation could not override an act of Congress. Despite conceding that "we cannot say that the statute is crystalline" (Was that meant as a pun?), the Court declined to apply the rule of lenity, explaining that "the statutory text allows us to make far more than 'a guess as to what Congress intended.'"

4. Federal law is not the only place where possession of crack cocaine is treated much more harshly than possession of powder cocaine. State drug laws, state sentencing guidelines, and state and local prosecutorial and police enforcement policies and practices also frequently target crack cocaine much more aggressively than they do powder cocaine, with similar consequences.

In one particularly egregious example of overly aggressive enforcement of crack cocaine laws, a study of drug law enforcement in the City of Seattle during a four-month period in 2005-06 found that two out of three (67 percent) of all those arrested for delivery of a serious drug were black—in a city where the black population is only 8 percent. Overall, the arrest rate of blacks for delivery of a serious drug was more than 21 times higher than the arrest rate of whites. What could be the cause of such extreme disparity? The same study revealed that 72.9 percent of all serious drug arrests in the city were for delivery of crack cocaine—and 73.4 percent of those arrested for delivery of crack cocaine were black. (For all other serious drugs, fewer than 20 percent of those arrested were black.) The study also concluded that this intense focus on crack cocaine was *not* the result of more crack cocaine crimes being committed in Seattle, or more citizen complaints about crack cocaine, or greater public health or public safety impacts of crack cocaine. See http://faculty.washington.edu/kbeckett/Race and Drug Law Enforcement in Seattle_2008.pdf. The study was conducted by Professor Katherine Beckett in connection with a lawsuit filed by the Racial Disparity Project (RDP) and the ACLU Drug Law Reform Project, alleging selective enforcement of drug laws based on race. Shortly before the study's public release, the City of Seattle agreed to settle with the plaintiffs and instituted a new program to divert eligible low-level drug offenders into community-based services in lieu of criminal prosecution. See http://rdp.defender. org/projects (describing RDP/ACLU lawsuit); http://leadkingcounty.org/ (describing diversion program).

D. DRUGS AND MEDICINE

United States v. Hurwitz
_____

United States Court of Appeals for the Fourth Circuit
459 F.3d 463 (2006)

Traxler, Circuit Judge.

A jury convicted Dr. William E. Hurwitz of multiple counts of drug trafficking for prescribing narcotic pain medicine in violation of 21 U.S.C. §§841(a)(1) and 846. Hurwitz appeals. . . . [W]e conclude that the district court did not properly instruct the jury on the controlling law. Accordingly, we vacate Hurwitz's convictions and remand for a new trial.

Hurwitz is a medical doctor who operated a practice in McLean, Virginia, dedicated to the treatment of patients suffering from pain. Hurwitz's approach to pain management involved the use of opioids, including methadone, oxycodone (typically Oxycontin, a brand-name version of a time-release form of oxycodone), and hydromorphone (usually the brand-name Dilaudid). Many of Hurwitz's patients were on a protocol that used very high doses of opioids to control their pain.

Hurwitz came to the attention of federal authorities in 2002, after several of his patients were arrested for attempting to sell illicit and prescription drugs. The patients identified Hurwitz as the source of their prescription drugs, and they began cooperating with the investigators. The information these patients provided eventually led to Hurwitz's indictment on numerous drug-related charges—one count of conspiracy to engage in drug trafficking, see 21 U.S.C. §846; one count of engaging in a continuing criminal enterprise, see 21 U.S.C. §848; two counts of healthcare fraud, see 18 U.S.C. §1347; and 58 counts of drug trafficking, including two counts each of drug-trafficking resulting in serious bodily injury and drug-trafficking resulting in death, see 21 U.S.C. §841(a)(1).

The government's evidence at trial painted a picture of a doctor who operated well outside the boundaries of usual medical practice. The government contended that Hurwitz was little more than a common drug dealer who operated out of a medical office rather than on a street corner. The government's expert witnesses testified that a doctor who knowingly prescribed opioids to an addict or to a patient the doctor knew was selling the drugs on the street was acting outside the bounds of legitimate medical practice, and the government presented compelling evidence suggesting that Hurwitz did just that—continued to prescribe large quantities of opioids to patients that he knew were selling the drugs or abusing them (for example, by injecting drugs that were directed to be taken orally).

Several of the patients who were cooperating with the authorities tape-recorded their appointments with Hurwitz. In one recording, Hurwitz indicated that it was "not inconceivable" to him that some patients were "selling part of their medicines so they could buy the rest." In another recording Hurwitz stated, "so I have kind of a huge conspiracy of silence because I, in fact, even, even knowing what I'll call the suspicious nature of you guys, assumed that you weren't stupid enough to — to not protect my practice and preserve your own . . . access to medications." Hurwitz told another patient to get an x-ray or an MRI "for the files to cover our butts."

The government presented evidence of what seemed to be extraordinarily high doses of opioids prescribed by Hurwitz. An expert witness for the government testified that high-dose opioid therapy typically involved doses of the equivalent of approximately 195 milligrams of morphine a day, although there had been a study involving doses of 350 milligrams a day and another involving doses of up to two grams a day.

The doses prescribed by Hurwitz, however, vastly exceeded those quantities. Hurwitz often wrote prescriptions calling for a patient to take thirty 80-milligram Oxycontins per day. For Hurwitz's patients in the high-dose program, a prescribed opioid dosage of 100 pills per day was not uncommon. Hurwitz testified that between 1998 and 2002, the median daily dosage for his patients was approximately 2000 milligrams (2 grams) of morphine or its equivalent. (Because Oxycontin is stronger than morphine, Hurwitz testified that 2000 milligrams of morphine would translate to about 1000 milligrams of Oxycontin.) Between July 1999 and October 2002, Hurwitz prescribed to one patient a total of more than 500,000 pills, which amounted to more than 400 pills per day. . . . Patients with limited visible sources of income spent tens of thousands of dollars a month on narcotics prescribed by Hurwitz.

The government also presented evidence showing that Hurwitz had previously been disciplined for improper prescribing practices. In 1992, the District of Columbia Board of Medicine had reprimanded Hurwitz and placed him on probation for prescribing drugs when not authorized to do so and for failing to conform to the prevailing standards of acceptable medical practice. In 1996, the Virginia Board of Medicine revoked his license upon finding that he had prescribed excessive amounts of controlled substances. The Virginia Board also required Hurwitz to attend classes on proper prescription practices and how to detect when patients were trying to use him as a source for prescription drugs rather than a doctor to treat pain.

Not surprisingly, the defense painted an entirely different picture. Hurwitz and his witnesses contended that the high-dose protocol was a proper medical procedure for treating patients with intractable pain. They testified that the body quickly develops resistance to the dangerous side-effects of opioids (such as respiratory depression), which then permits an escalation of the dosage until pain relief is obtained. One expert testified that once a patient becomes tolerant of the side-effects, there is effectively "no ceiling" on the quantity of opioids that can be prescribed if necessary to control pain. That expert also testified that many patients over time will require an increase in their opioid dosage in order to maintain control of their pain. Hurwitz's experts also testified that there is no medical reason to stop treating a patient for pain simply because that patient may be abusing illicit drugs and that, in some cases, stopping such treatment may even be more problematic.

Hurwitz testified about his practices and the patients he treated. He discussed how patients were generally asked to fill out questionnaires and submit medical records before receiving treatment and how he often included patients' family members during visits as a part of his approach to treating pain. Hurwitz participated in an e-mail discussion group with other professionals about how to approach various situations in pain treatment, and he would confer with other physicians concerning the treatment of certain patients. Hurwitz also discussed how he based his pain-management approach on what he learned at pain management conferences and what he understood other doctors would do.

Some of Hurwitz's patients testified on his behalf, explaining that Hurwitz was the only physician who had managed to relieve their debilitating pain. Molly Shaw, for example, discussed her futile attempts to treat what the Mayo Clinic had diagnosed as neuropathic pain, a pain so severe that it forced her to retire at age 47 and remain almost completely bedridden. She testified that Hurwitz's treatments allowed her to regain her life and live in considerably less pain. The patients' testimony, as well as the testimony of Hurwitz's staff, portrayed Hurwitz as a caring physician whose sole focus was providing pain relief for his patients.

Hurwitz was convicted of one count of drug trafficking conspiracy, one count of drug trafficking resulting in death, two counts of drug trafficking resulting in serious bodily injury, and forty-six counts of drug trafficking. The jury acquitted Hurwitz of six counts of drug trafficking, as well as one count of engaging in a continuing criminal enterprise and two counts of healthcare fraud. The jury failed to reach a decision on the remaining drug trafficking counts. The district court sentenced Hurwitz to 25 years in prison. This appeal followed. . . .

We turn now to Hurwitz's challenges to the jury instructions with regard to the charges he faced under 21 U.S.C. §841. . . .

Section 841 provides that, "[e]xcept as authorized by this subchapter, it shall be unlawful for any person knowingly or intentionally . . . to . . . distribute, or dispense, or possess with intent to . . . distribute, or dispense, a controlled substance." 21 U.S.C. §841(a)(1). Doctors who are "registered" by the Attorney General are authorized to write prescriptions for or to otherwise dispense controlled substances, so long as they comply with the requirements of their registration. See 21 U.S.C. §822(b).

As authorized by the Controlled Substances Act, the Attorney General has promulgated regulations addressing the conditions under which registrants are authorized to dispense controlled substances. The regulations provide that a prescription for a controlled substance is effective only if it is "issued for a legitimate medical purpose by an individual practitioner acting in the usual course of his professional practice." 21 C.F.R. §1306.04(a). The regulation further provides that:

> An order purporting to be a prescription issued not in the usual course of professional treatment or in legitimate and authorized research is not a prescription within the meaning and intent of section 309 of the Act (21 U.S.C. §829) and the person knowingly . . . issuing [such a purported prescription] shall be subject to the penalties provided for violations of the provisions of law relating to controlled substances.

Synthesizing the requirements of the relevant statutes and regulations, we have held that to convict a doctor for violating §841, the government must prove: (1) "that the defendant distributed or dispensed a controlled substance"; (2) that the defendant "acted knowingly and intentionally"; and (3) "that the defendant's actions were not for legitimate medical purposes in the usual course of his professional medical practice or were beyond the bounds of medical practice." United States v. Singh, 54 F.3d 1182, 1187 (4th Cir. 1995).

On appeal, Hurwitz raises several objections to the district court's instructions to the jury. He argues that the instructions required the jury to apply the knowledge requirement only to Hurwitz's act of writing a prescription, and that the instructions therefore permitted the jury to convict even if it concluded that Hurwitz did not know that any given prescription was not for a legitimate medical purpose or was beyond the bounds of medical practice. Hurwitz claims that the instructions thus improperly limited the statute's *mens rea* requirement and permitted the jury to convict him of a serious crime with little more than a finding of negligence. . . . . [I]n a related argument, Hurwitz contends that the district court erred by not including a good-faith instruction in connection with the §841 charges and by specifically instructing the jury that it could not consider Hurwitz's good faith as to any of the drug-trafficking charges. Hurwitz also argues that the district court erred by not defining the phrases "beyond the bounds of medical practice" or "not for a legitimate medical purpose." As we explain below, we conclude that a new trial is required because of the district court's error regarding the good-faith instruction. Given this conclusion, we need not consider and we express no opinion on Hurwitz's other challenges to the jury instructions. . . .

The district court agreed with the government's position that Hurwitz's good faith was legally irrelevant to the drug-trafficking charges . . . . However, as to the two healthcare fraud charges, the district court . . . instructed the jury that it could not convict Dr. Hurwitz if he "acted in good faith in dispensing any of the prescriptions alleged to constitute the crime of healthcare fraud." The court defined "good faith" to mean "good intentions in the honest exercise of best professional judgment as to a patient's needs. It means the doctor acted according to what he believed to be proper medical practice." The district court instructed the jury that "good faith applies only" to the healthcare fraud counts. . . .

In United States v. Moore, 423 U.S. 122 (1975), the seminal case addressing the prosecution of physicians under §841, the Supreme Court concluded that "registered physicians can be prosecuted under §841 when their activities fall outside the usual course of professional practice." Id. at 124. In the course of concluding that the evidence [sufficiently supported the defendant's conviction], the Court noted two good-faith instructions that had been given to the jury. The district court had instructed the jury that the defendant could be convicted if the jury found that he knowingly distributed controlled substances "other than in good faith for detoxification in the usual course of a professional practice . . . , [id.] at 139, and that the defendant "could not be convicted if he merely made 'an honest effort' to prescribe . . . in compliance with an accepted standard of medical practice." Id. at 142 n.20.

Building on the Supreme Court's approach in *Moore*, lower courts have concluded that when resolving the ultimate question in a §841 prosecution against a doctor—whether the doctor acted without a legitimate medical purpose or beyond the bounds of accepted medical practice—some latitude must be given to doctors . . . . See *Alerre*, 430 F.3d at 692 (noting that "the jury was correctly instructed on the applicable legal principles," and that the jury was instructed that the defendant-doctors "could not be convicted if they had dispensed the controlled substances at issue in good faith"); United States v. Hughes, 895 F.2d 1135, 1141-42 (6th Cir. 1990) (citing *Moore*'s standard that physicians cannot be convicted if they "dispens[e] controlled substances in the course of professional practice" and explaining that "[b]ecause Dudley was a licensed physician, the jury could not find him guilty of distributing controlled substances, as long as he acted in good faith"); United States v. Vamos, 797 F.2d 1146, 1151 (2d Cir. 1986) ("[T]he doctor must act in the good faith belief that his distribution of the controlled substance is for a legitimate medical purpose and in accordance with the usual course of generally accepted medical practice."); United States v. Hayes, 794 F.2d 1348, 1351-52 (9th Cir. 1986) (finding no error in charge that required jury to determine that physician acted other than in good faith and defined good faith as "an honest effort to prescribe for a patient's condition in accordance with the standard of medical practice generally recognized and accepted in the country"). Accordingly, the district court erred by concluding that good faith is not relevant when a registered physician is charged with violating §841. . . .

. . . [Nevertheless,] the government argues that Hurwitz is not entitled to reversal on this point because the good-faith instruction Hurwitz offered below was an incorrect statement of the law. . . . The good-faith instruction offered by Hurwitz at trial stated that:

> If a doctor dispenses a drug in good faith to medically treat a patient, then the doctor has dispensed the drug for a legitimate medical purpose and in the course of medical practice. That is, he has dispensed the drug lawfully. "Good faith" in this context means good intentions in the honest exercise of best professional judgment as to a patient's needs. It means the doctor acted according to what *he believed to be proper medical practice.*

J.A. 719 (emphasis added). This proposed instruction clearly sets forth a subjective standard, permitting Hurwitz to decide for himself what constitutes proper medical treatment. . . .

In *Moore,* the Supreme Court discussed the circumstances under which doctors could be prosecuted under §841 using language that strongly suggests the inquiry is an objective one. For example, the Court held that "registered physicians can be prosecuted under §841 when their activities fall outside the *usual course of professional practice." Moore,* 423 U.S. at 124 (emphasis added). The Court also noted that, when passing the Controlled Substances Act, Congress intended to "confine authorized medical practice within *accepted limits,"* id. at 142 (emphasis added), and that "physicians who go beyond *approved practice* remain subject to serious criminal penalties." Id. at 144 (emphasis added). . . .

. . . We believe that the inquiry must be an objective one, a conclusion that has been reached by every court to specifically consider the question. As the Second Circuit explained,

> "[P]rofessional practice" [as used in 21 C.F.R. §1306.04(a)] refers to generally accepted medical practice; a practitioner is not free deliberately to disregard prevailing standards of treatment. . . .
>
> To permit a practitioner to substitute his or her views of what is good medical practice for standards generally recognized and accepted in the United States would be to weaken the enforcement of our drug laws in a critical area.

Vamos, 797 F.2d at 1151, 1153; see also United States v. Williams, 445 F.3d 1302, 1309 (11th Cir. 2006) ("Williams's proposed instruction fails to introduce any objective standard by which a physician's prescribing behavior can be judged. Under Williams's proposed instruction, if it is a physician's subjective belief that he is meeting a patient's medical needs by prescribing that patient a controlled substance, then that physician cannot be convicted of violating the Controlled Substances Act even if he acts outside all accepted standards of medical practice. Thus, the proposed instruction is contrary to *Moore*.") . . .

The government contends that because Hurwitz's proposed instruction was not a correct statement of the law, any errors in the district court's good-faith instructions cannot justify a new trial. We disagree. The government's argument confuses two separate issues—whether the district court erred by refusing to use the good-faith charge proposed by Hurwitz, and whether the district court erred by affirmatively informing the jury that good faith was relevant only to the fraud charges. Hurwitz timely objected to that instruction, thus preserving that error of commission as a separate issue for review on appeal. The district court's incorrect instruction on good faith is not insulated from review on appeal simply because Hurwitz's proposed good-faith instruction was incorrect. . . .

Good faith was at the heart of Hurwitz's defense. Hurwitz did not dispute the bulk of the government's factual evidence—that is, he did not argue that he did not prescribe the narcotics that were the basis for the charges against him. Instead, Hurwitz argued that the manner in which he used narcotics to treat chronic and debilitating pain was a medically proper approach to a difficult medical issue. By concluding that good faith was not applicable to the §841 charges and affirmatively instructing the jury that good faith was not relevant to those charges, the district court effectively deprived the jury of the opportunity to consider Hurwitz's defense. . . .

To summarize, we conclude that good faith is relevant to §841 charges against a registered physician and that the district court erred by incorrectly instructing the jury that Hurwitz's good faith was relevant only to the health-care fraud charges. This error in the court's instructions to the jury cannot be considered harmless, and a new trial is therefore required. On remand, the district court shall include a good-faith instruction . . . , but that instruction must reflect an objective rather than subjective standard . . . .

. . . [F]or the foregoing reasons, we vacate Hurwitz's convictions under 21 U.S.C. §§841 and 846,[110] and we remand for a new trial in accordance with this opinion.

[The opinion of Judge WIDENER, concurring in part and dissenting in part, is omitted.]

---

10. The instructions on the §846 conspiracy count mirrored those for the substantive §841 counts, by requiring a determination that Hurwitz entered into an agreement to distribute controlled substances not for a legitimate medical purpose or beyond the bounds of medical practice. Thus, the error in connection with the good-faith instruction affects the conviction on the conspiracy count to the same extent as it does the §841 convictions.

Notes and Questions

1. After prevailing in the Fourth Circuit, Hurwitz was re-prosecuted on 45 counts of drug trafficking. A second federal jury in Alexandria, Virginia, convicted Hurwitz on 16 of the 45 counts and acquitted him on 17 others; the remaining 12 counts were dismissed by U.S. District Judge Leonie M. Brinkema.

At Hurwitz's re-sentencing in July 2007, federal prosecutors sought a life sentence, arguing that Hurwitz had "crossed the line from a healer to a dealer," and had prescribed clearly excessive amounts of opioids to addicts and others who often resold them on the streets. But Judge Brinkema gradually became persuaded by the testimony of numerous patient advocates and others—including Hurwitz himself—that Hurwitz mostly served legitimate pain patients in a manner that was consistent with a "new enlightenment" in the field of pain medication. According to Judge Brinkema: "An increasing body of respectable medical literature and expertise supports those types of high-dosage, opioid medications." Judge Brinkema also expressed the feeling that Hurwitz had been duped by a few unscrupulous patients who took advantage of his desire to ease patient suffering.

For more on the *Hurwitz* case, see Jerry Markon, "Va. Pain Doctor's Prison Term Is Cut to 57 Months; Originally Sentenced to 25 Years, Specialist Did More Good Than Harm, Judge Says," Washington Post, July 14, 2007, at B1.

2. The *Hurwitz* case is but one example of a highly publicized criminal case involving a pain doctor and opioid prescriptions. In 2016, the *Washington Post* reported another such case, involving a pain doctor in Michigan by the name of Hussein Awada. Dr. Awada was accused by the U.S. Drug Enforcement Agency and the U.S. Attorney's Office of running a "pill mill" through which, from 2010 until early 2012, he improperly prescribed 80,000 doses of Oxycodone, Roxicodone, and other narcotics and controlled substances to patients without a valid medical need for those medications. The patients were recruited to Dr. Awada's practice by James Lyons, a "marketer" who allegedly bought the pills back from the patients and then re-sold them on the streets. Dr. Awada was also accused of defrauding Medicare and Medicaid by billing those two government programs for ultrasounds, blood tests, and X-rays that either were medically unnecessary or were never performed at all (including some instances where the tests were ordered for patients who had already died).

In November 2015, Dr. Awada pleaded guilty to unlawful distribution of a controlled substance and conspiracy to commit health care fraud, and he received seven years in prison plus a requirement to pay about $2.3 million in restitution to the government. In September 2016, Dr. Awada settled a related civil claim, agreeing to pay $200,000 in damages. Dr. Awada's lawyer, Steve Fishman, explained that Dr. Awada had a plan to get his medical license reinstated after serving out his prison sentence, and he also wanted to settle the civil claim "so that when he comes home and goes back to work, he will not have this hanging over his head." See Kristine Guerra, The Pill Mill Doctor Who Prescribed Thousands of Opioids and Billed Dead Patients, Washington Post, Sept. 22, 2016, available online at https://www.washingtonpost.com/news/to-your-health/wp/2016/09/22/deceitful-pill-mill-doctor-who-prescribed-thousands-of-opioids-and-billed-dead-patients-settles-civil-lawsuit/).

3. The problem of addiction to opioids has reached epidemic proportions in America, and the individual and societal impacts are enormous. The Substance Abuse and Mental Health Services Administration reported in 2015 that more than one out of every three Americans—35 percent in all—were given painkiller prescriptions by medical providers during the preceding year. See https://www.washingtonpost.com/news/wonk/wp/2016/09/20/prescription-painkillers-are-more-widely-used-than-tobacco-new-federal-study-finds/?tid=a_inl. In November 2016, the U.S. Surgeon General, Dr. Vivek Murthy, stated:

> Over-prescription of powerful opioid pain relievers beginning in the 1990s led to a rapid escalation of use and misuse of these substances by a broad demographic of men and women across the country. This led to a resurgence of heroin use, as some users transitioned to using this cheaper street cousin of expensive prescription opioids. As a result, the number of people dying from opioid overdoses soared—increasing nearly four-fold between 1999 and 2014.
>
> Opioid analgesic pain relievers are now the most prescribed class of medications in the United States, with more than 289 million prescriptions written each year. The increase in prescriptions of opioid pain relievers has been accompanied by dramatic increases in misuse and by a more than 200 percent increase in the number of emergency department visits from 2005 to 2011. In 2014, 47,055 drug overdose deaths occurred in the United States, and 61 percent of these deaths were the result of opioid use, including prescription opioids and heroin. Heroin overdoses have more than tripled from 2010 to 2014. Heroin overdoses were more than five times higher in 2014 (10,574) then ten years before in 2004 (1,878).

See U.S. Department of Health and Human Services, Facing Addiction in America: The Surgeon General's Report on Alcohol, Drugs, and Health, available online at https://addiction.surgeongeneral.gov/.

According to Nora D. Volkow, M.D., testifying before the U.S. Senate Judiciary Committee on behalf of the National Institute on Drug Abuse (a component of the National Institutes of Health) in January 2016:

> The misuse of and addiction to opioids such as heroin and prescription pain medicines is a serious national problem that affects public health as well as social and economic welfare. An estimated 1.9 million people in the United

States suffered from substance use disorders related to prescription opioid pain medicines in 2014, and 586,000 suffered from a heroin use disorder. This issue has become a public health epidemic with devastating consequences including not just increases in opioid use disorders and related fatalities from overdoses, but also the rising incidence of newborns who experience neonatal abstinence syndrome because their mothers used these substances during pregnancy; and the increased spread of infectious diseases including HIV and hepatitis C (HCV), as was seen in 2015 in southern Indiana. . . .

The public-health consequences of opioid misuse are broad and profound. For example, use of many drugs including opioids by pregnant women can result in a withdrawal syndrome in newborns, referred to as neonatal abstinence syndrome, which increased by approximately 500 percent in the United States between 2000 and 2012. This increase was driven in part by the high rate of opioid prescriptions being given to pregnant women. An estimated 14.4 percent of pregnant women with private insurance and 21.6 percent of Medicaid enrolled pregnant women filled prescriptions for an opioid during their pregnancy between 2000 and 2007. Methadone has been the acknowledged standard for treating opioid use disorders in pregnant women and in infants born experiencing withdrawal. However, there is a growing literature supporting the efficacy of buprenorphine treatment for these conditions. These treatments, in combination with behavioral treatment, remain highly underused and present the best opportunities to treat opioid use disorder in pregnancy.

Another concern is the transmission of infectious diseases such as HIV and HCV due to injection of heroin or prescription opioids, which has risen as the number of individuals injecting opioids has increased. In 2015, we saw one of the fastest-spreading outbreaks of HIV in the U.S. since the inception of the epidemic with 184 cases reported in a small area in southeastern Indiana. This outbreak was driven by injection drug use—specifically, injection of the opioid painkiller oxymorphone. The high prevalence of opioid use also impacts public safety; from 1999 to 2010, there was a six-fold increase in positive opioid tests among drivers who died in car crashes.

See https://www.drugabuse.gov/about-nida/legislative-activities/testimony-to-congress/2016/what-science-tells-us-about-opioid-abuse-addiction.

Doctor Volkow also testified about the close relationship between prescription opioid abuse and heroin use:

Research has shown that prescription opioid misuse is a risk factor for heroin use. The incidence of heroin initiation is 19 times higher among those who report prior nonmedical pain-reliever use than among those who do not (0.39 percent vs. 0.02 percent). Indeed, eighty percent of new heroin users started by abusing prescription opioids. However, there are many more prescription opioid users than heroin users, and, overall, heroin use is rare among individuals who misuse prescription opioids. According to the National Survey on Drug Use and Health, fewer than four percent of people who had used prescription painkillers non-medically started using heroin within five years of their initiation of non-medical use of pain medication.

Heroin and prescription opioid pain relievers belong to a single class of drugs—but each is associated with distinct risks. The risk of overdose and negative consequences is greater with heroin due to the lack of control over the purity of the drug and its adulteration with other drugs, such as fentanyl—originally a potent prescription opioid but now often synthesized in clandestine labs. All of these factors increase the risk for overdose since users have no way of assessing the potency of the drug before taking it and, in the case of adulteration with fentanyl, users typically have no opportunity to become tolerant.

There also has been a shift in the demographic of opioid addiction over the last few decades. In the 1960s, more than 80 percent of people who began using opioids initiated with heroin; today, nearly 80 percent of opioid users reported that their first regular opioid was a prescription pain reliever. It also has been reported that current heroin users are more likely to be white, middle-class, and live in more suburban and rural areas; this is consistent with the population of people who report the largest increases in non-medical use of opioid pain relievers over the last decade.

The transition from misusing prescription opioids to using heroin may be part of the natural progression of disease in a subset of users. Evidence from interviews with individuals with heroin use disorder suggest that market forces, including the accessibility, cost, and high potency of heroin are driving increased use of heroin and transition from prescription opioids. Some individuals who have developed dependence on prescription opioids, when faced with the increasing difficulty of obtaining these medications through their providers and the cost of obtaining them illegally, have initiated heroin use, which is cheaper and in some communities easier to obtain than prescription opioids.

In aggregate, these data suggest that preventing the initiation of prescription opioid misuse is a crucial component of efforts to prevent heroin use.

Id.

Given these shocking facts and statistics, and the human carnage they reveal, should the criminal law take a tougher stance toward pain doctors like William Hurwitz who seem willing to run unreasonable risks by the relatively loose manner in which they prescribe opioids? Should the medical profession in general take greater responsibility for not only the initial prescribing of opioid drugs, but also the ongoing monitoring of opioid patients for possible signs of addiction?

Then again, doesn't the criminal law face a serious dilemma here, as evidenced by the twists and turns of the *Hurwitz* litigation? Surely, in the quest to prevent opioid abuse, we don't want to deprive truly needy and deserving patients from access to perhaps the only drugs that can ease their unbearable pain and suffering. Is it really possible for the criminal law to draw a line that allows pain relief for those who need it, but that also helps to prevent the tragic consequences of opioid addiction, including the increasingly deadly addiction to heroin? Is the criminal law really the best solution to this growing problem?

4. Might we be able to find a better solution by treating the problem of opioid addiction as a medical problem, rather than as a criminal problem? On December 13, 2016, President Obama signed into law the 21st Century Cures Act. One portion of this law authorizes $1 billion in new federal funding over two years to support state initiatives to prevent and treat the abuse of opioids and other addictive drugs like heroin. In his signing statement, President Obama explained:

> Over the last eight years, one of my highest priorities as President has been to unleash the full force of American innovation to some of the biggest challenges that we face. That meant restoring science to its rightful place. It meant funding the research and development that's always kept America on the cutting edge. It's meant investing in clean energy that's created a steady stream of good jobs and helped America become the world's leader in combatting climate change. It meant investing in the medical breakthroughs that have the power to cure disease and help all of us live healthier, longer lives.
>
> So I started the 2016 State of the Union address by saying we might be able to surprise some cynics and deliver bipartisan action on the opioid epidemic. And in that same speech, I put Joe in charge of mission control on a new Cancer Moonshot [to boost research to cure cancer]. And today, with the 21st Century Cures Act, we are making good on both of those efforts. We are bringing to reality the possibility of new breakthroughs to some of the greatest health challenges of our time. . . .
>
> [T]his legislation is going to combat the heroin and prescription opioid epidemic that is ravaging too many families across the country. This is an epidemic that can touch anybody—blue collar, white collar, college students, retirees, kids, moms, dads. I've had the chance to meet people from every stage of recovery who are working hard to sustain the progress that they're making. And I've met parents . . . who have worked tirelessly to help a child struggling with addiction.
>
> It could not be clearer that those of us called upon to lead this country have a duty on their behalf, that we have to stand by them; that, all too often, they feel as if they're fighting this fight alone instead of having the community gather around them and give them the resources and the access and the support that they need.
>
> So today, I could not be prouder that this legislation takes up the charge I laid out in my budget to provide $1 billion in funding so that Americans who want treatment can get started on the path to recovery. . . . It is the right thing to do, and families are ready for the support. . . .

See Remarks by the President at the 21st Century Cures Act Bill Signing, December 13, 2016, available online at https://www.whitehouse.gov/the-press-office/2016/12/13/remarks-president-and-vice-president-21st-century-cures-act-bill-signing.

E. LEGALIZATION OF MARIJUANA: THE NEXT FRONTIER OF FEDERALISM?

In Chapter 4, we learned about the constitutionally established (but ever-changing) balance of state and federal power to define and enforce criminal law, a balance of power that we call federalism. That balance is being tested by modern state statutes (and even state constitutional provisions) defining the possession and use of marijuana under certain circumstances as legal under state law, although the possession and sale of marijuana remains a serious crime under the federal Controlled Substances Act.

As of late 2016, at least 28 states and the District of Columbia had adopted so-called "medical marijuana" laws, allowing marijuana to be grown, harvested, sold, possessed, and used for certain medical purposes.* In addition, in 2012, two states—Colorado and Washington—officially legalized the possession and recreational use of relatively small amounts of marijuana by adults over the age of 21; six more states (Alaska, California, Oregon, Nevada, Massachusetts, and Maine) have since joined the list.** As noted earlier, however, marijuana is still classified as a "Schedule I controlled substance,"*** and marijuana possession thus remains illegal under federal law. How should this growing conflict between state and federal laws relating to marijuana be resolved?

Gonzales v. Raich

Supreme Court of the United States
545 U.S. 1 (2005)

Justice STEVENS delivered the opinion of the Court.

California is one of [the states] that authorize the use of marijuana for medicinal purposes. The question presented in this case is whether the

---

* Most of these states continue to impose civil regulations on the production, sale, and use of medical marijuana, including (in some states) rules about licensing and taxation of medical marijuana producers and distributors. Several states, including California, also permit individual users to grow their own medical marijuana.

** In four of the six new states—California, Nevada, Massachusetts, and Maine—ballot measures were approved by the voters in November 2016; in Arizona, a similar ballot measure was narrowly defeated.

In the first *month* (January 2014) of legal recreational marijuana sales in Colorado, the state reported total marijuana sales of $14.02 million—*not including* medical marijuana—which generated state tax revenues of $2.01 million. See http://nbcnews.to/PnOmhV. Do you think this might continue to influence other states to consider legalizing recreational marijuana?

*** On August 11, 2016, the U.S. Drug Enforcement Agency (DEA), after consulting with the U.S. Food and Drug Administration (FDA), rejected two petitions to reclassify marijuana under the Controlled Substances Act. See https://www.dea.gov/divisions/hq/2016/hq081116.shtml.

power vested in Congress by Article I, §8, of the Constitution "[t]o make all Laws which shall be necessary and proper for carrying into Execution" its authority to "regulate Commerce with foreign Nations, and among the several States" includes the power to prohibit the local cultivation and use of marijuana in compliance with California law.

I

California has been a pioneer in the regulation of marijuana. In 1913, California was one of the first States to prohibit the sale and possession of marijuana, and at the end of the century, California became the first State to authorize limited use of the drug for medicinal purposes. In 1996, California voters passed Proposition 215, now codified as the Compassionate Use Act of 1996. The proposition was designed to ensure that "seriously ill" residents of the State have access to marijuana for medical purposes, and to encourage Federal and State Governments to take steps towards ensuring the safe and affordable distribution of the drug to patients in need. The Act creates an exemption from criminal prosecution for physicians, as well as for patients and primary caregivers who possess or cultivate marijuana for medicinal purposes with the recommendation or approval of a physician. A "primary caregiver" is a person who has consistently assumed responsibility for the housing, health, or safety of the patient.

Respondents Angel Raich and Diane Monson are California residents who suffer from a variety of serious medical conditions and have sought to avail themselves of medical marijuana pursuant to the terms of the Compassionate Use Act. They are being treated by licensed, board-certified family practitioners, who have concluded, after prescribing a host of conventional medicines to treat respondents' conditions and to alleviate their associated symptoms, that marijuana is the only drug available that provides effective treatment. Both women have been using marijuana as a medication for several years pursuant to their doctors' recommendation, and both rely heavily on cannabis to function on a daily basis. Indeed, Raich's physician believes that forgoing cannabis treatments would certainly cause Raich excruciating pain and could very well prove fatal.

Respondent Monson cultivates her own marijuana, and ingests the drug in a variety of ways including smoking and using a vaporizer. Respondent Raich, by contrast, is unable to cultivate her own, and thus relies on two caregivers, litigating as "John Does," to provide her with locally grown marijuana at no charge. These caregivers also process the cannabis into hashish or keif, and Raich herself processes some of the marijuana into oils, balms, and foods for consumption.

On August 15, 2002, county deputy sheriffs and agents from the federal Drug Enforcement Administration (DEA) came to Monson's home. After a thorough investigation, the county officials concluded that her use of marijuana was entirely lawful as a matter of California law. Nevertheless, after a 3-hour standoff, the federal agents seized and destroyed all six of her cannabis plants.

Respondents thereafter brought this action against the Attorney General of the United States and the head of the DEA seeking injunctive and declaratory relief prohibiting the enforcement of the federal Controlled Substances Act (CSA), 84 Stat. 1242, 21 U.S.C. §801 *et seq.*, to the extent it prevents them from possessing, obtaining, or manufacturing cannabis for their personal medical use. In their complaint and supporting affidavits, Raich and Monson described the severity of their afflictions, their repeatedly futile attempts to obtain relief with conventional medications, and the opinions of their doctors concerning their need to use marijuana. Respondents claimed that enforcing the CSA against them would violate the Commerce Clause, the Due Process Clause of the Fifth Amendment, the Ninth and Tenth Amendments of the Constitution, and the doctrine of medical necessity.

The District Court denied respondents' motion for a preliminary injunction. Raich v. Ashcroft, 248 F. Supp. 2d 918 (ND Cal. 2003). Although the court found that the federal enforcement interests "wane[d]" when compared to the harm that California residents would suffer if denied access to medically necessary marijuana, it concluded that respondents could not demonstrate a likelihood of success on the merits of their legal claims. Id., at 931.

A divided panel of the Court of Appeals for the Ninth Circuit reversed and ordered the District Court to enter a preliminary injunction. Raich v. Ashcroft, 352 F.3d 1222 (2003). The court found that respondents had "demonstrated a strong likelihood of success on their claim that, as applied to them, the CSA is an unconstitutional exercise of Congress' Commerce Clause authority." Id., at 1227. The Court of Appeals distinguished prior Circuit cases upholding the CSA in the face of Commerce Clause challenges by focusing on what it deemed to be the "*separate and distinct class of activities*" at issue in this case: "the intrastate, noncommercial cultivation and possession of cannabis for personal medical purposes as recommended by a patient's physician pursuant to valid California state law." Id., at 1228. The court found the latter class of activities "different in kind from drug trafficking" because interposing a physician's recommendation raises different health and safety concerns, and because "this limited use is clearly distinct from the broader illicit drug market—as well as any broader commercial market for medicinal marijuana—insofar as the medicinal marijuana at issue in this case is not intended for, nor does it enter, the stream of commerce." Ibid.

The majority placed heavy reliance on our decisions in United States v. Lopez, 514 U.S. 549 (1995), and United States v. Morrison, 529 U.S. 598 (2000), as interpreted by recent Circuit precedent, to hold that this separate class of purely local activities was beyond the reach of federal power. In contrast, the dissenting judge concluded that the CSA, as applied to respondents, was clearly valid under *Lopez* and *Morrison*; moreover, he thought it "simply impossible to distinguish the relevant conduct surrounding the cultivation and use of the marijuana crop at issue in this case from the cultivation and use of the wheat crop that affected interstate commerce in Wickard v. Filburn." 352 F.3d, at 1235 (Beam, J., dissenting) (citation omitted).

The obvious importance of the case prompted our grant of certiorari. The case is made difficult by respondents' strong arguments that they will suffer irreparable harm because, despite a congressional finding to the contrary, marijuana does have valid therapeutic purposes. The question before us, however, is not whether it is wise to enforce the statute in these circumstances; rather, it is whether Congress' power to regulate interstate markets for medicinal substances encompasses the portions of those markets that are supplied with drugs produced and consumed locally. Well-settled law controls our answer. The CSA is a valid exercise of federal power, even as applied to the troubling facts of this case. We accordingly vacate the judgment of the Court of Appeals.

II

... [A]s early as 1906 Congress enacted federal legislation imposing labeling regulations on medications and prohibiting the manufacture or shipment of any adulterated or misbranded drug traveling in interstate commerce. Aside from these labeling restrictions, most domestic drug regulations prior to 1970 generally came in the guise of revenue laws, with the Department of the Treasury serving as the Federal Government's primary enforcer. For example, the primary drug control law, before being repealed by the passage of the CSA, was the Harrison Narcotics Act of 1914, 38 Stat. 785 (repealed 1970). The Harrison Act sought to exert control over the possession and sale of narcotics, specifically cocaine and opiates, by requiring producers, distributors, and purchasers to register with the Federal Government, by assessing taxes against parties so registered, and by regulating the issuance of prescriptions.

Marijuana itself was not significantly regulated by the Federal Government until 1937.... [See] Marihuana Tax Act, Pub. L. 75-238, 50 Stat. 551 (repealed 1970). Like the Harrison Act, the Marihuana Tax Act did not outlaw the possession or sale of marijuana outright. Rather, it imposed registration and reporting requirements for all individuals importing, producing, selling, or dealing in marijuana, and required the payment of annual taxes in addition to transfer taxes whenever the drug changed hands. Moreover, doctors wishing to prescribe marijuana for medical purposes were required to comply with rather burdensome administrative requirements. Noncompliance exposed traffickers to severe federal penalties, whereas compliance would often subject them to prosecution under state law. ...

Then in 1970, after declaration of the national "war on drugs," federal drug policy underwent a significant transformation. . . . [P]rompted by a perceived need to consolidate the growing number of piecemeal drug laws and to enhance federal drug enforcement powers, Congress enacted the Comprehensive Drug Abuse Prevention and Control Act.[19]

Title II of that Act, the CSA, repealed most of the earlier antidrug laws in favor of a comprehensive regime to combat the international and interstate traffic in illicit drugs. The main objectives of the CSA were to conquer drug abuse and to control the legitimate and illegitimate traffic in controlled substances.[20] Congress was particularly concerned with the need to prevent the diversion of drugs from legitimate to illicit channels.

To effectuate these goals, Congress devised a closed regulatory system making it unlawful to manufacture, distribute, dispense, or possess any controlled substance except in a manner authorized by the CSA. 21 U.S.C. §§841(a)(1), 844(a). The CSA categorizes all controlled substances into five schedules. §812. The drugs are grouped together based on their accepted medical uses, the potential for abuse, and their psychological and physical effects on the body. §§811, 812. Each schedule is associated with a distinct set of controls regarding the manufacture, distribution, and use of the substances listed therein. §§821-830. The CSA and its implementing regulations set forth

19. The Comprehensive Drug Abuse Prevention and Control Act of 1970 consists of three titles. Title I relates to the prevention and treatment of narcotic addicts through HEW (now the Department of Health and Human Services). 84 Stat. 1238. Title II, as discussed in more detail above, addresses drug control and enforcement as administered by the Attorney General and the DEA. Id., at 1242. Title III concerns the import and export of controlled substances. Id., at 1285.

20. In particular, Congress made the following findings:

"(1) Many of the drugs included within this subchapter have a useful and legitimate medical purpose and are necessary to maintain the health and general welfare of the American people. (2) The illegal importation, manufacture, distribution, and possession and improper use of controlled substances have a substantial and detrimental effect on the health and general welfare of the American people. (3) A major portion of the traffic in controlled substances flows through interstate and foreign commerce. Incidents of the traffic which are not an integral part of the interstate or foreign flow, such as manufacture, local distribution, and possession, nonetheless have a substantial and direct effect upon interstate commerce because—(A) after manufacture, many controlled substances are transported in interstate commerce, (B) controlled substances distributed locally usually have been transported in interstate commerce immediately before their distribution, and (C) controlled substances possessed commonly flow through interstate commerce immediately prior to such possession. (4) Local distribution and possession of controlled substances contribute to swelling the interstate traffic in such substances. (5) Controlled substances manufactured and distributed intrastate cannot be differentiated from controlled substances manufactured and distributed interstate. Thus, it is not feasible to distinguish, in terms of controls, between controlled substances manufactured and distributed interstate and controlled substances manufactured and distributed intrastate. (6) Federal control of the intrastate incidents of the traffic in controlled substances is essential to the effective control of the interstate incidents of such traffic."

21 U.S.C. §§801(1)-(6).

strict requirements regarding registration, labeling and packaging, production quotas, drug security, and recordkeeping. 21 CFR §1301 *et seq.* (2004).

In enacting the CSA, Congress classified marijuana as a Schedule I drug. 21 U.S.C. §812(c). This preliminary classification was based, in part, on the recommendation of the Assistant Secretary of HEW "that marihuana be retained within schedule I at least until the completion of certain studies now underway." Schedule I drugs are categorized as such because of their high potential for abuse, lack of any accepted medical use, and absence of any accepted safety for use in medically supervised treatment. §812(b)(1). These three factors, in varying gradations, are also used to categorize drugs in the other four schedules. For example, Schedule II substances also have a high potential for abuse which may lead to severe psychological or physical dependence, but unlike Schedule I drugs, they have a currently accepted medical use. §812(b)(2). By classifying marijuana as a Schedule I drug, as opposed to listing it on a lesser schedule, the manufacture, distribution, or possession of marijuana became a criminal offense, with the sole exception being use of the drug as part of a Food and Drug Administration pre-approved research study. §§823(f), 841(a)(1), 844(a); see also United States v. Oakland Cannabis Buyers' Cooperative, 532 U.S. 483, 490 (2001).

The CSA provides for the periodic updating of schedules and delegates authority to the Attorney General, after consultation with the Secretary of Health and Human Services, to add, remove, or transfer substances to, from, or between schedules. §811. Despite considerable efforts to reschedule marijuana, it remains a Schedule I drug.

III

. . . The Commerce Clause emerged as the Framers' response to the central problem giving rise to the Constitution itself: the absence of any federal commerce power under the Articles of Confederation. For the first century of our history, the primary use of the Clause was to preclude the kind of discriminatory state legislation that had once been permissible. Then, in response to rapid industrial development and an increasingly interdependent national economy, Congress "ushered in a new era of federal regulation under the commerce power," beginning with the enactment of the Interstate Commerce Act in 1887, 24 Stat. 379, and the Sherman Antitrust Act in 1890, 26 Stat. 209, as amended, 15 U.S.C. §2 *et seq.*[27]

Cases decided during that "new era," which now spans more than a century, have identified three general categories of regulation in which Congress is authorized to engage under its commerce power. First, Congress can regulate the channels of interstate commerce. Perez v. United States, 402 U.S. 146, 150 (1971). Second, Congress has authority to regulate and

---

27. *Lopez,* 514 U.S., at 554; see also Wickard v. Filburn, 317 U.S. 111, 121 (1942).

protect the instrumentalities of interstate commerce, and persons or things in interstate commerce. Ibid. Third, Congress has the power to regulate activities that substantially affect interstate commerce. Ibid.; NLRB v. Jones & Laughlin Steel Corp., 301 U.S. 1, 37 (1937). Only the third category is implicated in the case at hand.

Our case law firmly establishes Congress' power to regulate purely local activities that are part of an economic "class of activities" that have a substantial effect on interstate commerce. See, e.g., *Perez*, 402 U.S., at 151; Wickard v. Filburn, 317 U.S. 111, 128-29 (1942). As we stated in *Wickard*, "even if appellee's activity be local and though it may not be regarded as commerce, it may still, whatever its nature, be reached by Congress if it exerts a substantial economic effect on interstate commerce." Id., at 125. We have never required Congress to legislate with scientific exactitude. When Congress decides that the "total incidence" of a practice poses a threat to a national market, it may regulate the entire class. See *Perez*, 402 U.S., at 154-55. In this vein, we have reiterated that when "a general regulatory statute bears a substantial relation to commerce, the *de minimis* character of individual instances arising under that statute is of no consequence." E.g., *Lopez*, 514 U.S., at 558 (emphasis deleted).

Our decision in *Wickard*, 317 U.S. 111, is of particular relevance. In *Wickard*, we upheld the application of regulations promulgated under the Agricultural Adjustment Act of 1938, 52 Stat. 31, which were designed to control the volume of wheat moving in interstate and foreign commerce in order to avoid surpluses and consequent abnormally low prices. The regulations established an allotment of 11.1 acres for Filburn's 1941 wheat crop, but he sowed 23 acres, intending to use the excess by consuming it on his own farm. Filburn argued that even though we had sustained Congress' power to regulate the production of goods for commerce, that power did not authorize "federal regulation [of] production not intended in any part for commerce but wholly for consumption on the farm." *Wickard*, 317 U.S., at 118. Justice Jackson's opinion for a unanimous Court rejected this submission. He wrote:

> "The effect of the statute before us is to restrict the amount which may be produced for market and the extent as well to which one may forestall resort to the market by producing to meet his own needs. That appellee's own contribution to the demand for wheat may be trivial by itself is not enough to remove him from the scope of federal regulation where, as here, his contribution, taken together with that of many others similarly situated, is far from trivial." Id., at 127-28.

Wickard thus establishes that Congress can regulate purely intrastate activity that is not itself "commercial," in that it is not produced for sale, if it concludes that failure to regulate that class of activity would undercut the regulation of the interstate market in that commodity.

The similarities between this case and *Wickard* are striking. Like the farmer in *Wickard*, respondents are cultivating, for home consumption, a fungible commodity for which there is an established, albeit illegal, interstate market. Just as the Agricultural Adjustment Act was designed "to control the volume [of wheat] moving in interstate and foreign commerce in order to avoid surpluses . . ." and consequently control the market price, id., at 115, a primary purpose of the CSA is to control the supply and demand of controlled substances in both lawful and unlawful drug markets. In *Wickard*, we had no difficulty concluding that Congress had a rational basis for believing that, when viewed in the aggregate, leaving home-consumed wheat outside the regulatory scheme would have a substantial influence on price and market conditions. Here too, Congress had a rational basis for concluding that leaving home-consumed marijuana outside federal control would similarly affect price and market conditions.

. . . While the diversion of homegrown wheat tended to frustrate the federal interest in stabilizing prices by regulating the volume of commercial transactions in the interstate market, the diversion of homegrown marijuana tends to frustrate the federal interest in eliminating commercial transactions in the interstate market in their entirety. In both cases, the regulation is squarely within Congress' commerce power because production of the commodity meant for home consumption, be it wheat or marijuana, has a substantial effect on supply and demand in the national market for that commodity.

Nonetheless, respondents suggest that *Wickard* differs from this case in three respects: (1) the Agricultural Adjustment Act, unlike the CSA, exempted small farming operations; (2) *Wickard* involved a "quintessential economic activity"—a commercial farm—whereas respondents do not sell marijuana; and (3) the *Wickard* record made it clear that the aggregate production of wheat for use on farms had a significant impact on market prices. Those differences, though factually accurate, do not diminish the precedential force of this Court's reasoning.

The fact that Wickard's own impact on the market was "trivial by itself" was not a sufficient reason for removing him from the scope of federal regulation. 317 U.S., at 127. That the Secretary of Agriculture elected to exempt even smaller farms from regulation does not speak to his power to regulate all those whose aggregated production was significant, nor did that fact play any role in the Court's analysis. Moreover, even though Wickard was indeed a commercial farmer, the activity he was engaged in—the cultivation of wheat for home consumption—was not treated by the Court as part of his commercial farming operation. And while it is true that the record in the *Wickard* case itself established the causal connection between the production for local use and the national market, we have before us findings by Congress to the same effect.

. . . Respondents nonetheless insist that the CSA cannot be constitutionally applied to their activities because Congress did not make a specific finding that the intrastate cultivation and possession of marijuana for medical purposes based on the recommendation of a physician would substantially affect the larger interstate marijuana market. Be that as it may, we have never required Congress to make particularized findings in order to legislate, see *Lopez*, 514 U.S., at 562; *Perez*, 402 U.S., at 156, absent a special concern such as the protection of free speech. While congressional findings are certainly helpful in reviewing the substance of a congressional statutory scheme, particularly when the connection to commerce is not self-evident, and while we will consider congressional findings in our analysis when they are available, the absence of particularized findings does not call into question Congress' authority to legislate.

In assessing the scope of Congress' authority under the Commerce Clause, we stress that the task before us is a modest one. We need not determine whether respondents' activities, taken in the aggregate, substantially affect interstate commerce in fact, but only whether a "rational basis" exists for so concluding. *Lopez*, 514 U.S., at 557; see also Hodel v. Virginia Surface Mining & Reclamation Assn., Inc., 452 U.S. 264, 276-80 (1981); *Perez*, 402 U.S., at 155-56; Katzenbach v. McClung, 379 U.S. 294, 299-301 (1964); Heart of Atlanta Motel, Inc. v. United States, 379 U.S. 241, 252-53 (1964). Given the enforcement difficulties that attend distinguishing between marijuana cultivated locally and marijuana grown elsewhere, 21 U.S.C. §801(5), and concerns about diversion into illicit channels, we have no difficulty concluding that Congress had a rational basis for believing that failure to regulate the intrastate manufacture and possession of marijuana would leave a gaping hole in the CSA. Thus, as in *Wickard*, when it enacted comprehensive legislation to regulate the interstate market in a fungible commodity, Congress was acting well within its authority to "make all Laws which shall be necessary and proper" to "regulate Commerce . . . among the several States." U.S. Const., Art. I, §8. That the regulation ensnares some purely intrastate activity is of no moment. . . .

IV

. . . At issue in *Lopez*, 514 U.S. 549, was the validity of the Gun-Free School Zones Act of 1990, which was a brief, single-subject statute making it a crime for an individual to possess a gun in a school zone. 104 Stat. 4844-4845, 18 U.S.C. §922(q)(1)(A). The Act did not regulate any economic activity and did not contain any requirement that the possession of a gun have any connection to past interstate activity or a predictable impact on future commercial activity. . . . The statutory scheme that the Government is defending in this litigation is at the opposite end of the regulatory spectrum. As explained above, the CSA . . . was a lengthy and detailed statute creating a comprehensive framework for regulating the production, distribution, and possession of five classes of "controlled substances." Most of those substances—those listed in Schedules II through V—"have a useful and legitimate medical purpose and are necessary to maintain the health and general welfare of the American people." 21 U.S.C. §801(1). The regulatory scheme is designed to foster the beneficial use of those medications, to prevent their misuse, and to prohibit entirely the possession or use of substances listed in Schedule I, except as a part of a strictly controlled research project.

While the statute provided for the periodic updating of the five schedules, Congress itself made the initial classifications. It identified 42 opiates, 22 opium derivatives, and 17 hallucinogenic substances as Schedule I drugs. 84 Stat. 1248. Marijuana was listed as the 10th item in the third subcategory. That classification, unlike the discrete prohibition established by the Gun-Free School Zones Act of 1990, was merely one of many "essential part[s] of a larger regulation of economic activity, in which the regulatory scheme could be undercut unless the intrastate activity were regulated." *Lopez*, 514 U.S., at 561. Our opinion in *Lopez* casts no doubt on the validity of such a program.

Nor does this Court's holding in *Morrison*, 529 U.S. 598. The Violence Against Women Act of 1994, 108 Stat. 1902, created a federal civil remedy for the victims of gender-motivated crimes of violence. 42 U.S.C. §13981. The remedy was enforceable in both state and federal courts, and generally depended on proof of the violation of a state law. Despite congressional findings that such crimes had an adverse impact on interstate commerce, we held the statute unconstitutional because, like the statute in *Lopez*, it did not regulate economic activity. . . .

Unlike those at issue in *Lopez* and *Morrison*, the activities regulated by the CSA are quintessentially economic. . . . The CSA . . . regulates the production, distribution, and consumption of commodities for which there is an established, and lucrative, interstate market. Prohibiting the intrastate possession or manufacture of an article of commerce is a rational (and commonly utilized) means of regulating commerce in that product. Such prohibitions include specific decisions requiring that a drug be withdrawn from the market as a result of the failure to comply with regulatory requirements as well as decisions excluding Schedule I drugs entirely from the market. Because the CSA is a statute that directly regulates economic, commercial activity, our opinion in *Morrison* casts no doubt on its constitutionality.

The Court of Appeals was able to conclude otherwise only by isolating a "separate and distinct" class of activities that it held to be beyond the reach of federal power, defined as "the intrastate, noncommercial cultivation, possession and use of marijuana for personal medical purposes on the advice of a physician and in accordance with state law." 352 F.3d at 1229. The court characterized this class as "different in kind from drug trafficking." *Id.*, at 1228. The differences between the members of a class so defined and the principal traffickers in Schedule I substances might be sufficient to justify a policy decision exempting the narrower class from the coverage of the

CSA. The question, however, is whether Congress' contrary policy judgment . . . was constitutionally deficient. We have no difficulty concluding that Congress acted rationally. . . .

The exemption for cultivation by patients and caregivers can only increase the supply of marijuana in the California market.[41] The likelihood that all such production will promptly terminate when patients recover or will precisely match the patients' medical needs during their convalescence seems remote; whereas the danger that excesses will satisfy some of the admittedly enormous demand for recreational use seems obvious. . . . Taking into account the fact that California is only one of at least nine States to have authorized the medical use of marijuana, . . . Congress could have rationally concluded that the aggregate impact on the national market of all the transactions exempted from federal supervision is unquestionably substantial.

. . . [T]he case for the exemption comes down to the claim that a locally cultivated product that is used domestically rather than sold on the open market is not subject to federal regulation. Given the findings in the CSA and the undisputed magnitude of the commercial market for marijuana, our decisions in Wickard v. Filburn and the later cases endorsing its reasoning foreclose that claim.

V

Respondents also raise a substantive due process claim and seek to avail themselves of the medical necessity defense. These theories of relief were set forth in their complaint but were not reached by the Court of Appeals. We therefore do not address the question whether judicial relief is available to respondents on these alternative bases. We do note, however, the presence of another avenue of relief. As the Solicitor General confirmed during oral argument, the statute authorizes procedures for the reclassification of Schedule I drugs. But perhaps even more important than these legal avenues is the democratic process, in which the voices of voters allied with

---

41. The state policy allows patients to possess up to eight ounces of dried marijuana, and to cultivate up to 6 mature or 12 immature plants. Cal. Health & Safety Code Ann. §11362.77(a). However, the quantity limitations serve only as a floor. Based on a doctor's recommendation, a patient can possess whatever quantity is necessary to satisfy his medical needs, and cities and counties are given *carte blanche* to establish more generous limits. Indeed, several cities and counties have done just that. For example, patients residing in the cities of Oakland and Santa Cruz and in the counties of Sonoma and Tehama are permitted to possess up to 3 pounds of processed marijuana. Reply Brief for United States 19 (citing Proposition 215 Enforcement Guidelines). Putting that quantity in perspective, 3 pounds of marijuana yields roughly 3,000 joints or cigarettes. Executive Office of the President, Office of National Drug Control Policy, What America's Users Spend on Illegal Drugs 24 (Dec. 2001), http://www.whitehousedrugpolicy.gov/publications/pdf/american_users_spend_200 2.pdf. And the street price for that amount can range anywhere from $900 to $24,000. DEA, Illegal Drug Price and Purity Report (Apr. 2003) (DEA-02058).

these respondents may one day be heard in the halls of Congress. Under the present state of the law, however, the judgment of the Court of Appeals must be vacated. The case is remanded for further proceedings consistent with this opinion.

Justice SCALIA, concurring in the judgment.

. . . Since Perez v. United States, 402 U.S. 146 (1971), our cases have mechanically recited that the Commerce Clause permits congressional regulation of three categories: (1) the channels of interstate commerce; (2) the instrumentalities of interstate commerce, and persons or things in interstate commerce; and (3) activities that "substantially affect" interstate commerce. The first two categories are self-evident, since they are the ingredients of interstate commerce itself. The third category, however, is different in kind, and its recitation without explanation is misleading and incomplete.

It is *misleading* because, unlike the channels, instrumentalities, and agents of interstate commerce, activities that substantially affect interstate commerce are not themselves part of interstate commerce, and thus the power to regulate them cannot come from the Commerce Clause alone. Rather, as this Court has acknowledged since at least United States v. Coombs, 37 U.S. 72 (1838), Congress's regulatory authority over intrastate activities that are not themselves part of interstate commerce (including activities that have a substantial effect on interstate commerce) derives from the Necessary and Proper Clause. And the category of "activities that substantially affect interstate commerce," [United States v. Lopez, 514 U.S. 549, 559 (1995)], is *incomplete* because the authority to enact laws necessary and proper for the regulation of interstate commerce is not limited to laws governing intrastate activities that substantially affect interstate commerce. Where necessary to make a regulation of interstate commerce effective, Congress may regulate even those intrastate activities that do not themselves substantially affect interstate commerce.

. . . [T]he commerce power permits Congress not only to devise rules for the governance of commerce between States but also to facilitate interstate commerce by eliminating potential obstructions, and to restrict it by eliminating potential stimulants. See NLRB v. Jones & Laughlin Steel Corp., 301 U.S. 1, 36-37 (1937). That is why the Court has repeatedly sustained congressional legislation on the ground that the regulated activities had a substantial effect on interstate commerce. *Lopez* . . . recognized the expansive scope of Congress's authority in this regard: "[T]he pattern is clear. Where economic activity substantially affects interstate commerce, legislation regulating that activity will be sustained." *Lopez*, supra, at 560. . . .

Although this power "to make . . . regulation effective" commonly overlaps with the authority to regulate economic activities that substantially affect interstate commerce,[2] and may in some cases have been confused with that authority, the two are distinct. The regulation of an intrastate activity may be essential to a comprehensive regulation of interstate commerce even though the intrastate activity does not itself "substantially affect" interstate commerce. Moreover, . . . Congress may regulate even noneconomic local activity if that regulation is a necessary part of a more general regulation of interstate commerce. See *Lopez*, supra, at 561. The relevant question is simply whether the means chosen are "reasonably adapted" to the attainment of a legitimate end under the commerce power. See [United States v. Darby, 312 U.S. 100, 121 (1941)].

In *Darby*, for instance, the Court explained that "Congress, having . . . adopted the policy of excluding from interstate commerce all goods produced for the commerce which do not conform to the specified labor standards," 312 U.S., at 121, could not only require employers engaged in the production of goods for interstate commerce to conform to wage and hour standards, id., at 119-21, but could also require those employers to keep employment records in order to demonstrate compliance with the regulatory scheme, id., at 125. While the Court sustained the former regulation on the alternative ground that the activity it regulated could have a "great effect" on interstate commerce, id., at 122-23, it affirmed the latter on the sole ground that "[t]he requirement for records even of the intrastate transaction is an appropriate means to a legitimate end," id., at 125. . . .

. . . Unlike the power to regulate activities that have a substantial effect on interstate commerce, the power to enact laws enabling effective regulation of interstate commerce can only be exercised in conjunction with congressional regulation of an interstate market, and it extends only to those measures necessary to make the interstate regulation effective. As *Lopez* itself states, and the Court affirms today, Congress may regulate noneconomic intrastate activities only where the failure to do so "could . . . undercut" its regulation of interstate commerce. See *Lopez*, supra, at 561. This is not a power that threatens to obliterate the line between "what is truly national and what is truly local." *Lopez*, supra, at 567-68.

Lopez and [United States v. Morrison, 529 U.S. 598 (2000)], affirm that Congress may not regulate certain "purely local" activity within the States based solely on the attenuated effect that such activity may have in the interstate market. But those decisions do not declare noneconomic intrastate activities to be categorically beyond the reach of the Federal Government.

---

2. Wickard v. Filburn, 317 U.S. 111 (1942), presented such a case. Because the unregulated production of wheat for personal consumption diminished demand in the regulated wheat market, the Court said, it carried with it the potential to disrupt Congress's price regulation by driving down prices in the market. Id., at 127-29. This potential disruption of Congress's interstate regulation, and not only the effect that personal consumption of wheat had on interstate commerce, justified Congress's regulation of that conduct. Id., at 128-29.

Neither case involved the power of Congress to exert control over intra-state activities in connection with a more comprehensive scheme of regulation; *Lopez* expressly disclaimed that it was such a case, 514 U.S., at 561, and *Morrison* did not even discuss the possibility that it was. . . .

And there are other restraints upon the Necessary and Proper Clause authority. As Chief Justice Marshall wrote in McCulloch v. Maryland, [17 U.S. 316 (1819),] even when the end is constitutional and legitimate, the means must be "appropriate" and "plainly adapted" to that end. Id., at 421. Moreover, they may not be otherwise "prohibited" and must be "consistent with the letter and spirit of the constitution." Ibid. These phrases are not merely hortatory. . . .

The application of these principles to the case before us is straightforward. In the CSA, Congress has undertaken to extinguish the interstate market in Schedule I controlled substances, including marijuana. The Commerce Clause unquestionably permits this. The power to regulate interstate commerce "extends not only to those regulations which aid, foster and protect the commerce, but embraces those which prohibit it." *Darby*, 312 U.S., at 113; see also [Champion v. Ames,] 188 U.S. 321, 354 (1903). To effectuate its objective, Congress has prohibited almost all intrastate activities related to Schedule I substances — both economic activities (manufacture, distribution, possession with the intent to distribute) and noneconomic activities (simple possession). See 21 U.S.C. §§841(a), 844(a). That simple possession is a noneconomic activity is immaterial to whether it can be prohibited as a necessary part of a larger regulation. Rather, Congress's authority to enact all of these prohibitions of intrastate controlled-substance activities depends only upon whether they are appropriate means of achieving the legitimate end of eradicating Schedule I substances from interstate commerce.

By this measure, I think the regulation must be sustained. Not only is it impossible to distinguish "controlled substances manufactured and distributed intrastate" from "controlled substances manufactured and distributed interstate," but it hardly makes sense to speak in such terms. Drugs like marijuana are fungible commodities. As the Court explains, marijuana that is grown at home and possessed for personal use is never more than an instant from the interstate market — and this is so whether or not the possession is for medicinal use or lawful use under the laws of a particular State.[3] Congress need not accept on faith that state law will be effective in

---

3. The principal dissent claims that, if this is sufficient to sustain the regulation at issue in this case, then it should also have been sufficient to sustain the regulation at issue in *Lopez*. This claim founders upon the shoals of *Lopez* itself, which made clear that the statute there at issue was "*not* an essential part of a larger regulation of economic activity." *Lopez*, supra, at 561 (emphasis added). On the dissent's view of things, that statement is inexplicable. Of course it is in addition difficult to imagine what intelligible scheme of regulation of the interstate market in guns could have as an appropriate means of effectuation the prohibition of guns within 1000 feet of schools (and nowhere else). . . .

maintaining a strict division between a lawful market for "medical" marijuana and the more general marijuana market. "To impose on [Congress] the necessity of resorting to means which it cannot control, which another government may furnish or withhold, would render its course precarious, the result of its measures uncertain, and create a dependence on other governments, which might disappoint its most important designs, and is incompatible with the language of the constitution." *McCulloch,* supra, at 424.

Finally, neither respondents nor the dissenters suggest any violation of state sovereignty of the sort that would render this regulation "inappropriate," id., at 421,—except to argue that the CSA regulates an area typically left to state regulation. That is not enough to render federal regulation an inappropriate means. . . . At bottom, respondents' state-sovereignty argument reduces to the contention that federal regulation of the activities permitted by California's Compassionate Use Act is not sufficiently necessary to be "necessary and proper" to Congress's regulation of the interstate market. For the reasons given above and in the Court's opinion, I cannot agree. . . .

Justice O'CONNOR, with whom Chief Justice REHNQUIST and Justice THOMAS join as to all but [the final two paragraphs], dissenting.

We enforce the "outer limits" of Congress' Commerce Clause authority not for their own sake, but to protect historic spheres of state sovereignty from excessive federal encroachment and thereby to maintain the distribution of power fundamental to our federalist system of government. United States v. Lopez, 514 U.S. 549, 557 (1995); NLRB v. Jones & Laughlin Steel Corp., 301 U.S. 1, 37 (1937). One of federalism's chief virtues, of course, is that it promotes innovation by allowing for the possibility that "a single courageous State may, if its citizens choose, serve as a laboratory; and try novel social and economic experiments without risk to the rest of the country." New State Ice Co. v. Liebmann, 285 U.S. 262, 311 (1932) (Brandeis, J., dissenting).

This case exemplifies the role of States as laboratories. The States' core police powers have always included authority to define criminal law and to protect the health, safety, and welfare of their citizens. Exercising those powers, California (by ballot initiative and then by legislative codification) has come to its own conclusion about the difficult and sensitive question of whether marijuana should be available to relieve severe pain and suffering. Today the Court sanctions an application of the federal Controlled Substances Act that extinguishes that experiment, without any proof that the personal cultivation, possession, and use of marijuana for medicinal purposes, if economic activity in the first place, has a substantial effect on interstate commerce and is therefore an appropriate subject of federal regulation. . . .

What is the relevant conduct subject to Commerce Clause analysis in this case? . . . The Court's decision rests on two facts about the CSA: (1) Congress chose to enact a single statute providing a comprehensive prohibition on the production, distribution, and possession of all controlled substances, and (2) Congress did not distinguish between various forms of intrastate noncommercial cultivation, possession, and use of marijuana. See 21 U.S.C. §§841(a)(1), 844(a). Today's decision suggests that the federal regulation of local activity is immune to Commerce Clause challenge because Congress chose to act with an ambitious, all-encompassing statute, rather than piecemeal. In my view, allowing Congress to set the terms of the constitutional debate in this way, *i.e.*, by packaging regulation of local activity in broader schemes, is tantamount to removing meaningful limits on the Commerce Clause.

The Court's principal means of distinguishing *Lopez* from this case is to observe that the Gun-Free School Zones Act of 1990 was a "brief, single-subject statute," whereas the CSA is "a lengthy and detailed statute creating a comprehensive framework for regulating the production, distribution, and possession of five classes of 'controlled substances,'" ibid. Thus, according to the Court, it was possible in *Lopez* to evaluate in isolation the constitutionality of criminalizing local activity (there gun possession in school zones), whereas the local activity that the CSA targets (in this case cultivation and possession of marijuana for personal medicinal use) cannot be separated from the general drug control scheme of which it is a part. . . .

. . . I agree with the Court that we must look beyond respondents' own activities. Otherwise, individual litigants could always exempt themselves from Commerce Clause regulation merely by pointing to the obvious—that their personal activities do not have a substantial effect on interstate commerce. The task is to identify a mode of analysis that allows Congress to regulate more than nothing (by declining to reduce each case to its litigants) and less than everything (by declining to let Congress set the terms of analysis). The analysis may not be the same in every case, for it depends on the regulatory scheme at issue and the federalism concerns implicated.

A number of objective markers are available to confine the scope of constitutional review here. Both federal and state legislation—including the CSA itself, the California Compassionate Use Act, and other state medical marijuana legislation—recognize that medical and nonmedical (*i.e.*, recreational) uses of drugs are realistically distinct and can be segregated, and regulate them differently. See 21 U.S.C. §812; Cal. Health & Safety Code Ann. §11362.5. Respondents challenge only the application of the CSA to medicinal use of marijuana. Moreover, because fundamental structural concerns about dual sovereignty animate our Commerce Clause cases, it is relevant that this case involves the interplay of federal and state regulation in areas of criminal law and social policy, where "States lay claim by right of history and expertise." *Lopez*, supra, at 583 (Kennedy, J., concurring). California, like other States, has drawn on its reserved powers to distinguish the regulation of medicinal marijuana. To ascertain whether Congress' encroachment is constitutionally justified in this case, then, I would focus here on the personal cultivation, possession, and use of marijuana for medicinal purposes.

Having thus defined the relevant conduct, we must determine whether, under our precedents, the conduct is economic and, in the aggregate, substantially affects interstate commerce. Even if intrastate cultivation and possession of marijuana for one's own medicinal use can properly be characterized as economic, and I question whether it can, it has not been shown that such activity substantially affects interstate commerce. Similarly, it is neither self-evident nor demonstrated that regulating such activity is necessary to the interstate drug control scheme. . . .

The Court suggests that [Wickard v. Filburn, 317 U.S. 111 (1942)], . . . established federal regulatory power over any home consumption of a commodity for which a national market exists. I disagree. *Wickard* involved a challenge to the Agricultural Adjustment Act of 1938 (AAA), which directed the Secretary of Agriculture to set national quotas on wheat production, and penalties for excess production. 317 U.S., at 115-16. The AAA itself confirmed that Congress made an explicit choice not to reach—and thus the Court could not possibly have approved of federal control over—small-scale, noncommercial wheat farming. In contrast to the CSA's limitless assertion of power, Congress provided an exemption within the AAA for small producers. When Filburn planted the wheat at issue in *Wickard*, the statute exempted plantings less than 200 bushels (about six tons), and when he harvested his wheat it exempted plantings less than six acres. Id., at 130, n.30. *Wickard*, then, did not extend Commerce Clause authority to something as modest as the home cook's herb garden. . . .

Even assuming that economic activity is at issue in this case, the Government has made no showing in fact that the possession and use of homegrown marijuana for medical purposes, in California or elsewhere, has a substantial effect on interstate commerce. Similarly, the Government has not shown that regulating such activity is necessary to an interstate regulatory scheme. . . .

We would do well to recall how James Madison, the father of the Constitution, described our system of joint sovereignty to the people of New York: "The powers delegated by the proposed constitution to the federal government are few and defined. Those which are to remain in the State governments are numerous and indefinite. . . . The powers reserved to the several States will extend to all the objects which, in the ordinary course of affairs, concern the lives, liberties, and properties of the people, and the internal order, improvement, and prosperity of the State." The Federalist No. 45, at 292-93 (C. Rossiter ed. 1961).

Relying on Congress' abstract assertions, the Court has endorsed making it a federal crime to grow small amounts of marijuana in one's own home for one's own medicinal use. This overreaching stifles an express choice by some States, concerned for the lives and liberties of their people, to regulate medical marijuana differently. If I were a California citizen, I would not have voted for the medical marijuana ballot initiative; if I were a California legislator I would not have supported the Compassionate Use Act. But whatever the wisdom of California's experiment with medical marijuana, the federalism principles that have driven our Commerce Clause cases require that room for experiment be protected in this case. For these reasons I dissent.

Justice THOMAS, dissenting.

Respondents Diane Monson and Angel Raich use marijuana that has never been bought or sold, that has never crossed state lines, and that has had no demonstrable effect on the national market for marijuana. If Congress can regulate this under the Commerce Clause, then it can regulate virtually anything—and the Federal Government is no longer one of limited and enumerated powers. . . .

Even the majority does not argue that respondents' conduct is itself "Commerce among the several States." Art. I, §8, cl. 3. Monson and Raich neither buy nor sell the marijuana that they consume. They cultivate their cannabis entirely in the State of California—it never crosses state lines, much less as part of a commercial transaction. Certainly no evidence from the founding suggests that "commerce" included the mere possession of a good or some purely personal activity that did not involve trade or exchange for value. . . .

More difficult, however, is whether the CSA is a valid exercise of Congress' power to enact laws that are "necessary and proper for carrying into Execution" its power to regulate interstate commerce. Art. I, §8, cl. 18. The Necessary and Proper Clause is not a warrant to Congress to enact any law that bears some conceivable connection to the exercise of an enumerated power. Nor is it, however, a command to Congress to enact only laws that are absolutely indispensable to the exercise of an enumerated power.

In McCulloch v. Maryland, 17 U.S. 316 (1819), this Court, speaking through Chief Justice Marshall, set forth a test for determining when an Act of Congress is permissible under the Necessary and Proper Clause:

> "Let the end be legitimate, let it be within the scope of the constitution, and all means which are appropriate, which are plainly adapted to that end, which are not prohibited, but consist with the letter and spirit of the constitution, are constitutional." Id., at 421.

To act under the Necessary and Proper Clause, then, Congress must select a means that is "appropriate" and "plainly adapted" to executing an enumerated power; the means cannot be otherwise "prohibited" by the Constitution; and the means cannot be inconsistent with "the letter and spirit of the [C]onstitution." Ibid.; D. Currie, The Constitution in the Supreme Court: The First Hundred Years 1789-1888, at 163-64 (1985). The CSA, as applied to respondents' conduct, is not a valid exercise of Congress' power under the Necessary and Proper Clause. . . .

On its face, a ban on the intrastate cultivation, possession and distribution of marijuana may be plainly adapted to stopping the interstate flow of marijuana. Unregulated local growers and users could swell both the supply and the demand sides of the interstate marijuana market, making the market more difficult to regulate. But respondents do not challenge the CSA on its face. Instead, they challenge it as applied to their conduct. The question is thus whether the intrastate ban is "necessary and proper" as applied to medical marijuana users like respondents.

Respondents are not regulable simply because they belong to a large class (local growers and users of marijuana) that Congress might need to reach, if they also belong to a distinct and separable subclass (local growers and users of state-authorized, medical marijuana) that does not undermine the CSA's interstate ban. The Court of Appeals found that respondents' "limited use is distinct from the broader illicit drug market," because "th[eir] medicinal marijuana . . . is not intended for, nor does it enter, the stream of commerce." Raich v. Ashcroft, 352 F.3d 1222, 1228 (CA9 2003). If that is generally true of individuals who grow and use marijuana for medical purposes under state law, then even assuming Congress has "obvious" and "plain" reasons why regulating intrastate cultivation and possession is necessary to regulating the interstate drug trade, none of those reasons applies to medical marijuana patients like Monson and Raich. . . .

. . . Congress has encroached on States' traditional police powers to define the criminal law and to protect the health, safety, and welfare of their citizens.[5] Further, the Government's rationale—that it may regulate the production or possession of any commodity for which there is an interstate market—threatens to remove the remaining vestiges of States' traditional police powers. This would convert the Necessary and Proper Clause into precisely what Chief Justice Marshall did not envision, a "pretext . . . for the accomplishment of objects not intrusted to the government." *McCulloch*, supra, at 423. . . .

---

5. In fact, the Anti-Federalists objected that the Necessary and Proper Clause would allow Congress, inter alia, to "*constitute new Crimes*, . . . and extend [its] Power as far as [it] shall think proper; so that the State Legislatures have no Security for the Powers now presumed to remain to them; or the People for their Rights." Mason, Objections to the Constitution Formed by the Convention (1787), in 2 The Complete Anti-Federalist 11, 12-13 (H. Storing ed. 1981) (emphasis added). Hamilton responded that these objections were gross "misrepresentation[s]." The Federalist No. 33, at 204. He termed the Clause "perfectly harmless," for it merely confirmed Congress' implied authority to enact laws in exercising its enumerated powers. Id., at 205. According to Hamilton, the Clause was needed only "to guard against cavilling refinements" by those seeking to cripple federal power. The Federalist No. 33, at 205; id., No. 44, at 303-04 (J. Madison).

The majority prevents States like California from devising drug policies that they have concluded provide much-needed respite to the seriously ill. It does so without any serious inquiry into the necessity for federal regulation or the propriety of "displac[ing] state regulation in areas of traditional state concern," *Lopez*, supra, at 583 (Kennedy, J., concurring). The majority's rush to embrace federal power "is especially unfortunate given the importance of showing respect for the sovereign States that comprise our Federal Union." United States v. Oakland Cannabis Buyers' Cooperative, 532 U.S. 483, 502 (2001) (Stevens, J., concurring in judgment). Our federalist system, properly understood, allows California and a growing number of other States to decide for themselves how to safeguard the health and welfare of their citizens. I would affirm the judgment of the Court of Appeals. I respectfully dissent.

Notes and Questions

1. The trend toward state legalization of medical marijuana is clearly growing. At the time of the *Raich* case, 10 states were included; since that decision, 18 more have joined, along with the District of Columbia, meaning that medical marijuana is now legal under state law in a majority of U.S. states. See Marijuana Resource Center: State Laws Related to Marijuana, available at http://www.whitehouse.gov/ondcp/state-laws-related-to-marijuana. (Does it seem strange to you that the White House would maintain a "Marijuana Resource Center" on its official website?)

The District of Columbia presents a particularly interesting situation, because D.C. is not a state but a federal enclave, enjoying a kind of "home rule" but subject ultimately to the legal oversight and budgetary control of Congress. In 1998, D.C. voters approved the Legalization of Marijuana for Medical Treatment Initiative, but D.C. lawmakers were specifically banned by Congress from implementing the initiative. In December 2009, Congress finally lifted the ban, and a short while later, the D.C. Council enacted local legislation implementing the initiative. Congress then had 30 days to decide whether or not to overturn the new legislation. In July 2010, congressional inaction allowed the D.C. medical marijuana law to become effective.*

The D.C. law allows patients with cancer, glaucoma, HIV/AIDS, and other chronic illnesses to possess up to four ounces of marijuana, which

---

* Meanwhile, in November 2014, D.C. voters approved a ballot measure to legalize the possession and private use of small amounts of marijuana for *recreational* purposes. Shortly thereafter, Congress banned D.C. from taking any steps to set up legal, regulated markets (as exist in Colorado and Washington) where marijuana could be bought and sold. As a result, under D.C. law, marijuana may be cultivated for personal use, and may be transferred without any payment, but may not be bought or sold. Of course, all of these activities still remain illegal in D.C. under the *national* federal drug laws.

they may obtain from licensed dispensaries. Medical marijuana is subject to D.C.'s 6 percent sales tax; proceeds of the tax are used to help subsidize the cost of the drug for low-income users.

Does Congress' recent acquiescence in the D.C. medical marijuana law indicate that the federalism tide is turning? Might the outcome of the D.C. situation possibly influence the Supreme Court to hold, in some future case, that the federal Controlled Substances Act should be read to impliedly exempt medical marijuana from its criminal sanctions?

2. In Gonzalez v. Oregon, 546 U.S. 243 (2006), the Court held that the federal Controlled Substance Act's provisions that authorize the U.S. Attorney General to establish rules and procedures for the prescribing of controlled substances did *not* allow the Attorney General to bar registered physicians from prescribing such substances in order to carry out the purposes of the Oregon Death With Dignity Act (ODWDA), which legalized certain physician-assisted suicides. The Court held that the Controlled Substances Act was not intended to authorize federal regulation of the medical profession in general, and that the Attorney General was wrong to classify the use of controlled substances to carry out physician-assisted suicides under ODWDA as "drug abuse." The dissenters argued that the Court should have given greater deference to the Attorney General's interpretation of the Controlled Substances Act, and that the ruling was inconsistent with the overall tone and tenor of the *Raich* decision.

3. As a practical matter, federal prosecutors generally have chosen not to push the envelope, in terms of attempting to prosecute those who act in clear compliance with state medical marijuana laws. Instead, federal prosecutors have tended to keep a close and watchful eye, looking for evidence that such state laws are being abused by those seeking an end-run around the federal marijuana prohibition. Meanwhile, the medical marijuana movement continues to grow.

When Colorado and Washington in 2012 legalized the possession and use of small amounts of marijuana by all adults, the conflict between state and federal marijuana laws got kicked up a notch. On August 29, 2013, the U.S. Department of Justice issued a four-page memorandum specifically addressing this still-evolving conflict. The DOJ memo lists eight enforcement priorities that will guide federal prosecutors, including (1) preventing distribution of marijuana to minors; (2) preventing revenue from marijuana sales from reaching criminal organizations; (3) preventing diversion of marijuana to states where it is illegal under state law; (4) preventing marijuana activity from serving as a cover for other illegal drug activity; (5) preventing violence and use of firearms in connection with marijuana production and distribution; (6) preventing driving under the influence of marijuana; (7) preventing growing of marijuana on public lands; and (8) preventing possession or use of marijuana on federal property. The memo also notes that states that choose to legalize marijuana have a responsibility to develop and enforce their own laws and regulations about marijuana, which can help to minimize the need for federal intervention; but the federal government "may seek to challenge the regulatory structure itself" (in addition to bringing individual federal prosecutions) if "state enforcement efforts are not sufficiently robust" to protect against the eight harms listed in the memo. The memo concludes with a predictable disclaimer: "This memorandum does not alter in any way the Department's authority to enforce federal law, including federal laws relating to marijuana, regardless of state law." See U.S. Department of Justice, Office of the Deputy Attorney General, Memorandum for All United States Attorneys: Guidance Regarding Marijuana Enforcement, available online at http://www.justice.gov/iso/opa/resources/3052013829132756857467.pdf. In short, the new frontier of federalism remains an active one, and the end of the story has not yet been written.

At press time for the third edition of this casebook, there was no clear indication whether the above memorandum and its expression of federal prosecutorial restraint will survive the change of presidential administration that will occur in January 2017. In short, the new frontier of federalism remains an active one, and the end of the story—in terms of both medical marijuana (now legal in 28 states) and recreational marijuana (now legal in 8 states)—has not yet been written.

7

Inchoate Crimes and Accomplice Liability

In this chapter, we continue with our examination of drug crimes. In addition to their intrinsic interest as a subject of study, and their prevalence in the "real world" of criminal investigations and prosecutions, drug crimes also represent an extremely useful vehicle for learning about the nature, scope, and application of the so-called inchoate crimes—attempt, solicitation, and conspiracy—as well as the basic principles of accomplice (or "aiding and abetting") criminal liability. The inchoate crimes are ones that are committed somewhere along the way toward the commission of another crime that may never, in fact, be completed. Accomplice liability is a method by which one person—the accomplice—may be found guilty of a crime that is actually committed by a different person—the principal.

Both the inchoate crimes and accomplice liability are generally applicable doctrines that can be applied across most of the spectrum of substantive crimes. As such, these doctrines—like the doctrines of criminal conduct and criminal intent—belong to what is often called the "general part" of the criminal law (as opposed to the "special part," which refers to the definitions and applications of specific crimes). Indeed, we will encounter both the inchoate crimes and accomplice liability again later in this book—in Chapter 10, the homicide chapter.

The inchoate crimes and accomplice liability arise especially frequently, however, in connection with drug crimes. This is for two main reasons. First, drug crimes almost always involve the collaboration of multiple perpetrators (including "drug kingpins," manufacturers, importers, wholesale suppliers, transporters, enforcers, and retail street dealers). Drug crimes thus frequently raise issues of multi-party criminal liability, which invoke the doctrines of solicitation, conspiracy, and complicity (i.e., accomplice liability). The second reason is that it is extremely difficult for the government to prosecute successfully the completed crime of dealing in illegal drugs, because that crime involves a highly secretive consensual transaction between a willing perpetrator (the drug seller) and a willing victim (the drug buyer), and the government almost never catches the parties "in the act." Because of this inherent and intractable problem, if the government wants to get drug dealers off the streets and into prison, it must rely heavily on prosecutions for attempt and other inchoate crimes.

A. ATTEMPT

In this section, we examine both the traditional common law of attempt and the Model Penal Code's modern (and complicated!) version of attempt doctrine, which — to a greater extent than most of the rest of the Code — has managed to supplant the common law. We begin with a case from Arizona, where the legislature has enacted the Model Penal Code's version of attempt doctrine into state law.

State v. McElroy

Supreme Court of Arizona
128 Ariz. 315, 625 P.2d 904 (1981)

Opinion of CAMERON, J.

Defendant was found guilty by the court sitting without a jury of the crime of attempted possession of dangerous drugs in violation of Ariz. Rev. Stat. §§32-1996, 13-1001, 13-701, 13-801. The crime was treated as a misdemeanor, and defendant was placed on probation. . . .

We must answer only one question on appeal: May the defendant be charged with attempted possession of dangerous drugs when it was impossible for him to complete [that] crime . . . because the drugs were not, in fact, dangerous?

The facts necessary for a determination of this matter on appeal are as follows. At approximately 1:00 A.M. on 8 December 1978, the Yuma County Sheriff's Office received a call to investigate the presence of two suspicious persons near a residence on Highway 95 in Yuma County, Arizona. The two persons told the officer who came to investigate that they were hitchhiking. The defendant asked a deputy sheriff for a ride into Yuma. The deputy agreed and, pursuant to standard procedure, patted the defendant down for weapons. During the search, the deputy found a plastic bag in defendant's shirt. The deputy took the bag, looked at it, and found it contained white pills. The defendant stated that the pills were "speed" or amphetamines, and that he had purchased them earlier at a bar. Later the deputy found another plastic bag with more white pills in the back seat of the patrol vehicle after placing defendant in the back seat.

A field test showed positive for amphetamines, the defendant was advised of his *Miranda* rights, and defendant again stated that the pills were "speed." Later analysis by a chemist indicated that the pills were not amphetamines or dangerous drugs of any kind proscribed by statute.

[Defendant was found guilty at a non-jury trial and appealed.]

The defendant was charged with "attempt" to possess dangerous drugs. Our statute reads:

> "§13-1001. ATTEMPT; CLASSIFICATIONS
>
> "A. A person commits attempt if, acting with the kind of culpability otherwise required for the commission of an offense, such person:
>
> "1. Intentionally engages in conduct which would constitute an offense if the attendant circumstances were as such person believes them to be . . . ."

The courts are not in agreement as to when impossibility may be used as a defense to the crime of attempt. A distinction that has been made is whether the impossibility alleged is a legal impossibility or a factual impossibility. See Annotation, 37 A.L.R.3d 375 (1971). Where the act, if completed, would still not be a criminal act, then it is said to be legally impossible to commit and is a valid defense to the charge of attempt. For example, in Foster v. Commonwealth, 96 Va. 306, 31 S.E. 503 (1898), the defendant was under 14 years of age and by law was conclusively presumed to be incapable of committing rape. The court held that because of his age it was legally impossible for him to be convicted of rape, and he could not "as a plain legal deduction" be convicted of attempted rape. 96 Va. at 311, 31 S.E. at 505. Where the crime is impossible to complete because of some physical or factual condition unknown to the defendant, the impossibility is factual rather than legal. The courts have held that factual impossibility is not a valid defense. For example, the California Supreme Court has held that a person attempting to possess heroin, when in fact the substance was talcum powder, was nevertheless guilty of attempted possession of heroin. The court stated:

> "If there is an apparent ability to commit the crime in the way attempted, the attempt is indictable, although, unknown to the person making the attempt, the crime cannot be committed, because the means employed are in fact unsuitable, or because of extrinsic facts, such as the nonexistence of some essential object, or an obstruction by the intended victim or by a third person." People v. Siu, 126 Cal. App. 2d 41, 44, 271 P.2d 575, 576-77 (1954).

Our Court of Appeals has stated in upholding a conviction for attempt to receive stolen property where the property was not in fact stolen:

> "We therefore hold that legal impossibility is not a bar to prosecution for an attempt to receive stolen property. The rationale for this conclusion is that but for factors unknown to appellant, he committed acts which would have been sufficient to complete the substantive crime and exhibited the requisite intent." State v. Vitale, 530 P.2d 394, 401 (Ariz. App. 1975).

. . . [O]ur statute, Ariz. Rev. Stat. §13-1001, by the phrase "intentionally engages in conduct which would constitute an offense if the attendant circumstances were as such person believes them to be," reflects the intent of the legislature that factual impossibility is not a defense to the crime of attempt.

There can be no doubt that the defendant could never have been convicted of possession of dangerous drugs. However, if the pills were what defendant thought them to be, he could have been convicted of possession of drugs. The defendant believed he had the ability to accomplish the crime of possession, and the fact that the pills were not dangerous drugs does not erase his attempt to possess. Mere intent alone does not amount to an "attempt," People v. Siu, supra, but intent plus conduct toward the commission of a crime may be an attempt. In the instant case, defendant's conduct indicated not only intent, but an attempt to complete the crime of possession. We find no error.

Affirmed.

Notes on Attempt

1. The traditional common law of attempts reflects a simple and straightforward paradigm: the defendant who tries to commit a crime but fails, either because he fails to complete his conduct (e.g., an intended killer who is captured before he can actually fire the fatal shot), or because he completes his conduct but fails to cause his intended result (e.g., an intended killer who fires the shot and either misses the victim, or hits the victim but the victim nevertheless survives).

In common-law attempt doctrine, the *mens rea* element is also simple: As reflected in the above paradigm, a defendant satisfies the *mens rea* of attempt if he intends to commit the crime. The conduct element is only slightly more difficult: A defendant has committed an attempt if he comes "dangerously close" to completing the crime and actually causing the intended harm.

2. As is true in many states, Arizona's attempt statute is modeled on the Model Penal Code's attempt provision, which reads:

> (1) Definition of Attempt. A person is guilty of an attempt to commit a crime if, acting with the kind of culpability otherwise required for commission of the crime, he:
>
>> (a) purposely engages in conduct which would constitute the crime if the attendant circumstances were as he believes them to be; or
>>
>> (b) when causing a particular result is an element of the crime, does or omits to do anything with the purpose of causing or with the belief that it will cause such result without further conduct on his part; or
>>
>> (c) purposely does or omits to do anything which, under the circumstances as he believes them to be, is an act or omission constituting a substantial step in a course of conduct planned to culminate in his commission of the crime.
>
> (2) Conduct Which May Be Held Substantial Step Under Subsection (1)(c). Conduct shall not be held to constitute a substantial step under

Subsection (1)(c) of this Section unless it is strongly corroborative of the actor's criminal purpose. Without negativing the sufficiency of other conduct, the following, if strongly corroborative of the actor's criminal purpose, shall not be held insufficient as a matter of law:

     (a) lying in wait, searching for or following the contemplated victim of the crime;

     (b) enticing or seeking to entice the contemplated victim of the crime to go to the place contemplated for its commission;

     (c) reconnoitering the place contemplated for the commission of the crime;

     (d) unlawful entry of a structure, vehicle or enclosure in which it is contemplated that the crime will be committed;

     (e) possession of materials to be employed in the commission of the crime, which are specially designed for such unlawful use or which can serve no lawful purpose of the actor under the circumstances;

     (f) possession, collection or fabrication of materials to be employed in the commission of the crime, at or near the place contemplated for its commission, where such possession, collection or fabrication serves no lawful purpose of the actor under the circumstances;

     (g) soliciting an innocent agent to engage in conduct constituting an element of the crime.

MPC §5.01. The Code recognizes that there are three different reasons why an intended crime might not occur, which gives rise to three different kinds of attempts. The first is that—as in *McElroy*—the defendant might have thought he was committing the crime, but because of the failure of a circumstance element (e.g., the stuff that he bought wasn't really illegal drugs), he actually didn't commit the crime; this is covered by section 5.01(1)(a). The second reason is that the defendant might have done everything he thought would be necessary to cause a prohibited result, but that result never actually occurred; this kind of attempt is dealt with in section 5.01(1)(b). The third reason is that the defendant never managed to complete the conduct that would have resulted in the commission of the crime; such incomplete-conduct attempts are addressed in sections 5.01(1)(c) and 5.01(2).

    3. Under Arizona's attempt law, which is based on the Model Penal Code, the prosecution must prove two things in order to convict McElroy: first, that his conduct would "constitute an offense if the attendant circumstances were as [he] believe[d] them to be," and second, that he acted "intentionally" (i.e., with purpose)—meaning that he was trying to possess amphetamines. Notice the crucial role the defendant's mental state plays in the litigation: Without his purpose to buy speed and his belief that the pills *were* speed, he could not be convicted of attempt. And without his confession, neither the purpose nor the belief could be proved. Justice Cameron's opinion states that "[m]ere intent alone does not amount to an 'attempt.'" Is it clear that the state has proved more than McElroy's "mere intent"?

4. As Justice Cameron's opinion in *McElroy* states, courts that follow the common law of attempts usually hold that defendants are not liable for attempts that are legally impossible; factual impossibility, on the other hand, is no defense to attempt charges. What is meant by impossibility, and what distinguishes the legal kind from the factual kind?

In a nutshell, a crime is impossible if the defendant could not possibly have committed the completed offense, regardless of how hard he tried. Factual impossibility means that the obstacle to the crime's completion is a fact about which the defendant is ignorant: in *McElroy*, for example, the true character of the pills. Legal impossibility means that the reason the crime could not be completed lies in the law, not in the facts.

The New York Court of Appeals offered this example of a legally impossible crime:

> . . . [I]n People v. Teal, 196 N.Y. 372 (1909), a conviction for attempted subornation of perjury was overturned on the theory that the testimony attempted to be suborned was irrelevant to the merits of the case. Since it was not subornation of perjury to solicit false, but irrelevant, testimony, "the person through whose procuration the testimony is given cannot be guilty of subornation of perjury and, by the same rule, an unsuccessful attempt to that which is not a crime when effectuated, cannot be held to be an attempt to commit the crime specified." 196 N.Y., at 377.

People v. Dlugash, 363 N.E.2d 1155, 1160-61 (N.Y. 1977). Cases like *Teal* are rare. Cases of factual impossibility are more common:

> . . . For example, a man was held liable for attempted murder when he shot into the room in which his target usually slept and, fortuitously, the target was sleeping elsewhere in the house that night. State v. Mitchell, 170 Mo. 633 (1902). Although one bullet struck the target's customary pillow, attainment of the criminal objective was factually impossible. State v. Moretti, 52 N.J. 182 (1968), presents a similar instance of factual impossibility. The defendant agreed to perform an abortion, then a criminal act, upon a female undercover police investigator who was not, in fact, pregnant. The court sustained the conviction, ruling that "when the consequences sought by a defendant are forbidden by the law as criminal, it is no defense that the defendant could not succeed in reaching his goal because of circumstance unknown to him." 52 N.J., at 190.

Dlugash, 363 N.E.2d at 1160.

5. Some applications of impossibility doctrine seem more questionable. The Virginia Supreme Court's decision in Foster v. Commonwealth, 96 Va. 306, 31 S.E. 503 (1898) — *Foster* is cited and discussed in *McElroy* — is one example; the court held that 14-year-old males are conclusively presumed to be prepubescent and, therefore, incapable of sexual intercourse. Consequently, the court concluded, males of that age could neither commit nor attempt to commit rape. In State v. Guffey, 262 S.W.2d 152 (1953), the Missouri Court of Appeals held that a defendant could not be convicted of attempting to shoot a deer out of season when the object at which he shot was a stuffed animal, not a live one. In State v. Taylor, 133 S.W.2d 336 (1939), the Missouri Supreme Court found no liability for attempted bribery where the defendant bribed someone he believed, incorrectly, to be a juror.

6. "Sting" operations, in which the government uses undercover agents or cooperating compatriots to catch criminals, often give rise to impossible attempts. The Indiana Department of Natural Resources uses a robotic deer, nicknamed "Robo-Deer," to nab poachers and those who violate other hunting laws. Is shooting "Robo-Deer" outside of deer-hunting season, believing it to be a real deer, a factual impossibility (because Robo-Deer is not a real live deer) or a legal impossibility (because there's no illegal hunting season for robotic deer)? For a video about Indiana's Robo-Deer (other states, like California, also use the same technique), see http://www.youtube.com/watch?v=AgOipZyp4-g.

7. In United States v. Bernal, 90 F.3d 465 (11th Cir. 1996), federal authorities took the concept of a sting operation to a new level. As part of a joint U.S.-Mexico investigation of suspected primate smuggling by a Mexican zoo, an undercover U.S. Fish and Wildlife Service agent donned a fake gorilla outfit and was placed inside a real cage (complete with real gorilla dung!) supplied by the Miami Metrozoo. The cage was then "delivered" to the defendant at an airport in Opa-Locka, Florida. As Assistant U.S. Attorney Dan Gelber later explained, "[I]t's risky and dangerous to use a real animal, so we had to use a willing substitute . . . . It was a small gorilla, but he was a large agent." Bernal was convicted, inter alia, of two counts of attempted violation of the Endangered Species Act.

8. What is the point of impossibility doctrine? Does the doctrine make sense? The Model Penal Code's drafters didn't think so, and the Code essentially eliminates the doctrine—meaning that if, *in the defendant's mind*, he was committing the crime, then he is guilty of an attempt to do so without regard to whether or not it was impossible (factually *or* legally) for him actually to do so. The only (and very rare) exception is where the act the defendant *intended* to commit, or the result he *intended* to cause, is not defined as a crime at all; in such a case, there can be no attempt liability because there is no crime that the defendant could have attempted to commit. In other words, even under the Code, a defendant cannot be convicted of attempting to commit a non-existent crime.

9. According to the theory of attempt law adopted by the Model Penal Code, McElroy is no less culpable, and hence no less deserving of punishment, than one who actually buys a bag of speed. (Indeed, the Code drafters sought to punish attempts at the same level as the completed crime — but even states, like Arizona, that have adopted the MPC's attempt rules have flatly rejected that idea.) Is this theory right? Is there any reason to distinguish between unsuccessful defendants like McElroy and defendants who actually buy the drugs they intend to buy?

Although the Model Penal Code makes a defendant guilty of attempt (as well as the two other inchoate crimes, solicitation and conspiracy) based on what the defendant *thinks*, in his head, he is doing — and without regard to whether or not the crime *actually* could have been committed — the Code also provides judges with the discretion to reduce or dismiss such charges if a particular defendant's conduct "is so inherently unlikely to result or culminate in the commission of a crime that neither such conduct nor the actor presents a public danger warranting the grading of such offense." See MPC §5.05(2). This is intended to allow for mitigation in the case of a truly hapless defendant — for example, one who thinks that sticking pins into a voodoo doll will actually kill the intended victim.

Note on Solicitation

What happens if a defendant seeks to commit a crime by asking (or commanding, or cajoling, or encouraging, or paying) someone else to commit the crime for him? Common law treated this as the inchoate crime of solicitation. The Model Penal Code defines "criminal solicitation" as follows:

> (1) Definition of Solicitation. A person is guilty of solicitation to commit a crime if with the purpose of promoting or facilitating its commission he commands, encourages or requests another person to engage in specific conduct that would constitute such crime or an attempt to commit such crime or which would establish his complicity in its commission or attempted commission.
>
> (2) Uncommunicated Solicitation. It is immaterial under Subsection (1) of this Section that the actor fails to communicate with the person he solicits to commit a crime if his conduct was designed to effect such communication. . . .

MPC §5.02.

Notice that solicitation, as we have already seen with attempt (and as we will soon see with conspiracy), is a separate inchoate crime that can be committed even if the actual crime solicited is never committed. In addition, under the Model Penal Code, and depending on the particular crime being solicited, this could also be treated as an attempt under either section 5.01(1)(b) (because the defendant has done everything she believed necessary to bring about the desired result) or section 5.01(1)(c) (because the defendant has taken a "substantial step" toward the completion of the crime).

People v. Acosta

Court of Appeals of New York
80 N.Y.2d 665; 609 N.E.2d 518 (1993)

Opinion of KAYE, J.

A person who, with intent to possess cocaine, orders from a supplier, admits a courier into his or her home, examines the drugs and ultimately rejects them because of perceived defects in quality, has attempted to possess cocaine within the meaning of the Penal Law. As the evidence was legally sufficient to establish this sequence of events, we reinstate defendant's conviction of attempted criminal possession of a controlled substance in the first degree.

I

By jury verdict, defendant was convicted of conspiracy and attempted possession of cocaine. The latter charge—the only one at issue on this appeal—centers on the events of March 21, 1988.

Evidence at trial revealed that, commencing in November 1986, officers of the Manhattan North Narcotics Division began investigating the activities of defendant, his brother Miguel and others. Their investigation techniques included the use of an undercover officer to infiltrate the organization, stakeouts and court-authorized wiretaps. In July 1987 the undercover met with Miguel at a Manhattan apartment and purchased cocaine. At that time, Miguel introduced defendant to the officer, telling her that they "work together."

A wiretap on defendant's telephone at his Bronx apartment revealed that for several days prior to March 21, 1988, he was negotiating with Luis Rojas to purchase kilogram quantities of cocaine.[1] On March 21, at 11:37 A.M., Rojas called defendant and asked, "are you ready?" Defendant replied "come by here" and Rojas responded, "I'm going over." At 11:42, defendant called "Frank," an associate, and told him that he "spoke to the man" who would be "coming over here. . . . Right now."

About a half hour later, around 12:15, officers staking out defendant's six-floor apartment building saw a man pull up in a car, remove a black and white plastic bag from the trunk, and enter the building. The bag's handles were stretched, indicating that the contents were heavy. At 12:30, the man emerged from the building, carrying the same plastic bag which still appeared to be heavy. He placed the bag back in the trunk and drove off.

Minutes later, at 12:37, defendant called Frank, stating that he "saw the man" but "those tickets . . . were no good; they weren't good for the game man." Frank wondered whether "they got more expensive, the seats" and defendant explained that they were the "same price and all" but they were "not the same seats . . . some seats real bad, very bad, very bad." Defendant elaborated: "two pass tickets together on the outside stuck together, like a thing, like a ticket falsified. Then I told him to take it away, no, I don't want any problems and anything you see." Frank asked if defendant was

---

1. These conversations were routinely conducted in code words such as "tickets" or "tires" which the prosecution expert testified represented kilos of cocaine. Many such conversations were recorded in the weeks leading up to defendant's arrest.

told when the tickets would arrive, and defendant responded "No because who came was someone, somebody else, the guy, the messenger." Defendant acknowledged that he "want[s] to participate in the game but if you can't see it, you're going to come out upset."

At 12:50 P.M., Rojas called defendant and said something inaudible about "my friend." Defendant responded, "Oh yes, but he left because (inaudible) it doesn't fit me. . . . You told me it was the same thing, same ticket." Rojas rejoined, "No. We'll see each other at six."

Finally, at 1:26 P.M., defendant telephoned Hector Vargas, who wanted to know "what happened?" Defendant said, "Nothing. I saw something there, what you wanted, but I returned it because it was a shit there." Hector wanted to know, "like how?" but defendant simply responded, "No, no, a weird shit there." Vargas suggested that he might be able to obtain something "white and good.". . .

At trial, in motions before and after the verdict, defendant argued that the foregoing evidence was insufficient to establish that he attempted to possess cocaine on March 21. The trial court rejected those arguments and sentenced defendant, upon the jury's guilty verdict, to a prison term of 25 years to life, the maximum permitted by law.

On appeal, a sharply divided Appellate Division reversed and vacated the attempted possession conviction, the majority concluding that "[e]ven were we to accept [the] attenuated inference that the visitor actually reached defendant's apartment and offered his contraband to him, the remaining evidence shows defendant's flat rejection of that offer, and thus total abandonment of the criminal enterprise with respect to this particular quantity of cocaine." 172 App. Div. 2d 103, 105-106. One of the dissenting Justices granted the People leave to appeal, and we now reverse.

II

A person knowingly and unlawfully possessing a substance weighing at least four ounces and containing a narcotic drug is guilty of criminal possession of a controlled substance in the first degree, Penal Law §220.21(1). Under the Penal Law, "[a] person is guilty of an attempt to commit a crime when, with intent to commit a crime, he [or she] engages in conduct which tends to effect the commission of such crime." Penal Law §110.00. While the statutory formulation of attempt would seem to cover a broad range of conduct—anything "tend[ing] to effect" a crime—case law requires a closer nexus between defendant's acts and the completed crime.

In People v. Rizzo, 246 N.Y. 334, 337 (1927), we observed that in demarcating punishable attempts from mere preparation to commit a crime, a "line has been drawn between those acts which are remote and those which are proximate and near to the consummation." In *Rizzo*, this Court drew that line at acts "very near to the accomplishment of the intended crime." Id., at

337. Though apparently more stringent than the Model Penal Code "substantial step" test, Model Penal Code §5.01(1)(c) . . . [,] in this State we have adhered to *Rizzo*'s "very near" or "dangerously near" requirement, despite the later enactment of Penal Law §110.00. See People v. Mahboubian, 74 N.Y.2d 174, 191 (1989).[3]

A person who orders illegal narcotics from a supplier, admits a courier into his or her home and examines the quality of the goods has unquestionably passed beyond mere preparation and come "very near" to possessing those drugs. Indeed, the only remaining step between the attempt and the completed crime is the person's acceptance of the proffered merchandise, an act entirely within his or her control.

Our decision in People v. Warren, 66 N.Y.2d 831 (1985), is thus readily distinguishable. . . . In that case, an informant and an undercover officer posing as a cocaine seller met defendants in a hotel room and reached an agreement for the sale of about half a pound. The actual exchange, however, was to occur hours later, in another part of town, after repackaging and testing. Moreover, when defendants were arrested at that meeting, the sellers had insufficient cocaine on hand and defendants had insufficient funds. We concluded that since "several contingencies stood between the agreement in the hotel room and the contemplated purchase," defendants did not come "very near" to accomplishment of the intended crime. 66 N.Y.2d, at 833. The same cannot be said here.

Significantly, neither the Appellate Division nor the dissent in this Court disputes the proposition that a person who arranges for the delivery of drugs and actually examines them has come sufficiently close to the completed crime to qualify as an attempt. Rather, the Appellate Division relies on two other grounds for reversal: (i) the evidence was insufficient to establish that defendant in fact met with a drug courier and examined his wares; and (ii) in any event, defendant's ultimate rejection of the drugs constituted an abandonment of the criminal enterprise, vitiating the attempt. (The dissent in this Court is limited to the first ground.) Neither ground is persuasive.

Sufficiency of the Evidence

A jury . . . concluded from the evidence presented that defendant attempted to possess cocaine on March 21, 1988. In examining the record for legal

---

3. . . . [T]he statute interpreted in *Rizzo*, former Penal Law §2, is similar to the present version. The repealed statute provided: "An act, done with intent to commit a crime, and tending but failing to effect its commission, is an attempt to commit that crime."

Under the revised Penal Law, all attempts were initially classified for sentencing purposes at a lower grade than the completed crime, but subsequent legislation, premised on the belief that certain attempts—including attempted possession of a controlled substance in the first degree—were as serious as the completed crime, classified the attempt at the same grade as the consummated crime. See Penal Law §110.05(1).

sufficiency, "the evidence must be viewed in a light most favorable to the People . . . to determine whether there is a valid line of reasoning and permissible inferences from which a rational jury could have found the elements of the crime proved beyond a reasonable doubt." People v. Steinberg, 79 N.Y.2d 673, 681-82 (1992). This deferential standard is employed because the courts' role . . . is simply to determine whether enough evidence has been presented so that the resulting verdict was lawful. . . .

[W]e conclude that the evidence was legally sufficient to support the jury's finding that defendant met with a drug courier in his home on March 21. About a half-hour after defendant's supplier, Rojas, told defendant that he would be coming over, the police saw a man enter the apartment building with a weighted-down plastic bag and emerge 15 minutes later with the same heavy bag. Contemporaneously with the unidentified man's departure, defendant reported to an associate that he met with a messenger but that he rejected the offer because the "seats" were "very bad" and the "tickets" looked "falsified." When Rojas immediately called defendant asking about his "friend," defendant explained that "he left" and complained that Rojas misrepresented that the "same ticket" would be brought. And shortly thereafter, defendant called Vargas and told him that he "saw something there, what you wanted, but I returned it because it was a shit there.". . .

On the evidence presented, a rational jury could have found beyond a reasonable doubt that defendant, with the intent to possess more than four ounces of a controlled substance, met with Rojas' courier and examined cocaine, but rejected it because he was dissatisfied with the quality.

. . . [T]he jury knew from defendant's many earlier conversations about "tickets" and his meeting with the undercover that he was involved with drugs. Further, the jury knew that in the days immediately preceding March 21 defendant was negotiating with Rojas to buy kilos of cocaine and that on March 21 Rojas said that he was coming over. The unidentified man's visit to the apartment building with the parcel—coinciding to the minute with defendant's conversations—was fully consistent with defendant's several later admissions that he had met with a courier but rejected his merchandise. While the dissent would ignore the totality of this evidence, the jury most assuredly was not required to do so.

Rejection as Abandonment

. . . Penal Law §40.10(3) provides an affirmative defense to an attempt charge "under circumstances manifesting a voluntary and complete renunciation of [the] criminal purpose." To qualify for this defense, "the abandonment must be permanent, not temporary or contingent, not simply a decision to postpone the criminal conduct until another time" People v. Taylor, 80 N.Y.2d 1, 13-14 (1992).

An abandonment theory is inapposite here. . . . [T]he evidence revealed that even after rejecting the March 21 offer, defendant continued making efforts to obtain cocaine. Thus, while it may be true that there was an abandonment "with respect to [that] particular quantity of cocaine," 172 App. Div. 2d at 106, this is immaterial for purposes of the statutory renunciation defense. Rather, there must be an abandonment of [the] over-all criminal enterprise, see, People v. Taylor, 80 N.Y.2d at 14, which on this record plainly was not the case.

III

. . . Accordingly, the order of the Appellate Division should be reversed, the conviction for attempted criminal possession of a controlled substance in the first degree reinstated, and the case remitted to that court for [further proceedings]. . . .

Smith, J., dissenting.

To uphold defendant's conviction of an attempt, it must be shown beyond a reasonable doubt that his acts came "dangerously close" to committing the substantive crime. That someone got out of a car carrying a bag and entered the apartment building adds nothing to the proof of the attempted crime. There was no proof of who this man was, what was in the bag, where the man went inside the building or who owned the car. Any connection of this proof with defendant would necessarily be based on pure speculation. The critical question, then, is whether defendant's wiretapped phone calls, standing alone, or even in conjunction with the evidence of a man and his bag, could constitute sufficient evidence for a finding of guilt. Without more, these phone conversations, and other evidence submitted, were insufficient to show that defendant came "dangerously close" to possessing drugs. I, therefore, dissent. . . .

A police officer assigned to stakeout defendant's apartment building testified at trial that shortly after noon on March 21, 1988, he observed a small white four-door vehicle drive up to the front of the six-story apartment building in which defendant lived. The officer also testified that he saw a male Hispanic exit the car, remove a black and white plastic bag with long, completely stretched handles from the trunk, and enter the courtyard leading to the building. No one followed the person into the building to ascertain where he went. The officer testified further that the same man left the building 15 minutes later with the same bag with similarly stretched handles. According to the officer, the man walked to the rear of his vehicle, opened the trunk, placed the bag back inside, got into the vehicle, drove a few feet, made a U-turn, and drove back past the police vehicle in which he was seated. The officer testified that he never stopped the driver of the white vehicle or ascertained what was in the bag. This incident, along with overheard conversations of defendant that he had rejected "tickets" (allegedly cocaine), presented the sole basis for convicting defendant of attempted possession of a controlled substance in the first degree. . . .*

In [People v. Warren, 66 N.Y.2d 831 (1985)], this Court affirmed the dismissal of indictments charging two defendants with attempted criminal possession of a controlled substance where several contingencies stood between an earlier agreement to purchase and the contemplated purchase. The Grand Jury testimony showed that the defendants agreed to purchase cocaine from a police informant, but the transaction was not consummated because the informant did not have enough cocaine, the defendants did not have enough money, and the cocaine was not properly packaged. The informant agreed to meet the defendants later that evening to test the cocaine and effect the transaction. Before the informant departed, and while defendants were examining one-ounce bags of cocaine, police officers who were secretly watching the transaction entered the room and arrested them. This Court concluded that "the defendants did not come very near to the accomplishment of the intended crime." Id. at 833.

Here, too, the evidence adduced at trial does not establish that defendant came very near to the accomplishment of the crime of possession of a controlled substance in the first degree. According to the wiretap information, defendant had been anticipating a delivery of "tickets" from his suppliers for resale to a customer. The police observed an Hispanic male enter and leave the courtyard of the apartment building in which defendant lived carrying a heavy-laden shopping bag. . . . [T]he stakeout police officer did not stop and question the Hispanic male or ascertain what was in the shopping bag, nor did he observe the male approach or enter defendant's apartment. . . .

The sole basis for defendant's guilt was the wiretap conversations in which defendant told another individual that he had just rejected a delivery of "tickets" as unacceptable because it was "no good" and "stuck together." The evidence adduced simply does not establish beyond a reasonable doubt the attempted possession of cocaine by the defendant.

Notes and Questions

1. Acosta was convicted for attempting to possess cocaine, based on a transaction in which he refused to buy—in the law's terms, refused to possess—cocaine. How can that be right?

---

* . . . [A]lthough no objection to it was made by either party, the [trial court] erroneously charged the Federal standard on attempt in that a "substantial step" is required for the completion rather than the New York standard of a requirement that conduct come "very near" or "dangerously near" to completion.

2. Legally, it *is* right. Recall that attempts can be divided into three different conceptual categories, one of which consists of cases in which the defendant fails to complete the conduct that would have constituted the offense. Technically, *Acosta* falls into this category: The police arrested the defendant while he was still seeking to obtain cocaine. But the particular transaction for which the defendant was convicted of attempt doesn't quite fit the description. That transaction (better described as a failed negotiation) was already complete when the defendant was arrested. The defendant did not try and fail to possess cocaine; rather, he *chose* not to possess cocaine—at least not the cocaine his seller offered him. The case is akin to an attempted murder prosecution in which the defendant considers shooting the victim, then decides not to do so. Surely the law would not punish such a choice. Yet what else is there to punish?

The answer is that the attempted murder defendant can be punished for the conduct *before* his decision not to shoot—in effect, for almost making the attempt. So too, Acosta can be punished for almost possessing the cocaine: for arranging the deal, meeting his seller, and examining the drugs—that is, for everything that happened up to his decision not to accept delivery of those drugs.

3. Under the Model Penal Code, defendants like Acosta still might manage to avoid criminal liability if they abandon or "renounce" the relevant crime before they are apprehended:

> (4) Renunciation of Criminal Purpose. When the actor's conduct would otherwise constitute an attempt under Subsection (1)(b) or (1)(c) of this Section, it is an affirmative defense that he abandoned his effort to commit the crime or otherwise prevented its commission, under circumstances manifesting a complete and voluntary renunciation of his criminal purpose. The establishment of such defense does not, however, affect the liability of an accomplice who did not join in such abandonment or prevention.
>
> Within the meaning of this Article, renunciation of criminal purpose is not voluntary if it is motivated, in whole or in part, by circumstances, not present or apparent at the inception of the actor's course of conduct, that increase the probability of detection or apprehension or that make more difficult the accomplishment of the criminal purpose. Renunciation is not complete if it is motivated by a decision to postpone the criminal conduct until a more advantageous time or to transfer the criminal effort to another but similar objective or victim.

MPC §5.01(4). Acosta would not qualify for the renunciation defense, however, because his decision not to accept the drugs was "motivated by a decision to postpone the criminal conduct until a more advantageous time." Is that result fair? Can it be fair to punish a defendant for a choice (to possess drugs) he demonstrably did not make? On the other hand, the government had considerable evidence that Acosta was involved in the drug trade. Is it reasonable *not* to punish Acosta because, this one time, the deal did not go through?

4. Under the MPC, Acosta could be convicted if his conduct amounted to "a substantial step" toward completion of the crime, and if that conduct was "strongly corroborative of [Acosta's] criminal purpose." MPC §§5.01(1)(c), 5.01(2). New York's doctrinal formula for incomplete-conduct attempts, however, is more like the common law's approach. At common law, defendants could be convicted of criminal attempts only if their conduct went beyond "mere preparation." In New York, defendants can be convicted only if their conduct was "very near" or "dangerously near" to committing the completed crime. The MPC's approach looks to how much conduct the defendant has engaged in; New York looks instead to how little conduct remains to be done in order to commit the relevant offense.

This, by the way, is why the traditional common law of attempt was much less sanguine than is the Model Penal Code about defendants who initially cross the line of attempt and then think better of it. At common law, such defendants have already, by definition, come dangerously close to causing the harm of the completed crime; under such circumstances, it does not seem unfair to deny them the benefit of an abandonment defense.

The Code, by contrast, has two reasons to broaden the scope and availability of the renunciation defense. First, under the Code, a defendant becomes guilty of attempt much earlier in the chain of events leading up to the completed crime, so it seems more fair to give the defendant a chance to reconsider and opt out. Second, and more important, the Code's drafters argued (although no actual jurisdiction has ever agreed) that attempts generally should be punished at the exact same level as completed crimes; this was due to the Code's single-minded focus on culpability, rather than conduct or result, as the essence of criminality. But if a defendant who crosses the line of attempt by, say, shooting at his victim (and missing) has already "bought" all of the punishment he would get for the completed crime anyway, what incentive does he have not to reload and try again? The Code's renunciation defense gives him that incentive, which is important as a matter of public policy.

5. Reread the description of People v. Warren, 66 N.Y.2d 831 (1985), in Judge Smith's dissent. Is *Acosta* consistent with *Warren*? Did Acosta come dangerously close to possessing cocaine? Did Warren?

Kohlmeier v. State

Court of Appeals of Georgia
289 Ga. App. 709; 658 S.E.2d 261 (2008)

Opinion by PHIPPS, Judge.

After a traffic stop, Nicholas A. Kohlmeier and his two passengers were arrested; the vehicle was searched; and the three were charged with drug crimes. Kohlmeier appeals his conviction for criminal attempt to manufacture methamphetamine, contesting the sufficiency of the evidence and the lawfulness of the traffic stop and his arrest. We discern no error and affirm.

Kohlmeier contends that the evidence did not authorize the guilty verdict on the count of criminal attempt to manufacture methamphetamine. "A person commits the offense of criminal attempt when, with intent to commit a specific crime, he performs any act which constitutes a substantial step toward the commission of that crime."[2] An act constituting a "substantial step" is one

> done in pursuance of the intent, and more or less directly tending to the commission of the crime. In general, the act must be inexplicable as a lawful act, and must be more than mere preparation. Yet it can not accurately be said that no preparations can amount to an attempt. It is a question of degree, and depends upon the circumstances of each case. The phrase "inexplicable as a lawful act" does not mean that the act itself must be unlawful. Rather, it means that the act, in light of previous acts, constitutes a substantial step toward the commission of a crime. . . . [T]he "substantial step" requirement is intended to (1) ensure firmness of the defendant's criminal intent, (2) insulate from liability "very remote preparatory acts," and (3) allow for apprehension of offenders at an early stage. . . .[3]

The indictment alleged that Kohlmeier committed criminal attempt to manufacture methamphetamine by performing "an act constituting a substantial step toward the commission of said offense in that [he] did possess methanol, pseudoephedrine, a cookstove and approximately 1000 books of matches containing red phosphorus, essential elements in the manufacture of methamphetamine." . . .

. . . [T]he evidence showed that on the night of January 31, 2006, a county sheriff's department issued to its officers a BOLO ("be on the lookout") for a certain truck based upon a report from a local merchant, the Food Lion, that two of its customers had left in that truck after purchasing a large quantity of matches. The sheriff's department had requested area merchants to alert it of such a purchase, which the department considered an indication of possible impending methamphetamine manufacturing.

A patrol officer spotted at a Citgo gas station a truck that matched the description in the BOLO. The officer testified that, after the truck passed his patrol car as it left the Citgo parking lot, he "saw that the vehicle . . . didn't have a working tag light on the vehicle and it was dark, which is a violation of Georgia law," and he therefore "turned around and stopped the vehicle." Kohlmeier was the driver, and the male and

2. OCGA §16-4-1.
3. Dennard v. State, 243 Ga. App. 868, 871-72, 534 S.E.2d 182 (2000).

female passengers matched the descriptions in the BOLO of the two
recent purchasers of matches.

A K-9 unit arrived to assist in the traffic stop. As the patrol officer was
checking Kohlmeier's driving license, the drug dog alerted at the driver's
door seam. Kohlmeier and the passengers stepped out of the truck at the
officers' request. The search of the truck yielded a box of cold medicine containing pseudoephedrine, two full bottles of HEET brand fuel treatment, a
Coleman camping stove, and a can of kerosene. According to the patrol officer, the type of stove found could be used to make methamphetamine and
kerosene could be used to fuel that type of stove. No matches were found at
the scene, however.

Another officer, a former narcotics agent with special training regarding the clandestine manufacturing of methamphetamine, was summoned
to the scene for his opinion of whether Food Lion's report, coupled with
what had been discovered at the traffic stop scene, showed involvement in
the manufacture of methamphetamine. He testified that two of the three
main ingredients required for manufacturing the drug had been recovered:
pseudoephedrine and red phosphorus, the latter being contained in the
striker plates of the matchbooks. The officer further testified that HEET
was essentially methanol and often used in making the drug to extract the
red phosphorus from the striker plates and also to separate the pseudoephedrine out of certain types of cold medicines, including the type found
in the truck. Noting the stove, the officer explained that a heat source was
required to make methamphetamine. The former narcotics agent suspected
impending manufacturing of methamphetamine.

Kohlmeier was handcuffed, placed in the back of a patrol car with his
male passenger, and read his *Miranda* rights. Meanwhile, one of the officers
returned to the scene with a shopping bag of boxes containing about 5,000
matchbooks, which he had found on the road leading back to the Citgo, the
route Kohlmeier had just traveled. A device in the patrol car with Kohlmeier
recorded Kohlmeier stating to his male passenger that a store likely had
"ratted" about the matchbook purchases. Kohlmeier's female passenger was
also arrested and then placed in a separate patrol car. Receipts found in her
possession showed recent purchases at Food Lion and a CVS store.

At trial, the former narcotics agent further explained that those involved
in the clandestine manufacture of methamphetamine commonly gather the
required ingredients and materials surreptitiously to avoid arousing suspicion. To that end, the necessary items generally are not obtained within a
single purchase; rather, they are accumulated piecemeal.

In connection with the underlying incident, Kohlmeier's female passenger entered a negotiated guilty plea and then testified as a state witness as
follows. She, Kohlmeier, and the male passenger had been friends for years.

On several occasions before, the three of them had made and used methamphetamine. On the day in question, Kohlmeier and the male passenger had plans to make a small amount of the drug in a certain wooded area, where they previously had done so using the stove found on Kohlmeier's truck. When stopped by the patrol officer, the three of them were accumulating various items they needed to manufacture methamphetamine. She had purchased the cold medicine from CVS, two boxes of matches from Food Lion, and kerosene from Citgo. The male passenger had purchased three additional boxes of matches from Food Lion. And Kohlmeier had gone into a Fred's store and walked out, pulling from underneath his jacket two bottles of HEET. Somewhere "down the road," however, the male passenger had tossed the matches out the truck window. . . .

Kohlmeier's challenge to the sufficiency of the evidence on the ground that his conviction rests upon the "mere possession of a Coleman cooking stove and two (2) bottles of HEET" is without merit. The whole of the evidence, construed to uphold the verdict, authorized a finding that Kohlmeier was guilty beyond a reasonable doubt of criminal attempt to manufacture methamphetamine. . . .

Notes and Questions

1. Suppose Kohlmeier's conviction were reviewed under New York law, which holds that attempt defendants may be convicted only if their conduct comes dangerously close to completion. Would the conviction stand? Does *Kohlmeier* make you think differently about the merits of the MPC test for incomplete-conduct attempts?

2. How important is the testimony of the defendant's accomplice? Is the defendant's *mens rea* clear without that testimony?

3. In most jurisdictions, Kohlmeier could also be convicted of possessing "drug paraphernalia," meaning equipment commonly used to manufacture or consume illegal drugs. Statutes banning the possession of such items play much the same role in the criminal law of narcotics that laws banning the possession of burglars' tools play in the law of burglary. In both instances, the possession statutes largely displace the law of criminal attempts, and make conviction easier in borderline cases. Perhaps that is unproblematic if, as in *Kohlmeier*, the items are ones that, in combination, no one is likely to possess for legitimate reasons. But drug paraphernalia statutes also ban the possession of such ordinary items as bowls, spoons, and razor blades. Are convictions for possessing such items justifiable—even if the government proves criminal intent? Does possessing such items constitute an attempt to possess illegal drugs?

B. ACCOMPLICE LIABILITY AND CONSPIRACY

State v. Romero-Garcia

Court of Appeals of Idaho
139 Idaho 199, 75 P.3d 1209 (2003)

Opinion of PERRY, J.

Mario Romero-Garcia appeals from the judgments of conviction entered by the district court after a jury found him guilty of one count each of aiding and abetting trafficking in cocaine and aiding and abetting the failure to affix illegal drug tax stamps. We affirm.

I

On December 14, 2000, law enforcement officers met with a confidential informant (CI), who had arranged for a controlled cocaine purchase through Romero-Garcia. Pursuant to previous arrangements, officers followed the CI's vehicle to Hailey where the CI picked up Romero-Garcia at his residence. The CI and Romero-Garcia then drove to the parking lot of an apartment in Ketchum. While under law enforcement surveillance, Romero-Garcia exited the vehicle, walked to an apartment, and returned to the vehicle with another individual. The individual, a high-level drug dealer, agreed to sell the CI an ounce of cocaine, and walked back to the apartment to obtain the drugs. The drug dealer returned and gave the ounce of cocaine to the CI in exchange for $800. For his part in the transaction, Romero-Garcia was paid $200 and was returned to his residence. Ultimately, Romero-Garcia and the drug dealer were tried together on numerous drug-related offenses. The drug dealer was found guilty by a jury of trafficking in cocaine by knowingly and unlawfully delivering 28 grams or more to another person. The drug dealer was also found guilty of failing to affix illegal drug tax stamps to the cocaine he sold. As to both of these offenses, Romero-Garcia was charged with and found guilty of aiding and abetting trafficking in cocaine, Idaho Code §§37-2732B(a)(2)(A), 37-2732B(c), 18-204, and aiding and abetting the failure to affix drug tax stamps, Idaho Code §§63-4205(1), 63-4207(2), 18-204.

On appeal, Romero-Garcia . . . argues that the evidence was insufficient to support the verdict for aiding and abetting the failure to affix illegal drug tax stamps and that the district court improperly instructed the jury on that charge.

II

. . . We [first] address Romero-Garcia's challenges to the jury instructions given by the district court regarding aiding and abetting the failure to affix illegal drug tax stamps. Romero-Garcia argues that the jury was improperly required to find that he personally failed to affix the appropriate tax stamps. Romero-Garcia insists that he had no duty to personally affix tax stamps because he did not possess the cocaine. Romero-Garcia next contends that the jury instructions improperly failed to require the jury to find that Romero-Garcia knew the required tax stamps were not affixed to the cocaine. Additionally, Romero-Garcia argues that the district court erred by failing to instruct the jury, on the special verdict form, that it must find Romero-Garcia aided and abetted the failure to affix the tax stamps beyond a reasonable doubt. Finally, Romero-Garcia contends that the district court erred when it refused to give Romero-Garcia's proposed instruction regarding ignorance or mistake of fact. . . .

The state's evidence showed that cocaine was sold by the drug dealer to the CI in accordance with the arrangements made by Romero-Garcia. For these acts, the drug dealer was found guilty of trafficking in cocaine by delivery. Similarly, Romero-Garcia was found guilty of aiding and abetting trafficking in cocaine by delivery. Under the Idaho Illegal Drug Tax Act, illegal drug tax stamps were required to be permanently affixed to the cocaine sold. Because no stamps were attached, the drug dealer was charged with and found guilty of failure to affix the required tax stamps. Romero-Garcia was charged with and found guilty of aiding and abetting the failure to affix tax stamps.

The main dispute as to aiding and abetting the failure to affix the illegal drug tax stamps centers on the mental state required. An individual who participates in or assists the commission of an offense is guilty of aiding and abetting the crime. State v. Gonzalez, 134 Idaho 907, 909, 12 P.3d 382, 384 (Ct. App. 2002). The mental state required is generally the same as that required for the underlying offense—the aider and abettor must share the criminal intent of the principal and there must be a community of purpose in the unlawful undertaking. State v. Scroggins, 110 Idaho 380, 386, 716 P.2d 1152, 1158 (1985).

Idaho Code §63-4203(1) provides that "every person who in violation of Idaho law possesses a controlled substance shall be liable for payment of an excise tax on all of the controlled substance." When any person possesses a controlled substance subject to illegal drug taxes, the person must obtain illegal drug tax stamps and permanently affix them on the controlled substance to show that the required tax has been paid. Idaho Code §63-4205(1). Possession, in addition to its ordinary meaning, includes holding, selling, and transferring. Idaho Code §63-4202. Any person subject to the drug tax who distributes or possesses a controlled substance, without affixing the appropriate stamps, is guilty of a criminal offense. Idaho Code §63-4207(2).

The Illegal Drug Tax Act, as discussed above, does not specifically indicate the mental state necessary for commission of this crime. However, Idaho Code §18-114 requires that in every crime or public offense there must exist a union, or joint operation, of act and intent, or criminal negligence. Intent as used in that section means not an intent to commit a crime, but merely the intent to knowingly perform the interdicted act or, by criminal negligence, fail to perform the required act.

Pursuant to these statutes then, a person who fails to affix the illegal drug tax stamps becomes strictly liable for the omission. Accordingly, in order to find Romero-Garcia guilty of aiding and abetting the failure to affix the required drug tax stamps, the jury was required to find that: (1) Romero-Garcia knowingly participated in or assisted the drug dealer in the possession or distribution of cocaine; and (2) the necessary drug tax stamps had not been affixed. The jury was instructed that to prove Romero-Garcia's guilt, the state must show beyond a reasonable doubt that, on or about the alleged date in Blaine County, Romero-Garcia "intentionally aided and abetted the possession or distribution of seven grams or more of any controlled substance sold by weight" and that he failed to "permanently affix to it the appropriate Idaho tax stamp." Romero-Garcia insists that the instruction improperly imposed upon him the duty to affix tax stamps because he did not personally possess the cocaine and, therefore, had no duty to do so. Romero-Garcia also argues that the instructions erroneously failed to require proof that he knew that the appropriate tax stamps were not attached to the cocaine.

The Due Process Clause of the United States Constitution precludes conviction except upon proof beyond a reasonable doubt of every fact necessary to constitute the crime with which a defendant is charged. See In re Winship, 397 U.S. 358, 364 (1970). Each element of an offense must be found by a properly instructed jury. The instructions given in this case required the jury to find the two necessary elements. To aid and abet the failure to affix illegal drug tax stamps, Romero-Garcia needed only to participate or assist in the possession or distribution of cocaine for which the drug dealer failed to attach the appropriate stamps. Contrary to Romero-Garcia's argument, it was not necessary that he know that the cocaine lacked the required stamps in order to commit the offense of aiding and abetting the failure to affix drug tax stamps. Rather, the mental state necessary to that charge required only that Romero-Garcia knowingly participated in or assisted the drug dealer in the possession or distribution of cocaine. . . .

. . . Romero-Garcia asserts that the district court erred when it refused to give his requested instruction on the ignorance or mistake of law provisions found in Idaho Code §18-201(1). Romero-Garcia appears to argue that the intent element required for aiding and abetting the failure to affix illegal drug tax stamps was not met because he did not know tax stamps were not affixed. However, as discussed previously, knowledge that the necessary stamps were not attached was not required. Thus, the district court committed no error in refusing to give Romero-Garcia's requested jury instruction.

Romero-Garcia argues that the evidence at trial was insufficient to support a conviction for aiding and abetting the failure to affix illegal drug tax stamps because there was no substantial evidence that he intended that the tax stamps not be attached to the cocaine, that he knew tax stamps were not attached to the cocaine, that he participated in the drug dealer's failure to affix tax stamps to the cocaine, nor that he assisted or encouraged the drug dealer to not affix the tax stamps to the cocaine. This argument fails because this crime did not require proof of any of those elements. Rather, the state was required to show only that Romero-Garcia participated or assisted in the possession or distribution of cocaine lacking the required tax stamps.

The jury instructions in this case properly defined possession to include the sale of a controlled substance. The evidence showed that Romero-Garcia arranged the sale of cocaine to the CI and accompanied him to the drug dealer's residence where the sale took place. In return, Romero-Garcia was paid $200. Thus, the element of aiding and abetting possession or distribution of a controlled substance was supported by sufficient evidence. Likewise, the evidence showed that the drugs confiscated after the sale lacked the appropriate tax stamps. Thus, each element of aiding and abetting the failure to affix illegal drug tax stamps was sufficiently supported by the evidence presented at trial.

III

. . . Although the jury instructions given in this case could have more clearly set forth the applicable law, the jury was required to find, beyond a reasonable doubt, all of the required elements of aiding and abetting the failure to affix illegal drug tax stamps. The evidence presented at trial was sufficient to support the jury's verdict of guilty on that charge. We therefore affirm Romero-Garcia's judgments of conviction for aiding and abetting trafficking in cocaine and for aiding and abetting the failure to affix illegal drug tax stamps.

Notes on Accomplice Liability

1. Idaho Code §18-204 reads as follows:

> All persons concerned in the commission of a crime . . . whether they directly commit the act constituting the offense or aid and abet in its commission, or, not being present, have advised and encouraged its commission . . . or who, by threats, menaces, command or coercion, compel another to commit any crime, are principals in any crime so committed.

The federal accomplice liability statute is similar:

> (a) Whoever commits an offense against the United States or aids, abets, counsels, commands, induces or procures its commission, is punishable as a principal.
> (b) Whoever willfully causes an act to be done which if directly performed by him or another would be an offense against the United States, is punishable as a principal.

18 U.S.C. §2. Such statutes are common in the United States. The liability these statutes create travels under different labels: accomplice liability, complicity, liability for accessories, and liability for aiding and abetting, the two verbs that most commonly appear within such laws.

2. The Model Penal Code's accomplice liability statute appears in section 2, not in section 5 where the inchoate crimes appear, appropriately reflecting the fact that complicity is *not* a separate inchoate crime but instead a means to hold one person responsible for crimes actually committed by another person. The MPC's extremely (and perhaps unduly) complicated complicity provision reads as follows:

(1) A person is guilty of an offense if it is committed by his own conduct or by the conduct of another person for which he is legally accountable, or both.

(2) A person is legally accountable for the conduct of another person when:

. . .

(c) he is an accomplice of such other person in the commission of the offense.

(3) A person is an accomplice of another person in the commission of an offense if:

(a) with the purpose of promoting or facilitating the commission of the offense, he

(i) solicits such other person to commit it; or

(ii) aids or agrees or attempts to aid such other person in planning or committing it; or . . .

(b) his conduct is expressly declared by law to establish his complicity.

(4) When causing a particular result is an element of an offense, an accomplice in the conduct causing such result is an accomplice in the commission of that offense, if he acts with the kind of culpability, if any, with respect to that result that is sufficient for the commission of the offense.

. . .

(6) Unless otherwise provided by the Code or by the law defining the offense, a person is not an accomplice in an offense committed by another person if:

(a) he is a victim of that offense; or

(b) the offense is so defined that his conduct is inevitably incident to its commission; or

(c) he terminates his complicity prior to the commission of the offense and

(i) wholly deprives it of effectiveness in the commission of the offense; or

(ii) gives timely warning to the law enforcement authorities or otherwise makes proper effort to prevent the commission of the offense.

(7) An accomplice may be convicted on proof of the commission of the offense and of his complicity therein, though the person claimed to have committed the offense has not been prosecuted or convicted or has been convicted of a different offense or degree of offense or has an immunity to prosecution or conviction or has been acquitted.

MPC §2.06.

Notice that, under the Code's version of complicity, the act of *soliciting* or *conspiring* (i.e., agreeing) with another person to commit a crime will also make one an accomplice in that person's commission of the crime. Moreover, an *attempt* to aid another person makes one an accomplice of that person (i.e., actually providing aid is not required). Under the Code, one can be guilty as an accomplice for a crime that involves causing a result recklessly, or even negligently, if one is an accomplice in the *conduct* element of the crime and also satisfies the *mens rea* requirement for the result element. Finally, as with the inchoate crimes, the Code provides a renunciation defense, but with a twist: Because accomplice liability involves group criminality, it's not enough simply to change one's mind and stop; instead, to get the benefit of the renunciation defense, one must either eliminate entirely the effects of having been an accomplice (i.e., must make it so that the person actually committing the crime is truly on his or her own), or else notify the authorities (so that they can stop or catch the person actually committing the crime).

3. A simple example captures the idea behind these statutes. Suppose three thieves decided to break into a warehouse at night, and steal some of the more valuable (and portable) merchandise inside. The one in charge does the actual break-in, while a second stands lookout, and the third waits in a getaway car to drive the first two away when the offense is finished. Suppose the crime goes off as planned, but all three thieves are caught afterward. Which ones are guilty of burglary?

Without the law of accomplice liability, only the one who broke into the warehouse is guilty of burglary—the one whom the common law called "the principal." The driver of the getaway car did not actually enter a closed building, structure, or room with the intent to commit a felony (the usual elements of burglary). He had the requisite intent, but he did not commit the criminal act. The same is true of the lookout. Criminal liability is individual, not collective—but this hypothetical crime was collective, not individual. Consequently, two-thirds of this three-man team would avoid conviction for burglary.

The law of aiding and abetting is designed to address this problem. Not only may the thief who broke into the warehouse be convicted of burglary; criminal liability extends as well to anyone who helped him, lookouts and drivers of getaway cars included.

4. Notice the nature of the problem. Even simple criminal organizations operate on principles similar to those that drive legal organizations. One such principle is the division of labor: Different actors perform different tasks and together, they accomplish more than they could working singly. If criminal law adheres to its individualist model, criminal organizations can insulate most of their members from criminal liability. The problem extends beyond the number of actors who participate in criminal transactions. Most crimes are limited to a brief period in time. Transactional crimes like the manufacture and distribution of drugs are committed by multiple actors over an extended period of time. Liability for aiding and abetting extends criminal law's time horizon even as it enlarges the pool of criminal defendants.

5. The classic explanation of the doctrine of accomplice liability was delivered by Judge Learned Hand in United States v. Peoni, 100 F.2d 401 (2d Cir. 1938). Peoni was charged with aiding and abetting the passing of counterfeit currency:

> In the Borough of the Bronx Peoni sold counterfeit bills to one, Regno; and Regno sold the same bills to one, Dorsey, also in the Bronx. All three knew that the bills were counterfeit, and Dorsey was arrested while trying to pass them in the Borough of Brooklyn. The question is whether Peoni was guilty as an accessory to Dorsey's possession. . . .
>
> The prosecution's argument is that, as Peoni put the bills in circulation and knew that Regno would be likely, not to pass them himself, but to sell them to another guilty possessor, the possession of the second buyer was a natural consequence of Peoni's original act, with which he might be charged. If this were a civil case, that would be true; as innocent buyer from Dorsey could sue Peoni and get judgment against him for his loss. But the rule of criminal liability is not the same; since Dorsey's possession was not *de facto* Peoni's, and since Dorsey was not Peoni's agent, Peoni can be liable only as an accessory to Dorsey's act of possession. . . .
>
> The test of that must be found in the appropriate federal statute. . . . [Section] 550 of Title 18 U.S. Code, [which reads] as follows: "aids, abets, counsels, commands, induces, or procures." The substance of that formula goes back a long way. Pollock & Maitland, Vol. II, at 507, in speaking of the English law at the beginning of the 14th Century, say that already "the law of homicide is quite wide enough to comprise . . . those who have 'procured, counselled, commanded or abetted' the felony." . . . Blackstone, 1768, Book IV, at 36 & 37, described an accessory as "he who in any wise commands or counsels another to commit an unlawful act." . . .
>
> It will be observed that all these definitions have nothing whatever to do with the probability that the forbidden result would follow upon the accessory's conduct; and that they all demand that he in some sort associate himself with the venture, that he participate in it as in something that he wishes to bring about, that he seek by his action to make it succeed. All the words used — even the most colorless, "abet" — carry an implication of purposive attitude towards it. So understood, Peoni was not an accessory to Dorsey's possession; his connection with the business ended when he got his money from Regno, who might dispose of the bills as he chose; it was of no moment to him whether Regno passed them himself, and so ended the possibility of further guilty possession, or whether he sold them to a second possible passer. His utterance of the bills was indeed a step in the causal chain which ended in Dorsey's possession, but that was all. . . . [N]obody, so far as we can find, has ever held that a contract is criminal, because the seller has reason to know, not that the buyer will use the goods unlawfully, but that some one further down the line may do so.

100 F.2d at 401-03.

6. Plainly, Romero-Garcia was guilty of aiding and abetting the possession and distribution of cocaine: He set up the transaction between the buyer and seller, and received a commission for his efforts. Is it plain that Romero-Garcia also is guilty of aiding and abetting the failure to pay Idaho's tax on illegal drugs and to affix the requisite tax stamp on the drugs sold? On that charge, the *Romero-Garcia* court seems to impose accomplice liability because the defendant had "reason to know" that another transacting party would "use the goods unlawfully"—precisely the kind of liability Judge Hand barred in *Peoni*. Judge Perry presumably would respond by noting that the tax stamp rule imposes strict liability. But that cannot justify relaxing the *conduct* requirements for accomplice liability. How, exactly, did Romero-Garcia assist in the failure to attach the required stamp to the package? The court says that he assisted in the sale that triggered the requirement. Is that enough? Is *Romero-Garcia* consistent with *Peoni*?

7. Idaho's drug tax, and the tax stamps that go with it, may seem strange. But it is not without precedent. A half-century ago, federal law required gamblers to register with the Internal Revenue Service and pay an occupational tax, notwithstanding that gambling was a federal (and state) crime. See Marchetti v. United States, 390 U.S. 39 (1968). The Harrison Act—the original federal criminal prohibition of opium and its derivatives—required all those who sold opium or morphine to register and apply a tax stamp to the packages in which the drugs were sold. United States v. Balint, 258 U.S. 250 (1922). Such laws serve to make convictions easier, and the criminal law of controlled substances is already designed to make them easy.

8. The defendant in Cottman v. State, 886 A.2d 932 (Md. App. 2005), was convicted of aiding and abetting drug distribution; the defendant's role in the relevant transaction was to interview the "customer" to ensure that he was not an undercover agent—which he was. Even though the defendant failed to do his only job successfully, his conduct counted as aiding and abetting. The assistance of the defendant in Trapps v. United States, 887 A.2d 484 (D.C. 2005), was more successful but less active: Trapps knowingly permitted drug dealers to use the basement of his home as a location for drug sales. That sufficed to show aiding and abetting.

Consider the following jury instructions in *Trapps*:

> To find that the defendant aided and abetted in committing a crime, you must find that he knowingly associated himself with the person who committed the crime, that he participated in the crime as something he wished to bring about, and that he intended by his actions to make it succeed.
>
> Some affirmative conduct by the defendant to help in planning or carrying out the crime is necessary. Mere physical presence by the defendant at the place and time the crime is committed is not by itself sufficient to establish his guilt.

Did the provision of defendant's basement amount to "help in planning or carrying out the crime"?

9. Return to the burglary example in Note 3. In that example, neither the lookout nor the driver of the getaway car is likely to be the crew's boss. Accomplice liability began as a means of punishing underlings, not bosses. In drug cases, by contrast, underlings are usually the ones handling the merchandise; bosses have little or no physical contact with the drugs themselves. In drug cases, accomplice liability may be a means of convicting superiors, not subordinates. Yet when investigations of drug distribution networks lead to charges against whole organizations, conspiracy turns out to be a more common charge than aiding and abetting. Why might that be so?

United States v. Colon

United States Court of Appeals for the Seventh Circuit
549 F.3d 565 (2008)

POSNER, Circuit Judge.

The defendant was convicted by a jury of possessing cocaine with intent to sell it, conspiring to possess cocaine with intent to sell it, and aiding and abetting the conspiracy, and he was sentenced to 135 months in prison. The principal ground of his appeal is that he was not a conspirator or an aider and abettor of a conspiracy, but was merely a purchaser from a conspirator, and that the jury's contrary finding lacked sufficient basis in the evidence to stand. He also challenges on Fourth Amendment grounds his conviction of possession, and we start there.

The government was listening to the phone conversations of the defendant's supplier, Saucedo, and heard him tell Rodriguez (Saucedo's admitted co-conspirator) that "Dude" would be coming to a particular house in 15 minutes to pick up drugs that "Dude" had ordered. Sure enough, 15 minutes later, officers staking out the house saw a man enter it and emerge shortly afterwards, and they tried to stop him and after a chase caught him and found the cocaine he had just bought. The man was Colon. The cocaine was introduced into evidence against him at the trial. He argues that merely knowing that a house is one in which drugs are sold doesn't create probable cause to stop everyone who enters it. That is true in general, Ybarra v. Illinois, 444 U.S. 85, 94-96 (1979), but the police had reason to believe that the man who entered the house was indeed the expected buyer. He arrived when Saucedo told Rodriguez the buyer would arrive, and during the preceding 15 minutes no one else had entered the house from the street (some persons had entered from the porch of the house). So it was more than suspicion or a guess that the man the police seized was a buyer, and so the defendant's challenge to his conviction of possession fails.

His challenge to his conviction of conspiracy and of aiding and abetting a conspiracy has far more substance. The evidence of his guilt of these offenses, as summarized in the government's brief, is that the

> defendant regularly obtained distribution quantities of cocaine from Saucedo and Rodriguez. . . . The dealings between . . . [the defendant and Saucedo, with whom alone the defendant dealt] were standardized and exhibited mutual trust. Saucedo and Rodriguez had a stake in defendant's distribution activities as well as their ongoing arrangement, given that their profits depended on the success of defendant's distribution efforts. . . . [The defendant and Saucedo] conducted regular, standardized transactions through which defendant obtained cocaine in quantities of either 4.5 or 9 ounces at consistent prices, and distributed it to customers. Defendant and Saucedo regularly arranged deliveries by telephone, [with defendant being the caller, using Saucedo's cell-phone number].

The government's summary describes a routine buyer-seller relationship, as in United States v. Mercer, 165 F.3d 1331, 1336 (11th Cir. 1999), where the court remarked that "the evidence shows simply that his co-defendant Miller knew that Mercer sold drugs and that he had sources from which he could get drugs, that Mercer had a source for drugs and if that source failed he would 'go somewhere else,' that he bought quantities of cocaine from some unknown source and sold it to police agents presumably at a profit." The relationship in the present case was "standardized" only in the sense that because seller and buyer dealt regularly with each other, the sales formed a regular pattern, as one would expect in any repeat purchase, legal or illegal. The length of the sales relationship is unclear; it may have been as long as six weeks, but the total number of sales was no more than six or seven, involving a total of 30 to 35 ounces of cocaine.

In any event, how "regular" purchases on "standard" terms can transform a customer into a co-conspirator mystifies us. "[A]greement—the crime of conspiracy—cannot be equated with repeated transactions." United States v. Thomas, 150 F.3d 743, 745 (7th Cir. 1998). The government either is confusing buying with conspiring or believes that a seller and buyer who fail to wrangle over each sale aren't dealing at arms' length and therefore lack mutual trust. But "mutual trust" is already a factor in the conventional analysis of conspiracy; an act that is merely evidence of mutual trust cannot be a separate factor. And anyway repeat transactions need not imply greater mutual trust than is required in any buyer-seller relationship. If you buy from Wal-Mart your transactions will be highly regular and utterly standardized, but there will be no mutual trust suggestive of a relationship other than that of buyer and seller.

It is different if, as in United States v. Sax, 39 F.3d 1380, 1385-86 (7th Cir. 1994), a seller assists his customers in establishing the methods by which they will take delivery from him, for then he is more than just a seller; he is helping to create a distribution system for his illegal product. But the defendant in our case (a buyer, not a seller) did nothing to help Saucedo and Rodriguez establish a delivery system that would enable them to . . . serve him better.

The fact that in his conversations with Rodriguez, Saucedo referred to Colon as "Dude" or "Old Boy," rather than calling him by his name, is not, as the government believes, indicative of intimacy or a pre-existing relationship; it is for obvious reasons a convention in the drug trade not to refer to a customer by his real name. There were no sales on credit to the defendant, or other evidence of mutual trust or dependence, and he had no dealings with—indeed, he never met or spoke to—Rodriguez, Saucedo's unquestioned co-conspirator, although the defendant knew that they worked together. There is no suggestion that the defendant could expect to receive any part of the income that Saucedo obtained from selling cocaine to other customers. There was no "stimulation, instigation," or "encouragement" by the defendant of Saucedo and Rodriguez's business, Direct Sales Co. v. United States, 319 U.S. 703, 713 (1943), no "informed and interested cooperation" between that business and the defendant's retail drug business. Id. In his conversations with Rodriguez, Saucedo referred to the defendant only as a "customer," not as an associate, colleague, pal, or "one of us." The prosecutor in closing argument described the defendant as the conspirators' customer, and its own witnesses denied that Saucedo had ever asked the defendant to sell cocaine for him or Rodriguez.

Of course Saucedo and Rodriguez had, as the government says, "a stake in defendant's distribution activities." Every seller to a distributor has a stake in the distributor's activities; a person who buys for resale will not enrich his seller if his resale business dries up. Saucedo and Rodriguez had other customers; we do not know how many, or what the defendant's volume of purchases was relative to that of other customers.

Cases in this and other circuits list factors such as we have discussed . . . as indicative of participation in a conspiracy. But in every case such factors have to be placed in context before an inference of participation in a conspiracy can be drawn. In United States v. Hicks, 368 F.3d 801, 805 (7th Cir. 2004), for example, we listed a number of these factors but added "prolonged cooperation" between the parties (a quotation from Direct Sales Co. v. United States, supra, 319 U.S. at 713, the Supreme Court's leading case on the difference between a conspiracy and a mere buyer-seller relationship) and "sales on credit," factors that strengthen an inference of participation drawn from observing circumstances also found in a routine buyer-seller relationship. See also United States v. Hawkins, 547 F.3d 66 (2d Cir. 2008).

So the government's theory of conspiracy, when stripped of its redundancies and irrelevancies, reduces to an assertion that a wholesale customer of a conspiracy is a co-conspirator per se. The implication is that during Prohibition a speakeasy was a co-conspirator of the smuggler who provided it with its supply of booze. And the logic of the government's position does not stop with the customer who is a wholesale purchaser rather than a retail one. Had the defendant been purchasing for his personal consumption, he would still have had "regular, standardized" transactions with Saucedo, as in our Wal-Mart example, and Saucedo would have had a stake in whatever activity the defendant engaged in to obtain the money to buy cocaine. There would have been the same level of "mutual trust" as required in any illegal sale because either buyer or seller might be a government informant or turn violent. The mutual trust in this case was less than it would have been had Saucedo "fronted" cocaine to the defendant (a factor mentioned in almost all the cases) rather than being paid in cash at the time of sale. With fronting, the seller becomes the buyer's creditor, adding a dimension to the relationship that goes beyond a spot sale for cash.

There are practical reasons for not conflating sale with conspiracy. "A sale, by definition, requires two parties; their combination for that limited purpose does not increase the likelihood that the sale will take place, so conspiracy liability would be inappropriate." United States v. Townsend, 924 F.2d 1385, 1394 (7th Cir. 1991). As we put it in United States v. Manzella, 791 F.2d 1263, 1265 (7th Cir. 1986), "[a] conspiracy involves more people and can therefore commit more crimes; and it can do so more efficiently, by exploiting the division of labor and by arranging concealment more effectively—sometimes through suborning law enforcers." There is nothing like that here, so far as the defendant's involvement was concerned. And the situation is not altered just because he was a buyer for resale rather than for his personal consumption. As the plurality opinion in United States v. Lechuga, 994 F.2d 346 (7th Cir. 1993) (en banc), explains,

> "before today, it was widely assumed that a conviction for participation in a drug conspiracy could be affirmed with no more evidence than that the defendant had sold in a quantity too large to be intended for his buyer's personal consumption, though some of our cases . . . tugged the other way. Today we resolve the conflict in our cases by holding that large quantities of controlled substances, without more, cannot sustain a conspiracy conviction. What is necessary and sufficient is proof of an agreement to commit a crime other than the crime that consists of the sale itself."

Id. at 347. . . .

. . . This would be a different case . . . had the defendant agreed to look for other customers for Saucedo and Rodriguez, had received a commission on sales to those customers, had advised Saucedo and Rodriguez on the conduct of their business, or had agreed to warn them of threats to their business from competing dealers or from law-enforcement authorities. It would be a different case if "Lechuga [the seller] had told Pinto [the buyer] that he needed a good distributor on the south side of Chicago and wanted to enter into a long-term relationship with Pinto to that end. Then it would be as if Lechuga had hired Pinto to assist him in reaching his market." United States v. Lechuga, supra, 994 F.2d at 349.

. . . But in our case there is no evidence of a relationship other than a conventional sales relationship between the defendant and the conspiracy from which he bought drugs. It is true that after discarding, in his flight from the police, the cocaine he had just bought from Saucedo, the defendant called

Saucedo and told him what had happened. But there is no suggestion that he was warning Saucedo, in order to help the latter evade capture, rather than merely reporting an incident that might affect the defendant's future purchases. A drug runner employed by Saucedo phoned the defendant and told him he'd been stopped by the police after delivering cocaine to him, but that is not evidence of the defendant's participation in a conspiracy either.

The muddle that was the government's theory of the case was mirrored in the jury instructions, which after correctly noting that the defendant's purchase of drugs from another person for resale was insufficient evidence that the defendant had conspired with that person, told the jury to consider whether "the parties had an understanding that the cocaine would be sold" and whether "the transaction involved large quantities of cocaine." If the defendant was a middleman, as he was, the parties would understand that he would be reselling the cocaine; and as a middleman he would be likely to buy in quantities greater than one would buy for one's personal consumption, and therefore "large." The jury was also asked to consider whether the parties had "a standardized way of doing business over time," whether they had "a continuing relationship," "whether the sales were on credit or on consignment," and whether the seller had a "financial steak [*sic*] in a resale by the buyer." Only the question about credit or consignment was germane, for reasons that we've indicated, and that question could only have confused the jury, since all the transactions with the defendant were cash transactions. And the judge made no effort to relate the factors that she told the jury to consider to the difference between a customer and a conspirator. It is no surprise that the jury convicted; given the warped instructions, the conviction does nothing to advance the government's argument that the evidence of conspiracy was sufficient for a reasonable jury to convict.

Nor was the defendant proved to be an aider or abettor of the Saucedo-Rodriguez conspiracy. An aider and abettor is conventionally defined as one who knowingly assists an illegal activity, wanting it to succeed. E.g., United States v. Peoni, 100 F.2d 401, 402 (2d Cir. 1938) (L. Hand, J.). This is a general definition, however, and like most legal generalizations requires qualification in particular cases. Suppose you own and operate a store that sells women's clothing. Every month the same young woman buys a red dress from your store. You happen to know that she's a prostitute and wears the dress to signal her occupation to prospective customers. By selling her the dress at your normal price you assist her illegal activity, and probably you want the activity to succeed since if it fails she'll stop buying the dress and your income will be less. But you are not an aider and abettor of prostitution because if you refused to sell to her she would buy her red dress from another clothing store, one whose proprietor and staff didn't know her profession. See United States v. Falcone, 109 F.2d 579, 581 (2d Cir. 1940) (L. Hand, J.). So you're not *really* helping her or promoting prostitution, as you would be if you recommended customers to her in exchange for a commission.

It is the same here, so far as the record reveals. By buying from Saucedo, the defendant was assisting an illegal activity, which he doubtless wanted to be successful as otherwise he would have to find another seller. If that is enough to establish aiding and abetting, every buyer from a drug conspiracy is an aider and abettor of a conspiracy and is therefore to be treated by the law exactly as a member of the conspiracy would be treated. 18 U.S.C. §2(a). Yet as with the sale of the red dress, there is no basis for thinking that the defendant really helped Saucedo and Rodriguez's drug conspiracy—that he made a difference—because so far as appears they could have found another customer for the modest amount of cocaine that they sold to him.

The government relies on United States v. Kasvin, 757 F.2d 887 (7th Cir. 1985), but omits mention of the part of the opinion that shows how different that case is from this one. Kasvin, the buyer defendant,

> "for several years . . . had visited the headquarters of the conspiracy several times weekly, had been assigned a number just as some of the admitted members of the conspiracy had been assigned, his telephone number had been encoded, on occasion he provided the organization with marijuana for use in its business, his transactions with the conspiracy ran into hundreds of thousands of dollars annually but unlike an ordinary customer of a business, he simply picked up quantities of marijuana from headquarters, presumably disposed of it through a distribution network, and brought the money back from time to time in amounts which, so far as the records show, bore no definite relationship to the amounts of marijuana carried away at any particular time."

Id. at 891. There is nothing like that here. . . .

Even the government has its doubts whether the defendant was a member or an aider and abettor of the Saucedo-Rodriguez conspiracy. A conspirator is liable for the foreseeable crimes that his co-conspirators commit in furtherance of the conspiracy, Pinkerton v. United States, 328 U.S. 640, 646-47 (1946), yet the only drug quantity on which the government sought to base the defendant's sentence was the quantity that Saucedo sold him, though he knew that Saucedo and Rodriguez were selling cocaine to others as well as to him. One is led to wonder why the government added charges of conspiracy and of aiding and abetting to the charge of possession with intent to distribute. The guideline ranges were the same and the additional charges were likely to confuse the jury by making the defendant's conduct seem more ominous than it was. . . .

So probably the additional charges added nothing to the charge of possession with intent to distribute. But maybe the government was concerned that in the (unlikely) event that the evidence obtained when the defendant was caught at Saucedo's house was suppressed, the jury might acquit the defendant of possession or the sentence for possession might be based on a smaller quantity of cocaine and therefore be shorter.

Since the defendant was given concurrent sentences on the two counts, it may seem that reversing the conspiracy and aiding and abetting count

520 Inchoate Crimes and Accomplice Liability

could not alter his sentence. But the district judge sentenced him very near the top of the applicable guideline range, and in doing so may have been influenced by the fact that the jury had found the defendant guilty of conspiracy and aiding and abetting as well as of possession. So while the defendant's conviction of possession stands, he is entitled to be acquitted on the other count and he must therefore be resentenced.

Affirmed in part, vacated in part, and remanded with directions.

Notes on Drug Conspiracies

1. In Abuelhawa v. United States, 556 U.S. 816 (2009), the Supreme Court reached a similar conclusion under 21 U.S.C. §843(b), which makes it a felony crime "for any person knowingly or intentionally to use any communication facility in . . . facilitating the commission of any act or acts constituting a felony" under the Controlled Substances Act. The Court unanimously held that a misdemeanor drug buyer who telephones his dealer does not thereby "facilitate" the dealer's felony of drug distribution, because Congress could not have intended to convert all such misdemeanants into felons.

2. The federal criminal code has two main conspiracy statutes. The general conspiracy statute reads as follows:

> If two or more persons conspire either to commit any offense against the United States, or to defraud the United States, or any agency thereof in any manner or for any purpose, and one or more of such persons do any act to effect the object of the conspiracy, each shall be fined under this title or imprisoned not more than five years, or both.
>
> If, however, the offense, the commission of which is the object of the conspiracy, is a misdemeanor only, the punishment for such conspiracy shall not exceed the maximum punishment provided for such misdemeanor.

18 U.S.C. §371. The statute on drug conspiracies reads:

> Any person who attempts or conspires to commit any offense defined in this title shall be subject to the same penalties as those prescribed for the offense, the commission of which was the object of the attempt or conspiracy.

21 U.S.C. §846. As the aiding and abetting statute, 18 U.S.C. §2, fails to define "aid" or "abet," these conspiracy statutes likewise do not describe the governing doctrine; instead, they use the term that needs definition — "conspire" — without actually defining it.

3. The Model Penal Code defines conspiracy as follows:

> (1) Definition of Conspiracy. A person is guilty of conspiracy with another person or persons to commit a crime if with the purpose of promoting or facilitating its commission he:

(a) agrees with such other person or persons that they or one or more of them will engage in conduct which constitutes such crime or an attempt or solicitation to commit such crime; or

(b) agrees to aid such other person or persons in the planning or commission of such crime or of an attempt or solicitation to commit such crime.

. . .

(3) Conspiracy With Multiple Criminal Objectives. If a person conspires to commit a number of crimes, he is guilty of only one conspiracy so long as such multiple crimes are the object of the same agreement or continuous conspiratorial relationship.

. . .

(5) Overt Act. No person may be convicted of conspiracy to commit a crime, other than a felony of the first or second degree, unless an overt act in pursuance of such conspiracy is alleged and proved to have been done by him or by a person with whom he conspired.

(6) Renunciation of Criminal Purpose. It is an affirmative defense that the actor, after conspiring to commit a crime, thwarted the success of the conspiracy, under circumstances manifesting a complete and voluntary renunciation of his criminal purpose.

MPC §5.03.

Note that the Code's renunciation defense to the crime of conspiracy is the toughest of all the MPC renunciation defenses we have seen in this chapter. Under section 5.03(6), a person who has entered into a conspiracy and then wants out must, in order to earn the defense, actually prevent the other conspirators from committing the intended crime. This is a reflection of the seriousness of the crime of conspiracy; because group criminality is so much more dangerous than crimes committed by individuals, the Code insists that a would-be renouncer must do whatever it takes to thwart the success of the conspiracy.

4. Traditionally, conspiracy has two conduct elements: the criminal agreement, and an overt act in furtherance of the agreement. The overt act may be committed by any one of the conspirators, which means that, as to any particular defendant, the only conduct the government must prove is the agreement. And because the drug conspiracy statute doesn't specifically mention any overt act, the Supreme Court has held that an overt act plays no part in the definition of drug conspiracies under section 846. See United States v. Shabani, 513 U.S. 10 (1994). (It is also no part of the definition of antitrust conspiracies, for the same reason. See Nash v. United States, 229 U.S. 373 (1913).) In theory, conspiracies to distribute drugs are complete at the moment the agreement is reached.

5. That makes conspiracy charges a plausible substitute for criminal attempt charges. In attempt-like conspiracy cases, the presence or absence of the overt act requirement would appear to be crucial—without it, prosecutors might charge conspiracy based on nothing more than an agreement that someone, at some indefinite point in the future, should do something illegal. But such cases almost never happen. Prosecutors usually prove agreement by tying conspirators to completed crimes, which isn't possible if the crimes are incomplete. Conspiracy is not often used to move criminal liability backward in time, as attempt is. Instead, conspiracy plays two different roles. First, it substantially increases the punishment for crimes committed by groups. And second, conspiracy charges are a means by which the government can threaten fringe actors in criminal organizations with severe criminal punishment, in order to induce them to finger their more culpable colleagues.

6. For an example of the first role, see Pinkerton v. United States, 328 U.S. 640 (1946). The defendants in *Pinkerton* were two brothers who ran an illegal distillery, on which they did not pay federal taxes. The government charged one conspiracy count and ten counts of criminal tax evasion. Daniel Pinkerton was in prison when most of the behavior underlying the tax counts happened. Nevertheless, the Supreme Court held, Daniel was properly charged with his brother Walter's crimes: Each conspirator is criminally liable for all crimes committed by co-conspirators, as long as those crimes were in furtherance of the conspiracy — as Walter's tax evasion plainly was.

Because of *Pinkerton* doctrine, the aggregate punishment that may be imposed against co-conspirators is much greater than it would be if they had committed the same array of crimes as individuals.* If the government's theory had been accepted in *Colon*, for example, every regular drug buyer would become liable for all of the seller's drug crimes. What is the rationale for this increased punishment? Why should Daniel Pinkerton be punished for his brother's crimes? Is *Pinkerton* retributively fair? Is it a useful deterrent? What, exactly, does it deter?

Perhaps those are the wrong questions. The questions presuppose that the goal of the law of conspiracy, *Pinkerton* included, is to impose the proper level of punishment on deserving defendants. But that may not be the doctrine's goal. Instead, the primary reason for threatening (though not necessarily imposing) increased punishment may be to induce some conspirators to finger others — that is, conspiracy's second role may explain the first. (See Note 5 above.) If so, rules like the one in *Pinkerton* may be designed to impose too much punishment, not the right amount. The law may be unfair by choice, not by accident. In the law of contract, such rules are called "information-forcing defaults" or, sometimes, "penalty defaults." See, e.g., Ian Ayres & Robert Gertner, Strategic Contractual Inefficiency and the Optimal Choice of Legal Rules, 101 Yale L.J. 729 (1992). The party with privately held information is penalized in later litigation if she holds onto that information, and rewarded if she discloses it at the time of the bargain. So too in conspiracy cases.

---

* *Pinkerton* doctrine applies to conspiracy charges in some states, but a majority of states do not follow the federal rule.

7. The heart of the definition of conspiracy is the crime's *mens rea*. With respect to legal contracts, the precondition for a binding bargain is called a "meeting of the minds." What mental state must the government prove in order to establish that criminal minds have met? The answer comes in two parts: A defendant charged with conspiracy must knowingly enter into the agreement; in addition, the defendant must have "joined in the illegal agreement with the intent of helping it succeed in its criminal purpose." United States v. Svoboda, 347 F.3d 471, 479 (2d Cir. 2003). The second part of the formula explains why, under conventional conspiracy law, there is no such thing as a conspiracy to commit manslaughter: Manslaughter is reckless killing, and conspiracy requires a purpose to bring about the underlying crime. Conspiracy to commit murder is possible; conspiracy to commit lesser forms of homicide isn't.

8. Why wasn't Colon guilty of conspiring to distribute drugs? He appears to have had a long-term supply contract with Saucedo and Rodriguez. That contract was valuable to Colon only as long as Saucedo and Rodriguez remained in business; Colon thus had reason to want his contracting partners to succeed. Why is that insufficient to show membership in a conspiracy? Judge Posner's answer boils down to this: If Colon belongs to a conspiracy to distribute drugs, every regular buyer of drugs belongs to such a conspiracy. The difference between possession and distribution would be obliterated; buyers and sellers alike would be punished as sellers. The same is true, only more so, of accomplice liability. Every purchase aids and abets the sale of drugs: Sellers require a market, which buyers supply. Again, if that principle were given legal effect, buyers and sellers of drugs would be punished similarly.

In *Colon*, that possibility is treated as obviously wrong, perhaps absurd. Is it? Sellers do not create buyers, but buyers do, in essence, create sellers. If demand for illegal drugs disappeared, so would the supply. But if all current sellers were locked up, new sellers would soon take their place as long as willing buyers remained. What is wrong with punishing buyers for aiding and abetting drug distribution, or for conspiring with their suppliers to sell drugs?

9. The defendant in Direct Sales Co. v. United States, 319 U.S. 703 (1943), was a pharmaceutical corporation that sold drugs for medical use to individual doctors. One of those doctors received amounts of morphine greater than could possibly be used for legitimate medical reasons. The Supreme Court upheld the corporation's conspiracy conviction, in part on the ground that the corporation had a "stake in the venture" of the doctor/drug dealer: More sales to the doctor meant more profits for the business. Posner's opinion in *Colon* uses the same idea, noting that if the defendant had received loans or commissions from Saucedo and Rodriguez, the conspiracy charge would be appropriate.

Should the presence of a "stake in the venture" be a necessary condition of membership in a conspiracy to distribute drugs? Recall United States v. Hunte, 196 F.3d 687 (7th Cir. 1999), supra, at page 403. In a portion of the opinion not excerpted above, the court addressed the conspiracy charge against Cheryl Hunte:

> Conspiracy under 21 U.S.C. §846 requires that the Government establish the existence of an agreement between two or more persons "for the purpose of committing, by their joint efforts, a criminal act." United States v. Campbell, 985 F.2d 341, 344 (7th Cir. 1993). The Government must show a "participatory link" between the conspiracy and the defendant. United States v. Navarez, 954 F.2d 1375, 1380-81 (7th Cir. 1992). That link must be established by sufficient evidence demonstrating that the defendant knew of the conspiracy and intended to join its criminal purpose. However, unlike liability for attempt, conspiracy liability does not require evidence of an overt act by the defendant, see United States v. Shabani, 513 U.S. 10, 15 (1994), and the phrase "participatory link" should not be confused in that way. Rather, the link simply provides a way to show that the defendant joined the conspiratorial agreement.
>
> The evidence of Hunte's involvement in the conspiracy is slight. She appeared to have no role in planning the trip or securing any of the things necessary for its completion, such as the vehicles, cash or cohorts. She seemed to have no express understanding with Richards as to her involvement in the plan or share of the proceeds. She had no express responsibilities, did not negotiate the drug transaction and apparently was not needed to handle, weigh or transport the drugs.
>
> However, the jury may consider "overt acts in furtherance of the conspiracy as circumstantial evidence establishing knowing participation in a conspiracy." United States v. Burrell, 963 F.2d 976, 988 (7th Cir. 1992). The evidence shows that Hunte knew of the conspiracy's existence, as she spent several days traveling from New York to Arizona where the group picked up a large load of marijuana, sampled it, hid it in the minivan and returned toward New York. The question is whether she intended to join its criminal purpose, and the bare overt acts committed in furtherance of the conspiracy establish that intent. For instance, a jury could find a participatory link between Hunte and the conspiracy from Hunte's closing the window blinds to hide their activities from view, helping to roll a joint for sampling, registering for the hotel room where the group rested, driving one of the vehicles used for transportation of the co-conspirators and lying to police about their destination and about their association with Warwick and Gonzalez. The fact that she did not expect to share directly in the proceeds of the crime does not defeat a finding of knowing participation. A criminal without a profit motive is still a criminal as long as all elements of the crime are established.

196 F.3d at 691. Unlike Hunte, Colon had "a profit motive"; he resold the drugs he obtained from Saucedo and Rodriguez. Who deserves conspiracy liability more, Hunte or Colon?

10. Notice that the government charged Colon with aiding and abetting a conspiracy to distribute cocaine. Is there anything wrong with that charge? Attempt, solicitation, and conspiracy are called "inchoate" offenses because they impose criminal liability on people who haven't actually completed their intended crimes—based on the fact that they have tried to do so, or asked someone else do so, or agreed to do so. Should there be limits on the government's ability to combine accomplice liability with one or more inchoate crimes? If so, what should those limits be?

In answering that question, consider United States v. Partida, 385 F.3d 546 (5th Cir. 2004). Partida was a police officer working in Donna, Texas; he was also a longtime friend of Rigoberto Quintanilla, a local drug dealer whom the government used as a confidential informant. The rest of the facts were as follows:

With Quintanilla's consent, FBI agents commenced a reverse sting operation centered around Quintanilla, posing as a drug dealer, driving an empty vehicle which Partida was told would be carrying marijuana loads through Donna. Quintanilla would arrange for Partida, while on duty as a Donna police officer, to escort the load vehicle in a marked patrol vehicle to a destination outside the Donna city limits. Once the load vehicle reached the city limits, the patrol car would turn around, and the load vehicle would continue on. At a later point in time, Quintanilla would arrange a location to meet up with Partida and perform payment for the services rendered.

Pursuant to this operation, FBI agents began recording a series of meetings and conversations between Quintanilla and Partida, in which Partida pledged to assist in escorting bulks of marijuana through the city of Donna. In one recorded telephone conversation, Quintanilla and Partida spoke about how Quintanilla would be passing through the area with 300 pounds of marijuana in a red Suburban with tinted windows at "exactly uno." Partida replied, "OK. I'm going to be there."

In a recorded conversation on April 20, 2001, a staged event was arranged for Partida to follow a red Suburban through Donna while Partida was under the belief that he would be protecting the transport of 300 pounds of marijuana. Unbeknown to Partida, the Suburban actually contained no marijuana inside. Government agents provided Quintanilla with the Suburban (which had a video camera specially installed), and instructed Quintanilla to drive from McAllen to a location near the Donna city limits. Once Quintanilla arrived at the location near Donna, FBI agents switched on the camera. As the staged event unfolded, undercover FBI agents videotaped Partida's marked patrol vehicle "bumper locked" to the Suburban for two and a half miles as the Suburban, driven by Quintanilla, slowly drove through the city limit of Donna. Five days later, the two men met at Quintanilla's house, and in a recorded encounter Quintanilla paid Partida $500 for his assistance. As he took the money, Partida commented, "I'm in the wrong business. . . . That [was] the easiest money I ever made. Let's do it again."

As circumstances would have it, another ill fated opportunity arose for Partida to participate in drug trafficking. In May 2001, Quintanilla informed Partida of another "load coming through again." After learning of the time frame for the shipment, Partida responded "I'm there, Dude.". . . [B]y this time Partida had risen to the rank of acting chief of police. Partida's ascendance caused a problem because he no longer drove a marked patrol car. Quintanilla insisted that he needed a marked patrol car to follow the drug shipment in order to limit the risk of "getting the load ripped off" by a rival trafficking organization. Partida had someone in mind, and he discussed with Quintanilla how much Quintanilla would pay Partida and the other officer.

The person Partida had in mind was Donna police officer Vigil. After several phone calls between Quintanilla and Partida, a meeting was finally arranged. On November 7, 2001, Partida and Vigil met with Quintanilla in a videotaped meeting at a hotel in nearby Pharr, Texas. At the behest of government agents, Quintanilla asked Vigil whether Partida forced him to provide escort services to the drug shipment. Vigil responded, "Nah . . . I'm cool with it." Vigil also stated that prior to Partida requesting his services, he planned on asking Partida about the possibility of continuing drug escort activities a second time.

Two days later, on November 9, 2001, a similar "drill" was set up, with Vigil meeting Quintanilla (who was again driving a camera-equipped red Suburban without any drugs) at the southern city limits of Donna. Quintanilla phoned Partida ahead of time to tell him that he had 300 pounds of marijuana, and he later called both Partida and Vigil as he approached the designated meeting point. The operation went off as planned, and was captured on videotape as Quintanilla drove up FM 493 with Vigil following closely behind. Later that day, after the reverse sting operation was completed, Vigil and Quintanilla met again at the Comfort Inn in Pharr, Texas. Quintanilla paid Vigil $700 (he had already received $100 "up front"). Later, Partida arrived at the hotel room, Quintanilla paid him $2,200, and Partida placed the payment in his boot.

385 F.3d at 552-53. Partida was charged with extortion, conspiracy to possess marijuana with intent to distribute that drug, and attempt to aid and abet the possession of marijuana with intent to distribute. Vigil was charged with extortion and conspiracy. Both defendants were convicted of extortion; Partida was also convicted with conspiracy and attempt.

On appeal, Partida argued that attempting to aid and abet drug possession was not a federal crime—because neither the federal accomplice liability statute, 18 U.S.C. §2, nor the drug conspiracy statute, 18 U.S.C. §841, nor the federal statute governing attempts to commit drug crimes, 18 U.S.C. §846, expressly authorizes charges that combine attempt and aiding and abetting. The court acknowledged that point, but held that the charges were permissible, relying on MPC §5.01(3), which reads:

> A person who engages in conduct designed to aid another to commit a crime that would establish his complicity under Section 2.06 if the crime were committed by such other person, is guilty of an attempt to commit the crime, although the crime is not committed or attempted by such other person.

The official commentary to the MPC explains that provision as follows:

> Subsection (3) fills what would otherwise be a gap in complicity liability. Section 2.06 [of the Model Penal Code] covers accomplice liability in situations where the principal actor actually commits the offense, however, it is provided here that the accomplice will be liable if he engaged in conduct that would have established his complicity had the crime been committed.

Model Penal Code and Commentaries (Official Draft and Revised Comments), at 297-98 (1985) (explanatory note to §5.01(3)). Was Partida's conviction fair? Should a defendant be punished for assisting a drug crime that never actually happens?

C. UNDERCOVER DRUG BUYS

Given the secrecy and consensual nature of most illegal drug transactions, often the best (and sometimes the only) way for the government to catch and prosecute drug dealers is by setting up sham deals in which the drug buys (or drug sales) are actually made by undercover officers posing as buyers (or sellers). In many (but not all) such cases, the deals also involve fake rather than real drugs. These undercover operations generate interesting legal issues of inchoate crime liability.

In the first case below, *Freeman*, the defendant sold to an undercover officer two grams of a substance that the defendant believed to be illegal cocaine, but that actually turned out to be perfectly legal acetaminophen; the defendant was charged *not* with attempted possession with intent to distribute cocaine, but instead with violating an Iowa statute that created a new substantive crime for exactly such situations. In the second case, *Ruiz*, the defendant was charged with participating in a conspiracy to possess, with intent to distribute, 70 kilos of cocaine. The drugs were real, but the drug supplier was not; he was, in fact, an undercover agent. The defendant's claim is that the jury instructions prevented her from arguing effectively to the jury that she participated in the conspiracy only because she honestly believed that she was cooperating with a government agent in a way that would benefit her son-in-law's pending criminal case.

State v. Freeman

Supreme Court of Iowa
450 N.W.2d 826 (1990)

McGIVERIN, C.J.

The facts of this case are not disputed. The defendant, Robert Eric Freeman, agreed to sell a controlled substance, cocaine, to Keith Hatcher. Unfortunately for Freeman, Hatcher was cooperating with the government. Hatcher gave Freeman $200, and Freeman gave Hatcher approximately two grams of what was supposed to be cocaine. To everyone's surprise, the "cocaine" turned out to be acetaminophen. Acetaminophen is not a controlled substance.

Freeman was convicted at a bench trial of delivering a simulated controlled substance with respect to a substance represented to be cocaine, in violation of Iowa Code section 204.401(2)(a). The sole question presented by Freeman's appeal is whether he can be convicted of delivering a simulated controlled substance when, in fact, he believed he was delivering and intended to deliver cocaine.

. . . Iowa Code §204.401(2) provides, in relevant part: "It is unlawful for a person to create, deliver, or possess with intent to deliver . . . a simulated controlled substance. . . ." The term "simulated controlled substance" is defined by Iowa Code §204.101(27):

> "Simulated controlled substance" means a substance which is not a controlled substance but which is expressly represented to be a controlled substance, or a substance which is not a controlled substance but which is impliedly represented to be a controlled substance and which because of its nature, packaging, or appearance would lead a reasonable person to believe it to be a controlled substance.

Violation of section 204.401(2) with respect to a simulated controlled substance represented to be cocaine is a class "C" felony. Iowa Code §204.401(2)(a).

Our cases indicate that knowledge of the nature of the substance delivered is an imputed element of section 204.401(1) offenses. See, e.g., State v. Osmundson, 241 N.W.2d 892, 893 (Iowa 1976). Proof of such knowledge has been required to separate those persons who innocently commit the overt acts of the offense from those persons who commit the overt acts of the offense with scienter, or criminal intent. See Osmundson, 241 N.W.2d at 893 ("Scienter is an element of an offense such as this [violation of section 204.401(1)]."). In general, only the latter are criminally responsible for their acts. See Eggman v. Scurr, 311 N.W.2d 77, 78 (Iowa 1981) ("[A] basic premise of criminal liability . . . is that an act alone does not make one guilty unless his mind is also guilty.").

The Iowa Code prohibits delivery of controlled substances and imitation controlled substances, as well as delivery of counterfeit substances, in language nearly identical to that prohibiting delivery of simulated controlled substances. Compare Iowa Code §204.401(1) (prohibiting delivery of controlled substances) and §204.401(2) (prohibiting delivery of counterfeit substances and simulated controlled substances) with §204A.4 (prohibiting delivery of imitation controlled substances). The distinctions between these statutory classifications are not relevant to this case.

Seizing upon the similarity of the statutory prohibitions, Freeman argues that he cannot be convicted of delivering a simulated controlled substance because he mistakenly believed he was delivering and intended to deliver an actual controlled substance.

We disagree. Freeman's construction of section 204.401(2) would convert the offense of delivery of a simulated controlled substance into one requiring *knowing misrepresentation* of the nature of the substance delivered. The statute clearly does not require knowing misrepresentation of the nature of the substance delivered. Reading sections 204.401(2) and 204.101(27) together shows that the gist of this offense is *knowing representation* of a substance to be a controlled substance and delivery of a noncontrolled substance, rather than *knowing misrepresentation* and delivery. As one court explained under similar circumstances, statutes like section 204.401(2) are designed "to discourage anyone from engaging or appearing to engage in the narcotics traffic rather than to define the contractual rights of the pusher and his victim. . . ." People v. Ernst, 48 Cal. App. 3d 785, 791, 121 Cal. Rptr. 857, 861 (1975); see also State v. Marsh, 684 P.2d 459 (Kan. 1984) (statute prohibiting fraudulent delivery of noncontrolled substance does not require proof of specific intent to deliver noncontrolled substance; fact that defendant believed the substance he delivered was controlled is no defense).

Freeman's mistaken belief regarding the substance he delivered cannot save him from conviction. Mistake of fact is a defense to a crime of scienter or criminal intent only where the mistake precludes the existence of the mental state necessary to commit the crime. See, e.g., 21 Am. Jur. 2d Criminal Law §141 (1981) ("At common law an honest and reasonable belief in the existence of circumstances which, if true, *would have made the act done innocent,* is a good defense.") (emphasis added); Model Penal Code §2.04(2) (1962) ("Although ignorance or mistake would otherwise afford a defense to the offense charged, the defense is not available if the defendant would be guilty of another offense had the situation been as he supposed."). In this case, Freeman would not be innocent of wrongdoing had the situation been as he supposed; rather, he would be guilty of delivering a controlled substance. His mistake is no defense. The scienter required to hold him criminally responsible for committing the overt acts of the charged offense is present regardless of the mistake. Freeman knowingly represented to Hatcher that the substance he delivered was cocaine.

In conclusion, we hold that a person who delivers a substance that is not a controlled substance, but who knowingly represents the substance to be a controlled substance, commits the offense of delivery of a simulated controlled substance regardless of whether the person believed that the substance was controlled or not controlled.

Delivery of a simulated controlled substance is not a consumer fraud offense. Freeman attempted and intended to sell cocaine. The fact that Freeman was fooled as much as his customer is no defense to the charge in this case.

Affirmed.

United States v. Ruiz

United States Court of Appeals for the Eleventh Circuit
59 F.3d 1151 (1995)

DYER, Senior Circuit Judge.

The government indicted Ana Ruiz, Jose Aviles, and William Perez for conspiracy to possess with intent to distribute more than five kilograms of cocaine, in violation of 21 U.S.C. §846. This appeal followed the jury's guilty verdict as to all three defendants.[1] We find no merit in the arguments presented by Aviles and Perez, and affirm their convictions without opinion. Ruiz asserts the district court erroneously refused her jury instruction on a mistake of fact defense. We agree and reverse her conviction.

At trial the government presented evidence showing that Appellant Ruiz brokered the sale of seventy kilograms of cocaine by helping to arrange the ultimate meeting between the purchaser, Angel Santana, and the supplier, an undercover agent. Testimony revealed the following facts pertinent to this appeal.

On June 9, 1992, an undercover United States Customs agent, Victor Thompson, received a telephone call from a Colombian informant advising him to expect a beeper page from another man in Colombia named "Frank."[3] Frank contacted Agent Thompson shortly thereafter about purchasing seventy kilograms of cocaine that Thompson had "smuggled" to Tampa, Florida. . . . Frank said he would have his United States representative call Thompson within a few days. Frank indicated the contact person would either be Roke Julio (a/k/a Angel Santana) or a woman named "Lamento" (a/k/a Ana Ruiz). Appellant Ruiz asserts, and the government does not deny, that Angel Santana was the ultimate purchaser of the cocaine.

After several telephone calls to Chicago and Miami, Agent Thompson spoke with Santana. The parties agreed to meet on June 15, 1992 at a Circle K convenience store on Bayshore Boulevard in Tampa. . . . After the initial introductions Santana said he needed to take his family to a friend's house and that he would be right back to discuss the details of the buy. Thompson saw Santana enter a white, late-model Pontiac with two females and two children, who he later learned were Ana Ruiz, her

---

1. Charged also were Ana Ruiz' daughter, Alba Ruiz, and Angel Santana. The district court severed Santana's case prior to trial due to antagonistic defenses, and granted Alba Ruiz a judgment of acquittal at the close of the government's case.

3. "Frank" was Frank Burns, the husband of co-defendant Alba Ruiz and son-in-law of Appellant Ana Ruiz.

daughter and two grandchildren. . . . Santana did not return to the Circle K that day.

Three days later Ana Ruiz called Agent Thompson using the code name of "Lamento." She told Thompson she worked for "Roke Julio" and wanted to meet with him to negotiate the purchase of the seventy kilos. After several calls back and forth, Ana Ruiz and her daughter met Thompson on Franklin Street in Tampa on June 22nd. From there Thompson had the women follow him to his warehouse, an undercover site, to discuss the transaction. At the warehouse, Thompson told them that he was in fact a drug dealer, that he conducted his deals at the warehouse, and that he had received 250 kilos in his last transaction. They discussed some details of the pending buy, including the price of $13,000 per kilo.

After several days of negotiations between Appellant Ruiz and Agent Thompson about how and where to complete the transaction, the controlled delivery of cocaine took place on July 1, 1992 at the undercover site. Thompson met Ana Ruiz and Alba Ruiz in front of a Chili's restaurant. Co-defendants Perez and Aviles were present, driving an Oldsmobile and a Nissan minivan to consummate the deal. Ana Ruiz, Perez, and Aviles followed Thompson to the warehouse. On arrival Aviles accessed $300,000 from a false compartment in the Oldsmobile. Perez and Aviles then sampled the cocaine, and Aviles loaded it into a false compartment of the minivan. At this point the three defendants were arrested. Alba Ruiz was arrested a short while later as she waited at Chili's for her mother to return. Later that same day Angel Santana was arrested after having fled Tampa for his home in Miami.

Ana Ruiz testified at trial that she became involved in this drug deal to help her son-in-law, Frank Burns, resolve a pending federal drug charge so that he could return to his family in the United States.[4] Ruiz said she believed Santana was working as a government informant based on his statements to her. She testified she thought she was also assisting the government as an informant and, therefore, not committing a crime. Ruiz did not receive compensation for her involvement.[7] Aviles similarly testified that Santana told him that he (Santana) was working with the "federals."

At the close of all the evidence, Ruiz requested that the jury be instructed on a mistake of fact defense to better define the pattern instruction on the

---

4. Burns was arrested by an FBI special agent on March 27, 1991. After Burns was released on bond, he fled to Colombia and became a fugitive from justice.

7. She testified that the only benefit to her participation was "the credit that Frank Burns was [to be] able to come to this country because Angel Santana was going to report immediately [to] these people that that was Frank's credit. Therefore, the government will reduce a little his punishment and he could return to this country." She stated this made sense to her because Burns had been arrested for only six kilos of cocaine and a seventy kilo deal would certainly weigh heavily in his favor to return to the United States.

term "willfully."[8] The district court denied the instruction, stating that her theory was not a defense to the indictment and not justified by the facts. The jury returned a guilty verdict. . . . This appeal ensued.

. . . A trial court may not refuse to charge the jury on a . . . defense theory where the proposed instruction presents a valid defense and where there has been some evidence adduced at trial relevant to that defense. United States v. Middleton, 690 F.2d 820, 826 (11th Cir. 1982). The trial court is not free to determine the existence of such a defense as a matter of law. The threshold burden is extremely low: "The defendant . . . is entitled to have presented instructions relating to a theory of defense for which there is *any foundation* in the evidence." Perez v. United States, 297 F.2d 12, 15-16 (5th Cir. 1961) (emphasis added). . . .

Ruiz testified in her own behalf to prove her belief that she was assisting the government through Santana, who was, as far as she knew, also a government informant. She thus met the evidentiary burden. . . .

This Court has recognized that a defendant who thought he was performing legitimate law enforcement activities may lack the necessary criminal intent where he reasonably believed he acted in cooperation with the government. United States v. Juan, 776 F.2d 256 (11th Cir. 1985). Moreover, we have acknowledged that a defendant's "mistake of fact" may negate criminal intent, if believed by a jury properly instructed on the law, where the defendant did in fact engage in the conduct giving rise to the charged

---

8. The court ruled that guidance on "willful conduct" was all that was required by law and gave the following instruction:

> The word "willfully" as that term has been used from time to time in these instructions, means that the act was committed voluntarily and purposely, with the specific intent to do something the law forbids; that is with bad purpose either to disobey or disregard the law.

Ruiz requested the following supplemental instruction:

> An honest mistake of fact is a complete defense to the charge in the indictment because it is inconsistent with the existence of willfulness, which is an essential part of the charge. Such an honest mistake negates the criminal intent of a defendant when the defendant's acts would be lawful, if the facts were as she supposed them to be. . . . A defendant whose actions are based on her honest belief that she was acting lawfully is not chargeable with willful criminal conduct—even if her belief was erroneous or mistaken.

Alternatively, Ruiz requested that the court insert the following instruction after the instruction on "willfully":

> If you have a reasonable doubt as to whether the defendant acted in good faith, sincerely believing herself to be assisting the government, then she did not intentionally violate a known legal duty; that is she did not act "willfully," and that essential part of the offense would not be established.

offense. See United States v. Vicaria, 12 F.3d 195, 198-99 (11th Cir. 1994). We have reviewed the proposed instructions and conclude [that] either one is a substantially correct statement of the law that should have been given in some form.

The defense theory was not substantially covered by the instruction on "willfully," an element of the charged offense. The jury could have been misled by [that instruction, because] Ruiz . . . admitted to willfully participating in the drug deal to facilitate her son-in-law's return to the United States. The pattern instruction did not focus on the contention that criminal intent was negated by the defendant's honest but mistaken belief that the government, acting through Santana, had authorized the drug transaction. See *Vicaria*, 12 F.3d at 198-99. The pattern instruction as given failed to recognize that a series of unlawful acts may be intentionally, willfully, purposefully, and voluntarily committed without *criminal intent*. . . .

. . . Ruiz' beliefs were critical to her [theory of the case]. With no instruction on the legal effect of the erroneous belief that she was acting lawfully, in light of her admission[s] . . . , the jury was left with no legitimate and lawful alternative explanation for her conduct.

. . . Accordingly, we reverse and remand the case for a new trial.

Notes and Questions

1. Under *McElroy* or *Acosta*, Freeman would have been convicted of attempting to possess or distribute cocaine. But Iowa's statute on simulated controlled substances makes conviction easier. Is the statute fair? Should it be applied only to undercover drug sales like the one in *Freeman*, or should it also apply to mistakes like the one in *McElroy*?

2. Drug law is all about proxies: Possession serves as a proxy for purchase; possession of more-than-user-quantity is a proxy for sale; acetaminophen is sometimes a proxy for cocaine, as it was in *Freeman*. And the sham drug transactions in *Ruiz* are proxies for the many real drug transactions in which the defendants undoubtedly engaged outside the view of federal agents.

3. Because drug sales do happen outside the view of the police, undercover agents are a necessary means of enforcing the drug laws. Is the end worth the means? Because undercover agents and confidential informants are so widely used, the selection of drug defendants is very different than the choice of defendants charged with other crimes. When police officers investigate homicides, rapes, robberies, or burglaries, criminals decide where police resources are used: Officers go wherever the crimes happen. Drug enforcement is different. Drug crimes happen everywhere, so whom the police catch depends upon where they look—and where they look is almost entirely up to them. When informants and undercover agents are involved, the police select not only the places to investigate, but the individual suspects as well. Does that give too much power to law enforcers? On the other hand, can there be anything wrong with punishing defendants who participate in the sale of 70 kilograms of cocaine, as in *Ruiz*?

8

Gun Crimes

Most first-year criminal law casebooks do not include a chapter on gun crimes. That is a bit strange. The number of gun crimes in the United States each year is quite large—in 2015, almost 150,000 persons were arrested for illegal weapons possession. Moreover, that number does *not* include those arrested for some other crime who also happen to be carrying a gun. Many crimes involve the use, or at least the possession (and therefore the threatened or potential use), of guns. The Bureau of Justice Statistics estimates that about half of all robberies, a quarter of all assaults, and one-twelfth of all rapes and sexual assaults, are committed by an assailant who is armed. Surely most drug sellers also are armed, if only to help protect the merchandise. In many such instances, the presence of the gun will lead to enhanced criminal charges or enhanced penalties.

We have already encountered a number of cases involving gun crimes. Think back to *Marrero* (at page 157), involving state-law permits to carry a handgun; *Lopez* (at page 246), involving the federal crime of gun possession in a school zone; *Staples* (at page 262), involving mandatory federal registration of machine guns; and *Bryan* (at page 276), involving federal licensing requirements for gun sellers.

As we have seen with drug crimes, both the states and the federal government are deeply involved in the investigation and prosecution of gun crimes. The U.S. Code includes a relatively comprehensive set of firearm regulations that (1) prohibits the private ownership of some extremely dangerous weapons altogether (such as sawed-off shotguns with barrels shorter than 18 inches); (2) requires the registration of some firearms, as well as imposing various procedural requirements (such as background checks) for some firearm sales; (3) prohibits certain persons (including felons and those convicted of certain domestic assaults) from possessing firearms; (4) prohibits the transfer of firearms to a juvenile; and (5) provides for increased sentences for the use or possession of a gun in connection with some federal crimes (such as drug felonies or violent crimes). State firearm laws vary widely, but often include restrictions on the possession, method of carrying (i.e., concealed or open), possession in some locations (such as in some government buildings), discharge under some circumstances (such as within city limits unless in self-defense), and use or possession of a gun in connection with some other crimes. States also frequently impose their own registration and permit requirements, which can be quite complicated.

One key difference between gun crimes and the other kinds of crimes we have studied thus far is that gun crimes trigger (sorry!) a special constitutional concern. The Second Amendment to the U.S. Constitution provides: "A well-regulated Militia, being necessary to the security of a free State, the right of the people to keep and bear Arms, shall not be infringed." For more than 200 years, the application of the Second Amendment to private citizens not serving in an official "state militia" was unclear. Then, in District of Columbia v. Heller, 554 U.S. 570 (2008), the U.S. Supreme Court held that the Second Amendment *does* protect the gun rights of private citizens—at least in connection with "common" firearms that can be used for traditionally lawful purposes, such as self-defense. And in McDonald v. City of Chicago, 561 U.S. 742 (2010), the Court decided that the Second Amendment (which, like the rest of the Bill of Rights, originally was enacted *solely* to limit the powers of the then newly created federal government) is a "fundamental" right that limits the powers of state governments as well. In short, it is now clear that the Second Amendment can affect judicial decisions about the scope (sorry!) of many gun crimes.

This chapter is divided into two sections. Section A deals with "stand-alone" gun crimes—meaning gun crimes (based on various kinds of conduct, including possession, failure to register, public display, use, and discharge) that can be prosecuted independently of any other crime that the defendant might be committing at the same time. Section B is about gun "enhancements"—meaning statutes that bump up an underlying criminal charge, or that increase the defendant's sentence, based on the involvement of a gun in connection with the commission of another crime. As you will see, each category of gun crime raises its own interesting set of issues. Keep in mind that this chapter is not meant to be a comprehensive survey of gun crimes or the legal issues they present; that would require a separate book. Here, our aim (sorry!) is only to introduce the subject.

A. STAND-ALONE GUN CRIMES

Voisine v. United States

Supreme Court of the United States
579 U.S. ___ (2016)

Justice KAGAN delivered the opinion of the Court.

Federal law prohibits any person convicted of a "misdemeanor crime of domestic violence" from possessing a firearm. 18 U.S.C. §922(g)(9). That phrase is defined to include any misdemeanor committed against a domestic relation that necessarily involves the "use . . . of physical force." §921(a)(33)(A). The question presented here is whether misdemeanor assault convictions for reckless (as contrasted to knowing or intentional) conduct trigger the statutory firearms ban. We hold that they do.

I

Congress enacted §922(g)(9) some 20 years ago to "close [a] dangerous loophole" in the gun control laws. United States v. Castleman, 572 U.S. ___, ___ (2014) (quoting United States v. Hayes, 555 U.S. 415, 426 (2009)). An existing provision already barred convicted felons from possessing firearms. See §922(g)(1). But many perpetrators of domestic violence are charged with misdemeanors rather than felonies, notwithstanding the harmfulness of their conduct. And "[f]irearms and domestic strife are a potentially deadly combination." Hayes, 555 U.S., at 427. Accordingly, Congress added §922(g)(9) to prohibit any person convicted of a "misdemeanor crime of domestic violence" from possessing any gun or ammunition with a connection to interstate commerce. And it defined that phrase, in §921(a)(33)(A), to include a misdemeanor under federal, state, or tribal law, committed by a person with a specified domestic relationship with the victim, that "has, as an element, the use or attempted use of physical force."

Two Terms ago, this Court considered the scope of that definition in a case involving a conviction for a knowing or intentional assault. See Castleman, 572 U.S., at ___-___. In Castleman, we initially held that the word "force" in §921(a)(33)(A) bears its common-law meaning, and so is broad enough to include offensive touching. We then determined that "the knowing or intentional application of [such] force is a 'use' of force." But we expressly left open whether a reckless assault also qualifies as a "use" of force—so that a misdemeanor conviction for such conduct would trigger §922(g)(9)'s firearms ban. The two cases before us now* raise that issue.

---

* [Voisine was decided together with the companion case of Armstrong v. United States.—EDS.]

Petitioner Stephen Voisine pleaded guilty in 2004 to assaulting his girlfriend in violation of §207 of the Maine Criminal Code, which makes it a misdemeanor to "intentionally, knowingly or recklessly cause[ ] bodily injury or offensive physical contact to another person." Me. Rev. Stat. Ann., Tit. 17-A, §207(1)(A). Several years later, Voisine again found himself in legal trouble, this time for killing a bald eagle. See 16 U.S.C. §668(a). While investigating that crime, law enforcement officers learned that Voisine owned a rifle. When a background check turned up his prior misdemeanor conviction, the Government charged him with violating 18 U.S.C. §922(g)(9).[1]

Petitioner William Armstrong pleaded guilty in 2008 to assaulting his wife in violation of a Maine domestic violence law making it a misdemeanor to commit an assault prohibited by §207 (the general statute under which Voisine was convicted) against a family or household member. See Me. Rev. Stat. Ann., Tit. 17-A, §207-A(1)(A). A few years later, law enforcement officers searched Armstrong's home as part of a narcotics investigation. They discovered six guns, plus a large quantity of ammunition. Like Voisine, Armstrong was charged under §922(g)(9) for unlawfully possessing firearms.

Both men argued that they were not subject to §922(g)(9)'s prohibition because their prior convictions (as the Government conceded) could have been based on reckless, rather than knowing or intentional, conduct. The District Court rejected those claims. Each petitioner then entered a guilty plea conditioned on the right to appeal the District Court's ruling.

The Court of Appeals for the First Circuit affirmed the two convictions. . . . Voisine and Armstrong filed a joint petition for certiorari, and shortly after issuing *Castleman*, this Court (without opinion) vacated the First Circuit's judgments and remanded the cases for further consideration in light of that decision. On remand, the Court of Appeals again upheld the convictions. . . . We granted certiorari to resolve a Circuit split over whether a misdemeanor conviction for recklessly assaulting a domestic relation disqualifies an individual from possessing a gun under §922(g)(9). We now affirm.

II

The issue before us is whether §922(g)(9) applies to reckless assaults, as it does to knowing or intentional ones. To commit an assault recklessly is to take that action with a certain state of mind (or *mens rea*) — in the dominant

---

1. In United States v. Hayes, 555 U.S. 415, 418 (2009), this Court held that a conviction under a general assault statute like §207 (no less than one under a law targeting only domestic assault) can serve as the predicate offense for a §922(g)(9) prosecution. When that is so, the Government must prove in the later, gun possession case that the perpetrator and the victim of the assault had one of the domestic relationships specified in §921(a)(33)(A). See id., at 426.

formulation, to "consciously disregard[ ]" a substantial risk that the conduct will cause harm to another. ALI, Model Penal Code §2.02(2)(c); Me. Rev. Stat. Ann., Tit. 17-A, §35(3) (adopting that definition); see Farmer v. Brennan, 511 U.S. 825-837 (1994) (noting that a person acts recklessly only when he disregards a substantial risk of harm "of which he is aware"). For purposes of comparison, to commit an assault knowingly or intentionally (the latter, to add yet another adverb, sometimes called "purposefully") is to act with another state of mind respecting that act's consequences—in the first case, to be "aware that [harm] is practically certain" and, in the second, to have that result as a "conscious object." Model Penal Code §§2.02 (2)(a)-(b); Me. Rev. Stat. Ann., Tit. 17-A, §§35(1)-(2).

Statutory text and background alike lead us to conclude that a reckless domestic assault qualifies as a "misdemeanor crime of domestic violence" under §922(g)(9). Congress defined that phrase to include crimes that necessarily involve the "use . . . of physical force." §921(a)(33)(A). Reckless assaults, no less than the knowing or intentional ones we addressed in *Castleman*, satisfy that definition. Further, Congress enacted §922(g)(9) in order to prohibit domestic abusers convicted under run-of-the-mill misdemeanor assault and battery laws from possessing guns. Because fully two-thirds of such state laws extend to recklessness, construing §922(g)(9) to exclude crimes committed with that state of mind would substantially undermine the provision's design.

A

Nothing in the word "use"—which is the only statutory language either party thinks relevant—indicates that §922(g)(9) applies exclusively to knowing or intentional domestic assaults. Recall that under §921(a)(33)(A), an offense counts as a "misdemeanor crime of domestic violence" only if it has, as an element, the "use" of force. Dictionaries consistently define the noun "use" to mean the "act of employing" something. Webster's New International Dictionary 2806 (2d ed. 1954) ("[a]ct of employing anything"); Random House Dictionary of the English Language 2097 (2d ed. 1987) ("act of employing, using, or putting into service"); Black's Law Dictionary 1541 (6th ed. 1990) ("[a]ct of employing," "application"). On that common understanding, the force involved in a qualifying assault must be volitional; an involuntary motion, even a powerful one, is not naturally described as an active employment of force. See *Castleman*, 572 U.S., at ___ ("[T]he word 'use' conveys the idea that the thing used (here, 'physical force') has been made the user's instrument" (some internal quotation marks omitted)). But the word "use" does not demand that the person applying force have the purpose or practical certainty that it will cause harm, as compared with the understanding that it is substantially likely to do so. Or, otherwise said, that word is indifferent as to whether the actor has the mental state of intention, knowledge, or recklessness with respect to the harmful consequences of his volitional conduct.

Consider a couple of examples to see the ordinary meaning of the word "use" in this context. If a person with soapy hands loses his grip on a plate, which then shatters and cuts his wife, the person has not "use[d]" physical force in common parlance. But now suppose a person throws a plate in anger against the wall near where his wife is standing. That hurl counts as a "use" of force even if the husband did not know for certain (or have as an object), but only recognized a substantial risk, that a shard from the plate would ricochet and injure his wife. Similarly, to spin out a scenario discussed at oral argument, if a person lets slip a door that he is trying to hold open for his girlfriend, he has not actively employed ("used") force even though the result is to hurt her. But if he slams the door shut with his girlfriend following close behind, then he has done so—regardless of whether he thinks it absolutely sure or only quite likely that he will catch her fingers in the jamb. Once again, the word "use" does not exclude from §922(g)(9)'s compass an act of force carried out in conscious disregard of its substantial risk of causing harm. . . .

In sum, Congress's definition of a "misdemeanor crime of violence" contains no exclusion for convictions based on reckless behavior. A person who assaults another recklessly "use[s]" force, no less than one who carries out that same action knowingly or intentionally. The relevant text thus supports prohibiting petitioners, and others with similar criminal records, from possessing firearms.

B

So too does the relevant history. As explained earlier, Congress enacted §922(g)(9) in 1996 to bar those domestic abusers convicted of garden-variety assault or battery misdemeanors—just like those convicted of felonies—from owning guns. See *Castleman*, 572 U.S., at ___, ___; *Hayes*, 555 U.S., at 426-427. Then, as now, a significant majority of jurisdictions—34 States plus the District of Columbia—defined such misdemeanor offenses to include the reckless infliction of bodily harm. See Brief for United States 7a-19a (collecting statutes). That agreement was no coincidence. Several decades earlier, the Model Penal Code had taken the position that a *mens rea* of recklessness should generally suffice to establish criminal liability, including for assault. See §2.02(3), Comments 4-5, at 243-244 ("purpose, knowledge, and recklessness are properly the basis for" such liability); §211.1 (defining assault to include "purposely, knowingly, or recklessly caus[ing] bodily injury"). States quickly incorporated that view into their misdemeanor assault and battery statutes. So in linking §922(g)(9) to those laws, Congress must have known it was sweeping in some persons who had engaged in reckless conduct. See, e.g., United States v. Bailey, 9 Pet. 238, 256 (1835) (Story, J.) ("Congress must be presumed to have legislated under this known state of the laws"). And indeed, that was part of the point: to apply firearms restrictions to those abusers, along with all others, whom the States' ordinary misdemeanor assault laws covered.

What is more, petitioners' reading risks rendering §922(g)(9) broadly inoperative in the 35 jurisdictions with assault laws extending to recklessness—that is, inapplicable even to persons who commit that crime knowingly or intentionally. Consider Maine's statute, which (in typical fashion) makes it a misdemeanor to "intentionally, knowingly or recklessly" injure another. Me. Rev. Stat. Ann., Tit. 17-A, §207(1)(A). Assuming that provision defines a single crime (which happens to list alternative mental states)—and accepting petitioners' view that §921(a)(33)(A) requires at least a knowing *mens rea*—then, under Descamps v. United States, 570 U.S. ___ (2013), *no* conviction obtained under Maine's statute could qualify as a "misdemeanor crime of domestic violence." See id., at ___ (If a state crime "sweeps more broadly" than the federally defined one, a conviction for the state offense "cannot count" as a predicate, no matter what *mens rea* the defendant actually had). So in the 35 jurisdictions like Maine, petitioners' reading risks allowing domestic abusers of all mental states to evade §922(g)(9)'s firearms ban. . . .*

Petitioners respond that we should ignore the assault and battery laws actually on the books when Congress enacted §922(g)(9). In construing the statute, they urge, we should look instead to how the common law defined those crimes in an earlier age. And that approach, petitioners claim, would necessitate reversing their convictions because the common law "required a *mens rea* greater than recklessness."

But we see no reason to wind the clock back so far. Once again: Congress passed §922(g)(9) to take guns out of the hands of abusers convicted under the misdemeanor assault laws then in general use in the States. And by that time, a substantial majority of jurisdictions, following the Model Penal Code's lead, had abandoned the common law's approach to *mens rea* in drafting and interpreting their assault and battery statutes. Indeed, most had gone down that road decades before. That was the backdrop against which Congress was legislating. Nothing suggests that, in enacting §922(g)(9), Congress wished to look beyond that real world to a common-law precursor that had largely expired. To the contrary, such an approach would have undermined Congress's aim by tying the ban on firearms possession not to the laws under which abusers are prosecuted but instead to a legal anachronism.

---

* [The procedural problem to which the Court is alluding here is that criminal charging documents generally don't have to specify which particular term, in a list of terms that define a particular element of a crime, the defendant's behavior satisfied. And juries almost always issue general verdicts—meaning that there's also no good way to tell which particular term the jury found to be satisfied.—Eds.]

And anyway, we would not know how to resolve whether recklessness suf-ficed for a battery conviction at common law. Recklessness was not a word in the common law's standard lexicon, nor an idea in its conceptual frame-work; only in the mid- to late-1800's did courts begin to address reckless behavior in those terms. See Jerome Hall, Assault and Battery by the Reckless Motorist, 31 J. Crim. L. & C. 133, 138-139 (1940). The common law tradition-ally used a variety of overlapping and, frankly, confusing phrases to describe culpable mental states—among them, specific intent, general intent, pre-sumed intent, willfulness, and malice. See, e.g., Morissette v. United States, 342 U.S. 246, 252 (1952); Model Penal Code §2.02, Comment 1, at 230. Whether and where conduct that we would today describe as reckless fits into that obscure scheme is anyone's guess: Neither petitioners' citations, nor the Government's competing ones, have succeeded in resolving that counterfactual question. And that indeterminacy confirms our conclusion that Congress had no thought of incorporating the common law's treatment of *mens rea* into §921(a)(33)(A). That provision instead corresponds to the ordinary misdemeanor assault and battery laws used to prosecute domestic abuse, regardless of how their mental state requirements might—or, then again, might not—conform to the common law's.[6]

III

The federal ban on firearms possession applies to any person with a prior misdemeanor conviction for the "use . . . of physical force" against a domes-tic relation. §921(a)(33)(A). That language, naturally read, encompasses acts of force undertaken recklessly—i.e., with conscious disregard of a sub-stantial risk of harm. And the state-law backdrop to that provision, which included misdemeanor assault statutes covering reckless conduct in a sig-nificant majority of jurisdictions, indicates that Congress meant just what it said. Each petitioner's possession of a gun, following a conviction under Maine law for abusing a domestic partner, therefore violates §922(g)(9). We accordingly affirm the judgment of the Court of Appeals.

Justice THOMAS, with whom Justice SOTOMAYOR joins as to Parts I and II, dissenting.

Federal law makes it a crime for anyone previously convicted of a "mis-demeanor crime of domestic violence" to possess a firearm "in or affecting

---

6. Petitioners make two last arguments for reading §921(a)(33)(A) their way, but they do not persuade us. First, petitioners contend that we should adopt their construction to avoid creating a question about whether the Second Amendment permits imposing a life-time firearms ban on a person convicted of a misdemeanor involving reckless conduct. And second, petitioners assert that the rule of lenity requires accepting their view. But neither of those arguments can succeed if the statute is clear. . . . And as we have shown, §921(a)(33)(A) plainly encompasses reckless assaults.

commerce." 18 U.S.C. §922(g)(9). A "misdemeanor crime of domestic violence" includes "an offense that . . . has, as an element, the use or attempted use of physical force . . . committed by [certain close family members] of the victim." §921(a)(33)(A)(ii). In this case, petitioners were convicted under §922(g)(9) because they possessed firearms and had prior convictions for assault under Maine's statute prohibiting "intentionally, knowingly or recklessly caus[ing] bodily injury or offensive physical contact to another person." Me. Rev. Stat. Ann., Tit. 17-A, §207(1)(A) (2006). The question presented is whether a prior conviction under §207 has, as an element, the "use of physical force," such that the conviction can strip someone of his right to possess a firearm. In my view, §207 does not qualify as such an offense, and the majority errs in holding otherwise. I respectfully dissent.

I

. . . The Maine statute appears to lack, as a required element, the "use or attempted use of physical force." Maine's statute punishes at least some conduct that does not involve the "use of physical force." Section 207 criminalizes "recklessly caus[ing] bodily injury or offensive physical contact to another person." By criminalizing all reckless conduct, the Maine statute captures conduct such as recklessly injuring a passenger by texting while driving resulting in a crash. Petitioners' charging documents generically recited the statutory language; they did not charge intentional, knowing, and reckless harm as alternative counts. Accordingly, Maine's statute appears to treat "intentionally, knowingly, or recklessly" causing bodily injury or an offensive touching as a single, indivisible offense that is satisfied by recklessness. So petitioners' prior assault convictions do not necessarily have as an element the use of physical force against a family member. These prior convictions, therefore, do not qualify as a misdemeanor crime involving domestic violence under federal law, and petitioners' convictions accordingly should be reversed. At the very least, to the extent there remains uncertainty over whether Maine's assault statute is divisible, the Court should vacate and remand for the First Circuit to determine that statutory interpretation question in the first instance.

II

To illustrate where I part ways with the majority, consider different mental states with which a person could create and apply force. First, a person can create force intentionally or recklessly.[3] For example, a person can intentionally throw a punch or a person can crash his car by driving recklessly.

---

3. To simplify, I am using only those mental states relevant to the Court's resolution of this case. A person could also create a force negligently or blamelessly.

Second, a person can intentionally or recklessly harm a particular person or object as a result of that force. For example, a person could throw a punch at a particular person (thereby intentionally applying force to that person) or a person could swing a baseball bat too close to someone (thereby recklessly applying force to that person).

These different mental states give rise to three relevant categories of conduct. A person might intentionally create force and intentionally apply that force against an object (*e.g.,* punching a punching bag). A person might also intentionally create force but recklessly apply that force against an object (*e.g.,* practicing a kick in the air, but recklessly hitting a piece of furniture). Or a person could recklessly create force that results in damage, such as the car crash example.

The question before us is what mental state suffices for a "use of physical force" against a family member. In my view, a "use of physical force" most naturally refers to cases where a person intentionally creates force and intentionally applies that force against a family member. It also includes (at least some) cases where a person intentionally creates force but recklessly applies it to a family member. But I part ways with the majority's conclusion that purely reckless conduct—meaning, where a person recklessly creates force—constitutes a "use of physical force." In my view, it does not, and therefore, the "use of physical force" is narrower than most state assault statutes, which punish anyone who recklessly causes physical injury.

A

To identify the scope of the "use of physical force," consider three different types of intentional and reckless force resulting in physical injury.

1

The paradigmatic case of battery: A person intentionally unleashes force and intends that the force will harm a particular person. This might include, for example, punching or kicking someone. Both the majority and I agree that these cases constitute a "use of physical force" under §921(a)(33)(A)(ii).

This first category includes all cases where a person intentionally creates force and desires or knows with a practical certainty that that force will cause harm. This is because the law traditionally treats conduct as intended in two circumstances. First, conduct is intentional when the actor desires to produce a specific result. 1 W. LaFave, Substantive Criminal Law §5.2(a), pp. 340-342 (2d ed. 2003). But conduct is also traditionally deemed intentional when a person acts "knowingly": that is, he knows with practical certainty that a result will follow from his conduct. Ibid.; see also Restatement (Second) of Torts §8A, Comment *b*, at 15 ("If the actor knows that the consequences are certain, or substantially certain, to result from his act, and still goes ahead, he is treated by the law as if he had in fact desired to produce the result").

To illustrate, suppose a person strikes his friend for the purpose of demonstrating a karate move. The person has no desire to injure his friend, but he knows that the move is so dangerous that he is practically certain his friend will be injured. Under the common law, the person intended to injure his friend, even though he acted only with knowledge that his friend would be injured rather than the desire to harm him. Thus, even when a person acts knowingly rather than purposefully, this type of conduct is still a "use of physical force."

2

The second category involves a person who intentionally unleashes force that recklessly causes injury. The majority gives two examples:

1. The Angry Plate Thrower: "[A] person throws a plate in anger against the wall near where his wife is standing." The plate shatters, and a shard injures her.

2. The Door Slammer: "[A person] slams the door shut with his girlfriend following close behind" with the effect of "catch[ing] her fingers in the jamb."

The Angry Plate Thrower and the Door Slammer both intentionally unleashed physical force, but they did not intend to direct that force at those whom they harmed. Thus, they *intentionally* employed force, but *recklessly* caused physical injury with that force. The majority believes that these cases also constitute a "use of physical force," and I agree. The Angry Plate Thrower has used force against the plate, and the Door Slammer has used force against the door.

The more difficult question is whether this "use of physical force" comes within §921(a)(33)(A)(ii), which requires that the "use of physical force" be committed by someone having a familial relationship with the victim. The natural reading of that provision is that the use of physical force must be against a family member. In some cases, the law readily transfers the intent to use force from the object to the actual victim. Take the Angry Plate Thrower: If a husband throws a plate at the wall near his wife to scare her, that is assault. If the plate breaks and cuts her, it becomes a battery, regardless of whether he intended the plate to make contact with her person. See W. Keeton, D. Dobbs, R. Keeton, & D. Owens, Prosser and Keeton on Law of Torts §9, pp. 39-42 (5th ed. 1984) (Prosser and Keeton). Similarly, "if one person intends to harm a second person but instead unintentionally harms a third, the first person's criminal or tortious intent toward the second applies to the third as well." Black's Law Dictionary 1504 (defining transferred-intent doctrine); see also 1 LaFave, supra, §5.2(c)(4), at 349-350. Thus, where a person acts in a violent and patently unjustified manner, the law will often impute that the actor intended to cause the injury resulting from his conduct, even if he actually intended to direct his use of force elsewhere. Because we presume that Congress legislates against the backdrop of the common law, these cases would qualify as the "use of physical force" against a family member.

3

Finally, and most problematic for the majority's approach, a person could recklessly unleash force that recklessly causes injury. Consider two examples:

1. The Text-Messaging Dad: Knowing that he should not be texting and driving, a father sends a text message to his wife. The distraction causes the father to rear end the car in front of him. His son, who is a passenger, is injured.

2. The Reckless Policeman: A police officer speeds to a crime scene without activating his emergency lights and siren and careens into another car in an intersection. That accident causes the police officer's car to strike another police officer, who was standing at the intersection. See Seaton v. State, 385 S.W.3d 85, 88 (Tex. App. 2012).

In these cases, both the unleashing of the "force" (the car crash) and the resulting harm (the physical injury) were reckless. Under the majority's reading of §921(a)(33)(A)(ii), the husband "use[d] . . . physical force" against his son, and the police officer "use[d] . . . physical force" against the other officer.

But this category is where the majority and I part company. These examples do not involve the "use of physical force" under any conventional understanding of "use" because they do not involve an active employment of something for a particular purpose. In the second category, the actors intentionally use violence against property; this is why the majority can plausibly argue that they have "used" force, even though that force was not intended to harm their family members. But when an individual does not engage in any violence against persons or property—that is, when physical injuries result from purely reckless conduct—there is no "use" of physical force.

. . .

The "use of physical force" against a family member includes cases where a person intentionally commits a violent act against a family member. And the term includes at least some cases where a person engages in a violent act that results in an unintended injury to a family member. But the term does not include nonviolent, reckless acts that cause physical injury or an offensive touching. Accordingly, the majority's definition is overbroad. . . .

The majority blurs the distinction between recklessness and intentional wrongdoing by overlooking the difference between the *mens rea* for force and the *mens rea* for causing harm with that force. The majority says that "'use' does not demand that the person applying force have the purpose or practical certainty that it will cause harm" (namely, knowledge), "as compared with the understanding that it is [a substantial and unjustifiable risk that it will] do so" (the standard for recklessness).[5] Put in the language of

---

5. The majority's equation of recklessness with "the understanding" that one's actions are "substantially likely" to cause harm, misstates the standard for recklessness in States that follow the Model Penal Code. Recklessness only requires a "substantial and unjustifiable risk." ALI, Model Penal Code §2.02(2)(c) (1980). A "substantial" risk can include very small risks when there is no justification for taking the risk. See id., §2.02, Comment 1, at 237, n. 14. Thus, it would be reckless to play Russian roulette with a revolver having 1,000 chambers, even though there is a 99.9% chance that no one will be injured.

mens rea, the majority is saying that purposeful, knowing, and reckless applications of force are all equally "uses" of force.

But the majority fails to explain why mere recklessness in creating force—as opposed to recklessness in causing harm with intentional force—is sufficient. The majority gives the Angry Plate Thrower and the Door Slammer as examples of reckless conduct that are "uses" of physical force, but those examples involve persons who *intentionally* use force that *recklessly* causes injuries. Reckless assault, however, extends well beyond intentional force that recklessly causes injury. In States where the Model Penal Code has influence, reckless assault includes any recklessly caused physical injury. See ALI, Model Penal Code §211.1(1)(a) (1980). This means that the Reckless Policeman and the Text-Messaging Dad are as guilty of assault as the Angry Plate Thrower. See, e.g., *Seaton*, 385 S.W. 3d, at 89-90; see also People v. Grenier, 250 App. Div. 2d 874, 874-875, 672 N.Y.S. 2d 499, 500-501 (1998) (upholding an assault conviction where a drunk driver injured his passengers in a car accident).

The majority's examples are only those in which a person has intentionally used force, meaning that the person acts with purpose or knowledge that force is involved. As a result, the majority overlooks the critical distinction between conduct that is intended to cause harm and conduct that is not intended to cause harm. Violently throwing a plate against a wall is a use of force. Speeding on a roadway is not. That reflects the fundamental difference between intentional and reckless wrongdoing. An intentional wrong is designed to inflict harm. See Restatement (Second) of Torts §8A, at 15. A reckless wrong is not: "While an act to be reckless must be intended by the actor, the actor does not intend to cause the harm which results from it." Id., §500, Comment *f*, at 590.

All that remains of the majority's analysis is its unsupported conclusion that recklessness looks enough like knowledge, so that the former suffices for a use of force just as the latter does. That overlooks a crucial distinction between a "practical certainty" and a substantial risk. . . . [T]he distinction between intentional and reckless conduct is key for defining "use." When a person acts with a practical certainty that he will employ force, he intends to cause harm; he has actively employed force for an instrumental purpose, and that is why we can fairly say he "uses" force. In the case of reckless wrongdoing, however, the injury the actor has caused is just an accidental byproduct of inappropriately risky behavior; he has not actively employed force.

In sum, "use" requires the intent to employ the thing being used. And in law, that intent will be imputed when a person acts with practical certainty that he will actively employ that thing. Merely disregarding a risk that a harm will result, however, does not supply the requisite intent. . . .

. . .

If Congress wanted to sweep in all reckless conduct, it could have written §921(a)(33)(A)(ii) in different language. Congress might have prohibited the possession of firearms by anyone convicted under a state law prohibiting assault or battery. Congress could also have used language tracking the Model Penal Code by saying that a conviction must have, as an element, "the intentional, knowing, or reckless causation of physical injury." But Congress instead defined a "misdemeanor crime of domestic violence" by requiring that the offense have "the use of physical force." And a "use of physical force" has a well-understood meaning applying only to intentional acts designed to cause harm.

III

Even assuming any doubt remains over the reading of "use of physical force," the majority errs by reading the statute in a way that creates serious constitutional problems. The doctrine of constitutional avoidance "command[s] courts, when faced with two plausible constructions of a statute — one constitutional and the other unconstitutional — to choose the constitutional reading." Northwest Austin Municipal Util. Dist. No. One v. Holder, 557 U.S. 193, 213 (2009) (Thomas, J., concurring in judgment in part and dissenting in part) (internal quotation marks omitted). Section 922(g)(9) is already very broad. It imposes a lifetime ban on gun ownership for a single intentional nonconsensual touching of a family member. A mother who slaps her 18-year-old son for talking back to her — an intentional use of force — could lose her right to bear arms forever if she is cited by the police under a local ordinance. The majority seeks to expand that already broad rule to any reckless physical injury or nonconsensual touch. I would not extend the statute into that constitutionally problematic territory. . . .

Today the majority expands §922(g)(9)'s sweep into patently unconstitutional territory. Under the majority's reading, a single conviction under a state assault statute for recklessly causing an injury to a family member — such as by texting while driving — can now trigger a lifetime ban on gun ownership. And while it may be true that such incidents are rarely prosecuted, this decision leaves the right to keep and bear arms up to the discretion of federal, state, and local prosecutors.

We treat no other constitutional right so cavalierly. At oral argument the Government could not identify any other fundamental constitutional right that a person could lose forever by a single conviction for an infraction punishable only by a fine. Tr. of Oral Arg. 36-40. Compare the First Amendment. Plenty of States still criminalize libel. See, *e.g.,* Ala. Code. §13A-11-160 (2015); Fla. Stat. §836.01 (2015); La. Rev. Stat. Ann. §14:47 (West 2016); Mass. Gen. Laws, ch. 94, §98C (2014); Minn. Stat. §609.765 (2014); N. H. Rev. Stat. Ann. §644:11 (2007); Va. Code Ann. §18.2-209 (2014); Wis. Stat. §942.01 (2005). I have little doubt that the majority would strike down an absolute ban on publishing by a person previously convicted of misdemeanor libel. In construing the statute before us expansively so that causing a single minor reckless injury or offensive touching can lead someone to lose his right to bear arms forever, the Court continues to "relegat[e] the Second Amendment to a second-class right." *Friedman v. Highland Park*, 577 U.S. ___, ___ (2015) (Thomas, J., dissenting from denial of certiorari).

* * *

In enacting §922(g)(9), Congress was not worried about a husband dropping a plate on his wife's foot or a parent injuring her child by texting while driving. Congress was worried that family members were abusing other family members through acts of violence and keeping their guns by pleading down to misdemeanors. Prohibiting those convicted of intentional and knowing batteries from possessing guns—but not those convicted of reckless batteries—amply carries out Congress' objective.

Instead, under the majority's approach, a parent who has a car accident because he sent a text message while driving can lose his right to bear arms forever if his wife or child suffers the slightest injury from the crash. This is obviously not the correct reading of §922(g)(9). The "use of physical force" does not include crimes involving purely reckless conduct. Because Maine's statute punishes such conduct, it sweeps more broadly than the "use of physical force." I respectfully dissent.

Notes and Questions

1. The oral arguments before the Supreme Court in *Voisine* made headline news—not so much because of the facts or the legal issues, but because Justice Thomas asked several questions of the Assistant Solicitor General who was arguing the case for the government. That was the first time Justice Thomas had spoken during oral arguments in more than a decade. *Voisine* also happened to be one of the first cases orally argued before the Court after Justice Scalia's death on February 13, 2016.

2. Justice Kagan, speaking for the majority in *Voisine*, calls the common law of *mens rea* "obscure" and "confusing." But then she describes the Model Penal Code's recklessness standard as requiring a defendant to be aware that his conduct is "substantially likely" to cause harm. Is that really how the Code defines "recklessness"? Does the Code's definition require the harm to be "substantially likely" to occur, or merely that the risk of harm be both "substantial" and "unjustifiable"? See also footnote 5 in Justice Thomas' dissenting opinion. And why does Justice Kagan feel the need to emphasize that the defendant's conduct must be "volitional," rather than a mere accident? Those *mens rea* concepts don't appear in the Code—rather, they sound a lot more like how common-law courts would describe general intent.

For his part, Justice Thomas seems to have a rather idiosyncratic view about how to apply the mental states of "purpose" and "recklessness" to conduct elements and result elements. For example, he writes: "Finally, and most problematic for the majority's approach, a person could recklessly unleash force that recklessly causes injury." What does *that* mean? In the hypothetical case of the texting driver, the defendant's conduct (texting while driving) is clearly intentional, whereas the resulting injury to the victim is probably reckless. So what's the extra concept that Justice Thomas describes as "recklessly unleash[ing] force"? Where does *that* idea come from?

Based on *Voisine*, does anybody on the Court really seem to understand *mens rea*?

3. Who's got the better of the argument here? Does Justice Thomas adequately deal with the majority's concern that a victory for the defendants would make it virtually impossible—because of the way most contemporary state assault statutes are drafted, combined with the vagueness of most charging documents and the general verdicts rendered by juries—to keep domestic abusers in 34 states, plus the District of Columbia, from obtaining firearms? Could that really be what Congress intended? On the other hand, does Justice Kagan adequately deal with Justice Thomas' concern that the majority's interpretation will deny a basic constitutional right to persons whose misdemeanor assault crimes are so minor that they can't even be jailed for them?

4. Why do you think so many states amended their assault statutes to criminally punish the "reckless" causing of harm to close family members (and others)—as in the text-messaging-while-driving example provided by Justice Thomas? Keep in mind that, at common law, simple assault is a *general intent* crime—which means that *no* particular *mens rea*, with respect to the resulting harm, is required. On the other hand, common-law courts and legislatures always have had the option (as we have previously seen, in cases involving child abuse and arson) to require proof of either "malice" or "criminal negligence," in situations where the defendant's conduct alone doesn't seem bad enough to justify criminal punishment. Which approach makes more sense?

5. Although the constitutional issue was not part of the Court's grant of certiorari, and although Justice Kagan dismissed the issue in a brief footnote, the Second Amendment clearly lurks in the background in *Voisine*. But the Court has also made it perfectly clear that the Second Amendment does not invalidate all gun laws.

In District of Columbia v. Heller, 554 U.S. 570 (2008), the Court struck down the District's strict ban on handgun possession, as well as the requirement that all other guns legally owned must be "unloaded and dissembled or bound by a trigger lock or similar device," finding both restrictions to violate the Second Amendment. The Court's basic reasoning was that the Second Amendment protects the right of private citizens to possess "usable" handguns in their own home, for the purpose of self-defense. But the Court further explained:

Like most rights, the right secured by the Second Amendment is not unlimited. From Blackstone through the 19th-century cases, commentators and courts routinely explained that the right was not a right to keep and carry any weapon whatsoever in any manner whatsoever and for whatever purpose. For example, the majority of the 19th-century courts to consider the question held that prohibitions on carrying concealed weapons were lawful under the Second Amendment or state analogues. See, e.g., State v. Chandler, 5 La. Ann. 489, 490 (1850); Nunn v. State, 1 Ga. 243, 251 (1846); see generally 2 Kent *340, n. 2; The American Students' Blackstone 84, n. 11 (G. Chase ed. 1884). Although we do not undertake an exhaustive historical analysis today of the full scope of the Second Amendment, nothing in our opinion should be taken to cast doubt on longstanding prohibitions on the possession of firearms by felons and the mentally ill, or laws forbidding the carrying of firearms in sensitive places such as schools and government buildings, or laws imposing conditions and qualifications on the commercial sale of arms.

We also recognize another important limitation on the right to keep and carry arms. [W]e have explained, [in Miller v. United States, 307 U.S. 174 (1939),] that the sorts of weapons protected were those "in common use at the time." 307 U.S., at 179. We think that limitation is fairly supported by the historical tradition of prohibiting the carrying of "dangerous and unusual weapons." See 4 Blackstone 148-149 (1769); 3 B. Wilson, Works of the Honourable James Wilson 79 (1804); H. Stephen, Summary of the Criminal Law 48 (1840); F. Wharton, A Treatise on the Criminal Law of the United States 726 (1852). . . .

It may be objected that if weapons that are most useful in military service—M-16 rifles and the like—may be banned, then the Second Amendment right is completely detached from the prefatory clause [referring to the "well regulated Militia"]. But as we have said, the conception of the militia at the time of the Second Amendment's ratification was the body of all citizens capable of military service, who would bring the sorts of lawful weapons that they possessed at home to militia duty. It may well be true today that a militia, to be as effective as militias in the 18th century, would require sophisticated arms that are highly unusual in society at large. Indeed, it may be true that no amount of small arms could be useful against modern-day bombers and tanks. But the fact that modern developments have limited the degree of fit between the prefatory clause and the protected right cannot change our interpretation of the right. . . .

We are aware of the problem of handgun violence in this country, and we take seriously the concerns raised by the many *amici* who believe that prohibition of handgun ownership is a solution. The Constitution leaves the District of Columbia a variety of tools for combating that problem, including some measures regulating handguns . . . . But the enshrinement of constitutional rights necessarily takes certain policy choices off the table. These include the absolute prohibition of handguns held and used for self-defense in the home. Undoubtedly some think that the Second Amendment is outmoded in a society where our standing army is the pride of our Nation, where well-trained police forces provide personal security, and where gun violence is a serious problem. That is perhaps debatable, but what is not debatable is that it is not the role of this Court to pronounce the Second Amendment extinct.

554 U.S. at 626-28, 636.

And in McDonald v. City of Chicago, 561 U.S. 742 (2010), where the Court held that the Second Amendment is a "fundamental right" incorporated within the meaning of the Fourteenth Amendment's Due Process Clause, thus making it applicable to the states, the Court added:

> . . . Under our precedents, if a Bill of Rights guarantee is fundamental from an American perspective, then, unless stare decisis counsels otherwise, that guarantee is fully binding on the States and thus limits (but by no means eliminates) their ability to devise solutions to social problems that suit local needs and values. As noted by the 38 States that have appeared in this case as amici supporting petitioners, "[s]tate and local experimentation with reasonable firearms regulations will continue under the Second Amendment." Brief for State of Texas et al. 23. . . .
>
> As evidence that the Fourteenth Amendment has not historically been understood to restrict the authority of the States to regulate firearms, municipal respondents and supporting amici cite a variety of state and local firearms laws that courts have upheld. But what is most striking about their research is the paucity of precedent sustaining [complete handgun possession] bans comparable to those at issue here and in *Heller*. Municipal respondents cite precisely one case (from the late 20th century) in which such a ban was sustained. See Brief for Municipal Respondents 26-27 (citing Kalodimos v. Morton Grove, 103 Ill. 2d 483, 470 N.E.2d 266, 83 Ill. Dec. 308 (1984)); see also Reply Brief for Respondent NRA et al. 23, n. 7 (asserting that no other court has ever upheld a complete ban on the possession of handguns). It is important to keep in mind that *Heller*, while striking down a law that prohibited the possession of handguns in the home, recognized that the right to keep and bear arms is not "a right to keep and carry any weapon whatsoever in any manner whatsoever and for whatever purpose." 554 U.S., at 626, 678. We made it clear in *Heller* that our holding did not cast doubt on such longstanding regulatory measures as "prohibitions on the possession of firearms by felons and the mentally ill," "laws forbidding the carrying of firearms in sensitive places such as schools and government buildings, or laws imposing conditions and qualifications on the commercial sale of arms." Id., at 626-627. We repeat those assurances here. Despite municipal respondents' doomsday proclamations, incorporation does not imperil every law regulating firearms.

561 U.S. at 784-86.

What can be said with some certainty, after *Heller* and *McDonald*, is that complete state or federal bans on handgun possession (or on the possession of any other weapons "in common use" for the purpose of self-defense) inside the home cannot stand, in view of the Second Amendment. What about bans on such possession *outside* the home, such as in government buildings, in public parks, or on college campuses? What about bans on carrying concealed weapons in public places? Do felons, or those convicted of domestic assaults, forever forfeit their Second Amendment right to possess guns for self-defense? The Court seems to be leaving the door open to such legal restrictions, but only time will tell for sure.

Tafel v. State

Court of Appeals of Texas, Tenth District, Waco
2016 Tex. App. LEXIS 9703 (2016)

Opinion by Justice SCOGGINS (joined by Justice DAVIS):

In two cause numbers, the trial court convicted Mark Ken Tafel of the offense of unlawful carrying of a handgun by a license holder and assessed his punishment at thirty days confinement and a $500 fine. The trial court suspended imposition of the sentence and placed Tafel on community supervision for six months. We affirm.

BACKGROUND FACTS

Mark Ken Tafel was a County Commissioner for Hamilton County. Sheriff Gregg Bewley received complaints that Tafel was carrying a concealed handgun to meetings of the Commissioners Court. Sheriff Bewley met with Tafel and discussed those concerns. On February 23, 2011, Tafel gave Sheriff Bewley a written statement in which he stated that he understood he could not carry a handgun to the meetings of the Commissioners Court.

On April 14, 2011, County Judge Randy Mills issued a letter to Tafel purportedly authorizing Tafel to carry concealed handguns to the meetings. Judge Mills gave a copy of the letter to Tafel; however, Judge Mills did not file the letter in any court in Hamilton County.

Sheriff Bewley attended the November 14, 2011 meeting of the Hamilton County Commissioners Court and observed a bulge that he believed was a weapon under Tafel's jacket. Sheriff Bewley recovered a .45 caliber handgun and a .22 caliber revolver from Tafel, and he placed Tafel under arrest.

SUFFICIENCY OF THE EVIDENCE

In the first issue, Tafel argues that the evidence is insufficient to support the trial court's rejection of the defensive issue of lack of effective notice. We first will determine whether Section 46.035(i) of the Texas Penal Code is an exception or a defense. The Texas Penal Code provides that:

> A license holder commits an offense if the license holder intentionally, knowingly, or recklessly carries a handgun under the authority of Subchapter H, Chapter 411, Government Code, regardless of whether the handgun is concealed, at any meeting of a governmental entity.

Tex. Penal Code Ann. §46.035(c). The Texas Penal Code further provides that subsection (c) does "not apply if the actor was not given effective notice under Section 30.06." Tex. Penal Code Ann. §46.035(i).

Section 2.02(a) of the Penal Code provides, "An exception to an offense in this code is so labeled by the phrase: 'It is an exception to the application of . . . .'" Tex. Penal Code Ann. §2.02(a). Section 2.03(e) of the Penal Code states, "A ground of defense in a penal law that is not plainly labeled in accordance with this chapter has the procedural and evidentiary consequences of a defense." Tex. Penal Code Ann. §2.03(e). We agree with Tafel that Section 46.035(i) is a defense.

When a defendant challenges the legal sufficiency of the evidence to support rejection of a defense, we examine all of the evidence in the light most favorable to the verdict to determine whether a rational factfinder could have found the defendant guilty of all essential elements of the offense beyond a reasonable doubt and also could have found against the defendant on the defensive issue beyond a reasonable doubt. See Dudzik v. State, 276 S.W.3d 554, 557 (Tex. App.-Waco 2008, pet. ref'd).

Section 46.035(i) states that subsection (c) does "not apply if the actor was not given effective notice under Section 30.06." Tex. Penal Code Ann. §46.035(i). Section 30.06 provides that:

> (b) For purposes of this section, a person receives notice if the owner of the property or someone with apparent authority to act for the owner provides notice to the person by oral or written communication.
> (c) In this section:
>   (1) "Entry" has the meaning assigned by Section 30.05(b).
>   (2) "License holder" has the meaning assigned by Section 46.035(f).
>   (3) "Written communication" means:
>   (A) a card or other document on which is written language identical to the following: "Pursuant to Section 30.06, Penal Code (trespass by holder of license to carry a concealed handgun), a person licensed under Subchapter H, Chapter 411, Government Code (concealed handgun law), may not enter this property with a concealed handgun"; or
>   (B) sign posted on the property that:
>   (i) includes the language described by Paragraph (A) in both English and Spanish;
>   (ii) appears in contrasting colors with block letters at least one inch in height; and
>   (iii) is displayed in a conspicuous manner clearly visible to the public.

Tex. Penal Code Ann. §30.06(b)(c).

Tafel focuses on whether a rational factfinder could have found against him beyond a reasonable doubt on the issue of lack of effective notice. Section 30.06 provides that effective notice can be provided by oral or written communication. Judge Mills posted a sign in an attempt to comply with the provisions of Section 30.06. The record is unclear whether the sign was displayed in a conspicuous manner clearly visible to the public and whether it contained contrasting colors with block letters. The sign was printed only in English.

The record indicates that Tafel was aware of the sign after it was posted. Sheriff Bewley met with Tafel to discuss Tafel carrying weapons to the county commissioner's meetings. Tafel's statement to Sheriff Bewley is as follows:

My name is Mark Tafel and I am the Commissioner of Hamilton County Precinct Two. Sheriff Bewley asked me to come to his office today regarding concealed carry of a firearm. It has been brought to my attention questions have been raised from the past where I did not willingly or knowingly break any laws. On or prior to a Commissioner's Court meeting discussions from a gentleman, Dave Gustafson, asked questions of concealed carry. At that point in time no 30.06 sign was posted at the courtroom nor did I know that any laws were being broken. As questions arose weeks later I confirmed that I cannot carry a concealed weapon during court hours with proper signage displayed. Sheriff Bewley investigated Texas Penal Codes and determined that section 46.03 and 46.035 are applicable when Commissioner's Court is in session. From knowing this now I have not and will not carry a weapon until new laws are written from our state courts. In fact from that day forward, in talking to Sheriff Bewley, I have been pursuing our state representative and his aid where the state house is challenging and changing the validity of 46.03 and 46.035 to allow any elected officials in Commissioner's Court or any Justice Court to carry a concealed weapon as long as they are a CCL holder. The Sheriff has asked me about a conversation that occurred prior to a Commissioner's Court meeting between myself and Mr. Gustafson. A discussion I vaguely remember was about whether we, Dave and I, were legal to carry concealed weapons in the courthouse. Judge Mills had previously told me it didn't bother him that I carried in the courthouse. There was no positive outcome of Dave and mine's conversation till weeks later when Sheriff Bewley confirmed that according to Texas Penal Code section 46.03 and 46.035 that I would be breaking the law if I carried in the courtroom when in session. Back to the discussion with Dave Gustafson, in a conversation I vaguely remember, the Sheriff has referred to my patting my clothing and ankle with which I completely disagree that could have happened. Because, I have never carried a boot gun. I do however carry an underarm shouldered weapon or small of the back carry. Again though I must reiterate that no determination was made of what is legal and wasn't legal. Today however, we do know, and that is why I do not carry during court. I don't want to lie I believe I was carrying a concealed weapon on my first and second court date. Again after this conversation with Mr. Gustafson I brought the concern to our County Judge and he didn't care that I was carrying during court.

This issue seems to be very confusing to me and to others. We know state law says that a 30.06 sign must be posted to stop concealed carry with that building. At no time were signs ever present until recently, and now I know that I cannot carry a weapon past that sign. At no time did I intentionally or knowingly break any laws. In fact I pride myself in being an upstanding law abiding citizen. Being taught what is proper in concealed carry by my instructor, Carl Chandler, told me that it was my right to carry in the state capitol while it is in session. This has been confirmed by the state reps assistant that concealed carry is allowed at the state capitol but not in a county courtroom. This is why they are vigilantly trying to change the law. This is the end of my statement.

Tafel further consulted with County Attorney Mark Henke on carrying a concealed handgun in the courtroom and to the meetings of the Commissioners Court. Henke never advised Tafel that he was permitted to carry a concealed handgun to the meetings of the Commissioner's Court. Henke testified that his advice was consistently ". . . don't do it. You risk going to jail." Henke and Tafel also discussed the sign posted in an attempt to comply with Section 30.06. Tafel was aware of the written sign prohibiting him from carrying a handgun to the meetings, and Tafel received oral notice that he was prohibited from carrying a handgun to the meetings. Viewing the evidence in the light most favorable to the verdict, we find that a rational factfinder could have found against Tafel on the issue of lack of effective notice. We overrule the first issue.

MISTAKE OF LAW

In the second issue, Tafel argues that the evidence established as a matter of law the affirmative defense of mistake of law. To establish the affirmative defense of mistake of law, a defendant bears the burden of proving by a preponderance of the evidence that he reasonably believed the conduct charged did not constitute a crime and that he acted in reasonable reliance upon:

> (1) an official statement of the law contained in a written order or grant of permission by an administrative agency charged by law with responsibility for interpreting the law in question; or
> (2) a written interpretation of the law contained in an opinion of a court of record or made by a public official charged by law with responsibility for interpreting the law in question.

TEX. PENAL CODE ANN. §§2.04, 8.03(b).

The proper standard in criminal cases for review of legal sufficiency challenges to a factfinder's refusal to find on an issue that the defendant had the burden of proof is the same standard applied in civil cases. Reynolds v. State, 385 S.W.3d 93, 100-101(Tex. App.-Waco 2012, aff'd 423 S.W.3d 377 (Tex. Crim. App. 2014). That standard requires a two-step analysis. We first examine the record for any evidence that supports the factfinder's refusal to find while ignoring all evidence to the contrary. If no evidence supports the refusal to find, we then examine the entire record to determine whether the evidence establishes the affirmative defense as a matter of law.

Judge Mills wrote a letter addressed to "To Whom It May Concern" and states:

> Commissioner Mark Tafel is authorized by this office to exercise his authority under Texas Concealed Handgun laws to carry concealed handgun in Hamilton County Commissioners Court. This is to remain in effect until further notification.

Tafel contends that he relied on Judge Mill's authorization to bring concealed handguns to the commissioners meeting pursuant to Tex. Penal Code Ann. §8.03(b)(2).

Section 8.03 requires reliance on a narrow class of official statements or interpretations of the law. Hawkins v. State, 656 S.W.2d 70, 73 (Tex. Crim. App. 1983). The letter is not a written interpretation of the law contained in an opinion as set out in Section 8.03(b)(2). An interpretation is defined as an explanation. (Merriam Webster's Collegiate Dictionary (10th Edition 1993). The letter written by Judge Mills does not explain the applicable law, and it is not an opinion. Judge Mills testified that his letter did not constitute an opinion. We find that Tafel's reliance on the letter was not reasonable. Tafel did not establish the affirmative defense of mistake of law as a matter of law. We overrule the second issue.

CONCLUSION

We affirm the trial court's judgments.

Chief Justice Gray, dissenting.

The issues we decide today relate to how a concealed handgun license holder can be confident in the determination of where it is lawful to carry. The underlying right at issue was confirmed by the adoption of the second amendment to the United States Constitution. The scope of that right was discussed at length in the United States Supreme Court's opinion in District of Columbia v. Heller, 554 U.S. 570 (2008). And the right was confirmed as applicable to the States in the United States Supreme Court's opinion in McDonald v. City of Chicago, 561 U.S. 742 (2010).

As presented to this Court, the issue is narrower than the issue in *Heller* and *McDonald*; but due to the need to interpret various statutes and case law holdings, the issue is somewhat more complex. This is where the theory of the right to "keep and bear arms" runs into a maze of statutes and definitions that limit that right. . . .

In this case, we are called upon to review the sufficiency of the evidence to support the defendant's convictions. To do this, we must know the elements of the crime the State must prove to the requisite level of proof to obtain a conviction. But it does not stop there. We must also know whether there are circumstances that prevent the conduct from being criminal. Such circumstances can be broadly characterized as either exceptions or defenses. Moreover, exceptions and defenses can be further divided. For example, defenses can be ordinary defenses or they can be affirmative defenses. Analyzing what they are with precision is critical to understanding who, the State or the defendant, has to prove what, and to what level of certainty, for the State to obtain a valid criminal conviction. . . .

In this case, the indictment included the allegation that Tafel had received "effective notice" under section 30.06 of the Penal Code. . . . [T]he legislature decided that if a person was not given "effective notice" under section 30.06, the subsection did not apply. §46.035(i). It appears that the legislature meant that there is no offense without effective notice. Thus, whether or not a person was given effective notice seems to be a necessary part of the offense.

EFFECTIVE NOTICE

. . . What is "effective notice?" What seems like a simple question is not. The most difficult aspect of understanding the meaning of "effective notice" is to distinguish it from what it is not. "Effective notice" is not knowledge of section 46.035(c) of the Penal Code. It is not general familiarity with or understanding of the statute regarding where concealed carry is prohibited. It is not an awareness of a risk of criminal prosecution if the Penal Code provision is violated. The Penal Code elements of the crime, or overcoming the defense, are only satisfied if the defendant received "effective notice."

The fundamental flaw in the prosecution of Tafel was the prosecutor's, and ultimately the trial court's, belief that mere knowledge of the Penal Code provision was the equivalent of notice. This is evident in a question to County Attorney Henke when the prosecutor asked:

> And regardless of whether or not a notice was posted, if they had actual knowledge that they were not approved to do that, it really wouldn't matter if it [the 30.06 sign] was posted.

But it does matter. The Penal Code says it matters. Notice, not knowledge of the statute, is required.

But in this growing quagmire of legal analysis, "effective notice" of what? An excellent question! Let us return to the statute at issue: "(i) Subsections (b)(4), (b)(5), (b)(6), and (c) *do not apply* if the actor was not given *effective notice under Section 30.06*." See current version at TEX. PENAL CODE ANN. §46.035(i) (emphasis added). Thus, we turn our attention to section 30.06 of the Penal Code.

What does it mean to "receive notice?" The statute seems to provide the answer to this question; but upon further analysis the answer it provides is overly simplistic and leaves more questions than it answers. Subsection (b) of section 30.06 provides:

(b) For purposes of this section, a person receives notice if the owner of the property or someone with apparent authority to act for the owner provides notice to the person by oral or written communication.

The statute appears, at first glance, to be functionally defective because it seems to use the term "notice" to describe what it means to receive notice. This is worth further analysis. Because the license holder must "receive notice," this subsection is actually defining who can provide the notice and the form in which the notice must be provided. To be notice, the notice must be provided by either

1. The owner of the property; or
2. Someone with apparent authority to act for the owner.

In this proceeding, subdivision one is not at issue. The actual owner of the property was never identified. Hamilton County was apparently leasing the property as temporary space while the county's courthouse was being renovated. But let us not be unreasonable in our application of the statute. The County "owned" the lease that gave it the authority to occupy the property. Thus, I have no problem with the concept that the "owner" for purposes of the application of the statute was Hamilton County. Hamilton County is a governmental corporate entity. That entity is represented by the commissioners court. The evidence established that prior to Tafel's arrest, the commissioners court, as such, took no action to notify anyone, including Tafel, that a license holder could not enter upon the property with a concealed handgun.

Because the "owner" of the property did not provide notice to Tafel, we must consider whether "someone with apparent authority to act for the owner" provided notice to Tafel. The State contends that the required notice was provided by Sheriff Bewley, County Attorney Henke, or County Judge Mills. We will look at what oral or written communication was provided by each of these persons in turn but there are two issues that must be discussed first. The two issues are (1) what is the acceptable form of the communication and (2) what is the information that must be communicated.

a) Form of the Communication

There are two forms of communications that are authorized by the statute; oral and written. I will deal with written communications first.

i) Written Communications

There are two forms of written communication authorized by the statute. The statute dictates the form and content of both types of written communication. . . .

Whether a written communication that complied with the statute was provided to Tafel can be dispensed with quickly. There was not. However, this is where some confusion is created which must be addressed. There is no suggestion in the record of any card or other document having been provided to Tafel. There was, however, testimony that at some point the County Judge put up a sign at the public entrance to the room where commissioners court met. The State relies on the posted sign as notice.

. . . The testimony about the sign posted by Judge Mills is less than clear. It is not clear when it was posted, except that it was some time prior to the day of Tafel's arrest and prior to Tafel's meeting with Sheriff Bewley as will be discussed later. It is not clear when it was removed, except that it was removed sometime after Tafel's arrest. It is not clear precisely what the sign said or the size of the lettering, except that it did not comply with the requirements of the statute to be the written communication. See TEX. PENAL CODE ANN. §30.06(c)(3)(B). Specifically, the only testimony about the wording on the sign was that it had no Spanish content as required to meet the statutory definition of "Written Communication." Id.

Thus, it is undisputed, and the record contains no evidence to the contrary, that there was no "written communication" within the meaning of the statute that would have given Tafel, or any other concealed handgun license holder, the required notice to make entry on the property with a concealed handgun a criminal violation.

ii) Oral Communications

Because there was no "written communication," no written card and no compliant sign, the State now has to rely on an oral communication for section 30.06 notice. And we know the oral communication had to be from "someone with apparent authority to act for the owner." "Written communication" was expressly and meticulously defined by the statute. So now we turn to the statute to the definition of "oral communication." There is none.

Notwithstanding the detailed description of two different forms of what constitutes "written communication," the legislature provided absolutely nothing to define or describe an adequate or compliant "oral communication." It would, however, be unreasonable to require anything more to be communicated orally than in writing. Further, the oral communication should be adequate if communicated in English unless the person making the oral communication has reason to believe the person does not comprehend English.

There is nothing to suggest that Tafel cannot comprehend English and, as will be seen from the written statement he gave to Sheriff Bewley, he can speak English and is a college graduate. So we now turn to what the evidence shows was orally communicated in English to Tafel.

b) Means of Communication

Three people potentially communicated notice to Tafel. We will discuss each person's communication separately.

i) Sheriff Bewley

We will first examine what Sheriff Bewley communicated to Tafel. Tafel gave Sheriff Bewley a written statement. It is important to know the reason this statement was created. In response to a citizen complaint, Sheriff Bewley had confronted Tafel to get "his side of the story." Thus, Bewley confronted Tafel with the complaint. The record does not contain a recounting of the dialogue between Bewley and Tafel. The only evidence we have of what Bewley said or told Tafel is that which is contained in the statement Tafel gave Bewley as a result of the confrontation. In reading the statement, particular attention should be given to what oral notice was given to Tafel that would be the equivalent of what is required information in a written communication. In summary, that would be words to the effect that "Pursuant to Section 30.06, Penal Code, a person licensed under the concealed handgun law, may not enter this property with a concealed handgun."

There are a few specific passages [in the defendant's statement] that should be analyzed. We will discuss each in turn. There is a statement that: "Sheriff Bewley investigated Texas Penal Codes and determined that section 46.03 and 46.035 are applicable when commissioners court is in session." While they may be "applicable," that is not the issue. The issue is whether Sheriff Bewley provided the required oral communication to Tafel that he could not lawfully enter the premises. This portion of Tafel's statement does not support such a conclusion.

The statement later says, ". . . weeks later . . . Sheriff Bewley confirmed that according to Texas Penal Code section 46.03 and 46.035 that I would be breaking the law if I carried in the courtroom when in session." Unquestionably this portion of Tafel's statement is closer to documenting something that Sheriff Bewley may have provided to Tafel that would qualify as the required notice. But both forms of the written communication for notice require a specific reference to section 30.06 and that was not included in this implied oral communication from Sheriff Bewley. And each statement in the document must be considered in light of the language: "Again though I must reiterate that no determination was made of what is legal and what wasn't legal. Today, however, we do know, and that is why I do not carry during court." If these two sentences are isolated, it is clear that there was no determination made during the previous conversations with Sheriff Bewley but that, as of the date of the statement, they had determined it would be a violation.

But then there is the most important sentence in the entire statement: "We know state law says that a 30.06 sign must be posted to stop concealed carry within that building. At no time were any signs posted until recently, and now I know that I cannot carry a weapon past that sign." This brings home the need to reference section 30.06 in the oral communication—it informs the recipient of the basis for being excluded from the property whether it is an oral communication or a written sign.

The only reasonable inference from these statements in context is that because the purported 30.06 sign was now posted, as of the date the statement was given, which was February 23, 2011, Sheriff Bewley and Commissioner Tafel both thought that the presence of the sign was what made entry on the property by a license holder with a concealed handgun illegal. They were not relying on any type of oral notice. They were relying solely on the posted sign.

But, as discussed above, we know the purported section 30.06 sign did not comply with the required language of the statute. Because the sign did not comply with the statute, it was not a "written communication" as defined by the statute.

. . . This Penal Code provision defines conduct that is unlawful but only if a person provides notice to the actor. Thus, the conduct is not criminal without the required notice.[17] . . .

It is easy to get sucked into being comfortable with what Tafel "knew." And looking at all the back and forth and discussion, it is easy to conclude that Tafel "knew" he could not carry his concealed weapon past the posted sign. But regardless of what Tafel and the Sheriff thought they knew at the time, they were wrong on what made the conduct a violation. And what the State had to prove was that Tafel was given notice as required by section 30.06 that as a license holder he could not enter the property with a concealed handgun. That notice did not come from Sheriff Bewley. . . .

ii) County Attorney Henkes

The next potential source of an oral communication to Tafel relied on by the State was Tafel's discussion with the County Attorney, Mark Henkes. Probably the easiest way to approach the ineffectiveness of the State's position that Henkes could be the person providing an "oral communication" to Tafel is that Henkes does not appear to be a person that had apparent authority to provide the statutory notice for the County. Even if he had apparent authority, at no point in his testimony does Henkes testify that he provided oral notice that would comply with section 30.06 of the Penal Code. . . .

Henkes approached the issue from a risk management perspective that carrying a concealed handgun during a commissioners court meeting which was being held in a room that was also sometimes used as a district courtroom was not worth the risk of a felony prosecution and that he would

---

17. Compare the offense of "Left Lane for Passing Only" and the notice required to convict a driver thereof. See Abney v. State, 394 S.W.3d 542 (Tex. Crim. App. 2013). There are other crimes which require proof of some type of notice before the conduct is criminal. See generally Harvey v. State, 78 S.W.3d 368 (Tex. Crim. App. 2002) (notice of protective order); Ex parte Vetterick, 744 S.W.2d 598 (Tex. 1988) (notice of contempt); In re Moreno, 328 S.W.3d 915 (Tex. App. — Eastland 2010, orig. proceeding) (same).

advise against it. Henkes admitted he was not particularly familiar with the section 30.06 notice requirement because it related only to a possible misdemeanor violation and he was focused on the possibility of a felony violation. Accordingly, there was nothing to which he testified that could be construed as having been an "oral communication" that complied with the section 30.06 notice requirement.

iii) County Judge

This brings us to the County Judge, Randy Mills, and his testimony about whether he provided the notice required by section 30.06 to make the entry of a license holder on the property with a concealed handgun a violation. He did not. Judge Mills did not testify that the sign he posted complied with section 30.06. So, as discussed above, he provided no evidence of a written communication. Moreover, sometime after Tafel was confronted by Sheriff Bewley and after the discussion with County Attorney Henkes, Judge Mills provided a letter to Tafel on Hamilton County letterhead that expressly authorized Tafel to carry his handgun during commissioners court meetings. . . .

c) Summary—No 30.06 Notice Was Given

In summary, there is nothing in this record to show that Tafel was given the notice described in section 30.06 of the Penal Code that would make his carrying of a concealed handgun in commissioners court a violation of the Penal Code. But if I am mistaken on it being an exception and therefore the State's burden to negate such notice is an element of the offense; and instead, it was merely a defense and thus Tafel has the burden to raise the defense of lack of such notice, I would hold that Tafel raised the issue and the State failed to overcome the defense that section 30.06 notice was not provided. Alternately, I would hold Tafel proved the defense, even if not his burden, as a matter of law that the required notice was not given and that a reasonable fact finder could not have rejected Tafel's defense in that regard.

[In addition,] Judge Mills provided Tafel a letter on County letterhead that is quoted in full above. The operative portion of the letter for this discussion is as follows:

> Commissioner Mark Tafel is authorized by this office to exercise his authority under Texas Concealed Handgun laws to carry concealed handgun in Hamilton County Commissioners Court. This is to remain in effect until further notification.

. . . The issue thus framed is: Could the letter from Judge Mills override the assumed effectiveness of the oral notices? It has to. And why not? Any other result would leave the actor in the untenable position of not knowing whether it is lawful or unlawful to enter the property with his handgun under his concealed handgun license. Clarity is critical in determining when conduct is criminal. Laws are routinely held invalid for being vague.[20] In the fact pattern described with our assumption of the receipt of a compliant oral notice under section 30.06, the countermanding of the notice that otherwise makes the conduct criminal, has to have the effect of taking away the criminal nature of the otherwise lawful conduct.

. . . On the facts of this case, if we assume the section 30.06 sign posted by Judge Mills was a compliant sign even though it did not contain the required information and was not approved for posting by the commissioners court, then it seems inescapable that Judge Mills could issue a letter than authorizes a particular person with a concealed handgun license to enter the premises without that entry being a criminal act. Surely the person who can prohibit legal entry to all concealed handgun license holders can also authorize an exception. . . .

In summary, . . . I would hold that any person authorized to provide any of the forms or methods of notice under sections 46.035(i) and 30.06 that makes the conduct prohibited/criminal may also rescind, revoke, or withdraw the notice (in essence authorizing or permitting the conduct) by any of those same methods. Thus, because Judge Mills posted the sign on which the State relies to make the conduct of Tafel criminal, I believe Judge Mills also had the authority to give permission to Tafel that authorized his conduct that would otherwise be criminal. Judge Mills did so in writing.[22] Therefore, Tafel's conduct was not a criminal violation of section 46.035(c). . . .

Notes and Questions

1. Do you think that Commissioner Mark Ken Tafel was treated fairly here? Why wasn't the letter from County Judge Mills sufficient to authorize Tafel's carrying of his concealed handguns into the meetings of the Commissioner's Court? Even if the County Attorney and Sheriff told Tafel otherwise, shouldn't Judge Mills' letter take priority? Or, at the very least, shouldn't the letter be treated as sufficient for Tafel to raise a valid "mistake of law" defense?

On the other hand, what if many other law-abiding citizens of Hamilton County, Texas, felt threatened or intimidated by the suspected presence of concealed weapons at a meeting of the Commissioner's Court? Shouldn't their rights to attend a local government meeting without having to worry about who might be packing heat count for something, too?

20. See for example, Kolender v. Lawson, 461 U.S. 352 (1983) (California statute requiring loiterers to provide "credible and reliable" identification and account for his presence was unconstitutionally vague) . . . .

22. In this context, the written authorization from Judge Mills does not have to be a legal opinion as defined for a mistake-of-law defense.

Why do you think this case was prosecuted in the first place? Is this just a case of local political infighting run amok?

2. In addition to his misdemeanor conviction, Tafel also was subjected to the forfeiture of his two handguns to the government. This is a relatively common collateral consequence of a gun crime—sometimes as an adjunct to the criminal conviction, and sometimes pursuant to a separate civil forfeiture proceeding. Chief Justice Gray, in dissent, objected to the forfeiture as well:

> [T]he State moved to forfeit Tafel's two handguns pursuant to article 18.19(e). In relevant part, subsection (e) provides:
>
> > If the person found in possession of a weapon is convicted of an offense involving the use of the weapon, before the 61st day after the date of conviction the court entering judgment of conviction shall order destruction of the weapon, sale at public sale . . . , or forfeiture to the state. . . . If the court entering judgment of conviction does not order the destruction, sale, or forfeiture of the weapon within the period prescribed by this subsection, the law enforcement agency holding the weapon may request an order of destruction, sale, or forfeiture of the weapon from a magistrate.
>
> TEX. CODE CRIM. PROC. ANN. art. 18.19(e) (West 2015).
> . . . Here, it was not illegal for Tafel to carry a handgun. He was licensed to carry. It was the place into which he carried those handguns which arguably caused his conduct to be a criminal offense. The carrying of the handguns did not facilitate another offense, let alone a felony offense. Thus, according to the definitions used by the Court, there was no evidence that Tafel *used* the handguns which would authorize their forfeiture. The Court errs in holding otherwise.

Do you agree with Chief Justice Gray that Tafel did not "use" the two handguns, and therefore they were not properly subject to forfeiture? Or, as the majority concluded in upholding the forfeiture, did Tafel's physical carrying of the handguns into the meeting room constitute a prohibited "use" of those handguns?

B. GUN ENHANCEMENTS

Thompson v. State

Court of Appeals of Georgia
277 Ga. App. 323; 626 S.E.2d 825 (2006)

Opinion by MIKELL, Judge.

A Richmond County jury found Roger Thompson guilty of aggravated assault, possession of a firearm during the commission of a crime, and possession of a firearm by a convicted felon. Thompson appeals from his judgment of conviction and sentence, contending (i) that the evidence was insufficient to support the guilty verdict on the charge of aggravated assault, (ii) that the trial court erred by allowing testimony that Thompson's nickname was "Shotgun," and (iii) that the trial court erred by failing to instruct the jury on reckless conduct as a lesser included offense of aggravated assault. We affirm for the reasons set forth below.

Viewed in a light most favorable to the jury's verdict, the evidence shows that around 2:00 A.M. on April 1, 2000, the victim and two friends drove to the Hale Street Apartments in Augusta. There were more than 30 people in the apartment parking lot who were "having a good time." The victim became involved in an argument with another person in the parking lot. About two minutes after the argument began, the victim saw Thompson, who the victim only knew by the nickname "Shotgun," come out of an upstairs apartment. Thompson fired a gun three times, aiming "towards [the victim], towards the ground." The second shot grazed the victim over his left eye. The victim, who was scared, ran to the street to call for help on his cellphone.

1. Thompson claims the evidence was insufficient to support his conviction for aggravated assault because he did not intend to assault the victim. We disagree.

The indictment charged Thompson of aggravated assault with a deadly weapon by making "an assault upon the person of the [victim], with a certain handgun, a deadly weapon, by shooting him." See OCGA §16-5-21(a)(2) (a person commits the offense of aggravated assault when he or she assaults with a deadly weapon).

> The offense of aggravated assault has two essential elements: (1) that an assault, as defined in OCGA §16-5-20 be committed on the victim; and (2) that it was aggravated by (a) an intention to murder, rape, or to rob, or (b) use of a deadly weapon. OCGA §16-5-20 states: (a) a person commits the offense of simple assault when he either: (1) Attempts to commit a violent injury to the person of another; or (2) Commits an act which places another in reasonable apprehension of immediately receiving a violent injury.

(Citations, punctuation and emphasis omitted.) Williams v. State, 208 Ga. App. 12, 13, 430 S.E.2d 157 (1993).

The indictment only specifies that Thompson made an "assault" with a deadly weapon, and "[s]uch general language sufficiently charges an assault by way of either manner contained in the assault statute." (Footnote omitted.) Tucker v. State, 245 Ga. App. 551, 553, 538 S.E.2d 458 (2000). The trial court charged the jury that "assault is an intent to commit a violent injury to the person of another or an act which places another person in reasonable apprehension of immediately receiving a violent injury." Viewing the evidence in a light most favorable to the jury's verdict, a rational trier of fact could conclude that Thompson assaulted the victim with his gun, a deadly weapon, by shooting it toward the victim, an act which placed the victim in reasonable apprehension of receiving a violent injury. See Dukes v. State, 264 Ga. App. 820, 824, 592 S.E.2d 473 (2003) (a rational trier of fact could conclude that defendant committed the crime of aggravated assault by shooting his gun toward the victim).

Thompson argues that he did not intend to assault the victim, but that he fired the shots in order to quell the disturbance in the parking lot. However, the evidence showed that Thompson intended to commit the act which "place[d] another in reasonable apprehension of immediately receiving a violent injury," OCGA §16-5-20(a)(2). See *Williams*, supra, at 13-14 (victim's reasonable apprehension of receiving an immediate violent injury established crime of aggravated assault). "There is an intent of the accused that must be shown, but it is only the criminal intent to commit the acts which caused the victim to be reasonably apprehensive of receiving a violent injury, not any underlying intent of the accused in assaulting the victim." (Citation and footnote omitted.) Maynor v. State, 257 Ga. App. 151, 156, 570 S.E.2d 428 (2002). Accordingly, we find the evidence was sufficient to support Thompson's conviction for aggravated assault under the standard set forth in Jackson v. Virginia, 443 U.S. 307 (1979).

2. Thompson also claims that the trial court erred by denying his motion in limine to prevent the prosecution from presenting evidence that his nickname was "Shotgun." We disagree. A trial court's ruling on a motion in limine is reviewed for abuse of discretion. See Johnson v. State, 275 Ga. 650, 652, 571 S.E.2d 782 (2002).

Our Supreme Court has held that reference to a defendant by his nickname does not reflect on the defendant's bad character. Riley v. State, 268 Ga. 640, 643, 491 S.E.2d 802) (1997). See Burtts v. State, 269 Ga. 402-403, 499 S.E.2d 326 (1998) (trial court did not err in allowing witnesses to refer to defendant by his nickname, "Killer Corey," in defendant's murder trial). Thompson nevertheless relies on Justice Sears's suggestion in *Burtts*, supra, through her special concurrence, that "trial courts should consider whether the probative value associated with recitation of the street name in the jury's presence is outweighed by the prejudicial impact of the jury's hearing the defendant referred to by a nickname that explicitly suggests guilt." Id. at 404. However, even if we review the trial court's ruling in light of the approach suggested by Justice Sears, we must conclude that the trial court did not abuse its discretion in allowing testimony as to Thompson's street name. The testimony was probative of the issue of identification, and the nickname "Shotgun" did not explicitly suggest Thompson's guilt of aggravated assault. Accordingly, we conclude that the trial court did not abuse its discretion in denying Thompson's motion in limine.

3. Finally, Thompson claims the trial court erred by failing to give his requested jury charge on the lesser included offense of reckless conduct. Again, we disagree.

"[A] written request to charge a lesser included offense must always be given if there is any evidence that the defendant is guilty of the lesser included offense." State v. Alvarado, 260 Ga. 563, 564, 397 S.E.2d 550 (1990). "However, when the evidence establishes all of the elements of the indicted offense and there is no evidence [showing] the lesser offense, there is no error in refusing to charge the lesser offense." Anderson v. State, 264 Ga. App. 362, 365, 590 S.E.2d 729 (2003).

Thompson testified that he procured a gun from a neighbor in order to "get these folks attention, man, stop all the arguing," and then stepped in between the victim and the person the victim was arguing with, before firing the gun twice. While Thompson testified he "ain't . . . shot at" the victim, Thompson intentionally fired the gun, he was aware of the victim's location, and his testimony was consistent with the victim's testimony that Thompson aimed toward the victim, toward the ground. Thus, "[t]here was no evidence that [Thompson] was simply negligent in either pointing or firing the pistol and thus no evidence of reckless conduct." Anthony v. State, 276 Ga. App. 107, 110, 622 S.E.2d 450 (2005). See Tew v. State, 246 Ga. App. 270, 274-275, 539 S.E.2d 579 (2000) (where evidence showed that defendant pointed his gun at the victims and fired, and there was no evidence that he was negligent in doing so, it was not error for the court to refuse to charge on reckless conduct as lesser included offense of aggravated assault); Hall v. State, 235 Ga. App. 44, 46-47, 508 S.E.2d 703 (1998) (criminal negligence, which is an essential element of reckless conduct, was lacking where evidence showed defendant deliberately pointed a pistol at the victim). Shaw v. State, 238 Ga. App. 757, 519 S.E.2d 486) (1999), relied upon by Thompson, is factually distinguishable because the defendant in that case "might have merely fired a gun out of the car up into the air while the police were chasing the car in which he was riding." Id. at 759. Therefore, we conclude the trial court did not err in refusing to give a charge on reckless conduct as a lesser included offense of aggravated assault.

Judgment affirmed. Andrews, P.J., and Phipps, J., concur.

Notes and Questions

1. Did Roger Thompson (with his unfortunate nickname of "Shotgun") deserve a jury instruction on the lesser included offense of "reckless conduct" in this case? What does the Georgia court mean when it says, "criminal negligence . . . is an essential element of reckless conduct"? On the other hand, isn't it obvious—as the court ultimately concludes—that Thompson satisfies the statutory definition of the greater crime of "aggravated assault"?

2. What, exactly, is the *mens rea* required for the crime of aggravated assault in Georgia, pursuant to OCGA §16-5-20(a)? Is it a general intent crime, a specific intent crime, or some combination of the two? How does that affect your view of the result in *Thompson*?

Dean v. United States

Supreme Court of the United States
556 U.S. 568 (2009)

ROBERTS, C.J., delivered the opinion of the Court.

Accidents happen. Sometimes they happen to individuals committing crimes with loaded guns. The question here is whether extra punishment Congress imposed for the discharge of a gun during certain crimes applies when the gun goes off accidentally.

I

Title 18 U.S.C. §924(c)(1)(A) criminalizes using or carrying a firearm during and in relation to any violent or drug trafficking crime, or possessing a firearm in furtherance of such a crime. An individual convicted of that offense receives a 5-year mandatory minimum sentence, in addition to the punishment for the underlying crime. §924(c)(1)(A)(i). The mandatory minimum increases to 7 years "if the firearm is brandished" and to 10 years "if the firearm is discharged." §§924(c)(1)(A)(ii), (iii).

In this case, a masked man entered a bank, waved a gun, and yelled at everyone to get down. He then walked behind the teller counter and started removing money from the teller stations. He grabbed bills with his left hand, holding the gun in his right. At one point, he reached over a teller to remove money from her drawer. As he was collecting the money, the gun discharged, leaving a bullet hole in the partition between two stations. The robber cursed and dashed out of the bank. Witnesses later testified that he seemed surprised that the gun had gone off. No one was hurt.

Police arrested Christopher Michael Dean and Ricardo Curtis Lopez for the crime. Both defendants were charged with conspiracy to commit a robbery affecting interstate commerce, in violation of 18 U.S.C. §1951(a), and aiding and abetting each other in using, carrying, possessing, and discharging a firearm during an armed robbery, in violation of §924(c)(1)(A)(iii) and §2. At trial, Dean admitted that he had committed the robbery, and a jury found him guilty on both the robbery and firearm counts. The District Court sentenced Dean to a mandatory minimum term of 10 years in prison on the firearm count, because the firearm "discharged" during the robbery. §924(c)(1)(A)(iii).

Dean appealed, contending that the discharge was accidental, and that the sentencing enhancement in §924(c)(1)(A)(iii) requires proof that the defendant intended to discharge the firearm. The Court of Appeals affirmed, holding that separate proof of intent was not required. 517 F.3d 1224, 1229 (CA11 2008). That decision created a conflict among the Circuits over whether the accidental discharge of a firearm during the specified crimes gives rise to the 10-year mandatory minimum. See United States v. Brown,

449 F.3d 154 (CADC 2006) (holding that it does not). We granted certiorari to resolve that conflict. 555 U.S. 1028 (2008).

II

Section 924(c)(1)(A) provides:

> "[A]ny person who, during and in relation to any crime of violence or drug trafficking crime . . . uses or carries a firearm, or who, in furtherance of any such crime, possesses a firearm, shall, in addition to the punishment provided for such crime of violence or drug trafficking crime—
>> "(i) be sentenced to a term of imprisonment of not less than 5 years;
>> "(ii) if the firearm is brandished, be sentenced to a term of imprisonment of not less than 7 years; and
>> "(iii) if the firearm is discharged, be sentenced to a term of imprisonment of not less than 10 years."

The principal paragraph defines a complete offense and the subsections "explain how defendants are to 'be sentenced.'" Harris v. United States, 536 U.S. 545, 552 (2002). Subsection (i) "sets a catchall minimum" sentence of not less than five years. Subsections (ii) and (iii) increase the minimum penalty if the firearm "is brandished" or "is discharged." The parties disagree over whether §924(c)(1)(A)(iii) contains a requirement that the defendant intend to discharge the firearm. We hold that it does not.

A

"We start, as always, with the language of the statute." Williams v. Taylor, 529 U.S. 420, 431 (2000). The text of subsection (iii) provides that a defendant shall be sentenced to a minimum of 10 years "if the firearm is discharged." It does not require that the discharge be done knowingly or intentionally, or otherwise contain words of limitation. As we explained in Bates v. United States, 522 U.S. 23 (1997), in declining to infer an "'intent to defraud'" requirement into a statute, "we ordinarily resist reading words or elements into a statute that do not appear on its face." Id., at 29.

Congress's use of the passive voice further indicates that subsection (iii) does not require proof of intent. The passive voice focuses on an event that occurs without respect to a specific actor, and therefore without respect to any actor's intent or culpability. Cf. Watson v. United States, 552 U.S. 74, 81 (2007) (use of passive voice in statutory phrase "to be used" in 18 U.S.C. §924(d)(1) reflects "agnosticism . . . about who does the using"). It is whether something happened—not how or why it happened—that matters.

The structure of the statute also suggests that subsection (iii) is not limited to the intentional discharge of a firearm. Subsection (ii) provides a 7-year mandatory minimum sentence if the firearm "is brandished." Congress expressly included an intent requirement for that provision, by defining "brandish" to mean "to display all or part of the firearm, or otherwise make the presence of the firearm known to another person, *in order to intimidate* that person." §924(c)(4) (emphasis added). The defendant must have intended to brandish the firearm, because the brandishing must have been done for a specific purpose. Congress did not, however, separately define "discharge" to include an intent requirement. "[W]here Congress includes particular language in one section of a statute but omits it in another section of the same Act, it is generally presumed that Congress acts intentionally and purposely in the disparate inclusion or exclusion." Russello v. United States, 464 U.S. 16, 23 (1983) (internal quotation marks omitted).

Dean argues that the statute is not silent on the question presented. Congress, he contends, included an intent element in the opening paragraph of §924(c)(1)(A), and that element extends to the sentencing enhancements. Section 924(c)(1)(A) criminalizes using or carrying a firearm "during and in relation to" any violent or drug trafficking crime. In Smith v. United States, 508 U.S. 223 (1993), we stated that the phrase "in relation to" means "that the firearm must have some purpose or effect with respect to the drug trafficking crime; its presence or involvement cannot be the result of accident or coincidence." Id., at 238. Dean argues that the adverbial phrase thus necessarily embodies an intent requirement, and that the phrase modifies all the verbs in the statute—not only use, carry, and possess, but also brandish and discharge. Such a reading requires that a perpetrator knowingly discharge the firearm for the enhancement to apply. If the discharge is accidental, Dean argues, it is not "in relation to" the underlying crime.

The most natural reading of the statute, however, is that "in relation to" modifies only the nearby verbs "uses" and "carries." The next verb—"possesses"—is modified by its own adverbial clause, "in furtherance of." The last two verbs—"is brandished" and "is discharged"—appear in separate subsections and are in a different voice than the verbs in the principal paragraph. There is no basis for reading "in relation to" to extend all the way down to modify "is discharged." The better reading of the statute is that the adverbial phrases in the opening paragraph—"in relation to" and "in furtherance of"—modify their respective nearby verbs, and that neither phrase extends to the sentencing factors.

But, Dean argues, such a reading will lead to absurd results. The discharge provision on its face contains no temporal or causal limitations. In the absence of an intent requirement, the enhancement would apply "regardless of when the actions occur, or by whom or for what reason they are taken." Brief for Petitioner 11-12. It would, for example, apply if the gun used during the crime were discharged "weeks (or years) before or after the crime." Reply Brief for Petitioner 11.

We do not agree that implying an intent requirement is necessary to address such concerns. As the Government recognizes, sentencing factors such as the one here "often involve . . . special features of the manner in which a basic crime was carried out." Brief for United States 29 (quoting Harris, 536 U.S., at 553; internal quotation marks omitted). The basic crime here is using or carrying a firearm during and in relation to a violent or drug trafficking crime, or possessing a firearm in furtherance of any such crime. Fanciful hypotheticals testing whether the discharge was a "special featur[e]" of how the "basic crime was carried out," id., at 553 (internal quotation marks omitted), are best addressed in those terms, not by contorting and stretching the statutory language to imply an intent requirement.

B

Dean further argues that even if the statute is viewed as silent on the intent question, that silence compels a ruling in his favor. There is, he notes, a presumption that criminal prohibitions include a requirement that the Government prove the defendant intended the conduct made criminal. In light of this presumption, we have "on a number of occasions read a state-of-mind component into an offense even when the statutory definition did not in terms so provide." United States v. United States Gypsum Co., 438 U.S. 422, 437 (1978). "[S]ome indication of congressional intent, express or implied, is required to dispense with *mens rea* as an element of a crime." Staples v. United States, 511 U.S. 600, 606 (1994).

Dean argues that the presumption is especially strong in this case, given the structure and purpose of the statute. In his view, the three subsections are intended to provide harsher penalties for increasingly culpable conduct: a 5-year minimum for using, carrying, or possessing a firearm; a 7-year minimum for brandishing a firearm; and a 10-year minimum for discharging a firearm. Incorporating an intent requirement into the discharge provision is necessary to give effect to that progression, because an accidental discharge is less culpable than intentional brandishment. See *Brown*, 449 F.3d at 156.

It is unusual to impose criminal punishment for the consequences of purely accidental conduct. But it is not unusual to punish individuals for the unintended consequences of their *unlawful* acts. See 2 W. LaFave, Substantive Criminal Law §14.4, pp 436-437 (2d ed. 2003). The felony-murder rule is a familiar example: If a defendant commits an unintended homicide while committing another felony, the defendant can be convicted of murder. See 18 U.S.C. §1111. The Sentencing Guidelines reflect the same principle. See United States Sentencing Commission, Guidelines Manual §2A2.2(b)(3) (Nov. 2008) (USSG) (increasing offense level for aggravated assault according to the seriousness of the injury); §2D2.3 (increasing offense level for operating or directing the operation of a common carrier under the influence of alcohol or drugs if death or serious bodily injury results).

Blackstone expressed the idea in the following terms:

"[I]f any accidental mischief happens to follow from the performance of a *lawful* act, the party stands excused from all guilt: but if a man be doing any thing *unlawful*, and a consequence ensues which he did not foresee or intend, as the death of a man or the like, his want of foresight shall be no excuse; for, being guilty of one offence, in doing antecedently what is in itself unlawful, he is criminally guilty of whatever consequence may follow the first misbehaviour." 4 W. Blackstone, Commentaries on the Laws of England 26-27 (1769).

Here the defendant is already guilty of unlawful conduct twice over: a violent or drug trafficking offense and the use, carrying, or possession of a firearm in the course of that offense. That unlawful conduct was not an accident. See *Smith*, 508 U.S., at 238.

The fact that the actual discharge of a gun covered under §924(c)(1)(A)(iii) may be accidental does not mean that the defendant is blameless. The sentencing enhancement in subsection (iii) accounts for the risk of harm resulting from the manner in which the crime is carried out, for which the defendant is responsible. See *Harris*, supra, at 553. An individual who brings a loaded weapon to commit a crime runs the risk that the gun will discharge accidentally. A gunshot in such circumstances—whether accidental or intended—increases the risk that others will be injured, that people will panic, or that violence (with its own danger to those nearby) will be used in response. Those criminals wishing to avoid the penalty for an inadvertent discharge can lock or unload the firearm, handle it with care during the underlying violent or drug trafficking crime, leave the gun at home, or—best yet—avoid committing the felony in the first place.

Justice Stevens contends that the statute should be read to require a showing of intent because harm resulting from a discharge may be punishable under other provisions, such as the Sentencing Guidelines (but only if "bodily injury" results) (citing USSG §2B3.1(b)(3)). But Congress in §924(c)(1)(A)(iii) elected to impose a mandatory term, without regard to more generally applicable sentencing provisions. Punishment available under such provisions therefore does not suggest that the statute at issue here is limited to intentional discharges.

And although the point is not relevant under the correct reading of the statute, it is wrong to assert that the gunshot here "caused no harm." By pure luck, no one was killed or wounded. But the gunshot plainly added to the trauma experienced by those held during the armed robbery. See, e.g., App. 22 (the gunshot "shook us all"); ibid. ("Melissa in the lobby popped up and said, 'oh, my God, has he shot Nora?'").

C

Dean finally argues that any doubts about the proper interpretation of the statute should be resolved in his favor under the rule of lenity. "The simple existence of some statutory ambiguity, however, is not sufficient to warrant application of that rule, for most statutes are ambiguous to some degree." Muscarello v. United States, 524 U.S. 125, 138 (1998); see also *Smith*, supra, at 239 ("The mere possibility of articulating a narrower construction, however, does not by itself make the rule of lenity applicable"). "To invoke the rule, we must conclude that there is a grievous ambiguity or uncertainty in the statute." *Muscarello*, supra, at 138-139 (internal quotation marks omitted). In this case, the statutory text and structure convince us that the discharge provision does not contain an intent requirement. Dean's contrary arguments are not enough to render the statute grievously ambiguous.

* * *

Section 924(c)(1)(A)(iii) requires no separate proof of intent. The 10-year mandatory minimum applies if a gun is discharged in the course of a violent or drug trafficking crime, whether on purpose or by accident. The judgment of the Court of Appeals for the Eleventh Circuit is affirmed.

Justice STEVENS, dissenting.

Accidents happen, but they seldom give rise to criminal liability. Indeed, if they cause no harm they seldom give rise to any liability. The Court today nevertheless holds that petitioner is subject to a mandatory additional sentence—a species of criminal liability—for an accident that caused no harm. For two reasons, 18 U.S.C. §924(c)(1)(A)(iii) should not be so construed. First, the structure of §924(c)(1)(A) suggests that Congress intended to provide escalating sentences for increasingly culpable conduct and that the discharge provision therefore applies only to intentional discharges. Second, even if the statute did not affirmatively support that inference, the common-law presumption that provisions imposing criminal penalties require proof of *mens rea* would lead to the same conclusion. Cf. United States v. X-Citement Video, Inc., 513 U.S. 64, 70 (1994). Accordingly, I would hold that the Court of Appeals erred in concluding that petitioner could be sentenced under §924(c)(1)(A)(iii) absent evidence that he intended to discharge his gun.

I

It is clear from the structure and history of §924(c)(1)(A) that Congress intended §924(c)(1)(A)(iii) to apply only to intentional discharges. The statute's structure supports the inference that Congress intended to impose increasingly harsh punishment for increasingly culpable conduct. The lesser enhancements for carrying or brandishing provided by clauses (i) and (ii) clearly require proof of intent. Clause (i) imposes a 5-year mandatory minimum sentence for using or carrying a firearm "during and in relation to" a crime of violence or drug trafficking offense, or possessing a firearm "in furtherance" of such an offense. As we have said before, the provision's relational terms convey that it does not reach inadvertent conduct. See Smith v. United States, 508 U.S. 223, 238 (1993) ("The phrase 'in relation to' . . . at a minimum, clarifies that the firearm must have some purpose or effect with respect to the drug trafficking crime; its presence or involvement cannot be the result of accident or coincidence"). Similarly, clause (ii) mandates an enhanced penalty for brandishing a firearm only upon proof that a defendant had the specific intent to intimidate. See §924(c)(4). In that context, the most natural reading of clause (iii), which imposes the greatest mandatory penalty, is that it provides additional punishment for the more culpable act of intentional discharge.[1]

The legislative history also indicates that Congress intended to impose an enhanced penalty only for intentional discharge. In Bailey v. United States, 516 U.S. 137, 148 (1995), the Court held that "use" of a firearm for purposes of §924(c)(1) required some type of "active employment," such as "brandishing, displaying, bartering, striking with, and, most obviously, firing or attempting to fire." Congress responded to *Bailey* by amending §924(c)(1), making it an offense to "posses[s]" a firearm "in furtherance of" one of the predicate offenses and adding sentencing enhancements for brandishing and discharge. See Pub. L. 105-386, §1(a)(1), 112 Stat. 3469; see also 144 Cong. Rec. 26608 (1998) (remarks of Sen. DeWine) (referring to the amendments as the "*Bailey* Fix Act"). Given the close relationship between the *Bailey* decision and Congress' enactment of the brandishing and discharge provisions, those terms are best read as codifying some of the more culpable among the "active employment[s]" of a firearm that the Court identified in *Bailey*.

II

Even if there were no evidence that Congress intended §924(c)(1)(A)(iii) to apply only to intentional discharges, the presumption that criminal provisions include an intent requirement would lead me to the same conclusion. Consistent with the common-law tradition, the requirement of *mens rea* has long been the rule of our criminal jurisprudence. The concept of crime as a "concurrence of an evil-meaning mind with an evil-doing hand . . . took deep and early root in American soil." Morissette v. United States, 342 U.S. 246, 251-252 (1952). Legislating against that backdrop, States often omitted intent elements when codifying the criminal law, and "courts assumed that the omission did not signify disapproval of the principle but merely recognized that intent was so inherent in the idea of the offense that it required no statutory affirmation." Id., at 252. Similarly, absent a clear statement by Congress that it intended to create a strict-liability offense, a *mens rea*

---

1. Contrary to the Court's suggestion, Congress' provision of a specific intent element for brandishing and not for discharge only supports the conclusion that Congress did not intend enhancements under the discharge provision to require proof of specific intent; it supports no inference that Congress also intended to eliminate any general intent requirement and thereby make offenders strictly liable.

requirement has generally been presumed in federal statutes. See id., at 273; Staples v. United States, 511 U.S. 600, 605-606 (1994). With only a few narrowly delineated exceptions for such crimes as statutory rape and public welfare offenses, the presumption remains the rule today. See *Morissette*, 342 U.S., at 251-254, and n. 8; see also *Staples*, 511 U.S., at 606-607 (discussing United States v. Balint, 258 U.S. 250 (1922)).

Although mandatory minimum sentencing provisions are of too recent genesis to have any common-law pedigree, . . . there is no sensible reason for treating them differently from offense elements for purposes of the presumption of *mens rea*. Sentencing provisions of this type have substantially the same effect on a defendant's liberty as aggravated offense provisions. . . . If anything, imposition of a mandatory minimum sentence under §924(c)(1)(A) will likely have a greater effect on a defendant's liberty than will conviction for another offense because, unlike sentences for most federal offenses, sentences imposed pursuant to that section must be served consecutively to any other sentence. See §924(c)(1)(D)(ii).

. . . [M]andatory minimum sentencing provisions are in effect no different from aggravated offense provisions. The common-law tradition of requiring proof of *mens rea* to establish criminal culpability should thus apply equally to such sentencing factors. Absent a clear indication that Congress intended to create a strict-liability enhancement, courts should presume that a provision that mandates enhanced criminal penalties requires proof of intent. This conclusion is bolstered by the fact that we have long applied the rule of lenity—which is similar to the *mens rea* rule in both origin and purpose—to provisions that increase criminal penalties as well as those that criminalize conduct. See United States v. R.L.C., 503 U.S. 291, 305 (1992) (plurality opinion); Bifulco v. United States, 447 U.S. 381, 387 (1980); Ladner v. United States, 358 U.S. 169, 178 (1958). Accordingly, I would apply the presumption in this case and avoid the strange result of imposing a substantially harsher penalty for an act caused not by an "evil-meaning mind" but by a clumsy hand. . . .

[The dissenting opinion of Justice BREYER is omitted.]

Rosemond v. United States

Supreme Court of the United States
572 U.S. ___ (2014)

JUSTICE KAGAN delivered the opinion of the Court.*

A federal criminal statute, §924(c) of Title 18, prohibits "us[ing] or carr[ying]" a firearm "during and in relation to any crime of violence or drug trafficking crime." In this case, we consider what the Government

---

* Justice Scalia joins all but footnotes 7 and 8 of this opinion.

must show when it accuses a defendant of aiding or abetting that offense. We hold that the Government makes its case by proving that the defendant actively participated in the underlying drug trafficking or violent crime with advance knowledge that a confederate would use or carry a gun during the crime's commission. We also conclude that the jury instructions given below were erroneous because they failed to require that the defendant knew in advance that one of his cohorts would be armed.

I

This case arises from a drug deal gone bad. Vashti Perez arranged to sell a pound of marijuana to Ricardo Gonzales and Coby Painter. She drove to a local park to make the exchange, accompanied by two confederates, Ronald Joseph and petitioner Justus Rosemond. One of those men apparently took the front passenger seat and the other sat in the back, but witnesses dispute who was where. At the designated meeting place, Gonzales climbed into the car's backseat while Painter waited outside. The backseat passenger allowed Gonzales to inspect the marijuana. But rather than handing over money, Gonzales punched that man in the face and fled with the drugs. As Gonzales and Painter ran away, one of the male passengers—but again, which one is contested—exited the car and fired several shots from a semiautomatic handgun. The shooter then re-entered the vehicle, and all three would be drug dealers gave chase after the buyers-turned-robbers. But before the three could catch their quarry, a police officer, responding to a dispatcher's alert, pulled their car over. This federal prosecution of Rosemond followed.

The Government charged Rosemond with, *inter alia*, violating §924(c) by using a gun in connection with a drug trafficking crime, or aiding and abetting that offense under §2 of Title 18. Section 924(c) provides that "any person who, during and in relation to any crime of violence or drug trafficking crime[,] . . . uses or carries a firearm," shall receive a five-year mandatory-minimum sentence, with seven- and ten-year minimums applicable, respectively, if the firearm is also brandished or discharged. 18 U.S.C. §924(c)(1)(A). Section 2, for its part, is the federal aiding and abetting statute: It provides that "[w]hoever commits an offense against the United States or aids, abets, counsels, commands, induces or procures its commission is punishable as a principal."

Consistent with the indictment, the Government prosecuted the §924(c) charge on two alternative theories. The Government's primary contention was that Rosemond himself used the firearm during the aborted drug transaction. But recognizing that the identity of the shooter was disputed, the Government also offered a back-up argument: Even if it was Joseph who fired the gun as the drug deal fell apart, Rosemond aided and abetted the §924(c) violation.

The District Judge accordingly instructed the jury on aiding and abetting law. He first explained, in a way challenged by neither party, the rudiments of §2. Under that statute, the judge stated, "[a] person who aids or abets another to commit an offense is just as guilty of that offense as if he committed it himself." And in order to aid or abet, the defendant must "willfully and knowingly associate[ ] himself in some way with the crime, and . . . seek[ ] by some act to help make the crime succeed." The judge then turned to applying those general principles to §924(c) — and there, he deviated from an instruction Rosemond had proposed. According to Rosemond, a defendant could be found guilty of aiding or abetting a §924(c) violation only if he "intentionally took some action to facilitate or encourage the use of the firearm," as opposed to the predicate drug offense. But the District Judge disagreed, instead telling the jury that it could convict if "(1) the defendant knew his cohort used a firearm in the drug trafficking crime, and (2) the defendant knowingly and actively participated in the drug trafficking crime." In closing argument, the prosecutor contended that Rosemond easily satisfied that standard, so that even if he had not "fired the gun, he's still guilty of the crime." After all, the prosecutor stated, Rosemond "certainly knew [of] and actively participated in" the drug transaction. "And with regards to the other element," the prosecutor urged, "the fact is a person cannot be present and active at a drug deal when shots are fired and not know their cohort is using a gun. You simply can't do it."

The jury convicted Rosemond of violating §924(c) (as well as all other offenses charged). The verdict form was general: It did not reveal whether the jury found that Rosemond himself had used the gun or instead had aided and abetted a confederate's use during the marijuana deal. As required by §924(c), the trial court imposed a consecutive sentence of 120 months of imprisonment for the statute's violation.

The Tenth Circuit affirmed, rejecting Rosemond's argument that the District Court's aiding and abetting instructions were erroneous. The Court of Appeals acknowledged that some other Circuits agreed with Rosemond that a defendant aids and abets a §924(c) offense only if he intentionally takes "some action to facilitate or encourage his cohort's use of the firearm." 695 F.3d 1151, 1155 (2012).[3] But the Tenth Circuit had already adopted a different standard, which it thought consonant with the District Court's instructions. And the Court of Appeals held that Rosemond had presented no sufficient reason for departing from that precedent.

We granted certiorari, 569 U.S. ___ (2013), to resolve the Circuit conflict over what it takes to aid and abet a §924(c) offense. Although we disagree

3. See, e.g., United States v. Rolon-Ramos, 502 F.3d 750 (CA8 2007); United States v. Medina-Roman, 376 F.3d 1 (CA1 2004); United States v. Bancalari, 110 F.3d 1425 (CA9 1997).

with Rosemond's principal arguments, we find that the trial court erred in instructing the jury. We therefore vacate the judgment below.

II

The federal aiding and abetting statute, 18 U.S.C. §2, states that a person who furthers—more specifically, who "aids, abets, counsels, commands, induces or procures"— the commission of a federal offense "is punishable as a principal." That provision derives from (though simplifies) common-law standards for accomplice liability. See, e.g., Standefer v. United States, 447 U.S. 10, 14-19 (1980); United States v. Peoni, 100 F.2d 401, 402 (CA2 1938) (L. Hand, J.) ("The substance of [§2's] formula goes back a long way"). And in so doing, §2 reflects a centuries-old view of culpability: that a person may be responsible for a crime he has not personally carried out if he helps another to complete its commission. See J. Hawley & M. McGregor, Criminal Law 81 (1899).

We have previously held that under §2 "those who provide knowing aid to persons committing federal crimes, with the intent to facilitate the crime, are themselves committing a crime." Central Bank of Denver, N. A. v. First Interstate Bank of Denver, N. A., 511 U.S. 164, 181 (1994). Both parties here embrace that formulation, and agree as well that it has two components. As at common law, a person is liable under §2 for aiding and abetting a crime if (and only if) he (1) takes an affirmative act in furtherance of that offense, (2) with the intent of facilitating the offense's commission. . . .

The questions that the parties dispute, and we here address, concern how those two requirements—affirmative act and intent—apply in a prosecution for aiding and abetting a §924(c) offense. Those questions arise from the compound nature of that provision. Recall that §924(c) forbids "us[ing] or carr[ying] a firearm" when engaged in a "crime of violence or drug trafficking crime." The prosecutor must show the use or carriage of a gun; so too he must prove the commission of a predicate (violent or drug trafficking) offense. See Smith v. United States, 508 U.S. 223, 228 (1993). For purposes of ascertaining aiding and abetting liability, we therefore must consider: When does a person act to further this double-barreled crime? And when does he intend to facilitate its commission? We address each issue in turn.

A

Consider first Rosemond's account of his conduct (divorced from any issues of intent). Rosemond actively participated in a drug transaction, accompanying two others to a site where money was to be exchanged for a pound of marijuana. But as he tells it, he took no action with respect to any firearm. He did not buy or borrow a gun to facilitate the narcotics deal; he did not carry a gun to the scene; he did not use a gun during the subsequent events constituting this criminal misadventure. His acts thus advanced one part (the drug part) of a two-part incident—or to speak a bit more technically, one element (the drug element) of a two-element crime. Is that enough to satisfy the conduct requirement of this aiding and abetting charge, or must Rosemond, as he claims, have taken some act to assist the commission of the other (firearm) component of §924(c)?

The common law imposed aiding and abetting liability on a person (possessing the requisite intent) who facilitated any part—even though not every part—of a criminal venture. As a leading treatise, published around the time of §2's enactment, put the point: Accomplice liability attached upon proof of "*[a]ny* participation in a general felonious plan" carried out by confederates. 1 F. Wharton, Criminal Law §251, p. 322 (11th ed. 1912) (hereinafter Wharton) (emphasis added). Or in the words of another standard reference: If a person was "present abetting while *any* act necessary to constitute the offense [was] being performed through another," he could be charged as a principal—even "though [that act was] *not the whole thing necessary*." 1 J. Bishop, Commentaries on the Criminal Law §649, p. 392 (7th ed. 1882) (emphasis added). And so "[w]here several acts constitute[d] together one crime, if each [was] separately performed by a different individual[,] . . . all [were] principals as to the whole." Id., §650, at 392.[4] Indeed, as yet a third treatise underscored, a person's involvement in the crime could be not merely partial but minimal too: "The quantity [of assistance was] immaterial," so long as the accomplice did "*something*" to aid the crime. R. Desty, A Compendium of American Criminal Law §37a, p. 106 (1882) (emphasis added). After all, the common law maintained, every little bit helps—and a contribution to some part of a crime aids the whole.

That principle continues to govern aiding and abetting law under §2: As almost every court of appeals has held, "[a] defendant can be convicted as an aider and abettor without proof that he participated in each and every element of the offense." United States v. Sigalow, 812 F.2d 783, 785 (CA2 1987). In proscribing aiding and abetting, Congress used language that "comprehends all assistance rendered by words, acts, encouragement, support, or presence," Reves v. Ernst & Young, 507 U.S. 170, 178 (1993)—even if that aid relates to only one (or some) of a crime's phases or elements. So, for example, in upholding convictions for abetting a tax evasion scheme, this Court found "irrelevant" the defendants' "non-participation" in filing

4. The Wharton treatise gave the following example of how multiple confederates could perform different roles in carrying out a crime. Assume, Wharton hypothesized, that several persons "act in concert to steal a man's goods." Wharton §251, at 322. The victim is "induced by fraud to trust one of them[,] in the presence of [the] others[,] with the [goods'] possession." Ibid. Afterward, "another of the party entice[s] the owner away so that he who has the goods may carry them off." Id., at 322-323. Wharton concludes: "[A]ll are guilty as principals." Id., at 323.

a false return; we thought they had amply facilitated the illegal scheme by helping a confederate conceal his assets. United States v. Johnson, 319 U.S. 503, 515 (1943). "[A]ll who shared in [the overall crime's] execution," we explained, "have equal responsibility before the law, whatever may have been [their] different roles." Id., at 515. And similarly, we approved a conviction for abetting mail fraud even though the defendant had played no part in mailing the fraudulent documents; it was enough to satisfy the law's conduct requirement that he had in other ways aided the deception. See Pereira v. United States, 347 U.S. 1, 8-11 (1954). The division of labor between two (or more) confederates thus has no significance: A strategy of "you take that element, I'll take this one" would free neither party from liability.

Under that established approach, Rosemond's participation in the drug deal here satisfies the affirmative-act requirement for aiding and abetting a §924(c) violation. As we have previously described, the commission of a drug trafficking (or violent) crime is—no less than the use of a firearm—an "essential conduct element of the §924(c) offense." United States v. Rodriguez-Moreno, 526 U.S. 275, 280 (1999). In enacting the statute, "Congress proscribed both the use of the firearm *and* the commission of acts that constitute" a drug trafficking crime. *Rodriguez-Moreno*, 526 U.S., at 281. Rosemond therefore could assist in §924(c)'s violation by facilitating either the drug transaction or the firearm use (or of course both). In helping to bring about one part of the offense (whether trafficking drugs or using a gun), he necessarily helped to complete the whole. And that ends the analysis as to his conduct. It is inconsequential, as courts applying both the common law and §2 have held, that his acts did not advance each element of the offense; all that matters is that they facilitated one component.

Rosemond argues, to the contrary, that the requisite act here "must be directed at the use of the firearm," because that element is §924(c)'s most essential feature. Brief for Petitioner 33 (arguing that "it is the firearm crime" he was really charged with aiding and abetting, "not the drug trafficking crime"). But Rosemond can provide no authority for demanding that an affirmative act go toward an element considered peculiarly significant; rather, as just noted, courts have never thought relevant the importance of the aid rendered. And in any event, we reject Rosemond's premise that §924(c) is somehow more about using guns than selling narcotics. It is true enough, as Rosemond says in support of that theory, that §924(c) "establishes a separate, freestanding offense that is 'distinct from the underlying [drug trafficking crime].'" Brief for Petitioner 32 (quoting Simpson v. United States, 435 U.S. 6, 10 (1978)). But it is just as true that §924(c) establishes a freestanding offense distinct from any that might apply just to using a gun—say, for discharging a firearm in a public park. That is because §924(c) is, to coin a term, a combination crime. It punishes the temporal and relational conjunction of two separate acts, on the ground that together they pose an extreme risk of harm. See Muscarello v. United States, 524

U.S. 125, 132 (1998) (noting that §924(c)'s "basic purpose" was "to combat the dangerous combination of drugs and guns"). And so, an act relating to drugs, just as much as an act relating to guns, facilitates a §924(c) violation.

Rosemond's related argument that our approach would conflate two distinct offenses—allowing a conviction for abetting a §924(c) violation whenever the prosecution shows that the defendant abetted the underlying drug trafficking crime—fares no better. That is because, as we will describe, an aiding and abetting conviction requires not just an act facilitating one or another element, but also a state of mind extending to the entire crime. And under that rule, a defendant may be convicted of abetting a §924(c) violation only if his intent reaches beyond a simple drug sale, to an armed one. Aiding and abetting law's intent component—to which we now turn—thus preserves the distinction between assisting the predicate drug trafficking crime and assisting the broader §924(c) offense.

B

Begin with (or return to) some basics about aiding and abetting law's intent requirement, which no party here disputes. As previously explained, a person aids and abets a crime when (in addition to taking the requisite act) he intends to facilitate that offense's commission. An intent to advance some different or lesser offense is not, or at least not usually, sufficient: Instead, the intent must go to the specific and entire crime charged—so here, to the full scope (predicate crime plus gun use) of §924(c). See, e.g., ALI, Model Penal Code §2.06 Comment, p. 306 (1985).[7] And the canonical formulation of that needed state of mind—later appropriated by this Court and oft-quoted in both parties' briefs—is Judge Learned Hand's: To aid and abet a crime, a defendant must not just "in some sort associate himself with the venture," but also "participate in it as in something that he wishes to bring about" and "seek by his action to make it succeed." Nye & Nissen v. United States, 336 U.S. 613, 619 (1949) (quoting *Peoni*, 100 F.2d, at 402).

We have previously found that intent requirement satisfied when a person actively participates in a criminal venture with full knowledge of the circumstances constituting the charged offense. In *Pereira*, the mail fraud case discussed above, we found the requisite intent for aiding and abetting because the defendant took part in a fraud "know[ing]" that his confederate would take care of the mailing. 347 U.S., at 12. Likewise, in Bozza v. United States, 330 U.S. 160, 165 (1947), we upheld a conviction for aiding and abetting the

---

7. Some authorities suggest an exception to the general rule when another crime is the "natural and probable consequence" of the crime the defendant intended to abet. . . . That question is not implicated here, because no one contends that a §924(c) violation is a natural and probable consequence of simple drug trafficking. We therefore express no view on the issue.

evasion of liquor taxes because the defendant helped operate a clandestine distillery "know[ing]" the business was set up "to violate Government revenue laws." And several Courts of Appeals have similarly held—addressing a fact pattern much like this one—that the unarmed driver of a getaway car had the requisite intent to aid and abet armed bank robbery if he "knew" that his confederates would use weapons in carrying out the crime. See, e.g., United States v. Akiti, 701 F.3d 883, 887 (CA8 2012); United States v. Easter, 66 F.3d 1018, 1024 (CA9 1995). So for purposes of aiding and abetting law, a person who actively participates in a criminal scheme knowing its extent and character intends that scheme's commission.[8]

The same principle holds here: An active participant in a drug transaction has the intent needed to aid and abet a §924(c) violation when he knows that one of his confederates will carry a gun. In such a case, the accomplice has decided to join in the criminal venture, and share in its benefits, with full awareness of its scope—that the plan calls not just for a drug sale, but for an armed one. In so doing, he has chosen (like the abettors in *Pereira* and *Bozza* or the driver in an armed robbery) to align himself with the illegal scheme in its entirety—including its use of a firearm. And he has determined (again like those other abettors) to do what he can to "make [that scheme] succeed." *Nye & Nissen*, 336 U.S., at 619. He thus becomes responsible, in the typical way of aiders and abettors, for the conduct of others. He may not have brought the gun to the drug deal himself, but because he took part in that deal knowing a confederate would do so, he intended the commission of a §924(c) offense—i.e., an armed drug sale.

For all that to be true, though, the §924(c) defendant's knowledge of a firearm must be advance knowledge—or otherwise said, knowledge that enables him to make the relevant legal (and indeed, moral) choice. When an accomplice knows beforehand of a confederate's design to carry a gun, he can attempt to alter that plan or, if unsuccessful, withdraw from the enterprise; it is deciding instead to go ahead with his role in the venture that shows his intent to aid an *armed* offense. But when an accomplice knows nothing of a gun until it appears at the scene, he may already have completed his acts of assistance; or even if not, he may at that late point have no realistic opportunity to quit the crime. And when that is so, the defendant has not shown the requisite intent to assist a crime involving a gun. As even the Government concedes, an unarmed accomplice cannot aid and abet a §924(c) violation unless he has "foreknowledge that his confederate will commit the offense with a firearm." Brief for United States 38. For the

8. We did not deal in these cases, nor do we here, with defendants who incidentally facilitate a criminal venture rather than actively participate in it. A hypothetical case is the owner of a gun store who sells a firearm to a criminal, knowing but not caring how the gun will be used. We express no view about what sort of facts, if any, would suffice to show that such a third party has the intent necessary to be convicted of aiding and abetting.

reasons just given, we think that means knowledge at a time the accomplice can do something with it—most notably, opt to walk away.[9]

Both parties here find something to dislike in our view of this issue. Rosemond argues that a participant in a drug deal intends to assist a §924(c) violation only if he affirmatively desires one of his confederates to use a gun. The jury, Rosemond concedes, could infer that state of mind from the defendant's advance knowledge that the plan included a firearm. But according to Rosemond, the instructions must also permit the jury to draw the opposite conclusion—that although the defendant participated in a drug deal knowing a gun would be involved, he did not specifically want its carriage or use. That higher standard, Rosemond claims, is necessary to avoid subjecting persons of different culpability to the same punishment. Rosemond offers as an example an unarmed driver assisting in the heist of a store: If that person spent the drive "trying to persuade [his confederate] to leave [the] gun behind," then he should be convicted of abetting shoplifting, but not armed robbery. Reply Brief 9.

We think not. What matters for purposes of gauging intent, and so what jury instructions should convey, is that the defendant has chosen, with full knowledge, to participate in the illegal scheme—not that, if all had been left to him, he would have planned the identical crime. Consider a variant of Rosemond's example: The driver of a getaway car wants to help rob a convenience store (and argues passionately for that plan), but eventually accedes when his confederates decide instead to hold up a national bank. Whatever his original misgivings, he has the requisite intent to aid and abet *bank* robbery; after all, he put aside those doubts and knowingly took part in that more dangerous crime. The same is true of an accomplice who knowingly joins in an armed drug transaction—regardless whether he was formerly indifferent or even resistant to using firearms. The law does not, nor should it, care whether he participates with a happy heart or a sense of foreboding. Either way, he has the same culpability, because either way he has knowingly elected to aid in the commission of a peculiarly risky form of offense.

A final, metaphorical way of making the point: By virtue of §924(c), using a firearm at a drug deal ups the ante. A would-be accomplice might decide to play at those perilous stakes. Or he might grasp that the better course is to fold his hand. What he should not expect is the capacity to hedge his bets, joining in a dangerous criminal scheme but evading its penalties by leaving use of the gun to someone else. Aiding and abetting law prevents that outcome, so long as the player knew the heightened stakes when he decided to stay in the game.

___

9. Of course, if a defendant continues to participate in a crime after a gun was displayed or used by a confederate, the jury can permissibly infer from his failure to object or withdraw that he had such knowledge. In any criminal case, after all, the factfinder can draw inferences about a defendant's intent based on all the facts and circumstances of a crime's commission.

The Government, for its part, thinks we take too strict a view of when a defendant charged with abetting a §924(c) violation must acquire that knowledge. As noted above, the Government recognizes that the accused accomplice must have "foreknowledge" of a gun's presence. Brief for United States 38. But the Government views that standard as met whenever the accomplice, having learned of the firearm, continues any act of assisting the drug transaction. According to the Government, the jury should convict such a defendant even if he became aware of the gun only after he realistically could have opted out of the crime.

But that approach, we think, would diminish too far the requirement that a defendant in a §924(c) prosecution must intend to further an *armed* drug deal. Assume, for example, that an accomplice agrees to participate in a drug sale on the express condition that no one brings a gun to the place of exchange. But just as the parties are making the trade, the accomplice notices that one of his confederates has a (poorly) concealed firearm in his jacket. The Government would convict the accomplice of aiding and abetting a §924(c) offense if he assists in completing the deal without incident, rather than running away or otherwise aborting the sale. But behaving as the Government suggests might increase the risk of gun violence—to the accomplice himself, other participants, or bystanders; and conversely, finishing the sale might be the best or only way to avoid that danger. In such a circumstance, a jury is entitled to find that the defendant intended only a drug sale—that he never intended to facilitate, and so does not bear responsibility for, a drug deal carried out with a gun. A defendant manifests that greater intent, and incurs the greater liability of §924(c), when he chooses to participate in a drug transaction knowing it will involve a firearm; but he makes no such choice when that knowledge comes too late for him to be reasonably able to act upon it.[10]

III

Under these principles, the District Court erred in instructing the jury, because it did not explain that Rosemond needed advance knowledge of a firearm's presence. Recall that the court stated that Rosemond was guilty of aiding and abetting if "(1) [he] knew his cohort used a firearm in the drug

10. Contrary to the dissent's view, nothing in this holding changes the way the defenses of duress and necessity operate. Neither does our decision remotely deny that the "intent to undertake some act is . . . perfectly consistent with the motive of avoiding adverse consequences which would otherwise occur." Our holding is grounded in the distinctive intent standard for aiding and abetting someone else's act—in the words of Judge Hand, that a defendant must not just "in some sort associate himself with the venture" (as seems to be good enough for the dissent), but also "participate in it as in something that he wishes to bring about" and "seek by his action to make it succeed." Nye & Nissen v. United States, 336 U.S. 613, 619 (1949) (quoting *Peoni*, 100 F.2d, at 402). . . .

trafficking crime, and (2) [he] knowingly and actively participated in the drug trafficking crime." App. 196. We agree with that instruction's second half: As we have explained, active participation in a drug sale is sufficient for §924(c) liability (even if the conduct does not extend to the firearm), so long as the defendant had prior knowledge of the gun's involvement. The problem with the court's instruction came in its description of that knowledge requirement. In telling the jury to consider merely whether Rosemond "knew his cohort used a firearm," the court did not direct the jury to determine *when* Rosemond obtained the requisite knowledge. So, for example, the jury could have convicted even if Rosemond first learned of the gun when it was fired and he took no further action to advance the crime. For that reason, the Government itself describes the instruction's first half as "potentially misleading," candidly explaining that "it would have been clearer to say" that Rosemond had to know that his confederate "'would use' [a firearm] or something . . . that makes absolutely clear that you [need] foreknowledge." Tr. of Oral Arg. 48-49. We agree with that view, and then some: The court's statement failed to convey that Rosemond had to have advance knowledge, of the kind we have described, that a confederate would be armed. . . .

. . . Accordingly, we vacate the judgment below and remand the case for further proceedings consistent with this opinion.

Justice ALITO, with whom Justice THOMAS joins, concurring in part and dissenting in part.

I largely agree with the analysis in the first 12 pages of the opinion of the Court, but I strongly disagree with the discussion that comes after that point. Specifically, I reject the Court's conclusion that a conviction for aiding and abetting a violation of 18 U.S.C. §924(c) demands proof that the alleged aider and abettor had what the Court terms "a realistic opportunity" to refrain from engaging in the conduct at issue.[1] This rule represents an important and, as far as I am aware, unprecedented alteration of the law of aiding and abetting and of the law of intentionality generally.

. . . The Court imagines the following situation:

> "[A]n accomplice agrees to participate in a drug sale on the express condition that no one brings a gun to the place of exchange. But just as the parties are making the trade, the accomplice notices that one of his confederates has a (poorly) concealed firearm in his jacket."

---

1. I am also concerned that the Court's use, without clarification, of the phrase "advance knowledge" will lead readers astray. Viewed by itself, the phrase most naturally means knowledge acquired in advance of the commission of the drug trafficking offense, but this is not what the Court means. Rather, "advance knowledge," as used by the Court, may include knowledge acquired while the drug trafficking offense is in progress. Specifically, a defendant has such knowledge, the Court says, if he or she first learns of the gun while the drug offense is in progress and at that time "realistically could have opted out of the crime."

If the accomplice, despite spotting the gun, continues to assist in the completion of the drug sale, has the accomplice aided and abetted the commission of a violation of §924(c)?

The Court's answer is "it depends." Walking away, the Court observes, "might increase the risk of gun violence—to the accomplice himself, other participants, or bystanders; and conversely, finishing the sale might be the best or only way to avoid the danger." Moreover—and this is where the seriously misguided step occurs—the Court says that if the risk of walking away exceeds (by some unspecified degree) the risk created by completing the sale and if the alleged aider and abettor chooses to continue for that reason, the alleged aider and abettor lacks the *mens rea* required for conviction.

What the Court has done is to convert what has up to now been an affirmative defense into a part of the required *mens rea*, and this step has very important conceptual and practical consequences. It fundamentally alters the prior understanding of mental states that form the foundation of substantive criminal law, and it places a strange and difficult burden on the prosecution.

That the Court has taken a radical step can be seen by comparing what the Court now holds with the traditional defense of necessity. That defense excuses a violation of law if "the harm which will result from compliance with the law is greater than that which will result from violation of it." 2 W. LaFave, Substantive Criminal Law §10.1, p. 116 (2003) (hereinafter LaFave). This is almost exactly the balance-of-risks calculus adopted by the Court, but under the traditional approach necessity is an affirmative defense. See, e.g., United States v. Bailey, 444 U.S. 394, 416 (1980). Necessity and the closely related defense of duress are affirmative defenses because they almost invariably do not negate the *mens rea* necessary to incur criminal liability. See 2 LaFave §10.1(a), at 118 ("The rationale of the necessity defense is not that a person, when faced with the pressure of circumstances of nature, lacks the mental element which the crime in question requires"); id., §9.7(a), at 73 (same for duress). . . .

. . . [T]he Court, having refrained from deciding whether aiding and abetting requires purposeful, as opposed to knowing, conduct, quickly and without explanation jettisons the "knowing" standard and concludes that purposeful conduct is needed. This is a critical move because if it is enough for an alleged aider and abettor simply to know that his confederate is carrying a gun, then the alleged aider and abettor in the Court's hypothetical case (who spots the gun on the confederate's person) unquestionably had the *mens rea* needed for conviction.

. . . The Court confuses two fundamentally distinct concepts: intent and motive. It seems to assume that, if a defendant's *motive* in aiding a criminal venture is to avoid some greater evil, he does not have the *intent* that the venture succeed. But the intent to undertake some act is of course perfectly consistent with the motive of avoiding adverse consequences which would otherwise occur. We can all testify to this from our daily experience. People wake up, go to work, balance their checkbooks, shop for groceries—and yes, commit crimes—because they believe something bad will happen if they do not do these things, not because the deepest desire of their heart is to do them. A person may only go to work in the morning to keep his or her family from destitution; that does not mean he or she does not intend to put in a full day's work. In the same way, the fact that a defendant carries out a crime because he feels he must do so on pain of terrible consequences does not mean he does not intend to carry out the crime. When Jean Valjean stole a loaf of bread to feed his starving family, he certainly intended to commit theft; the fact that, had he been living in America today, he may have pleaded necessity as a defense does not change that fact. See V. Hugo, Les Misérables 54 (Fall River Press ed. 2012).

. . . [I]t seems inarguable to me that the existence of the purpose or intent to carry out a crime is perfectly compatible with facts giving rise to a necessity or duress defense. Once that proposition is established, the Court's error is readily apparent. The Court requires the Government to prove that a defendant in Rosemond's situation could have walked away without risking harm greater than he would cause by continuing with the crime—circumstances that traditionally would support a necessity or duress defense. It imposes this requirement on the Government despite the fact that such dangerous circumstances simply do not bear on whether the defendant intends the §924(c) offense to succeed, as (on the Court's reading) is required for aiding and abetting liability.

The usual rule that a defendant bears the burden of proving affirmative defenses is justified by a compelling, commonsense intuition: "[W]here the facts with regard to an issue lie peculiarly in the knowledge of a party, that party is best situated to bear the burden of proof." Smith v. United States, 568 U.S. ___, ___ (2013). By abandoning that rule in cases involving aiding and abetting of §924(c) offenses, the Court creates a perverse arrangement whereby the prosecution must prove something that is peculiarly within the knowledge of the defendant. Imagine that A aids B in committing a §924(c) offense and claims that he only learned of the gun once the crime had begun. If A had the burden of proof, he might testify that B was a hothead who had previously shot others who had crossed him. But under the Court's rule, the prosecution, in order to show the intent needed to convict A as an aider and abettor, presumably has the burden of proving that B was not such a person and that A did not believe him to be. How is the prosecution to do this? By offering testimony by B's friends and associates regarding his peaceful and easygoing nature? By introducing entries from A's diary in which he reflects on the sense of safety he feels when carrying out criminal enterprises in B's company? Furthermore, even if B were a hothead and A knew him to be such, A would presumably only be entitled to escape liability if he continued with the offense *because of* his fear of B's reaction if he walked away. Under the Court's rule, it is up to the Government to prove that A's continued participation was not on account of his fear of B—but how? By introducing footage of a convenient security camera demonstrating that A's eyes were not wide with fear, nor his breathing rapid?

The Court's rule breaks with the common-law tradition and our case law. It also makes no sense. I respectfully dissent from that portion of the Court's opinion which places on the Government the burden of proving that the alleged aider and abettor of a §924(c) offense had what the Court terms "a realistic opportunity" to refrain from engaging in the conduct at issue.

Notes and Questions

1. *Dean* and *Rosemond* both involve 18 U.S.C. §924(c)(1)(A), the federal statute that enhances criminal penalties for using or carrying a gun in connection with certain federal crimes. Both cases also involve accomplice liability under 18 U.S.C. §2, the federal aiding and abetting statute. Finally, both cases involve tricky issues of *mens rea*. The main difference between the two cases is that the focus in *Dean* is on the minimum required *mens rea* with respect to the fact that the gun "discharged" during the crime—an element that mandates a ten-year minimum sentence enhancement, consecutive to the sentence for the underlying crime—whereas in *Rosemond* the focus is on the defendant's *mens rea* with respect to the co-defendant's carrying of the gun. (*Rosemond* also involves the actus reus to be an accomplice to §924(c)(1)(A).) In *Dean*, the defendant loses. In *Rosemond*, it's a partial win and a partial loss for both sides. Did the Court get both cases right?

2. In *Dean*, do you agree that strict liability is the most appropriate *mens rea* with respect to the statutory element of the "discharge[ ]" of the gun? The Court analogizes the situation to the felony murder rule—a rule that has been roundly criticized by academics and legal reformers, and that the Model Penal Code drafters rejected. Are you persuaded? Does it seem fair for Dean to get a mandatory minimum of ten extra years in prison, just because he was a klutz?

3. In *Rosemond*, do you agree that the prosecution should be required to prove, in order to obtain the sentence enhancement, that the defendant had "advance knowledge" of the co-defendant's gun? According to the majority opinion, this means knowledge "at a time the accomplice can do something with it—most notably, opt to walk away." Isn't Justice Alito correct that this interpretation will make it prohibitively difficult for prosecutors to prevail in §924(c)(1)(A) cases involving accomplices? Should that matter? And isn't Justice Alito likewise correct that the *Rosemond* majority is confusing "intent" and "motive"? Should *that* matter?

4. What do you think about Justice Kagan's wry observation, in the majority opinion in *Rosemond*, that "[b]oth parties here find something to dislike in our view of this issue"? Do you think that makes it more, or less, likely that the Court found the right answer?

5. Note that Justice Scalia, who otherwise joins the majority opinion in *Rosemond*, declines to join footnotes 7 and 8. Why? Is he just being snarky? Does he think Justice Kagan is somehow implying an answer to the questions that she specifically declines, in those two footnotes, to answer? Or is it that Justice Scalia simply doesn't like any mention of questions that the Court is *not* going to answer?

9

Crimes of Sex and Sexual Violence

Sex has always occupied a large place in American criminal law. Not necessarily coerced sex: The common-law definition of rape was very restrictive, and that restrictive definition did not change much until the late 1970s. (It has changed a great deal since then.) For most of American history, rape convictions have been hard to obtain; consequently, they have been rarer events than they are today. But early American law criminalized a great deal of *consensual* sex — adultery and fornication, sodomy, and later prostitution accounted for the bulk of the many sex cases on criminal dockets. Until quite recently, sex that was the product of force or fraud was less likely to be punished than sex that was the product of bad morals.

Morals were the key to that older criminal law of sex; the law's chief focus was reinforcing the norm that sex should be reserved for heterosexual married couples. That norm has faded over the past two generations. The contemporary law of sex crimes has a very different focus: more the protection of sexual autonomy and the prohibition of sex-related violence than the promotion of sexual morality. But the change has been partial and incomplete; autonomy is better protected and violence more consistently punished in some legal spaces than in others. For example, the law of fraudulent sex continues to live (mostly) by the old rule of *caveat emptor* — let the buyer beware — save where the party doing the defrauding is HIV-positive or claims to offer medical treatment.

Keep these recent changes in mind as you read the cases that follow. The cases deal with four different types of sex crimes. Section A deals with the set of criminal prohibitions surrounding prostitution. The main case in that section is a California prosecution for "pimping" and "pandering"; the case deals with the legal line between permissible and impermissible sex businesses. Section B offers a pair of cases that explore the criminalization of fraudulent sex. Section C addresses three forms of sexual assault: sex by physical force or violence (or the threat thereof), sex through intoxication, and sex with an underage partner. Because the legal regulation of sex-related violence has changed so dramatically over the past few decades, Section C also includes the contemporary California statutes that govern the relevant topics; consider whether the California legislature has done a good job of drawing the legal lines fairly. Finally, Section D covers the crime of child pornography, which raises issues of vagueness (under the Due Process Clause) and overbreadth (under the First Amendment).

A. SEX FOR MONEY

Wooten v. Superior Court of San Bernardino County

Court of Appeal of California, Fourth Appellate District
93 Cal. App. 4th 422; 113 Cal. Rptr. 2d 195 (2001)

Opinion of WARD, J.

In the trial court, petitioners Brent Howard Wooten and Daniel Robert Mendoza (defendants) stand charged with pimping and pandering. According to the evidence at their preliminary hearing, they worked as managers at the Flesh Club. The Flesh Club appears to have been mainly a standard "strip joint." . . . [I]t also offered semiprivate rooms in which, for $240 plus an optional gratuity, a customer could watch two naked women perform sexual acts on each other for approximately nine minutes.

Defendants seek review of the trial court's refusal to set aside the information. They contend there was insufficient evidence of "prostitution," and hence insufficient evidence of either pimping or pandering, because the women sexually touched only each other and not the customer. . . . We agree . . . [and] hold that the definition of "prostitution" requires physical contact between the prostitute and the customer. Because there was no physical contact between the women and the customers, there can be no underlying crime of prostitution. Without prostitution, there is insufficient evidence of either pimping or pandering. Hence, defendants' motion to set aside the information should have been granted. . . .

. . . The main room of the Flesh Club consisted of a stage on which nude dancers performed. It was surrounded by chairs and couches; the couches were used for lap dances. A separate room, called the V.I.P. Room, included five to 10 booths. Each booth was about five feet square and furnished with two small couches and a lamp on a table. The entrance to each booth was partially covered by a sheer curtain. On May 4, 9, 16, 22, and 26, 2000, Officer Mark Aranda and Officer Jerry Valdivia visited the Flesh Club, posing as customers. Officer Valdivia was in a wheelchair, pretending to be disabled, to facilitate his operation of a hidden video camera.

During each visit, the officers went into one of the booths with two female dancers. For about nine minutes, the dancers performed sexual acts on each other.

On May 4, 2000, Officer Valdivia paid each of the dancers $100, plus a $10 tip. On May 9, 2000, he was told that the price had gone up to $120, of which the "house" would receive $45. . . . On May 4, 2000, the dancers involved were "Angel" and "Cat." Defendant Mendoza was a manager employed by the Flesh Club. From time to time, he looked into the booth and wrote something on a clipboard.

On May 22, 2000, the dancers involved were "Veronica" and "Anaya," and Veronica and "Malibu." Defendant Wooten was another manager employed by the Flesh Club. From time to time, Wooten came around with a clipboard and checked on the dancers. On May 26, 2000, the police executed a search warrant at the Flesh Club. Anaya and "Exotica" told police the charge for a V.I.P. Room show was $120 per dancer. Exotica said $75 of this went to the dancer and $45 went to the management at the end of the night. She said the managers kept track of how much the "house" should receive by walking around and taking notes on what each dancer was doing.

A felony complaint was filed charging Mendoza with four counts, all allegedly committed on May 4, 2000: pimping and pandering with respect to Angel, and pimping and pandering with respect to Cat. The same complaint also charged Wooten with six counts, all allegedly committed on May 22, 2000: pimping and pandering with respect to Veronica, Anaya and Malibu. . . . An information containing the same charges was filed. Defendants filed a motion to set aside the information. They argued that there was no underlying prostitution because "the customer d[id] not receive sex for his money." [The trial court denied the motion.] . . .

ANALYSIS

. . . Pimping is committed by

> "any person who, knowing another person is a prostitute, lives or derives support or maintenance in whole or in part from the earnings or proceeds of the person's prostitution, or from money loaned or advanced to or charged against that person by any keeper or manager or inmate of a house or other place where prostitution is practiced or allowed, or who solicits or receives compensation for soliciting for the person. . . ."[9]

Pandering . . . is committed by

> "any person who . . . :

---

9. [Cal. Penal Code §266h(a); section (b) prohibits "pimping a minor"—EDS.]

"(1) Procures another person for the purpose of prostitution. . . .

[(2) By promises, threats, violence, or by any device or scheme, causes, induces, persuades or encourages another person to become a prostitute.

(3) Procures for another person a place as an inmate in a house of prostitution or as an inmate of any place in which prostitution is encouraged or allowed within this state.]

"(4) By promises, threats, violence or by any device or scheme, causes, induces, persuades or encourages an inmate of a house of prostitution, or any other place in which prostitution is encouraged or allowed, to remain therein as an inmate."

[(5) By fraud or artifice, or by duress of person or goods, or by abuse of any position of confidence or authority, procures another person for the purpose of prostitution, or to enter any place in which prostitution is encouraged or allowed within this state, or to come into this state or leave this state for the purpose of prostitution.

(6) Receives or gives, or agrees to receive or give, any money or thing of value for procuring, or attempting to procure, another person for the purpose of prostitution, or to come into this state or leave this state for the purpose of prostitution.][10]

In People v. Freeman, [46 Cal. 3d 419, 424, 758 P.2d 1128 (1988),] the Supreme Court stated that the definition of prostitution is derived from section 647(b) because the pandering statute does not define prostitution. Section 647(b) states that "'prostitution' includes any lewd act between persons for money or other consideration." Hence, the definition of prostitution, and ultimately, the definition of pimping or pandering, depends on what sexual conduct is considered to be a "lewd act."

"Lewd conduct" has been defined by Pryor v. Municipal Court, [25 Cal. 3d 238, 599 P.2d 636 (1979),] and People v. Hill, [103 Cal. App. 3d 525, 163 Cal. Rptr. 99 (1980)]. . . . *Pryor* . . . defined "lewd conduct" as "touching of the genitals, buttocks, or female breast, for the purpose of sexual arousal, gratification, annoyance or offense" for purposes of section 647(a).[15] . . . [I]n *Hill*, [the Court of Appeal defined] "lewd act," for purposes of section 647(b), so as to require that "the genitals, buttocks, or female breast, of either the prostitute or the customer must come in contact with some part of the body of the other for the purpose of sexual arousal or gratification of the customer or of the prostitute."[16]

---

10. [*Id.* §§266i(a)(1)-(a)(6); section (b) prohibits "pandering" with a minor —EDS.]

15. Section 647(a) makes any person "[w]ho solicits anyone to engage in or who engages in lewd or dissolute conduct in any public place or in any place open to the public or exposed to public view" guilty of disorderly conduct, a misdemeanor. [Section 647(b) makes any person "[w]ho solicits or who agrees to engage in or who engages in any act of prostitution," where "prostitution" is defined to "include[] any lewd act between persons for money or other consideration . . . ," also guilty of disorderly conduct. —EDS.]

16. . . . *Hill*, 103 Cal. App. 3d 525, 534-35.

The People argue that the sexual conduct that occurred at the Flesh Club constitutes prostitution, as defined under section 647(b), because the statute does not state that there must be touching between the customer and the prostitute. Section 647(b) simply states that prostitution "includes any lewd act between persons for money or other consideration." Defendants, however, argue that the conduct does not satisfy the statutory definition of prostitution because courts have defined "lewd act," which was not defined by the Legislature, as requiring the touching between a customer and a prostitute. . . .

. . . There was evidence that the dancers touched each other's genitals; there was no evidence, however, that the dancers touched either of the officers except to shake hands with them. The issue, therefore, is whether a customer's observation of sexual conduct between two dancers, in exchange for consideration, constitutes a lewd act for purposes of prostitution.

[People v. Hill, 103 Cal. App. 3d 525, 535, 163 Cal. Rptr. 99 (1980),] stated that "bodily contact between the prostitute and the customer is required" to be a lewd act. In *Hill*, the defendant was charged with pimping and pandering. An undercover officer testified that the defendant agreed to supply him with a teenage boy in exchange for $300. The defendant showed up at the officer's hotel room with a teenage boy, commented that the boy "knew what to do sexually," and accepted a payment of $300. After the defendant left, the boy offered to engage in either oral copulation or sodomy. The defendant testified that it was his understanding that the officer wanted to use the boy only as a nude model for a photo session.

The appellate court reversed because the trial court had defined "prostitution" for the jury in terms of "lewd or dissolute acts" without defining "lewd or dissolute acts.". . . The court then stated that . . . "bodily contact *between the prostitute and the customer* is required to satisfy . . . section 647(b), which define[s] 'prostitution' as including 'any lewd act *between persons* for money or other consideration.' "[24]

. . . In *Freeman*, in the course of producing and directing an "adult" film called "Caught from Behind, Part II," the defendant hired and paid actors and actresses to perform sex acts, including sexual intercourse, oral copulation, and sodomy. As a result, the defendant was convicted of pandering. . . . [T]he Supreme Court relied upon *Hill*'s definition of prostitution, that "the genitals, buttocks, or female breast, *of either the prostitute or the customer* must come in contact with some part of *the body of the other* for the purpose of sexual arousal or gratification of the customer or of the prostitute."[26] *Freeman* itself, however, did not analyze whether any contact between the prostitute and the customer was necessary. Instead, *Freeman* [was decided]

24. *Hill*, 103 Cal. App. 3d [at 534-35], italics added.
26. *Freeman*, 46 Cal. 3d at 424, quoting *Hill*, 103 Cal. App. 3d at 534-35 (emphasis added).

on the second prong of *Hill*'s definition: that there was no evidence that the defendant paid the acting fees for the *purpose of sexual arousal or gratification* of the defendant or the actors.[27]

Applying the *Hill* definition of prostitution, the Supreme Court commented:

> "One contention of defendant is that requisite to the crime of prostitution is the existence of a 'customer' and there being no 'customer' here, no prostitution was involved and therefore no procurement for purposes of prostitution and no pandering. We find it unnecessary to address that contention. Whether or not prostitution must always involve a 'customer,' it is clear that in order to constitute prostitution, the money or other consideration must be paid for the purpose of sexual arousal or gratification."[28]

[The court concluded:]

> "There is no evidence that defendant paid the acting fees for the purpose of sexual arousal or gratification, his own or the actors. Defendant, of course, did not himself participate in any of the sexual conduct. Defendant, the payor, thus did not engage in either the requisite conduct nor did he have the requisite *mens rea* or purpose to establish procurement for purposes of prostitution."[29]

Then, the court went on to hold, alternatively, that: "[E]ven if defendant's conduct could somehow be found to come within the definition of 'prostitution' literally, the application of the pandering statute to the hiring of actors to perform in the production of a non-obscene motion picture would impinge unconstitutionally upon First Amendment values."[30] . . .

. . . [S]ection 647(b) defines "prostitution" as "any lewd act between persons for money or other consideration." Although this broad definition of "prostitution" could plausibly be interpreted to include sexual conduct between two dancers, for money or other consideration from a customer, *Hill* and *Freeman* support a different interpretation: that a lewd act, an element of prostitution, requires touching between the prostitute and the customer, even if the customer is simply an observer of sexual acts between two prostitutes.

We recognize that in *Hill*, the only two persons involved were the male prostitute and the undercover officer, and the court was not confronted with a situation where a customer would not be involved in sexual activity with the prostitute. We also recognize that, although *Freeman* adopted the *Hill* definition of "lewd act," *Freeman* limited its application of the *Hill* definition to the second prong—whether the defendant paid the acting fees for the purpose of sexual arousal or gratification of the defendant or the actors.

27. *Freeman*, 46 Cal. 3d at 424-25.
28. Id. at 424.
29. Id. at 424-25.
30. Id. at 424.

Nevertheless, there are no reported cases that deviate from or disapprove of the definition of "lewd act" espoused in *Hill* and relied upon in *Freeman*. . . .

. . . In light of the rule of lenity, . . . [and given] the ambiguity in the definition of "lewd act," defendants are entitled to a resolution of the ambiguity in their favor. . . .

Hence, we conclude that the definition of prostitution under section 647(b), as interpreted by *Hill* and applied by *Freeman*, requires sexual contact between the prostitute and the customer. In this case, it is undisputed that there was no sexual contact between the dancers and the officers. Without sexual contact, there can be no prostitution. Without the underlying crime of prostitution, there can be no pimping or pandering.

The People point to a Wisconsin case, State v. Kittilstad,[38] in support of the claim that the alleged conduct constitutes prostitution under California's statute. *Kittilstad* is distinguishable. In *Kittilstad*, the defendant, a Lutheran minister, let a series of young men stay at his home while they were studying at a local college. He repeatedly offered each of them money if they would have sex with a woman and let him watch. Each of them refused. The Wisconsin Supreme Court held that these actions . . . supported a charge of solicitation of prostitution. . . .

Wisconsin's statute states that a person is guilty of prostitution if that person "*requests to commit* an act of sexual gratification, in public or in private, . . . for anything of value" or "*requests to commit* an act of sexual contact for anything of value."[39] Hence, under the Wisconsin statute, the conduct alleged in *Kittilstad* constituted prostitution because the defendant *requested* that the young men engage in sexual conduct in exchange for money. If California's statute contained the language that was included in Wisconsin's statute, the sexual conduct alleged herein could constitute prostitution. California's statute, however, is different. Section 647(b) simply states that prostitution includes "any lewd act between persons for money or other consideration." And as discussed above, California courts have defined lewd acts as requiring physical contact between the prostitute and customer. . . .

. . . [T]he dissent . . . points to a number of hypotheticals in which a person pays to watch sex being performed. The dissent contends that "regardless of who the payor is, there is an exchange of sex for money. That is the quintessence of prostitution." . . .

For better or worse, our society has developed a tolerance for a wide variety of exchanges of sex for money. . . . Currently, there are numerous ways in which a person can pay money and see a performance of sex. Many of these circumstances are admittedly remote: pornographic home videos, pornographic computer websites, pay for view television, peep show theaters, and movie houses. Not so remote are the sex acts performed as a part of stage

---

38. 603 N.W.2d 732 (Wis. 1999).
39. Wisconsin Statutes, Crimes, §§944.30(2) and (5), italics added.

plays in front of live audiences. The performances in this case, by two women in a booth in a "theater," is different from the other performances only in degree. The dissent's definition of prostitution would include not only the Flesh Club presentations but any sex act performed on stage and, in theory, other presentations as well.

As objectionable as the performances are in this case, we are loath to find a public policy requirement that the acts be criminalized under existing law. Our Supreme Court found no public policy reason in *Freeman* to criminalize sex acts being recorded on film for distribution to potentially millions of people of all ages. While we offer no defense for the performances at the Flesh Club, at least it can be said that they are given to a small audience in an establishment which limits its clientele.

We agree with the dissent that section 647(b) does not require a completed act of prostitution, and that pimping and pandering do not require a completed act of prostitution. We . . . disagree with the dissent's conclusion that one of the dancers' offer of a "hand job" to an officer was sufficient to prove a pimping or pandering charge against defendants.

Pimping, under section 266h(a), is committed by "any person who, *knowing* another person is a prostitute, lives or derives support or maintenance in whole or in part from the earnings or proceeds of the person's prostitution. . . ." The dissent acknowledges that pimping requires that a defendant know that another person is a prostitute. . . . [P]andering, under section 266i(a)(4), is committed by any person who "[b]y promises, threats, violence or by any device or scheme, causes, induces, persuades or encourages an inmate of a house of prostitution, or any other place in which prostitution is encouraged or allowed, to remain therein as an inmate." Hence, pandering also requires that a defendant encourage prostitution, whether attempted or completed.

In this case, there is absolutely no evidence that defendants had knowledge that Malibu offered a "hand job" to Officer Aranda. At the preliminary hearing, Officer Aranda testified about his and Officer Valdivia's investigation of the Flesh Club on May 22, 2000. On that day, after Malibu and Veronica engaged in sexual activity and Officer Valdivia paid the dancers for their performance, Malibu stated that she was willing to perform a hand job on Officer Aranda. No further evidence was presented to follow up on Officer Aranda's testimony regarding this . . . offer. . . .

In sum, although Malibu's offer of a "hand job" could constitute prostitution, that offer—standing alone—is insufficient to support a charge of pimping or pandering because there was no evidence that defendants knew that Malibu had made such an offer. As stated above, defendants' knowledge of the prostitution, as alleged in the felony complaint, is an essential element of pimping and pandering.

. . . Let a peremptory writ of mandate issue directing respondent, the Superior Court of San Bernardino County, to set aside its order denying defendants' motion to set aside the information under section 995, and to enter a new order granting the motion and setting aside the information.

RICHLI, Presiding Judge, dissenting.

I respectfully dissent. The Legislature has broadly defined "prostitution" as "any lewd act between persons for money or other consideration," Pen. Code, §647(b), without specifying who the persons must be. The majority concludes, based on a dictum in People v. Hill, 103 Cal. App. 3d 525, 163 Cal. Rptr. 99 (1980), that this language is ambiguous. The "rule of lenity," however, applies only "[w]hen . . . the *language of a penal law* is reasonably susceptible of two interpretations. . . ." People v. Robles, 23 Cal. 4th 1106, 1115, 5 P.3d 176 (2000) (italics added). One errant dictum doth not an ambiguity make.

I would hold that the statutory definition of "prostitution" does require a sexual contact between at least two people, but not necessarily between the prostitute and the customer. In response to defendants' other contentions, I would also hold that the pimping and pandering statutes do not necessarily require a completed act of prostitution. The pimping statute can be satisfied by proof that the defendant derived support from money paid for another's agreement to perform an act of prostitution. Here, regardless of Officer Valdivia's actual intent, there was sufficient evidence that he paid the women for agreeing to perform an act of prostitution. Similarly, the pandering statute can be satisfied by proof that the defendant caused an inmate of a place where prostitution is encouraged or allowed to remain therein. Once again, regardless of Officer Valdivia's actual intent, there was sufficient evidence that prostitution was allowed or encouraged in the Flesh Club.

I need not repeat here the majority's generally excellent summary of the facts. I merely add that, no matter what the women whom the majority describes as "dancers" did on the main stage, their activities once inside the booth were not remotely terpsichorean. These included oral copulation, digital vaginal penetration, and vaginal penetration with a vibrator. Also, there was evidence that dancers at the Flesh Club sometimes made sexual contact with other customers and that defendants knew dancers sometimes made sexual contact with customers. Indeed, the dancer whose nom de guerre was "Malibu" offered to give Officer Aranda a "hand job," but he declined. . . .

My analysis, like the majority's, begins with the seminal case (no pun intended) of People v. Freeman, 46 Cal. 3d 419, 758 P.2d 1128 (1988). . . . *Freeman* . . . held that "in order to constitute prostitution, the money or other consideration must be paid *for the purpose of sexual arousal or gratification*." People v. Freeman, 46 Cal. 3d at 424. Thus, it adopted that portion of the *Hill* definition which required such a sexual purpose. However, it did not adopt that portion of the *Hill* definition which required the prostitute to touch the customer. To the contrary, it expressly refused to decide "[w]hether or not prostitution must always involve a 'customer' . . . " *Freeman*, supra, at 424. . . .

The statute itself requires only a "lewd act between persons for money or other consideration." Penal Code, §647(b). It does not specify that one of those persons must be the prostitute and another must be the customer. Indeed, the majority concedes that "this broad definition of prostitution could plausibly be interpreted to include sexual conduct between two dancers, for money or other consideration from a customer. . . ." It further concedes that the *Hill* definition requiring a touching between the prostitute and the customer was unnecessary to the decision and that *Freeman* declined to adopt any such requirement. Nevertheless, it concludes that, in light of *Freeman* and *Hill*, the statute is so ambiguous as to trigger the "rule of lenity."

Not so.

> "[T]his rule is inapplicable unless two reasonable interpretations of the same provision stand in relative equipoise, i.e., that resolution of the statute's ambiguities in a convincing manner is impracticable. . . . Courts will not construe an ambiguity in favor of the accused if such a construction is contrary to the public interest, sound sense, and wise policy."

People v. Williams, 49 Cal. App. 4th 1632, 1638-39, 57 Cal. Rptr. 2d 448 (1996). The statute itself is clear. Applying it to this case, there clearly were "lewd acts" (i.e., genital touching) "between persons" (i.e., the dancers). . . .

Just as I find no basis in the language of the statute for the majority's requirement that the customer touch the prostitute, I also find none in public policy. Under the majority's interpretation, if a father paid a woman to have sex with his son, or a businessman paid a woman to have sex with his client, there would be no prostitution, even though there would be if the son or the client paid the woman directly. Similarly, if a man paid another man to have sex with his wife while he watched, for his own sexual gratification, there would be no prostitution. If, however, the wife paid a man to have sex with her while her husband watched, so her husband could obtain sexual gratification, there would be prostitution. In each of these situations, regardless of who the payor is, there is an exchange of sex for money. That is the quintessence of prostitution. . . .

. . . [T]he majority opinion . . . minimizes the significance of Malibu's offer of a "hand job." Even if, as the majority holds, prostitution requires the prostitute to touch the customer, there was ample evidence that dancers did make sexual contact with other customers and that defendants were aware of this. Thus, her offer to commit prostitution would support a charge of pandering in connection with each date upon which she made this offer.

Defendants are also charged with pimping. Pimping requires that the defendant know that another person is a prostitute. People v. McNulty,

202 Cal. App. 3d 624, 630, 249 Cal. Rptr. 22 (1988). A "prostitute" for this purpose is a person who indiscriminately offers to perform sexual intercourse or other lewd acts between persons for hire. See People v. Schultz, 238 Cal. App. 2d 804, 812, 48 Cal. Rptr. 328 (1965). Pimping also requires either (1) deriving support from the earnings of another's act of prostitution or (2) soliciting. People v. McNulty, 202 Cal. App. 3d at 630. Under the deriving-support prong of the statute, the prostitute must have earnings from prostitution, and the defendant must knowingly derive support from such earnings. Under the soliciting prong of the statute, "there must be either the receipt of compensation for soliciting for a prostitute or the solicitation of compensation for soliciting for a prostitute." [Id.] at 630. . . .

Here . . . , there can be no doubt that the dancers intended to accept, and did accept, money for the sexual acts. Moreover, there was sufficient evidence that defendants *knew* the dancers had accepted money for the sexual acts. Once again, as far as either the dancers or defendants knew, the dancers completed acts of prostitution. Even assuming that, solely because of Officer Valdivia's hidden intent, they did not, they were "prostitutes," and the money they accepted were the earnings of "prostitution," within the meaning of the pimping statute. . . .

Notes on Prostitution and Related Crimes

1. What is the point of criminalizing prostitution? If the idea is that trading sex for money is abhorrent, isn't that exactly what the "dancers" at the defendants' club did—even if one puts aside the much-discussed offer of a "hand job"? Why is it permissible for two people to agree to have sex in exchange for money from a third person, but not for one person to have sex in exchange for money from his or her partner?

2. Perhaps the problem with the sex trade is not the conduct of the prostitutes, but the behavior of their bosses. Prostitutes are often abused and exploited by their employers; state statutes regularly impose harsher penalties on employers like Wooten and Mendoza than on employees like Angel, Cat, and Malibu. But that justification for criminal liability may get cause and effect backward: The business may be filled with exploitation and abuse in large part because of its illegality. State and federal law offer a wide range of protections against abusive behavior by employers. As a practical matter, such laws do not protect employees in illegal businesses—employees cannot report labor-law violations without admitting to criminal conduct themselves. Plus, illegal businesses attract different people than legal ones; the men—and, for the most part, they *are* men—who are charged under California's pimping and pandering statutes, and under similar laws in other states, tend to run their enterprises violently. If those businesses were legal, as in the case of Nevada's licensed brothels, the level of regulation would rise and the level of violence would likely fall. Does it make sense to criminalize a business and then punish it because it takes on the character of other criminal businesses?

3. Assuming the point of the pimping statute (though perhaps not the pandering statute) is to punish the coercion and violence that are common among those who run prostitution rings, shouldn't the government have to prove that Wooten and Mendoza ran their business through coercion and violence? Notice that the statute does not require such proof. The reason points to a problem common to all vice laws: Because all actors in the relevant business are criminals, and because the relevant transactions are at least nominally consensual, it is very hard for the government to gather detailed information about how the business is run. The consequence is that vice laws often criminalize different conduct than the legislature actually wishes to stamp out. Do the California statutes at issue in *Wooten* fit that description?

4. Historically, laws banning prostitution and associated enterprises arose out of a different impulse than the ones described in the preceding notes. The wrong that most concerned lawmakers of the late nineteenth and early twentieth centuries (most laws banning prostitution, pandering, and pimping date from that period) was not the commercialization of sex, but the tempting of prostitutes' customers to have sex outside marital relationships. That is the reason why prostitutes historically were punished more severely than their customers: The customers were just giving in to temptation, while the prostitutes were the ones doing the tempting. Similarly, concern for effects on marital relationships explains why, historically, adultery often was punished more severely than prostitution.

5. If the government wants to shut down businesses like the Flesh Club, why not punish buyers rather than sellers? If all those who ran such businesses were imprisoned, others would soon take their place. But if all the customers who frequent such businesses stopped doing so, the businesses would soon shut down. Sellers do not create buyers; buyers can and do generate sellers. Why isn't the morally and economically sound policy always to punish purchases more severely than sales?

Similar arguments are often made about illegal businesses like prostitution or the illegal drug trade. But criminal law overwhelmingly makes the opposite choice—in practice, selling is always punished more harshly than buying. At some times and for some vices, buying has not even been criminalized: During Prohibition, neither the possession of alcoholic beverages nor their purchase was a crime; only manufacturing and sales were forbidden. Why has that approach proved so popular? Assuming the sex trade is bad and/or socially harmful and ought to be criminally punished, which actors most deserve punishment? What is the most effective way to shut such businesses down?

B. FRAUDULENT SEX

State v. Bolsinger

Supreme Court of Iowa
709 N.W.2d 560 (Iowa 2006)

Opinion of Justice Larson:

John Michael Bolsinger appealed his convictions of third-degree sexual abuse under Iowa Code section 709.4(1) (2001), sexual exploitation by a counselor under Iowa Code section 709.15(2), and sexual misconduct with juvenile offenders under Iowa Code section 709.16(2). Bolsinger was sentenced to a combination of concurrent and consecutive sentences totaling a term not exceeding thirty-seven years. The court of appeals affirmed, and we granted further review. We vacate the decision of the court of appeals, reverse his conviction for sexual abuse, affirm the remainder of the convictions, and remand.

I. Facts and Prior Proceedings

Bolsinger was the program supervisor of a highly structured state facility for delinquent boys, the Wittenmyer Youth Center, in August 2001 when the Iowa Department of Human Services (DHS) conducted an investigation into allegations of sexual abuse by Bolsinger. The investigation revealed, through interviews with past and present youth at the camp, that Bolsinger would take boys into a private room and touch their genitals, saying he was checking for bruises, scratches, hernias, and testicular cancer. The testimony of the boys revealed that Bolsinger asked permission to touch them in this way and that he did not appear to them to be gaining any sexual gratification from the touching. The boys testified that they were not aware that they were being touched in a sexual manner, and they would not have consented if they had known the true reason for the touching. However, they also testified that, given the nature of the structured program, it was almost impossible for them to make choices of their own or to refuse the request of an instructor.

Following the DHS investigation, Davenport police officers obtained a search warrant for Bolsinger's home and seized a number of items, including the defendant's home computer. The computer's hard drive contained, among other things, numerous stories involving unidentified males engaging in sex acts with each other. Prior to trial, Bolsinger filed a motion to suppress evidence seized from his home, which was denied by the court.

II. Issues

Bolsinger's appeal raises three issues: (1) the court's interpretation of Iowa Code section 709.4(1) (third-degree sexual abuse), (2) its denial of his motion to suppress, and (3) its refusal to direct verdicts in his favor on all counts on the basis his acts were not "sex acts" under the Code. Bolsinger raises other issues, which we do not expressly discuss because their resolution is subsumed in other holdings in this case.

III. INTERPRETATION OF IOWA CODE SECTION 709.4(1) (THIRD-DEGREE SEXUAL ABUSE)

Under Iowa Code section 709.4,

> [a] person commits sexual abuse in the third degree when the person performs a sex act under any of the following circumstances:
>> 1. The act is done by force or against the will of the other person, whether or not the other person is the person's spouse or is cohabiting with the person.

In applying the "force or against the will" language of section 709.4, the court submitted Instruction No. 21:

> Concerning [the third-degree sexual abuse counts] the State must prove that the defendant committed a sex act "by force or against the will" of the alleged victim in that Instruction. In order to do so, however, the State does not have to prove that the alleged victim physically resisted the defendant's acts. The force used by the defendant does not have to be physical. *An act may be done "by force and against the will" of another if the other's consent or acquiescence is procured by:*
>
> (1) *threats of violence; or*
> (2) *deception, which may include deception concerning the nature of the act or deception concerning the defendant's right to exercise authority over the other under the circumstances.*
>
> You may consider all of the circumstances surrounding the defendant's act in deciding whether the act was done by force or against the will of the alleged victim.

(Emphasis added.)

The court stated that its authority for giving this instruction was found in Iowa Code section 709.5, which provides:

> Under the provisions of this chapter it shall not be necessary to establish physical resistance by a person in order to establish that an act of sexual abuse was committed by force or against the will of the person. *However, the circumstances surrounding the commission of the act may be considered in determining whether or not the act was done by force or against the will of the other.*

(Emphasis added.)

The court also relied on the case of State v. VanderEsch, 662 N.W.2d 689 (Iowa Ct. App. 2002). In *VanderEsch* the defendant, an owner of a pizza restaurant, employed teenage boys. He informed two of these employees that he was doing a scientific research project and asked them to provide him semen samples for this purpose. He promised to pay $50 for the samples should their sperm count be high enough. VanderEsch was present during the procedure and took possession of the semen samples. *VanderEsch*, 662 N.W.2d at 691. VanderEsch was not authorized by any scientific body to collect semen samples, and the victims indicated that they would not have consented to these acts had they known that no scientific research existed. *Id.* VanderEsch was charged with four counts of third-degree sexual abuse under Iowa Code section 709.4(1). He argued that the definition of sexual abuse, as set out in Iowa Code section 709.1(1), set forth the only means recognized in Iowa to negate consent and that neither fraud nor deceit did so. *Id.* at 691.

Our examination of the issue must begin with Iowa Code section 709.1(1), which defines sexual abuse and provides that certain circumstances will vitiate a victim's consent:

> Any sex act between persons is sexual abuse by either of the persons when the act is performed with the other person in any of the following circumstances:
>
> 1. The act is done by force or against the will of the other. If the consent or acquiescence of the other is procured by threats of violence toward any person or if the act is done while the other is under the influence of a drug inducing sleep or is otherwise in a state of unconsciousness, the act is done against the will of the other.

In *VanderEsch* the district court ruled that, in view of the fact that Iowa Code section 709.5 permits the consideration of all surrounding circumstances, section 709.1(1) is not exclusive and fraud and deception may vitiate consent. The court of appeals upheld that decision, classifying the fraud in question as fraud in fact, as opposed to fraud in the inducement (concepts we later discuss), and therefore, the act was done "by force or against the will" of the boys.

Bolsinger argues that the acts which occurred were hand-to-genital contact, which was expressly agreed to by the boys. He argues that his unexpressed purpose, apparently sexual gratification, was collateral to the act itself and, therefore, constituted fraud only in the inducement. As such, the fraud does not vitiate consent, according to him. Bolsinger also argues that *VanderEsch*, relied on by the court of appeals (which divided four to four on the question) and the district court in the present case, was incorrectly decided and should be overruled. Bolsinger argues that *VanderEsch* erroneously characterized the consent to semen sampling as being produced by fraud in fact, and therefore, any consent was vitiated.

If an act is done that is different from the act the defendant said he would perform, this is fraud in fact. If the act is done as the defendant stated it would be, but it is for some collateral or ulterior purpose, this is fraud in the inducement. Fraud in fact vitiates consent; fraud in the inducement does not. See Rollin M. Perkins & Ronald N. Boyce, Criminal Law ch. 9, §3, at 1079 (3d ed. 1982) [hereinafter Perkins & Boyce]. In other words,

> if deception causes a misunderstanding as to the fact itself (fraud in the *factum*) there is no legally-recognized consent because what happened is not that for which consent was given; whereas consent induced by fraud is as effective as other consent, so far as direct and immediate legal consequences are concerned, if the deception relates not to the thing done but merely to some collateral matter (fraud in the inducement).

Id.; *accord* Wayne R. LaFave, Substantive Criminal Law §6.5(a), at 506 (2d ed. 2003) (stating that "fraud in the factum involves a form of deception which results in a misunderstanding by the victim as to the very fact of the defendant's conduct").

Cases illustrating fraud in fact have often involved victims undergoing medical examination or treatment. In many cases, the victims consented to an examination, only to find that the doctor engaged in sex acts. See, e.g., People v. Ogunmola, 193 Cal. App. 3d 274, 238 Cal. Rptr. 300, 304 (Cal. Ct. App. 1987) (patient who consented to gynecological examination was in fact subjected to a sex act; consent held to be vitiated); McNair v. State, 108 Nev. 53, 825 P.2d 571, 575 (Nev. 1992) (sex acts under pretense of performing medical examination held to be against the will of the victim). See generally regarding fraud in fact in "doctor" cases, Jay M. Zitter, Annotation: "Conviction of Rape or Related Sexual Offenses on Basis of Intercourse Accomplished Under the Pretext of, or in the Course of, Medical Treatment," 65 A.L.R.4th 1064 (1988); 75 C.J.S. Rape §22, at 334 (2002). One treatise discusses fraud in these cases:

> In some of these cases the doctor has not hesitated to make it clear that he intended to have sexual intercourse with the patient, his fraud being in the deceitful suggestion that this was necessary to cure some malady, which was fraud in the inducement, since the patient knew exactly what was to be done and was deceived only in regard to a collateral matter—the reason why it was to be done. And here as usual the direct and immediate consequence of consent obtained by fraud in the inducement is the same as consent given in the absence of fraud, and since the patient consented to the intercourse it was not rape so long as she was over the statutory age.

Perkins & Boyce, ch. 9, at 1079-80.

Bolsinger argues that each of these young men was told what the touching would consist of and that they were then touched in the exact manner they expected. Thus, he argues, any fraud was fraud in the inducement, not fraud in fact.

In Bolsinger's case, if the boys had consented to acts such as massaging their legs and instead Bolsinger had touched their genital area, this would clearly be fraud in fact; they would have consented to one act but subjected to a different one. That is not the case, however. We conclude that the consents given here were based on fraud in the inducement, not on fraud in fact, as the victims were touched in exactly the manner represented to them. The consents, therefore, were not vitiated.

In reaching this conclusion, we do so based on the authorities discussed above and not on Bolsinger's alternative argument that Iowa's sex abuse law in effect provides no way to vitiate consent based on fraud. This argument, based on the doctrine of *inclusio unius est exclusio alterius*, is that the Code sets out a limited list of circumstances under which consent may be vitiated. These include the victim's age (Iowa Code section 709.4(2)(*b*) and (*c*)) a mental defect or incapacity (Iowa Code section 709.4(2)(*a*) and (4)), a physical incapacity (Iowa Code section 709.4(4)), and the influence of controlled substances (Iowa Code section 709.4(3)). Contrary to Bolsinger's argument, we believe that these are not the only circumstances in which consent can be vitiated and that fraud in fact should be held to vitiate consent in sexual abuse cases just as it does in any other criminal case. . . .

Our conclusion that the boys' consent in this case was based on fraud in the inducement and not fraud in fact calls into question the court of appeals case of *VanderEsch*. In fact, in the four-to-four decision by the court of appeals in Bolsinger's appeal, four members of that court urge us to overrule *VanderEsch*. We now hold that *VanderEsch* is no longer controlling because the facts on which that case was based clearly show fraud in the inducement, not fraud in fact.

IV. REMAINING ISSUES

A

. . . [T]he warrant was based on probable cause, was not based on false statements, and was not overbroad. Further, we conclude the officers properly executed the warrant. We reject Bolsinger's motion-to-suppress issue.

B

. . . We have already determined that Bolsinger's conviction of third-degree sexual abuse cannot stand. The remaining charges, sexual abuse by a counselor or therapist and sexual misconduct with offenders, both require proof of sex acts. Bolsinger argues that none of the young men testified there was anything sexual going on and that the evidence was insufficient to establish the existence of sex acts. The jury was instructed, based on Iowa Code section 702.17, that a "sex act" is

> any sexual contact between the fingers or hand of one person and the genitals or anus of another person. "Genitals" include the scrotum and penis. You may

consider the type of contact and the circumstances surrounding it in deciding whether the contact was sexual in nature.

We believe there was substantial evidence to support the jury's finding that sex acts had been committed. Direct evidence is not required.

> The sexual nature of the contact can be determined from the type of contact and the circumstances surrounding it. . . .
>
> . . . Other relevant circumstances include but are not limited to the relationship between the defendant and the victim; whether anyone else was present; the length of the contact; the purposefulness of the contact; whether there was a legitimate, nonsexual purpose for the contact; where and when the contact took place; and the conduct of the defendant and victim before and after the contact.

State v. Pearson, 514 N.W.2d 452, 455 (Iowa 1994). The evidence shows that Bolsinger was acting outside the scope of his duties, his actions took place in private, and he did not document these procedures, contrary to the policy at Wittenmyer. Bolsinger had no medical training other than information he had received in school on testicular cancer and self-examination and was in a position of power over the victims. Considered in light of this evidence a rational finder of fact could conclude that Bolsinger committed sex acts under the guise of performing medical examinations. The trial court did not err in overruling his motions for judgment of acquittal on the charges of sexual abuse by a counselor or sexual misconduct with offenders.

We reverse the convictions for third-degree sexual abuse and affirm the remaining convictions. We remand for resentencing without regard to the third-degree sexual abuse convictions under Iowa Code section 709.4(1).

Notes and Questions

1. *Bolsinger* states the longstanding rule in American criminal law: Fraudulent sex is a crime only when the victim is deceived about the sex act itself, not about the reasons for having sex. *Ogunmola* and *McNair* are classic examples of that rule in action. Ogunmola told his victim he would examine her gynecologically, using a speculum, but instead he used his penis. McNair's victims also consented to a gynecological exam, but instead McNair anally penetrated them with his penis. Both defendants lost.

Now consider two Illinois cases discussed in *VanderEsch*, the case *Bolsinger* overruled:

> In People v. Costello, 586 N.E.2d 742 (Ill. 1992), the defendant posed as a medical doctor and offered the victim a free medical examination, which including touching her breasts and vagina. The court stated, "There is no evidence to suggest that [the victim] would have consented to defendant's acts of sexual penetration if she was aware that defendant was not the doctor he

represented himself to be," and concluded, "undoubtedly this deception took away [the victim's] ability to give knowing consent to these acts." *Costello,* 586 N.E.2d at 748. In People v. Quinlan, 596 N.E.2d 28 (Ill. App. Ct. 1992), the defendant, a respiratory therapist, told the victim she needed a special test, in which he placed his fingers in her rectum and vagina. The court found the victim had consented to an invasive medical procedure, not to sexual acts, and concluded her consent was vitiated because it was received through deceit. *Quinlan,* 596 N.E.2d at 31.

VanderEsch, 662 N.W.2d, at 694.

Finally, compare Boro v. Superior Court, 210 Cal. Rptr. 122 (Cal. Ct. App. 1985). Boro, posing as a doctor (the press later nicknamed him "Dr. Feelgood"), told the victim that she had a "dangerous, highly infectious and perhaps fatal disease" that could be cured if she had sexual intercourse with a person who had been treated with a special serum—including Boro himself. The victim agreed to have sex with Boro, believing it would save her life. The court held that this was fraud in the inducement; the victim may have "succumbed to petitioner's fraudulent blandishments," but she knew the nature of the physical act to which she consented, and thus her consent was not vitiated by the fraud. Boro's conviction, like Bolsinger's, was therefore reversed.

Are these cases consistent? There seems to be a clear enough distinction between *Ogunmola* and *McNair* on the one hand, and *Boro* and *Bolsinger* on the other. Boro and Bolsinger may have acted with base motives, but the physical acts they committed were the exact ones to which their victims consented. Ogunmola and McNair, by contrast, committed different physical acts altogether.

But what about *Costello* and *Quinlan?* Did the Illinois courts reach the right results? Were those two defendants more like Boro and Bolsinger, or more like Ogunmola and McNair? Costello and Quinlan clearly acted with base motives, but didn't their victims consent to the exact physical acts that they actually performed? Or does the nature of the physical act change based on the motives of the actor? But if that is so, then shouldn't *Boro* and *Bolsinger* have come out differently?

2. The California legislature subsequently criminalized behavior like Boro's in California Penal Code §243.4(c), a provision of the state's "sexual battery" statute:

(c) Any person who touches an intimate part of another person for the purpose of sexual arousal, sexual gratification, or sexual abuse, and the victim is at the time unconscious of the nature of the act because the perpetrator fraudulently represented that the touching served a professional purpose, is guilty of sexual battery. A violation of this subdivision is punishable by imprisonment in a county jail for not more than one year, and by a fine not exceeding two thousand dollars ($2,000); or by imprisonment in the state prison for two, three, or four years, and by a fine not exceeding ten thousand dollars ($10,000).

Why are lies about "professional purpose[s]" worse than other lies that induce consent to sex? How were the false statements in, say, *Costello* ("I'm a doctor, and I'm going to help you") different from other false statements that might induce consent to sex ("I'm a doctor, I'm rich and single, and I love you")?

3. Does the traditional distinction between "fraud in the fact" and "fraud in the inducement" make sense? What is its rationale? Why not simply criminalize all fraudulent sex? The usual answer to the last question is: If fraudulent sex were criminalized generally, then lies about marital status, employment, and the nature of one's emotional commitments might all be criminally punished, if and when those lies lead to sex. Does that strike you as an obviously bad result? Why? As you saw in Chapter 5, frauds that induce victims to turn over money or property lead to prison terms—indeed, in some cases, frauds that cost victims nothing more than their intangible right of "honest services" can land the defrauder in prison. Is sex really less valuable than fiduciary duties and small sums of money?

4. Whatever the rationale may be for criminalizing prostitution, is it consistent with not criminalizing all fraudulent sex? If sex is too important to be left to consensual market transactions, doesn't it follow that it's also too important to permit victims to be cheated into providing it?

United States v. Bygrave

United States Court of Appeals for the Armed Forces
46 M.J. 491 (1997)

ARTERTON, District Judge.

Appellant was tried by a general court-martial, military judge alone, on March 23 and 25, 1992, and was convicted of two specifications of assault with a means likely to cause death or grievous bodily harm, in violation of Article 128(b)(1), Uniform Code of Military Justice, 10 U.S.C. §928(b)(1). Appellant was sentenced to a bad-conduct discharge, confinement for 4 years, total forfeitures, and reduction to pay grade E-1. . . . The . . . Court of Criminal Appeals affirmed the findings and the approved sentence in an unpublished opinion dated January 31, 1996. We granted review of the following issue: Whether the finding of guilty to aggravated assault can stand in light of the fact that the alleged victim consented to having sexual intercourse with appellant despite actual knowledge that appellant was HIV-positive.

FACTS

In 1986, appellant tested positive for the Human Immunodeficiency Virus (HIV), resulting in treatment at the HIV Ward of the Naval Hospital in San

Diego. Despite warnings of the risk of spreading the virus through sexual intercourse, appellant maintained a sexually active lifestyle involving at least two partners. The first partner, Petty Officer J, engaged in heterosexual sex with appellant over a year-long period, including acts of unprotected sex. Appellant did not warn Petty Officer J that he was HIV-positive. In June 1988, Petty Officer J herself tested positive for the virus.

Appellant's second partner, beginning in January 1990, was Boatswain's Mate Third Class (BM3) C. Prior to commencing sexual relations, appellant informed BM3 C of his HIV-positive status. Thereafter, appellant and BM3 C engaged in consensual sexual intercourse on a regular basis, using a condom on most, but not all, occasions. In July 1991, BM3 C tested positive for HIV. Six months later, BM3 C and appellant were married.

After a trial in March of 1992, a general court-martial convicted appellant on two specifications of aggravated assault, one arising from his sexual relationship with Petty Officer J; the other from his sexual relationship with BM3 C. Appellant has not challenged his conviction on the first specification. The only issue before us on the present appeal is whether BM3 C's informed consent constitutes a valid defense to the second specification.

DISCUSSION

This Court has made clear on numerous occasions that an HIV-positive servicemember commits an aggravated assault by having unprotected sexual intercourse with an uninformed partner.[3] United States v. Schoolfield, 40 M.J. 132 (CMA 1994); United States v. Joseph, 37 M.J. 392 (CMA 1993); United States v. Johnson, 30 M.J. 53 (CMA 1990). We have concluded that "under many circumstances, AIDS [Acquired Immune Deficiency Syndrome] is the natural and probable consequence of exposure to HIV." Id. at 57. Accordingly, we have held that any time a servicemember "willfully or deliberately" exposes another person to HIV, that servicemember may be found to have acted in a manner "likely to produce death or grievous bodily harm." *Joseph*, 37 M.J. at 396.

---

3. The elements of aggravated assault are as follows:

   i) That the accused attempted to do, offered to do, or did bodily harm to a certain person;
   ii) That the accused did so with a certain weapon, means, or force;
   iii) That the attempt, offer, or bodily harm was done with unlawful force or violence; and
   iv) That the weapon, means, or force was used in a manner likely to produce death or grievous bodily harm.

   ¶54b(4)(a), Part IV, Manual for Courts-Martial, United States (1995 ed.).

While appellant obviously can make no claim that informed consent by itself eliminates the risk of HIV transmission — indeed, the infection of appellant's wife would persuasively belie any argument to that effect — he offers a number of other reasons why he believes that informed consent either removes this case from the ambit of Article 128 or renders his prosecution under Article 128 unconstitutional.

. . . [T]he relevance of the victim's state of mind is not readily apparent on the face of the statute. We note that aggravated assault is not a crime like rape, in which lack of consent is an element of the offense. Moreover, the very nature of the offense invalidates, as a matter of law, any consent that has been given. Aggravated assault, of course, differs from simple assault in that the perpetrator has used a "means or force likely to produce death or grievous bodily harm." Art. 128(b)(1). As this Court has previously observed, "One cannot consent to an act which is likely to produce grievous bodily harm or death." United States v. Outhier, 45 M.J. 326, 330 (1996). Thus, while under certain circumstances consent may be a defense to simple assault, *Joseph*, 37 M.J. at 396 n.5, consent is generally not a valid defense to aggravated assault.[4] See, e.g., United States v. Outhier, supra.

At oral argument, appellant suggested that consent negates one of the required elements of aggravated assault, namely, that the act be perpetrated with "unlawful force or violence." However, our prior decisions make clear that an act of sexual intercourse may in some circumstances be an "offensive touching" subject to prosecution under Article 128, even in the absence of overt coercion or violence. See, e.g., *Joseph*, 37 M.J. at 395 n.4. In order for consent to be relevant to the "unlawful force or violence" element, the consent must be legally cognizable. For that reason, consent to sex secured without disclosure of HIV-positive status does not remove the act from the ambit of Article 128, for the consent has been improperly obtained. See id. at 395-96. By similar reasoning, even informed consent cannot save an accused in a case such as this one, for, as we have just noted, assault law does not recognize the validity of consent to an act that is likely to result in grievous injury or death, such as unprotected sex with an HIV-positive partner.[5] Given that appellant's unprotected sex acts with BM3 C were performed without legally valid consent, we must conclude

---

4. In this respect, aggravated assault is like numerous other crimes under the Uniform Code of Military Justice in which the consent of the immediate "victim" is irrelevant because of the broad military and societal interests in deterring the criminalized conduct. See, e.g., Arts. 114 (dueling), 120 (carnal knowledge), and 134 (bigamy), UCMJ, 10 U.S.C. §§914, 920, and 934, respectively.

5. Because appellant was only prosecuted for having unprotected sex, we need not, and do not, address [the question] whether one may validly consent to protected sex with an HIV-positive partner. . . .

that they amount to "unlawful force or violence" within the meaning of Article 128.[6]

Next, appellant points to the numerous states that have adopted specific criminal statutes addressing HIV transmission, including some that provide for a defense of informed consent. Appellant contends that the criminalization of HIV transmission, particularly in the context of informed consent, requires us to balance a number of highly sensitive public-policy concerns. Appellant argues that Congress should follow the lead of many state legislatures in passing a law to address this issue directly, and that this Court should refrain from holding that Article 128 encompasses informed, consensual sex until after Congress decides how to balance the competing interests. The problem with appellant's argument is that Congress has already established a mechanism for balancing the competing interests: Article 128. The Uniform Code of Military Justice provides for the prosecution of individuals who commit assault by "means or force likely to produce death or grievous bodily harm." Congress created no exceptions for cases in which the act likely to produce grievous bodily harm is sexual intercourse involving a person who is HIV-positive. Congress is certainly entitled to carve out exceptions for this class of cases, or subcategories thereof, and appellant has offered valid public-policy reasons in support of such legislation; however, until Congress acts to remove HIV transmission from the ambit of Article 128, the precedents of this Court clearly establish that conduct like appellant's, with or without the sex partner's informed consent, falls within the statutory meaning of "aggravated assault" under the UCMJ.

Having concluded that appellant could be found to have committed aggravated assault in violation of Article 128, the Court may now address the question of whether appellant's conviction violated his constitutional rights. Appellant argues that he had a fundamental right under the United States Constitution to engage in sexual intercourse, and that this right cannot be significantly burdened absent a showing of a compelling governmental interest. The Government readily concedes that its interpretation of Article 128 substantially burdens the sexual activity of military personnel who are HIV-positive. However, the Government contends that appellant has no constitutional right to sex, and that appellant's prosecution is therefore not subject to strict scrutiny. The Government further argues that its interests

6. Because there is no dispute that BM3 C was HIV-free prior to her relationship with appellant, we need not address the question of whether, or under what circumstances, one who is already HIV-positive may provide valid consent to sexual intercourse with another HIV-positive individual. If the added health risk of sexual intercourse between people who are already HIV-positive was shown to be minimal, then we might be more inclined to view informed consent as relevant to the Article 128 analysis. However, appellant has not argued that these circumstances are present in his case; nor have we been provided with an evidentiary record as to current medical knowledge of any increased health risks under these circumstances. . . .

are sufficiently weighty to survive strict scrutiny, if such heightened constitutional review is found to be applicable.[8]

There can be no doubt that certain aspects of reproductive behavior are safeguarded by a constitutional right to privacy, which has been variously located in the Due Process Clause, the Ninth Amendment, and the "penumbra" of the rights set forth in the Bill of Rights. See, e.g., Roe v. Wade, 410 U.S. 113 (1973); Griswold v. Connecticut, 381 U.S. 479 (1965). At the same time, the Supreme Court has made equally clear that there is no generalized constitutional right to sexual intimacy between consenting adults. See, e.g., Bowers v. Hardwick, 478 U.S. 186 (1986). However, between the poles of *Griswold* and *Bowers*, the constitutional terrain, at least insofar as it has been laid out by the Supreme Court, grows more difficult to negotiate. . . .

In such circumstances, when we are asked to recognize a fundamental constitutional right where neither the Supreme Court nor our own precedents have expressly done so in the past, we believe the most prudent course of action is to assess the governmental interests counterbalancing the proposed right before determining conclusively whether the right exists. See Cruzan v. Director, Missouri Dept. of Health, 497 U.S. 261, 279-82 (1990) (assuming, but not deciding, that the Constitution provides right "to refuse lifesaving hydration and nutrition," but upholding state regulations infringing this right [based on] weight of state's interests). . . .

Reviewing the Government's interests in the present case, we have little difficulty concluding that the Government has a legitimate interest in the health and life of appellant's wife. See *Cruzan*, 497 U.S. at 282 ("[A] state may . . . simply assert an unqualified interest in the preservation of human life to be weighed against the constitutionally protected interests of the individual."); *Roe*, 410 U.S. at 162 ("The State [has] an important and legitimate interest in preserving and protecting the health of the pregnant woman," which is "separate and distinct" from its "interest in protecting the potentiality of human life."). This interest is not negated by the fact that appellant's

8. We note a certain irony in the Government's present assertion of a compelling interest in celibacy by HIV-positive servicemembers: although the military provides extensive training and instruction to servicemembers when they contract the virus, the military has not in that context expressly mandated that HIV-positive servicemembers refrain from all sexual intercourse. Indeed, HIV-positive servicemembers are ordered to avoid unprotected sex and to notify prospective sex partners that they carry the virus, implicitly suggesting that safe sex with a properly forewarned partner is permissible. Thus, the prosecution of an HIV-positive servicemember for having safe sex after providing appropriate notice of his status to his or her partner might conceivably raise constitutional due process concerns. See United States v. Harriss, 347 U.S. 612, 617 (1954) ("The underlying principle is that no man shall be held criminally responsible for conduct which he could not reasonably understand to be proscribed."). In the present case, however, appellant does not dispute that he violated his safe-sex instruction on at least one or two occasions with BM3 C; nor has appellant raised a fair-notice argument in this appeal. . . .

wife chose to put her own health in danger by having unprotected sex with an HIV-positive partner. Indeed, the Government's interests are heightened by the nature of the risk assumed by BM3 C: infection by a contagious deadly disease. By compromising her own health, she also risked compromising the health of others. The Government's interests in the present case are not limited to the health of BM3 C, but also encompass the health of any sexual partners she may have in the future, any children she may bear, and anyone else to whom she may potentially transmit HIV through nonsexual contact.

Most crucially in the present case, however, is the fact that BM3 C was a member of the United States armed forces at the time of the sex acts in question. Where the life of one servicemember is put into serious jeopardy by the act of another servicemember, we must generally conclude that the Government has a compelling interest in proscribing the act and prosecuting the actor. As we have previously observed in reference to the military's efforts to stem the spread of AIDS, "The military, and society at large, have a compelling interest in having those who defend the nation remain healthy and capable of performing their duty." United States v. Womack, 29 M.J. 88, 90 (CMA 1989). When a member of the armed forces becomes infected with HIV, the military's duty-readiness is not merely reduced, but the Government must also bear the potentially extraordinary expenses of medical care associated with an AIDS patient. And, of course, as noted above, a newly-infected servicemember may then spread the disease to other noninfected servicemembers. . . .

Under the factual circumstances presented by this case, we need not, and do not, address the weight of the Government's interests in preventing the spread of HIV from a servicemember to a civilian. Nor need we consider whether our evaluation of the interests in the present case would differ if appellant had been prosecuted for sexual acts within the context of a marital relationship. We do conclude, however, that the Government has sufficiently compelling interests to proscribe unprotected sexual intercourse between HIV-positive servicemembers and uninfected, unmarried, noncivilian partners, even assuming that some sort of constitutional right to private heterosexual intercourse exists.

The decision of the United States Navy-Marine Corps Court of Criminal Appeals is affirmed.

Notes and Questions

1. In at least one important respect, *Bygrave* would be a more difficult case today than it was at the time. In *Bygrave*, the court relied on Bowers v. Hardwick, 478 U.S. 186 (1986), to conclude that "there is no generalized constitutional right to sexual intimacy between consenting adults." In Lawrence v. Texas, 539 U.S. 558 (2003), however, the Supreme Court

overruled Bowers v. Hardwick and held that the government may not criminalize the private, consensual sexual conduct of adult homosexuals:

> The present case does not involve minors. It does not involve persons who
> might be injured or coerced or who are situated in relationships where consent
> might not easily be refused. It does not involve public conduct or prostitution.
> It does not involve whether the government must give formal recognition to
> any relationship that homosexual persons seek to enter. The case does involve
> two adults who, with full and mutual consent from each other, engaged in
> sexual practices common to a homosexual lifestyle. The petitioners are enti-
> tled to respect for their private lives. The State cannot demean their exis-
> tence or control their destiny by making their private sexual conduct a crime.
> Their right to liberty under the Due Process Clause gives them the full right
> to engage in their conduct without intervention of the government. . . . The
> Texas statute furthers no legitimate state interest which can justify its intrusion
> into the personal and private life of the individual.

539 U.S. at 578.

In light of *Lawrence*, would *Bygrave* come out differently today? Could
the government still argue that, given the grave risks to Bygrave's partner,
she was incapable of giving the kind of "consent" referenced in *Lawrence*?
(Is this different from the issue of whether she could give valid consent to
conduct that would otherwise constitute an aggravated assault?) If that argument failed, could the government nevertheless prevail on the ground that
the military has what the *Bygrave* court called a "compelling interest" in protecting the health of its soldiers? Is that interest sufficient to overcome the
constitutional liberty interest recognized in *Lawrence*?

2. Statutes criminalizing the knowing transmission of the AIDS
virus are now common. Yet even in states that have such statutes, prosecutors sometimes charge defendants with assault, on a theory similar
to the theory the government used in *Bygrave*. For a recent example of
such a prosecution, see State v. Whitfield, 134 P.3d 1203 (Wash. Ct. App.
2006). Whitfield contracted HIV while in a prison in Oklahoma; after he
was released, he vowed to infect as many people as he could. Whitfield
moved to Washington, where he had sex with 17 different women and
fathered children with three of them. He did not tell his sex partners he
was infected, and he did not use condoms even when his partners asked
him to do so. A number of his partners became infected as well. Whitfield
was charged with multiple counts of aggravated assault; he was convicted
and sentenced to more than 178 years in prison: in effect, three consecutive life sentences. The Washington Court of Appeals affirmed the convictions and sentence.

Does the result in *Whitfield* seem right to you? What about the sentence?
Would your answer change if some or all of Whitfield's sex partners had
known he was HIV-positive?

3. Suppose Bygrave had told one of his sex partners that he was sterile, knowing that the claim was false; suppose the two then had unprotected sex, and Bygrave's partner got pregnant. Suppose further that Bygrave's partner did not want a pregnancy and would not have consented to unprotected sex had she known Bygrave could father a child. On those facts, is Bygrave guilty of aggravated assault? If Whitfield had falsely told his 17 sex partners that *he* was sterile, would he be guilty of assaulting all 17 of his partners, only the ones who became pregnant, or none of them?

4. What result if Bygrave and Whitfield were charged with violating the Iowa statute in *Bolsinger*? Does falsely denying that one is HIV-positive in order to obtain sex amount to fraud in the inducement, or is it fraud in the fact? Does the distinction make any sense in this context? In any context? Recall the California statute quoted in Note 2 after *Bolsinger*. Why should false claims to medical expertise be treated any differently than false claims about one's HIV-infected status? Which should be treated as worse?

C. COERCED SEX

1. Rape

Thanks in part to the rise of feminist legal theory and the reform movement it spawned, the definition of rape has changed more in the past three decades than in the two centuries before. The first main case below, Commonwealth v. Lopez, represents what has since become the prevailing view today about the legal definition of rape; along the way, the *Lopez* court also briefly discusses the definition that prevailed before the 1970s, and addresses an important issue on which states still differ today: the existence and content of a mistake-of-fact defense in rape cases. The second main case, In the Interest of M.T.S., represents the broadest definition of rape in any American court to date. The notes after the *M.T.S.* case are designed to prompt a serious discussion about the modern evolution of rape law, especially in the context of acquaintance rape and the recent debate about "no means no" and "yes means yes" policies about sexual consent. Following those notes are excerpts from California's current sexual assault and rape statutes, and then In re John Z., a California case that turns on the question whether and under what circumstances consent to sex, once given, can be withdrawn. After *John Z.* come sections on rape by intoxication and statutory rape, meaning sex with an underage partner.

You may find these cases upsetting to read. We found them so when preparing these materials. Still, they deserve careful and prolonged thought. The law of sexual assault has been the subject of a great deal of policy debate, which has led to substantial changes in the governing legal doctrine. This is a good time to consider which of the various reforms of the past generation are wise, and which ones may still need further rethinking.

Commonwealth v. Lopez

Supreme Judicial Court of Massachusetts
433 Mass. 722, 745 N.E.2d 961 (2001)

Opinion by SPINA, J.

The defendant, Kenny Lopez, was convicted on two indictments charging rape and one indictment charging indecent assault and battery on a person over the age of fourteen years. We granted his application for direct appellate review. The defendant claims error in the judge's refusal to give a mistake of fact instruction to the jury. He asks us to recognize a defendant's honest and reasonable belief as to a complainant's consent as a defense to the crime of rape, and to reverse his convictions and grant him a new trial. Based on the record presented, we decline to do so, and affirm the convictions.

BACKGROUND

We summarize facts that the jury could have found. On May 8, 1998, the victim, a seventeen year old girl, was living in a foster home in Springfield. At approximately 3 P.M., she started walking to a restaurant where she had planned to meet her biological mother. On the way, she encountered the defendant. He introduced himself, asked where she was going, and offered to walk with her. The victim met her mother and introduced the defendant as her friend. The defendant said that he lived in the same foster home as the victim and that "they knew each other from school." Sometime later, the defendant left to make a telephone call. When the victim left the restaurant, the defendant was waiting outside and offered to walk her home. She agreed.

The two walked to a park across the street from the victim's foster home and talked for approximately twenty to thirty minutes. The victim's foster sisters were within earshot, and the victim feared that she would be caught violating her foster mother's rules against bringing "a guy near the house." The defendant suggested that they take a walk in the woods nearby. At one point, deep in the woods, the victim said that she wanted to go home. The defendant said, "trust me," and assured her that nothing would happen and that he would not hurt her. The defendant led the victim down a path to a secluded area.

The defendant asked the victim why she was so distant and said that he wanted to start a relationship with her. She said that she did not want to "get into any relationship." The defendant began making sexual innuendos to which the victim did not respond. He grabbed her by her wrist and began kissing her on the lips. She pulled away and said, "No, I don't want to do this." The defendant then told the victim that if she "had sex with him, [she] would love him more." She repeated, "No, I don't want to. I don't want to do this." He raised her shirt and touched her breasts. She immediately pulled her shirt down and pushed him away.

The defendant then pushed the victim against a slate slab, unbuttoned her pants, and pulled them down. Using his legs to pin down her legs, he produced a condom and asked her to put it on him. The victim said, "No." The defendant put the condom on and told the victim that he wanted her to put his penis inside her. She said, "No." He then raped her, and she began to cry. A few minutes later, the victim made a "jerking move" to her left. The defendant became angry, turned her around, pushed her face into the slate, and raped her again. The treating physician described the bruising to the victim's knees as "significant." The physician opined that there had been "excessive force and trauma to the [vaginal] area" based on his observation that there was "a lot of swelling" in her external vaginal area and her hymen had been torn and was "still oozing." The doctor noted that in his experience it was "fairly rare" to see that much swelling and trauma.

The defendant told the victim that she "would get in a lot of trouble" if she said anything. He then grabbed her by the arm, kissed her, and said, "I'll see you later." The victim went home and showered. She told her foster mother, who immediately dialed 911. The victim cried hysterically as she spoke to the 911 operator.

The defendant's version of the encounter was diametrically opposed to that of the victim. He testified that the victim had been a willing and active partner in consensual sexual intercourse. Specifically, the defendant claimed that the victim initiated intimate activity, and never once told him to stop. Additionally, the defendant testified that the victim invited him to a party that evening so that he could meet her friends. The defendant further claimed that when he told her that he would be unable to attend, the victim appeared "mildly upset."

Before the jury retired, defense counsel requested a mistake of fact instruction as to consent.[1] The judge declined to give the instruction, saying that, based "both on the law, as well as on the facts, that instruction is not warranted." Because the defendant's theory at trial was that the victim actually consented and not that the defendant was "confused, misled, or mistaken" as to the victim's willingness to engage in sexual intercourse, the judge concluded that the ultimate question for the jury was simply whether they believed the victim's or the defendant's version of the encounter. The decision not to give the instruction provides the basis for this appeal.

---

1. The defendant proposed the following instruction: "If the Commonwealth has not proved beyond a reasonable doubt that the defendant was not motivated by a reasonable and honest belief that the complaining witness consented to sexual intercourse, you must find the defendant not guilty."

MISTAKE OF FACT INSTRUCTION

The defendant claims that the judge erred in failing to give his proposed mistake of fact instruction. The defendant, however, was not entitled to this instruction. In Commonwealth v. Ascolillo, 405 Mass. 456, 541 N.E.2d 570 (1989), we held that the defendant was not entitled to a mistake of fact instruction, and declined to adopt a rule that "in order to establish the crime of rape the Commonwealth must prove *in every case* not only that the defendant intended intercourse but also that he did not act pursuant to an honest and reasonable belief that the victim consented" (emphasis added). Id. at 463. Neither the plain language of our rape statute nor this court's decisions prior to . . . *Ascolillo* . . . warrant a different result.

A fundamental tenet of criminal law is that culpability requires a showing that the prohibited conduct (*actus reus*) was committed with the concomitant mental state (*mens rea*) prescribed for the offense. See, e.g., Morissette v. United States, 342 U.S. 246, 250 (1952) ("The contention that an injury can amount to a crime only when inflicted by intention is no provincial or transient notion"). The mistake of fact "defense" is available where the mistake negates the existence of a mental state essential to a material element of the offense. See Model Penal Code §2.04(1)(a) ("Ignorance or mistake as to a matter of fact or law is a defense if . . . the ignorance or mistake negatives the purpose, knowledge, belief, recklessness or negligence required to establish a material element of the offense"). In determining whether the defendant's honest and reasonable belief as to the victim's consent would relieve him of culpability, it is necessary to review the required elements of the crime of rape.

At common law, rape was defined as "the carnal knowledge of a woman forcibly and against her will." 4 W. Blackstone, Commentaries *210. Since 1642, rape has been proscribed by statute in this Commonwealth. While there have been several revisions to this statute, the definition and the required elements of the crime have remained essentially unchanged since its original enactment. The current rape statute, Gen. Laws ch. 265, §22(b), provides in pertinent part:

> "Whoever has sexual intercourse or unnatural sexual intercourse with a person and compels such person to submit by force and against his will, or compels such person to submit by threat of bodily injury, shall be punished by imprisonment in the state prison for not more than twenty years."

This statute follows the common-law definition of rape, and requires the Commonwealth to prove beyond a reasonable doubt that the defendant committed (1) sexual intercourse (2) by force or threat of force and against the will of the victim.

As to the first element, there has been very little disagreement. Sexual intercourse is defined as penetration of the victim, regardless of degree. The second element has proven to be more complicated. We have construed the element, "by force and against his will," as truly encompassing two separate elements each of which must independently be satisfied. See generally Commonwealth v. Caracciola, 409 Mass. 648, 653-654, 569 N.E.2d 774 (1991) (stating elements of "force" and "against his will" not superfluous, but instead must be read together). Therefore, the Commonwealth must demonstrate beyond a reasonable doubt that the defendant committed sexual intercourse (1) by means of physical force; nonphysical, constructive force; or threats of bodily harm, either explicit or implicit; and (2) at the time of penetration, there was no consent.

Although the Commonwealth must prove lack of consent, the "elements necessary for rape do not require that the defendant intend the intercourse be without consent." Commonwealth v. Grant, 391 Mass. 645, 650, 464 N.E.2d 33 (1984). Historically, the relevant inquiry has been limited to consent in fact, and no *mens rea* or knowledge as to the lack of consent has ever been required. See Commonwealth v. Lefkowitz, 20 Mass. App. Ct. 513, 519, 481 N.E.2d 227 (1985) ("the prosecution has proved rape if the jury concludes that the intercourse was in fact nonconsensual [that is, effectuated by force or by threat of bodily injury], without any special emphasis on the defendant's state of mind").

A mistake of fact as to consent, therefore, has very little application to our rape statute. Because Gen. Laws ch. 265, §22, does not require proof of a defendant's knowledge of the victim's lack of consent or intent to engage in nonconsensual intercourse as a material element of the offense, a mistake as to that consent cannot, therefore, negate a mental state required for commission of the prohibited conduct. Any perception (reasonable, honest, or otherwise) of the defendant as to the victim's consent is consequently not relevant to a rape prosecution. See Cavallaro, Big Mistake: Eroding the Defense of Mistake of Fact About Consent in Rape, 86 J. Crim. L. & Criminology 815, 818 (1996) (mistake of fact instruction is "available as a defense to a particular charge only where the definition of the offense makes a defendant's mental state as to a particular element material").

This is not to say, contrary to the defendant's suggestion, that the absence of any *mens rea* as to the consent element transforms rape into a strict liability crime. It does not. Rape, at common law and pursuant to Gen. Laws ch. 265, §22, is a general intent crime, and proof that a defendant intended sexual intercourse by force coupled with proof that the victim did not in fact consent is sufficient to maintain a conviction. See Bryden, Redefining Rape, 3 Buff. Crim. L. Rev. 317, 325 (2000) ("At common law, rape was a 'general intent' crime: The requisite intention was merely to perform the sexual act, rather than have nonconsensual intercourse").

Other jurisdictions have held that a mistake of fact instruction is necessary to prevent injustice. New Jersey, for instance, does not require the force necessary for rape to be anything more than what is needed to accomplish penetration. See [In the Interest of M.T.S.], ("physical force in excess of that inherent in the act of sexual penetration is not required for such penetration to be unlawful"). Thus, an instruction as to a defendant's honest and reasonable belief as to consent is available in New Jersey to mitigate the undesirable and unforeseen consequences that may flow from this construction. By contrast, in this Commonwealth, unless the putative victim has been rendered incapable of consent, the prosecution must prove that the defendant compelled the victim's submission by use of physical force; nonphysical, constructive force; or threat of force. Proof of the element of force, therefore, should negate any possible mistake as to consent.[4] See Estrich, Rape, 95 Yale L.J. 1087, 1098-1099 (1986) ("The requirement that sexual intercourse be accompanied by force or threat of force to constitute rape provides a [defendant] with some protection against mistakes as to consent").

We also have concerns that the mistake of fact defense would tend to eviscerate the longstanding rule in this Commonwealth that victims need not use any force to resist an attack. See Commonwealth v. McDonald, 110 Mass. 405, 406 (1872). A shift in focus from the victim's to the defendant's state of mind might require victims to use physical force in order to communicate an unqualified lack of consent to defeat any honest and reasonable belief as to consent. The mistake of fact defense is incompatible with the evolution of our jurisprudence with respect to the crime of rape.

We [recognize] that our interpretation is not shared by the majority of other jurisdictions. . . . "Lack of consent is a 'surrounding circumstance' which under the Revised Code, requires a complementary mental state as well as conduct to constitute a crime." Reynolds v. State, 664 P.2d 621, 625 (Alaska 1983). Because no specific mental state is mentioned in Alaska's statute governing sexual assault in the first degree, the State "must prove that the defendant acted 'recklessly' regarding his putative victim's lack of consent." Id. . . . [See also] Colo. Rev. Stat. §18-3-402(1) ("Any actor who knowingly inflicts sexual intrusion or sexual penetration on a victim commits sexual assault . . ."); Tex. Penal Code §22.021(a)(1)(A)(i) ("A person commits an offense if the person . . . intentionally or knowingly . . . causes . . . penetration . . . by any means, without that person's consent").

---

4. The trial judge properly instructed [the jury] as to the amount of force necessary to support a conviction. The judge, in essence, gave the model jury instruction as to the required element of force . . . :

> "The second element the Commonwealth must prove beyond a reasonable doubt is that the natural or unnatural sexual intercourse was accomplished by force or by threat of bodily injury and against the complainant's will. The force needed for rape may, depending on the circumstances, be constructive force, as well as physical force, violence or threat of bodily harm."

The New Jersey statute defines sexual assault (rape) as "any act of sexual penetration engaged in by the defendant without the affirmative and freely-given permission of the victim to the specific act of penetration." *M.T.S.*, supra, at [1277]. A defendant, by claiming that he had permission to engage in sexual intercourse, places his state of mind directly in issue. The jury must then determine "whether the defendant's belief that the alleged victim had freely given affirmative permission was reasonable." Id. at [1279].

The mistake of fact "defense" has been recognized by judicial decision in some States. In 1975, the Supreme Court of California became the first State court to recognize a mistake of fact defense in rape cases. See People v. Mayberry, 15 Cal. 3d 143, 542 P.2d 1337 (1975) (en banc). Although the court did not make a specific determination that intent was required as to the element of consent, it did conclude that, "if a defendant entertains a reasonable and bona fide belief that a prosecutrix voluntarily consented . . . to engage in sexual intercourse, it is apparent he does not possess the wrongful intent that is a prerequisite under Penal Code section 20 to a conviction of . . . rape by means of force or threat." Id. at 153. Thus, the intent required is an intent to engage in nonconsensual sexual intercourse, and the State must prove that a defendant intentionally engaged in intercourse and was at least negligent regarding consent.[5]

Other State courts have employed a variety of different constructions in adopting the mistake of fact defense. See State v. Smith, 210 Conn. 132, 142, 554 A.2d 713 (1989) (". . . whether a complainant should be found to have consented depends upon how her behavior would have been viewed by a reasonable person under the surrounding circumstances"); State v. Koonce,

---

5. Since that time, the Supreme Court of California has retreated from its original holding and steadily has eroded the defense. Today, the defense is available only if there is "substantial evidence of equivocal conduct that would have led a defendant to reasonably and in good faith believe consent existed where it did not." People v. Williams, 4 Cal. 4th 354, 362, 841 P.2d 961 (1992). Thus, as a threshold matter, the judge, not the jury, must find that the evidence with respect to consent is equivocal. Unless this showing is made, the "jury will be foreclosed from considering evidence that the defendant honestly and reasonably believed that there was consent, even if that jury would have credited such evidence." Cavallaro, supra, 86 J. Crim. L. & Criminology at 852. This requirement, in effect, virtually eliminates the mistake of fact doctrine because "those defendants who, as a factual matter, would present the strongest mistake case, by testifying to conduct that could be characterized as 'unequivocal,' are precluded by the rule of *Williams* from presenting that defense to the jury." Id. at 838. On the other hand, a "defendant who describes an encounter in which the complainant's conduct was admittedly equivocal as to consent essentially concedes that point and is doomed to almost certain conviction." Id. at 838-839.

In the present case, there was no evidence of equivocal conduct. The complaining witness testified that she had told the defendant, repeatedly and explicitly, that she did not want any form of sexual contact; that she tried to get away from the defendant; and that she cried during the forced intercourse. The defendant testified that the complaining witness was the one to initiate intimate contact; that she participated actively; and that she suggested they get together again later that evening.

731 S.W.2d 431, 437 n.2 (Mo. Ct. App. 1987) (construing rape statute to require [that] defendant acted at least recklessly as to consent).

However, the minority of States sharing our view is significant. See People v. Witte, 115 Ill. App. 3d 20, 26 n.2, 449 N.E.2d 966 (1983) ("whether the defendant intended to commit the offenses without the victim's consent is not relevant, the critical question being whether the victim did, in fact, consent. This involves her mental state, not the defendant's"); State v. Christensen, 414 N.W.2d 843, 845-846 (Iowa 1987) ("Defendant's awareness of a putative sexual abuse victim's lack of consent is not an element of third-degree sexual abuse. . . . It follows from this premise that a defendant's mistake of fact as to that consent would not negate an element of the offense"); State v. Reed, 479 A.2d 1291, 1296 (Me. 1984) ("The legislature, by carefully defining the sex offenses in the criminal code, and by making no reference to a culpable state of mind for rape, clearly indicated that rape compelled by force or threat requires no culpable state of mind"). See also People v. Hale, 142 Mich. App. 451, 453, 370 N.W.2d 382 (1985); State v. Elmore, 54 Wn. App. 54, 56, 771 P.2d 1192 (1989); Brown v. State, 59 Wis. 2d 200, 213-214, 207 N.W.2d 602 (1973). This case does not persuade us that we should recognize a mistake of fact as to consent as a defense to rape in *all* cases. See Commonwealth v. Ascolillo, supra, at 463. Whether such a defense might, in some circumstances, be appropriate is a difficult question that we may consider on a future case where a defendant's claim of reasonable mistake of fact is at least arguably supported by the evidence. This is not such a case. . . .

Notes on the Legal Definition of Rape

1. *Lopez* correctly quotes the common-law definition of rape: "the carnal knowledge of a woman forcibly and against her will." But that definition is missing an element that was key to the practical application of rape law in most jurisdictions throughout the nineteenth century and for most of the twentieth: the requirement that the victim physically resist the crime, even at risk of her survival. People v. Carey, 119 N.E. 83 (N.Y. 1918), describes the requirement:

> Rape is not committed unless the woman oppose the man to the utmost limit of her power. A feigned or passive or perfunctory resistance is not enough. It must be genuine and active and proportioned to the outrage. The record discloses a situation where conflicting inferences may be drawn whether resistance in that sense was offered.

Id. at 83. In *Carey*, the court reversed the defendant's conviction both because evidence of such physical resistance was lacking, and because the defendant "had taken liberties with her person" in the past, yet the victim "was again receiving him as a visitor in her rooms." Id. Notice: The crime was the defendant's, but the case turned on the victim's conduct. That was a common story in rape cases before the 1970s, as Susan Estrich has shown. Susan Estrich, Rape, 95 Yale L.J. 1087, 1121-32 (1986) (discussing the resistance rule).

2. Given the requirement of victim resistance, *mens rea* was traditionally a minor issue in rape prosecutions. Proof of force — which, in the past, usually meant extreme violence — and victim resistance precluded the possibility that the perpetrator might have believed the victim consented. Formally, rape was (and is) a general intent offense. Functionally, rape was a strict liability crime — because the relevant criminal conduct was defined in a manner that made accidental or mistaken conduct impossible.

3. In rejecting a mistake defense in rape cases, *Lopez* adopts a similar theory of the crime: By requiring proof that the defendant "compels [the victim] to submit by force," the Massachusetts legislature has made mistakes of fact a non-issue. If the defendant satisfied the force requirement, he must have known that consent was lacking. And if the sex act might have been consensual, the defendant's conduct must have been insufficiently violent to satisfy the force requirement. That theory works so long as force is defined to mean physical brutality, a definition courts often used in the late nineteenth and early twentieth centuries. See Estrich, 95 Yale L.J. at 1105-21. But that definition precludes prosecuting most so-called date (or acquaintance) rapes, where sex is coerced but the level of physical violence is usually lower than in stranger rapes.

On the other hand, if force is defined more broadly — if, for example, the amount of physical force inherent in sexual intercourse satisfies the force element, as per In the Interest of M.T.S., 609 A.2d 1266 (1992), the next main case — then the law risks criminalizing some genuinely consensual sex. How much of a problem is that? Is forcible sex ever consensual?

4. California's experience, as reported in footnote 5 in *Lopez*, suggests that a mistake-of-fact defense may not work to defendants' advantage. The California Supreme Court bars the defense save in cases in which the evidence shows "equivocal" conduct by the alleged victim — conduct suggesting that sex might or might not have been consensual. If, as in *Lopez*, the defendant claims that the victim's consent was unequivocal, the defense of mistake is unavailable. And if the defendant acknowledges that the victim might or might not have consented, the jury will likely assume the worst and convict. Either way, mistake is a non-issue.

5. Even if there were a mistake defense in rape cases in Massachusetts, mistake would have been a non-issue in *Lopez*. On the defendant's account of the facts, there was no need for a mistake defense, because the victim consented. The key to the case was the medical evidence, which corroborated the victim's account and was inconsistent with the defendant's. If cases like *Lopez* are the norm, the precise definition of rape matters less than first appears.

6. That is not the way things appeared a generation ago. Thanks in part to Estrich's article (see Note 1 supra), and also thanks to Susan Brownmiller, Against Our Will: Men, Women, and Rape (1975), and to Catherine MacKinnon, Toward a Feminist Theory of the State (1989), the conventional understanding of sexual assault was turned on its head in the 1970s and 1980s. State legislatures began enacting rape shield laws that prevented defendants from trying the victim's sexual history. In most states, court decisions and reformed rape statutes abolished the requirement that rape victims must resist their attackers "to the utmost limit of [their] power,"* and watered down the element that required proof of physical force in rape cases. All this came to pass because of a growing conviction that the law of sexual assault had become a means of protecting rapists rather than rape victims.

The response to that feeling, and the reaction to an apparently misogynist law of sexual assault, reached its peak in the next case.

In the Interest of M.T.S.

Supreme Court of New Jersey
609 A.2d 1266 (1992)

HANDLER, J., delivered the opinion of the Court.

Under New Jersey law a person who commits an act of sexual penetration using physical force or coercion is guilty of second-degree sexual assault. The sexual assault statute does not define the words "physical force." The question posed by this appeal is whether the element of "physical force" is met simply by an act of non-consensual penetration involving no more force than necessary to accomplish that result.

That issue is presented in the context of what is often referred to as "acquaintance rape." The record in the case discloses that the juvenile, a seventeen-year-old boy, engaged in consensual kissing and heavy petting with a fifteen-year-old girl and thereafter engaged in actual sexual penetration of the girl to which she had not consented. There was no evidence or suggestion that the juvenile used any unusual or extra force or threats to accomplish the act of penetration.

---

* Some version of the common law's "resistance" requirement remains a part of the law of rape in about a dozen states. But even in those states, the clear trend is to interpret the requirement so as to minimize its negative effects. See, e.g., State v. Jones, 154 Idaho 412, 299 P.3d 219 (Idaho S. Ct. 2013), where the court noted that "Idaho's forcible rape statute expressly requires resistance." Despite the fact that "this court has no authority to jettison the resistance requirement," and thus "some quantum of resistance is required," the court emphasized: "[I]n this State verbal resistance is sufficient for a charge of forcible rape." In other words, notwithstanding the continued existence in Idaho of the "resistance" requirement, "no" means "no," and a defendant who uses force to overcome the victim's verbal refusal is guilty of rape.

The trial court determined that the juvenile was delinquent for committing a sexual assault. The Appellate Division reversed the disposition of delinquency, concluding that non-consensual penetration does not constitute sexual assault unless it is accompanied by some level of force more than that necessary to accomplish the penetration. We granted the State's petition for certification.

I

. . . On Monday, May 21, 1990, fifteen-year-old C.G. was living with her mother, her three siblings, and several other people, including M.T.S. and his girlfriend. A total of ten people resided in the three-bedroom town-home at the time of the incident. M.T.S., then age seventeen, was temporarily residing at the home with the permission of the C.G.'s mother; he slept downstairs on a couch. C.G. had her own room on the second floor. At approximately 11:30 P.M. on May 21, C.G. went upstairs to sleep after having watched television with her mother, M.T.S., and his girlfriend. . . . At trial, C.G. and M.T.S. offered very different accounts concerning the nature of their relationship and the events that occurred after C.G. had gone upstairs. The trial court did not credit fully either teenager's testimony.

C.G. stated that earlier in the day, M.T.S. had told her three or four times that he "was going to make a surprise visit up in [her] bedroom." She said that she had not taken M.T.S. seriously and considered his comments a joke because he frequently teased her. She testified that M.T.S. had attempted to kiss her on numerous other occasions and at least once had attempted to put his hands inside of her pants, but that she had rejected all of his previous advances.

C.G. testified that on May 22, at approximately 1:30 A.M., she awoke to use the bathroom. As she was getting out of bed, she said, she saw M.T.S., fully clothed, standing in her doorway. According to C.G., M.T.S. then said that "he was going to tease [her] a little bit."

C.G. testified that she "didn't think anything of it"; she walked past him, used the bathroom, and then returned to bed, falling into a "heavy" sleep within fifteen minutes. The next event C.G. claimed to recall of that morning was waking up with M.T.S. on top of her, her underpants and shorts removed. She said "his penis was into [her] vagina." As soon as C.G. realized what had happened, she said, she immediately slapped M.T.S. once in the face, then "told him to get off [her], and get out." She did not scream or cry out. She testified that M.T.S. complied in less than one minute after being struck; according to C.G., "he jumped right off of [her]." . . .

C.G. said that after M.T.S. left the room, she "fell asleep crying" because "[she] couldn't believe that he did what he did to [her]." She explained that she did not immediately tell her mother or anyone else in the house of the events of that morning because she was "scared and in shock." . . .

At about 7:00 A.M., C.G. went downstairs and told her mother about her encounter with M.T.S. earlier in the morning and said that they would have to "get [him] out of the house." While M.T.S. was out on an errand, C.G.'s mother gathered his clothes and put them outside in his car. . . . C.G. and her mother then filed a complaint with the police.

According to M.T.S., he and C.G. had been good friends for a long time, and their relationship "kept leading on to more and more." He had been living at C.G.'s home for about five days before the incident occurred; he testified that during the three days preceding the incident they had been "kissing and necking" and had discussed having sexual intercourse. The first time M.T.S. kissed C.G., he said, she "didn't want him to, but she did after that." He said C.G. repeatedly had encouraged him to "make a surprise visit up in her room."

M.T.S. testified that at exactly 1:15 A.M. on May 22, he entered C.G.'s bedroom as she was walking to the bathroom. He said C.G. soon returned from the bathroom, and the two began "kissing and all," eventually moving to the bed. Once they were in bed, he said, they undressed each other and continued to kiss and touch for about five minutes. M.T.S. and C.G. proceeded to engage in sexual intercourse. According to M.T.S., who was on top of C.G., he "stuck it in" and . . . "[thrust] three times, and then the fourth time . . . that's when [she] pulled [him] off of her." M.T.S. said that as C.G. pushed him off, she said "stop, get off," and he "hopped off right away." According to M.T.S., after about one minute, he asked C.G. what was wrong; she replied with a back-hand to his face. He recalled asking C.G. what was wrong a second time, and her replying, "how can you take advantage of me or something like that." M.T.S. said that he proceeded to get dressed and told C.G. to calm down, but that she then told him to get away from her and began to cry. Before leaving the room, he told C.G., "I'm leaving . . . I'm going with my real girlfriend, don't talk to me . . . I don't want nothing to do with you or anything, stay out of my life . . . don't tell anybody about this . . . it would just screw everything up." He then walked downstairs and went to sleep.

On May 23, 1990, M.T.S. was charged with conduct that if engaged in by an adult would constitute second-degree sexual assault of the victim. . . .

Following a two-day trial on the sexual assault charge, M.T.S. was adjudicated delinquent. After reviewing the testimony, the court concluded that the victim had consented to a session of kissing and heavy petting with M.T.S. The trial court did not find that C.G. had been sleeping at the time of penetration, but nevertheless found that she had not consented to the actual sexual act. Accordingly, the court concluded that the State had proven second-degree sexual assault beyond a reasonable doubt. On appeal, following the imposition of suspended sentences on the sexual assault and the other remaining charges, the Appellate Division determined that the absence of force beyond that involved in the act of sexual penetration precluded a finding of second-degree sexual assault. It therefore reversed the juvenile's adjudication of delinquency for that offense.

II

The New Jersey Code of Criminal Justice, N.J.S.A. §2C:14-2c(1), defines "sexual assault" as the commission "of sexual penetration" "with another person" with the use of "physical force or coercion."[1] An unconstrained reading of the statutory language indicates that both the act of "sexual penetration" and the use of "physical force or coercion" are separate and distinct elements of the offense. Neither the definitions section . . . nor the remainder of the Code of Criminal Justice provides assistance in interpreting the words "physical force." . . .

   The parties offer two alternative understandings of the concept of "physical force" as it is used in the statute. The State would read "physical force" to entail any amount of sexual touching brought about involuntarily. A showing of sexual penetration coupled with a lack of consent would satisfy the elements of the statute. The Public Defender urges an interpretation of "physical force" to mean force "used to overcome lack of consent." That definition equates force with violence and leads to the conclusion that sexual assault requires the application of some amount of force in addition to the act of penetration. . . .

   . . . [A]s evidenced by the disagreements among the lower courts and the parties, and the variety of possible usages, the statutory words "physical force" do not evoke a single meaning that is obvious and plain. Hence, we must pursue avenues of construction in order to ascertain the meaning of that statutory language. Those avenues are well charted. When a statute is open to conflicting interpretations, the court seeks the underlying intent of the legislature, relying on legislative history and the contemporary context of the statute. Monmouth County v. Wissell, 68 N.J. 35, 41-42, 342 A.2d 199 (1975). With respect to a law like the sexual assault statute, that "alters or amends the previous law or creates or abolishes types of actions, it is important, in discovering the legislative intent, to ascertain the old law, the mischief and the proposed remedy." Grobart v. Grobart, 5 N.J. 161, 166, 74 A.2d 294 (1950). We also remain mindful of the basic tenet of statutory construction that penal statutes are to be strictly construed in favor of the accused. Nevertheless, the construction must conform to the intent of the Legislature.

   . . . The origin of the rape statute that the current statutory offense of sexual assault replaced can be traced to the English common law. Under the

---

1. The sexual assault statute, N.J.S.A. §2C:14-2c(1), reads as follows: "An actor is guilty of sexual assault [in the second degree] if he commits an act of sexual penetration with another person under any one of the following circumstances: (1) The actor *uses physical force or coercion*, but the victim does not sustain severe personal injury. . . ." (Emphasis added.)

common law, rape was defined as "carnal knowledge of a woman against her will." American jurisdictions generally adopted the English view, but over time states added the requirement that the carnal knowledge have been forcible, apparently in order to prove that the act was against the victim's will. As of 1796, New Jersey statutory law defined rape as "carnal knowledge of a woman, forcibly and against her will." Crimes Act of March 18, 1796 §8. Those three elements of rape—carnal knowledge, forcibly, and against her will—remained the essential elements of the crime until 1979.

Under traditional rape law, . . . the state had to show both that force had been used and that the penetration had been against the woman's will. . . . "Thus, the perpetrator's use of force became criminal only if the victim's state of mind met the statutory requirement. The perpetrator could use all the force imaginable and no crime would be committed if the state could not prove additionally that the victim did not consent." National Institute of Law Enforcement and Criminal Justice, Forcible Rape—An Analysis of Legal Issues 5 (March 1978). . . . As a Delaware court stated, "If sexual intercourse is obtained by milder means, or with the consent or silent submission of the female, it cannot constitute the crime of rape." State v. Brown, 83 A. 1083, 1084 (1912).

The presence or absence of consent often turned on credibility. To demonstrate that the victim had not consented to the intercourse, and also that sufficient force had been used to accomplish the rape, the state had to prove that the victim had resisted. According to the oft-quoted Lord Hale, to be deemed a credible witness, a woman had to be of good fame, disclose the injury immediately, suffer signs of injury, and cry out for help. 1 Matthew Hale, History of the Pleas of the Crown 633 (1st ed. 1847). . . . Evidence of resistance was viewed as a solution to the credibility problem. . . .

The resistance requirement had a profound effect on the kind of conduct that could be deemed criminal and on the type of evidence needed to establish the crime. Courts assumed that any woman who was forced to have intercourse against her will necessarily would resist to the extent of her ability. In many jurisdictions the requirement was that the woman have resisted to the utmost. "Rape is not committed unless the woman oppose the man to the utmost limit of her power." People v. Carey, 119 N.E. 83 (N.Y. 1918). . . .

. . . In State v. Harris, 70 N.J. Super. 9, 174 A.2d 645 (1961), the Appellate Division recognized that the "to the uttermost" test was obsolete. "The fact that a victim finally submits does not necessarily imply that she consented. Submission to a compelling force, or as a result of being put in fear, is not consent." Id. at 16-17. Nonetheless, the "resistance" requirement remained an essential feature of New Jersey rape law. Thus, in 1965 the Appellate Division stated: "[W]e have rejected the former test that a woman must resist 'to the uttermost.' We only require that she resist as much as she possibly can under the circumstances." State v. Terry, 89 N.J. Super. 445, 449, 215 A.2d 374. . . .

. . . Resistance was necessary not only to prove non-consent but also to demonstrate that the force used by the defendant had been sufficient to overcome the victim's will. The amount of force used by the defendant was assessed in relation to the resistance of the victim. See, e.g., Tex. Penal Code Ann. §21.02 (1974) (repealed 1983) (stating that "the amount of force necessary to negate consent is a relative matter to be judged under all the circumstances, the most important of which is the resistance of the female"). . . . Only if she resisted, causing him to use more force than was necessary to achieve penetration, would his conduct be criminalized. . . .

To refute the misguided belief that rape was not real unless the victim fought back, reformers emphasized empirical research indicating that women who resisted forcible intercourse often suffered far more serious injury as a result. Menachem Amir, Patterns in Forcible Rape, 164-65, 169-71 (1971). That research discredited the assumption that resistance to the utmost or to the best of a woman's ability was the most reasonable or rational response to a rape. . . . Susan Brownmiller, Against Our Will: Men, Women, and Rape 377 (1975). . . .

Critics of rape law agreed that the focus of the crime should be shifted from the victim's behavior to the defendant's conduct, and particularly to its forceful and assaultive, rather than sexual, character. Reformers also shared the goals of facilitating rape prosecutions and of sparing victims much of the degradation involved in bringing and trying a charge of rape. There were, however, differences over the best way to redefine the crime. Some reformers advocated a standard that defined rape as unconsented-to sexual intercourse; others urged the elimination of any reference to consent from the definition of rape. Nonetheless, all proponents of reform shared a central premise: that the burden of showing non-consent should not fall on the victim of the crime. . . .

Similarly, with regard to force, rape law reform sought to give independent significance to the forceful or assaultive conduct of the defendant and to avoid a definition of force that depended on the reaction of the victim. Traditional interpretations of force were strongly criticized for failing to acknowledge that force may be understood simply as the invasion of "bodily integrity." Susan Estrich, Rape, 95 Yale L.J. 1087, 1105 (1986). In urging that the "resistance" requirement be abandoned, reformers sought to break the connection between force and resistance.

III

. . . Since the 1978 reform, the Code has referred to the crime that was once known as "rape" as "sexual assault." The crime now requires "penetration," not "sexual intercourse." It requires "force" or "coercion," not "submission" or "resistance." It makes no reference to the victim's state of mind or attitude, or conduct in response to the assault. It eliminates the spousal exception based on implied consent. It emphasizes the assaultive character of the offense by defining sexual penetration to encompass a wide range of sexual contacts, going well beyond traditional "carnal knowledge." Consistent with the assaultive character, as opposed to the traditional sexual character, of the offense, the statute also renders the crime gender-neutral: both males and females can be actors or victims.

The reform statute defines sexual assault as penetration accomplished by the use of "physical force" or "coercion," but it does not define either "physical force" or "coercion" or enumerate examples of evidence that would establish those elements. . . . The task of defining "physical force" therefore was left to the courts. . . .

The Legislature's concept of sexual assault and the role of force was significantly colored by its understanding of the law of assault and battery. As a general matter, criminal battery is defined as "the unlawful application of force to the person of another." 2 Wayne LaFave & Austin Scott, Criminal Law, §7.15, at 301 (1986). The application of force is criminal when it results in either (a) a physical injury or (b) an offensive touching. Id. at 301-02. Any "unauthorized touching of another [is] a battery." Perna v. Pirozzi, 92 N.J. 446, 462, 457 A.2d 431 (1983). . . .

The understanding of sexual assault as a criminal battery, albeit one with especially serious consequences, follows necessarily from the Legislature's decision to eliminate nonconsent and resistance from the substantive definition of the offense. Under the new law, the victim no longer is required to resist and therefore need not have said or done anything in order for the sexual penetration to be unlawful. The alleged victim is not put on trial, and his or her responsive or defensive behavior is rendered immaterial. . . .

. . . We conclude, therefore, that any act of sexual penetration engaged in by the defendant without the affirmative and freely-given permission of the victim to the specific act of penetration constitutes the offense of sexual assault. . . . [P]hysical force in excess of that inherent in the act of sexual penetration is not required for such penetration to be unlawful. The definition of "physical force" is satisfied . . . if the defendant applies any amount of force against another person in the absence of what a reasonable person would believe to be affirmative and freely-given permission to the act of sexual penetration.

. . . [P]ermission to engage in sexual penetration must be affirmative and it must be given freely, but that permission may be inferred either from acts or statements reasonably viewed in light of the surrounding circumstances. Persons need not, of course, expressly announce their consent to engage in intercourse for there to be affirmative permission. Permission to engage in an act of sexual penetration can be and indeed often is indicated through physical actions rather than words. . . . Permission is demonstrated when the evidence, in whatever form, is sufficient to demonstrate that a reasonable person would have believed that the alleged victim had affirmatively and freely given authorization to the act. . . .

. . . The Legislature recast the law of rape as sexual assault to bring that area of law in line with the expectation of privacy and bodily control that long has characterized most of our private and public law. See Hennessey v. Coastal Eagle Paint Oil Co., 129 N.J. 81, 94-96, 609 A.2d 11 (1992) (recognizing importance of constitutional and common-law protection of personal privacy); id. at 106 (Pollock, J., concurring) (emphasizing that common-law right of privacy protects individual self-determination and autonomy). In interpreting "physical force" to include any touching that occurs without permission we seek to respect that goal. . . .

IV

. . . The definition of "permission" serves to define the "consent" that otherwise might allow a defendant to avoid criminal liability. Because "physical force" as an element of sexual assault in this context requires the *absence* of affirmative and freely-given permission, the "consent" necessary to negate such "physical force" under a defense based on consent would require the *presence* of such affirmative and freely-given permission. Any lesser form of consent would render the sexual penetration unlawful and cannot constitute a defense.

In this case, the Appellate Division concluded that non-consensual penetration accomplished with no additional physical force or coercion is not criminalized under the sexual assault statute. 247 N.J. Super. at 260, 588 A.2d 1282. It acknowledged that its conclusion was "anomalous" because it recognized that "a woman has every right to end [physically intimate] activity without sexual penetration." Ibid. Thus, it added to its holding that "[e]ven the force of penetration might . . . be sufficient if it is shown to be employed to overcome the victim's unequivocal expressed desire to limit the encounter." Ibid.

The Appellate Division was correct in recognizing that a woman's right to end intimate activity . . . is a protectable right the violation of which can be a criminal offense. However, it misperceived the purpose of the statute in believing that the only way that right can be protected is by the woman's unequivocally-expressed desire to end the activity. The effect of that requirement would be to import into the sexual assault statute the notion that an assault occurs only if the victim's will is overcome, and thus to reintroduce the requirement of . . . victim-resistance as a constituent material element of the crime. Under the reformed statute, a person's failure to protest or resist cannot be considered or used as justification for bodily invasion.

We acknowledge that cases such as this are inherently fact sensitive and depend on the reasoned judgment and common sense of judges and juries. The trial court concluded that the victim had not expressed consent to the act of intercourse, either through her words or actions. We conclude that the record provides reasonable support for the trial court's disposition.

Accordingly, we reverse the judgment of the Appellate Division and reinstate the disposition of juvenile delinquency for the commission of second-degree sexual assault.

Notes and Questions

1. *M.T.S.* was more famous than influential: The case is rarely cited in court opinions outside New Jersey. It is cited more often in the academic literature, where the case is chiefly known for two sentences in the court's opinion:

> [A]ny act of sexual penetration engaged in by the defendant without the affirmative and freely-given permission of the victim to the specific act of penetration constitutes the offense of sexual assault. . . . [P]hysical force in excess of that inherent in the act of sexual penetration is not required for such penetration to be unlawful.

What do those two sentences mean? Must "affirmative and freely-given permission" be explicit? If so, might *M.T.S.* condemn a large fraction of consensual sexual encounters? If not, what conduct would suffice to show such permission?

2. In *M.T.S.* as in *Lopez*, the defendant and the victim tell very different stories. C.G. claims that M.T.S. began having sex with her while she was still asleep, which would constitute sexual assault in most jurisdictions (though it was no crime under the common law). M.T.S. claims that intercourse followed several minutes of consensual kissing and petting; when C.G. objected—just after intercourse had begun—M.T.S. ended the encounter. Ordinarily in sexual assault cases, the defendant is convicted when the fact finder believes the victim. In *M.T.S.*, the trial judge seems to have found that the defendant's story was largely correct, but convicted the defendant nonetheless. Key to the latter finding was the court's determination that the physical force element of the crime was satisfied by the sex act itself. Under *M.T.S.*, sexual assault means not sex by force and without consent, but simply sex without consent.

The court's decision in *M.T.S.* was (and is) widely regarded as radical. Why? What could possibly be wrong with a legal standard holding that nonconsensual sex is a crime?

3. How should factual disputes like the ones in *Lopez* and *M.T.S.* be resolved? In *Lopez*, the resolution was fairly easy: The victim was examined shortly after the rape, and the examination corroborated the victim's account. Based on the New Jersey Supreme Court's opinion, what arguments might you make in support of C.G.'s account of the facts? What arguments might you make on behalf of M.T.S.'s account? Are there any common threads in your answers to those two questions?

4. Consider the facts in Commonwealth v. Berkowitz, 609 A.2d 1338, 1339-40 (Pa. Super. Ct. 1992):

At roughly 2:00 on the afternoon of April 19, 1988, after attending two morning classes, the victim returned to her dormitory room. There, she drank a martini to "loosen up a little bit" before going to meet her boyfriend. . . . Roughly ten minutes later she walked to her boyfriend's dormitory lounge to meet him. He had not yet arrived.

Having nothing else to do while she waited for her boyfriend, the victim walked up to appellant's room to look for Earl Hassel, appellant's roommate. She knocked on the door several times but received no answer. She therefore wrote a note to Mr. Hassel, which read, "Hi Earl, I'm drunk. That's not why I came to see you. I haven't seen you in a while. I'll talk to you later, [victim's name]." She did so, although she had not felt any intoxicating effects from the martini, "for a laugh."

After the victim had knocked again, she tried the knob on the appellant's door. Finding it open, she walked in. She saw someone lying on the bed with a pillow over his head, whom she thought to be Earl Hassel. After lifting the pillow from his head, she realized it was appellant. She asked appellant which dresser was his roommate's. He told her, and the victim left the note.

Before the victim could leave appellant's room, however, appellant asked her to stay and "hang out for a while." She complied because she "had time to kill" and because she didn't really know appellant and wanted to give him "a fair chance." Appellant asked her to give him a back rub but she declined, explaining that she did not "trust" him. Appellant then asked her to have a seat on his bed. Instead, she found a seat on the floor, and conversed for a while about a mutual friend. . . .

. . . [A]ppellant moved off the bed and down on the floor, and "kind of pushed [the victim] back with his body. It wasn't a shove, it was just kind of a leaning-type of thing." Next appellant "straddled" and started kissing the victim. The victim responded by saying, "Look, I gotta go. I'm going to meet [my boyfriend]." Then appellant lifted up her shirt and bra and began fondling her. The victim then said "no."

After roughly thirty seconds of kissing and fondling, appellant "undid his pants and he kind of moved his body up a little bit." The victim was still saying "no" but "really couldn't move because [appellant] was shifting at [her] body so he was over [her]." Appellant then tried to put his penis in her mouth. The victim did not physically resist, but rather continued to verbally protest, saying "No, I gotta go, let me go". . . .

Ten or fifteen more seconds passed before the two rose to their feet. Appellant disregarded the victim's continual complaints that she "had to go," and instead walked two feet away to the door and locked it so that no one from the outside could enter.

Then, in the victim's words, "[appellant] put me down on the bed. It was kind of like—he didn't throw me on the bed. It's hard to explain. It was kind of like a push but no.". . . "It wasn't slow like a romantic kind of thing, but it wasn't a fast shove either. It was kind of in the middle."

Once the victim was on the bed, appellant began "straddling" her again while he undid the knot in her sweatpants. He then removed her sweatpants and underwear from one of her legs. The victim did not physically resist in any way while on the bed because appellant was on top of her, and she "couldn't like go anywhere." She did not scream out at anytime because, "[i]t was like a dream was happening or something."

Appellant then used one of his hands to "guide" his penis into her vagina. At that point, after appellant was inside her, the victim began saying "no, no to him softly in a moaning kind of way . . . because it was just so scary." After about thirty seconds, appellant pulled out his penis and ejaculated onto the victim's stomach.

Immediately thereafter, appellant got off the victim and said, "Wow, I guess we just got carried away." To this the victim retorted, "No, we didn't get carried away, you got carried away." The victim then quickly dressed, grabbed her school books and raced downstairs to her boyfriend who was by then waiting for her in the lounge.

Once there, the victim began crying. Her boyfriend and she went up to his dorm room where, after watching the victim clean off appellant's semen from her stomach, he called the police.

The court reversed Berkowitz's rape conviction, on the ground that—whether or not the victim consented—the "force" element of rape was not satisfied:

Before us is not a case of mental coercion. There existed no significant disparity between the ages of appellant and the victim. They were both college sophomores at the time of the incident. Appellant was age twenty; the victim was nineteen. The record is devoid of any evidence suggesting that the physical or mental condition of one party differed from the other in any material way. Moreover, the atmosphere and physical setting in which the incident took place was in no way coercive. The victim walked freely into appellant's dorm room in the middle of the afternoon on a school day and stayed to talk of her own volition. There was no evidence to suggest that appellant was in any position of authority, domination or custodial control over the victim. Finally, no record evidence indicates that the victim was under duress. . . .

Even in the light most favorable to the Commonwealth, the victim's testimony as to the physical aspects of the encounter cannot serve as a basis to prove "forcible compulsion." The cold record is utterly devoid of any evidence regarding the respective sizes of either appellant or the victim. As such, we are left only to speculate as to the coercive effect of such acts as "leaning" against the victim or placing the "weight of his body" on top of her. This we may not do. Moreover, even if the record indicated some disparity in the respective weights or strength of the parties, such acts are not themselves inconsistent with consensual relations. Except for the fact that appellant was on top of the victim before and during intercourse, there is no evidence that the victim, if she had wanted to do so, could not have removed herself from appellant's bed and walked out of the room without any risk of harm or danger to herself whatsoever. These circumstances simply cannot be bootstrapped into sexual intercourse by forcible compulsion. . . .

The only evidence which remains to be considered is the fact that both the victim and appellant testified that throughout the encounter, the victim repeatedly and continually said "no." Unfortunately for the Commonwealth, under the existing statutes, this evidence alone cannot suffice to support a finding of "forcible compulsion."

609 A.2d at 1344, 1347. The Pennsylvania Supreme Court affirmed the reversal of the rape conviction, agreeing with the lower court's conclusion that Berkowitz did not use enough force to commit rape. See Commonwealth v. Berkowitz, 641 A.2d 1161 (Pa. S. Ct. 1994).

In which case is the evidence of force stronger, *M.T.S.* or *Berkowitz*? In which case would the defendant have a stronger argument that he mistakenly believed the victim consented to intercourse?

5. Was the *Berkowitz* case wrongly decided? After all, whether or not the defendant used sufficient "force" to satisfy the court's interpretation of the requirements of rape law, the victim clearly said "no"—multiple times—throughout the prolonged encounter. Why wasn't that enough to demonstrate her lack of consent to sex?

The law of rape has evolved significantly, from the "bad old days" when victims had to fight back against their assailants in order to express lack of consent, to the modern approach that shifts the focus from the victim's resistance to the amount of force used by the defendant. But decisions like *Berkowitz* illustrate why many believe that even this shift does not go nearly far enough. That is why "no means no" policies, with respect to sexual consent, have now become a pronounced trend. If the legal rule is "no means no," then *Berkowitz* becomes a pretty easy case.

So now let's make it more difficult. Imagine that all of the facts in *Berkowitz* happened exactly as they did in the real case—*except* that the victim, because she was too scared (and more than a little drunk), never said the word "no." How would you decide this alternate, hypothetical version of *Berkowitz*—a hypothetical version that seems all too real, in the context of sexual encounters that occur routinely on college campuses (not to mention before and after college)? If the victim never said "no," then would you still say that Berkowitz is a rapist?

6. Suppose M.T.S. and Berkowitz (either the actual version or the hypothetical version) were to testify that they had no idea they had done anything wrong, much less criminal. Suppose further that you believed their testimony. What conclusions would follow? If defendants are judged only by their own cultural norms, those norms may never change. On the other hand, is it fair to imprison defendants for conduct they didn't suspect might lead to prosecution and punishment?

Notes on Acquaintance Rape

1. *M.T.S.* and *Berkowitz* are instances of "acquaintance rape": In both cases, the victim and the defendant knew each other, and—at least to some extent and up to a certain point—willingly interacted with each other. Such cases present a challenge for the law of rape, in large part because they often (although certainly not always) involve lesser amounts of force (or threatened force) than the classic case of stranger rape. In addition, in cases of stranger rape, it's patently obvious that the victim would not have wanted to have sex with an unknown assailant; lack of consent is virtually a given. But in "acquaintance rape" cases—whether fairly or unfairly—the victim's lack of consent may seem to be less crystal clear.

For both of these reasons, acquaintance rape cases can be extremely difficult for the courts to resolve. In such cases, should the law err on the side of the defendant, or on the side of the victim? Think about that as you read the materials that follow.

2. Here are the actual facts of another, more recent acquaintance rape case from Pennsylvania, Commonwealth v. Clay, 64 A.3d 1049 (Pa. S. Ct. 2012):

> On February 7, 2009, at around 1:30 A.M., Jamel Clay, James Claybrook, and Rashid Lewis (collectively, "Appellees") visited R.B. at her college dormitory in West Chester, Pennsylvania. Upon their arrival at the dormitory, Appellees signed in and provided the security officer with photo identification. Appellees spent the next several hours socializing with R.B. and her friend, H.S., who lived in the same hall. Eventually, at approximately 3:30 A.M., the group discussed sleeping arrangements, and, according to Appellees, H.S. invited them to stay in her room. At trial, H.S. testified that Appellees "ended up" in her room because it was the one nearest to where the group was gathered at the time the socializing concluded, but she did not dispute that she allowed them to stay. There also was testimony at trial that H.S. had engaged in approximately 18 telephone calls with her friend Richard earlier in the evening, during which H.S. informed him that she was planning to allow Appellees to stay in her room, and Richard warned her not to do so.
>
> When Claybrook and Lewis first entered H.S.'s room, Lewis sat on her bed and Claybrook sat on H.S.'s roommate's bed. Clay either entered the room at the same time as Claybrook and Lewis, or shortly thereafter. At trial, H.S. testified that she asked Lewis to get off her bed, but he refused, and so she laid down next to him, back to back. H.S. stated that, after five to ten minutes, Lewis attempted to kiss her, and when she said no and attempted to get off the bed, he pulled her towards him, kissed her, and fondled her breasts. H.S. testified that, at some point, she scratched Lewis in an effort to resist him.

Lewis testified that, after he sat on H.S.'s bed, H.S. never asked him to get off the bed, and it was she who attempted to kiss him. At some point, after Clay entered the room and laid down in H.S.'s roommate's bed, Claybrook got into H.S.'s bed with H.S. and Lewis. Over the next hour, all three Appellees engaged in vaginal intercourse and oral sex with H.S., some of which involved all three of the men at the same time. H.S. also testified that each of the three men engaged in anal intercourse with her, although both Claybrook and Lewis denied having anal intercourse with H.S. Clay did not testify at trial. The hospital examination revealed ejaculate in H.S.'s rectum.

H.S. testified that Appellees initially restrained her, but conceded she was not held down the entire time. Appellees denied restraining H.S. at any time. Midway through the incident, Lewis and Clay left the room to obtain more condoms while Claybrook remained in the room with H.S. H.S. testified at trial that, during this time, Claybrook "was forcing me to have oral sex with him. . . . He had his hands on the side of my head and he forced his penis into my mouth." N.T. Trial, 10/26/09, at 162. When asked what kept her from leaving the room at that point, H.S. testified "I was just scared. I was really scared. I didn't know what was going to happen." Id. at 162-63. H.S. further testified that "they were three strangers that I didn't know, and they were forcing me to do these things with them." Id. at 163.

When Lewis and Clay returned, they each engaged in further sexual acts with H.S. H.S. testified that, except for the first time she told Lewis "no" when he tried to kiss her, she did not tell Appellees to stop, did not cry out for help, and did not attempt to leave the room. She explained in her trial testimony, when asked why she did not scream, that "[m]ost of the time I had somebody restrained over me, or I had somebod[y's] penis in my mouth." Id. at 165.

Thereafter, Appellees indicated they wanted to smoke, but H.S. asked them smoke outside so they would not set off the smoke alarm and get her in trouble. While Appellees were outside smoking, H.S. went down the hall to the bathroom and brushed her teeth. She then returned to her room and left the door open while she changed her sheets and picked up condoms from the floor. Appellees returned to the doorway of H.S.'s room[1] and Lewis asked for a clean shirt to wear, as the shirt he was wearing had blood on it. H.S. gave him a clean shirt.

Appellees then left, at which point H.S. called her friend Richard and assured him that everything was fine. Several minutes later, however, she sent Richard a text message telling him that she had lied, that everything was not okay, and that she had been raped. H.S. then told her friend, R.B., that Appellees had raped her. At R.B.'s suggestion, H.S. contacted her Resident Assistant and Resident Director about the incident. The Resident Director reported the incident to campus police on H.S.'s behalf. H.S. then went to the hospital to be examined. Karen Dougherty, a registered nurse in the Crozier Emergency Department,

---

1. There was a dispute at trial as to whether Appellees actually entered H.S.'s room when they returned from smoking, or merely stood in the doorway to her room.

examined H.S. Nurse Dougherty testified that she is a forensic nurse examiner and a sexual assault nurse examiner ("SANE") who had practiced nursing for 30 years and had conducted approximately 200 sexual assault exams. N.T. Trial, 10/27/09, at 484-86. Nurse Dougherty stated that, upon examining H.S., she observed a "suction mark" on her neck, a light scratch on her arm, a small abrasion on her inner elbow, and redness on her inner thighs. Id. at 491. The nurse also noted that H.S. told her she had scratched Lewis in self-defense.

All three defendants were charged with rape, involuntary deviate sexual intercourse, criminal conspiracy, sexual assault, indecent assault, and false imprisonment. At trial, all three were convicted of sexual assault,* indecent assault,** and false imprisonment, but the false imprisonment convictions were overturned by the trial judge.*** Each defendant received two to four years of imprisonment.

On appeal, the Superior Court unanimously reversed the convictions, finding them to be against the weight of the evidence. As the Superior Court's decision was later described by the Pennsylvania Supreme Court:

> [The Superior Court] noted: (1) at trial, H.S. denied inviting Appellees to sleep in her room, despite substantial evidence to the contrary; (2) when Lewis refused to get off her bed, H.S. did not demand Appellees leave her room, nor did she leave the room herself; (3) other than initially telling Lewis "no" when he attempted to kiss her and then scratching him, H.S. did not tell Appellees to stop, cry out for help, try to escape, or physically resist Appellees; (4) after the sexual activity ended, H.S. felt comfortable asking Appellees to smoke outside and, while Appellees were outside, H.S. did not lock her door to keep Appellees from coming back to her room; (5) the evidence established that Appellees returned to H.S.'s room after smoking, despite H.S.'s trial testimony to the contrary; and (6) H.S. suffered "minor" physical injuries. Based on these factors, the Superior Court concluded "despite [Trial] Judge MacElree's statement that the verdict did not shock *his* conscience, guilty verdicts based on the record before us should shock the conscience of *anyone* seeking to 'reach a dispassionate conclusion.'" The court thus held the trial court's decision was an abuse of discretion and vacated Appellees' convictions.

Commonwealth v. Clay, 64 A.3d at 1053. The Pennsylvania Supreme Court,

---

* 18 Pa. C.S.A. §3124.1. Sexual Assault. [A] person commits a felony of the second degree when that person engages in sexual intercourse or deviate sexual intercourse with a complainant without the complainant's consent.

** 18 Pa. C.S.A. §3126. Indecent Assault. (a) A person is guilty of indecent assault if the person has indecent contact with the complainant, causes the complainant to have indecent contact with the person or intentionally causes the complainant to come into contact with seminal fluid, urine or feces for the purpose of arousing sexual desire in the person or the complainant and (1) the person does so without the complainant's consent. . . .

*** Presumably the rape charges didn't stick because of the relative lack of physical force used by the defendants; note that sexual assault and indecent assault, as defined in Pennsylvania, require lack of consent but do not require the use or threatened use of force.

in turn, reversed the decision of the Superior Court on the ground that the decision was not sufficiently deferential to the trial court's conclusion that the guilty verdicts for sexual assault and indecent assault were *not* against the weight of the evidence presented at trial. The case was therefore remanded to the Superior Court for reconsideration under the proper standard of review.

How do you feel about the *Clay* case? Does it matter to you that the victim said "no" only once, and only with respect to a first attempt to kiss her? What about the fact that the victim didn't ever "cry out for help, try to escape, or physically resist" the defendants? Should that matter? Doesn't that sound a lot like the old, now-discredited "resistance" requirement? But on the other hand, in the absence of such victim resistance — either verbal *or* physical — is it really fair to convict the defendants of serious felony crimes that will send them to prison for years, not to mention likely stigmatizing them for the rest of their lives as sex offenders?

3. Maybe what we really need to change is not the law, but the culture. Speaking of changing cultural norms: In the early 1990s, in response to several reports of date rapes on campus, Antioch College officially adopted a new "Sexual Offense Policy." The policy, which attracted national media attention, provided (the following version dates from 1993):

THE ANTIOCH COLLEGE SEXUAL OFFENSE POLICY

All sexual contact and conduct on the Antioch College campus and/or occurring with an Antioch community member must be consensual. . . .

CONSENT

1. For the purpose of this policy, "consent" shall be defined as follows: the act of willingly and verbally agreeing to engage in specific sexual contact or conduct.

2. If sexual contact and/or conduct is not mutually and simultaneously initiated, then the person who initiates sexual contact/ conduct is responsible for getting the verbal consent of the other individual(s) involved.

3. Obtaining consent is an on-going process in any sexual interaction. Verbal consent should be obtained with each new level of physical and/or sexual contact/conduct in any given interaction, regardless of who initiates it. Asking "Do you want to have sex with me?" is not enough. The request for consent must be specific to each act.

4. The person with whom sexual contact/conduct is initiated is responsible to express verbally and/or physically her/his willingness or lack of willingness when reasonably possible.

5. If someone has initially consented but then stops consenting during a sexual interaction, she/he should communicate withdrawal verbally and/or through physical resistance. The other individual(s) must stop immediately.

6. To knowingly take advantage of someone who is under the influence of alcohol, drugs and/or prescribed medication is not acceptable behavior in the Antioch community.

7. If someone verbally agrees to engage in specific contact or conduct, but it is not of her/his own free will due to any of the circumstances stated in (a) through (d) below, then the person initiating shall be considered in violation of this policy if:

(a) the person submitting is under the influence of alcohol or other substances supplied to her/him by the person initiating;

(b) the person submitting is incapacitated by alcohol, drugs, and/or prescribed medication;

(c) the person submitting is asleep or unconscious;

(d) the person initiating has forced, threatened, coerced, or intimidated the other individual(s) into engaging in sexual contact and/or sexual conduct.

In a 2006 exchange on the well-known Volokh Conspiracy blog, a male commenter wrote:

Explicit verbal consent is not the same thing as consent. Every day we consent to things nonverbally. The government should not interfere in consensual relationships by declaring typical nonverbal indications of consent inoperative.

My wife would be creeped out if I asked her in advance before hugging or kissing her, and she would resent having to ask me. Certainly, she has never asked before doing it.

My guess is that these rules are enforced in the main the way the sodomy laws often used to be enforced: by one vindictive ex-partner using them to attack the other ex-partner for perfectly consensual conduct.

The fact that something was consensual at the time doesn't keep you from using it as a weapon later.

A female commenter responded:

Why are we so much more willing to HAVE sex than to talk about having sex??? What precisely is WRONG with asking permission before sticking parts of your body in mine?!

The complaint seems to be "it's creepy and unromantic." So? Ideas of what is romantic are constantly changing — in romance novels in the 70s & 80s there was never any mention of birth control — too creepy and unromantic! By the 90s, the sex scenes almost ALWAYS involved a condom — how romantic that he CARES enough to protect you! See? Is it really creepy and unromantic to say, "I'd really like to have sex with you, if that's what you want, too"?

The creepy-and-unromantic argument seems strongest when it applies to already-sexual relationships. But that presumes that such relationships never change, either. Just because she had sex with you last week—yesterday—this morning—10 minutes ago—doesn't necessarily mean she wants to have sex with you again. Do I have to list all the reasons why? (I haven't shaved my legs, I feel fat, I'm wearing unsexy underwear, you didn't bring me flowers, I didn't enjoy it last time, it's Lent and I promised I wouldn't. . . .). What's wrong with requiring a quick and oh-so-charming "Wanna do it?" before sex?

Admittedly, VERBAL agreement sounds pretty extreme for descendants of [P]uritans. We'd have to actually admit that we intended to have sex! And sure, it seems that in most cases nonverbal cues would be enough. But do you know how often men misunderstand NON-VERBAL cues that women are throwing out there? After all, no means yes, a hand pressed to your chest to keep you away means try harder, and struggle means persuade me, right?

I'm not saying all men are clueless—but an awful lot of them are. The question is simply one of who should have to assume the risk. Up 'til now, SHE has always assumed the risk, since the legal presumption has been that all women are consenting to sex all the time, unless she DOES something affirmatively to withdraw that consent (and that something might be earnest resistance, resistance to the utmost, or reasonable resistance, depending on the jurisdiction). The Antioch-type codes are simply reversing the presumption. And reversing the presumption is infinitely more protective of women.

Of course, it might be overly protective. Women have been taught the double standard quite well, and might get less sex than they want under the Antioch-type codes because of their unwillingness to seem too forward. So be it. I've frequently said that if a woman says no when she means yes, the man should teach her a lesson—walk away! Don't let her have what she wants!

See http://volokh.com/posts/1147374096.shtml.

4. The Antioch College policy may have seemed extreme in its day. But several states have now enacted statutes that require "affirmative consent" for any sexual activity that takes place on college campuses. These are not criminal statutes (at least not yet!), but they do set the governing rules for college disciplinary proceedings—which can lead to suspension and even expulsion. See, for example, California Education Code §67386, enacted in 2014, which now requires all California colleges that receive state funds for student financial aid (including independent colleges) to adopt policies that include the following:

(1) An affirmative consent standard in the determination of whether consent was given by both parties to sexual activity. "Affirmative consent" means affirmative, conscious, and voluntary agreement to engage in sexual activity. It is the responsibility of each person involved in the sexual activity to ensure

that he or she has the affirmative consent of the other or others to engage in the sexual activity. Lack of protest or resistance does not mean consent, nor does silence mean consent. . . .

(2) A policy that, in the evaluation of complaints in any disciplinary process, it shall not be a valid excuse to alleged lack of affirmative consent that the accused believed that the complainant consented to the sexual activity under either of the following circumstances:

(A) The accused's belief in affirmative consent arose from the intoxication or recklessness of the accused.

(B) The accused did not take reasonable steps, in the circumstances known to the accused at the time, to ascertain whether the complainant affirmatively consented.

Leaving aside the obvious strangeness of having a very different legal standard for sexual consent on college campuses from the legal standard that still governs both before and after college, does this new legal standard—"yes means yes"—make sense? Is it better than the traditional legal requirement of force in rape law? Is it preferable to a "no means no" approach? In the real world, is "yes means yes" a workable standard?

In this regard, consider the following anecdote: In 2015, California passed a new law requiring high school sex education classes to instruct students about the "yes means yes" affirmative consent standard. When a leading health educator, Shafia Zaloom, asked a group of tenth-grade students to come up with acceptable ways to ask for affirmative consent, the students quickly rejected options like "Can I touch you there?," "Do you want to do this?," and "Do you like that?" The solution preferred by most of the students was much simpler: "You good?" See Jennifer Medina, "Sex Ed Lesson: 'Yes Means Yes,' But It's Tricky," New York Times, Oct. 14, 2015.

5. Donald Dripps argues that defendants like M.T.S. and Berkowitz should be punished for "sexual expropriation," not sexual assault. In Dripps' view, the core problem with the contemporary law of rape is that it lumps sexually motivated violence together with conduct that is more akin to theft than to battery. Donald A. Dripps, Beyond Rape: An Essay on the Difference Between the Presence of Force and the Absence of Consent, 92 Colum. L. Rev. 1780 (1992). Using non-consent to distinguish criminal sexual assaults from legal sexual encounters, as the law increasingly does, puts more weight on consent and its absence than those facts can bear. Instead, Dripps contends, the law should focus on the different means used to obtain sex, and differentiate legitimate from illegitimate means—as the law does with the acquisition of property. With respect to the borderline cases in which the legitimacy of the encounter is unclear, Dripps has this to say:

> The burden of asking permission can be placed on the man, or the burden of expressing refusal can be placed on the woman. Granting that gender prejudice is implicated by either choice, I think the second alternative

is superior, because sexual encounters ought not to be lived or analyzed as sequences of particular touchings. In practice couples do not discuss in advance each specific sex act that one or another might initiate, and there is no strong reason why the law should attempt to compel them to do so. . . . If uncertainty and spontaneity can enhance the pleasures of lovemaking, people of either sex might prefer not being asked — so long as they can be sure that behavior they don't like will be stopped on demand. The interest in freedom from wrong guesses by one's bedmates is not so great as to call the criminal law into play.

92 Colum. L. Rev. at 1792 n.41. Is the relevant interest best described as "[t]he interest in freedom from wrong guesses"?

Robin West responded to Dripps' essay in Legitimating the Illegitimate: A Comment on Beyond Rape, 93 Colum. L. Rev. 1442 (1993):

Dripps's own analogy reveals the serious inadequacy of his construct. In trying to convey the "essence" of the expropriation offense, Dripps at one point analogizes it to the theft by a customer of a piece of jewelry off a counter while the merchant's back is turned. Nothing could be further from the experience of rape: rape is in no way like the near-instantaneous nonviolent theft of a piece of jewelry off a merchant's counter. Sex is not jewelry, and a woman's body is not a store. Unlike jewelry, sex cannot be "taken" quickly, cleanly, or painlessly. It can be "taken from," or "imposed on," a truly unwilling partner only with a great deal of force and considerable physical pain — a combination that in any other context we could quite readily recognize as violence.

Rape is sui generis. It is not accurately captured by any analogy, no matter how clever or elaborate. It is a primal experience to which other events might be meaningfully analogized — the "rape" of the land, the "rape" of a people. But rape itself cannot be reduced to other painful experiences. It certainly cannot be reduced to theft.

93 Colum. L. Rev. at 1448-49.

How should the law respond to that pain? What is the proper conception of rape? Is it primarily a crime of violence? Is it primarily a violation of the victim's sexual autonomy? Or is it both? How do the answers to those questions shape the crime's definition?

6. Notwithstanding modern expanded liability for sexual assault, the large majority of acquaintance rapes remain effectively unprosecutable. Ian Ayres and Katharine Baker offer a possible legal alternative to prosecution for sexual assault in such cases:

This Article . . . propos[es] a new crime of reckless sexual conduct, imposed for needlessly putting a sexual partner at such risk. The proposal is simple: a person would be guilty of reckless sexual conduct and subject to imprisonment for up to three months if, in a first-time sexual encounter with another specific person, he or she had sexual intercourse without using a condom.

Consent to unprotected intercourse would be an affirmative defense, to be established by the defendant by a preponderance of the evidence. The prosecution would have to prove beyond a reasonable doubt that this was the first time that the defendant had sexual intercourse with the accuser and that no condom was used. . . .

Unprotected first-time sexual encounters play a crucial role in exacerbating the prevalence of both sexually transmitted diseases (STDs) and acquaintance rape. While an increasing majority of people report and aspire to using condoms during casual sex, the unprotected residual of first-time sexual encounters may have a dramatic effect on the spread of infection. Unprotected first-time sexual encounters are also correlated with coercion. The lion's share of acquaintance rape (that is, nonstranger, nonrelative rape) occurs in unprotected first-time sexual encounters. Men who rape recklessly, by not finding the time or compassion to discern a partner's consent, rarely find time to use a condom.

Minimally regulating this small subset of sexuality can pay big dividends. Public policies designed to increase condom use will make progress with regard to both STD epidemics and acquaintance rape. Increased condom use in first-time sexual encounters will dramatically reduce the effective number of "nodes" in the network of potential infection for the simple reason that many sexual pairings do not result in subsequent sexual encounters. Increased condom use will also likely reduce the incidence of acquaintance rape. Giving men a new incentive to wear a condom in first-time sexual encounters should discourage the tragic lack of communication that often gives rise to the illusion of consent. The very act of stopping to put on a condom should increase deliberation and communication — the more deliberation and communication, the lesser the likelihood of acquaintance rape.

The crime of reckless sexual conduct will also be a powerful prosecutorial tool for the thousands of acquaintance rape cases that are simply not winnable under current law. It represents a way to partially overcome the "he said/she said" dilemma. A prosecutor who does not have enough objective evidence to go forward with a rape case could easily have enough objective evidence to prove reckless sexual conduct. Reasonable doubts can remain whether an alleged acquaintance rapist raped, but there is often no question that he engaged in an unprotected first-time sexual encounter. In such a case there could at least be a conviction, albeit for a much less serious offense. The threat of likely conviction can act as a significant deterrent to reckless conduct.

The message of our proposal is not necessarily to forgo one night stands, but rather to use a condom or communicate enough so that one can know one's partner is consenting to unprotected sex. The new crime of reckless sex would not replace current rape laws, and it would not immunize men who rape with condoms from prosecution under existing law. It also would not impose a punishment nearly as severe as rape. But, like laws prohibiting driving under the influence of alcohol, its very existence would send a clear message that society considers reckless sex both physically and emotionally damaging.

Ian Ayres & Katharine K. Baker, A Separate Crime of Reckless Sex, 72 U. Chi. L. Rev. 599, 601-03 (2005). What would be the likely effect of a statute like the one Ayres and Baker suggest? Does their proposal go too far toward criminalizing one-night stands? Not far enough?

7. According to Anne Coughlin, one reason why the common law defined rape so narrowly was fear of false accusations. See Anne M. Coughlin, Sex and Guilt, 84 Va. L. Rev. 1 (1998). In centuries past, adultery and fornication were more-than-nominal crimes. Extramarital sex raised the risk of prosecution for both parties. Rape allegations might have been one way to reduce that risk—which may explain why rape was defined such that the victim would have a duress defense against a prosecution for adultery or fornication. Rape's restrictive definition was designed not to separate legal conduct from the illegal kind, but to separate sex in which both parties are criminals from sex in which one party's criminal conduct harms an innocent victim.

That fear of false accusation was almost certainly exaggerated: There were, and are, many reasons not to concoct phony rape allegations, among them the stigma that long attached to the victims of this crime. But that stigma has declined in recent years. The definition of criminal sexual assault has broadened, making conviction easier than in the past. Has the pendulum swung too far? Are false accusations a greater problem today than decisions like *M.T.S.* imagined?

In that regard, consider the case of In re C.T., 991 N.E.2d 1171 (Ohio Ct. App. 2013), involving a charge of rape against a juvenile defendant:

> The trial court found C.T. delinquent for raping an acquaintance from his school. The pertinent facts of the case were set forth in [our earlier decision], which we adopt and repeat verbatim in the following:
>
> At trial, K.W. testified that she met C.T. in the high school band. As they traveled to a football game in different buses, K.W. initiated contact with C.T. by sending a text message to his cell phone. K.W. indicated she and her friends were reading about "sex and porn." K.W. and C.T. sat near each other during portions of the football game and then left on their separate buses where they resumed a text messaging phone conversation. They discussed "hanging out" together that night. C.T. suggested that they should "hang out" in K.W.'s car; to which K.W. replied, "We shall. [F]ind me."
>
> Both K.W. and C.T. testified that they met each other at a party after the football game as planned and that K.W.'s mother was acting as a chaperone. K.W.'s mother recalled extending her daughter's curfew that night.
>
> As C.T. was walking K.W. to her car, K.W. either agreed or offered to drive C.T. home. Both said C.T. was holding K.W.'s hand as she drove. According to C.T., they passed a street and wound up parking in a cul-de-sac with poor lighting. According to K.W., she initially believed C.T. lived in that area. In either case, both said they began talking.

C.T. and K.W. then described a similar course of events where K.W. moved (or was assisted by C.T.) into the passenger side of the vehicle where C.T. was sitting. They began kissing. K.W. helped remove her sweatshirt and shirt and C.T. removed his penis from his pants. He asked K.W. to perform oral sex, and she indicated she had never done so before; to which C.T. responded that there was a first time for everything. K.W. performed oral sex on C.T., and he penetrated her vaginally with his fingers.

K.W. testified that she told C.T. she did not want to engage in this activity and told C.T. to stop. C.T. testified that K.W. never said anything or gave any indication to him that the activity was anything other than consensual. K.W. said she complied because she was fearful of C.T. but admitted he did not threaten her verbally or physically.

At one point, K.W. returned to the driver's seat to check her phone. Her mother told her she needed to come home. According to C.T., K.W. said they could resume the sexual activity the next day. But, at C.T.'s request, she resumed performing oral sex upon C.T. K.W. said she did this just to get it over with and get out of the situation. C.T. wiped his hands with a tissue that he discarded out the window and onto the street.

C.T. testified that K.W. asked him if they were dating and seemed happy to know he was considering it. When K.W. returned home, she sent a cell phone text message to C.T. She invited C.T. to get together the next day but he said he could not because he was in trouble. Then, K.W. went to lunch with a friend and told her about her sexual encounter with C.T. Later that day, K.W. was on the bus with other band members when another teenager, B.T., called her outside to talk. B.T. asked K.W. about the allegations she had made against C.T. C.T. was standing nearby. C.T. denied that he forced K.W. to do anything. At this point, K.W. called her parents to pick her up and told her parents she had been raped by C.T.

K.W. was taken to the police station and then the hospital for an examination. As part of her statement to an examining nurse, K.W. indicated that she was aware that C.T. had "been in trouble with girls before, but [she] didn't want to believe it."

More than once during her testimony, K.W. confirmed that if C.T. had indicated to her that they were boyfriend and girlfriend, they would not be in court. On redirect examination, however, K.W. indicated that even if C.T. had said she was his girlfriend, she would still say she was raped by him.

991 N.E.2d at 1175-76. The legal issue before the Ohio Court of Appeals was whether or not evidence of C.T.'s prior bad acts—he had previously pleaded delinquent to a charge of gross sexual imposition after a girl accused him of forcefully making her perform oral sex on him and also digitally penetrating her—should have been admitted at his trial on the charge of raping K.W. The appellate court ultimately concluded that the evidence was too prejudicial and should not have been admitted: "Both parties in this case testified that sexual activity occurred. C.T. testified that K.W. consented. K.W. testified she did not. This is a classic 'he said she said' case, and the entire case hinges on the parties' credibility. The admission of evidence showing C.T.

had previously engaged in unconsented sexual conduct certainly tips the scales of credibility in favor of the prosecution's claim." Id. at 1178. The case was remanded to the juvenile court for a new hearing.

California Penal Code
§§243.4, 261, 261.5, 261.6, 261.7, 263

§243.4. Sexual Battery*

(a) Any person who touches an intimate part of another person while that person is unlawfully restrained by the accused or an accomplice, and if the touching is against the will of the person touched and is for the purpose of sexual arousal, sexual gratification, or sexual abuse, is guilty of sexual battery. . . .

(b) Any person who touches an intimate part of another person who is institutionalized for medical treatment and who is seriously disabled or medically incapacitated, if the touching is against the will of the person touched, and if the touching is for the purpose of sexual arousal, sexual gratification, or sexual abuse, is guilty of sexual battery. . . .

(c) Any person who touches an intimate part of another person for the purpose of sexual arousal, sexual gratification, or sexual abuse, and the victim is at the time unconscious of the nature of the act because the perpetrator fraudulently represented that the touching served a professional purpose, is guilty of sexual battery. . . .

(d) Any person who, for the purpose of sexual arousal, sexual gratification, or sexual abuse, causes another, against that person's will while that person is unlawfully restrained either by the accused or an accomplice, or is institutionalized for medical treatment and is seriously disabled or medically incapacitated, to masturbate or touch an intimate part of either of those persons or a third person, is guilty of sexual battery. . . .

(e)

(1) Any person who touches an intimate part of another person, if the touching is against the will of the person touched, and is for

---

* The punishment for sexual battery is either up to one year in a county jail plus a fine of up to $2,000; or two, three, or four years in state prison plus a fine of up to $10,000. The punishment for misdemeanor sexual battery is up to six months in county jail plus a fine of up to $2,000, unless the defendant was an employer and the victim an employee, in which case the maximum fine is $3,000.

the specific purpose of sexual arousal, sexual gratification, or sexual abuse, is guilty of misdemeanor sexual battery. . . .

(2) As used in this subdivision, "touches" means physical contact with another person, whether accomplished directly, through the clothing of the person committing the offense, or through the clothing of the victim.

(f) As used in subdivisions (a), (b), (c), and (d), "touches" means physical contact with the skin of another person whether accomplished directly or through the clothing of the person committing the offense.

§261. Rape**

(a) Rape is an act of sexual intercourse accomplished with a person not the spouse of the perpetrator, under any of the following circumstances:

(1) Where a person is incapable, because of a mental disorder or developmental or physical disability, of giving legal consent, and this is known or reasonably should be known to the person committing the act. . . .

(2) Where it is accomplished against a person's will by means of force, violence, duress, menace, or fear of immediate and unlawful bodily injury on the person or another.

(3) Where a person is prevented from resisting by any intoxicating or anesthetic substance, or any controlled substance, and this condition was known, or reasonably should have been known by the accused.

(4) Where a person is at the time unconscious of the nature of the act, and this is known to the accused. As used in this paragraph, "unconscious of the nature of the act" means incapable of resisting because the victim meets any one of the following conditions:

(A) Was unconscious or asleep.

(B) Was not aware, knowing, perceiving, or cognizant that the act occurred.

(C) Was not aware, knowing, perceiving, or cognizant of the essential characteristics of the act due to the perpetrator's fraud in fact.

** Rape of a spouse is defined separately in section 262, and includes the same circumstances designated in section 261(a)(2), (3), (4)(A), (4)(B), (4)(C), (6), and (7). The punishment for rape under sections 261 or 262 is up to three, six, or eight years in state prison plus a fine of up to $70, unless the rape is committed under section 261(a)(2) and the victim is under 14 (in which case the punishment is up to nine, eleven, or thirteen years in state prison) or at least 14 but below 18 (in which case the punishment is up to seven, nine, or eleven years in state prison).

(D) Was not aware, knowing, perceiving, or cognizant of the essential characteristics of the act due to the perpetrator's fraudulent representation that the sexual penetration served a professional purpose when it served no professional purpose.

(5) Where a person submits under the belief that the person committing the act is someone known to the victim other than the accused, and this belief is induced by any artifice, pretense, or concealment practiced by the accused, with intent to induce the belief.

(6) Where the act is accomplished against the victim's will by threatening to retaliate in the future against the victim or any other person, and there is a reasonable possibility that the perpetrator will execute the threat. As used in this paragraph, "threatening to retaliate" means a threat to kidnap or falsely imprison, or to inflict extreme pain, serious bodily injury, or death.

(7) Where the act is accomplished against the victim's will by threatening to use the authority of a public official to incarcerate, arrest, or deport the victim or another, and the victim has a reasonable belief that the perpetrator is a public official. . . . The perpetrator does not actually have to be a public official.

(b) As used in this section, "duress" means a direct or implied threat of force, violence, danger, or retribution sufficient to coerce a reasonable person of ordinary susceptibilities to perform an act which otherwise would not have been performed, or acquiesce in an act to which one otherwise would not have submitted. The total circumstances, including the age of the victim, and his or her relationship to the defendant, are factors to consider in appraising the existence of duress.

(c) As used in this section, "menace" means any threat, declaration, or act which shows an intention to inflict an injury upon another.

§261.5. Unlawful Sexual Intercourse With a Minor***

(a) Unlawful sexual intercourse is an act of sexual intercourse accomplished with a person who is not the spouse of the perpetrator, if the person is a minor. For the purposes of this section, a "minor" is a person under the age of 18 years and an "adult" is a person who is at least 18 years of age.

*** The punishment for felony unlawful sexual intercourse is either up to one year in a county jail (under section (c)), or up to one, two, three, or four years in a county jail (under section (d)), plus fines ranging from $2,000 to $25,000, depending on the particular section.

(b) Any person who engages in an act of unlawful sexual intercourse with a minor who is not more than three years older or three years younger than the perpetrator, is guilty of a misdemeanor.

(c) Any person who engages in an act of unlawful sexual intercourse with a minor who is more than three years younger than the perpetrator is guilty of either a misdemeanor or a felony. . . .

(d) Any person 21 years of age or older who engages in an act of unlawful sexual intercourse with a minor who is under 16 years of age is guilty of either a misdemeanor or a felony. . . .

§261.6. Consent

In prosecutions under Section 261, 262, 286, 288a, or 289, in which consent is at issue, "consent" shall be defined to mean positive cooperation in act or attitude pursuant to an exercise of free will. The person must act freely and voluntarily and have knowledge of the nature of the act or transaction involved.

A current or previous dating or marital relationship shall not be sufficient to constitute consent where consent is at issue in a prosecution under Section 261, 262, 286, 288a, or 289.

Nothing in this section shall affect the admissibility of evidence or the burden of proof on the issue of consent.

§261.7. Suggested Use of Condom

In prosecutions under Section 261, 262, 286, 288a, or 289, in which consent is at issue, evidence that the victim suggested, requested, or otherwise communicated to the defendant that the defendant use a condom or other birth control device, without additional evidence of consent, is not sufficient to constitute consent.

§263. Sexual Penetration for Rape

The essential guilt of rape consists in the outrage to the person and feelings of the victim of the rape. Any sexual penetration, however slight, is sufficient to complete the crime.

Several additional crimes involving sex and sexual violence are defined in California Penal Code §§285-289, including incest, sexual intercourse with a child 10 or younger, sexual assault of an animal, "sexual penetration" (i.e., by something other than a sex organ) without consent, certain "lewd and lascivious acts," and either sodomy or "oral copulation" with a minor or with an adult without consent.

The California statutes excerpted above illustrate an important trend in this area. While state courts have redefined rape, many state legislatures have chosen instead to add to it: to criminalize a wider variety of wrongful sex acts. Note, in particular, the list of crimes under the broad heading "Sexual

Battery." Would Berkowitz be guilty of violating any of the offenses in *that* list? Would M.T.S.?

In re John Z.

Supreme Court of California
29 Cal. 4th 756; 60 P.3d 183 (2003)

Opinion of CHIN, J.

We granted this case to settle a conflict in Court of Appeal decisions as to whether the crime of forcible rape is committed if the female victim consents to an initial penetration by her male companion, and then withdraws her consent during an act of intercourse, but the male continues against her will. Compare People v. Vela, 172 Cal. App. 3d 237, 218 Cal. Rptr. 161 (1985) (no rape committed) with People v. Roundtree, 77 Cal. App. 4th 846, 91 Cal. Rptr. 2d 921 (2000) (rape committed). We agree with *Roundtree* and the Court of Appeal in the present case that a withdrawal of consent effectively nullifies any earlier consent and subjects the male to forcible rape charges if he persists in what has become nonconsensual intercourse.

The juvenile court . . . found that [John Z. (the defendant)] committed forcible rape, Pen. Code, §261(a)(2). . . . On appeal, defendant contends the evidence is insufficient to sustain the finding that he committed forcible rape. We disagree.

The following facts are largely taken from the Court of Appeal opinion in this case. During the afternoon of March 23, 2000, 17-year-old Laura T. was working at Safeway when she received a call from Juan G., whom she had met about two weeks earlier. Juan wanted Laura to take him to a party at defendant's home and then return about 8:30 P.M. to pick him up. Laura agreed to take Juan to the party, but since she planned to attend a church group meeting that evening she told him she would be unable to pick him up.

Sometime after 6:00 P.M., Laura drove Juan to defendant's residence. Defendant and Justin L. were present. After arranging to have Justin L.'s stepbrother, P.W., buy them alcohol, Laura picked up P.W. and drove him to the store where he bought beer. Laura told Juan she would stay until 8:00 or 8:30 P.M. Although defendant and Juan drank the beer, Laura did not.

During the evening, Laura and Juan went into defendant's parents' bedroom. Juan indicated he wanted to have sex but Laura told him she was not ready for that kind of activity. Juan became upset and went into the bathroom. Laura left the bedroom and both defendant and Justin asked her why she "wouldn't do stuff." Laura told them that she was not ready.

About 8:10 P.M., Laura was ready to leave when defendant asked her to come into his bedroom to talk. She complied. Defendant told her that

Juan had said he (Juan) did not care for her; defendant then suggested that Laura become his girlfriend. Juan entered the bedroom and defendant left to take a phone call.

When defendant returned to the bedroom, he and Juan asked Laura if it was her fantasy to have two guys, and Laura said it was not. Juan and defendant began kissing Laura and removing her clothes, although she kept telling them not to. At some point, the boys removed Laura's pants and underwear and began "fingering" her, "playing with [her] boobs" and continued to kiss her. Laura enjoyed this activity in the beginning, but objected when Juan removed his pants and told defendant to keep fingering her while he put on a condom. Once the condom was in place, defendant left the room and Juan got on top of Laura. She tried to resist and told him she did not want to have intercourse, but he was too strong and forced his penis into her vagina. The rape terminated when, due to Laura's struggling, the condom fell off. Laura told Juan that "maybe it's a sign we shouldn't be doing this," and he said "fine" and left the room. (Although Juan G. was originally a codefendant, at the close of the victim's testimony he admitted amended charges of sexual battery, §243.4, and unlawful sexual intercourse, §261.5(b), a misdemeanor.)

Laura rolled over on the bed and began trying to find her clothes; however, because the room was dark she was unable to do so. Defendant, who had removed his clothing, then entered the bedroom and walked to where Laura was sitting on the bed and "he like rolled over [her] so [she] was pushed back down to the bed." Laura did not say anything and defendant began kissing her and telling her that she had "a really beautiful body." Defendant got on top of Laura, put his penis into her vagina "and rolled [her] over so [she] was sitting on top of him." Laura testified she "kept . . . pulling up, trying to sit up to get it out . . . [a]nd he grabbed my hips and pushed me back down and then he rolled me back over so I was on my back . . . and . . . kept saying, will you be my girlfriend." Laura "kept like trying to pull away" and told him that "if he really did care about me, he wouldn't be doing this to me and if he did want a relationship, he should wait and respect that I don't want to do this." After about 10 minutes, defendant got off Laura, and helped her dress and find her keys. She then drove home.

On cross-examination, Laura testified that when defendant entered the room unclothed, he lay down on the bed behind her and touched her shoulder with just enough pressure to make her move, a nudge. He asked her to lie down and she did. He began kissing her and she kissed him back. He rolled on top of her, inserted his penis in her and, although she resisted, he rolled her back over, pulling her on top of him. She was on top of him for four or five minutes, during which time she tried to get off, but he grabbed her waist and pulled her back down. He rolled her over and continued the sexual intercourse. Laura told him that she needed to go home, but he would not stop. He said, "just give me a minute," and she said, "no, I need to get home." He replied, "give me some time" and she repeated, "no, I have to go home." Defendant did not stop; "[h]e just stayed inside of me and kept like basically forcing it on me." After about a "minute, minute and [a] half," defendant got off Laura.

Defendant testified, admitting that he and Juan were kissing and fondling Laura in the bedroom, but claimed it was with her consent. He also admitted having sexual intercourse with Laura, again claiming it was consensual. He claimed he discontinued the act as soon as Laura told him that she had to go home.

Although the evidence of Laura's initial consent to intercourse with John Z. was hardly conclusive, we will assume for purposes of argument that Laura impliedly consented to the act, or at least tacitly refrained from objecting to it, until defendant had achieved penetration. But see §261.6 (defining the type of consent at issue under §261 as "positive cooperation in act or attitude pursuant to an exercise of free will"). As will appear, we conclude that the offense of forcible rape occurs when, during apparently consensual intercourse, the victim expresses an objection and attempts to stop the act and the defendant forcibly continues despite the objection.

Vela, supra, held that where the victim consents to intercourse at the time of penetration but thereafter withdraws her consent, any use of force by her assailant past that point is not rape. 172 Cal. App. 3d at 242-43. The court in *Vela* found "scant authority" on point, id. at 241, relying on two out-of-state cases which had held that if consent is given prior to penetration, no rape occurs despite the withdrawal of consent during intercourse itself. See Battle v. State, 414 A.2d 1266, 1268-70 (Md. 1980); State v. Way, 254 S.E.2d 760, 762 (N.C. 1979). . . .

Vela agreed with these cases, reasoning that

"the essence of the crime of rape is the outrage to the person and feelings of the female resulting from the nonconsensual violation of her womanhood. When a female willingly consents to an act of sexual intercourse, the penetration by the male cannot constitute a violation of her womanhood nor cause outrage to her person and feelings. If she withdraws consent during the act of sexual intercourse and the male forcibly continues the act without interruption, the female may certainly feel outrage because of the force applied or because the male ignores her wishes, but the sense of outrage to her person and feelings could hardly be of the same magnitude as that resulting from an initial nonconsensual violation of her womanhood. It would seem, therefore, that the essential guilt of rape as stated in . . . section 263 is lacking in the withdrawn consent scenario." *Vela*, 172 Cal. App. 3d at 243.

. . . [W]e find [this] reasoning unsound. First, . . . we have no way of accurately measuring the level of outrage the victim suffers from being subjected to continued forcible intercourse following withdrawal of her consent. We must assume the sense of outrage is substantial. More importantly,

§261(a)(2) defines rape as "an act of sexual intercourse . . . accomplished against a person's will by means of force, violence, duress, menace, or fear of immediate and unlawful bodily injury on the person or another." Nothing in section 261 conditions the act of rape on the degree of outrage of the victim. Section 263 states that "[t]he essential guilt of rape consists in the outrage to the person and feelings of the victim of the rape. Any sexual penetration, however slight, is sufficient to complete the crime." But no California case has held that the victim's outrage is an element of the crime of rape.

In *Roundtree*, 77 Cal. App. 4th 846, the court recognized that, by reason of sections 261 and 263,

> "[t]he crime of rape therefore is necessarily committed when a victim withdraws her consent during an act of sexual intercourse but is forced to complete the act. The statutory requirements of the offense are met as the act of sexual intercourse is forcibly accomplished against the victim's will. The outrage to the victim is complete." 77 Cal. App. 4th at 851.

Roundtree cited several cases from other states either criticizing *Vela* or reaching a contrary conclusion. See State v. Crims, 540 N.W.2d 860, 865 (Minn. App. 1995); State v. Siering, 644 A.2d 958, 963 (Conn. App. 1994); see also McGill v. State, 18 P.3d 77, 84 (Alaska 2001) (*Vela's* view that sexual assault statute is based on considerations of "outrage" [to the] victim's "womanhood" represents "archaic and outmoded social conventions").

As the Court of Appeal in this case stated,

> "while outrage of the victim may be the cause for criminalizing and severely punishing forcible rape, outrage by the victim is not an element of forcible rape. Pursuant to §261(a)(2), forcible rape occurs when the act of sexual intercourse is accomplished against the will of the victim by force or threat of bodily injury and it is immaterial at what point the victim withdraws her consent, so long as that withdrawal is communicated to the male and he thereafter ignores it."

In the present case, assuming arguendo that Laura initially consented to, or appeared to consent to, intercourse with defendant, substantial evidence shows that she withdrew her consent and, through her actions and words, communicated that fact to defendant. Despite the dissent's doubt in the matter, no reasonable person in defendant's position would have believed that Laura continued to consent to the act. See People v. Williams, 4 Cal. 4th 354, 360-61, 841 P.2d 961 (1992) (requiring reasonable and good faith belief, supported by substantial evidence, that the victim voluntarily consented to intercourse). As the Court of Appeal below observed, "Given [Laura's testimony], credited by the court, there was nothing equivocal about her withdrawal of any initially assumed consent."

Vela appears to assume that, to constitute rape, the victim's objections must be raised, or a defendant's use of force must be applied, *before* intercourse commences, but that argument is clearly flawed. One can readily imagine situations in which the defendant is able to obtain penetration before the victim can express an objection or attempt to resist. Surely, if the defendant thereafter ignores the victim's objections and forcibly continues the act, he has committed "an act of sexual intercourse accomplished . . . against a person's will by means of force . . ." §261(a)(2).

Defendant, candidly acknowledging *Vela*'s flawed reasoning, contends that, in cases involving an initial consent to intercourse, the male should be permitted a "reasonable amount of time" in which to withdraw, once the female raises an objection to further intercourse. As defendant argues, "By essence of the act of sexual intercourse, a male's primal urge to reproduce is aroused. It is therefore unreasonable for a female and the law to expect a male to cease having sexual intercourse immediately upon her withdrawal of consent. It is only natural, fair and just that a male be given a reasonable amount of time in which to quell his primal urge. . . ."

We disagree. . . . Aside from the apparent lack of supporting authority for defendant's "primal urge" theory, the principal problem with his argument is that it is contrary to the language of [the statute]: Nothing in the language of section 261 or the case law suggests that the defendant is entitled to persist in intercourse once his victim withdraws her consent.

. . . [E]ven were we to accept defendant's "reasonable time" argument, in the present case he clearly was given ample time to withdraw but refused to do so despite Laura's resistance and objections. Although defendant testified he withdrew as soon as Laura objected, . . . Laura testified that she struggled to get away when she was on top of defendant, but that he grabbed her waist and pushed her down onto him. At this point, Laura told defendant that if he really cared about her, he would respect her wishes and stop. Thereafter, she told defendant *three* times that she needed to go home and that she did not accept his protestations he just needed a "minute." Defendant continued the sex act for at least four or five minutes after Laura *first* told him she had to go home. According to Laura, after the *third* time she asked to leave, defendant continued to insist that he needed more time and "just stayed inside of me and kept like basically forcing it on me," for about a "minute, minute and [a] half.". . . [T]he force defendant exerted in resisting Laura's attempts to stop the act was clearly ample to satisfy section 261(a)(2). See People v. Mom, 80 Cal. App. 4th 1217, 1224, 96 Cal. Rptr. 2d 172 (2000) ([defining the required level of force as] force "substantially different from or substantially greater than that necessary to accomplish the rape itself"). . . .

. . . The judgment of the Court of Appeal is affirmed.

BROWN, J., dissenting.

. . . To the extent the majority holds the clear withdrawal of consent nullifies any earlier consent and forcible persistence in what then becomes nonconsensual intercourse is rape, not assault and battery as the Court of Appeal held in People v. Vela, 172 Cal. App. 3d 237, 218 Cal. Rptr. 161 (1985), I concur. . . . However, . . . I cannot concur in the rest of the majority opinion. The majority opinion is deficient in several respects. First, the opinion fails to consider whether the victim's statements in this case clearly communicated her withdrawal of consent. Second, there is no attempt to define what constitutes force in this context. Finally, questions about wrongful intent are given short shrift.

. . . Presumably, in a post-penetration rape case, the prosecution still has the burden of showing, beyond a reasonable doubt, that the victim clearly communicated withdrawal of consent and the defendant exercised some degree of force to continue. Moreover, a defendant's reasonable and good faith mistake of fact regarding a person's consent to sexual intercourse is a defense to rape. . . . The trial judge in this juvenile matter relied primarily on Laura's testimony and rejected John Z.'s testimony in its entirety. Even so, "assuming arguendo that Laura initially consented to, or appeared to consent to, intercourse with defendant," the facts in this case, as described solely by the prosecution witness, create doubt both about the withdrawal of consent and the use of force. . . .

. . . Around 8:00 P.M., Laura decided she was ready to leave [the party at John Z.'s home]. Before she walked out the door, John asked if he could talk to her. She walked back into the house and went into his bedroom, which was completely dark. She did not ask to turn on the light. She entered the room willingly and was not restrained from leaving. They sat in the dark, talking. John told her Juan never cared about her, was only "using [her] and anyone else could use [her] too." John said he really liked her; she should dump Juan and become John's girlfriend. When Juan came into the bedroom, Laura confronted him with what John had said. He denied it. The boys asked if she had ever fantasized about having "two guys." Laura said she had not, but she continued to sit on the bed in John's darkened bedroom with both Juan and John while one or both of them removed various items of her clothing. At first, she tried to replace her clothing, but after pulling her bra back into place a couple of times, she made no further efforts to retrieve her clothes. Asked why she did not leave, she responded: "There is no reason. I just didn't. I didn't think about it. I had already tried to leave once, and they asked me to go in the bedroom and talk."

Feeling there was "no point in fighting" because there was nothing she could do about it anyway, she laid back on the bed, with Juan on one side of her and John on the other. She did not say anything and she was not fighting or resisting while the rest of her clothing was removed. The boys were "fingering" her and playing with her "boobs" and kissing her and "like just trying to like keep me satisfied type of thing." She acknowledged that she enjoyed these activities, enjoyed it "because it was like a threesome"; she was laughing and liked being the center of attention.

After that prelude and after she had intercourse with Juan, which ended when the condom kept falling off and she told him perhaps that was a sign they "shouldn't be doing this," we come to the facts which form the basis of John Z.'s adjudication. According to Laura, she was sitting on the bed naked when John Z. came into the room, naked or partially unclothed. She had been unable to find her clothes in the dark. John sat on the bed behind her and touched her with one hand on her shoulder. . . . John began kissing her. She kissed him back. He climbed on top of her and achieved penetration. She did not say anything. She did not push him away, slap him or strike him. He made no threats and he did not hurt her. John asked her repeatedly "will you be my girlfriend?"

He rolled over so she was on top. She remained in that position for four to five minutes. Although he held her only with one hand on her waist—not hard enough for her to feel the pressure or to create a bruise—she was unable to extricate herself or break the connection. There was no conversation when intercourse began and she said nothing while she was on top of him. When she found herself on the bottom again, she said: "If he really did care about me, he wouldn't be doing this to me and if he really did want a relationship, he should wait and respect that I don't want to do this." John responded: "I really do care about you." . . .

Sometime later she said: "I should be going now." "I need to go home." John said: "Just give me a minute." Several minutes later, she said again: "I need to get home." He said: "[G]ive me some time." She said: "No. I have to go home." The third time she told him she had to go home she was a little more urgent. She [started to cry]. When asked if at anytime while having intercourse with John Z., she had told him "no," Laura [responded]: "No". . . . Calling a halt, her answers suggest, was entirely John Z.'s responsibility. He said he cared about her, "but he still just let it happen."

The majority finds Laura's "actions and words" clearly communicated withdrawal of consent in a fashion "no reasonable person in defendant's position" could have mistaken. But Laura's silent and ineffectual movements could easily be misinterpreted. And, none of her statements are unequivocal. While Laura may have felt these words clearly conveyed her unwillingness, they could reasonably be understood as requests for reassurance or demands for speed. . . . Indeed, Laura demonstrates a similar ambivalence. When asked if she had made it clear to John that she didn't want to have sex, Laura says "I thought I had," but she acknowledges she "never officially told him" she did not want to have sexual intercourse. When asked by the prosecutor on redirect why she told John "I got to go home," Laura [answered]: "Because I had to get home so my mom wouldn't suspect anything."

Furthermore, even if we assume that Laura's statements evidenced a clear intent to withdraw consent, sexual intercourse is not transformed into rape merely because a woman changes her mind. As the majority acknowledges, . . . "[t]he crime of rape therefore is necessarily committed when a victim withdraws her consent during an act of sexual intercourse but is *forced* to complete the act. The statutory requirements of the offense are met as the act of sexual intercourse is *forcibly* accomplished against the victim's will." (Quoting *Roundtree*, at 851, italics added.) . . . Under the facts of this case, however, it is not clear that Laura was forcibly compelled to continue. All we know is that John Z. did not instantly respond to her statement that she needed to go home. He requested additional time. He did not demand it. Nor did he threaten any consequences if Laura did not comply.

The majority relies heavily on John Z.'s failure to desist immediately. But, it does not tell us how soon would have been soon enough. Ten seconds? Thirty? A minute? Is persistence the same thing as force? And even if we conclude persistence should be criminalized in this situation, should the penalty be the same as for forcible rape? Such questions seem inextricably tied to the question of whether a reasonable person would know that the statement "I need to go home" should be interpreted as a demand to stop. Under these circumstances, can the withdrawal of consent serve as a proxy for both compulsion and wrongful intent? . . .

In reviewing a criminal conviction challenged as lacking evidentiary support we review the whole record in the light most favorable to the judgment to determine whether it discloses substantial evidence such that a reasonable trier of fact could find the defendant guilty beyond a reasonable doubt. Presumably, in determining guilt beyond a reasonable doubt, the juvenile court would have to consider and resolve the same questions the majority declines to address. Because the record contains no indication the juvenile court did so, I respectfully dissent.

Notes and Questions

1. Was consent in *John Z.* withdrawn, or was it never given in the first place?

2. Justices Chin and Brown offer different interpretations of the facts in *John Z.* Whose interpretation makes the most sense? Did the defendant behave forcibly? Did he have reason to believe Laura consented to sex? Did he have reason to believe that she withdrew her consent after intercourse began?

3. The character and consequences of withdrawn consent are major issues in the contemporary law of sexual assault. Consider how appellate courts in two other jurisdictions have resolved those issues.

The facts in State v. Bunyard, 133 P.3d 14 (Kan. 2006), were as follows:

The defendant was 21 years old when he met E.N. at a pool party at the home of a mutual friend. E.N., who was 17 years old, flirted with the defendant. She thought the defendant was "cool" so she invited him to a party at her friend's house the following night.

The defendant and friends attended the party the next night. After talking with E.N. for awhile, the defendant invited her to watch a movie in his car with another one of his friends. The defendant drove a Chrysler Sebring two-door convertible with a DVD player built in the dash. The defendant put the car's convertible top up before they began watching the movie.

After the defendant's friend left the car, the defendant and E.N. began kissing. E.N. did not object when the defendant removed her clothing. Likewise, she did not object when the defendant removed his clothing and placed a condom on his penis. However, after the defendant laid E.N. back in the seat and penetrated her vagina with his penis, E.N. said, "I don't want to do this." The defendant did not stop, replying, "Just a little bit longer." E.N. again stated that she did not "want to do this," but the defendant did not stop. E.N. testified that she unsuccessfully tried to sit up and roll over on her stomach to get away from the defendant. After 5 or 10 minutes had passed, E.N. began to cry, and the defendant stopped having sexual intercourse with her. . . .

The defendant testified that E.N. was on top of him during consensual intercourse and they were talking. E.N. asked him if he wanted a relationship and if he planned on calling her the next day. When the defendant said he was not interested in a relationship, E.N. became upset, got off of him, and told him about how she had been hurt by other guys in the past. E.N. wanted to continue kissing and wanted him to stay in the car and hold her, but the defendant did not stay in the car and told her to get dressed.

E.N. went back into the house visibly upset and told K.B. that she had been taken advantage of, that the defendant had gotten inside of her, and that she had said "no" more than once. M.B. also spoke with E.N., who was crying. M.B. testified that E.N. said, "I was raped. We had sex. I said no." E.N. did not want to report the incident to the police at that time because she did not want her parents to find out that she had been drinking.

Four days later, E.N. reported the incident to the police, and she was examined at the local hospital. The sexual assault examiner detected a cluster of abrasions consistent with blunt force trauma in E.N.'s vagina. The examiner testified that the location of the abrasions was consistent with mounting injuries. Although consensual sex could not be ruled out, the examiner testified that mounting injuries are more commonly found after nonconsensual sexual intercourse.

133 P.3d at 18-19. The defendant raised two arguments. First, he claimed that consent, once given, cannot be withdrawn until after the relevant act of intercourse has ended. Alternatively, the defendant maintained that he should have a "reasonable time" to cease having sex once the victim's consent was withdrawn. The Kansas Supreme Court rejected the first argument, but accepted the second—partly based on its reading of *John Z.*:

The defendant contends that even if rape can occur after consensual penetration, the State failed to prove that he did not cease sexual intercourse within a reasonable time after E.N. withdrew her consent. Relying upon In re John Z., 29 Cal. 4th 756, 60 P.3d 183 (2004), the Court of Appeals found that "when consent is withdrawn, continuing sexual intercourse for 5 to 10 minutes is not reasonable and constitutes rape." 31 Kan. App. 2d at 859. The majority opinion and the defendant's argument presume the issue we must decide—whether a defendant is entitled to a reasonable time to act on the victim's withdrawal of consent after consensual penetration.

In *John Z.*, the victim told the defendant three times that she "needed to go home," but the intercourse continued for an estimated 4 to 5 minutes after the . . . first [such statement]. The defendant argued that in cases involving an initial consent to intercourse, the male should be permitted a reasonable amount of time in which to withdraw once the female raises an objection to intercourse. The defendant reasoned: "By essence of the act of sexual intercourse, a male's primal urge to reproduce is aroused. . . . It is only natural, fair and just that the male be given a reasonable amount of time in which to quell his primal urge. . . ." 29 Cal. 4th at 762.

. . . [T]he California Supreme Court found that apart from the apparent lack of supporting authority for the "primal urge" theory, nothing in the language of its statute suggested that the defendant was entitled to persist in intercourse once his victim withdrew her consent. The court went on to find that even if it was to accept the "reasonable time" argument, the defendant was given ample time to withdraw but refused despite the victim's resistance and objections. The court declined to explore or recommend instructional language governing the point in time at which a defendant must cease intercourse once consent is withdrawn. . . .

The Court of Appeals' decision in this case seems to assume that a defendant should be given a reasonable amount of time to desist but concludes that continuation for an additional 5 to 10 minutes once consent is withdrawn was unreasonable. A recent law review article suggests the California Supreme Court's failure in *John Z.* to suggest what constitutes a "reasonable time" leads to the disturbing result that men are expected to control their sexual urges eventually, although not immediately, upon withdrawal of consent. Palmer, Antiquated Notions of Womanhood and the Myth of the Unstoppable Male: Why Post-Penetration Rape Should Be a Crime in North Carolina, 82 N.C. L. Rev. 1258, 1277 (2004). . . .

In the case of consensual intercourse and withdrawn consent, we agree that the defendant should be entitled to a reasonable time in which to act after consent is withdrawn and [the withdrawal is] communicated to the defendant. However, we conclude that the jury should determine whether the time between withdrawal of consent and the interruption of intercourse was reasonable. This determination must be based upon the particular facts of each case, taking into account the manner in which consent was withdrawn. We believe this conclusion balances our rejection of the primal urge theory per se with our recognition of the unique facts and circumstances of each individual case.

While the facts of this case may establish that the defendant's continuation of intercourse by placing the victim in fear or by forcing the victim to continue for 5 to 10 minutes was well beyond a reasonable time, we reiterate that this is a jury determination and not for the trial court or the appellate courts to decide. We [thus] conclude that the trial court had a duty to instruct the jury that post-penetration rape can occur under Kansas law and that the defendant has a "reasonable time" to respond to the withdrawal of consent.

133 P.3d at 29-30.

4. The second case is State v. Baby, 946 A.2d 463 (Md. 2008). The jury in *Baby* twice asked whether the victim had been raped if she consented to sex but later withdrew her consent. The trial judge refused to respond. The Maryland Court of Appeals had to decide whether that non-response constituted reversible error:

> During deliberations, the jury submitted to the trial court a note which asked, "If a female consents to sex initially and, during the course of the sex act to which she consented, for whatever reason, she changes her mind and the man continues until climax, does the result constitute rape?" While Baby's attorney argued that the court should respond to the note in the negative, the court found the question as phrased to be confusing and ambiguous, as it was unclear what was specifically meant by "during the course of the sex act," and viewed the note as potentially presenting a question of fact, rather than law. The judge, therefore, replied, "I am unable to answer this question as posed. Please reread the instructions as to each element and apply the law to the facts as you find them." The following morning, the jury submitted another note which read, "If at any time the woman says stop is that rape?" Baby's counsel requested that the court provide the jury with "the exact answer that you gave to the note last night." The court, characterizing the second question as a more simple variation of the first, instructed the jury, "This is a question that you as a jury must decide. I have given the legal definition of rape which includes the definition of consent."
>
> The definition which the trial judge had given was that, "Rape is unlawful vaginal intercourse with a female by force or threat of force and without her consent." The trial court also had supplied the jury with the descriptions of "vaginal intercourse," "force," and "consent" which were taken from the pattern jury instructions. . . .

946 A.2d 487-89. The court concluded that because the issue was "central to the case," the trial judge's failure to answer jurors' questions could not be harmless error. Elsewhere in its opinion, the court discussed the answer the trial judge should have given:

> . . . [W]e hold that a woman may withdraw consent for vaginal intercourse after penetration has occurred and that, after consent has been withdrawn, the continuation of vaginal intercourse by force or the threat of force may constitute rape. We iterate that force or the threat of force is, however, an essential element of the crime of rape.

Id. at 486. *Baby* did not address the "reasonable time" question raised in *John Z.* and *Bunyard.*

5. How should that question be answered? Should courts specify some period of time during which the defendant is obliged to respond? Or should the issue be left to jurors' discretion, as *Bunyard* suggests?

6. Is it realistic to expect either perpetrators or victims to remember the relevant facts in the level of detail that appears in the opinions in *John Z.?* The law of sexual assault requires judges and juries to draw fine lines.

The available evidence may not permit the accurate drawing of those lines. That is an especially large problem when one or more of the parties to the relevant transaction is intoxicated, as in the next two main cases.

People v. Giardino

Court of Appeal of California, Fourth Appellate District
98 Cal. Rptr. 2d 315 (2000)

Opinion of McKINSTER, J.

. . . In an 11-count information, the defendant was charged with committing rape by intoxication (Pen. Code §261(a)(3)) in counts 1, 2, and 3; with committing oral copulation by intoxication (§288a(i)) in counts 4 and 5; with committing oral copulation with a minor (§288a(b)(1)) in counts 6 and 7; with committing unlawful sexual intercourse (§261.5) in counts 8, 9 and 10; and with molesting a child (§647.6) in count 11. The jury found him guilty as charged in counts 2 through 7 and 9 through 11, but not guilty as to counts 1 and 8. [The defendant was sentenced] to a prison term of 13 years. . . .

The defendant contends that the convictions on counts 2 through 5 must be reversed because the trial court erred (1) by refusing to instruct the jury that lack of consent is an element of the charges of rape by intoxication and oral copulation by intoxication, (2) by failing to instruct the jury concerning the meaning of "prevented from resisting," and (3) by failing to instruct the jury concerning the effect of an honestly and reasonably held but mistaken belief in the victim's ability to give legal consent. . . .

DISCUSSION

A. Lack of Actual Consent Is Not an Element of Rape by Intoxication

The defendant asked the trial court to give a "consent instruction" regarding the charges of rape by intoxication and oral copulation by intoxication. In his oral request, the defendant did not describe the requested instruction in any detail, but the trial court interpreted him to be asking that the jury be instructed either that lack of consent was an element of those crimes or that consent is a defense. The trial court refused to do so.

Reasoning that lack of consent is an element of rape, or conversely that consent is a defense, the defendant contends that the trial court should have defined consent in accordance with section 261.6 and instructed the jury that lack of consent is an element of the offenses of rape by intoxication and oral copulation by intoxication.[2] He is mistaken.

---

2. For convenience, we shall discuss only rape by intoxication, but our analysis applies equally to both offenses.

In the context of rape and other sexual assaults, "consent" is defined as the "positive cooperation in act or attitude pursuant to an exercise of free will." §261.6. To give consent, a "person must act freely and voluntarily and have knowledge of the nature of the act or transaction involved." Ibid. . . . [T]hat definition describes consent that is actually and freely given without any misapprehension of material fact. We shall refer to this as "actual consent."[3]

By itself, the existence of actual consent is not sufficient to establish a defense to a charge of rape. That the supposed victim actually consented to sexual intercourse disproves rape only if he or she had "sufficient capacity" to give that consent. See People v. Mayberry, 15 Cal. 3d 143, 154, 542 P.2d 1337 (1975). For example, if the victim is so unsound of mind that he or she is incapable of giving legal consent, the fact that he or she may have given actual consent does not prevent a conviction of rape. People v. Griffin, 117 Cal. 583, 585-87, 49 P. 711 (1897), overruled on others grounds by People v. Hernandez, 61 Cal. 2d 529, 536, 393 P.2d 673 (1964). Hence, the consent defense fails if the victim either did not actually consent or lacked the capacity to give legally cognizable consent.

The distinction between actual consent and legal consent is further illustrated by the statutory definition of rape. Some of the various means of committing rape specified in the subdivisions of section 261 deal with the lack of the victim's actual consent while others deal with the victim's lack of capacity, i.e., with the lack of legal consent.

In the context of rape, "against the victim's will" is synonymous with "without the victim's consent." People v. Cicero, 157 Cal. App. 3d 465, 480, 204 Cal. Rptr. 582 (1984). Therefore, by specifically referring to intercourse accomplished against the victim's will, subdivisions (a)(2) (force or duress), (a)(6) (threat of retaliation), and (a)(7) (threat of detention or deportation) of section 261 describe instances in which the victim has not actually consented. The same is true when the victim is not aware of the nature of the act (§261(a)(4)(C)) or has been deceived into believing that the defendant is the victim's spouse (§261(a)(5)). In those cases, there is no actual consent because the victim lacks "knowledge of the nature of the act or transaction. . . ." §261.6. By contrast, subdivision (a)(1) of section 261 proscribes sexual intercourse with a person who lacks the capacity to give legal consent due to a mental disorder or a developmental or physical disability.

That distinction determines the instructions that are relevant to the charge. A charge that the defendant accomplished the act of sexual intercourse against the will of the victim . . . entitles the defendant to an

---

3. Actual consent must be distinguished from submission. For instance, a victim's decision to submit to an attacker's sexual demands out of fear of bodily injury is not consent, because the decision is not freely and voluntarily made. A selection by the victim of the lesser of two evils—rape versus the violence threatened by the attacker if the victim resists—is hardly an exercise of free will. See People v. Lay, 66 Cal. App. 2d 889, 893, 153 P.2d 379 (1944).

instruction that the act was not criminal if it was committed with the victim's actual consent. But if the charge is that the victim lacked the capacity to give legal consent (such as §261(a)(1)), then actual consent is irrelevant, and the jury instructions need not touch on that issue.

Unlike subdivisions (a)(2), (a)(6), and (a)(7) of section 261, section 261(a)(3) is not phrased in terms of the victim's "will." Nor does it employ the words "legal consent," as does subdivision (a)(1). Instead, section 261(a)(3) speaks in terms of the victim being "prevented from resisting. . . ."[5] Does that subdivision pertain to the victim's actual consent or to the victim's ability to give legal consent?

Although the language of section 261(a)(3) suggests that the victim's actual consent is at issue, our Supreme Court long ago rejected that notion. In discussing the elements of rape of a mentally incompetent person, the court said:

> "In this species of rape neither force upon the part of the man, nor resistance upon the part of the woman, forms an element of the crime. If, by reason of any mental weakness, she is incapable of legally consenting, resistance is not expected any more than it is in the case of one who has been drugged to unconsciousness, or *robbed of judgment by intoxicants.*"

People v. Griffin, 117 Cal. at 585, italics added. This emphasis on the effect of the intoxicants on the victim's powers of judgment rather than the victim's powers of resistance is consistent with the Model Penal Code, which provides that actual consent is not legal consent if "it is given by a person who by reason of youth, mental disease or defect, or intoxication is manifestly unable or known by the actor to be unable to make a reasonable judgment as to the nature or harmfulness of the conduct. . . ." Model Penal Code, §2.11(3)(b).

We conclude that, just as subdivision (a)(1) of section 261 proscribes sexual intercourse with a person who is not capable of giving legal consent because of a mental disorder or physical disability, section 261(a)(3) proscribes sexual intercourse with a person who is not capable of giving legal consent because of intoxication. In both cases, the issue is not whether the victim actually consented to sexual intercourse, but whether he or she was capable of exercising the degree of judgment a person must have in order to give legally cognizable consent.

---

5. The phrase dates from the original Penal Code of 1872, when the subdivision dealt with two types of rape: "Where she is prevented from resisting by threats of great and immediate bodily harm, accompanied by apparent power of execution, or by any intoxicating narcotic, or anesthetic, substance, administered by or with the privity of the accused. . . ." Former §261(4). The reference to threats was removed in 1980, but the "prevented from resisting" language was retained. The relevant subdivision now provides that a rape is committed "where a person is prevented from resisting by an intoxicating or anesthetic substance, or any controlled substance, and this condition was known, or reasonably should have been known by the accused." §261(a)(3).

In reaching that conclusion, we reject the defendant's contrary, more literal construction of section 261(a)(3). He notes that, prior to a 1980 amendment, the rape-by-force subdivision of section 261 expressly required evidence of resistance by the victim. Resistance was required to provide "an objective indicator of nonconsent," corroborating the victim's testimony that the act of intercourse was undertaken against the victim's will. People v. Barnes, 42 Cal. 3d 284, 299, 721 P.2d 110 (1984). In accordance with that purpose, the degree of resistance required "was only that which would reasonably manifest refusal to consent to the act of sexual intercourse." [Id.] at 297. The defendant asserts that, with that understanding of "resistance," it follows that "prevented from resisting" in section 261(a)(3) means that the victim is so intoxicated that he or she was physically incapable of manifesting a refusal to actually consent.

That construction is untenable. The case law interpreting the former resistance requirement demonstrates that the exertion of physical force by the victim against the defendant was not required; verbal protestations alone were sufficient to establish resistance. See, e.g., People v. Peckham, 232 Cal. App. 2d 163, 165-68, 42 Cal. Rptr. 673 (1965). Therefore, to be intoxicated to a degree that rendered the victim physically unable to resist would mean that the victim was unable to even speak. The line between that extreme level of intoxication and absolute unconsciousness is very thin. There is no indication in our decisional law that section 261(a)(3) has ever been interpreted to apply only to such severely incapacitated victims.

For instance, the evidence in People v. Ing, 65 Cal. 2d 603, 422 P.2d 590 (1967), was that the defendant, a medical doctor, had administered injections to the victim on several occasions; that after receiving the shots, the victim felt "light-headed" and "just didn't care about anything," id. at 607; that the doctor would then have intercourse with her; and that she would not have engaged in intercourse with him had she not been under the influence of the drugs. Ibid. There was apparently no evidence that the victim was unable to speak or otherwise communicate a refusal to consent; indeed, the evidence suggested that the victim actually consented to intercourse. Nevertheless, the court summarily rejected the defendant's contention that the evidence was insufficient to support his rape convictions. Id. at 612. . . .

Because section 261(a)(3) proscribes sexual intercourse with a person who is not capable of giving legal consent because of intoxication, the lack of actual consent is not an element of the crime. . . . [T]he trial court properly denied the defendant's request for an instruction to the contrary.

B. The Trial Court Prejudicially Erred by Failing to Explain to the Jury the Meaning of "Prevented from Resisting"

. . . [T]he jury was instructed that one of the elements of rape by intoxication was that "the alleged victim was prevented from resisting the act by an intoxicating substance." . . . [A]fter several hours of deliberation the jury asked the court for the legal definition of "resistance.". . . In response to the jury's request, . . . the trial court instructed the jury that "this is an area in which you must use your common sense and experience to determine the everyday meaning of resistance." . . .

. . . As demonstrated by its request for a definition of "resistance," the jury was having difficulty grasping the import of the statutory language, and understandably so. . . . [A]lthough the statutory language suggests that the factual issue is whether the intoxicating substance prevented the victim from physically resisting, the correct interpretation focuses on whether the victim's level of intoxication prevented him or her from exercising judgment. The defendant was entitled to have that concept correctly explained. . . . In particular, the jury should have been instructed that its task was to determine whether, as a result of her level of intoxication, the victim lacked the legal capacity to give "consent" as that term is defined in section 261.6. Legal capacity is the ability to exercise reasonable judgment, i.e., to understand and weigh not only the physical nature of the act, but also its moral character and probable consequences.

In deciding whether the level of the victim's intoxication deprived the victim of legal capacity, the jury shall consider all the circumstances, including the victim's age and maturity. It is not enough that the victim was intoxicated to some degree, or that the intoxication reduced the victim's sexual inhibitions. "Impaired mentality may exist and yet the individual may be able to exercise reasonable judgment with respect to the particular matter presented to his or her mind." People v. Peery, 26 Cal. App. 143, 145, 146 P. 44 (1914); accord, People v. Griffin, 117 Cal. at 585. Instead, the level of intoxication and the resulting mental impairment must have been so great that the victim could no longer exercise reasonable judgment concerning that issue.[6]

The trial court's response to the jury's inquiry did not help the jury to focus on the victim's ability to exercise that judgment. To the contrary, by instructing the jury "to determine the everyday meaning of resistance," the trial court erroneously implied that the meaning of the statute could be deciphered by giving the language of the statute its common meaning, and thus that the issue was the victim's ability to resist [physically]. . . .

. . . [Instructional error] . . . "does not warrant reversal unless prejudice is shown." People v. Beardslee, 53 Cal. 3d 68, 97, 806 P.2d 1311 (1991). This

---

6. In one sense, a minor is always legally incapable of giving consent. See §261.5 (unlawful sexual intercourse with a minor). But here the defendant was being prosecuted not only for unlawful sexual intercourse but also for the greater crime of rape by intoxication. In that event, the jury must set aside the statutory presumption that a person under 18 years of age is incapable of giving legal consent and must determine whether the elements of the more serious crime are met.

error did prejudice the defendant because the evidence supports conflicting conclusions regarding the victim's capacity.

Norliza G. lived with her mother and stepfather, the defendant. On December 27, 1996, Norliza's friend, the victim, was spending the night at Norliza's house. The victim had recently turned 16 years old. The victim testified that, on December 27, she consumed a single drink of bourbon over ice that the defendant had poured for her. She . . . described the drink as filling a 12-inch-tall glass "a little more than halfway". . . . Norliza testified that the victim had two drinks, the first poured by the defendant and the second poured by the victim herself. Norliza estimated the total amount of bourbon consumed by the victim to be five ounces.

According to the victim, she felt "woozy, very light headed" after consuming the alcohol. . . . Explaining that the victim had not had anything to eat, Norliza testified that the victim became "very giggly," slurred her speech, could not walk straight, and generally "wasn't altogether there." Norliza saw her fall several times. . . . However, she was never so intoxicated that she was close to passing out, that she did not know what she was doing, or that she could not physically resist. . . .

Lyles and the defendant said that they needed to get the victim out of the house to sober her up. She told the defendant that she did not want to leave the house, but he pulled her by the arm to his car. Lyles was with them. . . . The defendant stopped at a Motel 6 and rented a room. The victim stepped out of the car and the three of them climbed the stairs to the third floor motel room. Because she was so intoxicated, Lyles and the defendant were holding her by each arm to assist her up the stairs. Despite their help, as a result of the alcohol she tripped and fell on her knees near the top of the stairs. . . . The victim testified that, once in the motel room, she walked into the bathroom, disrobed, and started to take a shower. The defendant pulled her out of the shower, saying "we don't have time for this." The victim began to get dressed. . . .

The victim testified that after she had put on only the shirt, the defendant called to her. She came out of the bathroom to find both men naked. She began walking toward the door, and said, "I thought we were going home?" Lyles initially testified that she said something about wanting to go home, but later testified that she said "Let's get some liquor and have sex all night." Similarly, the defendant testified that as soon as she had disrobed, she came out of the bathroom and climbed onto one of the beds.

The victim testified that, in response to her comment about going home, the defendant said, "No. I want you to ride Tom." The defendant then pulled the victim by the arm on top of Lyles, who was lying down. While engaging in intercourse with Lyles, the defendant told her, "I want you to suck me." She then began to orally copulate the defendant. The defendant then took the victim to the other bed and pulled her on top of him. While engaging in intercourse with the defendant, the victim orally copulated Lyles. She testified that, during this time, she "was conscious a little bit." She felt like she "was just doing what they were saying to do."

The defendant then turned the victim on her back and again engaged in intercourse. While in that position, the defendant took a bottle of Rush (amyl nitrite inhalant), poured some onto a washcloth, and put it over the victim's face. She tried to hold her breath and push his hands away. Lyles recalled that she also told the defendant to stop applying it to her face. After the defendant ejaculated, he got up, started to dress, and instructed the victim to do the same. She was able to dress herself. As she was walking out, she still felt wobbly and light-headed, but she walked down the stairs without assistance. The defendant drove her to the corner of the block on which he lived and she walked the rest of the way to Norliza's house. . . .

The victim testified that she did not resist the defendant's actions that night because he was a lot bigger than she was, because she was afraid of him, and because she was intoxicated. Lyles testified that she never said she did not want to have sex. She never said "no," "don't," "stop," or anything else indicating that she did not consent. To the contrary, she said that she wanted to engage in sexual relations. According to the defendant, it did not appear that the victim was so drunk that she did not know what she was doing or that "she was prevented mentally from resisting."

The victim spent that night and the next day with Norliza at the defendant's house. At no time did she display any animosity toward Lyles or the defendant or express any displeasure to the defendant concerning the events of the prior evening.

Whether the victim possessed sufficient mental capacity to give legal consent despite her intoxication is a question of fact for the jury. Here, there is evidence from which the jury could have concluded that the victim was not capable of exercising reasonable judgment, but there is also evidence from which it could have concluded that she was capable. She voiced her objections both to leaving the house and to inhaling the Rush. Although unsteady on her feet, the victim was able to walk and to undress herself. . . . Shortly after engaging in the intercourse found by the jury, she dressed herself and walked down several flights of stairs unassisted. When she returned to the house, she was not drunk. And the next day, after she presumably was utterly sober, she amicably associated with both the defendant and Lyles without indicating in any fashion that she would have made different decisions the night before had she not been under the influence of alcohol.

In short, there is substantial evidence both that the victim actually consented and that she possessed the legal capacity to do so. There being evidence from which the jury could have concluded that the victim was not so intoxicated that she was deprived of the ability to exercise reasonable judgment, the trial court's erroneous failure to properly instruct the jury concerning the elements of section 261(a)(3) cannot be deemed to have been harmless. The conviction on counts 2 through 5 must be reversed.

C. An Honest and Reasonable But Mistaken Belief That a Sexual Partner Is Not Too Intoxicated to Give Legal Consent to Sexual Intercourse Is a Defense to Rape by Intoxication

. . . The Supreme Court explained in People v. Hernandez, [61 Cal. 2d 529, 532-33,] that unless the particular criminal statute at issue expresses a legislative intent . . . to impose strict criminal liability, a defendant's conduct is punished . . . only if it was committed with the necessary criminal intent.

> "There can be no dispute that a criminal intent exists when the perpetrator proceeds [to engage in sexual intercourse] with utter disregard of, or in the lack of grounds for, a belief that the female has reached the age of consent. But if he participates in a mutual act of sexual intercourse, believing his partner to be beyond the age of consent, with reasonable grounds for such belief, where is his criminal intent?"

Id. at 534. The court concluded that a reasonable and "bona fide but erroneous belief that a valid consent to an act of sexual intercourse has been obtained" is a defense to a charge of statutory rape. Id. at 535.

The same reasoning controls when the sexual partner's consent is invalid because of a lack of capacity due to brain damage rather than minority. People v. Dolly, 239 Cal. App. 2d 143, 146, 48 Cal. Rptr. 478 (1966). It also controls in this context, in which the lack of capacity is due to intoxication. As section 261(a)(3) itself provides, the accused is guilty only if the victim's incapacitating level of intoxication "was known, or reasonably should have been known by the accused." An honest and reasonable but mistaken belief that a sexual partner is not too intoxicated to give legal consent to sexual intercourse is a defense to rape by intoxication. . . .

DISPOSITION

The convictions on counts 2, 3, 4, 5, and 11 are reversed. . . . All other aspects of the judgment are affirmed. . . .

Notes and Questions

1. As the *Giardino* court determines, "prevented from resisting" means something akin to "unable to exercise judgment." Does that amount to a rewriting of the state's rape statute? Is the rewritten term defined appropriately?

2. The rule that actual consent is irrelevant when the victim crosses some threshold level of intoxication is common. States differ primarily in their definitions of the level of intoxication required to trigger the rule.

Here is the definition in Massachusetts:

> In determining whether a person is "incapable of consenting" to sexual inter-
> course as a result of intoxication, the inquiry focuses on whether that person
> is "wholly insensible . . . in a state of utter stupefaction . . . caused by drunken-
> ness . . . or drugs," a formulation derived from Commonwealth v. Burke, 105
> Mass. 376, 380-81 (1870). That is to say, the question is not merely whether
> a person is intoxicated, but whether due to intoxication, a person has been
> rendered physically or mentally "incapable of consenting." Id.

Commonwealth v. Urban, 853 N.E.2d 594, 596 (Mass. Ct. App. 2006). Is
Urban consistent with *Giardino*? What is the proper definition?

3. Notice that Giardino poured the first glass of bourbon the victim drank.
That fact seemingly was irrelevant to the decision that the sex acts qualified
as rape. Should the degree of intoxication in "rape by intoxication" cases
depend, at least in part, on who poured the drinks or supplied the drugs?

4. The American Law Institute (ALI) has been considering amendments to the Model Penal Code section defining rape and other forms of
sexual assault. See https://www.ali.org/projects/show/sexual-assault-and-
related-offenses/. In a Commentary to Draft MPC §213.6, released in 2015,
the drafters explained how the problem of determining consent in cases of
intoxication relates to the issue of sexual consent in general:

> The difficulty of identifying nonconsent in cases of heavy drinking flows
> directly from one fundamental but entirely unnecessary commitment—the
> law's prevalent assumption that passive or ambiguous behavior ordinarily can
> be treated as consent, until an individual has taken clear steps to
> indicate the contrary. Because the passive behavior of a sober person tradition-
> ally has been equated with consent and because the passive behavior of an
> extremely intoxicated person cannot be, the [current] law imposes upon itself
> the nearly impossible task of determining the genuine meaning of a person's
> behavior when docile or unresponsive actions occur under the influence of
> alcohol or drugs.
>   . . . Because the harm of erroneously presuming willingness in such cases
> vastly outweighs the harm of erroneously presuming unwillingness, the law
> should never treat ambiguous behavior as equivalent to consent, whether the
> individual in question is intoxicated or not.

Partly for the reasons explained in the Commentary, the initial version
of the proposed MPC amendments defined sexual consent as "affirmative
consent" (i.e., "yes means yes"). This proved highly controversial, and the
"affirmative consent" standard ultimately was rejected at the American Law
Institute's annual meeting in May 2016. The MPC amendments are now
being redrafted. See http://www.vice.com/en_ca/read/behind-the-scenes-
of-the-legal-group-that-could-change-americas-definition-of-sexual-consent.

Do you agree that the best way to solve the problem of intoxication and
consent is to redefine the meaning of sexual consent in general? Do you see
any potential problems with such an approach?

5. What if *both* parties to the relevant sex acts are intoxicated? Consider the next case.

State v. Smith

Court of Appeals of Kansas
39 Kan. App. 2d 204; 178 P.3d 672 (2008)

Opinion by GREENE, J.

Jesse Smith appeals his conviction and sentence for rape, arguing insufficiency of the evidence, error in the admission of certain evidence, error in applying the rape shield statute, instruction error, cumulative trial error, and sentencing error. We reject Smith's challenge to the sufficiency of the evidence. We conclude . . . that the district court erred in refusing to instruct the jury as to voluntary intoxication, but we conclude the error was harmless. Smith's remaining claims of error are rejected; thus, we affirm his conviction. . . .

FACTUAL AND PROCEDURAL BACKGROUND

On July 14, 2004, S.L. met Smith, her friend of 5 months, to have dinner and "a couple drinks." She considered him merely a friend, had no sexual or romantic interest in him, and was then dating another man. After dinner, they visited several bars and consumed a large quantity of beer; on the way home, S.L. passed out in Smith's vehicle. Upon arrival, Smith indicated it was not safe for her to drive and offered his bedroom, promising to sleep on the couch. Before she retired, however, she invited Smith to sleep on one side of the bed, but she did not intend to have sex with him.

According to S.L., she awakened in the night and felt something on her hips but went back to sleep until she awoke and discovered she had nothing on from the waist down. She also discovered what looked to be semen with a black pubic hair on her genital area. She tiptoed back to the bedroom, grabbed her clothes, and left. . . .

The next day, colleagues of S.L. urged her to see a physician, and the physician urged her to go to the hospital for an exam. Her father took her to the hospital, where she was examined and spoke to police about the incident.

Smith was charged with one count of rape in contravention of Kan. Stat. Ann. §21-3502(a)(1)(C), proscribing the act of sexual intercourse without consent under circumstances where the victim is incapable of giving a valid consent due to the effect of alcoholic liquor or narcotic drug, which condition is known by the defendant or reasonably apparent.

At trial, Smith testified that he went to sleep on the couch and did not remember anything else until he awoke the next morning. Smith requested an instruction on voluntary intoxication, but the district court refused to give the instruction and, instead, instructed the jury that "voluntary intoxication is not a defense to a charge of rape." Smith was found guilty by the jury, and he was sentenced to 184 months' imprisonment. . . .

Was the Evidence Sufficient to Support Smith's Conviction of Rape?

On appeal, Smith argues the evidence was insufficient to sustain his conviction because the State did not prove S.L. was unable to give consent and the State did not prove Smith had knowledge she was unable to give consent or that this was reasonably apparent. These arguments fail. . . .

Smith was charged and convicted of rape in contravention of Kan. Stat. Ann. §21-3502(a)(1)(C), which provides:

> "(a) Rape is (1) sexual intercourse with a person who does not consent to the sexual intercourse, under any of the following circumstances:
>
> . . .
>
> "(C) when the victim is incapable of giving consent because of mental deficiency or disease, or when the victim is incapable of giving consent because of the effect of any alcoholic liquor, narcotic, drug or other substance, which condition was known by the offender or was reasonably apparent to the offender."

. . . With regard to Smith's challenge to the evidence of S.L.'s condition, our review of the evidence shows that she was approximately 5'6" tall, weighed 117 pounds, drank 6 to 8 beers on the evening in question, and passed out from drinking. She unequivocally testified that she never gave consent to Smith to have sexual intercourse and would not have done so. Our Supreme Court has declined to define the degree of intoxication required to sustain a rape conviction under Kan. Stat. Ann. §21-3502(a)(1)(C) and has stated that "[l]ay persons are familiar with the effects of alcohol. If the jury concluded [the victim] was drunk enough to be unable to consent to sex, we should give great deference to that finding." State v. Chaney, 269 Kan. 10, 20, 5 P.3d 492 (2000).

With regard to Smith's challenge to the evidence of his knowledge of S.L.'s condition, our review of the evidence shows that Smith told her she was too intoxicated to drive home and that she should stay at his residence for the night. Moreover, S.L. testified that Smith did not attempt to wake her or otherwise seek consent before performing sexual intercourse. From this evidence, a reasonable inference can be drawn that Smith had knowledge that S.L. was unable to consent due to intoxication or that it was reasonably apparent to him. . . .

Viewing this evidence in the light most favorable to the State, we believe a rational jury could have found that S.L. was too intoxicated to give consent and that Smith had knowledge of this condition, or that it was reasonably apparent, and could therefore convict him beyond a reasonable doubt of the offense charged. We reject Smith's challenge to the sufficiency of the evidence for these reasons.

Did the District Court Err in Refusing to Instruct That Voluntary Intoxication Is a Defense to This Charge?

Smith next argues that the district court erred in refusing his request to instruct the jury on his defense of voluntary intoxication. . . .

The State argues that rape does not require specific intent on the part of the defendant, and that a defendant may not assert voluntary intoxication as a defense unless a particular intent or state of mind is a necessary element of the crime charged, citing State v. Gonzales, 253 Kan. 22, 23, 853 P.2d 644 (1993). . . . Smith argues, however, that Kan. Stat. Ann. §21-3502(a)(1)(C) is unlike the other statutory proscriptions of rape in that it requires knowledge by the defendant that the victim is incapable of giving consent. He argues generally that our Supreme Court has acknowledged that voluntary intoxication is a proper defense in a situation where the defendant is . . . incapable of forming the requisite state of mind for . . . the crime, citing State v. Ludlow, 256 Kan. 139, 883 P.2d 1144 (1994).

Our . . . Supreme Court has not faced the precise issue framed by this appeal, i.e., whether the knowledge requirement of Kan. Stat. Ann. §21-3502(a)(1)(C) justifies a voluntary intoxication defense. Even though rape has generally been held to be a crime of general intent, we do not find a case addressing the question in the context of the precise statutory subsection at issue here. . . .

. . . Based upon the statutory language, rape where the victim is unable to consent due to intoxication clearly requires, as an element of the offense, that the defendant have knowledge of this aspect of the victim's condition, or that this condition was reasonably apparent to him. This knowledge element is above and beyond whatever general intent may be required for the prohibited act of sexual intercourse. . . .

Kan. Stat. Ann. §21-3208 codifies the defense of voluntary intoxication. It states:

> "(1) The fact that a person charged with a crime was in an intoxicated condition at the time the alleged crime was committed is a defense only if such condition was involuntarily produced and rendered such person substantially incapable of knowing or understanding the wrongfulness of his conduct and of conforming his conduct to the requirements of law.
> "(2) An act committed while in a state of voluntary intoxication is not less criminal by reason thereof, but *when a particular intent or other state of mind is a necessary element to constitute a particular crime, the*

fact of intoxication may be taken into consideration in determining such intent or state of mind." (Emphasis added.)

We must determine whether the knowledge element of Kan. Stat. Ann. §21-3502(a)(1)(C), i.e., "which condition [the victim's intoxication] was known by the offender or was reasonably apparent to the offender" is an "other state of mind" under Kan. Stat. Ann. §21-3208 such that voluntary intoxication should have been recognized as a defense. We answer this question in the affirmative.

Our Supreme Court has provided a helpful discussion of "state of mind" for purposes of Kan. Stat. Ann. §21-3208 in *Ludlow*, 256 Kan. at 144-45. The court cited Black's Law Dictionary, which now defines "state of mind" as "the condition or capacity of a person's mind" or "a person's reasons or motive for committing an act, esp[ecially] a criminal act." Black's Law Dictionary 1446 (8th ed. 2004). Most notably for our purposes is the court's reference with apparent approval to United States v. Feola, 420 U.S. 671 (1975), where the Court noted the absence in a certain federal criminal statute of "any requirement for a particular state of mind such as 'knowingly'" in holding that in order to incur criminal liability under the statute, the actor must entertain merely a general criminal intent. See State v. Farris, 218 Kan. 136, 143, 542 P.2d 725 (1975). The corollary of this principle is that when a criminal statute *contains* a clear knowledge element, the crime proscribed requires a particular state of mind and makes it subject to a voluntary intoxication defense.

We recognize, however, that general criminal intent may be established by proof of intentional conduct, and that the term "knowingly" is included within the term "intentional" for these purposes. Kan. Stat. Ann. §21-3201. Nevertheless, when a criminal statute expressly requires specific knowledge of the victim's condition, above and beyond any general intent to commit the prohibited act, we believe this requirement is beyond any more general knowledge requirement for criminal intent. The distinction between a general intent crime and a crime of specific intent is whether, in addition to the intent required by Kan. Stat. Ann. §21-3201, the statute defining the crime in question identifies or requires a further particular intent which must accompany the prohibited act. See State v. Sterling, 235 Kan. 526, 528, 680 P.2d 301 (1984).

Examining Kan. Stat. Ann. §21-3502(a)(1)(C), the prohibited act is sexual intercourse with a victim incapable of giving consent, but the statute requires a *further* state of mind of the offender, i.e., knowledge of that condition if not reasonably apparent. This is a state of mind that is beyond the general criminal intent required for rape. Accordingly, we conclude [that] the knowledge requirement of §21-3502(a)(1)(C) justified a voluntary intoxication defense, and Smith was entitled to have the jury so instructed.

The erroneous instruction does not require reversal, however, because our review of the whole record shows that substantial justice has been done. Kan. Stat. Ann. §60-2105 requires that we disregard technical errors and irregularities which do not affirmatively appear to have prejudicially affected the substantial rights of the party complaining, where it appears upon the whole record that substantial justice has been done by the judgment. . . . [E]ven if Smith's claim was elevated to a constitutional deprivation, we need not reverse his judgment where the evidence of guilt is of such a direct and overwhelming nature that it cannot be said the error could have affected the result of the trial. See State v. Denney, 258 Kan. 437, 445, 905 P.2d 657 (1995).

Here, the evidence against Smith was indeed overwhelming. He testified that he was aware of S.L.'s inability to drive home, and he then drove her to his house. S.L. had passed out in his car, and he woke her upon reaching his house. He told the interviewing officer that he remembers telling an officer of brushing his teeth, taking his contacts out, and going to sleep. He also remembers being invited by S.L. to sleep on one side of the bed, but he claims to recall nothing thereafter, despite the clear DNA evidence of sexual intercourse with S.L. The fact that he remembers other details renders somewhat incredible his claim that he has no memory whatsoever of sexual intercourse with S.L. And, most damning, is the testimony of L.S. (detailed below), who testified to identical conduct by Smith, and which led to sexual intercourse with her after a night of mutual voluntary intoxication.

Reviewing all of this evidence, we conclude that the instruction error could not have affected the outcome of Smith's trial, and we therefore reject his contention that he is entitled to a new trial.

Did the District Court Err in Admitting Evidence of Defendant's Earlier Conduct?

Smith also argues that the district court erred in allowing a witness, L.S., to testify regarding Smith's conduct on another occasion that was similar to his purported conduct against S.L. The district court allowed the evidence on the grounds it showed plan and absence of mistake or accident. . . .

Prior to trial the State moved to present the testimony of L.S., who testified at trial that in December 2000 she was out with a group of people including Smith, when the group decided to go to a bar. They stayed until it closed, and she was very drunk. She was unable to drive home, so Smith suggested she come over to his house. He offered her the bed, agreeing to sleep on the couch. She did not remember how she got to Smith's apartment, but she remembered passing out once in Smith's bed. She awakened to find Smith having sexual intercourse with her, but was unable to move or speak. She testified that she did not consent in any manner to Smith's conduct, but she made no formal complaint of his conduct. They subsequently became a couple, lived together, and became engaged before breaking up in September 2003.

In examining a challenge to evidence of prior bad acts, our standard of review requires threshold determinations that (1) the evidence is relevant to . . . motive, opportunity, intent, preparation, plan, knowledge, identity, or absence of mistake or accident; and (2) the fact was a disputed material fact in the trial. State v. Tiffany, 267 Kan. 495, 498, 986 P.2d 1064 (1999). Here the evidence was clearly relevant to show motive, intent, plan, and absence of mistake or accident. We note that to show plan or *modus operandi* . . . , the evidence of the prior conduct must be so strikingly similar or so distinct to the allegations before the court that it is reasonable to conclude the same individual committed both acts. State v. Jones, 277 Kan. 413, 421, 85 P.3d 1226 (2004). . . . [T]he evidence presented by L.S. . . . appears, indeed, to be strikingly similar [to the evidence offered by S.L.].

Was motive, intent, plan, or absence of mistake or accident a disputed material fact in Smith's trial? Smith's defense was that he, too, was intoxicated and just did not remember having sex with L.S. This defense is potentially undermined by evidence of motive, intent, plan, and absence of mistake or accident. . . . [T]he offense requires an element of knowledge or state of mind, and Smith challenged this element, and the fact that Smith may have intended or planned the entire encounter, thus negating any mistake or accident, enhanced the materiality of this evidence. . . . There was no error in the admission of L.S.'s testimony. . . .

SUMMARY AND CONCLUSION

We reject Smith's challenge to the sufficiency of the evidence to support his conviction, together with all other claims of trial error, with the exception of the refusal of the district court to instruct on the defense of voluntary intoxication. This error does not entitle Smith to a new trial, however, because overwhelming evidence supports his conviction. . . .

Notes and Questions

1. Suppose L.S.'s testimony was not available. Is it obvious that Smith should be criminally liable? Why is S.L. protected against sex while intoxicated, while Smith is punished for sex while intoxicated? Is the answer that S.L. was more drunk than Smith? If a rape defendant could show a higher blood alcohol level than his intoxicated partner, should he be excused on that ground?

2. Does it matter that, after the incident she recounted in her testimony, L.S. lived with Smith and the two later became engaged? If so, how?

3. The *Smith* court held that the defendant can negate *mens rea* with evidence of his own intoxication, because the relevant Kansas statute bars sex with an intoxicated partner, "which condition *was known* by the offender or was reasonably apparent to the offender." Kan. Stat. Ann. §21-3502(a)(1)(C) (emphasis added). Suppose the prosecution alleges not that the defendant knew that S.L. was intoxicated, but that S.L.'s intoxication "was reasonably apparent." Would evidence of the defendant's intoxication then be admissible?

2. Statutory Rape

State v. Holmes

Supreme Court of New Hampshire
154 N.H. 723; 920 A.2d 632 (2007)

Opinion of DALIANIS, J.

The defendant, Martin Holmes, appeals his conviction by a jury for felonious sexual assault for engaging in sexual penetration with a person who was thirteen years of age or older but less than sixteen years of age. Rev. Stat. Ann. §632-A:3, II. He argues that the Superior Court erred when it ruled that the State did not have to prove that he knew that the victim was under the age of legal consent. We affirm.

The parties do not dispute the following facts: The defendant is twenty-four years old. The victim met the defendant while walking with a friend in Rochester. Although she was fifteen years old, she told the defendant that she was seventeen. The victim and the defendant exchanged telephone numbers and spoke on the phone a few days later. Approximately a week later, after consuming alcohol, the victim phoned the defendant and arranged to meet him at a local park, where they eventually had sexual intercourse.

The defendant was charged by grand jury indictment with felonious sexual assault for having engaged in sexual penetration with a person, other than his legal spouse, who was then fifteen years old. At the close of the State's case, he moved to dismiss the charge on the ground that the State had failed to prove that he knew that the victim was less than sixteen years of age. Relying upon our prior case law, the trial court denied the motion, ruling that the State did not have to prove beyond a reasonable doubt that the defendant knew that the victim was less than sixteen years old. See Goodrow v. Perrin, 119 N.H. 483, 488-89, 403 A.2d 864 (1979).

On appeal, the defendant invites us to overrule our prior precedent, which holds that the offense of felonious sexual assault with a person who is under the age of legal consent (statutory rape) "is a strict liability crime in that an accused cannot assert as a legal defense that he did not know the complainant was under the age of legal consent when penetration occurred." State v. Carlson, 146 N.H. 52, 58-59, 767 A.2d 421 (2001); see *Goodrow*, 119 N.H. at 488-89. For the reasons that follow, we decline his invitation.

The doctrine of *stare decisis* "demands respect in a society governed by the rule of law," because "when governing legal standards are open to revision in every case, deciding cases becomes a mere exercise of judicial will, with arbitrary and unpredictable results." Brannigan v. Usitalo, 134 N.H. 50, 53, 587 A.2d 1232 (1991). "[W]hen asked to reconsider a previous holding, the question is not whether we would decide the issue differently *de novo*, but whether the ruling has come to be seen so clearly as error that its enforcement was for that very reason doomed." State v. Gubitosi, 152 N.H. 673, 678, 886 A.2d 1029 (2005) (quotations omitted); see Planned Parenthood of Southeastern Pennsylvania v. Casey, 505 U.S. 833, 854 (1992). Several factors inform our judgment, including whether: (1) the rule has proven to be intolerable simply by defying practical workability; (2) the rule is subject to a kind of reliance that would lend a special hardship to the consequence of overruling; (3) related principles of law have so far developed as to have left the old rule no more than a remnant of abandoned doctrine; and (4) facts have so changed, or come to be seen so differently, as to have robbed the old rule of significant application or justification. Jacobs v. Director, N.H. Div. of Motor Vehicles, 149 N.H. 502, 505, 823 A.2d 752 (2003); *Casey*, 505 U.S. at 854-55.

. . . We will assume, without deciding, that factor (2) does not support adhering to *stare decisis*, and limit our discussion to factors (3) and (4).

The defendant first contends that we failed to interpret the statutory rape provision, Rev. Stat. Ann. §632-A:3, II and its predecessors, correctly in our prior cases because we did not take into account another provision of the Criminal Code, RSA 626:2, I (1996). Rev. Stat. Ann. §626:2, I, provides that a person may be found guilty of a crime only when he or she "acts purposely, knowingly, recklessly or negligently, as the law may require, with respect to each material element of the offense." The defendant asserts that §626:2, I, mandates proof of a culpable *mens rea* with respect to all material elements of the statutory rape statute, including the defendant's knowledge of the victim's age.

We interpreted §632-A:3, II in concert with §626:2, I, in State v. Goodwin, 140 N.H. 672, 671 A.2d 554 (1996). In that case, we held that "knowingly" is the *mens rea* for felonious sexual assault involving sexual penetration with a person under the age of legal consent. *Goodwin*, 140 N.H. at 675. We explained that "when a statute defining an offense is silent with respect to the *mens rea*, we will look to the common law origins of the crime." Id. at 674. We noted that the crime involved was rape, which "is generally considered to be a general intent, rather than a specific intent, crime." Id. "Whereas specific intent commonly refers to a special mental element above and beyond that required with respect to the criminal act itself, the general intent requirement for rape means that no intent is requisite other than that evidenced by the doing of the acts constituting the offense." Id. Thus, as the Criminal Code generally uses the term "purposely" in place of specific intent and "knowingly" in place of general intent, we ruled that "knowingly" was the *mens rea* for statutory rape. Id. at 674-75.

Although we did not discuss in *Goodwin* whether this *mens rea* applied to the defendant's knowledge of the victim's age, we had previously held, in effect, that a defendant's knowledge of the victim's age is *not* a material element of statutory rape. See *Goodrow*, 119 N.H. at 488-89. The plaintiff in *Goodrow* challenged the constitutionality of our statutory rape law, contending, in part, that the statute was invalid because it lacked the requirement of scienter. Id. at 487. We observed first that the statutory rape provision did not allow a defense of honest or reasonable mistake as to the victim's age. Id. at 488-89. We then ruled that the statute was not unconstitutional because it did not allow for such a defense. Id. at 489. . . .

Since we decided *Goodrow* in 1979, the legislature has amended the statutory rape law numerous times, but has not seen fit to add a *mens rea* or to make reasonable mistake of age a defense. The legislature most recently amended the statutory rape provision during this past legislative session. See Laws 2006, §162:1. As amended, the statutory rape provision makes it a felony to engage in sexual penetration with a person other than one's legal spouse who is thirteen years of age or older and less than sixteen years of age only where the age difference between the actor and the other person is three years or more. See id.

By amending the statutory rape provision, but failing to insert a *mens rea* or provide a reasonable mistake of age defense, the legislature has impliedly accepted our construction of that provision. See Del Norte, Inc. v. Provencher, 142 N.H. 535, 539, 703 A.2d 890 (1997). It is well settled that "when the legislature reenacts a statute on which a repeated practical construction has been placed by the Bench and Bar, that reenactment constitutes a legislative adoption of the long-standing construction." Id.; see also Commonwealth v. Miller, 432 N.E.2d 463, 465 (Mass. 1982). Although at oral argument, the defendant urged us to recognize an exception to this general rule, we decline to do so.

The defendant next asserts that because adult consensual sexual relationships are not as regulated as they were when we decided our prior cases, there is no longer any justification for permitting strict liability for statutory rape. The defendant notes, for instance, that fornication is no longer a crime. Additionally, since we decided *Goodrow*, the United States Supreme Court ruled in Lawrence v. Texas, 539 U.S. 558, 562, 564 (2003), that substantive due process precludes the State from criminalizing private consensual sexual conduct between adults. Thus, the defendant reasons, "Assuming that the accused has no reason to believe that a consensual sexual partner has not reached the age of consent, . . . his mental state is that of a person engaging in conduct that is not only lawful, but constitutionally protected." As he explains: "In an age where there is no fornication law and the federal constitution would forbid any such law, one who engages in sex with a person not his or her spouse cannot be said necessarily to have a 'culpable' *mens rea.*"

We decided *Goodrow*, however, assuming, without deciding, that the plaintiff *had* a constitutionally protected privacy right to engage in consensual heterosexual intercourse with other adults. *Goodrow*, 119 N.H. at 486. Specifically, we held:

> [E]ven assuming that the plaintiff has a federal privacy right to engage in consensual heterosexual intercourse with adults, the right does not require the invalidation of [the statutory rape statute]. The reason is that the United States Constitution does not require us to permit the defense of an honest and reasonable mistake to a charged violation of the statutory [rape] provisions.

Id. at 489. Thus, the developments in the law since we decided *Goodrow* would not change our analysis.

Moreover, intent to commit the then-legally wrongful act of fornication was only one of the rationales for statutory rape laws. See Collins v. State, 691 So. 2d 918, 923 (Miss. 1997). The other rationale concerned "the need for strict accountability to protect young [people]." Id. As we explained in *Goodrow*:

> The State, by enacting [the statutory rape provision], has fixed the age at which a minor person may consent to sexual intercourse. In essence, this provision prohibits an adult, such as the plaintiff, from engaging in sexual intercourse with a person who is below the fixed age of consent. It is well established that the State has an independent interest in the well-being of its youth. One reason for this heightened interest is the vulnerability of children to harm. Another reason for the State's concern is that minors below a certain age are unable to make mature judgments about important matters.

Goodrow, 119 N.H. at 486. This justification for making statutory rape a strict liability crime remains viable, despite decreased regulation of adult consensual sexual activity.

Statutory rape laws are based upon "a policy determination by the legislature that persons under the age of sixteen are not competent to consent to sexual contact or sexual intercourse." State v. Jadowski, 680 N.W.2d 810, 817 (Wis. 2004). "The statutes are designed to impose the risk of criminal penalty on the adult, when the adult engages in sexual behavior with a minor."

Jadowski, 680 N.W.2d at 817. In this way, these statutes accomplish deterrence. Owens v. State, 724 A.2d 43, 54 (Md. 1999). "The reason that mistake of fact as to the [child]'s age constitutes no defense is, not that these crimes like public welfare offenses require no *mens rea*, but that a contrary result would strip the victims of the protection which the law exists to afford." State v. Yanez, 716 A.2d 759, 769 (R.I. 1998). "If reasonable mistake were recognized as a defense, the very purpose of the [statutory rape] statute would be frustrated and the deterrent effect considerably diminished." *Collins*, 691 So. 2d at 923.

The defendant next suggests that *Goodrow* is contrary to the modern trend of judicial decisions in this area. He notes that "several state courts have overruled prior precedent and have required either a culpable *mens rea* or have allowed for some kind of reasonable mistake of age defense." To the contrary, "[i]n most states . . . a mistake of age, no matter how reasonable, is no defense." Loewy, Statutory Rape in a Post-*Lawrence v. Texas* World, 58 SMU L. Rev. 77, 88-89 (Winter 2005); see Carpenter, On Statutory Rape, Strict Liability, and the Public Welfare Offense Model, 53 Am. U. L. Rev. 313, 316-17 (2003). . . .

To the extent that a reasonable mistake of age defense exists in certain states, it is generally because the legislature has amended the applicable statute, not because the judiciary has engrafted this defense onto a statute that does not contain it. Indeed, at oral argument, the defendant conceded that hardly any states have a reasonable mistake of age defense. See Carpenter, supra, 53 Am. U. L. Rev. at 385-91 (legislatures in three states have enacted statutes in which reasonable mistake of age is a defense regardless of age of victim; legislatures in eighteen states have enacted statutes providing for defense of reasonable mistake of age depending upon relative age of victim and perpetrator; in remaining twenty-nine states, reasonable mistake of age is no defense to statutory rape). As one commentator has noted, the question whether there should be a reasonable mistake of age defense to statutory rape "is a policy matter that ought to be specifically addressed in the statutory definition of the crime." W. LaFave, Substantive Criminal Law §17.4(c) at 650 (2d ed. 2003).

For all of the above reasons, we conclude that the defendant has failed to demonstrate that our decision in *Goodrow* is "no more than a remnant of abandoned doctrine." *Jacobs*, 149 N.H. at 505.

The defendant next contends that changed circumstances have robbed *Goodrow* of significant application or justification. Specifically, he observes that the age of consent has risen while the age at which adolescents are becoming sexually active has declined over time. Further, he notes, the degree of punishment and social ostracism associated with the crime of statutory rape has escalated.

While these legitimate policy concerns might support a reasonable mistake of age defense, we believe that it is up to the legislature, not us, to create one. When we decided *Goodrow*, 119 N.H. at 489, we were "not concerned with the wisdom of the . . . law's policy in view of today's sexual mores. Instead, we [were] concerned only with whether the current law violate[d] the Constitution by not allowing for a defense of honest or reasonable mistake."

Affirmed.

Notes on Strict Liability and Statutory Rape

1. In Planned Parenthood of Southeastern Pennsylvania v. Casey, 505 U.S. 833 (1992), a case cited and discussed in *Holmes*, a fragmented Supreme Court decided to reaffirm Roe v. Wade, 410 U.S. 113 (1973). The key reason for the reaffirmation was *stare decisis*; *Roe* and the cases that followed it are precedents that merit respect:

> The obligation to follow precedent begins with necessity, and a contrary necessity marks its outer limit. With Cardozo, we recognize that no judicial system could do society's work if it eyed each issue afresh in every case that raised it. See Benjamin Cardozo, The Nature of the Judicial Process 149 (1921). Indeed, the very concept of the rule of law underlying our own Constitution requires such continuity over time that a respect for precedent is, by definition, indispensable. At the other extreme, a different necessity would make itself felt if a prior judicial ruling should come to be seen so clearly as error that its enforcement was for that very reason doomed.
>
> Even when the decision to overrule a prior case is not, as in the rare, latter instance, virtually foreordained, it is common wisdom that the rule of *stare decisis* is not an "inexorable command." . . . Rather, when this Court reexamines a prior holding, its judgment is customarily informed by a series of prudential and pragmatic considerations designed to test the consistency of overruling a prior decision with the ideal of the rule of law, and to gauge the respective costs of reaffirming and overruling a prior case. Thus, for example, we may ask whether the rule has proven to be intolerable simply in defying practical workability, Swift & Co. v. Wickham, 382 U.S. 111, 116 (1965); whether the rule is subject to a kind of reliance that would lend a special hardship to the consequences of overruling and add inequity to the cost of repudiation, e.g., United States v. Title Ins. & Trust Co., 265 U.S. 472, 486 (1924); whether related principles of law have so far developed as to have left the old rule no more than a remnant of abandoned doctrine, see Patterson v. McLean Credit Union, 491 U.S. 164, 173-174 (1989); or whether facts have so changed, or come to be seen so differently, as to have robbed the old rule of significant application or justification, e.g., [Burnet v. Coronado Oil & Gas Co., 285 U.S. 393, 412 (1932)] (Brandeis, J., dissenting).

505 U.S. at 854-55 (opinion of Justices O'Connor, Kennedy, and Souter). Is respect for precedent a powerful argument in *Holmes*? Historically, appellate courts have shaped the law of *mens rea*. Why is such shaping inappropriate in this context? On the other hand, the New Hampshire legislature has repeatedly amended the statute defining statutory rape, without altering the long-standing rule that the age element carries no *mens rea*. Legislative silence on this issue seems telling, does it not?

2. As recently as a half-century ago, the age of consent in most states was either 10 or 12. In the last generation, that age line has changed dramatically; now, the most common figures are 16 and 18. Does the change in the age of consent make the strict liability standard seem less appropriate today than in the past?

3. What did Holmes do that was wrong? What conduct does the statute that Holmes violated deter?

4. In State v. Loge, 608 N.W.2d 152 (Minn. 2000), excerpted at page 187, the court construed Minnesota's "open bottle" law to require strict liability. In State v. T.R.D., 942 A.2d 1000 (Conn. 2008), excerpted at page 194, the court interpreted a state Megan's Law to require strict liability as to the defendant's non-registration. The statute at issue in *Loge* imposed modest penalties; in *T.R.D.*, pre-release notification ensured that defendants knew about the registration requirement. The penalties for statutory rape, in New Hampshire and elsewhere, are severe; substantial prison terms are common in cases like *Holmes*. And there is no proceeding through which potential statutory rape defendants are informed about the state's age of consent. Do those facts render the rule in *Holmes* unfair?

5. With *Holmes*, compare State v. Jadowski, 680 N.W.2d 810 (Wis. 2004). The defendant in *Jadowski* was 35; the victim was 15. The defendant claimed he reasonably believed the victim to be 19:

> The defendant made an offer of proof that the victim was a chronic runaway; that the victim used what appeared to be a state-issued identification card showing her to be 19 years old; that the victim told the defendant and others that she was 19 years old; that the victim appeared to be 19 years old; and that the victim maintained in the defendant's presence that she was old enough to work as an exotic dancer.

680 N.W.2d at 813-14. The relevant state statute was essentially the same as in *Holmes*. The defendant proposed a defense for reasonable mistake as to the victim's age; the court rejected that proposal, for essentially the same reasons that *Holmes* rejected the defendant's proposed knowledge standard.

Is *Jadowski* a stronger case than *Holmes* for strict liability, or a weaker one? Do you think it mattered in *Jadowski* that the defendant was 35 years old? *Should* the age of the defendant matter in statutory rape cases? Note that in many states, modern statutory rape laws exclude (or substantially reduce the punishment for) cases in which the alleged perpetrator and the alleged victim are relatively close in age. These age-based exceptions to stat-utory rape laws are sometimes called "Romeo and Juliet" statutes. See, e.g., California Penal Code §261.5(b) (redefining sex with a minor who is "not more than three years older or three years younger than the perpetrator" as a misdemeanor crime).

6. In Collins v. State, 691 So. 2d 918, 923 (Miss. 1997), the court offered the following survey of the law of statutory rape:

> Historically, there have been two basic rationales for statutory rape laws. The first rationale is the need for strict accountability to protect young girls. The second rationale is the premise that the defendant's intent to commit statutory rape can be derived from his intent to commit the morally or legally wrongful act of fornication. Further, "the history of the offense of statutory rape indicates that from ancient times the law has afforded special protec-tion to those deemed too young to understand their actions." United States v. Ransom, 942 F.2d 775, 776 (10th Cir. 1991). The weight of authority in this country indicates that statutory rape has traditionally been viewed as a strict liability offense. Id.

> Despite the fact that statutory rape is historically a strict liability offense, "mistake of age" has been asserted successfully as a defense in several states[1] and is recognized by the Model Penal Code when the child is over the age of ten years. The basic premise of this defense is that a reasonable or good faith mistake as to the age of the victim is a valid defense to statutory rape.

> However, this defense remains the minority view. Far more states have rejected the defense. See Nelson v. Moriarty, 484 F.2d 1034 (1st Cir. 1973); U.S. v. Ransom, 942 F.2d 775 (10th Cir. 1991); People v. Green, 183 Colo. 25, 514 P.2d 769 (Colo. 1973); State v. Plude, 621 A.2d 1342 (Conn. 1993); State v. Sorakrai, 543 So. 2d 294 (Fla. 1989); Tant v. State, 281 S.E.2d 357 (Ga. 1981); State v. Silva, 491 P.2d 1216 (Haw. 1971); State v. Stiffler, 788 P.2d 220 (Idaho 1990); Toliver v. State, 372 N.E.2d 452 (Ind. 1978); State v. Tague, 310 N.W.2d 209 (Iowa 1981); Garnett v. State, 632 A.2d 797 (Md. 1993); Commonwealth v. Moore, 359 Mass. 509, 269 N.E.2d 636 (Mass. 1971); State v. Stokely, 842 S.W.2d 77 (Mo. 1992); State v. Campbell, 473 N.W.2d 420 (Neb. 1991); Jenkins v. State, 877 P.2d 1063 (Nev. 1994); State v. Davis, 229 A.2d 842 (N.H. 1967) rev'd on other grounds, 612 A.2d 923 (N.H. 1992); State v. Moore, 253 A.2d 579 (N.J. 1969); Guinyard v. State, 195 S.E.2d 392 (S.C. 1973); State v. Fulks, 160 N.W.2d 418 (S.D. 1968); State v. Randolph, 528 P.2d 1008 (Wash. 1974); Kelley v. State, 187 N.W.2d 810 (Wis. 1971).

> The "mistake of age" defense could hardly co-exist with our statutory rape statute which is intended to set forth the age of consent. As a result, children below this age are legally incapable of consenting to sexual relations. There is simply no indication by our legislature or by this Court that the defendant's knowledge the child's age is a factor to be considered. Rather, the knowledge or ignorance of the age of the child is irrelevant. If reasonable mistake were

---

1. Alaska, Arizona, California, Kentucky, Illinois, Maine, Minnesota, New Mexico, Ohio, Pennsylvania, Utah, Washington, West Virginia, Wyoming.

recognized as a defense, the very purpose of the statute would be frustrated and the deterrent effect considerably diminished.

Are the policy justifications offered in *Collins* persuasive? Defenders of strict-liability statutory rape laws sometimes argue that such laws are needed to protect against the coercion of teenage girls by adult men. Does that argument seem sound? If you were a prosecutor in New Hampshire, would you prosecute Holmes? If you were a Wisconsin district attorney, would you prosecute Jadowski? If you were a legislator in either state, would you seek to amend your state's statutory rape law? If so, what changes would you propose, and why?

D. CHILD PORNOGRAPHY

United States v. Williams

Supreme Court of the United States
553 U.S. 285 (2008)

Justice SCALIA delivered the opinion of the Court.

Section 2252A(a)(3)(B) of Title 18, United States Code, criminalizes, in certain specified circumstances, the pandering or solicitation of child pornography. This case presents the question whether that statute is overbroad under the First Amendment or impermissibly vague under the Due Process Clause of the Fifth Amendment.

I

A

We have long held that obscene speech—sexually explicit material that violates fundamental notions of decency—is not protected by the First Amendment. See Roth v. United States, 354 U.S. 476, 484-485 (1957). But to protect explicit material that has social value, we have limited the scope of the obscenity exception, and have overturned convictions for the distribution of sexually graphic but nonobscene material. See Miller v. California, 413 U.S. 15, 23-24 (1973); see also, e.g., Jenkins v. Georgia, 418 U.S. 153, 161 (1974).

Over the last 25 years, we have confronted a related and overlapping category of proscribable speech: child pornography. See Ashcroft v. Free Speech Coalition, 535 U.S. 234 (2002); Osborne v. Ohio, 495 U.S. 103 (1990); New York v. Ferber, 458 U.S. 747 (1982). This consists of sexually explicit visual portrayals that feature children. We have held that a statute which proscribes the distribution of all child pornography, even material that does not qualify as obscenity, does not on its face violate the First Amendment. See *id.*, at 751-753, 756-764. Moreover, we have held that the government may criminalize the possession of child pornography, even though it may not criminalize the mere possession of obscene material involving adults. Compare *Osborne, supra*, at 111, with Stanley v. Georgia, 394 U.S. 557, 568 (1969).

The broad authority to proscribe child pornography is not, however, unlimited. Four Terms ago, we held facially overbroad two provisions of the federal Child Pornography Protection Act of 1996 (CPPA). *Free Speech Coalition*, 535 U.S., at 258. The first of these banned the possession and distribution of " 'any visual depiction' " that " 'is, or appears to be, of a minor engaging in sexually explicit conduct,' " even if it contained only youthful-looking adult actors or virtual images of children generated by a computer. *Id.*, at 239-241 (quoting 18 U.S.C. §2256(8)(B)). This was invalid, we explained, because the child-protection rationale for speech restriction does not apply to materials produced without children. See 535 U.S., at 249-251, 254. The second provision at issue in *Free Speech Coalition* criminalized the possession and distribution of material that had been pandered as child pornography, regardless of whether it actually was that. See *id.*, at 257 (citing 18 U.S.C. §2256(8)(D)). A person could thus face prosecution for possessing unobjectionable material that someone else had pandered. 535 U.S., at 258. We held that this prohibition, which did "more than prohibit pandering," was also facially overbroad. *Ibid.*

After our decision in *Free Speech Coalition*, Congress went back to the drawing board and produced legislation with the unlikely title of the Prosecutorial Remedies and Other Tools to end the Exploitation of Children Today Act of 2003, 117 Stat. 650.* We shall refer to it as the Act. Section 503 of the Act amended 18 U.S.C. §2252A to add a new pandering and solicitation provision, relevant portions of which now read as follows:

"(a) Any person who—

. . .

"(3) knowingly—

. . .

"(B) advertises, promotes, presents, distributes, or solicits through the mails, or in interstate or foreign commerce by any means, including by computer, any material or purported material in a manner that reflects the belief, or that is intended to cause another to believe, that the material or purported material is, or contains—

"(i) an obscene visual depiction of a minor engaging in sexually explicit conduct; or

*[Note that the statute's odd title produces the catchy acronym, PROTECT. —Eds.]

"(ii) a visual depiction of an actual minor engaging in sexually explicit conduct, . . .

"shall be punished as provided in subsection (b)." §2252A(a)(3)(B).

Section 2256(2)(A) defines " 'sexually explicit conduct' " as

"actual or simulated—
"(i) sexual intercourse, including genital-genital, oral-genital, anal-genital, or oral-anal, whether between persons of the same or opposite sex;
"(ii) bestiality;
"(iii) masturbation;
"(iv) sadistic or masochistic abuse; or
"(v) lascivious exhibition of the genitals or pubic area of any person."

Violation of §2252A(a)(3)(B) incurs a minimum sentence of 5 years imprisonment and a maximum of 20 years. 18 U.S.C. §2252A(b)(1).

The Act's express findings indicate that Congress was concerned that limiting the child-pornography prohibition to material that could be *proved* to feature actual children, as our decision in *Free Speech Coalition* required, would enable many child pornographers to evade conviction. See §501(9), (10), 117 Stat. 677. The emergence of new technology and the repeated retransmission of picture files over the Internet could make it nearly impossible to prove that a particular image was produced using real children—even though "[t]here is no substantial evidence that any of the child pornography images being trafficked today were made other than by the abuse of real children," virtual imaging being prohibitively expensive. §501(5), (7), (8), (11), *id.,* at 676-678; see also Dept. of Justice, Office of Community Oriented Policing Services, R. Wortley & S. Smallbone, Child Pornography on the Internet 9 (May 2006), online at http://www.cops.usdoj.gov/mime/open.pdf?Item=1729 (hereinafter Child Pornography on the Internet) (as visited Jan. 7, 2008, and available in Clerk of Court's case file).

B

The following facts appear in the opinion of the Eleventh Circuit, 444 F.3d 1286, 1288 (2006). On April 26, 2004, respondent Michael Williams, using a sexually explicit screen name, signed in to a public Internet chat room. A Secret Service agent had also signed in to the chat room under the moniker "Lisa n Miami." The agent noticed that Williams had posted a message that read: "Dad of toddler has 'good' pics of her an [sic] me for swap of your toddler pics, or live cam." The agent struck up a conversation with Williams, leading to an electronic exchange of nonpornographic pictures of children. (The agent's picture was in fact a doctored photograph of an adult.) Soon thereafter, Williams messaged that he had photographs of men molesting his 4-year-old daughter. Suspicious that "Lisa n Miami" was a law-enforcement agent, before proceeding further Williams demanded that the agent produce additional pictures. When he did not, Williams posted the following public message in the chat room: "HERE ROOM; I CAN PUT UPLINK CUZ IM FOR REAL—SHE CANT." Appended to this declaration was a hyperlink that, when clicked, led to seven pictures of actual children, aged approximately 5 to 15, engaging in sexually explicit conduct and displaying their genitals. The Secret Service then obtained a search warrant for Williams's home, where agents seized two hard drives containing at least 22 images of real children engaged in sexually explicit conduct, some of it sadomasochistic.

Williams was charged with one count of pandering child pornography under §2252A(a)(3)(B) and one count of possessing child pornography under §2252A(a)(5)(B). He pleaded guilty to both counts but reserved the right to challenge the constitutionality of the pandering conviction. The District Court rejected his challenge, and imposed concurrent 60-month prison terms on the two counts and a statutory assessment of $100 for each count, see 18 U.S.C. §3013. No. 04-20299-CR-MIDDLEBROOKS, 2004 U.S. Dist. LEXIS 30603 (SD Fla., Aug. 20, 2004), App. B to Pet. for Cert. 46a-69a. The United States Court of Appeals for the Eleventh Circuit reversed the pandering conviction, holding that the statute was both overbroad and impermissibly vague. 444 F.3d at 1308-1309.

We granted certiorari. 549 U.S. 1304 (2007).

II

A

According to our First Amendment overbreadth doctrine, a statute is facially invalid if it prohibits a substantial amount of protected speech. The doctrine seeks to strike a balance between competing social costs. Virginia v. Hicks, 539 U.S. 113, 119-120 (2003). On the one hand, the threat of enforcement of an overbroad law deters people from engaging in constitutionally protected speech, inhibiting the free exchange of ideas. On the other hand, invalidating a law that in some of its applications is perfectly constitutional—particularly a law directed at conduct so antisocial that it has been made criminal—has obvious harmful effects. In order to maintain an appropriate balance, we have vigorously enforced the requirement that a statute's overbreadth be *substantial*, not only in an absolute sense, but also relative to the statute's plainly legitimate sweep. See Board of Trustees of State Univ. of N. Y. v. Fox, 492 U.S. 469, 485 (1989); Broadrick v. Oklahoma,

413 U.S. 601, 615 (1973). Invalidation for overbreadth is "'"strong medicine"'" that is not to be "casually employed." Los Angeles Police Dept. v. United Reporting Publishing Corp., 528 U.S. 32, 39 (1999) (quoting *Ferber*, 458 U.S., at 769).

The first step in overbreadth analysis is to construe the challenged statute; it is impossible to determine whether a statute reaches too far without first knowing what the statute covers. Generally speaking, §2252A(a)(3)(B) prohibits offers to provide and requests to obtain child pornography. The statute does not require the actual existence of child pornography. In this respect, it differs from the statutes in *Ferber, Osborne,* and *Free Speech Coalition,* which prohibited the possession or distribution of child pornography. Rather than targeting the underlying material, this statute bans the collateral speech that introduces such material into the child-pornography distribution network. Thus, an Internet user who solicits child pornography from an undercover agent violates the statute, even if the officer possesses no child pornography. Likewise, a person who advertises virtual child pornography as depicting actual children also falls within the reach of the statute.

The statute's definition of the material or purported material that may not be pandered or solicited precisely tracks the material held constitutionally proscribable in *Ferber* and *Miller*: obscene material depicting (actual or virtual) children engaged in sexually explicit conduct, and any other material depicting actual children engaged in sexually explicit conduct. See *Free Speech Coalition,* 535 U.S., at 245-246 (stating that the First Amendment does not protect obscenity or pornography produced with actual children); *id.,* at 256 (holding invalid the challenged provision of the CPPA because it "cover[ed] materials beyond the categories recognized in *Ferber* and *Miller*").

A number of features of the statute are important to our analysis:

First, the statute includes a scienter requirement. The first word of §2252A(a)(3)—"knowingly"—applies to both of the immediately following subdivisions. . . . We think that the best reading of the term in context is that it applies to every element of the two provisions. . . .

Second, the statute's string of operative verbs—"advertises, promotes, presents, distributes, or solicits"—is reasonably read to have a transactional connotation. That is to say, the statute penalizes speech that accompanies or seeks to induce a transfer of child pornography—via reproduction or physical delivery—from one person to another. . . .

Third, the phrase "in a manner that reflects the belief" includes both subjective and objective components. [It] suggests that the defendant must actually have held the subjective "belief" that the material or purported material was child pornography. . . . The statement or action

[also] must objectively manifest a belief that the material is child pornography . . . .

Fourth, the other key phrase, "in a manner . . . that is intended to cause another to believe," contains only a subjective element: The defendant must "intend" that the listener believe the material to be child pornography, and must select a manner of "advertising, promoting, presenting, distributing, or soliciting" the material that *he* thinks will engender that belief—whether or not a reasonable person would think the same. . . .

Fifth, the definition of "sexually explicit conduct" . . . is very similar to the definition of "sexual conduct" in the New York statute we upheld against an overbreadth challenge in *Ferber*. . . . If anything, the fact that the defined term here is "sexually *explicit* conduct," rather than (as in *Ferber*) merely "sexual conduct," renders the definition more immune from facial constitutional attack. "[S]imulated sexual intercourse" (a phrase found in the *Ferber* definition as well) is even less susceptible here of application to the sorts of sex scenes found in R-rated movies—which suggest that intercourse is taking place without explicitly depicting it, and without causing viewers to believe that the actors are actually engaging in intercourse. "Sexually *explicit* conduct" connotes actual depiction of the sex act rather than merely the suggestion that it is occurring. And "simulated" sexual intercourse is not sexual intercourse that is merely suggested, but rather sexual intercourse that is explicitly portrayed, even though (through camera tricks or otherwise) it may not actually have occurred. The portrayal must cause a reasonable viewer to believe that the actors actually engaged in that conduct on camera. Critically, unlike in *Free Speech Coalition*, §2252A(a)(3)(B)(ii)'s requirement of a "visual depiction of an actual minor" makes clear that, although the sexual intercourse may be simulated, it must involve actual children (unless it is obscene). This change eliminates any possibility that virtual child pornography or sex between youthful-looking adult actors might be covered by the term "simulated sexual intercourse."

B

We now turn to whether the statute, as we have construed it, criminalizes a substantial amount of protected expressive activity.

Offers to engage in illegal transactions are categorically excluded from First Amendment protection. . . . One would think that this principle resolves the present case, since the statute criminalizes only offers to provide or requests to obtain contraband—child obscenity and child pornography involving actual children, both of which are proscribed, see 18 U.S.C. §1466A(a), §2252A(a)(5)(B), and the proscription of which is constitutional, see *Free Speech Coalition*, 535 U.S., at 245-246, 256. The Eleventh Circuit, however, believed that the exclusion of First Amendment protection extended only to *commercial* offers to provide or receive contraband. . . .

This mistakes the rationale for the categorical exclusion. It is based not on the less privileged First Amendment status of commercial speech, see Central Hudson Gas & Elec. Corp. v. Public Serv. Comm'n of N.Y., 447 U.S. 557, 562-563 (1980), but on the principle that offers to give or receive what it is unlawful to possess have no social value and thus, like obscenity, enjoy no First Amendment protection. . . . Many long established criminal proscriptions—such as laws against conspiracy, incitement, and solicitation—criminalize speech (commercial or not) that is intended to induce or commence illegal activities. See, *e.g.*, ALI, Model Penal Code §5.02(1) (1985) (solicitation to commit a crime); §5.03(1)(a) (conspiracy to commit a crime). Offers to provide or requests to obtain unlawful material, whether as part of a commercial exchange or not, are similarly undeserving of First Amendment protection. It would be an odd constitutional principle that permitted the government to prohibit offers to sell illegal drugs, but not offers to give them away for free.

To be sure, there remains an important distinction between a proposal to engage in illegal activity and the abstract advocacy of illegality. See Brandenburg v. Ohio, 395 U.S. 444, 447-448 (1969) (*per curiam*); see also NAACP v. Claiborne Hardware Co., 458 U.S. 886, 928-929 (1982). The Act before us does not prohibit advocacy of child pornography, but only offers to provide or requests to obtain it. There is no doubt that this prohibition falls well within constitutional bounds. The constitutional defect we found in the pandering provision at issue in *Free Speech Coalition* was that it went *beyond* pandering to prohibit possession of material that could not otherwise be proscribed. 535 U.S., at 258.

In sum, we hold that offers to provide or requests to obtain child pornography are categorically excluded from the First Amendment. . . .

The Eleventh Circuit found "particularly objectionable" the fact that the "reflects the belief" prong of the statute could ensnare a person who mistakenly believes that material is child pornography. *Ibid*. This objection has two conceptually distinct parts. First, the Eleventh Circuit thought that it would be unconstitutional to punish someone for mistakenly distributing virtual child pornography as real child pornography. We disagree. Offers to deal in illegal products or otherwise engage in illegal activity do not acquire First Amendment protection when the offeror is mistaken about the factual predicate of his offer. The pandering and solicitation made unlawful by the Act are sorts of inchoate crimes—acts looking toward the commission of another crime, the delivery of child pornography. As with other inchoate crimes—attempt and conspiracy, for example—impossibility of completing the crime because the facts were not as the defendant believed is not a defense. "All courts are in agreement that what is usually referred to as 'factual impossibility' is no defense to a charge of attempt." 2 W. LaFave, Substantive Criminal Law §11.5(a)(2) (2d ed. 2003). See also ALI, Model Penal Code §5.01, Comment, p. 307 (in attempt prosecutions "the defendant's conduct should be measured according to the circumstances as he believes them to be, rather than the circumstances as they may have existed in fact").

. . . [T]he Eleventh Circuit also thought that the statute could apply to someone who subjectively believes that an innocuous picture of a child is "lascivious." (Clause (v) of the definition of "sexually explicit conduct" is "lascivious exhibition of the genitals or pubic area of any person." §2256(2)(A). That is not so. The defendant must believe that the picture contains certain material, and that material in fact (and not merely in his estimation) must meet the statutory definition. Where the material at issue is a harmless picture of a child in a bathtub and the defendant, knowing that material, erroneously believes that it constitutes a "lascivious exhibition of the genitals," the statute has no application.

Williams and *amici* raise other objections, which demonstrate nothing so forcefully as the tendency of our overbreadth doctrine to summon forth an endless stream of fanciful hypotheticals. Williams argues, for example, that a person who offers non-pornographic photographs of young girls to a pedophile could be punished under the statute if the pedophile secretly expects that the pictures will contain child pornography. Brief for Respondent 19-20. That hypothetical does not implicate the statute, because the offeror does not hold the belief or intend the recipient to believe that the material is child pornography.

Amici contend that some advertisements for mainstream Hollywood movies that depict underage characters having sex violate the statute. Brief for Free Speech Coalition et al. as *Amici Curiae* 9-18. We think it implausible that a reputable distributor of Hollywood movies, such as Amazon.com, believes that one of these films contains *actual* children engaging in *actual or simulated* sex on camera; and even more implausible that Amazon.com would *intend* to make its customers believe such a thing. The average person understands that sex scenes in mainstream movies use nonchild actors, depict sexual activity in a way that would not rise to the explicit level necessary under the statute, or, in most cases, both.

There was raised at oral argument the question whether turning child pornography over to the police might not count as "present[ing]" the material. See Tr. of Oral Arg. 9-11. An interpretation of "presents" that would include turning material over to the authorities would of course be self-defeating in a statute that looks to the prosecution of people who deal in child pornography. . . .

It was also suggested at oral argument that the statute might cover documentary footage of atrocities being committed in foreign countries, such as soldiers raping young children. See Tr. of Oral Arg. 5-7. Perhaps so, if the material rises to the high level of explicitness that we have held is required. That sort of documentary footage could of course be the subject of an as-applied challenge. The courts presumably would weigh the educational interest in the dissemination of information about the atrocities against the government's interest in preventing the distribution of materials that constitute "a permanent record" of the children's degradation whose dissemination increases "the harm to the child." *Ferber, supra,* at 759. . . .

. . . According to the dissent, Congress has made an end run around the First Amendment's protection of virtual child pornography by prohibiting proposals to transact in such images rather than prohibiting the images themselves. But an offer to provide or request to receive virtual child pornography is not prohibited by the statute. A crime is committed only when the speaker believes or intends the listener to believe that the subject of the proposed transaction depicts *real* children. . . . Simulated child pornography will be as available as ever, so long as it is offered and sought *as such,* and not as real child pornography. The dissent would require an exception from the statute's prohibition when, unbeknownst to one or both of the parties to the proposal, the completed transaction would not have been unlawful because it is (we have said) protected by the First Amendment. We fail to see what First Amendment interest would be served by drawing a distinction between two defendants who attempt to acquire contraband, one of whom happens to be mistaken about the contraband nature of what he would acquire. Is Congress prohibited from punishing those who attempt to acquire what they believe to be national-security documents, but which are actually fakes? To ask is to answer. There is no First Amendment exception from the general principle of criminal law that a person attempting to commit a crime need not be exonerated because he has a mistaken view of the facts.

III

As an alternative ground for facial invalidation, the Eleventh Circuit held that §2252A(a)(3)(B) is void for vagueness. Vagueness doctrine is an outgrowth not of the First Amendment, but of the Due Process Clause of the Fifth Amendment. A conviction fails to comport with due process if the statute under which it is obtained fails to provide a person of ordinary intelligence fair notice of what is prohibited, or is so standardless that it authorizes or encourages seriously discriminatory enforcement. Hill v. Colorado, 530 U.S. 703, 732 (2000); see also Grayned v. City of Rockford, 408 U.S. 104, 108-109 (1972). Although ordinarily "[a] plaintiff who engages in some conduct that is clearly proscribed cannot complain of the vagueness of the law as applied to the conduct of others," we have relaxed that requirement in the First Amendment context, permitting plaintiffs to argue that a statute is overbroad because it is unclear whether it regulates a substantial amount of protected speech. Village of Hoffman Estates v.

Flipside, Hoffman Estates, Inc., 455 U.S. 489, 494-495, and nn.6 and 7 (1982); see also Reno v. American Civil Liberties Union, 521 U.S. 844, 870-874 (1997). But "perfect clarity and precise guidance have never been required even of regulations that restrict expressive activity." Ward v. Rock Against Racism, 491 U.S. 781, 794 (1989).

The Eleventh Circuit believed that the phrases "'in a manner that reflects the belief'" and "'in a manner . . . that is intended to cause another to believe'" are "so vague and standardless as to what may not be said that the public is left with no objective measure to which behavior can be conformed." 444 F.3d at 1306. The court gave two examples. First, an e-mail claiming to contain photograph attachments and including a message that says "'little Janie in the bath—hubba, hubba!'" *Ibid.* According to the Eleventh Circuit, given that the statute does not require the actual existence of illegal material, the Government would have "virtually unbounded discretion" to deem such a statement in violation of the "'reflects the belief'" prong. *Ibid.* The court's second example was an e-mail entitled "'Good pics of kids in bed'" with a photograph attachment of toddlers in pajamas asleep in their beds. *Ibid.* The court described three hypothetical senders: a proud grandparent, a "chronic forwarder of cute photos with racy tongue-in-cheek subject lines," and a child molester who seeks to trade the photographs for more graphic material. *Id.*, at 1306-1307. According to the Eleventh Circuit, because the "manner" in which the photographs are sent is the same in each case, and because the identity of the sender and the content of the photographs are irrelevant under the statute, all three senders could arguably be prosecuted for pandering. *Id.*, at 1307.

We think that neither of these hypotheticals, without further facts, would enable a reasonable juror to find, beyond a reasonable doubt, that the speaker believed and spoke in a manner that reflected the belief, or spoke in a manner intended to cause another to believe, that the pictures displayed actual children engaged in "sexually explicit conduct" as defined in the Act. The prosecutions would be thrown out at the threshold.

But the Eleventh Circuit's error is more fundamental than merely its selection of unproblematic hypotheticals. Its basic mistake lies in the belief that the mere fact that close cases can be envisioned renders a statute vague. That is not so. Close cases can be imagined under virtually any statute. The problem that poses is addressed, not by the doctrine of vagueness, but by the requirement of proof beyond a reasonable doubt. See In re Winship, 397 U.S. 358, 363 (1970).

What renders a statute vague is not the possibility that it will sometimes be difficult to determine whether the incriminating fact it establishes has been proved; but rather the indeterminacy of precisely what that fact is. Thus, we have struck down statutes that tied criminal culpability to whether the defendant's conduct was "annoying" or "indecent"—wholly subjective judgments without statutory definitions, narrowing context, or settled legal meanings. See Coates v. Cincinnati, 402 U.S. 611, 614 (1971); *Reno, supra*, at 870-871, and n.35.

There is no such indeterminacy here. The statute requires that the defendant hold, and make a statement that reflects, the belief that the material is child pornography; or that he communicate in a manner intended to cause another so to believe. Those are clear questions of fact. Whether someone held a belief or had an intent is a true-or-false determination, not a subjective judgment such as whether conduct is "annoying" or "indecent." Similarly true or false is the determination whether a particular formulation reflects a belief that material or purported material is child pornography. To be sure, it may be difficult in some cases to determine whether these clear requirements have been met. "But courts and juries every day pass upon knowledge, belief and intent—the state of men's minds—having before them no more than evidence of their words and conduct, from which, in ordinary human experience, mental condition may be inferred." American Communications Ass'n v. Douds, 339 U.S. 382, 411 (1950) (citing 2 J. Wigmore, Evidence §§244, 256 *et seq.* (3d ed. 1940)). And they similarly pass every day upon the reasonable import of a defendant's statements—whether, for example, they fairly convey a false representation, see, e.g., 18 U.S.C. §1621 (criminalizing perjury), or a threat of physical injury, see, e.g., §115(a)(1) (criminalizing threats to assault federal officials). Thus, the Eleventh Circuit's contention that §2252A(a)(3)(B) gives law-enforcement officials "virtually unfettered discretion" has no merit. No more here than in the case of laws against fraud, conspiracy, or solicitation.

*   *   *

Child pornography harms and debases the most defenseless of our citizens. Both the State and Federal Governments have sought to suppress it for many years, only to find it proliferating through the new medium of the Internet. This Court held unconstitutional Congress's previous attempt to meet this new threat, and Congress responded with a carefully crafted attempt to eliminate the First Amendment problems we identified. As far as the provision at issue in this case is concerned, that effort was successful.

The judgment of the Eleventh Circuit is reversed. It is so ordered.

Justice STEVENS, with whom Justice BREYER joins, concurring.

My conclusion that this statutory provision is not facially unconstitutional is buttressed by two interrelated considerations on which the Court finds it unnecessary to rely. First, I believe the result to be compelled by the principle that "every reasonable construction must be resorted to, in order to save a statute from unconstitutionality," Hooper v. California, 155 U.S. 648, 657 (1895). . . .

Second, to the extent the statutory text alone is unclear, our duty to avoid constitutional objections makes it especially appropriate to look beyond the text in order to ascertain the intent of its drafters. It is abundantly clear from the provision's legislative history that Congress' aim was to target materials advertised, promoted, presented, distributed, or solicited with a lascivious purpose—that is, with the intention of inciting sexual arousal. The provision was described throughout the deliberations in both Houses of Congress as the "pandering" or "pandering and solicitation" provision, despite the fact that the term "pandering" appears nowhere in the statute. See, *e.g.,* 149 Cong. Rec. 4227 (2003) ("[T]he bill criminalizes the pandering of child pornography, creating a new crime to respond to the Supreme Court's recent ruling [in Ashcroft v. Free Speech Coalition, 535 U.S. 234 (2002)]" (statement of Sen. Leahy, bill's cosponsor)). . . . [O]ur cases have explained that "pandering" is " 'the business of purveying textual or graphic matter openly advertised to appeal to the erotic interest,' " Ginzburg v. United States, 383 U.S. 463, 467, and n.7 (1966) (quoting Roth v. United States, 354 U.S. 476, 495-496 (1957)).

It was against this backdrop that Congress crafted the provision we uphold today. Both this context and the statements surrounding the provision's enactment convince me that in addition to the other limitations the Court properly concludes constrain the reach of the statute, the heightened scienter requirements described *ante,* at 295-296, contain an element of lasciviousness. . . .

The dissent argues that the statute impermissibly undermines our First Amendment precedents insofar as it covers proposals to transact in constitutionally protected material. It is true that proof that a pornographic but not obscene representation did not depict real children would place that representation on the protected side of the line. But any constitutional concerns that might arise on that score are surely answered by the construction the Court gives the statute's operative provisions; that is, proposing a transaction in such material would not give rise to criminal liability under the statute unless the defendant actually believed, or intended to induce another to believe, that the material in question depicted real children.

Accordingly, when material which is protected—particularly if it possesses serious literary, artistic, political, or scientific value—is advertised, promoted, presented, distributed, or solicited for some lawful and nonlascivious purpose, such conduct is not captured by the statutory prohibition. Cf. Miller v. California, 413 U.S. 15, 24-25 (1973).

Justice SOUTER, with whom Justice GINSBURG joins, dissenting.

Dealing in obscenity is penalized without violating the First Amendment, but as a general matter pornography lacks the harm to justify prohibiting it. If, however, a photograph (to take the kind of image in this case) shows an actual minor child as a pornographic subject, its transfer and even its possession may be made criminal. New York v. Ferber, 458 U.S. 747, 765-766 (1982); Osborne v. Ohio, 495 U.S. 103, 110-111 (1990). The exception to the general rule rests not on the content of the picture but on the need to foil the exploitation of child subjects, *Ferber,* 458 U.S., at 759-760, and the justification limits the exception: only pornographic photographs of actual children may be prohibited, see *id.,* at 763, 764; Ashcroft v. Free Speech Coalition, 535 U.S. 234, 249-251 (2002). Thus, just six years ago the Court struck down a statute outlawing particular material merely represented to be child pornography, but not necessarily depicting actual children. *Id.,* at 257-258.

The Prosecutorial Remedies and Other Tools to end the Exploitation of Children Today Act of 2003 (Act), 117 Stat. 650, was enacted in the wake of *Free Speech Coalition.* The Act responds by avoiding any direct prohibition of transactions in child pornography when no actual minors may be pictured; instead, it prohibits proposals for transactions in pornography when a defendant manifestly believes or would induce belief in a prospective party that the subject of an exchange or exhibition is or will be an actual child, not an impersonated, simulated or "virtual" one, or the subject of a composite created from lawful photos spliced together. The Act specifically prohibits three types of those proposals. It outlaws solicitation of child pornography, as well as two distinct kinds of offers: those "advertis[ing]" or "promot[ing]" prosecutable child pornography, which recommend the material with the implication that the speaker can make it available, and those "present[ing]" or "distribut[ing]" such child pornography, which make the material available to anyone who chooses to take it. 18 U.S.C. §2252A(a)(3)(B).

The Court holds it is constitutional to prohibit these proposals, and up to a point I do not disagree. In particular, I accept the Court's explanation that Congress may criminalize proposals unrelated to any extant image. I part ways from the Court, however, on the regulation of proposals made with regard to specific, existing representations. Under the new law, the elements of the pandering offense are the same, whether or not the images are of real children. As to those that do not show real children, of course, a transaction in the material could not be prosecuted consistently with the First Amendment, and I believe that maintaining the First Amendment protection of expression we have previously held to cover fake child pornography requires a limit to the law's criminalization of pandering proposals. In failing to confront the tension between ostensibly protecting the material pandered while approving prosecution of the pandering of that same material, and in allowing the new pandering prohibition to suppress otherwise protected speech, the Court undermines *Ferber* and *Free Speech Coalition* in both reasoning and result. This is the significant element of today's holding, and I respectfully dissent from it. . . .

Notes and Questions

1. We first encountered the concepts of overbreadth and vagueness back in Chapter 1, at page 43, supra. *Williams* demonstrates how overbreadth takes on special constitutional significance in the First Amendment context. Because the Supreme Court does not wish to "chill" the exercise of First Amendment speech rights, the Court will closely scrutinize any law that might apply in an overbroad manner. If the law impacts a "substantial" amount of protected speech, then it will be held facially unconstitutional and invalid. If it does not, then the law will survive the facial challenge, although it could later be held unconstitutional "as applied" to particular facts and circumstances.

In *Williams*, Justice Scalia concludes that—at least so long as the PROTECT Act is construed carefully in certain respects—there is no First Amendment overbreadth problem, and the statute is not facially unconstitutional. Do you agree?

2. As for the due process vagueness argument, *Williams* shows how the First Amendment affects that argument as well. As Scalia notes, even a defendant whose behavior clearly falls within the ambit of a statute (and who, outside of the First Amendment context, would thus be barred from complaining about the possible vagueness of the statute as applied to other defendants) may challenge the statute as vague, if the statute's lack of clarity would allow it to be read to regulate a "substantial" amount of protected speech. In other words, in the First Amendment context, the possibility of overbroad application of a statute can lead indirectly to the conclusion that the statute is unconstitutionally vague.

Scalia finds no vagueness problem with the PROTECT Act, either, mostly because it is no more vague than many other criminal statutes that are based on the reasonableness of a defendant's statements—statements that would otherwise enjoy the full protection of the First Amendment. That conclusion seems right, doesn't it? Are you persuaded?

3. The PROTECT Act is an odd statute, is it not? The statute criminalizes, *inter alia*, transactions in materials that are not themselves obscene, and that might not even involve real children at all—that is, materials that are protected by the First Amendment—as long as the person proposing the transaction either *believes* the materials to be child pornography, or intends to try to *persuade* the other party to the transaction that it is so. Isn't the PROTECT Act actually a form of attempt law? Or maybe the better analogy is to one of those drug statutes that prohibits dealing in "simulated" controlled substances—after all, it's not illegal to sell (or to possess) baggies full of powdered sugar, but the legislature surely can make it illegal to sell a baggie full of powdered sugar while representing it to be cocaine.

4. Take another close look at the language of the PROTECT Act. Now consider the increasingly popular practice of "sexting"—in which students, including those in high school and even junior high, take sexually explicit photos of themselves with their cell phone cameras and send those photos to their boyfriends or girlfriends. Assuming that the "sexters" are minors, does sexting violate child pornography laws? In 2010, a Harrisburg, Pennsylvania prosecutor charged eight teens with felony violations of that state's child pornography law. The defendants, who ranged from 13 to 17 years old, had sent nude photos to each other (and, in one case, a short video of an oral sex encounter). In an interview, the prosecutor explained, "That was the only charge that really fits what they were doing. . . . What would have been the best thing to charge would be something that would have been a little less severe but would still draw these teenagers' attention to the wrongness of their acts." A local civil rights attorney representing one of the charged students asked, "Should they be crimes at all? This is an over-zealous and inappropriate application of the criminal law. . . . Are you going to stop kids from sexting that way? Maybe you should try talking to mom and dad." See CBS News, "Sexting Leads to Child Porn Charges for Teens," June 5, 2010, available online at http://www.cbsnews.com/stories/2010/06/05/eveningnews/main6552438.shtml.

In the wake of such episodes, a number of states have begun the process of amending their criminal statutes to treat sexting as a separate, and much less serious, crime than child pornography. Should it be a crime at all? How should the law distinguish sexting from the kind of behavior that the PROTECT Act was designed to prohibit?

10

Homicide Crimes

Of all the criminal offenses that are frequently punished, homicide is the most serious. Homicide is also the most consistently punished class of crimes. In some states at some times, more than 80 percent of non-vehicular homicides lead to an arrest and prosecution. The analogous figure for other crimes is vastly lower.

All of which would seem to make the clear definition of homicide particularly important. Yet there may be no frequently punished offense that is so poorly, and so strangely, defined. Most criminal statutes specify the relevant criminal conduct with great precision while leaving criminal intent vague. The law of homicide does the opposite. As you will see, the *mens rea* for homicide—in particular, the *mens rea* for murder—is statutorily defined in great detail. (Whether that detail produces much clarity is open to question.) But the relevant criminal conduct is remarkably open-ended: Homicide statutes usually prohibit *any* act or omission that causes the death of another human being, leaving the meaning of causation to the relevant jurisdiction's courts. Attempted murder, conspiracy to commit murder, solicitation of murder—the conduct required to prove these inchoate crimes is more undefined still, as are the requirements to prove aiding and abetting manslaughter or murder.

Section A of this chapter covers the criminal conduct that must be proved in order to convict defendants of one of the various forms of homicide. The cases in Section A fall into two categories: cases that explore the meaning of "causing death," and cases that involve the definitions of attempt, conspiracy, solicitation, and aiding and abetting when those doctrines are attached to homicide crimes. Section B constitutes the bulk of the chapter; it covers the *mens rea* for the different degrees of homicide.

By way of introduction, traditionally there are five such degrees. They are defined primarily by the mental states that the government must prove to convict:

First-degree murder includes premeditated killings and most felony murders. Premeditation means, basically, that the killer made a rational, as opposed to an impulsive, decision to kill. This is often established by proving some degree of advance planning—although, as you will see below, the extent of planning may be slight. Felony murder is, as the label suggests, homicide committed during the course of a qualifying felony; the necessary intent attaches to the qualifying felony, not to the killing. Most state statutes define certain "enumerated" felonies that, if their commission causes a death, will authorize a conviction for first-degree murder; the enumerated felonies usually include rape, robbery, burglary, arson, and kidnapping.*

Second-degree murder consists of homicides committed with one of several mental states that fall short of premeditated intent to kill. These several mental states are described, in the aggregate, as "malice aforethought." The list includes intent to kill that is *not* premeditated (i.e., impulsive rather than rational intent); intent to cause serious (i.e., likely to be lethal) bodily injury; and extreme recklessness, which is also described as acting with a "depraved heart," an "abandoned and malignant heart," or "depraved indifference to human life." Some felony murders also fall within the scope of second-degree murder, if the felony is not enumerated in the first-degree murder statute, but is nevertheless judged to be "inherently dangerous to human life."

Voluntary manslaughter means intentional killings committed while the defendant is in the "heat of passion" due to some event that the law considers "adequate provocation"; or (under the Model Penal Code's version) "extreme mental or emotional disturbance" (or EMED, for short) for which there is "reasonable explanation or excuse." Provocation and EMED combine two very different concepts: that homicides are less blameworthy (1) when they are the product of intense passion that leads the defendant to act out of character, and (2) when they are prompted by the victim's aggression or wrongdoing.

Involuntary manslaughter usually means homicide committed with ordinary recklessness, but not with malice or depravity. In some jurisdictions, causing death through criminal negligence can also lead to an involuntary manslaughter conviction.

Negligent homicides are committed, as the name suggests, with criminal negligence (in those jurisdictions where that is not considered to be involuntary manslaughter).

These five traditional categories of homicide are punished in descending order of severity: First-degree murder is punished most harshly, followed by second-degree murder, voluntary manslaughter, and involuntary

---

* Felony escape from the commission of any of these crimes, or sometimes from prison, is often also included on the list of enumerated felonies.

manslaughter; where it exists as a separate crime, negligent homicide receives the least punishment.

As you read the cases that follow, pay attention to the rank ordering of criminal homicides. Are the killings that are punished most harshly actually the worst killings? Are the killings that are punished the least (or maybe not at all) actually the least culpable ones, or are they simply the ones that we find the easiest to understand? Does the law of homicide make moral sense? Does it make practical sense?

A. CRIMINAL CONDUCT

1. Causing Death

Kuntz v. Thirteenth Judicial District Court

Supreme Court of Montana
995 P.2d 951 (2000)

Justice NELSON delivered the Opinion of the Court.

. . . On January 8, 1999, the District Court for the Thirteenth Judicial District, Yellowstone County, issued an Order denying Bonnie Kuntz's motion to dismiss or strike an amended information. The amended information alleged, under one charge, that Kuntz negligently caused the death of Warren Becker by stabbing [him] and then failing to call for medical assistance. Kuntz contended that her affirmative defense of justifiable use of force nullified any conceivable duty she had to render aid to Becker following the stabbing, and therefore the portion of the information pertaining to her failure to summon medical aid should be amended or stricken. . . . [The District Court denied Kuntz's motion. Both Kuntz and the state then sought a "writ of supervisory control" under Montana Rule of Appellate Procedure 17—an advisory opinion by the state supreme court clarifying the relevant legal issues.] . . .

FACTUAL AND PROCEDURAL BACKGROUND

According to the amended information and supporting affidavit, Yellowstone County Sheriffs deputies were dispatched on April 19, 1998, to the home of Bonnie Kuntz and Warren Becker to investigate a reported stabbing. When the deputies arrived at the trailer house, Becker was dead from a single stab wound to the chest. . . .

The alleged facts indicate that Kuntz and Becker, who had never married but had lived together for approximately six years, were in the process of ending what is described as a stormy relationship. When Kuntz arrived at the mobile home [on the night of April 18], she discovered that many of her personal belongings had been destroyed, the interior of the home "trashed," and the phone ripped from the wall. Kuntz told the deputies that she then went into the kitchen. There, allegedly, Becker physically attacked her, and at one point grabbed her by the hair, shook her, and slammed her into the stove.

Kuntz told the deputies that she could not clearly remember what happened, only that she had pushed Becker away and had then gone outside by the kitchen door to "cool off." When she thought that the fight was over, and that it was safe to go back inside, she returned to the kitchen. She discovered a trail of blood leading from the kitchen through the living room and out onto the front porch where she found Becker collapsed face-down on the porch. She alleges that she rolled him over. Becker was unresponsive.

Kuntz then alleges that she found Becker's car keys in one of his pockets, got in his vehicle, drove to a friend's house several miles away, and called her mother. Kuntz does not allege that she personally contacted medical or law enforcement personnel; rather, authorities were apparently summoned by Kuntz's sister-in-law, who lived next door to Kuntz's mother, sometime within an hour after the stabbing. Kuntz did return, however, to the trailer home where she waited for the deputies and medics to arrive.

On June 23, 1998, Bonnie Kuntz was charged with negligent homicide for causing the death of Warren Becker by stabbing him once in the chest. Although she admitted stabbing Becker and causing his death, Kuntz entered a plea of not guilty based on the defense of justifiable use of force.

On November 6, 1998, shortly before the scheduled trial date, the State filed an amended information charging the same offense but alleging that Kuntz caused the death of Becker by stabbing him once in the chest with a knife *and* by failing to call for medical assistance. Kuntz again entered a plea of not guilty. On December 18, 1998, Kuntz filed a motion to dismiss the amended information or in the alternative to strike the allegation that the failure to seek medical assistance constituted negligent homicide. Following a hearing and briefing, the District Court issued an Order and Memorandum on January 8, 1999, denying Bonnie Kuntz's motion to dismiss the amended information. . . .

DISCUSSION

. . . For criminal liability to be based upon a failure to act, there must be a duty imposed by the law to act, and the person must be physically capable of performing the act. As a starting point in our analysis, the parties here have identified what is often referred to as "the American bystander rule." This rule imposes no legal duty on a person to rescue or summon aid for another person who is at risk or in danger, even though society recognizes that a moral obligation might exist. This is true even "when that aid can be rendered without danger or inconvenience to" the potential rescuer. Pope v. State, 396 A.2d 1054, 1064 (Md. 1979). Thus, an Olympic swimmer may be deemed by the community as a shameful coward, or worse, for not rescuing a drowning child in the neighbor's pool, but she is not a criminal. See LaFave & Scott, Substantive Criminal Law §3.3(a) (1986).

But this rule is far from absolute. Professors LaFave and Scott have identified seven common-law exceptions to the American bystander rule: (1) a duty based on a personal relationship, such as parent-child or husband-wife; (2) a duty based on statute; (3) a duty based on contract; (4) a duty based upon voluntary assumption of care; (5) a duty based on creation of the peril; (6) a duty to control the conduct of others; and (7) a duty based on being a landowner. See [id.] §3.3, at 283-89. A breach of one of these legal duties by failing to take action, therefore, may give rise to criminal liability. Our review of the issues presented here can accordingly be narrowed to two of the foregoing exceptions as briefed by the parties and identified by the District Court: a duty based on a personal relationship, and a duty based on creation of the peril.

. . . In the widely cited case of State v. Mally, 366 P.2d 868 (Mont. 1961), this Court held that under certain circumstances a husband has a duty to summon medical aid for his wife and breach of that duty could render him criminally liable. The facts of the case described how Kay Mally, who was suffering from terminal kidney and liver diseases, fell and fractured both her arms on a Tuesday evening. Her husband, Michael Mally, put her to bed and did not summon a doctor until Thursday morning. "During this period of time, as she lay there with only the extended arm of death as a companion, she received but one glass of water." *Mally*, 366 P.2d at 873. Although his wife ultimately died of kidney failure, Mally was found guilty of involuntary manslaughter, a forerunner of Montana's negligent homicide statute, because his failure to act hastened his wife's death. See [id.] at 874. See also Territory v. Manton, 19 P. 387 (Mont. 1888) (finding husband criminally culpable for leaving intoxicated and inadequately clothed wife outside in winter conditions overnight).

In *Mally*, however, we alluded to a limitation of this rule which is a point of contention between the parties here. We cited to People v. Beardsley, 113 N.W. 1128 (Mich. 1907) . . . , [in which the] Michigan Supreme Court concluded that the legal duty imposed on the personal relationship of husband and wife could not be extended to a temporary, non-family relationship. The court held that a married defendant had no duty to summon medical help for his mistress, who was staying in his house for the weekend, after she took morphine following a bout of heavy drinking and fell into a "stupor." *Beardsley*, 113 N.W. at 1131.

We agree with the State, as well as myriad commentators over the years, that . . . *Beardsley* is indeed "outmoded." . . . See, e.g., Note, Criminal Omissions, 55 Harv. L. Rev. 615, 625 (1942) (suggesting that the law should protect the expectation found in certain personal relationships that "in an emergency a limited faith or trust will be honored"); Graham Hughes, Criminal Omissions, 67 Yale L.J. 590, 624 (1958) (stating that *Beardsley* "proclaims a morality which is smug, ignorant and vindictive"). See also State v. Miranda, 715 A.2d 680, 682 (Conn. 1998) (concluding that person who is not biological or legal parent of a child but who establishes a "familial relationship" with live-in girlfriend has duty to protect child from abuse).

Applying the foregoing to the facts here, we conclude that Kuntz and Becker, having lived together for approximately six years, owed each other the same "personal relationship" duty as found between spouses under our holding in *Mally*. This duty, identified as one of "mutual reliance" by LaFave and Scott, would include circumstances involving "two people, though not closely related, [who] live together under one roof." LaFave & Scott, §3.3(a)(1), at 285-86. To hold otherwise would result in an untenable rule that would not, under the factual circumstances found in *Mally*, impose a legal duty to summon medical aid on persons in a relationship involving cohabitation. Nevertheless, this holding is far from dispositive in establishing a legal duty under the facts presented.

We agree with the District Court that the duty based on "creation of the peril" is far more closely aligned with the factual circumstances here. Undoubtedly, when a person places another in a position of danger, and then fails to safeguard or rescue that person, and the person subsequently dies as a result of this omission, such an omission may be sufficient to support criminal liability. See LaFave & Scott, §3.3(a)(5), at 288; State v. Morgan, 936 P.2d 20, 23 (Wash. App. 1997) (imposing criminal liability for supplying cocaine leading to victim's overdose).

This duty may include peril resulting from a defendant's criminal negligence, as alleged here. See generally *Mally*, 366 P.2d at 872 (stating that failure to obtain medical aid for one who is owed a duty is a sufficient degree of negligence as to constitute involuntary manslaughter). . . .

The legal duty based on creation of the peril has been extended . . . to cases involving self-defense. See King v. Commonwealth, 148 S.W.2d 1044 (Ky. App. 1941). . . . The court in *King* . . . reversed a conviction of voluntary manslaughter that was based on the appellant's refusal to give or permit others to give aid or medical attention. The court, in finding that jury instructions were improper and prejudicial, stated:

> Since the shooting was justified, appellant could not have been guilty of voluntary or involuntary manslaughter unless he had committed *some subsequent act* which converted a non-fatal injury into a fatal one. If the injury was fatal, nothing which appellant might have done could have changed the result, or lessened or increased his responsibility.

King, 148 S.W.2d at 1047 (emphasis added). The facts do not reveal how the use of force came about, only that the appellant shot the decedent in the leg with a shotgun in the "necessary defense of appellant's father." *King*, 148 S.W.2d at 1046. Following the shooting, the Kings (father and son) carried the victim to their front porch and, futilely, attempted to stop the bleeding.

The Kings did not have access to a phone or an automobile. Consequently, "some hours elapsed before the first-aid man and the constable arrived, and about 11:30 A.M. an automobile was procured [approximately five hours after the shooting]." *King,* 148 S.W.2d at 1046. . . . [T]he court concluded that the Kings had not committed a "subsequent act" in that they did not actually refuse to render or seek medical attention for the victim, and thus could not have been found guilty of voluntary manslaughter, which required an unlawful, willful act. *King,* 148 S.W.2d at 1046-47. . . .

As *King* [suggests], the legal duty imposed on personal relationships and those who create peril are not absolute; i.e., there are exceptions to these exceptions. The personal relationship legal duty, for example, does not require a person to jeopardize his own life. See State v. Walden, 293 S.E.2d 780, 786 (N.C. 1982) (stating that although a parent has a legal duty to prevent harm to his or her child, "this is not to say that parents have the legal duty to place themselves in danger of death or great bodily harm in coming to the aid of their children"). Furthermore, the duty does not arise unless the spouse "unintentionally entered a helpless state," or was otherwise incompetent to summon medical aid on his or her own behalf. Commonwealth v. Konz, 450 A.2d 638, 642 (Pa. 1982).

Similarly, the law does not require that a person, who places another person in a position of peril, risk bodily injury or death in the performance of the legally imposed duty to render assistance. . . . Therefore, where self-preservation is at stake, the law does not require a person to "save the other's life by sacrificing his own," and therefore no crime can be committed by the person who "in saving his own life in the struggle for the only means of safety," causes the death of another. 40 Am. Jur. Homicide §116 (1999). Even states such as Vermont that have adopted a "Good Samaritan Doctrine" which—contrary to the American bystander rule—imposes a legal duty to render or summon aid for imperiled strangers, do not require that the would-be rescuer risk bodily injury or death. See, e.g., State v. Joyce, 433 A.2d 271, 273 (Vt. 1981) (holding that Vermont's Duty to Aid the Endangered Act did not require bystanders to intervene in a fight, because such intervention would expose person to risk of sustaining an injury). . . .

With these general principles in place, we now turn to the [issue] subject to the writ of supervisory control[:] Does one who justifiably uses deadly force in defense of her person nevertheless have a legal duty to summon aid for the mortally wounded attacker?

Our analysis of this issue is narrowed to whether the legal duty to summon aid, based on the defendant's personal relationship or creation of peril, extends into circumstances where the defendant's alleged use of justifiable force places his or her aggressor in need of medical attention. The State contends that even if Kuntz's use of force was justified, a proven subsequent failure by her to summon aid could constitute a gross deviation from ordinary care. Thus, the State's amended information charging Kuntz with negligent homicide for stabbing Becker and then failing to immediately call for medical assistance was proper and should not be stricken. Although the use of force may be justified, to not hold such a person criminally account-able for the subsequent omission would, according to the State, "encourage revenge and retaliation."

Whether inflicted in self-defense or accidentally, a wound that causes a loss of blood undoubtedly places a person in some degree of peril, and therefore gives rise to a legal duty to either (1) personally provide assistance; or (2) summon medical assistance. Even so, the performance of this legal duty, as discussed above, does not require that a person place herself at risk of serious bodily injury or death.

Accordingly, . . . we hold that when a person justifiably uses force to fend off an aggressor, that person has no duty to assist her aggressor in any manner that may conceivably create the risk of bodily injury or death to herself, or oth-er persons. This absence of a duty necessarily includes any conduct that would require the person to remain in, or return to, the zone of risk created by the original aggressor. We find no authority that suggests that the law should require a person, who is justified in her use of force, to subsequently check the pulse of her attacker, or immediately dial 911, before retreating to safety.

Under the general factual circumstances described here, we conclude that the victim has but one duty after fending off an attack, and that is the duty owed to one's self — as a matter of self-preservation — to seek and secure safety away from the place the attack occurred. Thus, the person who justifiably acts in self-defense is temporarily afforded the same status as the innocent bystander under the American rule. See LaFave & Scott, §3.3(a)(5), at 288 (suggesting that "one who innocently creates danger is on principle in the same position as that of a bystander who happens by when a situation of danger has developed").

Finally, we conclude that the duty to summon aid may in fact be "revived" as the State contends, but only after the victim of the aggressor has fully exercised her right to seek and secure safety from personal harm. Then, and only then, may a legal duty be imposed to summon aid for the person placed in peril by an act of self-defense. We further hold that preliminary to imposing this duty, it must be shown that (1) the person had knowledge of the facts indicating a duty to act; and (2) the person was physically capable of performing the act. See LaFave & Scott, §3.3(b), at 289 (stating prevail-ing view that person may not be held criminally liable where defendant is unaware of the facts giving rise to the duty to act); Mont. Code Ann. §45-2-202 (stating that a "material element of every offense is a voluntary act, which includes an omission to perform a duty which the law imposes on the offender and which he is physically capable of performing").

It must be emphasized, however, that once imposed, a proven breach of this legal duty may still fall far short of negligent homicide, which requires a gross deviation from an ordinary or reasonable standard of care. . . .

Justice TRIEWEILER, with whom Justice HUNT joins, concurring and dissenting.

. . . The majority has concluded that although circumstances occur which are so extreme that a woman is justified in the use of deadly force to defend herself, a jury can, after the fact, in the safe confines of the jury room, conclude that at some subsequent point she was sufficiently free from danger that she should have made an effort to save her assailant and that because she didn't she is still criminally liable for his death even though at some previous point in time she was justified in taking his life. This result is simply unworkable as a practical matter and makes poor public policy.

Montana Code Annotated §45-3-102 provides that a person is justified in the use of deadly force only when necessary to prevent imminent death or serious bodily harm to herself or another, or to prevent commission of a [forcible] felony. . . . It is inherently contradictory to provide by statute that under certain circumstances deadly force may be justified, but that having so acted, a victim has a common law duty to prevent the death of her assailant. . . .

Notes on Criminal Omissions

1. As Justice Nelson states in *Kuntz*, "[f]or criminal liability to be based upon a failure to act, there must be a duty imposed by the law to act." Criminal liability for omissions is legally disfavored—the presumption is that one may not be punished for inaction but only for affirmative conduct.

At least in theory. In practice, the exceptions to that general principle tend to swallow the rule. Courts usually list four exceptions to the general rule of non-liability for omissions. First, omissions liability may be based on statute. Defendants are routinely prosecuted and punished for failing to file tax returns; those prosecutions are permissible because the tax code specifies the relevant affirmative obligation. In other words, the general principle that omissions liability is disfavored is a principle rather than a binding rule, and certainly not a rule that binds legislatures. Second, omissions liability may be based on contract. Employees of nursing homes and other assisted-living facilities may be prosecuted for homicide when their inattention leads to the death of someone in their care; the theory in such cases is usually that the defendant assumed a contractual obligation to care for the victim. Third, omissions liability may be based on a qualifying relationship or status. When a child dies due to lack of food or medical care, the child's parents or legal guardians can be held criminally liable for the death. Fourth and finally, a defendant may be liable for failing to assist someone whom the defendant has "secluded," or placed in a worse position, so that others are less likely to be able to offer such assistance. The famous case of Regina v. Instan, 1 Q.B. 450 (1893), may be an example of this last category. Instan was the victim's niece, and was living in the victim's house at the time of the death.

The victim died of gangrene over an extended period of time; the defendant never summoned aid. The defendant was convicted of manslaughter, and the Queen's Bench affirmed the conviction.

Taken together, these four exceptions cover a great many cases. Consequently, criminal liability for inaction is more common than the language in hornbooks and appellate opinions would lead one to believe. It is especially common in homicide cases. Homicide is one of the few crimes in which the offense consists of causing a particular result. In that sense, homicide resembles many civil liability regimes — legal liability is triggered when the defendant causes injury. Just as liability for inaction is common in civil cases (think of the many tort cases in which a defendant is held liable for failing to take some precaution), it is common in criminal cases as well.

2. *Instan* illustrates the flexibility of the omissions doctrine. The defendant did not remove the victim from public circulation; the victim's illness did that. But it was clear to the defendant that if she did not seek help, no one else would be in a position to do so; the victim was essentially secluded in the defendant's house, which sufficed to establish criminal liability. Is that an adequate definition of criminal homicide? The boundaries of criminal conduct are ordinarily specified in some detail; not so when a failure to act causes the victim's death. Does that fact create the potential for surprising criminal liability? For unfair criminal liability?

3. At any given time, the list of things one is physically doing is quite small. The list of things one is *not* doing, by contrast, is limitless. It follows that the odds that a given criminal defendant chose to do what she did are high; the odds that she chose to abstain from one of the countless activities in which she *didn't* engage are much lower. Criminal law ordinarily seeks to impose liability only on those who choose to do something the law forbids. Such choices are absent in many omissions cases. Thus, disfavoring omissions liability might be seen as a close relative of the principle that strict liability is disfavored in criminal law, and perhaps also the principle that criminal liability without fair notice is wrong.

Does *Kuntz* make sense on the theory that omissions and some combination of intent and notice are closely related? Was Kuntz's failure to summon help for the victim the product of inattention? Of fear? Of anger? Should the answer matter?

4. Consider Commonwealth v. Konz, 450 A.2d 638, 642 (Pa. 1982), one of the cases cited in *Kuntz*. The two defendants in *Konz* were the victim's wife and a close friend; the victim was a diabetic who died because he had abstained, or was prevented, from using insulin. The defendants claimed that the victim was following the dictates of his faith, which precluded medical intervention in such cases, and that they merely helped him carry out his own wish to avoid medical assistance of any sort. The government claimed the defendants' role in the victim's death was more active; the government also argued that the defendants had an obligation to assist the victim once it became clear that his condition was worsening. The defendants were convicted of involuntary manslaughter. On appeal, the convictions were overturned. Is the result in *Konz* sound? Suppose the victim had been a child, and the parents refused to seek medical help on the ground that their religious convictions forbade doing so. Should the result change? Does your answer depend on your assumptions about the reasonableness of the relevant religious doctrine?

Commonwealth v. Carlson

Supreme Judicial Court of Massachusetts
849 N.E.2d 790 (2006)

GREANEY, Justice.

We transferred this case here on our own motion to consider the scope of criminal liability for the negligent operation of a motor vehicle that results, in the circumstances described below, in death. A jury . . . convicted the defendant on a complaint charging motor vehicle homicide by negligent operation.[1] The evidence at trial demonstrated that Carol Suprenant (victim) was hospitalized with chest and lung injuries suffered as a result of an accident caused by the defendant's negligent operation of an automobile and died of respiratory failure four days later after her doctors, at her request, removed her from a ventilator that allowed her to breathe and might have ensured her survival. The defendant appeals from her conviction, challenging (as she did at trial) the sufficiency of the evidence proving causation and claiming (for the first time on appeal) that the trial judge's instructions to the jury on the concept of superseding causes were inadequate. We affirm the conviction.

The jury could have found the following facts. On July 4, 2002, the victim and her husband, Robert Suprenant, left their home in Spencer to attend a cookout at their daughter's home. At about noon, the Suprenants were traveling south on Mechanic Street and had just entered the intersection of Mechanic and Chestnut Streets, when their automobile was struck on the passenger side by an automobile traveling east on Chestnut Street operated by the defendant. The force of impact pushed the Suprenants' automobile a distance of approximately fifteen to twenty feet, across the road, over a sidewalk, and into a chain link fence. Traffic entering the intersection from the defendant's direction was controlled by both a stop sign and blinking

---

1. The defendant was sentenced to twelve months in a house of correction, suspended for thirty-six months, and six months of electronically monitored house arrest, and her driver's license was revoked for ten years. Execution of her sentence was stayed pending appeal by a single justice of the Appeals Court.

red light. A jury could infer that the defendant had failed to stop (or yield the right of way) at the intersection and, thus, was negligent. The victim was transferred from the accident scene by emergency medical personnel to St. Vincent's Hospital at Worcester Medical Center.

As a result of the accident, the victim suffered multiple chest wall fractures, including fractures of the ribs and sternum and a lung contusion. The victim had suffered for several years prior to the accident from chronic obstructive pulmonary disease, a condition which makes it difficult to breathe and, thus, to supply oxygen to the bloodstream, and had required the use of an oxygen tank in her home to assist in her breathing.[2] The trauma to her chest compromised her ability to breathe as she had before the accident, to the point where she could no longer oxygenate her blood by normal breathing. That night in the intensive care unit, the victim was intubated and placed on a ventilator.[3] The next morning, the doctors removed the victim from the ventilator, and she was transferred from the intensive care unit to a medical floor in the hospital.

Over the next few days, the victim's breathing difficulties increased. Three doctors separately advised the victim of the need to reintubate her and place her again on a ventilator in order to assist her breathing. At first the victim, who had in the past repeatedly told her daughter-in-law . . . that she never wanted to be kept alive by a ventilator, refused permission for the doctors to do so. After speaking with family members and her doctors, however, the victim acquiesced and allowed herself to be reintubated, at least temporarily, in order to determine if her health would improve.

The next morning the victim's kidneys began to fail, and doctors advised the victim that her worsening condition would require dialysis. At this point, the victim stated that she no longer wished to be attached to a ventilator. Two doctors on the medical staff of the hospital met separately with the victim to discuss the nature of the circumstances facing her and the probable consequences of forgoing mechanical ventilation. The victim's personal physician also spoke with her at great length about her decision and encouraged her to remain on the breathing tube and ventilator to allow her situation time to improve. The victim understood (a jury could infer) that her death was probable if she did not allow intubation and that, conversely, her injuries were potentially survivable if she remained on the ventilator. The victim was

---

2. The victim's primary care physician testified at trial that the victim's condition would have gradually deteriorated over time and that the disease would have shortened her life. He opined that, based on the severity of her disease, the victim could have expected to enjoy only three to six more years of "good quality" life.

3. Intubation is a procedure where a hollow tube, one-half to three-quarters of an inch in circumference, is inserted into the mouth and approximately six to eight inches into the windpipe. The tube enables oxygen to be delivered directly into the lungs by means of a ventilator. A ventilator was described at trial as a "mechanical breathing machine" that pushes air into and out of the lungs by way of a pressure piston.

adamant that she did not want to be intubated. On July 8, she was taken off the ventilator and the intubation tube was removed. She died a few hours later from respiratory failure.

At trial one doctor testified that, if the accident had not happened, the victim probably would not have needed a ventilator and could have continued being on home oxygen in her usual fragile state of health, but that the chest injuries suffered in the accident "tipped the scales against her." He also opined that the victim's decision not to be intubated "likely played a role in her death." Another doctor stated his opinion "to a reasonable degree of medical certainty" that the victim would have survived her injuries if she had agreed to mechanical ventilatory support, and might even have returned to the state she was in before the accident, but conceded as well that the victim might have required "chronic and continuous ventilatory support." The victim's daughter-in-law assessed the situation as follows: "We all knew that it was a possibility that she might not make it, but [the doctors] couldn't give us a guarantee that she would make it without . . . hav[ing] to be on a [ventilator] for the rest of her life, and she didn't want to live like that, and we couldn't force her to do that." The victim's primary care physician testified, "I do think her mind was made up."

The judge denied the defendant's motions for the entry of a required finding of not guilty presented at the close of the Commonwealth's case and at the close of all the evidence. The defendant argues that the Commonwealth's proof was insufficient to sustain the conviction because no rational jury could have determined, beyond a reasonable doubt, that the victim's death from respiratory failure was proximately caused by the defendant's negligence.[4] The defendant asserts that the victim's death was a direct result of her independent decision not to undertake medical procedures that could be considered appropriate for a person in her condition and that would, in all probability, have allowed her to survive the accident. The defendant concedes that the victim had the right to make an informed decision to forgo life support, but argues that the victim's choice broke the chain of causation and relieved the defendant of criminal responsibility for the victim's death. We disagree.

. . . The standard of causation under Gen. Laws ch. 90, §24G, is the same as that employed in tort law. See Commonwealth v. Berggren, 398 Mass. 338, 340, 496 N.E.2d 660 (1986). Conduct is a proximate cause of death if the conduct, "by the natural and continuous sequence of events, causes the death

---

4. Conviction under Gen. Laws ch. 90, §24G(b), requires proof by the Commonwealth beyond a reasonable doubt that (1) the defendant operated a motor vehicle, (2) on a public way, (3) in a negligent manner to endanger lives and public safety, (4) thereby causing the death of another person. The focus at trial was on whether the defendant was negligent and whether her negligence caused the victim's death. Only the latter element is at issue in this appeal.

and without which the death would not have occurred." Commonwealth v. Rosado, 434 Mass. 197, 202, 747 N.E.2d 156 (2001). There is no question that the defendant's negligent failure to stop, or yield the right of way, at the intersection . . . set in motion a chain of events that resulted in the victim's death. The victim's injuries from the accident exacerbated serious preexisting health problems and required her to be intubated and placed on the ventilator. Her ultimate decision to be removed from life support was not an independent occurrence but the final step in the continuous sequence of events that began with the defendant's negligent operation of her automobile. "But for" the negligence, the accident would not have occurred, and the victim would not have been forced into the position of having to make what was, in retrospect, a true life-or-death decision.

The general rule is that intervening conduct of a third party will relieve a defendant of culpability for antecedent negligence only if such an intervening response was not reasonably foreseeable. "This is just another way of saying that an intervening act of a third party that was not reasonably foreseeable in the circumstances would prevent the victim's death from following naturally and continuously from the defendant's conduct." Commonwealth v. Askew, 404 Mass. 532, 534, 536 N.W.2d 341 (1989). Whether an intervening act was reasonably foreseeable and, thus, followed naturally from the defendant's conduct, or unforeseeable and, thus, broke the chain of causation . . . is a question of fact for the jury to decide based on an assessment of the circumstances. See Restatement (Second) of Torts §453 comment b (1965) (if either facts or reasonable foreseeability of intervening act are subject to reasonable difference of opinion, question of proximate cause must go to jury).

Here, the victim's choice was between invasive life support that might have assured her survival, but could also have led to a life of ventilator dependence (and, we may assume, continued pain and suffering), or acceptance of "comfort measures" only. The record shows that the victim was intelligent and coherent at all times. She had an absolute right to make the decision that she did. Modern medicine can sometimes prolong or sustain life by way of invasive procedures, but it is common knowledge that some patients will refuse to consent to such procedures. The jury were warranted in determining, in the circumstances of this case, that the victim's decision to forgo invasive life support was reasonably foreseeable.[6]

6. The defendant's attempt to assign blame to the victim for her own death, because she "made the deliberate choice to . . . engage in irrational and self-destructive behavior" is not persuasive. There is no contributory negligence in the law of motor vehicle homicide. See Commonwealth v. Campbell, 394 Mass. 77, 87, 474 N.E.2d 1062 (1985), and cases cited. We also reject the defendant's attempt to apply the tort doctrine of "avoidable consequences" to this criminal matter.

The defendant poses the question: "In the realm of crimes of negligence, should the tort concept of 'you take your victim as you find him' apply . . . even though, by pure chance and coincidence, it has the effect of turning an act of simple negligence into a serious crime?" The answer to this question is "yes."

Through the enactment of Gen. Laws ch. 90, §24G(b), the Legislature has decided . . . to deter acts of reckless driving by making the killing of another human being by means of negligent operation of a motor vehicle an offense punishable by up to two and one-half years' imprisonment and a $3,000 fine. Prior to the statute's enactment, prosecutors presented with facts like those before us had to choose between prosecution of a misdemeanor, such as driving so as to endanger, Gen. Laws ch. 90, §24(2)(a), or of the far more serious crime of involuntary manslaughter, Gen. Laws ch. 265, §13, which carries a maximum penalty of twenty years' imprisonment. We have concluded that the Legislature intended the statute "to provide a middle ground between the felony of manslaughter and the misdemeanor of driving so as to endanger." Commonwealth v. Jones, 382 Mass. 387, 390-91, 416 N.E.2d 502 (1981). A finding of ordinary negligence is sufficient to establish a violation of the statute. See id. at 389, and cases cited. The defendant's insistence that this standard is not fair, or leaves "nothing to soften the blow," is irrelevant.

The defendant's suggestion that she should not be held accountable for the victim's death, because the same injuries would have been minor if inflicted on a healthy young person, has no merit. Our long-standing rule in Massachusetts, in criminal law as well as in tort, is that "the wrongdoer takes the victim as he or she finds him." Commonwealth v. Tevlin, 433 Mass. 305, 313, 741 N.E.2d 827 (2001). See Commonwealth v. Fox, 73 Mass. 585, 7 Gray 585, 58687 (1856) (if the act hastened the death, then the death was caused by the act).

We now consider the defendant's argument that the judge's instructions to the jury on causation were so inadequate and confusing as to require a new trial. The defendant asserted no challenge to the judge's instructions at trial. She is entitled to relief only if she demonstrates error in the instructions that created a substantial risk of a miscarriage of justice, namely, "a substantial danger that the jury was misled by [an] erroneous instruction, and that the instruction may have materially influenced their appraisal of the [evidence]." Commonwealth v. Freeman, 352 Mass. 556, 564, 227 N.E.2d 3 (1967). There was no error.

The judge properly charged the jury on the elements of negligent motor vehicle homicide. He advised the jury that there may be more than one cause of a person's death, but that the Commonwealth is required to prove beyond a reasonable doubt that the defendant "directly and substantially set in motion a chain of events that produced the death in a natural and continuous sequence," and that the death would not have occurred without the defendant's actions. This is a correct statement of the law.

The judge instructed the jury on the law of intervening events and superseding causes, as set forth in the margin,[8] in accordance with what has been said in this opinion. The judge emphasized that the jury must acquit the defendant "if the death would not have occurred without the intervention of another person or event, and a reasonable person in the same circumstances would not have foreseen the likely possibility of such a result." There was no possibility that the jury did not understand that they must find beyond a reasonable doubt that the defendant's negligence directly set in motion a continuous chain of events that produced the death, and that they must acquit the defendant if the death would not have occurred without the intervention of some other person or event that was not reasonably foreseeable. The judge's instructions focused the jury's attention on the issue of causation and correctly left the issue of foreseeability to the jury.

The order staying the defendant's sentence on her conviction of homicide by negligent operation of a motor vehicle is vacated. The judgment of conviction is affirmed.

Notes and Questions

1. Is the result in *Carlson* (including the sentence, see footnote 1) just? If you were the prosecutor responsible for the case, what charge would you have filed? If you were free to choose what sentence to suggest to the court, what sentence would you recommend?

2. *Carlson* accurately describes the conventional law of causation in homicide cases. Note in particular the statement that in criminal law, as in tort, defendants take their victims as they find them: the familiar "eggshell skull" doctrine. Is the doctrine sensible? Perhaps so, when the question is who should pay for the victim's medical expenses—it's better for injurers to pay the extra doctors' bills than for their victims to have to do so. *Carlson*, however, presents a different question: whether a criminal defendant should be punished for negligent *driving* or for negligent *homicide*. Should the victim's medical condition matter when answering *that* question? What about the victim's decision to forgo life-saving medical treatment?

3. At some points in the court's opinion, Justice Greaney suggests that either the defendant or the victim should be blamed for the victim's death. But those are not the only options. People often die without legal fault on

8. "If the defendant's actions would not have brought about the death all by themselves without the intervention of some other person or event, the defendant is still held responsible as the cause of death if two conditions are met. First, the defendant's actions directly and substantially set in motion a natural, continuous sequence of events to cause the death. And second, a reasonable person in the defendant's position would have foreseen that her actions could easily result in serious injury or death to someone like the victim."

anyone's part. There is no inconsistency between holding that the victim has an unqualified right to decline to be intubated again, and holding that the defendant is not criminally liable for the consequences of the victim's decision. The real question ought to be whether, in these circumstances, it is fair to punish this defendant for killing this victim. Should the answer to that question turn on causation? On intent? Something else?

4. Philosophers have a phrase for causal scenarios like the one in *Carlson*: "moral luck." As to Carlson, Carol Suprenant's medical condition was a piece of bad fortune—the wrong person in the wrong place at the wrong time. Carlson's bad luck (or perhaps Suprenant's bad luck) says nothing about the degree of her indifference toward the interests of others. It follows, defendants like Carlson routinely argue, that she should be punished no more than would a luckier defendant who behaved similarly but caused no serious harm. How powerful does that argument seem?

Consider the concept of moral luck and the criminal law of drunk driving. The large majority of intoxicated drivers cause no harm to anyone; a smaller but substantial number cause injury only to themselves and their automobiles. But *some* drunk drivers cause enormous harm to others: Roughly 10,000 people die each year in accidents caused by intoxicated drivers. How should the law treat drunk drivers who kill?

There are three possible ways to separate drunk driving cases that deserve more severe punishment from cases that deserve less. First, one might decide based on how intoxicated the defendant was. Second, one might examine the defendant's driving and determine how incompetently or dangerously the defendant handled his or her vehicle. Third, one might look to the harm the defendant actually caused, and punish those who cause death or serious injury more severely than those whose misconduct does not produce such tragic results. In practice, American criminal law uses the first method when no one is killed or seriously injured, and the third method when the drunk driver causes death or serious injury. Is that the fairest way to punish drunk drivers? Might it be the most effective way to deter drunk driving?

5. The defendants in United States v. Martinez, 16 F.3d 202 (7th Cir. 1994), were charged with having bombed several pornographic bookstores; one of the conspirators accidentally killed himself in the course of setting off one of the bombs. Judge Posner had this to say about moral luck and criminal responsibility:

> . . . It is true that in a system of morality in which only intentions and behaviors, but not consequences, count, there is no moral distinction between dangerous conduct that causes harm and otherwise identical dangerous conduct that does not. The only difference is luck, not usually considered a moral attribute. But "moral luck," as philosophers refer to distinctions in culpability that are based on consequences rather than intentions, is, rightly or wrongly, a pervasive characteristic of moral thought in our society, at least the moral

thought that informs the criminal law. Two people drive at the same unlawful speed under identical road conditions. One hits a child; one hits no one. The first is guilty of involuntary manslaughter; the second of a violation of the highway code. The only difference between their conduct is the consequence. The difference, though fortuitous, counts for the severity of the punishment deemed appropriate for the defendants' behavior.

So there is no anomaly in the fact that the appellants in this case received heavier punishments "merely" because of the accident that Mares blew himself up with one of his bombs. The greater anomaly would be if his death had not affected their punishment in the slightest. Not everyone would agree. Hamlet thought it poetic justice that a bomber should be blown up by his own bomb—hoist by his own petard ("petard" means bomb).

Id. at 205-06. Posner went on to explain that federal law did not take Hamlet's position.

In the scene from *Hamlet* to which Judge Posner refers, the Prince of Denmark is traveling to England with his friends Rosencrantz and Guildenstern, who carry a letter from Denmark's King Claudius to the English king. The letter is a warrant for Hamlet's execution. Hamlet discovers the plot and alters the letter so it permits his friends' execution, not his:

> There's letters seal'd, and my two schoolfellows,
> Whom I will trust as I will adders fang'd—
> They bear the mandate, they must sweep my way
> And marshal me to knavery. Let it work;
> For 'tis the sport to have the engineer
> Hoist with his own petard, an't shall go hard
> But I will delve one yard below their mines
> And blow them at the moon.

William Shakespeare, *Hamlet*, Act III, scene iv. Should those who make and plant bombs be punished as severely when the bombs fail as when they kill? Should punishment be as severe when the bombs kill one of the bombers as when they kill their intended victims? Is moral luck moral? Is it lucky?

6. The defendant in Baraka v. Commonwealth, 194 S.W.3d 313 (Ky. 2006), sought to suppress the testimony of the government's expert medical witness, who would have testified that the victim died of "homicide by heart attack." The trial court denied the motion to suppress. On appeal, Justice Cooper noted that the medical expert's conclusion had a good deal of supporting precedent:

> Virtually every jurisdiction that has considered the issue has held that a homicide conviction can be predicated upon death by heart attack caused by stress resulting from actions of the defendant provided the prosecution proves both cause and effect. E.g., People v. Stamp, 82 Cal. Rptr. 598, 602-03 (Cal. Dist. Ct. App. 1969) (conviction of felony murder affirmed where pathologist testified that severe stress experienced during robbery by defendant caused

victim's fatal heart attack); State v. Spates, 405 A.2d 656, 658-60 (Conn. 1978) (conviction of manslaughter affirmed where medical testimony established that cause of death was heart attack brought on by emotional stress occurring during robbery); Maynard v. State, 660 So. 2d 293, 296 (Fla. Dist. Ct. App. 1995) (conviction of manslaughter upheld where defendant's physical assault of victim produced no discernible physical injuries but victim died of heart attack, and medical examiner testified that the altercation caused the fatal heart attack); Cromartie v. State, 620 S.E.2d 413, 416 (Ga. Ct. App. 2005) (conviction of vehicular homicide affirmed where intoxicated driver struck pedestrian who died of heart attack, and medical examiner testified that collision "directly and materially contributed" to pedestrian's death); Thomas v. State, 436 N.E.2d 1109, 1112 (Ind. 1982) (conviction of murder affirmed where pathologist testified hypothetically that stress resulting from being robbed by the defendant would have been the primary cause of death); State v. Vaughn, 707 S.W.2d 422, 426 (Mo. Ct. App. 1986) (conviction of second-degree murder upheld where medical examiner testified that victim's cardiac arrest resulted from stress induced by defendant's assault); State v. Dixon, 387 N.W.2d 682, 689 (Neb. 1986) (conviction of felony murder upheld where pathologist testified that cause of cardiac arrhythmia was shock experienced during burglary of victim's home by defendant); In re Anthony M., 471 N.E.2d 447, 450, 452 (N.Y. 1984) (two cases) (juvenile adjudication of manslaughter in the second degree upheld where defendant snatched purse of elderly woman who fell and broke her hip and subsequently died of heart attack . . .); id. at 451-52 (felony murder conviction upheld where victim of burglary and robbery died next day of myocardial infarction and forensic pathologist testified it was reasonably certain "that the emotional and physical trauma of the burglary caused [the victim's] heart attack"); State v. Atkinson, 259 S.E.2d 858, 864 (N.C. 1979) (conviction of felony murder upheld where medical examiner testified that victim died of heart attack and that injuries and stress caused by defendant's assault of victim contributed to and accelerated victim's death), overruled on other grounds by State v. Jackson, 273 S.E.2d 666 (N.C. 1981): cf. Commonwealth v. Evans, 343 Pa. Super. 118, 494 A.2d 383, 389-90 (Pa. Super. Ct. 1985) (counsel was not ineffective in failing to assert insufficiency of evidence to sustain conviction of felony murder where forensic pathologist had testified that stress caused by defendant's robbery and kidnapping of victim aggravated victim's arteriosclerotic heart disease, resulting in his death).

Id. at 316-17 (Cooper, J., concurring). Consider the facts in *Baraka*:

Appellant allegedly engaged in a vocal and physical altercation with her father, following which her father died. Dr. Rolf was the medical examiner who performed the postmortem examination. . . . Dr. Rolf testified that her postmortem examination revealed that the decedent was thin and frail and had suffered from coronary artery disease and pulmonary emphysema. She also found abrasions and contusions on his body which were not in themselves life-threatening. She concluded that the cause of the decedent's death was a heart attack. . . .

Id. at 316 (Cooper, J., concurring). Notice the non-life-threatening abrasions and contusions; notice, too, that violent felonies triggered the heart attacks in the cases Justice Cooper cited. Does that make you think differently about criminal liability for death by heart attack? When is such liability appropriate?

Baraka is not the only close-to-the-line causation opinion Justice Cooper has written. Consider the next case.

Robertson v. Commonwealth

Supreme Court of Kentucky
82 S.W.3d 832 (2002)

Justice COOPER delivered the opinion of the Court.

Michael Partin, a police officer employed by the city of Covington, Kentucky, was killed when he fell through an opening between the roadway and the walkway of the Clay Wade Bailey Bridge and into the Ohio River while in foot pursuit of Appellant Shawnta Robertson. Following a trial by jury in the Kenton Circuit Court, Appellant was convicted of manslaughter in the second degree for wantonly causing Partin's death, Ky. Rev. Stat. §507.040(1), and was sentenced to imprisonment for six years. The Court of Appeals affirmed, and we granted discretionary review to further consider the circumstances under which criminal liability can be imposed upon a defendant for injuries or death directly caused by the volitional act of another.

At about 2:00 A.M. on January 4, 1998, Officer Brian Kane of the Kenton County Police Department attempted to arrest Appellant in Covington for possession of marijuana. Appellant broke free of Kane's grasp and began running north on Fourth Street toward the Clay Wade Bailey Bridge which spans the Ohio River between Covington and Cincinnati, Ohio. Kane radioed for assistance and pursued Appellant on foot "at a sprint." When Appellant reached the bridge, he vaulted over the concrete barrier between the roadway and the walkway and began running north on the walkway toward Cincinnati. Kane, who, at that point, was running on top of the concrete barrier jumped down to the walkway and continued his pursuit.

Meanwhile, Partin and two other Covington police officers, Steve Sweeney and Cody Stanley, responded to Kane's request for assistance and arrived at the bridge almost simultaneously in three separate vehicles. . . . Partin's vehicle was the first of the three police cruisers to reach the bridge. He stopped in the right northbound lane just beyond where Appellant was running on the walkway. Stanley stopped his vehicle directly behind Partin's vehicle, and Sweeney stopped in the left northbound lane, also behind Partin's vehicle. Sweeney and Stanley testified that they . . . saw Partin exit his vehicle, proceed to the concrete barrier, place his left hand on the barrier, then vault over the barrier "as if he had done it a million times before," and disappear. The concrete barrier was thirty-two inches high. The railing of the walkway was forty-three inches high. There was a forty-one-inch-wide open space between the concrete barrier and the walkway railing. Partin fell through the open space into the river ninety-four feet below. His body was recovered four months later.

No one will ever know why Partin fell through the opening between the concrete barrier and the pedestrian walkway. Perhaps, he did not realize the opening was there. Perhaps, he knew it was there and miscalculated his vault. Either way, . . . his death resulted from his own volitional act and not from any force employed against him by Appellant. Whether Appellant's act of resisting arrest by unlawful flight from apprehension was a legal cause of Partin's death requires application of the provisions of Ky. Rev. Stat. §§501.020(3) (definition of "wantonly"), 501.020(4) (definition of "recklessly"), and 501.060 ("causal relationships").

Ky. Rev. Stat. §501.020(3) defines "wantonly" as follows:

A person acts wantonly with respect to a result or to a circumstance described by a statute defining an offense when he is aware of and consciously disregards a substantial and unjustifiable risk that the result will occur or that the circumstance exists. The risk must be of such nature and degree that disregard thereof constitutes a gross deviation from the standard of conduct that a reasonable person would observe in the situation. . . .

Ky. Rev. Stat. §501.020(4) defines "recklessly" as follows:

A person acts recklessly with respect to a result or to a circumstance described by a statute defining an offense when he fails to perceive a substantial and unjustifiable risk that the result will occur or that the circumstance exists. The risk must be of such nature and degree that the failure to perceive it constitutes a gross deviation from the standard of care that a reasonable person would observe in the situation.

Thus, wantonness is the awareness of and conscious disregard of a risk that a reasonable person in the same situation would not have disregarded, and recklessness is the failure to perceive a risk that a reasonable person in the same situation would have perceived.

Ky. Rev. Stat. §501.060 provides in pertinent part:

> (1) Conduct is the cause of a result when it is an antecedent without which the result in question would not have occurred. . . .
> (3) When wantonly or recklessly causing a particular result is an element of the offense, the element is not established if the actual result is not within the risk of which the actor is aware or, in the case of recklessness, of which he should be aware unless:
>> (a) The actual result differs from the probable result only in the respect that a different person or different property is injured or affected or that the probable injury or harm would have been more serious or more extensive than that caused; or

(b) The actual result involves the same kind of injury or harm as the probable result and occurs in a manner which the actor knows or should know is rendered substantially more probable by his conduct.

(4) The question of whether an actor knew or should have known the result he caused was rendered substantially more probable by his conduct is an issue of fact.

Obviously, Appellant's unlawful act of resisting arrest by fleeing from apprehension was a "but for" cause of Partin's fatal attempt to pursue him by vaulting from the roadway of the bridge to the walkway. As noted by the 1974 Commentary to Ky. Rev. Stat. §501.060, the issue then becomes primarily one of *mens rea.*

> Once an act is found to be a cause in fact of a result and a substantial factor in bringing about that result, it is recognized as the proximate cause unless another cause, independent of the first, intervenes between the first and the result. And even then the first cause is treated as the proximate cause if the harm or injury resulting from the second is deemed to have been reasonably foreseeable by the first actor.

Thus, the fact that Partin vaulted over the concrete barrier of his own volition does not exonerate Appellant if Partin's act was either foreseen or foreseeable by Appellant as a reasonably probable result of his own unlawful act of resisting arrest by fleeing from apprehension. . . .

In Phillips v. Commonwealth, 17 S.W.3d 870 (Ky. 2000), we [upheld] the wanton murder conviction of a defendant who fired shots at an intended victim from inside a vehicle and thereby induced the intended victim to return fire and kill a passenger in the defendant's vehicle. We held that it was reasonably foreseeable that, if shots were fired at another person from inside a vehicle, the other person would return fire in the direction of the vehicle, thus endangering the lives of its other occupants. 17 S.W.3d at 875. Also illustrative is the pre-code case of Sanders v. Commonwealth, 50 S.W.2d 37 (Ky. 1932), which upheld the manslaughter conviction of a defendant who had threatened his wife with a deadly weapon while they were in a moving vehicle, causing her to jump from the vehicle to her death—clearly a volitional act by the victim but a probable and reasonably foreseeable consequence of the unlawful act of the defendant.

In both *Phillips* and *Sanders,* a defendant applied unlawful force against another whose volitional response to that force caused the victim's death. The case sub judice is conceptually more similar to Lofthouse v. Commonwealth, 13 S.W.3d 236 (Ky. 2000), which reversed the reckless homicide conviction of a defendant who applied no force against the victim but supplied cocaine and heroin to the victim whose self-ingestion of those drugs caused his death. The result reached by the plurality opinion in *Lofthouse* did not turn on the fact that the victim died as a result of his own volitional act. Rather, in reversing the conviction, the opinion emphasized the absence of any evidence that the defendant knew or should have known that ingestion of those drugs under those circumstances would probably cause the victim's death. Id. at 241. Here, as in *Lofthouse*, Appellant's *mens rea*, i.e., what he knew or should have known with respect to the probable consequences of his conduct, is crucial to determining the issue of his criminal liability.

Analogous to this set of facts is the case where a person pursued by the police in a high speed motor vehicle chase is held criminally liable for the death of an innocent bystander accidentally struck by a pursuing police vehicle. E.g., People v. Schmies, 51 Cal. Rptr. 2d 185 (Cal. Ct. App. 1996). In *Schmies*, the California Court of Appeal directly addressed the effect of the police officers' conduct vis-à-vis the criminal liability of the defendant.

> The negligence or other fault of the officers is not a defense to the charge against defendant. The fact that the officers may have shared responsibility or fault for the accident does nothing to exonerate defendant for his role. In short, whether the officers' conduct could be described with such labels as negligent, careless, tortious, cause for discipline, or even criminal, in an action against them, is not at issue with respect to the defendant here. . . .
>
> The issue with respect to defendant focuses upon his point of view, that is, whether the harm that occurred was a reasonably foreseeable consequence of his conduct at the time he acted. Since the officers' conduct was a direct and specific response to defendant's conduct, the claim that their conduct was a superseding cause of the accident can be supported only through a showing that their conduct was so unusual, abnormal, or extraordinary that it could not have been foreseen.

51 Cal. Rptr. 2d at 193-94. Although California does not have a statutory equivalent of Ky. Rev. Stat. §501.060, this common law analysis of causation is consistent with the principles embodied in our statute. . . . The fault or negligence of the officer is not determinative of the defendant's guilt. However, the reasonableness of the officer's response is relevant in determining whether the response was foreseeable by the defendant. The more reasonable the response, the more likely that the defendant should have foreseen it. It is immaterial that the ultimate victim was the officer, himself, as opposed to an innocent bystander. Here, the conduct that supports Appellant's conviction is not, as the Commonwealth suggests, his own act of vaulting over the concrete barrier. Partin was not present when that act occurred; thus, it was not reasonably foreseeable that he would have vaulted over the barrier in reliance on the fact that Appellant had done so without incident. (That analysis might have been appropriate if Officer Kane had fallen from the bridge when he followed Appellant onto the walkway.) The conduct that supports Appellant's conviction is the continuation of his unlawful flight when he obviously knew that Partin intended to pursue him . . . and that, to do so, Partin would be required to cross the open space between the roadway and the walkway and thereby risk falling to his death.

"The question of whether [Appellant] knew or should have known [that Partin's death] was rendered substantially more probable by his conduct is an issue of fact." Ky. Rev. Stat. §501.060(4). There was sufficient evidence in this case to present that fact to a jury. . . .

Accordingly, the judgment of conviction and the sentence imposed by the Kenton Circuit Court are affirmed.

Justice GRAVES, concurring.

. . . The act of vaulting the gap between the roadway and the sidewalk is sufficiently wanton to support the jury's verdict in this case. Appellant was aware of the danger of the gap and consciously disregarded it when he jumped. Knowing he was being pursued by at least one officer on foot, Appellant had to assume any pursuing officer would attempt to follow him, also becoming susceptible to the risk. A gap of nearly 4 feet across a drop of 94 feet into moving water cannot be described as anything but a substantial [and] unjustifiable risk. It is certainly logical for the jury to conclude that, when Appellant disregarded this risk to which he was subjecting those lawfully pursuing him, he grossly deviated from the standard of conduct that a reasonable person would observe.

[The dissenting opinion of Justice KELLER, joined by Chief Justice LAMBERT and Justice STUMBO, is omitted.]

Notes on the Relationship Between Causation and Mens Rea

1. In *Carlson*, the defendant's *mens rea* appears not to affect causation analysis. In *Robertson*, the court holds that *mens rea* is the key to causation analysis. What explains the inconsistency?

2. Perhaps the intent that matters in *Robertson* is the victim's. Consider: The central issue, as the court defines it, is whether Officer Partin's death was foreseeable, given the defendant's decision to flee across the bridge. Foreseeability, in turn, would seem to depend on just how foolish Partin was to try to jump over the gap. If the victim's decision was seriously foolish—say, because it posed a large risk of death in order to apprehend an offender for a minor crime—then it would appear to be unforeseeable: How could Robertson have known whether Partin would behave foolishly?

Is that analysis right? If it is, then why should the victim's negligence govern the defendant's criminal liability? Does that seem like inappropriate victim-blaming?

3. Compare *Robertson* with People v. Cervantes, 26 Cal. 4th 860, 29 P.3d 225 (2001). The facts in *Cervantes* are as follows:

Shortly after midnight on October 30, 1994, defendant and fellow Highland Street gang members went to a birthday party in Santa Ana thrown by the Alley Boys gang for one of their members. Joseph Perez, the prosecution's gang expert, testified the Highland Street and Alley Boys gangs were not enemies at the time. Over 100 people were in attendance at the party, many of them gang members.

Outside of the house, defendant approached a woman he knew named Grace. She was heavily intoxicated and declined defendant's invitation to go to another party with him, which prompted him to call her a "ho," leading, in turn, to an exchange of crude insults. Juan Cisneros, a member of the Alley Boys, approached and told defendant not to "disrespect" his "homegirl." Richard Linares, also an Alley Boy, tried to defuse the situation, but Cisneros drew a gun and threatened to "cap [defendant's] ass." Defendant responded by brandishing a handgun of his own, which prompted Linares to intervene once again, pushing or touching defendant on the shoulder in an effort to separate him from Cisneros. In response, defendant stated "nobody touches me" and shot Linares through the arm and chest.

A crowd of some 50 people was watching these events unfold. Someone yelled, "Why did you shoot my home boy?" or "your home boy shot your own homeboy," to which someone responded "Highland [Street] is the one that shot." A melee erupted, and gang challenges were exchanged.

A short time later a group of Alley Boys spotted Hector Cabrera entering his car and driving away.[2] Recognizing him as a member of the Highland Street gang, they fired a volley of shots, killing him. A variety of shell casings recovered from the street evidenced that at least five different shooters had participated in the murder of Cabrera.

Perez testified that although the Highland Street and Alley Boys gangs were not enemies at the time of the shootings, both gangs would be expected to be armed. He opined that the Alley Boys would consider defendant's conduct in shooting Linares to be an act of "major disrespect" to their gang. To avenge the shooting, they would be expected to respond quickly with equal or greater force against defendant or another member of his gang. Therefore, Perez opined, Cabrera's death was a reasonably foreseeable consequence of defendant's actions.

Defendant testified he did not intend to shoot Linares, but was simply trying to protect himself from Cisneros, who drew his weapon first. He was surprised when his gun went off, because he did not feel it fire or see any flash. He testified, "I don't know if I shot [Linares] or somebody else shot [him], but what I do know is that if I [had] attempted to murder anybody, I would have shot [him] while he was on the floor." In the confusion following the shooting of Linares, defendant heard someone say, "[Y]our home boy shot your own home boy," and then he heard someone say "Highland's the one that shot." Realizing he was in danger, defendant ran from the party and sped off with several others. He heard shots being fired as they drove away. He was stopped by police and arrested a short distance away.

Defendant was charged with murdering Cabrera. The relevant instructions informed the jury that murder is unlawful homicide with malice aforethought, that malice could be implied from the deliberate doing of a dangerous act with indifference to human life, and that the doing of a provocative act that resulted in death could be such an act.

---

2. The witnesses' time estimates varied from several seconds to a minute or two.

The court held that "provocative act" causation did not extend so far:

> The provocative act murder doctrine has traditionally been invoked in cases in which the perpetrator of the underlying crime instigates a gun battle, either by firing first or by otherwise engaging in severe, life-threatening, and usually gun-wielding conduct, and the police, or a victim of the underlying crime, responds with privileged lethal force by shooting back and killing the perpetrator's accomplice or an innocent bystander. . . .
>
> Turning to the facts at hand, we agree with defendant that the evidence introduced below is insufficient as a matter of law to support his conviction of provocative act murder, for it fails to establish the essential element of proximate causation. The facts of this case are distinguishable from the classic provocative act murder case in a number of respects. Defendant was not the initial aggressor in the incident that gave rise to the provocative act. There was no direct evidence that Cabrera's unidentified murderers were even present at the scene of the provocative act, i.e., in a position to actually witness defendant shoot Linares. Defendant himself was not present at the scene where Cabrera was fatally gunned down; the only evidence introduced on the point suggests he was already running away from the party or speeding off in his car when the victim was murdered.
>
> But the critical fact that distinguishes this case from other provocative act murder cases is that here the actual murderers were not responding to defendant's provocative act by shooting back at him or an accomplice, in the course of which someone was killed. . . .
>
> To the contrary, the acts of the actual murderers here were themselves criminal, felonious, and perpetrated with malice aforethought. The fatal shots were fired, not at the defendant or an accomplice, but instead at a third party (Cabrera) who was not a party to the initial provocative act. It can further be said that the murderers of Cabrera "intend[ed] to exploit the situation created by [defendant], but [were] not acting in concert with him," a circumstance that is "normally held to relieve the first actor [defendant] of criminal responsibility." Hart & Honore, Causation in the Law 326 (2d ed. 1985). In short, nobody forced the Alley Boys' murderous response in this case, if indeed it was a direct response to defendant's act of shooting Linares. The willful and malicious murder of Cabrera at the hands of others was an independent intervening act on which defendant's liability for the murder could not be based.
>
> The circumstance that the murder occurred a very short time after defendant shot Linares, and the opinion of prosecution gang expert Perez that Cabrera's murder was a foreseeable consequence of defendant's shooting of Linares in the context of a street gang's code of honor mentality, was essentially the only evidence on which the jury was asked to find that Cabrera's murder was "a direct, natural, and probable consequence" of defendant's act of shooting Linares. Given that the murder of Cabrera by other parties was itself felonious, intentional, perpetrated with malice aforethought, and directed at a victim who was not involved in the original altercation between defendant and Linares, the evidence is insufficient as a matter of law to establish the requisite proximate causation to hold defendant liable for murder.

Cervantes and *Robertson* seem to be in some tension. Robertson's intent was to flee, not to kill anyone. Cervantes shot a gang rival; he may not have intended the ultimate victim's death, but he certainly intended to harm *someone*. Yet the defendant with the less culpable intent gets convicted, while the one who fired a gun is not. Are those results fair? Are they wise?

2. Inchoate Crimes and Accomplice Liability

The causation cases excerpted above raise the question whether the government has proved enough conduct, and the right sort of conduct, to justify punishment for homicide. Another class of cases raises that question: cases in which defendants are charged with attempted murder, conspiracy to commit murder, solicitation of murder, or aiding and abetting one or another form of criminal homicide.

In this section, we take a second look at inchoate crimes and complicity, doctrines that we encountered initially back in Chapter 7. In *Decker*, the defendant hired a hit man to kill his sister; fortunately for the sister, the hit man was a police officer working undercover. Over a strong dissent, the California Supreme Court found that the defendant had done enough—barely—to justify liability for attempted murder. In *Clark*, the defendant and a political associate, both would-be members of the Black Panther Party, allegedly conspired to murder a white police officer 35 years before charges were filed. Over another strong dissent, the Minnesota Supreme Court found that the evidence supported both the conspiracy charge and a separate charge of aiding and abetting the officer's murder. As you read these two cases, consider whether the conduct the government proved should have triggered the punishments the defendants received.

People v. Superior Court of Los Angeles County (*Decker*)

Supreme Court of California
41 Cal. 4th 1; 157 P.3d 1017 (2007)

Opinion by BAXTER, J.

Defendant and real party in interest Ronald Decker has been charged with the attempted willful, deliberate, and premeditated murder of his sister, Donna Decker, and her friend, Hermine Riley Bafiera. According to the evidence offered at the preliminary hearing, Decker did not want to kill these women himself—as he explained, "he would be the prime suspect" and "would probably make a mistake somehow or another"—so he sought the services of a hired assassin.

Decker located such a person (or thought he did). He furnished the hired assassin with a description of his sister, her home, her car, and her workplace, as well as specific information concerning her daily habits. He also advised the assassin to kill Hermine if necessary to avoid leaving a witness behind. Decker and the hired assassin agreed on the means to commit the murder, the method of payment, and the price. The parties also agreed that Decker would pay $5,000 in cash as a down payment. Before Decker handed over the money, the assassin asked whether Decker was "sure" he wanted to go through with the murders. Decker replied, "I am absolutely, positively, 100 percent sure, that I want to go through with it. I've never been so sure of anything in my entire life." All of these conversations were recorded and videotaped because, unknown to Decker, he was talking with an undercover police detective posing as a hired assassin.

Decker does not dispute that the foregoing evidence was sufficient to hold him to answer to the charge of solicitation of the murder of Donna and Hermine but argues that this evidence was insufficient to support a charge of their attempted murder. The magistrate and the trial court, believing themselves bound by People v. Adami, 36 Cal. App. 3d 452, 111 Cal. Rptr. 544 (1973), reluctantly agreed with Decker and dismissed the attempted murder charges. The Court of Appeal disagreed with *Adami* and issued a writ of mandate directing the respondent court to reinstate the dismissed counts. We granted review to address the conflict and now affirm.

BACKGROUND

Ronald Decker was charged by felony complaint with the attempted willful, deliberate, and premeditated murder of his sister, Donna Decker, and her friend, Hermine Riley Bafiera; the solicitation of Detective Wayne Holston to commit these murders; and the solicitation of Russell Wafer to murder Donna Decker. The undisputed evidence presented at the preliminary hearing revealed the following:

On August 20, 2003, Ronald Decker (identifying himself only as "Ron") placed a telephone call to Russell Wafer, a gunsmith at Lock, Stock and Barrel in Temple City (Los Angeles County). Decker said he was looking for someone to do some "work" for him and arranged to meet privately with Wafer the following week. During that meeting, Decker explained that he had been in contact with Soldier of Fortune Magazine, had done some research, and came up with Wafer's name as a possible "contractor" for a local "job" — "basically it was that he wanted someone taken care of." Decker added that he could not kill the victim himself because he would be a prime suspect. Wafer advised that while he could not handle the job, his friend "John" from Detroit might be interested. After Decker offered to pay the killer $35,000 and an additional $3,000 to Wafer as a finder's fee, Wafer said he would try to contact John. He instructed Decker to call him back the following week.

. . . Wafer instead called the Los Angeles County Sheriff's Department, spoke to Detective Wayne Holston, and agreed to assist in a sting operation. When Decker called Wafer on September 2, Wafer claimed he had been in contact with "John," who was coming to town shortly. . . . At Holston's request, Wafer arranged a meeting with Decker for the evening of September 5 at a golf course parking lot in Arcadia. Holston accompanied Wafer to the meeting and was introduced as "John" from Detroit. . . . [T]he encounter was both videotaped and recorded.

After Wafer left the two men alone, Decker explained that a "lady" owed him a lot of money and that the only way for him to get it back was "to take her out." Decker subsequently identified the target as his sister, Donna Decker, and provided descriptions of her person, her mode of dress, her residence, her office, her car, and her daily habits. Decker offered Holston $25,000 to perform the execution, with a $10,000 bonus if it were a "nice, neat, clean job." Decker reiterated that he could not do it himself, as "he would be the prime suspect," and might "slip up" somewhere. . . . When Holston then proposed killing Donna during a staged robbery or carjacking, Decker said that would be "great" and urged Holston to "shoot her in the heart and head both, just to make sure." Decker added that Donna spent a lot of time with her friend and coworker, Hermine Riley Bafiera, and that Holston might need to "take out" Hermine as well to avoid having a witness. . . .

When Holston said he could complete the job within a week, Decker replied, "Marvelous. . . . The sooner the better." Holston also asked for some money up front, and Decker said he could supply him with $5,000 in cash as a down payment in a couple of days "so you can start right away." . . .

Decker and Holston met again at the golf course on September 7. This meeting was also videotaped and recorded. Decker gave Holston $5,000 in cash, wrapped in two plastic bundles. He reiterated that Holston, after Donna had been murdered, should use a pay phone to leave him a voice-mail message — Holston was to say that "the paint job has been completed" — and that Holston would get the rest of the money about a month later. Decker also reiterated that "if Hermine is in the car, with her . . . [y]ou have to take her out too. . . . But don't charge me double."

Holston told Decker that he had already performed some intelligence work, that he was "convinced" he would see the victim the next day, and that he could get this "job" done quickly — eliciting another "marvelous" from Decker — and explained that "once I leave here, it's done. So, you sure you want to go through with it?" Decker replied, "I am absolutely, positively, 100 percent sure, that I want to go through with it. I've never been so sure of anything in my entire life. . . . [D]o it very fast . . . as fast as you can." At the end of the conversation, Decker seemed "very pleased" and thanked Holston and Wafer. A short time after Holston and Wafer drove off, Decker was arrested.

DISCUSSION

. . . Attempted murder requires the specific intent to kill and the commission of a direct but ineffectual act toward accomplishing the intended killing. Penal Code §21a. The uncontradicted evidence that Decker harbored the specific intent to kill his sister (and, if necessary, her friend Hermine) was overwhelming. Decker expressed to both Wafer and Holston his desire to have Donna killed. He researched [finding] a hired assassin. He spent months accumulating cash in small denominations to provide the hired assassin with a down payment and had also worked out a method by which to pay the balance. He knew the layout of his sister's condominium and how one might enter it surreptitiously. He had tested the level of surveillance in the vicinity of her home and determined it was "not really that sharp." He chronicled his sister's daily routine at both her home and her office. . . . And, at both meetings with Holston, he insisted that Hermine, if she were present, be killed as well, so as to prevent her from being a witness.

The controversy in this case, as the parties readily concede, is whether there was also a direct but ineffectual act toward accomplishing the intended killings. For an attempt, the overt act must go beyond mere preparation and show that the killer is putting his or her plan into action; it need not be the last proximate or ultimate step toward commission of the crime or crimes, nor need it satisfy any element of the crime. People v. Dillon, 34 Cal. 3d 441, 454, 668 P.2d 697 (1983). However, as we have explained, "[b]etween preparation for the attempt and the attempt itself, there is a wide difference. The preparation consists in devising or arranging the means or measures necessary for the commission of the offense; the attempt is the direct movement toward the commission after the preparations are made." People v. Murray, 14 Cal. 159 (1859).

. . . Although a definitive test has proved elusive, we have long recognized that "[w]henever the design of a person to commit crime is clearly shown, slight acts in furtherance of the design will constitute an attempt." People v. Anderson, 1 Cal. 2d 687, 690, 37 P.2d 67 (1934) (attempted robbery); see also People v. Memro, 38 Cal. 3d 658, 698, 700 P.2d 446 (1985) (attempted lewd conduct); People v. Dillon, supra, 34 Cal. 3d at 455 (attempted robbery); People v. Morales, 5 Cal. App. 4th 917, 926, 7 Cal. Rptr. 2d 358 (1992) (attempted murder). Viewing the entirety of Decker's conduct in light of his clearly expressed intent, we find sufficient evidence under the slight-acts rule to hold him to answer to the charges of attempted murder.

Decker's plan was to get rid of his sister so that he could recover money that she owed him. He was concerned, however, that he would be considered an obvious suspect in her murder, so he sought out someone else to carry out his plan. To that end, he conducted research into the underworld of professional killers, he budgeted to pay for those services, he evaluated how and where the murder should be done, he tested the level of security around his sister's condominium, and he considered the possibility that there might be a witness and what should be done in that event. Once he met Detective Holston, whom he believed was a professional assassin, they agreed Holston would kill Donna and (if necessary) her friend Hermine, they agreed on a price, and they agreed it would be done within the week.

Decker provided Holston with all of the necessary information concerning his sister, her home and office, and her habits and demeanor. He also gave Holston the agreed-on down payment of $5,000 cash. Before he did, Holston warned him, "I want you to know, once I leave here, it's done. So, you sure you want to go through with it?" Decker replied, "I am absolutely, positively, 100 percent sure, that I want to go through with it. I've never been so sure of anything in my entire life."

Accordingly, at the time Decker handed Holston the down payment on the murder, Decker's intention was clear. It was equally clear that he was "actually putting his plan into action." People v. Dillon, supra, 34 Cal. 3d at 453. . . . [Decker's conduct] would lead a reasonable person to "believe a crime is about to be consummated absent an intervening force"—and thus that "the attempt is underway." Id. at 455. . . . Although Decker did not himself point a gun at his sister, he did aim at her an armed professional who had agreed to commit the murder.

As contrary authority, Decker relies on *Adami*, supra, 36 Cal. App. 3d 452, which affirmed the dismissal of an attempted murder charge on similar facts, and relies also on the small number of out-of-state majority and minority opinions that have followed *Adami*. See Braham v. State, 571 P.2d 631, 651 (Alaska 1977) (Connor, J., concurring in part and dissenting in part); State v. Otto, 629 P.2d 646, 649 (Idaho 1981); see also State v. Disanto, 688 N.W.2d 201, 208-209 (S.D. 2004). In *Adami*, the defendant sought to have his wife killed because she had stolen money from him. He agreed on a price with an undercover police agent posing as an assassin and supplied the agent with a photograph of the victim, a description of the victim and her residence and vehicles, and other pertinent information. The defendant gave the police agent $500 as a down payment and announced he was not going to change his mind. *Adami*, supra, 36 Cal. App. 3d at 454-455. *Adami* declared that these acts "consisted solely of solicitation or mere preparation" and concluded, in accordance with the "weight of authority," that "solicitation alone is not an attempt." Id. at 457.

We perceive several flaws in *Adami*'s analysis.

First, the opinion makes no mention of the slight-acts rule, which has long been the rule for attempted crimes in California. . . . Decker argues that the slight-acts rule should not be applied to the crime of attempted murder, but his argument lacks legal or logical support. Our adoption of the slight-acts rule in People v. Anderson, supra, 1 Cal. 2d at page 690, was supported by a citation to Stokes v. State, 46 So. 627, 629 (Miss. 1908), which is one of the leading cases in the United States on attempt . . . and which (like the present case) involved a defendant who hired another to perform a murder. The cases on which Decker relies . . . conflict not only with California law, see, e.g., People v. Morales, supra, 5 Cal. App. 4th at 926, but also with the "fairly general agreement . . . that slight acts are enough when the intent to murder is clearly shown." Annotation, What Constitutes Attempted Murder,

54 A.L.R.3d 612, 617-618 (1974). Indeed, where (as here) the crime involves concerted action—and hence a greater likelihood that the criminal objective will be accomplished—there is a *greater* urgency for intervention by the state at an *earlier* stage in the course of that conduct. Had Decker struck an agreement with and paid earnest money to a real hired killer, he could have been prosecuted for conspiracy to commit murder, which is punishable to the same extent as the completed crime of first degree murder. Because of the fortuity that Decker's hired killer was actually an undercover detective, Decker faces the much less serious charge of attempted murder. Neither Decker nor the dissent has offered any reason for us to create an exception to the slight-acts rule for attempted murder, especially . . . where the attempt involves concerted action with others, merely so that Decker's maximum potential punishment may be further reduced.

Second, *Adami* has misconceived the issue under these circumstances to be "whether the solicitation itself was sufficient to establish probable cause to believe that defendant attempted the murder." *Adami*, supra, 36 Cal. App. 3d at 455. Decker similarly expends considerable effort to convince us that

> solicitation of another to commit a crime is an attempt to commit that crime if, but only if, it takes the form of urging the other to join with the solicitor in perpetrating that offense, not at some future time or distant place, but here and now, and the crime is such that it cannot be committed by one without the cooperation and submission of another.

Perkins, Criminal Law 519 (1957); see also *Adami*, supra, 36 Cal. App. 3d at 457. But a solicitation requires only that a person invite another to commit or join in an enumerated crime (including murder) with the intent that the crime be committed. Penal Code §653f.* The solicitation is complete once the request is made, and is punishable "irrespective of the reaction of the person solicited." In re Ryan N., 92 Cal. App. 4th 1359, 1377, 112 Cal. Rptr. 2d 620 (2001). In this case, the solicitation was complete early in Decker's first conversation with Holston, when he asked Holston to kill Donna. But the People do not contend that this request was sufficient to prosecute Decker for attempted murder. They argue instead that the solicitation, in combination with Decker's subsequent conduct, revealed his plan to have Holston murder Donna (and, if necessary, her friend Hermine) and that Decker put this plan into operation no later than the point at which he completed the agreement with Holston, finalized the details surrounding the murders, and paid Holston $5,000 in earnest money.

The issue, then, is not whether solicitation alone is sufficient to establish an attempt but whether a solicitation to commit murder, combined with

---

* [California Penal Code §653f(b) provides: "Every person who, with the intent that the crime be committed, solicits another to commit or join in the commission of murder shall be punished by imprisonment in the state prison for three, six, or nine years."—EDS.]

a completed agreement to hire a professional killer and the making of a down payment under that agreement, can establish probable cause to believe Decker attempted to murder these victims. A substantial number of our sister states have held that it can. E.g., State v. Mandel, 278 P.2d 413, 415-416 (Ariz. 1954); Howell v. State, 278 S.E.2d 43, 46-48 (Ga. App. 1981); State v. Montecino, 906 So. 2d 450, 454 (La. App. 2005); State v. Manchester, 331 N.W.2d 776, 780 (Neb. 1983); State v. Kilgus, 519 A.2d 231, 235-236 (N.H. 1986); People v. Sabo, 687 N.Y.S.2d 513, 519-520 (N.Y. Sup. Ct. 1998); Ashford v. Commonwealth, 626 S.E.2d 464, 467-468 (Va. App. 2006); State v. Burd, 419 S.E.2d 676, 680 (W. Va. 1991). Additional jurisdictions have held that a solicitation to murder, in combination with a completed agreement to hire a professional killer and further conduct implementing the agreement, can similarly constitute an attempted murder. E.g., Braham v. State, supra, 571 P.2d at 638 (completed agreement, plus a visit by the hired killer to the victim to "foster[] a relationship of trust and confidence"); State v. Group, 781 N.E.2d 980, 996 (Ohio 2002) ("Group did more than merely solicit the firebombing of Mrs. Lozier's house. He took all action within his power, considering his incarceration, to ensure that the crime would be committed."). We find these authorities persuasive.

Third, *Adami* mistakenly assumes that there can be no overlap between the evidence that would tend to prove solicitation to murder and that which would tend to prove attempted murder. . . . But it could not be plainer, as Chief Justice Holmes put it, that while "preparation is not an attempt," nonetheless "*some* preparations may amount to an attempt." Commonwealth v. Peaslee, 59 N.E. 55, 56 (Mass. 1901) (emphasis added). Conduct that qualifies as mere preparation and conduct that qualifies as a direct but ineffectual act toward commission of the crime exist on a continuum, "since all acts leading up to the ultimate consummation of a crime are by their very nature preparatory." State v. Sunzar, 751 A.2d 627, 630 (N.J. Super. Ct. 1999). The difference between them "is a question of degree." *Peaslee*, supra, 59 N.E. at 56. There is thus no error in resting a finding of attempted murder in part on evidence that *also* tends to establish solicitation to commit murder. . . .

Fourth, we reject the contention, endorsed by Decker and by *Adami*'s progeny, that there is "no persuasive reason" why a solicitation to commit murder "should be treated differently under the law merely because part of the agreed upon fee has passed hands. . . ." State v. Otto, supra, 629 P.2d at 650. As the People point out, . . . a down payment on a contract to murder serves the same purpose as a down payment on any other type of contract. It evidences the solicitor's "seriousness of purpose" and makes the object of the contract "closer to fruition." State v. Molasky, 765 S.W.2d 597, 602 (Mo. 1989). It blinks reality to equate the threat posed by an individual who has merely invited another, perhaps unsuccessfully, to commit murder with the threat posed by an individual who has already reached an agreement with a hired killer to commit murder, finalized the plans, and made the down payment under the contract to kill. But for Holston's status as an undercover detective, it is likely that Decker's conduct would have resulted in the murder of these victims. Where, as here, the defendant's intent is unmistakable, "the courts should not destroy the practical and common-sense administration of the law with subtleties as to what constitutes preparation and what constitutes an act done toward the commission of a crime." People v. Memro, supra, 38 Cal. 3d at 698. . . .

In finding the record sufficient to hold Decker to answer to the charges of attempted murder here, we do not decide whether an agreement to kill followed by a down payment is *always* sufficient to support a charge of attempted murder. Whether acts done in contemplation of the commission of a crime are merely preparatory or whether they are instead sufficiently close to the consummation of the crime is a question of degree and depends upon the facts and circumstances of a particular case. A different situation may exist, for example, when the assassin has been hired and paid but the victims have not yet been identified. In this case, however, Decker had effectively done all that he needed to do to ensure that Donna and her friend be executed. Accordingly, he should have been held to answer to the charges of attempted murder. We disapprove People v. Adami, supra, to the extent it is inconsistent with this opinion.

The judgment of the Court of Appeal is affirmed.

WERDEGAR, J., dissenting.

. . . "An attempt to commit a crime consists of two elements: a specific intent to commit the crime, and a direct but ineffectual act done toward its commission." Penal Code §21a. Defendant's conduct in this case does not include "a direct but ineffectual act" done toward the murder's commission. Accordingly, he cannot be guilty of attempted murder.

As we have long recognized, the required act for an attempt under California law must be "directed towards immediate consummation," People v. Dillon, 34 Cal. 3d 441, 454, 668 P.2d 697 (1983), of the crime attempted. As the majority details, defendant's conduct included numerous *indirect* acts toward accomplishing the murder of his sister: he sought the services of a hired assassin; he located a person (actually an undercover police detective) he thought would act as such; he furnished the supposed assassin with a description of his sister, her home, her car and her workplace, as well as specific information concerning her daily habits; he discussed how the murder would be done and how and when he would pay for the work, agreeing to furnish $5,000 in cash as a down payment; and, finally, just before he was arrested, he stated he was "absolutely, positively, 100 percent sure, that I want to go through with it" and urged the supposed assassin to do it "as fast as you can."

I agree with the majority that as evidence defendant harbored the specific intent to kill his sister, these facts are overwhelming. None of them, however, constitutes a *direct* but ineffectual act done toward the murder's commission. As the majority states, defendant "did not himself point a gun at his sister"; neither did he otherwise directly menace her. Instead, he relied on the person he thought had agreed to commit the murder to do the actual deed.[1] The direct object of defendant's preparatory acts was the person he sought to engage as his agent—not the ultimate, intended victim of the scheme.

We previously have stated that for attempt, it must be "clear from a suspect's acts what *he* intends to do. . . ." People v. Dillon, supra, 34 Cal. 3d at 455 (emphasis added). In this case, what defendant intended to do was have his sister killed *by someone else*. Defendant's own conduct did not include even "slight" acts toward actual commission of the murder. That he hired another, supplied him with information, and paid him a down payment only highlights his intention not to perform the act himself.

The California cases the majority purports to rely on generally involve single actors, i.e., defendants who acted directly on their victims.[2] These cases simply confirm that for attempt a defendant must have committed a direct act toward commission of the crime. Defendant here committed no direct act toward commission of the murder, since his scheme interposed a third party between himself and his intended victim, and the third party never acted. The majority goes astray in applying to this solicitation-of-murder case, where action by another person was required to effectuate (or attempt) the intended killing, principles applicable when an offense is intended and attempted by a single individual.

Although defendant's conduct went beyond the minimum required for solicitation, for purposes of attempt law his arrangements constitute mere preparation. Reprehensible as they were, his acts "did not amount to any more than the mere arrangement of the proposed measures for [the] accomplishment" of the crime. People v. Adami, 36 Cal. App. 3d 452, 457-458, 111 Cal. Rptr. 544 (1973). . . . To do all one can to motivate and encourage

---

1. Although the majority asserts defendant "did aim at [his sister] an armed professional who had agreed to commit the murder," the armed professional referred to . . . only *pretended* to agree so that in fact there was no agreement, though defendant thought there was. This absence of actual agreement presumably is why the case was not prosecuted as a conspiracy. . . .

2. See, e.g., People v. Memro, 38 Cal. 3d 658, 699, 700 P.2d 446 (1985) (ushering a boy into a room and standing close by during a strobe display were direct acts sufficient for the attempted commission of a lewd or lascivious act on a minor); People v. Dillon, supra, 34 Cal. 3d at 456 (arriving on land armed and disguised, and dividing into groups to encircle a field, were direct acts sufficient for the attempted robbery of a marijuana farm); People v. Anderson, 1 Cal. 2d 687, 690, 37 P.2d 67 (1934) (approaching a ticket office and pulling out a gun were direct acts sufficient for the attempted armed robbery of a theater); People v. Morales, 5 Cal. App. 4th 917, 926-927, 7 Cal. Rptr. 2d 358 (1992) (threatening twice to "get" the victim, going home, loading a gun, driving to the victim's neighborhood, and hiding in a position with a clear shot were direct acts sufficient for attempted murder).

another to accomplish a killing—even to make a down payment on a contract to kill—while blameworthy and punishable, is neither logically nor legally equivalent to attempting the killing oneself. In concluding to the contrary, the majority blurs the distinction between preparation and perpetration the Legislature intended by requiring that an attempt include a direct act. . . .

The majority's criticisms of People v. Adami, supra, are unpersuasive. The majority faults *Adami* for not mentioning the slight acts rule, but since the *Adami* court concluded no "appreciable fragment of the crime charged was accomplished," 36 Cal. App. 3d at 457, the rule had no application. Nor, contrary to the majority's account, did *Adami* assume that evidence of solicitation cannot also be evidence of attempt. *Adami* simply held that hiring a murderer, planning the murder, and making a down payment logically constitute "solicitation or mere preparation," id., not attempted murder.

Confronted with statutory language and judicial precedent contrary to its conclusion, the majority relies on out-of-state cases. Several of these interpret attempt statutes distinguishable from our own.[4] Others involve more than a completed agreement with a hired killer, including a direct act *toward the victim.*[5] The remaining cases are in my view mistaken for the same reason the majority is mistaken: they implicitly allow that a defendant may be guilty of attempt when no direct act toward the commission of the crime has been done. . . .

Had the supposed assassin hired to kill defendant's sister actually attempted to kill her, defendant would be punishable under Penal Code section 31 as a principal in the offense, either as an aider and abettor or as a coconspirator.[8] But in this case, neither defendant nor the supposed assassin took a direct act toward commission of the offense. . . . There was no attempt.

For the foregoing reasons, I dissent.

4. See, e.g., Howell v. State, 278 S.E.2d 43, 46 (Ga. Ct. App. 1981) ([statute required a] "substantial step toward the commission of that crime"); State v. Molasky, 765 S.W.2d 597, 600 (Mo. 1989) (noting "[a]n act of perpetration [is] no longer required, and instead a defendant need only do an act which [is] a 'substantial step' toward commission"); State v. Gay, 486 P.2d 341, 345 (Wash. Ct. App. 1971) ([statute required an] "act . . . tending but failing to accomplish" the crime).

5. See, e.g., State v. Mandel, 278 P.2d 413, 415-416 (Ariz. 1954) (defendant planned to entice victim to murder scene and drove assassin in her car to view victim's home and arroyo where body was to be disposed of); State v. Kilgus, 519 A.2d 231, 234-236 (N.H. 1986) (defendant said he was "going to have to get involved" and made arrangements for the victim to be alone); State v. Burd, 419 S.E.2d 676, 680 (W. Va. 1991) (defendant offered to drive the assassin to show him the victim's house and provided a fake suicide note to leave at the crime scene and money for a gun).

8. Penal Code section 31 states that "[a]ll persons concerned in the commission of a crime, . . . whether they directly commit the act constituting the offense, or aid and abet in its commission, or, not being present, have advised and encouraged its commission . . . are principals in any crime so committed."

Notes on Attempted Murder

1. Reread California's solicitation statute, quoted in an editor's note in Justice Baxter's majority opinion. Such laws are common; they were enacted to cover scenarios like the one in *Decker*. Why, then, is attempt liability at issue? There is no debate about Decker's liability for soliciting the murder of his sister. Consequently, the stakes in *Decker* are modest: The only question is whether the defendant will be punished for attempt *in addition to* solicitation. Why should the addition be permitted? Why aren't attempt and solicitation treated as mutually exclusive crimes? Note that the Model Penal Code—unlike the common law—specifically prohibits convicting a defendant of more than one inchoate crime (attempt, solicitation, or conspiracy) with respect to the same intended actual crime. See MPC §5.05.

2. Consider the "slight acts rule" discussed in *Decker*. That rule holds that even slight acts may suffice to show attempt where the government has proved that the defendant had the requisite specific intent. If the rule makes sense, it must be on the assumption that requiring proof of affirmative conduct in attempt cases is simply a means of proving *mens rea*—that the conduct element in criminal attempts has no independent significance. Is that assumption correct? Notice that slight acts and even omissions will suffice in cases where the defendant causes the victim's death. Is proof of affirmative conduct more important in attempted murder cases than in completed homicides?

3. Recall *Robertson*, excerpted supra at page 722. The defendant in that case was charged with manslaughter because he fled onto a bridge over the Ohio River while being pursued by a police officer for a low-level drug charge. Because the bridge was under construction, the defendant had to leap over a gap in the walkway to continue fleeing; when the pursuing officer tried the same maneuver, the officer fell to his death. At the least, the *Robertson* defendant's conduct was ambiguous, was it not? Decker's conduct, by contrast, was anything but: He hired an assassin, discussed the method the assassin planned to use, and paid a portion of the money owed for the hit. Robertson was probably shocked to learn that he was charged with manslaughter. Decker may have expected to get away with his crime, but once caught, he cannot have been surprised to find attempted murder charges filed against him. Robertson's behavior did not show a murderous intent (which is why he was charged with manslaughter rather than murder). Decker's conduct plainly shows his intent to murder his sister. Why is conduct like Robertson's punished when death results, while some courts refuse to punish behavior like Decker's when attempted murder is the charge?

4. One reason for the difference has to do with the law of *mens rea*: Solicitation of murder and attempted murder both require proof of specific intent to kill. Negligent homicide, involuntary manslaughter, second-degree murder, and felony murder require different mental states: criminal negligence, recklessness, "malice aforethought" (which, despite the word "aforethought," does not require a purposeful choice to kill), and either strict liability or criminal negligence, respectively. A great many homicides, in other words, are reckless or negligent rather than purposeful. Consequently, many defendants will be liable for murder, manslaughter, or negligent homicide if their victims die — but may be liable for no crime at all if their victims survive or if the defendants are caught before the danger materializes. Why?

5. Because attempt is a specific intent offense, there can be no such charge as attempted involuntary manslaughter (the usual *mens rea* for which is recklessness) or attempted negligent homicide (the *mens rea* for which is, as the name suggests, criminal negligence). In nearly every state, attempted homicides are always either attempted murders or attempted voluntary manslaughters.**

6. The conduct gap between attempted murder and completed homicide is nicely captured by Thacker v. Commonwealth, 114 S.E. 504 (Va. 1922). The defendant in *Thacker* was charged with and convicted of attempted murder, on these facts:

> The accused, in company with two other young men . . . was attending a church festival in Allegheny County, at which all three became intoxicated. They left the church between ten and eleven o'clock at night, and walked down the county road about one and one-half miles, when they came to a sharp curve. Located in this curve was a tent in which the said Mrs. J.A. Ratrie, her husband, four children and a servant were camping for the summer. The husband, though absent, was expected home that night, and Mrs. Ratrie, upon retiring, had placed a lighted lamp on a trunk by the head of her bed. After eleven o'clock she was awakened by the shots of a pistol and loud talking in the road near by, and heard a man say, "I am going to shoot that God-damned light out"; and another voice said, "Don't shoot the light out." The accused and his friends then appeared at the back of the tent, where the flaps of the tent were open, and said they were from Bath County and had lost their way, and asked Mrs. Ratrie if she could take care of them all night. She informed them she was camping for the summer and had no room for them. One of the three thanked her, and they turned away, but after passing around the tent the accused used some vulgar language and did some cursing and singing. When they got back in the road, the accused said again he was going to shoot the light out, and fired three shots, two of which went through the tent, one passing through the head of the bed in which Mrs. Ratrie was lying, just missing her head and the head of her baby, who was sleeping with her. The accused did not know Mrs. Ratrie and had never seen her before. He testified he did not know any of the parties in the tent and had no ill will against either of them; that he simply shot at the light, without any intent to harm Mrs. Ratrie or anyone else; that he would not have shot had he been sober, and regretted his action.

** The Model Penal Code proposed the creation of a new crime, "reckless endangerment," for situations where a defendant recklessly creates a substantial risk of death, but no death actually results. See MPC §211.2. At least a few states, especially those like Washington and New York where the Model Penal Code has had substantial influence on the criminal law, have adopted this proposed new crime.

Id. at 505. The Virginia Supreme Court overturned Thacker's conviction, relying on the following discussion of attempts from a then-leading treatise:

> "The act must be done with the specific intent to commit a particular crime. This specific intent at the time the act is done is essential. To do an act from general malevolence is not an attempt to commit a crime, because there is no specific intent, though the act according to its consequences may amount to a substantive crime. To do an act with intent to commit one crime cannot be an attempt to commit another crime though it might result in such other crime. To set fire to a house and burn a human being who is in it, but not to the offender's knowledge, would be murder, though the intent was to burn the house only; but to attempt to set fire to the house under such circumstances would be an attempt to commit arson only and not an attempt to murder. A man actuated by general malevolence may commit murder though there is no actual intention to kill; to be guilty of an attempt to murder there must be a specific intent to kill."

Clark & Marshall, On the Law of Crimes 111 (2d ed. 1905), quoted in *Thacker*, 114 S.E. at 506. In most jurisdictions at the time, Thacker would have been liable for attempted destruction of property, a low-level misdemeanor, or he would have been guilty of no crime at all. Yet if Mrs. Ratrie had sat up in bed or had she picked up her baby, she or the child might easily have been killed, in which case Thacker would have been convicted of murder. Why does the law require such different results for such similar conduct? Recall the discussion of moral luck, supra at pages 719-720. Is the result in *Thacker* morally sound?

7. Here is one way to make sense of the restrictive definition of attempted murder: For the most part, criminal law punishes blameworthy conduct; the key concept distinguishing crime from non-crime is fault, and the key legal means by which fault is determined is *mens rea*. The law of homicide may operate on a different principle: responsibility, with those responsible for untimely deaths punished for those deaths. On that principle, the key doctrine is not *mens rea* but causation — since causation determines which defendants are responsible for which bad outcomes.

That principle may seem wrong in cases like *Thacker*, in which the defendant's blameworthy conduct did not cause death. But the principle is hardly strange: Most of the civil justice system, for example, depends on responsibility, not fault. If Putney kicks Vosburg and no injury results, there is no liability; if, as in the actual case, Vosburg must have his leg amputated, Putney is liable for the cost of the amputation. See Vosburg v. Putney, 56 N.W. 480 (Wis. 1893).

Which of these two principles seems best suited to criminal law? Does the law of attempted murder produce just results?

8. Look again at footnote 4 in Justice Werdegar's dissent. Two of the three cases cited in that footnote interpreted attempt statutes that were modeled on Model Penal Code §5.01 — which requires that, in attempt cases, the government prove that the defendant took a "substantial step" toward completion of the relevant crime, and that the defendant's conduct was "strongly corroborative of [his] criminal purpose." California's attempt statute is phrased differently; under that statute, the prosecution must prove "a direct but ineffectual act done toward [the] commission" of the crime in question. California Penal Code §21a. Which formula requires the government to prove more conduct? Which formula is more likely to produce fair results? Recall the common law's conduct test in attempt cases. Under the common law, the defendant's conduct must come dangerously close to completion; conduct that fails to meet this test is called "mere preparation" and is insufficient for attempt liability. Which of these three approaches — "substantial step," "direct but ineffectual act," or coming dangerously close to the completed offense — best defines the conduct for criminal attempts generally? Which does the best job of defining attempted murder?

State v. Clark

Supreme Court of Minnesota
755 N.W.2d 241 (2008)

Opinion by ANDERSON, J.

A Ramsey County jury found Larry Larue Clark guilty of [conspiracy to commit] first-degree premeditated murder [and of] aiding and abetting [first-degree premeditated murder] . . . for the 1970 shooting death of Saint Paul Police Officer James Sackett. The district court . . . sentenced [Clark] to life in prison. In this direct appeal Clark raises [the question whether the evidence is sufficient to support the jury's verdicts, as well as the question whether the trial judge's failure to give an accomplice instruction requires reversal]. . . . We conclude . . . that the court's failure to give . . . an accomplice instruction was plain error requiring remand for a new trial, [and that the evidence may be sufficient to support the conviction if that error is corrected]. . . . Therefore, we reverse Clark's conviction and remand for a new trial.

In 1969, . . . Clark and his friend Ronald Reed were teenagers living in the Selby-Dale neighborhood of Saint Paul, Minnesota. Clark and Reed frequented the Inner City Youth League, along with other young people from the neighborhood. Reed emerged as the leader of a group of these young people. According to Joseph Garrett, the group's self-described "minister of information," the group used the name United Black Front. At their meetings, the group discussed black-empowerment and self-protection from the police. At this time, the tension between the police and these young people was high. In the months preceding the murder of Saint Paul police officer James Sackett, at least two of the neighborhood's young men had been shot by the police. . . . As a result, the rhetoric at the United Black Front's meetings became more inflammatory. At Clark's trial there was testimony that Reed and others in the group wanted authority from the Black Panther Party to organize a chapter in Saint Paul and that members of the group thought that if they got national attention by killing a police officer it would increase their chances of success. Witness testimony indicated that Reed was a strong advocate for killing a police officer and that Clark agreed with Reed. Several of the group's members carried guns, and Reed and Clark were seen together with a bolt-action rifle on a number of occasions.

Just after midnight on Friday, May 22, 1970, the Saint Paul police received an emergency telephone call requesting assistance for a woman in labor at 859 Hague Avenue in the Selby-Dale neighborhood. Officer Sackett and his partner, Officer Glen Kothe, responded to the call, parked their police car in front of 859 Hague, went to the front door, and knocked. When no one in the house came to the door, Kothe walked to the back door and knocked. Hearing a dog bark inside, Kothe started to warn Sackett about the dog, and, as he did so, he saw a bright flash, heard a loud bang, and heard a scream. Running to the front of the house, Kothe found Sackett lying on the ground, bleeding. Kothe realized that Sackett had been shot and radioed for assistance. At some point, a crowd, including Reed and other members of the United Black Front, gathered at the scene. Clark was not identified as having been present in the crowd. Sackett later died as a result of a gunshot wound to the chest.

In the ensuing investigation, the police determined that no one at the 859 Hague address had placed the emergency call or was involved in the shooting. They also concluded that the shot that killed Officer Sackett came from a southwesterly direction. . . . Although no weapon or shell casing was found in the area, the police determined that the shot that killed Sackett probably came from a single-shot, bolt-action rifle. The police also determined that the emergency call that preceded the shooting was made from a telephone booth one block away at the corner of Selby Avenue and Victoria Street. No fingerprints or other useable evidence were found on or in the booth. At the time of the shooting, Clark lived at 882 Hague, which was approximately 102 yards west of 859 Hague on the south side of the street. The house at 859 Hague is located on the north side of the street.

Through voice-print analysis, the police were eventually able to identify Constance Trimble as the person who made the May 22nd telephone call. Trimble was Reed's girlfriend and the mother of his child. Trimble was arrested in October 1970 and, after a 1972 jury trial, she was acquitted of Sackett's murder. At her trial, Trimble testified that she had been told the telephone call was being made as a ruse to set up Gerald Starling for a drug bust in retaliation for Starling having allegedly threatened Trimble's family. Trimble refused, both during and after her trial, to identify the person who asked her to make the call. As a result, she was held in contempt of court and remained in jail for a period of time after her acquittal. . . .

In October 1970, Reed and Clark, along with Horace Myles, were involved in an attempted armed bank robbery in Omaha, Nebraska. An off-duty police officer, working as a security guard at the bank, was shot by

Myles when the officer tried to thwart the robbery. Reed and Clark also fired weapons during the robbery attempt. Clark was arrested for the attempted robbery 10 days later. Reed was arrested roughly two weeks after Clark at an acquaintance's apartment in Minneapolis. The police found Reed lying on a bed, with a handgun under the bed within his reach. . . . A search of the apartment produced a handgun, a flare, a sawed-off shotgun, and a duffel bag holding walkie-talkies. In 1971, Reed and Clark were convicted of the attempted bank robbery in Omaha. . . . [N]either Reed, Clark, nor anyone else was arrested in connection with Sackett's murder. . . .

In 1994, a television reporter interviewed Trimble about Officer Sackett's murder. Trimble refused to disclose who had asked her to make the false emergency telephone call. In 1995, the Saint Paul police contacted Trimble, at which time she admitted that Reed was with her when she made the call, but she refused to provide any further information. In 2004, at her request, Trimble met with the police and disclosed for the first time that Reed had asked her to make the call and had given her a script to read. She told the police that Reed drove the two of them, along with their baby, to the telephone booth. She also stated that after the call was made, Reed drove them directly from the booth to Clark's house to get some marijuana.

Following this subsequent investigation, a grand jury was convened to determine whether there was probable cause to indict Reed and Clark. . . . In 2005, Reed and Clark were indicted for aiding and abetting each other (count 1) and for conspiring with each other (count 2) to kill Officer Sackett. . . . Reed was tried first and was found guilty on both counts. We affirmed Reed's conviction on direct appeal. See State v. Reed, 737 N.W.2d 572, 590 (Minn. 2007).

Clark went to trial on April 10, 2006. At Clark's trial, Donald Walker testified that he frequented the Inner City Youth League in the late 1960s and early 1970s. He also attended "so-called Black Panther Party meetings" at a neighborhood church, at which Reed and Clark would make intense, motivational statements of hatred toward white people, the government, and the police. Walker did not recall any times when the discussions turned to plans of violence or to killing police officers, but he did testify that he "transported" a single-shot, bolt-action rifle for Reed and Clark on at least two occasions when he gave them a ride. . . .

Anthony Foster also testified that he attended the United Black Front meetings. Foster stated that at the meetings Reed talked about killing a police officer to attract national attention in order to get permission to start a Black Panther chapter in Saint Paul. He further testified that Reed [and] Arthur Harper . . . came to his apartment a few days after Officer Sackett was shot and that Reed would not respond to his attempts to discuss the shooting. . . .

. . . [Trimble] testified that Reed drove her directly to Clark's house after she placed the false emergency telephone call, that Clark was waiting outside the back door of his house when they arrived, and that she and

Reed remained there for five to seven minutes before driving home. At her own trial, Trimble testified that she went to buy cigarettes after making the call and that Reed was home asleep when she returned. At both Reed's and Clark's trials, she testified that neither Reed nor Clark left Clark's house while she was there. During her grand jury testimony, however, Trimble testified [that] . . . "[t]hey could have [left], you know. Now that I think about it, they could have, you know." Trimble did not provide any explanation for the inconsistencies in her statements.

Joseph Garrett, the "minister of information" for the United Black Front, also testified at Clark's trial. Garrett testified that Reed and others at the United Black Front meetings advocated protecting themselves from the police "by any means necessary." Garrett further testified that he, together with Clark and others, agreed with that proposition. According to Garrett, members of the United Black Front "tended to be armed." He testified that he had access to several bolt-action, 30-caliber rifles that he had stolen and later sold, but, as far as he knows, none of the stolen rifles went to anyone else in the group. Garrett testified that Reed had approached him a few weeks before Sackett's murder about being involved in "bring[ing] down the first pig." Garrett understood this to mean killing a police officer. . . .

Arthur Harper testified that he, Day, Reed, and Clark often socialized at Day's apartment, located at 844 Dayton Avenue. The apartment was less than two blocks from where Officer Sackett was shot. According to Harper, Reed often made statements, with which Clark agreed, that the police were the oppressors and needed to be taught a lesson. Harper further testified that . . . he saw Reed and Clark leave Day's apartment at about 11:30 P.M. the night of Sackett's murder and that, at the time, Reed appeared to be carrying a bolt-action rifle. . . . Harper also testified that he heard a gunshot 15 to 20 minutes later and that a few minutes later he walked south on Selby, in the direction the police cars were heading. Harper further testified that he joined Day, who was standing in front of the Inner City Youth League, and they were joined by Reed sometime later. . . .

. . . [T]he district court, over the defense's objection, allowed evidence of Clark's and Reed's 1971 bank robbery convictions to prove intent and motive to shoot a police officer. The court gave a limiting instruction to the jury about the use of this other crimes evidence both immediately before the jury heard the testimony about the convictions and at the end of Clark's trial. Clark also objected to the court's jury instruction on conspiracy. Clark argued that the jury should be instructed that the State must prove he conspired with Reed to shoot a police officer because that was how the indictment read, rather than having to prove simply that he conspired with an unknown person to shoot an officer.

The jury found Clark guilty [of both aiding and abetting premeditated murder, and of conspiracy to commit premeditated murder]. The district court . . . sentenced him to life in prison. . . .

[Justice Anderson's opinion proceeded to discuss and reject a variety of challenges to Clark's conviction, and to discuss and accept Clark's claim that the trial judge should have instructed the jury that Trimble was a probable accomplice, and that accomplice testimony is suspect given the incentive to blame others for the witnesses' own crimes. That error, the majority concluded, required reversal of Clark's convictions. — EDS.]

SUFFICIENCY OF THE EVIDENCE

Clark argues that the evidence presented at his trial was insufficient to support the jury's guilty verdicts of aiding and abetting . . . and conspiracy. . . . In Burks v. United States, the United States Supreme Court held that "[t]he Double Jeopardy Clause forbids a second trial for the purpose of affording the prosecution another opportunity to supply evidence which it failed to muster in the first proceeding." 437 U.S. 1, 11 (1978). Accordingly, where the evidence at a trial was "legally insufficient" to support a conviction, "the only just remedy . . . is the direction of a judgment of acquittal." Id. at 18. Thus, even though we conclude that Clark's conviction must be reversed based on the district court's failure to instruct the jury on accomplice testimony, we must also . . . determine whether the appropriate remedy is to remand for a new trial or [to order the entry of] a judgment of acquittal. . . .

The first count for which the jury found Clark guilty is aiding and abetting first-degree premeditated murder. A person is liable for aiding and abetting a crime if he "intentionally aids, advises, hires, counsels, or conspires with or otherwise procures the other to commit the crime." Minn. Stat. §609.05(1). In order to prove aiding and abetting, the State has to prove that the defendant had knowledge of the crime and "intended his presence or actions to further the commission of that crime." State v. Mahkuk, 736 N.W.2d 675, 682 (Minn. 2007).

The jury also found Clark guilty of conspiracy to commit first-degree premeditated murder. A person is guilty of conspiracy if he "conspires with another to commit a crime and in furtherance of the conspiracy one or more of the parties does some overt act in furtherance of such conspiracy." Minn. Stat. §609.175(2). In order to prove conspiracy, the State's evidence must "objectively indicate[. . .] an agreement" between the defendant and another person to commit a crime. State v. Hatfield, 639 N.W.2d 372, 376 (Minn. 2002).

The State's theory of Officer Sackett's murder is that on the night of the shooting, Reed and Clark walked to Clark's house, where they stored the murder weapon. Reed then picked up Trimble, drove her to the public telephone booth where she made the false emergency call to lure a police officer to the scene, and then returned to Clark's house. Either Reed or Clark retrieved the murder weapon, left the house, and shot Sackett. The shooter then returned to the house, and Reed drove Trimble home.

At Clark's trial, Arthur Harper testified that Reed was seen carrying a rifle and walking with Clark toward Clark's house approximately one-half hour before Officer Sackett's murder. Voice-print analysis showed that, shortly before the shooting, Trimble made a false emergency call from a public telephone booth on the corner of Victoria Street and Selby Avenue. According to Trimble's testimony, Reed then drove her to Clark's house, which was only one block away. When they arrived, Clark was standing outside waiting to meet them. Although Trimble testified that she did not see either Reed or Clark leave the house, her grand jury testimony indicated that she went into the house to use the restroom and that the two men could have left the house during that time. Trimble also testified that she did not see a rifle in the car.

The State's evidence showed that Officer Sackett was shot with a 30-caliber, bolt-action rifle, that Reed and Clark had been seen in possession of a similar weapon on multiple occasions in the months before the murder, that Clark's house was located . . . 102 yards from the murder scene, which is within the range of a rifle like that used in the murder, and that Clark's house was located in the general direction from where the fatal shot was fired. Finally, the State's evidence showed that Reed and Clark were close friends and that they shared a common motive for the shooting—Reed had previously advocated killing a police officer as part of an attempt to bring a Black Panther chapter to Saint Paul, and Clark had openly agreed with those views. . . .

. . . [T]he fact that Reed and Clark were seen together with a rifle in Reed's possession one-half hour before the shooting would not be sufficient to support either an aiding and abetting or a conspiracy conviction. But we conclude that Trimble's testimony is sufficient to fill the gaps in the chain of evidence. . . . Trimble's testimony places Reed and Clark together in the area where the fatal shot was fired and, if the jury credited her grand jury testimony, this gave the two men an opportunity to commit the crime. Trimble's testimony also leads to an inference that Reed and Clark had arranged to meet behind Clark's house after the false emergency call was placed, and that the two men had stored the murder weapon at Clark's house before the false emergency call. . . . [W]e conclude that a reasonable jury could have found beyond a reasonable doubt that Reed and Clark agreed to murder a police officer and that Clark's actions were intended to further the commission of that crime. Accordingly, we conclude that the evidence presented at Clark's trial . . . was sufficient to support the jury's verdicts of aiding and abetting first-degree premeditated murder and conspiracy to commit first-degree murder.

Having concluded that the district court committed plain error when it failed to instruct the jury on accomplice testimony, that Clark was substantially prejudiced by the error, and that the evidence is sufficient to corroborate

Trimble's testimony and to support the jury's verdicts, the appropriate remedy is to remand for a new trial. . . .

PAGE, J., dissenting.

. . . Because I believe, as a matter of law, that Trimble's testimony lacks corroboration, I conclude that Clark's conviction cannot rest on that testimony. Given the nature of the remaining evidence, I also conclude that the failure to give the accomplice instruction . . . require[s] reversal of Clark's convictions. . . .

Having concluded that Clark's convictions must be reversed, the next question is whether we should remand for a new trial. . . . The answer to that question . . . turns on whether, absent Trimble's testimony, there is otherwise sufficient evidence to sustain Clark's convictions. . . .

CONSPIRACY TO COMMIT FIRST-DEGREE PREMEDITATED MURDER

In order to convict Clark of conspiracy to commit first-degree murder, the State was required to prove, among other things, that Clark was part of a conspiracy. Under our law, "[w]hoever conspires with another to commit a crime and in furtherance of the conspiracy one or more of the parties does some overt act in furtherance of such conspiracy" is guilty of conspiracy. Minn. Stat. §609.175(2). To establish a conspiracy, the State must provide evidence "that objectively indicates an agreement" between the defendant and another to commit the crime. State v. Hatfield, 639 N.W.2d 372, 376 (Minn. 2002). Generally, when there is evidence of "a common plan, concerted conduct, or prior involvement with the alleged co-conspirator," it is reasonable to infer that there was an agreement. Id. at 377.

The State's theory of the case at trial was that on the night that Officer Sackett was shot, Reed, along with Clark, followed through with Reed's previously stated desire to kill a police officer. According to the State, Reed, carrying a bolt-action rifle, walked with Clark from Day's apartment to Clark's house, where they stored the rifle. Reed then picked up Trimble and drove her to make the false emergency phone call. Then Reed, along with Trimble, drove to Clark's house to retrieve the rifle, at which point either Reed or Clark or both left Clark's house and carried out the shooting of Officer Sackett. The shooter then returned to Clark's house after which Reed drove Trimble home.

According to the State, the evidence supporting Clark's conspiracy conviction includes evidence: (1) that Clark was present at group meetings at which Reed advocated killing a police officer; (2) of Clark's apparent agreement with Reed's statements about killing a police officer, self-defense, and black power; (3) that Clark made statements about black power and self-defense; (4) that Clark had a close relationship with Reed; and (5) that Clark was seen shortly before the shooting walking with Reed, who was carrying a rifle, in the direction of Clark's house and the location of the shooting. The State also argues that evidence of Clark and Reed's involvement in the shooting of a police officer during the Nebraska bank robbery supports the element of intent. . . .

All of the evidence that the State contends supports Clark's guilt is circumstantial. The question that must be answered is whether this circumstantial evidence when viewed in a light most favorable to the verdict points "unerringly" to Clark's guilt. I conclude that it does not. First, the evidence of Clark's presence at United Black Front meetings, his agreement with Reed's statements about killing a police officer, statements of his own about black power and self-defense, and Clark's close relationship with Reed, standing alone, does nothing more than suggest that Clark is guilty because of his association with Reed. Without more, this evidence is insufficient because "mere association with an individual engaged in an illegal enterprise does not make a person a conspirator." United States v. Moss, 591 F.2d 428, 435 (8th Cir. 1979). . . .

The strongest evidence against Clark is Harper's testimony that he saw Clark, along with a rifle-carrying Reed, leave Day's apartment walking in the direction of Clark's house and the location of the shooting. The State argues that the inference to be drawn from this evidence is that Reed and Clark were on their way to carry out the shooting. The State further argues that this evidence supports not only an agreement to shoot a police officer, but also action by the two men in furtherance of that agreement, which goes beyond mere association. However, based on other evidence in the record indicating that Reed and Clark had been seen together on a number of occasions with a rifle in their possession without anyone being shot, it is equally possible to infer that Clark did not know of Reed's plan to shoot a police officer that evening. This inference leads to a rational hypothesis other than guilt. Absent a showing that Clark had knowledge of Reed's plan, an agreement to be part of the plan cannot be inferred. . . . [W]hile Reed, Day, Harper, and Garrett were seen immediately after the shooting near the scene, there is no evidence in the record that Clark was seen after Officer Sackett was shot, either with Reed or near the crime scene. . . .

The State also suggests that Clark's guilt can be inferred from the proximity of Clark's house to 859 Hague, the location where Officer Sackett was shot. . . . Other than establishing that Clark lived in close proximity to those locations, the location of Clark's house, without more, sheds no light on Clark's involvement, if any, in Officer Sackett's shooting. . . . [M]ere proximity to the crime scene is insufficient to support the inference that Clark conspired with Reed and/or others to carry out the shooting.

Finally, the State asserts that Reed's and Clark's convictions for the Nebraska bank robbery, which occurred five months after Officer Sackett's shooting and during which an off-duty police officer was shot, evidence Clark's intentional involvement in Officer Sackett's shooting. . . . To the extent that [the State argues] that Reed's and Clark's intent to engage in a conspiracy to shoot Officer Sackett can be inferred from the intentional shooting of the police officer during the bank robbery, that argument fails. The fact that Reed and Clark, during a bank robbery, shot a security guard who happened to be an off-duty police officer after the guard attempted to thwart the robbery [sheds no light] on any agreement that Clark and Reed may have had five months earlier to shoot Officer Sackett. . . . I therefore conclude that Clark's involvement in the bank robbery does not either by itself or in combination with the other evidence provide sufficient evidentiary support for Clark's conspiracy conviction.

AIDING AND ABETTING FIRST-DEGREE PREMEDITATED MURDER

. . . [I]n order for Clark to be convicted of aiding and abetting first-degree murder, the State had to prove that Clark intentionally aided, advised, hired, counseled, or conspired with "or otherwise procure[d] the other to commit the crime." Minn. Stat. §609.05. If a defendant plays a "knowing role" in the commission of a crime and [takes] no steps to thwart it, he is guilty of aiding and abetting. State v. Ostrem, 535 N.W.2d 916, 924 (Minn. 1995). To show that Clark played a knowing role in the shooting, the State had to prove that Clark knew that his accomplice, in this case Reed, was going to shoot Officer Sackett and that Clark "intended his presence or acts to encourage or further the completion of the crime." State v. Mahkuk, 736 N.W.2d 675, 682 (Minn. 2007). Intentional presence at or near the scene of the crime alone is insufficient to support a conviction for aiding and abetting.

The evidence the State relies on to support Clark's aiding and abetting conviction is the same circumstantial evidence the State relies on in support of Clark's conspiracy conviction. Again, there is no direct evidence of Clark's involvement in Officer Sackett's shooting. As discussed above, the evidence of Clark's presence at United Black Front meetings, his agreement with Reed's statements about killing a police officer, statements of his own about black power and self-defense, and Clark's close relationship with Reed, standing alone, does nothing more than suggest that Clark is guilty because of his association with Reed. . . .

Moreover, Harper's testimony that Reed and Clark were seen leaving Day's apartment establishes nothing more than Clark's mere presence in Reed's company some 15 to 30 minutes before the shooting. That evidence does not, however, place Clark in Reed's company at the time of or after the shooting. Nor does it lead unerringly to the conclusion that Clark knew of the plan to shoot a police officer that night or that he played a knowing role in the plan. Further, the record is silent with respect to any action taken by Clark at anytime in furtherance of Officer Sackett's shooting. Finally, for the same reasons discussed above, the Nebraska bank robbery evidence is also insufficient to support the conclusion that Clark played a knowing role in the shooting of Officer Sackett or took any actions in furtherance of that crime.

Having concluded that Trimble's uncorroborated accomplice testimony cannot be used to support Clark's convictions and that the remaining evidence is insufficient to support Clark's convictions for conspiracy to commit first-degree murder and for aiding and abetting first-degree murder, I conclude that Clark's convictions must be reversed outright. . . .

Notes and Questions

1. Notice the dates of Clark's crime, and of his prosecution. Ordinarily, a statute of limitations will bar prosecution for a crime after several years have passed without charges having been filed, much less several decades. But there is no statute of limitations for murder—the state may prosecute at any time up to the defendant's death. Were prosecutors right to charge Clark and Reed more than 30 years after Officer Sackett was shot and killed?

2. Two traditional rules of evidence figure prominently in the opinions in *Clark*. First, no criminal defendant may be convicted on accomplice testimony alone; the testimony must be corroborated by other evidence or it should receive no weight. The reason for that principle is straightforward: Accomplices have an incentive to shift blame from themselves to their partners in crime; their testimony is thus inherently suspect. Which leads to the second rule: When accomplices do testify, the trial judge must give a cautionary instruction to the jurors, telling them that accomplices like Trimble have good reason to lie, and that they should consider that fact when judging credibility. Clark's conviction was overturned because the trial judge violated the second rule. On appeal, Justice Page argued that the first rule was violated as well; because Trimble's testimony was not corroborated, Page maintained, it could not be considered when deciding whether the evidence was strong enough to allow a reasonable jury to convict.

3. One more piece of legal background is important to the decision in *Clark*. The Double Jeopardy Clause of the Fifth Amendment states: ". . . nor shall any person be subject for the same offence to be twice put in jeopardy of life or limb." One might suppose that, when a criminal conviction gets reversed, a second criminal trial is impermissible—two trials for "the same offence" would seem to amount to two distinct jeopardies for purposes of the Fifth Amendment. Double jeopardy law does not so hold. Instead, as is explained in *Clark*, the law permits retrials after appellate reversals as long as the evidence introduced in the first trial was legally sufficient for a reasonable jury to convict. Justice Anderson and his colleagues in the *Clark* majority thought the government satisfied this test; Justice Page thought not. Based on the descriptions in the two opinions, who had it right? Would you have voted to convict Clark based on the evidence described by Justices Anderson and Page?

4. Clark and Reed both sympathized with and sought to join the Black Panther Party. That party was founded in the mid-1960s by Huey Newton and Bobby Seale. Among the Black Panthers' expressed goals was an end to police brutality; some of the witnesses in *Clark* testified that the killing of Officer Sackett was designed to impress the Panthers' leaders and to induce them to let Reed and Clark join the party. A number of the Panthers' members were charged with violent felonies, though there was a good deal of dispute in the late 1960s and early 1970s about the evidentiary basis of those charges. The Panthers' critics saw them as a terrorist organization. The Panthers' supporters saw them as a political organization that law enforcement agencies, in particular the FBI, sought to harass.

Notes on Conspiracy, Complicity, and the Law of Homicide

1. Proof of conspiracy relies heavily on inference. Conspirators do not reduce their agreements to writing; usually, there is no express agreement at all, written or oral. Because criminal agreements are usually tacit, judges and juries must decide whether the circumstances suggest that the relevant parties agreed to commit the relevant crime. In *Clark*, the inference of agreement rests on two evidentiary sources: Clark's close association with Reed, and the testimony of their co-conspirator Trimble. Taken together, are those facts enough to prove conspiracy? Was Clark punished for conspiring to murder a police officer, or for having the wrong friends—and, perhaps, the wrong political beliefs as well?

2. The *mens rea* for conspiracy is specific intent. In order to prove conspiracy to commit murder, the government must prove, first, that the defendant knowingly joined the relevant agreement, and second, that the defendant had the purpose to kill the conspiracy's target. Because of that standard, there is no crime of conspiracy to commit manslaughter or negligent homicide; just as with attempt and solicitation, all homicidal conspiracies are conspiracies to commit murder.

3. State v. Greene, 874 A.2d 750 (Conn. 2005), involved a challenge to the above proposition. Mashawn Greene was charged with murder and conspiracy to commit murder; the jury convicted him of manslaughter and conspiracy to commit manslaughter. The Connecticut Supreme Court overturned both convictions; following is the discussion of the conspiracy charge:

> In State v. Beccia, 199 Conn. 1, 5, 505 A.2d 683 (1986), this court held that conspiracy to commit arson in the third degree . . . was not a cognizable offense under Connecticut law. We observed that
>
> > "conspiracy is a specific intent crime, with the intent divided into two elements: (a) the intent to agree or conspire and (b) the intent to commit

the offense which is the object of the conspiracy. . . . To sustain a conviction for conspiracy to commit a particular offense, the prosecution must show not only that the conspirators intended to agree but also that they *intended to commit the elements of the offense.*"

Id. at 3-4 (emphasis in original). We further noted that "the essential elements of the crime of arson in the third degree are the intentional starting of a fire or causing of an explosion thereby recklessly causing damage or destruction to a building." Id. at 4. Thus, the arson statute proscribed reckless conduct and "one who acts recklessly does not have a conscious objective to cause a particular result." Id. We concluded that conspiracy to commit arson was not a cognizable offense because "conspirators cannot agree to accomplish a result recklessly when that result is an essential element of the crime. . . . There is . . . no such crime as would require proof that one intended a result that accidentally occurred. . . ." Id. at 5.

Manslaughter in the first degree . . . , like arson, is a crime defined in terms of recklessly causing a result. . . . A person is guilty of manslaughter in the first degree in violation of [Conn. Gen. Stat.] §53a-55(a)(1) when "with intent to cause serious physical injury to another person, he causes the death of such person or of a third person. . . ." We previously have held that manslaughter in the first degree . . . is "committed without an intent to cause the death of another." . . . State v. Almeda, 189 Conn. 303, 308, 455 A.2d 1326 (1983).

Accordingly, we conclude that conspiracy to commit manslaughter in the first degree . . . is not a cognizable crime because it "requires a logical impossibility, namely, that the actor . . . [agree and] intend that an unintended death result." Id. at 309 (crime of attempted manslaughter in violation of §53a-55(a)(1) does not exist under Connecticut law because one cannot logically attempt to bring about unintended result). Therefore, we reverse the defendant's judgment of conviction for conspiracy to commit manslaughter in the first degree. . . .

874 A.2d at 770-71.

4. Accomplice liability for manslaughter is another matter. The crime of involuntary manslaughter usually requires proof of some degree of recklessness. In Riley v. State, 60 P.3d 204 (2002), the Alaska Court of Appeals considered whether defendants may be convicted of crimes of recklessness by means of complicity. The facts in *Riley* are as follows:

Richard L. Riley and another man, Edward F. Portalla, opened fire on an unsuspecting crowd of young people who were socializing around a bonfire on the Tanana River near Fairbanks. Two of the young people were seriously wounded. Riley and Portalla were indicted on two counts of first-degree assault (recklessly causing serious physical injury by means of a dangerous instrument) and six counts of third-degree assault (recklessly placing another person in fear of imminent serious physical injury by means of a dangerous instrument). Riley was ultimately convicted of all eight charges. In this appeal, Riley challenges his two convictions for first-degree assault.

The State faced a problem in prosecuting Riley and Portalla for first-degree assault: the physical evidence (in particular, the ballistics analysis) did not reveal which of the defendants' weapons had fired the wounding shots. The bullet recovered from the body of one victim was so deformed that it could not be matched to either Riley's or Portalla's weapon, and the bullet that wounded the other victim passed through the victim's body and was never recovered. Thus, with respect to each victim, the State could prove that the wound was inflicted by one of the two defendants, but the State could not easily prove which one.

60 P.3d at 205-06. Riley was convicted as an accomplice in the wounding of both injured victims. On appeal, he argued that Echols v. State, 818 P.2d 691 (Alaska App. 1991), barred such convictions. The court in *Riley* rejected that argument, and overruled *Echols*:

In *Echols*, . . . a wife was charged as an accomplice to first-degree assault committed by her husband. The State's evidence showed that the defendant summoned her husband to discipline their child, then stood by and watched while the husband inflicted serious physical injury on the child by whipping her with an electric cord. The question was whether the wife's conduct was sufficient to establish her accountability as an accomplice to the assault.

The underlying crime of first-degree assault required proof that the principal (the husband) acted recklessly with respect to the result (the infliction of serious physical injury). The State argued that the wife could be convicted as an accomplice to the first-degree assault because (1) she solicited her husband to discipline the child and (2) she acted with the culpable mental state required for the crime — i.e., she acted recklessly with respect to the possibility that the beating would result in serious physical injury to the child.

But this Court held that the wife's complicity could not be premised on recklessness. Rather, we held that the wife could be held accountable as an accomplice to the first-degree assault only if the State proved that she acted *intentionally* with respect to the prohibited result — i.e., that her conscious objective was to have the child suffer serious physical injury. . . .

. . . [T]he State asks us to re-examine our holding in *Echols*. We have done so and . . . we conclude that we misstated the law of complicity in *Echols*.

We were wrong when we said in *Echols* that liability for assault or criminal homicide under a complicity theory always requires proof that the defendant intended to cause the injury or the death, even though the underlying crime requires proof of only a lesser culpable mental state (extreme indifference to the value of human life, recklessness, or criminal negligence). When a defendant solicits, encourages, or assists another to engage in conduct, and does so with the intent to promote or facilitate that conduct, the defendant becomes accountable under Alaska Stat. §11.16.110(2) for that conduct. If that conduct leads to unintended injury or death, the defendant can be convicted of assault or criminal homicide if the government additionally proves that the defendant acted with the culpable mental state required for the charged crime.

Thus, to establish Riley's guilt of first-degree assault in the present case, the State did not have to prove that Riley acted with the intention of causing serious physical injury. Rather, the State had to prove that Riley acted recklessly with respect to the possibility that serious physical injury would be inflicted on another person through (1) Riley's own conduct or (2) the conduct of another for which Riley was accountable under Alaska Stat. §11.16.110. And, to prove that Riley was accountable for Portalla's conduct, the State had to prove (1) that Riley solicited, encouraged, or assisted Portalla's act of shooting at the victims, and (2) that Riley did so with the intent to promote or facilitate this conduct.

To summarize: when two or more people are jointly accountable for conduct under Alaska's complicity statute, and if, on the basis of that conduct, they are charged with a crime that is defined in terms of an unintended injury or death . . . , that same culpable mental state—whether it be "extreme indifference to the value of human life," "recklessness," or "criminal negligence"—applies to the State's prosecution of all participants, whether they acted as principals or accomplices, and regardless of whether the resulting injury or death can be linked beyond a reasonable doubt to a particular defendant's conduct.

60 P.3d at 206-07.

Riley's conviction seems unproblematic: After all, he fired into a crowd, and his conduct easily could have caused multiple deaths. What about the conviction in *Echols*? The defendant's conduct in that case consisted of one act—"summon[ing] her husband to discipline their child"—and one omission: watching while the husband beat the child. Assume for the sake of argument that the defendant did not know how her husband would behave when she summoned him. In that event, her conviction would rest wholly on her failure to intervene to protect her child. But Echols' non-intervention might have been motivated by fear for *her own* safety—not an admirable motive, to be sure, but hardly the sort of conduct for which one expects to go to prison. Should the government have to prove that Echols was not motivated by fear of her husband, in order to convict her as an accomplice in the beating? How can the state possibly prove that? On the other hand, is it fair to punish Echols for protecting herself?

B. CRIMINAL INTENT

1. Premeditation and Deliberation

Commonwealth v. Coleman

Supreme Judicial Court of Massachusetts
747 N.E.2d 666 (2001)

MARSHALL, Chief Justice.

The defendant was convicted of murder in the first degree on a theory of deliberate premeditation, and of unlawful possession of a firearm. The trial judge denied the defendant's motion to set aside the verdict and to enter a finding of not guilty or to order a new trial, or, in the alternative, to reduce the verdict to manslaughter. The defendant's motion to reconsider that ruling was also denied. The defendant appeals from his conviction of murder. He challenges the sufficiency of the evidence of deliberate premeditation. . . . We affirm the defendant's conviction of murder in the first degree. . . .

FACTS

The jury could have found that at approximately 2 A.M. on May 25, 1997, the defendant was involved in an altercation involving several persons outside a nightclub in Worcester. The fight began when two men attacked the defendant. At some point during or after the fight in which several persons had thrown punches, the defendant left the brawl and went to a nearby automobile where he retrieved a gun from the trunk. He then turned in the direction from which he had come and shot the victim at close range. There was evidence that the victim had followed the defendant to the automobile, but no evidence that the victim was armed at the time of the shooting. There was evidence that the defendant also shot the victim a second time as he lay on the ground. After the shooting, the defendant and three other men jumped into an automobile and sped away.

Paramedics arrived at the scene shortly after the shooting and found the victim with a gunshot wound to his chest. The victim was transported to a hospital, where he died approximately two hours later. A medical examiner located a single bullet that killed the victim lodged in his lower right chest. The gun used in the shooting was not recovered.

SUFFICIENCY OF THE EVIDENCE

The defendant asserts that the evidence was insufficient to permit the jury to find that the element of deliberate premeditation had been proved beyond a reasonable doubt because there was insufficient time for the defendant to have planned the killing. . . . There was no error.

. . . To convict the defendant of murder in the first degree, the Commonwealth was required to prove beyond a reasonable doubt that the defendant unlawfully killed the victim, with deliberate premeditation and malice aforethought. Commonwealth v. Judge, 420 Mass. 433, 437, 650 N.E.2d 1242 (1995). Because the defendant challenges the sufficiency of the evidence as to one element only—deliberate premeditation—we examine the sufficiency of evidence relevant to that element alone. The Commonwealth was required to establish beyond a reasonable doubt that the defendant "reflected on his resolution to kill," Commonwealth v. Ruci, 409 Mass. 94, 96, 564 N.E.2d 1000 (1991), and that the defendant's decision to kill was the product of "cool reflection," Commonwealth v. Davis, 403

Mass. 575, 582, 531 N.E.2d 577 (1988).[2] "Cool reflection merely requires that the purpose [be] resolved upon and the mind determined to do it before the blow is struck[;] then it is, within the meaning of the law, deliberately premeditated malice aforethought." Id.

The defendant recognizes that no particular period of reflection is required, and that a plan to murder may be formed in seconds. He argues that, because the fighting started when two men attacked the defendant and thereafter "everything was spontaneous," there was not enough time for the defendant to plan the killing. We disagree. Three witnesses testified that, during or after a brief fistfight, the defendant walked to the trunk of a nearby automobile and obtained a gun. One witness testified that, as the defendant walked toward an automobile, he overheard another man say, "It ain't over. It ain't over. Pop the trunk. Pop the trunk." This witness saw the trunk pop open, and the man hand something to the defendant, who then turned toward and shot the victim. A rational jury could infer that as the defendant walked toward the automobile, he formed the plan to kill. See Commonwealth v. Whipple, 377 Mass. 709, 714-15, 387 N.E.2d 575 (1979) (sufficient evidence of premeditation where defendant disengaged from fistfight, obtained gun from nearby automobile, returned and shot victim).

One witness also testified that, after the defendant shot at the victim once, the victim fell to the ground, and the defendant "stepped back like a foot or so, and . . . shot at him again." Other witnesses also heard more than one shot. Because only one bullet wound was located in the victim's body and the victim fell to the ground after the first shot, the defendant argues that this evidence cannot support a finding of deliberate premeditation, as the fatal shot had already been fired. But the jury could have inferred in these circumstances that the multiple shots fired at the victim were evidence of deliberate premeditation, even if only one shot killed the victim. Commonwealth v. Good, 409 Mass. 612, 618, 568 N.E.2d 1127 (1991) (evidence that defendant approached victim and at close range fired three bullets at victim sufficient to support finding that "before the shooting, the defendant at least briefly reflected on his resolution to kill").

The defendant points to testimony that he claims undermines the evidence of deliberate premeditation, namely that the victim chased the defendant as he approached the automobile from which he obtained the gun. But there was no evidence that the victim was armed, or that the defendant

---

2. As the defendant recognizes, the judge correctly instructed that

"deliberate premeditation excludes action which is taken so quickly that there is no time to reflect on the action and then decide to do it. The Commonwealth must show that the defendant's resolution to kill was, at least for some short period of time, the product of reflection."

shot the victim to protect himself from the victim. In any event, the defendant's reliance on contradictory evidence is misplaced. "Once sufficient evidence is presented to warrant submission of the charges to the jury, it is for the jury alone to determine what weight will be accorded to the evidence." Commonwealth v. Ruci, supra at 97. . . .

POST-CONVICTION MOTION [TO REDUCE] THE VERDICT

. . . The defendant also argues that the judge abused his discretion by not reducing the verdict because the "verdict was against the weight of the evidence and a manslaughter verdict would be more consonant with justice." Mass. R. Crim. P. 25(b)(2). The defendant points to the evidence that he did not start the fight, but became involved after being attacked by two unknown men. He notes that there was evidence that the victim was walking or running behind him when the defendant retrieved the gun.[4] He suggests that, because the shooting occurred during a "free-for-all" during which he and the victim exchanged blows, the crime should more properly be seen as manslaughter as the result of provocation or sudden combat. . . .

Rule 25(b)(2) empowers a judge to reduce a jury's verdict when, in the judge's discretion, the lesser verdict is required in the interests of justice. We have noted, however, that a judge should exercise this broad power sparingly. See Commonwealth v. Woodward, 427 Mass. 659, 667, 694 N.E.2d 1277 (1998). The judge concluded that "considering the weight and credibility of the Commonwealth's case, the verdict was consonant with justice" and "in the interest of justice." On our own review of the evidence, without benefit of the judge's superior information regarding the credibility of the witnesses, we cannot conclude that he abused his discretion. . . . [T]here is no evidence suggesting that the defendant killed the victim because he was provoked or engaged in sudden combat.

The verdict in this case is consistent with similar cases that have resulted in verdicts of murder in the first degree. See, e.g., Commonwealth v. Whipple, 377 Mass. 709, 711-15, 387 N.E.2d 575 (1979) (verdict not reduced where defendant left brief fistfight to obtain gun and returned to shoot victim); Commonwealth v. Watkins, 373 Mass. 849, 852-53, 370 N.E.2d 701 (1977) (verdict not reduced where evidence showed that during argument defendant ran to another room, retrieved knife, returned, and stabbed victim). The judge applied the proper legal standards, and did not abuse his discretion in denying the defendant's motion. . . .

Judgment affirmed.

---

4. The defendant insists that he did not shoot the victim but recognizes that the evidence warranted a jury finding to that effect.

Notes and Questions

1. Premeditation is a variant of specific intent. Recall that, at common law, specific intent was chiefly used as the *mens rea* standard for property crimes: theft, fraud, and similar offenses. Violent felonies—murder, rape, arson—were usually general intent crimes. As you may recall from the cases in Chapter 3, that basic structure endures. Sometimes, though, specific intent is used to distinguish ordinary violence from especially culpable violence. The law of assault and battery offers a prime example: In addition to simple assault, nearly all state criminal codes punish assault with intent to rape, assault with intent to kill, and assault with intent to cause serious bodily harm—all specific intent crimes, and all punished more severely than ordinary assault and battery. So using specific intent to kill as a means of distinguishing the most serious murders from the rest is hardly a novel idea. Nor is it a recent idea: The first use of premeditation in American murder cases dates to the 1790s in Pennsylvania.

The innovative part of premeditation (or, as some state statutes term it, "premeditation and deliberation"—the difference in terminology does not seem to make much of a difference in practice, see Note 5, infra) is the part that is at issue in *Coleman*: the requirement that the government prove not just purpose, but a particular *kind*, or *quality*, of purposeful thought. This was demonstrated in *Coleman* by the presence (at least according to the court, which found that it could have formed during the brief moments while the defendant walked to the car to get the gun) of a plan or rational design to kill.

As one well-known opinion from the D.C. Circuit explained it, in reversing a first-degree murder conviction based on improper jury instructions:

> Our concern is that there was no straight-forward explanation to the jury of the difference between the two degrees of murder—that first degree murder, with its requirement of premeditation and deliberation, covers calculated and planned killings, while homicides that are unplanned or impulsive, even though they are intentional and with malice aforethought, are murder in the second degree.
>
> In homespun terminology, intentional murder is in the first degree if committed in cold blood, and is murder in the second degree if committed on impulse or in the sudden heat of passion. These are the archetypes, that clarify by contrast. The real facts may be hard to classify and may lie between the poles. A sudden passion, like lust, rage, or jealousy, may spawn an impulsive intent yet persist long enough and in such a way as to permit that intent to become the subject of a further reflection and weighing of consequences and hence to take on the character of a murder executed without compunction and "in cold blood." The term "in cold blood" does not necessarily mean the assassin lying in wait, or the kind of murder brilliantly depicted by Truman Capote in *In Cold Blood* (1965). Thus the common understanding might find both passion and cold blood in the husband who surprises his wife in adultery,

leaves the house to buy a gun at a sporting goods store, and returns for a deadly sequel. The analysis of the jury would be illuminated, however, if it is first advised that a typical case of first degree is the murder in cold blood; that murder committed on impulse or in sudden passion is murder in the second degree; and then instructed that a homicide conceived in passion constitutes murder in the first degree only if the jury is convinced beyond a reasonable doubt that there was an appreciable time after the design was conceived and that in this interval there was a further thought, and a turning over in the mind—and not a mere persistence of the initial impulse of passion.

Austin v. United States, 382 F.2d 129, 137 (D.C. Cir. 1967).

The basic premise of the premeditation standard seems to be that, all else equal, killings that are based on rational thought (as evidenced by planning) are more blameworthy than impulsive or spontaneous killings. Is this premise correct? Does the answer depend on the motive behind the killing?

2. Was Coleman's conduct actually planned, or was it spontaneous? The court notes that "[t]he fight began when two men attacked the defendant." The defendant then ran to his car—and the victim followed, at which point the defendant grabbed a gun and shot the victim. Did the defendant plan on getting into a fight? Did he plan on being followed? Do the facts as stated in *Coleman* sound more like a calculated killing based on cool reflection, or do they instead paint the picture of an unplanned fight that quickly escalated out of control?

3. Note that although planning may be *sufficient*, it is not *necessary* in order to prove premeditation. If evidence of planning is not present, what other kinds of evidence might suffice to establish premeditation? If cases like *Coleman*, *Whipple*, and *Watkins* are all instances of premeditated first-degree murder, are there any purposeful killings that *aren't* premeditated first-degree murder?

4. Notice the high level of factual uncertainty in *Coleman*. Witnesses claimed that Coleman shot the victim more than once, but the victim suffered only one gunshot wound. The gun was never found. The degree of threat the victim posed was unclear, as was the role of the man who said to Coleman, "it ain't over" and "pop the trunk." Yet the fight, and the killing to which it led, happened in front of multiple witnesses. If these facts seem unclear, how likely is it that courts—and juries—will be able to figure out what happened in the many cases in which no one save the defendant and the victim was present when the victim was killed? How should the law of homicide respond to that uncertainty?

5. In Nika v. State, 198 P.3d 839 (Nev. 2008), the Nevada Supreme Court discussed the meaning of premeditation and deliberation, both past and present:

> Since the days of territorial law, first-degree murder in Nevada has included killings that are "willful, deliberate, and premeditated." The meaning of the terms or the phrase as a whole has never been addressed legislatively. . . .

[T]here is no indication that the terms have anything other than their ordinary dictionary meanings. But those ordinary dictionary meanings have varied. In different sources and at different times, the terms have been used to define each other, suggesting synonyms or overlapping connotations,[19] or as similar concepts of mental operation differing in degree.[20]

. . . For example, in its 1877 decision in State v. Harris, 12 Nev. 414, 422-23 (1877), this court . . . approved of an instruction that explained the class of first-degree murder based on a "willful, premeditated and deliberate killing." The instruction considered in *Harris* informed the jury that to fit this class of first-degree murder, the unlawful killing must be the result of a "deliberate and preconceived intent to kill." Id. at 416. The instruction further informed the jury that "[t]he unlawful killing must be accompanied with a deliberate and clear intent to take life" and "[t]he intent to kill must be the result of deliberate premeditation," "formed upon a preexisting reflection, and not upon a sudden heat of passion sufficient to preclude the idea of deliberation." Id.

Three years later, in State v. Lopez, 15 Nev. 407, 414 (1880), this court observed that the words "premeditation" and "deliberation" "are of similar import, each being held to imply the other." . . .

. . . In Powell v. State, 108 Nev. 700, 838 P.2d 921 (1992), vacated on other grounds, 511 U.S. 79 (1994), the court considered a challenge to the [standard jury instruction, which stated that "if the jury believes . . . that the act constituting the killing has been preceded by and has been the result of premeditation . . . , it is willful, deliberate and premeditated murder."] . . . In rejecting that challenge, this court observed that prior decisions . . . used "premeditated and deliberate" as a single term and that other courts had treated the terms "willful, deliberate, and premeditated" as "a single phrase, meaning simply that the

19. *Compare* The American Heritage Dictionary of the English Language 349 (1981) (defining "deliberate" as "[t]o consider (a matter) by carefully weighing alternatives or the like," "[p]remeditated; intentional," "[c]areful and slow in deciding or determining," "[n]ot rashly or hastily determined"), *and* Black's Law Dictionary 438 (7th ed. 1999) (defining "deliberate" as "[i]ntentional; premeditated; fully considered" and "[u]nimpulsive; slow in deciding"), *with* The American Heritage Dictionary of the English Language 1033 (1981) (defining "premeditate" as "[t]o meditate or deliberate beforehand"), *and* Webster's Seventh New Collegiate Dictionary 671 (1969) (defining "premeditate" as "to think, consider, or deliberate beforehand"), *and* Webster's Third New International Dictionary 1789 (2002) (defining "premeditation" as "previous deliberation as to action; planning and contriving; forethought; consideration or planning of an act beforehand that shows intent to commit that act").

20. Black's Law Dictionary 513-14 (4th ed. rev. 1968) ("'Deliberation' and 'premeditation' are of the same character of mental operations, differing only in degree. Deliberation is but prolonged premeditation. In other words, in law, deliberation is premeditation in a cool state of the blood, or, where there has been heat of passion, it is premeditation continued beyond the period within which there has been time for the blood to cool, in the given case. Deliberation is not only to think of beforehand, which may be but for an instant, but the inclination to do the act is considered, weighed, pondered upon, for such a length of time after a provocation is given as the jury may find was sufficient for the blood to cool. One in a heat of passion may premeditate without deliberating. Deliberation is only exercised in a cool state of the blood, while premeditation may be either in that state of the blood or in the heat of passion.").

actor intended to commit the act and intended death to result." Id. at 708-09, 838 P.2d at 927. On these grounds, this court concluded that as long as the jury is properly instructed on premeditation, "it is not necessary to separately define deliberateness or willfulness." Id. at 709-10, 838 P.2d at 927. . . .

. . . Nevada was not alone in the view espoused by [*Powell*] that the terms "willful," "deliberate," and "premeditated" need not be separately defined, but rather those terms constituted a single phrase. . . . The Alabama courts [concluded] that "'[p]remeditation' and 'deliberation' are synonymous terms, which, as elements of first degree murder, mean simply that the accused, before he committed the fatal act, intended that he would commit the act at the time that he did, and that death would be the result of the act." Sanders v. State, 392 So. 2d 1280, 1282 (Ala. Crim. App. 1980). Maryland . . . reached a similar conclusion, stating that "[t]he trilogy of terms [willful, deliberate, and premeditated] connotes the same general idea — the intention to kill." Brown v. State, 410 A.2d 17, 22 (Md. Ct. Special App. 1979). The *Brown* court further reasoned that "[t]he use of all three words seems to us to serve no purpose other than to shroud the intention in an aura of redundancy so as to convey the seriousness of the matter." Id. More recently, the Mississippi Supreme Court "held that malice aforethought, premeditated design and deliberate design all mean the same thing." Wilson v. State, 936 So. 2d 357, 363 (Miss. 2006).

In Byford v. State, 116 Nev. 215, 235, 994 P.2d 700, 713-14 (2000), however, this court concluded that "willfulness," "deliberation," and "premeditation" are distinct elements of the *mens rea* required for this category of first-degree murder. In doing so, the court abandoned the line of cases starting with *Powell* . . . because those cases had reduced "deliberation" to a synonym of "premeditation" and then had further reduced "premeditation and deliberation" to "intent." . . . Because the [traditional jury] instruction defining premeditation "underemphasized the element of deliberation," this court set forth instructions with distinct definitions for willfulness, deliberation, and premeditation. Id. at 234, 994 P.2d at 713.

198 P.3d at 845-47. Jury instructions ultimately determine what terms like premeditation and deliberation mean in litigated cases. Here are the revised jury instructions the court wrote in *Byford*:

Murder of the first degree is murder which is perpetrated by means of any kind of willful, deliberate, and premeditated killing. All three elements — willfulness, deliberation, and premeditation — must be proven beyond a reasonable doubt before an accused can be convicted of first-degree murder.

Willfulness is the intent to kill. There need be no appreciable space of time between formation of the intent to kill and the act of killing.

Deliberation is the process of determining upon a course of action to kill as a result of thought, including weighing the reasons for and against the action and considering the consequences of the action.

A deliberate determination may be arrived at in a short period of time. But in all cases the determination must not be formed in passion, or if formed in passion, it must be carried out after there has been time for the passion to subside and deliberation to occur. A mere unconsidered and rash impulse is not deliberate, even though it includes the intent to kill.

Premeditation is a design, a determination to kill, distinctly formed in the mind by the time of the killing.

Premeditation need not be for a day, an hour, or even a minute. It may be as instantaneous as successive thoughts of the mind. For if the jury believes from the evidence that the act constituting the killing has been preceded by and has been the result of premeditation, no matter how rapidly the act follows the premeditation, it is premeditated.

The law does not undertake to measure in units of time the length of the period during which the thought must be pondered before it can ripen into an intent to kill which is truly deliberate and premeditated. The time will vary with different individuals and under varying circumstances.

The true test is not the duration of time, but rather the extent of the reflection. A cold, calculated judgment and decision may be arrived at in a short period of time, but a mere unconsidered and rash impulse, even though it includes an intent to kill, is not deliberation and premeditation as will fix an unlawful killing as murder of the first degree.

994 P.2d at 713-15.

Different parts of the *Byford* instruction seem to send different messages. Willfulness requires no elapsed time; the same appears to be true of premeditation, which may be "as instantaneous as successive thoughts of the mind." Deliberation is another story. There, the instruction seems to require the weighing of arguments, the consideration of consequences, and the opportunity for passion to cool—all things that happen over time, not instantaneously. Query whether deliberating juries properly understand the definition of deliberation—or whether, instead, that term becomes a synonym for premeditation and willfulness, both of which appear to mean purpose or design. Why not require that all first-degree murders be deliberate, and excise willfulness and premeditation from the definition of the crime? Would that make the law of homicide more lawlike? More just?

6. The defendant in State v. Texieira, 944 A.2d 132 (R.I. 2008), was charged with first-degree murder under a statute that covers "[e]very murder perpetrated by poison, lying in wait, or any other kind of willful, deliberate, malicious, and premeditated killing." Rhode Island General Laws §11-23-1. There was no doubt that the killing in *Texieira* was malicious—see the discussion of "malice aforethought" in the next subsection—but the named defendant claimed it was not premeditated. Here are the facts:

The events that led to [the murder] began on August 30, 2003, when [Edgar] Ortega and three of his friends, Rigoberto Gomez, Victor Alonzo, and Jonathan Peguero, decided to spend the evening at "The Keg Room," a Providence nightclub. The impetus for the fight occurred after they arrived at that nightclub [at about 11:30 P.M.] when a club patron, later identified as Jonas Chattelle, walked by and bumped Mr. Ortega from behind while he was dancing with a female friend. The two men stared at each other ominously, but apparently did not confront each other at that time.

. . . [A]t approximately 2:00 A.M., as the club was closing, Mr. Ortega began to argue with Mr. Chattelle, saying, "[H]it me, hit me. I don't care that the bouncers are here." As they continued to verbally quarrel, some bouncers came over to the two men and attempted to separate them. Mr. Ortega struggled with the bouncers; the bouncers then physically ushered Mr. Ortega out of the nightclub. The bouncers also directed several other patrons out of the club through its back entrance.

Mr. Ortega met up with his friends outside of the club and warned them that they should "watch out because there might be [a fight]." Immediately after making that statement, Mr. Ortega saw Mr. Chattelle and they began to fight on the sidewalk. . . . As the two men continued their physical confrontation, a sizeable crowd began to surround them. . . . [R]ecognizing that it was an unfair fight (Mr. Ortega was a large man who stood over six feet tall and weighed over three hundred pounds, whereas Mr. Chattelle weighed only about 180 pounds), the crowd became rowdier, yelling at the two men. Mr. Gomez heard defendant, a friend of Mr. Chattelle's, say: "This is not going to be fair. This is not going to be fair. This is my boy. He's not going to go down like that." . . .

Eventually, the fight between Mr. Chattelle and Mr. Ortega evolved into a melee involving friends of both men. At some point, Mr. Ortega was brought down to the ground, at which time Mr. Heredia proceeded to hit and kick him in the abdominal area. Mr. Ortega attempted to get up and was on all fours; at that point, in the descriptive words of [one witness], defendant "kicked Ortega in the face . . . [h]ard, like he was trying to kick [a football] thirty yards." . . .

At that time, Mr. Ortega was struck in the head by a bottle, possibly thrown by Mr. Heredia. After being struck by the bottle, Mr. Ortega attempted to stand up, but he was "confused" and was moving like a "punch drunk boxer" and was "walking wobbly." It appears that at this point the police arrived and began to take action to disperse the crowd.

It is here that the several accounts of the events . . . begin to diverge. According to Mr. Alonzo, he and Mr. Ortega attempted to flee the scene; however, they were spotted by Mr. Chattelle and several others, including defendant, and the fighting resumed. Mr. Alonzo testified that defendant attacked him and that he and defendant were "struggling" when he felt someone hit the back of his head. Mr. Alonzo then saw defendant run toward his friends, who were in a circle "kicking" Mr. Ortega. Mr. Alonzo testified that he saw defendant enter the circle, but that he could not see what, if anything, [the defendant] was doing.

Another friend of Mr. Ortega's, Rigoberto Gomez, testified that, during the second phase of the fight, he saw defendant, among others, kicking and stomping on Mr. Ortega. According to Mr. Gomez, he witnessed defendant kick Mr. Ortega in the head "about three times." . . .

Dylan Andrews, a bystander who had been at the club and who did not know Mr. Ortega or any of the other individuals involved in the fight, testified that . . . he saw Mr. Texieira run approximately three to four steps and then kick Mr. Ortega in the face. Mr. Andrews stated that the noise was jarring and sounded "like [Mr. Ortega's] face broke." At that point, Mr. Ortega's head went back, his hands came off the ground, and he collapsed on the ground without further movement.

The police found Mr. Ortega unconscious, and medical aid was summoned. He was taken by ambulance to the hospital, but he was pronounced dead shortly thereafter.

Doctor Dorota Latuszynski, the Acting Chief Medical Examiner who performed the autopsy on Mr. Ortega, testified that Mr. Ortega suffered multiple blunt force traumas to the head and body. She identified a contusion and abrasions above the right eye and a further abrasion on the cheekbone. She also testified that Mr. Ortega had a black eye, hemorrhaging of the eye, and a laceration to the tissue that connects the lips with the gums. Mr. Ortega had additional contusions on his left shoulder and back, on his right hand and right elbow, as well as abrasions on his wrist, armpit, and knees. Doctor Latuszynski listed the cause of death as cerebral edema (swelling of the brain) and subarachnoid hemorrhage of the brain due to blunt force trauma.

944 A.2d at 134-36. The Rhode Island Supreme Court found the evidence sufficient to prove Texieira guilty of premeditated murder. Was that result correct? How much planning does it take to show premeditation? How deliberate must deliberation be?

7. What if a defendant intentionally (and, let's assume, with premeditation) tries to kill one victim (say, a gang rival), but accidentally misses the intended victim and instead kills an innocent bystander? The common law developed the doctrine of "transferred intent" to handle such situations. Under transferred intent, the defendant's intent to kill one victim (who survived) transfers to the other victim (who died), and the defendant is guilty of premeditated first-degree murder; he may also be found guilty of attempted murder for the failed try. See, e.g., People v. Shabazz, 38 Cal. 4th 55; 130 P.3d 519; 40 Cal. Rptr. 3d 750 (Cal. S. Ct. 2006). Sharad Shabazz, a member of the West Boulevard Crips, walked up to a car in a drive-through lane at a Popeye's Chicken restaurant and fired repeatedly into the car, in an effort to kill a member of the rival Black P Stone Bloods. He missed his intended target, but killed another passenger in the car. The passenger who died was Lori Gonzalez, a 20-year-old college student and the granddaughter of the Los Angeles Chief of Police, Bernard Parks. (Gonzalez was not affiliated with either gang; according to the court, "her death was simply attributable to being in the wrong place at the wrong time.") Shabazz was convicted of first-degree murder for the killing of Gonzalez, and attempted first-degree murder for the attempt to kill his gang rival; he was sentenced to life without parole. The court, relying on transferred intent, affirmed both of the convictions.

Note that the same theory of transferred intent also can be applied to other homicide crimes, such as second-degree intentional murder and voluntary manslaughter.

2. "Malice Aforethought"

At common law, the *mens rea* for murder (there were no degrees of murder back then) was "malice," or as the term was more commonly stated, "malice aforethought." After a half-century of reform in state criminal codes, that phrase remains the *mens rea* for second-degree murder in most states. One clear example of malice aforethought (indeed, the paradigmatic example of second-degree murder) is when the defendant acts with the intent to kill (but without premeditation). Three other *mens rea* phrases from the common law—"depraved heart," "abandoned and malignant heart," and "depraved indifference"—also play a large role in defining the scope of malice aforethought, and thus the scope of second-degree murder, because the criminal law treats them as the moral equivalent of intent to kill. What do malice aforethought and "depraved heart" mean in this context? How does the government prove that a given killer displayed those characteristics? Do these vague phrases help or hinder the effort to distinguish the worst homicides from the rest?

State v. Porter

Supreme Court of Idaho
142 Idaho 371; 128 P.3d 908 (2005)

SCHROEDER, Chief Justice.
. . . Michael S. Porter met D.J. Flett during an evening of drinking in a bar. A conflict erupted between Porter and Flett outside the bar at approximately 2:00 A.M. Porter punched Flett, who fell. Porter hit him two or three more times in the face as Flett lay on the ground. Flett suffered extensive injuries to his face and head, including brain damage likely caused by his head hitting the pavement after he was knocked unconscious. He died from the injuries.

The State conceded at preliminary hearing that the evidence did not support a finding of intent to kill, but argued that the evidence did show malice aforethought which supported the charge of second degree murder. The magistrate judge held that the State had met its burden to show malice aforethought although there was insufficient evidence to show intent to kill. The magistrate judge bound Porter over for trial on the second degree murder. Porter moved to dismiss the charge in district court or, in the alternative, that the charge be reduced from second degree murder to involuntary manslaughter. The district court reduced the charge to voluntary manslaughter, concluding that the intent to kill was an essential element for second degree murder but not for voluntary manslaughter.

Both parties appealed. The Court of Appeals ruled that neither second degree murder nor voluntary manslaughter requires [that] the defendant possess the intent to kill the victim. The Court of Appeals reversed the district court's order reducing the charge and remanded with instructions to reinstate the second degree murder charge. Porter petitioned this Court for review. . . .

Porter contends that the intent to kill is an element of second degree murder, and therefore, a charge of second degree murder is inappropriate since there was insufficient evidence to show Porter had the intent to kill Flett. The State argues that the intent to kill is not a necessary element of second degree murder and the charge against Porter should stand. Murder is defined in Idaho as follows:

> *Murder is the unlawful killing of a human being* including, but not limited to, a human embryo or fetus, *with malice aforethought* or the intentional application of torture to a human being. . . . The death of a human being caused by such torture is murder irrespective of proof of specific intent to kill; torture causing death shall be deemed the equivalent of intent to kill.

Idaho Code §18-4001 (emphasis added). Porter contends that the legislature's inclusion of language that murder by torture does not require a specific intent to kill indicates that the legislature intended a finding of specific intent to kill when a murder occurs with malice aforethought. Idaho Code §18-4002 defines malice:

> Such malice may be express *or* implied. It is express when there is manifested a deliberate intention unlawfully to take away the life of a fellow creature. *It is implied when* no considerable provocation appears, or when *the circumstances attending the killing show an abandoned and malignant heart.*

(Emphasis added). . . .

. . . In State v. Aragon, 690 P.2d 293 (Idaho 1984), this Court held that the instructions given in the district court properly defined malice and did not blur the distinction between first and second degree murder. The instructions provided in part:

> As set forth in the preceding instructions on murder, any unlawful killing of a human being with malice aforethought is murder. If nothing further characterizes the killing, the murder is of the second degree. To constitute the higher offense of murder in the first degree, there must be willfulness, deliberation and premeditation in addition to malice aforethought. Willfulness means that there was manifested a clear intent to take life. Deliberation and premeditation means done with reflection and conceived beforehand and not done upon a sudden heat of passion or other condition precluding the idea of deliberation.

Aragon, 690 P.2d at 297. The Court held that malice was properly distinguished from "intent to take life, premeditation, conceived beforehand, and deliberation, done with reflection" and the instructions properly set forth "the additional elements necessary to prove first degree murder, and thus there was no error." Id. at 298. . . .

. . . The elements of express and implied malice that will support a charge of murder are set forth in Idaho Criminal Jury Instruction No. 703:

> Malice may be express or implied. Malice is express when there is manifested a deliberate intention unlawfully to kill a human being. Malice is implied when:
>
> 1. The killing resulted from an intentional act,
> 2. The natural consequences of the act are dangerous to human life, and
> 3. The act was deliberately performed with knowledge of the danger to, and with conscious disregard for, human life.
>
> When it is shown that a killing resulted from the intentional doing of an act with express or implied malice, no other mental state need be shown to establish the mental state of malice aforethought. The mental state constituting malice aforethought does not necessarily require any ill will or hatred of the person killed. The word "aforethought" does not imply deliberation or the lapse of time. It only means that the malice must precede rather than follow the act.

. . . Porter contends that involuntary manslaughter is the appropriate charge in this case because, as with murder, intent to kill is an essential element of voluntary manslaughter. He relies on State v. Ransom, 50 P.3d 1055 (Idaho App. 2002), in which the Idaho Court of Appeals stated, "The key distinction between voluntary manslaughter and involuntary manslaughter is that voluntary manslaughter requires an intent to kill, while involuntary manslaughter does not." *Ransom*, 50 P.3d at 1061. . . . [T]he *Ransom* court cited State v. Atwood, 669 P.2d 204, 207 (Idaho App. 1983), for the following elements of voluntary manslaughter: "(a) an unlawful killing, with (b) the intent to kill, but without malice." The Court of Appeals' decision in this case rejects the prior case law stating that voluntary manslaughter requires an intent to kill. The Court of Appeals' analysis is correct. To the extent that prior cases state that the intent to kill is a necessary element of voluntary manslaughter, those cases are disavowed. . . .

The decision of the district court is vacated and the case is remanded for proceedings under the charge of second degree murder.

Notes on the Meaning of Malice Aforethought

1. The facts in *Porter* sound eerily similar to the facts in State v. Texieira, 944 A.2d 132 (R.I. 2008), supra at page 763, do they not? Why was Texieira guilty of first-degree murder based on premeditation, while Porter was guilty only of second-degree murder based on malice aforethought?

2. Two generations ago, Herbert Wechsler and Jerome Michael described malice aforethought as "a term of art signifying neither malice nor forethought." Herbert Wechsler & Jerome Michael, A Rationale of the Law of Homicide: Part I, 37 Colum. L. Rev. 701, 707 (1937). American courts generally use the term as it is used in *Porter*, to describe killings with any of three distinct mental states. Killings with "express malice" are intentional killings. Killings with "implied malice" fall into one of two subcategories: homicides in which the defendant intended to cause the victim serious injury (typical examples include shooting the victim anywhere in the torso, or otherwise inflicting injuries of such a nature and degree that they might be expected to be fatal), and homicides in which the circumstances of the killing reveal that the defendant acted with a "depraved heart" or with "depraved indifference." In most states, as in *Porter*, killings with implied malice constitute second-degree murder, even absent proof that the defendant actually intended to kill the victim.

3. The definition of manslaughter plays off the definition of murder. Ordinarily, voluntary manslaughter covers intentional killings committed in the "heat of passion" as a result of provocation (see pages 798-812 below), while involuntary manslaughter covers reckless killings that do not rise to the level of depravity required by the law of second-degree murder. In other words, intentional homicides end up as either first-degree murder, second-degree murder, or voluntary manslaughter, depending on the culpability of the defendant; reckless homicides will be either second-degree murder or involuntary manslaughter. Do the cases you have read thus far convince you that this doctrinal structure makes sense? Does the outcome in *Porter* make sense? How should killings that arise from bar fights—historically, a common fact pattern (apparently, fighting is what men in bars mostly did before ESPN and beer pong came along)—be categorized? How severely should such killings be punished?

4. Consider the definition of malice aforethought used in Iowa jury instructions:

> "Malice" is a state of mind which leads one to intentionally do a wrongful act to the injury of another out of actual hatred, or with an evil or unlawful purpose. Malice may be established by evidence of actual hatred, or by proof of a deliberate or fixed intent to do injury. Malice may be found from the act and conduct of the defendant, and the means used in doing the wrongful and injurious act.

State v. Bentley, 757 N.W.2d 257, 265 (Iowa 2008). The Iowa Supreme Court explains that definition this way:

> Our law provides that malice to support a conviction for first-degree murder must be "formed before and continue[] to exist at the time of the injury." State v. Hofer, 28 N.W.2d 475, 482 (Iowa 1947). This statement captures the essential meaning of the "aforethought" component of the malice requirement. Importantly, "[t]he relationship that must be shown between the state of mind that is malice aforethought and the homicidal act is more accurately characterized as a causal relationship than as a temporal relationship." State v.

Lee, 494 N.W.2d 706, 707 (Iowa 1993). In other words, the malice must result in the homicidal act. This concept is the critical aspect expressed by "malice aforethought."

757 N.W.2d at 265.

5. Under English law, the first of the two subcategories of implied malice — killings in which the defendant intended to cause serious injury — constitutes murder. The second subcategory — killings under circumstances that show the defendant acted with a "depraved heart" — does not: Killings that are merely reckless, even extremely so, fall within the definition of manslaughter, not murder. But the two categories may not really be as distinct as that description suggests. Consider the facts of this English murder case:

> The appellant lost his temper and threw his three-month-old son on to a hard surface. His son sustained a fractured skull and died. The appellant was charged with murder. The Crown did not contend that the appellant desired to kill his son or to cause him serious injury. The issue was whether the appellant nevertheless had the intention to cause serious harm. The appellant denied that he had any such intention.

Regina v. Woollin, 4 All E.R. 103 (1998) (opinion of Lord Steyn). Don't you wish American judges wrote such pithy descriptions of facts and arguments?

Jury instructions in English cases differ from those used in American cases. Here in America, judges tend to follow standard form instructions governing the definitions of relevant legal terms, and try to say as little as possible about the facts of the case at hand. English judges likewise follow form instructions on the law, but are more willing to comment on the evidence than their American cousins. There were two key passages in the trial judge's instructions in *Woollin*. Here is the first, as quoted in Lord Steyn's opinion:

> In looking at this, you should ask yourselves two questions and I am going to suggest that you write them down. First of all, how probable was the consequence which resulted from his throw, the consequence being, as you know, serious injury? How probable was the consequence of serious injury which resulted from his throw? Secondly, did he foresee that consequence in the second before or at the time of throwing?
>
> The second question is of particular importance, members of the jury, because he could not have intended serious harm could he, if he did not foresee the consequence and did not appreciate at the time that serious harm might result from his throw? If he thought, or may have thought, that in throwing the child he was exposing him to only the slight risk of being injured, then you would probably readily conclude that he did not intend to cause serious injury, because it was outside his contemplation that he would be seriously injured. But the defence say here that he never thought about the consequence at all when he threw the child. He did not give it a moment's

thought. Again, if that is right, or may be right, you may readily conclude that he did not appreciate that serious harm would result. It follows from that, if that is how you find, that you cannot infer that he intended to do Karl really serious harm unless you are sure that serious harm was a virtual certainty from what he was doing and he appreciated that that was the case.

And here is the second:

> If you think that he had not given any thought to the consequences of what he was doing before he did it, then the Crown would have failed to prove the necessary intent, the intent to cause really serious harm, for murder and you should acquit him of murder and convict him of manslaughter.
>
> If, on the other hand, you reject that interpretation and are quite satisfied that he was aware of what he was doing and must have realised and appreciated when he threw that child that there was a substantial risk that he would cause serious injury to it, then it would be open to you to find that he intended to cause injury to the child and you should convict him of murder.

The first of these passages suggests that Woollin was guilty of murder only if he knew that "serious harm was a virtual certainty" when he threw the child down. The second suggests that Woollin's conduct constituted murder if he "appreciated when he threw the child that there was a substantial risk that he would cause serious injury." Which standard was correct? The Law Lords decided that "virtual certainty" more accurately described the governing law. As Lord Steyn put the point:

> By using the phrase "substantial risk" the judge blurred the line between intention and recklessness, and hence between murder and manslaughter. The misdirection enlarged the scope of the mental element required for murder. It was a material misdirection. At one stage it was argued that the earlier correct direction "cured" the subsequent incorrect direction. A misdirection cannot by any means always be cured by the fact that the judge at an earlier or later stage gave a correct direction. After all, how is a jury to choose between a correct and an incorrect direction on a point of law? . . .
>
> That is, however, not the end of the matter. For my part, I have given anxious consideration to the observation of the Court of Appeal that, if the judge had used the phrase "a virtual certainty," the verdict would have been the same. In this case there was no suggestion of any other ill-treatment of the child. It would also be putting matters too high to say that on the evidence before the jury it was an open-and-shut case of murder rather than manslaughter. In my view the conviction of murder is unsafe. The conviction of murder must be quashed.

Is *Woollin* rightly decided? If the defendant had been charged with and convicted of "depraved heart" murder in an American court, would your answer change? See the next case.

State v. Robinson

Supreme Court of Kansas
261 Kan. 865; 934 P.2d 38 (1997)

The opinion of the court was delivered by ABBOTT, J.

This is a direct appeal by the defendant, Jerry Lee Robinson, from a jury conviction for depraved heart second-degree murder in violation of Kan. Stat. Ann. §21-3402(b). Robinson was 14 years of age when he killed Clyde Richard Crowley by striking him in the head with a golf club. Robinson contends . . . that the evidence is insufficient to prove depraved heart murder. . . .

. . . On the day of his death, Crowley went to the Ottawa Police Department because he felt the police were not responding to two separate incidents in which his sons had been threatened by Jeremy Hendrickson and his friends. Crowley was upset and told the police that if they did not take care of the problem, then he would.

From the police department, Crowley drove to Forest Park, where he inquired as to whether Jeremy Hendrickson was at the park. Upon receiving a negative response, Crowley went home. Crowley later returned to Forest Park where he spotted Jeremy Hendrickson, Eddie Carter, Tony Surber, and Robinson. . . . Crowley approached Hendrickson, yelling at him to leave his sons alone. . . . Then Surber made a comment and Crowley yelled at Surber, "I am [Richard Crowley] and you don't know who you're fucking with." Crowley hit Surber twice in the face. At this point, Surber took a knife from Robinson, which Robinson had been using to clean his nails. Surber held up the knife and Crowley stated, "Oh, you want to play games." Crowley returned to his truck and obtained a metal baseball bat. Crowley began to chase the boys with the bat, swinging at them when he got close. While running away from Crowley, the boys spotted golf clubs hanging out of a window of a car in the park and each boy grabbed a club. The boys began chasing Crowley and eventually surrounded him. The boys taunted Crowley by calling him names and swinging their clubs at him, although they did not actually hit him. At this point, Crowley . . . was using the bat defensively, trying to avoid being struck with the golf clubs. . . .

Later, while the boys and Crowley were still "fencing," Victoria Bond drove her car through Forest Park. Scott Renyer, a passenger in the car, saw the altercation and heard someone from the boys' group yell, "I'll teach you to hit my brother again, mother fucker!" Crowley then broke free from the boys, running towards Bond's moving vehicle. According to Renyer, Crowley "hollered" for help. . . .

. . . Renyer testified that he saw one of the boys, Surber, hit Crowley in the back with a golf club. Crowley then chased Surber, with the other three boys chasing Crowley. Surber tripped, fell to the ground, and Crowley hit Surber twice with the bat. Griffin, a witness for the State, testified that Hendrickson ran up to Crowley and struck Crowley twice in the back or in the ribs with a golf club. After Hendrickson hit him, Crowley turned away from Surber to see who was hitting him. With this opportunity, Surber rolled away from Crowley and began to get off the ground. At this time, Robinson fatally struck Crowley in the head with his golf club. Robinson testified that he was not trying to hit Crowley in the head, but was trying to hit Crowley in the arms in order to make him stop hitting Surber with the bat. Robinson testified that he could not remember if his eyes were open or shut when he hit Crowley. After Robinson struck Crowley in the head, he let go of the club because it was stuck in Crowley's head. Crowley fell to the ground, and Robinson ran home.

The police arrived and removed the baseball bat from Crowley's hands before transporting him to the hospital, with the golf club still impaled in his head. Crowley died shortly thereafter in the emergency room of Ransom Hospital due to the blow to his head. The autopsy revealed that the club directly struck Crowley's head and was not deflected by his arm. The autopsy also showed numerous defensive wounds on Crowley's hands, but did not show any bruising on his back or ribs.

A few hours after the altercation, Robinson, along with his mother and his mother's boyfriend, returned to the park where the police were investigating the scene. Robinson asked to talk to a police officer, and he told the officer his version of what occurred.

Upon completing its investigation of the altercation, the State charged Robinson with depraved heart second-degree murder in violation of Kan. Stat. Ann. §21-3402(b). The jury was instructed on depraved heart second-degree murder and on the lesser included offense of involuntary manslaughter. The jury convicted Robinson of depraved heart second-degree murder. The presumptive guidelines sentence for this crime is 68 to 77 months in prison. Robinson filed a motion for a downward departure in sentencing. The trial court granted this motion, based on Robinson's young age and the fact Crowley was the initial aggressor. The trial court sentenced Robinson to a term of 55 months. Robinson timely filed a notice of appeal from his conviction to the Court of Appeals. . . .

Robinson argues that depraved heart second-degree murder, the unintentional but reckless killing under circumstances manifesting extreme indifference to the value of human life, Kan. Stat. Ann. §21-3402(b),* is indistinguishable from reckless involuntary manslaughter, which is the unintentional killing of a human being committed recklessly, Kan. Stat. Ann. §21-3404(a).** . . . Thus, . . . Robinson argues that prosecutors and jurors

---

* [Kan. Stat. Ann. §21-3402 reads: "Murder in the second degree is the killing of a human being committed: (a) intentionally; or (b) unintentionally but recklessly under circumstances manifesting extreme indifference to the value of human life."—EDS.]

** [Kan. Stat. Ann. §21-3404 reads: "Involuntary manslaughter is the unintentional killing of a human being committed: (a) recklessly; (b) in the commission of, or attempt to commit, or flight from any felony, other than an inherently dangerous felony . . . ; or (c) during the commission of a lawful act in an unlawful manner."—EDS.]

may decide to punish one defendant for depraved heart second-degree murder, a severity level 2 crime, but punish a different defendant for reckless involuntary manslaughter, a severity level 5 crime, for the same conduct, based on discriminatory, arbitrary and subjective reasons. This results in an unconstitutional . . . [denial of both "due process of law" and "equal protection of the laws," both guaranteed by the Fourteenth Amendment to the Constitution of the United States.] . . .

The depraved heart second-degree murder statute, the reckless involuntary manslaughter statute, and the definition of recklessness in Kansas are all patterned after the Model Penal Code. See Model Penal Code §§210.2(1)(b), 210.3(1)(a), and 2.02(2)(c), respectively.*** . . .

Based on the plain language of the depraved heart second-degree murder statute . . . , the legislature intended for the depraved heart murder statute to carry a higher degree of culpability than the reckless involuntary manslaughter statute, thereby making the two statutes distinguishable. This intent is further supported by the commentary to the Model Penal Code, which provides:

> "Ordinary recklessness . . . is made sufficient for a conviction of manslaughter under Section 210.3(1)(a). In a prosecution for murder, however, the Code calls for the further judgment whether the actor's conscious disregard of the risk, under the circumstances, manifests extreme indifference to the value of human life. . . . Whether recklessness is so extreme that it demonstrates similar indifference is not a question, it is submitted, that can be further clarified. It must be left directly to the trier of fact under instructions which make it clear that recklessness that can fairly be assimilated to purpose or knowledge should be treated as murder and that less extreme recklessness should be punished as manslaughter." A.L.I., Model Penal Code & Commentaries, Part II §210.2, Comment 4, at 21-22 (1980). . . .

. . . Both depraved heart murder and reckless involuntary manslaughter require recklessness—that the killing be done under circumstances showing a realization of the imminence of danger and a conscious disregard of

---

*** [Model Penal Code §210.2(1)(b) states that "criminal homicide constitutes murder when . . . (b) it is committed recklessly under circumstances manifesting extreme indifference to the value of human life." MPC §210.3(1)(a) states that "[c]riminal homicide constitutes manslaughter when (a) it is committed recklessly." Finally, MPC §2.02(2)(c) defines recklessness as follows:

> A person acts recklessly with respect to a material element of an offense when he consciously disregards a substantial and unjustifiable risk that the material element exists or will result from his conduct. The risk must be of such a nature and degree that, considering the nature and purpose of the actor's conduct and the circumstances known to him, its disregard involves a gross deviation from the standard of conduct that a law-abiding person would observe in the actor's situation.

—Eds.]

that danger. Depraved heart murder requires the additional element that the reckless killing occur under circumstances manifesting extreme indifference to the value of human life.

The question is whether the jury, from looking at the instructions, would know that the two statutes, depraved heart murder and reckless involuntary manslaughter, do not punish the same thing. The phrase in the depraved heart murder statute requiring the "extreme indifference to the value of human life" indicates, as the legislature intended, that this statute requires a higher degree of recklessness than that required by the reckless involuntary manslaughter statute. If a jury is given a lesser included instruction on reckless involuntary manslaughter, then the jury must assume that some killings fall under this crime. Thus, the jury is put on notice that it must determine whether a reckless killing involves an extreme degree of recklessness and is depraved heart murder or involves a lower degree of recklessness and is involuntary manslaughter. . . . [T]he two statutes (depraved heart murder and involuntary manslaughter) are distinguishable and do not unconstitutionally violate due process or equal protection.

Finally, when the jury is determining whether a reckless killing indicates an extreme indifference to the value of human life beyond that indifference present in all reckless killings, the question is whether the jury can determine what "extreme indifference to the value of human life" is. . . . The comments to the Model Penal Code depraved heart statute, [the model for] the Kansas depraved heart statute . . . , state:

> "Given the Model Code definition of recklessness, the point involved is put adequately and succinctly by asking whether the recklessness rises to the level of 'extreme indifference to the value of human life.' As has been observed, it seems undesirable to suggest a more specific formulation. [Other] variations . . . retain in some instances greater fidelity to the common-law phrasing but they do so at great cost in clarity. . . . The result of these formulations is that the method of defining reckless murder is impaired in its primary purpose of communicating to jurors in ordinary language the task expected of them. The virtue of the Model Penal Code language is that it is a simpler and more direct method by which this function can be performed." A.L.I., Model Penal Code & Commentaries, Part II §210.2, Comment 4, at 25-26 (1980).

A jury is expected to decipher many difficult phrases without receiving specific definitions, such as the term "reasonable doubt." The phrase "extreme indifference to the value of human life" is not so vague as to be [unconstitutional]. . . .

Robinson [also] contends that the phrase "manifesting extreme indifference to the value of human life" in the depraved heart second-degree murder statute refers to a grave indifference to the value of human life *in general*, not to a particular or specific human life. Under this interpretation of the statute, Robinson contends that the evidence was insufficient to convict him of depraved heart murder because, if he manifested an extreme indifference to the value of human life at all, the evidence showed his indifference was only directed at one specific person, Crowley, and was not directed at human life in general. . . .

The Judicial Council's Comments regarding the proposed depraved heart murder statute provide:

> "Depraved heart murder includes extremely reckless killings and killings resulting from actions which were intended to inflict serious bodily injury. Examples of depraved heart murder include: (1) killing a child while target shooting at school windows during school hours; and (2) killing a person while beating him with a baseball bat with intent to severely injure him." 41 Kan. L. Rev., at 78.

The Kansas depraved heart statute is patterned after the Model Penal Code's depraved heart statute. The commentary to the Model Penal Code . . . refer[s] to the classic example of depraved heart murder when a defendant unintentionally kills a friend through the game of Russian roulette. In such a case, the defendant demonstrated extreme indifference to the value of only one specific human life, the friend with which he was playing Russian roulette, but the defendant's conduct still qualified as depraved heart murder under the Model Penal Code.

. . . Although general indifference is often present in crimes prosecuted as depraved heart murders, it is not required under the Model Penal Code. The Kansas Legislature did not indicate that it intended to part with the Model Penal Code and require general indifference to the value of human life as a requirement of depraved heart second-degree murder. Thus, it appears that the Kansas Legislature intended for the elements of depraved heart murder to be met if the defendant manifested an extreme indifference to the value of one specific human life.

The evidence was sufficient in this case for the jury to find that Robinson recklessly killed a person while manifesting an extreme indifference to the value of one specific human life — Crowley's life. . . .

[The opinion of Justice LOCKETT, joined by Justices ALLEGRUCCI and SIX, concurring in part and dissenting in part, is omitted.]

Notes on the Meaning of Depraved Heart Murder

1. The phrase "depraved heart" appears 35 times in the portions of *Robinson* excerpted above, 65 times in the full opinion. Yet that phrase does not appear anywhere in Kansas' second-degree murder statute. The crime of which Robinson was convicted defines murder as killing "unintentionally but recklessly under circumstances manifesting extreme indifference to the value of human life." Kan. Stat. Ann. §21-3402(b). Save for the words "unintentionally but," the analogous Model Penal Code provision is identical. MPC §210.1(1)(b). What accounts for the durability of "depraved heart" murder, a phrase that seems to survive all legislative efforts to bury it?

2. According to the Model Penal Code comment quoted in *Robinson*, murder (the MPC, unlike most state laws, does not distinguish first-degree from second-degree murder) should be characterized by "recklessness that can fairly be assimilated to purpose or knowledge," while "less extreme recklessness should be punished as" manslaughter (again, the MPC, unlike most state laws, does not distinguish voluntary from involuntary manslaughter). Model Penal Code & Commentaries, Part II §210.2, Comment 4, at 21-22 (1980).

What does "recklessness that can fairly be assimilated to purpose or knowledge" mean? Recall the key line in the approved portion of the jury instructions in *Regina v. Woollin*, excerpted supra at page 770. The *Woollin* jury was told not to convict "unless you are sure that serious harm was a virtual certainty from what [the defendant] was doing and he appreciated that that was the case." "Virtual certainty" sounds closer to knowledge than to recklessness. Was it virtually certain when Robinson began to swing his golf club that Crowley would die from the blow? If so, do you think Robinson "appreciated that that was the case"? (How could you tell?) If not, why does Robinson's recklessness deserve to be treated like purposeful killing?

3. *Woollin* and the Model Penal Code commentary would define murder committed with "extreme indifference to the value of human life" roughly as follows: The state must prove that the defendant's conduct was very likely—the Law Lords would say "virtually certain"—to cause the victim's death, *and* that the defendant knew it. Focus on the second half of that formula. Jurors have no way of knowing for sure what was in the mind of a defendant like Robinson at the time he struck the fatal blow. The chief reason to conclude that Robinson knew that he might kill Crowley is that he *did* kill Crowley, and that any blow hard enough to leave a golf club implanted in the victim's head seems likely to cause the victim's death. In other words, Robinson's intent is inferred from his conduct.

4. Which leads back to the likelihood that death would result from the defendant's conduct. If that likelihood is the key to the definition of "depraved heart" murder, then the fault standard in cases like *Robinson* is primarily objective, not subjective: Liability for murder is based, in large measure, on the degree of the defendant's negligence. Can that be right? English courts have struggled with this question; the following passage from Lord Steyn's opinion in *Woollin* traces the history of the struggle:

> My Lords, since the early [1960s] the House has on a number of occasions considered the *mens rea* required to establish murder. It would be right to acknowledge that none of these decisions satisfactorily settled the law. In Director of Public Prosecutions v. Smith, [1961] A.C. 290, the defendant tried to avoid arrest and killed a policeman by driving off with the policeman clinging to the car. The House ruled (1) that the defendant committed murder

because death or grievous bodily harm was foreseen by him as a "likely" result of his act and (2) that he was deemed to have foreseen the risk a reasonable person in his position would have foreseen. There was widespread and severe criticism of the second part of the decision in *Smith.* In retrospect it is now clear the criminal law was set on a wrong course. By section 8 of the Criminal Justice Act 1967 Parliament reversed the effect of *Smith.* Since then one thing at least has been clear: the mental element of murder is concerned with the subjective question of what was in the mind of the man accused of murder. In *Regina v. Hyam,* [1975] A.C. 55, the House of Lords had an opportunity to consider what state of mind, apart from the case where a defendant acts with the purpose of killing or causing serious injury, may be sufficient to constitute the necessary intention. The defendant had burnt down the house of her rival in love, thereby killing her children. The judge directed the jury to convict the defendant of murder if she knew that it was highly probable that her act would cause death or serious bodily harm. The jury convicted her of murder. The House upheld the conviction by a majority of three to two. But the Law Lords constituting the majority gave different reasons: one adopted the "highly probable" test; another thought a test of probability was sufficient; and a third thought it was sufficient if the defendant realised there was "a serious risk." The law of murder was in a state of disarray. . . .

. . . The [disarray took an] acute form in *Regina v. Hancock,* [1986] A.C. 455. Two miners on strike had pushed a concrete block from a bridge onto a three-lane highway on which a miner was being taken to work by taxi. The concrete block hit the taxi and killed the driver. The defendants were charged with murder. The defendants said that they merely intended to block the road and to frighten the non-striking miner. . . . [T]he judge directed the jury to ask themselves: "Was death or serious injury a natural consequence of what was done? Did a defendant foresee that consequence as a natural consequence?" The jury convicted the defendants of murder. . . . [In the Court of Appeal, the] conviction of murder was quashed. There was an appeal to the House of Lords. . . . Lord Scarman observed:

> ". . . [T]he greater the probability of a consequence the more likely it is that the consequence was foreseen and . . . if that consequence was foreseen[,] the greater the probability . . . that consequence was also intended. But juries also require to be reminded that the decision is theirs to be reached upon a consideration of all the evidence."

Id. at 473. . . .

In *Hancock,* . . . Lord Scarman [stated] that where explanation is required the jury should be directed as to the relevance of probability without expressly stating the matter in terms of any particular level of probability. The manner in which trial judges were to direct juries was left unclear. Moreover, in practice juries sometimes ask probing questions which cannot easily be ignored by trial judges. For example, imagine that in a case such as *Hancock* the jury sent a note to the judge to the following effect:

> "We are satisfied that the defendant, though he did not want to cause serious harm, knew that it was probable that his act would cause serious

bodily harm. We are not sure whether a probability is enough for murder. Please explain."

One may alter the question by substituting "highly probable" for "probable." Or one may imagine the jury asking whether a foresight of a "substantial risk" that the defendant's act would cause serious injury was enough. What is the judge to say to the jury? . . . [*Hancock*] does not explain how such questions are to be answered. . . .

In Regina v. Nedrick, [1986] 1 W.L.R. 1025, the appellant poured paraffin through the front door of a house and set it alight. In the fire a child died. . . . The trial judge in *Nedrick* framed his direction in terms of foresight of a high probability that the act would result in serious bodily injury. Lord Lane observed (at 1028):

> "When determining whether the defendant had the necessary intent, it may therefore be helpful for a jury to ask themselves two questions. (1) How probable was the consequence which resulted from the defendant's voluntary act? (2) Did he foresee that consequence?
>
> "If he did not appreciate that death or serious harm was likely to result from his act, he cannot have intended to bring it about. . . . On the other hand, if the jury are satisfied that at the material time the defendant recognised that death or serious harm would be virtually certain (barring some unforeseen intervention) to result from his voluntary act, then that is a fact from which they may find it easy to infer that he intended to kill or do serious bodily harm, even though he may not have had any desire to achieve that result. . . .
>
> "Where the charge is murder and in the rare cases where the simple direction is not enough, the jury should be directed that they are not entitled to infer the necessary intention, unless they feel sure that death or serious bodily harm was a virtual certainty (barring some unforeseen intervention) as a result of the defendant's actions and that the defendant appreciated that such was the case.
>
> "Where a man realises that it is for all practical purposes inevitable that his actions will result in death or serious harm, the inference may be irresistible that he intended that result, however little he may have desired or wished it to happen."

Save for *Smith*, all the cases discussed in the excerpt just quoted were decided after Parliament passed the Criminal Justice Act of 1967, section 8 of which reads:

A court or jury, in determining whether a person has committed an offence,

> (a) shall not be bound in law to infer that he intended or foresaw a result of his actions by reasons only of its being a natural and probable consequence of those actions; but
>
> (b) shall decide whether he did intend or foresee that result by reference to all the evidence, drawing such inferences from the evidence as appear proper in the circumstances.

Is the *mens rea* for murder in England subjective, objective, or a mix of the two? Same question, different jurisdiction: What is the mix of objective and subjective in the standard articulated in *Robinson*?

5. In England, "depraved heart" murder does not exist; Lord Steyn's opinion seeks to define the bounds of murder committed with intent to cause the victim serious physical injury. One might think the difference in categories would produce different legal analyses. Yet *Woollin* and *Robinson* look to the same basic facts and arguments, weighed in similar ways. What conclusion should be drawn from this similarity? What is the source of defendants' culpability in "depraved heart" murder cases? How does one decide whose heart is depraved?

6. The defendant in *Robinson* claimed that "extreme indifference to the value of human life" requires proof that the defendant acted indifferently toward human life in general. What intuition lies behind that argument? Save for drunk driving and acts of terrorism, generalized indifference to human life characterizes very few homicides. Are drunk drivers the moral equivalent of terrorists? Should all other unintentional killings be excluded from the definition of murder?

7. Consider the following explanation of what New York law calls "depraved indifference" murder, from the case of People v. Suarez, 6 N.Y.3d 202, 844 N.E.2d 721 (N.Y. Ct. App. 2005):

DISTINCTION FROM RECKLESS MANSLAUGHTER

Reckless homicide cannot be elevated into depraved indifference murder merely because the actions of the defendant created a risk of death, however grave or substantial that risk may have been. Otherwise, manslaughter in the second degree would routinely and automatically become depraved indifference murder inasmuch as the victim (who was, after all, killed) was necessarily exposed to a grave or substantial risk of death. The critical statutory language that separates second-degree manslaughter from depraved indifference murder is the defendant's underlying *depraved indifference*. "[C]ircumstances evincing a depraved indifference to human life" are not established by recklessness coupled only with actions that carry even an inevitable risk of death.

We therefore make clear that depraved indifference is best understood as an utter disregard for the value of human life—a willingness to act not because one intends harm, but because one simply doesn't care whether grievous harm results or not. Reflecting wickedness, evil or inhumanity, as manifested by brutal, heinous and despicable acts, depraved indifference is embodied in conduct that is "so wanton, so deficient in a moral sense of concern, so devoid of regard of the life or lives of others, and so blameworthy" as to render the actor as culpable as one whose conscious objective is to kill. . . . Quintessential examples are firing into a crowd, driving an automobile along a crowded sidewalk at high speed, opening the lion's cage at the zoo, placing a time bomb in a public place, poisoning a well from which people are accustomed to draw water, opening a drawbridge as a train is about to pass over it and dropping stones from an overpass onto a busy highway.

Oftentimes it will not be easy to determine whether a defendant's conscious objective was to kill or merely to injure a victim. But those are the hard choices to be weighed by the trier of fact. Depraved indifference murder was never meant as a fallback crime enabling courts and juries to avoid making these difficult decisions. We therefore make clear that the statutory provision that a defendant act "[u]nder circumstances evincing a depraved indifference to human life" constitutes an additional requirement of the crime — beyond mere recklessness and risk — which in turn comprises both depravity and indifference, and that a jury considering a charge of depraved indifference murder should be so instructed.

844 N.E.2d at 730-31. Among the "depraved indifference" cases cited with approval by the *Suarez* court was People v. Roe, 74 N.Y.2d 20, 542 N.E.2d 610 (1989), where the victim died during a game of "Polish Roulette"; the defendant loaded a shotgun with a mixture of live and dummy shells, aimed it at the victim without knowing which kind of shell was in the chamber, and pulled the trigger, killing the victim.

8. Here's an idea: Maybe the key to this kind of murder is not the magnitude of the risk, nor the degree of the defendant's recklessness, but instead the value the defendant placed on the victim's life. Some premeditated murders happen under great pressure; the perpetrator may attach a high value to the victim's life, but not high enough to overcome whatever motivated the killing. Some reckless killers, by contrast, seem to attach no value at all to their victims' lives. *That* sounds like depravity.

In thinking about the kinds of cases that generally lead to "depraved heart" murder convictions when someone dies — hitting someone in the head with a golf club, throwing a rock off a bridge or a tall building, shooting into a house (without knowing, or caring, whether there might be someone inside), playing Russian (or Polish) Roulette, "opening the lion's cage at the zoo," and (in an increasing number of states today) driving while drunk**** — one is struck by the utter lack of social utility of the underlying conduct that led to the death. Such cases make one want to slap the defendant upside the head and ask, "What in the world were you thinking? Why would you *do* such a thing?" Maybe that's the true meaning of the term "depraved heart": when the defendant's conduct is so devoid of any possible socially redeeming value that engaging in the conduct, and thereby creating even a relatively small amount of lethal risk to the victim, demonstrates that the defendant really did place no value at all on the life of the victim.

**** One of the leading cases on the subject is People v. Watson, 30 Cal. 3d 290, 637 P.2d 279 (1981), where the California Supreme Court upheld a second-degree murder charge in a case of drunk driving that killed two people. The *Watson* court quoted from an earlier decision in Taylor v. Superior Court, 24 Cal. 3d 890, 598 P.2d 854 (1979): "One who wilfully consumes alcoholic beverages to the point of intoxication, knowing that he thereafter must operate a motor vehicle, thereby combining sharply impaired physical and mental faculties with a vehicle capable of great force and speed, reasonably may be held to exhibit a conscious disregard of the safety of others."

3. Felony Murder

Another way to establish "malice aforethought," and thereby obtain a conviction for either first-degree or second-degree murder, is to show that the death was caused by the defendant's intentional commission of another dangerous felony crime.

People v. Billa

Supreme Court of California
31 Cal. 4th 1064; 79 P.3d 542 (2003)

Opinion by CHIN, J.

Defendant conspired with two others to commit arson of his truck for purposes of insurance fraud. All three conspirators were present at the scene of the burning. While committing the arson, one of the conspirators caught fire and burned to death. We must decide whether defendant is guilty of murdering that coconspirator under the felony-murder rule. We conclude, as did the Court of Appeal, that the felony-murder rule applies to all arsonists at the scene of the arson. In so doing, we distinguish People v. Ferlin, 203 Cal. 587, 265 P. 230 (1928), which held that the rule does not apply to a conspirator who was never at the scene. We leave for another day the question whether *Ferlin* was correctly decided on its facts.

THE FACTS

The prosecution presented evidence from which the jury could reasonably find the following. Defendant purchased a truck and insured it for physical damage. On August 26, 1997, defendant and two others, including Manoj Bhardwaj, drove from Yuba City towards Sacramento, with defendant and Bhardwaj in defendant's truck and the third person following in a car. They intended to burn defendant's truck and obtain the insurance proceeds. Near Wheatland, defendant drove his truck onto a gravel road and stopped about two-tenths of a mile down the road around a bend. There the three set the truck on fire, using either kerosene or diesel fuel.

During these events, Bhardwaj's clothing somehow became saturated with the fuel. It is not clear exactly what happened, but evidence suggested he might have held a leaky canister of the fuel on his lap during the drive. While the three were setting the truck on fire, Bhardwaj's clothing caught fire, and he was severely burned. He died later of his injuries.

A jury convicted defendant of the second degree murder of Bhardwaj (Penal Code §§187, 189), arson causing great bodily injury (§451(a)), and making a false or fraudulent insurance claim (§550(a)(4)). The trial court had instructed the jury solely on the felony-murder rule as a basis for finding defendant guilty of murder. The Court of Appeal . . . affirmed. . . . We granted defendant's petition for review to decide whether the felony-murder rule applies on these facts.

Discussion

"All murder . . . which is committed in the perpetration of, or attempt to perpetrate, [specified felonies, including arson] . . . is murder of the first degree." [Penal Code §189].[2] This felony-murder rule covers "a variety of unintended homicides resulting from reckless behavior, or ordinary negligence, or pure accident. . . ." People v. Dillon, 34 Cal. 3d 441, 477, 668 P.2d 697 (1983). We must decide whether it includes the unintended death of one of the perpetrators during the commission of arson.

Two overarching principles guide us. First, "we are not concerned here with the wisdom of the first degree felony-murder rule itself, or with the criticisms—and defenses—directed at it by judicial and academic commentators; section 189 is the law of California, and we are not free to ignore or alter it if we would." People v. Pulido, 15 Cal. 4th 713, 724, 936 P.2d 1235 (1997). Second, "[n]evertheless, when the rule as ordained by the Legislature requires detailed delineation, this court properly considers policy and consistency. In particular, we have held the first degree felony-murder rule 'should not be extended beyond any rational function that it is designed to serve.'" Ibid., quoting People v. Washington, 62 Cal. 2d 777, 783, 402 P.2d 130 (1965).

Analysis of this question must begin with *Ferlin*, supra. In that case, the defendant hired Skala to commit arson and purchased gasoline used in the arson, but he apparently did not otherwise actively participate in the crime and was not present at the scene of the arson. Skala burned to death while committing the arson. [203 Cal.] at 590. We held that the defendant was improperly convicted of felony murder.

> It would not be seriously contended that one accidentally killing himself while engaged in the commission of a felony was guilty of murder. If the defendant herein is guilty of murder because of the accidental killing of his co-conspirator then it must follow that Skala was also guilty of murder, and if he had recovered from his burns that he would have been guilty of an attempt to commit murder. . . . It cannot be said from the record in the instant case that defendant and deceased had a common design that deceased should accidentally kill himself. Such an event was not in furtherance of the conspiracy, but entirely opposed to it.

[Id. at 596-97.] Several Court of Appeal cases have followed *Ferlin* under similar facts. In Woodruff v. Superior Court, 237 Cal. App. 2d 749, 47 Cal. Rptr. 291 (1965), the defendant procured another to burn the defendant's cafe but was not present at the actual burning. The other person died in

---

2. Although the prosecution proceeded on a felony-murder theory with arson the underlying felony, it only sought conviction for second degree murder, possibly, as the Court of Appeal suggested, "out of a belief that a charge of first degree murder would be unduly harsh under the circumstances. . . ."

the arson. The court described the question as "whether a person who aids, counsels or procures another to maliciously set fire to a building, but who is not physically present at the scene of the arson, is guilty of murder when his confederate negligently or accidentally burns himself to death while setting the fire." [Id. at 750]. It followed *Ferlin* in concluding the felony-murder rule did not apply. Id. at 750-52. In People v. Jennings, 243 Cal. App. 2d 324, 52 Cal. Rptr. 329 (1966), three persons, including the defendants, hired another to burn a building for insurance purposes. That person caught fire himself while setting the fire and died later. The Court of Appeal also found no liability for felony murder. Id. at pp. 327-29.

In People v. Earnest, 46 Cal. App. 3d 792, 120 Cal. Rptr. 485 (1975), the defendant conspired with Munoz to burn the defendant's house for the insurance proceeds. "Munoz, acting alone, attempted to set fire to the then unoccupied home, an explosion occurred and Munoz was killed." Id. at p. 794. The court also found no felony-murder liability. "It is settled California law that where, as here, an accomplice in a conspiracy to commit arson for the purpose of defrauding an insurer accidentally burns himself to death, his co-conspirator[s] may not be charged with murder under the felony-murder rule." Ibid. The court interpreted *Ferlin* and its progeny as

> clearly express[ing] the rule that the accomplice's accidental self-destruction is not in furtherance of the common design. It is not the fact that the accomplice killed himself that precludes application of the theory of vicarious responsibility, but the fact that his was the sole human agency involved in his death.

People v. Earnest, supra, at 796-97.

We have not confronted similar facts since *Ferlin*, but we have cited that case a number of times. In the landmark decision of People v. Washington, supra, 62 Cal. 2d 777, we held that the robbery [portion of the] felony-murder rule does not apply when someone other than a robber, such as the police or a victim, does the killing. We cited *Ferlin* for the proposition that "for a defendant to be guilty of murder under the felony-murder rule the act of killing must be committed by the defendant or by his accomplice acting in furtherance of their common design." *Washington*, supra, at 783. In People v. Antick, 15 Cal. 3d 79, 539 P.2d 43 (1975), we held that one robber cannot be vicariously liable for the death of an accomplice due to the deceased robber's actions because people cannot murder themselves. We discussed *Ferlin* and said its "holding was aptly explained by the Court of Appeal in Woodruff v. Superior Court, 237 Cal. App. 2d 749, 47 Cal. Rptr. 291 (1965)":

> We believe the rationale of that decision to be that section 189 was inapplicable because there was no killing by the accused felon and no killing of another by one for whose conduct the accused was vicariously responsible. . . . [I]n *Ferlin* "the coconspirator killed himself while he alone was perpetrating the felony he conspired to commit" and "it was held in substance and effect that

inasmuch as [the deceased] killed himself Ferlin could not be held criminally responsible for his death."

People v. Antick, supra, at 89 (quoting *Woodruff*, at 751). More recently, we cited *Ferlin* for the proposition that to be guilty of murder for a killing attributable to the act of an accomplice, "the accomplice must cause the death of another human being by an act committed in furtherance of the common design." People v. Caldwell, 36 Cal. 3d 210, 217 n.2, 681 P.2d 274 (1984).

Defendant argues primarily that *Ferlin* and its progeny are on point here: Bhardwaj killed himself, and his death was not in furtherance of the conspiracy but entirely opposed to it. In deciding this question, we must consider the purpose behind the felony-murder rule, for we have said the rule should not be extended beyond its purpose. People v. Pulido, supra, 15 Cal. 4th at 724. The rule's primary purpose is "to deter felons from killing negligently or accidentally by holding them strictly responsible for killings they commit." *Washington*, supra, 62 Cal. 2d at 781; accord, People v. Hansen, 9 Cal. 4th 300, 310, 885 P.2d 1022 (1994). In *Washington*, we found this purpose not applicable when a *third person* kills a robber. "This purpose is not served by punishing [felons] for killings committed by their victims." *Washington*, supra, at 781. However, here no third person killed Bhardwaj. Making arsonists guilty of murder if anyone, including an accomplice, dies in the arson gives them an incentive to do whatever is necessary to make sure no one dies. Defendant argues that felons already have a natural incentive not to kill themselves or their accomplices while committing their crimes. To the extent this is so, making felons strictly liable for deaths maximizes this incentive, thus furthering the purpose of the felony-murder rule.

The felony-murder rule applies to the death of a cohort as much as to the death of an innocent person. People v. Johnson, 28 Cal. App. 3d 653, 656-58, 104 Cal. Rptr. 807 (1972) (defendant's gun discharged, apparently accidentally, killing an accomplice who was running [toward] one of the victims; felony-murder rule applies); People v. Cabaltero, 31 Cal. App. 2d 52, 55-56, 87 P.2d 364 (1939) (one accomplice shot and killed another accomplice, apparently out of anger that that accomplice had fired his gun; felony-murder rule applies). Defendant cites language in People v. Jennings, supra, 243 Cal. App. 2d at 328-29, [stating] that the felony-murder rule exists to protect the public, not to benefit lawbreakers. . . . But we said the felony-murder rule does not benefit lawbreakers in order to *extend* the rule; we did not suggest it fails to *protect* lawbreakers. People v. Chavez, [37 Cal. 2d 656, 669-70, 234 P.2d 632 (1951)]. One may have less sympathy for an arsonist who dies in the fire he is helping to set than for innocents who die in the same fire, but an accomplice's participation in a felony does not make his life forfeit or compel society to give up all interest in his survival.

One rationale of *Ferlin* and its progeny is that the accomplice's death "was not in furtherance of the conspiracy, but entirely opposed to it." *Ferlin,*

203 Cal. at 597. This reasoning is flawed.[4] The death of the accomplice in People v. Johnson, supra, 28 Cal. App. 3d 653, and possibly also People v. Cabaltero, supra, 31 Cal. App. 2d 52, was similarly not in furtherance of the conspiracy. . . . Nevertheless, the courts found felony-murder liability in those cases. As the Attorney General argues, there is a difference between *acts* done in furtherance of the conspiracy and the *results* of those acts. We have said that the "*act* of killing" must be in furtherance of the conspiracy. *Washington*, 62 Cal. 2d at 783 (italics added). But the result need not further the conspiracy. In this case, all three conspirators, including Bhardwaj, were *acting* in furtherance of the conspiracy, including committing the acts that *resulted* in Bhardwaj's death. Although the unintended result—Bhardwaj's death—was opposed to the conspiracy, the acts causing that result were in furtherance of it. One can hypothesize many killings that harm a conspiracy—killing the only person who knows the combination to a safe, for example—but felony-murder liability would extend to such [killings]. *Washington*, which found no felony-murder liability for killings by third persons, is distinguishable in this regard.

> When a killing is not committed by a robber or by his accomplice but by his victim, malice aforethought is not attributable to the robber, for the killing is not committed by him in the perpetration or attempt to perpetrate robbery. . . . Section 189 requires that the felon or his accomplice commit the killing, for if he does not, the killing is not committed to perpetrate the felony. Indeed, in the present case the killing was committed to thwart a felony.

Washington, supra, at 781. Here, no third party contributed to the death. Bhardwaj's death was attributable solely to the arsonists' acts in furtherance of the arson.

Another rationale of *Ferlin* is that the victim killed himself. Defendant would distinguish *Johnson* and *Cabaltero* on this basis. He argues that in those cases, an accomplice killed the victim; here Bhardwaj, like the victim in *Ferlin*, simply killed himself. We disagree. Whether the deceased was solely responsible for his own death is questionable even under *Ferlin*'s facts. After all, Ferlin hired the deceased to commit the arson and procured the gasoline, acts that contributed to the death. But even if *Ferlin*'s rationale applied to its facts, this case is different. Although Bhardwaj may have played a more active role in his own death than did the accomplice victims in *Johnson* and *Cabaltero*, he did not just kill himself. All three conspirators, including

4. *Ferlin* was also incorrect in another part of its analysis, although one not critical to its conclusion. It stated that if the defendant were guilty of Skala's murder, then Skala must also be guilty of murder, "and if he had recovered from his burns . . . he would have been guilty of an attempt to commit murder." [203 Cal.] at 596. The reference to attempted murder is incorrect. California has no crime of attempted felony murder. People v. Bland, 28 Cal. 4th 313, 328, 48 P.3d 1107 (2002); see also People v. Mize, 80 Cal. 41, 43, 22 P. 80 (1889) (attempted murder requires specific intent to kill).

defendant, were at the crime scene and active participants in the events immediately causing his death. Ferlin's connection to his accomplice's death was more attenuated than defendant's connection to Bhardwaj's death.

We agree with the Court of Appeal's assessment:

> In this case, Bhardwaj did not act alone in perpetrating the arson that was the cause of his death. Defendant was present and an active participant in the crime. And his active conduct was a direct cause of Bhardwaj's death. In short, regardless of whether the death was accidental or not, defendant's act of arson killed Bhardwaj. Under the circumstances, *Ferlin* is inapposite, and the felony-murder rule may be applied to defendant's conduct. . . . [Even if] there is no killing "of another" when an accomplice acts alone in causing his own death, there is a killing upon which murder liability may attach when the defendant or other accomplices actively participate in the events causing death.

We conclude that felony-murder liability for any death in the course of arson attaches to all accomplices in the felony at least where, as here, one or more surviving accomplices were present at the scene and active participants in the crime. We need not decide here whether *Ferlin* was correct on its facts.

Defendant argues that "any retroactive weakening of the *Ferlin* rule to expand felony-murder liability would be unconstitutionally ex post facto." We disagree. "[A]n unforeseeable judicial enlargement of a criminal statute, applied retroactively, operates in the same manner as an ex post facto law." People v. Davis, 7 Cal. 4th 797, 811, 872 P.2d 591 (1994). In this case, however, we are not retroactively enlarging a criminal statute but merely *interpreting* one. *Ferlin* and its progeny are factually distinguishable. Our holding is a routine interpretation of existing law, not an overruling of controlling authority or a sudden, unforeseeable enlargement of a statute.

We affirm the judgment of the Court of Appeal.

Notes and Questions

1. In *Billa*, the victim (actually one of the co-perpetrators) was killed during the commission of the felony of arson. Arson is one of those extremely serious felonies that—together with rape, robbery, burglary, kidnapping, and (often) escape—usually appears on the list of statutorily enumerated felonies that in most states (including California) trigger the first-degree felony murder rule. In *Billa*, however, the prosecution declined to pursue a first-degree murder conviction, and the defendant instead was convicted of second-degree murder.

2. In place of intent to kill or reckless disregard of the risk of death, the felony murder rule substitutes the intent to commit a dangerous felony. Is the substitution fair? The Michigan Supreme Court in People v. Aaron, 299 N.W.2d 304 (1980), thought not. Here is the edited syllabus of the *Aaron* court's opinion:

The common-law felony-murder doctrine which allows the element of malice required for murder to be satisfied by the intent to commit the under-lying felony is [hereby] abrogated. In order to convict a defendant of murder, it must be shown that he acted with intent to kill or to inflict great bodily harm, or with a wanton and willful disregard of the likelihood that the natural tendency of his behavior was to cause death or great bodily harm. Further, the issue of malice must be submitted to the jury. The first-degree murder statute continues to operate: all *murder* committed in the perpetration or attempted perpetration of the enumerated felonies is first-degree murder. . . .

Felony murder has never been a static, well-defined doctrine at common law, but throughout its history has been characterized by judicial reinterpre-tation to limit the harshness of its application. Historians and commentators have concluded that it is of questionable origin and that the reasons for the doctrine no longer exist, making it an anachronistic remnant for which there is no logical or practical basis. . . . At early common law[,] the felony-murder doctrine went unchallenged because practically all felonies were punishable by death and it was of no moment whether the condemned was hanged for the initial felony or for the death accidentally resulting from the felony. . . . During the nineteenth and twentieth centuries the doctrine was continuously modified and restricted in England until it was ultimately rejected by an act of Parliament in 1957.

Even though the felony-murder doctrine survives in the United States, the numerous modifications and restrictions of it by courts and legislatures reflect dissatisfaction with the harshness and injustice of the doctrine. To the extent that these modifications reduce the scope and significance of the common-law doctrine, they also call into question its continued existence.

The felony-murder doctrine violates the basic principle of criminal law that criminal liability for causing a result is not justified in the absence of some culpable mental state in respect to it. The doctrine punishes all homicides committed in the perpetration or attempted perpetration of proscribed felo-nies, whether intentional, unintentional, or accidental, without the necessity of proving the relation between the homicide and the perpetrator's state of mind. The [doctrine thus] . . . ignores the concept of guilt on the basis of indi-vidual misconduct, and . . . erodes the relation between criminal liability and moral culpability. . . . The purpose of the statutes creating degrees of murder is to punish more severely the more culpable forms of murder, but an acciden-tal killing occurring during the perpetration of a felony would be punished more severely than a second-degree murder requiring intent to kill. . . . When the felony-murder doctrine originated, proof of the intention to commit a felony met the test of criminal culpability based on the vague definition of malice aforethought governing at that time, but today malice is a term of art which does not include the nebulous definition of intentional wrongdoing. Thus, although the felony-murder doctrine did not broaden the definition of murder at early common law, it does so now. This enlargement of the scope of murder is . . . based on a [mistaken] concept of culpability. . . .

It is no longer acceptable to equate the intent to commit a felony with the intent to kill, intent to do great bodily harm, or wanton and willful disregard of the likelihood that the natural tendency of a person's behavior is to cause death or great bodily harm. Malice requires an intent to cause the very harm that results or some harm of the same general nature, or an act done in wanton or willful disregard of the plain and strong likelihood that such harm will result. . . . The intent to commit the felony, of itself, does not connote a man-endangering state of mind. Hence, it does not constitute a sufficient *mens rea* to establish the crime of murder. . . .

Abrogation of the category of malice arising from the intent to commit the underlying felony does not make irrelevant the fact that a death occurred in the course of a felony. A jury can properly *infer* malice from evidence that a defendant intentionally set in motion a force likely to cause death or great bodily harm. . . . [But] the jury may not find malice from the intent to commit the underlying felony alone. The defendant will be permitted to assert any of the applicable defenses relating to *mens rea* which he would be allowed to assert if he were charged with premeditated murder.

Notice the characterization of the historical definition of "malice aforethought": "[T]oday malice is a term of art which does not include the nebulous definition of intentional wrongdoing." Many English and American judges in the nineteenth century would say that the intentional commission of a dangerous felony constituted "intentional wrongdoing," and that such intentional wrongdoing in turn constituted malice — so that homicide committed during the course of a dangerous felony was murder, with or without the felony murder doctrine.

Aaron characterized that older definition of malice aforethought as "nebulous"; its abandonment was, in the court's view, a sign of moral progress. Do you agree? Is the result in *Billa* morally defensible?

3. *Billa* is an example of a common felony murder fact pattern: The felony leads to the death of someone whom the defendant did not wish to kill. If ordinary intent principles applied in such cases, it would be difficult to justify liability for murder, perhaps for any form of homicide. After all, Bhardwaj's death was not part of Billa's plan. Nor did Billa's recklessness or negligence lead to his colleague's demise — Bhardwaj apparently spilled fuel on his own clothing; the direct cause of death was *his* negligence, not Billa's.

What is the basis for murder liability in such a case? One answer is deterrence: Felony murder liability raises the "price" of dangerous felonies, by raising the risk that, if something inadvertently goes wrong, defendants who commit such felonies will wind up convicted not just of the underlying felonies but of murder as well. Another possibility is that felony murder doctrine imposes additional costs not just upon the commission of dangerous felonies by individuals, but also upon their commission by groups of criminals rather than by solo actors. It is no accident that *Billa* and *Mitchell* (see below) both arose out of crimes committed by more than one person. Many felony murder cases share that characteristic.

4. There are other deterrence stories one might tell about felony murder doctrine. Are there any retributive explanations for the doctrine? The literature on the subject mostly assumes the answer is no, but that assumption may be wrong. For one thing, defendants who commit violent felonies in ways that lead to death may be likely to have committed many serious crimes in the past. Perhaps the felony murder doctrine is a proxy for the commission of multiple crimes, not during the incident in question but cumulatively over the course of the defendant's criminal career.

Consider also the following possibility: Homicides are committed for a wide range of reasons, some heinous and others understandable, occasionally even virtuous. When death is caused during the course of a crime like rape, robbery, or arson, it is exceedingly unlikely that the defendant was acting virtuously. If the underlying felony was dangerous—either because it is inherently so or because the circumstances made it so in the particular case at hand—then its commission tends to suggest that the defendant was willing to run sizeable risks of killing people in order to advance his own interests. This suggests that the felony murder rule might be viewed as nothing more than a specialized, rule-based application of "depraved heart" murder.

This is, in essence, the position taken by the Model Penal Code. The Code does not include a felony murder rule as such, but it creates a presumption of recklessness plus "extreme indifference to the value of human life" (the Code's formulation of "depraved heart" murder) whenever a death is caused "in the commission of" robbery, rape, arson, burglary, kidnapping, or felonious escape. See §210.2.*

Ex parte Mitchell

Court of Criminal Appeals of Alabama
936 So. 2d 1094 (2006)

PER CURIAM.

The petitioner, Oronde Kenyatt Mitchell, filed a petition for a writ of prohibition/mandamus directing Judge Truman Hobbs of the Montgomery Circuit Court to dismiss the felony-murder charges against him. In June 2004, a Montgomery County grand jury indicted Mitchell for felony murder. The predicate felony named in the indictment was the unlawful distribution of a controlled substance. Mitchell moved to dismiss the felony-murder charge because, he argued, the underlying felony was not "clearly dangerous to human life." The circuit court denied the motion; this extraordinary petition followed. . . .

---

* Note that, under Francis v. Franklin, 471 U.S. 307 (1985), the use of such a "presumption" to satisfy an element of a crime would be unconstitutional today; as a result, any state that tried to adopt the Code's provision would need to use the word "inference" instead. See the discussion of Francis v. Franklin, supra, at page 137.

Felony murder is defined in §13A-6-2, Ala. Code:

"(a) A person commits the crime of murder if: ... (3) He commits or attempts to commit arson in the first degree, burglary in the first or second degree, escape in the first degree, kidnapping in the first degree, rape in the first degree, robbery in any degree, sodomy in the first degree, *or any other felony clearly dangerous to human life* and, in the course of and in furtherance of the crime that he is committing or attempting to commit, or in immediate flight therefrom, he, or another participant if there be any, causes the death of any person."

(Emphasis added.)

Mitchell argues that Count I of the two-count indictment fails to charge a crime and is void; therefore, he argues, the circuit court has no jurisdiction to proceed on the charges. Specifically, he argues that the predicate felony named in the indictment—the unlawful distribution of a controlled substance—is not a felony recognized under §13A-6-2(a)(3), because it is not "clearly dangerous to human life." Count I of the indictment charged:

"The Grand Jury of said County charge that, before the finding of this indictment, Oronde Kenyatt Mitchell ... did commit or attempt to commit a felony clearly dangerous to human life: unlawful distribution of a controlled substance, to wit: marijuana, and, in the course of and in furtherance of the said felony that the said Mitchell was committing or attempting to commit, or in immediate flight therefrom, the said Mitchell or another participant: Jaquin Deaudrey Jones ... caused the death of ... Cedric Tolbert, ... by shooting the said Tolbert with a pistol, in violation of Section 13A-6-2 of the Code of Alabama, against the peace and dignity of the State of Alabama."[2]

Mitchell also argues that other states have held that only offenses that are "inherently dangerous" can constitute the predicate felony for felony murder. He cites State v. Anderson, 666 N.W.2d 696 (Minn. 2003); State v. Wesson, 802 P.2d 574 (Kan. 1990); People v. Taylor, 8 Cal. Rptr. 2d 439 (Cal. App. 1992), in support of his assertion. In essence, Mitchell argues that we should follow the abstract approach used by Minnesota, Kansas, and California when determining whether the unlawful distribution of a controlled substance is a felony that is "clearly dangerous to human life."

The State asserts that distributing controlled substances is a felony that is clearly dangerous to human life. Alternatively, it asserts that whether the charge of distributing controlled substances meets the statutory definition of "clearly dangerous to human life" should be decided on a case-by-case basis based on the facts in each case.

The issue presented in this petition is an issue of first impression in Alabama. Because there is no Alabama law on this issue, we have looked to other states for guidance.

2. In this case it appears that Mitchell and the victim, Cedric Tolbert, were in a vehicle attempting to sell marijuana to Jaquin Deaudrey Jones when Jones attempted to rob Mitchell and Tolbert with a gun.

In State v. Mora, 950 P.2d 789 (N.M. 1997),[3] the New Mexico Supreme Court considering whether criminal sexual contact of a minor could support a felony-murder charge, stated:

"In [State v.] Harrison, [564 P.2d 1321 (N.M. 1977)], this Court considered two approaches in determining whether a felony is inherently dangerous for felony murder purposes. Under the first approach, 'the felony is examined in the abstract to determine whether it is inherently dangerous to human life.' Id. The abstract approach involves a two-step process by which the court first examines the 'primary element' of the offense at issue to determine whether it involves the requisite danger to life. Id. The court then looks to the 'factors elevating the offense to a felony' to determine whether the felony, taken in the abstract, is inherently dangerous to human life. Id. . . .

"Under the second possible approach cited by *Harrison*, 'both the nature of the felony and the circumstances surrounding its commission may be considered to determine whether it was inherently dangerous to human life.' Id. at 1324. . . . When applying the factual approach, a court looks to the particular facts of the case to decide whether the defendant carried out the predicate felony in a manner dangerous to human life. Thus, a proscribed offense which on its face does not appear to be a dangerous felony, may be carried out in a manner which would allow it to serve as a predicate felony for felony murder.

"In *Harrison*, this Court adopted the factual approach. Id. We see no reason to deviate from that ruling today. We cannot say as a matter of law whether a particular felony is or is not inherently dangerous to human life. This decision is necessarily fact-specific. We cannot say as a matter of law that criminal sexual contact of a minor is never an inherently dangerous felony. As stated in *Harrison*, it is for the jury to decide, subject to appellate review, whether a felony is inherently dangerous. In this case, it was for the jury to decide whether the facts of the case warranted a conclusion that the criminal sexual contact of a minor was committed under inherently dangerous circumstances."

950 P.2d at 796-97.

The Rhode Island Supreme Court in State v. Stewart, 663 A.2d 912, 916 (R.I. 1995), considered whether "permitting a child to be a habitual sufferer" was an "inherently dangerous felony" sufficient to support a charge of felony murder in the second degree.[4] The Rhode Island Supreme Court stated:

3. New Mexico defines felony murder in N.M. Stat. Ann. §30-2-1.A to include a murder committed "in the commission of or an attempt to commit any felony; or . . . by any act greatly dangerous to the lives of others, indicating a depraved mind regardless of human life."

4. The state of Rhode Island defines murder in degrees. Murder in the first degree is defined as a murder committed during the course of specific enumerated felonies. One of the felonies enumerated in R.I. Gen. Laws §11-23-1 is the felony manufacture, sale, or delivery of a controlled substance. If the felony is not enumerated in R.I. Gen. Laws §11-23-1, then the murder is murder in the second degree. To serve as the predicate felony for murder in the second degree the felony must be an "inherently dangerous felony."

"In advancing her argument, defendant urges this court to adopt the approach used by California courts to determine if a felony is inherently dangerous. This approach requires that the court consider the elements of the felony 'in the abstract' rather than look at the particular facts of the case under consideration. See, e.g., People v. Patterson, 778 P.2d 549, 553 (Cal. 1989). With such an approach, if a statute can be violated in a manner that does not endanger human life, then the felony is not inherently dangerous to human life. People v. Caffero, 255 Cal. Rptr. 22, 25 (Cal. App. 1989). Moreover, the California Supreme Court has defined an act as 'inherently dangerous to human life' when there is 'a high probability that it will result in death.' *Patterson*, 778 P.2d at 558.

"In *Caffero*, a two-and-one-half-week-old baby died of a massive bacterial infection caused by lack of proper hygiene that was due to parental neglect. The parents were charged with second-degree felony murder and felony child abuse, with the felony-child-abuse charge serving as the predicate felony to the second-degree-murder charge. Examining California's felony-child-abuse statute in the abstract, instead of looking at the particular facts of the case, the court held that because the statute could be violated in ways that did not endanger human life, felony child abuse was not inherently dangerous to human life. *Caffero*, 255 Cal. Rptr. at 25. By way of example, the court noted that a fractured limb, which comes within the ambit of the felony-child-abuse statute, is unlikely to endanger the life of an infant, much less of a seventeen-year-old (the statute applied to all minors below the age of eighteen years, not only to young children). Because felony child abuse was not inherently dangerous to human life, it could not properly serve as a predicate felony to a charge of second-degree felony murder. *Caffero*, 255 Cal. Rptr. at 24-25.

"The defendant urges this court to adopt the method of analysis employed by California courts to determine if a felony is inherently dangerous to life. Aside from California, it appears that Kansas is the only other state which looks at the elements of a felony in the abstract to determine if such felony is inherently dangerous to life. See, e.g., State v. Wesson, 802 P.2d 574, 581 (Kan. 1990) (holding that the sale of crack cocaine when viewed in the abstract is not inherently dangerous to human life); State v. Underwood, 615 P.2d 153, 161 (Kan. 1980) (holding that the unlawful possession of a firearm by an ex-felon when viewed in the abstract is not inherently dangerous to human life). The case of Ford v. State, 423 S.E.2d 255 (Ga. 1992), cited in defendant's brief for the proposition that possession of a firearm by an ex-felon is not an inherently dangerous felony which can support a felony-murder conviction, actually holds that the attendant circumstances of the particular case should be considered in determining whether the underlying felony 'created a foreseeable risk of death.' In *Ford* the defendant . . . had previously been convicted of the felony of possession of cocaine with intent to distribute. Ford was visiting the home of his girlfriend's mother and had brought with him a semiautomatic pistol. While there he attempted to unload the pistol, but in so doing, he discharged the weapon, sending a bullet both through the floor and through the ceiling of a basement apartment located in the house. The bullet struck and killed the occupant of the basement apartment. There was no evidence that at the time of the shooting the defendant was aware of the existence of the apartment or of the victim's presence in it. Ford was charged with and convicted of felony murder, with the underlying felony being the possession of a firearm by a convicted felon.

"The Georgia Supreme Court reversed the conviction for felony murder holding that a status felony, including the possession of a firearm by a previously-convicted felon, is not inherently dangerous. The court explained that there could indeed be circumstances in which such a felony could be considered dangerous (for example when the possession of the firearm was coupled with an aggravated assault or other dangerous felony) but that such circumstances were absent in that case. It held that in that particular case, which did not involve an assault or other criminal conduct, the underlying felony of possession of a firearm by a previously convicted felon was not inherently dangerous and thus could not serve as a predicate to the charge of felony murder. 423 S.E.2d at 256.

"We decline defendant's invitation to adopt the California approach in determining whether a felony is inherently dangerous to life and thus capable of serving as a predicate to a charge of second-degree felony murder. We believe that the better approach is for the trier of fact to consider the facts and circumstances of the particular case to determine if such felony was inherently dangerous in the manner and the circumstances in which it was committed, rather than have a court make the determination by viewing the elements of a felony in the abstract. We now join a number of states that have adopted this approach. See, e.g., Jenkins v. State, 230 A.2d 262 (Del. 1967); State v. Wallace, 333 A.2d 72 (Me. 1975); Commonwealth v. Ortiz, 560 N.E.2d 698 (Mass. 1990); State v. Harrison, 564 P.2d 1321 (N.M. 1977); State v. Nunn, 297 N.W.2d 752 (Minn. 1980). . . ."

663 A.2d at 918-19. See also Smith v. State, 596 N.W.2d 661, 664 (Minn. Ct. App. 1999) ([holding that the lower court] "misinterpreted the statute and abused its discretion by concluding a sale of cocaine that results in a shooting death was an invalid predicate felony for second-degree felony murder."); Malaske v. State, 89 P.3d 1116, 1117 n.2 (Okla. Crim. App. 2004) ("The act of . . . trafficking in illegal drugs may serve as [a] predicate crime[] for first-degree felony murder.").

Our research revealed little law to support Mitchell's argument that Alabama should use an abstract approach in determining whether the crime of unlawful distribution of a controlled substance is "clearly dangerous to human life." Though states define the predicate offense to felony murder differently—"an act greatly dangerous to the lives of others," or "an inherently dangerous felony"—they appear to be in agreement in their approach to analyzing whether the offense fits within the felony-murder law. . . .

Mitchell . . . relies on . . . State v. Wesson, 802 P.2d 574 (Kan. 1990). In *Wesson*, the Kansas Supreme Court held that the sale of cocaine could never be a predicate felony for felony murder in Kansas. . . . [I]n State v. Mitchell, 942 P.2d 1 (1997), [the Kansas Supreme Court said] the following concerning post-*Wesson* Kansas law:

"The legislative overhaul of the felony-murder statute in 1992 requires us to reexamine the reasoning applied in *Wesson* and the 'abstract approach' announced in State v. Underwood, 615 P.2d 153 (Kan. 1980). If the felony sale of cocaine is viewed in the abstract, as it was in *Wesson*, then it does not fit within the catchall definition of a forcible felony. The elements of that crime do not involve any threat or use of physical force or violence against any person, although threat, force, or violence may frequently be involved in cocaine sales on the street. Courts no longer have the task of determining whether a crime is inherently dangerous. . . . Either the crime fits within one of the K.S.A. §21-3436 categories or it does not. Comparison of the crime to those listed in K.S.A. §21-3110(8) (definition of forcible felony), or to the catchall portion of the definition, is no longer required. In determining whether sale of cocaine is a forcible felony, we find consideration of the circumstances of the commission of the crime, in addition to the elements of the crime in the abstract, appropriate because the legislature has determined a cocaine sale to be inherently dangerous. . . .

The significant changes to the felony-murder statute after *Wesson*, with the legislature having expressly defined sale of cocaine as an inherently dangerous felony, justify reconsideration of our reasoning. . . . The abstract approach, first taken in *Underwood*, is not controlling in the determination of whether a felony is forcible because the legislature has now statutorily defined inherently dangerous felonies."

942 P.2d at 6. . . .

We believe that the fact-based approach is the more logical approach and is consistent with the evolution of the offense of felony murder in Alabama. Alabama originally separated murder into degrees. First-degree murder was defined in §13-1-70, . . . [which] provided, in part:

> "Every homicide perpetrated by poison, lying in wait or any other kind of willful, deliberate, malicious and premeditated killing; or committed in the perpetration of, or the attempt to perpetrate, any arson, rape, robbery or burglary . . . is murder in the first degree. . . ."

In 1977, the Alabama criminal code was . . . rewritten. Murder was no longer separated into degrees, and felony murder was defined in §13A-6-2(a)(3). The legislature . . . increased the number of felonies that could serve as the basis for felony murder and added the additional proviso to §13A-6-2(a)(3): "or any other felony clearly dangerous to human life. . . ."

Based on the evolution of felony murder in Alabama and the overwhelming consensus that a fact-based approach should be used to determine whether an offense can furnish the predicate felony for felony murder, we join the majority of jurisdictions that have considered this issue. We agree with the Rhode Island Supreme Court: "The better approach is for the trier of fact to consider the facts and circumstances of the particular case to determine if such felony was inherently dangerous in the manner and the circumstances in which it was committed." State v. Stewart, 663 A.2d at 919.

Accordingly, the indictment issued by the Montgomery County grand jury is not void. This petition is due to be, and is hereby, denied.

Notes on Qualifying Felonies

1. When an unintended death is caused by the commission of a felony that does not appear on the relevant state's statutory list of enumerated felonies that can lead to a first-degree murder conviction, the application of the felony murder rule—and the defendant's liability for second-degree murder—depends upon whether the felony is judged to be "inherently dangerous to human life" (or, in Alabama, "clearly dangerous"). Reread footnote 2 in *Mitchell*. Based on that description, how would you argue that the felony was "clearly dangerous to human life"? How would you argue that it wasn't?

2. Under the fact-bound approach to dangerousness that the *Mitchell* court adopts, a given felony triggers the felony murder doctrine in some cases but not in others. Suppose, for example, that Mitchell and Tolbert met Jones, who bought a large stash of marijuana. Just after the drug deal, Mitchell was driving back home when he struck and killed a bicyclist. Should the felony murder rule apply? Presumably not: Marijuana distribution does not dramatically raise the risk of such accidents. In fact, it may even *lower* the risk—drug dealers have good reason to drive carefully, lest the police pull them over and find the drugs and/or cash they carry. Notice the nature of the argument. Evaluating the dangerousness of the relevant felony under the fact-bound approach is similar to—the same as?—assessing proximate cause. In both cases, the question is whether this behavior raised the risk of that result and, if so, by how much. Is that the right way to decide cases like *Mitchell*?

3. Consider the approach taken by California courts and by the Kansas Supreme Court in *Wesson*. How do those courts decide whether a given felony is "inherently dangerous"? The court in *Caffero* (the felony child abuse case discussed in State v. Stewart, 663 A.2d 912 (R.I. 1995), which is extensively quoted in *Mitchell*) suggests that if the felony can be committed without risk of killing someone, it lacks inherent danger. Save for homicide and attempted homicide, *any* felony can be committed in a manner that poses little or no risk of death. The question must be whether the relevant felony creates substantial risks of death *in many cases*—not in *every* case.

How many cases are enough? According to the FBI's annual Uniform Crime Reports, roughly 400,000 robberies are reported each year in the United States. There are roughly 15,000 non-vehicular homicides in the United States each year. The large majority of those homicides do not happen during the course of robberies. Fewer than one percent of all robberies lead to a homicide. *Caffero*'s reasoning suggests that robbery is not inherently dangerous, and hence is not the kind of felony that triggers the felony murder rule. But if that conclusion holds, *no* felony is dangerous enough to trigger the rule, and the rule simply disappears.

4. If the felony in *Mitchell* qualifies as "clearly dangerous," where does the danger come from? Presumably the answer is guns, not marijuana. If so, *Mitchell* might stand for the proposition that *any* felony committed while in possession of a firearm is sufficiently dangerous to trigger the felony murder doctrine. Since most homicides are committed with guns, that stance would dramatically increase the number of homicides treated as murder, and would sharply reduce the number treated as manslaughter. Is that fair? Is it wise?

5. Some felonies, even though they may (and, indeed, often do) cause deaths, are nevertheless exempted from the felony murder rule by virtue of the "merger" doctrine. This doctrine applies whenever the nature or essence of the felony is so closely connected to the resulting homicide that the felony "merges" with the homicide. In such cases, the defendant can still be convicted of a homicide crime, but the conviction must be based on the standard *mens rea* analysis for homicides, and not on the felony murder rule.

A clear (and obvious) example would be the crime of involuntary manslaughter. Involuntary manslaughter is a felony crime, and by definition, *every* instance of the crime causes a death, which proves that the crime is "inherently dangerous to human life." If there were no merger doctrine, every case of involuntary manslaughter would thus automatically become a case of second-degree murder by means of the felony murder rule.

Another relatively clear example is the crime of assault. Most homicides — including the criminally negligent or reckless ones that lead to convictions of negligent homicide or involuntary manslaughter — involve an assault (i.e., an unwanted physical touching of the victim). Without the merger doctrine, all such cases would be bootstrapped into second-degree murders; the crimes of negligent homicide and involuntary manslaughter would largely cease to exist. It is in this sense that one might say that the merger doctrine serves to protect the integrity of the criminal law's carefully developed distinctions between the various different homicide crimes.**

Courts have had more difficulty with the crime of felony child abuse, as charged in the *Caffero* case. Is felony child abuse similar to assault, in that the essence of the criminal conduct is so closely related to the conduct that actually causes the victim's death that it should be held to merge with the homicide? Isn't it true that almost all cases in which a defendant's wrongful act or omission causes the death of a child could be characterized as child abuse? In *Caffero*, the California court held that felony child abuse is not even a dangerous enough felony to qualify for the felony murder rule at all. In State v. Lucas, 759 P.2d 90 (1988), however, the Kansas Supreme Court held that — although felony child abuse *is* an "inherently dangerous"

** The "merger" doctrine also arises occasionally outside the context of the felony murder rule, whenever two crimes are necessarily so connected that it would be inconsistent with legislative intent, or otherwise inappropriate, to punish for both. See, e.g., State v. Freeman, 153 Wash. 2d 765 (Wash. S. Ct. 2005), where a defendant was convicted of first-degree robbery (statutorily defined as a robbery where the perpetrator either (i) "is armed with a deadly weapon," (ii) "displays what appears to be a firearm or other deadly weapon," or (iii) "inflicts bodily injury") and also second-degree assault, based on evidence that he punched a woman and stole her cash and casino chips. The court reversed the second-degree assault conviction based on the merger doctrine, because "without the conduct amounting to assault, [he] would be guilty of only second degree robbery."

felony—it is not sufficiently distinct from the conduct that causes the victim's death, and thus merges with the resulting homicide, rendering the felony murder rule inapplicable. The Kansas legislature subsequently took the *Lucas* court's explicit suggestion to clarify the law of felony murder, and overturned the result in *Lucas*. Given society's prevailing views about the crime of felony child abuse, is that surprising?

4. Provocation and "Extreme Mental or Emotional Disturbance"

Like the law of murder, the law of manslaughter divides into two main categories, called voluntary and involuntary manslaughter. The names are misleading; the distinction between the two categories has little to do with voluntariness or its absence. Voluntary manslaughter is usually defined as intentional killing plus either provocation or what the Model Penal Code calls "extreme mental or emotional disturbance." Involuntary manslaughter, by contrast, usually refers to reckless homicides that do not rise to the level of "depraved heart" murder. The next two cases deal with the first category; the case after that deals with the second category.

Commonwealth v. Acevedo

Supreme Judicial Court of Massachusetts
845 N.E.2d 274 (2006)

Spina, Justice.

The defendant was indicted for murder in the first degree for the stabbing death of Charles McCullough during a fight. At trial, defense counsel argued for acquittal based on self-defense, and the trial judge instructed the jury on self-defense, voluntary manslaughter based on excessive force in self-defense, and involuntary manslaughter. The jury convicted the defendant of murder in the second degree. The defendant appealed from the conviction and filed a motion for a new trial, arguing that the failure of the judge to instruct the jury on voluntary manslaughter based on reasonable provocation created a substantial risk of a miscarriage of justice. . . . This motion was denied. . . . The defendant's appeal from the order denying his motion for a new trial was consolidated with his direct appeal, and . . . the Appeals Court affirmed the order and the conviction. We granted the defendant's application for further appellate review, and we now reverse both the order and the conviction.

Background

On November 17, 2000, Crystal Graham, a high school student, hosted a party at her home in Lowell after a school dance. Charles McCullough,

Graham's former boyfriend, attended the party.[1] When the defendant and four of his friends arrived at the party, they argued with McCullough, who accused them of stealing his headlights. Graham told the defendant and his friends to leave if they were going to fight, and they left the party.

Approximately forty-five minutes later, the defendant and his friends returned to the party.[2] Another argument involving the defendant and McCullough ensued. The argument escalated into a physical confrontation when two of the defendant's friends punched McCullough. Graham demanded that everyone leave, and the defendant and his friends suggested taking the fight outside. Once outside, McCullough challenged the defendant to fight "one on one," and they stepped toward each other, into the middle of a circle of people. McCullough, who was unarmed, punched the defendant in the head, and the defendant appeared to be punching McCullough's chest: no one else was involved in the fight. After ten seconds, McCullough fell back, holding his chest, and shouted that the defendant had stabbed him.

Although none of the Commonwealth's witnesses had seen a knife, McCullough had been stabbed five times. One wound penetrated his heart, and another perforated his liver: both injuries caused McCullough to lose a significant amount of blood quickly. McCullough collapsed in the street, and the defendant and his friends fled. When police arrived on the scene, at approximately 3 A.M., McCullough, still alive, was able to tell an officer that the defendant had stabbed him. He was pronounced dead when he arrived at a hospital. . . .

. . . Testifying on his own behalf at trial, the defendant explained that he and his friends went to Graham's party, but they left because McCullough was "trying to start" trouble. They returned to the party later, hoping that more people had arrived. They again encountered McCullough, who started an argument with two of the defendant's friends that escalated into a physical confrontation. After McCullough challenged them to "rumble," the defendant decided to leave the party and ran outside, followed by his friends and other party guests. He tried to get into a friend's car, but, finding it locked, he joined his friends in the crowd that had gathered on the street. The defendant and his friends walked backward across the street as McCullough and his friends approached them. The defendant saw McCullough look at him, bite his lip, make a fist, and run toward him. Someone hit the side of the defendant's face, knocking him to the ground. He felt people beating

1. McCullough was drinking beer at the party and had taken the drug commonly known as "ecstasy." Several of the Commonwealth's witnesses testified that McCullough appeared to be in a good mood that night, but the medical examiner testified that large amounts of "ecstasy" may cause paranoia or aggressive behavior.

2. The defendant and his friends later testified that they drove around, drank beer, and smoked marijuana at one of their homes during this time.

him about the head and attempted to push them away, but could not. The defendant then pulled his knife from his pocket, opened it, and swung it several times. After he heard McCullough cry out that he had been stabbed, he ran to his friend's car. The defendant threw the knife out the window as they drove over a bridge.

The defendant explained that he feared for his life because he was outnumbered and could not get away from his attackers: by his estimation, there were at least fifteen men, including McCullough, involved in the confrontation. On cross-examination, the defendant admitted that he could have run after discovering the cars were locked, but he did not want to leave his friends. He also acknowledged that McCullough was not the first person to hit him, and that when he fell backward, he could not see who was punching him.

Two of the defendant's friends who attended the party with him that night also testified for the defense. They corroborated the defendant's testimony that he left the party after a fight started; that a large crowd gathered outside; and that a group of men, including McCullough, surrounded the defendant, knocked him to the ground, and hit him. Both witnesses testified that they saw McCullough punch the defendant twice before the group closed in on him.

At the close of evidence, defense counsel orally requested jury instructions on manslaughter, without specifying a theory, and involuntary manslaughter. The Commonwealth argued that jury instructions on any theory of manslaughter were not warranted because, even in the light most favorable to the defendant, the evidence did not show that he acted based on heat of passion, reasonable provocation, or sudden combat. The Commonwealth also argued that the defendant was not entitled to an instruction on self-defense. Over the Commonwealth's objection, the judge instructed the jury on self-defense, voluntary manslaughter based on excessive force in self-defense, and involuntary manslaughter. The judge did not provide instructions on reasonable provocation or sudden combat. Defense counsel did not object to the instructions. . . .

On the third day of deliberations, the jurors submitted [a] question[: "Could you elaborate on malice? Please define all mitigating circumstances which should be considered in deciding malice. In other words, other than excessive force in self-defense, are there any other mitigating circumstances that would eliminate malice?"] After discussing the issue with counsel, the judge reinstructed the jury on malice and informed them, again without objection, that there were no mitigating circumstances to consider other than excessive force in self-defense. The jury returned their verdict finding the defendant guilty of murder in the second degree approximately forty minutes after the judge answered their . . . question.

The defendant timely appealed from his conviction. Later, represented by new counsel, he filed a motion for a new trial, arguing that the omission of a jury instruction on reasonable provocation created a substantial risk of a miscarriage of justice. . . . [T]he judge denied the motion, concluding that the evidence at trial, viewed in the light most favorable to the defendant, would not have warranted an instruction on reasonable provocation, even if that instruction had been requested. . . .

The defendant's direct appeal was consolidated with his appeal from the judge's order denying his motion for a new trial. [The Appeals Court] affirm[ed] both the conviction and the order, . . . conclud[ing] that the absence of a jury instruction on reasonable provocation was not error because [defense counsel] did not request the instruction, and the trial judge was not obligated to provide one sua sponte. . . .

DISCUSSION

. . . As a threshold matter, we must determine whether the defendant would have been entitled to a jury instruction on reasonable provocation had he requested one. See, e.g., Commonwealth v. DeMarco, 444 Mass. 678, 685, 830 N.E.2d 1068 (2005) (counsel not ineffective in failing to request instruction to which defendant not entitled). If requested, "[a] manslaughter instruction is required if, on any view of the evidence, regardless of the credibility, manslaughter may be found." Commonwealth v. Carrion, 407 Mass. 263, 266-67, 552 N.E.2d 558 (1990). We therefore view the evidence in the light most favorable to the defendant to determine whether an instruction on reasonable provocation was warranted. . . .

Voluntary manslaughter is an unlawful killing "arising not from malice, but from . . . sudden passion induced by reasonable provocation, sudden combat, or excessive force in self-defense." Commonwealth v. Carrion, supra, at 267. Reasonable provocation is provocation that "would have been likely to produce in an ordinary person such a state of passion, anger, fear, fright, or nervous excitement as would eclipse his capacity for reflection or restraint." Commonwealth v. Walden, 380 Mass. 724, 728, 405 N.E.2d 939 (1980). A jury instruction on reasonable provocation is warranted "if there is evidence of provocation deemed adequate in law to cause the accused to lose his self-control in the heat of passion, and if the killing followed the provocation before sufficient time had elapsed for the accused's temper to cool." Commonwealth v. Andrade, 422 Mass. 236, 237, 661 N.E.2d 1308 (1996). The defendant's actions must be "both objectively and subjectively reasonable. That is, the jury must be able to infer that a reasonable person would have become sufficiently provoked and would not have 'cooled off' by the time of the homicide, and that in fact a defendant was provoked and did not cool off." Commonwealth v. Groome, 435 Mass. 201, 220, 755 N.E.2d 1224 (2001).

The defendant presented adequate evidence of reasonable provocation. He testified that, as he left the party, he was surrounded by McCullough and his friends, who repeatedly punched him in the head. He further testified that these men knocked him to the ground, and that he feared for his life because he was outnumbered by his attackers. Such testimony, if credited, could demonstrate "fear, fright, or nervous excitement" on the part of the defendant, sufficient to overcome a reasonable person's "capacity for reflection or restraint."[13] See Commonwealth v. Walden, supra.

It is well established that "provocation must come from the victim." Commonwealth v. Ruiz, 442 Mass. 826, 838-39, 817 N.E.2d 771 (2004), and cases cited. The Commonwealth contends that the defendant was not entitled to an instruction on provocation because, even considering the defendant's own testimony, there was no evidence of adequate provocation from McCullough: the defendant could state with certainty only that McCullough looked at him, made a fist, and ran toward him, not that he actually struck him. We do not agree with the Commonwealth's contention. Several defense witnesses, including the defendant, testified that McCullough was part of a group of young men who surrounded the defendant, knocked him down, and beat him. Although the defendant testified that he could not see which of the men struck the blows, two defense witnesses testified that they saw McCullough strike the defendant twice. At times, even a single blow from the victim can constitute reasonable provocation. See Commonwealth v. Maskell, 403 Mass. 111, 116-117, 526 N.E.2d 756 (1988); Commonwealth v. Weaver, 395 Mass. 307, 312, 479 N.E.2d 682 (1985). "Whether the contact is sufficient will depend on whether a reasonable person under similar circumstances would have been provoked to act out of emotion rather than reasoned reflection." Model Jury Instructions on Homicide 29 (1999). A jury could conclude that a reasonable person in the defendant's position would have felt an "immediate and intense" threat, and lashed out in fear as a result. Commonwealth v. Amaral, 389 Mass. 184, 189, 450 N.E.2d 142 (1983). . . .

A substantial risk of a miscarriage [of justice] exists "if we have a serious doubt whether the result of the trial might have been different had the error not been made." Commonwealth v. LeFave, 430 Mass. 169, 174, 714 N.E.2d 805 (1999). Although we cannot be certain that the jury would

13. The Commonwealth claims that the actual provoking fact in this case was McCullough's accusation that the defendant stole his headlights, and that any provocation arising from that accusation should have dissipated by the time the defendant returned to the party forty-five minutes later. In other words, the Commonwealth, citing Commonwealth v. Amaral, 389 Mass. 184, 189, 450 N.E.2d 142 (1983), argues that a reasonable person would have "cooled off" by the time he returned to the party, and therefore the defendant's actions were not objectively reasonable. . . . The defendant maintains that the provocation occurred not when words were exchanged at the party earlier in the night, but outside in the street, when McCullough and his friends charged at him, knocked him to the ground, and punched him in the head. According to defense witnesses, this occurred immediately before the stabbing, and if their testimony is credited, the defendant's emotions would not have had time to cool.

have returned a verdict of voluntary manslaughter had they been instructed on reasonable provocation, it appears to be a real possibility in this case. The jury need not have been convinced beyond a reasonable doubt that the defendant reasonably was provoked: they only would need to harbor a reasonable doubt on the issue. . . . The Commonwealth's case was strong but not overwhelming: the Commonwealth's witnesses testified that the fight involved only McCullough and the defendant, and that the defendant was the instigator, whereas defense witnesses testified that the defendant was attacked by McCullough and others.[19] The jury's . . . question strongly suggests their willingness to consider other mitigating factors, the evidence supported an instruction on reasonable provocation, and the theory of provocation was consistent with the other defense theories. Accordingly, we conclude that trial counsel's failure to request an instruction on reasonable provocation . . . created a substantial risk of a miscarriage of justice.

CONCLUSION

For the foregoing reasons, the judgment is reversed, the verdict set aside, and the order denying the defendant's motion for a new trial is reversed. . . .[20]

Notes on Provocation

1. Following is a conventional definition of the "heat of passion" or provocation doctrine:

> "Heat of passion" has been defined as a state of violent and uncontrollable rage engendered by a blow or certain other provocation given, which will reduce a homicide from the grade of murder to that of manslaughter. . . . The term includes an emotional state of mind characterized by anger, rage, hatred, furious resentment or terror. The passion felt by the person committing the act should be superinduced by some insult, provocation, or injury, which would naturally and instantly produce, in the minds of ordinarily constituted men, the highest degree of exasperation.

McClendon v. State, 748 So. 2d 814 (Miss. Ct. App. 1999). Notice the reference to "ordinarily constituted *men*." The gendered language is no accident — the law of provocation seems to have been designed with testosterone-driven male defendants in mind. Susan Estrich's famous comment

---

19. The jury's decision to convict the defendant of murder in the second degree, rather than murder in the first degree, shows that they rejected the Commonwealth's theory of deliberate premeditation. . . .

20. The defendant may not be retried for murder in the first degree because he effectively was acquitted of that charge when the jury found him guilty of murder in the second degree. See Commonwealth v. Berry, 431 Mass. 326, 336 n.13, 727 N.E.2d 517 (2000).

about American criminal law applies with special force in this context: "Most of the time[,] criminal law that reflects male views and male standards imposes its judgment on men who have injured other men. It is 'boys' rules' applied to a boy's fight." Susan Estrich, Real Rape 60 (1987). As you read the materials that follow, consider whether the law grants too much leeway to violent young men doing battle with one another—and, perhaps, too little to women who seek to defend themselves against those young men.

2. As the quote from *McClendon* suggests, successful provocation claims require two showings: that the defendant in fact acted in "an emotional state of mind characterized by anger, rage, hatred, furious resentment or terror," and that this state of mind was prompted by "some insult, provocation, or injury, which would naturally and instantly produce, in the minds of ordinarily constituted men, the highest degree of exasperation." That is, provocation claims must clear two hurdles, one subjective (the defendant was actually provoked), and the other objective (a reasonable person in the defendant's circumstances would have been provoked).

The meaning of "reasonable" in this context is unclear. Provocation is not a complete defense—a valid provocation claim does not eliminate criminal liability, but merely reduces the level of liability from murder to manslaughter. If the defendant's behavior was reasonable in the ordinary sense of that word, why hold the defendant criminally liable at all? As you will see later, self-defense doctrine provides a complete excuse for defendants who respond reasonably to a wrongful threat of harm. (Self-defense doctrine is discussed infra, at pages 827-874.) It would seem to follow that reasonableness must have a specialized meaning in this setting. It does. In provocation cases, reasonableness generally refers only to the defendant's emotional state—his fear or rage, and not his conduct. If a reasonable person in the defendant's shoes would have experienced the same "heat of passion" as the defendant—think about situations so extremely provoking that almost anyone would be moved to think homicidal thoughts, even though the reasonable person would never act on those thoughts—then the provocation was reasonable, even though the defendant's homicidal conduct was excessive and therefore unreasonable.

3. The government attacks the reasonableness of defendants' provocation claims in two primary ways. First, prosecutors argue that the provoking event was not legally sufficient to trigger the "heat of passion." Second, they argue that too much time elapsed between the provoking event and the homicide—that a reasonable person would have "cooled off" in the relevant period of time. These two arguments—the sufficiency of the provoking event and the presence or absence of what courts call "cooling time"—have prompted a great deal of litigation.

With respect to the legal sufficiency of the provoking event, three propositions seem fairly clear. First, violence (even if it does not give rise to a valid claim of self-defense) is a sufficient provoking event, as *Acevedo* suggests.* Second, "mere words," no matter how egregious, generally do *not* suffice to show provocation (at least not at common law—modern versions of the doctrine, such as the Model Penal Code's, tend to be more inclusive). Third, neither does a trespass on the defendant's property, if unaccompanied by any threat of violence or further crimes.

With respect to "cooling time," the law is somewhat murkier. In general, the government tends to prevail when the defendant leaves the scene of the provoking event and later returns—even if the departure and return take only a couple of minutes. "Cooling time" may, in practice, have more to do with *place* than with *time*. Courts seem disinclined to accept provocation claims when the provoking event and the homicide happen in different places. The idea appears to be that, if the defendant had enough sense to leave the scene of the provoking event, he could and should have avoided the subsequent encounter that led to the homicide.

4. What is the point of these doctrines? On the surface, provocation doctrine appears to be a species of the law of criminal intent. "Heat of passion" obviously refers to the defendant's mental state, as does the idea of "cooling time." But there is another, very different thread running through provocation doctrine, one that has little to do with the defendant. In practice, defendants who raise provocation claims seek to show that the *victim* is at least partly to blame for the incident in question. Acevedo argues, in effect, that McCullough had it coming to him—perhaps he didn't deserve to die, but it's at least as much his fault as Acevedo's that the incident in question escalated out of control.

Should the law of homicide pay attention to such arguments? Does granting Acevedo's provocation claim devalue McCullough's life? Should the killing of more morally upright victims be punished more severely than killings like the one in *Acevedo*?

State v. Shumway

Supreme Court of Utah
63 P.3d 94 (2002)

Howe, Justice.

Defendant Brookes Colby Shumway appeals from a judgment of conviction for murder, a first degree felony under section 76-5-203 of the Utah Code, and for tampering with evidence, a second degree felony under section 76-8-510.

---

* Older cases suggest that witnessing adultery is likewise a legally sufficient provoking event. Nineteenth- and early-twentieth-century provocation cases are filled with examples of defendants (nearly always men) who killed their spouses and/or their spouses' lovers immediately upon discovering the infidelity. There are fewer such cases today—perhaps because society's mores have changed with respect to extramarital sex—but they still do occur.

BACKGROUND

On January 22, 2000, then fifteen-year-old Brookes Colby Shumway spent much of the day with his friend, fourteen-year-old Christopher Ray. That evening, Brookes "slept over" at Christopher's trailer home. Brookes and Christopher were up until 5:30 A.M. playing video games. At about 7 A.M., Brookes went to Christopher's mother's room and awoke her by exclaiming that Christopher had tried to stab him and that he stabbed Christopher back and thought that he might be dead. Christopher's mother came out of her room and found Christopher lying on his back on the floor in the front room with a butcher knife covered in blood next to him. She called 911, and the police and paramedics arrived shortly thereafter. After trying to revive Christopher, the paramedics declared him dead at the scene. The police searched the trailer and took into evidence the butcher knife, along with other knives from the kitchen.

The police also found that blankets the boys had been using had blood stains and stab patterns in them and were rolled up in the corner of the front room. A gym bag in Christopher's bedroom contained bloody socks. Later that day, after the police finished their search and investigation, a crime scene cleanup company cleaned out the trailer. The next day, the state medical examiner reported that Christopher had been stabbed thirty-nine times and that some of the stab wounds, including the fatal neck wound to the carotid artery, apparently had been inflicted with an instrument other than the butcher knife found by police. That instrument was never found.

Brookes was subsequently charged with murder and with tampering with the evidence. The juvenile court certified him to stand trial as an adult in the district court. Following deliberations, the jury convicted Brookes of both charges. He now appeals.

ANALYSIS

Brookes contends that the trial court erred in giving jury instruction 26, which mandated the order of deliberation on the murder charge. That instruction stated:

> Before you can convict the defendant, Brookes Colby Shumway, of the offense of Manslaughter, a lesser included offense in count I of the information, you must have found that the evidence fails to establish one or more of the elements of Murder, as charged in count I of the information, beyond a reasonable doubt. . . .

Brookes' trial counsel made no objection to the jury instruction. Brookes now contends, and the State concedes, that the instruction was erroneous. . . . [T]he jury should have been allowed to consider extreme emotional disturbance manslaughter even if they determined that all the elements of murder had been proved. In State v. Piansiaksone, 954 P.2d 861 (Utah 1998), we wrote:

It was theoretically possible that the jury could have found that every necessary element for murder had been satisfied and yet that manslaughter was the crime committed if the jury found that the killing was committed under the influence of extreme emotional disturbance for which there is a reasonable explanation or excuse.

Id. at 870. . . . [D]efendant's counsel at trial made no objection to jury instruction 26. However, defendant now contends that it was plain error on the part of the trial court. . . .

Our case law requires that to establish plain error, a defendant must show that (1) the instruction was erroneous; (2) the error should have been obvious to the trial court; and (3) but for the error, there would be a reasonable likelihood for a more favorable outcome for the defendant. State v. Dunn, 850 P.2d 1201, 1208-09 (Utah 1993). The State concedes that the jury instruction was erroneous and does not dispute that the error should have been obvious to the trial court, but counters that any error caused thereby was harmless because there is no evidence which would support the conclusion beyond a reasonable doubt that defendant killed the victim as a result of an extreme emotional disturbance or in imperfect self-defense, either of which would justify a verdict of manslaughter.

The State's contention that the trial court's error was harmless requires us to examine the evidence that might support a verdict of manslaughter. Utah Code Ann. section 76-5-203(3) provides two circumstances where a charge of murder can be reduced to manslaughter:

> (3)(a) It is an affirmative defense to a charge of murder or attempted murder that the defendant caused the death of another or attempted to cause the death of another:
>
> > (i) under the influence of extreme emotional distress for which there is a reasonable explanation or excuse. . . .
> >
> > (b) Under subsection (3)(a)(i), emotional distress does not include . . . distress that is substantially caused by the defendant's own conduct.
> >
> > (c) The reasonableness of an explanation or excuse under subsection (3)(a)(i) . . . shall be determined from the viewpoint of a reasonable person under the then existing circumstances.

Extreme Emotional Distress Manslaughter

Turning first to consideration under subsection (3)(a)(i), we explained in State v. Bishop, 753 P.2d 439, 471 (Utah 1988), overruled on other grounds by State v. Menzies, 889 P.2d 393 (Utah 1994), that a person suffers from an extreme emotional disturbance "when he is exposed to extremely unusual and overwhelming stress" such that

> the average reasonable person under that stress would have an extreme emotional reaction to it, as a result of which he would experience a loss of self-control and that person's reason would be overborne by intense feelings such as passion, anger, distress, grief, excessive agitation, or other similar emotions.

Id. However, an extreme emotional disturbance will not serve to reduce murder to manslaughter if the actor brought about his own mental disturbance. *Gardner*, 789 P.2d at 282-83; §76-5203(3)(b)(ii).

One interpretation of the evidence supports the necessity for a manslaughter instruction under subsection (3)(a)(i). Brookes disclosed to police that on the morning of the altercation Christopher was irritated at him for beating Christopher at video games. As the boys went to bed, Christopher went to the kitchen and retrieved a knife that he began to throw in the air and catch. Christopher then lunged at Brookes and began poking him with the knife. The boys wrestled over control of the knife and in his anger, Brookes stabbed Christopher. Brookes also suffered stab wounds to his hand. There was evidence that Christopher had a reputation for being a "hothead" and losing his temper, while Brookes was known to be cooperative and peaceful. Other evidence supported the argument that Brookes had been bullied and pushed around by his peers since he was in the third grade, and that all of this "came out on Chris" when the boys fought over the knife.

Under this interpretation of the evidence, Brookes arguably did not bring about the disturbance by his own conduct, but rather Christopher initiated a violent and traumatic act by attacking Brookes with the knife. Christopher's aggressive conduct could be found by a jury to provide a reasonable excuse or explanation for Brookes' stress and rage that resulted in Brookes stabbing Christopher in the throat and chest. According to the medical examiner, "the lethal wound to the victim's throat was inflicted early in the struggle, while the victim's blood pressure was still good." There is evidence that the wounds other than the two potentially fatal stabs would not have been deadly. At the end of the encounter, Brookes went to Christopher's mother's bedroom to awake her and told her twice that Christopher had tried to stab him. Brookes assisted her in her efforts to resuscitate Christopher. He was peaceful and sobbing. Police officers who responded testified that Brookes was not violent or a danger, but was cooperative and nonthreatening.

The State responds that the plain intent of our statutory scheme is to mitigate the crime of murder where a defendant's conduct was clearly wrong but where the circumstances were so provocative that even a reasonable person might have reacted similarly. But, the State asserts, even assuming the truthfulness of defendant's version of the incident, those facts would not constitute a "reasonable explanation or excuse" for the stabbing of Christopher. The State asserts that no reasonable person under the then existing circumstances, teased by a good friend playing with a knife during a sleepover, would have become so enraged or experience such an extreme emotional disturbance as to cause him to kill that person by cutting his throat and stabbing him thirty-nine times.

We conclude that defendant was entitled to an instruction under subsection (3)(a)(i) because a jury could conclude that Brookes caused the death of Christopher "under the influence of extreme emotional distress for which there is a reasonable explanation or excuse." In holding that the defendant was entitled to an instruction under subsection (3)(a)(i), we do not suggest that Brookes' version of the events that took place is the only reasonable interpretation of the evidence. Most disturbing, of course, is the fact that the medical examiner testified that Christopher had been stabbed thirty-nine times. However, in State v. Standiford, 769 P.2d 254, 264, 266 (Utah 1988), we approved of the giving of instructions for manslaughter and self-defense based on the defendant's theory of the case where he had stabbed the victim 107 times. See also State v. Cloud, 722 P.2d 750, 753-55 (Utah 1986), in which we held that the defendant would be entitled to an instruction on extreme emotional distress manslaughter where the victim had been stabbed twenty-seven times and died of multiple critical wounds. . . .

[The court proceeded to find the evidence at trial legally insufficient to sustain the conviction for evidence tampering. — EDS.]

CONCLUSION

Brookes' conviction of murder is reversed, and the case is remanded for a new trial. His conviction for tampering with evidence is reversed, and the charge is dismissed for insufficiency of the evidence.

Notes on Extreme Mental or Emotional Disturbance

1. The Model Penal Code suggested replacing provocation doctrine with a partial excuse for "extreme mental or emotional disturbance" (EMED), sometimes called (as in *Shumway*) "extreme emotional distress":

> Criminal homicide constitutes manslaughter when . . . a homicide which would otherwise be murder is committed under the influence of extreme mental or emotional disturbance for which there is reasonable explanation or excuse. The reasonableness of such explanation or excuse shall be determined from the viewpoint of a person in the actor's situation under the circumstances as he believes them to be.

MPC §210.3(b). About a dozen states eventually adopted some form of the EMED defense in place of traditional provocation doctrine.*

2. The key difference between EMED and provocation doctrine lies in the last phrase of the Model Penal Code provision quoted above: "under the circumstances as he believes them to be." That phrase makes the standard for EMED arguments significantly more subjective than the conventional provocation standard. On the one hand, a more subjective standard would seem to follow from the nature of the claim—if, in fact, acting in a highly emotional state is less blameworthy than acting after cool reflection, the

---

* Note that the Utah statute cited in *Shumway* changed EMED from a lesser-included crime into an "affirmative defense," thus shifting the burden of proof on EMED to the defendant. In 2009, post-*Shumway*, the Utah legislature abolished the EMED defense altogether. See Utah Code Ann. §76-5-203.

legal inquiry should focus on the defendant's emotional state. On the other hand, the Model Penal Code's EMED standard seems to raise the problem that so concerned the majority in People v. Marrero (see Chapter 3, page 157). Marrero claimed that his error about the scope of New York's criminal gun possession law should give him a legal excuse; Judge Bellacosa's majority opinion rejected that claim, arguing that Marrero should be bound by the same rules as the rest of the population. If each of us defines the legal standard by which we are judged, Bellacosa contended, then each of us is a law unto himself. Might the same be true if defendants define not the *legal rules* by which they are judged, but the *factual circumstances* to which those legal rules are applied?

3. According to Victoria Nourse, the more subjective EMED standard mostly serves to make it easier for male defendants to (partially) excuse the killing of girlfriends who seek to end their relationships. See Victoria Nourse, Passion's Progress: Modern Law Reform and the Provocation Defense, 106 Yale L.J. 1331 (1997). Nourse's interesting article discusses a number of cases in which defendants raised EMED claims that would have been rejected as a matter of law under conventional provocation doctrine—that is, the jury would not even have been permitted to decide the claim—but that made it to the jury in jurisdictions with statutes similar to MPC §210.3(b). In reported decisions, these claims nearly all lost, but that may well be a consequence of the fact that the government is not allowed to appeal successful provocation claims. (When a defendant's provocation claim succeeds, the jury convicts the defendant of manslaughter; that conviction is deemed the legal equivalent of an acquittal on the more serious murder charge. Under the Double Jeopardy Clause, such acquittals are unappealable.)

One example Nourse discusses is People v. Casassa, 49 N.Y.2d 668, 404 N.E.2d 1310 (1980). Casassa and the victim dated for a few months in the fall of 1976; in November of that year, the victim told him that she was not in love with him and did not want to pursue a relationship. Three months later, Casassa broke into the victim's apartment seeking (he claimed) to renew the relationship. When the victim refused him, Casassa stabbed her several times, then drowned her in the bathtub. At his murder trial, a mental health expert testified that Casassa was obsessed with the victim, and was not fully in control of his actions. (Casassa was convicted of second-degree murder; his conviction was affirmed on appeal.) Should juries be permitted to hear such testimony? Should the legal system punish impulsive homicides by emotionally disturbed defendants—actually, it isn't even clear that Casassa's killing *was* impulsive; he brought the knife with him to the victim's apartment—less severely than other homicides? If so, why? If not, why not?

4. How should the provocation (or EMED) defense apply to battered spouses (usually, women) who kill their batterers (usually, men)? Battered spouse cases have proven difficult for many courts. On the one hand, they tend not to fit well within the traditional parameters of self-defense (because the battered spouse usually does not kill while she is being attacked, but instead waits for a later—and safer—time to do so).** But on the other hand, they also seem problematic under the provocation doctrine. One reason is that women so rarely kill under any circumstances, which can make the homicidal response of a battered spouse appear inherently less "reasonable" to judges and juries than the homicidal reaction of a man who, say, comes home to find his wife in bed with another man (one of the traditional paradigms of voluntary manslaughter).

A second reason is that most battered spouses who kill tend to do so at least as much due to extreme fear than as a product of extreme anger. The traditional "heat of passion" provocation defense (which is only a partial defense, remember—indeed, many advocates for battered spouses reject the provocation defense out of hand, believing that such women deserve complete exoneration, not reduced criminal punishment) arose from situations involving anger (usually male), and continues even today to be applied most frequently to such situations.

It may even be the case that the metaphorical name of the doctrine (the "heat of passion" defense) helps to constrain our thinking about the doctrine, making it harder to apply in cases involving defendants who, like battered spouses, kill out of fear. Anger is a "hot" emotion ("he burned with rage") that we can easily understand as giving rise to the "heat of passion" and causing an "explosion" of lethal violence. Fear, on the other hand, is a "cold" emotion ("an icy chill ran down her spine") that is rarely thought to generate much action at all, other than perhaps running away from whatever scares us. This folk theory of emotion may partially explain why the law of voluntary manslaughter has tended to resist most efforts (including the Model Penal Code's) to broaden its scope to include battered spouses and other defendants motivated by fear. See Elise J. Percy, Joseph L. Hoffmann & Steven J. Sherman, "Sticky Metaphors" and the Persistence of the Traditional Voluntary Manslaughter Doctrine, 44 Mich. J. L. Reform 383 (2011).

5. Notice that Utah's EMED statute does not contain the closing phrase from MPC §210.3(b). Instead, the statute says that reasonableness "shall be determined from the viewpoint of a reasonable person under the then existing circumstances." Does the difference matter? Only Shumway knows the circumstances surrounding the killing—Ray knew, but he is dead. In practice, an objective standard that turns on the defendant's testimony (either to the police shortly after the crime or at the defendant's trial) may be no different than a subjective standard.

One reason why police interrogation plays an especially important role in homicide cases is that the circumstances surrounding many homicides

---

** We will discuss the "battered spouse" defense more fully in Chapter 11, in connection with the law of self-defense—which is the legal context in which the "battered spouse" defense usually arises. See infra, at page 848.

are known only to the perpetrators. Often, if the police cannot obtain a confession, the defendant is unconvictable. Should crimes be defined in such a manner? What is the alternative?

6. In addition to Ray's death, two other facts in *Shumway* are clear: The defendant stabbed the victim more than three dozen times, and the defendant used more than one weapon to inflict the stab wounds. What do you make of those two facts? Do the number of weapons and wounds suggest that Shumway consciously chose to kill Ray, or do they suggest the opposite — that Shumway acted in an emotional state for which he is not fully responsible?

5. Reckless Manslaughter

State ex rel. Thomas v. Duncan

Court of Appeals of Arizona, Division One
216 Ariz. 260; 165 P.3d 238 (2007)

Opinion of BARKER, Judge.

This special action presents the issue of whether evidence of justification in a manslaughter case that would be prohibited . . . if a justification defense were sought, may be admissible if it is relevant on a separate issue. The State of Arizona, Petitioner, asks this court to reverse the trial court's order permitting William Joseph Reagan, Jr. . . . to present such evidence to a jury. For the reasons that follow, we accept jurisdiction and deny relief.

FACTS AND PROCEDURAL HISTORY

On October 29, 2005, Reagan was driving his truck with his brother seated in the passenger seat. Reagan alleges that he was involved in a road rage incident. He claims that the occupants of the other vehicle involved in the incident "made threats that led him to believe that he and his brother were in danger of being seriously injured or perhaps killed." Reagan tried to drive away, but alleges that the other vehicle chased him. Reagan was "fearful and remembers driving quickly because they were being chased and he wanted to get away from the danger." During later investigation, witnesses claimed to have seen another truck either racing with or chasing Reagan's car. Reagan ran a red light while driving approximately seventy-nine to eighty-four miles per hour in a forty mile per hour zone and struck the victim's car, killing her. Reagan had a blood alcohol content of .093 at the time.

The State filed a motion to preclude Reagan from introducing evidence of the chase, arguing it went to the justification defense and was prohibited pursuant to Ariz. Rev. Stat. §§13-401(A), 13-412(C), and 13-417(C). Following oral argument, the trial court denied the State's motion to preclude. The State filed this special action.

Special action jurisdiction is highly discretionary. *See State ex rel. McDougall v. Superior Court*, 186 Ariz. 218, 219-20, 920 P.2d 784, 785-86 (App. 1996). Jurisdiction is appropriate when there is no adequate remedy by way of appeal. *Sun Health Corp. v. Myers*, 205 Ariz. 315, 317, P2, 70 P.3d 444, 446 (App. 2003). . . . Should Reagan be acquitted, the State could not appeal the trial court's order. Under these circumstances, the State does not have an adequate remedy by way of appeal. Furthermore, this special action presents a purely legal issue of first impression that is of statewide importance. Accordingly, special action jurisdiction is appropriate here.

DISCUSSION

The State raises two issues. First, does Ariz. Rev. Stat. §13-401(A) preclude the admission of evidence that is relevant to a justification defense when the defendant is seeking to use the evidence for other legitimate purposes? Second, did the trial court err in its determination that the disputed evidence in this case was relevant to the *mens rea* element of reckless manslaughter?

. . . [T]he justification defense here is an affirmative defense that the defendant must prove by a preponderance of the evidence. A justification defense is unavailable in certain instances, as provided for in Ariz. Rev. Stat. §13-401(A):

> Even though a person is justified under this chapter in threatening or using physical force or deadly physical force against another, if in doing so such person recklessly injures or kills an innocent third person, the justification afforded by this chapter is unavailable in a prosecution for the reckless injury or killing of the innocent third person.

The unavailability provision applies to the defense of self-defense and other justification defenses. The defenses of duress and necessity are two of the justification defenses set forth in that chapter that are also specifically made unavailable "for offenses involving homicide or serious physical injury." Ariz. Rev. Stat. §§13-412(C), 13-417(C). Duress and necessity are therefore unavailable in this case [regardless] of §13-401(A).

Reagan . . . does not claim that he should be able to raise an affirmative defense of justification, be it one of duress, necessity or otherwise. Rather, he asserts that the evidence of the chase is relevant to the *mens rea* element of reckless manslaughter. The State argues that by introducing evidence that is relevant to a justification defense, Reagan is raising the defense despite his assertion to the contrary. The State urges this court to hold that §13-401, in prosecutions for the reckless injury or killing of an innocent third person, is an absolute bar to admitting evidence that might support a justification defense even if the evidence is properly admissible for other purposes. We do not agree.

The language in the statutes cited by the State bars the use of *defenses* to a charged offense. *See* Ariz. Rev. Stat. §§13-412(C) ("*the defense* provided by subsection A [duress] is unavailable for offenses involving homicide or serious physical injury"); 13-417(C) ("An accused person may not assert *the defense* under subsection A [necessity] for offenses involving homicide or serious physical injury.") (emphasis added). Thus, by the statutes' own terms, they only restrict the availability of *defenses*. They do not bar the use of all *evidence* when admission of that evidence is sought for a separate, but permissible purpose.

The idea that a court may admit evidence for a legitimate purpose even though the evidence is inadmissible for another purpose is not foreign to the law of evidence. Thus, we hold that the trial court may admit evidence tending to show justification in prosecutions for the reckless injury or killing of an innocent third person if that evidence is otherwise admissible for a separate purpose. . . .

Having determined that Ariz. Rev. Stat. §§13-401(A), 13-412(C), and 13-417(C) do not bar evidence of justification when it is admissible for a separate, permissible purpose, we now turn to whether such a purpose exists in this case. Reagan argues that the evidence is admissible as to the issue of *mens rea*. . . .

The crime of manslaughter, with which Reagan is charged, is defined as "[r]ecklessly causing the death of another person." Ariz. Rev. Stat. §13-1103(A)(1). The term "recklessly" is defined to include the requirement that "a person is *aware of* and *consciously disregards* a substantial and unjustifiable risk." Ariz. Rev. Stat. §13-105(9)(c) (emphasis added).[6]

Reagan argues that . . . because of the chase he was not "aware of" nor did he "consciously disregard" the [relevant] risk. If the State cannot satisfy this element, then acquittal on the manslaughter charge would be required.[7]

---

6. The full definition of "recklessly" is as follows:

"Recklessly" means, with respect to a result or to a circumstance described by a statute defining an offense, that a person is aware of and consciously disregards a substantial and unjustifiable risk that the result will occur or that the circumstance exists. The risk must be of such nature and degree that disregard of such risk constitutes a gross deviation from the standard of conduct that a reasonable person would observe in the situation. A person who creates such a risk but is unaware of such risk solely by reason of voluntary intoxication also acts recklessly with respect to such risk.

Ariz. Rev. Stat. §13-105(9)(c).

7. A lesser included offense to manslaughter is negligent homicide. A person is guilty of negligent homicide "if with criminal negligence the person causes the death of another person." Ariz. Rev. Stat. §13-1102(A).

"Criminal negligence" means, with respect to a result or to a circumstance described by a statute defining an offense, that a person fails to perceive a substantial and unjustifiable risk that the result will occur or that the circumstance exists. The risk must be of such nature and degree that the failure to perceive it constitutes a gross deviation from the standard of care that a reasonable person would observe in the situation.

Ariz. Rev. Stat. §13-105(9)(d). "Negligent homicide is distinguished from reckless manslaughter in that for the latter offense, the defendant is aware of the risk of death and consciously disregards it, whereas, for the former offense, he is unaware of the risk." State v. Walton, 133 Ariz. 282, 291, 650 P.2d 1264, 1273 (App. 1982). Thus, the lesser included offense would still be applicable.

In Commonwealth v. Papadinis, 503 N.E.2d 1334, 1335-36 (Mass. App. Ct. 1987), reversed on other grounds, 520 N.E.2d 1300 (Mass. 1988), the defendant was convicted of involuntary manslaughter, which required a culpable mental state of recklessness. The trial court refused to admit evidence that the defendant feared for his safety to disprove the element of awareness of a risk of causing death by his actions. The appellate court reversed, holding that "[t]he jury might have accepted the defendant's explanation that he was much afraid, beclouded by panic, and consequently drove off unaware [of the risk]." Id. at 1337.

Similarly, . . . evidence of the alleged chase at the time Reagan ran the red light is evidence the jury may consider in determining whether the State has met its burden to show that Reagan was "aware of and consciously disregard[ed]" the risk at issue here. Being "aware" of the risk and the "justifiability" of the risk are also separate and distinct inquiries. The use for this purpose is thus for a purpose different from that prohibited by the justification statutes.

In sum, the trial court did not err in admitting the evidence of the chase. We need not consider the defendant's constitutional grounds for the admissibility of the evidence as we resolve the case on other grounds.

For the foregoing reasons, we accept jurisdiction and deny relief.

Notes and Questions

1. In most jurisdictions, the crime charged in *Thomas* would be called involuntary manslaughter. The crime's defining feature is a degree of recklessness that isn't extreme enough to deserve the label of murder. As voluntary manslaughter is first-degree murder's junior partner, involuntary manslaughter—or, as the crime is known in Arizona, reckless manslaughter—has the same relationship with second-degree murder.

2. Reagan could not claim self-defense because the *victim* did not threaten him; self-defense claims are available in homicide cases only when the decedent was the aggressor. Necessity and duress are not so limited. In duress cases, the defendant commits the relevant crime under the compulsion of a third party; in necessity cases, the compulsion comes from the surrounding circumstances. Because those defenses do not require proof of misconduct by crime victims, duress and necessity historically were not permitted in homicide cases, as *Thomas* suggests. Both English and American law have traditionally barred all defenses that would excuse the killing of innocent victims—recall *Dudley & Stephens*, supra at page 5, in which that principle received its most famous explanation. All of which explains why Reagan sought to use the evidence of the car chase not to raise an affirmative defense, but to negate *mens rea*.

3. Why, exactly, does the evidence of the chase make Reagan seem less culpable? According to Judge Barker's opinion, the answer is that, because of the chase, Reagan might not have been conscious of the risk of harm his conduct imposed on other drivers. Notice footnote 7 in Barker's opinion: If Reagan were charged with negligent homicide, the evidence in question would be inadmissible, since criminal negligence does not require awareness of the relevant risks. Is that analysis sound? Suppose Reagan testified that he understood perfectly that running a red light posed a risk of harm to other drivers; it also posed a risk of harm to Reagan and his brother. Suppose further that Reagan claimed he ran the red light in spite of those risks because not doing so posed an even greater risk of harm — the risk that the motorist chasing him might kill him and his brother. That hypothetical testimony would seem to bear on the question whether Reagan's conduct constituted "a gross deviation from the standard of conduct that a reasonable person would observe" in similar circumstances — part of the definition of *both* recklessness *and* negligence under Arizona law. Yet the evidence at issue in *Thomas* would have been inadmissible to support that defense theory. Why?

To put the point another way, evidence of the car chase that led to the accident in *Thomas* helps Reagan in two distinct ways: It tends to support his claim that he wasn't aware of the risks his conduct posed to others, and it tends to suggest that his conduct was not as blameworthy as one might suppose. *Thomas* accepts the first of those arguments, but rejects the second. Again, why?

4. Reagan's blood alcohol content placed him just under the level required for driving while intoxicated, in Arizona and in most jurisdictions. Should that fact bear on the issue in *Thomas*? If so, how?

6. Negligent Homicide

People v. Cabrera

Court of Appeals of New York
10 N.Y.3d 370; 887 N.E.2d 1132 (2008)

Opinion by READ, J.

Late in the afternoon on a bright, summer June day in 2004, a group of Sullivan County youths set out for a local lake to go swimming. They piled into two vehicles to make the trip. One was operated by 19-year-old Monica Mendoza, with her younger sister as a passenger; the other, by defendant Brett Cabrera, a 17-year-old with a junior "class DJ" license. Cabrera was driving his parents' 2004 Mercury Mountaineer, a midsized SUV; the Mountaineer had no mechanical defects and nearly new tires. Cabrera was transporting four teenage passengers; none were family members.

Cabrera's junior license imposed several restrictions: as relevant here, the holder of a class DJ license . . . may not operate a vehicle with more than two passengers under 21 years of age who are not members of the junior licensee's immediate family, and must ensure that all passengers have buckled their seat belts. See Vehicle and Traffic Law §501-b(2) *et seq.* But on this trip to the lake, none of Cabrera's four passengers—a 14-year-old, a 15-year-old, a 17-year-old and an 18-year-old—wore a seat belt. Cabrera himself did.

Because she did not know the way to the lake, Monica followed Cabrera. . . . [The two cars] eventually turned onto Sackett Lake Road, where the posted speed limit was 55 mph. At a point where the roadway curved to the right, Monica "slowed down" . . . because she was "not always used to driving" that type of hilly, winding road. When she reduced her speed, Cabrera "just kept on the same speed[,] so he pulled away . . . from [her] a little. . . . " "[B]y the time [Monica] was getting into" a second curve (presumably the curve to the left before the accident scene), she "just saw the back of the car [Cabrera was driving] . . . and then [she] lost" sight of it "for . . . a second or two and then when [she] saw the car again[,] it was . . . losing control . . . going to the side of the road" before crashing. Three of the passengers in the Cabrera vehicle died in this accident, and one was critically injured. Cabrera suffered noncritical injuries. He tested free of drugs and alcohol.

Santiago Mendoza, the only surviving passenger in Cabrera's vehicle, testified at trial about "what was going on in [Cabrera's] car" leading up to the accident. The passengers were talking amongst themselves and listening to rap music; they were not interacting with Cabrera. When asked what Cabrera was doing, Santiago answered simply: "Driving." Asked by the prosecutor if "there [was] any conversation in the car about how fast or speed or where your sisters were, or anything about that," he answered "No." Indeed, the first time Santiago noticed anything distinctive about Cabrera's driving was when he "felt the car lose control" and "felt the back end slide . . . [and] hit the dirt on the opposite side of the road."

According to Deputy Sheriff Amanda Cox, the first quarter of a mile or so on the stretch of Sackett Lake Road leading to the accident scene is flat or uphill; the road crests and goes down along a straightaway past a turnoff. The road then goes up slightly before bending to the left and sloping downhill. At the bottom of this descent is a dip in the road before it starts back uphill and slants to the right; the accident occurred "right at the dip."

There is a "40 mph curve" sign near the point at which Sackett Lake Road veers left into the downhill slope. Deputy Cox authored a police accident report concluding that the operator of Vehicle One[, the SUV driven by Cabrera,]

"while traveling westbound on Sackett Lake Road at a rate of speed unsatisfactory for the roadway[,] failed to negotiate a curve. Vehicle One then crossed over the double yellow line into the eastbound lane [and] went off the eastbound shoulder striking a . . . utility pole [and] a tree and coming to rest on the [driver's] side of the vehicle."

When Cabrera's vehicle went off the left-hand side of the road, it slid down a 25-to-30 foot embankment. Deputy Cox knew of other accidents at this location. Similarly, Detective Don Starner had "investigated several accidents . . . most of them caused by either speed or alcohol" on Sackett Lake Road near the crash site.

Trooper Shane Conklin, a collision reconstructionist for the New York State Police, "observed two tire marks that [began] in the westbound lane to the right of the center line and . . . progressed in a westerly direction through the westbound lane back across the double solid line into the eastbound lane and ended on the edge of the asphalt," at which point the rear of the Cabrera vehicle fell down the embankment on the left side of the road (followed by the rest of the vehicle). The distance from the point at which the tire marks started until the point at which the vehicle left the road was approximately 230 feet. . . .

According to Trooper Conklin, the tire marks from the Cabrera vehicle were made by "critical speed yaw." This occurs when a vehicle begins spinning on its central axis and the tires are "side slipping" while rotating; in other words, the tire marks were caused by the vehicle as it spun out of control, not by skidding upon braking. Using the yaw marks, Trooper Conklin calculated a speed of 70-72 mph upon entry into the critical speed yaw and opined that the left side of Cabrera's vehicle had crossed the double-yellow center line by that point.

Trooper Conklin ultimately concluded that Cabrera's "vehicle was attempting to negotiate the curve at a speed that was too great to be negotiated . . . [a]nd the speed was between 70 and 72 miles per hour," causing the SUV to enter into critical speed yaw. He observed that once a critical speed yaw is entered, "it is very difficult to bring the car back under control."

Cabrera was charged with three counts of criminally negligent homicide, Penal Law §125.10, one count of assault in the third degree, Penal Law §120.00(3), reckless driving, Vehicle and Traffic Law §1212, and various traffic infractions. At his subsequent jury trial, he sought to dismiss the homicide and assault charges on the ground that his actions, as proved by the People, were insufficient as a matter of law to establish criminal negligence. The judge was unpersuaded. Cabrera also was unable to convince the trial judge to advise the jury that excessive speed is by itself not enough to support criminal negligence, and that junior license violations are not evidence of criminal negligence. . . .

The jury convicted Cabrera on all counts and the trial judge sentenced him to the maximum term allowed by statute—an aggregate term of [16 months] to 4 years in prison—and fined him $800. Cabrera was then remanded to the custody of the New York State Department of Correctional Services, and served out his sentence in a maximum security prison.

The Appellate Division . . . affirmed the conviction [by a three-to-two vote], with one of the two dissenting justices granting Cabrera leave to appeal to us. Cabrera advances two arguments on appeal: that the evidence adduced at trial was insufficient as a matter of law to sustain his convictions for criminally negligent homicide and third-degree assault; and, in the alternative, that he is entitled to a new trial because the trial judge's instructions were erroneous.

"A person is guilty of criminally negligent homicide when, with criminal negligence, he causes the death of another person." Penal Law §125.10. Similarly, a person is guilty of third-degree assault when "[w]ith criminal negligence, he causes physical injury to another person by means of . . . a dangerous instrument." Penal Law §120.00(3). Since an automobile is concededly "a dangerous instrument" for purposes of Penal Law §120.00(3), and Cabrera "cause[d] the death of" three of his passengers insofar as he may have been criminally negligent, the parties contest only whether he acted with the requisite *mens rea.* Under section 15.05(4) of the Penal Law,

> "[a] person acts with criminal negligence with respect to a result . . . when he fails to perceive a substantial and unjustifiable risk that such result will occur or that such circumstance exists. The risk must be of such nature and degree that the failure to perceive it constitutes a gross deviation from the standard of care that a reasonable person would observe in the situation."

We have examined section 15.05(4) . . . on numerous occasions, most recently in People v. Conway, 6 N.Y.3d 869, 849 N.E.2d 954 (2006). There, we explained that

> "the carelessness required for criminal negligence is appreciably more serious than that for ordinary civil negligence, and that the carelessness must be such that its seriousness would be apparent to anyone who shares the community's general sense of right and wrong. Moreover, criminal negligence requires a defendant to have engaged in some blameworthy conduct creating or contributing to a substantial and unjustifiable risk of a proscribed result; nonperception of a risk, even if [the proscribed result occurs], is not enough."

Id. at 872.

Cabrera protests that excessive speed is never enough to make out a case of criminally negligent homicide, citing People v. Bearden, 290 N.Y. 478, 49 N.E.2d 785 (1943), and People v. Eckert, 2 N.Y.2d 126, 138 N.E.2d 794 (1956), two decades-old cases decided under Penal Law §1053-a, the predecessor statute to Penal Law §125.10. While Cabrera reads *Bearden* and *Eckert* as, in effect, establishing a *per se* rule, our more recent cases take a slightly different tack.

In 1990, for example, we decided two companion cases involving criminally negligent homicide arising out of automobile accidents: People v. Boutin, 75 N.Y.2d 692, 555 N.E.2d 253 (1990), and People v. Paul V.S., 75 N.Y.2d 944, 554 N.E.2d 1273 (1990). In *Boutin*, we reversed a conviction for criminally negligent homicide where the defendant—traveling near, and possibly under, the speed limit—struck a marked police car stopped in the right-hand travel lane of Interstate 87 on a rainy, foggy night. In *Paul V.S.*, . . . we affirmed a conviction for criminally negligent homicide where the defendant was traveling 90 mph in a 55 mph "radar zone," accelerated after being warned by his passenger to slow down, continued past a line of cars that had been stopped by police, and ultimately struck and killed a State Trooper attempting to direct him off the highway.

When discussing our precedents in *Boutin*, we observed that the common thread was the "creation," rather than the "nonperception," of risk. *Boutin* [involved] noncriminal "risk nonperception" because the defendant had simply "fail[ed] to see the vehicle stopped in the lane ahead of him[,] result[ing] in the fatal accident." 75 N.Y.2d at 697. This was to be distinguished from cases where there was "criminally culpable risk creating conduct—e.g., *dangerous* speeding, racing, failure to obey traffic signals, *or* any other misconduct that created or contributed to a 'substantial and unjustifiable' risk of death." Id. at 697-98 (emphases added).

In short, it takes some additional affirmative act by the defendant to transform "speeding" into "dangerous speeding"; conduct by which the defendant exhibits the kind of "serious[ly] blameworth[y]" carelessness whose "seriousness would be apparent to anyone who shares the community's general sense of right and wrong." *Boutin*, 75 N.Y.2d at 696. Thus, in the cases where we have considered the evidence sufficient to establish criminally negligent homicide, the defendant has engaged in some other "risk-creating" behavior in addition to driving faster than the posted speed limit. *Compare* People v. Haney, 30 N.Y.2d 328, 284 N.E.2d 564 (1972) (defendant was speeding on city street and failed to stop at red light before killing pedestrian crossing street with green light in her favor); People v. Soto, 44 N.Y.2d 683, 376 N.E.2d 907 (1978) (defendant, who was speeding and drag racing on city street, struck and killed driver stopped at red light); People v. Ricardo B., 73 N.Y.2d 228, 535 N.E.2d 1336 (1989) (defendant was drag racing at between 70 and 90 mph on a busy metropolitan street, ran a red light and struck vehicle crossing intersection with light in its favor); People v. Loughlin, 76 N.Y.2d 804, 807, 559 N.E.2d 656 (1990) (intoxicated defendant was speeding on obstructed street under construction in residential neighborhood in Queens); People v. Maher, 79 N.Y.2d 978, 980, 594 N.E.2d 915 (1992) (intoxicated defendant drove at speeds of 50 to 100 mph in 35 mph zone in Manhattan, disobeying several traffic signals); [and] People v. Harris, 81 N.Y.2d 850, 851-52, 613 N.E.2d 526 (1993) ("defendant, while legally intoxicated, drove his motor vehicle in the dark of night from a public highway into an unfamiliar farmer's field, . . . and suddenly and forcefully drove through a hedgerow of small trees and shrubs, not knowing what obstacles and dangers lurked on the other side") *with* People v. Perry, 123 App. Div. 2d 492, 507 N.Y.S.2d 90 (4th Dept. 1986), aff'd, 70 N.Y.2d 626, 512 N.E.2d 540 (1987) (no criminal negligence present where defendant was driving approximately 80 mph in a 55 mph zone "on a rural road, on a dark night," struck a utility pole, and killed two passengers; defendant's "conduct . . . d[id] not constitute a gross deviation from the ordinary standard of care held by those who share the community's general sense of right and wrong").

The question on this appeal is therefore whether, when viewed in the light most favorable to the People, the evidence adduced at trial showed that Cabrera's conduct constituted "not only a failure to perceive a risk of death, but also some serious blameworthiness in the conduct that caused it." *Boutin*, 75 N.Y.2d at 696. Measured by this standard, the evidence falls short.

There was testimony and forensic evidence that Cabrera, a young and inexperienced but sober driver, entered a tricky downhill curve, the site of other accidents, at a rate of speed well in excess of the posted warning sign. This behavior is certainly negligent, and unquestionably "blameworthy." But our decisions have uniformly looked for some kind of morally blameworthy component to excessive speed in determining criminal negligence; for example, consciously accelerating in the presence of an obvious risk. See People v. Paul V.S., 75 N.Y.2d 944, 554 N.E.2d 1273. No such morally blameworthy behavior could be inferred from the testimony in this case.[2] For a 17-year-old to badly misgauge his ability to handle road conditions is not the kind of . . . behavior that the Legislature envisioned when it defined "criminal negligence," even though the consequences here were fatal. This crash resulted from noncriminal failure to perceive risk; it was not the result of criminal risk creation.

Next, at the time of the accident, Cabrera was transporting more than two teenagers who were nonfamily members, and his passengers were not wearing seat belts. As an initial matter, we reject Cabrera's contention that these license violations are "logically irrelevant" because criminal negligence may not turn on whether (holding everything else equal) the accident happened on the day it did or several months later, when Cabrera reached the age of 18 and these restrictions would no longer have been in force. . . . The Legislature adopted a graduated licensing scheme to reduce the level of teen automobile crashes—the leading cause of death among teenagers—by making full drivers' licensing privileges contingent upon a period of safe driving during which various restrictions apply. . . . Yet even if, as the dissent argues, New York's graduated licensing scheme was meant to reduce the likelihood of "risky driving behavior to impress peers" . . . , Santiago

---

2. The dissent argues that "there was ample evidence for the jury to find that defendant was attempting to achieve a racing car-type stunt as he drove into the curve." Yet even the prosecution—which asserted every possible inference in a seventy-two page closing argument—never made such a claim. To the contrary, the prosecution argued: "I'm not going to stand here and tell you he intentionally did it. I'm not going to look you in the eye and tell you he intended to do it. I'm telling you he *failed to perceive* the great risk [of] harm he was creating." (Emphasis added.)

Mendoza's trial testimony does not support the inference that Cabrera was showing off or was distracted by conversation with his passengers in the moments prior to the accident. Simply put, Cabrera's failure to ensure that his passengers wore seat belts was not conduct causing or contributing to the risk of an automobile accident; the fact that Cabrera's passengers were teenagers likewise did not cause or contribute to the crash.

In sum, even when viewed in the light most favorable to the People, the evidence adduced at Cabrera's trial was insufficient as a matter of law to sustain his convictions for criminally negligent homicide and third-degree assault. . . .

Accordingly, the Appellate Division's order should be modified by dismissing the three counts of criminally negligent homicide and the count of assault in the third degree and vacating the sentences imposed thereon and, as so modified, affirmed.

GRAFFEO, J., joined by CIPARICK and SMITH, JJ., dissenting.

. . . [E]ven excluding consideration of the evidence relating to defendant's junior license violations, I believe that this case falls within the ambit of our precedents sustaining convictions for criminally negligent homicide. Viewing the evidence in a light most favorable to the People, this case involved much more than excessive speed. Defendant was familiar with Sackett Lake Road, a two-lane country byway divided by a double yellow line with a posted speed limit of 55 miles per hour. A warning sign with a recommended speed limit of 40 miles per hour preceded the left-hand curve where the accident occurred. . . . [A]s defendant approached the curve, he partially crossed the double yellow line into the oncoming lane of traffic before losing control of his vehicle. The evidence demonstrated that defendant did not apply his brakes as he approached the curve or even when he attempted to negotiate it. Rather, he drove 70 to 72 miles per hour into the curve, at which point his SUV entered "critical speed yaw," rotated and slid off the road, crashing into and severing a utility pole.

Giving the People all the favorable inferences from the proof presented, as we must, there was ample evidence for the jury to find that defendant was attempting to achieve a racing car-type stunt as he drove into the curve. Trooper Conklin . . . testified that defendant's excessive speed and decision to cross the double yellow line in anticipation of the curve were consistent with an attempt "to negotiate the curve inside and in other words flatten[] out the curve." Investigator Scalia, another collision reconstruction expert employed by the State Police, . . . defined "flattening out a curve" to mean "when you come on [a] turn, you are cutting, you are bringing over [the] yellow or center line a little bit [so] you can flatten that turn out with [the] car." The proof—that defendant crossed the double line prior to entry, came into the curve at 70 to 72 miles per hour and failed to apply the brakes—supports this inference. Hence, contrary to the majority's conclusion, the People did present legally sufficient evidence of excessive speed coupled with independently culpable, "blameworthy conduct creating or contributing to a substantial and unjustifiable risk of a proscribed result." People v. Conway, 6 N.Y.3d 869, 872, 849 N.E.2d 954 (2006), beyond what the majority characterizes as a mere "failure to perceive risk" by an inexperienced driver.

. . . In their opening statement, the People clearly advanced this concept, commenting that the evidence would show that defendant viewed the bend as a "NASCAR curve" and that he sought "to flatten that curve out like [a] NASCAR driver." Echoing this contention in the closing statement, the prosecutor remarked that defendant intentionally cut the curve and tried to take it at 70 to 72 miles per hour even though he was "no NASCAR driver." . . .

As the holder of a class DJ license, defendant was not authorized to operate a vehicle with more than two passengers under the age of 21 unless the other passengers were family members or he was accompanied by a parent or guardian, and he was required to ensure that all occupants of the vehicle wore seat belts. See Vehicle and Traffic Law §501-b(2). The Legislature enacted this provision in 2002 as part of an overall graduated licensing system, and these restrictions were designed, at least in part, for the purpose of "limiting [teenagers'] exposure to hazardous driving situations" due to their inexperience and tendency to be easily distracted. . . . Sponsor's Memorandum, 2002 McKinney's Session Laws of N.Y., at 2114. The Legislature recognized that the national crash rate for teens is four times higher than that for adults . . . due to "the propensity of young drivers to take risks, their belief that they are invincible and their susceptibility to peer pressure." Id. . . .

It is logical to conclude that a young driver would be less likely to drive carelessly if a parent was in the vehicle and more likely to engage in risky driving behavior to impress peers when there is no parental supervision. . . . The facts here well illustrate this point. Had defendant's parent been in the SUV with the four teen passengers, it seems unlikely that he would have attempted to take the turn at 70 to 72 miles per hour. . . . [T]he statutory obligation placed on defendant to ensure that his passengers wore their seat belts also factors into whether his [conduct was criminally negligent].[4] Certainly, contrary to defendant's argument, the jury was not required to ignore these license violations in assessing defendant's culpability. . . .

---

4. . . . [F]ailure to comply with seat belt requirements is, by statute, not admissible on the question of liability in civil negligence cases. See Vehicle and Traffic Law §1229-c(8). That statute, however, contains no similar restriction for criminal cases. Furthermore, the statute provides that a failure to use seat belts is admissible on the issue of civil damages. This makes sense because ordinarily a driver's failure to comply with seat belt requirements does not cause an accident[, but] it can make injuries more severe. This distinction between liability and damages does not exist in a criminal case.

Notes and Questions

1. Cabrera's conduct seems a good deal worse than the conduct of the defendant in *State ex rel. Thomas v. Duncan*, excerpted supra at page 812. After all, Cabrera entered the fateful turn at an excessive speed simply because he wanted to do so; Reagan ran the fateful red light because he was being chased by (he feared) someone who wished to do him harm. Yet Cabrera is deemed innocent of negligent homicide as a matter of law, while Reagan might be guilty of manslaughter. Why the difference?

2. Perhaps the answer is that Reagan was an adult, whereas Cabrera was only a teenager. Recall this statement in Judge Read's opinion: "For a 17-year-old to badly misgauge his ability to handle road conditions is not the kind of . . . behavior that the Legislature envisioned when it defined 'criminal negligence.' . . ." That sentence has a "boys will be boys" flavor, does it not? Should the fact that 17-year-old males cause a vastly disproportionate number of accidental deaths serve as a mitigating factor in cases like *Cabrera*? An aggravating factor? Neither?

3. The next sentence of Judge Read's opinion reads: "This crash resulted from noncriminal failure to perceive risk; it was not the result of criminal risk creation." What do you make of *that* sentence? One might suppose that driving 30 miles per hour above the posted speed limit on a dangerous curve amounts to "criminal risk creation." Evidently, that supposition is wrong—but why? Plainly, Cabrera was driving dangerously fast; equally plainly, that conduct caused the accident that, in turn, caused three deaths. Yet the opinions in *Cabrera* (*both* opinions; Judge Graffeo's dissent does the same thing) go to great lengths to establish that the defendant either did or did not engage in some negligent conduct *other than* driving at a wildly excessive speed. Why doesn't driving at a wildly excessive speed suffice to establish criminal liability?

4. Recall the cases on criminal drug possession in Chapter 6. Those cases do not permit defendants to argue that they should be excused because drug use is common among people their age. Yet drug possession and drug use harm those who possess and use drugs, while dangerous driving regularly kills innocent victims, as it did in *Cabrera*. Is *Cabrera* wrongly decided? Are the drug cases in Chapter 6 wrongly decided? Both? Neither?

5. In a number of states, legislatures—partly in response to judicial decisions like *Cabrera*, as well as jury acquittals under similar circumstances—have created a new and even less serious category of homicide, "vehicular homicide." Vehicular homicide means causing death, with criminal negligence, through the operation of a motor vehicle. In such states, causing another's death by criminally negligently shooting them, or knocking them off a bridge, or dropping a piano on their head (as in the Saturday morning cartoon shows) is negligent homicide; causing death by criminally negligently driving over them is a different crime carrying a much lower punishment.

Ask yourself, which kind of behavior causes more deaths: criminally negligent transporting of pianos, or criminally negligent driving? Then why should criminally negligent driving be punished less? Maybe the answer is that most of us do not really believe that we would ever be negligent in transporting a piano (or shooting a gun, or walking across a bridge), but we all realize that we all drive negligently much of the time. (Random exhortation: Please don't talk—or, heaven forbid, text—on a cell phone while driving!) In other words, maybe the real problem is that nobody wants to convict and severely punish a defendant who—in terms of both conduct and culpability, albeit not in terms of the resulting death—looks pretty much like us.

6. Criminal liability is sometimes justified as a means of changing destructive cultural norms. Expanded liability for sexual assault in the 1980s and 1990s was often defended on that ground; so were heightened punishments for drunk driving. Those exercises in "norm reform" appear to have worked. The number of reported sexual assaults is down sharply in the last decade; so is the number of deaths attributable to drunk driving. Is it possible that the same approach might work with teenage drivers who drive too fast?

11

Defenses

If the government proves, beyond a reasonable doubt, all the conduct elements plus the relevant *mens rea* of any given criminal charge, the defendant is convicted—unless he raises a valid defense. Below, we consider six such defenses: self-defense, duress, necessity, entrapment, public authority, and insanity. The first three are of a type: All either justify or excuse the defendant's crime because it was committed in response to a threat of great harm. In self-defense cases, the crime victim (i.e., the person actually killed) is the threat's source. Duress claims arise from threatened harm at the hands of a third party. Necessity or "choice of evils" claims usually involve threatened harm that flows from natural forces—recall Dudley and Stephens, stranded and dying in the South Atlantic (see page 5 supra). The last three defenses are of a different character. Entrapment and public authority claims seek to excuse the defendant's crime due to government misconduct. Last but not least, insanity claimants argue that mental illness renders them non-responsible for their criminal behavior. As you read each of the cases that follow, ask yourself: Does this defendant deserve to be free from punishment for his crime? On what ground?

A. SELF-DEFENSE

United States v. Biggs

United States Court of Appeals for the Ninth Circuit
441 F.3d 1069 (2006)

Opinion by BEEZER, Circuit Judge.

Donzell Wayne Biggs . . . pleaded guilty to assault with a dangerous weapon in violation of 18 U.S.C. §113(a)(3) and possession of contraband in prison in violation of 18 U.S.C. §1791(a)(2). He was sentenced to 84 months in prison. The guilty plea reserved the right to argue on appeal that the district court erred by precluding Biggs from presenting evidence and arguing to a jury that he was acting in self-defense. We conclude that the district court failed to properly define the elements of a claim of self-defense.

Biggs has been in federal custody serving a life sentence for first degree murder since 1977. In 2001, Biggs was incarcerated at Lompoc, United States Penitentiary and was being housed in its administrative segregation unit. In the segregation unit, inmates are left in their two-person cells twenty-three hours a day. During the twenty-fourth hour, four prisoners at a time are allowed access to a recreation cage. Prisoners are walked handcuffed to the cage and, once inside, are instructed to put their hands through the bars so that officers can remove the handcuffs.

On April 26, 2001, Biggs attacked a fellow inmate, Michael Smith, with an 8-inch homemade knife while they were inside the recreation cage. Biggs stabbed Smith in the arm and ear. Biggs alleges that he was acting in self-defense because he knew that Smith had been attempting to procure a knife from other inmates and had threatened him on the way to the cage. The district court concluded that Biggs had not made out a prima facie claim of self-defense because he could not show that there were no reasonable alternatives to the use of force.

In order to make a prima-facie case of self-defense, a defendant must make an offer of proof as to two elements: (1) a reasonable belief that the use of force was necessary to defend himself or another against the immediate use of unlawful force and (2) the use of no more force than was reasonably necessary in the circumstances. See United States v. Keiser, 57 F.3d 847, 851 (9th Cir. 1995). The district court erred by requiring Biggs to present evidence of a third element, that there were "no reasonable alternatives to the use of force," in order to make out a prima facie case of self-defense.

Evidence that a defendant had no reasonable opportunity to avoid the use of force is relevant only to a defense of justification, whether labeled duress, coercion or necessity,[2] and is not an element of a claim of self-defense. Justification defenses are significantly more constrained than the defense of self-defense and require showing both that the defendant had no reasonable opportunity to escape the harm and that he had not recklessly placed himself in a dangerous situation. [See] United States v. LaFleur, 971 F.2d 200, 206 (9th Cir. 1991) (duress is not a defense to murder, nor will it mitigate murder to manslaughter). Self-defense is distinct from these other justification defenses and is a viable defense for any defendant who presents

---

2. "Necessity is the defense one pleads when circumstances force one to perform a criminal act. Duress, or coercion, applies when human beings force one to act." United States v. Nolan, 700 F.2d 479, 484 n.1 (9th Cir. 1983).

evidence that he had a reasonable belief that the use of force was necessary to defend himself against the immediate use of unlawful force.

We reject the reasoning of the Seventh Circuit that "absence of lawful alternatives is an element of all lesser-evil defenses, of which self-defense is one." United States v. Haynes, 143 F.3d 1089, 1090-91 (7th Cir. 1998); see also United States v. Bello, 194 F.3d 18, 26-27 (1st Cir. 1999) (citing *Haynes*).

The district court's application of the incorrect legal standard for self-defense requires reversal because we cannot conclude that the error was harmless. . . .[3]

Notes on the Definition of Self-Defense

1. *Biggs* turns on the court's classification of self-defense: Is it a justification or an excuse? As the name suggests, successful justification defenses show that the defendant's conduct was proper under the circumstances; the defendant escapes punishment because he did nothing wrong. Excuse defenses presuppose that the defendant behaved wrongly, but grant the defendant his freedom on the ground that—under the circumstances—the wrong is not reason enough to impose criminal sanctions. As *Biggs* suggests, courts disagree about which label best fits self-defense.

2. Courts likewise disagree about the proper list of elements of a successful self-defense claim. Consider the following list:

(1) The accused must have had reasonable grounds to believe himself in apparent imminent or immediate danger of death or serious bodily harm from his assailant or potential assailant;
(2) The accused must have in fact believed himself in this danger;
(3) The accused claiming the right of self-defense must not have been the aggressor or provoked the conflict; and
(4) The force used must have not been unreasonable and excessive, that is, the force must not have been more force than the exigency demanded.

Dykes v. State, 571 A.2d 1251, 1254 (Md. 1990). Notice element (3); in *Biggs*, Judge Beezer stated that the threat the defendant faced must have been unlawful. Do the two formulations mean the same thing? Can a threat from an aggressor be lawful?

3. Claims that a threat from one prisoner justified violence by another are common. Judge Easterbrook's opinion in United States v. Haynes, 143 F.3d 1089 (7th Cir. 1998), takes a different approach to such cases than Judge Beezer took in *Biggs*. Here are the facts in *Haynes*:

---

3. We do not address whether Biggs' offer of proof is sufficient to allow a self-defense claim to be presented to a jury. . . .

Nelson Flores-Pedroso was playing dominoes after lunch in the cafeteria of the federal prison in Oxford, Wisconsin, when Charles Haynes emerged from the kitchen and poured scalding oil on his head. Severely burned over 18 percent of his body, Flores-Pedroso is disfigured for life. . . . Haynes pleaded guilty to assault, in violation of 18 U.S.C. §113(a)(6), and was sentenced to 33 months' imprisonment (consecutive to the 10-year term he was serving for a drug offense). The guilty plea reserved the right to argue on appeal that the district judge erred in foreclosing Haynes from arguing to the jury that the attack was justified as a measure of self-defense.

Self-defense? How can a sneak attack be self-defense? Haynes made an offer of proof that Flores-Pedroso was a bully who had a reputation for coercing smaller inmates (such as Haynes) to provide favors of all kinds—food, commissary items, and sex. About a month before the incident in the cafeteria, Flores-Pedroso began pressuring Haynes to use Haynes' position . . . in the kitchen to do favors for him. Haynes refused, and in response Flores-Pedroso threatened to make Haynes his "bitch." . . . For the next month staredowns and jostling occurred, while Flores-Pedroso kept up a stream of threats. One time Flores-Pedroso cornered Haynes in a bathroom, and Haynes thought that rape was imminent, but another inmate entered and Flores-Pedroso left. A day before Haynes poured the oil, Flores-Pedroso picked up Haynes and slammed him to the ground within sight of a guard, who did nothing. On the day of the oil incident, Flores-Pedroso told Haynes that as soon as food service was closed for the afternoon he would "finish what he started." Haynes contends that he believed that he would be attacked as soon as he left the cafeteria, and that he struck first in order to protect himself.

143 F.3d at 1089-90. The government argued that Haynes should have reported the threats to the guards rather than protecting himself. As a practical matter, Haynes argued, that option was unavailable to him:

He could not go to "the police"—a term used to describe the guards. If the guards elected to take him out of population, he would be forced to stay in administrative segregation which meant twenty-four hour per day lock-up. If his protective custody status resulted in a transfer, all the inmates of the receiving institution would know that he was in protective custody, for being victimized by another inmate and by being a "snitch," which would result in further victimization and perhaps invite an assault by not just one inmate, but several. If Haynes went to the guards and they did not believe him and left him in population, things would only get worse. He would certainly be attacked, not only by Flores-Pedroso, but by others who labeled him a "snitch."

Id. at 1090. Nevertheless, Judge Easterbrook dismissed Haynes' claim:

Under the law of the jungle a good offense may be the best defense. But although prisons are nasty places, they are not jungles—and it is the law of the United States rather than Hobbes' state of nature that regulates inmates' conduct. Haynes concedes that he never reported Flores-Pedroso to the guards or sought protection—protection a prison is constitutionally obliged to provide. . . .

. . . The evidence and line of defense Haynes wanted to pursue, as the district court saw things, was just a request for jury nullification—a plea to jurors to let the Davids of federal prisons smite the Goliaths, to give the predators a taste of their own medicine, without legal consequences. The judge ruled that an inmate must use available, lawful options to avoid violence, even if they find those options unpalatable. Haynes asks us to hold that the existence of lawful alternatives is irrelevant to a claim of self-defense.

All doubts about the role of lawful alternatives to one side, it is hard to see how Haynes' offer of proof conforms to the normal understanding of self-defense: a use of force necessary to defend against an imminent use of unlawful force. Haynes was not faced with an imminent use of force by Flores-Pedroso. There was a threat of action later that afternoon, but Flores-Pedroso had made unfulfilled threats before, and anyway "later" and "imminent" are opposites. A judge may, and generally should, block the introduction of evidence supporting a proposed defense unless all of its elements can be established. United States v. Bailey, 444 U.S. 394, 415-17 (1980). But we need not dwell on timing, because we agree with the district judge's reason: absence of lawful alternatives is an element of all lesser-evil defenses, of which self-defense is one.

Bailey establishes this point. Four men who escaped from a federal prison argued that their acts were justified by duress. They offered to establish that they feared injury if they remained—not simply because there were ruffians among the inmates, but because they had actually been beaten up; and, according to the four escapees, the guards were among the aggressors. 444 U.S. at 398-99. The Court held that "whatever defenses of duress or necessity are available . . . [,] one principle remains constant: if there was a reasonable, legal alternative to violating the law, a chance both to refuse to do the criminal act and also to avoid the threatened harm, the defense will fail." Id. at 410. The prisoners in *Bailey* had options other than escaping and remaining at large; even the option of escape followed by immediate surrender to the FBI was enough to foreclose a duress defense. Haynes asks us not to extend the approach of *Bailey* to claims of self-defense. . . . [But] *Bailey* is not about duress so much as it is about the set of lesser-evil defenses that includes duress, necessity, and self-defense. Each rests on the belief that a person facing harm is justified in performing an act, otherwise illegal, less injurious than the impending loss. . . . Differences in nomenclature have more to do with the source of the threat than with the nature of the justification. For example, "duress" is the name used when A credibly threatens to hit B unless B hits C (or destroys C's property); B responds that the damage done to C is justified because it is less than the injury B himself would have received had he not complied. When A is inanimate (a flood, for example), the defense takes the name "necessity." When A threatens B, and B hits A, the defense receives the name "self-defense." . . . But in all of these cases, the defense fails if the use of force was unjustified. This is the idea behind the "imminence" requirement (if the threat is not imminent, a retreat or similar step avoids injury) as well as the requirement that the object of the threat prefer a lawful response to an unlawful one.

Prisons collect violent persons who have little respect for the law, which makes them hard to control without the use of devices such as segregation that are unpleasant in their own right. If prisoners could decide for themselves when to seek protection from the guards and when to settle matters by violence, prisons would be impossible to regulate. The guards might as well throw the inmates together, withdraw to the perimeter, and let them kill one another. . . . Perhaps Haynes was hoping that a jury would have this view of the right way to manage prisons. But it is not the view reflected in the United States Code or the United States Constitution. A prisoner who requests protection from the guards without success (or who lacks time to do so) may defend himself with force proportioned to the threat. But Haynes, who listened to Flores-Pedroso's menaces for a month without seeking help, had no conceivable justification for a preemptive strike. The district judge correctly barred Haynes from making his proposed defense.

143 F.3d at 1090-91. Note that Haynes could have raised his self-defense claim had he reported the victim's threats to the guards "without success" — meaning, presumably, that Haynes could have defended himself *after* Flores-Pedroso attacked him. Why not before? If Haynes could show that the guards did not protect inmates from one another, shouldn't he be able to raise his defense? Hasn't Haynes already made that showing?

4. Easterbrook's view that self-defense, duress, and necessity constitute a single doctrine of justification is widely accepted in federal courts (though not in state courts). For two recent decisions taking that tack, see United States v. Butler, 485 F.3d 569 (10th Cir. 2007); United States v. Leahy, 473 F.3d 401 (1st Cir. 2007). The defendants in *Butler* and *Leahy* were charged under the federal felon-in-possession statute, which bars possession of firearms by those with felony convictions. Both defendants claimed they needed their weapons for self-defense. Such claims are fairly common, though rarely successful. In an opinion rejecting one such claim, Judge Posner explained why:

> Perez's felony, conviction of which deprived him of the right to possess a gun, was for drug offenses, and he was suspected of having resumed the drug trade after his release from prison. The DEA decided to conduct a surveillance of Perez. Three agents, in two unmarked cars, watched his apartment from various vantage points in the street and alley next to the apartment building. Perez saw them from the window of his apartment one afternoon and he contends . . . that he thought they were crooks planning to rob him. As it happened, he wanted to go to the bank that afternoon and deposit $600 in cash and checks. Fearful of being robbed when he left the apartment and got into his car, Perez took his girlfriend's pistol from the bedroom dresser of the apartment (which they shared) and slipped it into his waistband before leaving. The agents had just learned that there was an outstanding warrant for Perez's arrest, so when they saw him get into his Cadillac and start to drive off they arrested him. . . .
>
> Even crediting fully Perez's assertion that he genuinely believed the men in the cars would try to rob him when he left the apartment, he has not come close to satisfying the elements of the defense of necessity. If ex-felons who feel endangered can carry guns, felon-in-possession laws will be dead letters. Upon release from prison most felons return to their accustomed haunts. . . . Many of them will not go straight, but will return to dangerous activities such

as the drug trade. Every drug dealer has a well-grounded fear of being robbed or assaulted, so that if Perez's defense were accepted felon-in-possession laws would as a practical matter not apply to drug dealers.

The defense of necessity will rarely lie in a felon-in-possession case. . . . Rarely does not mean never; for a pertinent illustration, see United States v. Panter, 688 F.2d 268, 271-72 (5th Cir. 1982). But only in the most extraordinary circumstances, illustrated by United States v. Gomez, 92 F.3d 770 (9th Cir. 1996), where the defendant had sought protection from the authorities without success, will the defense entitle the ex-felon to arm himself in advance of the crisis merely because he fears, however sincerely and reasonably, that he is in serious danger of deadly harm. More often than not the basis of his fear will be his own involvement in illegal activities; and when the danger that gives rise to the fear results from engaging in such activities—from "looking for trouble"—the defense is barred.

United States v. Perez, 86 F.3d 735, 736-37 (7th Cir. 1996).

5. The two cases Judge Posner cited have extreme facts: If they are representative of the cases in which defendants have valid justification defenses, such cases will be very rare indeed. In *Panter*, the defendant shot an assailant who had already stabbed him, though the government claimed he possessed the weapon before that threat materialized. *Gomez*'s facts were worse—or better, from the defendant's point of view. Gomez volunteered to serve as a government informant in an attempted murder-for-hire case. After the government disclosed his identity (with no warning), the man on whom Gomez informed put a contract on his life. Gomez asked to be placed in protective custody but the government refused, whereupon he obtained a shotgun. Two days later he was arrested for violating his parole; prosecutors then added the felon-in-possession charge (Gomez had a state felony conviction). As Judge Kozinski put it: "This case gives fresh meaning to the phrase, 'I'm from the government and I'm here to help you.'" 92 F.3d at 772.

Gomez claimed he acted out of necessity and in self-defense; the government contended that those defenses did not apply to the felon-in-possession statute, and the district court appears to have bought the government's argument. The Ninth Circuit reversed. In a footnote, Judge Kozinski opined that the felon-in-possession statute "might not pass constitutional muster were it not subject to a justification defense," on the ground that "[t]he Second Amendment embodies the right to defend oneself and one's home against physical attack." Id. at 774 n.7.

6. How much should the victim's culpability matter in self-defense cases? Consider the case of Cory Maye:

On the evening of December 26, 2001, Officer Ron Jones of the Prentiss Police Department secured two search warrants for a duplex located on Mary Street in Prentiss, Mississippi. Officer Ron Jones presented two affidavits and search warrants to Municipal Judge Donald Kruger. Officer Ron Jones signed the affidavits in the presence of Judge Kruger. The affidavits indicated that Officer Ron Jones had received information from a confidential informant who had within the prior twenty-four hours seen a large amount of marijuana stored in the duplex. Officer Ron Jones also attested that he had information from various sources that drugs were being sold out of the duplex. Officer Ron Jones attested that he had conducted surveillance of the duplex and had seen large amounts of traffic there at unusual hours. Judge Kruger discussed the search warrant with Officer Ron Jones, and later testified, "Yes, I talked with him about it. He said that he was reliable, a person, that the informant was, and that one or two arrests had been made because of this reliable, this so-called reliable informant." Based on Officer Ron Jones's affidavit, Judge Kruger issued two search warrants for the Mary Street duplex, one for the left side of the duplex identifying Jamie Smith and/or persons unknown as the occupants and one for the right side of the duplex, which listed persons unknown as the occupants.

After securing the search warrants, Officer Ron Jones selected a team . . . to assist him in executing the search warrants. The officers were separated into two teams: one team to search the left side of the duplex and the other team to search the right side of the duplex. Agent Darrell Graves led Officers Mike Brown, Earl Bullock, Allen Allday, and Terrence Cooley in executing the search warrant on Smith's apartment, which was the left side of the duplex. Officer Ron Jones led Officers Stephen Jones, Darrell Cooley, and Phillip Allday in executing the search warrant on Maye's apartment, which was the right side of the duplex.

The officers arrived at the Mary Street duplex in marked police cars. The officers parked the cars directly in front of the duplex. Officer Ron Jones's team was the first to arrive at Maye's side of the duplex. Officers Ron Jones, Stephen Jones, and Darrell Cooley took the front door with Officer Phillip Allday guarding the back door.

Maye testified that he was asleep on the "chair right beside the front door." The officers testified that they went to the front door and loudly announced, "police, search warrant," three times. Officer Darrell Cooley testified that he arrived at the door first. The front porch light was on. Officer Darrell Cooley testified that he loudly announced, "police," then someone behind him announced, "search warrant." He then kicked at the door. Officer Darrell Cooley testified that he yelled "police" a second time, then someone behind him announced "search warrant" loudly. Again, Officer Darrell Cooley kicked at the door.

Officer Stephen Jones reported that at this point he could see a light in the house through the cracked blinds. He testified that "[t]he blinds opened, it appeared that somebody opened the blinds and looked out." When the blinds were opened, he noticed the light on inside of Maye's apartment. Officer Darrell Cooley testified that this was the first time that he noticed a light on inside the apartment. Officer Darrell Cooley testified that he looked "back in toward the window on the door, and [he] could see a light back to the left side of the door."

After noticing the light, Officer Darrell Cooley yelled, "police," a third time with someone behind him announcing "search warrant." When the door would not open, the officers decided to go to the back of the duplex to gain entry.

Officers Phillip Allday and Terrence Cooley were at the back of the duplex. Officer Terrence Cooley testified that he could "clearly hear" his fellow officers at the front of the house announce police, search warrant three times while he was at the back steps.

Officer Graves was in charge of executing the search warrant on Smith's apartment (left side). Officer Graves confirmed that the officers on Maye's side of the duplex had announced, "police, search warrant," as Officer Graves approached Smith's apartment. The occupants of Smith's apartment (left side) responded to the announcements and opened their door to allow the officers to execute the search warrant.

Unable to gain entry through Maye's front door, Officers Ron Jones and Stephen Jones went to the back door of Maye's apartment, leaving Officer Terrence Cooley to guard the front door. Officer Stephen Jones testified that upon reaching the back door, Officer Ron Jones checked to see if the back door would open, and then announced, "search warrant, police, search warrant." When the door would not open, Officers Ron Jones and Stephen Jones proceeded to the front of the house. Officers at the back of the duplex kicked the back door open. A couple of minutes passed between the officers' first announcement at the front door and the back door being kicked in. After the back door was opened, Officer Ron Jones was called to the back of the house. He proceeded to enter the house, yelling "police." He was met by shots fired from Maye's gun. Officer Ron Jones immediately left Maye's apartment stating that he had been shot. He was taken by Officer Stephen Jones to the hospital, where Officer Ron Jones died shortly after arrival. Officer Cooley apprehended Maye. A search of Maye's apartment conducted later by officers yielded small amounts of marijuana.

Maye, who admittedly was asleep on a chair right by the front door, testified that he was wakened by the banging on the front door. Maye denied hearing the police announce "police, search warrant" or looking out the window. Maye testified that he awoke frightened and ran to the bedroom in the back of the house. Maye testified that he grabbed his gun, loaded it, and laid it on the floor by the foot of his bed. His fourteen-month-old daughter was asleep in the middle of the bed. Maye testified that he heard kicks to the back door. He testified that he fired when he heard someone entering the house. Maye testified that after he fired the shots, he heard the other officers yell, "police, police, you just shot a[n] officer." Maye testified that he immediately put his weapon down and slid it away.

49 So. 3d 1124 (Miss. S. Ct. 2010). Maye was charged with and convicted of capital murder, and was sentenced to death; the trial judge set aside the death sentence and substituted a sentence of life imprisonment without the possibility of parole.

The *Maye* case attracted a good deal of attention in the blogosphere. Here is what one e-reporter had to say about the case:

To convict Maye, the jury had to believe, beyond a reasonable doubt, that a man with no criminal record, a man who had just moved out of his parents' home to make a life with his daughter and girlfriend, a man who had only a minuscule amount of marijuana in his apartment, looked out the window to see a team of police officers was about to enter; decided to take them on, even though he had done nothing wrong; waited for them to forcibly enter his home; fired three shots, killing *just one* of them; and then surrendered, leaving four bullets still in his gun. . . .

There are more troubling details in the case against Maye. To begin with, there is no record of Ron Jones' investigation of Jamie Smith and the Mary Street duplex. Nobody knows the identity of the confidential informant who tipped Jones off. There are no written records of the informant's past tips or his reliability, or of any surveillance or corroborating investigation Jones did to supplement the informant's tip. Judge Kruger testified at the trial that he merely took Jones at his word and didn't press him for details about the informant's record or Jones' investigation. But if the informant lied about seeing marijuana in the Maye-Longino half of the duplex, or if Jones misinterpreted what the informant said, it raises the possibility that the raid on Cory Maye's home was illegal, in which case he had every right to defend himself under Mississippi law. The absence of Maye's name from the warrants and his lack of a criminal record reinforce the possibility. When District Attorney McDonald [was asked] what happened to Jones' records, he replie[d], "Any record of Jones' investigation died with Jones."

Radley Balko, "The Case of Cory Maye," Reason, October 2006, available online at http://reason.com/archives/2006/10/01/the-case-of-cory-maye.

In December 2010, the Mississippi Supreme Court awarded Maye a new trial on the ground that the trial court did not properly instruct the jury on either self-defense or the related, but distinct, theory of "defense of others" (in this case, Maye's infant daughter).* According to the Mississippi Supreme Court, the trial court should have given the jury the following proper instruction, proffered by Maye's trial lawyer:

The Court instructs the jury that you are not to judge the actions of Cory J. Maye in the cool, calm light of after-developed facts, but instead you are to judge his actions in the light of the circumstances confronting Cory J. Maye at the time, as you believe from the evidence that those circumstances reasonably appeared to him on that occasion; and if you believe that under those circumstances it reasonably appeared to Cory J. Maye, at the instant that he took up a weapon, that Cory J. Maye then and there had reasonable ground to apprehend a design on the part of Ron Jones to kill Cory J. Maye or his daughter or to do Cory J. Maye and his daughter some great personal injury, and there

---

* The variant of self-defense known as "defense of others" (or "defense of another") historically was limited to the use of force to defend members of one's own family. Modern law, now usually codified in statutes, has greatly expanded the doctrine to include the use of force (including deadly force, if necessary) to defend anyone whom the actor reasonably believes to be threatened with death or serious bodily injury. Here is the relevant Mississippi statute:

> (1) The killing of a human being by the act, procurement or omission of another shall be justifiable in the following cases:
>   (f) When committed in the lawful defense of one's own person or any other human being, where there shall be reasonable ground to apprehend a design to commit a felony or to do some great personal injury, and there shall be imminent danger of such design being accomplished[.]

See Miss. Code §97-3-15.

> reasonably appeared to Cory J. Maye to be imminent danger of such designs
> being accomplished; then Cory J. Maye was justified in anticipating an attack
> and using reasonable means to defend such attack; then you must find Cory J.
> Maye not guilty of the murder of Ron Jones.

Maye v. State, 49 So. 3d at 1131. After the decision, Cory Maye pleaded guilty
to manslaughter and received a new prison sentence of ten years; shortly
thereafter, he was released from prison because he had already served longer
than ten years. See Radney Balko, "Cory Maye to Be Released from Prison,"
available online at www.huffingtonpost.com/2011/07/01/cory-maye-to-be-
released-_n_888454.html.

Had Officer Ron Jones and his colleagues actually been illegal intruders,
Maye would likely have had a valid claim of either self-defense or defense
of another. Moreover, even if Maye made a mistake—but a reasonable
one—about who the men really were, he would still have been entitled,
under Mississippi law, to use "reasonable means" to defend against what
he reasonably perceived as an attack. Assume for the sake of argument the
truth of the factual claim that Maye did not hear Jones identify himself. Was
Maye's response justified? Should Maye be excused?

People v. Goetz

Court of Appeals of New York
68 N.Y.2d 96; 497 N.E.2d 41 (1986)

Chief Judge WACHTLER delivered the opinion of the Court.

A Grand Jury has indicted defendant on attempted murder, assault,
and other charges for having shot and wounded four youths on a New York
City subway train after one or two of the youths approached him and asked
for $5. The lower courts, concluding that the prosecutor's charge to the
grand jury on the defense of justification was erroneous, have dismissed the
attempted murder, assault and weapons possession charges. We now reverse
and reinstate all counts of the indictment.

I

The precise circumstances of the incident giving rise to the charges against
defendant are disputed, and ultimately it will be for a trial jury to determine
what occurred. We feel it necessary, however, to provide some factual background to properly frame the legal issues before us. Accordingly, we have
summarized the facts as they appear from the evidence before the grand
jury. . . .

On Saturday afternoon, December 22, 1984, Troy Canty, Darryl Cabey,
James Ramseur, and Barry Allen boarded an IRT express subway train in
The Bronx and headed south toward lower Manhattan. The four youths
rode together in the rear portion of the seventh car of the train. Two of the

four, Ramseur and Cabey, had screwdrivers inside their coats, which they said were to be used to break into the coin boxes of video machines.

Defendant Bernhard Goetz boarded this subway train at 14th Street in Manhattan and sat down on a bench towards the rear section of the same car occupied by the four youths. Goetz was carrying an unlicensed .38 caliber pistol loaded with five rounds of ammunition in a waistband holster. The train left the 14th Street station and headed towards Chambers Street.

It appears from the evidence before the [g]rand jury that Canty approached Goetz, possibly with Allen beside him, and stated "give me five dollars." Neither Canty nor any of the other youths displayed a weapon. Goetz responded by standing up, pulling out his handgun and firing four shots in rapid succession. The first shot hit Canty in the chest; the second struck Allen in the back; the third went through Ramseur's arm and into his left side; the fourth was fired at Cabey, who apparently was then standing in the corner of the car, but missed, deflecting instead off of a wall of the conductor's cab. After Goetz briefly surveyed the scene around him, he fired another shot at Cabey, who then was sitting on the end bench of the car. The bullet entered the rear of Cabey's side and severed his spinal cord.

All but two of the other passengers fled the car when, or immediately after, the shots were fired. The conductor, who had been in the next car, heard the shots and instructed the motorman to radio for emergency assistance. The conductor then went into the car where the shooting occurred and saw Goetz sitting on a bench, the injured youths lying on the floor or slumped against a seat, and two women who had apparently taken cover, also lying on the floor. Goetz told the conductor that the four youths had tried to rob him.

While the conductor was aiding the youths, Goetz headed towards the front of the car. The train had stopped just before the Chambers Street station and Goetz went between two of the cars, jumped onto the tracks and fled. Police and ambulance crews arrived at the scene shortly thereafter. Ramseur and Canty, initially listed in critical condition, have fully recovered. Cabey remains paralyzed, and has suffered some degree of brain damage.

On December 31, 1984, Goetz surrendered to police in Concord, New Hampshire, identifying himself as the gunman being sought for the subway shootings in New York nine days earlier. Later that day, after receiving *Miranda* warnings, he made two lengthy statements, both of which were tape recorded with his permission. In the statements, which are substantially similar, Goetz admitted that he had been illegally carrying a handgun in New York City for three years. He stated that he had first purchased a gun in 1981 after he had been injured in a mugging. Goetz also revealed that twice between 1981 and 1984 he had successfully warded off assailants simply by displaying the pistol.

According to Goetz's statement, the first contact he had with the four youths came when Canty, sitting or lying on the bench across from him, asked "how are you," to which he replied "fine." Shortly thereafter, Canty, followed by one of the other youths, walked over to the defendant and stood to his left, while the other two youths remained to his right, in the corner of the subway car. Canty then said "give me five dollars." Goetz stated that he knew from the smile on Canty's face that they wanted to "play with me." Although he was certain that none of the youths had a gun, he had a fear, based on prior experiences, of being "maimed."

Goetz then established "a pattern of fire," deciding specifically to fire from left to right. His stated intention at that point was to "murder [the four youths], to hurt them, to make them suffer as much as possible." When Canty again requested money, Goetz stood up, drew his weapon, and began firing, aiming for the center of the body of each of the four. Goetz recalled that the first two he shot "tried to run through the crowd [but] they had nowhere to run." Goetz then turned to his right to "go after the other two." One of these two "tried to run through the wall of the train, but . . . he had nowhere to go." The other youth (Cabey) "tried pretending that he wasn't with [the others]" by standing still, holding on to one of the subway hand straps, and not looking at Goetz. Goetz nonetheless fired his fourth shot at him. He then ran back to the first two youths to make sure they had been "taken care of." Seeing that they had both been shot, he spun back to check on the latter two. Goetz noticed that the youth who had been standing still was now sitting on a bench and seemed unhurt. As Goetz told the police, "I said '[you] seem to be all right, here's another,'" and he then fired the shot which severed Cabey's spinal cord. Goetz added that "if I was a little more under self-control . . . I would have put the barrel against his forehead and fired." He also admitted that "if I had had more [bullets], I would have shot them again, and again, and again."

II

. . . The matter was presented to a grand jury in January 1985, with the prosecutor seeking an indictment for attempted murder, assault, reckless endangerment, and criminal possession of a weapon. Neither the defendant nor any of the wounded youths testified before his grand jury. On January 25, 1985, the grand jury indicted defendant on one count of criminal possession of a weapon in the third degree (Penal Law §265.02), for possessing the gun used in the subway shootings, and two counts of criminal possession of a weapon in the fourth degree (Penal Law §265.01), for possessing two other guns in his apartment building. It dismissed . . . the attempted murder and other charges stemming from the shootings themselves.

. . . [T]he People . . . moved for an order authorizing them to resubmit the dismissed charges to a second grand jury. [The motion was granted.]

. . . Two of the four youths, Canty and Ramseur, testified. Among the other witnesses were four passengers from the seventh car of the subway who had seen some portions of the incident. Goetz again chose not to testify, though the tapes of his two statements were played for the grand jurors. . . .

On March 27, 1985, the second grand jury filed a 10-count indictment, containing four charges of attempted murder, Penal Law §§110.00, 125.25(1), four charges of assault in the first degree, Penal Law §120.10(1), one charge of reckless endangerment in the first degree, Penal Law §120.25, and one charge of criminal possession of a weapon in the second degree, Penal Law §265.03 (possession of loaded firearm with intent to use it unlawfully against another). . . .

. . . Goetz moved to dismiss the charges contained in the second indictment alleging, among other things, that the evidence before the second grand jury was not legally sufficient to establish the offenses charged, and that the prosecutor's instructions to that grand jury on the defense of justification were erroneous and prejudicial to the defendant so as to render its proceedings defective.

. . . [W]hile the motion to dismiss was pending before Criminal Term, a column appeared in the New York Daily News containing an interview which the columnist had conducted with Darryl Cabey the previous day in Cabey's hospital room. The columnist claimed that Cabey had told him in this interview that the other three youths had all approached Goetz with the intention of robbing him. The day after the column was published, a New York City police officer informed the prosecutor that he had been one of the first police officers to enter the subway car after the shootings, and that Canty had said to him "we were going to rob [Goetz]." . . . [N]one of the police reports filed on the incident contained any such information. Goetz then orally expanded his motion to dismiss, asserting that resubmission of the charges voted by the second grand jury was required . . . because it appeared, from this new information, that Ramseur and Canty had committed perjury.

In an order dated January 21, 1986, Criminal Term granted Goetz's motion to the extent that it dismissed all counts of the second indictment, other than the reckless endangerment charge, with leave to resubmit these charges to a third grand jury. The court, after inspection of the grand jury minutes, first rejected Goetz's contention that there was not legally sufficient evidence to support the charges. It held, however, that the prosecutor, in a supplemental charge elaborating upon the justification defense, had erroneously introduced an objective element into this defense by instructing the grand jurors to consider whether Goetz's conduct was that of a "reasonable man in [Goetz's] situation." The court . . . concluded that the statutory test for whether the use of deadly force is justified to protect a person should be wholly subjective, focusing entirely on the defendant's state of mind when he used such force. It concluded that dismissal was required for this error because the justification issue was at the heart of the case. . . .

On appeal by the People, a divided Appellate Division affirmed Criminal Term's dismissal of the charges. The plurality opinion by Justice Kassal . . . agreed with Criminal Term's reasoning on the justification issue, stating that the grand jurors should have been instructed to consider only the defendant's subjective beliefs as to the need to use deadly force. Justice Kupferman concurred in the result reached by the plurality on the ground that the prosecutor's charge did not adequately apprise the grand jurors of the need to consider Goetz's own background. . . .

Justice Asch, in a dissenting opinion in which Justice Wallach concurred, disagreed. . . . On the justification question, he opined that the statute requires consideration of both the defendant's subjective beliefs and whether a reasonable person in defendant's situation would have had such beliefs. Accordingly, he found no error in the prosecutor's introduction of an objective element into the justification defense. . . .

. . . We agree with the dissenters that neither the prosecutor's charge to the grand jury on justification nor the information which came to light while the motion to dismiss was pending required dismissal of any of the charges in the second indictment.

III

Penal Law article 35 recognizes the defense of justification, which "permits the use of force under certain circumstances." See People v. McManus, 67 N.Y.2d 541, 545. One such set of circumstances pertains to the use of force in defense of a person, encompassing both self-defense and defense of a third person. Penal Law §35.15(1) sets forth the general principles governing all such uses of force:

> "[a] person may . . . use physical force upon another person when and to the extent he *reasonably believes* such to be necessary to defend himself or a third person from what he *reasonably believes* to be the use or imminent use of unlawful physical force by such other person" (emphasis added).[3]

Section 35.15(2) sets forth further limitations on these general principles with respect to the use of "deadly physical force":

> "A person may not use deadly physical force upon another person under circumstances specified in subdivision one unless (a) He *reasonably believes* that such other person is using or about to use deadly physical force . . .[4] or

---

3. Subdivision (1) contains certain exceptions to this general authorization to use force, such as where the actor himself was the initial aggressor.

4. Section 35.15(2)(a) further provides, however, that even under these circumstances a person ordinarily must retreat "if he knows that he can with complete safety as to himself and others avoid the necessity of [using deadly physical force] by retreating."

(b) He *reasonably believes* that such other person is committing or attempting to commit a kidnapping, forcible rape, forcible sodomy or robbery" (emphasis added).

Thus, consistent with most justification provisions, Penal Law §35.15 permits the use of deadly physical force only where requirements as to triggering conditions and the necessity of a particular response are met. See Robinson, Criminal Law Defenses §121(a), at 2. As to the triggering conditions, the statute requires that the actor "reasonably believes" that another person either is using or about to use deadly physical force or is committing or attempting to commit one of certain enumerated felonies, including robbery. As to the need for the use of deadly physical force as a response, the statute requires that the actor "reasonably believes" that such force is necessary to avert the perceived threat.[5]

Because the evidence before the second grand jury included statements by Goetz that he acted to protect himself from being maimed or to avert a robbery, the prosecutor correctly chose to charge the justification defense in section 35.15 to the grand jury. The prosecutor properly instructed the grand jurors to consider whether the use of deadly physical force was justified to prevent either serious physical injury or a robbery, and, in doing so, to separately analyze the defense with respect to each of the charges. He elaborated upon the prerequisites for the use of deadly physical force essentially by reading or paraphrasing the language in Penal Law §35.15. The defense does not contend that he committed any error in this portion of the charge.

When the prosecutor had completed his charge, one of the grand jurors asked for clarification of the term "reasonably believes." The prosecutor responded by instructing the grand jurors that they were to consider the circumstances of the incident and determine "whether the defendant's conduct was that of a reasonable man in the defendant's situation." It is this response by the prosecutor—and specifically his use of "a reasonable man"—which is the basis for the dismissal of the charges by the lower courts. As expressed repeatedly in the Appellate Division's plurality opinion, because section 35.15 uses the term "*he* reasonably believes," the appropriate test, according to that court, is whether a defendant's beliefs and reactions were "reasonable *to him*." . . . Such an interpretation defies the ordinary meaning and significance of the term "reasonably" . . . and misconstrues the clear intent of the Legislature, in enacting section 35.15, to retain an objective element as part of any provision authorizing the use of deadly physical force. . . .

---

5. While the portion of section 35.15(2)(b) pertaining to the use of deadly physical force to avert a felony such as robbery does not contain a separate "retreat" requirement, it is clear from reading subdivisions (1) and (2) of section 35.15 together, as the statute requires, that the general "necessity" requirement in subdivision (1) applies to all uses of force under section 35.15, including the use of deadly physical force under subdivision (2)(b).

In 1961 the Legislature established a Commission to undertake a complete revision of the Penal Law and the Criminal Code. The impetus for the decision to update the Penal Law came in part from the drafting of the Model Penal Code by the American Law Institute, as well as from the fact that the existing law was poorly organized and in many aspects antiquated. See, e.g., Criminal Law Revision Through a Legislative Commission: The New York Experience, 18 Buff. L. Rev. 213; Note, Proposed Penal Law of New York, 64 Colum. L. Rev. 1469. Following the submission by the Commission of several reports and proposals, the Legislature approved the present Penal Law in 1965, and it became effective on September 1, 1967. The drafting of the general provisions of the new Penal Law, including the article on justification, was particularly influenced by the Model Penal Code. See Wechsler, Codification of Criminal Law in the United States: The Model Penal Code, 68 Colum. L. Rev. 1425, 1428. While using the Model Penal Code provisions on justification as general guidelines, however, the drafters of the new Penal Law did not simply adopt them verbatim.

The provisions of the Model Penal Code with respect to the use of deadly force in self-defense reflect the position of its drafters that any culpability which arises from a mistaken belief in the need to use such force should be no greater than the culpability such a mistake would give rise to if it were made with respect to an element of a crime. Accordingly, under Model Penal Code §3.04(2)(b), a defendant charged with murder (or attempted murder) need only show that he "[believed] that [the use of deadly force] was necessary to protect himself against death, serious bodily injury, kidnapping or [forcible] sexual intercourse" to prevail on a self-defense claim. If the defendant's belief was wrong, and was recklessly or negligently formed, . . . he may be convicted of the type of homicide charge requiring only a reckless or negligent, as the case may be, criminal intent. See Model Penal Code §3.09(2). . . .

New York did not follow the Model Penal Code's equation of a mistake as to the need to use deadly force with a mistake negating an element of a crime, choosing instead to use a single statutory section which would provide either a complete defense or no defense at all to a defendant charged with any crime involving the use of deadly force. The drafters of the new Penal Law adopted in large part the structure and content of Model Penal Code §3.04, but, crucially, inserted the word "reasonably" before "believes."

The plurality below agreed with defendant's argument that the change in the statutory language from "reasonable ground," used prior to 1965, to "he reasonably believes" in Penal Law §35.15 evinced a legislative intent to conform to the subjective standard contained in Model Penal Code §3.04. This argument, however, ignores the plain significance of the insertion of "reasonably." . . . Interpreting the statute to require only that the defendant's belief was "reasonable to *him*," as done by the plurality below, would hardly be different from requiring only a genuine belief; in either case, the defendant's own perceptions could completely exonerate him from any criminal liability.

We cannot lightly impute to the Legislature an intent to fundamentally alter the principles of justification to allow the perpetrator of a serious crime to go free simply because that person believed his actions were reasonable and necessary to prevent some perceived harm. To completely exonerate such an individual, no matter how aberrational or bizarre his thought patterns, would allow citizens to set their own standards for the permissible use of force. It would also allow a legally competent defendant suffering from delusions to kill or perform acts of violence with impunity, contrary to fundamental principles of justice and criminal law.

We can only conclude that the Legislature retained a reasonableness requirement to avoid giving a license for such actions. The plurality's interpretation, as the dissenters below recognized, excises the impact of the word "reasonably." . . .

The change from "reasonable ground" to "reasonably believes" is better explained by the fact that the drafters of section 35.15 were proposing a single section which, for the first time, would govern both the use of ordinary force and deadly force in self-defense or defense of another. Under the 1909 Penal Law and its predecessors, the use of ordinary force was governed by separate sections which, at least by their literal terms, required that the defendant was *in fact* responding to an unlawful assault, and not just that he had a reasonable ground for believing that such an assault was occurring. See People v. Young, 11 N.Y.2d 274. . . . [T]he drafters of section 35.15 eliminated this sharp dichotomy between the use of ordinary force and deadly force in defense of a person. . . . [T]he integrated section reflects the wording of Model Penal Code §3.04, with the addition of "reasonably" to incorporate the long-standing requirement of "reasonable ground" for the use of deadly force and apply it to the use of ordinary force as well. See Note, 64 Colum. L. Rev. at 1500. . . .

In People v. Collice, 41 N.Y.2d 906, we rejected the position that section 35.15 contains a wholly subjective standard. The defendant in *Collice* asserted, on appeal, that the trial court had erred in refusing to charge the justification defense. We upheld the trial court's action because we concluded that, even if the defendant had actually believed that he was threatened with the imminent use of deadly physical force, the evidence clearly indicated that "his reactions were not those of a reasonable man acting in self-defense." Id., at 907. . . .

Goetz . . . argues that the introduction of an objective element [in self-defense doctrine] will preclude a jury from considering factors such as the prior experiences of a given actor. . . . This argument, however, falsely presupposes that an objective standard means that the background and other relevant characteristics of a particular actor must be ignored. To the contrary, we have frequently noted that a determination of reasonableness must be based on the "circumstances" facing a defendant or his "situation." See, e.g., People v. Ligouri, 284 N.Y. 309, 316; People v. Lumsden, 201 N.Y. 264, 268. Such terms encompass more than the physical movements of the potential assailant. As just discussed, these terms include any relevant knowledge the defendant had about that person. They also necessarily bring in the physical attributes of all persons involved, including the defendant. Furthermore, the defendant's circumstances encompass any prior experiences he had which could provide a reasonable basis for a belief that another person's intentions were to injure or rob him or that the use of deadly force was necessary under the circumstances.

Accordingly, a jury should be instructed to consider this type of evidence in weighing the defendant's actions. The jury must first determine whether the defendant had the requisite beliefs under section 35.15, that is, whether he believed deadly force was necessary to avert the imminent use of deadly force or the commission of one of the felonies enumerated therein. If the People do not prove beyond a reasonable doubt that he did not have such beliefs, then the jury must also consider whether . . . , in light of all the "circumstances," as explicated above, . . . a reasonable person could have had these beliefs.

The prosecutor's instruction to the second grand jury . . . was thus essentially an accurate charge. It is true that the prosecutor did not elaborate on the meaning of "circumstances" or "situation" and inform the grand jurors that they could consider, for example, the prior experiences Goetz related in his statement to the police. We have held, however, that a grand jury need not be instructed on the law with the same degree of precision as the petit jury. This lesser standard is premised upon the different functions of the grand jury and the petit jury: the former determines whether sufficient evidence exists to accuse a person of a crime and thereby subject him to criminal prosecution; the latter ultimately determines the guilt or innocence of the accused, and may convict only where the People have proven his guilt beyond a reasonable doubt. . . .

. . . The grand jury has indicted Goetz. It will now be for the petit jury to decide whether the prosecutor can prove beyond a reasonable doubt that Goetz's reactions were unreasonable and therefore excessive. . . .

Accordingly, the order of the Appellate Division should be reversed, and the dismissed counts of the indictment reinstated.

Notes and Questions

1. At trial, Bernhard Goetz was acquitted on all save the weapons charges. He served eight months in jail. For more details about the *Goetz* case and its aftermath, see George P. Fletcher, A Crime of Self-Defense: Bernhard Goetz and the Law on Trial (1990).

2. The central issue in *Goetz* is the mix of subjective and objective components in the legal standard by which the shooting is to be judged. Did the New York Court of Appeals treat Goetz fairly? Recall People v. Marrero, supra, at page 157. Like *Goetz*, *Marrero* raised the question whether the defendant would be judged based on his own experience and understanding, or whether he would be held to the standard of conduct the law defines. In *Marrero*, the court rejected the defendant's mistake-of-law claim; Goetz's claim of self-defense was judged more generously. Did the court decide these two cases properly? Does it surprise you that Chief Judge Wachtler, author of the court's opinion in *Goetz*, dissented in *Marrero*?

3. Goetz has a much stronger claim with respect to his initial flurry of shots than with respect to the last shot he fired, the one that paralyzed Darryl Cabey. Recall that Goetz returned to Cabey, who had already been shot once; said to him, "[you] seem to be all right, here's another"; and then fired the last shot into Cabey's spine. That doesn't seem much like self-defense—in fact, it seems more like premeditation, doesn't it? Should the shots be analyzed differently, or should the entire incident—the relevant events happened within a few seconds—be treated as a single course of conduct? How finely can the law slice such events? What is the proper time horizon in a case like *Goetz*? See Mark Kelman, Interpretive Construction in the Substantive Criminal Law, 33 Stan. L. Rev. 591 (1981) (arguing, inter alia, that the criminal law often makes "hidden" choices between narrow and broad time frames that end up determining the outcomes of particular cases).

4. The defendant in People v. Wesley, 563 N.E.2d 21 (N.Y. 1990), was convicted of second-degree manslaughter on these facts:

> . . . [D]efendant, a 19-year-old college student, was on the porch of a house in Buffalo with Diane Jackson, Jelean McMillan, and Arlene Woods. Woods, who had a knife in her possession, got into an argument with Jackson. The argument continued as Jackson and Woods walked away from each other. Suddenly, Woods doubled back after Jackson and threatened to stab her. Defendant managed to get the knife away from Woods and placed it in a paper bag.
>
> At about that time, three male teen-agers arrived on the scene. Two of these youths—Eric Stone and Keith Robinson—began calling defendant "faggot" and Woods a lesbian. Despite defendant's pleas to be left alone, Stone, Robinson and others continued shouting epithets at defendant as he walked down the street. Stone and Robinson also threatened defendant, saying "We'll fuck you up" and "We'll kick your ass."
>
> Stone left the scene for a few minutes and returned carrying a stick (sometimes referred to as a pipe), 2 to 2½ feet in length and 1 to 3 inches in diameter. After more argument, Stone struck defendant with the stick, and defendant stabbed him in the chest. Stone fell to the ground and dropped the stick. Robinson then picked up the stick and began chasing defendant out of the area where the stabbing had taken place. When Robinson returned, he had been stabbed in the hand. Stone died as a result of the stab wound.

563 N.E.2d at 22-23. Wesley's conviction was reversed because the jury instructions did not make clear that his self-defense claim was to be judged by the standard of a reasonable person in the defendant's circumstances, with the defendant's characteristics and vulnerabilities.

5. Some states—less than a majority—have adopted a doctrine called "imperfect self-defense." The Maryland Court of Appeals explained that doctrine as follows:

> Perfect self-defense requires not only that the killer subjectively believed that his actions were necessary for his safety but, objectively, that a reasonable man would so consider them. Imperfect self-defense, however, requires no more than a subjective honest belief on the part of the killer that his actions were necessary for his safety, even though, on an objective appraisal by a reasonable man, they would not be found to be so.

State v. Marr, 765 A.2d 645, 648 (Md. 2001). Imperfect self-defense does not excuse a defendant from a homicide charge; instead, it reduces murder to manslaughter (and, presumably, aggravated assault to simple assault). The doctrine is thus a variant on provocation, but with a twist: Provocation requires that the homicide take place very soon after the provoking event and usually in the same place. Imperfect self-defense claims can arise after "cooling time." *Marr* is an example; here are the facts of that case:

> . . . The shooting of [Arthur Carroll] stemmed from an incident that occurred three days earlier, . . . when Carroll, Kevin Jackson, and Jerome Wright went to Marr's home with the intent to rob him. Marr was not at home, but the three came upon Marr's cousin, Ronald Muse, with whom Marr lived. In the course of searching for drugs and money, one or more of the trio shot and killed Muse. Marr later went looking for Carroll and Jackson, allegedly to inquire about their involvement in the killing of Muse. On December 2, he caught up with Carroll; on December 4, he found Jackson, who was luckier than Carroll and managed to escape in a hail of gunfire.

Id. at 646. Does Marr deserve a partial defense on these facts? Is his conduct more excusable than Goetz's, or less so?

6. Recall Lon Fuller's hypothetical Case of the Speluncean Explorers, supra at page 13. Justice Foster had this to say about Newgarth's law of self-defense:

> The true reconciliation of the excuse of self-defense with the statute making it a crime to kill another is to be found in the following line of reasoning. One of the principal objects underlying any criminal legislation is that of deterring men from crime. Now it is apparent that if it were declared to be the law that a killing in self-defense is murder such a rule could not operate in a deterrent manner. A man whose life is threatened will repel his aggressor, whatever the law may say. Looking therefore to the broad purposes of criminal legislation, we may safely declare that this statute was not intended to apply to cases of self-defense.

Justice Tatting's explanation was different:

> The taught doctrine of our law schools . . . runs in the following terms: The statute concerning murder requires a "willful" act. The man who acts to repel an aggressive threat to his own life does not act "willfully," but in response to an impulse deeply ingrained in human nature.

Does the law of self-defense fit Foster's rationale? Tatting's? Or is the reason for the defense different than either of these arguments suggest?

State v. Gartland

Supreme Court of New Jersey
694 A.2d 564 (1997)

Per Curiam.

This appeal concerns the statutory duty to retreat before resorting to the use of deadly force in self-defense. In this case a woman killed her husband in a bedroom of their home. The jury convicted her of reckless manslaughter. She died while her appeal was pending. Three issues were argued in the case: (1) whether her appeal should be dismissed because it became moot upon her death; (2) whether the trial court erred in instructing the jury under the circumstances that she had a duty to retreat from her separate bedroom before using deadly force; and (3) whether the trial court should have specifically instructed the jury that it could consider the history of spousal abuse to determine (in addition to whether she might have killed in the heat of passion arising from a reasonable provocation) whether she honestly and reasonably believed that deadly force was necessary to protect herself against death or serious bodily injury. From the evidence in the case, a jury could have found the following facts.

I

The killing occurred on February 8, 1993. The jury heard evidence of long-standing physical and emotional abuse inflicted by the victim on defendant. Witnesses portrayed John Gartland as a violent and threatening husband obsessed with jealousy.

On the afternoon of the killing, the Gartlands stopped at a tavern in Newark. There, they began to argue. When the Gartlands returned home at about 5:00 p.m., a neighbor heard Mr. Gartland (John) threaten his wife. Other neighbors heard similar abuse and threats. The argument continued when John could not find the remote control for the television and accused Ellen of hiding it. Angered, he left the home. When he returned, he renewed the argument about the remote control. Ellen asked him to leave her alone and went upstairs to her bedroom. For over ten years, she and her husband had had separate bedrooms.

Previously, John had left her alone in this room. On this evening, he followed her into her bedroom. She told him to go to bed and to leave her alone. He approached her, threatening to strike her. One of them, the parties dispute which, said "I'm going to hurt you" as he approached her.

Ellen took her son's hunting shotgun from her bedroom closet. She pointed it at her husband and told him to stop. He said, "You're not going to do [anything] to me because you, bitch, I'm going to kill you." He lunged at her with his fists clenched. She pulled the trigger. The shotgun blast hit her husband. He stepped into the hallway and fell.

Ellen dropped the gun, called an operator, and asked for an ambulance, saying that she had just shot her husband. She then called her son as well as John Gartland's son. She told the responding officers that she had feared for her life. She said that she would never forget the look on his face and that he approached her looking "like a devil."

At trial, the jury had asked twice during its deliberations for clarification of the court's charge on self-defense. On both occasions the trial court repeated its initial instructions. The instruction never specifically apprised the jury that it could consider the seventeen years of spousal abuse suffered by Mrs. Gartland in determining whether she honestly and reasonably believed that deadly force was necessary to protect herself against her husband. The trial [judge] . . . told the jury that "[a] reasonable belief is one which is to be held by a person of ordinary prudence and intelligence situated as Mrs. Gartland was on February 8, 1993."

Prior to the charge, defense counsel objected to the court's intent to charge that Ellen had a duty to retreat before resorting to deadly force. Counsel renewed his objection immediately after the charge. Before the first recharge on self-defense, defense counsel again objected. He noted that because Ellen had been in her own room, one that her husband never occupied, he was not a cohabitant and under the law she had no duty to retreat from her own separate dwelling. The trial court ruled that "under the statute, there was a duty to retreat." The court gave the Model Jury Charge:

> And even if you find the use of deadly force was reasonable, there are limitations on the use of deadly force. . . . If you find that Mrs. Gartland knew that she could avoid the necessity of using deadly force by retreating from that house, providing Mrs. Gartland knew that she could do so with complete safety, then the defense is not available to her.

The jury convicted Mrs. Gartland of reckless manslaughter. Two jurors later contacted the court describing confusion and indecision in their deliberations. After denying a motion for a new trial, the court sentenced Mrs. Gartland to a five-year term with a mandatory three years imprisonment. . . . She was freed on bail pending appeal.

The Appellate Division affirmed the conviction. . . . Defendant died after her petition for certification was filed. We granted the petition, and reserved decision on the State's motion to dismiss the appeal.

II

. . . The power to entertain a criminal appeal even after death should be sparingly exercised. A conviction should not be set aside unless the record shows palpably that there has been a fundamental miscarriage of justice, an error that "cut mortally into the substantive rights of the defendant . . . [or impaired] a defendant's ability to maintain a defense on the merits." State v. Harper, 128 N.J. Super. 270, 277, 319 A.2d 771 (App. Div. 1974). Such caution is required because there is an intrinsic imbalance in the conduct of a criminal appeal on behalf of a deceased defendant. The contest is one-sided. The defendant can no longer be retried for the crime. The State and the victims of the crime cannot win. If the conviction is set aside, the State is realistically deprived of the opportunity to vindicate the public interest in enforcement of the law. On the other hand, important interests of the defendant or society at large may be at stake if an erroneous conviction is left standing. We find those important interests present here.

III

. . . The drafters of our Code originally approached the concept of justification in terms of the subjective attitudes of the criminal actor. However, in the course of legislative modifications the self-defense provisions of the Code were altered to reestablish objective standards of self-defense:

> . . . Subject to the provisions of this section and of section 2C:3-9, the use of force upon or toward another person is justifiable when the actor reasonably believes that such force is immediately necessary for the purpose of protecting [the actor] against the use of unlawful force by such other person on the present occasion.

N.J. Stat. Ann. §2C:3-4a.

. . . Concerning deadly force, the Code provides: "The use of deadly force is not justifiable under this section unless the actor reasonably believes that such force is necessary to protect [the actor] against death or serious bodily harm. . . ." Id. §2C:3-4b(2). Even if deadly force is permissible, the actor still has the duty to retreat from the scene if the actor can do so safely. Id. §2C:3-4b(2)(b). One exception to this duty to retreat is if the actor is in his or her own home at the time of the attack (the so-called "castle doctrine"), unless the attacker is a cohabitant. N.J. Stat. Ann. §2C:3-4b(2)(b)(i) states that "[t]he actor is not obliged to retreat from [the] dwelling, unless [the actor] was the initial aggressor or is assailed in [the actor's own] dwelling by another person whose dwelling the actor knows it to be." N.J. Stat. Ann. §2C:3-4c provides special rules for the use of deadly force on an intruder into one's dwelling. For example, under this provision, deadly force may be used against an intruder to counter *any* level of unlawful force threatened by the intruder.

[According to the Public Defender,] it is ironic that Ellen Gartland could have used the shotgun against a burglar who intended to do her no serious harm but was precluded from using the same force against the true threat in her life, her husband. Instead, the law requires her to flee from her bedroom, which she had described as the only sanctuary in her chaos-filled home.

The retreat doctrine is one of several related legal doctrines affecting battered women as criminal defendants. See generally Holly Maguigan, Battered Women and Self-Defense: Myths and Misconceptions in Current Reform Proposals, 140 U. Pa. L. Rev. 379 (1991). . . .

> Under the common law regime, even if faced with immediate danger of death or great bodily harm, an individual could use only equal force to repel the danger. The doctrine of equal force, developed on a prototype of two males of equal size and strength, held that, if attacked without a deadly weapon, one could not respond with a deadly weapon. This doctrine obviously disadvantaged women, who are generally smaller and lack the same upper-body strength as men.
>
> Traditional common law self-defense imposes no duty to retreat, except for co-occupants of the same house. Given that most men are assaulted and killed outside their homes by strangers, while most women are assaulted and killed within their homes by male intimates, this doctrine also disadvantaged women.

Marina Angel, Criminal Law and Women: Giving the Abused Woman Who Kills a Jury of Her Peers Who Appreciate Trifles, 33 Am. Crim. L. Rev. 229, 320 (1996). . . .

Imposition of the duty to retreat on a battered women who finds herself the target of a unilateral, unprovoked attack in her own home is inherently unfair. During repeated instances of past abuse, she has "retreated," only to be caught, dragged back inside, and severely beaten again. If she manages to escape, other hurdles confront her. Where will she go if she has no money, no transportation, and if her children are left behind in the "care" of an enraged man? . . .

These are grave concerns. . . . However, . . . [a]s presently structured, the Code of Criminal Justice requires that a cohabitant who can safely leave the home to avoid violence should do so before resorting to deadly force. We have invariably adhered to the Code's concepts of self-defense. We have insisted, as the Code requires, that the belief of the person wielding deadly force must be a reasonable belief, not simply an honest belief. State v. Kelly, 97 N.J. 178, 204, 478 A.2d 364 (1984). . . . [W]e have declined to create new justifications for criminal conduct. See State v. Bowens, 108 N.J. 622, 532 A.2d 215 (1987) (holding that Code did not provide independent category of imperfect self-defense); State v. Tate, 102 N.J. 64, 505 A.2d 941 (1986) (holding that Code did not provide defense of medical necessity to illegal possession of drugs). Only when we have been satisfied that the structure of the Code makes a defense available have we allowed it to be asserted.

There is no comparable basis for departing from . . . the Code requirement that an actor may not use deadly force against a cohabitant if an actor may safely retreat. "The Legislature and the Executive do not decide cases . . . the judiciary does not pass laws. One of the categories of legislation that the judiciary has no power to adopt is that [of] defining crimes and providing for their punishment." State v. Cannon, 128 N.J. 546, 560, 608 A.2d 341 (1992). Although we find present the statutory duty to retreat, we commend to the Legislature consideration of the application of the retreat doctrine in the case of a spouse battered in her own home. There are arguments to be made on each side of the issue. See majority and dissenting opinions in State v. Thomas, 673 N.E.2d 1339 (Ohio 1997) (holding that domestic partner assaulted in her own home has no duty to retreat before using deadly force in self defense).

That leaves for resolution whether John Gartland could be considered a cohabitant of Ellen's bedroom. Put the other way, the question is whether the upstairs bedroom in which Ellen slept was a separate dwelling. It is a close question on this record but we agree with the courts below that the bedroom was not a separate dwelling. . . .

It is true that one building may have separate apartments. However, the idea of a dwelling is that one has an "exclusive right to occupy" a portion of a building. State v. Silva, 684 A.2d 725, 728 (Conn. App. 1996). In State v. Pontery, 19 N.J. 457, 117 A.2d 473 (1955), an estranged couple jointly owned a summer home. The wife went there to be away from her husband. When he and other family members joined her over the weekend, she could not claim that she was under no duty to retreat from the jointly-owned dwelling before inflicting deadly force. In contrast, in State v. Lamb, 71 N.J. 545, 366 A.2d 981 (1976), the Court exempted a wife from a duty to retreat from her husband's attack within an apartment that she exclusively occupied. He had burst in uninvited through an unlocked door. The Court stated: "In the circumstances of this case [the] defendant's estranged husband did not have as much right to be in the apartment as [the] defendant. It was her home. [The husband] was in fact an intruder and [the] defendant was under no duty to retreat." 71 N.J. at 549.

In this case, there is simply no evidence that the door to the bedroom had normally been kept locked or that John Gartland did not generally have access to the room. Defendant merely testified that because of sexual dysfunction, the couple slept in separate rooms. We cannot say that Ellen had the exclusive right to occupy this room. Hence, we agree, on this record, that the court correctly charged the statutory duty to retreat.

IV

Did the trial court err in failing specifically to instruct the jury that the evidence that defendant was abused by the decedent could be considered in assessing her claim of self-defense?

In *Kelly*, supra, this Court held that evidence of domestic abuse is relevant to a claim of self-defense. Specifically, the Court held that expert testimony concerning the battered women syndrome is relevant to the jury's determination of subjective honesty and the objective reasonableness of a defendant's belief that deadly force was necessary to protect herself against death or serious bodily harm. *Kelly*, 97 N.J. at 202-04. The Court recognized that evidence of prior abuse has the potential to confuse the jury and that expert testimony is useful to clarify and refute common myths and misconceptions about battered women. . . . [D]efendant argues that because evidence of prior abuse is relevant to the issue of self-defense and because evidence of prior abuse is potentially confusing, it follows that the jury must be properly instructed concerning how to consider and give effect to such evidence. . . . The trial court specifically instructed the jury to consider the evidence of prior abuse in determining the question of provocation. However, it did not specifically instruct the jury to consider evidence of prior abuse in determining the question of self-defense.

We agree that a better charge would have instructed the jury to consider the history of prior abuse in assessing the honesty and reasonableness of defendant's belief in the need to use deadly force. . . . The issue arises in this case as one of plain error and the question is whether the absence of the specific instruction . . . was clearly capable of producing an unjust result. . . . Taken as a whole, the instruction could not be understood to foreclose the jury's full and appropriate consideration of the prior abuse in assessing the honesty and reasonableness of defendant's belief.

The possibility that the jury might not have considered the prior abuse in assessing the self-defense claim appears highly attenuated in this case. A major focus of the opening and closing remarks of defense counsel was that the jury could and should consider the long-standing abuse of defendant by her husband in assessing her claim of self-defense. . . .

. . . The court's instructions did not foreclose the jury's consideration of that prior abuse; nor were its instructions so erroneous as to confuse or mislead the jury in its consideration of self-defense. The instructions gave the members of the jury an opportunity to consider fully whether an honest and reasonable belief in the necessity to use deadly force was present. The trial court explicitly told the jurors . . . that they could not find the defendant guilty of murder or any of the lesser-included offenses if they had a reasonable doubt as to whether or not the defendant had killed her victim in the honest and reasonable belief that the use of deadly force was necessary. . . .

V

We now turn to consider other aspects of this case that have been neither raised nor argued by the parties, that would have been grounds for retrial in the case of a living defendant.

In a long series of cases, we have held that an essential ingredient to a fair trial is that adequate and understandable instructions be given to the jury. The "charge is a road map to guide the jury and without an appropriate charge a jury can take a wrong turn in its deliberations." State v. Martin, 119 N.J. 2, 15, 573 A.2d 1359 (1990). We have regularly insisted that courts give content to statutory language in their charges to juries. "[A]n instruction solely in the terms of the language of the statute will [sometimes] not give sufficient guidance to the jury." State v. Olivio, 123 N.J. 550, 567, 589 A.2d 597 (1991)....

The instructions in this case were largely devoid of reference to the specific circumstances of the case. As noted, the trial court instructed the jury that if Mrs. Gartland "knew that she could avoid the necessity of using deadly force by retreating from that house, providing . . . [that] she could do so with complete safety, then the defense is not available to her." We intend no criticism of the trial court because neither party requested a charge tailored to the facts. However, an abstract charge on the duty to retreat could only have been confusing in the circumstances of this case. Exactly where could she retreat? As we understand the record, there was no other way out of the bedroom other than the doorway where her assailant stood. The charge should have asked whether, armed with a weapon, she could have safely made her way out of the bedroom door without threat of serious bodily injury to herself. In the similar circumstances of *Thomas*, supra, 673 N.E.2d 1339, a woman trapped in her trailer retreated to the bathroom. Unable to escape, she ran to a closet and took out a gun. She fired two warning shots and even after being shot her assailant continued to threaten her. The concurring judge asked, "[h]ad the defendant gotten around [her cohabitant] to the door of the small trailer, would her attempt to escape the altercation have increased the risk of her death? Would [the cohabitant] have become further enraged and tried to kill her?" 673 N.E.2d at 1346 (Stratton, J., concurring). These are the circumstances that a jury must evaluate. One of the problems in applying the retreat doctrine to the case of a battered woman is that the jurors may confuse the question of leaving the abusive partner with the duty to retreat on the occasion. See Maguigan, 140 U. Pa. L. Rev. at 419 (noting "there is a tendency to blur the definition of the retreat rule with the question of whether the woman could have escaped the relationship")....

The charge on self-defense should also have been tailored to the circumstances of the case. In State v. Wanrow, 559 P.2d 548 (Wash. 1977), the Washington Supreme Court recognized that its traditional self-defense standard failed to account for the perspective of abused women. Any limitation of the jury's consideration of the surrounding acts and circumstances to those occurring at or immediately before the killing would be an erroneous statement of the applicable law. Id. at 556. . . . At a minimum, the jury in Ellen Gartland's case should have been asked to consider whether, if it found such to be the case, a reasonable woman who had been the victim of years of domestic violence would have reasonably perceived on this occasion that the use of deadly force was necessary to protect herself from serious bodily injury.

In another context, the failure to relate to the facts of the case the duty to retreat and right of self-defense might not have cut so mortally into a defendant's ability to maintain a defense on the merits. However, the persistent stereotyping of the victims of domestic violence requires special concern. Both partners to the domestic tragedy are now deceased. Although we cannot fully right past wrongs, we can correct errors in the charge that were clearly capable of producing an unjust result.

The judgment of the Appellate Division is reversed and the conviction of manslaughter is set aside.

Notes and Questions on the Battered Spouse Defense

1. As *Gartland* suggests, self-defense doctrine was one of the key legal battlegrounds in the women's movement. According to the conventional wisdom, the key doctrinal issue in "battered spouse" cases is the meaning of the requirement that the defendant face a threat of "imminent" harm. The classic example of this problem was the case of Judy Norman; Victoria Nourse describes the case as follows:

> Norman killed her husband while he was asleep, hours after the last bout, after enduring years of degrading abuse in which she was prostituted, deprived of food, made to sleep on the floor, and driven to attempt suicide. The North Carolina court denied a jury instruction based on self-defense. State v. Norman, 378 S.E.2d 8, 9-10, 19 (1989).

V.F. Nourse, Self-Defense and Subjectivity, 68 U. Chi. L. Rev. 1235, 1241 n.28 (2001).

2. But it turns out that cases like *Norman* are the exception. *Gartland* is closer to the norm:

> The problem with the law of self-defense is neither new nor limited to the battered woman; it is as old and as persistent as the law's search for an objective meaning for necessity. Based on a survey of twenty years of self-defense cases, I sought to "test" claims of objectivity by focusing on what purports to be one of the most objective of self-defense rules: the requirement that the threat must have been "imminent" for the defendant's response to have been permissible. . . .
>
> . . . The case law shows that imminence has many meanings; indeed, imminence often operates as a proxy for any number of other self-defense factors — for example, strength of threat, retreat, proportionality, and aggression. Perhaps more importantly, my survey shows that the conventional image of imminence may be incorrect. It is widely believed by scholars that the

"problem" of imminence is one of too much time between the threat and the killing. If my survey is right, however, most judicial opinions raising imminence do not involve long periods of time between the threat and the killing. They are cases of weak threats and extended fights, cases in which the defendant is struggling with the victim, is faced with a gun, believes that the victim is advancing, or hears a stranger in the woods outside his home. This should confound traditional doctrinal understandings of the term "imminence." . . .

This has important implications for both the law of self-defense [and] the problem of battered women. The law of self-defense, if I am right, is far from as settled or coherent as it is assumed to be. . . . Indeed, it is even possible that the law, through imminence, contradicts itself: for example, if imminence is really asking whether the defendant had a means to escape the violence, it may function as a retreat rule in jurisdictions that do not require retreat. . . .

. . . [T]he battered woman cases in my survey . . . raise imminence most often in confrontational situations, where the defendant kills when she sees a gun, where the victim is advancing, or during an actual brawl. If that is right, then the problem of the battered woman case may not be one of fact, but of law. We do not ask of the man in the barroom brawl that he leave the bar before the occurrence of an anticipated fight, but we do ask the battered woman threatened with a gun why she did not leave the relationship. If, when courts are saying "imminence," they import meanings that demand retreat before the confrontation, they are applying a rule that the law itself disavows. . . .

68 U. Chi. L. Rev. at 1236-38. As Nourse notes, the law of self-defense does not require retreat *in advance of* the relevant threat. Was any other kind of retreat possible in *Gartland*?

3. Another important issue in "battered spouse" cases is the extent to which the defendant should be entitled to a "subjective," rather than an "objective," evaluation of the reasonableness of her conduct under the circumstances. In State v. Frei, 831 N.W.2d 70 (Iowa S. Ct. 2013), the defendant, Denise Frei, killed her longtime boyfriend (and purported common-law husband), Curtis Bailey, in the home they both shared. She was assisted in the killing by her 18-year-old son and his girlfriend. After initially trying to blame the murder on a drug deal gone bad, Frei eventually changed her story. She claimed that she had been subjected to years of humiliating and degrading emotional, verbal, and sexual abuse, and that Bailey—whom she described as extremely jealous and controlling—had threatened to kill her children and grandchild if she ever left him. She said that she had even tried to kill Bailey on three prior occasions by giving him morphine and insulin. On the day of the actual killing, Frei, her son, and the girlfriend began to implement a plan (devised more than a week earlier) to get Bailey drunk on vodka, and then wrap his face tightly with plastic wrap to suffocate him. As they tried to wrap his face, however, Bailey woke up and struggled to get free. Frei, her son, and the girlfriend then beat Bailey to death.

Frie was charged with first-degree murder. At trial, she argued self-defense, and introduced expert testimony that she suffered from depression, post-traumatic stress syndrome, and "battered women's syndrome." The jury, however, convicted her. On appeal, Frei challenged the jury instructions on her defense of justification. Here is what the Iowa Supreme Court had to say:

Iowa Code section 704.3 (2011) prescribes the elements of a justification defense.

> A person is justified in the use of reasonable force when the person reasonably believes that such force is necessary to defend oneself or another from any imminent use of unlawful force.

Iowa Code §704.3. "Reasonable force" is defined as

> that force and no more which a reasonable person, in like circumstances, would judge to be necessary to prevent an injury or loss and can include deadly force if it is reasonable to believe that such force is necessary to avoid injury or risk to one's life or safety or the life or safety of another, or it is reasonable to believe that such force is necessary to resist a like force or threat. Reasonable force, including deadly force, may be used even if an alternative course of action is available if the alternative entails a risk to life or safety, or the life or safety of a third party, or requires one to abandon or retreat from one's dwelling or place of business or employment.

Id. §704.1.

When interpreting and applying these statutes, we have explained that "the test of justification is both subjective and objective. The actor must actually believe that he is in danger and that belief must be a reasonable one." State v. Elam, 328 N.W.2d 314, 317 (Iowa 1982). Frei takes issue with this characterization of the justification defense. She contends the "objective" element of the justification—requiring the defendant to act and perceive as a reasonable person—is incompatible with the requirement that the State must prove the defendant possessed the level of culpability required to support a conviction for the charged crime. She asserts that if the defendant possesses the subjective belief that her actions are justified, then "the objective reasonableness of that belief should not matter." Accordingly, she contends the district court erred when it rejected her proposed instruction defining "reasonable force" as "only the amount of force a reasonable person *or a person with the Defendant's alleged degree of mental illness* would find necessary to use under the circumstances." Frei contends the district court further erred in denying her requested justification instruction, which would have permitted the jurors to acquit her if they found she subjectively believed her actions were justified without considering whether her perception of danger or belief regarding the availability of an alternative course of action was reasonable. The given justification instruction, by contrast, retained an objective reasonableness requirement.

. . . As applied to a battered woman, an appropriately specific reasonableness inquiry might consider objective facts about the batterer, any history of violence, any failed attempts to escape abuse, and any other facts relevant under the circumstances. Further, expert testimony can aid in cautioning jurors that the behavior of battered women should not be lightly dismissed as inherently unreasonable. The[] cases [cited by Frei] do not, however, establish that an appropriate reasonableness inquiry extends only as far as a specific defendant's actual, subjective beliefs regarding the surrounding circumstances. Accordingly, Frei's reliance on [those cases] does not support her argument for a purely subjective test for justification.

    The State argues that the jury instructions given by the court in this case accurately express the legal elements of a justification defense as provided by sections 704.1 and 704.3 and interpreted by our prior caselaw. We agree. Frei's proposal for an entirely subjective test of justification is incompatible with the clear mandate of sections 704.1 and 704.3 requiring the actions and perceptions of the defendant be tested against a reasonableness standard. The district court did not err in instructing the jury as it did.

Id. at 74-75. The court also rejected several other appellate claims raised by Frei, and affirmed her first-degree murder conviction.

    Notice that Frei's argument essentially sought to blur the line (if, indeed, there is such a line) between "justification" and "excuse": She sought to have the jury consider her claim of self-defense, i.e., a justified killing, but under a "subjective" approach that would evaluate her behavior from the perspective of a person suffering from mental illness. The court, in turn, ultimately agreed with Frei that a certain amount of "subjectivization" is appropriate in a "battered spouse" case; at the same time, the court felt that Frei's "purely subjective" version of the defense would go too far. In the court's view, it's fine to highlight the "objective facts" about a troubled and abusive relationship that leads to a killing, but in the end, the defendant's behavior still must be judged against an "objective reasonableness" standard.

    Do you agree with the court's decision? Does it make sense to draw a line between "subjectifying" the "objective facts," on the one hand, while still applying an "objective reasonableness" standard to the defendant's behavior, on the other hand? If the jury is not allowed to evaluate a battered spouse's behavior *from the perspective of a battered spouse*, then what good will it do to tell the jury about the "objective facts" of the battering?

    4. The *Gartland* case involved both the "retreat" doctrine in New Jersey's law of self-defense and the related "castle" doctrine (applicable to persons attacked or threatened within their own homes); the Iowa statute on "reasonable force," quoted in *Frei*, also talks about a duty to retreat. But the requirement that a person confronted by a potentially lethal threat must retreat, if possible, before using potentially lethal force in self-defense is *not* the law in most American jurisdictions; fewer than 20 states (including both New Jersey and Iowa) have some version of the "retreat" doctrine. A century ago, the Missouri Supreme Court offered one explanation for the absence of a retreat requirement:

> It is true, human life is sacred, but so is human liberty. One is as dear in the eye of the law as the other, and neither is to give way and surrender its legal status in order that the other may exclusively exist, supposing for a moment that such an anomaly to be possible. In other words, the wrongful and violent act of one man shall not abolish or even temporarily suspend the lawful and constitutional right of his neighbor. And this idea of the non-necessity of retreating from any locality where one has the right to be is growing in favor, as all doctrines based upon sound reason inevitably will. . . . [No] man, because he is the physical inferior of another, from whatever cause such inferiority may arise, is, because of such inferiority, bound to submit to a public horsewhipping. We hold it a necessary self-defense to resist, resent, and prevent such humiliating indignity—such a violation of the sacredness of one's person—and that, if nature has not provided the means for such resistance, art may; in short, a weapon may be used to effect the unavoidable necessity.

State v. Bartlett, 71 S.W. 148, 151-52 (Mo. 1902), quoted in Dan M. Kahan, The Secret Ambition of Deterrence, 113 Harv. L. Rev. 413, 429 (1999). Justice Oliver Wendell Holmes offered a different explanation:

> The law has grown, and even if historical mistakes have contributed to its growth, it has tended in the direction of rules consistent with human nature. . . . Detached reflection cannot be demanded in the presence of an uplifted knife. Therefore, in this court, at least, it is not a condition of immunity that one in that situation should pause to consider whether a reasonable man might not think it possible to fly with safety, or to disable his assailant rather than to kill him.

Brown v. United States, 256 U.S. 335, 343 (1921), quoted in Kahan, 113 Harv. L. Rev. at 429.

Dan Kahan has this to say about those different accounts of the law:

> Although they get to the same place, these two justifications for the "no retreat" rule travel along strikingly different normative paths. The position of the Missouri Supreme Court is unapologetically expressive. The man who stands his ground and fights has done nothing wrong because his "resentment" reveals that he appropriately attaches more value to his "rights," "liberty," and "sacredness of . . . person" than he does to the life of a "wrongful" aggressor. Indeed, other courts of the day defended the same result on the ground that "a true man"—one whose character and values are straight rather than warped—cannot be expected "to fly from an assailant, who, by violence or surprise, maliciously seeks to take his life or do him enormous bodily harm." Extending the privilege to use deadly force to repel such an attack is the appropriate way for the law to acknowledge the courage of the defender's decision to stand firm; indeed, punishing him for killing the aggressor would send the "anomalous" message that the law values the sanctity of "human life"

but not the goods—from "liberty" to "rights" to "dignity" to honor—that make life sacred.

Justice Holmes's argument, in contrast, is a concession to futility. A deadly attack triggers an unthinking impulse to fight; it disregards "human nature" to believe that the threat of subsequent criminal punishment will induce "detached reflection" on the prospects for safe retreat. Although there is certainly more than one way to interpret Holmes's argument, Holmes . . . can plausibly be read . . . as making a deterrence argument. Because punishment cannot be expected to influence behavior in such circumstances, it would be a waste to punish a man for not taking flight in the face of deadly aggression.

As an exercise in normative justification, Holmes's account is manifestly less satisfying than the Missouri Supreme Court's. For one thing, Holmes's defense of the "no retreat" doctrine displays the characteristic empirical speculativeness of deterrence arguments. Why so quickly assume that "human nature" makes it impossible for a person confronted with aggression to hear a legal directive to retreat? Physically threatened people run in fear all the time; adding the prospect of being killed down the road by the state to the prospect of being killed instantly by the attacker should only make running in fear all the more likely. . . .

These empirical issues are much less of a problem for the Missouri Supreme Court, because it doesn't see maximizing lives per se as the goal. Life has sacred value only because liberty, dignity, and honor do; legally obliging a person either to "retreat[] from [a] locality where [he] has the right to be" or "to submit to a public horsewhipping" when he could effectively repel the attack would express contempt for these values. If we accept this account, then it doesn't much matter whether the "true man" doctrine leads to the unnecessary taking of aggressors' lives, for the virtue of the "true men" would be worth much more than the lives of wrongful aggressors.

113 Harv. L. Rev. at 429-31.

5. Kahan goes on to offer the following history of the retreat doctrine:

From the end of the Civil War well into the early part of this century, the duty to retreat was an unsettled and fiercely contested issue in American criminal law. . . . The judicial proponents of the "true man" doctrine—which constituted a sharp break with English common law—were located in the South and West. By virtue of the slave culture in the former and the frontier culture in the latter, both of these regions had inherited rich systems of honor that put a premium on physical displays of courage and on violent reactions to slights. Opponents of the "true man" doctrine . . . tended to come from the East, which viewed traditional honor norms with alarm and contempt in part because of their historical association with slavery. Western judges derided the English common law requirement that a man "retreat to the wall" before using deadly force as contrary to "the tendency of the American mind"; in fact, the dispute over the "true man" doctrine was about whose minds—those of the aristocratic South and the ruggedly individualistic West, on the one hand, or those of the more egalitarian and cosmopolitan East, on the other—would be proclaimed genuinely "American" by the law.

Id. at 432-33. Perhaps it is to be expected that the obligation to retreat, seen as so onerous to "true men," is more readily imposed today on defendants like Gartland. Is self-defense doctrine sexist? Under what circumstances should defendants be obliged to flee rather than fight?

Mobley v. State

Court of Appeal of Florida, Third District
132 So. 3d 1160 (2014)

Opinion by WELLS, J.

We have jurisdiction to review the instant petition for writ of prohibition seeking to preclude the court below from proceeding further in adjudicating criminal charges against petitioner, Gabriel Mobley, on the grounds that Mobley is immune from prosecution under the provisions of Chapter 776 of the Florida Statutes (Florida's Stand Your Ground Law). . . .

The standard of review applicable to this case is the same as that which is applied to the denial of a motion to suppress. . . . Under this standard, the trial court's findings of fact are "presumed correct and can be reversed only if they are not supported by competent substantial evidence," while the trial court's legal conclusions are reviewed de novo. . . . For the reasons that follow, we grant the petition but withhold issuance of our writ confident that the court below will comply with this court's order.

FACTS

Gabriel Mobley, the petitioner here, was charged with two counts of second degree murder following a shooting which took place outside a local Chili's restaurant on February 27, 2008. The day of the fatal shooting, Mobley finished work around 3:00 P.M. at his pressure cleaning business, and after going home to shower and change, went to work at the tax preparation office of high school friend, Jose (Chico) Correa.[1] After working several hours at Chico's business, Mobley was invited by Chico to join him and his staff at a local Chili's to unwind. Mobley agreed to join them but drove his own car intending to go home from the restaurant. When Mobley arrived at the restaurant, he removed the handgun that he was carrying and stowed the gun in the glove compartment of his car.[2] He did so because he believed from the training that he had received to secure a concealed carry license that firearms could not be brought into any establishment where food and

---

1. Mobley testified that he was temporarily working two jobs to earn extra money because his wife, a school teacher, was soon to go on maternity leave following the birth of the couple's second child.

2. It is conceded that Mobley was properly licensed to carry a concealed firearm.

alcohol are served. By the time Mobley got to the restaurant, a number of Chico's female employees had arrived and were sitting at a booth located near one end of the restaurant's bar. Because the booth was crowded, Mobley, Chico, and another of Chico's employees (another man) sat at the bar nearest the booth.

Sometime after food and drinks were ordered, Mobley and Chico went outside to smoke. They returned to the bar where they ate, drank and conversed without incident. However, things changed after Mobley and Chico went outside a second time for a smoke. This time when they reentered the restaurant, they found two men, later identified as Jason Gonzalez and Rolando (Roly) Carranza, talking to Chico's female employees. According to Chico, the women seemed to be uncomfortable so he told the men to leave. This sparked a verbal altercation between Chico and the two men which continued until the two men returned to their table at the other end of the bar. The altercation, which lasted only a few minutes, was loud enough to attract the attention of the restaurant's security guard and its manager, who asked the guard to keep an eye on Jason and Roly.

Mobley was not involved in the argument but acted as peacemaker instead, going to Jason's and Roly's table to ask them to forget what he described as a petty misunderstanding. He even shook Jason's hand and gave him a friendly pat on the back. Mobley also spoke to a third person seated at the bar who appeared to be with Jason and Roly about forgetting this petty disagreement.

Although the altercation appeared to have ended, Mobley testified that he began to feel uncomfortable after he noticed Roly staring in the direction of Chico's party with a "mean, cold [look] on his face."[5] He decided it was time to leave. But before he left, he and Chico went to the restroom where he expressed his concerns to his friend. As Mobley and Chico were returning from the bathroom, they passed the front of the restaurant where Mobley saw Jason, with Roly nearby, banging aggressively on the restaurant's window and pointing toward them. When Mobley and Chico reached their seats, Mobley suggested that after Jason and Roly left, they should all go home. Approximately ten to fifteen minutes later, after Jason and Roly appeared to have left, Mobley left the restaurant alone while Chico settled the check.

The events that transpired next were captured on a security camera recording made outside the restaurant, and, for the most part, are beyond dispute. The recording shows that at 23:52:15, Mobley, wearing only a sleeveless tee shirt, exited the Chili's front door and went to his vehicle parked only feet away, but mostly outside the security camera's viewing range. There,

5. Alexandra Martinez, a server at the restaurant called by the State to testify, confirmed that Jason and Roly continued to be angry after the initial shouting match had ended and appeared to become angrier as the evening wore on.

Mobley, as subsequent footage confirms, donned a sweat shirt, because, according to Mobley, it was chilly that night. He also retrieved his gun and put it in a holster that he wore around his waist. Less than a minute after Mobley left the restaurant, Chico and the third man in their party exited the front door. Chico was joined by Mobley who walked with Chico to his near-by car.[8] There the two remained for approximately thirty seconds until, at 23:53:38, Mobley stepped onto the sidewalk near the front fender of Chico's car. Approximately twenty seconds later, Chico joined him on the sidewalk where the two smoked a cigarette.

Four seconds after Chico joined Mobley on the sidewalk, Jason Gonzalez can be seen rapidly approaching from Mobley's and Chico's right. Four seconds after that, Jason delivered a vicious punch to Chico's face which fractured Chico's eye socket. Jason then can be seen to dance backward, hands raised in a fighter's pose, and within four seconds of landing the punch on Chico advance forward toward Mobley. Mobley reacted by raising his arm and hand to ward Jason off. Two seconds later, as Jason steps back from Mobley, Roly can be seen rushing up from the rear of the restaurant to join Jason in what Mobley testified he believed to be a renewed attack on both himself and Chico. At this juncture, as Roly neared Jason, who was only feet from both Mobley and Chico, Mobley testified that he saw Roly reach under his long, baggy shirt. Believing that Roly was reaching for a weapon to use in an attack, Mobley drew his gun and shot at Roly hitting both Roly and Jason.

This entire series of events, from the time Jason first comes into view on the sidewalk until the first shot was fired, took only twelve seconds. After being shot, Jason turned and fled toward his (or Roly's) car to collapse with a gunshot wound to the chest and die. Roly, hit four times, fell to the ground near the restaurant's door where he was assisted by the third man in their party who had been sitting at the bar. Roly later died at a local hospital. Although no weapons were found on Roly's body, two knives were found on the ground near where he fell.[9]

Following the shooting, Mobley remained at the scene and had the other members of his party, who by then were leaving in their cars, return to wait for the authorities. When police officers arrived only minutes later, Mobley told them that he was armed and otherwise fully cooperated with them. After being held in a police car for a number of hours, he was transported to the police station where he was read and waived his *Miranda* rights. While there, he gave both an unsworn and a sworn statement. He was then released but not charged.

8. The third man walked to his car parked next to Chico's and remained there until after the shooting occurred.
9. According to Ms. Martinez, the man who went to Roly's aid after he was shot took a knife with him when he left the restaurant.

Several weeks later, after a new lead investigator had been assigned to the case, Mobley agreed to be and was re-interviewed. While there is no indication that his version of the events changed in any manner during this interview, he subsequently was arrested and charged with two counts of second degree murder. Mobley claimed below and now claims here that these facts are undisputed and demonstrate that he is immune from prosecution as provided by sections 776.012 and 776.032 of the Florida Statutes. We agree in part that the pertinent facts are not in dispute and that Mobley is entitled to immunity from prosecution.

ANALYSIS

Florida law confers immunity from criminal prosecution and civil liability, without the obligation to retreat, on those who use deadly force reasonably believing that the use of such force is necessary to either prevent imminent death or great bodily harm to self or others or to prevent the imminent commission of a forcible felony. See §776.032, Fla. Stat. (2013) (providing that a "person who uses force as permitted in §776.012, §776.013, or §776.031 is justified in using such force and is immune from criminal prosecution and civil action for the use of such force"); see also §776.012(1), (2), Fla. Stat. (2013) (providing that a "person is justified in the use of deadly force . . . and does not have a duty to retreat if: (1) [h]e or she reasonably believes that such force is necessary to prevent imminent death or great bodily harm to himself or herself or another or to prevent the imminent commission of a forcible felony; or (2) [u]nder those circumstances permitted pursuant to §776.013").

An objective standard is applied to determine whether the immunity provided by these provisions attaches. See Montanez v. State, 24 So. 3d 799, 803 (Fla. 2d DCA 2010) (confirming that in determining whether the immunity accorded by section 776.032 attaches, "the objective, reasonable person standard by which claims of justifiable use of deadly force are measured" should be applied). That standard requires the court to determine whether, based on circumstances as they appeared to the defendant when he or she acted, a reasonable and prudent person situated in the same circumstances and knowing what the defendant knew would have used the same force as did the defendant. See Toledo v. State, 452 So. 2d 661, 663 (Fla. 3d DCA 1984) ("[A] person in the exercise of his right of self-defense may use 'only such force as a reasonable person, situated as he was and knowing what he knew, would have used under like circumstances.'"; see also Chaffin v. State, 121 So. 3d 608 (Fla. 4th DCA 2013) (confirming that the standard to be applied for determining whether a person is justified in using deadly force in self-defense is not a subjective standard as to the defendant's state of mind, but an objective standard as to a reasonably prudent person's state of mind); Price v. Gray's Guard Service, Inc., 298 So. 2d 461, 464 (Fla. 1st DCA 1974) ("The conduct of a person acting in self defense is measured by an objective standard, but the standard must be applied to the facts and circumstances as they appeared at the time of the altercation to the one acting in self defense.").

Here, the court below determined that Mobley did not "reasonably" believe that deadly force was "necessary" to prevent "imminent" death, great bodily harm, or commission of a forcible felony. In doing so, the court discounted the totality of the circumstances facing Mobley and concluded that the use of deadly force was not reasonable, first, because Mobley "never saw a weapon and did not know anything about the possibility of a weapon," with him only seeing "the second attacker appear to be reaching for something under his shirt," and second, because Mobley should have brandished his gun, fired a warning shot or told the attackers to stop because he had a gun. We disagree for the following reasons.

As a preliminary matter, Mobley was not required to warn that he had a gun. Section 776.012(1), (2), clearly states where the danger of death, great bodily harm or the commission of a forcible felony is "imminent," the use of deadly force is justified. The statute contains no warning requirement. See T.P. v. State, 117 So. 3d 864, 866 (Fla. 4th DCA 2013) (". . . [U]nder section 776.013, a person who is attacked is allowed to stand his or her ground and 'meet force with force.' It appears that the new law places no duty on the person to avoid or retreat from danger, so long as that person is not engaged in an unlawful activity and is located in a place where he or she has a right to be. §776.013(3), Fla. Stat. (2005).").

As to the primary reason given by the court for rejecting Mobley's "Stand Your Ground" defense—that Mobley did not see a weapon, this likewise cannot be deemed determinative. The record reflects that Mobley observed Jason viciously attack his friend Chico outside the Chili's. Mobley then saw Jason's friend Roly approach and reach under his shirt. It was then that Mobley became afraid for his safety and life and for that of his friend and he pulled his gun:

Q. Okay. So, as soon as he [Roly] was coming towards you, you shot?
A. Yes.
Q. Why did you first pull your firearm?
A. Why[?]
Q. Yes.
A. By this time, you know, I didn't know what they had done—I didn't know what Chico had got hit with, and it was so much blood, I freaked, I was scared and I seen [sic] this other guy coming up from the back. And he reached up under his shirt. So, I was scared, I thought, they were going to shoot or kill us or stab us or something. So I was scared.

The shooting at issue did not occur in a vacuum. Mobley did not shoot two innocent bystanders who just happened upon him on a sidewalk. The record—as corroborated by a video of the events—is that (1) Mobley found himself in the middle of a violent, unprovoked attack on a companion who was standing right next to him, by one of two men who earlier had engaged in an altercation to which he was a witness; (2) after the initial violent attack on Mobley's friend, the attacker immediately turned his attention to Mobley; (3) less than four seconds after that, the first attacker was joined by the second man involved in the altercation inside the restaurant; and (4) when the second man reached under his shirt after rushing up to join his companion who had not abandoned the field, Mobley believed the second man was reaching for a weapon to continue the attack. With these facts at hand, and with Mobley's knowledge of these two assailants, the issue for determination was not whether Mobley knew a weapon was possible or whether he actually saw one, but whether a reasonably prudent person in those same circumstances and with the same knowledge would have used the force Mobley used.

Rather than applying the objective standard required, the court below instead focused on the events that transpired inside the Chili's to entirely discount Mobley's "expressed beliefs or intentions" about what occurred outside the Chili's. The court found that because Mobley was not directly involved in the earlier altercation inside the restaurant between Chico and Jason/Roly, but had acted as peacemaker, he could not have feared for his own life during the events which happened later outside the restaurant. However the events that occurred inside the Chili's are relevant only insofar as they provide the context for Mobley's actions when the attack outside the restaurant occurred.

It may have been more prudent for Mobley and Chico to skitter to their cars and hightail it out of there when they had the chance; however, as even the State concedes and the court below recognized, Mobley and Chico had every right to be where they were, doing what they were doing and they did nothing to precipitate this violent attack. The only relevant inquiry was whether, given the totality of the circumstances leading up to the attack, the appearance of danger was so real that a reasonably cautious and prudent person under the same circumstances would have believed that the danger could be avoided only through the use of deadly force.

Because the preponderance of the evidence demonstrates that had the proper standard been applied, Mobley's use of deadly force was justified, the motion to dismiss should have been granted . . . . Petition granted.

SHEPHERD, C.J., concurs.

SALTER, J., dissenting.

I respectfully dissent. . . .

Regarding the facts, four judges have now split evenly on whether the defendant's decisions to (1) take his Glock .45 out of the glove compartment of his truck, following a verbal altercation within the restaurant, and (2) fire five shots into the two decedents, after a single punch was thrown outside the restaurant, met the requirements for Stand Your Ground (SYG) immunity. One was the trial judge who actually heard and observed thirteen witnesses under oath and subjected to cross-examination. This Court was of course required to conduct its review of the testimony by reading it and without observing the witnesses as they testified.

The facts are also ambiguous when it comes to the surveillance video recorded by the camera affixed to the outside of the restaurant. Did deceased victim Carrazana appear to be reaching for a weapon, as the defendant testified? The video has only two frames per second (human vision is equivalent to 60 frames per second), and the camera caught the action from above and behind the incident. As described below, the few video freeze-frames of the incident seem to me to disprove, rather than prove the defendant's testimony. These uncertainties confirm that the defendant's claim is a classic, fact-based issue for the jury at trial.

Nor do I agree that the trial court committed any error of law in ruling on the defendant's motion. The trial court's reference to the defendant's conflicting statements regarding the fear that purportedly caused him to shoot both decedents—whether a fear of imminent death or great bodily harm to (a) himself, (b) Chico Correa, or (c) both of them—is a reflection (and not the only one) on the defendant's disparate accounts of the incident, going to credibility, and not a legal error (application of a "subjective" standard regarding the defendant's state of mind as opposed to an "objective" standard regarding a reasonably prudent person's state of mind), as characterized by the majority. For these reasons, we should deny the defendant's petition without prejudice to his right to present SYG immunity and self-defense as affirmative defenses at trial.

ADDITIONAL FACTS

A number of additional facts in the record before us warrant specific consideration. The first is that the defendant and his friend Mr. Correa went outside to smoke cigarettes three times during their visit to the restaurant on the evening in question. During the first and second of those cigarette breaks, the defendant was unarmed—his firearm was inside the glove compartment of his truck—and he was wearing a sun shirt. Only at the time of his third exit from the restaurant (after the verbal exchanges inside the restaurant, and after the defendant had told others that he planned to return home to his pregnant wife), did he instead unlock his truck, put on a sweatshirt, retrieve his firearm and holster from the glove compartment, and tuck the holstered firearm into his belt under the sweatshirt. Instead of going home to his wife as he had said, the defendant lingered on the sidewalk with Mr. Correa for a third, fateful smoke.

It was a cool February evening in Miami when the defendant had first arrived at the restaurant (well after 9:00 P.M.), but he had not put on his sweatshirt for the first and second cigarette breaks. He did not unlock his truck and put on his sweatshirt until the sweatshirt was used to cover his holster and Glock .45.

A second factual point for consideration is the punch thrown by Mr. Gonzalez at Mr. Correa's right eye. The testimony established that: Mr. Correa did not fall to the ground; his injury was treated with an ice pack at the scene; his vital signs were normal when he was checked by a fire rescue lieutenant at the scene after the incident; and he declined to be transported to an emergency room or other medical provider for treatment that night. Mr. Gonzalez's blow drew blood and, according to Mr. Correa's description of a later diagnosis, fractured his eye socket, but ordinarily an assessment of "great bodily harm" is a jury issue. . . .

A third factual consideration involves the surveillance video of the incident and freeze-frame images from that video. The images do not corroborate the testimony by Mr. Correa and the defendant that the second decedent, Mr. Carrazana, seemed to be reaching under a jacket as if for a weapon. To the contrary, Mr. Carrazana is not fully visible in the images until time stamp label 23:54:09. In that image, the defendant was off the sidewalk, three feet or so into a vacant parking place, and Mr. Carrazana had both hands well away from his waistline, extended as in a normal gait. Both hands were visible and neither held a weapon. His sleeves were rolled up.

In the next frame, stamped 23:54:10, the defendant's line of sight to Mr. Carrazana was blocked by Mr. Gonzalez. In the very next frame, 23:54:11, both Mr. Gonzalez and Mr. Carrazana are staggering from the first gunshot or gunshots that hit them.[15] The evidence at the SYG hearing did not establish that either decedent carried a knife, displayed a knife, or that Mr. Correa or the defendant ever saw a knife before the defendant opened fire. The two restaurant knives later found outside the door (after the incident) were not shown by the defense to have been obtained, displayed, or held by either decedent at any time.

The fourth and final factual point warranting additional discussion is also pertinent in self-defense and SYG cases — the relative size and weight of the parties involved in an attack claimed to justify the use of deadly force. In the present case, the decedents were five feet, eight inches, and 217 pounds (Mr. Gonzalez), and five feet, six inches, and 156 pounds (Mr. Carrazana).

---

15. The forensic evidence confirmed that one gunshot, fired from several feet away, hit Mr. Gonzalez (who had been in front of Mr. Carrazana and was closest to the defendant), who then turned and staggered several steps away from Mr. Mobley before collapsing and dying. Additional gunshots (also fired from several feet away) hit, and ultimately killed, Mr. Carrazana.

Mr. Correa, punched by Mr. Gonzalez, was six feet, one inch, and 285 pounds, while the defendant was six feet, two inches, and weighed 285 pounds.

Having addressed these four additional factual points that were part of the record before the trial court, I next turn to the majority's conclusion that the trial court applied the incorrect legal standard to the evidence. . . .

MONTANEZ AND THE "OBJECTIVE, REASONABLE PERSON" STANDARD

While I agree with the majority that the "objective, reasonable person" standard applies to an assessment of whether the use of deadly force is justifiable (under Montanez v. State, 24 So. 3d 799, 803 (Fla. 2d DCA 2010), and Fla. Std. Jury Instr. (Crim.) 3.6(f)), I disagree with the majority's further conclusions regarding the trial court's adherence to that standard. . . .

As to the argument that the trial court erroneously applied a subjective, state-of-the-defendant's mind standard, it must be remembered that the "objective, reasonable person" is not a hypothetical, unknowing stranger dropped into the altercation and the defendant's shoes a microsecond before Mr. Gonzalez punched Mr. Correa. The "objective, reasonable person" is a person situated in the same circumstances as the defendant and knowing what the defendant knew. *Montanez* at 803 n.6; Slip Op. at 9-10.

In the present case, the trial court correctly assessed those circumstances and the defendant's state of knowledge; the trial court did not otherwise dwell on the defendant's subjective state of mind or intentions. The fact-intensive determination of whether a reasonable and prudent person in the defendant's shoes might have perceived that Mr. Carrazana was reaching for a deadly weapon turned on the court's assessment of the defendant's credibility. The defendant and his friend of 17 years were the only living eyewitnesses to that important fact. The video and freeze-frame images did not definitively prove or disprove the reasonableness of that alleged perception—an alleged perception which turned out to be erroneous.

Simply stated, the justifiability of this defendant's use of force, or of a hypothetical "reasonably prudent person's" use of force, turns on a fact dependent on the defendant's credibility. The majority disagrees with the trial court regarding the trial court's assessment of the defendant's credibility, but that is an assessment to which we should defer. There is competent, substantial evidence in this record to support the trial court's determination that the defendant failed to prove his entitlement to immunity. . . .

CONCLUSION

For these reasons, I respectfully dissent. I would deny the defendant's petition for prohibition without prejudice to his rights to raise self-defense and SYG immunity as affirmative defenses and issues for resolution by a jury. . . .

Notes and Questions on "Stand Your Ground" Laws

1. "Stand Your Ground" laws, like the one in Florida, are based on a premise that is more or less the opposite of the "retreat" doctrine: If you have a right to be where you are (including in a public place), and if you are doing nothing wrong, then you should not have to yield or "retreat" in the face of a threat. Instead, you should be entitled to "stand your ground" and repel the threat with force—even lethal force, if you reasonably believe you are in danger of death or great bodily harm, or if you reasonably believe you are about to become the victim of a felony crime. That doesn't seem unreasonable, does it? Especially if the law requires people to act only upon a "reasonable" belief?

2. But think about this: Who gets to decide whether or not a particular situation qualifies for "Stand Your Ground" use of lethal force? In the end, of course, it's a jury or court that will decide the question. But in the first instance, don't "Stand Your Ground" laws encourage individuals to make those decisions for themselves—with potentially deadly consequences? To put it another way, "Stand Your Ground" laws authorize an individual, caught up in a moment of extreme anger and/or extreme fear, to decide whether or not their own lethal response is "reasonable"—with that decision subject to later review by a court, but only after there's already a (possibly innocent) dead body on the ground. Does that seem like a good rule? Might your reaction to such a rule depend, at least in part, on whether you think that other people are more (or less) likely to perceive someone who looks like you to be threatening?

3. More than half of the states currently have some form of "Stand Your Ground" law on the books. (In several additional states, judicial interpretations of state self-defense law have reached the same result.) Most of these statutes are similar—indeed, most are based on a model law that was developed by the American Legislative Exchange Council, a conservative think tank, in conjunction with the National Rifle Association. Florida's statute was the original archetype for the model law:

§776.012. Use of force in defense of person.—A person is justified in using force, except deadly force, against another when and to the extent that the person reasonably believes that such conduct is necessary to defend himself or herself or another against the other's imminent use of unlawful force. However, a person is justified in the use of deadly force and does not have a duty to retreat if:

(1) He or she reasonably believes that such force is necessary to prevent imminent death or great bodily harm to himself or herself or another or to prevent the imminent commission of a forcible felony; or

(2) Under those circumstances permitted pursuant to §776.013.

§776.013. Home protection; use of deadly force; presumption of fear of death or great bodily harm.—

(1) A person is presumed to have held a reasonable fear of imminent peril of death or great bodily harm to himself or herself or another when using defensive force that is intended or likely to cause death or great bodily harm to another if:

(a) The person against whom the defensive force was used was in the process of unlawfully and forcefully entering, or had unlawfully and forcibly entered, a dwelling, residence, or occupied vehicle, or if that person had removed or was attempting to remove another against that person's will from the dwelling, residence, or occupied vehicle; and

(b) The person who uses defensive force knew or had reason to believe that an unlawful and forcible entry or unlawful and forcible act was occurring or had occurred.

(2) The presumption set forth in subsection (1) does not apply if:

(a) The person against whom the defensive force is used has the right to be in or is a lawful resident of the dwelling, residence, or vehicle, such as an owner, lessee, or titleholder, and there is not an injunction for protection from domestic violence or a written pretrial supervision order of no contact against that person; or

(b) The person or persons sought to be removed is a child or grandchild, or is otherwise in the lawful custody or under the lawful guardianship of, the person against whom the defensive force is used; or

(c) The person who uses defensive force is engaged in an unlawful activity or is using the dwelling, residence, or occupied vehicle to further an unlawful activity; or

(d) The person against whom the defensive force is used is a law enforcement officer, as defined in § 943.10(14), who enters or attempts to enter a dwelling, residence, or vehicle in the performance of his or her official duties and the officer identified himself or herself in accordance with any applicable law or the person using force knew or reasonably should have known that the person entering or attempting to enter was a law enforcement officer.

(3) A person who is not engaged in an unlawful activity and who is attacked in any other place where he or she has a right to be has no duty to retreat and has the right to stand his or her ground and meet force with force, including deadly force if he or she reasonably believes it is necessary to do so to prevent death or great bodily harm to himself or herself or another or to prevent the commission of a forcible felony.

(4) A person who unlawfully and by force enters or attempts to enter a person's dwelling, residence, or occupied vehicle is presumed to be doing so with the intent to commit an unlawful act involving force or violence.

(5) As used in this section, the term:

(a) "Dwelling" means a building or conveyance of any kind, including any attached porch, whether the building or conveyance is temporary or permanent, mobile or immobile, which has a roof over it, including a tent, and is designed to be occupied by people lodging therein at night.

(b) "Residence" means a dwelling in which a person resides either temporarily or permanently or is visiting as an invited guest.

(c) "Vehicle" means a conveyance of any kind, whether or not motorized, which is designed to transport people or property.

Recall that fewer than 20 states today recognize the retreat doctrine that traditionally prevailed in English (and Eastern U.S.) self-defense law. See supra, at page 858. Florida was one of those states, until the "Stand Your Ground" law was enacted there in 2005. In those states across the West and South that have already rejected the retreat doctrine, would adoption of a "Stand Your Ground" law change anything?

4. Note that under §776.013(2)(d) of the Florida statute, even police officers might well find themselves subject to "Stand Your Ground" use of lethal force by someone in a home or car—if, for example, they seek to enter the home (acting pursuant to a warrant), but do not announce their presence and identity loudly enough, and assuming that the resident of the home doesn't otherwise have reason to know it's a police officer. (Recall the facts of the Cory Maye case, supra at page 833.) Once again, this rule might seem reasonable enough at first glance—until you consider that the decision about exactly what kind of defensive behavior is "reasonable" initially rests entirely with the resident, subject to later review by a court (but only after there's a very real possibility that a police officer has been shot dead).

In March 2012, Indiana amended its "Stand Your Ground" statute—with the lobbying support of the National Rifle Association—to emphasize the existence of a legal right, under limited circumstances, to use force (including lethal force) even against police officers:

IC 35-41-3-2. Use of force to protect person or property.

. . .

(i) A person is justified in using reasonable force against a public servant if the person reasonably believes the force is necessary to:

(1) protect the person or a third person from what the person reasonably believes to be the imminent use of unlawful force;

(2) prevent or terminate the public servant's unlawful entry of or attack on the person's dwelling, curtilage, or occupied motor vehicle; or

(3) prevent or terminate the public servant's unlawful trespass on or criminal interference with property lawfully in the person's possession, lawfully in possession of a member of the person's immediate family, or belonging to a person whose property the person has authority to protect.

(j) Notwithstanding subsection (i), a person is not justified in using force against a public servant if:

(1) the person is committing or is escaping after the commission of a crime;

(2) the person provokes action by the public servant with intent to cause bodily injury to the public servant;

(3) the person has entered into combat with the public servant or is the initial aggressor, unless the person withdraws from the encounter and communicates to the public servant the intent to do so and the public servant nevertheless continues or threatens to continue unlawful action; or

(4) the person reasonably believes the public servant is:
    (A) acting lawfully; or
    (B) engaged in the lawful execution of the public servant's official duties.
  (k) A person is not justified in using deadly force against a public servant whom the person knows or reasonably should know is a public servant unless:
    (1) the person reasonably believes that the public servant is:
      (A) acting unlawfully; or
      (B) not engaged in the execution of the public servant's official duties; and
    (2) the force is reasonably necessary to prevent serious bodily injury to the person or a third person.

The last part of the amendment, section (k), was added in an effort to reassure police officers that they would not face an increased risk of encountering lethal resistance when serving warrants or making traffic stops. If you were a police officer, would you feel reassured? The president of the Indiana State Fraternal Order of Police, Tim Downs, didn't; he canceled his NRA membership over the amendment. See http://www.bloomberg.com/news/2012-06-05/nra-backed-law-spells-out-when-indianans-may-open-fire-on-police.html.

5. Florida's version of "Stand Your Ground" became the subject of national controversy in connection with the Feb. 26, 2012, shooting death of Trayvon Martin, an unarmed black teenager, in a gated community in Sanford, Florida, by George Zimmerman, head of the local neighborhood watch program. It's important to recognize that, although "Stand Your Ground" was originally cited by the local police as a reason why Zimmerman was initially released from custody, the Florida "Stand Your Ground" law was never *directly* implicated in the Zimmerman case. That's because George Zimmerman claimed that he was jumped, forced to the ground, held there, and pummeled by Trayvon Martin, and thus he did not have any *opportunity* to retreat. For this reason, Zimmerman's defense at trial was based entirely on traditional self-defense. The prosecution, of course, argued that Trayvon Martin was not the aggressor at all, and that George Zimmerman was a self-appointed vigilante who provoked the fight that ultimately led to Trayvon's death. The trial was a classic case of "he said, he said"—that is, a credibility battle over exactly what really happened before the shooting—except, of course, that one of the two participants was dead and could not speak for himself. On July 13, 2013, the jury acquitted George Zimmerman on the charge of second-degree murder, as well as the lesser charge of manslaughter. See http://www.cnn.com/2013/07/13/justice/zimmerman-trial/.

6. In January 2014, another racially charged Florida case of alleged self-defense hit the national media. Michael Dunn, a white, 47-year-old software developer, fired ten gunshots at an SUV occupied by four black teenagers in a convenience-store parking lot in Jacksonville, Florida (about 125 miles from where the Zimmerman case arose). One of the four teens, Jordan Davis, was killed. Davis was unarmed. Dunn claimed, however, that he acted in self-defense, after Davis verbally threatened him and began to emerge from the car holding something that Dunn believed to be a shotgun. The altercation started when Dunn asked the teens to turn down the "thug music" booming from their car stereo, thus leading the media to refer to the case as the "Loud Music Case." At trial, prosecutors argued that Dunn acted not out of reasonable fear, but instead because he was "disrespected" by the four teenagers. Dunn was convicted by a jury of three counts of attempted second-degree murder, plus one count of shooting into an occupied vehicle, but the jury could not reach a verdict on the charge of first-degree murder of Jordan Davis, thus leading to a mistrial on that particular charge. See http://www.huffingtonpost.com/2014/02/15/michael-dunn-verdict_n_4796068.html.

Once again, as in the George Zimmerman case, the Florida "Stand Your Ground" was never *directly* implicated in the Michael Dunn case. That's because, as in the *Zimmerman* case, Dunn argued at trial that he simply had no *opportunity* to retreat—he was facing an imminent and deadly threat, and needed to act in self-defense to protect his life. Nevertheless, the two cases have prompted a national debate over "Stand Your Ground," and whether recognizing a legal right to respond with lethal force to a threat that could be avoided simply by running away might lead to unnecessary deaths of innocent people. See Dan Abrams, ABC News, "No, Florida's Stand Your Ground Law Did Not Determine Either Zimmerman or Dunn Cases," available online at http://abcnews.go.com/US/floridas-stand-ground-law-determine-zimmerman-dunn-cases/story?id=22543929.

B. PUBLIC AUTHORITY

1. Police Use of Force

Tennessee v. Garner

Supreme Court of the United States
471 U.S. 1 (1985)

JUSTICE WHITE delivered the opinion of the Court.

This case requires us to determine the constitutionality of the use of deadly force to prevent the escape of an apparently unarmed suspected felon. We conclude that such force may not be used unless it is necessary to prevent the escape and the officer has probable cause to believe that the suspect poses a significant threat of death or serious physical injury to the officer or others.

I

At about 10:45 P.M. on October 3, 1974, Memphis Police Officers Elton Hymon and Leslie Wright were dispatched to answer a "prowler inside call." Upon arriving at the scene, they saw a woman standing on her porch and gesturing toward the adjacent house. She told them she had heard glass breaking and that "they" or "someone" was breaking in next door. While Wright radioed the dispatcher to say that they were on the scene, Hymon went behind the house. He heard a door slam and saw someone run across the backyard. The fleeing suspect, who was appellee-respondent's decedent, Edward Garner, stopped at a 6-feet-high chain link fence at the edge of the yard. With the aid of a flashlight, Hymon was able to see Garner's face and hands. He saw no sign of a weapon, and, though not certain, was "reasonably sure" and "figured" that Garner was unarmed. He thought Garner was 17 or 18 years old and about 5' 5" or 5' 7" tall.[2] While Garner was crouched at the base of the fence, Hymon called out "police, halt" and took a few steps toward him. Garner then began to climb over the fence. Convinced that, if Garner made it over the fence, he would elude capture,[3] Hymon shot him. The bullet hit Garner in the back of the head. Garner was taken by ambulance to a hospital, where he died on the operating table. Ten dollars and a purse taken from the house were found on his body.

In using deadly force to prevent the escape, Hymon was acting under the authority of a Tennessee statute and pursuant to Police Department policy. The statute provides that

"[i]f, after notice of the intention to arrest the defendant, he either flee or forcibly resist, the officer may use all the necessary means to effect the arrest."

Tenn. Code Ann. 40-7-108 (1982). The Department policy was slightly more restrictive than the statute, but still allowed the use of deadly force in cases of burglary. The incident was reviewed by the Memphis Police Firearm's Review Board and presented to a grand jury. Neither took any action.

---

2. In fact, Garner, an eighth-grader, was 15. He was 5' 4" tall and weighed somewhere around 100 or 110 pounds.

3. When asked at trial why he fired, Hymon stated:

"Well, first of all it was apparent to me from the little bit that I knew about the area at the time that he was going to get away because, number 1, I couldn't get to him. My partner then couldn't find where he was because, you know, he was late coming around. He didn't know where I was talking about. I couldn't get to him because of the fence here, I couldn't have jumped this fence and come up, consequently jumped this fence and caught him before he got away because he was already up on the fence, just one leap and he was already over the fence, and so there is no way that I could have caught him."

He also stated that the area beyond the fence was dark, that he could not have gotten over the fence easily because he was carrying a lot of equipment and wearing heavy boots, and that Garner, being younger and more energetic, could have outrun him.

Garner's father then brought this action in the Federal District Court for the Western District of Tennessee, seeking damages under 42 U.S.C. §1983* for asserted violations of Garner's constitutional rights. The complaint alleged that the shooting violated the Fourth, Fifth, Sixth, Eighth, and Fourteenth Amendments of the United States Constitution. It named as defendants Officer Hymon, the Police Department, its Director, and the Mayor and City of Memphis. After a three-day bench trial, the District Court entered judgment for all defendants. It dismissed the claims against the Mayor and the Director for lack of evidence. It then concluded that Hymon's actions were authorized by the Tennessee statute, which in turn was constitutional. Hymon had employed the only reasonable and practicable means of preventing Garner's escape. Garner had "recklessly and heedlessly attempted to vault over the fence to escape, thereby assuming the risk of being fired upon."

[The U.S. Court of Appeals for the Sixth Circuit affirmed the judgment in favor of Officer Hymon, based on his "good faith reliance" on the Tennessee statute, but remanded for reconsideration of the city's possible liability based on the notion that the city might have a "policy or custom" that led to an unconstitutional use of force by Officer Hymon. On remand, the District Court once again ruled in favor of the city, finding no constitutional violation. The Court of Appeals then reversed, finding that the Tennessee statute unconstitutionally authorized the use of deadly force without regard to the facts of an individual encounter between a police officer and a fleeing felon. The State of Tennessee intervened to defend the statute, and the Supreme Court agreed to review the case. — EDS.]

II

Whenever an officer restrains the freedom of a person to walk away, he has seized that person. United States v. Brignoni-Ponce, 422 U.S. 873, 878 (1975). While it is not always clear just when minimal police interference becomes a seizure, see United States v. Mendenhall, 446 U.S. 544 (1980), there can be no question that apprehension by the use of deadly force is a seizure subject to the reasonableness requirement of the Fourth Amendment.

A

A police officer may arrest a person if he has probable cause to believe that person committed a crime. E.g., United States v. Watson, 423 U.S. 411

---

* This federal statute, enacted shortly after the end of the Civil War, provides: "Every person who, under color of any statute, ordinance, regulation, custom, or usage, of any State or Territory or the District of Columbia, subjects, or causes to be subjected, any citizen of the United States or other person within the jurisdiction thereof to the deprivation of any rights, privileges, or immunities secured by the Constitution and laws, shall be liable to the party injured in an action at law, suit in equity, or other proper proceeding for redress . . . ." — EDS.

(1976). Petitioners and appellant argue that, if this requirement is satisfied, the Fourth Amendment has nothing to say about how that seizure is made. This submission ignores the many cases in which this Court, by balancing the extent of the intrusion against the need for it, has examined the reasonableness of the manner in which a search or seizure is conducted. To determine the constitutionality of a seizure,

> "[w]e must balance the nature and quality of the intrusion on the individual's Fourth Amendment interests against the importance of the governmental interests alleged to justify the intrusion."

United States v. Place, 462 U.S. 696, 703 (1983). We have described "the balancing of competing interests" as "the key principle of the Fourth Amendment." Michigan v. Summers, 452 U.S. 692, 700, n.12 (1981). Because one of the factors is the extent of the intrusion, it is plain that reasonableness depends on not only when a seizure is made, but also how it is carried out. . . .

B

The same balancing process. . . demonstrates that, notwithstanding probable cause to seize a suspect, an officer may not always do so by killing him. The intrusiveness of a seizure by means of deadly force is unmatched. The suspect's fundamental interest in his own life need not be elaborated upon. The use of deadly force also frustrates the interest of the individual, and of society, in judicial determination of guilt and punishment. Against these interests are ranged governmental interests in effective law enforcement.[8] It is argued that overall violence will be reduced by encouraging the peaceful submission of suspects who know that they may be shot if they flee. Effectiveness in making arrests requires the resort to deadly force, or at least the meaningful threat thereof. "Being able to arrest such individuals is a condition precedent to the state's entire system of law enforcement." Brief for Petitioners 14.

---

8. . . . In lamenting the inadequacy of later investigation, the dissent relies on the report of the President's Commission on Law Enforcement and Administration of Justice. It is worth noting that, notwithstanding its awareness of this problem, the Commission itself proposed a policy for use of deadly force arguably even more stringent than the formulation we adopt today. See President's Commission on Law Enforcement and Administration of Justice, Task Force Report: The Police 189 (1967). The Commission proposed that deadly force be used only to apprehend

> "perpetrators who, in the course of their crime, threatened the use of deadly force, or if the officer believes there is a substantial risk that the person whose arrest is sought will cause death or serious bodily harm if his apprehension is delayed."

In addition, the officer would have "to know, as a virtual certainty, that the suspect committed an offense for which the use of deadly force is permissible."

Without in any way disparaging the importance of these goals, we are not convinced that the use of deadly force is a sufficiently productive means of accomplishing them to justify the killing of nonviolent suspects. The use of deadly force is a self-defeating way of apprehending a suspect and so setting the criminal justice mechanism in motion. If successful, it guarantees that that mechanism will not be set in motion. And while the meaningful threat of deadly force might be thought to lead to the arrest of more live suspects by discouraging escape attempts, the presently available evidence does not support this thesis. The fact is that a majority of police departments in this country have forbidden the use of deadly force against nonviolent suspects. If those charged with the enforcement of the criminal law have abjured the use of deadly force in arresting nondangerous felons, there is a substantial basis for doubting that the use of such force is an essential attribute of the arrest power in all felony cases. Petitioners and appellant have not persuaded us that shooting nondangerous fleeing suspects is so vital as to outweigh the suspect's interest in his own life.

The use of deadly force to prevent the escape of all felony suspects, whatever the circumstances, is constitutionally unreasonable. It is not better that all felony suspects die than that they escape. Where the suspect poses no immediate threat to the officer and no threat to others, the harm resulting from failing to apprehend him does not justify the use of deadly force to do so. It is no doubt unfortunate when a suspect who is in sight escapes, but the fact that the police arrive a little late or are a little slower afoot does not always justify killing the suspect. A police officer may not seize an unarmed, nondangerous suspect by shooting him dead. The Tennessee statute is unconstitutional insofar as it authorizes the use of deadly force against such fleeing suspects.

It is not, however, unconstitutional on its face. Where the officer has probable cause to believe that the suspect poses a threat of serious physical harm, either to the officer or to others, it is not constitutionally unreasonable to prevent escape by using deadly force. Thus, if the suspect threatens the officer with a weapon or there is probable cause to believe that he has committed a crime involving the infliction or threatened infliction of serious physical harm, deadly force may be used if necessary to prevent escape, and if, where feasible, some warning has been given. As applied in such circumstances, the Tennessee statute would pass constitutional muster.

III

A

It is insisted that the Fourth Amendment must be construed in light of the common law rule, which allowed the use of whatever force was necessary to effect the arrest of a fleeing felon, though not a misdemeanant. As stated in Hale's posthumously published Pleas of the Crown:

> "[I]f persons that are pursued by these officers for felony or the just suspicion thereof. . . shall not yield themselves to these officers, but shall either resist or fly before they are apprehended or being apprehended shall rescue themselves and resist or fly, so that they cannot be otherwise apprehended, and are upon necessity slain therein, because they cannot be otherwise taken, it is no felony."

2 M. Hale, Historia Placitorum Coronae 85 (1736). See also 4 W. Blackstone, Commentaries *289. Most American jurisdictions also imposed a flat prohibition against the use of deadly force to stop a fleeing misdemeanant, coupled with a general privilege to use such force to stop a fleeing felon. . . .

The State and city argue that, because this was the prevailing rule at the time of the adoption of the Fourth Amendment and for some time thereafter, and is still in force in some States, use of deadly force against a fleeing felon must be "reasonable." It is true that this Court has often looked to the common law in evaluating the reasonableness, for Fourth Amendment purposes, of police activity. On the other hand, it

> "has not simply frozen into constitutional law those law enforcement practices that existed at the time of the Fourth Amendment's passage."

Payton v. New York, 445 U.S. 573, 591, n.33 (1980). Because of sweeping change in the legal and technological context, reliance on the common law rule in this case would be a mistaken literalism that ignores the purposes of a historical inquiry.

B

It has been pointed out many times that the common law rule is best understood in light of the fact that it arose at a time when virtually all felonies were punishable by death.

> "Though effected without the protections and formalities of an orderly trial and conviction, the killing of a resisting or fleeing felon resulted in no greater consequences than those authorized for punishment of the felony of which the individual was charged or suspected."

American Law Institute, Model Penal Code 3.07, Comment 3, p. 56 (Tentative Draft No. 8, 1958) (hereinafter Model Penal Code Comment). Courts have also justified the common law rule by emphasizing the relative dangerousness of felons.

Neither of these justifications makes sense today. Almost all crimes formerly punishable by death no longer are or can be. See, e.g., Enmund v. Florida, 458 U.S. 782 (1982); Coker v. Georgia, 433 U.S. 584 (1977). And while in earlier times "the gulf between the felonies and the minor offences was broad and deep," 2 Pollock & Maitland 467, n.3, today the distinction is minor, and often arbitrary. Many crimes classified as misdemeanors, or nonexistent, at common law are now felonies. These changes have undermined the concept, which was questionable to begin with, that use of deadly force against a fleeing felon is merely a speedier execution of someone who has already forfeited his life. They have also made the assumption that a "felon" is more dangerous than a misdemeanant untenable. Indeed, numerous misdemeanors involve conduct more dangerous than many felonies.

There is an additional reason why the common law rule cannot be directly translated to the present day. The common law rule developed at a time when weapons were rudimentary. Deadly force could be inflicted almost solely in a hand-to-hand struggle during which, necessarily, the safety of the arresting officer was at risk. Handguns were not carried by police officers until the latter half of the last century. L. Kennett & J. Anderson, The Gun in America 150-151 (1975). Only then did it become possible to use deadly force from a distance as a means of apprehension. As a practical matter, the use of deadly force under the standard articulation of the common law rule has an altogether different meaning — and harsher consequences — now than in past centuries. See Wechsler & Michael, A Rationale for the Law of Homicide: I, 37 Colum. L. Rev. 701, 741 (1937). . . .

In short, though the common law pedigree of Tennessee's rule is pure on its face, changes in the legal and technological context mean the rule is distorted almost beyond recognition when literally applied.

C

In evaluating the reasonableness of police procedures under the Fourth Amendment, we have also looked to prevailing rules in individual jurisdictions. The rules in the States are varied. See generally Comment, 18 Ga. L. Rev. 137, 140-144 (1983). Some 19 States have codified the common law rule, though in two of these the courts have significantly limited the statute. Four States, though without a relevant statute, apparently retain the common law rule. Two States have adopted the Model Penal Code's provision verbatim. Eighteen others allow, in slightly varying language, the use of deadly force only if the suspect has committed a felony involving the use or threat of physical or deadly force, or is escaping with a deadly weapon, or is likely to endanger life or inflict serious physical injury if not arrested. Louisiana and Vermont, though without statutes or case law on point, do forbid the use of deadly force to prevent any but violent felonies. The remaining States either have no relevant statute or case law or have positions that are unclear.

It cannot be said that there is a constant or overwhelming trend away from the common law rule. In recent years, some States have reviewed their laws and expressly rejected abandonment of the common law rule. Nonetheless, the long-term movement has been away from the rule that deadly force may be used against any fleeing felon, and that remains the rule in less than half the States.

This trend is more evident and impressive when viewed in light of the policies adopted by the police departments themselves. Overwhelmingly, these are more restrictive than the common law rule. C. Milton, J. Halleck, J. Lardner, & G. Abrecht, Police Use of Deadly Force 45-46 (1977). The Federal Bureau of Investigation and the New York City Police Department, for example, both forbid the use of firearms except when necessary to prevent death or grievous bodily harm. Id. at 40-41. For accreditation by the Commission on Accreditation for Law Enforcement Agencies, a department must restrict the use of deadly force to situations where

> "the officer reasonably believes that the action is in defense of human life . . . or in defense of any person in immediate danger of serious physical injury."

Commission on Accreditation for Law Enforcement Agencies, Inc., Standards for Law Enforcement Agencies 1-2 (1983) (italics deleted). A 1974 study reported that the police department regulations in a majority of the large cities of the United States allowed the firing of a weapon only when a felon presented a threat of death or serious bodily harm. Overall, only 7.5% of departmental and municipal policies explicitly permit the use of deadly force against any felon; 86.8% explicitly do not. See generally W. Geller & K. Karales, Split-Second Decisions 33-42 (1981); Brief for Police Foundation et al. as Amici Curiae. In light of the rules adopted by those who must actually administer them, the older and fading common law view is a dubious indicium of the constitutionality of the Tennessee statute now before us.

D

Actual departmental policies are important for an additional reason. We would hesitate to declare a police practice of long standing "unreasonable" if doing so would severely hamper effective law enforcement. But the indications are to the contrary. There has been no suggestion that crime has worsened in any way in jurisdictions that have adopted, by legislation or departmental policy, rules similar to that announced today. . . .

Nor do we agree with petitioners and appellant that the rule we have adopted requires the police to make impossible, split-second evaluations of unknowable facts. We do not deny the practical difficulties of attempting to assess the suspect's dangerousness. However, similarly difficult judgments must be made by the police in equally uncertain circumstances. Nor is there any indication that, in States that allow the use of deadly force only against dangerous suspects, the standard has been difficult to apply or has led to a rash of litigation involving inappropriate second-guessing of police officers' split-second decisions. Moreover, the highly technical felony/misdemeanor distinction is equally, if not more, difficult to apply in the field. An officer is in no position to know, for example, the precise value of property stolen, or whether the crime was a first or second offense. Finally, as noted above, this claim must be viewed with suspicion in light of the similar self-imposed limitations of so many police departments.

IV

The District Court concluded that Hymon was justified in shooting Garner because state law allows, and the Federal Constitution does not forbid, the use of deadly force to prevent the escape of a fleeing felony suspect if no alternative means of apprehension is available. This conclusion made a determination of Garner's apparent dangerousness unnecessary. The court did find, however, that Garner appeared to be unarmed, though Hymon could not be certain that was the case. Restated in Fourth Amendment terms, this means Hymon had no articulable basis to think Garner was armed.

In reversing, the Court of Appeals accepted the District Court's factual conclusions and held that "the facts, as found, did not justify the use of deadly force." 710 F.2d at 246.

We agree. Officer Hymon could not reasonably have believed that Garner—young, slight, and unarmed—posed any threat. Indeed, Hymon never attempted to justify his actions on any basis other than the need to prevent an escape. . . . Hymon did not have probable cause to believe that Garner, whom he correctly believed to be unarmed, posed any physical danger to himself or others.

The dissent argues that the shooting was justified by the fact that Officer Hymon had probable cause to believe that Garner had committed a nighttime burglary. While we agree that burglary is a serious crime, we cannot agree that it is so dangerous as automatically to justify the use of deadly force. The FBI classifies burglary as a "property," rather than a "violent," crime. See Federal Bureau of Investigation, Uniform Crime Reports, Crime in the United States 1 (1984). Although the armed burglar would present a different situation, the fact that an unarmed suspect has broken into a dwelling at night does not automatically mean he is physically dangerous. This case demonstrates as much. In fact, the available statistics demonstrate that burglaries only rarely involve physical violence. During the 10-year period from 1973-1982, only 3.8% of all burglaries involved violent crime. Bureau of Justice Statistics, Household Burglary 4 (1985).[23] . . .

___

23. . . . The dissent also points out that this 3.8% adds up to 2.8 million violent crimes over a 10-year period, as if to imply that today's holding will let loose 2.8 million violent burglars. The relevant universe is, of course, far smaller. At issue is only that tiny fraction of cases where violence has taken place and an officer who has no other means of apprehending the suspect is unaware of its occurrence.

V

. . . We hold that the statute is invalid insofar as it purported to give Hymon the authority to act as he did. As for the policy of the Police Department, the absence of any discussion of this issue by the courts below, and the uncertain state of the record, preclude any consideration of its validity.

The judgment of the Court of Appeals is affirmed, and the case is remanded for further proceedings consistent with this opinion.

Justice O'Connor, with whom Chief Justice Burger and Justice Rehnquist join, dissenting.

. . . Although the circumstances of this case are unquestionably tragic and unfortunate, our constitutional holdings must be sensitive both to the history of the Fourth Amendment and to the general implications of the Court's reasoning. By disregarding the serious and dangerous nature of residential burglaries and the longstanding practice of many States, the Court effectively creates a Fourth Amendment right allowing a burglary suspect to flee unimpeded from a police officer who has probable cause to arrest, who has ordered the suspect to halt, and who has no means short of firing his weapon to prevent escape. I do not believe that the Fourth Amendment supports such a right, and I accordingly dissent.

. . . For purposes of Fourth Amendment analysis, I agree with the Court that Officer Hymon "seized" Garner by shooting him. Whether that seizure was reasonable, and therefore permitted by the Fourth Amendment, requires a careful balancing of the important public interest in crime prevention and detection and the nature and quality of the intrusion upon legitimate interests of the individual. United States v. Place, 462 U.S. 696, 703 (1983). In striking this balance here, it is crucial to acknowledge that police use of deadly force to apprehend a fleeing criminal suspect falls within the "rubric of police conduct. . . necessarily [involving] swift action predicated upon the on-the-spot observations of the officer on the beat." Terry v. Ohio, 392 U.S. 1, 20 (1968). The clarity of hindsight cannot provide the standard for judging the reasonableness of police decisions made in uncertain and often dangerous circumstances. . . .

Because burglary is a serious and dangerous felony, the public interest in the prevention and detection of the crime is of compelling importance. Where a police officer has probable cause to arrest a suspected burglar, the use of deadly force as a last resort might well be the only means of apprehending the suspect. With respect to a particular burglary, subsequent investigation simply cannot represent a substitute for immediate apprehension of the criminal suspect at the scene. . . .

Against the strong public interests justifying the conduct at issue here must be weighed the individual interests implicated in the use of deadly force by police officers. The majority declares that "[t]he suspect's fundamental interest in his own life need not be elaborated upon." This blithe assertion hardly provides an adequate substitute for the majority's failure to acknowledge the distinctive manner in which the suspect's interest in his life is even exposed to risk. For purposes of this case, we must recall that the police officer, in the course of investigating a nighttime burglary, had reasonable cause to arrest the suspect and ordered him to halt. The officer's use of force resulted because the suspected burglar refused to heed this command and the officer reasonably believed that there was no means short of firing his weapon to apprehend the suspect. Without questioning the importance of a person's interest in his life, I do not think this interest encompasses a right to flee unimpeded from the scene of a burglary. . . .

. . . Admittedly, the events giving rise to this case are, in retrospect, deeply regrettable. No one can view the death of an unarmed and apparently nonviolent 15-year-old without sorrow, much less disapproval. Nonetheless, the reasonableness of Officer Hymon's conduct for purposes of the Fourth Amendment cannot be evaluated by what later appears to have been a preferable course of police action. . . .

The Court's silence on critical factors in the decision to use deadly force simply invites second-guessing of difficult police decisions that must be made quickly in the most trying of circumstances. . . . We can expect an escalating volume of litigation as the lower courts struggle to determine if a police officer's split-second decision to shoot was justified by the danger posed by a particular object and other facts related to the crime. Thus, the majority opinion portends a burgeoning area of Fourth Amendment doctrine concerning the circumstances in which police officers can reasonably employ deadly force.

. . . I cannot accept the majority's creation of a constitutional right to flight for burglary suspects seeking to avoid capture at the scene of the crime. Whatever the constitutional limits on police use of deadly force in order to apprehend a fleeing felon, I do not believe they are exceeded in a case in which a police officer has probable cause to arrest a suspect at the scene of a residential burglary, orders the suspect to halt, and then fires his weapon as a last resort to prevent the suspect's escape into the night. I respectfully dissent.

Notes and Questions

1. Four years after the decision in *Garner*, the Court—in another §1983 case, involving police use of non-deadly force that injured a man whom the police believed to be acting suspiciously, but who actually was a diabetic suffering from an insulin reaction—tried to clarify the governing constitutional standard. The case was Graham v. Connor, 490 U.S. 386 (1989). According to Chief Justice Rehnquist's majority opinion:

. . . In addressing an excessive force claim brought under §1983, analysis begins by identifying the specific constitutional right allegedly infringed by the challenged application of force. . . . In most instances, that will be either the Fourth Amendment's prohibition against unreasonable seizures of the person or the Eighth Amendment's ban on cruel and unusual punishments, which are the two primary sources of constitutional protection against physically abusive governmental conduct. The validity of the claim must then be judged by reference to the specific constitutional standard which governs that right, rather than to some generalized "excessive force" standard. See Tennessee v. Garner, 471 U.S. at 7-22 (claim of excessive force to effect arrest analyzed under a Fourth Amendment standard); Whitley v. Albers, 475 U.S. 312, 318-326 (1986) (claim of excessive force to subdue convicted prisoner analyzed under an Eighth Amendment standard).

Where, as here, the excessive force claim arises in the context of an arrest or investigatory stop of a free citizen, it is most properly characterized as one invoking the protections of the Fourth Amendment, which guarantees citizens the right "to be secure in their persons. . . against unreasonable. . . seizures" of the person. This much is clear from our decision in Tennessee v. Garner. . . .

. . . Today we make explicit what was implicit in *Garner's* analysis, and hold that all claims that law enforcement officers have used excessive force—deadly or not—in the course of an arrest, investigatory stop, or other "seizure" of a free citizen should be analyzed under the Fourth Amendment and its "reasonableness" standard, rather than under a "substantive due process" approach. Because the Fourth Amendment provides an explicit textual source of constitutional protection against this sort of physically intrusive governmental conduct, that Amendment, not the more generalized notion of "substantive due process," must be the guide for analyzing these claims.

Determining whether the force used to effect a particular seizure is "reasonable" under the Fourth Amendment requires a careful balancing of "the nature and quality of the intrusion on the individual's Fourth Amendment interests" against the countervailing governmental interests at stake. [Garner,] 471 U.S. at 8. Our Fourth Amendment jurisprudence has long recognized that the right to make an arrest or investigatory stop necessarily carries with it the right to use some degree of physical coercion or threat thereof to effect it. See Terry v. Ohio, 392 U.S. 1, 22-27 (1968). Because "[t]he test of reasonableness under the Fourth Amendment is not capable of precise definition or mechanical application," Bell v. Wolfish, 441 U.S. 520, 559 (1979), however, its proper application requires careful attention to the facts and circumstances of each particular case, including the severity of the crime at issue, whether the suspect poses an immediate threat to the safety of the officers or others, and whether he is actively resisting arrest or attempting to evade arrest by flight. See Garner, 471 U.S. at 8-9 (the question is "whether the totality of the circumstances justifie[s] a particular sort of. . . seizure").

The "reasonableness" of a particular use of force must be judged from the perspective of a reasonable officer on the scene, rather than with the 20/20 vision of hindsight. The Fourth Amendment is not violated by an arrest based on probable cause, even though the wrong person is arrested,

Hill v. California, 401 U.S. 797 (1971), nor by the mistaken execution of a valid search warrant on the wrong premises, Maryland v. Garrison, 480 U.S. 79 (1987). With respect to a claim of excessive force, the same standard of reasonableness at the moment applies: "Not every push or shove, even if it may later seem unnecessary in the peace of a judge's chambers," Johnson v. Glick, 481 F.2d 1028, 1033 (2d Cir. 1973), violates the Fourth Amendment. The calculus of reasonableness must embody allowance for the fact that police officers are often forced to make split-second judgments—in circumstances that are tense, uncertain, and rapidly evolving—about the amount of force that is necessary in a particular situation.

As in other Fourth Amendment contexts, however, the "reasonableness" inquiry in an excessive force case is an objective one: the question is whether the officers' actions are "objectively reasonable" in light of the facts and circumstances confronting them, without regard to their underlying intent or motivation. See Scott v. United States, 436 U.S. 128, 137-139 (1978); see also Terry v. Ohio, 392 U.S. at 21 (in analyzing the reasonableness of a particular search or seizure, "it is imperative that the facts be judged against an objective standard"). An officer's evil intentions will not make a Fourth Amendment violation out of an objectively reasonable use of force; nor will an officer's good intentions make an objectively unreasonable use of force constitutional. See Scott v. United States, supra, at 138, citing United States v. Robinson, 414 U.S. 218 (1973).

Because petitioner's excessive force claim is one arising under the Fourth Amendment, the Court of Appeals erred in consider[ing] whether the individual officers acted in "good faith" or "maliciously and sadistically for the very purpose of causing harm" . . . . We do not agree with the Court of Appeals' suggestion that the "malicious and sadistic" inquiry is merely another way of describing conduct that is objectively unreasonable under the circumstances. . . . The Fourth Amendment inquiry is one of "objective reasonableness" under the circumstances, and subjective concepts like "malice" and "sadism" have no proper place in that inquiry.[12]

490 U.S. at 394-99. Does *Graham* succeed in clarifying the standard? If you were a police officer, would you feel like you understood the Fourth Amendment limits on your use of force?

2. The question of police use of deadly force has erupted onto the national scene in connection with the police-action shooting deaths of a number of

---

12. Of course, in assessing the credibility of an officer's account of the circumstances that prompted the use of force, a factfinder may consider, along with other factors, evidence that the officer may have harbored ill-will toward the citizen. See Scott v. United States, 436 U.S. 128, 139, n.13 (1978). Similarly, the officer's objective "good faith"—that is, whether he could reasonably have believed that the force used did not violate the Fourth Amendment—may be relevant to the availability of the qualified immunity defense to monetary liability under §1983. See Anderson v. Creighton, 483 U.S. 635 (1987). Since no claim of qualified immunity has been raised in this case, however, we express no view on its proper application in excessive force cases that arise under the Fourth Amendment.

unarmed black men, including Michael Brown in Ferguson, Missouri; Eric Harris in Tulsa, Oklahoma; Samuel DuBose in Cincinnati, Ohio; Jonathan Ferrell in Charlotte, North Carolina; Walter Scott in Charleston, South Carolina; and 12-year-old Tamir Rice in a public park in Cleveland, Ohio. These deaths and several others (as well as the killings of Trayvon Martin and Jordan Davis by white civilians, see supra at page 873) gave rise to the "Black Lives Matter" political movement. In at least some of the cases, the police officers responsible for the shootings eventually were charged with homicide crimes. In most, they were not.

Perhaps the most prominent of the cases was the shooting death of Michael Brown by white police officer Darren Wilson in Ferguson, Missouri, a poor and largely black suburb of St. Louis, on August 9, 2014. The killing of Michael Brown led to weeks of protests, some peaceful and some not so peaceful. The county prosecutor, Robert P. McCullough, convened a grand jury to consider criminal charges against Darren Wilson; after hearing testimony from 60 witnesses over the course of three months of hearings, on November 24, 2014, the grand jury declined to indict Wilson. Federal authorities also investigated, trying to decide whether to charge Wilson with a federal civil rights crime.** On March 4, 2015, the U.S. Department of Justice issued a lengthy report clearing Wilson, finding insufficient credible evidence to contradict Wilson's account of the facts: that Brown reached into Wilson's patrol car, punched him, and tried to grab his gun, before first running away but then charging back at Wilson, at which point Wilson—fearing for his life—shot Brown at least six times, including twice in the head.

3. How, exactly, does the criminal law apply to police use of deadly force? The answer is surprisingly opaque—possibly because the common law of crimes and defenses evolved long before the creation of modern, professionalized police departments. In an era when private citizens frequently had to enforce their own remedies for crimes, the common law had to devise rules to govern the private use of force. "The oddity is that with the rise of professional police forces and the constitutionalization of excessive force regulation, the federal law governing police uses of force has remained poorly developed." See Rachel A. Harmon, When Is Police Violence Justified?, 102 Nw. U. L. Rev. 1119, 1149 (2008).

** See 18 U.S.C. §242: "Whoever, under color of any law, statute, ordinance, regulation, or custom, willfully subjects any person . . . to the deprivation of any rights, privileges, or immunities secured or protected by the Constitution or laws of the United States, or to different punishments, pains, or penalties, on account of such person being an alien, or by reason of his color, or race, than are prescribed for the punishment of citizens, shall be fined under this title or imprisoned not more than one year, or both. . . ." Substantially greater penalties apply in cases involving bodily injury or death, or the use or threatened use of a dangerous weapon.

As a starting point, police officers often can benefit from the same defenses to criminal liability that would apply to civilians. We have already seen that civilians may use deadly force in self-defense (or defense of another), as well as when the "castle" or "Stand Your Ground" doctrines apply. The same is true for police officers—indeed, self-defense was the primary ground upon which the decision was made not to prosecute Darren Wilson for the killing of Michael Brown. Even here, however, there are important differences—such as the fact that police officers are legally obligated *not* to retreat in situations where civilians might have to. There are also interesting questions without clear answers. For example: In the context of self-defense, should the behavior of police officers be judged by the same standard as that of civilians? Or should police officers be held to a higher standard because of their training and experience—which, one might imagine, should make them more capable of responding to possible threats in a controlled manner that can help to preserve and protect the lives of both the police officer *and* the suspect? (This question may be especially relevant in the all-too-common context of police interactions with disruptive and potentially violent persons who are suffering from mental illnesses, drug addictions, or—as in Graham v. Connor—insulin reactions.) On the other hand, should police officers be allowed to use deadly force in situations where a civilian might not—precisely because, based on their training and experience, they might perceive a particular threat as more dangerous than a civilian would?

In addition, police officers also can benefit from a specialized "public authority" defense that would not normally apply to private citizens (but see Section B.2, supra). The "public authority" defense originated in the common law, but is often written into modern state criminal statutes. Here's one traditional example of such a statute, from the Mississippi Code (note that this statute also contains provisions about self-defense, defense of another, defense of property, the "castle" doctrine, and "Stand Your Ground"):

§97-3-15. Homicide; justifiable homicide; use of defensive force; duty to retreat

(1) The killing of a human being by the act, procurement or omission of another shall be justifiable in the following cases:

(a) When committed by public officers, or those acting by their aid and assistance, in obedience to any judgment of a competent court;

(b) When necessarily committed by public officers, or those acting by their command in their aid and assistance, in overcoming actual resistance to the execution of some legal process, or to the discharge of any other legal duty;

(c) When necessarily committed by public officers, or those acting by their command in their aid and assistance, in retaking any felon who has been rescued or has escaped;

(d) When necessarily committed by public officers, or those acting by their command in their aid and assistance, in arresting any felon fleeing from justice;

(e) When committed by any person in resisting any attempt unlawfully to kill such person or to commit any felony upon him, or upon or in any dwelling, in any occupied vehicle, in any place of business, in any place of employment or in the immediate premises thereof in which such person shall be;

(f) When committed in the lawful defense of one's own person or any other human being, where there shall be reasonable ground to apprehend a design to commit a felony or to do some great personal injury, and there shall be imminent danger of such design being accomplished;

(g) When necessarily committed in attempting by lawful ways and means to apprehend any person for any felony committed;

(h) When necessarily committed in lawfully suppressing any riot or in lawfully keeping and preserving the peace; and

(i) When necessarily committed in the performance of duty as a member of a church or place of worship security program as described in Section 45-9-171.

(2)(a) As used in subsection (1)(c) and (d) of this section, the term "when necessarily committed" means that a public officer or a person acting by or at the officer's command, aid or assistance is authorized to use such force as necessary in securing and detaining the felon offender, overcoming the offender's resistance, preventing the offender's escape, recapturing the offender if the offender escapes or in protecting himself or others from bodily harm; but such officer or person shall not be authorized to resort to deadly or dangerous means when to do so would be unreasonable under the circumstances. The public officer or person acting by or at the officer's command may act upon a reasonable apprehension of the surrounding circumstances; however, such officer or person shall not use excessive force or force that is greater than reasonably necessary in securing and detaining the offender, overcoming the offender's resistance, preventing the offender's escape, recapturing the offender if the offender escapes or in protecting himself or others from bodily harm.

(b) As used in subsection (1)(c) and (d) of this section the term "felon" shall include an offender who has been convicted of a felony and shall also include an offender who is in custody, or whose custody is being sought, on a charge or for an offense which is punishable, upon conviction, by death or confinement in the Penitentiary.

(c) As used in subsections (1)(e) . . . of this section, "dwelling" means a building or conveyance of any kind that has a roof over it, whether the building or conveyance is temporary or permanent, mobile or immobile, including a tent, that is designed to be occupied by people lodging therein at night, including any attached porch.

Here is the Washington version (note that Washington is, generally speaking, a Model Penal Code state):

§9A.16.040. Justifiable homicide or use of deadly force by public officer, peace officer, person aiding.

(1) Homicide or the use of deadly force is justifiable in the following cases:

(a) When a public officer is acting in obedience to the judgment of a competent court; or

(b) When necessarily used by a peace officer to overcome actual resistance to the execution of the legal process, mandate, or order of a court or officer, or in the discharge of a legal duty.

(c) When necessarily used by a peace officer or person acting under the officer's command and in the officer's aid:

(i) To arrest or apprehend a person who the officer reasonably believes has committed, has attempted to commit, is committing, or is attempting to commit a felony;

(ii) To prevent the escape of a person from a federal or state correctional facility or in retaking a person who escapes from such a facility; or

(iii) To prevent the escape of a person from a county or city jail or holding facility if the person has been arrested for, charged with, or convicted of a felony; or

(iv) To lawfully suppress a riot if the actor or another participant is armed with a deadly weapon.

(2) In considering whether to use deadly force under subsection (1)(c) of this section, to arrest or apprehend any person for the commission of any crime, the peace officer must have probable cause to believe that the suspect, if not apprehended, poses a threat of serious physical harm to the officer or a threat of serious physical harm to others. Among the circumstances which may be considered by peace officers as a "threat of serious physical harm" are the following:

(a) The suspect threatens a peace officer with a weapon or displays a weapon in a manner that could reasonably be construed as threatening; or

(b) There is probable cause to believe that the suspect has committed any crime involving the infliction or threatened infliction of serious physical harm. Under these circumstances deadly force may also be used if necessary to prevent escape from the officer, where, if feasible, some warning is given.

(3) A public officer or peace officer shall not be held criminally liable for using deadly force without malice and with a good faith belief that such act is justifiable pursuant to this section.

(4) This section shall not be construed as . . . [p]reventing a law enforcement agency from adopting standards pertaining to its use of deadly force that are more restrictive than this section.

And Missouri—where the Ferguson incident occurred—has amended its statute, effective January 1, 2017, to impose new limits on the police use of force:

1. A law enforcement officer need not retreat or desist from efforts to effect the arrest, or from efforts to prevent the escape from custody, of a

person he or she reasonably believes to have committed an offense because of resistance or threatened resistance of the arrestee. In addition to the use of physical force authorized under other sections of this chapter, a law enforcement officer is, subject to the provisions of subsections 2 and 3, justified in the use of such physical force as he or she reasonably believes is immediately necessary to effect the arrest or to prevent the escape from custody.

2. The use of any physical force in making an arrest is not justified under this section unless the arrest is lawful or the law enforcement officer reasonably believes the arrest is lawful, and the amount of physical force used was objectively reasonable in light of the totality of the particular facts and circumstances confronting the officer on the scene, without regard to the officer's underlying intent or motivation.

3. In effecting an arrest or in preventing an escape from custody, a law enforcement officer is justified in using deadly force only:

(1) When deadly force is authorized under other sections of this chapter; or

(2) When the officer reasonably believes that such use of deadly force is immediately necessary to effect the arrest or prevent an escape from custody and also reasonably believes that the person to be arrested:

(a) Has committed or attempted to commit a felony offense involving the infliction or threatened infliction of serious physical injury; or

(b) Is attempting to escape by use of a deadly weapon or dangerous instrument; or

(c) May otherwise endanger life or inflict serious physical injury to the officer or others unless arrested without delay.

4. The defendant shall have the burden of injecting the issue of justification under this section.

See Mo. Rev. Stat. §563.046.1.

4. So what is the relationship between the "public authority" defense under state law and the Supreme Court's constitutional decisions in *Garner* and *Graham*? The answer is, perhaps somewhat less than one might expect. The *Garner* Court, in particular, clearly believed that police use of deadly force should be much more limited, in modern times, than it was historically at common law. But *Garner* and *Graham* are not criminal cases; instead, they are about when police officers can be sued successfully for violating a person's Fourth Amendment constitutional rights. (In addition, because *Garner* and *Graham* deal with the governing legal standard for Fourth Amendment violations, they also help to determine when evidence seized from a suspect following an unlawful police use of force may be barred from a subsequent criminal trial of the suspect, pursuant to the Fourth Amendment's Exclusionary Rule.) And although the states must obey the U.S. Constitution, they are not required to criminalize every instance of unconstitutional behavior—even by state officials such as police officers.

As the *Garner* Court explained, by 1985, almost half of the states had abandoned the old common-law rule that allowed police to use deadly force to apprehend *any* "fleeing felon." Since 1985, about a dozen more states have chosen, by legislation or by court interpretation, to conform their criminal laws more closely to the new Fourth Amendment standard for "fleeing felon" cases articulated in *Garner.* But not all states have done so—roughly a dozen states still adhere to the old common-law rule (including, for example, Mississippi—see the statute reproduced in Note 3 above). And some states that abandoned the common-law approach decided not to go quite as far as the *Garner* Court in restricting police use of deadly force—or to go even further. The result is a totally confusing patchwork of differing state laws about police use of deadly force. See generally Chad Flanders & Joseph C. Welling, Police Use of Deadly Force: State Statutes 30 Years After *Garner*, St. Louis U. L.J. Online, http://www.slu.edu/colleges/law/journal/police-use-of-deadly-force-state-statues-30-years-after-garner/ (posted Jan. 15, 2016). Moreover, prosecutorial (and grand jury) discretion virtually guarantees that at least some unconstitutional uses of force by the police will go unpunished by the criminal law—even in those states where the relevant state statute would allow for criminal charges against the police officer.

The unfortunate bottom line is that decisions about charging police officers with crimes in situations involving the allegedly unlawful police use of force are likely to remain—for the foreseeable future—wildly inconsistent, hugely controversial, and heavily influenced by shifting political winds.

2. Private Citizens and the Public Authority Defense

United States v. Burt

United States Court of Appeals for the Ninth Circuit
410 F.3d 1100 (2005)

BRIGHT, Circuit Judge.

The government filed a two-count indictment charging appellant Marnie Ann Burt with conspiracy to transport illegal aliens and transportation of illegal aliens. Burt requested jury instructions on her apparent public authority defense. The district court refused to give Burt's requested jury instructions, and the jury found Burt guilty on both counts. Burt appeals and argues the district court erred in refusing to instruct the jury on her public authority defense. . . . We reverse and remand for a new trial.

On May 22, 2003, Border Patrol Agents Mike Van Edwards and Brian Brown arrested Burt for transporting illegal aliens. Burt told the agents that she had information regarding a plan to transport illegal aliens in a semi-trailer that coming weekend. The agents were interested in this information. Agent Brown decided not to recommend that Burt be prosecuted, and Agent Van Edwards contends he told Burt she would not be prosecuted. Burt agreed to come back the next day to meet with the agents regarding her knowledge of the semi-trailer plan. Burt contends that the agents told her that a warrant would be issued for her arrest if she did not attend the meeting.

The next day, May 23, 2003, Agent George Scott interviewed Burt. Agents Brown, Van Edwards, and Mark Friend were also present at the interview. . . . Agent Scott contends he told Burt that she was not a confidential informant, that she should not do anything illegal, and that she should contact him with any information. Burt claims that the agents instructed her to get information and told her not to do anything illegal. Burt contends, however, that the agents told her that she would not be doing anything illegal as long as she was gathering information for the agents. Burt never contacted the agents after the interview.

On May 28, 2003, border patrol agents arrested Burt for transporting illegal aliens in a van. Burt told the agents that she was working for Agent Van Edwards. Shortly after Agent Scott heard that Burt had been arrested, he destroyed his notes of the May 23 meeting.

The government filed an indictment, charging Burt with conspiracy to transport illegal aliens and transportation of illegal aliens. At trial, Burt testified that she believed she was properly collecting information for the agents. At the close of evidence, Burt's counsel and the district court discussed Burt's requested jury instructions, which included the model Ninth Circuit public authority instruction. . . . The district court refused to give Burt's requested public authority jury instruction.[1] The jury found Burt guilty of both counts in the indictment.

---

1. Burt's other defenses, including equitable estoppel and entrapment by estoppel, had been rejected . . . [by] the district court's pretrial order. During trial, however, the only issue raised on jury instructions was Burt's requested public authority instruction. The Ninth Circuit Model Criminal Jury Instruction [on] Public Authority or Government Authority Defense reads:

> If a defendant engages in conduct violative of a criminal statute at the request of a government enforcement officer, with the reasonable belief that the defendant is acting as an authorized government agent to assist in law enforcement activity, then the defendant may not be convicted of violating the criminal statute, because the requisite criminal intent is lacking. The government must prove beyond a reasonable doubt that the defendant did not have a reasonable belief that [he] [she] was acting as an authorized government agent to assist in law enforcement activity at the time of the offense charged in the indictment.

The district court rejected Burt's requested public authority instruction, noting that Burt's theory is "covered by the offense instructions."

Burt filed a motion for a new trial, challenging the district court's decision not to give her requested instructions. The district court denied Burt's motion. The district court sentenced Burt to concurrent terms of thirty-six months in prison on both charges, to be followed by thirty-six months of supervised release. Burt filed a timely notice of appeal, and this appeal followed.

. . . Burt contends that the district court erred in refusing to give her requested apparent public authority jury instruction. Burt argues that a jury with appropriate instructions should decide whether her belief, that her conduct on May 28 was for the sole purpose of gathering information for the agents, was reasonable.

The district court erred in refusing to give Burt's requested jury instructions on the public authority defense. At trial, Burt testified that the agents told her that as long as she was gathering information for the agents her actions would not be illegal. Burt also noted that the agents gave her no instructions on how to conduct herself. Agent Scott testified at the evidentiary hearing that Burt "should not be committing an offense if she's working for me." A jury could believe Burt and interpret Agent Scott's statement to mean that if Burt was working for Scott her actions would not be illegal. In addition, Agent Scott destroyed his notes from his interview with Burt, which was the only contemporaneous record of the interview. The magistrate judge correctly noted that "when government agents destroy evidence, they place their own credibility in serious jeopardy."

Although Burt's evidence may not be strong, Burt has presented sufficient evidence to justify jury instructions on her public authority defense. The evidence, taken in its best light for Burt, could indicate that Burt's participation in the May 28 transportation of illegal aliens served the purpose of Burt gathering information about the crime, which could be reported to the agents. Burt's arrest, however, terminated her opportunity to make such a report. A jury could have determined, based on the evidence presented, that on May 28 Burt reasonably believed that she was working for the agents. Burt was, therefore, entitled to instructions relating to her public authority defense, and the district court erred in refusing to instruct the jury on the defense.[2]

---

2. As noted in footnote 1, the district court, in its pretrial order, rejected Burt's other defenses, including Burt's entrapment by estoppel defense. . . . We note that the difference between the defenses of entrapment by estoppel and public authority are "not great"; however, there are some differences between the defenses. United States v. Burrows, 36 F.3d 875, 882 (9th Cir. 1994). The defense of entrapment by estoppel is available when "a government official commits an error and the defendant relies on [the error] and thereby violates the law." Id. The public authority defense is available when "a government official makes some statement or performs some act and the defendant relies on it, possibly mistakenly, and commits an offense" by relying on the government official. Id.

Based on the instructions given, the jury would have to find Burt guilty even if the jury believed Burt was working for the agents, because Burt had the intent to transport illegal aliens into the United States. Therefore, the district court's error in refusing to instruct the jury on Burt's public authority defense was prejudicial. . . .

People v. Chacon

Supreme Court of California
40 Cal. 4th 558; 150 P.3d 755 (2007)

Opinion by CORRIGAN, J.

Maria Socorro Chacon was charged with violating Government Code section 1090 by holding a financial interest in a contract made by the public agency of which she was a member.[1] The trial court ruled in limine that defendant could assert the defense of entrapment by estoppel. As a result, the People announced they could not proceed and the court dismissed the case. . . . On appeal, the People challenged the recognition of entrapment by estoppel, a question of first impression. The Court of Appeal held it was error to allow the defense, and reversed the dismissal order. We granted defendant's petition for review to consider . . . whether the entrapment by estoppel defense is available under the circumstances of this case.

We conclude that . . . an entrapment by estoppel defense is not available in this case. Accordingly, we affirm the judgment of the Court of Appeal.

FACTUAL AND PROCEDURAL BACKGROUND

Defendant, while a member of the Bell Gardens City Council, sought and obtained appointment as city manager. Her conduct in securing that position resulted in criminal charges under Government Code section 1090.

Defendant solicited the support of fellow Councilmember Rogelio Rodriguez, advising him of her desired salary and terms. However, the Bell Gardens Municipal Code provided that a council member was ineligible for appointment for one year following his or her departure from the council. City Attorney Arnoldo Beltran drafted an ordinance eliminating the waiting period, and Councilmember Pedro Aceituno placed it on the council agenda. Defendant joined the other council members in voting unanimously for the ordinance.

---

1. Government Code section 1090 states in pertinent part: "Members of the Legislature, state, county, district, judicial district, and city officers or employees shall not be financially interested in any contract made by them in their official capacity, or by any body or board of which they are members."

The council met in a special closed session to choose a city manager. Defendant excused herself from this session, but remained in a nearby office. During a break, City Attorney Beltran asked Councilmember Aceituno to meet with defendant and the mayor to discuss defendant's appointment and contract terms. After Aceituno returned to the session, the council approved defendant's appointment, but modified her requested terms. The council then announced its decision in a public session. Defendant accepted the appointment, resigned from the council and signed an employment contract, approved by Beltran.

Defendant was charged with violating Government Code section 1090 because, as a city council member, she had "participated in making or causing to be made . . . for the Bell Gardens City Council [an employment contract] in which she was financially interested or had the expectation of financial interest." By pretrial motion, defendant informed the court she sought to call Beltran as a witness. She represented that Beltran advised her on the legality of her efforts to become city manager and was actively involved in the appointment process. Concerned that Beltran might invoke his Fifth Amendment privilege not to testify, defendant asked the court to grant him use immunity. By separate motion, the prosecutor sought to exclude evidence of Beltran's advice as irrelevant, arguing that because defendant was charged with a general intent crime, advice of counsel was not a defense.

On the eve of trial, defendant advised the court that she intended to assert the defense of "entrapment by estoppel." Citing United States v. Tallmadge, 829 F.2d 767 (9th Cir. 1987), she contended that the defense, based on federal due process, applied because she relied on advice from a government official that her conduct was legal. The court declined to confer immunity on the city attorney, and took the novel question of the defense under submission.

The court ultimately denied the motion to exclude evidence of Beltran's advice and ruled that defendant could present evidence of entrapment by estoppel. The court expressed doubt that a city official's advice could bind the state, but felt compelled to follow Cox v. Louisiana, 379 U.S. 559 (1965). In Cox, the United States Supreme Court reversed a conviction because the defendant had acted at the direction of the local police chief. Applying Cox, the court ruled that it would "permit" the defense, noting the jury must determine whether defendant reasonably relied on Beltran's advice.

The prosecutor called the ruling a "devastating development," and asked for a continuance to seek writ review. Defendant objected that she was ready for trial immediately. The court agreed that its recognition of entrapment by estoppel in these circumstances was a "fair question for appeal," but expressed concern at granting a continuance over defendant's objection.

When the prosecutor asked whether the court intended to instruct on the newly recognized defense, the court replied that it would do so if warranted by the evidence. The prosecutor responded, "[T]he People are announcing that we're going to be unable to proceed to trial." The court then dismissed the case. . . .

The trial court incorporated its ruling in the minutes: "The court denies the People's motion to exclude testimony regarding advice of counsel to defendant by the Bell Gardens City Attorney. As a general matter, advice of counsel is not a defense in actions under Government Code sections 1090 and 1097," which the court determined were general intent crimes.[5] "However, in this case defendant has asserted the defense of entrapment by estopp[el]." The minutes also reflect that the court had "not settle[d] upon the language of any jury instructions, but if defendant's evidence established the necessary elements of the defense the court would give the jury an appropriate instruction. The People then announced they were unable to proceed."

The People appealed . . . from "the orders denying the People's motion to exclude evidence and dismissing the case. . . ." The Court of Appeal considered the merits of the in limine ruling. It assumed without deciding that the defense of entrapment by estoppel is recognized in California and that defendant would present sufficient evidence at trial to warrant an appropriate instruction. Unlike the trial court, the Court of Appeal distinguished Cox v. Louisiana, supra, 379 U.S. 559, on the basis that the police official in Cox was responsible for administering and enforcing the particular statute at issue. The Court of Appeal concluded that the Bell Gardens City Attorney has neither enforcement nor regulatory authority over criminal conflict of interest statutes. Thus, as a matter of law, the city attorney did not have the power to bind the state to an erroneous interpretation of the conflict of interest statutes. The Court of Appeal reversed the order of dismissal. It then directed the trial court to exclude evidence of, and deny instruction on, the defense.

DISCUSSION

. . . In a pretrial memorandum, defendant argued, ". . . Mrs. Chacon relied upon the legal advice and actions of the Bell Garden's [sic] City Attorney when she entered into that employment contract [as city manager.]"

At oral argument, defense counsel requested immunity for City Attorney Beltran by making an offer of proof as to what Beltran "could say" at trial. Defense counsel recounted Beltran's anticipated testimony as follows:

> ". . . I was asked whether this waiting period was essential under state law, or whether we could adopt the ordinance that we finally adopted. I ordered my subordinate . . . to do a memo on that. I took that memo . . . and drafted a statute. I put that statute on the agenda. I had the council vote on it. I was

---

5. Government Code §1097 prescribes criminal penalties for persons who "willfully" violate Government Code §1090.

there to explain anything they wanted. . . . [A]s I drafted the statute and as I said in the statute, the waiting period was not required by state law.[9] And if we got rid of the waiting period, we would be in accordance with state law. I checked with other municipalities. They didn't have a waiting period. I put it on the agenda for a first reading. After it was put on for first reading, we had a waiting period. It was put on for a second reading. There were comments. *I spoke to Mrs. Chacon about whether or not this statute was a legal statute, and her actions, if she became city manager or any council member became city manager, whether that would be legal. I authorized that as yes, it would be in compliance with state law. And actions were taken with regard to my advice.* . . . [O]n December 7th, I placed on the agenda the appointment of Mrs. Chacon to be . . . City Manager. I always do that. I asked Mr. Aceituno to see what she wanted as far as salary. I was in a closed session with the rest of the council members talking about the legality of a city councilman becoming city manager, about the terms and contracts of employment, about what the requirements were for city manager."

(Italics added.) According to the defense offer of proof, Beltran relayed the council's salary offer and contract terms to defendant and drafted the employment contract.

Defense counsel also said Beltran would testify:

"I urged Mrs. Chacon to become city manager. I thought she would be a good city manager. I thought it would be good for the city of Bell Gardens, and I prevailed upon her to sign the contract and give it a try. I told her that if she became city manager, that was an automatic resignation from the city council, and *I never gave any indication that there was anything improper about this entire situation.*"

(Italics added.) Defense counsel advised the trial court that witnesses other than Beltran could provide some, but not all of this information.

Entrapment by estoppel, based on principles of federal due process, has been recognized by the federal courts and in some sister states. The defense evolved from three United States Supreme Court opinions, although none used the term "entrapment by estoppel." The concept was first applied in Raley v. Ohio, 360 U.S. 423 (1959). Defendants there were convicted of contempt for refusing to answer questions before Ohio's Un-American Activities Commission. The defendants had invoked their privilege against self-incrimination after being advised of their right to do so by the commission chairman. Id. at 424-425. The advice, however, was contrary to the Ohio immunity statute, which eliminated the availability of the privilege for persons testifying before legislative committees. Id. at 431. The United States Supreme Court held that the contempt convictions violated due process: "After the Commission, speaking for the State, acted as it did, to sustain the Ohio Supreme Court's judgment would be to sanction an indefensible sort

---

9. The People do not dispute that elimination of the one-year waiting period was lawful.

of entrapment by the State—convicting a citizen for exercising a privilege which the State had clearly told him was available to him." Id. at 425-426.

In Cox v. Louisiana, the Supreme Court applied *Raley* to reverse the convictions of protestors arrested for picketing across the street from a courthouse. The leader of the demonstration had been given permission by the police chief to demonstrate at the location. The demonstrators were nevertheless arrested and convicted under a state statute barring certain demonstrations "near" any courthouse. *Cox*, supra, 379 U.S. at 568-571. In reversing the convictions, the Supreme Court observed:

> "[T]he highest police officials of the city, in the presence of the Sheriff and Mayor, in effect told the demonstrators that they could meet where they did. . . . [A]ppellant was advised that a demonstration at the place it was held would not be one 'near' the courthouse within the terms of the statute. . . . The Due Process Clause does not permit convictions to be obtained under such circumstances."

379 U.S. at 571.

In United States v. Pennsylvania Chemical Corp., 411 U.S. 655 (1973), the court considered the defense in a regulatory setting involving a corporate defendant found to have discharged refuse into navigable waters. The Supreme Court, relying on *Raley* and *Cox*, held the defendant should have been allowed to present a defense that it had been misled by administrative regulations which appeared to permit the defendant's actions. Id. at 670-675.

Federal cases applying the entrapment by estoppel defense, while varying slightly in their formulation, rest on the premise that the government may not actively provide assurances that conduct is lawful, then prosecute those who act in reasonable reliance on those assurances.[10] Under these

---

10. See, e.g., United States v. Batterjee, 361 F.3d 1210, 1216 (9th Cir. 2004) (a defendant asserting the defense of entrapment by estoppel has the burden of proving that an authorized government official, empowered to render the asserted erroneous advice, and who has been made aware of all the relevant necessary facts, affirmatively told the defendant the proscribed conduct was permissible and that defendant reasonably relied on the erroneous advice); United States v. Funches, 135 F.3d 1405, 1407 (11th Cir. 1998) (to successfully assert this defense, a defendant must actually and reasonably rely on a point of law misrepresented by an official of the state); United States v. West Indies Transport, Inc., 127 F.3d 299, 313 (3d Cir. 1997) (entrapment by estoppel applies when the defendant establishes that a government official told him the conduct was legal; the defendant relied on the official's statements; and the defendant's reliance was reasonable and in good faith based on the identity of the official, the point of law represented, and the substance of the official's statement); United States v. Trevino-Martinez, 86 F.3d 65, 69 (5th Cir. 1996) (criminal defendant may be entitled to raise a defense of entrapment by estoppel only when a government official or agent actively assures a defendant that certain conduct is legal and the defendant, reasonably relying on that advice, continues or initiates the conduct); United States v. Levin, 973 F.2d 463, 468 (6th Cir. 1992) ("To determine the availability of the defense, the court must conclude that (1) a government must have announced that the charged criminal act was legal; (2) the defendant relied on the government announcement; (3) the defendant's reliance was reasonable; and (4) given the defendant's reliance, the prosecution would be unfair").

limited circumstances, fundamental fairness supports the defense, even when the prosecution can prove each element of the crime. . . .

. . . [T]he trial court's *recognition* of the entrapment by estoppel defense and its concomitant refusal to exclude supporting evidence was not tentative. . . . [D]efendant was then required to present sufficient evidence to support the defense she was allowed to interpose.[11] Regardless of whether she succeeded in this effort, however, the trial court had made a final legal ruling that the defense was available and, therefore, evidence of Beltran's advice was admissible.

We assume, as do the parties, that defendant would have produced evidence consistent with the offer of proof described above. Under these facts, the defense of entrapment by estoppel is not available as a matter of law.

We also assume, but do not decide, that defendant's conduct would fall within the proscription of Government Code section 1090. A contract made in violation of that section may be voided by any party except the financially interested official. Gov. Code §1092. To incur criminal liability, an official must act both willfully and knowingly. Gov. Code §1097; People v. Honig, 48 Cal. App. 4th 289, 333-336, 55 Cal. Rptr. 2d 555 (1996). An official who [purposely] makes the prohibited contract acts "willfully." *Honig*, at 334. To act "knowingly" the official must be aware "there is a reasonable likelihood that the contract may result in a personal financial benefit to him." Id. at 337, 338. An official is *not* required to know that his conduct is unlawful. Id. at 336-337. Therefore, reliance on advice of counsel as to the lawfulness of the conduct is irrelevant.

Nevertheless, defendant argues that she is entitled to assert the defense of entrapment by estoppel because City Attorney Beltran is a *government* lawyer, authorized to advise the city council on legal matters.[12] Defendant's attempt to rely on existing authority fails. Unlike those charged in Cox v. Louisiana, supra, and Raley v. Ohio, supra, defendant was not an ordinary citizen confronting the power of the state. Defendant was a member of the executive branch of government. A public office is a position held for the benefit of the people; defendant was obligated to discharge

---

11. Defendant's proposed jury instruction stated:

"Entrapment by estoppel occurs when a government official such as the City Attorney of Bell Gardens, acts in such a way or represents to the defendant that certain conduct is legal and the defendant reasonably relies on the representation. In order for Entrapment by Estoppel to apply, the evidence must establish that the reliance on the official's misleading advice was reasonable — in the sense that a person sincerely desirous of obeying the law would have accepted the advice as true, and would not have been put on notice to make further inquiries. . . . [T]he City Attorney of Bell Gardens is a government official duly licensed and authorized to render a legal opinion to a Bell Gardens Council Member."

12. Government Code section 41801 provides: "The city attorney shall advise the city officials in all legal matters pertaining to city business."

her responsibilities with integrity and fidelity. The law in question regulates the very manner in which defendant was empowered to exercise her governmental authority. "For over a hundred years our courts have consistently held that that our conflict-of-interest statute, now embodied in [Government Code] section 1090, is intended to enforce the government's right to the absolute, undivided, uncompromised allegiance of public officials by proscribing any personal interest." People v. Honig, supra, 48 Cal. App. 4th at 324-325. "In our society, people of ordinary sensibility should recognize, *without the intervention of a criminal proscription*, that a public official is a trustee and that it is wrong for such a trustee to engage in self-dealing, including the contingent feathering of one's own nest." Id. at 338 (italics added).

For these reasons, we are reluctant to extend the defense to public officials who seek to defend conflict of interest accusations by claiming reliance on the advice of public attorneys charged with counseling them and advocating on their behalf. Recognizing entrapment by estoppel in such circumstances is antithetical to the strong public policy of strict enforcement of conflict of interest statutes and the attendant personal responsibility demanded of our officials.

The defense is particularly inappropriate here. Bell Gardens is a general law city, in which the city attorney is a subordinate officer of the city council, appointed by and serving at its pleasure. An official cannot escape liability for conflict of interest violations by claiming to have been misinformed by an employee serving at her pleasure. If permitted to rely on the defense of entrapment by estoppel, such an official could insulate herself from prosecution by influencing an appointee to provide the advice she seeks. The appointee would be forced to choose between two masters: the official in whose hands his continued employment rests and the public that both are sworn to serve. Obviously, this circumstance is not in the public interest.[14]

Additional policy considerations also support our conclusion. City Attorney Beltran is authorized to give legal advice to the city council on

---

14. Defendant cites United States v. Hedges, 912 F.2d 1397 (11th Cir. 1990), in which Hedges, an Air Force colonel, was convicted under a federal conflict of interest statute for negotiating employment with a defense contractor while still serving in the military. Hedges offered evidence that he had consulted his "Standards of Conduct" officer, who, by regulations and order of General McCarthy, was specifically charged with the "duty and responsibility of precluding any conflict of interest that might arise." Id. at 1404. The Eleventh Circuit Court of Appeals reversed the conviction, concluding the trial court erroneously refused an entrapment by estoppel defense. Id. at 1405. *Hedges* is not binding on us. Further, the *Hedges* court specifically noted that "this is not a reliance on advice of counsel case." Ibid. Instead, the *Hedges* court based its analysis on the express role of this military ethics officer.

matters related to city business. He is not similarly situated to those public officials whose actions have been found to bind the state. In Cox v. Louisiana, supra, 379 U.S. at 568, the police chief was charged with administering and enforcing the statute at issue, and in United States v. Pennsylvania Chemical Corp., supra, 411 U.S. at 674, the Army Corp of Engineers was the administrative agency promulgating regulations "as to the meaning and requirements of the statute." In Raley v. Ohio, supra, 360 U.S. at 437, the commission chairman conducting the hearing "clearly appeared to be the agent of the State." Legal advice regarding the application of a statute must be distinguished from the authority to bind the government. Any lawyer may be asked to provide an opinion as to the meaning of a statute. However, only certain government authorities are empowered to administer or enforce particular statutes. Officials like the police chief [in *Cox*] or the commission chairman [in *Raley*] are designated to apply and implement the law in question. . . .

The city attorney offering an interpretation of Government Code section 1090 to council members in the course of his daily responsibilities acts simply as a lawyer advising a client. Government Code section 1090 applies statewide to "[m]embers of the Legislature, state, county, district, judicial district, and city officers or employees." City Attorney Beltran's clients are the officials of Bell Gardens. Section 1090 is one of the myriad of state statutes he and other city attorneys must advise upon in the course of their daily responsibilities. Beltran is not authorized to criminally enforce or administer this law.[15]

Private attorneys interpret and advise their clients on the application of statutes under all kinds of circumstances. Yet the average citizen cannot rely on a private lawyer's erroneous advice as a defense to a general intent crime. See People v. Vineberg, 125 Cal. App. 3d 127, 137, 177 Cal. Rptr. 819 (1981); People v. Aresen, 91 Cal. App. 2d 26, 35, 204 P.2d 389 (1949).

> "The defense of action taken in good faith, in reliance upon the advice of a reputable attorney that it was lawful, has long been rejected. The theory is that this would place the advice of counsel above the law and would place a premium on counsel's ignorance or indifference to the law."

---

15. The city attorney has a limited power to prosecute misdemeanors with the consent of the district attorney. Government Code section 41803.5, subdivision (a) provides: "With the consent of the district attorney of the county, the city attorney . . . may prosecute any misdemeanor committed within the city arising out of violation of state law. . . ." At the *in limine* hearing, the deputy district attorney represented that the Bell Gardens City Attorney does not prosecute misdemeanors. The power to prosecute felonies, such as those charged against defendant, is retained by the district attorney.

1 Witkin & Epstein, California Criminal Law: Defenses §38, at 369 (3d ed. 2000). Defendant cannot evade that rule by asserting the attorney who mistakenly advised her happened to hold a governmental position.

We express no view as to whether defendant's conduct violated Government Code section 1090. We hold only that the defense of entrapment by estoppel is not available under the offer of proof contained in this record.

For the foregoing reasons, we affirm the judgment of the Court of Appeal.

Notes and Questions

1. Reread footnote 2 in *Burt*, at page 894. What, exactly, is the difference between the "public authority" defense offered in that case and the "entrapment by estoppel" defense in *Chacon*?

2. Originally, public authority defenses were reserved for those actually in positions of authority—they were meant to be used by government officials (including, but not limited to, police officers) charged with committing crimes while doing their jobs. United States v. Ehrlichman, 546 F.2d 910 (D.C. Cir. 1976), and United States v. Barker, 546 F.2d 940 (D.C. Cir. 1976), are classic examples. John Ehrlichman was President Richard Nixon's domestic policy advisor, one of the President's top aides. Nixon gave Ehrlichman the responsibility of finding the source of what became known as "the Pentagon Papers"—classified, "top secret" government documents on the Vietnam War that the *New York Times* obtained and published. In the course of carrying out that mission, Ehrlichman ordered a team of "plumbers" (so named because they fixed leaks) to break into the office of Dr. Louis Fielding, psychiatrist for Daniel Ellsberg, the man who had leaked a copy of the Pentagon Papers to the Times reporter who broke the story. The *Barker* defendants were two of the underlings who carried out the break-in. Both they and Ehrlichman were convicted of conspiring to deny Dr. Fielding his civil rights. All the defendants claimed that they were following superiors' orders, and therefore acted legally.

The D.C. Circuit split the difference, affirming Ehrlichman's conviction and reversing the two underlings' convictions in *Barker*. Ehrlichman claimed that his actions were permissible—or, in the alternative, that he lacked the requisite *mens rea*—because he was following the President's orders on a matter that concerned the nation's security. Unfortunately for Ehrlichman, Nixon did not actually order the break-in; he simply told his aide to find the leak. The defendants in *Barker* were better positioned to advance a public authority defense, since they *did* follow orders (namely,

Ehrlichman's). Judge Wilkey's opinion concluded that, as long as the defendants reasonably believed their superior had the legal authority to order the relevant action, they had a valid defense. *Barker*, 546 F.2d at 947-49 (Wilkey, J., concurring).

3. Under 18 U.S.C. §2340A, the torture of a prisoner is a federal crime carrying a sentence of up to 20 years in prison. Torture is defined as "an act committed by a person acting under the color of law specifically intended to inflict severe physical or mental pain or suffering (other than pain or suffering incidental to lawful sanctions) upon another person within his custody or physical control." 18 U.S.C. §2340. Suppose a CIA employee were charged with violating this statute in the course of questioning one or more suspected terrorists; suppose further that the employee used interrogation tactics that were deemed legal by an opinion of the Office of Legal Counsel—one of the famous, or infamous, "torture memos" issued during the Bush Administration. Finally, suppose that the relevant OLC opinion is determined by a court of competent jurisdiction to be incorrect. Does the employee have a valid public authority defense? The bottom line is unclear, but the likely answer is yes. For a thorough analysis, see Note, The Immunity-Conferring Power of the Office of Legal Counsel, 121 Harv. L. Rev. 2086 (2008).

4. Consider that Burt made no effort to obtain specific instructions concerning what she was and wasn't permitted to do as part of her alleged understanding with her police handlers. Chacon, meanwhile, sought the advice of the city attorney, and did not sit as a council member when the council determined the terms of her future employment. As between the two defendants, it seems clear that Chacon took more and better precautions against future legal liability. Yet Burt's defense is apparently viable, while Chacon's isn't. Why?

5. Should the result in *Chacon* be the same if the defendant's colleagues on the city council were charged with conspiring to violate California Government Code §§1090 and 1097?

6. Perhaps the scope of the defenses in *Burt* and *Chacon* depends on the need to take legal risks. If federal agents are to enforce the laws against the smuggling of illegal immigrants, those agents must have the cooperation of some of the smugglers. To obtain that cooperation, the agents must give a pass to a few offenders like Burt. A similar principle might apply to the low-level flunkies who participated in the burglary in the Pentagon Papers case. By contrast, there is no clear need for deals like the one struck in *Chacon*: It is unlikely that any of the council members was a far better fit for the job of city manager than any other job applicant would be. Any possible benefits to the town are outweighed by the risk of harm from self-dealing politicians.

Are you persuaded? Was *Chacon* rightly decided? Was *Burt*?

C. DURESS

Williams v. State

Court of Special Appeals of Maryland
101 Md. App. 408; 646 A.2d 1101 (1994)

Opinion by ALPERT, J.

. . . Marvin Larvae Williams, appellant, was charged with attempted robbery with a deadly weapon, daytime housebreaking, and the use of a handgun in the commission of a crime of violence. Williams waived his right to a jury trial and a court trial commenced in the Circuit Court for Baltimore County on February 23, 1993, at the close of which, the trial judge requested memoranda concerning the defense of duress. The case was resumed on May 4, 1993, at which time Williams was convicted of the charged offenses. He was sentenced to eight years imprisonment for attempted robbery with a deadly weapon, eight years for daytime housebreaking, and five years imprisonment, without possibility of parole, for the use of a handgun in the commission of a crime of violence. All sentences were to run concurrently. . . .

The victim, the Reverend Chris Glenn Hale, lived at 8601 Gray Fox Road, Apartment 102 in Randallstown, Maryland at the time of the incident. On March 1, 1990 at or about 4:45 P.M., Hale heard a knock on his apartment door. He went to the door, looked through the keyhole, and saw Williams standing at the door. Hale asked who was there and Williams answered by mumbling, asking if a certain person resided at Hale's residence. Hale could not understand Williams so he partially opened the door, whereupon four men, including Williams, rushed through. One of the men, not Williams, proceeded to hold a gun to Hale's face. Hale noticed that three of the men were armed, but did not see if Williams was armed.

After the men entered Hale's apartment, they spread out around the apartment to search for other persons, and the apparent leader demanded that Hale divulge the location of "the money" and "the dope." Williams, in the meantime, kept telling the men that the "dope" was in Hale's apartment, that he and Hale were friends, and that he had been in the apartment the previous day where he had used the "dope" with Hale. After searching unsuccessfully for the "dope," Williams was forced to kneel next to Hale, and the three men made more demands of the both of them as to where the money and the dope were located. The men then allowed Williams to get up from the floor to make a telephone call. Williams spoke on the phone for about ten minutes, and when he got off the phone, he walked out of the bedroom with two of the men (including the leader), where they talked for about five minutes. Hale was then tied up and the men, including Williams, left shortly. Nothing was taken from Hale's apartment.

At the trial, Williams testified that he was abducted by the three men because they believed that he knew the whereabouts of the drug stash of one

Chuckie Eubanks, a reputed drug dealer. Williams had borrowed money from Chuckie's brother, Rodney, and had been induced to make a drug run to New York in order to help repay his debt. The Eubanks organization required Williams to make a second trip to New York, during which Williams cooperated with the police and obtained the names, phone numbers, addresses, and license tag numbers of the parties involved in the drug deal. Apparently, the three abductors, who were former members of Eubanks's drug organization, knew of Williams' relationship with Eubanks and believed that he would know the location of the stash house. When Williams was abducted by the men, he told them that he did not know the location of the stash house. The men did not believe Williams and threatened to kill him if he did not disclose its location. Williams led the men to Hale's apartment, told them it was the stash house, and knocked on the door. Once inside Hale's apartment, Williams testified that he pretended to participate in the search of the premises. Williams also said that the phone call he made was to his mother and was done at the request of one of the abductors who instructed him to say that "everything was all right," the abductors being concerned because Williams' sister had witnessed the abduction.

. . . [T]he trial court heard the testimony of all the witnesses and concluded that

> the [Appellant] wants you to believe that he was victimized, that he was taken off the street, and by point of gun, forced to commit an armed robbery. That simply is not true. No one forced him to commit an armed robbery. No one forced him to go to the Reverend's house and demand money. The only thing these three persons wanted was to have the debt repaid, and they didn't care how it was done. The [Appellant] said, I don't care how I repay the debt, I just want to save my own soul, and I will commit an armed robbery to do it, and I will assist in the commission of an armed robbery if that satisfies the debt, if that appeases you and I am safe.

The court went on to find that the testimony taken as a whole did "lend[] some corroboration to [Appellant's] suggestion that, at least to some degree, [Appellant] was under duress." The court however, did qualify its finding by noting that the duress was not "to go to the stash house" but rather "duress to pay the debt." Accordingly, the court aptly focused on a very narrow issue: "whether the fact that [appellant] was under duress to repay the debt, and thereby created the scenario for this offense, operates as a complete defense. . . ." The court requested additional memoranda on this issue and concluded that facts of this case did not support a finding of duress. Accordingly, we are faced with the question . . . whether the appellant's conduct presents an exception to the applicability of the duress defense. We conclude that it does. . . .

Chief Judge Orth, speaking for this court nearly a quarter of a century ago, explained that

> in order to constitute a defense, the duress . . . must be present, imminent, and impending, and of such a nature as to induce well grounded apprehension of

death or serious bodily injury if the act is not done. It must be of such a character as to leave no opportunity to the accused for escape. Mere fear or threat by another is not sufficient nor is a threat of violence at some prior time. The defense cannot be raised if the apprehended harm is only that of property damage or future but not present personal injury.

Frasher v. State, 8 Md. App. 439, 449, 260 A.2d 656 (1970) (citing 1 Wharton's Criminal Law and Procedure §123, at 262-264). Additionally, we noted that the defense of duress is not successful if the "compulsion arose by the defendant's own fault, negligence, or misconduct." *Frasher*, 8 Md. App. at 449.

Our research has not disclosed any controlling Maryland cases on this [issue, and the Maryland General Assembly has not enacted a statute defining the duress defense]. Accordingly, we examine the legal reasoning and analysis from other [states].

In Commonwealth v. Knight, 611 A.2d 1199 (Pa. Super. Ct. 1992), the appellant, Terrence Knight, attempted to rob a bar at gunpoint. When the owner of the bar pulled a gun, Knight said that there were other men outside, and ran out the door. Knight was later picked up by police and identified by the bar owner as the man who tried to rob the bar. At trial, Knight . . . asserted that he was forced to rob the bar by two men from whom he bought $60 worth of drugs earlier that day. Knight claimed that the drug dealers, armed with a knife and a baseball bat, found him at his girlfriend's house, and forced him under the threat of death to go to the bar and rob it. Id. at 1201.

The court, citing 18 Pa. Cons. Stat. Ann. §309(b),[3] which was adopted from the Model Penal Code, stated that the duress defense is unavailable if the actor "recklessly placed himself in a situation in which it was probable that he would be subjected to duress," or if the actor was "negligent in placing himself in such a situation, whenever negligence suffices to establish culpability to the offense charged." Id. at 1203. . . . The court . . . affirmed his conviction.

---

3. The Pennsylvania statute defined the duress defense, and the exception thereto, as follows:

§309. DURESS

(a) General Rule. — It is a defense that the actor engaged in the conduct charged to constitute an offense because he was coerced to do so by the use of, or threat to use, unlawful force against his person or the person of another, which a person of reasonable firmness in his situation would have been unable to resist.

(b) Exception. — The defense provided by subsection (a) of this section is unavailable if the actor recklessly placed himself in a situation in which it was probable that he would be subjected to duress. The defense is also unavailable if he was negligent in placing himself in such a situation, whenever negligence suffices to establish culpability to the offense charged.

[Quoted in] *Knight*, 611 A.2d at 1202-03.

. . . [I]n Walker v. State, 674 P.2d 825, 830 (Alaska App. 1983), . . . the defendant and his cohorts knocked on the door of a residence they planned to burglarize to make sure no one was home. When the owner's son opened the door, the three men claimed they had car trouble and were in need of a telephone. The men entered the dwelling, robbed it and later kidnapped and killed the owner and her son. Id. at 827. At trial, Walker claimed that he agreed to participate in the burglary, but from the moment his companions drew a gun, he had to go along with the other greater crimes out of fear for his well-being. Walker was tried for two counts of first-degree murder, two counts of kidnapping, one count of robbery, one count of burglary, and two counts of theft. Walker was convicted on all counts except the murder counts. Id. . . . [U]nder Alaska Stat. §11.81.440(b),[4] duress is an affirmative defense and therefore the burden was on Walker to establish this defense. . . . [The Alaska Court of Appeals affirmed the defendant's conviction.] . . .

In People v. Merhige, 180 N.W. 418 (Mich. 1920), three bank robbers had defendant Merhige, a public taxi driver, drive them to and from the bank they robbed. At trial, Merhige pled guilty and was convicted of bank robbery. On appeal, Merhige stated that the robbers were total strangers and that he was not aware of their intentions to rob a bank. He further asserted that throughout the robbery, he was afraid for his life and that the robbers forced him to acquiesce to their demands. In reversing Merhige's conviction the Supreme Court of Michigan cited [this] definition of the duress defense . . . :

> An act which would otherwise constitute a crime may also be excused on the grounds that it was done under compulsion or duress. The compulsion which will excuse a criminal act, however, must be present, imminent, and impending, and of such a nature as to induce a well-grounded apprehension of death or serious bodily harm if the act is not done. A threat of future injury is not enough. Such compulsion must have arisen without the negligence or fault of the person who insists upon it as a defense.

Id. at 422 (citation omitted). . . .

In addition to the case law mentioned above, we also note that the Model Penal Code defines duress as follows:

---

4. The Alaska statute defined duress and an exception thereto as follows:

(a) In any prosecution for an offense, it is an affirmative defense that the defendant engaged in the proscribed conduct because he was coerced to do so by the use of unlawful force upon him or a third person, which force a reasonable person in his situation would have been unable to resist.

(b) The defense of duress is not available when a person recklessly places himself in a situation where it is probable that he will be subject to duress.

[Quoted in] *Walker*, 674 P.2d at 827.

(1) It is an affirmative defense that the actor engaged in the conduct charged to constitute an offense because he was coerced to do so by the use of, or threat to use, unlawful force against his person or the person of another, which a person of reasonable firmness in his situation would have been unable to resist.

(2) The defense provided by this Section is unavailable if the actor recklessly placed himself in a situation in which it was probable that he would be subjected to duress. The defense is also unavailable if he was negligent in placing himself in such a situation, whenever negligence suffices to establish culpability for the offense charged.

Model Penal Code §2.09. . . .

In 1 Wharton's Criminal Law §52 (15th ed. 1993), the author notes that "the defense of duress is not available if the defendant intentionally or recklessly placed himself in a situation in which it was reasonably foreseeable that he would be subjected to coercion." See also 1 Wayne R. LaFave and Austin W. Scott, Jr., Substantive Criminal Law §5.3 (1986); 22 C.J.S., Criminal Law §52 (1989 & Supp. 1994).

The reasoning of these cases and other authorities is persuasive. . . . Additionally, we note that many of the statutes enacting the defense of duress substantially adopt the Model Penal Code definition of duress. See, e.g., *Knight*, 611 A.2d at 1202-03 (quoting 18 Pa. Cons. Stat. Ann. §309(b)); *Walker*, 674 P.2d at 827 (quoting Alaska Stat. §11.81.440(b)). As noted above, the Maryland General Assembly has not codified the defense of duress. Based upon the authorities cited above, we hold that where an actor recklessly (as defined in the Model Penal Code) places himself or herself in a situation where it is probable that he or she would be subjected to duress, the defense of duress is unavailable. In so holding we are particularly mindful of the Model Penal Code drafters' reasoning that

> though this provision may have the effect of sanctioning conviction of a crime of purpose when the actor's culpability was limited to recklessness, we think the substitution is permissible in view of the exceptional nature of the defense. The provision will have its main room for operation in the case of persons who connect themselves with criminal activities, in which case too fine a line need not be drawn.

ALI, Model Penal Code §2.09 (Tentative Draft No. 10, 1960).

Because Williams' prior conduct contributed mightily to the predicament in which he later found himself, the trial court did not err in concluding that the defense of duress was inapplicable. . . . Here, the evidence reveals that Williams voluntarily became involved with the Eubanks' drug organization. . . . Williams borrowed money from Rodney Eubanks. Because of his inability to repay promptly, Williams allegedly was forced to make the first drug run up to New York. He also participated in another drug run. In other words, the evidence does not suggest that he was forced to make these runs, he did this of his own volition to help pay off his debt. By becoming involved with this drug ring, Williams through his own recklessness made others aware of his connection with Eubanks, including his abductors. Williams was readily identifiable to those in the organization, including his abductors, and the abductors acted accordingly. This was a situation that would not have occurred but for Williams' association with the drug organization. Considering these facts and the applicable law, we conclude that Williams' assertion [of] the defense of duress . . . is unavailing. . . .

Notes on the Duress Defense

1. *Williams* is an example of what is often called "causing the conditions" doctrine, which bars a defense for one who is, at least in part, responsible for the pressure brought to bear on him — the same pressure the defendant relies on when claiming duress. For the classic discussion of causing the conditions doctrine, see Paul H. Robinson, Causing the Conditions of One's Own Defense: A Study in the Limits of Theory in Criminal Law Doctrine, 71 Va. L. Rev. 1 (1985). Robinson argues, basically, that a defendant should retain his defense unless he anticipates the relevant threats when he engages in the behavior that causes those threats. By that standard, what is the proper result in *Williams*?

2. Given the rule in *Williams*, ex-gang members who wish not to participate in the gang's criminal activities are subject to different legal standards than the rest of the population: They are criminally liable even if their former associates coerce them. Is that result fair? Shouldn't criminal law encourage gang members to quit their gangs? Does "causing the conditions" doctrine send the opposite signal?

3. Successful duress claims are exceedingly rare. (Why might that be so?) Claims that succeed at trial do not produce appellate opinions, since acquittals are not appealable. Defendants raising duress claims who are convicted usually lose on appeal: *Williams* is very much the norm. For a rare exception, see State v. Nieto, 761 So. 2d 467 (Fla. 3d Dist. Ct. App. 2000). Nieto claimed he was forced to smuggle drugs:

> Defendant is a Colombian national who arrived at the Miami airport having swallowed forty pellets containing 1.17 pounds of heroin. As his defense to the charge of drug trafficking, he offers the defense of duress. Defense counsel represents that defendant will testify that he is a Colombian businessman who has a multi-entry-exit visa which allows regular travel to and from the United States. Defendant will testify that he was threatened and put in fear of imminent harm if he did not comply with the instructions of a Colombian drug trafficking cartel to swallow the drug pellets and smuggle them into the United States.
>
> Defendant intends to call an expert witness at trial, Dr. Bruce Bagley, professor of international studies at the University of Miami, whose area of concentration is the operations of drug cartels in Colombia and Mexico. . . . Defendant desires to have Dr. Bagley testify about the methods used by Colombian drug

cartels, and in substance, that those methods are consistent with what happened in this case: that a person with the defendant's characteristics, a multi-entry-exit visa and legitimate business and/or personal reasons to travel to and from the United States, may become targeted and threatened with harm to himself or his family if he does not consent to smuggle contraband.

Id. at 467-68. The trial court suppressed Dr. Bagley's testimony; that decision was overturned on appeal.

4. Meir Dan-Cohen suggests that the duress defense is best understood as a "decision rule" that defendants like Williams are not meant to "hear," lest they manipulate the evidence to exempt themselves from criminal liability. Here is Professor Dan-Cohen's explanation of the basic idea:

> Imagine a universe consisting of two groups of people—the general public and officials. The general public engages in various kinds of conduct, while officials make decisions with respect to members of the general public. Imagine further that each of the two groups occupies a different, acoustically sealed chamber. This condition I shall call "acoustic separation." Now think of the law as a set of normative messages directed to both groups. In such a universe, the law necessarily contains two sets of messages. One set is directed at the general public and provides guidelines for conduct. These guidelines are what I have called "conduct rules." The other set of messages is directed at the officials and provides guidelines for their decisions. These are "decision rules." . . .
>
> A concrete example . . . may [be helpful]. For centuries criminal lawyers have been troubled by the question whether duress should operate as a defense to a criminal charge. Some have maintained that, even when external pressures impel an individual toward crime, the law should by no means relax its demand that the individual make the socially correct choice. If anything, the opposite is the case: "[I]t is at the moment when temptation to crime is strongest that the law should speak most clearly and emphatically to the contrary."[16] Proponents of the defense, by contrast, have emphasized the unfairness of punishing a person for succumbing to pressures to which even his judges might have yielded. These conflicting arguments seem to impale the law on the horns of an inexorable dilemma. The law faces a hopeless trade-off between the competing values of deterrence and compassion (or fairness); whichever way it resolves the question of duress, it must sacrifice one value to the other.
>
> The impasse dissolves, however, if we analyze the problem in terms of the distinction between conduct rules and decision rules and consider to which of the two categories the defense of duress properly belongs. To answer this question, we again resort to our mental experiment: we locate duress in the imaginary world of acoustic separation. When we do so, it becomes obvious that the policies advanced by the defense would lead to its use as a decision

---

16. 2 J. Stephen, A History of the Criminal Law of England 107 (1883).

rule—an instruction to the judge that defendants who under duress committed acts that would otherwise amount to offenses should not be punished. Just as obviously, no comparable rule would be included among the conduct rules of the system: knowledge of the existence of the defense of duress would not be permitted to shape individual conduct; conduct would be guided exclusively by the relevant criminal proscriptions.

Meir Dan-Cohen, Decision Rules and Conduct Rules: On Acoustic Separation and the Criminal Law, 97 Harv. L. Rev. 625, 630, 632-33 (1984). As Dan-Cohen goes on to explain, the core problem criminal-law makers face is that both conduct rules and decision rules send signals that are "heard" by potential criminal defendants.

Dan-Cohen's construct helps to explain an otherwise puzzling feature of the criminal justice system. Some two million felony charges are filed each year. Nearly half of those cases are dismissed; the overwhelming majority of the dismissals are voluntary—meaning, the prosecutor drops the charges on her own, not in response to any judicial ruling. In the remaining cases, the conviction rate is 99 percent. In short, defendants win a great many victories—but nearly all of those defense victories are invisible; they happen outside public view. In the transparent portions of the criminal justice system, defense victories are rare at best.

Dixon v. United States

Supreme Court of the United States
548 U.S. 1 (2006)

Justice STEVENS delivered the opinion of the Court.

In January 2003, petitioner Keshia Dixon purchased multiple firearms at two gun shows, during the course of which she provided an incorrect address and falsely stated that she was not under indictment for a felony. As a result of these illegal acts, petitioner was indicted and convicted on one count of receiving a firearm while under indictment in violation of 18 U.S.C. §922(n) and eight counts of making false statements in connection with the acquisition of a firearm in violation of §922(a)(6). At trial, petitioner admitted that she knew she was under indictment when she made the purchases and that she knew doing so was a crime; her defense was that she acted under duress because her boyfriend threatened to kill her or hurt her daughters if she did not buy the guns for him.

Petitioner contends that the trial judge's instructions to the jury erroneously required her to prove duress by a preponderance of the evidence instead of requiring the Government to prove beyond a reasonable doubt that she did not act under duress. The Court of Appeals rejected petitioner's contention, 413 F.3d 520 (CA5 2005); given contrary treatment of the issue by other federal courts, we granted certiorari.

I

At trial, in her request for jury instructions on her defense of duress, petitioner contended that she "should have the burden of production, and then that the Government should be required to disprove beyond a reasonable doubt the duress." . . . [T]he judge's instructions to the jury defined the elements of the duress defense[2] and stated that petitioner has "the burden of proof to establish the defense of duress by a preponderance of the evidence."

Petitioner argues here, as she did in the District Court and the Court of Appeals, that federal law requires the Government to bear the burden of disproving her defense beyond a reasonable doubt and that the trial court's erroneous instruction on this point entitles her to a new trial. . . .

II

The crimes for which petitioner was convicted require that she have acted "knowingly" or "willfully." As we have explained, "unless the text of the statute dictates a different result, the term 'knowingly' merely requires proof of knowledge of the facts that constitute the offense." Bryan v. United States, 524 U.S. 184, 193 (1998). And the term "willfully" in §924(a)(1)(D) requires a defendant to have "acted with knowledge that his conduct was unlawful." Ibid. In this case, then, the Government bore the burden of proving beyond a reasonable doubt that petitioner knew she was making false statements in connection with the acquisition of firearms and that she knew she was breaking the law when she acquired a firearm while under indictment. See In re Winship, 397 U.S. 358, 364 (1970). . . . [T]he Government . . . clearly met its burden when petitioner testified that she knowingly committed certain acts—she put a false address on the forms she completed to purchase the firearms, falsely claimed that she was the actual buyer of the firearms, and falsely stated that she was not under indictment at the time of the purchase—and when she testified that she knew she was breaking the law when, as an individual under indictment at the time, she purchased a firearm.

Petitioner contends, however, that she cannot have formed the necessary *mens rea* for these crimes because she did not freely choose to commit the acts in question. But even if we assume that petitioner's will was

---

2. There is no federal statute defining the elements of the duress defense. We have not specified the elements of the defense, see, e.g., United States v. Bailey, 444 U.S. 394, 409-10 (1980), and need not do so today. Instead, we presume the accuracy of the District Court's description of these elements: (1) The defendant was under an unlawful and imminent threat of such a nature as to induce a well-grounded apprehension of death or serious bodily injury; (2) the defendant had not recklessly or negligently placed herself in a situation in which it was probable that she would be forced to perform the criminal conduct; (3) the defendant had no reasonable, legal alternative to violating the law, that is, a chance both to refuse to perform the criminal act and also to avoid the threatened harm; and (4) that a direct causal relationship may be reasonably anticipated between the criminal act and the avoidance of the threatened harm.

overborne by the threats made against her and her daughters, she still *knew* that she was making false statements and *knew* that she was breaking the law by buying a firearm. The duress defense, like the defense of necessity that we considered in United States v. Bailey, 444 U.S. 394, 409-10 (1980), may excuse conduct that would otherwise be punishable, but the existence of duress normally does not controvert any of the elements of the offense itself.[4] As we explained in *Bailey*, "[c]riminal liability is normally based upon the concurrence of two factors, an evil-meaning mind [and] and evil-doing hand. . . ." Id., at 402. Like the defense of necessity, the defense of duress does not negate a defendant's criminal state of mind when the applicable offense requires a defendant to have acted knowingly or willfully; instead, it allows the defendant to "avoid liability . . . because coercive conditions or necessity negates a conclusion of guilt even though the necessary *mens rea* was present." [Ibid.]

. . . Congress defined the crimes at issue to punish defendants who act "knowingly," §922(a)(6), or "willfully," §924(a)(1)(D). It is these specific mental states, rather than some vague "evil mind" or "criminal intent" that the Government is required to prove beyond a reasonable doubt. The jury instructions in this case were consistent with this requirement and, as such, did not run afoul of the Due Process Clause when they placed the burden on petitioner to establish the existence of duress by a preponderance of the evidence.

III

. . . [U]ntil the end of the 19th century, common-law courts generally adhered to the rule that "the proponent of an issue bears the burden of persuasion on the factual premises for applying the rule." Fletcher, Two Kinds of Legal Rules: A Comparative Study of Burden-of-Persuasion Practices in Criminal Cases, 77 Yale L.J. 880, 898 (1967-1968). In petitioner's view, however, two important developments have established a contrary common-law rule that now prevails in federal courts: this Court's decision in Davis v. United States, 160 U.S. 469 (1895), which placed the burden on the Government to prove a defendant's sanity, and the publication of the Model Penal Code in 1962. . . .

Davis . . . does not support petitioner's position. In that case, we reviewed a defendant's conviction for having committed murder "feloniously, wilfully, and of his malice aforethought." 160 U.S., at 474. It was undisputed that the

---

4. As the Government recognized at oral argument, there may be crimes where the nature of the *mens rea* would require the Government to disprove the existence of duress beyond a reasonable doubt. See Tr. of Oral Arg. 26-27; see also, *e.g.*, 1 W. LaFave, Substantive Criminal Law §5.1, p. 333 (2d ed. 2003) (hereinafter LaFave) (explaining that some common-law crimes require that the crime be done "maliciously"); Black's Law Dictionary 968 (7th ed. 1999) (defining malice as "[t]he intent, without justification or excuse, to commit a wrongful act").

prosecution's evidence "if alone considered, made it the duty of the jury to return a verdict of guilty of the crime charged"; the defendant, however, adduced evidence at trial tending to show that he did not have the mental capacity to form the requisite intent. Id., at 475. At issue before the Court was the correctness of the trial judge's instruction to the jury that the law "presumes every man is sane, and the burden of showing it is not true is upon the party who asserts it." Id., at 476. . . .

In reversing the defendant's conviction, we found ourselves "unable to assent to the doctrine that *in a prosecution for murder* . . . it is the duty of the jury to convict where the evidence is equally balanced on the issue as to the sanity of the accused at the time of the killing." Id., at 484 (emphasis added). . . . Our opinion focused on the "definition of murder," explaining that "it is of the very essence of that heinous crime that it be committed by a person of sound memory and discretion, and with malice aforethought." Ibid. . . . *Davis* . . . interpreted a defendant's sanity to controvert the necessary *mens rea* for the crime of murder committed "feloniously, wilfully, and of his malice aforethought," id., at 474, as "[o]ne who takes human life cannot be said to be actuated by malice aforethought, or to have deliberately intended to take life, or to have 'a wicked, depraved, and malignant heart,' . . . unless at the time he had sufficient mind to comprehend the criminality or the right and wrong of such an act," id., at 485. . . . [T]his reasoning . . . does not help petitioner: The evidence of duress she adduced at trial does not contradict or tend to disprove any element of the statutory offenses that she committed. . . .

. . . [P]etitioner's reliance on *Davis* ignores the fact that federal crimes "are solely creatures of statute," [Liparota v. United States, 471 U.S. 419, 424 (1985)], and therefore that we are required to effectuate the duress defense as Congress "may have contemplated" it in the context of these specific offenses, United States v. Oakland Cannabis Buyers' Cooperative, 532 U.S. 483, 491, n.3 (2001). The offenses at issue in this case were created by statute in 1968, when Congress enacted the Omnibus Crime Control and Safe Streets Act. See 82 Stat. 197. There is no evidence in the Act's structure or history that Congress actually considered the question of how the duress defense should work in this context. . . . Assuming that a defense of duress is available to the statutory crimes at issue, then, we must determine what that defense would look like as Congress "may have contemplated" it.

As discussed above, the common law long required the defendant to bear the burden of proving the existence of duress. Similarly, even where Congress has enacted an affirmative defense in the proviso of a statute, the "settled rule . . . [is] that it is incumbent on one who relies on such an exception to set it up and establish it." McKelvey v. United States, 260 U.S. 353, 357 (1922). Even though the Safe Streets Act does not mention the defense of duress, we can safely assume that the 1968 Congress was familiar with both the long-established common-law rule and the rule applied in *McKelvey* and that it would have expected federal courts to apply a similar approach to any affirmative defense that might be asserted as a justification or excuse for violating the new law. . . .

. . . Petitioner cites only one federal case decided before 1968 for the proposition that it has been well established in federal law that the Government bears the burden of disproving duress beyond a reasonable doubt. But that case involved a defendant's claim that he "lacked the specific intent to defraud required by the statute for the reason that he committed the offense under duress and coercion." Johnson v. United States, 291 F.2d 150, 152 (CA8 1961). Thus, when the Court of Appeals explained that "there is no burden upon the defendant to prove his defense of coercion," id., at 155, that statement is best understood in context as a corollary to the by-then-unremarkable proposition that "the burden of proof rests upon the Government to prove the defendant's guilt beyond a reasonable doubt," ibid. Properly understood, *Johnson* provides petitioner little help. . . .

. . . [F]or us [to accept petitioner's argument], we would need to find an overwhelming consensus among federal courts that it is the Government's burden to disprove the existence of duress beyond a reasonable doubt. The existence today of disagreement among the Federal Courts of Appeals on this issue . . . demonstrates that no such consensus has ever existed. Also undermining petitioner's argument is the fact that, in 1970, the National Commission on Reform of Federal Criminal Laws proposed that a defendant prove the existence of duress by a preponderance of the evidence. See 1 Working Papers 278. . . .

It is for a similar reason that we give no weight to the publication of the Model Penal Code in 1962. As petitioner notes, the Code would place the burden on the government to disprove the existence of duress beyond a reasonable doubt. See Model Penal Code §1.12 (stating that each element of an offense must be proved beyond a reasonable doubt); §1.13(9)(c) (defining as an element anything that negatives an excuse for the conduct at issue); §2.09 (establishing affirmative defense of duress). . . . [E]ven if we assume Congress' familiarity with the Code and the rule it would establish, there is no evidence that Congress endorsed the Code's views or incorporated them into the Safe Streets Act.

In fact, the Act itself provides evidence to the contrary. Despite the Code's careful delineation of mental states, see Model Penal Code §2.02, the Safe Streets Act attached no explicit *mens rea* requirement to the crime of receiving a firearm while under indictment, §924(a), 82 Stat. 233 ("Whoever violates any provision of this chapter . . . shall be fined not more than $5,000 or imprisoned not more than five years, or both"). And when Congress amended the Act to impose a *mens rea* requirement, it punished people who "willfully" violate the statute, see 100 Stat. 456, a mental state that has not been embraced by the Code. . . .

IV

Congress can, if it chooses, enact a duress defense that places the burden on the Government to disprove duress beyond a reasonable doubt. In light of Congress' silence on the issue, however, it is up to the federal courts to effectuate the affirmative defense of duress as Congress "may have contemplated" it in an offense-specific context. In the context of the firearms offenses at issue—as will usually be the case, given the long-established common-law rule—we presume that Congress intended the petitioner to bear the burden of proving the defense of duress by a preponderance of the evidence. Accordingly, the judgment of the Court of Appeals is affirmed.

Justice KENNEDY, concurring.

. . . When issues of congressional intent with respect to the nature, extent, and definition of federal crimes arise, we assume Congress acted against certain background understandings set forth in judicial decisions in the Anglo-American legal tradition. Those decisions, in turn, consult sources such as legal treatises and the [American Law Institute's] Model Penal Code. All of these sources rely upon the insight gained over time. . . . Absent some contrary indication in the statute, we can assume that Congress would not want to foreclose the courts from consulting these newer sources and considering innovative arguments in resolving issues not confronted in the statute and not within the likely purview of Congress. . . .

While the Court looks to the state of the law at the time the statute was enacted, the better reading of the Court's opinion is that isolated authorities or writings do not control unless they were indicative of guiding principles upon which Congress likely would have relied. Otherwise, it seems altogether a fiction to attribute to Congress any intent one way or the other in assigning the burden of proof. It seems unlikely, moreover, that Congress would have wanted the burden of proof for duress to vary from statute to statute depending upon the date of enactment. Consistent with these propositions, the Court looks not only to our precedents and common-law traditions, but also to the treatment of the insanity defense in a 1984 statute and a proposal of the National Commission on Reform of Federal Criminal Laws, even though they both postdated the passage of the [Omnibus Crime Control and Safe Streets Act].

As there is no reason to suppose that Congress wanted to depart from the traditional principles for allocating the burden of proof, the proper approach is simply to apply these principles to the context of duress. The facts needed to prove or disprove the defense "lie peculiarly in the knowledge of" the defendant. 2 K. Broun, McCormick on Evidence §337, at 475 (6th ed. 2006). The claim of duress in most instances depends upon conduct that takes place before the criminal act; and, as the person who allegedly coerced the defendant is often unwilling to come forward and testify, the prosecution may be without any practical means of disproving the defendant's allegations. There is good reason, then, to maintain the usual rule of placing the burden of production and persuasion together on the party raising the issue. The analysis may come to a different result, of course, for other defenses.

With these observations, I join the Court's opinion.

Justice ALITO, with whom Justice SCALIA joins, concurring.

I join the opinion of the Court with the understanding that it does not hold that the allocation of the burden of persuasion on the defense of duress may vary from one federal criminal statute to another.

Duress was an established defense at common law. See 4 W. Blackstone, Commentaries on the Laws of England *30 (1769). When Congress began to enact federal criminal statutes, it presumptively intended for those offenses to be subject to this defense. Moreover, Congress presumptively intended for the burdens of production and persuasion to be placed, as they were at common law, on the defendant. Although Congress is certainly free to alter this pattern and place one or both burdens on the prosecution, either for all or selected federal crimes, Congress has not done so but instead has continued to revise the federal criminal laws and to create new federal crimes without addressing the issue of duress. Under these circumstances, I believe that the burdens remain where they were when Congress began enacting federal criminal statutes.

I do not assume that Congress makes a new, implicit judgment about the allocation of these burdens whenever it creates a new federal crime or, for that matter, whenever it substantially revises an existing criminal statute. It is unrealistic to assume that on every such occasion Congress surveys the allocation of the burdens of proof on duress under the existing federal case law and under the law of the States and tacitly adopts whatever the predominant position happens to be at the time. . . . If the allocation differed for different offenses, there might be federal criminal cases in which the trial judge would be forced to instruct the jury that the defendant bears the burden of persuasion on this defense for some of the offenses charged in the indictment and that the prosecution bears the burden on others.

I would also not assume, as Justice Breyer does, that Congress has implicitly delegated to the federal courts the task of deciding in the manner of a common-law court where the burden of persuasion should be allocated. The allocation of this burden is a debatable policy question with an important empirical component. In the absence of specific direction from Congress, I would not assume that Congress has conferred this authority on the Judiciary.

Justice BREYER, with whom Justice SOUTER joins, dissenting.

Courts have long recognized that "duress" constitutes a defense to a criminal charge. Historically, that defense "excuse[d] criminal conduct" if (1) a "threat of imminent death or serious bodily injury" led the defendant to commit the crime, (2) the defendant had no reasonable, legal alternative to breaking the law, and (3) the defendant was not responsible for creating the threat. United States v. Bailey, 444 U.S. 394, 409-10 (1980). . . . The Court decides today in respect to *federal* crimes that the defense must bear the burden of both producing evidence of duress and persuading the jury. I agree with the majority that the burden of production lies on the defendant, that here the burden of persuasion issue is not constitutional, and that Congress may allocate that burden as it sees fit. But I also believe that, in the absence of any indication of a different congressional intent, the burden of persuading the jury beyond a reasonable doubt should lie where such burdens normally lie in criminal cases, upon the prosecution.

My disagreement with the majority in part reflects my different view about how we should determine the relevant congressional intent. Where Congress speaks about burdens of proof, we must, of course, follow what it says. But suppose, as is normally the case, that the relevant federal statute is silent? The majority proceeds on the assumption that Congress wished courts to fill the gap by examining judicial practice *at the time that Congress enacted the particular criminal statute in question.* I would not follow that approach.

To believe Congress intended the placement of such burdens to vary from statute to statute and time to time is both unrealistic and risks unnecessary complexity, jury confusion, and unfairness. It is unrealistic because the silence could well mean only that Congress did not specifically consider the "burden of persuasion" in respect to a duress defense. . . . Had it done so, would Congress have wanted courts to freeze current practice statute-by-statute? Would it have wanted to impose different burden-of-proof requirements where claims of duress are identical, where statutes are similar, where the *only* relevant difference is the time of enactment? Why? Indeed, individual instances of criminal conduct often violate several statutes. In a trial for those violations, is the judge to instruct the jury to apply different standards of proof to a duress defense depending upon when Congress enacted the particular statute in question? . . .

I would assume instead that Congress' silence typically means that Congress expected the courts to develop [burden of proof] rules governing affirmative defenses as they have done in the past, by beginning with the common law and taking full account of the subsequent need for that law to evolve through judicial practice informed by reason and experience. That approach would produce uniform federal practice across different affirmative defenses, as well as across statutes passed at different points in time.

My approach leads me to conclude that in federal criminal cases, the prosecution should bear the duress defense burden of persuasion. The issue is a close one. In Blackstone's time the accused bore the burden of proof for all affirmative defenses. See 4 W. Blackstone, Commentaries *201. And 20th-century experts have taken different positions on the matter. The Model Penal Code, for example, recommends placing the burden of persuasion on the prosecution. The Brown Commission recommends placing it upon the defendant. National Commission on Reform of Federal Criminal Laws, 1 Working Papers 278 (1970). And the proposed revision of the federal criminal code, agnostically, would have turned the matter over to the courts for decision. S. 1722, 96th Cong., 1st Sess., §501 (1979). Moreover, there is a practical argument that favors the Government's position here, namely that defendants should bear the burden of persuasion because defendants often have superior access to the relevant proof.

Nonetheless, several factors favor placing the burden on the prosecution. For one thing, in certain respects the question of duress resembles that of *mens rea,* an issue that is always for the prosecution to prove beyond a reasonable doubt. . . .

. . . [W]here a defendant acts under duress, she lacks any semblance of a meaningful choice. . . . As Blackstone wrote, the criminal law punishes "abuse[s] of th[e] free will"; hence "it is highly just and equitable that a man should be excused for those acts, which are done through unavoidable force and compulsion." 4 Commentaries *27. And it is in this "force and compulsion," acting upon the will, that the resemblance to lack of *mens rea* lies. Davis v. United States, [160 U.S. 469 (1895),] allocated the federal insanity defense burden to the Government partly for these reasons. That case, read in light of Leland v. Oregon, 343 U.S. 790, 797 (1952), suggests that, even if insanity does not always show the absence of *mens rea,* it does show the absence of a "*vicious* will." *Davis,* supra, at 484 (citing Blackstone; emphasis added).

For another thing, federal courts . . . have imposed the federal-crime burden of persuasion upon the prosecution in respect to self-defense, insanity, and entrapment, which resemble the duress defense in certain relevant ways. In respect to both duress and self-defense, for example, the defendant's illegal act is voluntary . . . but the circumstances deprive the defendant of any meaningful ability or opportunity to act otherwise, depriving the defendant of a choice that is free. Insanity . . . may involve circumstances that resemble, but are not identical to, a lack of *mens rea.* And entrapment requires the prosecution to prove that the defendant was "predisposed" to commit the crime—a matter sometimes best known to the defendant. . . .

It is particularly difficult to see a practical distinction between this affirmative defense and, say, self-defense. The Government says that the prosecution may "be unable to call the witness most likely to have information bearing on the point," namely, the defendant. Brief for United States 21. But what is the difference in this respect between the defendant here, who says her boyfriend threatened to kill her, and a battered woman who says that she killed her husband in self-defense, where the husband's evidence is certainly unavailable? Regardless, unless the defendant testifies, it could prove difficult to satisfy the defendant's burden of *production*; and, of course, once the defendant testifies, cross-examination is possible.

In a word, I cannot evaluate the claim of practicality without somewhat more systematic evidence of the existence of a problem, say, in those Circuits that for many years have imposed the burden on the prosecutor. And, of course, if I am wrong about the Government's practical need (and were my views to prevail), the Government would remain free to ask Congress to reallocate the burden.

Finally, there is a virtue in uniformity, in treating the federal statutory burden of persuasion similarly in respect to *actus reus, mens rea,* mistake, self-defense, entrapment, and duress. The Second Circuit, when imposing the burden of persuasion for duress on the prosecution, wrote that differences in this respect create "a grave possibility of juror confusion." United States v. Mitchell, 725 F.2d 832, 836 (1983) (Newman, J., joined by Feinberg, C. J., and Friendly, J.). They risk unfairness as well.

For these reasons I believe that, in the absence of an indication of congressional intent to the contrary, federal criminal law should place the burden of persuasion in respect to the duress defense upon the prosecution, which, as is now common in respect to many affirmative defenses, it must prove beyond a reasonable doubt. With respect, I dissent.

Notes on the Federal Law of Defenses

1. Federal defenses to crime are almost entirely non-statutory. Insanity is the exception: There, Congress acted to narrow the common-law federal defense in the wake of John Hinckley's acquittal for shooting then-President Reagan. Post-*Hinckley*, federal criminal defendants claiming insanity must prove the defense by clear and convincing evidence. 18 U.S.C. §17. The same federal statute also removed that portion of the insanity defense based on irresistible impulses, and added a required showing that the defendant's "mental disease or defect" be "severe." Id.; see infra at page 955. Do these legislative moves affect your view of *Dixon*?

2. Congress has not exactly been loath to define new federal crimes. Why has it been so slow to define defenses?

3. None of the Justices in *Dixon* doubted the existence of a duress defense, even though Congress has never codified it. Instead, there are three interpretive positions in *Dixon*, none of which appears to have the allegiance of a majority of the Court. First, Justice Stevens and at least some of his colleagues take the view that the existence of such a defense and its appropriate contours are to be determined statute by statute: The existence and scope of a duress defense to a given federal gun crime is akin to the existence and scope of an "exculpatory no" exception to the false statements statute in *Brogan*. Second, Justices Kennedy, Breyer, and Souter would define the bounds of duress and other criminal defenses for federal criminal law as a whole, through common-law reasoning. Justices Alito and Scalia take a third approach: They accept the existence of the duress defense not because state legislatures and state and federal judges adopt and apply it *now*, but because it existed at common law "[w]hen Congress began to enact federal criminal statutes." On this view, the federal law of duress is frozen as of 1789.

Which of those positions seems most consistent with congressional intent? Which represents the wisest exercise of judicial power? Are your answers the same?

4. Two issues divide the Justices in *Dixon*. The first concerns the scope of judicial power over federal criminal law. The second is less obvious, but no less important: The Justices also disagree about which doctrines are appropriately seen as *trans-substantive*—that is, which doctrines should apply across the board to all federal crimes, or at least to all save for a small number of exceptions. Historically, the law of defenses, including the burden of proof that applies to duress claims, has been trans-substantive. Should it be? Different intent standards apply to different crimes—why not make different defenses available for different criminal charges? In effect, that is what the "exculpatory no" doctrine did: It established a limited defense for federal misrepresentation cases.

The authors of the concurring and dissenting opinions seem to think that's the wrong model to follow in *Dixon*. Are they right? Suppose Keshia Dixon were charged with shooting and killing a federal officer; suppose further that her boyfriend threatened to kill her and her daughters unless she pulled the trigger. Should the burden of proving duress be different in that case than in the real *Dixon*?

5. Whatever the rule in that case should be, at common law and in most jurisdictions today, the duress defense is unavailable in homicide cases—thereby proving that the law of defenses is not *always* trans-substantive. See, e.g., People v. Anderson, 50 P.3d 368 (Cal. 2002); State v. Glass, 455 So. 2d 659 (La. 1984). In People v. Son, 93 Cal. Rptr. 2d 871 (Ct. App. 2000), the court rejected a defense argument to establish an "imperfect duress" defense that, paralleling imperfect self-defense, defendants might use to reduce the grade of homicide from murder to manslaughter.

6. In Davis v. United States, 160 U.S. 469 (1895), a case discussed extensively in *Dixon*, the Supreme Court treated the assertion of an insanity defense as a *mens rea* argument: If the defendant could show that his mental condition made him unable to know right from wrong, he could not have acted with the requisite criminal intent. Should all defenses be so treated? One might argue that a defendant acting in self-defense or under duress did not truly intend his physical acts; the defendant's only intent was to escape the relevant harm. Is there anything wrong with that argument? Why do you suppose such arguments have not prevailed, aside from a few unusual cases like *Davis*?

D. NECESSITY

Muller v. State

Court of Appeals of Alaska
196 P.3d 815 (2008)

Opinion by Coats, Chief Judge.

Don G. Muller was convicted of criminal trespass after he entered United States Senator Ted Stevens' office to protest the war in Iraq and then refused to leave when it was time for the office to close for the day. Muller argues that his conviction should be reversed because the district court wrongly instructed the jury on the necessity defense. We conclude that Muller was not entitled to a necessity defense and therefore affirm his conviction.

On February 20, 2007 at about 1:10 p.m., Muller and eight or nine other protesters arrived at Senator Stevens' Fairbanks office to protest the war in Iraq. Senator Stevens was not there at the time. Muller told Diane Hutchison, who ran the Fairbanks office for Stevens, that the protesters planned to read a list of 6000 names of civilians killed in the Iraq war. Another protester said he had an additional 3200 names of American soldiers who had been killed. The protesters proceeded to read the names. At 4:00 p.m., the office's normal closing time, the protesters still had about 8500 names to read. Hutchison asked the protesters to come back the following morning. One of the protesters then said: "[It] wouldn't be civil disobedience if we left when you asked, would it?" A security guard then asked the protesters to leave. When they refused, the guard called the police, and the police arrived at about 4:15 p.m. Three of the protesters, including Muller, were arrested. Muller was charged with the misdemeanor offense of second-degree criminal trespass.

Muller appeared *pro se*. Before trial, he gave notice that he intended to raise the defense of necessity, and he proposed the pattern jury instruction on the necessity defense. He also sought admission of thirteen articles he claimed showed that his protest was aimed at stopping an illegal war.

District Court Judge Jane F. Kauvar denied Muller's request to admit the articles on the war. She did, however, allow Muller to present a necessity defense, though she rejected the pattern jury instruction and substituted her own. Muller did not object to Judge Kauvar's substitute instruction.

In his testimony at trial, Muller admitted that he stayed in Senator Stevens' office after closing. He testified that he did so to stop a significant harm—what he believed was an illegal war in Iraq—and that he believed he had no adequate alternative to bring about an end to the war. He said he had pursued other activities, from education to films to non-violence training, and that none of these activities had ended the war. He also testified that he believed the Iraq war was an "infinitely greater harm" than staying past closing in a government office.

The jury rejected Muller's defense and convicted him of trespass. He appeals.

To establish a necessity defense the defendant must show that: (1) the act charged was done to prevent a significant evil; (2) there was no adequate alternative; and (3) the harm caused was not disproportionate to the harm avoided. The first two elements are established if the defendant shows that he reasonably believed at the time of acting that those elements were present, even if that belief was mistaken. As to the third element, which involves balancing the harm caused against the harm sought to be avoided, the court must make "an objective determination . . . as to whether the defendant's value judgment was correct, given the facts as [the defendant] reasonably perceived them."[4]

A defendant is not entitled to a jury instruction on the defense of necessity and is not entitled to argue that defense to the jury unless there is "some evidence" of necessity.[5] "In this context, 'some evidence' is a term of art; it means evidence which, if viewed in the light most favorable to the defendant, is sufficient to allow a reasonable juror to find in the defendant's favor on each element of the defense."[6]

Muller argues that Judge Kauvar's instruction on the necessity defense was flawed because it did not inform the jury that the first two elements of the defense—that the criminal trespass was done to prevent a significant evil and that there were no adequate alternatives to bring about an end to the war in Iraq—were proved as long as he *reasonably believed* those elements were present, even if his belief was mistaken.

Muller is right that the jury was not properly instructed on the mental state he had to prove to establish the first two elements of the necessity defense. The record suggests that Judge Kauvar intended to instruct the jury in line with our decision in Bird v. Anchorage,[7] which clearly states that the first two elements of the defense only require proof that the defendant reasonably believed those elements were present. But this language was not in the instruction read and submitted to the jury. Muller argued to the jury that he held these beliefs and that his beliefs were reasonable. But

4. Seibold v. State, 959 P.2d 780, 782 (Alaska App. 1998).
5. Lacey v. State, 54 P.3d 304, 306, 308 (Alaska App. 2002). . . .
6. *Lacey*, 54 P.3d at 308.
7. 787 P.2d 119 (Alaska App. 1990).

given the erroneous instruction, the jurors may not have understood that Muller's reasonable beliefs were enough to satisfy the first two elements of the defense.

Even so, Muller never objected to Judge Kauvar's instruction, so he cannot prevail on appeal unless he shows he was substantially prejudiced by the court's error. We conclude that Muller cannot show substantial prejudice because, as a matter of law, he was not entitled to raise the defense of necessity in the circumstances of his case.

The Alaska Supreme Court addressed a similar situation in Cleveland v. Anchorage.[10] In *Cleveland*, anti-abortion protesters sought to raise a necessity defense after they were charged with criminal trespass for disrupting the operations of an abortion clinic by blocking the doorways and refusing to leave. The supreme court found that the necessity defense was unavailable in this circumstance for several reasons. First, the defense cannot be raised if the human harm sought to be avoided is a legal act, and abortion is lawful in Alaska. Second, a protest aimed at political change does not generally present the type of emergency situation that entitles a defendant to a necessity defense.

In reaching this latter conclusion, the supreme court adopted the reasoning of the Hawaii Supreme Court in State v. Marley.[14] In *Marley*, the defendants were charged with criminal trespass for entering the offices of Honeywell Corporation in an effort to stop what they believed were "war crimes" being committed by Honeywell. The protest was non-violent, but it disrupted normal business operations. The supreme court found that two of the Hawaii Supreme Court's grounds for rejecting the necessity defense in *Marley* were applicable in *Cleveland*: (1) the defendants had other forms of non-criminal protest available "to enable them to dramatize, and hence hopefully terminate, conduct which they may view [as] harmful," and (2) the defendants' actions " 'were not reasonably designed to actually prevent the threatened greater harm. . . . Under any possible set of hypotheses, defendants could foresee that their actions would fail to halt' the practices to which they objected."[17]

In *Cleveland*, the defendants attempted to distinguish *Marley*, arguing that the alleged harm in *Marley*—the manufacture of weapons for use in the Vietnam War—"was spatially and temporally remote from the site of the trespass," while their protest halted abortions "scheduled in the very rooms [they] blocked, within minutes of the time of their entry."[18] The supreme court found that this distinction was not determinative:

10. 631 P.2d 1073 (Alaska 1981).
14. 509 P.2d 1095 (Hawaii 1973).
17. *Cleveland*, 631 P.2d at 1079 (quoting *Marley*, 509 P.2d at 1109).
18. Id. at 1079.

In both cases, it was obvious to the trespassers that their actions could not halt the alleged greater harm to which society had given its imprimatur, but rather that, at best, the harm could be only postponed for a brief interval, following which society's normal operations would reassert themselves. This was simply not the kind of emergency situation contemplated by the defense of necessity.

Further, in spite of appellants' protestations to the contrary, their acts, like the acts of the *Marley* defendants, are much more appropriately characterized as protesting with the intent to "dramatize, and hence hopefully terminate, conduct which they may view [as] harmful," [than], as appellants describe their own behavior, "directly intervening to avert an imminent threat to human life." Appellants' protest was, in fact, part of a nationwide protest that resulted in several similar arrests in other cities. Appellants appear to concede that if their actions are best described as a protest, the necessity defense would be unavailable. We think it manifest that it would be inappropriate to characterize these trespasses as anything other than a protest, and that appellants' argument of necessity must therefore be rejected.[19]

This reasoning is even more applicable in the circumstances of this case. Although Muller testified that he believed the only adequate alternative to halting the Iraq War was staying in Senator Stevens' office after closing—because he had already tried other types of protest and they had failed—he offered no evidence that coming back at 8:00 A.M. the following morning to finish reading the names of Iraq War casualties would have been any less effective. Moreover, Muller offered no evidence that, "[u]nder any possible set of hypotheses," his actions had any realistic hope of ending the war in Iraq.[20] And, unlike the protesters in *Cleveland*, Muller has not asserted, much less shown, that his acts were anything other than a symbolic protest intended to "dramatize, and hence hopefully terminate" conduct he viewed as harmful. Thus, Muller had no right to a necessity defense: he offered no evidence that he reasonably believed his protest could prevent a significant evil or that he reasonably believed there were no adequate alternatives to criminal trespass to achieve his goal.

Because Muller offered no evidence that his actions had any realistic hope of ending the war in Iraq, the harm caused by disrupting normal operations in Stevens's office, objectively viewed, was disproportionate to the harm Muller could realistically hope to avoid by his trespass.

And lastly, because Muller as a matter of law was not entitled to raise a necessity defense, the court did not abuse its discretion by refusing to admit the articles he argued would show he reasonably believed the war in Iraq was a "significant harm." Even if Muller reasonably believed the war in Iraq was illegal and morally wrong, he offered no evidence that his protest had any

---

19. Id. at 1080 (quoting *Marley*, 509 P.2d at 1109).
20. See id. at 1079 (quoting *Marley*, 509 P.2d at 1109).

realistic hope of ending the war, or that it would be any less effective if it was completed during normal business hours.

Muller's conviction is affirmed.

Notes and Questions

1. Most reported opinions on the scope of the necessity defense look like *Muller.* Protesters of some sort have been charged with trespass for carrying out their protest; the defendants claim that their objective justifies their relatively minor crime. *Muller* suggests that those cases don't qualify for the defense, because the defendants offer no reason to believe that their protests would be effective—hence the balance of harms tilts against them.

Carrying this line of reasoning one step farther, the Ninth Circuit held in United States v. Schoon, 971 F.2d 193 (1992), that *no* act of "indirect civil disobedience"—in which the law violated is not the real target of the defendant's protest—can *ever* qualify for the necessity defense:

> [Defendants] gained admittance to the IRS office in Tucson, where they chanted "keep America's tax dollars out of El Salvador," splashed simulated blood on the counters, walls, and carpeting, and generally obstructed the office's operation. After a federal police officer ordered the group, on several occasions, to disperse or face arrest, appellants were arrested [and charged with obstruction of the IRS and failure to comply with a police order].
>
> At a bench trial, appellants proffered testimony about conditions in El Salvador as the motivation for their conduct. They attempted to assert a necessity defense, essentially contending that their acts in protest of American involvement in El Salvador were necessary to avoid further bloodshed in that country. While finding appellants motivated solely by humanitarian concerns, the court nonetheless precluded the defense as a matter of law, relying on Ninth Circuit precedent. The sole issue on appeal is the propriety of the court's exclusion of a necessity defense as a matter of law. . . .
>
> What all the traditional necessity cases have in common is that the commission of the "crime" averted the occurrence of an even greater "harm." In some sense, the necessity defense allows us to act as individual legislatures, amending a particular criminal provision or crafting a one-time exception to it, subject to court review, when a real legislature would formally do the same under those circumstances. . . .
>
> Because the necessity doctrine is utilitarian, however, strict requirements contain its exercise so as to prevent nonbeneficial criminal conduct. . . .
>
> Analysis of three of the necessity defense's four elements leads us to the conclusion that necessity can never be proved in a case of indirect civil disobedience. . . .
>
> *1. Balance of Harms*
>
> It is axiomatic that, if the thing to be averted is not a harm at all, the balance of harms necessarily would disfavor any criminal action. Indirect

civil disobedience seeks first and foremost to bring about the repeal of a law or a change of governmental policy, attempting to mobilize public opinion through typically symbolic action. These protestors violate a law, not because it is unconstitutional or otherwise improper, but because doing so calls public attention to their objectives. Thus, the most immediate "harm" this form of protest targets is the *existence* of the law or policy. However, the mere existence of a constitutional law or governmental policy cannot constitute a legally cognizable harm. . . . There may be, of course, general harms that result from the targeted law or policy. Such generalized "harm," however, is too insubstantial an injury to be legally cognizable. . . . The law could not function were people allowed to rely on their *subjective* beliefs and value judgments in determining which harms justified the taking of criminal action.

2. Causal Relationship Between Criminal Conduct and Harm to Be Averted
. . . In the traditional cases, a prisoner flees a burning cell and averts death, or someone demolishes a home to create a firebreak and prevents the conflagration of an entire community. The nexus between the act undertaken and the result sought is a close one. Ordinarily it is the volitional illegal act alone which, once taken, abates the evil.

In political necessity cases involving indirect civil disobedience against congressional acts, however, the act alone is unlikely to abate the evil precisely because the action is indirect. . . . [I]t takes another *volitional* actor not controlled by the protestor to take a further step; Congress must change its mind.

3. Legal Alternatives
A final reason the necessity defense does not apply to these indirect civil disobedience cases is that legal alternatives will never be deemed exhausted when the harm can be mitigated by congressional action. As noted above, the harm indirect civil disobedience aims to prevent is the continued existence of a law or policy. Because congressional action can *always* mitigate this "harm," lawful political activity to spur such action will always be a legal alternative. . . .

The real problem here is that litigants are trying to distort to their purposes an age-old common law doctrine meant for a very different set of circumstances. What these cases are really about is gaining notoriety for a cause—the defense allows protestors to get their political grievances discussed in a courtroom. . . . Because these attempts to invoke the necessity defense "force the courts to choose among causes they should make legitimate by extending the defense of necessity," and because the criminal acts, themselves, do not maximize social good, they should be subject to a *per se* rule of exclusion.

Under *Schoon*, illegal sit-ins at racially segregated lunch counters during the Civil Rights Era could have qualified for the necessity defense, but illegal marches protesting segregation could not. Does the distinction make sense?

2. Note the logic of protests like the one in *Muller*: Often, the goal is not to obtain an acquittal but to get one's argument before a jury in a public trial. Why should that result be barred? If a local jury sufficiently sympathizes with Muller's view of the Iraq War and wishes to excuse Muller on the trespass charge, why not permit that result? Technically, the law *does* permit that result—juries may acquit for any reason, and such acquittals are not appealable even if they amount to "nullification" of the governing law—but this permission is more sham than real, since trial judges routinely instruct jurors not to grant defenses like Muller's. Is that the right result? Does your answer depend on the crime charged?

3. Recall Regina v. Dudley & Stephens, supra at page 5. As reflected in that famous decision, necessity traditionally is not a defense to homicide charges (although the Model Penal Code and some states would allow it). As you have already seen, the duress defense likewise does not apply in homicide cases. But self-defense does apply to homicide. Put those three rules together, and one gets the following picture: Killing in response to some great pressure or threat is excused only when the victim had it coming to him. Is that an accurate picture of the doctrine? Is the doctrine fair?

4. The Oakland Cannabis Buyers' Cooperative was a non-profit organization, staffed by doctors and nurses, that provided marijuana to cancer patients. (For some kinds of cancer treatment, marijuana is an effective anti-nausea drug.) Federal officials sought and obtained an injunction ordering the Cooperative to cease its activities. The Cooperative violated the injunction, was charged with criminal contempt, and asserted a defense of "medical necessity." The District Court denied the defense. The Ninth Circuit reversed, and the Supreme Court reversed the Ninth Circuit's decision, unanimously. Justice Thomas wrote the majority opinion:

> As an initial matter, we note that it is an open question whether federal courts ever have authority to recognize a necessity defense not provided by statute. A necessity defense "traditionally covered the situation where physical forces beyond the actor's control rendered illegal conduct the lesser of two evils." United States v. Bailey, 444 U.S. 394, 410 (1980). Even at common law, the defense of necessity was somewhat controversial. See, e.g., Queen v. Dudley & Stephens, 14 Q.B. 273 (1884). And under our constitutional system, in which federal crimes are defined by statute rather than by common law, it is especially so. As we have stated: "Whether, as a policy matter, an exemption should be created is a question for legislative judgment, not judicial inference." United States v. Rutherford, 442 U.S. 544, 559 (1979). Nonetheless, we recognize that this Court has discussed the possibility of a necessity defense without altogether rejecting it. See, e.g., *Bailey*, supra, at 415.

> We need not decide, however, whether necessity can ever be a defense when the federal statute does not expressly provide for it. In this case, to resolve the question presented, we need only recognize that a medical necessity exception for marijuana is at odds with the terms of the Controlled Substances Act. The statute, to be sure, does not explicitly abrogate the defense. But its provisions leave no doubt that the defense is unavailable.

> . . . [The Controlled Substances Act] divides drugs into five schedules, depending in part on whether the particular drug has a currently accepted medical use. The Act then imposes restrictions on the manufacture and

distribution of the substance according to the schedule in which it has been placed. Schedule I is the most restrictive schedule. The Attorney General can include a drug in schedule I only if the drug "has no currently accepted medical use in treatment in the United States," "has a high potential for abuse," and has "a lack of accepted safety for use . . . under medical supervision." §§812(b)(1)(A)-(C). . . .

The Cooperative . . . argues that use of schedule I drugs . . . can be medically necessary, notwithstanding that they have "no currently accepted medical use." According to the Cooperative, a drug may not yet have achieved general acceptance as a medical treatment but may nonetheless have medical benefits to a particular patient or class of patients. We decline to parse the statute in this manner. . . .

For these reasons, we hold that medical necessity is not a defense to manufacturing and distributing marijuana. . . .

532 U.S. at 490-94. Justice Stevens joined the judgment in *Oakland Cannabis Buyers*, but objected to the language casting doubt on common-law defenses in federal cases:

. . . [T]he Court takes two unwarranted and unfortunate excursions that prevent me from joining its opinion. First, the Court reaches beyond its holding, and beyond the facts of the case, by suggesting that the defense of necessity is unavailable for anyone under the Controlled Substances Act. Because necessity was raised in this case as a defense to distribution, the Court need not venture an opinion on whether the defense is available to anyone other than distributors. Most notably, whether the defense might be available to a seriously ill patient for whom there is no alternative means of avoiding starvation or extraordinary suffering is a difficult issue that is not presented here.

Second, the Court gratuitously casts doubt on "whether necessity can ever be a defense" to any federal statute that does not explicitly provide for it, calling [the existence of] such a defense . . . an "open question." By contrast, our precedent has expressed no doubt about the viability of the common-law defense. . . . See, e.g., United States v. Bailey, 444 U.S. 394, 415 (1980) ("We therefore hold that, where a criminal defendant is charged with escape and claims that he is entitled to an instruction on the theory of duress or necessity, he must proffer evidence of a bona fide effort to surrender or return to custody as soon as the claimed duress or necessity had lost its coercive force"); id. at 415, n.11 ("Our principal difference with the dissent, therefore, is not as to the *existence* of such a defense but as to the importance of surrender as an element of it" (emphasis added)). . . .

532 U.S. at 500-01 (Stevens, J., concurring in the judgment). Justices Ginsburg and Souter agreed; Justice Breyer took no part in the case. Along with *Dixon v. United States*, supra at page 912, *Oakland Cannabis Buyers* suggests that the Supreme Court has yet to resolve the legal status of defenses to federal crimes.

E. ENTRAPMENT

The entrapment defense dates (at least) to the eighteenth century, but it was first ensconced in American law in Sorrells v. United States, 287 U.S. 435 (1932). *Sorrells* arose near the end of the nation's brief experience with criminalizing the manufacture and sale of alcoholic beverages. The facts were as follows:

> For the Government, one Martin, a prohibition agent, testified that having resided for a time in Haywood County, North Carolina, where he posed as a tourist, he visited defendant's home near Canton, on Sunday, July 13, 1930, accompanied by three residents of the county who knew the defendant well. He was introduced as a resident of Charlotte who was stopping for a time at Clyde. The witness ascertained that defendant was a veteran of the World War and a former member of the 30th Division [American Expeditionary Force]. Witness informed defendant that he was also an ex-service man and a former member of the same Division, which was true. Witness asked defendant if he could get the witness some liquor and defendant stated that he did not have any. Later, there was a second request without result. One of those present, one Jones, was also an ex-service man and a former member of the 30th Division, and the conversation turned to the war experiences of the three. After this, witness asked defendant for a third time to get him some liquor, whereupon defendant left his home and after a few minutes came back with a half gallon of liquor for which the witness paid defendant five dollars. Martin also testified that he was "the . . . only person among those present at the time who said anything about securing some liquor," and that his purpose was to prosecute the defendant for procuring and selling it. The Government rested its case on Martin's testimony.
>
> Defendant called as witnesses the three persons who had accompanied the prohibition agent. In substance, they corroborated the latter's story but with some additions. Jones, a railroad employee, testified that . . . witness told defendant that the agent was "an old 30th Division man" and the agent thereupon said to defendant that he "would like to get a half gallon of whiskey to take back to Charlotte to a friend of his that was in the furniture business with him," and that defendant replied that he "did not fool with whiskey"; that the agent and his companions were at defendant's home "for probably an hour or an hour and a half and that during such time the agent asked the defendant three or four or probably five times to get him, the agent, some liquor." Defendant said "he would go and see if he could get a half gallon of liquor" and he returned with it after an absence of "between twenty and thirty minutes." Jones added that at that time he had never heard of defendant being in the liquor business, that he and the defendant were "two old buddies," and that he believed "one former war buddy would get liquor for another."

287 U.S. at 439-40. Writing for a unanimous Court, Chief Justice Hughes found the defendant's claim sufficiently strong to go to the jury:

. . . [T]he defense of entrapment is not simply that the particular act was committed at the instance of government officials. That is often the case where the proper action of these officials leads to the revelation of criminal enterprises. The predisposition and criminal design of the defendant are relevant. But the issues raised and the evidence adduced must be pertinent to the controlling question whether the defendant is a person otherwise innocent whom the Government is seeking to punish for an alleged offense which is the product of the creative activity of its own officials. If that is the fact, common justice requires that the accused be permitted to prove it. . . .

. . . The defense is available, not in the view that the accused though guilty may go free, but that the Government cannot be permitted to contend that he is guilty of a crime where the government officials are the instigators of his conduct. . . . [T]he question is whether the defense, if the facts bear it out, takes the case out of the purview of the statute because it cannot be supposed that the Congress intended that the letter of its enactment should be used to support such a gross perversion of its purpose.

We are of the opinion that upon the evidence produced in the instant case the defense of entrapment was available and that the trial court was in error in holding that as a matter of law there was no entrapment and in refusing to submit the issue to the jury.

Id. at 451-52.

As Hughes' language makes clear, predisposition is the key to the entrapment defense. If the defendant was predisposed to commit the crime, the defendant was not "a person otherwise innocent whom the Government is seeking to punish for an alleged offense which is the product of the creative activity of its own officials." In most cases, predisposition is shown by the character of the crime: for example, in a simple buy-and-bust, an undercover police officer proposes a drug buy, gives the seller the money, and receives the drugs. The routinized nature of the transaction suggests that the defendant has sold drugs on many other occasions—unlike the defendant in *Sorrells*, who apparently took part in the illegal liquor trade only to do a favor for a fellow ex-soldier.

What if the government has abundant evidence that the defendant was predisposed to commit a wide variety of crimes, but not the crime charged? See the next case.

United States v. Luisi

United States Court of Appeals for the First Circuit
482 F.3d 43 (2007)

LYNCH, Circuit Judge.

Defendant Robert C. Luisi, Jr., an admitted member of [a] "La Cosa Nostra" (LCN) crime family, appeals his convictions on three cocaine-related charges. These convictions stemmed from an FBI investigation that employed a paid cooperating witness and LCN member, Ronald Previte.

At trial, Luisi testified and admitted his involvement in the cocaine transactions. His defense was entrapment, on intertwined theories. He claimed that Previte, acting for the government along with undercover FBI agent Michael McGowan, had improperly tried to induce him to commit drug crimes. He further claimed that when he resisted, Previte persuaded Philadelphia LCN boss Joseph Merlino to order Luisi to engage in the charged drug transactions. Merlino was Luisi's superior in the LCN, and the government was aware of the serious consequences Luisi would face if he refused to follow Merlino's order.

The district court instructed the jury on the entrapment defense. However, the court's supplemental instructions—given in response to a jury question—foreclosed the jury from considering Merlino's role in the asserted government entrapment of Luisi. We conclude that those instructions were erroneous, and we vacate the convictions and remand the case.

I

In July 1999, a grand jury in the District of Massachusetts indicted Luisi and three co-defendants on three charges: one count of conspiracy to possess cocaine with intent to distribute, see 21 U.S.C. §§841(a)(1), 846, and two counts of possession of cocaine with intent to distribute, see id. §841(a). The conspiracy was alleged to have run from February 1999 through June 28, 1999. The two possession counts stemmed from transactions on April 30, 1999, and June 3, 1999. . . .

In the late 1990s, the FBI conducted a major investigation into the operations of the Philadelphia LCN. Previte, a captain or "capo regime" in the LCN, assisted the FBI investigation by working as a cooperating witness under a personal services contract with the FBI. He was paid a substantial sum of money in return.

The FBI came to learn that Luisi was working for the Philadelphia LCN as a captain, and that he was supervising the criminal activity that the organization undertook in Boston. Eager to get evidence against Luisi, the FBI had Previte introduce Luisi to McGowan, who posed as a source of illegal money-making opportunities.

. . . McGowan operated under the pseudonym "Michael O'Sullivan" and purported to be in the import/export business. He told Luisi he had previously worked with Capo Previte in Philadelphia, and said he had now relocated to Boston. McGowan explained to Luisi that as part of his business he was sometimes presented with "opportunities" and that sometimes he needed help taking advantage of these "deals." Luisi agreed that he would look at future deals with McGowan. Unbeknownst to Luisi, this conversation was being recorded by the FBI—as were the vast majority of the future conversations Luisi would have with McGowan.

The first "opportunity" occurred on February 10, 1999, when McGowan presented Luisi with several "stolen" furs. Luisi was not sure if he would be able to sell them, but he stated he would look into it. He also inquired whether McGowan had other items; when McGowan mentioned the possibility of obtaining jewelry, Luisi expressed more interest in that, and particularly in diamonds. There was no mention of any drugs at this point.

Several days later, Luisi and Previte spoke to each other at a party in Philadelphia. Merlino was also present at the party. Luisi testified that Previte proposed a "swap" of cocaine for diamonds, and that Luisi's response was that he would "try" to get the deal done. He testified that he gave this response because "at the party [Merlino] . . . made it very clear to me that he wanted these drugs," although Luisi later clarified that he did not at that time understand Merlino to be giving an "order" to do the deal, but merely "permission." . . . Luisi testified that at or shortly after the party he chose not to do the deal.

On March 8, 1999, McGowan again met with Luisi, along with two of Luisi's associates. McGowan referred to Previte's proposed swap and stated that he (McGowan) knew a guy with diamonds, and that the guy was looking to exchange them for "three bricks." Luisi's immediate response was: "I want to get them, I want to bring them to [a jeweler friend of mine], if he likes it, boom. We'll do the deal and I'll do it that way, whatever [Previte] wants." McGowan interpreted this to mean that Luisi wanted to see the diamonds, and that he would be willing to exchange cocaine for them.

Several minutes later, however, Luisi took McGowan aside privately. This part of the conversation was not recorded. According to McGowan, Luisi told him that because Previte had referred McGowan to him, Luisi would make "every effort" to get the cocaine, but it would be difficult and it would take time. Luisi testified that he did not actually agree to do a drugs-for-diamonds swap. Also during the March 8th conversation, McGowan asked Luisi what items, other than the diamonds, he would be interested in. Luisi responded that he would be interested in jewelry, watches, and cigarettes, and some of his associates mentioned film and razor blades.

McGowan's next meeting with Luisi and his associates came on March 11, 1999. McGowan had some "stolen" Polaroid film, and the participants discussed how it was to be sold. Luisi reported on his only partially successful attempts to sell fur coats, and the participants also discussed diamonds and jewelry. Later during the meeting, McGowan mentioned that Previte was coming up to Boston in a few days, and Luisi agreed to meet with both Previte and McGowan then. Luisi and his associates left with the film.

Previte came to Boston, and on March 16, 1999, he met with McGowan, Luisi, and some of Luisi's associates. The participants had a cryptic conversation during which, according to McGowan, Luisi confirmed that he would get the cocaine-for-diamonds deal done. The following day, McGowan talked to Luisi over the phone, and again inquired into the status of the cocaine deal with Previte. Luisi replied that he would work on it, but indicated that the deal would not happen immediately.

During this time, Luisi had also been trying to sell the film that McGowan had given him on March 11th. He was unable to do so at a price that McGowan was willing to accept, and so on March 19th Luisi returned the film. After Luisi again expressed his preference for jewelry, and after McGowan again reaffirmed his ability to get jewelry, the conversation turned back to the proposed diamonds-for-cocaine deal. Luisi made comments that, if taken at face value, expressed a reluctance to go ahead with the deal and indicated that Luisi had "nothing to do with" the cocaine business. Luisi also explained to McGowan that "in the last . . . three years I lost over a dozen and a half guys to that. . . . And I have to make a stern, a firm stand here. . . . I don't wanna have nothing to do with it." . . .

Luisi and McGowan had no contact with each other for the next three weeks. On April 19, 1999, McGowan initiated a phone conversation with Luisi. McGowan turned the discussion to dealings with Previte, and Luisi responded that "[e]verything's gonna be okay soon." McGowan understood this to be a reference to the cocaine transaction.

McGowan initiated another phone conversation with Luisi on April 23, 1999. McGowan told him that Previte would be coming to Boston on April 28th, and he asked Luisi to be available then. . . . On April 27, 1999, one day before Previte's planned trip to Boston, Previte had a conversation with Merlino, his superior in the LCN. Previte was wearing a wire, and the conversation was recorded. As revealed by the tape, Previte complained to Merlino that Luisi had not yet done the cocaine transaction, despite Luisi's representations. Previte explained to Merlino that he had "big money sittin[g] on the line," and that Merlino would also make money from the transaction. He directly asked Merlino if there was "any way you could just tell [Luisi] to do what he gotta do." Merlino agreed to do so. Previte and Merlino then agreed that when Previte went to Boston the next day, Previte would put Luisi on the phone with Merlino, at which point Merlino would tell Luisi to do the cocaine deal. As Merlino put it on the tape: "I'll say [to Luisi:] whatever [Previte] says to do[,] just do it."

Previte was still cooperating with the FBI at the time he had the conversation with Merlino, and a jury could conclude that the FBI had in fact directed Previte's request of Merlino. Previte did not testify, nor did any of the Philadelphia FBI agents who had worked with him. But McGowan was asked if the FBI had arranged the meeting between Previte and Merlino, and his response was that while he did not know, he "assume[d] so because Previte was cooperating."

Previte flew to Boston on the morning of April 28th, the day after his conversation with Merlino. He went to McGowan's office, and McGowan arranged for Previte to make a three-way call with LCN boss Merlino and Capo Luisi, Merlino's underling. The call was recorded in its entirety. . . . Once Luisi was on the line, Previte brought Merlino into the conversation. After an exchange of preliminaries, Merlino (somewhat cryptically) got down to business.[5] Luisi testified that he understood Merlino to be ordering him to get the cocaine deal done, and that he agreed to do the deal as a result of this.

McGowan, who had been listening in to the conversation, testified to having a similar understanding. As he put it, "[a]fter this phone conversation, I expected to receive cocaine." His hopes were soon realized.

Within an hour after Merlino spoke to Luisi, Luisi met with Previte and McGowan to confirm details of the drug transaction. Initially, Previte and Luisi had a private conversation to work out certain points, and Previte explained that McGowan wanted to do multiple cocaine deals. Luisi agreed, and the private conversation ended shortly thereafter. With Luisi looking on, Previte then informed McGowan that . . . Shawn Vetere, one of Luisi's associates, [would be playing a role in the deal]. Vetere promptly put McGowan in touch with Bobby Carrozza. McGowan worked out more details with Carrozza. On April 30, 1999 — two days after the call with Merlino — Carrozza sold two kilograms of cocaine to McGowan. Carrozza told McGowan that the cocaine came "right from [Luisi and Vetere]. I wouldn't be able to do it any other way."

Two weeks later, McGowan gave Luisi a $1,000 "tribute" payment for arranging the transaction. McGowan and Luisi also engaged in preliminary discussions about a future cocaine deal, and Luisi told McGowan to work the rest out with Carrozza. McGowan did so.

The next cocaine delivery was not immediately forthcoming, however. On May 24, 1999, McGowan complained to Luisi, who told him to be patient. On June 1, 1999, Luisi proposed certain changes to the impending cocaine transaction; McGowan agreed to the revised cocaine deal the next day, and he paid Luisi the $24,000 cash price. On June 3, 1999, Carrozza and Tommy Wilson (another of Luisi's associates) came to McGowan's office to deliver one kilogram of cocaine. McGowan later gave Luisi a $500 "tribute" payment for arranging the deal.

Luisi was the sole witness to testify for the defense. He testified to several additional pertinent points. He admitted that he had been a captain in the LCN since the fall of 1998, and he agreed that the LCN was properly described as "the Mafia" and as "the mob." As a captain, one of his jobs

---

5. As recorded, the relevant portions of the conversation were as follows:

MERLINO: Bob, can that guy, you know, do what he's got to do over there for him?
LUISI: Oh, yeah.
MERLINO: All right.
LUISI: Yeah, that's, that's gonna, ah, that's gonna be.
PREVITE: Okay.
MERLINO: All right.
LUISI: You know?
MERLINO: You got it.

had been to make "tribute" payments to Merlino, and these payments had come out of Luisi's earnings from the criminal enterprises conducted by his "crew" in Boston. Luisi explained that the LCN was extremely hierarchical, and he stated that when the head of the LCN ordered him to do the cocaine transaction, he felt that he had no alternative other than to fulfill the order. He was also asked why he had engaged in the second cocaine transaction; while he did not specifically reference Merlino's order, he responded that he had not wanted to do the drug deal, and he did so because he "had to bring money to Philadelphia" and so he "was desperate." . . .

Luisi also offered an explanation for why he had seemed receptive to the cocaine deal, even before receiving the order from Merlino on April 28th. He claimed he had been trying to "pal off" McGowan and Previte; that is, he politely pretended to be cooperating with them on the drug deal, while in fact he had no intention of ever delivering drugs to them.

Before the jury was instructed, Luisi's attorney asked the district court to dismiss the case on the ground that the government had engaged in allegedly outrageous conduct, thereby violating Luisi's due process rights. The court never ruled on that motion; such a motion is an issue for the judge and not the jury. See United States v. Bradley, 820 F.2d 3, 7 n.5 (1st Cir. 1987). However, over the government's objection, the district court did agree that Luisi was entitled to an entrapment instruction.

The district court's entrapment instructions correctly informed the jury that the government had the burden to prove, beyond a reasonable doubt, that Luisi had not been entrapped. See United States v. Walter, 434 F.3d 30, 37 (1st Cir. 2006). The district court further explained that the government had to prove, beyond a reasonable doubt, that at least one of two things was true: either (1) "no government agent[9] or person acting on behalf [of] or . . . under [the] auspices of the government persuaded or induced the defendant to commit" the charged crimes; or (2) "the defendant was ready and willing to commit the [charged] crime[s] without persuasion from the government." This was also a correct statement of the law. See United States v. Gamache, 156 F.3d 1, 9 (1st Cir. 1998) (explaining that the two prongs of an entrapment defense are improper government inducement and lack of predisposition).

Luisi specifically asked for an instruction indicating that if the jury found that Previte had induced Merlino, that meant that Merlino's order could be considered government action. The district court refused, stating that the instruction was improper because there was a factual dispute over whether the government's responsibility ended due to the presence of an intermediary.

---

9. The district court did not provide a definition for the term "government agent."

Shortly after commencing deliberations, the jury sent the court a question that revealed it was considering Merlino's role and how it related to the entrapment defense. The jury asked:

> "Is Merlino's request of Luisi, if determined to be excessive pressure, considered to be government persuasion or inducement because the contact between Merlino and Luisi resulted from the government agent Previte and Merlino?"

The court and the parties researched the issue overnight, and returned in the morning to discuss the proper response. Luisi contended that because Previte had spoken to Merlino about the cocaine transaction, and because Merlino's order had been facilitated by Previte and McGowan (the latter of whom had actually placed the three-way call to Merlino), the actions of Merlino, Previte, and McGowan together could be attributed to the government. . . . The government described Luisi's asserted defense as "derivative entrapment," . . . claimed that [only one case had recognized that defense, and distinguished that case.]

The court took a different route, and it ultimately concluded that a case from this circuit, United States v. Bradley, was controlling. In *Bradley* a prison inmate named Constanza, who could have been deemed to have been acting as a government agent, directly threatened an intermediary named Brenner to do a drug deal on pain of physical harm. 820 F.2d at 5-6. The intermediary was unable to do the deal on his own, and he in turn pressured his friend — the defendant Bradley — to assist him. See id. at 7-8. We found the evidence sufficient to support an entrapment instruction for the intermediary Brenner, as the government agent had directly threatened him. Id. But we held that Brenner's friend, defendant Bradley, was not entitled to an entrapment instruction: while Brenner could claim duress, Bradley had "only an appeal to sympathy, which he was free to reject." Id. at 7. We stated that we "would not extend the [entrapment] defense to a remote defendant without, at least, a showing that pressure had been put upon him by the intermediary at the instruction of the government agent." Id. at 8.

Thus in *Bradley* this court rejected defendant Bradley's argument that the government's improper inducement of Brenner could be an indirect entrapment of Bradley, as the agent (Constanza) had neither ordered nor expected Brenner to entrap other persons. See id. at 7. We said that a "quite different case would be presented if Constanza had targeted a putative seller and had instructed Brenner to put the arm on him." Id. We then added a footnote to "suggest that such a case, though argued to be a third-party case, is not really a third-party case at all. The intermediary in such instance is really acting under instructions, as a government subagent — a quite different situation." Id. at 7 n.6.

The district court focused upon *Bradley*'s use of the word "instructions," and it read that case as concerned with whether the government agent (Previte) had "instructed" the intermediary (Merlino) to pressure Luisi.

The court concluded that because Previte ranked below Merlino in the LCN hierarchy, Previte was in no position to "instruct" Merlino to do anything. Although Luisi argued for a broader reading of the word "instruct," the district court rejected such a reading of *Bradley*. In the alternative, Luisi asked that the jury be allowed to determine whether Merlino had been "instructed," but the court rejected that option as well.

The district court then called the jury back into the courtroom and answered the jury's question as follows:

> [I]n your consideration of the entrapment question, you should focus your attention on the relationship—the direct relationship between Mr. Previte . . . and Mr. McGowan on the one hand, and Mr. Luisi on the other hand. You should consider evidence as [it] relates to the direct contact between and among those people.

Because the district court omitted Merlino from this statement, while simultaneously mentioning other individuals, the jury likely concluded that it could not consider Merlino's role in any inducement of Luisi. This was particularly so since the jury's question specifically asked about Merlino, and the court told the jury to focus on individuals other than Merlino. As a result, and as the government has not disputed, the jury was precluded from finding that Merlino's order to Luisi could be deemed improper governmental inducement.

Later that day, the jury convicted Luisi on all three counts of the indictment.

II

Luisi's primary contention on appeal is that the district court's jury instructions, as supplemented by its answer to the jury's question, were incorrect as a matter of law. We review that issue de novo here. See United States v. Buttrick, 432 F.3d 373, 376 (1st Cir. 2005). . . .

. . . The Supreme Court has explained that the "function of law enforcement is the prevention of crime and the apprehension of criminals. Manifestly, that function does not include the manufacturing of crime. . . . Congress could not have intended that its statutes were to be enforced by tempting innocent persons into violations." Sherman v. United States, 356 U.S. 369, 372 (1958). A successful entrapment defense requires that there be a reasonable doubt on both prongs of a two-pronged test.

The first prong necessitates a showing of improper government inducement. See *Gamache*, 156 F.3d at 9. This aspect of the defense plainly seeks to deter improper government conduct. United States v. Gendron, 18 F.3d 955, 961 (1st Cir. 1994). Indeed, a defendant cannot claim entrapment when government conduct played no causal role in the defendant's inducement. See *Sherman*, 356 U.S. at 372. Nevertheless, the entrapment defense only deters government misbehavior in cases where the defendant would otherwise be law-abiding. *Gendron*, 18 F.3d at 962. That is because the second prong requires that the defendant have a lack of predisposition to commit the charged offense. See id.; see also Sorrells v. United States, 287 U.S. 435, 448 (1932).

These two prongs, and the policy concerns behind them, play important roles in delimiting the scope of the entrapment defense. But they are not the only considerations that matter. This court and the Supreme Court have taken account of the practical problems facing law enforcement, particularly in the prosecution of "victimless" crimes where "significant governmental involvement in illegal activities" is often required [to catch and punish offenders]. *Bradley*, 820 F.2d at 6-8; see also United States v. Russell, 411 U.S. 423, 432 (1973); *Gendron*, 18 F.3d at 961. We must be mindful that "the defense of entrapment . . . [does] not . . . give the federal judiciary a 'chancellor's foot' veto over law enforcement practices of which it [does] not approve." *Russell*, 411 U.S. at 435. . . .

. . . It is beyond dispute that an individual like Previte, hired by the government as an informant, is a "government agent" for entrapment purposes. See *Sherman*, 356 U.S. at 373-75. Nor can there be any dispute that Merlino's order to Luisi, with its implied threat of physical harm or other serious retribution, could be found by a jury to be improper inducement if attributed to the government. See *Gendron*, 18 F.3d at 961; *Bradley*, 820 F.2d at 7.

It is also clear that Luisi's case does not fit the pattern of what has come to be known as "vicarious entrapment." In "vicarious entrapment" an unknowing middleman merely tells the defendant about an inducement that the government had used to target the middleman. See United States v. Valencia, 645 F.2d 1158, 1168-69 (2d Cir. 1980) (recognizing the vicarious entrapment defense). Here, the target was not the middleman Merlino, but the defendant Luisi. Further, a jury could find that Merlino had himself threatened Luisi. . . . Merlino [did not repeat] to Luisi a threat that Previte had made against Merlino. Indeed, Previte did not threaten Merlino at all.

Instead, this case is much closer to what has been called "derivative entrapment," a situation in which a government agent "uses the unsuspecting middleman as a means of passing on an inducement" to the defendant. 2 W. LaFave, Substantive Criminal Law, §9.8(a), at 93 (2d ed. 2003). Yet even within this category, further refinement is required.

We have before us a situation in which a jury could find that Previte specifically targeted Luisi, and then "induced" Merlino to give an order to Luisi when Merlino might not have otherwise done so. But Previte's inducement of Merlino does not appear to have itself been improper. Previte simply helped set up a drug transaction, explained to Merlino that Merlino would profit from the transaction's execution, and then encouraged Merlino to order Luisi's assistance. Cf. *Gendron*, 18 F.3d at 961-62 (explaining that improper inducement "goes beyond providing an ordinary 'opportunity to commit a crime,'" and providing examples (quoting Jacobson v. United States, 503 U.S. 540, 550 (1992))). A jury would presumably find that Previte merely provided an "ordinary" inducement to Merlino; it was Merlino's inducement of Luisi that a jury could find improper.

This is an unusual entrapment situation. Under the original, correct instructions given, it is evident that the jury was considering the possibility that Merlino had put excessive pressure on Luisi, and that the jurors were unsure whether Merlino's order could be considered "government persuasion or inducement. . . ." The effect of the court's response was the same as if it had instructed the jury, as a matter of law, that Merlino's order could not be considered *government* inducement or persuasion. We must decide whether the issue was correctly removed from the jury's consideration. . . .

The *Bradley* court ultimately held that it "would not extend the [entrapment] defense to a remote defendant without, at least, a showing that pressure had been put upon him by the intermediary at the instruction of the government agent." Id. at 8. The government reads "instruct" to mean "command," such that Previte is not responsible for Merlino's threats against Luisi unless Previte had commanded Merlino to order Luisi into the cocaine deal. Luisi reads "instruct" to mean "convince" or "inform." But the dispute about the use of particular language in *Bradley* is largely beside the point. *Bradley* was a case in which the government agent neither "commanded," "convinced," nor "informed" the middleman (Brenner) to target Bradley. . . . [Unlike] *Bradley*, [in this case] the government's actions were specifically designed to pressure Luisi. . . .

. . . [T]he law in this circuit permits an entrapment instruction involving a middleman when there is evidence that (1) a government agent specifically targeted the defendant in order to induce him to commit illegal conduct; (2) the agent acted through the middleman after other government attempts at inducing the defendant had failed; (3) the government agent requested, encouraged, or instructed the middleman to employ a specified inducement, which could be found improper, against the targeted defendant; (4) the agent's actions led the middleman to do what the government sought, even if the government did not use improper means to influence the middleman; and (5) as a result of the middleman's inducement, the targeted defendant in fact engaged in the illegal conduct.[13] . . .

In light of our understanding of the law, we think a properly instructed jury could conclude that the government was responsible for Merlino's order

13. Contrary to our precedent, several circuits categorically deny the entrapment defense in *all* third-party situations where the middleman is unaware that he is helping the government. See United States v. Squillacote, 221 F.3d 542, 574 (4th Cir. 2000); United States v. Thickstun, 110 F.3d 1394, 1398 (9th Cir. 1997); United States v. Martinez, 979 F.2d 1424, 1432 (10th Cir. 1992). The Third Circuit's law varies. *Compare* United States v. Klosterman, 248 F.2d 191, 195-96 (3d Cir. 1957) (concluding that the third-party entrapment defense was available in a case where the defendant was specifically targeted and the middleman was unwitting), *with* United States v. Beverly, 723 F.2d 11, 12 (3d Cir. 1983) (*per curiam*) (failing to cite *Klosterman* and claiming that the third-party entrapment defense is categorically unavailable when the middleman is unwitting). With the possible exception of the Ninth Circuit's opinion in United States v. Emmert, 829 F.2d 805 (9th Cir. 1987), we are unaware of any cases in which these circuits have rejected the third-party defense when confronted with the kind of fact pattern we face here. As for *Emmert*, we respectfully disagree with the Ninth Circuit's conclusions.

to Luisi. . . . [S]uch a jury could decide that: (1) Previte specifically requested that Merlino order Luisi to engage in the cocaine deal; (2) Previte's request came after earlier government efforts to ensnare Luisi, without a middle-man, had not been fruitful; (3) Previte, as an LCN captain, understood that the order he requested from Merlino would contain an implied threat of death, physical harm, or [other] serious retribution if Luisi failed to comply; (4) Merlino's order to Luisi was exactly what Previte had requested; and (5) Merlino would not have given the order if Previte had not encouraged him to do so. As a result, we think that the district court incorrectly answered the jury's question. . . .

. . . We do not suggest that a jury would necessarily have concluded that Luisi was entrapped through Merlino. We hold only that the defendant was entitled to have a properly instructed jury consider the issue.

As a fallback argument, the government contends that Luisi failed to present sufficient evidence of his lack of predisposition, and thus was not entitled to any entrapment instruction at all. We readily dispose of this argument.

A judge may only instruct the jury on entrapment if the defendant meets his entry-level burden of production. That is, a defendant is entitled to an entrapment instruction only if there is "some evidence," on both elements of the entrapment defense, sufficient to raise a reasonable doubt that the defendant was merely an unwary innocent. See United States v. Joost, 92 F.3d 7, 12 (1st Cir. 1996). The defendant must show "more than a scintilla of evidence, more than mere creation of an opportunity for criminal activity." Id. . . .

Luisi made the requisite entry-level showing. We have already explained why a jury could find improper governmental inducement. Additionally, Luisi introduced "some evidence" of his lack of predisposition. . . . Luisi . . . stalled the drug transaction for several months to "pal off" McGowan, thereby indefinitely delaying a drug deal to which Luisi was opposed. Indeed, a jury could find that this two-*month* delay stood in stark contrast to the two-*day* lag between when Merlino gave Luisi the order, and when McGowan received drugs from Luisi's colleagues. . . . Accordingly, we find that Luisi introduced sufficient evidence of his lack of predisposition to entitle him to an entrapment instruction. . . .

III

. . . The judgments of conviction are vacated and the case is remanded for further proceedings consistent with this opinion.

Notes on Entrapment

1. Even the clearest threats by his fellow mobsters cannot give rise to a duress defense for someone in Luisi's position: Recall Williams v. State, supra at page 905. Why, then, does Merlino's oblique order—see footnote 5 in the court's opinion—suffice to raise a plausible claim of entrapment?

2. Consider another comparison. Had Merlino been the sole source of the order Luisi received, Luisi would have no colorable entrapment claim—it is no defense that one committed a crime to which one was not predisposed in response to the bribe or threat of a private individual. Why should the result change if the bribe or threat comes from the government?

3. The defendant in Wyatt v. Commonwealth, 219 S.W.3d 751 (Ky. 2007), was convicted of soliciting murder; the supposed hit man was an undercover police officer and the party who arranged the phony transaction was a police informant. Here is the court's account of the key conversation:

> Agent Thielhorn began the conversation by telling Appellant he had heard that she was willing to pay with drugs for two police officers to be killed. He told Appellant that he had come in from Illinois and he did not have a gun or anything so he asked her how she wanted them killed. Appellant told him that she didn't care, "dead is dead." Appellant then said, "the easiest way," but she immediately stated that she had no money. Agent Thielhorn said that the easiest way to do it was to shoot the two officers with a gun, but he did not have one. At Ferguson's urging, Appellant admitted that she had a sawed-off shotgun and Ferguson asked if it could be used for the crime. Agent Thielhorn told Appellant that she would not get the gun back because he would have to dispose of it. Appellant again stated that she had no money, but Agent Thielhorn suggested that pills (Lortabs) would be acceptable payment. A discussion of payment amounts and methods began between Agent Thielhorn and Ferguson. Appellant responded, "I don't know, I'll have to think about it." Eventually, Agent Thielhorn arrived at a down payment amount of one-hundred pills. When specifically asked by Agent Thielhorn, Appellant agreed that it was a fair down payment.

219 S.W.3d at 754. Noting that "[a]ppellant had no history of engaging in crimes similar to those charged" and that the chief instigator of the plot to kill the officers was Ferguson, the police informant, the court held that the defendant was entitled to have the jury instructed on the entrapment defense.

4. The defendant in United States v. Holmes, 421 F.3d 683 (8th Cir. 2005), was convicted of conspiracy to distribute cocaine, based in part on sales to a police informant. The defendant claimed entrapment. The court dismissed the claim:

> . . . [W]e have stated that the entrapment defense "should not preclude officers from using stealth or strategy to trap an unwary criminal, or from providing a criminal with the opportunity to commit a crime." United States v. Hinton, 908 F.2d 355, 358 (8th Cir. 1990). . . . [T]he officers involved in the investigation testified that Holmes exhibited a working knowledge of terms used in the drug trade, conducted herself during the transactions in a manner comporting with one who deals narcotics out of the home, and discussed with [the buyer] her

dealings with other customers, her desire to engage in future deals, and her ability to secure certain quantities of crack. These facts establish not only that the government merely provided Holmes the opportunity to engage in illicit drug transactions, but also that Holmes was predisposed to do so. Although the government was not able to specifically name any of Holmes's other drug customers, such an identification was unnecessary because Holmes's own statements . . . establish the existence of other customers. Accordingly, she was not entitled to submit her entrapment defense to the jury.

421 F.3d at 686-87.

5. A standard federal jury instruction on predisposition asks jurors to decide whether the defendant "was ready and willing to commit crimes such as are charged in the indictment . . . and that government officers or their agents did no more than offer the opportunity" to commit those crimes. Quoted in Louis Michael Seidman, The Supreme Court, Entrapment, and Our Criminal Justice Dilemma, 1981 Sup. Ct. Rev. 111, 118. But, as Seidman explains,

> whether a person is "ready and willing" to break the law depends on what the person expects to get in return — that is, on the level of inducement. Like the rest of us, criminals do not generally work for free. . . .
>
> . . . [S]o long as one equates "predisposition" with a readiness to commit crime, no definition of "predisposition" can be complete without [specifying] the level of inducement to which a "predisposed" defendant would respond. Furthermore, the "predisposed" cannot be distinguished from the "nondisposed" without focusing on the propriety of the government's conduct — the very factor that the subjective approach professes to ignore.

Id. at 118-19. What does predisposition mean? Is it an appropriate basis for criminal liability?

F. INSANITY

State v. Arriola

Court of Criminal Appeals of Tennessee
2009 Tenn. Crim. App. LEXIS 728 (Aug. 26, 2009)

Opinion by WEDEMEYER, J.

After conducting a bench trial, the trial court found the Defendant, Richard Anthony Arriola, guilty of one count of first degree murder, one count of attempted first degree murder, and two counts of attempted second degree murder. The trial court sentenced the Defendant to an effective sentence of life imprisonment plus fifteen years. This Court remanded the case to the trial court for an order clarifying its findings on the insanity defense. On appeal, the Defendant claims: (1) the trial court erred when it used an improper legal standard for the insanity defense; and (2) the evidence presented at trial proved by clear and convincing evidence that the Defendant was not guilty by reason of insanity. After a thorough review of the record and the applicable law, we conclude that the trial court applied an improper legal standard for the insanity defense. Therefore, we reverse the convictions and remand for a new trial.

OPINION

I. FACTS

A. Trial

In our remand to the trial court for clarification of its findings on the insanity defense, we summarized the relevant facts:

> This case arises from a standoff between the Defendant and the Davidson County Sheriff's Department on September 22, 1995, which resulted in the death of Officer Jerry Newsome. The Defendant was indicted on charges of one count of first degree murder, one count of attempted first degree murder, and two counts of attempted second degree murder. The Defendant waived his right to a jury trial. At his trial, the relevant evidence included: the Defendant was a well-adjusted and active young man as he completed high school. After enrolling in college at the University of Tennessee-Martin, he began exhibiting symptoms of mental illness. According to his mother, Viola Couser, and his brother, John Arriola, the Defendant became reclusive and paranoid. After completing only one trimester, the Defendant left college and moved back home to Nashville. He then traveled around the world, later claiming to have visited Jerusalem and to have joined a religious group in Florida. When the Defendant would "travel," he would leave home for months at a time, taking only a "pack on his back" and not tell his family his plans. The Defendant also enlisted in the Navy (and was discharged after three to four months for an unknown reason) and got married for less than a month. When he was in Nashville, he worked at his step-father's restaurant peeling potatoes. While he was at home, he engaged in peculiar activities like preaching on street corners and on his front porch when no one was near him to listen. He always carried a Bible with him, and he repeatedly tried to baptize his family. The Defendant was even arrested once for preaching outside in the rain.
>
> According to Couser, the Defendant was first hospitalized for mental health treatment in 1987. He remained at Middle Tennessee Mental Health Institute (MTMHI) for thirty days, where the doctors diagnosed him with paranoid schizophrenia. The Defendant was released with orders to stay on his medicine and continue treatment, but he did neither. The Defendant was hospitalized at MTMHI for another thirty days in 1988, where he was treated again for paranoid schizophrenia. Similar to before, upon release, he refused to take his medication. Around 1989 or 1990, the Defendant moved from the upstairs of his parents' house into their basement, which he kept "cluttered up," according to his mother. The Defendant was hospitalized a third time in

1991 at Baptist Hospital as a result of judicial order. The Defendant had gotten into a fist fight with his older brother, John, over the issue of the Defendant not bathing regularly. John agreed to drop the charges if the Defendant entered an inpatient treatment facility. He was kept for thirty days, treated for paranoid schizophrenia, and released. According to Couser, after the Defendant was released, he stopped his treatment; when describing one manifestation of her son's illness when he stopped his medication, she said, he "wasn't keeping himself clean. He grew the beard and he wasn't getting his hair cut."

In September 1995, the Defendant began posting signs for his "businesses" in his neighborhood. The Defendant thought he ran a scuba diving business, an electrician business, and an advertising business. When the police served his parents with a warrant, ordering that the signs be removed or they pay a fine, the Defendant threatened the police with his neighbor's dogs. The Defendant's parents took down his signs to avoid paying a fine, but the Defendant replaced the signs and refused to remove them. The Defendant's parents both thought if they served the Defendant with an eviction warrant, the judge could commit the Defendant for treatment or, at least, have the Defendant agree to treatment, similar to what happened in 1991.

On September 22, 1995, Officer Johnnie Spears and Officer Jerry Newsome arrived at the Defendant's house to serve him with the eviction warrant. Officer Spears wore his badge in a visible location, and Officer Newsome wore a green and tan Sheriff's Department uniform. They knocked on the door with their night sticks, to avoid another threat involving the neighbor's dogs. The Defendant "came out sideways with his hand behind his back. . . . He was cussing." Officer Spears said he dropped the warrant on the ground, and as he started to turn, "that's when [the Defendant] shot me in the midsection, and it knocked me down." Officer Spears also saw Officer Newsome "grab his chest and fall." Officer Spears said the Defendant was originally firing a handgun, but as he made his way back to his police cruiser to call for help, the Defendant began using a camouflaged shotgun. Officer Spears thought Officer Newsome was dead because he never saw him move after falling. Officer Spears made a radio call signaling that a "police officer [was] in serious danger."

Officer Mike Hagar arrived at the scene after hearing the radio call. He saw Officer Newsome lying in the grass and not moving. After additional police arrived, they realized the Defendant was still in the basement, and they called for the SWAT team. Officer Hagar stated that the Defendant's brother, John Arriola, came to the scene and warned them that the Defendant was schizophrenic. Officer Hagar said that, while he was at the scene, no shots were fired before the SWAT team went into the house.

When the SWAT team arrived, they divided up into two teams: one for the upstairs portion of the house and one for the basement portion of the house. They initially tried negotiating with the Defendant, but there was no response. After the negotiation failed, the SWAT team began to move into the house. Before the basement team made it into the house, they began "drawing fire" from the Defendant after throwing two "distraction devices" into the house. Distraction devices are stun grenades that "cause[] a concussion. . . . And if [a person is] looking at it the flash will temporarily blind them." After throwing in the second device, the SWAT team heard gun shots. According to Officer Randy Hickman, one of the SWAT team members on the "upstairs" team, "once we dropped the devices, [the Defendant] fire[d] two, approximately two shots, at us, up the staircase there. Then we g[a]ve commands to come out, and at which time he fired about, approximately, two more shots at us, up the steps. I could see the rounds ricochet."

As the SWAT team was "thinking of what [it was] going to do next, that's when the suspect came out" of the house. Officer Hyde said the basement was "filled with smoke," and, as the Defendant came out cursing, one SWAT team member kicked the Defendant's lower body to knock him on the ground. At that point, the Defendant tried grabbing the officer's weapon, but only managed to grab the strap. Eventually, the Defendant was arrested and put into a van for transport to the hospital to check on his injuries.

Officer Pat Postiglione, an officer on the murder squad, helped transport the Defendant to the hospital. He described the Defendant as "very subdued" and said the Defendant refused to give a statement because "he didn't trust the government." Officer Larry Flair, another officer of the murder squad, characterized the Defendant as "coherent, conscious." In fact, the Defendant chose not to waive his *Miranda* rights when they were given to him, and he refused to give consent to search his property. Once the Defendant was out of the basement, various officers of the murder squad searched the basement for weapons. Officer Bill Pridemore described the basement as "very disarrayed. Things [were] scattered throughout the floor." The officers found a handgun in a hole in the drywall.

Doctor Bruce Levy, the current medical examiner for Nashville and a specialist in forensic pathology, testified that Officer Jerry Newsome was shot five times: three times with a handgun and two times with a shotgun. Three of the shots were quickly fatal.

Since the arrest, the Defendant has been housed at MTMHI and undergoing therapy and treatment for paranoid schizophrenia. Some of the Defendant's delusions included that his mother did not give birth to him; rather, he believed she found him at an airport. The Defendant also had a fascination with religion, and he believed he needed to baptize his family members in his bathtub. Dr. Rokeya Farooque, one of the Defendant's doctors at MTMHI, testified that the Defendant "[believed] that he would be the next Pope. He owned the government world bank. He owned the government of the United States." Additionally, he believed he invented the bar code. Dr. Farooque discussed the Defendant's "gradual deteriorating function" at great length. She said he was diagnosed again with paranoid schizophrenia in 1996, which took into account his bizarre behaviors, religious ideas, loose speech, hallucinations, delusional thinking, grandiose delusional thinking, and persecutorial delusional thinking. Dr. Farooque testified that on September 22, 1995, the Defendant was psychotic and was not able to appreciate the wrongfulness of his actions. In fact, she said he felt justified to defend himself because he thought he owned everything.

The Defendant was also treated by Dr. Samuel Craddock, who echoed Dr. Farooque's opinion that the Defendant could not appreciate the wrongfulness of his actions. Dr. Craddock described the Defendant as "suspicious of just about everybody that he encountered." He also stated that the Defendant believed he owned Palm Beach, Florida. Speaking of the September 1995 shooting incident, Dr. Craddock said, "I think even if [the Defendant] were a spectator, though, across the street watching what was occurring, I am not so sure that he could comprehend even what was going on he was so mentally ill, much less being able to participate and having the emotional involvement." Whenever the Defendant was asked about the shooting incident, he complained of "burning sensations." He also suffered from those sensations when the doctors suggested that he take some psychological tests. Moreover, Dr. Craddock conveyed that the Defendant told him that he would not have done anything illegal, implying that he did not know his shooting the police was illegal.

Dr. Patricia Corry explained that the Defendant had two "plans" as part of his mental illness. "Plan A" included all of his purely delusional thoughts, such as, he was going to become King Richard. "Plan B" included his thoughts and memories concerning the September 22, 1995, shooting. When talking about the shooting, the Defendant only recalls "intruding thoughts that—really voices, or feelings, or things that—he thought he could float around outside his body, things that he could feel inside his body as well." The Defendant told Dr. Corry that he heard "voices that told him to shoot and kill anybody that messed with him." Dr. Corry said the Defendant thought the ship the Queen Mary II was on its way to Florida to take him and Vanessa Corona, one of the characters the Defendant created in his mind, to the Vatican. He believed that Corona was the District Attorney in Miami, Florida and that she would leave the United States with him when he became King Richard, the President of the United States, or the first American Jewish Pope. While in treatment, the Defendant planned which eighty-five countries he was going to conquer and rule when he became king. The Defendant consistently believed himself to be either a saint or a preacher. Dr. Corry also elaborated that the Defendant believed one of the deputies had a virus that "was just kind of free-flow" and it could move from computers to humans in the Defendant's thoughts. The Defendant was afraid of contracting this virus when the police came to his door. Additionally, the Defendant believed the CIA met in a church on West End Avenue in Nashville, Tennessee two months prior to the shooting.

The Defendant was in custody from 1995 until 2006 before he was deemed competent to stand trial. Dr. Ronnie Stout, another of the Defendant's doctors at MTMHI, said that the Defendant's treatment progress was very slow, partially due to the difficulty of ascertaining the proper medication for him.

After hearing this testimony, the trial court found the Defendant guilty of first degree murder, attempted first degree murder, and two counts of attempted second degree murder. It sentenced the Defendant to an effective sentence of life imprisonment plus fifteen years.

State v. Richard Anthony Arriola, No. M2007-00428-CCA-R3-CD, 2008 Tenn. Crim. App. LEXIS 577, 2008 WL 1991098, at *1-4 (May 8, 2008) (herein *Arriola I*). . . .

II. ANALYSIS

On appeal, the Defendant contends that: (1) the trial court erred when it used an improper legal standard for the insanity defense; and (2) the evidence presented at trial clearly and convincingly supported an insanity defense.

A. Insanity Defense Legal Standard

The Defendant claims that the trial court applied the wrong legal standard for the insanity defense because the trial court understood the Defendant's ability to appreciate the nature of his actions to encompass his ability to appreciate the wrongfulness of his actions, and, accordingly, required the Defendant to prove he appreciated neither the nature nor the wrongfulness of his actions. The State argues that the trial court did not err because, although it stated that "wrongfulness is part and parcel of the word nature," the trial court later "look[ed] further at the specific facts to discern whether the [D]efendant could appreciate the wrongfulness of his actions."

We discussed the statutorily-based insanity standard in *Arriola I*, and we concluded that for a defendant to successfully prove an insanity defense, he need only prove that, as a result of a severe mental disease or defect, *either* he did not appreciate the nature of his actions *or* he did not appreciate that his actions were wrongful:

> The statutory requirements for an insanity defense are described in Tennessee Code Annotated section 39-11-501:
>
>> It is an affirmative defense to prosecution that, at the time of the commission of the acts constituting the offense, the defendant, as a result of a severe mental disease or defect, was unable to appreciate the nature *or* wrongfulness of the defendant's acts. Mental disease or defect does not otherwise constitute a defense. The defendant has the burden of proving the defense of insanity by clear and convincing evidence.

(emphasis added) (1995). When interpreting a statute, courts should use the "natural and ordinary meaning[s of the statutory language], unless the legislature used [the words] in a specialized, technical sense." BellSouth Telecomm., Inc. v. Green, 972 S.W.2d 663, 673 (Tenn. App. 1997). The word at issue here is "or." There is no indication that the legislature used it in a specialized, technical way, therefore, we will assign it its natural and ordinary meaning. According to *Black's Law Dictionary*, "or" is "a disjunctive particle used to express an alternative or to give a choice of one among two or more things." *Black's Law Dictionary* 1095 (6th ed. 1990). We contrast that with the definition of "and," which is "a conjunction connecting words or phrases expressing the idea that the latter is to be added to or taken along with the first." *Black's Law Dictionary* 86 (6th ed. 1990). Applying the correct definition of "or" to this statute, the plain meaning shows two distinct ways that the defendant may present a successful insanity defense: proving either that he could not appreciate the nature of his acts or, in the alternative, that he could not appreciate the wrongfulness of his acts. Moreover, to prevail, the Defendant need not prove both that he could not appreciate the nature of his act and that he could not appreciate the wrongfulness of his acts.

Arriola I, 2008 Tenn. Crim. App. LEXIS 577, 2008 WL 1991098, at *5. In *Arriola I*, we remanded the case to the trial court and instructed it to clarify its factual findings with respect to the Defendant's insanity defense. 2008 Tenn. Crim. App. LEXIS 577, [WL] at *8.

Complying with our request, the trial court issued a written order clarifying its findings on the issue of insanity. It concluded that the concept of "wrongfulness" is a narrower part of the concept of "nature":

> As the [c]ourt stated in its original ruling, the experts testified that the defendant could not appreciate the wrongfulness of his actions. However, they could not say that the defendant could not appreciate the nature of his actions.
>
> The [c]ourt believes that *because the defendant could not prove that he was unable to appreciate the nature of his actions he therefore could not prove that he was unable to appreciate the wrongfulness of his actions.* Although the words "nature" and "wrongfulness" are distinctly different words, *"wrongfulness" is encompassed in the word "nature."* The plain meaning of the word "nature" is that "it is the essential character of something." Since terms such as "rightfulness" and "wrongfulness" speak to the essence of character, it follows that *wrongfulness is part and parcel of the word nature, and is simply more narrowly defined than the word nature.* The [c]ourt thus had to look further at the specific facts to discern whether the defendant could appreciate the wrongfulness of his actions.

(emphasis added). The trial court then listed facts from the case that, in its view, demonstrated the Defendant knew his actions were wrong:

> Initially, when the defendant was contacted by the deputies, he hid his weapon behind his back, thus indicating not only his intent but his knowledge of the wrongfulness of his action. After the defendant shot and wounded one deputy and killed another deputy, he demonstrated that he knew that it was wrong by barricading himself in his apartment and refusing to come out even after being surrounded by the police. He had to be forced out through the use of distraction devices. The defendant further demonstrated the wrongfulness of his actions by hiding his pistol. If he truly believed that he owned the world and could do no wrong, he would not have attempted to hide himself or one of his weapons. Moreover, the defendant refused to discuss with the police or his treatment providers the acts that he committed that day, again implying that he knew that his actions were wrong. It was not until sometime later that he began to discuss the events of that day with his treatment providers.

After that discussion, the trial court concluded that "the defendant did not carry his burden of proving by clear and convincing evidence that he was unable to appreciate the nature or wrongfulness of his acts."

Whether the trial court used the proper legal standard for the insanity defense is a question of law, which we review *de novo* with no presumption of correctness. We conclude that the trial court applied the wrong legal standard. First, the trial court clearly stated that the concept of "wrongfulness" is encompassed in the concept of "nature." We respectfully disagree. "Wrongfulness" goes to whether a defendant understands whether the actions were wrong, or, in other words, it addresses a moral capacity, whereas "nature" goes to whether a defendant understands what the actions were, or, in other words, it addresses a cognitive capacity. *See* Clark v. Arizona, 548 U.S. 735, 747-48, 753-54 (2006) (interpreting Arizona's insanity defense statute,[1] which has similar language to Tennessee's statute); *see also* State v. Holder, 15 S.W.3d 905 (Tenn. Crim. App. 1999) (holding that the defendant knew the nature of his actions because he knew he stabbed a man and that he knew the wrongfulness of those actions because he knew stabbing a person was wrong). Additionally, as we stated in *Arriola I*, the Legislature listed "wrongfulness" and "nature" as independent grounds of supporting a defense of insanity. *See* T.C.A. §39-11-501 (1995). Thus, the two words must be mutually exclusive and not "part and parcel," as the trial court found.

Second, a defendant need only successfully prove that he, "as a result of a severe mental disease or defect, was unable to appreciate the nature *or* wrongfulness of [his] acts." T.C.A. §39-11-501. The trial court wrote that "*because* the defendant could not prove that he was unable to appreciate the *nature* of his actions he *therefore* could not prove that he was unable to appreciate the *wrongfulness* of his actions." (emphasis added.) Again, we respectfully disagree. A defendant need only prove that, as a result of a severe mental disease or defect, *either* he could not appreciate the nature of his actions *or* he could not appreciate the wrongfulness of those actions. T.C.A. §39-11-501. In addition to the discussion we have already presented from *Arriola I*, we add that the nature or wrongfulness language of the Tennessee insanity defense statute corresponds to a portion of the *M'Naughten* standard, a well-known insanity defense rule.[2] *Arriola I*, 2008 Tenn. Crim. App. LEXIS 577, 2008 WL 1991098, at *5; 8 Eng. Rep. 718. *M'Naughten* reads, in relevant part, that the defendant "was labouring under such a defect of

---

1. The relevant portion of the Arizona insanity defense statute reads that a "person was suffering from such a mental disease or defect as not to know the nature and quality of the act or, if such person did know, that such person did not know that what he was doing was wrong." Ariz. Rev. Stat. Ann. §13-502 (West 1978).

2. The Tennessee insanity defense statute was formally adopted from the Federal Insanity Defense Reform Act of 1984, and the same nature and wrongfulness language is in both the Federal insanity statute and the Tennessee insanity statute. See State v. Flake, 88 S.W.3d 540, 550-51 (Tenn. 2002); see also 18 U.S.C. §17. That same nature and wrongfulness language is also found in *M'Naughten*, and while there are obvious differences between the Tennessee statute and the *M'Naughten* standard, such as who bears the burden of proof, we look only to the similar clauses between them which discuss the nature and wrongfulness of a defendant's actions. *See* 8 Eng. Rep. 718.

reason, from disease of the mind, as not to know the nature and quality of the act he was doing; or, if he did know it, that he did not know he was doing what was wrong." 8 Eng. Rep. 718. In Graham v. State, the Tennessee Supreme Court analyzed that particular language of the *M'Na[u]ghten* insanity standard, and it parsed out the requirements of the two-prong test:

> There are two *M'Na[u]ghten* tests: (1) knowledge of the nature and quality of the act and (2) knowledge of its wrongfulness. These criteria are expressed in the conjunctive in that it must be shown that the defendant knew right from wrong and knew the nature and quality of the act, in order to convict of a crime while laboring under a defect of reason or disease of the mind. If a defendant does not know the nature and quality of the act he is insane; if he knows this but does not know right from wrong, he is insane.
>
> The failure to recognize and apply both prongs of this two-prong test operates to narrow the rules.

Graham v. State, 547 S.W.2d 531, 539 (Tenn. 1977). In other words, if a defendant proves by clear and convincing evidence either prong (that he cannot appreciate the nature of his acts or that he cannot appreciate the wrongfulness of his acts), he has met the burden of the insanity defense. Given the marked similarities between the *M'Naughten* standard and the current Tennessee insanity defense statute, we see no reason not to impute the Tennessee Supreme Court's previous conclusion to the current statute. As such, there are two separate prongs of the Tennessee insanity defense: whether the defendant understood the nature of his actions or whether he understood the wrongfulness of his actions. And, a defendant need only prove one prong to be successful in his defense. Thus, the trial court erred in the legal standard it applied, and we must turn to address whether, applying the correct legal standard, the evidence was sufficient to prove the insanity defense.

B. Remedy

The Defendant argues that he has proven by clear and convincing evidence that, as a result of a severe mental disease, he was unable to appreciate the wrongfulness of his conduct. The Defendant asks this Court to rely on the trial court's factual findings but to apply the correct legal standard to those findings. The State argues that this Court must rely on the trial court's factual findings and that these findings, taken in the light most favorable to the State, do not sufficiently support the Defendant's insanity defense.

After a careful consideration, we conclude that we cannot grant the relief sought by either side, rather, we must remand this case for a new trial. Although this case was a bench trial, we conclude that the appropriate remedy to be the same as for a jury trial. Generally, a jury would resolve all factual issues and apply the appropriate legal principles, as instructed by the trial court. Similarly, if in a bench trial, the trial court merely issued a finding of guilt, all factual findings would be based on that determination. This case is not that simple. In this case, the trial court, acting as the finder of fact, twice explained his factual findings and conclusions of law with respect to the Defendant's insanity defense. Because he enunciated these findings, this Court may not ignore them. . . .

In our view, the trial court's application, in this bench trial, of an erroneous legal standard for insanity should be analyzed just as we would analyze a jury trial in which the jury was given this erroneous legal standard for determining the applicability of the insanity defense. We conclude that this error affected the verdict, was not harmless, and prevented the Defendant from receiving a fair trial. See State v. Hodges, 944 S.W.2d 346, 352 (Tenn. 1997). . . . Because the Defendant's conviction is based on the trial court's application of an erroneous legal standard, the Defendant did not receive a fair trial. *See Hodges*, 944 S.W.2d at 352 ("A jury instruction is considered 'prejudicially erroneous,' only 'if it fails to fairly submit the legal issues or if it misleads the jury as to the applicable law.' "). Considering the Defendant's constitutional right to a fair trial, we remand this case for a new trial.

The Defendant argues that he proved by clear and convincing evidence that he is entitled to a verdict of "not guilty by reason of insanity" and that this Court should modify the trial court's judgment to that effect. We respectfully decline to do so. To a large extent, whether the Defendant met his burden of proof as to the insanity defense depends upon the credibility of the Defendant's expert witnesses. Because we are a reviewing court, without, in most situations, the means of assessing the credibility of witnesses, we have concluded that a new trial is the appropriate remedy in this case. Because a new trial dictates the utilization of a new finder of facts, we also conclude that the interests of justice require that a different trial judge be assigned this case upon remand.

In sum, we conclude the Defendant did not receive a fair trial, and the proper remedy is to order a new trial.

Notes and Questions

1. The insanity defense as we know it today started with the 1843 attempted assassination of British Prime Minister Robert Peel by one Daniel M'Naghten (the spelling of his last name has varied over the years). M'Naghten, who was psychotic, believed that Peel was persecuting him; however, he actually shot Peel's assistant, Edward Drummond in the back. Drummond survived the initial attack reasonably well, but after being bled and leeched by doctors for five days, he died. (Could M'Naghten perhaps have argued that he wasn't the "proximate cause" of Drummond's death?) M'Naghten's murder trial focused on the issue of his alleged insanity. The prosecution argued that, despite his apparent "partial" insanity, he was able to plan the attack, knew the difference between right and wrong, and knew that he was committing a crime. The defense claimed that M'Naghten had lost his moral sense and self-control, and was not a responsible actor at the time of the attack. Much medical testimony was introduced by the defense, but none by the prosecution; at the close of the evidence, the prosecutor admitted to the jury, "I cannot press for a verdict against the prisoner," and the jury, without even retiring to deliberate, returned a verdict of not guilty by reason of insanity. M'Naghten was transferred to the State Criminal Lunatic Asylum; he remained in confinement until his death in 1865.

After the controversial *M'Naghten* verdict, Queen Victoria and the House of Lords convened a special panel of judges to review and determine the proper legal standard for claims of insanity. The results of that review became known as the "*M'Naghten* test":

> To establish a defence on the ground of insanity it must be clearly proved, that, at the time of committing the act, the party accused was labouring under such a defect of reason from disease of the mind, as not to know the nature and quality of the act he was doing, or if he did know it, that he did not know that what he was doing was wrong.

The *M'Naghten* test served as at least a portion of the governing legal standard for the insanity defense in a large majority of American jurisdictions for more than a hundred years, until the promulgation of the Model Penal Code in 1962.

2. In the early twentieth century, advances in psychology led to the development of a second, supplementary test for legal insanity: the so-called "irresistible impulse" test. Under this test, a defendant should also be found not guilty by reason of insanity if, by reason of his mental illness, he could not control an "irresistible impulse" to commit the crime. By the mid-1950s, almost half of American jurisdictions had adopted some version of the irresistible impulse test to go with the *M'Naghten* test.

3. In 1962, the Model Penal Code proposed a new test for the insanity defense:

> A person is not responsible for criminal conduct if at the time of such conduct as a result of mental disease or defect he lacks substantial capacity either to appreciate the criminality of his conduct or to conform his conduct to the requirements of the law.

MPC §4.01(1). The Code's drafters essentially combined the *M'Naghten* and "irresistible impulse" tests into one (two-part) legal standard. At the same time, the Code's version of the standard slightly broadened both the previous tests, applying to all defendants whose mental illness deprived them of "substantial capacity" either to appreciate the nature of their conduct or to act in conformity with the law. These changes were thought necessary to modernize the test, by taking into account what psychologists and psychiatrists had learned about the effects of serious mental illness.

Within a decade or so, the MPC's new version of the insanity defense was adopted by a majority of American states and by the federal government. Subsequent world events, however, would soon overtake the Code drafters' efforts to reform the law of insanity, and would lead to a large-scale retreat from the MPC's reformist version of the insanity test.

4. On March 30, 1981, John Hinckley, Jr., attempted to assassinate President Ronald Reagan, as part of a bizarre scheme to impress the actress Jodie Foster, with whom Hinckley had become seriously obsessed after watching the movie *Taxi Driver* (which featured Foster as well as a lead character, played by actor Robert DeNiro, who plotted to assassinate a U.S. Senator running for president). The Hinckley assassination attempt, which was caught on videotape and replayed endlessly on TV, seriously injured President Reagan (hit in the chest by a ricocheting bullet), Press Secretary James Brady (paralyzed for life by a shot to the head), police officer Thomas Delahanty, and Secret Service officer Timothy McCarthy.

On June 21, 1982, John Hinckley, Jr., was found not guilty, by reason of insanity, of all crimes growing out of the assassination attempt. The verdict produced a firestorm of public criticism, and led to major changes in the law of insanity. Within a few years, numerous states shifted the burden of proof on the insanity defense to the defendant (previously, prosecutors often were required to *disprove* insanity, once the issue had been properly raised), and one state (Utah) abolished the insanity defense altogether (Montana and Idaho would do so a bit later). In addition, a number of states created the new verdict of "guilty but mentally ill," allowing juries to convict a defendant of a crime notwithstanding the effects of the defendant's mental illness (such defendants, in theory, are supposed to receive psychiatric treatment while serving their prison sentences). And in 1984, Congress enacted, and President Reagan signed into law, the federal Insanity Defense Reform Act:

> It is an affirmative defense to a prosecution under any federal statute that, at the time of the commission of the acts constituting the offense, the defendant as a result of a severe mental disease or defect, was unable to appreciate the nature and quality or the wrongfulness of his acts. Mental disease or defect does not otherwise constitute a defense.

18 U.S.C. §17. The new version of the federal insanity defense requires the defendant to prove, by "clear and convincing evidence," that the statutory standard is satisfied. This federal burden of proof is even more difficult than the one imposed by most of the states (today, more than two-thirds of the states treat insanity as an affirmative defense) upon defendants who claim to be insane.

Today, we can say that the *M'Naghten* test, or some variant of it, has returned to the forefront of American insanity law. Most states (and the federal government) no longer use the MPC's version; instead, they have returned to a test that focuses primarily on the defendant's ability to appreciate the nature or wrongfulness of his conduct. The defense is usually limited to those who suffer from severe mental illnesses, but the notion of an "irresistible impulse" has been excised from the insanity test in most jurisdictions. And the law of insanity today generally requires the defendant to prove that he was legally insane at the time of the crime.

5. There is another way that a defendant's mental illness at the time of the crime can affect the outcome of a criminal case. Sometimes a defendant claims that, due to mental illness, he was incapable of forming the *mens rea* that the charged crime requires. This claim is often called a "diminished capacity" claim. Properly understood, the claim is nothing more than an indirect way of challenging the prosecution's proof that the defendant satisfied the *mens rea* for the crime charged; in essence, the defendant's claim is, "I *did* not satisfy that *mens rea* standard, because—as a result of my mental illness—I *could* not have satisfied the standard." See MPC §4.02(1). One example would be a defendant charged with theft who claims that, due to a mental illness, she was incapable of understanding that the property in question did not belong to her. If such a claim ultimately is believed (and that's a very big "if"—jurors are understandably highly skeptical about such claims), then in some (but not most) jurisdictions, the defendant must be found not guilty of the crime—not by virtue of some special "defense," but simply because she lacks the *mens rea* for the crime charged.

The "diminished capacity" defense was first recognized in a 1948 California case, People v. Wells, 202 P.2d 53 (1949). But California later became one of the leading states to abolish the doctrine, after the infamous 1978 murders of San Francisco Mayor George Moscone and Supervisor Harvey Milk, the first openly gay elected public official in the state. The man accused of the murders, Dan White (who had recently resigned as Supervisor but wanted his job back), was acquitted in 1981 of first-degree murder, based on the "diminished capacity" claim that he was too mentally depressed to have formed the requisite *mens rea* for the crime. (Part of the evidence offered at trial in support of this claim was that White, a known health-food devotee, had consumed large quantities of junk food during the days and nights before the killings; this was later misdescribed in the media as the "Twinkie defense." White's chief defense lawyer later stated that he did not recall Twinkies ever being mentioned at the trial; rather, the trial evidence referred to "HoHos and Ding Dongs." See Carol Pogash, "Myth of the 'Twinkie Defense,'" San Francisco Chronicle, Nov. 23, 2003, available at http://www.sfgate.com/cgi-bin/article.cgi?f=/c/a/2003/11/23/INGRE 343501.DTL&hw=twinkie+defense&sn=001&sc=1000.) White was convicted instead of voluntary manslaughter, and he was sentenced to less than eight years in prison. One year later, angry and frustrated California voters approved a ballot initiative providing: "The defense of diminished capacity is hereby abolished. . . ."

Can you think of any logical reason why a defendant should not be allowed to raise a "diminished capacity" defense, assuming the evidence would support the claim? Doesn't it seem as if an inherent incapacity to form the *mens rea* required to commit a particular crime would be the strongest *mens rea* argument a defendant could possibly make—and certainly stronger than the typical self-serving declaration that the defendant "didn't mean to do it"?

12

Sentencing

A. LAW AND DISCRETION

State v. Thompson

Nebraska Court of Appeals
735 N.W.2d 818 (2007)

SIEVERS, Judge.

Richard W. Thompson pled no contest to two counts of sexual assault of a child, and the district court for Cheyenne County sentenced Thompson to 5 years' intensive supervised probation on each count, to run consecutively. The State of Nebraska appeals the sentences imposed on Thompson as excessively lenient. . . .

FACTUAL BACKGROUND

On October 31, 2005, Thompson was charged with count I, sexual assault of a child; count II, sexual assault of a child; and count III, first degree sexual assault. Thompson was arraigned on November 8 and entered a plea of not guilty. Thereafter, a plea agreement was reached. Thompson's counsel put the plea agreement on the record, stating: "Thompson is prepared to enter a no contest plea to counts I and II, in exchange count III is going to be dismissed and at the time of sentencing the county attorney is going to remain silent." The Cheyenne County Attorney affirmed that such was the plea agreement by the simple statement, "That's right." And, upon inquiry by the court as to whether such was "your agreement," Thompson responded affirmatively on the record. Thompson pled no contest to the two counts of sexual assault of a child, a factual basis was provided on the record, and the trial court accepted the plea and scheduled the sentencing hearing. . . .

On May 23, 2006, a sentencing hearing was held. When the court asked if there was any evidence or recommendations to present, the State said that there was "no argument from the State." The State noted that this was "part of [the plea] agreement." The district court then sentenced Thompson as stated above, and the State has timely appealed. . . .

ANALYSIS

We begin with Thompson's assertions that the State, by complaining on appeal that his sentences were excessively lenient after agreeing to stand silent at the sentencing hearing, is in violation of the parties' plea agreement. . . .

The simple and straightforward agreement of the prosecutor to remain silent at the time of sentencing does not in any way implicate . . . the prosecutor's statutory right to seek appellate review of a sentence that he or she believes is excessively lenient. . . . Thompson's approach would create a waiver from thin air when none was expressed or even implied. The effect of such a position is that a prosecutor who agrees only to stand silent . . . at sentencing has somehow blithely agreed to accept whatever sentence the sentencing judge hands down — no matter how inappropriate it might be in a particular case for a particular defendant. . . . [W]e hold that the State did not waive its statutory right to appellate review of the trial court's sentences.

We cannot pretend to be unaware that the sentences imposed, in conjunction with certain comments made by the trial judge at sentencing, created a brief nationwide firestorm of critical publicity. After a complete review of the record, particularly the presentence investigation report (PSI), we find that the sentences were not an abuse of the trial judge's discretion, and we therefore affirm the district court's sentences. . . .

When the State appeals from a sentence, contending that it is excessively lenient, an appellate court reviews the record for an abuse of discretion, and a grant of probation will not be disturbed unless there has been an abuse of discretion by the sentencing court. State v. Detweiler, 544 N.W.2d 83 (Neb. 1996). . . . A judicial abuse of discretion exists only when the reasons or rulings of a trial judge are clearly untenable, unfairly depriving a litigant of a substantial right and denying a just result in matters submitted for disposition. . . .

. . . The State's principal arguments [are] that (1) the trial judge [considered] an improper factor — Thompson's physical stature, (2) Thompson is a sexual predator who "groomed" his victim, (3) Thompson is at risk to reoffend, (4) Thompson is an abuser of his girlfriend and did not complete the counseling he was to get to avoid prosecution for that offense, and (5) Thompson is unrepentant.

After listening to comments from defense counsel at the sentencing hearing, the district judge commented as follows before imposing the probationary sentences:

> What you have done is absolutely inexcusable. Absolutely wrong. You will never have any idea of how deeply you have harmed this child. You are an

adult. You betrayed the trust and you betrayed it not only at a psychological but a physical level. . . . You've earned your way to prison. So, I'm sitting here thinking this guy has earned his way to prison but then I look at you and I look at your physical size. I look at your basic ability to cope with people and, quite frankly, I shake to think of what might happen to you in prison because I don't think you'll do well in prison. . . . I was relieved to know that the people who evaluated you—you are a sex offender, okay. You did this and you did it to a child. That means that at some level you have a sexual preference to children. That doesn't make you a hunter, the predator that we hear about on [television] all the time. I was very relieved to know that you do not fit in that category of human being because that gives me more leeway to not send you to prison. But you need to understand I am going to try to put together some kind of order that will keep you out of prison. But you need to understand that if you don't follow it right to the "T" I have to put you in prison. If you can't structure your behavior so that you are safe and other people are safe out in the community then I have to structure it with prison.

Neb. Rev. Stat. §29-2322 states in relevant part:

> [T]he appellate court, upon a review of the record, shall determine whether the sentence imposed is excessively lenient, having regard for:
> (1) The nature and circumstances of the offense;
> (2) The history and characteristics of the defendant;
> (3) The need for the sentence imposed:
> (a) To afford adequate deterrence to criminal conduct;
> (b) To protect the public from further crimes of the defendant;
> (c) To reflect the seriousness of the offense, to promote respect for the law, and to provide just punishment for the offense; and
> (d) To provide the defendant with needed educational or vocational training, medical care, or other correctional treatment in the most effective manner; and
> (4) Any other matters appearing in the record which the appellate court deems pertinent.

Neb. Rev. Stat. §29-2261(3) provides that "[t]he presentence investigation and report shall include . . . the offender's . . . physical and mental condition. . . ." And, §29-2322(2) mandates consideration of the "characteristics of the defendant." Therefore, the State's [claim] that the trial court improperly considered Thompson's physical stature, or that we cannot, is simply incorrect. . . .

Thompson stands 5 feet 2 inches tall and weighs 125 to 130 pounds. Thompson's size and how that "physical condition" will affect him in a prison setting is a relevant consideration. However, given other matters found in the PSI, which matters we will detail shortly, we have no doubt that Thompson's physical stature, although specifically mentioned, was but a minor point in the trial court's sentencing decision. . . .

[B]ecause probation rather than imprisonment was imposed, Neb. Rev. Stat. §29-2260 is implicated. [That section] provides in pertinent part:

[T]he court may withhold sentence of imprisonment unless, having regard to the nature and circumstances of the crime and the history, character, and condition of the offender, the court finds that imprisonment of the offender is necessary for protection of the public because:

(a) The risk is substantial that during the period of probation the offender will engage in additional criminal conduct;

(b) The offender is in need of correctional treatment that can be provided most effectively by commitment to a correctional facility; or

(c) A lesser sentence will depreciate the seriousness of the offender's crime or promote disrespect for law.

(3) The following grounds, while not controlling the discretion of the court, shall be accorded weight in favor of withholding sentence of imprisonment:

(a) The crime neither caused nor threatened serious harm;

(b) The offender did not contemplate that his or her crime would cause or threaten serious harm;

(c) The offender acted under strong provocation;

(d) Substantial grounds were present tending to excuse or justify the crime, though failing to establish a defense;

(e) The victim of the crime induced or facilitated commission of the crime;

(f) The offender has compensated or will compensate the victim of his or her crime for the damage or injury the victim sustained;

(g) The offender has no history of prior delinquency or criminal activity and has led a law-abiding life for a substantial period of time before the commission of the crime;

(h) The crime was the result of circumstances unlikely to recur;

(i) The character and attitudes of the offender indicate that he or she is unlikely to commit another crime;

(j) The offender is likely to respond affirmatively to probationary treatment; and

(k) Imprisonment of the offender would entail excessive hardship to his or her dependents.

. . . Thompson was born out of wedlock in Sidney, Nebraska, on July 10, 1955. He never knew his father and had no siblings. His mother never married and died in late 2005 at the age of 80. Thompson described a good and loving relationship with his mother and said that her passing was extremely hard on him. Thompson is a high school graduate, but according to testing, he has less than average intelligence. He has been employed throughout his life since age 17, and his employer at the time of the PSI indicated that if Thompson was not incarcerated, he would retain his employment with them. He was earning approximately $1,100 per month.

Before these convictions, Thompson had two convictions in the 1980s for driving under the influence, but no conviction since 1988 for even so much as a traffic ticket. In April 2005, as a result of a domestic altercation between Thompson and the woman with whom he was living, C.G., he was charged with third degree assault and cruelty toward a child, but he was not prosecuted on the condition that he seek counseling and abide by the counselor's recommendations. The record indicates that during this domestic altercation, Thompson pushed C.G., causing her to fall and sustain a bruise; shook his fist at her; and pushed C.G.'s daughter when she tried to intervene. While the State argues that Thompson's failure to complete this required counseling militates against probation in this case, the record shows that he contacted a counselor and had four sessions with the counselor before the current situation arose in October 2005.

The victim in this case, E.G., was the daughter of C.G., the woman who began dating Thompson and subsequently lived with him upon moving to Sidney with her two children in April 2004. E.G. was 12 years old at the time she, her younger brother, and her mother began living with Thompson. E.G. reported six occasions of sexual contact by Thompson between July 2005 and September of that year, when the living arrangement between Thompson, C.G., and her children ended.

E.G. recounted that Thompson rubbed her vaginal area outside of her clothing on two occasions and that during one such occasion, he attempted to briefly penetrate her digitally, but he stopped when she asked him to stop. There were three occasions recounted by E.G. when Thompson, who was clothed, laid on top of her and rubbed against her genital area through her clothes. E.G. recounted that on two of those occasions, Thompson kissed her breasts. Thompson also kissed E.G. on the mouth a number of times. E.G. did not describe any attempt at penile penetration. E.G. described Thompson as gentle and said that he did not threaten her in any way. She also described these encounters as being very brief in duration and stated that such ended when he voluntarily stopped and left. . . .

E.G. completed a victim impact statement in which she recounted the following:

> I don't trust men. I worry about what they want to do to me. I'm afraid to live with mom and her new boyfriend because of what [Thompson] did to me. . . . I worry about other kids knowing what [Thompson] did to me. This makes me feel different. . . . I think [Thompson] should go to prison so he doesn't do it to any other girls.

A licensed mental health professional who saw E.G.—although we cannot discern from the PSI the nature, length, or frequency of any therapy—also completed a victim impact statement form, on which she stated:

> [E.G.] does not trust her own judgment. This is directly related to [Thompson's] gradual grooming and seduction of [E.G., who] truly believed

[Thompson] cared about her and would not harm her or do anything that was wrong. [E.G.] is also having a multitude of social problems that stem from her feelings of being different now that this has happened. She is still suffering from feelings of shame, embarrassment and guilt that will take a great deal of time to work through. [E.G.] was horrifically used, abused and betrayed by this man and will continue to need extensive therapy to help her recover from this tragic violation. He not only violated her physically but emotionally and spiritually.

This therapist also offered the following opinions to the trial court on the victim impact statement form:

I think that [Thompson] should be sentenced to 10 years in prison. I realize that this is his first offense that he has been arrested for but I have every reason to believe that this is not the first time that he has molested a child. After listening in great detail to [E.G.'s account of her] seduction and molestation[,] I have no doubt that [Thompson] has molested other children in the past. If he is not held accountable for this he will continue to molest other girls. But rest assured he will get better at it.

Other than this statement, there is absolutely no evidence to support the conclusion that Thompson has victimized any other child or adult female, and the claim that he purposefully "groomed" E.G. is contradicted by others involved in the presentence evaluation of Thompson.

The psychologist who performed a mental status examination of Thompson . . . stated as follows regarding the result of such testing:

. . . [Thompson's] tendency is to act without thinking in a rather immature reaction style. He does not appear to meet criteria for pedophilia. The present offense appears to be one more of impulse control and lack of judgment and does not appear to include any violence or "grooming." There are no known previous sexual offenses with adults or children. It is noted that the victim in this case is post pubescent. Testing shows [Thompson] to be rather immature and self-centered, but he does not show indications of psychopathy or psychosis. Sexual offenders with this profile are usually best managed by requiring no unsupervised contact with vulnerable potential victims, requirement of lack of use of drugs and alcohol to prevent further diminishment of judgment, and long term probation/parole oversight to ensure compliance. He can be characterized as an immature/opportunistic offender rather than an aggressive offender. Ongoing counseling services may be of benefit to this individual. . . . As noted in the diagnostic impression this patient does not appear to meet criteria for classification as a sexual psychopath, sexual predator, or similar classifications.

. . . Within the PSI is Thompson's handwritten statement that contains his admission of wrongdoing and his acknowledgment that he hurt E.G. as well as family and friends. It contains a number of assertions that he will never repeat this mistake. The State argues that his letter is overly focused on his own pain and suffering from these events rather than on that of his victim. There is certainly an element of that in his letter. For example, he stated:

> I know that I will never ever do something like this again [be]cause what it has done to me mentally and how bad it has hurt me, and it isn't worth the pain to go through it again because I have suffered in my mind and hurt so much that I know I would not do it again.

However, his letter expresses his remorse and acknowledges that he hurt E.G. For example, he wrote: "And knowing that I have also hurt [E.G.] too because the way she loved me as her dad[d]y. . . ."

Finally, we quote in part the "Summary/Evaluation" section of the report by the district probation officer:

> With [respect] to the sentence in this case, it does not appear a term of imprisonment at the Nebraska Correctional Complex would be required, rather [Thompson] may benefit from services that could be provided during a term of Intensive Supervised Probation (ISP). In addition to the standard terms of ISP, this officer would ask the Court that specific conditions of probation be included. [Thompson] should be ordered to complete a letter of apology to the victim and her family. Additional conditions would include [Thompson's] being prohibited from becoming involved in a relationship with someone who has young children or with someone who is around and/or caring for young children. A condition of probation that prohibits [Thompson] from purchasing or being in possession of pornographic material would also be recommended.

We now turn to §29-2260, which provides that the trial court may withhold a sentence of imprisonment unless, having regard for the nature and circumstances of the crime as well as the history, character, and condition of the offender, the court finds that imprisonment is necessary for protection of the public because (1) there is a substantial risk that during the period of probation, the offender will engage in additional criminal conduct; (2) the offender is in need of correctional treatment that can be provided most effectively by commitment to a correctional facility; or (3) a lesser sentence will depreciate the seriousness of the offender's crime or promote disrespect for the law.

. . . [T]he only assertion that Thompson will reoffend is that made by E.G.'s counselor, but she has had no contact with Thompson and her information comes solely from the victim. In contrast, the psychologist who evaluated Thompson found no evidence of violence or grooming and found no known previous sexual offenses with either adults or children. The psychologist concluded that Thompson is not a pedophile, but, rather, that Thompson's offenses in this case stem from poor judgment and a lack of impulse control. The psychologist unequivocally stated that Thompson does not meet the criteria for classification "as a sexual psychopath, sexual predator, or similar classifications." . . .

The second factor under §29-2260 is that the offender is in need of correctional treatment that can be provided most effectively by commitment to a correctional facility. The PSI reveals and the probation officer specifically recommends that intensive supervised probation, not incarceration, is appropriate in this case. There is no showing in the PSI that the assistance Thompson needs is most effectively provided at a correctional facility.

The third factor addresses whether a lesser sentence will depreciate the seriousness of the offender's crime or promote disrespect for the law. Of the statutory considerations to withhold imprisonment, this is obviously the most subjective. Clearly, the victim and her counselor seek imprisonment, and we assume that they would hold the view that anything less than imprisonment depreciates the seriousness of Thompson's crimes and promotes disrespect for the law. However, . . . [Thompson] is not a person who has led an irresponsible life; nor does the PSI suggest that at his core, he is an inherently bad, evil, or dangerous person. He did, however, commit horrific acts violating a young girl's trust and affection for him.

. . . It has long been recognized that a sentence should fit the offender and not merely the crime. See Williams v. New York, 337 U.S. 241 (1949). As stated by the Nebraska Supreme Court in State v. Harrison, 588 N.W.2d 556, 565 (Neb. 1999):

> A sentence not involving confinement is to be preferred to a sentence involving partial or total confinement in the absence of affirmative reasons to the contrary. Thus, "justice" may certainly be served by a sentence of probation. Whether justice is so served is a matter that is, in the first instance, properly left to the trial court.

Section 29-2260(3) contains considerations which [weigh] in favor of withholding a sentence of imprisonment, including . . . whether the crime neither caused nor threatened serious harm, whether the offender acted under strong provocation, whether substantial grounds were present tending to excuse or justify the crime, and whether the victim induced or facilitated the commission of the crime. The record does not support a conclusion that any of these factors are present, . . . and thus, the probationary sentences are not justified by these factors. But the inquiry does not end here. . . .

. . . Under the terms of Thompson's probation, he must be employed or attend school and he must avoid contact with persons having criminal records. He cannot leave Cheyenne County without the permission of his probation officer. He must abstain from the use and possession of alcohol and submit, upon request of his probation officer, to a chemical test of his blood, breath, or urine. He cannot associate with anyone who possesses firearms. He must serve up to 180 days of electronic monitoring. He is subject to a curfew set by his probation officer. He cannot frequent premises specializing in the sale or consumption of alcohol. He shall enroll in and successfully complete counseling for sexual behavior, as directed by his probation officer. He shall write an apology to his victim. He shall never be unsupervised when a person under the age of 18 is present. He cannot have a dating relationship with anyone who has children under the age of 18 or who cares for children under such age, nor can he live with anyone under the age of 18. He shall not possess any pornography and shall have no computer access in his home. Finally, Thompson is to serve 30 days in the Cheyenne County jail, which was to begin January 1, 2007, and serve another 30 days beginning on January 1 of each year that he is on probation, although such imprisonment may be waived by his probation officer. If Thompson violates the terms of his probation . . . [,] he is subject to the filing of a motion to revoke his probation and be sentenced anew. Thompson has agreed to each and every one of these conditions of his probation.

CONCLUSION

The PSI that was in the hands of the district judge before imposition of these sentences contains abundant . . . justification for ordering probation — the terms of which are strict and demanding — rather than incarceration. After our review of the crimes, the sentences, and the information in the PSI, we have no hesitancy in saying that the sentences are not an abuse of discretion and, therefore, are not excessively lenient. . . .

Because the trial judge did not abuse her discretion in sentencing Thompson, we affirm.

[The concurring opinion of Chief Judge INBODY is omitted.]

Notes and Questions

1. As the court notes, the trial judge's sentencing decision in *Thompson* made national headlines; more than 500 newspapers (including the *New York Times* and the *Washington Post*) reported about the case, and CNN covered the controversy on more than one occasion. See Reuters News Service, "Nebraska Will Appeal Man's Sentence," New York Times, May 27, 2006; Scott Bauer (Associated Press), "Sentence for Short Sex Offender Draws Fire," Washington Post, May 26, 2006; "Paula Zahn Now," CNN, June 15 2006; "Nancy Grace," CNN, May 26, 2006.

The judge's decision also proved extremely controversial in Nebraska. Within days after the sentencing, large crowds were protesting on the courthouse lawn in Sidney, and petitions (eventually including more than 1000 signatures) were being circulated seeking Judge Kristine Cecava's resignation or removal from office.

In June 2006, two separate complaints against Judge Cecava—who had previously received consistently above-average evaluations from local attorneys—were filed before the Nebraska Commission on Judicial Qualifications. One was brought by a Nebraska state legislator who claimed he didn't really want Judge Cecava to be disciplined, but felt that a public hearing would help reduce the "crescendo of anger-driven demands" for her resignation. The other complaint was filed by a local citizen and day-care manager, who argued that Judge Cecava should have imposed "the stiffest penalty she can for people who harm our children." See Paul Hammel, "Date Set for Complaints About Judge," Omaha World-Herald, June 21, 2006.

Judge Cecava managed to avoid disciplinary sanctions; the Commission ultimately decided that an error in judgments could not be the basis for disciplining a judge. But in November 2008, Judge Cecava was removed from office anyway; by 52 percent to 48 percent, she lost a judicial retention election, becoming only the eighth Nebraska judge in nearly 50 years to do so. See "Judge Who Gave Short Man Probation Ousted," North Platte Bulletin, November 6, 2008.

As the above suggests, the feature of the case that attracted the most attention was Judge Cecava's comment about the defendant's small size. Was the judge wrong to take account of that fact? The comment preceded the judge's statement that "I shake to think of what might happen to you in prison because I don't think you'll do well in prison"—a clear reference to the likelihood that Thompson would be the victim of repeated rapes if he served time in prison. Rape is a serious problem in American prisons, and some classes of inmates—including small men and prisoners punished for molesting children, two categories to which Thompson would belong if incarcerated—are victimized disproportionately. (See Report, National Prison Rape Elimination Commission, June 2009, available online at https://www.ncjrs.gov/pdffiles1/226680.pdf.) Again, should judges consider that fact when imposing sentences? If not, why not?

2. Given Thompson's vulnerability, would a prison sentence of, say, five years amount to the same punishment as the same length of prison time imposed on a less vulnerable defendant? For an argument that the answer is clearly "no," see Adam J. Kolber, The Subjective Experience of Punishment, 109 Colum. L. Rev. 182 (2009). Assuming Kolber is right, how should judges approach prison sentences—by looking to the sentences other convicted defendants received, or by looking to the vulnerability (or lack thereof) of the defendant in the case at hand? The first approach seems heartless, while the second is lawless. Is there any way out of this box?

3. The process that produced Thompson's sentence was fairly typical. As is true of the large majority of felony convictions, Thompson's conviction was by guilty plea. As with most pleas, the parties reached a plea agreement. In most plea agreements, the government promises to drop specified charges, to recommend a particular sentence, or to "stand mute" when defense counsel recommends a particular sentence. In *Thompson*, the prosecutor made the first and third of those promises. One of the two legal issues the case raised was whether the government waived its right to appeal the sentencing decision by declining to offer any recommended sentence.

4. The second legal issue was the permissibility of the sentence that Judge Cecava imposed. Based on the facts as specified in Judge Sievers' opinion, did Judge Cecava get it wrong? Was Thompson treated too leniently? Shortly after the trial judge's sentencing decision, Thompson tried and failed to commit suicide. Does that affect your answer to the previous question?

5. For most of American history, sentencing decisions like the one in *Thompson* were unreviewable. Criminal statutes specified large sentencing ranges and either did not specify the factors sentencing judges were to take into account, or listed factors pliable enough to justify any sentence within the range. Appellate opinions discussing the legality of non-capital sentences were all but unknown. Since the mid-1970s, that state of affairs has changed radically. About half of the states adopted some form of sentencing guidelines: rules that usually trigger either mandatory sentences or narrow sentencing ranges. The other half continued to permit broad sentencing discretion — but state statutes and court decisions required appellate review of those discretionary decisions. Which leads to cases like *Thompson*, with discretionary sentencing decisions reviewed for compliance with vague statutory standards. Judging by this case, how well do such systems work?

6. There is no equivalent to the rule of lenity in cases like *Thompson*, but there are several substitutes. Judge Cecava's decision appears to have been based on the belief that probation should be the norm and incarceration the exception. The idea of such a presumption is an old one. The Declaration of the Rights of Man and of the Citizen, adopted in the summer of 1789 by the French National Assembly, stated the principle that "[t]he law shall provide for such punishments only as are strictly and obviously necessary." (This is sometimes referred to as the "principle of parsimony.") *Thompson* is the natural product of the principle. Is the principle wise? Or should incarceration be the norm and probation the exception, at least when offenders commit crimes as serious as the ones Thompson committed?

Vandergriff v. State

Court of Appeals of Alaska
125 P.3d 360 (2005)

Opinion by STEWART, Judge.

From December 2003 through February 2004, Norman L. Vandergriff burglarized remote residences outside of Petersburg. He stole several items including boats, an outboard motor, and firearms. He forged a check made payable to himself and purportedly signed by one of the victims. The grand jury indicted Vandergriff on nine felony counts.

The parties reached a plea agreement that called for Vandergriff to plead to three class C felonies: second-degree theft; second-degree forgery;

and second-degree burglary. There was no agreement on the sentence to be imposed. Under the sentencing law that applied to Vandergriff's case, he faced a presumptive 3-year term on each count because he had five prior felony convictions.

The superior court imposed a composite 9-year term with 3 years suspended, a net 6-year term to serve. In this sentence appeal, Vandergriff advances several reasons why the superior court erred by imposing this sentence. We reject each claim and affirm the judgment of the superior court.

BACKGROUND FACTS AND PROCEEDINGS

The grand jury indicted Vandergriff on four counts of second-degree theft, one count of second-degree forgery, two counts of first-degree burglary, and two counts of first-degree vehicle theft. These charges arose after an investigation by the Alaska State Troopers showed that from December 2003 through February 2004, Vandergriff broke into two remote cabins near Petersburg, stole three firearms, stole two boats, stole an outboard motor, and forged a check bearing the purported signature of one of the victims.

The State and Vandergriff negotiated a plea agreement. Vandergriff agreed to plead to three counts: second-degree theft; second-degree burglary; and second-degree forgery. The State agreed not to pursue any aggravating factors, and the parties agreed not to restrict the court's power to impose the sentences on any count concurrent with or consecutive to any other count.

Vandergriff had five prior felony convictions. His first felony conviction occurred in 1970 in Virginia. His most recent felony conviction occurred in 2003 in Florida. Two of the five convictions were burglary charges; three were forgery charges.

Superior Court Judge Michael A. Thompson imposed a 3-year term for second-degree theft, a consecutive 3-year term for second-degree burglary, and a consecutive 3-year term, [suspended], for forgery. Thus, Judge Thompson imposed a composite 9-year term with 3 years suspended. Vandergriff appeals.

DISCUSSION

Vandergriff argues that the United States Supreme Court's decision in Blakely v. Washington, 542 U.S. 296 (2004), restricts a sentencing judge's authority to impose consecutive sentences exceeding the prescribed presumptive term for the defendant's most serious offense or the maximum term for the defendant's most serious offense. But under former Alaska Stat. §12.55.025(e) and (g), a sentencing judge's authority to impose consecutive sentences did not require proof of aggravating factors or other special factual circumstances.

Blakely rests on a principle that the Supreme Court recently repeated in United States v. Booker, 543 U.S. 220, 244 (2005): "Any fact (other than a prior conviction) which is necessary to support a sentence . . . must be admitted by the defendant or proved to a jury beyond a reasonable doubt." . . . But Judge Thompson's authority to impose consecutive sentences did not depend on proof of additional facts. His authority to impose consecutive sentences was governed by former Alaska Stat. §12.55.025(e) and (g).[9] [Apart from] exceptions not applicable here, those subsections gave Judge Thompson the discretion to impose the sentences consecutively or concurrently.

We recently addressed the application of *Blakely* to consecutive sentencing in Edmonds v. State, 118 P.3d 17 (Alaska App. 2005). We held that *Blakely* did not limit a judge's authority to impose consecutive sentences with the exception of one potential issue that we did not decide in Edmonds' case: Is the fact finding called for by the *Neal-Mutschler* rule subject to the procedural requirements of *Blakely*? The *Neal-Mutschler* rule is a common-law sentencing rule announced by our supreme court; before a sentencing judge imposes consecutive sentences that total more than the maximum sentence for a defendant's most serious offense, the judge must expressly find that the total sentence is necessary to protect the public.[11] . . .

. . . [T]he *Neal-Mutschler* rule is a judicially created common-law rule that guides a sentencing judge's analysis when imposing consecutive sentencing. The rule directs a judge to explain the rationale for imposing a term . . . greater than the maximum term for the single most serious offense. This [rule] promotes the legislature's mandate to eliminate unjustified disparity and attain reasonable uniformity in sentencing because the [rule enables appellate review of sentencing]. The rule does not increase the potential sentence a defendant may receive beyond the statutory range . . . already specified by the legislature. . . .

. . . [W]e conclude that, when a sentencing judge applying the *Neal-Mutschler* rule assesses whether a composite term . . . exceeding the maximum term for the defendant's single most serious crime is necessary to protect the public, the judge is not required to submit this issue to a jury.

---

9. These two sections were repealed in 2004 and replaced with Alaska Stat. §12.55.127, which went into effect on July 1, 2004. Although Vandergriff was sentenced in August 2004, Alaska Stat. §12.55.127 applies to offenses committed on or after July 1, 2004.

11. See Neal v. State, 628 P.2d 19, 21 (Alaska 1981) ("Our past decisions imply that where consecutive sentences for two or more counts exceed the maximum sentence for any single count, the sentencing judge should make a formal finding that confinement for the combined term is necessary to protect the public.") (citing Mills v. State, 592 P.2d 1247, 1248 (Alaska 1979), and Mutschler v. State, 560 P.2d 377, 381 (Alaska 1977)); Powell v. State, 88 P.3d 532, 537 (Alaska App. 2004) (applying the *Neal-Mutschler* rule based on belief defendant was a poor candidate for rehabilitation).

Vandergriff argues that Judge Thompson improperly applied the *Neal-Mutschler* rule. Vandergriff claims, without citation to authority, that "when a court speaks of protecting the public, it generally means protecting the public against violent crimes." Vandergriff argues that a sentence in excess of the maximum term for the most serious offense is not justified because Vandergriff's present offenses and past offenses were property offenses.

This is not the rule illustrated by our case law. For example, in O'Brannon v. State, 812 P.2d 222 (Alaska App. 1991), we affirmed the superior court's sentence of 1500 days' imprisonment with 1125 days suspended on eighteen counts of criminal contempt, [each of] which had a maximum penalty of 180 days imprisonment. And in Montes v. State, 669 P.2d 961 (Alaska App. 1983), we affirmed the superior court's imposition of a composite 7-year term, a term that exceeded the 5-year maximum term for each of the five counts of second-degree theft for which Montes had been convicted. We concluded that the superior court imposed the term to protect the public. Id. at 967-68.

We conclude that Judge Thompson properly applied the *Neal-Mutschler* rule to impose a composite term that exceeds the maximum 5-year term for Vandergriff's individual crimes. . . .

Vandergriff's sentence is affirmed.

MANNHEIMER, Judge, concurring.

I write separately to explain my analysis of the *Blakely* issue presented in this appeal.

In Neal v. State, 628 P.2d 19 (Alaska 1981), the Alaska Supreme Court announced a rule that governs consecutive sentencing in this state. The supreme court held that when a judge sentences a defendant for two or more crimes, and when the law authorizes the judge to impose consecutive sentences for these crimes, the judge should not [impose a sentence] that exceeds the maximum term of imprisonment for the defendant's most serious offense unless the judge makes "a formal finding that confinement for [this composite] term is necessary to protect the public." *Neal*, 628 P.2d at 21.

Vandergriff's appeal presents the question of whether the Sixth Amendment right to jury trial, as construed by the United States Supreme Court in Apprendi v. New Jersey, 530 U.S. 466 (2000), Blakely v. Washington, 542 U.S. 296 (2004), and United States v. Booker, 543 U.S. 220 (2005), applies to the sentencing finding required by *Neal*. . . . To [answer that question], it is necessary to examine the principle underlying the decisions in *Apprendi*, *Blakely*, and *Booker*, and then assess whether that principle is violated when a sentencing court makes the finding required by *Neal*.

In *Apprendi*, the Supreme Court assessed the constitutionality of a provision of state law (New Jersey's "hate crime" law) which increased the maximum sentence for various offenses. The defendant in *Apprendi* was convicted of possessing a firearm for an unlawful purpose. The normal maximum sentence for this crime was 10 years' imprisonment, but the hate crime law authorized a sentencing judge to impose an "extended term" of 20 years if the judge found (by a preponderance of the evidence) that the defendant had acted for the purpose of intimidating other people based on their race, religion, ethnic background, [or] sexual orientation. . . . 530 U.S. at 469-70.

. . . [T]he Supreme Court declared that this type of sentencing provision implicated a defendant's right to notice, to trial by jury, and to proof beyond a reasonable doubt. Id. at 476-77. The Court explained:

> Any possible distinction between an "element" of a felony offense and a "sentencing factor" was unknown to the practice of criminal indictment, trial by jury, and judgment by court as it existed during the years surrounding our Nation's founding. As a general rule, criminal proceedings were submitted to a jury after being initiated by an indictment containing "all the facts and circumstances which constitute the offence, . . . stated with such certainty and precision, that the defendant . . . may [. . .] determine the species of offence they constitute [and] prepare his defence accordingly . . . and *that there may be no doubt as to the judgment which should be given*, if the defendant be convicted."

Apprendi, 530 U.S. at 478 (quoting J. Archbold, Pleading and Evidence in Criminal Cases 44 (15th ed. 1862)) (emphasis in the *Apprendi* opinion).

The Supreme Court italicized this last portion of the quote from Archbold to emphasize that, in the eighteenth and nineteenth centuries, there was an "invariable linkage of punishment with crime." In the words of Blackstone (quoted in *Apprendi*), a sentencing court was obliged to "pronounce that judgment, which the law hath annexed to the crime." 530 U.S. at 478-79.

The Court explained that it was compelled to take action because, in recent years, new forms of sentencing statutes had begun to erode "the historic link between verdict and judgment." Id. at 482. The problem, as explained by the Court, was that these statutes introduced "the novelty of a . . . scheme that removes the jury from the determination of a fact that, if found, exposes the criminal defendant to a penalty exceeding the maximum he [might] receive if punished according to the facts reflected in the jury verdict alone." Id. at 482-83. "We do not suggest that trial practices cannot change. . . . But [criminal] practice must . . . adhere to the basic principles undergirding the requirements of trying to a jury *all facts necessary to constitute a statutory offense*, and proving those facts beyond a reasonable doubt." Id. at 483-84.

This italicized language is, I believe, key to understanding the *Apprendi* decision. The Supreme Court viewed the New Jersey hate crime law as, in essence, creating a new group of statutory offenses—new, aggravated versions of the various underlying offenses to which the hate crime law applied. The Court declared that, whatever might be said in favor of

> the constitutionally novel and elusive distinction between "elements" [of an offense] and "sentencing factors," . . . the relevant inquiry is one not of form,

but of effect—does the required finding [i.e., the defendant's motive for committing the underlying offense] expose the defendant to a greater punishment than that authorized by the jury's . . . verdict [finding the defendant guilty of that underlying offense]?

Id. at 494.

Having reached the conclusion that New Jersey's hate crime law actually created a new, aggravated form of the underlying crime of possession of a firearm for an unlawful purpose, the Supreme Court then (naturally) declared that it was unconstitutional for the government of New Jersey to segregate one element of this offense, call it a "sentencing factor," and then have that element tried to the sentencing judge under a preponderance of the evidence standard. Id. at 494-97.

In *Blakely*, the Supreme Court extended the rationale of *Apprendi* to the context of [binding sentencing guidelines. The defendant in *Blakely* pleaded guilty to second-degree kidnapping, a crime that carried a statutory maximum sentence of 10 years' imprisonment. On the facts as admitted in the guilty plea in *Blakely*, Washington's sentencing guidelines permitted the sentencing judge to impose a sentence of 49 to 53 months in prison. Those same guidelines allowed the judge to increase the sentence beyond the 53-month limit if the judge found, by a preponderance of the evidence, one or more of a list of aggravating factors. The judge found that the defendant had acted with "deliberate cruelty," and sentenced the defendant to 90 months in prison. 542 U.S. at 299-301.] . . .

. . . [U]nder Washington's sentencing laws, the finding of deliberate cruelty was legally necessary to support the punishment that Blakely received—and . . . for this reason, Blakely was entitled to have a jury decide whether the state had proved this fact beyond a reasonable doubt:

> The "statutory maximum" [sentence] for *Apprendi* purposes is the maximum sentence a judge may impose *solely on the basis of the facts reflected in the jury verdict or admitted by the defendant.* . . . In other words, the relevant "statutory maximum" is not the maximum sentence a judge may impose after finding additional facts, but the maximum he may impose *without* any additional findings. When a judge inflicts punishment that the jury's verdict alone does not allow, . . . the judge exceeds his proper authority.

Blakely, 542 U.S. at 303-04 (emphasis in the original). . . .

Justice Scalia then emphasized that the problem was not judicial factfinding *per se*, but rather legislative encroachment on the right to jury trial. "The Sixth Amendment . . . is not a limitation on judicial power, but a reservation of jury power. It limits judicial power only to the extent that the claimed judicial power infringes on the province of the jury." Id. at 308. Thus, under a system of *indeterminate* sentencing—i.e., a sentencing scheme in which the judge has the discretion to impose any term of imprisonment within a [specified range—judicial fact-finding does not violate the Sixth Amendment]:

Indeterminate sentencing . . . increases judicial discretion, . . . but not at the expense of the jury's traditional function of finding the facts essential to the lawful imposition of the penalty. . . . Indeterminate [sentencing] schemes involve judicial factfinding, in that a judge . . . may implicitly rule on those facts he deems important to the exercise of his sentencing discretion. But [these] facts do not pertain to whether the defendant has a legal *right* to a lesser sentence—and that makes all the difference . . . In a system that says the judge may punish burglary with [a sentence of] 10 to 40 years, every burglar knows he is risking 40 years in jail. [But in] a system that punishes burglary with a 10-year sentence, with another 30 added for use of a gun, the burglar who enters a home unarmed is *entitled* to no more than a 10-year sentence—and by reason of the Sixth Amendment[,] the facts [that authorize any higher sentence] must be found by a jury.

Id. at 309 (emphasis in the original).

The Supreme Court's most recent decision in this area, United States v. Booker, 543 U.S. 220, contains an even more explicit explanation of the rationale underlying *Apprendi* and *Blakely*. Justice Stevens, writing for the majority, emphasized that the key constitutional problem was the erosion of the jury's traditional role in determining a criminal defendant's level of guilt, as more and more states (and the federal government) adopted determinate sentencing schemes—sentencing schemes that gave judges the power to resolve the factual disputes that would determine the upper limit of the defendant's punishment. . . .

Justice Stevens explained that, given this development in sentencing law, "the Court was faced with the issue of preserving the ancient guarantee [of jury trial] under a new set of circumstances":

The new sentencing practice forced the Court to address the question [of] how the right of jury trial could be preserved [so that it would continue to guarantee], in a meaningful way[,] . . . that the jury would still stand between the individual and the power of the government under the new sentencing regime. It is the new circumstances . . . that have led us to the answer . . . developed in *Apprendi* and subsequent cases. . . . It is an answer not motivated by Sixth Amendment formalism, but by the need to preserve Sixth Amendment substance.

Id. at 237.

. . . The Supreme Court's decisions in *Apprendi*, *Blakely*, and *Booker* all ultimately deal with the same issue: the limitation that the Sixth Amendment places on the government's power to define criminal offenses. To preserve the right to jury trial guaranteed by the Sixth Amendment, the Supreme Court has ruled that governments can not define criminal offenses in a manner that allows the prosecutor to present a stripped-down case to the jury and then, following the defendant's conviction, allows the sentencing judge to decide other factual issues which (if proved) will lift the sentencing ceiling—effectively convicting the defendant of an aggravated degree of the underlying offense.

But as the Supreme Court has repeatedly emphasized, this trilogy of cases does not affect the legality of judicial fact-finding in the context of indeterminate sentencing—that is, in a sentencing scheme where the penalty for a crime is a range of imprisonment, and the judge's task is to decide how to exercise [discretion within that range]. In this context, as Justice Scalia explained in *Blakely*, the facts found by the sentencing judge "do not pertain to whether the defendant has a legal *right* to a lesser sentence—and that makes all the difference" as to whether the judge's fact-finding "impinges upon the traditional role of the jury." *Blakely*, 542 U.S. at 309.

Under Alaska law, the fact that a defendant has been found guilty of two or more crimes automatically subjects the defendant to the possibility of consecutive sentences. No further fact-finding is necessary to invest the sentencing judge with the authority to impose consecutive terms of imprisonment. . . .

Thus, when an Alaska judge decides whether, or to what extent, a defendant's sentences should be imposed consecutively, the judge is performing a task analogous to the task a judge would face when sentencing a defendant for a single offense under an indeterminate sentencing scheme. Except in those instances where Alaska law expressly *requires* consecutive sentencing, the judge's sentencing discretion does not hinge on any particular fact relating to the defendant's conduct, mental state, or criminal history, or to any other circumstance surrounding the defendant's crimes. When the sentencing judge engages in fact-finding on any of these issues, this fact-finding is not done to establish the judge's legal authority to impose the selected sentence. Rather, this fact-finding is done to explain—to the defendant, to the public, and ultimately to a reviewing court—why the judge exercised [his or her] sentencing discretion in a particular manner.

[Here is the argument] that could be made in favor of Vandergriff's position in this appeal. . . . An Alaska sentencing judge's discretion to impose consecutive sentences is not unbounded. In *Neal*, our supreme court established a ceiling (albeit a flexible ceiling) that applies to consecutive sentencing decisions, and the court defined the question that must be addressed before this ceiling is exceeded: whether the protection of the public requires a composite sentence beyond the maximum term for the defendant's single most serious offense. Because this question must be answered in the affirmative before a judge may properly impose consecutive sentences that exceed this ceiling, a defendant has the right to demand that a jury decide this question, and the right to demand that the government prove its position (i.e., the necessity of such a lengthy sentence) beyond a reasonable doubt.

I reject this argument for three reasons.

First, the rule announced in *Neal* does not implicate the constitutional concern addressed in *Apprendi*, *Blakely*, and *Booker*. As explained above, these three decisions are aimed at preventing the government from subverting the right to jury trial by artificially dividing crimes into "elements" (facts that must be proved to a jury beyond a reasonable doubt) and "sentencing factors" (facts which increase the defendant's maximum punishment and which can be proved to a judge under some lesser standard). The *Neal* rule has nothing to do with reshaping the role of the jury in the criminal justice process. Rather, *Neal* is the supreme court's attempt to regulate the expansive consecutive sentencing power that the legislature has given to judges. *Neal* requires sentencing judges to think, and to explain, before they utilize the full extent of their consecutive sentencing power.

Second, the finding required by *Neal* is not the same type of finding that was at issue in *Apprendi, Blakely,* and *Booker.* . . . The constitutional problem in *Apprendi, Blakely,* and *Booker* was the attempt by various governments to segregate certain aspects of a crime—facts that would traditionally be viewed as elements of the crime (facts relating to the defendant's conduct, mental state, or criminal history, or to other circumstances surrounding the crime)—and assign the decision of these facts to the sentencing judge by declaring these facts to be "sentencing factors."

In contrast, the finding required by *Neal* does not turn on any factual aspect of the defendant's present offenses. Although a sentencing judge who complies with the *Neal* rule may mention or even rely on the facts of the [charged] offenses, the ultimate question posed by *Neal* is not one of historical fact. Rather, . . . the finding required by *Neal* (that a lengthy sentence is required to protect the public) is partly a weighing of imponderables and partly a prediction of the defendant's future behavior, based on the judge's assessment of the underlying causes of the defendant's criminal behavior, the defendant's likelihood of recidivism, and the defendant's amenability to rehabilitative efforts. In other words, this finding does not look like any of the findings that are traditionally entrusted to the jury under our system of justice. . . . Accord: People v. Black, 113 P.3d 534, 548-50 (Cal. 2005); State v. Rivera, 102 P.3d 1044, 1054-58, 1059-62 (Haw. 2004); People v. Rivera, 833 N.E.2d 194, 199-200 (N.Y. 2005); State v. Lett, 829 N.E.2d 1281, 1290-92 (Ohio App. 2005) (en banc); State v. Hughes, 110 P.3d 192, 202 (Wash. 2005).

Third, and finally, it makes no sense to require the government to prove the necessity of a particular sentence beyond a reasonable doubt. Alaska law recognizes that sentencing is not an exact science. As our supreme court has said, appellate sentence review in this state "is founded on two concepts: first, that reasonable judges, confronted with identical facts, can and will differ on what constitutes an appropriate sentence; second, that society is willing to accept these sentencing discrepancies, so long as a judge's sentencing decision falls within a permissible range of reasonable sentences." State v. Hodari, 996 P.2d 1230, 1232 (Alaska 2000). Because [application of the *Neal* rule] involves the weighing of imponderables and a prediction of future behavior, it [would be] self-defeating and fruitless to ask the government to prove that, beyond any reasonable doubt, a particular sentence is necessary to protect the public.

For these reasons, I conclude that the *Neal* rule does not implicate the Sixth Amendment concerns expressed in *Apprendi*, *Blakely*, and *Booker*. Accordingly, I concur with my colleagues that a defendant has no right to have a jury decide the sentencing question posed by *Neal*.

Notes and Questions

1. The Alaska rule at issue in *Vandergriff*—concurrent sentences are presumed; consecutive sentences require special justification—is another substitute for a rule of lenity in sentencing. Does it work? The rule's target is one of the most important and least understood features of American criminal justice: Even in cases unlike *Vandergriff*, in which all charges stem from a single criminal incident, the government usually files and can prove several different criminal charges. The *Neal-Mutschler* doctrine might be seen as a norm that, however many overlapping charges the government brings, a single crime merits a single punishment.

2. If, as Judge Mannheimer maintains, appellate review of sentencing decisions amounts to "a weighing of imponderables," how is such review to be conducted? Can sentencing be imposed according to *law* without being imposed according to *rules*?

3. Judge Mannheimer's opinion accurately summarizes the *Apprendi* line of decisions in the Supreme Court. Those decisions—especially Blakely v. Washington, 542 U.S. 296 (2004)—have upended state sentencing and—especially United States v. Booker, 543 U.S. 220 (2005)—federal sentencing as well. *Booker* is particularly complicated. The Justices there faced two issues: first, whether the operation of the Federal Sentencing Guidelines violated the Sixth Amendment; and second, if so, what was to be done to remedy the violation. Justice Stevens' majority opinion, joined by Justices Scalia, Souter, Thomas, and Ginsburg, answered the first question affirmatively. Justice Stevens' opinion reaffirmed *Blakely*, decided only seven months before: Legally binding sentencing guidelines that, on the basis of facts found by the sentencing judge, raise the maximum sentence the defendant can receive violate the Sixth Amendment's right to a jury trial.

4. The second question in *Booker* was answered by a second majority opinion, this one authored by Justice Breyer and joined by Chief Justice Rehnquist and Justices O'Connor, Kennedy, and Ginsburg. (Note that Justice Ginsburg was the only member of the Court to join both opinions—eight of the nine Justices objected to the result in *Booker*.*) This opinion is usually called the "remedial majority"; Justice Stevens' majority opinion is called the

---

* To make the story stranger still, both Justice Stevens and Justice Breyer also filed *dissenting* opinions in *Booker*, each objecting to the other's majority opinion.

"liability majority." *Booker*'s remedial majority rewrote the major federal sentencing statutes, as Justice Breyer's summary of his own opinion indicates:

> We answer the question of remedy by finding the provision of the federal sentencing statute that makes the Guidelines mandatory, 18 U.S.C. §3553(b)(1), incompatible with today's constitutional holding. We conclude that this provision must be severed and excised, as must one other statutory section, §3742(e), which depends upon the Guidelines' mandatory nature. So modified, the Federal Sentencing Act, see Sentencing Reform Act of 1984, as amended, 18 U.S.C. §3551 *et seq.*, 28 U.S.C. §991 *et seq.*, makes the Guidelines effectively advisory. It requires a sentencing court to consider Guidelines ranges, but it permits the court to tailor the sentence in light of other statutory concerns as well, see §3553(a).

These non-mandatory guidelines, Breyer reasoned, did not run afoul of the Sixth Amendment because judges were not required to find any facts in addition to the facts found by a jury (or admitted by the defendant in a guilty plea) in order to justify defendants' sentences.

The key to Breyer's system of advisory guidelines was the standard by which sentencing decisions would be made and reviewed. Under 18 U.S.C. §3742(e), Guidelines decisions had been reviewed de novo: When any of the Guidelines' many rules were not followed, appellate courts reversed the relevant sentencing decisions. Under Breyer's majority opinion in *Booker*, sentencing decisions are judged instead by their reasonableness. Under the Court's later decisions in Rita v. United States, 551 U.S. 338 (2007), and Gall v. United States, 552 U.S. 38 (2007), these sentencing decisions must be reviewed on appeal for abuse of discretion. The meaning of this combined reasonableness/abuse of discretion standard is the subject of *Gall*, the next case.

Gall v. United States

Supreme Court of the United States
552 U.S. 38 (2007)

Justice STEVENS delivered the opinion of the Court.

In two cases argued on the same day last Term we considered the standard that courts of appeals should apply when reviewing the reasonableness of sentences imposed by district judges. The first, Rita v. United States, 551 U.S. 338 (2007), involved a sentence *within* the range recommended by the Federal Sentencing Guidelines; we held that when a district judge's discretionary decision in a particular case accords with the sentence the United States Sentencing Commission deems appropriate "in the mine run of cases," the court of appeals may presume that the sentence is reasonable. Id., at 351.

The second case, Claiborne v. United States, involved a sentence *below* the range recommended by the Guidelines, and raised the converse question whether a court of appeals may . . . require that a sentence that constitutes a substantial variance from the Guidelines be justified by extraordinary circumstances. We did not have the opportunity to answer this question because the case was mooted by Claiborne's untimely death. Claiborne v. United States, 549 U.S. 1016 (2007) (*per curiam*). We granted certiorari in the case before us today in order to reach that question. . . . We now hold that, while the extent of the difference between a particular sentence and the recommended Guidelines range is surely relevant, courts of appeals must review all sentences — whether inside, just outside, or significantly outside the Guidelines range — under a deferential abuse-of-discretion standard. We also hold that the sentence imposed by the experienced District Judge in this case was reasonable.

I

In February or March 2000, petitioner Brian Gall, a second-year college student at the University of Iowa, was invited by Luke Rinderknecht to join an ongoing enterprise distributing a controlled substance popularly known as "ecstasy." Gall — who was then a user of ecstasy, cocaine, and marijuana — accepted the invitation. During the ensuing seven months, Gall delivered ecstasy pills, which he received from Rinderknecht, to other conspirators, who then sold them to consumers. He netted over $30,000.

A month or two after joining the conspiracy, Gall stopped using ecstasy. A few months after that, in September 2000, he advised Rinderknecht and other co-conspirators that he was withdrawing from the conspiracy. He has not sold illegal drugs of any kind since. He has, in the words of the District Court, "self-rehabilitated." App. 75. He graduated from the University of Iowa in 2002, and moved first to Arizona, where he obtained a job in the construction industry, and later to Colorado, where he earned $18 per hour as a master carpenter. He has not used any illegal drugs since graduating from college.

After Gall moved to Arizona, he was approached by federal law enforcement agents who questioned him about his involvement in the ecstasy distribution conspiracy. Gall admitted his limited participation in the distribution of ecstasy, and the agents took no further action at that time. On April 28, 2004 — approximately a year and a half after this initial interview, and three and a half years after Gall withdrew from the conspiracy — an indictment was returned in the Southern District of Iowa charging him and seven other defendants with participating in a conspiracy to distribute ecstasy, cocaine, and marijuana, that began in or about May 1996 and continued through October 30, 2002. The Government has never questioned the truthfulness of any of Gall's earlier statements or contended that he played any role in, or had any knowledge of, other aspects of the conspiracy described in the indictment. When he received notice of the indictment, Gall moved back to Iowa and surrendered to the authorities. While free on his own recognizance, Gall started his own business in the construction industry, primarily engaged in subcontracting for the installation of windows and doors. In his first year, his profits were over $2,000 per month.

Gall entered into a plea agreement with the Government, stipulating that he was "responsible for, but did not necessarily distribute himself, at least 2,500 grams of [ecstasy], or the equivalent of at least 87.5 kilograms of marijuana." Id., at 25. In the agreement, the Government acknowledged that by "on or about September of 2000," Gall had communicated his intent to stop distributing ecstasy to Rinderknecht and other members of the conspiracy. Ibid. The agreement further provided that recent changes in the Guidelines that enhanced the recommended punishment for distributing ecstasy were not applicable to Gall because he had withdrawn from the conspiracy prior to the effective date of those changes.

In her presentence report, the probation officer concluded that Gall had no significant criminal history; that he was not an organizer, leader, or manager; and that his offense did not involve the use of any weapons. The report stated that Gall had truthfully provided the Government with all of the evidence he had concerning the alleged offenses, but that his evidence was not useful because he provided no new information to the agents. The report also described Gall's substantial use of drugs prior to his offense and the absence of any such use in recent years. The report recommended a sentencing range of 30 to 37 months of imprisonment.

The record of the sentencing hearing held on May 27, 2005, includes a "small flood" of letters from Gall's parents and other relatives, his fiance, neighbors, and representatives of firms doing business with him, uniformly praising his character and work ethic. . . . The [federal prosecutor] did not contest any of the evidence concerning Gall's law-abiding life during the preceding five years, but urged that "the Guidelines are appropriate and should be followed," and requested that the court impose a prison sentence within the Guidelines range. Id., at 93. He mentioned that two of Gall's co-conspirators had been sentenced to 30 and 35 months, respectively, but upon further questioning by the District Court, he acknowledged that neither of them had voluntarily withdrawn from the conspiracy.

The District Judge sentenced Gall to probation for a term of 36 months. In addition to making a lengthy statement on the record, the judge filed a detailed sentencing memorandum explaining his decision, and provided the following statement of reasons in his written judgment:

> "The Court determined that, considering all the factors under 18 U.S.C. 3553(a), the Defendant's explicit withdrawal from the conspiracy almost four years before the filing of the Indictment, the Defendant's post-offense

conduct, especially obtaining a college degree and the start of his own successful business, the support of family and friends, lack of criminal history, and
his age at the time of the offense conduct, all warrant the sentence imposed,
which was sufficient, but not greater than necessary to serve the purposes of
sentencing." Id., at 117.

At the end of both the sentencing hearing and the sentencing memorandum, the District Judge reminded Gall that probation, rather than "an
act of leniency," is a "substantial restriction of freedom." Id., at 99, 125. In
the memorandum, he emphasized:

> "[Gall] will have to comply with strict reporting conditions along with a three-
> year regime of alcohol and drug testing. He will not be able to change or
> make decisions about significant circumstances in his life, such as where to
> live or work, which are prized liberty interests, without first seeking authoriza-
> tion from his Probation Officer. . . . Of course, the Defendant always faces the
> harsh consequences that await if he violates the conditions of his probationary
> term." Id., at 125.

Finally, the District Judge explained why he had concluded that the sentence of probation reflected the seriousness of Gall's offense and that no
term of imprisonment was necessary:

> "Any term of imprisonment in this case would be counter effective by depriv-
> ing society of the contributions of the Defendant who, the Court has found,
> understands the consequences of his criminal conduct and is doing everything
> in his power to forge a new life. The Defendant's post-offense conduct indi-
> cates neither that he will return to criminal behavior nor that the Defendant
> is a danger to society. In fact, the Defendant's post-offense conduct was not
> motivated by a desire to please the Court or any other governmental agency,
> but was the pre-Indictment product of the Defendant's own desire to lead a
> better life." Id., at 125-126.

II

The Court of Appeals reversed and remanded for resentencing. Relying
on its earlier opinion in United States v. Claiborne, 439 F.3d 479 (8th Cir.
2006), it held that a sentence outside of the Guidelines range must be supported by a justification that "is proportional to the extent of the difference
between the advisory range and the sentence imposed." 446 F.3d 884, 889
(8th Cir. 2006). Characterizing the difference between a sentence of probation and the bottom of Gall's advisory Guidelines range of 30 months as
"extraordinary" because it amounted to "a 100% downward variance," 446
F.3d at 889, the Court of Appeals held that such a variance must be—and
here was not—supported by extraordinary circumstances.

Rather than making an attempt to quantify the value of the justifications provided by the District Judge, the Court of Appeals identified what

it regarded as five separate errors in the District Judge's reasoning: (1) He gave "too much weight to Gall's withdrawal from the conspiracy"; (2) given that Gall was 21 at the time of his offense, the District Judge erroneously gave "significant weight" to studies showing impetuous behavior by persons under the age of 18; (3) he did not "properly weigh" the seriousness of Gall's offense; (4) he failed to consider whether a sentence of probation would result in "unwarranted" disparities; and (5) he placed "too much emphasis on Gall's post-offense rehabilitation." Id., at 889-890. As we shall explain, we are not persuaded that these factors, whether viewed separately or in the aggregate, are sufficient to support the conclusion that the District Judge abused his discretion. As a preface to our discussion of these particulars, however, we shall explain why the Court of Appeals' rule requiring "proportional" justifications for departures from the Guidelines range is not consistent with our remedial opinion in United States v. Booker, 543 U.S. 220 (2005).

III

In *Booker* we invalidated both the statutory provision, 18 U.S.C. §3553(b)(1), which made the Sentencing Guidelines mandatory, and §3742(e), which directed appellate courts to apply a *de novo* standard of review to departures from the Guidelines. As a result of our decision, the Guidelines are now advisory, and appellate review of sentencing decisions is limited to determining whether they are "reasonable." Our explanation of "reasonableness" review in the *Booker* opinion made it pellucidly clear that the familiar abuse-of-discretion standard of review now applies to appellate review of sentencing decisions. See 543 U.S., at 260-262.

It is also clear that a district judge must give serious consideration to the extent of any departure from the Guidelines and must explain his conclusion that an unusually lenient or an unusually harsh sentence is appropriate in a particular case with sufficient justifications. For even though the Guidelines are advisory rather than mandatory, they are, as we pointed out in *Rita*, the product of careful study based on extensive empirical evidence derived from the review of thousands of individual sentencing decisions. Id., at 349.

In reviewing the reasonableness of a sentence outside the Guidelines range, appellate courts may therefore take the degree of variance into account and consider the extent of a deviation from the Guidelines. We reject, however, an appellate rule that requires "extraordinary" circumstances to justify a sentence outside the Guidelines range. We also reject the use of a rigid mathematical formula that uses the percentage of a departure as the standard for determining the strength of the justifications required for a specific sentence.

As an initial matter, the approaches we reject come too close to creating an impermissible presumption of unreasonableness for sentences outside the Guidelines range. See [*Rita*], 551 U.S. at 354-55 ("The fact that we permit courts of appeals to adopt a presumption of reasonableness does not mean that courts may adopt a presumption of unreasonableness"). Even the Government has acknowledged that such a presumption would not be consistent with *Booker.* See Brief for United States in Rita v. United States, O.T. 2006, No. 06-5754, at 34-35.

The mathematical approach also suffers from infirmities of application. On one side of the equation, deviations from the Guidelines range will always appear more extreme—in percentage terms—when the range itself is low, and a sentence of probation will always be a 100% departure regardless of whether the Guidelines range is 1 month or 100 years. Moreover, quantifying the variance as a certain percentage of the maximum, minimum, or median prison sentence recommended by the Guidelines gives no weight to the "substantial restriction of freedom" involved in a term of supervised release or probation. App. 95.

We recognize that custodial sentences are qualitatively more severe than probationary sentences of equivalent terms. Offenders on probation are nonetheless subject to several standard conditions that substantially restrict their liberty. . . . Probationers may not leave the judicial district, move, or change jobs without notifying, and in some cases receiving permission from, their probation officer or the court. They must report regularly to their probation officer, permit unannounced visits to their homes, refrain from associating with any person convicted of a felony, and refrain from excessive drinking. Most probationers are also subject to individual "special conditions" imposed by the court. Gall, for instance, may not patronize any establishment that derives more than 50% of its revenue from the sale of alcohol, and must submit to random drug tests as directed by his probation officer.

On the other side of the equation, the mathematical approach assumes the existence of some ascertainable method of assigning percentages to various justifications. Does withdrawal from a conspiracy justify more or less than, say, a 30% reduction? Does it matter that the withdrawal occurred several years ago? Is it relevant that the withdrawal was motivated by a decision to discontinue the use of drugs and to lead a better life? What percentage, if any, should be assigned to evidence that a defendant poses no future threat to society, or to evidence that innocent third parties are dependent on him? The formula is a classic example of attempting to measure an inventory of apples by counting oranges.

Most importantly, both the exceptional circumstances requirement and the rigid mathematical formulation reflect a practice—common among courts that have adopted "proportional review"—of applying a heightened standard of review to sentences outside the Guidelines range. This is inconsistent with the rule that the abuse-of-discretion standard of review applies to appellate review of all sentencing decisions—whether inside or outside the Guidelines range.

As we explained in *Rita*, a district court should begin all sentencing proceedings by correctly calculating the applicable Guidelines range. See 551 U.S. at 351. As a matter of administration and to secure nationwide consistency, the Guidelines should be the starting point and the initial benchmark. The Guidelines are not the only consideration, however. Accordingly, after giving both parties an opportunity to argue for whatever sentence they deem appropriate, the district judge should then consider all of the §3553(a) factors to determine whether they support the sentence requested by a party. In so doing, he may not presume that the Guidelines range is reasonable. See id., at 351. He must make an individualized assessment based on the facts presented. If he decides that an outside-Guidelines sentence is warranted, he must consider the extent of the deviation and ensure that the justification is sufficiently compelling to support the degree of the variance. We find it uncontroversial that a major departure should be supported by a more significant justification than a minor one. After settling on the appropriate sentence, he must adequately explain the chosen sentence to allow for meaningful appellate review and to promote the perception of fair sentencing. Id., at 356.

Regardless of whether the sentence imposed is inside or outside the Guidelines range, the appellate court must review the sentence under an abuse-of-discretion standard. It must first ensure that the district court committed no significant procedural error, such as failing to calculate (or improperly calculating) the Guidelines range, treating the Guidelines as mandatory, failing to consider the §3553(a) factors, selecting a sentence based on clearly erroneous facts, or failing to adequately explain the chosen sentence — including an explanation for any deviation from the Guidelines range. Assuming that the district court's sentencing decision is procedurally sound, the appellate court should then consider the substantive reasonableness of the sentence imposed under an abuse-of-discretion standard. When conducting this review, the court will, of course, take into account the totality of the circumstances, including the extent of any variance from the Guidelines range. If the sentence is within the Guidelines range, the appellate court may, but is not required to, apply a presumption of reasonableness. Id., at 347. But if the sentence is outside the Guidelines range, the court may not apply a presumption of unreasonableness. It may consider the extent of the deviation, but must give due deference to the district court's decision that the §3553(a) factors, on a whole, justify the extent of the variance. The fact that the appellate court might reasonably have concluded that a different sentence was appropriate is insufficient to justify reversal of the district court. . . .

"It has been uniform and constant in the federal judicial tradition for the sentencing judge to consider every convicted person as an individual and every case as a unique study in the human failings that sometimes mitigate, sometimes magnify, the crime and the punishment to ensue." [Koon

v. United States, 518 U.S. 81, 113 (1996).] The uniqueness of the individual case, however, does not change the deferential abuse-of-discretion standard of review that applies to all sentencing decisions. As we shall now explain, the opinion of the Court of Appeals in this case does not reflect the requisite deference and does not support the conclusion that the District Court abused its discretion.

IV

As an initial matter, we note that the District Judge committed no significant procedural error. He correctly calculated the applicable Guidelines range, allowed both parties to present arguments as to what they believed the appropriate sentence should be, considered all of the §3553(a) factors, and thoroughly documented his reasoning. The Court of Appeals found that the District Judge erred in failing to give proper weight to the seriousness of the offense, as required by §3553(a)(2)(A), and failing to consider whether a sentence of probation would create unwarranted disparities, as required by §3553(a)(6). We disagree.

. . . The Court of Appeals concluded that "the district court did not properly weigh the seriousness of Gall's offense" because it "ignored the serious health risks ecstasy poses." 446 F.3d at 890. Contrary to the Court of Appeals' conclusion, the District Judge plainly did consider the seriousness of the offense. . . . It is true that the District Judge did not make specific reference to the (unquestionably significant) health risks posed by ecstasy, but the prosecutor did not raise ecstasy's effects at the sentencing hearing. Had the prosecutor raised the issue, specific discussion of the point might have been in order, but it was not incumbent on the District Judge to raise every conceivably relevant issue on his own initiative.

The Government's legitimate concern that a lenient sentence for a serious offense threatens to promote disrespect for the law is at least to some extent offset by the fact that seven of the eight defendants in this case have been sentenced to significant prison terms. Moreover, the unique facts of Gall's situation provide support for the District Judge's conclusion that, in Gall's case, "a sentence of imprisonment may work to promote not respect, but derision, of the law if the law is viewed as merely a means to dispense harsh punishment without taking into account the real conduct and circumstances involved in sentencing." Id., at 126.

Section 3553(a)(6) requires judges to consider "the need to avoid unwarranted sentence disparities among defendants with similar records who have been found guilty of similar conduct." . . . [A]voidance of unwarranted disparities was clearly considered by the Sentencing Commission when setting the Guidelines ranges. Since the District Judge correctly calculated and carefully reviewed the Guidelines range, he necessarily gave significant weight and consideration to the need to avoid unwarranted disparities.

Moreover, . . . it seems that the judge gave specific attention to the issue of disparity when he inquired about the sentences already imposed by a different judge on two of Gall's codefendants. . . . [I]t is perfectly clear that the District Judge considered the need to avoid unwarranted disparities, but also considered the need to avoid unwarranted *similarities* among other co-conspirators who were not similarly situated. The District Judge regarded Gall's voluntary withdrawal as a reasonable basis for giving him a less severe sentence than the three codefendants . . . , who neither withdrew from the conspiracy nor rehabilitated themselves as Gall had done. We also note that neither the Court of Appeals nor the Government has called our attention to a comparable defendant who received a more severe sentence.

Since the District Court committed no procedural error, the only question for the Court of Appeals was whether the sentence was reasonable — i.e., whether the District Judge abused his discretion in determining that the §3553(a) factors supported a sentence of probation and justified a substantial deviation from the Guidelines range. As we shall now explain, the sentence was reasonable. The Court of Appeals' decision to the contrary was incorrect and failed to demonstrate the requisite deference to the District Judge's decision.

V

The Court of Appeals gave virtually no deference to the District Court's decision that the §3553(a) factors justified a significant variance in this case. Although the Court of Appeals correctly stated that the appropriate standard of review was abuse of discretion, it engaged in an analysis that more closely resembled *de novo* review of the facts presented and determined that, in its view, the degree of variance was not warranted.

The Court of Appeals thought that the District Court "gave too much weight to Gall's withdrawal from the conspiracy because the court failed to acknowledge the significant benefit Gall received from being subject to the 1999 Guidelines."[10] 446 F.3d at 889. This criticism is flawed in that it ignores the critical relevance of Gall's voluntary withdrawal, a circumstance that distinguished his conduct not only from that of all his codefendants, but from the vast majority of defendants convicted of conspiracy in federal court. The District Court quite reasonably attached great weight to the fact that Gall voluntarily withdrew from the conspiracy after deciding, on his own initiative, to change his life. This lends strong support to the District Court's conclusion that Gall is not going to return to criminal behavior and is not a danger to society. See 18 U.S.C. §§3553(a)(2)(B), (C). Compared

---

10. The Court of Appeals explained that under the current Guidelines, which treat ecstasy more harshly, Gall's base offense level would have been 32, eight levels higher than the base offense level imposed under the 1999 Guidelines.

to a case where the offender's rehabilitation occurred after he was charged with a crime, the District Court here had greater justification for believing Gall's turnaround was genuine, as distinct from a transparent attempt to build a mitigation case.

The Court of Appeals thought the District Judge "gave significant weight to an improper factor" when he compared Gall's sale of ecstasy when he was a 21-year-old adult to the "impetuous and ill-considered" actions of persons under the age of 18. 446 F.3d at 890. The appellate court correctly observed that the studies cited by the District Judge do not explain how Gall's "specific behavior in the instant case was impetuous or ill-considered." Ibid.

In that portion of his sentencing memorandum, however, the judge was discussing the "character of the defendant," not the nature of his offense. App. 122. He noted that Gall's criminal history included a ticket for underage drinking when he was 18 years old and possession of marijuana that was contemporaneous with his offense in this case. In summary, the District Judge observed that all of Gall's criminal history "including the present offense, occurred when he was twenty-one-years old or younger" and appeared "to stem from his addictions to drugs and alcohol." Id., at 123. . . . Given the dramatic contrast between Gall's behavior before he joined the conspiracy and his conduct after withdrawing, it was not unreasonable for the District Judge to view Gall's immaturity at the time of the offense as a mitigating factor, and his later behavior as a sign that he had matured and would not engage in such impetuous and ill-considered conduct in the future. . . .

Finally, the Court of Appeals thought that, even if Gall's rehabilitation was dramatic and permanent, a sentence of probation for participation as a middleman in a conspiracy distributing 10,000 pills of ecstasy "lies outside the range of choice dictated by the facts of the case." 446 F.3d at 890. If the Guidelines were still mandatory, and assuming the facts did not justify a Guidelines-based downward departure, this would provide a sufficient basis for setting aside Gall's sentence because the Guidelines state that probation alone is not an appropriate sentence for comparable offenses. But the Guidelines are not mandatory, and thus the "range of choice dictated by the facts of the case" is significantly broadened. Moreover, the Guidelines are only one of the factors to consider when imposing sentence, and §3553(a)(3) directs the judge to consider sentences other than imprisonment. . . .

The Court of Appeals clearly disagreed with the District Judge's conclusion that consideration of the §3553(a) factors justified a sentence of probation; it believed that the circumstances presented here were insufficient to sustain such a marked deviation from the Guidelines range. But it is not for the Court of Appeals to decide *de novo* whether the justification for a variance is sufficient or the sentence reasonable. On abuse-of-discretion review, the Court of Appeals should have given due deference to the District Court's reasoned and reasonable decision that the §3553(a) factors, on the whole, justified the sentence. Accordingly, the judgment of the Court of Appeals is reversed.

[Justice SCALIA's concurring opinion, Justice SOUTER's concurring opinion, and Justice THOMAS' dissenting opinion are omitted.]

Justice ALITO, dissenting.

The fundamental question in this case is whether, under the remedial decision in United States v. Booker, 543 U.S. 220 (2005), a district court must give the policy decisions that are embodied in the Sentencing Guidelines at least some significant weight in making a sentencing decision. I would answer that question in the affirmative and would therefore affirm the decision of the Court of Appeals.

In *Booker*, . . . the lower federal courts were instructed that the Guidelines must be regarded as "effectively advisory," *Booker*, 543 U.S., at 245, and that individual sentencing decisions are subject to appellate review for "reasonableness." Id., at 262. . . . [I]n the remedial opinion, the Court expressed confidence that appellate review for reasonableness would help to avoid "excessive sentencing disparities" and "would tend to iron out sentencing differences." Id., at 263. Indeed, a major theme of the remedial opinion, as well as our decision last Term in Rita v. United States, 551 U.S. 338 (2007), was that the post-*Booker* sentencing regime would still promote the Sentencing Reform Act's goal of reducing sentencing disparities. . . .

It is unrealistic to think this goal can be achieved over the long term if sentencing judges need only give lip service to the Guidelines. The other sentencing factors set out in §3553(a) are so broad that they impose few real restraints on sentencing judges. Thus, if judges are obligated to do no more than consult the Guidelines before deciding upon the sentence that is, in their independent judgment, sufficient to serve the other §3553(a) factors, . . . sentencing disparities will gradually increase. Appellate decisions affirming sentences that diverge from the Guidelines (such as the Court's decision today) will be influential, and the sentencing habits developed during the pre-*Booker* era will fade. . . .

Notes and Questions

1. Voluntary abandonment is a defense to a conspiracy charge — but only if the abandonment prevents the conspiracy from achieving its object. Decisions like Gall's to abandon conspiracies that have been functioning for a considerable time are no defense. Should they be? If not, why does Gall's abandonment justify his sentence?

2. For more than two decades, federal judges have criticized the Federal Sentencing Guidelines on the ground that the Guidelines make federal sentencing too harsh. One might suppose, therefore, that in *Booker*'s aftermath, federal sentences dropped sharply as federal judges exercised the discretion that Stephen Breyer and his colleagues gave them. Not so: Average federal sentences have remained essentially unchanged. Why so little change? One answer lies in the incentives *Gall*'s standard of review creates. Sentencing decisions that conform to the no-longer-binding Guidelines are deemed presumptively reasonable, meaning that those decisions carry essentially no risk of reversal on appeal. Sentencing decisions like the one in *Gall* are *not* presumed reasonable—Gall's sentence was upheld, but only because the Supreme Court overturned the Court of Appeals that found Gall's sentence too lenient. The message to trial judges is clear: The risk-minimizing move is to stick within Guidelines ranges.

3. Assume for the sake of argument that Gall's sentence was just. Which system best ensures that such a sentence is imposed—a system built on sentencing rules, a system built on sentencing standards, or a system built on sentencing discretion?

4. One category of rigid sentencing rules that remained outside the scope of *Apprendi* doctrine, at least for a while, was the category of mandatory minimum sentences. Statutes imposing mandatory minimum sentences became popular with legislators (state and federal) in the 1980s, especially for drug crimes and crimes involving the sexual abuse of children. Because mandatory minimum sentences don't actually raise the *maximum* punishment that can be imposed against a defendant—the trial judge could always have chosen to impose a sentence above the mandatory minimum level anyway—the Supreme Court initially held that the factors that trigger such sentences fall outside of *Apprendi* and need not be found by a jury beyond reasonable doubt. The Court reversed course, however, in Alleyne v. United States, 570 U.S. __ (2013). In *Alleyne*, the Court extended *Apprendi* to include those factors that trigger mandatory minimum sentences. Justice Scalia objected, finding the extension to be inconsistent with the theory (at least with *his* theory) behind *Apprendi* and its progeny.

Mandatory minimum sentences are controversial, for a variety of reasons. One important reason is that they require the lengthy imprisonment of offenders who might be seen as less dangerous (e.g., low-level drug offenders) than those who commit other serious crimes—such as murder and rape—that generally are not subject to mandatory minimum sentences. Mandatory minimum sentencing statutes thus can be blamed for at least part of the dramatic increases in imprisonment rates in the United States since the 1980s. Moreover, because drug crimes are prosecuted disproportionately against the poor and people of color, see supra Chapter 6, at page 399, the same mandatory minimum sentencing statutes contribute significantly to the disproportionality by race and socioeconomic class of American prison populations. See Michael Tonry, "Racial Disparities Getting Worse in U.S. Prisons and Jails," in Sentencing Reform in Overcrowded Times 223 (Michael Tonry & Kathleen Hatlestad eds. Oxford U. Press, 1997).

5. *Booker, Gall,* and even *Alleyne* might be viewed as calling into question the fundamental premises underlying *Apprendi* and *Blakely,* because they approved a remedial scheme or (in the case of *Alleyne*) adopted a theoretical approach that (at least in the view of Justice Scalia, the author of *Blakely* and thus the chief architect of the prevailing doctrine) is incompatible with those premises. But those cases did not directly challenge the *Apprendi/Blakely* doctrine itself. The first such direct challenge might be the case of Oregon v. Ice, 555 U.S. 160 (2009). Under Oregon law, Ice—who was convicted of multiple crimes in a single trial—was subject to consecutive rather than concurrent sentences only if the trial judge made a factual finding that the crimes involved separate incidents, or if (in the same incident) the defendant manifested a "willingness to commit more than one criminal offense" or the crimes created a risk of "greater or qualitatively different loss, injury or harm to the victim."* The judge made such findings in Ice's case, and Ice was given consecutive sentences that totaled 340 months in prison.

The Court held that Ice's consecutive sentencing did not violate *Apprendi* and *Blakely*. In a majority opinion by Justice Ginsburg, joined by Justices Stevens, Kennedy, Breyer, and Alito, the Court explained:

> This case concerns the scope of the Sixth Amendment's jury-trial guarantee, as construed in Apprendi v. New Jersey, 530 U.S. 466 (2000), and Blakely v. Washington, 542 U.S. 296 (2004). Those decisions are rooted in the historic jury function—determining whether the prosecution has proved each element of an offense beyond a reasonable doubt. They hold that it is within the jury's province to determine any fact (other than the existence of a prior conviction) that increases the maximum punishment authorized for a particular offense. Thus far, the Court has not extended the *Apprendi* and *Blakely* line of decisions beyond the offense-specific context that supplied the historic grounding for the decisions. The question here presented concerns a sentencing function in which the jury traditionally played no part: When a defendant has been tried and convicted of multiple offenses, each involving discrete sentencing prescriptions, does the Sixth Amendment mandate jury determination of any fact declared necessary to the imposition of consecutive, in lieu of concurrent, sentences?
>
> Our application of *Apprendi*'s rule must honor the "long-standing common-law practice" in which the rule is rooted. . . . The rule's animating principle is the preservation of the jury's historic role as a bulwark between the State and the accused at the trial for an alleged offense. See *Apprendi*, 530 U.S., at 477. Guided by that principle, our opinions make clear that the Sixth Amendment does not countenance legislative encroachment on the jury's traditional domain. See *id.*, at 497. We accordingly considered whether the finding of a particular fact was understood as within "the domain of the jury . . . by those who framed the Bill of Rights." Harris v. United States, 536 U.S. 545, 557 (2002) (plurality opinion). In undertaking this inquiry, we remain cognizant

---

* This is a rather unusual kind of statute. In most American jurisdictions, the decision whether to have criminal sentences run concurrently or consecutively lies within the sound discretion of the trial judge. Often this remains true even in a modern determinate (or guideline-based) sentencing system. See, e.g., 18 U.S.C. §3584(b), which authorizes federal trial judges to impose either concurrent or consecutive sentences, with the only requirement being that the judge "shall consider, as to each offense for which a term of imprisonment is being imposed, the [general sentencing] factors set forth [at the beginning of the Sentencing Reform Act]."

that administration of a discrete criminal justice system is among the basic sovereign prerogatives States retain. See, *e.g.*, Patterson v. New York, 432 U.S. 197, 201 (1977).

These twin considerations—historical practice and respect for state sovereignty—counsel against extending *Apprendi*'s rule to the imposition of sentences for discrete crimes. The decision to impose sentences consecutively is not within the jury function that "extends down centuries into the common law." *Apprendi*, 530 U.S., at 477. Instead, specification of the regime for administering multiple sentences has long been considered the prerogative of state legislatures.

Members of this Court have warned against "wooden, unyielding insistence on expanding the *Apprendi* doctrine far beyond its necessary boundaries." Cunningham [v. California], 549 U.S. [270], 295 (Kennedy, J., dissenting). The jury-trial right is best honored through a "principled rationale" that applies the rule of the *Apprendi* cases "within the central sphere of their concern." 549 U.S., at 295. Our disposition today—upholding an Oregon statute that assigns to judges a decision that has not traditionally belonged to the jury—is faithful to that aim.

Justice Scalia, predictably, was not amused:

> [T]he Court attempts to distinguish Oregon's sentencing scheme by reasoning that the rule of *Apprendi* applies only to the length of a sentence for an individual crime and not to the total sentence for a defendant. I cannot understand why we would make such a strange exception to the treasured right of trial by jury. Neither the reasoning of the *Apprendi* line of cases, nor any distinctive history of the factfinding necessary to imposition of consecutive sentences, nor (of course) logic supports such an odd rule. . . .
>
> To support its distinction-without-a-difference, the Court puts forward the same (the *very* same) arguments regarding the history of sentencing that were rejected by *Apprendi*. Here, it is entirely irrelevant that common-law judges had discretion to impose either consecutive or concurrent sentences, just as there it was entirely irrelevant that common-law judges had discretion to impose greater or lesser sentences (within the prescribed statutory maximum) for individual convictions. . . . Our concern here is precisely the same as our concern in *Apprendi*: What happens when a State breaks from the common-law practice of discretionary sentences and permits the imposition of an elevated sentence only upon the showing of extraordinary facts? In such a system, the defendant "is *entitled* to" the lighter sentence "and by reason of the Sixth Amendment[,] the facts bearing upon that entitlement must be found by a jury." *Blakely*, 542 U.S., at 309. . . .
>
> Today's opinion muddies the waters, and gives cause to doubt whether the Court is willing to stand by *Apprendi*'s interpretation of the Sixth Amendment's jury-trial guarantee.

Does *Ice* truly represent the beginning of the end for the *Apprendi/Blakely* doctrine? Or is it a one-off exception that will leave the core of the rule unscathed? Only time will tell.

B. MEASURING PUNISHMENT

1. The Rule Against Multiplicity

United States v. Buchanan

United States Court of Appeals for the Fifth Circuit
485 F.3d 274 (2007)

PRISCILLA R. OWEN, Circuit Judge.

Following a jury trial, Joseph Buchanan was convicted of four counts of receiving child pornography transported in interstate commerce by computer and one count of possession of child pornography. [18 U.S.C. §§2252(a)(2), 2252(a)(4)(A).] Buchanan appeals his conviction and sentence on numerous grounds. Because the first four counts against Buchanan are multiplicitous, we vacate them and remand with instructions to reinstate only one of the convictions and to resentence him consistent with this opinion. All of Buchanan's other claims lack merit.

I

Joseph Buchanan was employed by the United States Army Corps of Engineers as a park ranger and served at its Lake Texoma location. Each ranger was assigned an individual computer that required a unique password for access and would log the actions on the computer to a record tied to the specific ranger. In early 2001, a Corps system administrator in Tulsa received a complaint from the Texoma station that the office's internet access was slow. The administrator used a program to determine that Buchanan's computer was slowing down the office's access by connecting to "an X-rated porn site." The Corps began monitoring Buchanan's computer use and determined that he continued to view pornography on his office computer.

When confronted, Buchanan admitted the misuse and stated he would never do it again. In March 2002, Ron Jordan, the Lake Texoma manager, received a report that Buchanan was again viewing pornography. Using the network administrator's password, Jordan accessed Buchanan's computer and discovered pornographic photographs and movies involving adults as well as bestiality. Jordan printed out an image and questioned Buchanan, who again admitted to viewing the pornography and promised to cease these activities. In April, Jordan received another report about Buchanan, found pornographic images on a scan of Buchanan's computer, and suspended Buchanan for two days.

In August 2002, Jordan resumed monitoring Buchanan's computer use after receiving another report that Buchanan was viewing pornography on his work computer. On August 28, Jordan found pornographic images in

Buchanan's temporary internet folder—the location on the hard drive in which data from accessed webpages, including images, are automatically stored. Jordan copied some of the temporary internet folder files from Buchanan's computer to his computer. The next day, Jordan saw that more files had been added to Buchanan's temporary internet folder. Some of these files were images of nude, prepubescent children. Jordan noticed that files were being added and deleted as he viewed the folder. A number of graphic files with sexually explicit names were automatically downloaded—showing that someone was viewing a webpage or webpages containing these images on the internet—over a span of several minutes during a single computer session. Jordan copied some of the files, including both child and adult pornography, onto a compact disc that was later turned over to law enforcement officials.

FBI Agent Wes Wheeler investigated Buchanan's computer use and found that four large images on the CD depicted children from 10 to 12 years old engaged in sexually explicit conduct. Wheeler met with Buchanan on September 12, 2002 and showed him images printed from the CD. Buchanan admitted that he had visited internet sites containing child pornography and that he had in the past saved such images, viewed them, and later deleted them. He said the sites he typically visited contained both adult and child pornography.

An FBI computer forensic examiner determined that the CD contained 127 images, including 54 depicting minors from 7 to 15 years old. The examiner found fifty small, "thumbnail" images depicting minors—pictures displayed on a web page to preview an image, which a viewer could click to access a larger, higher-resolution version of the same image—in addition to the four larger images of child pornography Agent Wheeler had earlier identified. The examiner also used sophisticated software to find a number of encrypted files on Buchanan's hard drive. The files were password-protected and buried nine directories deep through the creation of multiple subdirectories. The examiner further found an encryption program, called Scramdisk, designed to disguise files. After a thorough sweep of the hard drive with various software programs, the examiner found over 3,000 pornographic images on the hard drive, including more than 300 images of children from 3 to 15 years old engaged in sexually explicit conduct, each of which was hidden and password-protected.

[The] indictment charged four separate counts of receipt and attempted receipt of child pornography under 18 U.S.C. §§2252(a)(2) and 2252(b)(1)—one count for each of the four larger images from the CD provided by Jordan. A fifth count charged Buchanan with possession of child pornography under 18 U.S.C. §2252(a)(4)(A) based on eleven images found on Buchanan's hard drive.

Following a jury trial, Buchanan was convicted on all five counts and sentenced to 71 months in prison for each of the first four counts and 60 months for the fifth count, all to be served concurrently. Buchanan was also assessed a $100 special assessment for each count and a $5,000 fine — $5,500 total. Buchanan appeals both his convictions and sentence.

II

Buchanan argues that the convictions for receipt of child pornography in counts one through four of the . . . indictment are multiplicitous. Convictions are multiplicitous when the prosecution charges "a single offense in more than one count." [United States v. De La Torre, 634 F.2d 792, 794 (5th Cir. 1981).] The . . . indictment alleged that Buchanan had knowingly received and attempted to receive one or more visual depictions of minors engaging in sexually explicit conduct by means of a computer and the internet, and the indictment then listed the four counts in a table with information about four images, as follows:

Count	Image	Description
1	andy — 1[1].jpg	[omitted][4]
2	hard 11[1].jpg	[omitted]
3	matt [1].jpg	[omitted]
4	Boyshard4[1].jpg	[omitted]

. . . Buchanan maintains that the indictment does not allege that his receipt of the four images was the result of four separate transactions. He also contends that the four images were automatically downloaded by the computer he was using into temporary internet folders while he was viewing images of adults contained on the same, single webpage.

The rule against multiplicity is grounded in the Fifth Amendment's prohibition against double jeopardy, intending "to prevent multiple punishments for the same act." [United States v. Kimbrough, 69 F.3d 723, 729 (5th Cir. 1995).] We have held that "[t]he test for determining whether the same act or transaction constitutes two offenses or only one is whether conviction under each statutory provision requires proof of an additional fact which the other does not." [United States v. Reedy, 304 F.3d 358, 363 (5th Cir. 2002).] We have said, "Where a multipart transaction raises the prospect of multiplicity under a single statute, the question becomes whether separate and distinct prohibited acts, made punishable by law, have been committed." [Id. at 363-64.] When "the jury is allowed to return convictions on multiplicitous counts, the remedy is to remand for resentencing, with the government dismissing the count(s) that created the multiplicity" because

---

4. The description of the content of each image is not at issue and has been omitted as unnecessary to our decision.

"[t]he chief danger raised by a multiplicitous indictment is the possibility that the defendant will receive more than one sentence for a single offense." [United States v. Galvan, 949 F.2d 777, 781 (5th Cir. 1991).]

Buchanan was convicted in counts one through four of four separate violations of 18 U.S.C. §2252(a)(2), which provides:

> (a) Any person who—
>> (2) knowingly receives, or distributes, any visual depiction that has been mailed, or has been shipped or transported in interstate or foreign commerce, or which contains materials which have been mailed or so shipped or transported, by any means including by computer, or knowingly reproduces any visual depiction for distribution in interstate or foreign commerce or through the mails, if—
>>> (A) the producing of such visual depiction involves the use of a minor engaging in sexually explicit conduct; and
>>> (B) such visual depiction is of such conduct. . . .

At the time of the offense, the penalty for violating or attempting to violate this section was imprisonment for not more than 15 years, unless there has been a prior conviction for certain crimes, in which event the penalty was imprisonment for not less than 5 years and not more than 30 years.

We have specifically addressed multiplicity and §2252 on at least two occasions. [See United States v. Reedy, 304 F.3d 358, 367 (5th Cir. 2002); United States v. Gallardo, 915 F.2d 149 (5th Cir. 1990).] In *Gallardo*, a defendant was convicted under §2252 of four counts of mailing child pornography. The defendant had mailed three envelopes to different locations at one time and a fourth envelope on a later date. He was charged with a separate count for each envelope. On appeal, the defendant asserted that the three counts stemming from the three envelopes mailed at the same time should have been reduced to a single count. Applying a previous holding regarding mail fraud, [see United States v. Blankenship, 746 F.2d 233, 236 (5th Cir. 1984),] we held that "each separate use of the mail to transport or ship child pornography should constitute a separate crime because it is the act of either *transporting or shipping* that is the central focus of this statute." *Gallardo*, 915 F.2d at 151. "The number of photographs in each envelope is irrelevant" for determining the appropriate number of counts. Id. . . . [By analogy,] "a defendant arrested with one binder containing numerous photographs has committed only one act of transportation," [id., just as] "a single transportation of two women is but one violation of the Mann Act." [Id. (citing Bell v. United States, 349 U.S. 81, 84 (1955)).] The four convictions were upheld because the defendant mailed four envelopes. Id.

In United States v. Reedy, this court held that §2252 "does not speak to the question" of "what 'unit of prosecution' should apply" and therefore, that the rule of lenity governed the outcome. [304 F.3d 358, 361 (5th

Cir. 2002).] The defendants in that case were convicted of multiple counts of violating §2252 for transporting visual depictions of minors engaged in sexually explicit conduct. The defendants operated a sign-on, screening and age verification system for pornographic websites, and charged subscribers by website. The defendants contended that they should have been charged with only ten counts because there were only ten websites containing child pornography. The district court "used the total number of images appearing on all the websites as the relevant unit of prosecution for determining the number of counts for violating §2252." [Id. at 365.] This court disagreed, concluding that "the rule of lenity require[d] resentencing based on the number of websites rather than the number of individual images." [Id. at 361.]

In *Reedy*, this court began its analysis by explaining that "the 'unit of prosecution' for a crime is the *actus reus*, the physical conduct of the defendant." [Id. at 365.] In examining §2252, *Reedy* considered whether "a 'visual depiction' is neatly confined to an individual image or encompasses a broader set of items, such as books, magazines, movies, or other collections." [Id. at 366.] The court observed that 18 U.S.C. §2256, which defines terms used in §2252, provides that "visual depiction" includes "any photograph, film, video, picture, or computer or computer-generated image or picture, whether made or produced by electronic, mechanical, or other means." [Id. (quoting former 18 U.S.C. §2256(8)).] This court recognized that this definition "includes both items that may be classified as a single shot of a single scene, such as a still photograph, and series of shots of several scenes or ongoing action, such as a film or video" and that §2252 therefore "contemplates 'visual depictions' as constituting both single images and more than one image." [Id.] This court also noted that §2252(c)(1) "creates an affirmative defense for persons possessing 'less than three matters containing any visual depiction,'" and reasoned that "a 'matter' is larger and inclusive of a 'visual depiction,'" but that the terms used in the statute "do not explain the size or inclusiveness of a 'visual depiction.'" [Id.]

The *Reedy* decision then turned to precedent regarding related issues and focused on the defendants' physical conduct, which was bundling images by website:

> Consider the Reedys' actions. . . . The Reedys chose to bundle their service by website; they charged for subscriptions to individual websites. . . . As the defendant in *Gallardo* chose to collect several pictures in an envelope, or the publisher of a magazine of child pornography chooses to collect several images in a periodical, the Reedys chose to bundle in this manner. *Gallardo* cuts slightly in favor of the Reedys' interpretation.

[Id. at 367.]

This court expressed its dismay at the government's suggestion that it could hold the Reedys criminally liable for each time that a customer downloaded an image.[36] Ultimately, this court concluded that it had reached the "same impasse," [id.,] that the Supreme Court had reached in Bell v. United States, in which the Mann Act's prohibition of transporting "any woman or girl" in interstate commerce for immoral purposes was found to be ambiguous. [349 U.S. 81, 82 (1955).] Quoting *Bell*, this court said that "argumentative skill" "'could persuasively and not unreasonably reach' either interpretation" offered by the parties and therefore, that "the 'ambiguity should be resolved in favor of lenity.'" *Reedy*, 304 F.3d at 367. . . .

It is in light of these precedents that we examine the record before us and conclude that the government failed to allege or prove with regard to counts one through four that Buchanan engaged in more than one transaction in violation of 18 U.S.C. §2252. As in other contexts, the government bore the burden of establishing multiple counts by charging and proving separate receipts of child pornography.[42] The indictment failed to allege separate receipt of the four images identified.

Nor did the expert or other testimony at trial establish that Buchanan took more than one action to receive the four images made the basis of counts one through four. The evidence showed only that when Buchanan visited a webpage, his computer automatically downloaded the images on that webpage to his computer's temporary internet folder. The differing times shown on the compact disc to which some of the temporary internet files were copied did not establish that the images had come from different webpages or that Buchanan had to take any action other than navigating to a single webpage for the images to be captured in the temporary internet file folders. There was also uncontroverted testimony that the date and time stamps on the copied files were not necessarily the actual times that the images were automatically downloaded to Buchanan's temporary internet folder due to the machinations of some computer programs.

The fact that the four images made the basis of counts one through four were larger than thumbnail images on the compact disc to which some of Buchanan's temporary internet file folders were copied was not explained at

---

36. [304 F.3d] at 365 n.6:

> Take, hypothetically, one website with 100 child pornographic pictures. If each of 100 subscribers were to download each of the 100 pictures just once, the defendant could be charged with 10,000 counts, for a potential sentence of 150,000 years. Such an extreme interpretation of Congressional intent undermines the reliability and credibility of the government's case on appeal.

42. See United States v. Hodges, 628 F.2d 350, 351-52 (5th Cir. 1980) (holding that under former 18 U.S.C. §922(h)(1), which prohibited a felon from receiving in interstate commerce "any firearm," simultaneous possession or receipt of multiple firearms can only be charged as a single offense and that [in order to convict for distinct offenses,] the government must establish that a defendant "received the firearms at different times or stored them in separate locations"); United States v. Rosenbarger, 536 F.2d 715, 721 (6th Cir. 1976) (stating that "it was the Government's burden to establish separate offenses under the statute").

trial. The record was silent as to whether Buchanan would have had to have "clicked on" each of the four larger images separately to enlarge them or whether they were larger on the webpage itself. . . . We do not resolve today whether a separate mouse click on an image to maximize its size would suffice as a separate receipt of child pornography.

Based on the facts before us, the government did not offer any proof that Buchanan took more than one action to receive the four images that were the basis of his convictions under §2252(a)(2). His convictions were therefore multiplicitous. . . .

BENAVIDES, Circuit Judge, concurring.

. . . There are many ways in which a defendant might receive four "visual depiction[s]" from the web. In the simplest example, he could visit a single page that contains four large images, all of which are automatically displayed on the screen and downloaded to his hard drive. In such a case, we could debate whether the defendant had committed four separate acts of receiving an individual image, or the single act of receiving one web page. Our holding in *Reedy* strongly suggests that such a defendant has "bundled" his conduct by website, rather than by individual image, and should face only a single conviction. In a more complicated example, however, a defendant might visit a web page that has thumbnails of various images, and then individually select some of those thumbnails to enlarge them on screen. In that case, would we focus on the receipt of the first page, or the subsequent receipt of each image, or both? And what if the defendant views the same image twice during one visit? How many receipts is that?

These various scenarios—and one could easily imagine others—demonstrate that conceptualizing the "knowing receipt of any visual depiction" via the internet is much more complicated than it is in cases involving regular mail. Even with complete information about what the defendant did and what he knew at the time he did it, categorizing the criminal behavior is challenging. Our opinion in *Reedy* illustrates this difficulty well, and handles it with great skill. In this case, however, we are not well situated to do the same.

As the majority correctly states, the government's burden is to prove that Buchanan took more than one action to receive the four images at issue. After combing through the record, we are left with insufficient proof of exactly what Buchanan did to receive the four images for which he was charged, and as a result we are unable to classify the defendant's conduct as one criminal act or four. We cannot be sure, for example, if the defendant visited a single website that had four large images on it, or if the images were selected and received individually. This is not to say that the former is necessarily a single criminal act, nor that the latter is necessarily more than one. It falls to future panels to decide these issues when they are adequately presented by the record. It is to say, however, that if the "'unit of prosecution' for a crime is the *actus reus*, the physical conduct of the defendant," United States v. Reedy, 304 F.3d 358, 365 (5th Cir. 2002), as it surely is, then we need to know more about the conduct of this particular defendant before we can sustain his four convictions.

We can be sure of the fact that Buchanan violated 18 U.S.C. §2252. What we do not know is whether he violated it once, twice, or four times. Accordingly, I agree with the majority that it would be multiplicitous to sustain four separate convictions in this case.

Notes and Questions

1. In civil liability systems, the remedy is nearly always tied to the injury that the defendant's conduct caused. No matter how many distinct acts of negligence the defendant committed, no matter how many different legal theories the plaintiff advances in support of her claim for relief, the total recovery must match the plaintiff's injury. No analogous principle operates in criminal sentencing. Instead, a criminal defendant's sentence usually depends on the number and nature of the distinct criminal acts the defendant has committed. Which leads to cases like *Buchanan*, in which judges and lawyers debate how finely to slice a particular course of criminal conduct.

2. Does the slicing make sense? There is abundant evidence that Buchanan engaged in many more distinct acts of receipt than four. What, then, is the court's concern?

3. In part, the rule of multiplicity replicates double jeopardy law. The constitutional ban on double jeopardy bars two successive prosecutions for "the same offence." The test for sameness appears in Blockburger v. United States, 284 U.S. 299, 304 (1932), where Justice Sutherland wrote these words for a unanimous Court: "The applicable rule is that where the same act of transaction constitutes a violation of two distinct statutory provisions, the test to be applied to determine whether there are two offenses or only one, is whether each provision requires proof of a fact which the other does not." Thus, in a case like People v. Hood, 462 P.2d 370 (Cal. 1969), see page 142 supra, the defendant may be charged with battery upon a police officer, assault with a deadly weapon, *and* assault with intent to kill—the first crime requires proof that the victim was a police officer, the second requires proof that the defendant used a deadly weapon, and to convict of the third, the government must prove intent to kill. Since each crime has at least one unique element, the government may punish the defendant for all three.

When the government prosecutes a defendant serially, the *Blockburger* test is a constitutional requirement. When, as in *Hood*, all the relevant charges are brought in a single proceeding, *Blockburger* becomes a mere rule of statutory construction. The California legislature is free to decide how severely to punish Hood, and how much prison time to assign to the various pieces of Hood's conduct—as long as the relevant punishment is imposed after a single prosecution. Still, while *Blockburger*'s test is not constitutionally required in individual prosecutions, it is nearly always observed.

The last two paragraphs deal with cases in which the defendant is charged with violating more than one criminal statute. *Blockburger*'s test also applies to multiple charges brought under the same criminal statute, that is, to cases like *Buchanan*. There too, the question is whether the government has proved a distinct act for each charge—in *Buchanan*, a distinct receipt of child pornography.

4. But while the rule against multiplicity bars punishments that violate *Blockburger*, it extends further. In Bell v. United States, 349 U.S. 81 (1955), the defendant was convicted of two counts of violating the Mann Act, which forbade the interstate transportation of women "for the purpose of prostitution." The government proved a single act of transportation; two women were transported. Plainly, punishment for two separate counts satisfied *Blockburger*, since there were two victims. Nevertheless, the Court in *Bell* held that the defendant could be punished only for a single count.

5. The defendant in Bedard v. State, 48 P.3d 46 (Nev. 2002), was convicted of ten counts of burglary for breaking into ten offices in Templeton Plaza, an office building in Las Vegas. The defendant argued that this amounted to multiple punishment for a single offense. The Nevada Supreme Court disagreed:

> There is no doubt that if the premises had been located in [ten] separate buildings defendant could have been punished for [ten] separate burglaries; he is not entitled to [nine] exempt burglaries merely because his victims chose the same landlord. If the rule were otherwise, a thief who broke into and ransacked every store in a shopping center under one roof, or every apartment in an apartment building, or every room or suite in a hotel, could claim immunity for all but one of the burglaries thus perpetrated.

48 P.3d at 48.

6. State v. Kujawa, 929 So. 2d 99 (La. App. 1st Cir. 2006), raised essentially the same question as *Buchanan*, under a state statute that punished not the receipt of child pornography but its possession. The court described the facts as follows:

> . . . The defendant, a Catholic priest, was assigned to Holy Cross Catholic Church in Morgan City in St. Mary Parish. On January 4, 2000, Bishop Michael Jarrell of the Diocese of Houma-Thibodaux issued a press release stating that the defendant had been found in possession of pornographic material, some of which involved pictures of minors.
>
> Based on that information, on January 11, 2000 Detective Eric DeLaune and other city police investigators obtained a warrant and searched the defendant's living area at the rectory. They seized, among other things, the defendant's computer, a second computer hard drive, [and] computer disks. . . .

Sergeant Travis Crouch and Detective DeLaune examined the materials in a box obtained in the seizure. They found hundreds of pages of printed text and pictures. They removed 220 pages of pictures of nude persons, believed to be juveniles, in various poses and engaged in sexual acts.

On January 10, 2000, the pictures were viewed by Dr. Scott Benton, an assistant professor of pediatrics and Director of Pediatric Forensic Medicine at Louisiana State University Medical School. Dr. Benton found that 62 pages contained pictures of minor children, which, in his opinion, constituted child pornography. The other pages also depicted child pornography, according to Dr. Benton, but less clearly so.

929 So. 2d at 103. The defendant was charged with 62 counts of illegally possessing child pornography; eventually, the defendant pled guilty to 15 counts, reserving the right to appeal the question whether those charges impermissibly punished the defendant multiple times for a single course of conduct.

The Louisiana Court of Appeal thought not. Judge Gaidry's opinion summarized the relevant case law, beginning with a decision about hunting deer out of season:

> . . . In State v. Freeman, 411 So. 2d 1068 (La. 1982), two defendants were each convicted on three counts of hunting deer at night and three counts of hunting or taking deer in closed season. The statute at issue prohibited the hunting of "deer" at certain proscribed times. The defendants argued that finding them both guilty of six violations of the statute, when in fact only two existed, subjected them to triple punishment for each of the two violations. . . . The court found that if the legislative aim had been to make the taking of each individual deer an offense, it would have clearly expressed that intent, and to construe the statutory provisions otherwise would permit prosecutors to create multiple offenses without a legislative grant of authority. Id. at 1072.

929 So. 2d at 106. The *Kujawa* court then turned to child pornography cases like *Buchanan*:

> In United States v. Esch, [832 F.2d 531 (10th Cir. 1987),] the defendants were charged with sixteen counts of sexual exploitation of children for photographing their children and themselves engaged in sexually explicit conduct. The codefendants then sold these photographs. The applicable statutory provision, 18 U.S.C. §2251(a), proscribed the use of a minor to engage in "any sexually explicit conduct for the purpose of producing any visual depiction of such conduct." In construing the statute, the Tenth Circuit found that each use of a minor to create a visual depiction constituted a separate and distinct violation. . . . The fact that multiple photographs were sequentially produced during a single photographing session was deemed irrelevant because each photograph depended upon a separate and distinct use of the children. 832 F.2d at 542. The court distinguished United States v. Meyer, 602 F. Supp. 1480 (S.D. Cal. 1985). In *Meyer*, the transportation and importation of a binder of pornographic pictures were simultaneous, while the criminal acts in *Esch*,

according to the court, were not simultaneous. The court concluded that the indictment properly charged separate counts for each of the photographs produced. Id. . . .

In State v. Mather, 646 N.W.2d 605 (Neb. 2002), the defendant was convicted of eighteen counts of visual depiction of sexually explicit conduct which had a child as one of its participants in violation of the applicable statute, which provided . . . that it "shall be unlawful for a person to knowingly make, publish, direct, create, provide, or in any manner generate any visual depiction of sexually explicit conduct which has a child as one of its participants or portrayed observers." "Visual depiction" was defined by the applicable statute as a "live performance or photographic representation." The defendant, a photographer, had photographed a nude or partially nude seventeen-year-old female. The defendant argued that his conduct amounted to one count because all eighteen photographs were taken of the same subject the same day as part of one ongoing or continuous act. The court found the plain language of the statute focused on "*any* visual depiction." It further found that the singular form of "photographic representation" in the statute read in conjunction with the term "any" indicated that the legislature intended prosecution for each differing photographic representation. 646 N.W.2d at 610-11. Thus, . . . the defendant was held to have committed multiple offenses. . . .

In State v. Multaler, 643 N.W.2d 437 (Wis. 2002), the defendant pleaded guilty to 28 counts of child pornography. The pornographic images were found on two computer disks labeled "Child Pornography" and "Child Pornography II." The defendant argued that the legislatively intended unit of prosecution was determined by the number of disks, not the number of images. The applicable statute provided that whoever possessed "any undeveloped film, photographic negative, photograph . . . or other pictorial reproduction . . . of a child engaged in sexually explicit conduct . . . is guilty of a Class E felony. . . ." The defendant contended the legislature intended punishment based not upon an image but rather upon the medium on which the images were found. The court disagreed and found that nothing in the plain language of the statute supported the defendant's position that the legislature intended that a computer disk, rather than an image, was the intended unit of prosecution. 643 N.W.2d at 451. . . .

In Commonwealth v. Davidson, 860 A.2d 575 (Pa. Super. 2004), authorities found approximately 500 images of child pornography on the defendant's computer hard drive. The defendant was convicted of 28 counts of sexual abuse of children. . . . The defendant argued that there was a single possessory offense. The court disagreed, finding that the offenses charged stemmed from 28 different criminal acts. The 28 pornographic pictures found involved different children or, in some cases, the same children photographed multiple times. The court reasoned that each photograph of each child victimized that child and subjected him or her to precisely the type of harm the statute seeks to prevent. 860 A.2d at 583.

929 So. 2d at 108-10. Were the cases summarized in *Kujawa* rightly decided? Was *Kujawa* rightly decided?

Recall that in drug cases, punishment usually tracks the quantity of drugs possessed or sold. Should crimes like those described above be punished in the same fashion? What is the best measure of the harm the defendants' conduct causes? What is the best measure of defendants' culpability?

2. Recidivist Sentencing

Clines v. State

Supreme Court of Florida
912 So. 2d 550 (2005)

Opinion by CANTERO, J.

We review Clines v. State, 881 So. 2d 721 (Fla. 1st DCA 2004), which certified conflict with Works v. State, 814 So. 2d 1198 (Fla. 2d DCA 2002), and Oberst v. State, 796 So. 2d 1263 (Fla. 4th DCA 2001). The issue on which they disagree is whether the recidivist sentencing statute allows a court to sentence a defendant as both a habitual felony offender and a violent career criminal. In the case we review, the First District [Court of Appeals] held that it does, see *Clines*, 881 So. 2d at 722, while the conflicting courts held it does not. *Works*, 814 So. 2d at 1199; *Oberst*, 796 So. 2d at 1265. . . .

I. THE STATUTE

The defendant, Michael Ray Clines, was sentenced under Florida's recidivist sentencing statute. That statute, section 775.084, Florida Statutes, establishes four categories of recidivists whose sentences may be enhanced. They are, in order of increasing punishment, habitual felony offenders, habitual violent felony offenders, three-time violent felony offenders, and violent career criminals. Fla. Stat. §775.084(1). These categories have different but overlapping definitions. To be sentenced as a habitual felony offender, a defendant must have two prior felony convictions and must have committed his current felony within a certain time frame: either (a) while serving a prison sentence or while under supervision as the result of one of the prior convictions that qualified him for this category, or (b) within five years of his last conviction, prison release, or release from supervision attributable to one of those qualifying convictions. §775.084(1)(a). To be sentenced as a habitual violent felony offender, a defendant must have been convicted of one prior enumerated felony and must have committed his current felony within the above time frame. §775.084(1)(b). To be sentenced as a three-time violent felony offender, a defendant must have been convicted twice as an adult of certain violent felonies . . . and must have committed another such offense within the above time frame. §775.084(1)(c). Finally, to be sentenced as a violent career criminal, a defendant must have been previously incarcerated in state or federal prison, must have been convicted three times as an adult of certain violent felonies . . . , and must have committed another such offense within the above time frame. §775.084(1)(d).

Recidivists within these categories are subject to enhanced punishment, which generally increases with each category. The two habitual offender categories are permissive; such offenders "may" be sentenced more harshly than otherwise. §775.084(4)(a)-(b). The other two categories are mandatory. Three-time violent felony offenders "must" be sentenced to mandatory minimum terms. §775.084(4)(c). Violent career criminals "shall" be sentenced to lengthy minimum terms and may also be sentenced to even longer maximum terms, with no eligibility for discretionary early release. §775.084(4)(d), (4)(k)2. The following table summarizes the specific punishments authorized by each category:

	3rd-Degree Felonies	2nd-Degree Felonies	1st-Degree Felonies	Life Felonies
Habitual Felony Offenders	Up to 10 Years	Up to 30 years	Life imprisonment	Life imprisonment
Habitual Violent Felony Offenders	Up to 10 years; not eligible for release for 5 years	Up to 30 years; not eligible for release for 10 years	Life imprisonment; not eligible for release for 15 years	Life imprisonment; not eligible for release for 15 years
Three-Time Violent Offenders	Mandatory minimum of 5 years	Mandatory minimum of 15 years	Mandatory minimum of 30 years	Mandatory minimum of life imprisonment
Violent Career Criminals	Up to 15 years, with a mandatory minimum of 10 years	Up to 40 years, with a mandatory minimum of 30 years	Life imprisonment; no discretionary early release	Life imprisonment; no discretionary early release

See §775.084(4)(a)-(k).

Because of the substantial overlap among the four recidivist categories, a defendant may meet the criteria of more than one category. For instance, a violent career criminal (one who has been convicted three times as an adult of certain violent felonies, and committed another such offense within the specified time frame) will always be a habitual felony offender (because he will have two prior felony convictions and will have committed his current felony within the same time frame). Compare §775.084(1)(a) with §775.084(1)(d).

II. PROCEEDINGS BELOW

Clines was charged with resisting arrest with violence, grand theft, and two counts of battery on a law enforcement officer. The State filed notices of its intent to seek both habitual felony offender sentencing and violent career criminal sentencing under section 775.084. Clines later pled *nolo contendere* to the resisting arrest and grand theft charges, while the State dropped the two counts of battery on a law enforcement officer. The punishment was left for the trial court to determine.

At the sentencing hearing, the State introduced evidence showing that Clines qualified as a habitual felony offender and a violent career criminal. The trial court applied both designations. As to the resisting arrest charge, having designated Clines a habitual felony offender, the court sentenced him to ten years in prison; and having designated him a violent career criminal, the court imposed a ten-year mandatory minimum term.[2] Clines later filed a motion to correct a sentencing error . . . , arguing that he could not be designated as both a habitual felony offender and a violent career criminal. The trial court denied the motion. . . .

On appeal, Clines argued that his dual designation violated double jeopardy protections and conflicted with the Legislature's intent in adopting the recidivist sentencing statute. The First District affirmed, concluding that dual designation "violates neither double jeopardy protections nor legislative intent." *Clines*, 881 So. 2d at 722. According to the First District, "the entire statutory scheme of section 775.084 readily contemplates, in the case of a single criminal charge, a sentence under the habitual felony offender provision, with the mandatory minimum term provisions provided for by the violent career criminal designation." Id. at 724. The First District certified conflict, however, with the Second District's decision in *Works*, 814 So. 2d at 1199, and the Fourth District's decision in *Oberst*, 796 So. 2d at 1265, both of which interpreted section 775.084 to prohibit the sentencing of a defendant under more than one recidivist category. *Clines*, 881 So. 2d at 724. Clines now asks us to resolve the conflict.

III. ANALYSIS

Clines argues that the trial court violated section 775.084 by sentencing him as both a violent career criminal and a habitual felony offender. According to Clines, the statute permits the court to sentence under only one category. The State responds that the Legislature intended to allow sentencing under multiple categories. The disputed provision is subsection (4)(f), which states:

---

2. On the grand theft charge, Clines received a concurrent five-year sentence.

At any time when it appears to the court that the defendant is eligible for sentencing under this [recidivist sentencing] section, the court shall make that determination as provided in paragraph (3)(a), paragraph (3)(b), *or* paragraph (3)(c).

§775.084(4)(f) (emphasis added). The cross-referenced paragraphs cover different recidivist categories. Each provides that "[i]n a separate proceeding, the court shall determine" whether the defendant qualifies for designation within that category. §775.084(3)(a), (3)(b), (3)(c).

The parties disagree about whether the "or" in subsection (4)(f) is disjunctive or conjunctive. If disjunctive, as Clines advocates, then trial courts may sentence defendants under only one category. But if the "or" is conjunctive, as the State proposes, defendants may be sentenced under multiple categories. . . .

. . . [I]t would be a rare circumstance for the word "or" to have the plain meaning "and." In this case, if the Legislature had been aware of the grammatical dilemma and had wanted to make its conjunctive meaning clear, it would not have relied on the typically disjunctive word "or" to do so. Instead, the Legislature would have added an explicitly clarifying phrase, such as "or any combination thereof," to the end of the sentence. That it did not [do so suggests] that the Legislature either intended a disjunctive meaning, or simply did not anticipate the grammatical dilemma that this case raises. We doubt that the latter is true, because the dilemma is so readily apparent. . . .

The [State argues] that various provisions in the recidivist sentencing statute reveal the Legislature's obvious intent to punish career criminals with the most severe sanction possible. The State emphasizes two provisions: one expressly stating that the Legislature's intent in enacting these provisions was "to incarcerate [recidivists] for extended terms," §775.0841; and another demanding that "[a]ll reasonable prosecutorial efforts shall be made to persuade the court to impose the most severe sanction authorized upon a person convicted after prosecution as a career criminal." §775.0843(2)(d).

We see nothing in these two provisions that clarifies whether multiple recidivist categories may be applied to a single criminal sentence. The provisions speak generally of "extended terms" and "severe sanction[s]," but do not direct the severity of the punishment when more than one recidivist category applies. The Legislature has ordered prosecutors to pursue "the most severe sanction authorized"—not the most severe sanction *possible*, as the State suggests. Whether a sentence imposed under multiple recidivist categories is, in fact, authorized by section 775.084 is unclear from these general statements of legislative intent. Moreover, designation of a defendant under more than one category would not necessarily increase the severity of a sentence. For example, a defendant who commits a third-degree felony and is designated as both a habitual felony offender and a habitual violent felony offender is subject to ten years' imprisonment as a habitual felony offender; but he is already subject to the same term as a habitual violent felony offender, with a minimum five-year term. Similarly, a defendant sentenced as both a habitual felony offender and a violent career criminal receives no greater punishment than if he were sentenced solely as a violent career criminal. Therefore, designation within more than one category does not always (or even often) result in greater punishment. . . .

. . . We believe that the recidivist categories are designed to be hierarchical, not complementary. . . . [A]nyone whose pattern of recidivism meets the stringent requirements for designation as a violent career criminal will also qualify for designation as a habitual felony offender. But designation as a violent career criminal renders superfluous any other designation. . . . [T]he mandatory *minimum* prison term for a violent career criminal in Clines's position is as long as the *maximum* prison term for a habitual felony offender. We doubt the Legislature intended a trial court to apply both categories when one encompasses the other.

Based on the above analysis, we conclude that section 775.084 is ambiguous about whether multiple recidivist categories may be applied to a single criminal sentence. Although the Legislature certainly intended for recidivists to be sentenced "for extended terms," §775.0841, there is no clear evidence that the Legislature intended for sentences to be extended under multiple recidivist categories, only one of which ultimately matters. . . .

We therefore apply the rule of lenity. Florida has codified the rule as follows: "The provisions of this [criminal] code and offenses defined by other statutes shall be strictly construed; when the language is susceptible of differing constructions, it shall be construed most favorably to the accused." §775.021(1). We have explained that the rule "is applicable to sentencing provisions" if they "create ambiguity or generate differing reasonable constructions." Nettles v. State, 850 So. 2d 487, 494 (Fla. 2003). Because section 775.084 generates differing reasonable constructions, we endorse the construction that favors the defendant and hold that only one recidivist category in section 775.084 may be applied to any given criminal sentence.

IV. Conclusion

We hold that subsection 775.084 permits the application of only one recidivist category to the defendant's sentence. . . . We therefore quash the First District's decision in this case and remand to the trial court for resentencing in light of our ruling. We note that the original sentence given to Clines for resisting arrest—a ten-year term of imprisonment with a ten-year mandatory minimum—would be authorized on remand by the violent career criminal category alone. See §775.084(4)(d)3.

It is so ordered.

[Justice Wells' concurring opinion is omitted.]

Notes and Questions

1. Laws like Florida's are common in the United States. The last decades of the twentieth century saw a wave of "three strikes" laws, many of them harsher than the ones at issue in *Clines*. As Victoria Nourse has explained, these late-twentieth-century recidivist sentencing laws were not an innovation. More like a tradition:

> . . . [T]hree-strikes laws—then called habitual offender laws—swept the nation in the period from the mid-1920s until the mid-1930s. These laws were so popular that manuals on them were created for debating societies. One of the reasons that these laws have gone unnoticed is because they went by a particular name, after their "inventor," a New York legislator named Caleb Baumes. To be sure, not all legislatures adopted Baumes's mandatory-life solution, and some laws were harsher than others, but this is a difference in degree, not kind. The conclusion remains the same: contrary to widespread scholarly assumption, today's three-strikes laws are not unprecedented. . . . [L]aws mandating or permitting life imprisonment for repeat felonies (two, three, or four prior offenses) were passed or operative in more than twenty states. . . .

> These laws created their share of controversy, inciting disagreement not only among lawyers and judges, but in the public as well. Just as we see with mandatory sentencing guidelines today, judges who were forced to apply the Baumes laws were sometimes resistant. Also as we see today, unjust applications of these laws yielded public uproar and demands, in some cases, to limit the law's applications, as in cases where grandmothers could find themselves sentenced to jail for life for fairly trivial offenses.[31] As they do today, commentators rightly asked why legislatures were passing such laws given the existence of already harsh penalties. . . . And it was only upon crisis—serious overcrowding and riots in New York prisons—that the Baumes laws themselves were softened to a mandatory minimum penalty. . . .

> Contrast this political and legislative story with the story that is typically told by academics about the criminal law of the 1920s and 1930s. Most academics remember it as . . . an era of realism and the injection of social science into the legal curriculum, when criminal law professors were happily recruited from the ranks of criminologists and psychiatrists. This was the era in which Dean Pound excoriated the academy for failing to study and reform the criminal law and in particular criminal procedure. This was the era of the great "studies" and "crime commissions." . . . The recommendations of these commissions were all quite forward-looking, often focusing on streamlining criminal procedure, opposing [coercive police interrogation], and impaling crass public assumptions such as the idea, then quite prevalent, that the "foreign-born" were responsible for crime.

> To remember this story is to focus on intellectual history. . . . For the people of the 1920s and 1930s, crime was a part of real life, as real as machine gun

---

31. See, e.g., "Woman, 85, Escapes Life Term as Thief: State Permits Mrs. La Touche to Plead Guilty to Minor Charge Because of Her Age," N.Y. Times (Sept. 1, 1931).

shootings, motorcars, and children being gunned down in the streets. This fear was in part a panic — fear of crime always is. But in this, there is less that is different about crime and crime legislation than is conventionally thought. Laws are frequently passed because of panic or even sheer anecdote — because of a flood or a hurricane, because of the impending close of government, or because of a terrorist bombing. This exaggerates, but only a bit, particularly if one remembers how extraordinarily difficult it is to pass any piece of legislation, how easy it is to block legislation (a single vote may be enough), and how fear is a powerful galvanizing factor in many political matters. . . .

In the early 1930s, there were some reasons to panic, and they were more than the public celebrities we remember or the film noir they inspired. At the height of the Depression scare, two-and-a-half-year-old Dorette Zeitlow was "snatched" by a thirteen-year-old and left to die in an icehouse outside Chicago. Ten thousand mobbed her funeral. In April 1934, five thousand men searched the Arizona desert for the body of six-year-old June Robles, who had been kidnapped and buried alive in a box (she survived). . . . [Five] months earlier, in San Jose, California, a mob lynched two white kidnappers, and the Governor pardoned them on the spot, thanking them for their vengeance. Is it a surprise in this world that federalism objections to national intervention (which were made) were given short shrift, and that Congress in May of 1934 put its final stamp of approval on expansive new federal criminal laws in two hours on a Saturday?[49]

V.F. Nourse, Rethinking Crime Legislation: History and Harshness, 39 Tulsa L. Rev. 925, 930-34 (2004).

2. That earlier era of crime waves and three-strikes laws ended with the century's largest decade-long crime drop, beginning in 1934. The more recent age of three-strikes laws ended with the second-largest decade-long crime drop, this one beginning in 1992. Perhaps that is a coincidence. Or, perhaps not. For what it's worth, leading criminologists tend to agree that increasing the certainty of criminal punishment has far greater deterrent effect than increasing the severity of punishment — meaning that three-strikes laws probably have little deterrent value.

3. For what, exactly, is Clines being punished? The answer is, both the crimes charged now and the crimes for which he has already been convicted (which the Florida Supreme Court declined to specify). But Clines has already been punished for his priors. That sounds like impermissible double punishment of the sort that double jeopardy, not to mention the rule against multiplicity, forbids. How can such multiple punishments be permissible? In theory, the answer is that the prior crimes serve as reasons to enhance the punishment for the *current* crimes, so there is no multiplicity or double jeopardy problem. In practice, the answer is that the earlier crimes serve as

---

49. Dillinger Causes House to Pass 10 Anti-Crime Bills: Sweeping Power Voted to Federal Agents, with Roosevelt Applying the Goad, Muskogee Daily Phoenix 1 (May 6, 1934).

stand-ins or substitutes—if a given defendant has several prior convictions, he likely has committed many other serious crimes that have gone undiscovered. Is it legitimate to punish defendants for crimes they very probably committed, but that have never been proved in court or admitted in a guilty plea?

Here is another way to describe recidivist sentencing laws: Criminal liability is usually imposed for conduct that happens in a specific place in a brief period of time. Criminal punishment is based partly on that snippet of conduct, and partly based on the defendant's behavior over the course of his lifetime—including, but not limited to, his criminal record. Is criminal law's narrow focus appropriate? Is the broader view the law of sentencing takes fair? Are both approaches sound?

4. Notice that the rule of lenity is part of Florida's criminal code. That is unusual, which may have something to do with the state's unusual adoption of the rule in sentencing cases like *Clines*, and not just in cases in which the issue is the scope of criminal liability.

5. Most states' recidivist sentencing laws bind judges, but not prosecutors. Consider Bordenkircher v. Hayes, 434 U.S. 357 (1978). Paul Hayes stole a check from a local business in Lexington, Kentucky. Forging the signature, Hayes wrote the check to a grocery store; the amount was $88.30. Hayes was arrested and charged with "uttering a forged check," a felony carrying a sentence of two to ten years in prison. That was not Hayes' first felony charge; he had prior convictions for robbery and for "detaining a female," a lower grade of sexual assault. The local prosecutor, Glen Bagby, suggested a guilty plea with a five-year prison sentence attached; if Hayes refused the offer, Bagby promised to charge Hayes under Kentucky's three-strikes statute, which carried a mandatory life sentence. When Hayes turned down the offer, Bagby carried out his threat. Hayes was tried, convicted, and sentenced to life in prison.

Hayes' lawyer argued that this chain of events amounted to "vindictive prosecution": The three-strikes charge was filed because Hayes had asserted his right to a criminal trial; prior case law suggested that prosecutors may not punish defendants for the exercise of constitutional rights. See Blackledge v. Perry, 417 U.S. 21 (1974). But Hayes' argument lost. Justice Stewart's majority opinion emphasized the importance of plea bargaining to the operation of the criminal justice system. If Hayes' claim won, the Justices feared, a constitutional shadow might be cast on plea negotiations—many of which involve an agreement to forgo filing more serious charges in exchange for the defendant's plea.

Notice the role Kentucky's three-strikes law played in *Bordenkircher*. That law was the tool Bagby used to extract a guilty plea from Hayes. The tool failed in *Bordenkircher*—but given the result in that case, it was bound to succeed afterward: Had Hayes known that his vindictive prosecution claim would lose, he plainly would have taken Bagby's offer. That captures a key consequence of recidivist sentencing laws. Those laws' largest effects happen in cases in which the laws are not invoked — cases in which prosecutors use them to induce guilty pleas, not to define defendants' sentences.

6. Keep in mind that recidivist sentencing statutes have been the subject of several of the United States Supreme Court's modern Eighth Amendment proportionality decisions. See, e.g., Rummel v. Estelle, 445 U.S. 263 (1980); Solem v. Helm, 463 U.S. 277 (1983); and Ewing v. California, 538 U.S. 11 (2003). The *Ewing* decision is discussed in Chapter 1, supra, at page 35.

3. Victim Restitution

United States v. Chalupnik

United States Court of Appeals for the Eighth Circuit
514 F.3d 748 (2008)

LOKEN, Chief Judge.

BMG Columbia House ("BMG") sells CDs and DVDs by mail. Many BMG discs prove to be undeliverable. During the time in question, BMG arranged with the United States Postal Service ("USPS") to gather and discard undeliverable discs, as it was less costly for BMG to produce replacement discs than to pay for the return and restocking of undeliverable discs. James Chalupnik, a janitorial supervisor at the downtown post office in Fargo, North Dakota, took several thousand undeliverable CDs and DVDs from the post office trash and sold them to used record stores. Initially charged with felony mail theft, Chalupnik pleaded guilty to misdemeanor copyright infringement in violation of 17 U.S.C. §506(a) and 18 U.S.C. §2319(b)(3). The district court sentenced Chalupnik to two years probation and ordered him to pay BMG restitution in an amount equal to his documented sales proceeds, $78,818. Chalupnik appeals the restitution award. We conclude that the government failed to prove the amount of loss to BMG proximately caused by Chalupnik's offense. Accordingly, we vacate the restitution award and remand for resentencing.

I

Chalupnik supervised disabled persons who provided janitorial services at the downtown post office in Fargo. In October 2001, he began removing undeliverable CDs and DVDs from the post office trash and selling the discs to used record stores. In June 2006, USPS began investigating the disappearance of undeliverable CDs and DVDs at the Fargo post office. A surveillance camera revealed Chalupnik hiding discs in a telephone closet, and 3,580 CDs and 125 DVDs were found in his possession. He admitted selling the discs to used record stores in Moorhead and St. Cloud, Minnesota, and

Sioux Falls, South Dakota. Store records reflected purchases of several thousand discs and payments to Chalupnik totaling $78,818. The stores had no record of what CD and DVD titles they purchased from Chalupnik, but one store owner told investigators that most if not all were BMG products.

Chalupnik pleaded guilty to a charge that he willfully infringed numerous copyrighted sound recordings for private financial gain between October 2001 and July 2006 in violation of 17 U.S.C. §506(a) and 18 U.S.C. §2319(b)(3). At the change of plea hearing, he admitted selling discs for $78,818 without authority from the copyright owners. At sentencing, the government recommended a sentence of probation. The district court agreed and sentenced Chalupnik to two years probation.

The presentence investigation report (PSR) recommended that Chalupnik be ordered to pay BMG mandatory restitution in the amount of $78,818 because his offense conduct deprived BMG of "the option of returning the CD's to the market or destroying them." Chalupnik submitted a Sentencing Memorandum opposing restitution. Noting the absence of evidence that BMG owned any copyright interest in the discs, Chalupnik argued that BMG was not a victim of his offense. He further argued that the government could not prove actual loss because BMG threw away or destroyed undeliverable discs, and because customers of used music stores will not buy new products by mail so BMG cannot show it lost sales on account of his offense conduct. In response, the government submitted a letter from BMG's senior counsel asserting that USPS "routinely returns DVDs" to BMG for restocking, that BMG accepts CDs returned by customers and "most likely" returns a portion to inventory for resale, that BMG competes with used record stores in the "larger music market," and that Chalupnik's offense conduct resulted in no royalty payments being made to the copyright owners. The government's Sentencing Memorandum argued that BMG is a victim because it owns the discs, sells them with permission of the copyright owners, and controls the disposition of undeliverable discs; that each time Chalupnik sold an undeliverable disc, the artist lost a royalty and BMG lost a potential sale; and that the amount of those losses is conservatively estimated by Chalupnik's gross revenues, $78,818.

At sentencing, the government introduced no additional evidence relating to BMG's actual loss. Chalupnik testified that all undeliverable discs were discarded in the post office trash. . . . Agreeing with the government and the PSR, the district court ordered Chalupnik to pay $78,818 in restitution to BMG. The court explained: "I do believe that there is in fact a lost opportunity to . . . BMG, that the people that bought those CDs . . . would likely have bought new CDs, and that that represents a real and substantial loss to . . . BMG in the amount of $78,818." The court further noted that, in a civil lawsuit by BMG, Chalupnik's liability would include disgorgement of his profits from converting BMG property; therefore, imposing a fine payable to the United States instead of restitution might well increase Chalupnik's total liability.

II

The Mandatory Victims Restitution Act ("MVRA") provides that a sentencing court "shall order" a defendant convicted of "an offense against property under this title" to pay restitution to a "victim." 18 U.S.C. §§3663A(a)(1), (c)(1). The restitution award in this case raises two distinct issues: whether BMG is a "victim" entitled to mandatory restitution under the MVRA and, if so, what is the proper amount of restitution to be awarded. The first is primarily an issue of law that we review *de novo*. In resolving the second issue, we review a finding as to the amount of loss for clear error and the district court's decision to award restitution for abuse of discretion. See United States v. Petruk, 484 F.3d 1035, 1038 (8th Cir. 2007). The government has the burden of proof on both issues.

A. Is BMG a Victim?

In Hughey v. United States, 495 U.S. 411, 416 (1990), the Supreme Court held that the Victim and Witness Protection Act of 1982 ("VWPA") was "intended to compensate victims only for losses caused by the conduct underlying the offense of conviction." Therefore, restitution may be awarded only to victims of the offense of conviction, and a victim may not be compensated for conduct unrelated to the offense of conviction, even if that unrelated conduct was the subject of criminal charges dropped by the government in exchange for the defendant's guilty plea. Id. at 420-21. . . .

When Congress enacted the MVRA in 1996, it included a definition of "victim" that . . . incorporated the core principle of *Hughey*:

> (2) For the purposes of this section, the term "victim" means a person directly and proximately harmed as a result of the commission of an offense for which restitution may be ordered including, in the case of an offense that involves as an element a scheme, conspiracy, or pattern of criminal activity, any person directly harmed by the defendant's criminal conduct in the course of the scheme, conspiracy, or pattern. . . .
>
> (3) The court shall also order, if agreed to by the parties in a plea agreement, restitution to persons other than the victim of the offense.

18 U.S.C. §3663A(a)(2)-(3). Consistent with *Hughey*, the Senate Judiciary Committee Report explained that, unless a plea agreement provides otherwise, the "mandatory restitution provisions apply only in those instances where a named, identifiable victim suffers a physical injury or pecuniary loss directly and proximately caused by the course of conduct under the count or counts for which the offender is convicted." S. Rep. No. 104-179, at 19 (1996). Congress also amended the VWPA so that the two statutes would

contain identical definitions of the term "victim" and substantively identical plea agreement provisions. See 18 U.S.C. §3663(a)(2)-(3).

Chalupnik argues that the government failed to prove that BMG was a "victim" for purposes of the MVRA because it presented no evidence that BMG, a retail mail-order seller of CDs and DVDs, had an interest in the infringed copyrights sufficient to make BMG a victim of his copyright infringement offense. This is a novel and intriguing contention. We agree with a number of its underlying premises. First, restitution is "essentially a civil remedy created by Congress and incorporated into criminal proceedings for reasons of economy and practicality." United States v. Carruth, 418 F.3d 900, 904 (8th Cir. 2005). Therefore, restitution, at least in theory, "tracks the recovery to which the victim would have been entitled in a civil suit against the criminal." United States v. Behrman, 235 F.3d 1049, 1052 (7th Cir. 2000). Second, copyright law generally limits standing to seek a civil remedy for copyright infringement to the owner of the copyright or to a person who holds an *exclusive* license to one of the owner's exclusive rights in the copyrighted work. See 17 U.S.C. §§106, 501(b); 3 Nimmer on Copyright §12.02(B) (2007). . . . [I]t appears that BMG could not bring a civil action against Chalupnik for copyright infringement unless it was the exclusive licensee of the copyright owners, and the government does not argue to the contrary. Third, the government offered no evidence that BMG was an owner or exclusive licensee of any of the infringed copyrights. . . .

Though we agree with Chalupnik's underlying premises, we agree with the government that BMG was a victim under the MVRA as a matter of law. The issue posed by Chalupnik is whether, to be a victim for purposes of the MVRA, a person must have standing to bring a civil action for the injury the criminal statute is intended to remedy — here, copyright infringement — or whether MVRA victims include persons who have other injuries proximately caused by, in the words of *Hughey*, "the conduct underlying the offense of conviction." 495 U.S. at 416. The MVRA does not use the term, "conduct underlying the offense of conviction." Instead, it defines a victim as a person "proximately harmed as a result of the commission of" the offense. 18 U.S.C. §3663A(a)(2). But the word "commission" reflects an intent to include the defendant's total conduct in committing the offense, an intent confirmed by the Senate Judiciary Committee Report, which paraphrased *Hughey* in referring to "the course of conduct under the count or counts for which the offender is convicted." S. Rep. No. 104-179, at 19.

For this reason, we conclude that the relevant analogy is not whether BMG could sue Chalupnik for copyright infringement. Rather, the relevant analogy is whether BMG would have a civil cause of action against Chalupnik for his conduct in committing the copyright infringement offense of conviction. As the district court noted at sentencing, the answer to that question is clearly yes, because Chalupnik's offense conduct included stealing or converting BMG property from BMG's bailee, USPS.[3] That qualifies BMG as an MVRA victim, just as the bank customer who suffered lost wages as a result of witnessing an attempted bank robbery was an MVRA victim in *Moore v. United States*, 178 F.3d 994, 1001 (8th Cir. 1999). The bank customer could not have sued the defendant for attempting to rob the bank, but the customer was an MVRA victim because he suffered pecuniary damage as a result of the defendant's commission of the offense.

B. Did the Government Prove a BMG Loss?

When an MVRA victim is identified, the government must prove "the amount of the loss sustained by [the] victim as a result of the offense" by a preponderance of the evidence. 18 U.S.C. §3664(e). Chalupnik argues that the government failed to prove that BMG suffered lost profits, or any other actual loss, as a result of his committing the offense of conviction. On this barren record, we agree.

In concluding that BMG was an MVRA victim, the district court commented that it was appropriate to award restitution in the amount of Chalupnik's $78,818 in sale proceeds because BMG could recover these ill-gotten gains in a civil lawsuit. The government stresses this disgorgement concept on appeal. However, we rejected this approach to criminal restitution some two months after the district court ruled:

> The modern trend in private civil litigation endorses use of the common law remedy of restitution to punish intentional wrongdoers by compelling the disgorgement of all ill-gotten gain. See Restatement (Third) of Restitution and Unjust Enrichment §51 (Tentative Draft No. 5, Mar. 12, 2007). . . . However, while restitution under the MVRA may be a form of [criminal punishment] . . . it is clear that Congress intended that restitution be a compensatory remedy from the victim's perspective. Therefore . . . MVRA victims should be limited to compensation for their actual losses.

Petruk, 484 F.3d at 1038. In other words, while the availability of a civil remedy is relevant in determining *who* is an MVRA victim, the *amount* of restitution that may be awarded is limited to the victim's provable actual loss, even if more punitive remedies would be available in a civil action. Thus, while the fact that a defendant profited from the crime without causing actual loss to an identifiable victim may be an appropriate reason to increase his punishment, *Petruk* and the plain language of the MVRA confirm that punishment of a federal criminal defendant must be imposed by means of criminal penalties—fines, criminal forfeitures, and imprisonment. Restitution to

---

3. The court commented: "Isn't it a bailment [between BMG and USPS]? . . . You've [Chalupnik] converted the property to your own use. . . . And you've made a profit. . . . If the property can't be specifically recovered, then there's a constructive trust that's created in the proceeds of . . . that property. Which would be what? The $78,000. Just ordinary property principles, that would happen, right?"

MVRA victims "must be based on the amount of loss *actually caused* by the defendant's offense." Id. at 1036 (emphasis in original).

Stripped of a disgorgement rationale, it is clear that the government proved no actual loss to BMG. The PSR recommended, and the district court agreed, that BMG suffered a "lost opportunity" when Chalupnik stole BMG's undeliverable discs and sold them to competing retail sellers. The PSR's lost opportunity rationale is valid in the sense that all authorized retailers of the copyrighted discs—Wal-Mart, Best Buy, iTunes, BMG, and countless others—as well as the copyright owners, suffered collective financial injury when infringer Chalupnik sold purloined discs at cut-rate prices to used record stores. But it would be a windfall to award BMG this entire collective "injury to the market." And the large number of victims and the difficulty of determining each victim's actual loss make the collective injury inappropriate for MVRA restitution.

The government argues that the price at which Chalupnik sold the stolen discs is a reasonable, indeed conservative estimate of BMG's lost sales. One problem with this argument is that, for goods held by a merchant for sale, lost profits rather than lost sales revenues are the proper measure of "actual loss." A more fundamental problem is that proof of lost sales, like proof of lost profits, may not be "based entirely upon speculation." United States v. Young, 272 F.3d 1052, 1056 (8th Cir. 2001). Here, the letter from BMG's senior counsel asserted that Chalupnik sold discs to used record stores whose customers "theoretically could have purchased them [from BMG], resulting in lost sales to BMG." But BMG's practice of destroying rather than restocking undeliverable discs meant that the discs Chalupnik stole would not have been sold by BMG, and there is no evidence that Chalupnik's sales diverted specific business from BMG. From this standpoint, BMG's position resembles that of the purported MVRA victims whose restitution awards were reversed because the government failed to prove actual loss through lost sales in United States v. Hudson, 483 F.3d 707, 710-11 (10th Cir. 2007), where counterfeit Microsoft software was turned over to the government by the infringing defendant's customer before any payment to the infringer. . . .

Finally, the government argues that BMG should receive restitution *on behalf of* the unidentified copyright owners who would have been paid royalties had BMG sold the purloined discs. This argument is without merit because restitution to each victim is limited to "the full amount of each victim's losses." 18 U.S.C. §3664(f)(1)(A). The letter from BMG's senior counsel admitted that Chalupnik's criminal conduct "resulted in no royalty payments being made [by BMG] to the artists, record labels, music publishers, and movie studios," so there was no proof of actual loss to BMG arising out of its unproven relationships with copyright owners.

For the foregoing reasons, we vacate the restitution portion of the district court's judgment and remand for resentencing. Because our decision in *Petruk* clarified the applicable law after the district court entered the judgment, we leave to the district court's discretion on remand whether to reconsider the restitution issue on an expanded sentencing record as well as its previous decision not to impose a fine.

Notes and Questions

1. Victim restitution laws like the one in *Chalupnik* have become common-place today. Historically, "restitution" was a civil remedy for what the common law called "unjust enrichment." Such claims sought the disgorgement of the defendant's gains from his wrongful conduct, and were used mostly where those gains were easier to calculate than the victim's losses. Criminal victim restitution is not analogous to civil restitution — rather, it's the criminal justice system's version of civil damages.

2. Ironically, *Chalupnik* fits the civil model of restitution better than the criminal model. Figuring out how much money the defendant wrong-fully acquired is easy. Answering two other questions is a good deal harder. First, whom did the defendant's crime harm? Second, how much harm did that victim suffer? The aggregate injury may be fairly easy to determine—it equals Chalupnik's revenues from selling the undeliverable CDs and DVDs. Had Chalupnik not sold those discs, that revenue would have been available to someone else. But which someone else?

3. Perhaps the better question is, how many someone elses? If Chalupnik did not take money from BMG, he took money from would-be sellers of used CDs and DVDs. The number of those would-be sellers is large, and the amount any one individual lost is probably small. That is good news for Chalupnik—without a victim who has large enough losses to be worth prov-ing, there will be no victim restitution order. Does that make sense? Why not just give BMG the money the defendant gained?

4. Put yourself in Chalupnik's shoes. He sold perfectly good CDs and DVDs that, had he not sold them, would have been left in a landfill. Is it obvious that his behavior was wrong? More to the point, was it obvious to Chalupnik when he decided to go into the music and movie businesses? Chalupnik may deserve to lose the $78,818 he made on the sales, but does he deserve any other punishment? Should this really be a criminal case?

5. *Chalupnik* involved the problem of multiple victims; similar problems can arise in cases with multiple perpetrators. In Paroline v. United States, 572 U.S. ___ (2014), the Supreme Court held that the statutory obligation under 18 U.S.C. §2259 for convicted possessors of child pornography to pay restitution to their victims must be limited by the particular defendant's "relative role" in the overall harm caused, given that the defendant may have been only one of thousands to have possessed the same image(s) of the victim.

13

Constitutional Limits

Constitutional law extensively regulates America's criminal justice system. Police investigations are limited by both the Fourth Amendment, which bars "unreasonable searches and seizures," and the Fifth, which forbids (among many other things) compelled self-incrimination. The Sixth Amendment gives criminal defendants the right to "the assistance of counsel." Nearly every aspect of criminal trials is subject to elaborate bodies of constitutional doctrine, many of them based on the Sixth Amendment's jury trial guarantee. Due process (under the Fifth Amendment, for federal cases, or the Fourteenth Amendment, for state cases) requires that defendants' guilt be proved beyond a reasonable doubt, and that the government give defendants material exculpatory evidence in its possession. Recently, the Supreme Court has applied both the reasonable-doubt proof standard and the jury trial guarantee to a wide range of sentencing factors. For defendants charged with capital murder, the Eighth Amendment establishes detailed rules governing the process by which death sentences are imposed. And that is only a partial list.

Yet constitutional law has surprisingly little to say about the definition of crimes, or about the (non-capital) sentences that attach to those crimes. Constitutional rules and texts dominate criminal procedure. Those same rules and texts barely touch substantive criminal law. This chapter explores some of the reasons why, by surveying the major lines of argument for imposing constitutional limits on crime definition. For the most part, those arguments have failed—but not completely, and never definitively. The cases that follow are best seen as a series of doors not fully open, but not quite closed either. As you read them, ask yourself which arguments hold the most promise, and why.

Section A begins with the relevant portions of the Constitution's text. Section B briefly reviews the two constitutional doctrines that were introduced back in Chapter 1: that due process prohibits the government from defining crimes in a "vague" manner, in order to provide defendants with fair notice and also to properly limit the discretion of police, prosecutors, judges, and juries; and that criminal punishment must be at least roughly "proportional" to the crime and to the defendant's culpability. Section C examines the most famous constitutional right of our time, but one that to date has had relatively little impact on criminal law: the right not to be punished for private conduct (defined to include reproductive choices and sex with consenting adults). Section D discusses an argument that, 50 years ago, was widely expected to shake the foundations of the field: that the Constitution requires the government to prove some substantial form of fault or intent in every criminal case. Last but not least, Section E explores the relationship between criminal law and the Fourteenth Amendment's guarantee of "the equal protection of the laws."

A. THE CONSTITUTIONAL TEXT

The main body of the Constitution says little about crime and criminal justice. Article I, Section 8—the section that lists the permissible subjects of federal legislation—gives Congress the power "[t]o provide for the Punishment of counterfeiting the Securities and current Coin of the United States," and "[t]o define and punish Piracies and Felonies committed on the high Seas, and Offences against the Law of Nations." The following section expressly forbids ex post facto laws (retroactive criminal legislation) and bills of attainder (legislation imposing punishment on specified individuals). Article II, Section 3 requires the President to "take Care that the Laws be faithfully executed": a constitutional provision that might have proved important but has been largely ignored. Section 4 of the same Article permits the impeachment and removal of the President or Vice-President for "Treason, Bribery, or other high Crimes and Misdemeanors." Article III, Section 2 orders that trials of federal crimes "shall be by Jury; and [that] such Trial[s] shall be held in the State where the said Crimes shall have been committed." Article III, Section 3 defines treason, and bars conviction of that crime save on the testimony of at least two witnesses. The jury trial right aside, none of the texts just mentioned has produced any substantial body of legal doctrine.

The Bill of Rights is another story: Four of the first ten Amendments deal expressly with criminal justice, and all four have spawned large bodies of decisional law. The relevant texts follow:

Amendment IV. The right of the people to be secure in their persons, houses, papers, and effects, against unreasonable searches and seizures, shall not be violated, and no Warrants shall issue, but upon probable cause, supported by Oath or affirmation, and particularly describing the place to be searched, and the persons or things to be seized.

Amendment V. No person shall be held to answer for any capital, or otherwise infamous crime, unless on a presentment or indictment of a Grand Jury, . . . nor shall any person be subject for the same offence to be twice put in jeopardy of life or limb; nor shall be compelled in any criminal case to be a witness against himself, nor be deprived of life, liberty, or property, without due process of law. . . .

Amendment VI. In all criminal prosecutions, the accused shall enjoy the right to a speedy and public trial, by an impartial jury of the State and district where in the crime shall have been committed, . . . and to be informed of the nature and cause of the accusation; to be confronted with the witnesses against him; to have compulsory process for obtaining witnesses in his favor, and to have the Assistance of Counsel for his defense.

Amendment VIII. Excessive bail shall not be required, nor excessive fines imposed, nor cruel and unusual punishments inflicted.

Procedure dominates these provisions. Save for the First Amendment's protection of speech and religion, nothing in the Bill of Rights directly limits legislators' ability to criminalize whatever they wish. Save for the mild constraints of the Eighth Amendment, nothing in the Bill limits the severity of criminal punishment. Meanwhile, the Fourth, Fifth, and Sixth Amendments contain 14 separate procedural guarantees for criminal suspects and defendants. The Constitution's procedural focus shapes the allocation of power over criminal justice. Because there are few constitutional limits on the definition of crimes and sentences, those forms of lawmaking are left in the hands of elected state legislators and members of Congress. Because the Bill of Rights includes so many procedural guarantees, defining the bounds of those guarantees is chiefly the work of appellate judges — the chief interpreters of constitutional texts.

One more constitutional provision reinforces that allocation of lawmaking power. The Fourteenth Amendment — enacted following the Civil War as a means of protecting the civil rights of newly freed slaves — requires that state-court criminal proceedings (and any other state action that takes away a person's "life, liberty, or property") conform to "due process of law," and also guarantees that all persons receive "the equal protection of the laws." Unsurprisingly given the textual language (Justice Scalia likes to say there is no such thing as a "due substance clause"), the law of due process has focused mostly on process, not substance. More surprisingly, the same is also true of the law of equal protection.

To twenty-first-century Americans, that bottom line may seem natural. *Of course* constitutional rights focus on procedures, like the right to be free of unreasonable searches and seizures, the privilege against self-incrimination, the right to the assistance of counsel and to trial by an impartial jury. What else could written constitutions do? Actually, however, the procedural focus of American constitutional law is not as natural and inevitable as it first appears. Near the end of the eighteenth century, at a time when written constitutions were still a novelty, two sets of constitutional authors took a stab at defining the core legal rights essential to a just criminal justice system. Those authors worked independently and simultaneously: James Madison introduced his draft of what would become the American Bill of Rights in June 1789; 11 weeks later, the French National Assembly adopted the Declaration of the Rights of Man and of the Citizen. To make the comparison more interesting still, Madison's friend and political mentor—Thomas Jefferson, then the United States' Ambassador to France and soon to be George Washington's Secretary of State—may have contributed to the drafting of the French Declaration through conversations with his friend the Marquis de Lafayette, then an influential figure in the National Assembly.

Five of the French Declaration's 17 Articles deal with criminal justice, in whole or in part. In English, they read as follows:

> 4. Liberty consists in the freedom to do everything which injures no one else; hence the exercise of the natural rights of each man has no limits except those which assure to the other members of the society the enjoyment of the same rights. These limits can only be determined by law.
>
> 5. Law can only prohibit such actions as are hurtful to society. Nothing may be prevented which is not forbidden by law, and no one may be forced to do anything not provided for by law.
>
> 7. No person shall be accused, arrested, or imprisoned except in the cases and according to the forms prescribed by law. Any one soliciting, transmitting, executing, or causing to be executed, any arbitrary order, shall be punished. But any citizen summoned or arrested in virtue of the law shall submit without delay, as resistance constitutes an offense.
>
> 8. The law shall provide for such punishments only as are strictly and obviously necessary, and no one shall suffer punishment except it be legally inflicted in virtue of a law passed and promulgated before the commission of the offense.
>
> 9. As all persons are held innocent until they shall have been declared guilty, if arrest shall be deemed indispensable, all harshness not essential to the securing of the prisoner's person shall be severely repressed by law.

Roughly speaking, the Declaration is the Bill of Rights' mirror image. In the Bill of Rights, substance is governed lightly but procedure is extensively regulated. In the Declaration, procedure is governed lightly, and substantive law is seriously constrained.

Taken together with the second sentence of Article 5, Article 7 of the French Declaration covers the same ground as the Due Process Clause, but helpfully adds that lawless behavior by law enforcers "shall be punished." (The text of the Bill of Rights establishes no remedy for constitutional violations.) Article 9 defines two crucial procedural guarantees missing from the Bill of Rights: the presumption of innocence and a ban on police torture. The rest of the quoted provisions deal with substance, not process. Article 4 guarantees "the freedom to do everything that injures no one else"; Article 5 declares that "[l]aw can only prohibit such actions as are hurtful to society." These Articles endorse John Stuart Mill's harm principle, 70 years before Mill himself defended that principle in his famous book, On Liberty. Mill argued that legal punishments should be triggered only when defendants have injured others; policing public morals, Mill believed, is not an appropriate function of criminal law. Mill's argument was too radical for his native Britain and for the United States, neither of which has ever adopted that view in its criminal codes. All the more reason to marvel at the French revolutionaries who embraced the harm principle nearly two decades before Mill was born.

Article 8 is the French Declaration's counterpart to the Eighth Amendment, which bars both "excessive fines" and "cruel and unusual punishments." But instead of banning only the most extreme criminal sanctions as American law does in the Eighth Amendment (existing punishments, including branding and whipping, were grandfathered by the word "unusual"), Article 8 forbids *all* punishments that are not "strictly and obviously necessary." As Articles 4 and 5 command that doubts be resolved against criminalization, Article 8 requires that, for those convicted of crime, doubts be resolved against severity. Freedom and lenity are to be the legal norms, criminal liability and severe punishment the carefully limited exceptions. American law knows nothing like these limits on substantive government power: Recall that the rule of lenity is a rule of statutory construction, not a piece of constitutional law, and that so-called rule has little bite even within its limited domain.

The French Declaration's limits on substantive criminal law have been mostly a historical anomaly; even French law did not adhere to those limits until the late twentieth century. Madison's Bill of Rights has proved far more influential. Limits on police searches and seizures and a ban on compelled self-incrimination—both present in the Bill of Rights, both absent from the French Declaration—are common features of the many written constitutions adopted since the fall of the Soviet Union and South African apartheid. So are lists of required trial procedures akin to the lists Madison included in the Fifth and Sixth Amendments. One of the hot topics of today's comparative law scholarship is convergence: Scholars argue that code-based justice systems like those used throughout Continental Europe and South America increasingly resemble common-law systems like those used in Great Britain and the United States. That is, code-based justice systems are becoming more proceduralized; the law under which those systems operate resembles, more and more, American law. Meanwhile, Mill-type bans on criminalizing harmless conduct or on punishments that are less than "obviously necessary" are largely absent from the world's constitutions. One wonders whether the rest of the world is following the right model.

B. REVIEW: DUE PROCESS VAGUENESS AND EIGHTH AMENDMENT PROPORTIONALITY

Back in Chapter 1, we introduced two constitutional doctrines of special relevance to the criminal law. The first is "vagueness": the idea that, as a matter of constitutional due process (guaranteed by the Fifth Amendment for federal crimes, and by the Fourteenth Amendment for state crimes), the definitions of crimes must be reasonably clear, in order to provide fair notice to defendants of what is being prohibited, and also in order to avoid the related problem of granting too much discretion to police, prosecutors, judges, and juries to determine who is, and who is not, a criminal. The primary concern about too much discretion is that it may be abused on personal, political, or legally impermissible grounds, such as race or class.

The second doctrine is "proportionality": the idea that criminal punishments that are grossly excessive, in relation to the crime and the culpability of the defendant, violate the Eighth Amendment's ban on "cruel and unusual punishments." The proportionality doctrine has been used frequently by the Supreme Court to regulate the scope and application of the death penalty, but has been used only rarely to invalidate non-capital punishments.

If you have forgotten the relevant portions of Chapter 1, at pages 34-52, supra, you may want to return to them now for a more complete discussion of these two constitutional limits on the definition and application of the criminal law.

C. PRIVACY

Today, probably the best-known doctrine in American constitutional law holds that private conduct having to do with sex and reproduction must be free of intrusive government regulation. That doctrine's origins lie in the next main case: Griswold v. Connecticut, 381 U.S. 479 (1965), which overturned a criminal ban on the use of contraceptives. Today, we know that *Griswold* spawned (pun intended) both Roe v. Wade, 410 U.S. 113 (1973), and Lawrence v. Texas, 539 U.S. 558 (2003), which established the constitutional rights to be free of government bans on abortion and on consensual adult sex. When it was decided, *Griswold* seemed likely to produce two other sorts of privacy doctrine, either of which would have had large effects on substantive criminal law. The first of those doctrines would have protected geographic privacy, limiting the government's power to criminalize consensual conduct that takes place inside private homes. The second of the doctrines would have protected physical privacy, limiting the power to criminalize voluntary decisions concerning the use of one's own body.

Each of those doctrinal "roads not taken" might have substantially limited the scope of permissible drug crimes. Many drug cases are proved on the basis of drugs found (or, in the case of methamphetamines, manufactured) inside defendants' homes. And the use of illegal drugs, like sex and reproduction, implicates individuals' freedom to do as they wish with their own bodies. Should constitutional law protect the purchase, possession, and use of illegal drugs? Why are some pleasurable uses of our bodies constitutionally protected, while others can lead to a long stay in the nearest penitentiary?

Griswold v. Connecticut

Supreme Court of the United States
381 U.S. 479 (1965)

Justice DOUGLAS delivered the opinion of the Court.

Appellant Griswold is Executive Director of the Planned Parenthood League of Connecticut. Appellant Buxton is a licensed physician and a professor at the Yale Medical School who served as Medical Director for the League at its Center in New Haven—a center open and operating from November 1 to November 10, 1961, when appellants were arrested.

They gave information, instruction, and medical advice to married persons as to the means of preventing conception. They examined the wife and prescribed the best contraceptive device or material for her use. Fees were usually charged, although some couples were serviced free.

The statutes whose constitutionality is involved in this appeal are §§53-32 and 54-196 of the General Statutes of Connecticut. The former provides: "Any person who uses any drug, medicinal article or instrument for the purpose of preventing conception shall be fined not less than fifty dollars or imprisoned not less than sixty days nor more than one year or be both fined and imprisoned." Section 54-196 provides: "Any person who assists, abets, counsels, causes, hires or commands another to commit any offense may be prosecuted and punished as if he were the principal offender."

The appellants were found guilty as accessories and fined $100 each, against the claim that the accessory statute as so applied violated the Fourteenth Amendment. The Appellate Division of the Circuit Court affirmed. The Supreme Court of Errors affirmed that judgment. . . .

We think that appellants have standing to raise the constitutional rights of the married people with whom they had a professional relationship. Tileston v. Ullman, 318 U.S. 44, is different, for there the plaintiff seeking to represent others asked for a declaratory judgment. In that situation we thought that the requirements of standing should be strict, lest the standards of "case or controversy" in Article III of the Constitution become blurred. Here those doubts are removed by reason of a criminal conviction for serving married couples in violation of an aiding-and-abetting statute. Certainly the accessory should have standing to assert that the offense which he is charged with assisting is not, or cannot constitutionally be, a crime. . . .

. . . We do not sit as a super-legislature to determine the wisdom, need, and propriety of laws that touch economic problems, business affairs, or social conditions. This law, however, operates directly on an intimate relation of husband and wife and their physician's role in one aspect of that relation.

The association of people is not mentioned in the Constitution nor in the Bill of Rights. The right to educate a child in a school of the parents' choice—whether public or private or parochial—is also not mentioned. Nor is the right to study any particular subject or any foreign language. Yet the First Amendment has been construed to include certain of those rights.

By Pierce v. Society of Sisters, 268 U.S. 510, the right to educate one's children as one chooses is made applicable to the States by the force of the First and Fourteenth Amendments. By Meyer v. Nebraska, 262 U.S. 390, the same dignity is given the right to study the German language in a private school. In other words, the State may not, consistently with the spirit of the First Amendment, contract the spectrum of available knowledge. The right of freedom of speech and press includes not only the right to utter or to print, but the right to distribute, the right to receive, the right to read and freedom of inquiry, freedom of thought, and freedom to teach. . . . Without those peripheral rights the specific rights would be less secure. And so we reaffirm the principle of the *Pierce* and the *Meyer* cases.

In NAACP v. Alabama, 357 U.S. 449, 462, we protected the "freedom to associate and privacy in one's associations," noting that freedom of association was a peripheral First Amendment right. Disclosure of membership lists of a constitutionally valid association, we held, was invalid "as entailing the likelihood of a substantial restraint upon the exercise by petitioner's members of their right to freedom of association." Ibid. In other words, the First Amendment has a penumbra where privacy is protected from governmental intrusion. In like context, we have protected forms of "association" that are not political in the customary sense but pertain to the social, legal, and economic benefit of the members. NAACP v. Button, 371 U.S. 415, 430-431. . . .

Those cases involved more than the "right of assembly"—a right that extends to all irrespective of their race or ideology. The right of "association," like the right of belief, is more than the right to attend a meeting; it includes the right to express one's attitudes or philosophies by membership in a group or by affiliation with it or by other lawful means. Association in that context is a form of expression of opinion; and while it is not expressly included in the First Amendment its existence is necessary in making the express guarantees fully meaningful.

The foregoing cases suggest that specific guarantees in the Bill of Rights have penumbras, formed by emanations from those guarantees that help give them life and substance. Various guarantees create zones of privacy. The right of association contained in the penumbra of the First Amendment is one, as we have seen. The Third Amendment in its prohibition against the quartering of soldiers "in any house" in time of peace without the consent of the owner is another facet of that privacy. The Fourth Amendment explicitly affirms the "right of the people to be secure in their persons, houses, papers, and effects, against unreasonable searches and seizures." The Fifth Amendment in its Self-Incrimination Clause enables the citizen to create a zone of privacy which government may not force him to surrender to his detriment. The Ninth Amendment provides: "The enumeration in the Constitution, of certain rights, shall not be construed to deny or disparage others retained by the people."

The Fourth and Fifth Amendments were described in Boyd v. United States, 116 U.S. 616, 630, as protection against all governmental invasions "of the sanctity of a man's home and the privacies of life." We recently referred in Mapp v. Ohio, 367 U.S. 643, 656, to the Fourth Amendment as creating a "right to privacy, no less important than any other right carefully and particularly reserved to the people." . . .

The present case, then, concerns a relationship lying within the zone of privacy created by several fundamental constitutional guarantees. And it concerns a law which, in forbidding the use of contraceptives rather than regulating their manufacture or sale, seeks to achieve its goals by means having a maximum destructive impact upon that relationship. Such a law cannot stand in light of the familiar principle, so often applied by this Court, that a "governmental purpose to control or prevent activities constitutionally subject to state regulation may not be achieved by means which sweep unnecessarily broadly and thereby invade the area of protected freedoms." NAACP v. Alabama, 377 U.S. 288, 307. Would we allow the police to search the sacred precincts of marital bedrooms for telltale signs of the use of contraceptives? The very idea is repulsive to the notions of privacy surrounding the marriage relationship.

We deal with a right of privacy older than the Bill of Rights—older than our political parties, older than our school system. Marriage is a coming together for better or for worse, hopefully enduring, and intimate to the degree of being sacred. It is an association that promotes a way of life, not causes; a harmony in living, not political faiths; a bilateral loyalty, not commercial or social projects. Yet it is an association for as noble a purpose as any involved in our prior decisions. . . .

[Justice GOLDBERG's concurring opinion, joined by Chief Justice WARREN and Justice BRENNAN, is omitted, as is Justice WHITE's opinion concurring in the judgment.]

Justice HARLAN, concurring in the judgment.

. . . In my view, the proper constitutional inquiry in this case is whether this Connecticut statute infringes the Due Process Clause of the Fourteenth Amendment because the enactment violates basic values "implicit in the concept of ordered liberty," Palko v. Connecticut, 302 U.S. 319, 325. For reasons stated at length in my dissenting opinion in Poe v. Ullman, 367 U.S. 497, I believe that it does. While the relevant inquiry may be aided by resort to one or more of the provisions of the Bill of Rights, it is not dependent on them or any of their radiations. The Due Process Clause of the Fourteenth Amendment stands, in my opinion, on its own bottom. . . .

Justice BLACK, with whom Justice STEWART joins, dissenting.

. . . The Court talks about a constitutional "right of privacy" as though there is some constitutional provision or provisions forbidding any law ever to be passed which might abridge the "privacy" of individuals. But there is not. There are, of course, guarantees in certain specific constitutional provisions which are designed in part to protect privacy at certain times and places with respect to certain activities. Such, for example, is the Fourth Amendment's guarantee against "unreasonable searches and seizures." But I think it belittles that Amendment to talk about it as though it protects nothing but "privacy." . . . The average man would very likely not have his feelings soothed any more by having his property seized openly than by having it seized privately and by stealth. He simply wants his property left alone. And a person can be just as much, if not more, irritated, annoyed and injured by an unceremonious public arrest by a policeman as he is by a seizure in the privacy of his office or home.

One of the most effective ways of diluting or expanding a constitutionally guaranteed right is to substitute for the crucial word or words of a constitutional guarantee another word or words, more or less flexible and more or less restricted in meaning. This fact is well illustrated by the use of the term "right of privacy" as a comprehensive substitute for the Fourth Amendment's guarantee against "unreasonable searches and seizures." "Privacy" is a broad, abstract and ambiguous concept which can easily be shrunken in meaning but which can also, on the other hand, easily be interpreted as a constitutional ban against many things other than searches and seizures. . . .

. . . [T]his Court does have power, which it should exercise, to hold laws unconstitutional where they are forbidden by the Federal Constitution. My point is that there is no provision of the Constitution which either expressly or impliedly vests power in this Court to sit as a supervisory agency over acts of duly constituted legislative bodies and set aside their laws because of the Court's belief that the legislative policies adopted are unreasonable, unwise, arbitrary, capricious or irrational. The adoption of such a loose, flexible, uncontrolled standard for holding laws unconstitutional, if ever it is finally achieved, will amount to a great unconstitutional shift of power to the courts which I believe and am constrained to say will be bad for the courts and worse for the country. Subjecting federal and state laws to such an unrestrained and unrestrainable judicial control as to the wisdom of legislative enactments would, I fear, jeopardize the separation of governmental powers that the Framers set up and at the same time threaten to take away much of the power of States to govern themselves which the Constitution plainly intended them to have.

I realize that many good and able men have eloquently spoken and written, sometimes in rhapsodical strains, about the duty of this Court to keep the Constitution in tune with the times. The idea is that the Constitution must be changed from time to time and that this Court is charged with a duty to make those changes. For myself, I must with all deference reject that philosophy. The Constitution makers knew the need for change and provided for it. Amendments suggested by the people's elected representatives can be submitted to the people or their selected agents for ratification. That method of change was good for our Fathers, and being somewhat old-fashioned I must add it is good enough for me. . . .

The late Judge Learned Hand, after emphasizing his view that judges should not . . . invalidate legislation offensive to their "personal preferences," made the statement, with which I fully agree, that: "For myself it would be most irksome to be ruled by a bevy of Platonic Guardians, even if I knew how to choose them, which I assuredly do not." So far as I am concerned, Connecticut's law as applied here is not forbidden by any provision of the Federal Constitution as that Constitution was written, and I would therefore affirm.

Justice STEWART, whom Justice BLACK joins, dissenting.

Since 1879 Connecticut has had on its books a law which forbids the use of contraceptives by anyone. I think this is an uncommonly silly law. As a practical matter, the law is obviously unenforceable, except in the oblique context of the present case. As a philosophical matter, I believe the use of contraceptives in the relationship of marriage should be left to personal and private choice, based upon each individual's moral, ethical, and religious beliefs. As a matter of social policy, I think professional counsel about methods of birth control should be available to all, so that each individual's choice can be meaningfully made. But we are not asked in this case to say whether we think this law is unwise, or even asinine. We are asked to hold that it violates the United States Constitution. And that I cannot do.

In the course of its opinion the Court refers to no less than six Amendments to the Constitution: the First, the Third, the Fourth, the Fifth, the Ninth, and the Fourteenth. But the Court does not say which of these Amendments, if any, it thinks is infringed by this Connecticut law.

. . . [T]he Due Process Clause of the Fourteenth Amendment [does not require the result] in this case. . . . There is no claim that this law, duly enacted by the Connecticut Legislature, is unconstitutionally vague. There is no claim that the appellants were denied any of the elements of procedural due process at their trial, so as to make their convictions constitutionally invalid. . . .

As to the First, Third, Fourth, and Fifth Amendments, I can find nothing in any of them to invalidate this Connecticut law, even assuming that all those Amendments are fully applicable against the States. It has not even been argued that this is a law "respecting an establishment of religion, or prohibiting the free exercise thereof." And surely, unless the solemn process of constitutional adjudication is to descend to the level of a play on words, there is not involved here any abridgment of "the freedom of speech, or of the press; or the right of the people peaceably to assemble, and to petition the Government for a redress of grievances." No soldier has been quartered in any house. There has been no search, and no seizure. Nobody has been compelled to be a witness against himself. . . .

What provision of the Constitution, then, does make this state law invalid? The Court says it is the right of privacy "created by several fundamental constitutional guarantees." With all deference, I can find no such general right of privacy in the Bill of Rights, in any other part of the Constitution, or in any case ever before decided by this Court. . . .

. . . It is the essence of judicial duty to subordinate our own personal views, our own ideas of what legislation is wise and what is not. If, as I should surely hope, the law before us does not reflect the standards of the people of Connecticut, the people of Connecticut can freely exercise their true Ninth and Tenth Amendment rights to persuade their elected representatives to repeal it. That is the constitutional way to take this law off the books.

Note on Poe v. Ullman

Justice Harlan's concurring opinion refers to Poe v. Ullman, 367 U.S. 497 (1961), in which the Court had declined to consider the constitutionality of the same Connecticut statute at issue in *Griswold*. In *Poe*, Justice Harlan discussed his view of the relevant constitutional questions at some length. Following are some excerpts:

> Precisely what is involved here is this: the State is asserting the right to enforce its moral judgment by intruding upon the most intimate details of the marital relation with the full power of the criminal law. Potentially, this could allow the deployment of all the incidental machinery of the criminal law, arrests, searches and seizures; inevitably, it must mean at the very least the lodging of criminal charges, a public trial, and testimony as to the corpus delicti. Nor could any imaginable elaboration of presumptions, testimonial privileges, or other safeguards, alleviate the necessity for testimony as to the mode and manner of the married couples' sexual relations, or at least the opportunity for the accused to make denial of the charges. In sum, the statute allows the State to enquire into, prove and punish married people for the private use of their marital intimacy. . . .

> That aspect of liberty which embraces the concept of the privacy of the home receives explicit Constitutional protection at two places only. These are the Third Amendment, relating to the quartering of soldiers,[13] and the Fourth Amendment, prohibiting unreasonable searches and seizures.[14] While these Amendments reach only the Federal Government, this Court has held in the strongest terms, and today again confirms, that the concept of "privacy" embodied in the Fourth Amendment is part of the "ordered liberty" assured against state action by the Fourteenth Amendment. See Wolf v. Colorado, 338 U.S. 25; Mapp v. Ohio, [367 U.S. 643]. . . .

> It is clear, of course, that this Connecticut statute does not invade the privacy of the home in the usual sense, since the invasion involved here may . . . be accomplished without any physical intrusion whatever into the home. What the statute undertakes to do, however, is to create a crime which is grossly offensive to this privacy. . . .

> Perhaps the most comprehensive statement of the principle of liberty underlying these aspects of the Constitution was given by Mr. Justice Brandeis, dissenting in Olmstead v. United States, 277 U.S. 438, at 478:

> > ". . . The makers of our Constitution undertook to secure conditions favorable to the pursuit of happiness. They recognized the significance of man's spiritual nature, of his feelings and of his intellect. They knew that only a part of the pain, pleasure and satisfactions of life are to be found in material things. They sought to protect Americans in their beliefs, their thoughts, their emotions and their sensations. They conferred, as against the Government, the right to be let alone—the most

13. "No Soldier shall, in time of peace be quartered in any house, without the consent of the Owner, nor in time of war, but in a manner to be prescribed by law."

14. "The right of the people to be secure in their persons, houses, papers, and effects, against unreasonable searches and seizures, shall not be violated, and no Warrants shall issue, but upon probable cause, supported by Oath or affirmation, and particularly describing the place to be searched, and the persons or things to be seized."

comprehensive of rights and the right most valued by civilized men. To protect that right, every unjustifiable intrusion by the Government upon the privacy of the individual, whatever the means employed, must be deemed a violation of the Fourth Amendment. . . ."

I think the sweep of the Court's decisions, under both the Fourth and Fourteenth Amendments, amply shows that the Constitution protects the privacy of the home against all unreasonable intrusion of whatever character. "[These] principles . . . affect the very essence of constitutional liberty and security. They reach farther than [a] concrete form of the case . . . before the court, with its adventitious circumstances; they apply to all invasions on the part of the government and its employees of the sanctity of a man's home and the privacies of life. . . ." Boyd v. United States, 116 U.S. 616, 630. "The security of one's privacy against arbitrary intrusion by the police — which is at the core of the Fourth Amendment — is basic to a free society." Wolf v. Colorado, supra, at 27. . . .

. . . [H]ere we have not an intrusion into the home so much as on the life which characteristically has its place in the home. But to my mind such a distinction is so insubstantial as to be captious: if the physical curtilage of the home is protected, it is surely as a result of solicitude to protect the privacies of the life within. Certainly the safeguarding of the home does not follow merely from the sanctity of property rights. The home derives its pre-eminence as the seat of family life. And the integrity of that life is something so fundamental that it has been found to draw to its protection the principles of more than one explicitly granted Constitutional right. Thus, Mr. Justice Brandeis, writing of a statute which made "it punishable to teach [pacifism] in any place [to] a single person . . . no matter what the relation of the parties may be," found such a "statute invades the privacy and freedom of the home. Father and mother may not follow the promptings of religious belief, of conscience or of conviction, and teach son or daughter the doctrine of pacifism. If they do any police officer may summarily arrest them." Gilbert v. Minnesota, 254 U.S. 325, 335-336 (dissenting opinion). . . . These decisions, as was said in Prince v. Massachusetts, 321 U.S. 158, at 166, "have respected the private realm of family life which the state cannot enter." . . .

Though undoubtedly the States are and should be left free to reflect a wide variety of policies, and should be allowed broad scope in experimenting with various means of promoting those policies, I must agree with Mr. Justice Jackson that "There are limits to the extent to which a legislatively represented majority may conduct . . . experiments at the expense of the dignity and personality" of the individual. Skinner v. Oklahoma, 316 U.S. 535. In this instance these limits are, in my view, reached and passed. . . .

Notes on Privacy and Substantive Criminal Law

1. Assume, for the sake of argument, that *some* sphere of private conduct should be free from regulation by substantive criminal law. What should that constitutionally protected zone of privacy include? The decision to use (or not to use) contraceptives? To obtain an abortion? To have sex? To use drugs? All of the above?

2. Though much of the language in *Griswold* dealt with the right of married couples to buy and use contraceptives, the right is not limited to married couples, nor even to couples. In Eisenstadt v. Baird, 405 U.S. 438 (1972), the Supreme Court struck down a law barring the provision of contraceptives to unmarried persons:

> It is true that in *Griswold* the right of privacy in question inhered in the marital relationship. . . . If the right of privacy means anything, it is the right of the *individual*, married or single, to be free from unwarranted governmental intrusion into matters so fundamentally affecting a person as the decision whether to bear or beget a child.

Id. at 453. The Court extended *Eisenstadt* in Carey v. Population Services International, 431 U.S. 678 (1977), which invalidated a state statute barring the distribution of contraceptives to persons younger than 16 years of age.

3. Recall the two key doctrines that flow from *Griswold*. First, pregnant women have a constitutionally protected right to seek an abortion; the government can regulate the practice of abortion, but not in a manner that unduly burdens exercise of the right. See Roe v. Wade, 410 U.S. 113 (1973); Planned Parenthood of Southeastern Pennsylvania v. Casey, 505 U.S. 833 (1992). Second, adults—gay and straight alike—have the constitutional right to have consensual sex with one another in private homes, without government interference. See Lawrence v. Texas, 539 U.S. 558 (2003). As with abortion, the government retains the power to regulate consensual sex: That power plainly includes the authority to ban prostitution and incest, for example, and probably also extends to the prohibition of bigamy and adultery. Those categories aside, and absent force or fraud, the government may not forbid sex between consenting adults.

Those broadly defined rights are often said to protect individuals' physical autonomy—the right to do with one's body as one sees fit. But autonomy does not extend to all uses of one's body. With *Roe*, compare United States v. Hurwitz, 459 F.3d 463 (4th Cir. 2006), excerpted supra at page 453. *Roe* grants broad protection to medical decisions made by pregnant women in consultation with their doctors. *Hurwitz* interprets the federal Controlled Substances Act to authorize the imprisonment of doctors who prescribe larger-than-customary doses of opioid pain killers for patients with various sorts of chronic pain. With *Lawrence*, compare United States v. Hunte, 196 F.3d 687 (7th Cir. 1999), excerpted supra at page 403. *Lawrence* invalidates criminal sodomy laws because, through such laws, the government "seek[s] to control a personal relationship that, whether or not entitled to formal recognition in the law, is within the liberty of persons to choose without being punished as criminals." Cheryl Hunte's relatively minor drug crimes were intertwined with her relationship with Joseph Richards. As the decision in *Hunte* illustrates, the government regularly punishes parties to sexual relationships who refuse to testify to their lovers' drug offenses. Constitutional rights involving physical autonomy and intimacy seem to disappear when drugs enter the picture.

4. The Texas statute at issue in *Lawrence* expressly barred gay sex. Such statutes had been deemed constitutionally permissible as recently as 1986. See Bowers v. Hardwick, 478 U.S. 186 (1986). Justice Kennedy's majority opinion in *Lawrence* explained why, in the Justices' view, *Bowers* should be overruled:

> When sexuality finds overt expression in intimate conduct with another person, the conduct can be but one element in a personal bond that is more enduring. The liberty protected by the Constitution allows homosexual persons the right to make this choice. . . .
>
> . . . [T]here is no longstanding history in this country of laws directed at homosexual conduct as a distinct matter. Beginning in colonial times there were prohibitions of sodomy derived from the English criminal laws passed in the first instance by the Reformation Parliament of 1533. The English prohibition was understood to include relations between men and women as well as relations between men and men. Nineteenth-century commentators similarly read American sodomy, buggery, and crime-against-nature statutes as criminalizing certain relations between men and women and between men and men. . . . [A]ccording to some scholars the concept of the homosexual as a distinct category of person did not emerge until the late 19th century. See, e.g., J. Katz, The Invention of Heterosexuality 10 (1995); J. D'Emilio & E. Freedman, Intimate Matters: A History of Sexuality in America 121 (2d ed. 1997) ("The modern terms *homosexuality* and *heterosexuality* do not apply to an era that had not yet articulated these distinctions"). Thus, early American sodomy laws were not directed at homosexuals as such but instead sought to prohibit nonprocreative sexual activity more generally. . . .
>
> Laws prohibiting sodomy do not seem to have been enforced against consenting adults acting in private. A substantial number of sodomy prosecutions and convictions for which there are surviving records were for predatory acts against those who could not or did not consent, as in the case of a minor or the victim of an assault. As to these, one purpose for the prohibitions was to ensure there would be no lack of coverage if a predator committed a sexual assault that did not constitute rape as defined by the criminal law. . . . Instead of targeting relations between consenting adults in private, 19th-century sodomy prosecutions typically involved relations between men and minor girls or minor boys, relations between adults involving force, relations between adults implicating disparity in status, or relations between men and animals.
>
> To the extent that there were any prosecutions for the acts in question, 19th-century evidence rules imposed a burden that would make a conviction more difficult to obtain even taking into account the problems always inherent in prosecuting consensual acts committed in private. Under then-prevailing standards, a man could not be convicted of sodomy based upon testimony of a consenting partner, because the partner was considered an accomplice.

A partner's testimony, however, was admissible if he or she had not consented to the act or was a minor, and therefore incapable of consent. See, e.g., F. Wharton, Criminal Law 512 (8th ed. 1880). The rule may explain in part the infrequency of these prosecutions. In all events that infrequency makes it difficult to say that society approved of a rigorous and systematic punishment of the consensual acts committed in private and by adults. The longstanding criminal prohibition of homosexual sodomy upon which the *Bowers* decision placed such reliance is as consistent with a general condemnation of nonprocreative sex as it is with an established tradition of prosecuting acts because of their homosexual character. . . .

. . . [F]ar from possessing "ancient roots," *Bowers,* 478 U.S., at 192, American laws targeting same-sex couples did not develop until the last third of the 20th century. The reported decisions concerning the prosecution of consensual, homosexual sodomy between adults for the years 1880-1995 are not always clear in the details, but a significant number involved conduct in a public place. It was not until the 1970s that any State singled out same-sex relations for criminal prosecution, and only nine States have done so. . . . Post-*Bowers* . . . , States with same-sex prohibitions have moved toward abolishing them. See, e.g., Jegley v. Picado, 80 S.W.3d 332 (Ark. 2002); Gryczan v. State, 942 P.2d 112 (Mont. 1997); Campbell v. Sundquist, 926 S.W.2d 250 (Tenn. App. 1996); Commonwealth v. Wasson, 842 S.W.2d 487 (Ky. 1992); see also 1993 Nev. Stats. at 518 (repealing Nev. Rev. Stat. §201.193). . . .

It must be acknowledged, of course, that . . . for centuries there have been powerful voices to condemn homosexual conduct as immoral. The condemnation has been shaped by religious beliefs, conceptions of right and acceptable behavior, and respect for the traditional family. For many persons these are not trivial concerns but profound and deep convictions accepted as ethical and moral principles to which they aspire and which thus determine the course of their lives. These considerations do not answer the question before us, however. The issue is whether the majority may use the power of the State to enforce these views on the whole society through operation of the criminal law. "Our obligation is to define the liberty of all, not to mandate our own moral code." Planned Parenthood of Southeastern Pa. v. Casey, 505 U.S. 833, 850 (1992).

Chief Justice Burger joined the opinion for the Court in *Bowers* and further explained his views as follows: "Decisions of individuals relating to homosexual conduct have been subject to state intervention throughout the history of Western civilization. Condemnation of those practices is firmly rooted in Judeao-Christian moral and ethical standards." 478 U.S., at 196. . . . [S]cholarship casts some doubt on the sweeping nature of the statement by Chief Justice Burger as it pertains to private homosexual conduct between consenting adults. See, e.g., Eskridge, *Hardwick* and Historiography, 1999 U. Ill. L. Rev. 631, 656. In all events we think that our laws and traditions in the past half century are of most relevance here. These references show an emerging awareness that liberty gives substantial protection to adult persons in deciding how to conduct their private lives in matters pertaining to sex. . . .

This emerging recognition should have been apparent when *Bowers* was decided. In 1955 the American Law Institute promulgated the Model Penal

Code and made clear that it did not recommend or provide for "criminal penalties for consensual sexual relations conducted in private." ALI, Model Penal Code §213.2, Comment 2, at 372 (1980). It justified its decision on three grounds: (1) The prohibitions undermined respect for the law by penalizing conduct many people engaged in; (2) the statutes regulated private conduct not harmful to others; and (3) the laws were arbitrarily enforced and thus invited the danger of blackmail. ALI, Model Penal Code, Commentary 277-80 (Tent. Draft No. 4, 1955). In 1961 Illinois changed its laws to conform to the Model Penal Code. Other States soon followed. . . .

The sweeping references by Chief Justice Burger to the history of Western civilization and to Judeo-Christian moral and ethical standards did not take account of other authorities pointing in an opposite direction. A committee advising the British Parliament recommended in 1957 repeal of laws punishing homosexual conduct. The Wolfenden Report: Report of the Committee on Homosexual Offenses and Prostitution (1963). Parliament enacted the substance of those recommendations 10 years later. Sexual Offences Act 1967, §1.

Of even more importance, almost five years before *Bowers* was decided the European Court of Human Rights considered a case with parallels to *Bowers* and to today's case. An adult male resident in Northern Ireland alleged he was a practicing homosexual who desired to engage in consensual homosexual conduct. The laws of Northern Ireland forbade him that right. He alleged that he had been questioned, his home had been searched, and he feared criminal prosecution. The court held that the laws proscribing the conduct were invalid under the European Convention on Human Rights. Dudgeon v. United Kingdom, 45 Eur. Ct. H.R. (1981) ¶52. Authoritative in all countries that are members of the Council of Europe (21 nations then, 45 nations now), the decision is at odds with the premise in *Bowers* that the claim put forward was insubstantial in our Western civilization.

In our own constitutional system the deficiencies in *Bowers* became even more apparent in the years following its announcement. The 25 States with laws prohibiting the relevant conduct referenced in the *Bowers* decision are reduced now to 13, of which 4 enforce their laws only against homosexual conduct. In those States where sodomy is still proscribed, . . . there is a pattern of nonenforcement with respect to consenting adults acting in private. . . .

The stigma this criminal statute imposes, moreover, is not trivial. The offense, to be sure, is but a class C misdemeanor, a minor offense in the Texas legal system. Still, it remains a criminal offense with all that imports for the dignity of the persons charged. The petitioners will bear on their record the history of their criminal convictions. Just this Term we rejected various challenges to state laws requiring the registration of sex offenders. Smith v. Doe, 538 U.S. 84 (2003). We are advised that if Texas convicted an adult for private, consensual homosexual conduct under the statute here in question the convicted person would come within the registration laws of at least four States were he or she to be subject to their jurisdiction. This underscores the consequential nature of the punishment and the state-sponsored condemnation attendant to the criminal prohibition. . . .

Lawrence, 539 U.S. at 567-76. Justice Kennedy's citation of British and European law excited a good deal of controversy when the decision in *Lawrence* was announced. Is it reasonable to rely on other countries' legal rules when determining the meaning of American constitutional law, which in turn defines the permissible boundaries of American criminal law? Which countries' laws should American judges examine?

5. Note Justice Kennedy's reference to the common law of rape. As you may recall, before the 1970s, proof of rape in most jurisdictions required proof of a high degree of violence apart from the relevant sex acts—violence sufficient to overcome the victim's physical resistance. Those requirements effectively permitted a great deal of coercive, even violent sex. Sodomy laws like the one at issue in *Lawrence* were sometimes used to mitigate the effects of rape doctrine, since proof of force and victim resistance was not required in sodomy cases. At the same time, sodomy laws could not always function as a substitute for hard-to-prove rape charges, since sodomy laws usually covered only certain sex acts—most commonly, oral and anal sex (both gay and straight).

6. Recall United States v. Bygrave, 46 M.J. 491 (Ct. App. 1997), excerpted supra at page 610, and In the Interest of M.T.S., 609 A.2d 1266 (N.J. 1992), excerpted supra at page 626. Are those decisions in tension with *Lawrence*? Under *Lawrence*, sex between willing adults is constitutionally protected, at least in most instances. The sex in *Bygrave* was apparently wholly consensual, yet it was also criminally punishable. As for *M.T.S.*, that decision has been both widely applauded and widely criticized—and the critics' chief complaint is that, by treating ordinary sexual intercourse as forcible, the New Jersey Supreme Court risked criminalizing consensual sex as well as the truly coercive kind. The decisions in *Bygrave* and *M.T.S.* (and many others like them) suggest a long-term trend, prompted by shifting social norms, toward the increasing criminalization of sex that would not clearly qualify as either assaultive or coercive. At some point, that trend may run afoul of *Lawrence*. Stay tuned.

D. CONSTITUTIONALIZED INTENT

Lambert v. California

Supreme Court of the United States
355 U.S. 225 (1957)

Justice DOUGLAS delivered the opinion of the Court.

Section 52.38(a) of the Los Angeles Municipal Code defines "convicted person" as follows:

"Any person who, subsequent to January 1, 1921, has been or hereafter is convicted of an offense punishable as a felony in the State of California, or who has been or who is hereafter convicted of any offense in any place other than the State of California, which offense, if committed in the State of California, would have been punishable as a felony."

Section 52.39 provides that it shall be unlawful for "any convicted person" to be or remain in Los Angeles for a period of more than five days without registering; it requires any person having a place of abode outside the city to register if he comes into the city on five occasions or more during a 30-day period; and it prescribes the information to be furnished the Chief of Police on registering.

Section 52.43(b) makes the failure to register a continuing offense, each day's failure constituting a separate offense.

Appellant, arrested on suspicion of another offense, was charged with a violation of this registration law. The evidence showed that she had been at the time of her arrest a resident of Los Angeles for over seven years. Within that period she had been convicted in Los Angeles of the crime of forgery, an offense which California punishes as a felony. Though convicted of a crime punishable as a felony, she had not at the time of her arrest registered under the Municipal Code. At the trial, appellant asserted that §52.39 of the Code denies her due process of law and other rights under the Federal Constitution, unnecessary to enumerate. The trial court denied this objection. The case was tried to a jury which found appellant guilty. The court fined her $250 and placed her on probation for three years. Appellant, renewing her constitutional objection, moved for arrest of judgment and a new trial. This motion was denied. On appeal the constitutionality of the Code was again challenged. The Appellate Department of the Superior Court affirmed the judgment, holding there was no merit to the claim that the ordinance was unconstitutional. The case is here on appeal. . . . [W]e now hold that the registration provisions of the Code as sought to be applied here violate [due process]. . . .

The registration provision, carrying criminal penalties, applies if a person has been convicted "of an offense punishable as a felony in the State of California" or, in case he has been convicted in another State, if the offense "would have been punishable as a felony" had it been committed in California. No element of willfulness is by terms included in the ordinance nor read into it by the California court as a condition necessary for a conviction.

We must assume that appellant had no actual knowledge of the requirement that she register under this ordinance, as she offered proof of this defense which was refused. The question is whether a registration act of this character violates due process where it is applied to a person who has no actual knowledge of his duty to register, and where no showing is made of the probability of such knowledge.

We do not go with Blackstone in saying that "a vicious will" is necessary to constitute a crime, 4 Blackstone's Commentaries *21, for conduct alone without regard to the intent of the doer is often sufficient. There is wide latitude in the lawmakers to declare an offense and to exclude elements of knowledge and diligence from its definition. But we deal here with conduct that is wholly passive — mere failure to register. It is unlike the commission of acts, or the failure to act under circumstances that should alert the doer to the consequences of his deed. Cf. United States v. Balint, 258 U.S. 250; United States v. Dotterweich, 320 U.S. 277, 284. The rule that "ignorance of the law will not excuse" is deep in our law, as is the principle that of all the powers of local government, the police power is "one of the least limitable." District of Columbia v. Brooke, 214 U.S. 138, 149. On the other hand, due process places some limits on its exercise. Engrained in our concept of due process is the requirement of notice. Notice is sometimes essential so that the citizen has the chance to defend charges. Notice is required before property interests are disturbed, before assessments are made, before penalties are assessed. Notice is required in a myriad of situations where a penalty or forfeiture might be suffered for mere failure to act. Recent cases illustrating the point are Mullane v. Central Hanover Trust Co., 339 U.S. 306; Covey v. Town of Somers, 351 U.S. 141; Walker v. Hutchinson City, 352 U.S. 112. These cases involved only property interests in civil litigation. But the principle is equally appropriate where a person, wholly passive and unaware of any wrongdoing, is brought to the bar of justice for condemnation in a criminal case.

Registration laws are common and their range is wide. Many such laws are akin to licensing statutes in that they pertain to the regulation of business activities. But the present ordinance is entirely different. Violation of its provisions is unaccompanied by any activity whatever, mere presence in the city being the test. Moreover, circumstances which might move one to inquire as to the necessity of registration are completely lacking. . . . [T]his appellant on first becoming aware of her duty to register was given no opportunity to comply with the law and avoid its penalty, even though her default was entirely innocent. She could but suffer the consequences of the ordinance, namely, conviction with the imposition of heavy criminal penalties thereunder. We believe that actual knowledge of the duty to register or proof of the probability of such knowledge and subsequent failure to comply are necessary before a conviction under the ordinance can stand. As Holmes wrote in The Common Law, "A law which punished conduct which would not be blameworthy in the average member of the community would be too severe for that community to bear." Id., at 50. Its severity lies in the absence of an opportunity either to avoid the consequences of the law or to defend any prosecution brought under it. Where a person did not know of the duty to register and where there was no proof of the probability of such knowledge, he may not be convicted consistently with due process. Were it otherwise, the evil would be as great as it is when the law is written in print too fine to read or in a language foreign to the community. . . .

Justice BURTON dissents because he believes that, as applied to this appellant, the ordinance does not violate her constitutional rights.

Justice FRANKFURTER, whom Justice HARLAN and Justice WHITTAKER join, dissenting.

The present laws of the United States and of the forty-eight States are thick with provisions that command that some things not be done and others be done, although persons convicted under such provisions may have had no awareness of what the law required or that what they did was wrongdoing. The body of decisions sustaining such legislation, including innumerable registration laws, is almost as voluminous as the legislation itself. The matter is summarized in United States v. Balint, 258 U.S. 250, 252: "Many instances of this are to be found in regulatory measures in the exercise of what is called the police power where the emphasis of the statute is evidently upon achievement of some social betterment rather than the punishment of the crimes as in cases of *mala in se.*"

Surely there can hardly be a difference as a matter of fairness, of hardship, or of justice, if one may invoke it, between the case of a person wholly innocent of wrongdoing, in the sense that he was not remotely conscious of violating any law, who is imprisoned for five years for conduct relating to narcotics [as in *Balint*], and the case of another person who is placed on probation for three years on condition that she pay $250, for failure . . . to register under a law passed as an exercise of the State's "police power." Considerations of hardship often lead courts, naturally enough, to attribute to a statute the requirement of a certain mental element — some consciousness of wrongdoing and knowledge of the law's command — as a matter of statutory construction. . . .

But what the Court here does is to draw a constitutional line between a State's requirement of doing and not doing. What is this but a return to Year Book distinctions between feasance and nonfeasance — a distinction that may have significance in the evolution of common-law notions of liability, but is inadmissible as a line between constitutionality and unconstitutionality. . . .

If the generalization that underlies . . . this decision were to be given its relevant scope, a whole volume of the United States Reports would be required to document in detail the legislation in this country that would fall or be impaired. I abstain from entering upon a consideration of such legislation . . . because I feel confident that the present decision will turn out to be an isolated deviation from the strong current of precedents — a derelict on the waters of the law. Accordingly, I content myself with dissenting.

Notes and Questions

1. So far, *Lambert* is the closest the Supreme Court has ever come to holding that due process requires the government to prove some form of *mens rea* in order to convict a person of a crime. How close is it? The decision appears to bar convictions of those who are "wholly passive and unaware of any wrongdoing," which sounds important. But the first part of the phrase just quoted limits the second. At most, the Court's decision forbids punishing defendants for failure to fulfill some affirmative legal obligation when the defendant is reasonably unaware of the obligation.

That principle would not apply to cases like United States v. Dotterweich, 320 U.S. 277 (1943), excerpted supra at page 248, or United States v. Hong, 242 F.3d 528 (4th Cir. 2001), discussed supra at page 251. Like *Lambert*, *Dotterweich* and *Hong* involved a form of strict liability, but the defendants in the latter two cases were punished for affirmative conduct—shipping adulterated drugs in *Dotterweich*, releasing untreated waste into the local sewage system in *Hong*—not for omissions. Moreover, the defendants in *Dotterweich* and *Hong* might reasonably have been expected to know—at least more so than *Lambert*—about their legal obligations.

Nor does *Lambert* cast any doubt on People v. Marrero, 507 N.E.2d 1068 (N.Y. 1987), excerpted supra at page 157. *Marrero* is a classic application of the principle that ignorance of criminality is no defense. *Lambert* is at odds with that principle, but only in omissions cases. And *Marrero* is not a pure omissions case: The defendant committed the act of bringing a gun to a New York City club. It seems reasonably clear that Justice Frankfurter exaggerated when he claimed that "a whole volume of the United States Reports would be required to document" the legislation *Lambert* would invalidate.

2. Another Frankfurter claim has proved prescient. Judging by the infrequency with which the case is cited, *Lambert* has indeed become "a derelict on the waters of the law." No substantial line of cases rests on *Lambert*; no body of law has arisen from Justice Douglas' opinion. *Lambert* remains a source not of legal doctrine but of legal arguments—a signpost that marks a doctrinal road not taken.

3. In light of *Lambert*, consider United States v. Wilson, 159 F.3d 280 (7th Cir. 1998). During the course of a traffic stop, police officers found two guns in Wilson's pickup truck and a third on his person. Having physically abused and threatened his soon-to-be ex-wife in the past, Wilson was subject to a protective order at the time he was stopped. He was subsequently charged with violating 18 U.S.C. §922(g)(8), which reads, in relevant part:

> It shall be unlawful for any person . . . who is subject to a court order that (A) was issued after a hearing of which such person received actual notice, and at which such person had an opportunity to participate; (B) restrains such

person from harassing, stalking, or threatening an intimate partner of such person or child of such intimate partner or person, or engaging in other conduct that would place an intimate partner in reasonable fear of bodily injury to the partner or child; and (C)(i) includes a finding that such person represents a credible threat to the physical safety of such intimate partner or child; or (ii) by its terms explicitly prohibits the use, attempted use, or threatened use of physical force against such intimate partner or child that would reasonably be expected to cause bodily injury . . . [to] possess in or affecting commerce, any firearm. . . .

18 U.S.C. §924(a)(2) authorizes prison terms for all who "knowingly" violate section 922(g). Wilson plainly had notice of the protective order, which he did not oppose. But he was not told that the law required him to dispose of any firearms in his possession. Nevertheless, Wilson was convicted and sentenced to 41 months in prison.

On appeal, Wilson argued that his conviction was unconstitutional under *Lambert*. Writing for two of the three members of a Seventh Circuit panel, Judge Bauer disagreed:

> To the extent that Wilson is arguing that language used in §922(g)(8) does not give adequate notice of the conduct it makes illegal, he is incorrect. . . . A statute must be struck down when it is not "sufficiently explicit to inform those who are subject to it what conduct on their part will render them liable to its penalties." Bouie v. Columbia, 378 U.S. 347, 351 (1964). An examination of the language of §922(g)(8) shows that it does not suffer from any such deficiencies. It clearly specifies that individuals subject to certain types of protective orders may not ship or transport firearms or ammunition in or affecting commerce. The class of affected individuals is explicitly defined, as is the conduct sought to be regulated, and the statute is not unconstitutionally vague.
>
> To the extent that Wilson is arguing that he was unaware of the law and that his conviction therefore cannot stand, he is [again] incorrect. The traditional rule in American jurisprudence is that ignorance of the law is no defense to a criminal prosecution. Cheek v. United States, 498 U.S. 192, 199 (1991); see also Bryan v. United States, 524 U.S. 184 (1998) (traditional rule is that "ignorance of the law is no excuse"); Lambert v. California, 355 U.S. 225, 228 (1957) (rule that "ignorance of the law will not excuse" is deeply rooted in American law). Wilson has not shown that the present statute falls into an exception to this general rule, see *Bryan*, 524 U.S. at 194 (noting exception for "highly technical statutes that present[] the danger of ensnaring individuals engaged in apparently innocent conduct"), and *Lambert*, 355 U.S. at 228 (notice required when penalty may be exacted for failing to act), and the fact that he was unaware of the existence of §922(g)(8) does not render his conviction erroneous.

159 F.3d at 288-89. Chief Judge Posner concluded that Wilson's argument had merit:

[Section 922(g)] was enacted in 1994 and the number of prosecutions for violating it has been minuscule (perhaps fewer than 10, though I have not been able to discover the exact number, which is not a reported statistic) in relation to the probable number of violations. I estimate that every year the law has been in effect almost one hundred thousand restraining orders against domestic violence have been issued (estimated from Patricia Tjaden & Nancy Thoenes, Stalking in America: Findings From the National Violence Against Women Survey 3, 6, 12 (U.S. Dept. of Justice, April 1998); Adele Harrell & Barbara E. Smith, "Effects of Restraining Orders on Domestic Violence Victims," in Do Arrests and Restraining Orders Work? 219 (Eve S. Buzawa & Carl G. Buzawa eds. 1996)). Since 40 percent of U.S. households own guns, there can be very little doubt that a large percentage of those orders were issued against gun owners.

How many of these gun owners, when they got notice of the restraining order, dispossessed themselves of their guns? I doubt that any did. The law is *malum prohibitum*, not *malum in se*; that is, it is not the kind of law that a lay person would intuit existed because the conduct it forbade was contrary to the moral code of his society. Yet the Department of Justice took no steps to publicize the existence of the law until long after Wilson violated it. . . . At argument the prosecutor told us that the Office of the U.S. Attorney for the Southern District of Illinois has made no effort to advise the local judiciary of the law. . . .

The federal criminal code contains thousands of separate prohibitions, many ridiculously obscure, such as the one against using the coat of arms of Switzerland in advertising, 18 U.S.C. §708, or using "Johnny Horizon" as a trade name without the authorization of the Department of the Interior. 18 U.S.C. §714. The prohibition in section 922(g)(8) is one of the most obscure. A person owns a hunting rifle. He knows or should know that if he is convicted of a felony he will have to get rid of the gun; if he doesn't know, the judge or the probation service will tell him. But should he be made subject to a restraining order telling him to keep away from his ex-wife, whom he has *not* ever threatened with his hunting rifle . . . , it will not occur to him that he must give up the gun unless the judge issuing the order tells him. The judge didn't tell Wilson; so far as appears, the judge was unaware of the law. Wilson's lawyer didn't tell him either—Wilson didn't have a lawyer. No one told him. . . .

. . . The purpose of criminal laws is to bring about compliance with desired norms of behavior. In the present case it is to reduce domestic violence by getting guns out of the hands of people who are behaving menacingly toward (in the usual case) an estranged or former spouse. This purpose is ill served by keeping the law a secret, which has been the practical upshot of the Department of Justice's failure—until too late, at least for Wilson—either to enforce the law vigorously or to notify the relevant state officials of the law's existence. In such circumstances the law is not a deterrent. It is a trap.

159 F.3d at 294-95 (Posner, C.J., dissenting). Posner concluded that convictions in cases like *Wilson* should be upheld only if the government proved knowledge of illegality—which it could not possibly prove in *Wilson*. Was Posner right? Was Wilson's conviction fair?

4. If proof of some form of criminal intent were constitutionally necessary, what intent would be required? Knowledge of illegality is not the most common form of *mens rea* prosecutors must prove. Should due process instead require proof of intentional conduct? Criminal negligence? Something else? Recall Staples v. United States, 511 U.S. 600 (1994), excerpted at page 262, and Cheek v. United States, 498 U.S. 192 (1991), discussed at page 274. Roughly speaking, and whenever *Staples* and *Cheek* apply, those two decisions hold that, in order to convict, federal prosecutors must prove knowledge of all facts as well as the law that rendered the defendant's conduct illegal. Formally, *Staples* and *Cheek* are statutory interpretation decisions, meaning that Congress is free to overrule them (as Congress actually did with respect to the nearly identical decision in Ratzlaf v. United States, 510 U.S. 65 (1994), see supra, at page 276). Should the *mens rea* holdings in *Staples* and *Cheek* instead define a constitutional standard that Congress is *not* free to overturn?

Montana v. Egelhoff

Supreme Court of the United States
518 U.S. 37 (1996)

Justice SCALIA announced the judgment of the Court and delivered an opinion in which Chief Justice REHNQUIST, Justice KENNEDY, and Justice THOMAS join.

We consider in this case whether the Due Process Clause is violated by Montana Code Annotated §45-2-203, which provides, in relevant part, that voluntary intoxication "may not be taken into consideration in determining the existence of a mental state which is an element of [a criminal] offense."

I

In July 1992, while camping out in the Yaak region of northwestern Montana to pick mushrooms, respondent made friends with Roberta Pavola and John Christenson, who were doing the same. On Sunday, July 12, the three sold the mushrooms they had collected and spent the rest of the day and evening drinking, in bars and at a private party in Troy, Montana. Some time after 9 P.M., they left the party in Christenson's 1974 Ford Galaxy station wagon. The drinking binge apparently continued, as respondent was seen buying beer at 9:20 P.M. and recalled "sitting on a hill or a bank passing a bottle of Black Velvet back and forth" with Christenson. 900 P.2d 260, 262 (1995).

At about midnight that night, officers of the Lincoln County, Montana, sheriff's department, responding to reports of a possible drunk driver, discovered Christenson's station wagon stuck in a ditch along U.S. Highway 2. In the front seat were Pavola and Christenson, each dead from a single gunshot to the head. In the rear of the car lay respondent, alive and yelling obscenities. His blood-alcohol content measured .36 percent over one hour later. On the floor of the car, near the brake pedal, lay respondent's .38 caliber handgun, with four loaded rounds and two empty casings; respondent had gunshot residue on his hands.

Respondent was charged with two counts of deliberate homicide, a crime defined by Montana law as "purposely" or "knowingly" causing the death of another human being. Mont. Code Ann. §45-5-102. A portion of the jury charge, uncontested here, instructed that "[a] person acts purposely when it is his conscious object to engage in conduct of that nature or to cause such a result," and that "[a] person acts knowingly when he is aware of his conduct or when he is aware under the circumstances his conduct constitutes a crime; or, when he is aware there exists the high probability that his conduct will cause a specific result." Respondent's defense at trial was that an unidentified fourth person must have committed the murders; his own extreme intoxication, he claimed, had rendered him physically incapable of committing the murders, and accounted for his inability to recall the events of the night of July 12. Although respondent was allowed to make this use of the evidence that he was intoxicated, the jury was instructed, pursuant to Mont. Code Ann. §45-2-203, that it could not consider respondent's "intoxicated condition . . . in determining the existence of a mental state which is an element of the offense." The jury found respondent guilty on both counts, and the court sentenced him to 84 years' imprisonment.

The Supreme Court of Montana reversed. It reasoned (1) that respondent "had a due process right to present and have considered by the jury all relevant evidence to rebut the State's evidence on all elements of the offense charged," 900 P.2d, at 266, and (2) that evidence of respondent's voluntary intoxication was "clearly . . . relevant to the issue of whether [respondent] acted knowingly and purposely," id., at 265. Because §45-2-203 prevented the jury from considering that evidence with regard to that issue, the court concluded that the State had been "relieved of part of its burden to prove beyond a reasonable doubt every fact necessary to constitute the crime charged," id., at 266, and that respondent had therefore been denied due process. We granted certiorari.

II

The cornerstone of the Montana Supreme Court's judgment was the proposition that the Due Process Clause guarantees a defendant the right to present and have considered by the jury "*all relevant evidence* to rebut the State's evidence on all elements of the offense charged." 900 P.2d, at 266 (emphasis added). Respondent does not defend this categorical rule; he acknowledges that the right to present relevant evidence "has not been viewed as absolute." Brief for Respondent 31. That is a wise concession, since the proposition that the Due Process Clause guarantees the right to introduce all relevant evidence is simply indefensible. As we have said: "The accused does not have an unfettered right to offer [evidence] that is incompetent, privileged, or otherwise inadmissible under standard rules of evidence." Taylor v. Illinois, 484 U.S. 400, 410 (1988). . . . [A]ny number of familiar and unquestionably constitutional evidentiary rules also authorize the exclusion of relevant evidence. For example, Federal (and Montana) Rule of Evidence 403 provides: "*Although relevant*, evidence may be excluded if its probative value is substantially outweighed by the danger of unfair prejudice, confusion of the issues, or misleading the jury, or by considerations of undue delay, waste of time, or needless presentation of cumulative evidence" (emphasis added). Hearsay rules similarly prohibit the introduction of testimony which, though unquestionably relevant, is deemed insufficiently reliable. Of course, to say that the right to introduce relevant evidence is not absolute is not to say that the Due Process Clause places *no* limits upon restriction of that right. But it is to say that the defendant asserting such a limit must sustain the usual heavy burden that a due process claim entails:

> "Preventing and dealing with crime is much more the business of the States than it is of the Federal Government, and . . . we should not lightly construe the Constitution so as to intrude upon the administration of justice by the individual States. Among other things, it is normally within the power of the State to regulate procedures under which its laws are carried out, . . . and its decision in this regard is not subject to proscription under the Due Process Clause unless it offends some principle of justice so rooted in the traditions and conscience of our people as to be ranked as fundamental." Patterson v. New York, 432 U.S. 197, 201-02 (1977).

Respondent's task, then, is to establish that a defendant's right to have a jury consider evidence of his voluntary intoxication in determining whether he possesses the requisite mental state is a "fundamental principle of justice."

Our primary guide in determining whether the principle in question is fundamental is, of course, historical practice. Here that gives respondent little support. By the laws of England, wrote Hale, the intoxicated defendant "shall have no privilege by this voluntary contracted madness, but shall have the same judgment as if he were in his right senses." 1 M. Hale, Pleas of the Crown *32-33. . . . Blackstone, citing Coke, explained that the law viewed intoxication "as an aggravation of the offence, rather than as an excuse for any criminal misbehaviour." 4 W. Blackstone, Commentaries *25-26. This stern rejection of inebriation as a defense became a fixture of early

American law as well. . . . In an opinion citing the foregoing passages from Blackstone and Hale, Justice Story rejected an objection to the exclusion of evidence of intoxication as follows:

> "This is the first time, that I ever remember it to have been contended, that the commission of one crime was an excuse for another. Drunkenness is a gross vice, and in the contemplation of some of our laws is a crime; and I learned in my earlier studies, that so far from its being in law an excuse for murder, it is rather an aggravation of its malignity." United States v. Cornell, 25 F. Cas. 650, 657-58 (C.C.R.I. 1820).

The historical record does not leave room for the view that the common law's rejection of intoxication as an "excuse" or "justification" for crime would nonetheless permit the defendant to show that intoxication prevented the requisite *mens rea*. Hale, Coke, and Blackstone were familiar, to say the least, with the concept of *mens rea*, and acknowledged that drunkenness "deprive[s] men of the use of reason," 1 Hale, supra, at *32. . . . Hale's statement that a drunken offender shall have the same judgment "as if he were in his right senses" must be understood as precluding a defendant from arguing that, because of his intoxication, he could not have possessed the *mens rea* required to commit the crime. . . .

Against this extensive evidence of a lengthy common-law tradition decidedly against him, the best argument available to respondent is the one made by his *amicus* and conceded by the State: Over the course of the 19th century, courts carved out an exception to the common law's traditional across-the-board condemnation of the drunken offender, allowing a jury to consider a defendant's intoxication when assessing whether he possessed the mental state needed to commit the crime charged, where the crime was one requiring a "specific intent." . . .

On the basis of this historical record, respondent's *amicus* argues that "the old common-law rule . . . was no longer deeply rooted at the time the Fourteenth Amendment was ratified." Brief for National Association of Criminal Defense Lawyers as Amicus Curiae 23. That conclusion is questionable, but we need not pursue the point, since the argument of *amicus* mistakes the nature of our inquiry. It is not the State which bears the burden of demonstrating that its rule is "deeply rooted," but rather respondent who must show that the principle of procedure *violated* by the rule (and allegedly required by due process) is "so rooted in the traditions and conscience of our people as to be ranked as fundamental." *Patterson*, 432 U.S. at 202. . . . The burden remains upon respondent to show that the "new common-law" rule—that intoxication may be considered on the question of intent—was so deeply rooted at the time of the Fourteenth Amendment (or perhaps has become so deeply rooted since) as to be a fundamental principle which that Amendment enshrined.

That showing has not been made. Instead of the uniform and continuing acceptance we would expect for a rule that enjoys "fundamental principle" status, we find that fully one-fifth of the States either never adopted the "new common-law" rule at issue here or have recently abandoned it.[2] . . .

It is not surprising that many States have held fast to or resurrected the common-law rule prohibiting consideration of voluntary intoxication in the determination of *mens rea*, because that rule has considerable justification. . . . A large number of crimes, especially violent crimes, are committed by intoxicated offenders; modern studies put the numbers as high as half of all homicides, for example. Disallowing consideration of voluntary intoxication has the effect of increasing the punishment for all unlawful acts committed in that state, and thereby deters drunkenness or irresponsible behavior while drunk. The rule also serves as a specific deterrent, ensuring that those who prove incapable of controlling violent impulses while voluntarily intoxicated go to prison. And finally, the rule comports with and implements society's moral perception that one who has voluntarily impaired his own faculties should be responsible for the consequences. . . .

In sum, not every widespread experiment with a procedural rule favorable to criminal defendants establishes a fundamental principle of justice. Although the rule allowing a jury to consider evidence of a defendant's voluntary intoxication where relevant to *mens rea* has gained considerable acceptance, it is of too recent vintage, and has not received sufficiently uniform and permanent allegiance, to qualify as fundamental, especially since it displaces a lengthy common law tradition which remains supported by valid justifications today.

III

. . . In re Winship, 397 U.S. 358, 364 (1970), announced the proposition that the Due Process Clause requires proof beyond a reasonable doubt of every fact necessary to constitute the charged crime, and Sandstrom v. Montana, 442 U.S. 510, 524 (1979), established a corollary, that a jury instruction which shifts to the defendant the burden of proof on a requisite element of mental state violates due process. These decisions simply are not implicated here because, as the Montana court itself recognized, "the burden is not shifted" under §45-2-203. 900 P.2d, at 266. The trial judge instructed the

2. Besides Montana, those States are Arizona, see Ariz. Rev. Stat. Ann. §13-503 (voluntary intoxication "is not a defense for any criminal act or requisite state of mind"); Arkansas, see White v. State, 717 S.W.2d 784, 786-88 (1986) (interpreting Ark. Code Ann. §5-2-207); Delaware, see Wyant v. State, 519 A.2d 649, 651 (1986) (interpreting Del. Code. Ann., Tit. 11, §421); Georgia, see Foster v. State, 374 S.E.2d 188, 194-96 (1988) (interpreting Ga. Code Ann. §16-3-4); Hawaii, see Haw. Rev. Stat. §702-230(2); Mississippi, see Lanier v. State, 533 So. 2d 473, 478-79; Missouri, see Mo. Rev. Stat. §562.076; South Carolina, see State v. Vaughn, 232 S.E.2d 328, 330-31 (1977); and Texas, see Hawkins v. State, 605 S.W.2d 586, 589 (Tex. Crim. App. 1980) (interpreting Tex. Penal Code Ann. §8.04).

jury that "the State of Montana has the burden of proving the guilt of the Defendant beyond a reasonable doubt," and that "[a] person commits the offense of deliberate homicide if he purposely or knowingly causes the death of another human being." Thus, failure by the State to produce evidence of respondent's mental state would have resulted in an acquittal. That acquittal did not occur was presumably attributable to the fact . . . that the State introduced considerable evidence from which the jury might have concluded that respondent acted "purposely" or "knowingly." For example, respondent himself testified that, several hours before the murders, he had given his handgun to Pavola and asked her to put it in the glove compartment of Christenson's car. That he had to retrieve the gun from the glove compartment before he used it was strong evidence that it was his "conscious object" to commit the charged crimes; as was the execution-style manner in which a single shot was fired into the head of each victim. . . .

. . . The people of Montana have decided to resurrect the rule of an earlier era, disallowing consideration of voluntary intoxication when a defendant's state of mind is at issue. Nothing in the Due Process Clause prevents them from doing so, and the judgment of the Supreme Court of Montana to the contrary must be reversed.

Justice GINSBURG, concurring in the judgment.

The Court divides in this case on a question of characterization. The State's law, Mont. Code Ann. §45-2-203, prescribes that voluntary intoxication "may not be taken into consideration in determining the existence of a mental state which is an element of [a criminal] offense.". . . If §45-2-203 is simply a rule designed to keep out "relevant, exculpatory evidence," Justice O'Connor maintains, Montana's law offends due process. If it is, instead, a redefinition of the mental state element of the offense, on the other hand, Justice O'Connor's due process concern "would not be at issue," for "[a] state legislature certainly has the authority to identify the elements of the offenses it wishes to punish," and to exclude evidence irrelevant to the crime it has defined.

Beneath the labels (rule excluding evidence or redefinition of the offense) lies the essential question: Can a State, without offense to the Federal Constitution, make the judgment that two people are equally culpable where one commits an act stone sober, and the other engages in the same conduct after his voluntary intoxication has reduced his capacity for self-control? . . .

Section 45-2-203 does not appear in the portion of Montana's Code containing evidentiary rules (Title 26), the expected placement of a provision regulating solely the admissibility of evidence at trial. Instead, Montana's intoxication statute appears in Title 45 ("Crimes"), as part of a chapter entitled "General Principles of Liability." Mont. Code Ann., Tit. 45, ch. 2. No less than adjacent provisions governing duress and entrapment, §45-2-203 embodies a legislative judgment regarding the circumstances under which individuals may be held criminally responsible for their actions.

As urged by Montana and its *amici*, §45-2-203 "extract[s] the entire subject of voluntary intoxication from the *mens rea* inquiry," Reply Brief for Petitioner 2. . . . Thus, in a prosecution for deliberate homicide, the State need not prove that the defendant "purposely or knowingly caused the death of another," Mont. Code Ann. §45-5-102[(1)](a), in a purely subjective sense. To obtain a conviction, the prosecution must prove only that (1) the defendant caused the death of another with actual knowledge or purpose, *or* (2) that the defendant killed "under circumstances that would otherwise establish knowledge or purpose but for [the defendant's] voluntary intoxication." Brief for American Alliance for Rights and Responsibilities et al. as *Amici Curiae* 6. Accordingly, §45-2-203 does not "lighten the prosecution's burden to prove [the] mental state element beyond a reasonable doubt," as Justice O'Connor suggests, for "the applicability of the reasonable-doubt standard . . . has always been dependent on how a State defines the offense that is charged," Patterson v. New York, 432 U.S. 197, 211, n.12 (1977).

Comprehended as a measure redefining *mens rea*, §45-2-203 encounters no constitutional shoal. States enjoy wide latitude in defining the elements of criminal offenses, particularly when determining "the extent to which moral culpability should be a prerequisite to conviction of a crime," Powell v. Texas, 392 U.S. 514, 545 (1968) (Black, J., concurring). When a State's power to define criminal conduct is challenged under the Due Process Clause, we inquire only whether the law "offends some principle of justice so rooted in the traditions and conscience of our people as to be ranked as fundamental." *Patterson*, 432 U.S. at 202. Defining *mens rea* to eliminate the exculpatory value of voluntary intoxication does not offend a "fundamental principle of justice," given the lengthy common-law tradition and the adherence of a significant minority of the States to that position today. . . .

Justice O'CONNOR, with whom Justice STEVENS, Justice SOUTER, and Justice BREYER join, dissenting.

. . . Due process demands that a criminal defendant be afforded a fair opportunity to defend against the State's accusations. Meaningful adversarial testing of the State's case requires that the defendant not be prevented from raising an effective defense, which must include the right to present relevant, probative evidence. To be sure, the right to present evidence is not limitless; for example, it does not permit the defendant to introduce any and all evidence he believes might work in his favor, nor does it generally invalidate the operation of testimonial privileges. Nevertheless, "an essential component of procedural fairness is an opportunity to be heard. That opportunity would be an empty one if the State were permitted to exclude competent, reliable evidence" that is essential to the accused's defense. Crane v. Kentucky, 476 U.S. 683, 690 (1986).

Section 45-2-203 forestalls the defendant's ability to raise an effective defense by placing a blanket exclusion on the presentation of a type of evidence that directly negates an element of the crime, and by doing so, it lightens the prosecution's burden to prove that mental-state element beyond a reasonable doubt.

. . . A state legislature certainly has the authority to identify the elements of the offenses it wishes to punish, but once its laws are written, a defendant has the right to insist that the State prove beyond a reasonable doubt every element of an offense charged. "The Due Process Clause protects the accused against conviction except upon proof beyond a reasonable doubt of every fact necessary to constitute the crime with which he is charged." In re Winship, 397 U.S. 358, 364 (1970). Because the Montana Legislature has specified that a person commits "deliberate homicide" only if he "purposely or knowingly causes the death of another human being," Mont. Code Ann. §45-5-102(1)(a), the prosecution must prove the existence of such mental state in order to convict. That is, unless the defendant is shown to have acted purposely or knowingly, *he is not guilty of the offense of deliberate homicide.* The Montana Supreme Court found that it was inconsistent with the legislature's requirement of the mental state of "purposely" or "knowingly" to prevent the jury from considering evidence of voluntary intoxication. . . . 900 P.2d, at 265-66.

Where the defendant may introduce evidence to negate a subjective mental-state element, the prosecution must work to overcome whatever doubts the defense has raised about the existence of the required mental state. On the other hand, if the defendant may *not* introduce evidence that might create doubt in the factfinder's mind as to whether that element was met, the prosecution will find its job so much the easier. A subjective mental state is generally proved only circumstantially. If a jury may not consider the defendant's evidence of his mental state, the jury may impute to the defendant the culpability of a mental state he did not possess.

In Martin v. Ohio, 480 U.S. 228 (1987), the Court considered an Ohio statute providing that a defendant bore the burden of proving, by a preponderance of the evidence, an affirmative defense such as self-defense. We held that placing that burden on the defendant did not violate due process. The Court noted in explanation that it would nevertheless have been error to instruct the jury that "self-defense evidence could not be considered in determining whether there was a reasonable doubt about the State's case" where Ohio's definition of the intent element made self-defense evidence relevant to the State's burden. Id., at 233-34. "Such an instruction would relieve the State of its burden and plainly run afoul of *Winship*'s mandate." Id., at 234. In other words, the State's right to shift the burden of proving an affirmative defense did not include the power to prevent the defendant from attempting to prove self-defense in an effort to cast doubt on the State's case. . . .

. . . I would afford more weight to principles enunciated in our case law than is accorded in the plurality's opinion today. It seems to me that a State may not first determine the elements of the crime it wishes to punish, and then thwart the accused's defense by categorically disallowing the very evidence that would prove him innocent. . . .

Justice BREYER, with whom Justice STEVENS joins, dissenting.

. . . As [Justice O'Connor's] dissent says, . . . the Montana Supreme Court did not understand Montana's statute to have redefined the mental element of deliberate homicide. In my view, however, this circumstance is not simply . . . a technical matter that deprives us of the power to uphold that statute. To have read the statute differently—to treat it as if it had redefined the mental element—would produce anomalous results. A statute that makes voluntary intoxication the legal equivalent of purpose or knowledge *but only where external circumstances would establish purpose or knowledge in the absence of intoxication*, is a statute that turns guilt or innocence not upon state of mind, but upon irrelevant external circumstances. An intoxicated driver stopped at an intersection who unknowingly accelerated into a pedestrian would likely be found guilty, for a jury unaware of intoxication would likely infer knowledge or purpose. An identically intoxicated driver racing along a highway who unknowingly sideswiped another car would likely be found innocent, for a jury unaware of intoxication would likely infer negligence. Why would a legislature want to write a statute that draws such a distinction, upon which a sentence of life imprisonment, or death, may turn? If the legislature wanted to equate voluntary intoxication, knowledge, and purpose, why would it not write a statute that plainly says so, instead of doing so in a roundabout manner that would affect, in dramatically different ways, those whose minds, deeds, and consequences seem identical? I would reserve the question of whether or not such a hypothetical statute might exceed constitutional limits.

[Justice SOUTER's dissenting opinion is omitted.]

Notes and Questions

1. *Egelhoff* begins with two constitutional guarantees and one state power. Due process requires that, in order to convict, the government prove criminal defendants' guilt beyond a reasonable doubt. In re Winship, 397 U.S. 358 (1970). According to the defendant, Montana's bar on intoxication evidence amounts to an evasion of the beyond-a-reasonable-doubt standard: The government gets to prove *mens rea* without the need to address contrary evidence. Due process also requires that the defendant be permitted to introduce relevant evidence in his defense. Chambers v. Mississippi, 410

U.S. 284 (1973). Intoxication evidence is obviously relevant in *Egelhoff*, so the state's ban on that evidence prevents the defendant from contesting the homicide charges. The state power is familiar: Legislators may define crimes, including *mens rea* standards, as they wish. According to the state, Montana Code §45-2-203 merely defines the governing *mens rea* standard: Behavior that would count as intentional if done by a sober person still counts as intentional if done by one who is drunk.

   2. Consider the argument in Justice Breyer's dissent. Should Egelhoff be punished as severely as a defendant who killed when sober? If so, why? If not, what role should intoxication evidence play in murder cases?

   3. Imagine the following rule: State legislatures may define the mental state required for criminal conviction however they wish—but criminal defendants may offer whatever evidence and arguments *they* wish to negate that mental state. Would that rule work? What result would it produce in *Egelhoff?*

E. THE "EQUAL PROTECTION OF THE LAWS"

The constitutional right that might have had the largest effect on American criminal justice concerns neither the law of *mens rea*, nor the vagueness of criminal prohibitions, nor the privacy of choices having to do with sex and reproduction. The chief concern of the right to the "equal protection of the laws" is race, not sex; the right's intended beneficiaries were crime victims, not criminal defendants. Had that right been construed and applied as its authors expected, the consequences for criminal law enforcement might have been large indeed. But the law followed another path—so the story of equal protection is another story of what might have been.

   The heart of that story took place in the dozen years after the Civil War ended. Section 1 tells the tale, briefly. Sections 2 and 3 turn to contemporary legal doctrine, exploring the meaning of "equal" and of the phrase it modifies: the "protection of the laws."

1. The Rise and Fall of Equal Protection

On May 1, 1866—just over a year after the Civil War's end—two carriages collided in Memphis, Tennessee. One of the two drivers was black. This thoroughly ordinary accident triggered a three-day riot in which four dozen people were killed, several women raped, and a host of houses and businesses destroyed. Nearly all the victims of this violence were black; the perpetrators included a large fraction of the city's white police officers and firemen. The following July 30, a similar riot took place in New Orleans. Louisiana's Governor had called the state's Unionist constitutional convention back into session. (Near the war's conclusion, that convention had drafted the state constitution that Abraham Lincoln saw as a model for a reconstructed South.) New Orleans blacks were marching toward the convention center in support of black suffrage, which the convention was expected to endorse. Some of the blacks were armed. When local whites threw bricks at the marchers, a few responded by firing into the white crowd. At that point, white police officers attacked the marchers, killing 34 blacks and wounding more than one hundred. Four whites were killed in the mêlée.

Six weeks after the Memphis massacre and a month before the one in New Orleans, Congress voted to submit the Fourteenth Amendment to the states for ratification. Section One of the Amendment reads as follows:

> All persons born or naturalized within the United States, and subject to the jurisdiction thereof, are citizens of the United States and of the State wherein they reside. No State shall make or enforce any law which shall abridge the privileges or immunities of citizens of the United States; nor shall any State deprive any person of life, liberty, or property without due process of law; nor deny to any person within its jurisdiction the equal protection of the laws.

Section Two declared that, in any state in which blacks are denied the right to vote, the number of representatives and electoral votes must be reduced in proportion to the number of voters disenfranchised. (Section Two would have had large consequences for twentieth-century American politics had it been enforced—which it never was.) Section Three barred ex-Confederate officials from holding political office, absent a congressional pardon. Section Four forbade payment of Confederate government debts, and Section Five authorized Congress "to enforce, by appropriate legislation, the provisions of this [Amendment]." At the time the Amendment was written and ratified—it became law in 1868—Sections Two and Three were its most contested provisions. Section One turned out to matter most.

In part, Section One of the Fourteenth Amendment was designed to undo the South's Black Codes. In the Civil War's wake, ex-Confederate states enacted legislation binding ex-slaves to their employers in the manner of indentured servants. Blacks were not allowed to quit their jobs, and their employers could use physical punishments to discipline them: a form of quasi-slavery to take the place of the institution that Lincoln's proclamation abolished.* In March 1866, Congress enacted the first Civil Rights Act, which did overturn the Black Codes, by guaranteeing blacks and whites the same rights to make contracts and own property. Then-President Andrew Johnson vetoed the Act, after which Congress overrode his veto on April 9. By that

---

* Before the Thirteenth Amendment abolished slavery nationwide, the Emancipation Proclamation abolished it in the portions of the Confederacy that Union armies did not hold in January 1863. As a practical matter, the Proclamation applied to 9 of the Confederacy's 11 states—all save for Tennessee and Louisiana, most of which Union armies then occupied.

time, the Fourteenth Amendment was already in the works. Along with many of his colleagues, the Amendment's chief author—Ohio Congressman John Bingham—was concerned about the constitutionality of the Civil Rights Act while that legislation was still being drafted. The Amendment's "Privileges or Immunities" and Due Process Clauses, plus Section Five's grant of power to Congress to enforce those clauses, were intended to render the Civil Rights Act immune to constitutional challenge.

The Equal Protection Clause had another purpose: to address mob "justice" of the sort embodied by the Memphis and New Orleans massacres. In both of those murderous incidents, white police officers' job was to protect black residents of the cities they patrolled; instead of doing that job, officers killed those they were supposed to serve. Note: The murders themselves did not violate the equal protection guarantee, at least not directly. Rather, the constitutional violation was the failure to prevent those murders from happening—the officers' failure to enforce the law to protect black victims against violence the officers themselves perpetrated.

Even in 1866, the idea that the government owed all its citizens the "protection of the laws" was an old one. As Blackstone had put the point a century before: "[T]he community should guard the rights of each individual member, and . . . (in return for the protection) each individual should submit to the laws of the community." 1 William Blackstone, Commentaries on the Law of England *124 (1769). To use a leading legal historian's more compact terms: "In the shorthand of the era, allegiance is the obligation of the citizen and protection the obligation of the sovereign." Earl M. Maltz, The Concept of Equal Protection of the Laws—A Historical Inquiry, 22 San Diego L. Rev. 499, 507 (1985). Mass murders like those in Memphis and New Orleans plainly denied that right. When white police officers did the killing, there was no doubt about the government's complicity in the massacre of ex-slaves.

Government officials' responsibility was less clear when private citizens were the murderers—as happened increasingly often when, beginning in the late 1860s, Republican governments took control of southern cities and towns. A congressional investigation found that from the spring of 1868 through that year's November presidential election, more than one thousand political murders—nearly all of them by white killers against black victims—were committed in Louisiana alone. Charles Lane, The Day Freedom Died: The Colfax Massacre, the Supreme Court, and the Betrayal of Reconstruction 18-19 (2008). Counting only those killings, the state had an annual murder rate in excess of 178 per 100,000 population: more than 16 times the nation's peak twentieth-century murder rate, a staggering 31 times today's murder rate. Those thousand-plus murders happened when the state and most of its parishes were governed, at least officially, by Republicans. Government officials and their allies were not the perpetrators of this crime wave. They were its victims.

That set the pattern for the southern violence of the 1870s, as the most famous Reconstruction massacre illustrates. In the Red River valley in central Louisiana, Republicans had carved a new black-majority parish from sections of neighboring jurisdictions, naming the parish after President Grant and its capital after Grant's first Vice-President, Schuyler Colfax. After the 1872 elections, both Republicans and Democrats claimed control of the state and of Grant Parish. Hoping to forestall a Democratic takeover, approximately 150 black men and several dozen black women occupied the parish courthouse, along with two white men named Shaw and Register who then served as local sheriff and judge, respectively. The two whites and most of the women left the courthouse before the killing began, but not before Shaw deputized the black men who remained behind to protect parish property. These temporary deputies—agents of the lawful local government—were armed with shotguns and a few pistols. They dug a shallow trench around the courthouse for protection. Several hundred whites, armed with Enfield rifles and a cannon, took up positions near the courthouse.

On April 13, 1873—Easter Sunday—the whites attacked. Cannon fire on the shallow trench drove black defenders back into the building. The whites then set the courthouse on fire, and shot blacks as they fled the building. The final death toll is unknown; Charles Lane's book on the massacre and its aftermath places the number of blacks killed between 62 and 81. Three white men died, two of them killed by friendly fire. Most of the black dead were murdered either after surrendering or while trying to do so. Some died in the course of a game the killers played: lining up two or three black prisoners in a row to see how many could be executed with a single bullet. Two days after this slaughter, black bodies still littered the courthouse grounds. Passengers on a nearby steamboat reported being overwhelmed by the smell of rotting flesh. Several days after the massacre, a Deputy United States Marshal and his assistant arrived from New Orleans and turned the trench outside the courthouse into a mass grave. Louisiana officials later put up a plaque commemorating the massacre; the plaque stated that the murders at Colfax "marked the end of carpetbag misrule in the South."

Those murders did not fit the simple pattern of the police riots in Memphis and New Orleans. The perpetrators were not government officials—on the contrary, they killed government officials. At a deeper level, these three murderous rampages had much in common, with one another and with Klan violence in the Reconstruction South more generally. (The Colfax killers belonged to the White League, Louisiana's version of the Klan.) The white perpetrators of that violence sought to deprive government officials of the ability to exercise their lawful power so the perpetrators might exercise that power themselves, and use it to destroy blacks' hopes of freedom and political equality. The killers had two goals: to put an end to Republican rule by forcibly ejecting the rulers from office, and to stop blacks from voting so that Republicans could not win office again. Once they seized power in

Grant Parish, the Colfax killers did precisely what the white police officers of Memphis and New Orleans had done: killed those who most needed the law's protection.

Judged in those terms, slaughters like the one in Colfax amounted to a clear violation of the Fourteenth Amendment. Unsurprisingly, defendants in Klan prosecutions argued otherwise. Section One of the Amendment bars "any state" from denying its residents "equal protection of the laws." Klan defendants contended that neither the Amendment nor any legislation based on it could possibly apply to their behavior, since they did not exercise government power. They might be guilty of murder, arson, and assault: all state-law crimes (for which they would never be prosecuted, as they understood). But, those defendants argued, they were innocent of the federal charges brought against them under the Enforcement Act and the Ku Klux Klan Act, both of which authorized criminal punishment for violations of ex-slaves' right to equal protection. Those Acts, like the Amendment that authorized them, could apply only to government officials, not to private citizens like the Colfax killers.

That defense argument lost in a series of Klan cases in the early 1870s, most of them in South Carolina and Alabama. The leading case was United States v. Hall, 26 Fed. Cases 79 (1871), a judicial opinion authored by then-Circuit Judge and future Supreme Court Justice William Woods. Judge Woods wrote:

> [T]he Fourteenth Amendment . . . prohibits the states from denying to all persons within its jurisdiction the equal protection of the laws. Denying includes inaction as well as action, and denying the equal protection of the laws includes the omission to protect. . . . [T]o guard against the invasion of the citizen's fundamental rights, and to insure their adequate protection, as well against state legislation as state inaction, or incompetency, the Amendment gives Congress the power to enforce its provisions by appropriate legislation. And as it would be unseemly for Congress to interfere directly with state enactments, and as it cannot compel the activity of state officials, the only appropriate legislation it can make is that which will operate directly on offenders and offenses. . . .

In other words, if local officials could not stop the intimidation of black voters, the federal government could punish the intimidators. If southern blacks were victimized by violence that local authorities could neither prevent nor prosecute, federal officials could do the prosecuting. The only alternative was to have federal judges order local police to make arrests and local prosecutors to file charges — a legal impossibility in the nineteenth century.

By the end of 1872, 65 Klan members were incarcerated in federal prison, most of them put there on Woods' legal theory. Those few dozen prison sentences had large behavioral effects. Klan leaders were not like ordinary thieves and murderers; they wanted to be men of status in their society. Even a small chance of prison time was bound to be a serious deterrent to such men. Klan violence was thus a solvable problem: not like the culture wars of the twentieth century, when America's justice system sought to suppress mass markets for gambling, prostitution, alcohol, and cocaine. Those fights were destined to fail; this one was winnable. South Carolina, locus of the largest number of prosecutions, was pacified for the first time since the Civil War's end. Across the South, violence levels declined. Reconstruction appeared to have been a law enforcement success. Judging by the fall elections in 1872, it was also a political success: Pro-Reconstruction Republicans gained 63 House seats that year, and Republican President Grant won reelection by the most lopsided vote in 40 years.

Then, the political winds shifted—thanks to the economy, not changed attitudes toward Reconstruction. Less than a month after the Colfax massacre, Vienna's stock market collapsed; four months later, Jay Cooke & Company (Cooke had sold the bonds that financed the Civil War) went bankrupt. Cooke's company was the Lehman Brothers of its time; its bankruptcy triggered a panic that in turn led to a decade-long depression. As such events often do, the depression transformed American politics. The House of Representatives elected in 1872 included 199 Republicans and 88 Democrats; the 1874 election changed those figures to 103 Republicans and 182 Democrats, plus 8 members who belonged to neither party. Democrats would control the House for the next 6 years, and for 16 of the next 20. In order to regain power, Republican politicians needed to win votes now cast for Democrats. Narrowing the gap between their agenda and the agenda of their Democratic opponents was a natural political move. Reconstruction was the chief issue on which the two parties differed. So, after the 1874 elections, Republican politicians began to suggest an end to federal control of the ex-Confederate South. Two Republican Presidents—Ulysses S. Grant and Rutherford B. Hayes—pulled the last federal soldiers from the region. A depression that had nothing to do with federal policy toward the South dramatically changed that policy, and all but destroyed southern blacks' civil rights in the process.

These shifting political winds affected supposedly apolitical federal courts. Following the massacre in Colfax, United States Attorney James Beckwith obtained 90 indictments but a mere nine arrests. (Most of the massacre's participants—including its ringleader, a man named Christopher Columbus Nash—evaded federal capture.) Defendants were charged with 32 counts of intimidating black voters, denying their victims the law's protection, and conspiring to do the same. The case went to trial in February 1874: five months after depression struck the United States. One defendant was acquitted; the other eight received a hung jury. A second trial in May produced five acquittals and a mere three convictions: of Bill Cruikshank, John Hadnot, and Bill Irwin, three of Nash's lieutenants.

For the prosecution, the story worsened from there. Sitting as Circuit Judge, Supreme Court Justice Joseph Bradley nominally presided over the Colfax trial along with his friend Judge Woods: Bradley was on the bench when the trial opened and again when post-verdict motions were heard; in between, Woods presided alone. Two years earlier, Bradley had written Woods a letter praising his ruling in *Hall*. Now, Bradley concluded that the three convictions in *Cruikshank* should be overturned, reasoning that the Fourteenth Amendment applied only to government officials, not to private citizens like Cruikshank and his friends. Woods disagreed. The Supreme Court had to choose between the two.**

The Court followed Bradley, unanimously. See United States v. Cruikshank, 92 U.S. 542 (1876). Chief Justice Morrison Waite's opinion emphasized the Fourteenth Amendment's limits, not its broad scope:

> The Fourteenth Amendment prohibits a State from denying to any person within its jurisdiction the equal protection of the laws; but this provision does not . . . add any thing to the rights which one citizen has under the Constitution against another. The equality of the rights of citizens is a principle of republicanism. Every republican government is in duty bound to protect all its citizens in the enjoyment of this principle, if within its power. That duty was originally assumed by the States; and it still remains there.

Id. at 554-55. The quoted passage begins with the proposition that the Equal Protection Clause cannot support the prosecution of private citizens: "[T]his provision does not . . . add any thing to the rights which one citizen has . . . against another." It ends with the proposition that enforcing equal protection is chiefly the obligation of the states, not of the federal government: "That duty was originally assumed by the States; and it still remains there." The first proposition made federal prosecutions in cases like the Colfax massacre impossible. The second made such prosecutions difficult even in cases like the police riots in Memphis and New Orleans.*** A more complete defense victory is hard to imagine.

Waite's opinion in *Cruikshank* remains good law today. The notion that victims of violent crimes have a constitutional right to the "protection of

---

** Four procedural practices followed in *Cruikshank* seem strange to twenty-first-century lawyers. First, Circuit Judges sat as trial judges in civil rights cases; today, federal Circuit Judges hear appeals but, with rare exceptions, do not try cases. Second, Supreme Court Justices "rode circuit" in the nineteenth century, frequently sitting as Circuit Judges within their assigned Circuits, as Bradley did in *Cruikshank*. Today's Justices hear and decide only the cases that come to them on the Supreme Court. Third, at the time of *Cruikshank*, appeals to the Supreme Court were allowed in cases in which two Circuit Judges—here, Bradley (a Justice sitting as a Circuit Judge) and Woods—divided, leaving the relevant case undecided absent appellate review. Today, the Courts of Appeals of the nation's 13 circuits sit in panels of 3, so equal division is impossible. Fourth, Supreme Court Justices routinely reviewed their own decisions made when sitting as Circuit Judges, again as Bradley did in *Cruikshank*. Today's practice is to recuse in such cases—which rarely arise, since the Justices no longer ride circuit.

*** The relevance of this second proposition to the modern-day controversy over police shootings of unarmed black men, which has given rise to the "Black Lives Matter" political movement, should be self-evident. The Equal Protection Clause could have been used by the federal courts to review local prosecutorial decisions not to charge police officers with crimes in such cases; thanks largely to *Cruikshank*, however, it has not.

the laws" is no part of American law. And since *Cruikshank*, private citizens cannot be found to have violated the Equal Protection Clause; that clause binds only government officials. Those propositions have enormous consequences. But for *Cruikshank*, American law might include a requirement that prosecutors prosecute serious crimes when they can do so. Such a requirement would in turn shape the definition of the crimes prosecuted: If legislators knew that the criminal prohibitions they enact would be enforced to the limits of the law, they would take greater care when defining the boundaries of those prohibitions—lest their constituents face unmerited criminal liability. Federal criminal law might have been devoted to punishing the crimes local officials refuse to punish. And pre-*Cruikshank* equal protection doctrine would be at odds with today's common-law enforcement practices. At the least, the large gaps between the clearance rate (i.e., the percentage of crimes in which a suspect is arrested) for homicides in poor city neighborhoods and the clearance rate for suburban homicides would raise a serious constitutional issue; at the most, those gaps would be cause for federal judges to order more and better policing of high-crime city neighborhoods. The common practice of using drug offenses to punish suspected violent crimes in those same city neighborhoods—but not elsewhere—would be forbidden, with large consequences for drug law and drug enforcement.

None of these things came to pass. Instead, prosecutors' discretion not to charge remains virtually absolute. See Inmates of Attica Correctional Facility v. Rockefeller, infra at page 1073. The quantity and quality of policing varies widely between poor neighborhoods and rich ones, and such economic variation often correlates with race. Drug enforcement is regularly used as a substitute for enforcing the laws that forbid violent felonies—but again, only in some neighborhoods. *Cruikshank* continues to cast a large shadow on the law of criminal justice.

2. "Equal"

In the wake of *Cruikshank*, the Equal Protection Clause was a constitutional afterthought: Justice Oliver Wendell Holmes once described the clause as "the last resort of constitutional arguments." Buck v. Bell, 274 U.S. 200, 205 (1927).**** Not until the 1980s did the Supreme Court discuss the necessary components of a claim that criminal prosecution or punishment constituted unconstitutional discrimination. The defendant in McCleskey v. Kemp, 481 U.S. 279 (1987), a black man who killed a white police officer in the course of a robbery, was convicted of capital murder in Georgia and sentenced to

---

**** Holmes wrote those words in a case whose name is synonymous with injustice: Buck v. Bell, 274 U.S. 200 (1927), authorized the state-mandated sterilization of mentally retarded adults. The most famous line from Holmes's opinion is not the Justice's expression of contempt for equal protection claims, but his expression of contempt for the plaintiffs: "Three generations of imbeciles are enough." Id. at 207.

death. On federal habeas corpus, he argued that Georgia's death penalty was administered in a discriminatory fashion. To support this claim, the defendant relied on a statistical study of Georgia murder cases known as the Baldus Study, after David Baldus, the law professor who conducted it.

The study found that "the death penalty was assessed in 22 percent of the cases involving black defendants and white victims; 8 percent of the cases involving white defendants and white victims; 1 percent of the cases involving black defendants and black victims; and 3 percent of the cases involving white defendants and black victims." 481 U.S. at 286. The study also found that "prosecutors sought the death penalty in 70 percent of the cases involving black defendants and white victims; 32 percent of the cases involving white defendants and white victims; 15 percent of the cases involving black defendants and black victims; and 19 percent of the cases involving white defendants and black victims." Id. at 287. Even after adjusting for some 230 variables, the study concluded that in "mid-range" cases (a category that included McCleskey's case), 34 percent of killers of whites, but only 14 percent of killers of blacks, received death sentences. Id. at 287 n.5.

Discussing the relevance of these statistics for a finding of intentional discrimination, Justice Powell, author of the *McCleskey* majority opinion, wrote:

> . . . [T]o prevail under the Equal Protection Clause, McCleskey must prove that the decisionmakers in his case acted with discriminatory purpose. He offers no evidence specific to his own case that would support an inference that racial considerations played a part in his sentence. Instead, he relies solely on the Baldus study. McCleskey argues that the Baldus study compels an inference that his sentence rests on purposeful discrimination. . . .
>
> The Court has accepted statistics as proof of intent to discriminate in certain limited contexts. First, this Court has accepted statistical disparities as proof of an equal protection violation in the selection of the jury venire in a particular district. Although statistical proof normally must present a "stark" pattern to be accepted as the sole proof of discriminatory intent under the Constitution,[12] Arlington Heights v. Metropolitan Housing Dev. Corp., 429 U.S. 252, 266 (1977), "because of the nature of the jury-selection task, . . . we have permitted a finding of constitutional violation even when the statistical

---

12. Gomillion v. Lightfoot, 364 U.S. 339 (1960), and Yick Wo v. Hopkins, 118 U.S. 356 (1886), are examples of those rare cases in which a statistical pattern of discriminatory impact demonstrated a constitutional violation. In *Gomillion*, a state legislature violated the Fifteenth Amendment by altering the boundaries of a particular city "from a square to an uncouth twenty-eight-sided figure." 364 U.S., at 340. The alterations excluded 395 of 400 black voters without excluding a single white voter. In *Yick Wo*, an ordinance prohibited operation of 310 laundries that were housed in wooden buildings, but allowed such laundries to resume operations if the operator secured a permit from the government. When laundry operators applied for permits to resume operation, all but one of the white applicants received permits, but none of the over 200 Chinese applicants were successful. In those cases, the Court found the statistical disparities "to warrant and require," *Yick Wo v. Hopkins*, supra, at 373, a "conclusion [that was] irresistible, tantamount for all practical purposes to a mathematical demonstration," *Gomillion v. Lightfoot*, supra, at 341, that the State acted with a discriminatory purpose.

pattern does not approach [such] extremes." Id., at 266, n.13. Second, this Court has accepted statistics in the form of multiple-regression analysis to prove statutory violations under Title VII of the Civil Rights Act of 1964. . . .

But the nature of the capital sentencing decision, and the relationship of the statistics to that decision, are fundamentally different from the corresponding elements in the venire-selection or Title VII cases. Most importantly, each particular decision to impose the death penalty is made by a petit jury selected from a properly constituted venire. Each jury is unique in its composition, and the Constitution requires that its decision rest on consideration of . . . factors that vary according to the characteristics of the individual defendant and the facts of the particular capital offense. . . . Thus, the application of an inference drawn from the general statistics to a specific decision in a trial and sentencing simply is not comparable to the application of an inference drawn from general statistics to a specific venire-selection or Title VII case. In those cases, the statistics relate to fewer entities, and fewer variables are relevant to the challenged decisions.[15] . . .

Finally, McCleskey's statistical proffer must be viewed in the context of his challenge. McCleskey challenges decisions at the heart of the State's criminal justice system. "One of society's most basic tasks is that of protecting the lives of its citizens and one of the most basic ways in which it achieves the task is through criminal laws against murder." Gregg v. Georgia, 428 U.S. 153, 226 (1976) (White, J., concurring). Implementation of these laws necessarily requires discretionary judgments. Because discretion is essential to the criminal justice process, we would demand exceptionally clear proof before we would infer that the discretion has been abused. The unique nature of the decisions at issue in this case also counsels against adopting such an inference from the disparities indicated by the Baldus study. Accordingly, we hold that the Baldus study is clearly insufficient to support an inference that any of the decisionmakers in McCleskey's case acted with discriminatory purpose.

481 U.S. at 291-97.

Reread the last quoted paragraph above, along with footnote 12 in *McCleskey*. The Court seems to be saying that, absent extreme disparities of the sort seen in *Yick Wo*, prosecutorial charging decisions cannot be deemed discriminatory. Note also the Court's requirement of "exceptionally clear proof" when deciding whether prosecutors' and juries' discretionary decisions were discriminatory. In practice, prosecutors are subject to a less rigorous standard of discrimination than other government officials. For a stinging criticism of this position, along with an argument that the standard for prosecutorial discrimination should be tougher rather than more

15. We refer here not to the number of entities involved in any particular decision, but to the number of entities whose decisions necessarily are reflected in a statistical display such as the Baldus study. The decisions of a jury commission or of an employer over time are fairly attributable to the commission or the employer. Therefore, an unexplained statistical discrepancy can be said to indicate a consistent policy of the decisionmaker. The Baldus study seeks to deduce a state "policy" by studying the combined effects of the decisions of hundreds of juries that are unique in their composition. It is incomparably more difficult to deduce a consistent policy by studying the decisions of these many unique entities. . . .

lenient than the standards for other sorts of state discrimination, see Randall Kennedy, *McCleskey v. Kemp*: Race, Capital Punishment, and the Supreme Court, 101 Harv. L. Rev. 1388 (1988).

United States v. Armstrong

Supreme Court of the United States
517 U.S. 456 (1996)

Chief Justice Rehnquist delivered the opinion of the Court.

In this case, we consider the showing necessary for a defendant to be entitled to discovery on a claim that the prosecuting attorney singled him out for prosecution on the basis of his race. We conclude that respondents failed to satisfy the threshold showing: They failed to show that the Government declined to prosecute similarly situated suspects of other races.

In April 1992, respondents were indicted in the United States District Court for the Central District of California on charges of conspiring to possess with intent to distribute more than 50 grams of cocaine base (crack) and conspiring to distribute the same, in violation of 21 U.S.C. §§841 and 846, and federal firearms offenses. For three months prior to the indictment, agents of the Federal Bureau of Alcohol, Tobacco, and Firearms and the Narcotics Division of the Inglewood, California, Police Department had infiltrated a suspected crack distribution ring by using three confidential informants. On seven separate occasions during this period, the informants had bought a total of 124.3 grams of crack from respondents and witnessed respondents carrying firearms during the sales. The agents searched the hotel room in which the sales were transacted, arrested respondents Armstrong and Hampton in the room, and found more crack and a loaded gun. The agents later arrested the other respondents as part of the ring.

In response to the indictment, respondents filed a motion for discovery or for dismissal of the indictment, alleging that they were selected for federal prosecution because they are black. In support of their motion, they offered only an affidavit by a "Paralegal Specialist," employed by the Office of the Federal Public Defender representing one of the respondents. The only allegation in the affidavit was that, in every one of the 24 §841 or §846 cases closed by the office during 1991, the defendant was black. Accompanying the affidavit was a "study" listing the 24 defendants, their race, whether they were prosecuted for dealing cocaine as well as crack, and the status of each case.

The Government opposed the discovery motion, arguing, among other things, that there was no evidence or allegation "that the Government has acted unfairly or has prosecuted non-black defendants or failed to prosecute them." The District Court granted the motion. It ordered the Government (1) to provide a list of all cases from the last three years in which the Government charged both cocaine and firearms offenses, (2) to identify the race of the defendants in those cases, (3) to identify what levels of law enforcement were involved in the investigations of those cases, and (4) to explain its criteria for deciding to prosecute those defendants for federal cocaine offenses.

The Government moved for reconsideration of the District Court's discovery order. With this motion it submitted affidavits and other evidence to explain why it had chosen to prosecute respondents and why respondents' study did not support the inference that the Government was singling out blacks for cocaine prosecution. The federal and local agents participating in the case alleged in affidavits that race played no role in their investigation. An Assistant United States Attorney explained in an affidavit that the decision to prosecute met the general criteria for prosecution, because

> "there was over 100 grams of cocaine base involved, over twice the threshold necessary for a ten-year mandatory minimum sentence; there were multiple sales involving multiple defendants, thereby indicating a fairly substantial crack cocaine ring; . . . there were multiple federal firearms violations intertwined with the narcotics trafficking; the overall evidence in the case was extremely strong, including audio and videotapes of defendants; . . . and several of the defendants had criminal histories including narcotics and firearms violations." Id., at 81.

The Government also submitted sections of a published 1989 Drug Enforcement Administration report which concluded that "large-scale, interstate trafficking networks controlled by Jamaicans, Haitians and Black street gangs dominate the manufacture and distribution of crack." J. Featherly & E. Hill, Crack Cocaine Overview 1989.

In response, one of respondents' attorneys submitted an affidavit alleging that an intake coordinator at a drug treatment center had told her that there are "an equal number of caucasian users and dealers to minority users and dealers." Id., at 138. Respondents also submitted an affidavit from a criminal defense attorney alleging that in his experience many nonblacks are prosecuted in state court for crack offenses, id., at 141, and a newspaper article reporting that Federal "crack criminals . . . are being punished far more severely than if they had been caught with powder cocaine, and almost every single one of them is black," Newton, Harsher Crack Sentences Criticized as Racial Inequity, Los Angeles Times, Nov. 23, 1992, at 1.

The District Court denied the motion for reconsideration. When the Government indicated it would not comply with the court's discovery order, the court dismissed the case.[2]

---

2. We have never determined whether dismissal of the indictment, or some other sanction, is the proper remedy if a court determines that a defendant has been the victim of prosecution on the basis of his race. Here, "it was the government itself that suggested dismissal of the indictments to the district court so that an appeal might lie." 48 F.3d 1508, 1510 (CA9 1995).

A divided three-judge panel of the Court of Appeals for the Ninth Circuit reversed, holding that, because of the proof requirements for a selective-prosecution claim, defendants must "provide a colorable basis for believing that 'others similarly situated have not been prosecuted'" to obtain discovery. 21 F.3d 1431, 1436 (1994). The Court of Appeals voted to rehear the case en banc, and the en banc panel affirmed the District Court's order of dismissal, holding that "a defendant is not required to demonstrate that the government has failed to prosecute others who are similarly situated." 48 F.3d 1508, 1516 (1995) (emphasis deleted). We granted certiorari to determine the appropriate standard for discovery for a selective-prosecution claim. . . .

A selective-prosecution claim asks a court to exercise judicial power over a "special province" of the Executive. Heckler v. Chaney, 470 U.S. 821, 832 (1985). The Attorney General and United States Attorneys retain "broad discretion" to enforce the Nation's criminal laws. Wayte v. United States, 470 U.S. 598, 607 (1985). They have this latitude because they are designated by statute as the President's delegates to help him discharge his constitutional responsibility to "take Care that the Laws be faithfully executed." U.S. Const., Art. II, §3; see 28 U.S.C. §§516, 547. As a result, "the presumption of regularity supports" their prosecutorial decisions and "in the absence of clear evidence to the contrary, courts presume that they have properly discharged their official duties." United States v. Chemical Foundation, 272 U.S. 1, 14-15 (1926). In the ordinary case, "so long as the prosecutor has probable cause to believe that the accused committed an offense defined by statute, the decision whether or not to prosecute, and what charge to file or bring before a grand jury, generally rests entirely in his discretion." Bordenkircher v. Hayes, 434 U.S. 357, 364 (1978).

Of course, a prosecutor's discretion is "subject to constitutional constraints." United States v. Batchelder, 442 U.S. 114, 125 (1979). One of these constraints, imposed by the equal protection component of the Due Process Clause of the Fifth Amendment, is that the decision whether to prosecute may not be based on "an unjustifiable standard such as race, religion, or other arbitrary classification," Oyler v. Boles, 368 U.S. 448, 456 (1962). A defendant may demonstrate that the administration of a criminal law is "directed so exclusively against a particular class of persons . . . with a mind so unequal and oppressive" that the system of prosecution amounts to "a practical denial" of equal protection of the law. Yick Wo v. Hopkins, 118 U.S. 356, 373 (1886).

In order to dispel the presumption that a prosecutor has not violated equal protection, a criminal defendant must present "clear evidence to the contrary." *Chemical Foundation*, supra, at 14-15. We explained in *Wayte* why courts are "properly hesitant to examine the decision whether to prosecute." 470 U.S. at 608. Judicial deference to the decisions of these executive officers rests in part on an assessment of the relative competence of prosecutors and courts. "Such factors as the strength of the case, the prosecution's general deterrence value, the Government's enforcement priorities, and the case's relationship to the Government's overall enforcement plan are not readily susceptible to the kind of analysis the courts are competent to undertake." Id., at 607. It also stems from a concern not to unnecessarily impair the performance of a core executive constitutional function. "Examining the basis of a prosecution delays the criminal proceeding, threatens to chill law enforcement by subjecting the prosecutor's motives and decisionmaking to outside inquiry, and may undermine prosecutorial effectiveness by revealing the Government's enforcement policy." Ibid.

The requirements for a selective-prosecution claim draw on "ordinary equal protection standards." Id., at 608. The claimant must demonstrate that the federal prosecutorial policy "had a discriminatory effect and that it was motivated by a discriminatory purpose." Ibid. To establish a discriminatory effect in a race case, the claimant must show that similarly situated individuals of a different race were not prosecuted. This requirement has been established in our case law since Ah Sin v. Wittman, 198 U.S. 500 (1905). Ah Sin, a subject of China, petitioned a California state court for a writ of habeas corpus, seeking discharge from imprisonment under a San Francisco county ordinance prohibiting persons from setting up gambling tables in rooms barricaded to stop police from entering. Id., at 503. He alleged in his habeas petition "that the ordinance is enforced 'solely and exclusively against persons of the Chinese race and not otherwise.'" Id., at 507. We rejected his contention that this averment made out a claim under the Equal Protection Clause, because it did not allege "that the conditions and practices to which the ordinance was directed did not exist exclusively among the Chinese, or that there were other offenders against the ordinance than the Chinese as to whom it was not enforced." Id., at 507-508.

The similarly situated requirement does not make a selective-prosecution claim impossible to prove. Twenty years before *Ah Sin*, we invalidated an ordinance, also adopted by San Francisco, that prohibited the operation of laundries in wooden buildings. *Yick Wo*, 118 U.S. at 374. The plaintiff in error successfully demonstrated that the ordinance was applied against Chinese nationals but not against other laundry-shop operators. The authorities had denied the applications of 200 Chinese subjects for permits to operate shops in wooden buildings, but granted the applications of 80 individuals who were not Chinese subjects to operate laundries in wooden buildings "under similar conditions." Ibid. We explained in *Ah Sin* why the similarly situated requirement is necessary:

> "No latitude of intention should be indulged in a case like this. There should be certainty to every intent. Plaintiff in error seeks to set aside a criminal law of the State, not on the ground that it is unconstitutional on its face, not that it is discriminatory in tendency and ultimate actual operation as the ordinance was

which was passed on in the *Yick Wo* case, but that it was made so by the manner of its administration. This is a matter of proof, and no fact should be omitted to make it out completely, when the power of a Federal court is invoked to interfere with the course of criminal justice of a State." 198 U.S. at 508.

. . . Having reviewed the requirements to prove a selective-prosecution claim, we turn to the showing necessary to obtain discovery in support of such a claim. If discovery is ordered, the Government must assemble from its own files documents which might corroborate or refute the defendant's claim. Discovery thus imposes many of the costs present when the Government must respond to a prima facie case of selective prosecution. It will divert prosecutors' resources and may disclose the Government's prosecutorial strategy. The justifications for a rigorous standard for the elements of a selective-prosecution claim thus require a correspondingly rigorous standard for discovery in aid of such a claim.

The parties, and the Courts of Appeals which have considered the requisite showing to establish entitlement to discovery, describe this showing with a variety of phrases, like "colorable basis," "substantial threshold showing," "substantial and concrete basis," or "reasonable likelihood." However, the many labels for this showing conceal the degree of consensus about the evidence necessary to meet it. The Courts of Appeals "require some evidence tending to show the existence of the essential elements of the defense," discriminatory effect and discriminatory intent. United States v. Berrios, 501 F.2d 1207, 1211 (CA2 1974).

In this case we consider what evidence constitutes "some evidence tending to show the existence" of the discriminatory effect element. The Court of Appeals held that a defendant may establish a colorable basis for discriminatory effect without evidence that the Government has failed to prosecute others who are similarly situated to the defendant. 48 F.3d at 1516. We think it was mistaken in this view. The vast majority of the Courts of Appeals require the defendant to produce some evidence that similarly situated defendants of other races could have been prosecuted, but were not, and this requirement is consistent with our . . . case law. . . .

The Court of Appeals reached its decision in part because it started "with the presumption that people of all races commit all types of crimes—not with the premise that any type of crime is the exclusive province of any particular racial or ethnic group." 48 F.3d at 1516-17. It cited no authority for this proposition, which seems contradicted by the most recent statistics of the United States Sentencing Commission. Those statistics show that: More than 90% of the persons sentenced in 1994 for crack cocaine trafficking were black, United States Sentencing Comm'n, 1994 Annual Report 107 (Table 45); 93.4% of convicted LSD dealers were white, ibid.; and 91% of those convicted for pornography or prostitution were white, id., at 41 (Table 13). Presumptions at war with presumably reliable statistics have no proper place in the analysis of this issue.

The Court of Appeals also expressed concern about the "evidentiary obstacles defendants face." 48 F.3d at 1514. But . . . respondents could have investigated whether similarly situated persons of other races were prosecuted by the State of California, were known to federal law enforcement officers, but were not prosecuted in federal court. We think the required threshold—a credible showing of different treatment of similarly situated persons—adequately balances the Government's interest in vigorous prosecution and the defendant's interest in avoiding selective prosecution.

In the case before us, respondents' "study" did not constitute "some evidence tending to show the existence of the essential elements of" a selective-prosecution claim. The study failed to identify individuals who were not black, could have been prosecuted for the offenses for which respondents were charged, but were not so prosecuted. This omission was not remedied by respondents' evidence in opposition to the Government's motion for reconsideration. The newspaper article, which discussed the discriminatory effect of federal drug sentencing laws, was not relevant to an allegation of discrimination in decisions to prosecute. Respondents' affidavits, which recounted one attorney's conversation with a drug treatment center employee and the experience of another attorney defending drug prosecutions in state court, recounted hearsay and reported personal conclusions based on anecdotal evidence. The judgment of the Court of Appeals is therefore reversed, and the case is remanded for proceedings consistent with this opinion.

Justice STEVENS, dissenting.

. . . I am persuaded that the District Judge did not abuse her discretion when she concluded that the factual showing was sufficiently disturbing to require some response from the United States Attorney's Office. Perhaps the discovery order was broader than necessary, but I cannot agree with the Court's apparent conclusion that no inquiry was permissible.

The District Judge's order should be evaluated in light of three circumstances that underscore the need for judicial vigilance over certain types of drug prosecutions. First, the Anti-Drug Abuse Act of 1986 and subsequent legislation established a regime of extremely high penalties for the possession and distribution of so-called "crack" cocaine. Those provisions treat one gram of crack as the equivalent of 100 grams of powder cocaine. The distribution of 50 grams of crack is thus punishable by the same mandatory minimum sentence of 10 years in prison that applies to the distribution of 5,000 grams of powder cocaine. The Sentencing Guidelines extend this ratio to penalty levels above the mandatory minimums: for any given quantity of crack, the guideline range is the same as if the offense had involved 100 times that amount in powder cocaine. These penalties result in sentences for crack offenders that average three to eight times longer than sentences for comparable powder offenders.

Second, the disparity between the treatment of crack cocaine and powder cocaine is matched by the disparity between the severity of the punishment imposed by federal law and that imposed by state law for the same conduct. For a variety of reasons, often including the absence of mandatory minimums, the existence of parole, and lower baseline penalties, terms of imprisonment for drug offenses tend to be substantially lower in state systems than in the federal system. The difference is especially marked in the case of crack offenses. The majority of States draw no distinction between types of cocaine in their penalty schemes; of those that do, none has established as stark a differential as the Federal Government. For example, if respondent Hampton is found guilty, his federal sentence might be as long as a mandatory life term. Had he been tried in state court, his sentence could have been as short as 12 years, less worktime credits of half that amount.

Finally, it is undisputed that the brunt of the elevated federal penalties falls heavily on blacks. While 65% of the persons who have used crack are white, in 1993 they represented only 4% of the federal offenders convicted of trafficking in crack. Eighty-eight percent of such defendants were black. . . . Those figures represent a major threat to the integrity of federal sentencing reform, whose main purpose was the elimination of disparity (especially racial) in sentencing. The Sentencing Commission acknowledges that the heightened crack penalties are a "primary cause of the growing disparity between sentences for Black and White federal defendants." [United States Sentencing Commission,] Special Report [to Congress: Cocaine and Federal Sentencing Policy] 145 [(Feb. 1995)]. . . .

Respondents submitted a study showing that of all cases involving crack offenses that were closed by the Federal Public Defender's Office in 1991, 24 out of 24 involved black defendants. To supplement this evidence, they submitted affidavits from two of the attorneys in the defense team. The first reported a statement from an intake coordinator at a local drug treatment center that, in his experience, an equal number of crack users and dealers were caucasian as belonged to minorities. The second was from David R. Reed, counsel for respondent Armstrong. . . . Reed stated that he did not recall "ever handling a [crack] cocaine case involving non-black defendants" in federal court, nor had he even heard of one. Id., at 140. He further stated that "there are many crack cocaine sales cases prosecuted in state court that do involve racial groups other than blacks." Id., at 141. . . .

The criticism that the affidavits were based on "anecdotal evidence" is . . . unpersuasive. I thought it was agreed that defendants do not need to prepare sophisticated statistical studies in order to receive mere discovery in cases like this one. Certainly evidence based on a drug counselor's personal observations or on an attorney's practice in two sets of courts, state and federal, can "tend to show the existence" of a selective prosecution.

Even if respondents failed to carry their burden of showing that there were individuals who were not black but who could have been prosecuted in federal court for the same offenses, it does not follow that the District Court abused its discretion in ordering discovery. There can be no doubt that such individuals exist, and indeed the Government has never denied the same. In those circumstances, I fail to see why the District Court was unable to take judicial notice of this obvious fact and demand information from the Government's files to support or refute respondents' evidence. The presumption that some whites are prosecuted in state court is not "contradicted" by the statistics the majority cites, which show only that high percentages of blacks are convicted of certain federal crimes, while high percentages of whites are convicted of other federal crimes. Those figures are entirely consistent with the allegation of selective prosecution. The relevant comparison, rather, would be with the percentages of blacks and whites who commit those crimes. But, as discussed above, in the case of crack far greater numbers of whites are believed guilty of using the substance. The District Court, therefore, was entitled to find the evidence before her significant and to require some explanation from the Government.

. . . In this case, the evidence was sufficiently disturbing to persuade the District Judge to order discovery that might help explain the conspicuous racial pattern of cases before her Court. I cannot accept the majority's conclusion that the District Judge either exceeded her power or abused her discretion when she did so. I therefore respectfully dissent.

Notes and Questions

1. The federal sentencing disparity between crack cocaine and powder cocaine that was implicated in *Armstrong* was substantially reduced—though not eliminated—by the Fair Sentencing Act of 2010, signed into law by President Barack Obama in August of that year. The Act reduced the disparity between the two crimes from 100-to-1 down to roughly 18-to-1. See "Fair Sentencing Act Signed By President Obama," The Sentencing Project (Aug. 3, 2010), available at http://www.sentencingproject.org/detail/news.cfm?news_id=984&id=164.

2. The Fourteenth Amendment applies to the states, and to local governments that are the legal creation of the states in which they reside. So what is the source of the *federal* government's obligation to provide the "equal protection of the laws"? The answer comes from Bolling v. Sharpe, 347 U.S. 497 (1954), a companion case to Brown v. Board of Education of Topeka, 347 U.S. 483 (1954). In *Brown*, the Supreme Court held that segregated public schools in Kansas violated the Fourteenth Amendment's Equal Protection Clause. In *Bolling*, the Court held that the District of Columbia's segregated school system—which was governed by federal law—violated the equal protection guarantee that, according to the Justices, was implicit in the Fifth Amendment's Due Process Clause. Under *Bolling*, the equal protection doctrine that binds federal officials is the same as the doctrine that applies to the acts of state and local government officials. Technically, *Armstrong* is a Fifth Amendment case, even though the law it applies is based on the Fourteenth Amendment.

3. Consider Wayte v. United States, 470 U.S. 598 (1985), cited and quoted in *Armstrong*. The defendant in *Wayte* was one of 16 violators of the federal draft registration law whom the federal government prosecuted for intentional failure to register. The total number of non-registrants was approximately 674,000. Even allowing for the likelihood that a large fraction of those offenders had failed to register because they did not know about the registration requirement (might criminal conviction in such cases violate *Lambert?*), the number of intentional violations was probably in the hundreds of thousands. In the few cases federal officials chose to prosecute, defendants had announced their violation publicly. The government's enforcement pattern was called the "beg policy," because those prosecuted, in effect, begged the government to prosecute them. Wayte himself did so; at one point, he wrote the Selective Service System, saying:

> "Last August I wrote to inform you of my intention not to register for the draft. Well, I did not register, and still plan never to do so, but thus far I have received no reply to my letter, much less any news about your much-threatened prosecutions."
>
> "I must interpret your silence as meaning you are too busy or disorganized to respond to letters or keep track of us draft-age youth. So I will keep you posted of my whereabouts."

470 U.S. at 601 n.2.

Somewhat churlishly, Wayte contended that prosecuting him in part because he wrote such letters amounted to discrimination on the basis of protected speech. The Supreme Court disagreed:

> It is appropriate to judge selective prosecution claims according to ordinary equal protection standards. . . . [T]hese standards require petitioner to show both that the passive enforcement system had a discriminatory effect and that it was motivated by a discriminatory purpose. All petitioner has shown here is that those eventually prosecuted, along with many not prosecuted, reported themselves as having violated the law. He has not shown that the enforcement policy selected nonregistrants for prosecution on the basis of their speech. . . . The Government did not prosecute those who reported themselves but later registered. Nor did it prosecute those who protested registration but did not report themselves or were not reported by others. In fact, the Government did not even investigate those who wrote letters to Selective Service criticizing registration unless their letters stated affirmatively that they had refused to comply with the law. . . . These facts demonstrate that the Government treated all reported nonregistrants similarly. It did not subject vocal nonregistrants to any special burden. Indeed, those prosecuted in effect selected themselves. . . .

470 U.S. at 608-10. Notice: Wayte did not argue that selecting 16 violators from a pool of hundreds of thousands was unconstitutionally arbitrary. That argument was not raised because it had no chance of success. Longstanding legal doctrine holds that prosecutors are free to prosecute no non-registrants, all non-registrants, or any number in between—as long as prosecutors do not discriminate on the basis of suspects' race, sex, or political beliefs. Is that doctrinal stance appropriate? Does it treat suspects equally?

4. The data mentioned in Justice Stevens' dissent in *Armstrong* suggest that discriminatory drug punishment is primarily a feature of federal criminal justice. But the situation is not much better in the states. African Americans comprise roughly 13 percent of the overall U.S. population, and the best available evidence strongly suggests that rates of illegal drug possession and drug use are roughly comparable between whites and blacks. Yet in September 2014, 38.7 percent of all federal prisoners incarcerated for drug offenses were black. The comparable ratio in state prisons, at year-end 2013, was 38.4 percent. See Bureau of Justice Statistics, U.S. Department of Justice, "Prisoners in 2014," Tables 11 & 12 (September 2015).

5. The defendants in *Armstrong* probably would have lost even if they had received the discovery they sought. Under *McCleskey*, equal protection claims cannot succeed without proof of discriminatory intent. If federal prosecutors could offer a credible non-racial explanation for their charging decisions, the court would be bound to rule for the government. Such explanations are easy to come by: Prosecutors need only say that Armstrong and his colleagues were charged because of the amounts they possessed, or because of their prior arrests or convictions, or because of their violation of federal gun registration laws, or because of the violence of the drug markets in which they participated. Defendants could prevail only if they could prove that such explanations are pretextual. Proof of pretext is nearly impossible. Which is why successful claims of discriminatory prosecution were nearly unheard of before *Armstrong*, and remained so afterward.

6. It is hard, maybe impossible to know for sure the reasons for the prosecutorial patterns at issue in *Armstrong*. But some part of the reason has to do with the behavior of the police—both local cops and federal agents. As Daniel Richman has noted, police and prosecutors constitute what antitrust lawyers would call a "bilateral monopoly": Each must deal with the other, and neither side of this relationship can achieve its goals without the other side's cooperation. Daniel C. Richman, Prosecutors and Their Agents, Agents and Their Prosecutors, 103 Colum. L. Rev. 749 (2003). Prosecutors cannot prosecute unless the police bring them cases, and the police cannot see their suspects punished without a decision to prosecute.

In some classes of federal criminal cases—including drug cases like the ones in *Armstrong*—the relationship is more complicated. Federal prosecutors ordinarily get their cases from federal agents. (Richman writes: "One often hears rookie prosecutors refer to 'my agents.' Most soon learn to drop the possessive." Id. at 756.) But many federal drug cases begin with an arrest by local police; the case is turned over to federal prosecutors because the local district attorney lacks needed manpower, or because the arrest arose out of a local-federal task force, or because local police are trying to play off one prosecutor's office against the other, or for a variety of other reasons. In these cases, the bilateral monopoly does not hold. In most cases, though, it *does* hold. Which means that the biggest check on the power of prosecutors may be the police officers with whom they must deal—and vice versa.

Prosecutors decline to prosecute a large fraction of the cases police officers bring them. Richman's article noted that in the six months after the terrorist attacks on September 11, 2001, federal prosecutors declined to prosecute 61 percent of the terrorism cases federal agents brought them. Id. at 765. Perhaps those declinations mean that federal agents were bringing weak cases. Or perhaps prosecutors were offering non-prosecution in return for information in other cases. Or maybe post-September 11 Assistant U.S. Attorneys were especially afraid, given the heightened public attention to everything related to terrorism, of *losing* terrorism cases, and so refused to prosecute unless they were absolutely certain of a conviction. One of the largest consequences of the legal doctrine we see in *McCleskey* and *Armstrong* is that only prosecutors know why they pursue the cases they pursue, and decline the ones they decline. The decision to file criminal charges (or not) is one of the most important ways government officials exercise power. It is also one of the least transparent.

3. The "Protection of the Laws"

In the years between 1868 (when the Fourteenth Amendment was ratified) and 1876 (when the Supreme Court decided United States v. Cruikshank, 92 U.S. 542 (1876); see supra page 1059), the government's obligation to provide the "protection of the laws" was both real and substantial. With its decision in *Cruikshank*, the Supreme Court put an end to that obligation. The consequence is decisions like the next one.

Inmates of Attica Correctional Facility v. Rockefeller

United States Court of Appeals for the Second Circuit
477 F.2d 375 (1973)

Judge MANSFIELD delivered the opinion of the court.

This appeal raises the question of whether the federal judiciary should, at the instance of victims, compel federal and state officials to investigate and prosecute persons who allegedly have violated certain federal and state criminal statutes. Plaintiffs in the purported class suit, which was commenced in the Southern District of New York against various state and federal officers, are certain present and former inmates of New York State's Attica Correctional Facility ("Attica"), the mother of an inmate who was killed when Attica was retaken after the inmate uprising in September 1971, and Arthur O. Eve, a New York State Assemblyman and member of the Subcommittee on Prisons. They appeal from an order of the district court, Lloyd F. MacMahon, Judge, dismissing their complaint. We affirm.

The complaint alleges that before, during, and after the prisoner revolt at and subsequent recapture of Attica in September 1971, which resulted in the killing of 32 inmates and the wounding of many others, the defendants, including the Governor of New York, the State Commissioner of Correctional Services, the Executive Deputy Commissioner of the State Department of Correctional Services, the Superintendent at Attica, and certain State Police, Corrections Officers, and other officials, either committed, conspired to commit, or aided and abetted in the commission of various crimes against the complaining inmates and members of the class they seek to represent. It is charged that the inmates were intentionally subjected to cruel and inhuman treatment prior to the inmate riot, that State Police, Troopers, and Correction Officers (one of whom is named) intentionally killed some of the inmate victims without provocation during the recovery of Attica, that state officers (several of whom are named and whom the inmates claim they can identify) assaulted and beat prisoners after the prison had been successfully retaken and the prisoners had surrendered, . . . that personal property of the inmates was thereafter stolen or destroyed, and that medical assistance was maliciously denied to over 400 inmates wounded during the recovery of the prison.

The complaint further alleges that Robert E. Fischer, a Deputy State Attorney General specially appointed by the Governor . . . with a specially convened grand jury, to investigate crimes relating to the inmates' takeover of Attica and the resumption of control by the state authorities, . . . "has not investigated, nor does he intend to investigate, any crimes committed by state officers." Plaintiffs claim, moreover, that because Fischer was appointed by the Governor he cannot neutrally investigate the responsibility of the Governor and other state officers said to have conspired to commit the crimes alleged. It is also asserted that since Fischer is the sole state official currently authorized under state law to prosecute the offenses allegedly committed by the state officers, no one in the State of New York is investigating or prosecuting them.

With respect to the sole federal defendant, the United States Attorney for the Western District of New York, the complaint simply alleges that he has not arrested, investigated, or instituted prosecutions against any of the state officers accused of criminal violation of plaintiffs' federal civil rights, 18 U.S.C. §§241, 242, and he has thereby failed to carry out the duty placed upon him by 42 U.S.C. §1987, discussed below.

As a remedy for the asserted failure of the defendants to prosecute violations of state and federal criminal laws, plaintiffs request relief in the nature of mandamus (1) against state officials, requiring the State of New York to submit a plan for the independent and impartial investigation and prosecution of the offenses charged against the named and unknown state officers, and insuring the appointment of an impartial state prosecutor and state judge to "prosecute the defendants forthwith," and (2) against the United States Attorney, requiring him to investigate, arrest and prosecute the same state officers for having committed the federal offenses defined by 18 U.S.C. §§241 and 242. The latter statutes punish, respectively, conspiracies against a citizen's free exercise or enjoyment of rights secured by the Constitution and laws of the United States, . . . and the willful subjection of any inhabitant, under color of law, to the deprivation of such rights or to different punishment or penalties on account of alienage, color, or race than are prescribed for the punishment of citizens. . . .

The motions of the federal and state defendants to dismiss the complaint for failure to state claims upon which relief can be granted . . . were granted by Judge MacMahon without opinion. We agree that the extraordinary relief sought cannot be granted in the situation here presented. . . .

With respect to the defendant United States Attorney, plaintiffs seek mandamus to compel him to investigate and institute prosecutions against state officers, most of whom are not identified, for alleged violations of 18 U.S.C. §§241 and 242. Federal mandamus is . . . available only "to compel an officer or employee of the United States . . . to perform a duty owed to the plaintiff." 28 U.S.C. §1361. And the legislative history of §1361 makes it clear that ordinarily the courts are "not to direct or influence the exercise of discretion of the officer or agency in the making of the decision," United States ex rel. Schonbrun v. Commanding Officer, 403 F.2d 371, 374 (2d Cir. 1968). More particularly, federal courts have traditionally and, to our knowledge, uniformly refrained from overturning, at the instance of a private person, discretionary decisions of federal prosecuting authorities not to prosecute persons regarding whom a complaint of criminal conduct is made. [There follows a long string of case citations. —Eds.]

This judicial reluctance to direct federal prosecutions at the instance of a private party asserting the failure of United States officials to prosecute alleged criminal violations has been applied even in cases such as the present one where, according to the allegations of the complaint, which we must accept as true for purposes of this appeal, serious questions are raised as to the protection of the civil rights and physical security of a definable class of victims of crime and as to the fair administration of the criminal justice system. . . .

The primary ground upon which this traditional judicial aversion to compelling prosecutions has been based is the separation of powers doctrine.

"Although as a member of the bar, the attorney for the United States is an officer of the court, he is nevertheless an executive official of the Government, and it is as an officer of the executive department that he exercises a discretion as to whether or not there shall be a prosecution in a particular case.

It follows, as an incident of the constitutional separation of powers, that the courts are not to interfere with the free exercise of the discretionary powers of the attorneys of the United States in their control over criminal prosecutions." United States v. Cox, 342 F.2d 167, 171 (5th Cir. 1965).

. . . [In addition, in] the absence of statutorily defined standards governing reviewability, or regulatory or statutory policies of prosecution, the problems inherent in the task of supervising prosecutorial decisions do not lend themselves to resolution by the judiciary. The reviewing courts would be placed in the undesirable and injudicious posture of becoming "superprosecutors." In the normal case of review of executive acts of discretion, the administrative record is open, public and reviewable on the basis of what it contains. The decision not to prosecute, on the other hand, may be based upon the insufficiency of the available evidence, in which event the secrecy of the grand jury and of the prosecutor's file may serve to protect the accused's reputation from public damage based upon insufficient, improper, or even malicious charges. In camera review would not be meaningful without access by the complaining party to the evidence before the grand jury or U.S. Attorney. Such interference with the normal operations of criminal investigations, in turn, based solely upon allegations of criminal conduct, raises serious questions of potential abuse by persons seeking to have other persons prosecuted. Any person, merely by filing a complaint containing allegations in general terms . . . of unlawful failure to prosecute, could gain access to the prosecutor's file. . . .

Nor is it clear what the judiciary's role of supervision should be were it to undertake such a review. At what point would the prosecutor be entitled to call a halt to further investigation as unlikely to be productive? What evidentiary standard would be used to decide whether prosecution should be compelled? How much judgment would the United States Attorney be allowed? Would he be permitted to limit himself to a strong "test" case rather than pursue weaker cases? What collateral factors would be permissible bases for a decision not to prosecute, e.g., the pendency of another criminal proceeding elsewhere against the same parties? What sort of review should be available in cases like the present one where the conduct complained of allegedly violates state as well as federal laws? With limited personnel and facilities at his disposal, what priority would the prosecutor be required to give to cases in which investigation or prosecution was directed by the court?

These difficult questions engender serious doubts as to the judiciary's capacity to review and as to the problem of arbitrariness inherent in any judicial decision to order prosecution. On balance, we believe that substitution of a court's decision to compel prosecution for the U.S. Attorney's decision not to prosecute, even upon an abuse of discretion standard of review and even if limited to directing that a prosecution be undertaken in good faith, would be unwise.

Plaintiffs urge, however, that Congress withdrew the normal prosecutorial discretion for the kind of conduct alleged here by providing in 42 U.S.C. §1987[4] that the United States Attorneys are "authorized and required . . . to institute prosecutions against all persons violating any of the provisions of [18 U.S.C. §§241, 242]," and, therefore, that no barrier to a judicial directive to institute prosecutions remains. This contention must be rejected. The mandatory nature of the word "required" as it appears in §1987 is insufficient to evince a broad Congressional purpose to bar the exercise of executive discretion in the prosecution of federal civil rights crimes. . . .

Such language has never been thought to preclude the exercise of prosecutorial discretion. Indeed the same contention made here was specifically rejected in Moses v. Kennedy, 219 F. Supp. 762, 765 (D.D.C. 1963), aff'd, 342 F.2d 931 (1965), where seven black residents and one white resident of Mississippi sought mandamus to compel the Attorney General of the United States and the Director of the F.B.I. to investigate, arrest, and prosecute certain individuals, including state and local law enforcement officers, for willfully depriving the plaintiffs of their civil rights. There the Court noted that "considerations of judgment and discretion apply with special strength to the area of civil rights, where the Executive Department must be largely free to exercise its considered judgment on questions of whether to proceed by means of prosecution, injunction, varying forms of persuasion, or other types of action."

. . . It therefore becomes unnecessary to decide whether, if Congress were by explicit direction and guidelines to remove all prosecutorial discretion with respect to certain crimes or in certain circumstances we would properly direct that a prosecution be undertaken. . . .

With respect to the state defendants, plaintiffs also seek prosecution of named and unknown persons for the violation of state crimes. However, they have pointed to no statutory language even arguably creating any mandatory duty upon the state officials to bring such prosecutions. To the contrary, New York law reposes in its prosecutors a discretion to decide whether or not to prosecute in a given case, which is not subject to review in the state courts. . . . Yet the federal district court is asked to compel state prosecutions and appoint an "impartial" state prosecutor and state judge to conduct them, as well as to require the submission of a plan for impartial investigation and prosecution of the alleged offenses, . . . in the context of a continuing grand jury investigation into criminal conduct connected with the

---

4. "§1987. PROSECUTION OF VIOLATION OF CERTAIN LAWS"
"The United States attorneys, marshals, and deputy marshals . . . are authorized and required, at the expense of the United States, to institute prosecutions against all persons violating any of the provisions of [various criminal statutes barring the intentional violation of citizens' constitutional rights], and to cause such persons to be arrested, and imprisoned or bailed, for trial before the court of the United States . . . having cognizance of the offense."

Attica uprising, and where the state itself on September 30, 1971, appointed a Special Commission on Attica which has now published its findings. The very elaborateness of the relief believed by plaintiffs to be required indicates the difficulties inherent in judicial supervision of prosecutions, federal or state, which render such a course inadvisable. . . .

Notes on Prosecutorial Discretion and the Protection of the Laws

1. If plaintiffs' allegations are correct, the relevant events in *Inmates of Attica* resemble the facts in the Memphis and New Orleans massacres in 1866. See page 1053 supra. In all three instances, those charged with enforcing the law assaulted and murdered those they were obliged to protect. Current equal protection doctrine does not provide a criminal justice remedy for such cases. Should it? What ought to have happened in the wake of the violent retaking of the prison?

2. Race played a large role in the events at issue in *Inmates of Attica*. At the time of the riot, all but two members of the more-than-five-hundred-person prison staff were white, while more than 60 percent of the prison's inmates were black. See Leo Carroll, "Race, Ethnicity and the Social Order of the Prison," in The Pains of Imprisonment 184 (Robert Johnson & Hans Toch eds., 1982). Black prisoners believed, with reason, that white guards treated them with special brutality. Anger at such treatment was one of the causes of the prisoners' riot. The guards were angry too: During the riot, a number of guards were taken prisoner, several were beaten, and one was killed. The extreme violence with which the prison was retaken was, in part, a response to the violence of the prisoners' takeover, with guards taking vengeance for their colleagues' mistreatment. That vengeance had a racial cast, as did the violence—on both sides—that prompted it.

3. If you find the decision not to prosecute in *Inmates of Attica* unfair, what about a decision (by state officials) to prosecute for manslaughter or negligent homicide rather than murder, or simple assault instead of aggravated assault? Is anything less than maximum criminal liability unfair? If not, what criteria should prosecutors use when deciding to charge less severe crimes than the evidence would support?

4. The relevant facts in Moses v. Kennedy, 219 F. Supp. 762 (D.D.C. 1963), cited and discussed in *Inmates of Attica*, are as follows:

> Plaintiffs' complaint lists a number of incidents in which these plaintiffs allegedly have been intimidated, arrested, beaten, and prosecuted by public officials of the State of Mississippi while plaintiffs were engaged in constitutionally protected activities such as drives to register voters for Federal elections. . . . The complaint further alleges that a number of Federal statutes, [including 42 U.S.C. §1987], authorize and require United States Marshals, agents of the F.B.I., and United States Attorneys to arrest, imprison, and

institute prosecutions against all persons who willfully subject any inhabitant of any state to the deprivation of any rights, privileges or immunities secured or protected by the Constitution or laws of the United States. Defendants have made no contention that this allegation is defective, and the Court will therefore assume, for the purposes of this motion, that plaintiffs could establish this proposition. Plaintiffs have further alleged, and these allegations must also be assumed to be true, that defendants "have been repeatedly requested by plaintiffs and others to perform [their] statutory duties . . . , but they have refused and failed to do so."

Id. at 763-64. Notwithstanding those allegations, the court in *Moses* held that there was no legal remedy for the alleged official misconduct:

> This complaint must be dismissed because it seeks remedies which, in the context of the above pleadings, this Court has no power to grant.
>
> First, plaintiffs seek a court order directing the defendants to direct their agents to arrest, cause to be imprisoned, and institute criminal prosecutions against "those state and local law enforcement officials and any other persons, public or private, responsible for the deprivations of plaintiffs' rights". . . . Such actions on the part of defendants, however, are clearly discretionary, and decisions respecting such actions are committed to the Executive branch of the Government, not to the courts. . . .
>
> . . . "[T]he duty to prosecute [does not follow] automatically from the presentation of a complaint. The United States Attorney is not a rubber stamp. His problems are not solved by the strict application of an inflexible formula. Rather, their solution calls for the exercise of judgment. . . ." Pugach v. Klein, 193 F. Supp. 630, 635 (D.D.C., 1961). Such considerations apply to investigations, arrests, and imprisonments, just as much as they do to actual prosecutions.

219 F. Supp. at 764-65.

Judicial opinions like those in *Moses* and *Inmates of Attica* are unusual: Courts rarely discuss the scope of prosecutorial discretion—because that discretion is so rarely challenged. Few litigants offer claims like those made by the plaintiffs in these two cases, since such claims face certain defeat. There is more than a little irony in that proposition. If there was one scenario John Bingham and his colleagues wished to prevent when they drafted and voted on the Fourteenth Amendment's Equal Protection Clause, it is the scenario at issue in these two cases. Today, equal protection doctrine guards against many types of official misconduct. But not the type for which that doctrine was originally designed.

Table of Cases

Principal cases are indicated by italics.

Table of Statutes and Acts

Model Penal Code

Index